PSYCHOLOGY: PERSPECTIVES ON BEHAVIOR

PSYCHOLOGY: PERSPECTIVES ON BEHAVIOR

PETER D. SPEAR
University of Wisconsin-Madison

STEVEN D. PENROD
University of Wisconsin-Madison

TIMOTHY B. BAKER
University of Wisconsin-Madison

WILEY

JOHN WILEY & SONS
New York   Chichester   Brisbane   Toronto   Singapore

This book is dedicated to our families:

Meredith, Eli, and Jessica
Joan and Rachel
Linda and Hannah

Cover and text design by Karin Gerdes Kincheloe
Cover painting by Roy Wiemann
Photo research by Stella Kupferberg
Production supervision by Lucille Buonocore

Library of Congress Cataloging in Publication Data:

Spear, Peter D.
  Psychology: perspectives on behavior.

  Includes indexes.
  1. Psychology. I. Penrod, Steven. II. Baker,
Timothy B. III. Title. [DNLM: 1. Behavior.
2. Psychology. BF 121 S741p]

BF121.S64 1988   150   87-25340
ISBN 0-471-82425-9

Printed in the United States of America

10 9 8 7 6 5 4 3 2 1

ABOUT THE AUTHORS

Peter D. Spear received his B.A. degree in 1966 from Rutgers University, where he majored in psychology. He went on to Yale University, where he received his Ph.D. in psychology in 1970. His major area was physiological and sensory psychology, his minor area was learning and motivation. Dr. Spear then spent two years as a Postdoctoral Fellow at Stanford University. From 1972–1976, he was a member of the faculty in the psychology department at Kansas State University. He joined the faculty at the University of Wisconsin-Madison in 1976, where he currently is a Professor of Psychology and a member of the faculty of the Neurosciences Train-

Steven D. Penrod received his B.A. in 1969 from Yale University, where he majored in political science. He received his J.D. degree in 1974 from Harvard Law School, with some time out for military service. While in law school, Dr. Penrod became interested in the psychological aspects of the law. Upon completing his law degree, he went on to graduate school and received his Ph.D. in psychology from Harvard in 1979. Dr. Penrod joined the faculty at the University of Wisconsin-Madison in 1979, and he is currently an Associate Professor of Psychology. He was a visiting professor at Indiana University in 1985. Dr. Penrod carries

Timothy B. Baker received his B.A. degree in 1972 from the University of California at Riverside, where he majored in psychology. He obtained his Ph.D. in psychology in 1978 from the University of Utah, where he specialized in clinical psychology. Dr. Baker joined the faculty at the University of Wisconsin-Madison in 1979, and he is currently a Professor of Psychology and Director of Clinical Training. His research centers on addiction and the behavioral and physiological effects of addictive drugs. He studies drug tolerance in animals as well as the nature of addiction motivation in humans. In addition, Dr. Baker carries out research on psy-

Peter D. Spear

Steven D. Penrod

Timothy B. Baker

ing Program. Dr. Spear carries out an active research program concerned with the brain mechanisms of vision and the effects of early visual experience on neural and behavioral development. He also conducts research on the effects of brain damage and the neural mechanisms of recovery from brain damage in infants and adults. He has published over 60 papers on these topics in journals such as the *Journal of Neuroscience, Journal of Comparative Neurology, Behavioural Brain Research,* and *Journal of Neurophysiology.* In addition, Dr. Spear is on the editorial board of the *Journal of Neuroscience* and *Vision Research.* Dr. Spear teaches undergraduate and graduate courses in physiological psychology and graduate courses concerned with sensory processes and neural development. In addition, he taught introduction to psychology at Kansas State University and currently teaches the course at the University of Wisconsin-Madison.

out an active research program concerned with psychology and the law, decision making, eyewitness reliability, media effects, and behavioral medicine. He has published over 40 papers on these topics in journals such as the *Journal of Personality and Social Psychology, Journal of Applied Social Psychology, Law and Human Behavior,* and *Psychological Review.* In addition, he is coauthor of the books *Inside the Jury* and *The Question of Pornography,* and he is the author of a textbook entitled *Social Psychology.* Dr. Penrod is also on the editorial boards of the journals *Law and Human Behavior, Social Behavior: An International Journal of Applied Social Psychology,* and *Forensic Reports.* Dr. Penrod is a recent recipient of the American Psychological Association's Distinguished Scientific Award for an Early Career Contribution to Applied Psychology. He teaches undergraduate and graduate courses in social psychology, psychology and law, social cognition research methods, and introduction to psychology.

chological treatments for addiction. He has published over 50 papers on these topics in books and journals such as the *Nebraska Symposium on Motivation, Journal of Consulting and Clinical Psychology, Behavioral Neuroscience,* and *Psychological Review.* Dr. Baker also has served as editor of the special issue of the *Journal of Abnormal Psychology,* "Models of Addiction." He teaches undergraduate and graduate courses in addiction, neuropsychology, psychopathology, and assessment, and he supervises clinical psychology graduate students in psychotherapy. In addition, Dr. Baker regularly teaches introduction to psychology.

PREFACE

Why Write an Introductory Psychology Textbook?

As we wrote this book, friends and colleagues often asked why we were writing an introduction to psychology textbook when there already are so many introductory textbooks available. One reason is the fun and excitement of introducing students to a whole new realm of information about their world and of guiding students to think about their world in new ways. We have taught the introductory psychology course to thousands of college students over the past 10 to 15 years, and we continue to find it a stimulating and enlightening experience. The enjoyment of teaching psychology led us to write the book, and we hope the book reflects that.

A second reason for writing this book is that when teaching the introductory psychology course we often felt dissatisfied with the textbooks that were available. We found that high-level, scholarly texts were dry and lost the student's interest, whereas texts that captured the student's interest were too simplistic and superficial. In addition, the available texts tended to artificially divide the field into separate disciplines without integrating the various "areas" of psychology or showing how they are related. This book is an attempt to remedy these shortcomings by presenting an introduction to psychology that is scholarly, integrated, and interesting.

Specific Goals of the Book

One goal of the book is to provide a balanced, up-to-date, and scholarly overview of psychology. The field of psychology encompasses a broad range of inquiry, from the operation of the brain in controlling behavior to the nature of complex social interactions. Obviously, it is not possible to cover everything that is known about psychology in an introductory text. However, we have taken care to give a comprehensive overview of classic research, major theories, and the most important and active modern research. Our own research interests span the field of psychology, from neuroscience, sensation and perception, and development (P.D.S.), to learning, motivation, and clinical psychology (T.B.B.), to memory, information processing, and social psychology (S.D.P.). This background, plus a continued active involvement in research, has helped us bring a critical and contemporary perspective to the range of material that is discussed in the book. A balanced and rigorous overview of psychology is the foundation on which our other goals rest.

A second goal is to give students an appreciation of the *process* by which knowledge about psychology is obtained. Psychology is presented not merely as a collection of facts, but as an exciting and dynamic science that continues to broaden and enrich our knowledge of human behavior. The book describes the research process that leads to new observations, it provides critical discussions of research, and it recognizes and discusses controversies in the field. By doing this, we hope to lead students to *think* about how psychologists know what they know. We hope to teach students to have critical minds, not just fact-filled ones.

A third goal is to provide a more integrated view of psychology than is presented in other books. Introductory psychology texts tend to isolate the topics that are presented in each chapter. Topics such as developmental psychology, physiological psychology, learning, motivation, social psychology, and so on, often are presented as separate disciplines that are relegated almost entirely to separate, unrelated chapters. But these are not isolated disciplines; in many ways the different areas of psychology are simply different perspectives on thought and behavior. Any particular phenomenon or behavior (such as perception, learning, or psychopathology) can be analyzed in terms of its physiological bases, its functional significance from an evolutionary standpoint, how it changes during development and aging, the extent to which it is influenced by genetic and environmental factors, how it is affected by cognitive processes, how it is influenced by and expressed in social psychological phenomena, and so on. One of the main themes of this book is that behavior and psychological phenomena can be understood best by viewing them from a variety of different perspectives, or levels of analysis. This "levels of analysis" approach helps to integrate the topics that are discussed in the book and helps the student gain a deeper understanding of psychology than is possible otherwise.

Our fourth major goal is to stimulate and maintain the student's interest in psychology. The other goals can be met adequately only if the student's interest is sustained. We do this in part by using examples that relate to the student's everyday life and by providing self-demonstrations that make phenomena being discussed relevant to the student's own experience. In addition, we engage the student in the process of psychology as a live and dynamic science. Topics are introduced in a way that stimulates the student's curiosity about questions to be answered, and the student is led progressively through the research that answers these questions and in turn raises new questions. We try to tell a story of psychology that ties together past and present findings and shows how each new discovery builds on previous ones. We believe that telling an integrated and progressive story of psychology leads to greater interest as well as greater understanding.

Organization of the Book

The book contains 17 chapters plus appendixes on research methods in psychology, the use of statistics in psychology, and careers in psychology. We have organized the chapters into a sequence that progresses from phenomena that relate primarily to individuals to phenomena that involve wider social interactions among individuals. In addition, the chapter sequence progresses from how people gather information about the world, to how people process information and change, to how people act on and interact with others. This organizational sequence corresponds to that used by most instructors in their courses. We have used it in the book because we believe the sequence makes sense and also because it will allow instructors to easily integrate the book with their already established course organization.

Nevertheless, there are several distinctive features of the book's organization that we have incorporated because we believe they reflect modern psychology and help the student to understand psychology. In keeping with the levels of analysis approach, developmental psychology is considered throughout the book, not just in a single chapter. Although a chapter on this topic (Chapter 9) is included to discuss the fundamental concepts of developmental psychology, developmental aspects of psychological phenomena are discussed in virtually all of the chapters. Furthermore, we recognize that development refers to the process of change throughout life and, accordingly, we have taken a life-span approach (including aging).

Physiological psychology also is considered throughout the book. A chapter on Biological Foundations (Chapter 2) is included to give students the foundations of biology and neuroscience necessary to understand how people behave. However, physiological psychology is not limited to this chapter. Biological bases of behavior are considered throughout the book in the context of the topics that are discussed in each chapter (for example, sensation and perception, learning, memory, psychopathology, aggression, interpersonal attraction, and so on). This reflects the fact that the brain and body are an integral part of all behavior, and it reflects the recent trend in psychology to consider biological along with psychological mechanisms of thought and behavior.

Methods of psychology also are integrated with content material throughout the book. Appendix A presents an overview of conceptual issues in experimental design and methods of doing psychological research. However, specific methods and experimental designs that are used by researchers in particular areas of psychology are presented where they are relevant to the substance and content of psychological knowledge that is being discussed. This avoids a long and tedious section on methods and makes methods in psychology more concrete and relevant to the student.

Another distinctive aspect of the book's organization is the treatment of sensation and perception. Other texts have one chapter (or section of a chapter) on sensation and a second on perception, which tends to artificially dichotomize the two topics. Furthermore, the discussion of perception is almost always devoted exclusively to *visual* perception; little or nothing is said about perception in other sensory systems. We have organized these topics into one chapter on visual sensation and perception (Chapter 3) and a second chapter on sensation and perception in the other senses (hearing, taste, smell, touch, and so on) (Chapter 4). This gives greater continuity to the discussion of each sensory system. In addition, we have included three to four times more coverage of the nonvisual senses than other texts, and this is virtually the only text that discusses *perception* as well as sensation in the nonvisual sensory systems.

The coverage in the two social psychology chapters (16 and 17) gives a stronger emphasis than other texts to the contemporary application of cognitive psychology to understanding social psychological phenomena. The growth of social-cognition research is reflected not only in discussions of self and social perception, but also in discussions of traditional social psychological questions such as attitude change, social influence, aggression, and pro-social behavior.

When writing a textbook or deciding whether to adopt one for a course, an important consideration is the length of the book. For several reasons, this textbook is slightly longer than other introduction to psychology texts. Psychology is an active empirical science, and new research *adds* information to the existing body of knowledge; it does not simply change or replace old information. We have tried to include new information without shortchanging the foundations on which it is based. In addition, instead of giving superficial statements of important psychological concepts, we have chosen to explain them and to provide examples that will help make the concepts clear and interesting to students. We have also used illustrations (line-drawings and photographs) extensively, and these have been printed in a large format that makes them easy to see and understand. These choices have combined to make each chapter an average of 3 to 4 pages longer than comparable chapters in other texts. We believe students would rather read chapters that may be slightly longer, but are clear and interesting than slightly shorter chapters that are cursory and more difficult to understand.

Instructors may organize their courses somewhat differently depending on the time available (e.g., one semester or one quarter), the type of students, and the objectives of the course. For shorter courses, we believe it is better to cover less material fully than to attempt to cover everything and do it superficially. Shorter courses could omit Chapters 4 (Sensation and Perception: Auditory, Chemical, and Body Senses), 8 (Language and Thought), 10 (Basic Models of Motivation), 14 (Assessment of Personality, Behavior, and Intelligence), 17 (Social Interaction), and/or the appendixes. The remaining chapters still provide the important concepts of psychology; for example, Chapter 3 covers the basic concepts of sensation and perception in the context of vision. Chapters that are not assigned can be read by interested students and can be used for reference.

Learning Aids

Throughout the book we have incorporated a variety of features intended to make psychology interesting and alive to the student and to help the student understand what he or she has read. One such feature is the liberal use of relevant examples and self-demonstrations that are chosen to make the material meaningful to the student as well as to help clarify concepts that are discussed. We use these examples and demonstrations in our own classes and find that they help engage the student and show him or her how research and theory in psychology applies to everyday life and experience.

As noted earlier we also have used illustrations extensively throughout the book. For example, Chapters 2 (Biological Foundations) and 7 (Memory) contain over 30 figures each and Chapter 3 (Sensation and Perception: Vision) contains approximately 50 figures. The figures are chosen to clarify and illuminate and not simply as window-dressing. In the text itself, we have taken care to indicate when the student should refer to a figure so that the figures are well integrated with the material they are intended to illustrate.

Within each chapter, there are separate "boxes" in which special aspects of the topic under consideration are discussed. The boxes are designed to draw students into psychology by providing detailed information about theories and research findings that form the basis of conclusions drawn in the text or by discussing special applications related to material in the text. The number and placement of the boxes within the text have been considered carefully so that the boxes do not distract the student or break the flow of the text, but rather illuminate material being discussed.

Within the text, reference citations are given for major statements of results or conclusions. This is done to give investigators credit for their observations and also to provide a concrete reminder to students that findings discussed in the text are made by scientists carrying out research. The reference citations also make it possible for students to look up specific papers on a subject if they wish. The number and placement of the citations have been chosen carefully to avoid clutter and disruption of the flow of the text. At the end of each chapter there also is an annotated list of further readings for interested students.

Frequent summaries and statements of major conclusions are woven into the text within each chapter. In addition, each chapter ends with a thorough summary of the material that has been discussed. These chapter summaries are overviews of the main content, conceptual issues, and conclusions and not simply cursory statements of a few facts.

Important terms are printed in **bold** when they first appear in the text and they are defined in the glossary at the end of the book. A unified glossary at the end of the book makes it easy for students to look up terms that reappear from chapter to chapter.

A *Study Guide* is available that includes chapter outlines and reviews, key terms and concepts, and statements of the main learning objectives for each chapter. The Study Guide also provides interesting and easy exercises to help the student understand the main concepts of the book. Practice test questions, with an answer key, also are provided.

An *Instructor's Manual* is available for the teacher. This manual includes an overview and detailed summary of each chapter. Suggestions for discussion topics and classroom demonstrations also are provided. In addition, the manual includes a list of suggested lecture topics that can be used to supplement the material covered in the text. Source materials are given for these topics as well as for topics that are discussed in the text. A list of relevant films and film sources also is given.

A set of color *slides and overhead transparencies* also is available. Background and descriptive material for each of these illustrations is included in the *Instructor's Manual* so that the illustrations can be easily integrated with the instructor's lectures.

The *Test Bank* has been written with special care. The most common complaint that students have about multiple-choice questions is that they are "too picky" or that they are too ambiguous. We have made an effort to include questions that are clear and a list of answers that are unambiguous. In addition, we have included many questions that test the student's understanding of concepts and his or her ability to integrate material. We believe that tests are an important opportunity to encourage students to think about what they have learned, and we have tried to devise test questions that stimulate that thinking.

All three authors have taken an active part in developing and writing these supplements. We believe that the supplements are an important part of the learning package and should be of the same high quality as the text itself. In addition, we have tried to integrate the supplements with the text so that the text and supplements can be used interactively.

ACKNOWLEDGMENTS

A large number of colleagues at the University of Wisconsin and at other colleges and universities have made helpful suggestions and comments on the manuscript. Some of these people are specialists on topics covered in specific chapters and have helped to ensure that the material is up-to-date and accurate. In addition, some of these people have had extensive experience in teaching introductory psychology and have made useful suggestions for improving the flow and overall integration of material in the book. These colleagues are: Christopher Coe, Nancy Denney, Robert Goy, Richard Keesey, Gregg Oden, Jack Sherman, and Frederic Wightman, all at the University of Wisconsin, John Cavanaugh, Bowling Green State University; John Bargh, New York University; Vaida Thompson, University of North Carolina at Chapel Hill; Michael Epstein, Rider College; Edward Gavurin, Lehman College–CUNY; Janet Proctor, Auburn University, AL; Michael McCloskey, Johns Hopkins University; Richard Sanders, University of North Carolina–Wilmington; John Carroll, Northwestern University; Kirk Howard Smith, Bowling Green State University; Nancy S. Anderson, University of Maryland; Julia E. Wallace, University of N. Iowa; Donald Meyer, University of Pittsburgh; Sarah O'Dowd, CCRI–Community College of Rhode Island; Larry Hjelle, SUNY @ Brockport; William Ghiselli, University of Missouri–Kansas City; Don Herrin, University of Utah; Paul Wellman, Texas A & M University; Roger Moss, California State University–Northridge; Martin Moss, Wright State University; Jim Council, North Dakota State University; Deborah Balogh, Ball State University; Michael Siegel, SUNY, Oneonta; John Mueller, University of Missouri; Gregory Murphy, Brown University; Bonnie Wright, St. Olaf College; Arnold Buss, University of Texas–Austin; Katherine Hoyenga, Western Illinois University; Rex Bierley, North Dakota State University; Paul Kaplan, Suffolk County Community College; Carl Baffi, Vanderbilt University; Ned Schultz, California Polytechnic State University–San Luis Obispo; Russ Green, University of Missouri; Steve Prentice-Dunn, University of Alabama; Ellen Strommen, Michigan State University; Paul Shinkman, University of North Carolina; George Hampton, University of Houston–Downtown; Martin Covington, University of California–Berkeley.

We also thank the many people at John Wiley & Sons whose thoughtful, conscientious, and creative contributions helped to make this a high-quality book that we are all proud of. These people include Suzanne Ingrao, Director of College Production; Lucille Buonocore, Senior Production Supervisor; Karin Kincheloe, Senior Designer; Stella Kupferberg, Photo Research Manager; and Gilda Stahl, Senior Copyeditor. Thanks also go to our editors Mark Mochary, who convinced us that Wiley was the best publisher for our book and Warren Abraham, who guided us through the long process of writing, reviewing, and producing the book. Finally, special thanks go to Susan Friedman and her excellent depth editing.

CONTENTS

PSYCHOLOGY: PERSPECTIVES ON BEHAVIOR

1

INTRODUCTION

THE DEVELOPMENT
OF MODERN
PSYCHOLOGY _____

LEVELS OF ANALYSIS IN
PSYCHOLOGY

THE PHILOSOPHICAL
BASES OF PSYCHOLOGY

PHYSIOLOGICAL
FOUNDATIONS OF
PSYCHOLOGY
[*The Physiological Perspective*]

INTROSPECTIONISM

GESTALT PSYCHOLOGY

COGNITIVE PSYCHOLOGY
[*The Cognitive Perspective*]

FUNCTIONALIST
PSYCHOLOGY
[*The Sociobiological Perspective*]

BEHAVIORISM
[*The Learning and Behavioral Perspectives*]

PSYCHOANALYSIS

HUMANIST PSYCHOLOGY
[*The Clinical Perspective*]

DEVELOPMENTAL
PSYCHOLOGY
[*The Developmental Perspective*]

SOCIAL PSYCHOLOGY
[*The Social Psychological Perspective*]

THE VIEW OF THIS TEXT:
MULTIPLE LEVELS AND
MULTIPLE PERSPECTIVES

PSYCHOLOGY AS A
SCIENCE _____

THE SCIENTIFIC ASSUMP-
TIONS OF PSYCHOLOGY

SCIENTIFIC GOALS OF
PSYCHOLOGY

What do you expect to find between the covers of this volume? You have no doubt formed some impressions of what psychology is about. Perhaps you have seen psychologists on television ("The Bob Newhart Show"? Dr. Joyce Brothers? Dr. Ruth Westheimer?). Perhaps you have heard of some of the big names in psychology such as Sigmund Freud or B. F. Skinner. Perhaps you know that some psychologists study and provide therapy to people with mental illnesses, that other psychologists counsel people with family and work problems, that some psychologists advise students and adults about career choices, that other psychologists work as personnel directors for businesses, that some psychologists study learning in humans and animals, that some psychologists study child development, that some psychologists study group behavior, that some psychologists study communication—even communication with other species. The list could go on and on. Though it may never have occurred to you, all of these psychologists have things in common even though they may be engaged in very different activities. If they are all psychologists, then what is psychology? One of the major objectives of this chapter is to establish what it is that these many types of psychologists have in common.

Although it is tempting to define psychology in simple terms such as "the science of the mind" or "the science of behavior," such definitions are rather vague. Without further explanation these definitions fail to convey the complexity and richness of psychology. Psychology does not really lend itself to a simple definition, so in this chapter we provide an introduction to psychology that will touch upon its many facets. We will highlight some of the ways in which psychologists differ, but we also will emphasize the things they share. Among the things that psychologists share are a common set of assumptions and values about how psychology should and does develop as a *science*. This means that psychologists share a belief in the value of scientific research methods and scientific theories. Psychologists also share a common and fairly recent history, for the scientific discipline of psychology is only slightly more than a century old.

FIGURE 1-1   WILHELM WUNDT (1832–1920).
Wundt established one of the first psychological laboratories at the University of Leipzig, Germany, in 1879. Wundt was a professor of philosophy, but had been trained as a physician. In 1874 he published Principles of Physiological Psychology *and in 1881 he founded a journal entitled* Philosophische Studien, *which was devoted to studies of sensation and perception.*

THE DEVELOPMENT OF MODERN PSYCHOLOGY

Historians of psychology generally agree that scientific research in the discipline started just over a century ago in Europe and the United States. Among the most important early developments in the discipline were Wilhelm Wundt's (Figure 1-1) establishment, in 1879 in Leipzig, Germany, of a laboratory for the study of psychology. At approximately the same time in Cambridge, Massachusetts, William James (Figure 1-2) opened a laboratory and taught his first course in psychology at Harvard University. Although scientific laboratories for research on psychological issues are only a little more than a century old, the fundamental questions addressed by psychology have a longer history. Indeed, it is likely that since time immemorial humans have been trying to figure out why people behave as they do.

FIGURE 1-2   WILLIAM JAMES (1842–1910).

James opened the first psychological laboratory in the United States at Harvard University in the late 1870s. In 1879 James became one of the nation's first "Professors of Psychology" and in 1890 published his highly influential Principles of Psychology.

Levels of Analysis in Psychology

One of the most important characteristics of the field of psychology is that there is no single, universally agreed upon approach to psychology. Rather, there are a variety of perspectives and levels of analysis from which psychologists approach their research problems and develop their theories. In this section, we briefly discuss the historical foundations of the most important perspectives. This discussion has several objectives. First, we would like to familiarize you with these perspectives because we will repeatedly encounter them throughout the textbook. Second, although psychology is not an entirely unified field, these perspectives do encompass the major theories and methods employed in psychology, and so they serve an important unifying function both for psychology and for this textbook. Third, the fact that there are several major perspectives within psychology makes it clear that research in psychology can be viewed from a number of levels of analysis.

Because human behavior is so complex, psychologists have found that analyzing particular forms of behavior at many different levels helps them to capture this complexity. Take a behavior like language, for example. Why and how do you communicate with language? To understand those questions, psychologists need answers at a number of levels. They might want to know about the functions that language serves. In the broadest sense, language has clear practical value. For example, it enables you to manage effectively in your environment by helping you to communicate your desires to other people and to fulfill certain needs (e.g., asking for directions to the nearest fast food outlet). At the **molecular** level, that is, at the level of the smallest elements or component parts of language, psychologists might want to know about the physiological components of language. They would study the structure of the mouth and throat, the ear, and the brain; how the neurons in the ear respond to sound and communicate with one another, and recognize words. Some scientists seek explanations at the molecular level and reduce phenomena to their biological or chemical underpinnings. Although most psychologists favor research of psychological phenomena at this level, they also reject a radical **reductionism** that holds a molecular analysis is sufficient to understand psychological phenomena. Most psychologists prefer to work toward a multileveled understanding.

The complement to the molecular level of analysis is the **molar** level of analysis. In investigating language, psychologists working at the molar level might consider that newborn infants cannot speak, and thus a full understanding of language requires some knowledge about human development. They might ask which developmental changes take place in infants that allow them to learn to communicate effectively once they are four to five years old. Among other things, children must learn how to articulate speech sounds and assemble them into words and sentences. Some of this development involves physiological maturation and some of it involves cognitive development—study of both is necessary to get a complete picture.

Psychologists working at the molar level also might be interested in studying the acquisition of language. It is clear that language is not an inborn reflex, and it is also clear that most other organisms do not learn

FIGURE 1-3 ARISTOTLE (384–322 B.C.).
Many ancient Greek and Roman philosophers were interested in the problems now addressed by psychologists. Aristotle made many original contributions to theories of sensation, perception, memory and thinking, and human and animal behavior.

FIGURE 1-4 RENÉ DESCARTES (1596–1650).
The French philosopher Descartes wrote extensively on human physiology, human thinking, and memory.

language (though they may learn other complex behaviors). The understanding of language would certainly be enriched by an understanding of basic learning processes and by a comparison of communication in humans and other organisms. It is also clear that language abilities require sophisticated cognitive or mental skills. Understanding the words we hear or read requires that people have memories for the meaning of words and the symbols for those words. This memory must not only include the information necessary for recognizing words, but it must also contain a fairly elaborate base of knowledge—including social and cultural knowledge—that allows people to comprehend, interpret, and act upon words after they recognize them. Some psychologists may be interested in abnormalities in language such as dyslexia and aphasia—their research may both shed light on the treatment of such abnormalities and provide a better understanding of normal language. Other psychologists may be interested in the social aspects of language and attempt to determine the relationship between language and social phenomena such as aggression, altruism, social influence, and interpersonal attraction. One of the harder questions in unraveling the mysteries of language concerns how people put together all of these processes, molecular and molar, into smooth acts of communication. In other words, how do physiology, development, learning, cognitive abilities, and social experiences combine to produce language?

Why are there multiple levels of analysis within psychology? What are the objectives of psychologists conducting research at these different levels and what sorts of research methods do they employ? One especially helpful way to understand the objectives and methods of modern psychological perspectives is to examine their historical foundations. In the remainder of this section we briefly survey the development of psychology as a scientific discipline and identify the major contemporary perspectives within psychology.

The Philosophical Bases of Psychology

Some of the first recorded systematic thinking about psychological questions comes from ancient Greece of the late sixth and fifth centuries B.C. In the writings of Aristotle (Figure 1-3), we find evidence of systematic observation of the world and the formation of a system of knowledge based on observation rather than mythology. Aristotle was, of course, a philosopher rather than a psychologist, but before psychology developed as a separate science, it was philosophers who, among others, were interested in questions such as what is the basic nature of humans? how do the five senses work? and how does memory function?

Aristotle, for example, recognized that sensory information was integrated by a "common sense" (today we ascribe it to brain function). His theory of memory included distinctions, held valid today, between the retention of information in memory and the retrieval of that information, and he recognized the importance to memory of the associations between experiences.

In seventeenth-century Europe rapid intellectual developments began that would culminate in the birth of the science of psychology. One of

FIGURE 1-5 JOHN STUART MILL (1806–1873).
A Scottish philosopher, Mill wrote A System of Logic in which he offered a very influential theory of how memory operates.

FIGURE 1-6 JOHANNES MÜLLER (1801–1858).
Müller was a professor of physiology at the University of Berlin. He was a pioneering researcher in neuropsychology and published a widely used Handbook of Physiology during the period 1833–1840.

the important figures of that era was René Descartes (Figure 1-4), a philosopher and mathematician, who saw such inspiring advances in machinery all around him that he likened the human body to an elaborate machine. Descartes was particularly fascinated by the problem of how the "mind" (which he thought was not physical) controlled the "matter" of the body.

Through the next two centuries a number of philosophers significantly advanced the development of science and of human behavior. John Stuart Mill (Figure 1-5), another eighteenth-century philosopher, rejected Descartes' mind/body distinction and argued that the mind, too, was mechanical. Although the proposal represented a sharp break with the philosophical past, Mill's views were soon supported by advances in physiological research.

Physiological Foundations of Psychology

With the work of Johannes Müller (Figure 1-6), physiology and psychology began a mutually beneficial journey that continues to this day. Müller advanced the doctrine of "specific nerve energies." He argued that nerves in all the sensory systems transmit messages through electrical impulses but that different types of nerves generate signals of different energies. Thus light-sensitive nerves transmit only information about light, even though the nerve might have been stimulated by electricity rather than light. Because these different messages had to be sorted out somewhere, Müller postulated that specific areas of the brain were specialized to interpret them. One implication of his work was that people gain knowledge about the world through their nerves.

Experimental work by a number of physiologists confirmed many of Müller's hypotheses about specialized brain functions. Soon brain research was directed to more "psychological" questions, and foremost among the researchers in this area was a student of Müller named Hermann von Helmholtz (Figure 1-7). His research on hearing and color vision still forms the foundation of modern theories of sensation (as you will see in Chapters 2 and 3). Another German physiologist (and physicist) of this era was Gustav Theodor Fechner (Figure 1-8), whose interest in the mind/body problem led him to investigate the manner in which physical stimuli are translated into psychological experiences. His research led to precise measurements of both the intensity of stimuli and the intensity of the psychological experiences they produce. These German physiologists laid the groundwork for the modern physiological perspective in psychology.

Introspectionism

Wilhelm Wundt, credited with having established the first true psychological laboratory, had an immense influence on modern psychology. Wundt studied with Müller and worked as assistant to Helmholtz. Wundt was a remarkable man: he wrote an extremely influential textbook in psychology (1873), published over 500 other works, established the first

THE PHYSIOLOGICAL PERSPECTIVE

Physiologists have traditionally studied the physiological bases of a wide variety of behaviors such as sensation, perception, sleep, emotion, learning, motivation, and sexual behavior. Their studies concentrate upon understanding the role that chemistry, biology, and physical structure play in complex behavior, such as aggression and memory, and they pay closest attention to the operation of the brain,

other parts of the nervous system, and the endocrine system.

Traditionally, most physiological experiments were conducted with animals because the methods used by these researchers—the creation of lesions or damaged areas in the brain, dissection, electrical stimulation of the brain, injection of chemicals, and so forth—could not be ethically used in humans. However, as physiological research methods become increasingly sophisticated and benign, more of this research is conducted with humans. Indeed, physiological psychology has become a highly specialized field in which complex methods of research are used to study narrowly defined research questions. Research methods range from the use of microscopic electrodes to measure the activity of single neurons to the use of computer scanners that can make three-dimensional records of the electrical, chemical, and even magnetic activity of the brain. Of course, physiological psychologists are not merely interested in examining behavior at the biological level and their methods can be used to examine behaviors ranging from the least to most complex.

psychology journal (1881), and was an ardent advocate for official recognition of psychology as a separate discipline.

Wundt's interests were wide ranging, spanning physiology, sensation, perception, memory, attention, and even social psychology. Along with other psychologists of the time, Wundt is remembered as a **structuralist**, that is, one who is interested in the interrelationships of the various parts of the brain and how they operate together in sensation, perception, and conscious experience. One of Wundt's students, Edward Titchener, an Englishman who emigrated to the United States, established a laboratory at Cornell University in 1892. Titchener is remembered as an ardent advocate of **introspective** methods. Although many psychologists had rejected the idea of examining their own experiences as a basis for psychology, Titchener attempted to develop introspection into a scientific method by training his subjects to carefully observe and report the operation of their own mental functions. Titchener wrote a number of influential volumes on research methods and several textbooks. Despite Titchener's efforts, introspectionism fell into disfavor at the turn of the century. However, introspection has enjoyed something of a revival in the recent development of cognitive psychology.

Gestalt Psychology

One major school of German psychology that has substantially influenced general psychology can be traced to the work of three men, Max Wertheimer, Wolfgang Kohler, and Kurt Koffka, who began working together in Frankfurt, Germany, in 1911 and continued to influence one another's work for three decades. Together, they developed what has been termed the **Gestalt** school of psychology. The major theoretical thrust behind the Gestalt school can be found in the translation of the German word *gestalt,* which refers to "whole forms" or "patterns."

FIGURE 1-7 HERMANN VON HELMHOLTZ (1821–1894). Helmholtz studied medicine with Müller and combined interests in physiology, chemistry, and physics in his studies of sensation. His book Sensations of Tone *(1863) and his three-volume work* Physiological Optics *(1856–1866) were standard references for many decades.*

FIGURE 1-8 GUSTAV THEODOR FECHNER (1801–1887). After studying medicine at the University of Leipzig Fechner held a professorship of physics there from 1834 to 1839. In 1860 he published the highly influential volume Elements of Psychophysics. *Fechner strongly advocated the use of experimental methods in psychology.*

Unlike the introspectionists, who were determined to understand the structure of the mind by analyzing its component, molecular parts, the Gestaltists were interested in the overarching or molar aspects of experience. The Gestaltists wanted to examine the whole of experience—the larger patterns, structure, and organization of behavior. They sought to understand the full richness of experience rather than breaking it into tiny constituent parts. Their argument was that the whole is different from the sum of its parts and that something essential is lost when only the parts are examined. Thus, a song is more than just musical notes and words—it includes, among other things, the configuration and patterning of the notes, the juxtapositioning of the words and music, the expressiveness of the singer and the musicians, and the experience engendered in the listener.

Cognitive Psychology

Although Titchener's introspective methods have fallen into disfavor and Gestalt theories are no longer as popular as they once were, both of these earlier schools of scientific psychology have influenced subsequent research and theory. This fact is nowhere more evident than in the development, over the past 40 years, of an active and influential school of psychology loosely encompassed by the term **cognitive psychology**.

Part of the impetus for cognitive research was supplied by World War II and the need to understand better the interactions of humans and machines. In particular, researchers were interested in improving the effectiveness of pilots, gunners, bombardiers, radar operators, and so on. Pioneering work on the flow of information between machines and humans—feedback—was conducted by Kenneth J. W. Craik. In 1958, Donald E. Broadbent stirred further interest in cognitive functioning with the publication of his *Perception and Communication,* a summary of Broadbent's research on the role of attention in human perception (discussed more fully in Chapter 4). Broadbent was particularly interested in understanding how humans select from the broad and potentially overwhelming range of stimuli available to them.

The advent of the modern computer also played a role in encouraging researchers to think about analogies between the functioning of computers, computer programs, and the human brain. Herbert Simon was one of the first researchers to undertake analysis of human "information processing." Today those who investigate thought and memory from the perspective of the information processing school form an important part of the field of cognitive psychology. Simon's research was strongly influenced by analogies to computers and spawned interest in **artificial intelligence**, the use of computers to simulate complex human thought processes. Other researchers have been interested in determining how humans store and use information and have devised new information processing techniques to explore old questions about learning and memory. Many of these researchers are actively working to understand the mental processes involved in collecting, organizing, interpreting, remembering, and using information.

THE COGNITIVE PERSPECTIVE

Cognitivists are interested in the higher forms of mental functioning such as thinking and problem solving. Although there is a substantial body of comparative cognitive research (which compares, for instance, human problem-solving strategies with the problem-solving strategies of primates such as chimpanzees), most cognitive research is conducted with humans.

Cognitive researchers seek to understand how information is processed in thinking and decision making. Thus, much cognitive research is addressed to problems such as information acquisition (e.g., how do we use language to communicate and acquire information about our environment), information storage (how does memory operate? what can be done to assure that information reaches memory? how is information lost from memory or forgotten?), and information

use (how is our knowledge and experience with the world organized and stored? and how do we use it to interpret and understand new information?).

Although most cognitive psychologists are interested in understanding the cognitive capacities that all humans share, a number also are interested in individual differences in cognitive functioning. These psychologists examine how humans vary in the way they process information.

FIGURE 1-9 CHARLES DARWIN (1809–1882).

Darwin was a naturalist who is best known for his works on natural selection and evolution (Origin of Species, published in 1859, and The Descent of Man, published in 1871). Darwin's theories of natural selection have had an enduring influence on psychologists interested in the relationship between behavior and genetics.

Functionalist Psychology

In 1859 Charles Darwin (Figure 1-9) published his pioneering volume, *On the Origin of Species by Means of Natural Selection.* Darwin's theory of evolution emphasized the **functional** significance of biological characteristics. In Darwin's theory characteristics that confer survival value on the organism help to assure that the organism's genes and the characteristics expressed by those genes will be passed along to the next generation—a process Darwin termed **natural selection**. In his later volume on *The Expression of the Emotions in Man and Animals* (1872), Darwin further demonstrated that behaviors could be analyzed to determine their functional significance or role in promoting the survival of an organism and the reproduction of its genes. Darwin's view of behavior departed dramatically from that of the structuralists. Functional analysis emphasized overt (rather than covert), observable aspects of behavior (rather than private mental activity) and sought to determine the survival value of behaviors rather than to determine the structure of the mind and brain.

The American psychologist William James was very interested in human consciousness and was strongly influenced by the functionalist theories advanced by Darwin. James challenged Titchener's introspectionist methods and sought to establish the functions of consciousness. He wanted, for example, to understand the functional role of emotions and learning. James did not advance a well-developed research method, as did Wundt and Titchener, but articulated a point of view toward psychological questions. In contrast to the structuralist school, which fell out of favor, the functionalist school associated with James did not. The basic orientation of the functional analysis of behaviors continues to influence modern psychological thinking.

One contemporary functionalist school of research and theory that has strongly influenced psychology is **ethology**. Konrad Lorenz (Figure 1-10) is a Nobel prizewinning biologist (he won the prize in 1973) who has championed the functional analysis of behaviors. Lorenz argues that

THE SOCIOBIOLOGICAL PERSPECTIVE

A contemporary functionalist perspective on behavior—also strongly influenced by Darwin's evolutionary theories—has been termed **sociobiology**. Perhaps the best known advocate of this theory is zoologist Edward O. Wilson, whose *Sociobiology: The New Synthesis* (1975), stirred a controversy when it was published. Wilson's provocative argument is that many behaviors, including some complex human social behaviors, are under the control of genes. The sociobiological approach emphasizes the analysis of behavior at the level of the gene. When Darwin's doctrine of natural selection is put in its starkest terms, organisms and species are both seen merely as carriers of the genes and the genetic codes that produce the characteristics of particular species. Natural selection operates to select both the physical characteristics and the behaviors that maximize the likelihood that organisms will successfully reproduce their genes.

Sociobiologists attempt to explain even complex human behaviors such as aggression and altruism in genetic terms. In very simple terms, sociobiologists argue that aggressive behaviors that assure an animal's survival (so that it can reproduce the genes that provide the basis for the aggressive behavior) are favored by natural selection. But how can altruistic or self-sacrificing behaviors serve reproductive needs? Sociobiologists answer that because all organisms share genes with their family members, altruistic acts that preserve family members even at the cost of the life of the altruist help assure the survival of the family members and, most important, assure the reproduction of the shared genes. Thus, the "selfish gene" benefits from altruistic acts that preserve family members.

every species shows characteristic patterns of behavior necessary to survival, behavior such as reproducing behavior, rearing offspring, showing aggression, and eating. These behaviors reflect the end products of evolutionary pressures and have developed as a result of natural selection. The ethological approach emphasizes the study of species within their natural environments and uses comparisons across species to determine the functional significance of behaviors.

Behaviorism

The Darwinian revolution prompted many nineteenth-century scientists (biologists, physiologists, and zoologists) to undertake investigations of animal behavior and abilities. By the turn of the century, debates were raging over questions such as whether animals possessed consciousness, how much of animal behavior was innate and instinctive, whether animals learned and, if so, how. A number of psychologists also were interested in these questions. At Harvard, for example, E. L. Thorndike (Figure 1-11) was using experimental methods to study animal (particularly cat) learning and realized that animals learned from experience by associating their actions with the satisfaction or relief from annoyance produced by those actions. His early analyses of learning were reported in his *Animal Intelligence* (1898). By 1911 Thorndike had explicitly formulated his **Law of Effect**, which held that the strength of a behavioral **response** was a function of the number of times the response had been associated with a **stimulus** (any change in the environment that can be detected by an organism) and the strength and duration of the association.

FIGURE 1-10 KONRAD LORENZ (b. 1903).
An Austrian zoologist and ethologist, Lorenz has made major contributions to the study of genetic and environmental influences on behavior. He was a co-winner of the Nobel Prize for medicine/physiology in 1973. His comparative analysis of aggression in animals and humans (On Aggression, 1966) has been quite controversial.

FIGURE 1-11 EDWARD L. THORNDIKE (1874–1949).
Thorndike conducted some of the earliest experimental research on animal learning and helped lay the theoretical groundwork for the behaviorist perspective on behavior. In addition to his work with animals, he also made early contributions to mental assessment—e.g., Mental and Social Measurements, *published in 1904.*

FIGURE 1-12 IVAN PAVLOV (1849–1936).
A Russian physiologist and experimental psychologist, Pavlov received a Nobel Prize in physiology/medicine in 1904 for his research on the digestive system. His discovery of the conditioned reflex (discussed in Chapter 6) influenced the development of behaviorism.

FIGURE 1-13 JOHN B. WATSON (1878–1958).
Watson drew upon early learning research to found the school of thought known as behaviorism. His emphasis on the study of behavior through observation and his rejection of the study of consciousness and mind contributed to the downfall of introspectionist methods. Though Watson spent most of his career outside the academic world, his contributions to psychology were recognized by a gold medal awarded by the American Psychological Association in 1957.

At about the same time in Russia, the physiologist Ivan Pavlov (Figure 1-12) also was conducting research on animal learning, and gradually his writings found their way to the United States. The work of learning researchers such as Thorndike and Pavlov had a major influence on a young psychologist at Johns Hopkins University. That psychologist, John B. Watson (Figure 1-13), is generally credited with founding, almost singlehandedly, one of the most influential schools of modern psychology: **behaviorism**. Watson had started his education in philosophy, but while studying at the University of Chicago he grew interested in animal learning. In 1913 Watson published a short paper titled "Psychology as the Behaviorist Views It," which profoundly influenced the course of psychology. In that and later writings, Watson adopted a radically functionalist approach to behavior, strongly rejected the introspectionist approach to psychology, and argued vehemently that only directly observable behavior was the proper subject for psychological study. To Watson, consciousness, the mind, and mental activity were the wrong things to study. Indeed, he denied that these things existed except as mirrors of overt behavior and reduced them to muscular behavior. Mental activity or thinking, he said, was simply silent talking to the self. It used the same muscles as talking, but on a miniature scale. Indeed, one of the enduring contributions to general psychology of Watson's learning theories is the emphasis on clear and measurable definitions of abstract ideas.

Watson's position was quickly embraced by large numbers of American psychologists who began to study the relationship between the **stimuli** presented to people and other animals, and the **responses** to those stimuli. In the 1930s behaviorism acquired a new champion in the person of B. F. Skinner (Figure 1-14). Skinner originally wanted to be a writer (and in fact has become a highly successful one) but grew frustrated with his early efforts. After reading Watson's work, Skinner returned to graduate school at Harvard, where he earned a Ph.D. in experimental psychology in 1931. Over the next half century, Skinner produced a tremendous volume of research and other writings. He,

THE LEARNING AND BEHAVIORAL PERSPECTIVES

Behaviorists today still are interested in understanding how organisms learn behavior. They are primarily interested in overt behavior, rather than mental operations that cannot be observed, and in the relationships between an organism's actions and the feedback provided to the organism by its environment. Research on the physiological bases of learning is left to other researchers, for behaviorists are more intrigued by the problem of describing the lawful manner in which an organism's behavior is shaped by its environment. (Chapter 6 provides a detailed discussion of learning.) Learning theories explain how simple and complex organisms learn simple and complex behaviors.

more than any other behaviorist, supplied both the theoretical and scientific substance of behaviorism. Skinner strongly endorsed the basic tenets of Watson's behaviorism such as the emphasis on **observable** behavior and on the role of learning in behavior. Skinner's key contributions to behaviorism have been the principles of **operant conditioning**, which, as we shall see in Chapter 6, provides a broad set of theoretical and applied insights into learning.

Psychoanalysis

Sigmund Freud (Figure 1-15) is the man who almost singlehandedly established the **psychoanalytic** school. Freud was trained as a physician and maintained a private practice in clinical neurology in Vienna. He would, today, be called a psychiatrist. Freud's thinking about human behavior was profoundly influenced by the psychological difficulties or **psychopathologies** presented to him by his patients. Freud explored a variety of methods to treat the problems he encountered. In some of his early work, he used hypnosis. Freud came to believe that some symptoms (for example, paralysis of a limb or blindness in the absence of any physical causes) occurred because patients had failed to fully experience earlier traumatic events (such as rejection by a parent) and instead had

FIGURE 1-14 B(URRHUS) F(REDERIC) SKINNER (b. 1904). The leading exponent of behaviorism and the experimental analysis of behavior, Skinner has been a prolific writer. He has produced scholarly volumes on his learning theories (e.g., The Behavior of Organisms, *published in 1938, and* Verbal Behavior, *1957), popular volumes explaining his theories to the general public (e.g.,* Science and Human Behavior, *1957), and even a work of fiction (*Walden Two, *1948) that was strongly influenced by his learning theories.*

FIGURE 1-15 SIGMUND FREUD (1856–1939). An Austrian psychiatrist, Freud spent the early years of his medical career treating patients suffering from hysteria. His experiences convinced him these patients were the victims of early traumas that had been pushed from consciousness. Freud developed not only methods to treat hysteria but also a very broad theory of human development and behavior that had a profound influence on psychology, psychiatry, and other fields during the first half of the twentieth century. Among his many important works are The Interpretation of Dreams *(1900),* The Ego and the Id *(1923), and* New Introductory Lectures on Psychoanalysis *(1933).*

FIGURE 1-16   ABRAHAM MASLOW (1908–1970).

Maslow emphasized normal rather than abnormal development. He studied successful and well-adjusted individuals in an effort to determine how therapists could assist others to become fully "self-actualized." His Toward a Psychology of Being *(1969) describes what it is like to be self-actualized.*

FIGURE 1-17   CARL ROGERS (b. 1902).

Like Maslow, Rogers emphasizes the personal growth of his clients. Rogers advocates "client-centered therapy" (the title of his 1951 book) in which the therapist assists the client in the client's search for increased self-regard and self-respect.

pushed the trauma out of their conscious experience. Instead of experiencing and adjusting to these traumas, the patients were wasting psychic energy on keeping the memories unconscious. Because the traumatic events could not be readily brought to consciousness by the patients, Freud tried to help them through hypnosis. Later, Freud abandoned hypnosis and instead adopted a method of **free association**—the uncensored reporting of thoughts as they occur—which he believed would help him to guide the patient in uncovering the traumatic memories.

Freud ultimately developed an elaborate theory concerning the structure, development, and relationships between the conscious and unconscious minds. He was very interested in the instinctual side of mental life (which he associated with that part of unconscious mental energy he called the **id**), in how instinctual needs are governed by the development of a conscience (the **superego**, which reflects the rules of society), and in how the conflicts between id and superego are managed by the conscious, integrating aspect of the mind (the self or **ego**).

Humanist Psychology

Most psychologists work with the scientific assumption that human behavior is caused by an interaction of environmental and internal factors that can be discovered through systematic study. This perspective implies that humans do not possess "free will." Most psychologists probably feel a certain amount of conflict between the scientific assumption that human behavior is entirely determined and the personal sense that we all make choices. Some psychologists have been troubled by the implications of deterministic scientific assumptions and have chosen to emphasize an alternative view of human psychology. In the humanistic or existentialist perspective on human behavior, what is important and valuable about people is such things as their self-determination, experiences, feelings, problems, and their potential to enjoy a fulfilling life.

Abraham Maslow (Figure 1-16) called this perspective the "third force" in an effort to distinguish it from behaviorism and psychoanalysis. Maslow and Carl Rogers (Figure 1-17) are two psychologists whose work has significantly advanced the humanist perspective. Maslow emphasized the concept of "self-actualization" and sought methods that would allow psychologists to help people to realize their potential. In contrast to Freud's emphasis on internal conflicts between the instinctual forces of the id and the superego, Maslow emphasized the positive aspects of human nature and believed that people are good and responsible, and innately wish to improve.

Carl Rogers has long endorsed a perspective similar to Maslow's. Rogers' influence has probably been most profound in settings where psychologists counsel others. Rogers believes that it is important for counselors to help *clients* (not "patients," for Rogers strongly rejects a medical model for counseling) to define themselves rather than to impose definitions or interpretations on the clients. Rogers has termed his approach to counseling **client-centered therapy** to emphasize that it is the client's view of himself or herself and the world that matter and that the therapist must see the world through the client's eyes.

THE CLINICAL PERSPECTIVE

Freud, Maslow, and Rogers conducted much of their research and theoretical work in clinical settings, where they worked with patients and clients seeking assistance for psychological problems. Many psychologists work and conduct research in clinical settings such as hospitals, community health centers, private clinics, and clinical research centers. Many other clinical psychologists offer psycho-

therapy in private practice. Many clinicians conduct research on and offer therapy for a wide range of cognitive and behavioral problems. These problems range from speech and cognitive deficiencies produced by causes such as birth defects, disease, aging, and traumatic injury to debilitating psychological disturbances such as depression and schizophrenia, adjustment problems produced by life events such as job loss, the death of family members, and physical illness. Throughout this text we will draw upon research and theories developed

in clinical settings. This research is important first of all because it often offers patients hope of recovery. Second, the research is important because it often provides insights into normal functioning. We will see, for instance, that clinical research with brain-damaged patients has helped us understand memory, language, and consciousness. We will also see that clinical research has generated promising treatments for mental disturbances such as depression and schizophrenia.

Developmental Psychology

Among the psychologists who have had the most profound influences on modern psychology is the Swiss biologist and psychologist Jean Piaget (Figure 1-18). As the director of the Jean-Jacques Rousseau Institute in Geneva, Piaget produced more than 30 books and 150 articles over a 60-year period. Piaget was interested in the ways in which children develop into adults, and his studies of children (ranging in age from newborn to late adolescence) have provided psychologists with a complex set of theories and research findings. Piaget was interested in topics ranging from language development and the development of logic, to motor development—learning to control the body as progress is made from lying to sitting, crawling, walking, and running.

Most of Piaget's work was based upon the systematic study of children. In a typical experiment, Piaget presented a child with a problem to solve. For example, Piaget was interested in the development of infants of **object constancy**—the knowledge that an object continues to exist even though it may be out of sight behind a screen (where Piaget or one of his researchers had placed it). By observing many children and their efforts to find such hidden objects, Piaget determined the age at which most children attain object constancy. As a result of huge numbers of such studies in which children were presented with all kinds of tasks and problems, Piaget formulated his theories of cognitive development. You will read about a number of such studies and Piaget's stage theories of development in Chapter 9.

FIGURE 1-18   JEAN PIAGET (1896–1980).
Piaget conducted research on cognitive development in children over a period of six decades. Piaget closely examined the patterns of adaptations children make to their environment. Among his many influential works are The Language and Thought of the Child *(1926),* The Moral Judgment of the Child *(1933), and* The Origins of Intelligence in Children *(1952).*

Social Psychology

Just as cognitive psychology is a recent development within psychology, so is social psychology. Social psychologists address questions such as why does a person like some people and not others? why do people act aggressively or altruistically? why do groups behave the way they do? and

THE DEVELOPMENTAL PERSPECTIVE

The research of Piaget is a good illustration of the developmental perspective. As Piaget's research makes clear, infants (especially human infants) bear only a crude resemblance to fully developed adults. What happens as an infant matures into an adult? Developmental psychologists tackle this question by studying physical maturation and social, emotional, and cognitive changes in individuals over the whole life span.

Some developmental psychologists study the development of the nervous system, sensation, and perception (they not only share this interest with physiological psychologists, they also share research methods). Some developmental psychologists are interested in the development of cognitive abilities (as was Piaget) and thus share research methods and theories with cognitive psychologists. Other developmentalists are interested in the acquisition of and changes in social behaviors and thus share research methods and theories with social psychologists.

Although many developmental psychologists are primarily interested in children, not all are. In recent years there has been rapid growth in the study of adult development. It has become increasingly clear that maturation does not simply end at puberty (sexual maturation) or at some particular age. Contemporary developmental research is life-span oriented, and developmental psychologists are just as interested in psychological development in the elderly as they are in psychological development of the child.

FIGURE 1-19 KURT LEWIN (1890–1947).

Lewin was trained in Germany and his social psychological theories were heavily influenced by Gestalt psychology. Lewin spent the final years of his career in the United States. His work emphasized applied social psychology.

how do social and cultural factors influence individual and group behavior?

Experimental study of social behavior is sometimes traced back to Norman Triplett of Indiana University, who initiated research on how the presence of groups benefited an individual's performance, a process called **social facilitation**. Others like to point to Floyd H. Allport, a Harvard psychologist, whose 1924 book *Social Psychology* was influenced by behaviorism and elaborated on Triplett's research.

Social psychologists also credit Kurt Lewin (Figure 1-19) with a major role in shaping modern social psychology. Lewin was born in Germany and was heavily influenced by the Gestalt psychologists with whom he studied. After Lewin fled Nazi Germany, he taught at Cornell, Iowa, and the Massachusetts Institute of Technology. Lewin was interested in practical social problems such as the effects of prejudice, the behavior of small groups, and industrial psychology. Lewin's students have made significant contributions to social psychology.

Lewin's students produced some of the most important social psychological research of the 1950s and 1960s as they applied Lewin's theories and methods. Their research included the study of attitudes and attitude change—especially examining the ways in which people resolve inconsistencies in their attitudes; studies of social influences on people's interpretation of their emotional arousal; exploration of the relationships between groups and deviant group members; and work on social inferences—the attributions people make based on their observations of other people's behavior.

The research conducted by Lewin and his students helped to launch what has come to be a major body of social psychological research on social perception, social memory, and social judgment.

THE SOCIAL PSYCHOLOGICAL PERSPECTIVE

Social psychologists are also interested in social and cultural influences on nonsocial behavior. Among the topics that have received the greatest attention from social psychologists over the last half-century are the formation and change of attitudes and their relationship to behavior; interpersonal attraction; leadership and social influence processes; group behavior; aggression and altruism; the development of the "self"; the nature and development of moral behavior; and recently, cognitive aspects of the ways in which people perceive their social world. We will examine this research in the last two chapters of the text.

The View of This Text: Multiple Levels and Multiple Perspectives

In essence, any complex behavior can be analyzed from a number of different perspectives. Any complex behavior can be examined at the level of its constituent parts, at the level of its most global characteristics, or at an intermediate level. No level of analysis is inherently better or more informative than another, although some perspectives and some levels of analysis yield more fruitful results in the research of some phenomena rather than others. Each perspective provides different insights into a phenomenon, and each perspective is essential to the overall picture. Throughout this textbook we place special emphasis on looking at psychological phenomena from a variety of perspectives and levels, for we believe that a full understanding of psychology can be achieved only by taking a broad view of psychological theories and research.

PSYCHOLOGY AS A SCIENCE

We should emphasize that the reason we have included this test is, not to demonstrate how little you know about psychology, but to alert you to the fact that common sense and everyday experience can lead people astray when they try to understand the causes of the human behavior we observe. Part of the problem with everyday, commonsense efforts to understand the world is that they lack a number of the qualities that a true science requires. As you read this text, you will come to see that psychology is a science and how it differs, therefore, from common sense.

The Scientific Assumptions of Psychology

All scientists, psychologists included, share a number of assumptions about the world and about the way in which research ought to be conducted. Once you understand these assumptions, you will find it much easier to see how psychology is a science.

BOX 1-1
COMMON SENSE PSYCHOLOGY

Take the true and false test reproduced here and then use the scoring key at the bottom of the page to assess your performance on this test of "commonsense" psychological knowledge. This test is based on a larger test of psychological knowledge administered by Eva Vaughan to 119 students at the University of Pittsburgh. The original test had 80 items and those reproduced here were the ones on which the students performed least well—in fact, over 50% of the students answered these questions incorrectly. The number at the end of each question indicates the percentage of students who answered the question incorrectly. As you read this textbook, you will learn the correct answers to most of these questions and why the answers are correct.

____ 1. To change people's behavior toward members of ethnic minority groups, we must first change their attitudes. 92%

____ 2. Memory can be likened to a storage chest in the brain into which we deposit material and from which we can withdraw it later if needed. Occasionally, something gets lost from the "chest," and then we say we have forgotten. 87%

____ 3. The basis of the baby's love for its mother is the fact that the mother fills its physiological needs for food, etc. 84%

____ 4. The more highly motivated you are, the better you will do at solving a complex problem. 80%

____ 5. The best way to ensure that a desired behavior will persist after training is completed is to reward the behavior every single time it occurs throughout training (rather than intermittently). 77%

____ 6. A schizophrenic is someone with a split personality. 77%

____ 7. Fortunately for babies, human beings have a strong maternal instinct. 73%

____ 8. Biologists study the body; psychologists study the mind. 71%

____ 9. Psychiatrists are defined as medical people who use psychoanalysis. 67%

____ 10. Children memorize much more easily than adults. 66%

____ 11. Boys and girls exhibit no behavioral differences until environmental influences begin to produce such differences. 61%

____ 12. Genius is closely akin to insanity. 53%

____ 13. The unstructured interview is the most valid method for assessing someone's personality. 52%

____ 14. Under hypnosis, people can perform feats of physical strength which they could never do otherwise. 51%

____ 15. Children's IQ scores have very little relationship with how well they do in school. 50%

DETERMINISM Psychologists and other scientists assume that the world proceeds in an orderly and systematic fashion and that by employing the proper methods, we can come to understand that order. The **determinist** point of view holds that events are caused by other events. Through the systematic study of events and their relationships to one another, psychologists seek to establish the laws that govern behavior. Psychologists assume that if the causal laws underlying human behavior can be understood, it is possible, in principle at least, to predict all human behavior. If we were to assume that the world proceeded in a random fashion, there would be little reason to study it systematically. It is worth emphasizing that psychology is far from being able to account for (let alone predict) all human actions.

EMPIRICISM Psychology is grounded on direct observation of the world. This means that psychologists, like other scientists, understand the world by directly experiencing and testing it, an approach known as

empiricism. Psychologists collect their observations or **data** through systematic observation. Empiricism can be contrasted with other methods of studying the world that do not involve direct observation. For example, the armchair philosopher who seeks to understand the world by staying at home and thinking or reasoning about the world can rely on intuition and imagination. But because the nonempirical thinker does not subject his or her theories to testing in the real world, there is no guarantee that these theories reflect the true state of the world.

INVARIANCE   The notion of invariance is linked to that of determinism. The basic concept is that the causal relationships studied by scientists are orderly and enduring and do not change with the passage of time or changes in location. You can imagine the consternation that would result if—all other conditions being the same—the outcome of chemical reactions changed each time an experiment was carried out. You can readily see the importance of invariance in the operation of our senses. Imagine our consternation if an everyday object such as a house or a person produced dramatically different experiences in different people or if the same object produced dramatically different experiences in the same person from one occasion to the next. Clearly our ability to function in the world depends on everyone sharing generally similar experiences when confronted by similar events and objects and also requires that we repeatedly and reliably recognize familiar events and objects.

The concept of invariance in causal relationships leads us to predict, for example, that the social or other behaviors we observe in one social setting will be the same as the behaviors in another social setting, but only if all other conditions are equal. If something about the setting changes, the effects on behavior should also be lawful or invariant. Just as chemists have determined the effects that changes in temperature will have upon chemical reactions, social psychologists are working hard to determine the effects that changes in social culture and the social environment (including such aspects of the environment as temperature!) have on social behavior. In both chemistry and social psychology, the causal laws are presumed to remain constant: if the same chemicals or social settings are involved, the changes in temperature should invariably produce the same chemical or social reactions. As you will see later, psychologists use certain research methods precisely because they can control conditions so that invariant causal relationships can be detected.

OPERATIONISM   Often psychologists are interested in very abstract concepts such as motivation, depression, anxiety, obedience to authority, and love. But these concepts mean different things to different people. One of the major tasks confronting a research psychologist is to find definitions that are not only widely acceptable to others, but definitions that allow reliable scientific observation and measurement. Operationism refers to the scientific method of specifying how concepts can be observed and measured.

Operational definitions are definitions that specify how a concept is to be measured. If, for example, we are interested in assessing whether two people love one another, we might operationally define love in terms of the amount of time two people spend together, the extent to which they say they like one another, the strength of their desire to live together, the extent to which they share resources, and so on. Notice that psychologists *can* measure all of these. They can count the hours that people in love spend together. They can ask them specific questions about their liking one another. Part of the creativity of psychology rests in the imaginative ways in which psychologists have taken complex aspects of human behavior and devised operational definitions that allow systematic study of that behavior.

OBJECTIVITY All scientists including psychologists seek to maintain an objective approach to their work. As a practical matter, objectivity means a variety of things. It means that psychologists attempt to devise theories, make predictions, collect, analyze, and interpret data in a fair and impartial manner. Scientists make concerted efforts to assure that their preconceptions about human behavior and their personal beliefs and experiences do not shape their work. Ideally, psychology should proceed in a manner that is understood by and acceptable to all other scientists regardless of their personal beliefs and expectations. Thus an objective assessment of love should be acceptable to scientists who personally believe that people should not commit themselves to living together outside of marriage, as well as to scientists who personally believe the opposite.

Not all of psychology proceeds along a strictly objective path. All psychologists have had personal experiences that cause them to be interested in some problems and not others. All psychologists find some theories more credible than other theories, and some psychologists have theories in which they have personal investments (at least investments of pride). All psychologists are trained in some methods of research, but not others, and in some theories but not others. Psychologists' training and experiences influence the types of questions they pose, the methods they use to seek answers, and the interpretations they give to findings. Despite these obstacles, all psychologists strive for objectivity. Much of training to be a psychologist is concerned with learning to formulate operational definitions; learning methods of data collection, measurement, and analysis; and studying how to develop and test theories in ways that help psychologists to maintain an objective stance toward their work.

Scientific Goals of Psychology

Although almost all psychologists would readily acknowledge that they study behavior because they find it intrinsically interesting, as scientists, psychologists possess a set of goals that are more important than satisfying their personal interests. The scientific apparatus we have been discussing is really directed toward four basic goals: description, explanation, prediction, and control. These goals can be thought of as a kind of hierarchy that describes how far a science has progressed.

DESCRIPTION A basic task confronting the psychologist who is interested in a new problem or phenomenon is that of describing what the problem or phenomenon is. The importance of accurate description can be illustrated by reference to the physical sciences, in which some of the most important early advances consisted of systematic descriptions or taxonomies. Physics and chemistry were significantly advanced by the insights provided by the periodic table of elements. Biology and paleontology were advanced by the development of classification systems for plants and animals. Medicine was advanced dramatically by the descriptive work of early anatomists.

Similarly, within psychology major advances in the understanding (and, later, prediction and control) of important aspects of human behavior have depended on accurate descriptions. For example, it was only after psychologists undertook the task of systematically observing and collecting facts about mental illness—its incidence, its symptoms, its response or lack of response to therapies—that they could detect and tentatively classify types of mental illness (see Figure 13-1). The objective of the descriptive phase of research is to observe a phenomenon systematically and to identify, collect, and systematize the facts that characterize the phenomenon.

EXPLANATION   Once a phenomenon has been systematically described, researchers can tackle the problem of explaining it. Once they observe a pattern of relationships, that is, that certain behaviors or characteristics occur together, they may begin to investigate causal relationships. Their central objective is to establish the causal relationships that produce the patterns they observe. Although their early explanations may be tentative, these initial explanations are essential to the understanding of a phenomenon.

PREDICTION   A good scientific theory is one that makes accurate predictions. The theory must also be falsifiable. This means that it must be *possible* to test the theory and determine whether its predictions are correct or incorrect. If theories did not make testable predictions, it would be impossible for researchers to prove that defective or inadequate theories are wrong. The rejection of poor theories makes it possible—indeed, necessary—to develop better theories. A psychological theory must make specific predictions about what behaviors will occur under a specific set of conditions. Furthermore, the conditions and the behavior must be observable and measurable. If we have conducted a test properly and the predicted behavior occurs, confidence in the theory is increased. As we shall see, however, it is important to recognize that the theory might have made the "right" prediction even though the theory is not entirely correct. If a test has been conducted properly but the predicted behavior does *not* occur, confidence in the theory is shaken, and it may be the time to go back to the explanation stage and reformulate the theory.

In some areas of psychology, predictive accuracy is still limited. For instance, psychologists cannot often accurately predict the social or emotional behavior of individuals in particular situations. We still, for example, cannot accurately predict the school achievement of a 20-year-old from the intelligence test administered when he was 1 year old, and we cannot predict whether the people who are in love today will still be in love next year. However, there also are many areas of psychology—for example, certain domains of physiology, cognition, learning, and clinical psychology—where knowledge and theories are sufficiently well developed to allow for accurate predictions. Indeed, in some areas of psychology our knowledge is sufficiently deep and our theories sufficiently well developed that it can be argued that psychologists are realizing the fourth goal of science: control.

CONTROL At first thought the notion of scientists in control of behavior may be rather menacing. It may conjure images of mad dictatorial doctors or human clones existing in a heartless "brave new world." But psychologists' interests in controlling behavior are far more benign than these images. Just as meteorologists are working hard to develop detailed theories of weather that will allow them to make accurate, long-term forecasts and ultimately help them exercise control over the weather, psychologists are working to find ways to constructively control human behaviors. Just as it would help humankind for meteorologists to find ways to relieve droughts and predict devastating storms, it would help if psychologists could find ways to relieve mental illness, help people to change their destructive and dangerous behavior—stop smoking, lose weight, and the like—reduce international hostilities, and foster cooperation.

How do psychologists realize these lofty goals? How do psychologists avoid the pitfalls of commonsense reasoning? By adopting scientific methods of theory building and research (see Appendix A), scientists can describe, explain, predict, and control. In the remaining chapters of this book we take a close-up look at psychologists' scientific theories and research findings.

SUMMARY

THE DEVELOPMENT OF MODERN PSYCHOLOGY

1. *Levels of Analysis in Psychology.* Psychologists study behavior from a variety of levels of analysis. Some psychologists examine behavior at a molecular level where they examine the smallest elements or units that make up the behavior. Thus, their contribution to the study of thinking might concentrate on the biochemistry of the brain and the role of neurons in thinking. Psychologists who approach thinking from a molar level might be interested in how people acquire and make use of knowledge and how language and social experiences influence thinking.

2. *Perspectives within Psychology.* Although psychology has its roots in ancient philosophy, it has been little more than a century since researchers first began applying scientific methods to the study of behavior. The first scientific breakthroughs were produced by physiologists who sought to understand the operation of the nervous system and its role in perception. The legacy of this early research is the **physiological perspective**, which emphasizes the role of chemical and biological processes in behavior. Early efforts to explore the structure of mental experiences and perception have given way to the **cognitive perspective** and its emphasis on how information is acquired, stored, and used. A legacy of the early functionalist analysis of behavior is the contemporary **sociobiological perspective**, which emphasizes the influence of genes on behavior. The pioneering theories of John Watson and B. F. Skinner continue to play an important role in the **learning and behavioral perspective**.

Sigmund Freud's psychoanalytic theory, his methods, and his emphasis on psychopathology had a broad influence on psychology and particularly helped to shape the **clinical perspective** on normal and abnormal functioning. The **developmental perspective** also takes a broad view of behavior and changes over the life span. Developmental psychologists are interested in changes in such diverse areas as perception, cognition, learning, memory, personality, and social behavior. Finally, the **social psychological perspective** examines the relationships between individual behavior and the social environment in such areas as interpersonal attestation, leadership, group behavior, aggression, and the "self."

PSYCHOLOGY AS A SCIENCE

3. *Scientific Assumptions.* Psychologists make certain basic scientific assumptions about the world. First, psychologists assume we live in a deterministic universe—that the world proceeds in an orderly and systematic fashion and that if the causal laws underlying human behavior can be understood, it is possible, in principle at least, to predict all human behavior. Psychologists are empiricists—they seek to understand the world through direct observation, measurement, and testing. Psychologists assume that the causal relationships they study are invariant. They assume, for example, that the laws of psychological nature are invariant and if "all other conditions are the same," behavior will be same. Psychologists subscribe to operationism. Even though psychologists conduct research on abstract problems such as "love" and "stress," they use operational definitions of these abstract constructs in order to assure reliable measurement and reproducibility. Psychologists assume that the most effective way to learn the truth about behavior is to proceed objectively. Psychologists strive to assure that their preconceptions about human behavior and their personal beliefs and experiences do not shape their work.

4. *Scientific Goals of Psychology.* Scientific psychological research is directed to four goals. First, psychologists seek to adequately describe the phenomena they are interested in. Second, once adequate descriptions have been made, psychologists look for patterns and relationships in their observations. These patterns aid psychologists in the detection of causal relationships and help them to explain the phenomena they observe. Third, psychologists formulate testable theories and predictions about the world. When tests confirm predictions, confidence in the theories is enhanced. Finally, psychologists draw upon their theories in order to help people control undesirable behaviors and promote desirable behaviors.

FURTHER READINGS

There are a number of volumes on the history of psychology that provide an overview of the development of modern psychology and the contributions made by individual psychologists. These volumes include *A History of Modern Psychology* (4th Ed.) by Duane Schultz and Sydney Schultz (1987); *A Brief History of Psychology* (3rd Ed.) by Michael Wertheimer (1987); and *A History of Psychology* by Howard Kendler (1987). Volumes with somewhat different approaches to the history of psychology include *Three Psychologies: Perspectives from Freud, Skinner, and Rogers* (3rd Ed.) by Robert Nye (1986) and *The Lewin Legacy* by Eugene Stivers and Susan Wheelan (1986).

To complement the chapter's materials on psychological theories and research perspectives, readers might turn to any of several volumes, such as *Theories and Systems of Psychology* by Robert Lunden (1987); and *Systems and Theories in Psychology* (4th Ed.) by Melvin Marx and William Hillix (1986). A most interesting approach to the history of psychology can be found in *A Source Book in the History of Psychology* edited by Richard Herrnstein and Edwin Boring—the volume contains commentary and excerpts from the writings of many of the psychologists mentioned in this chapter.

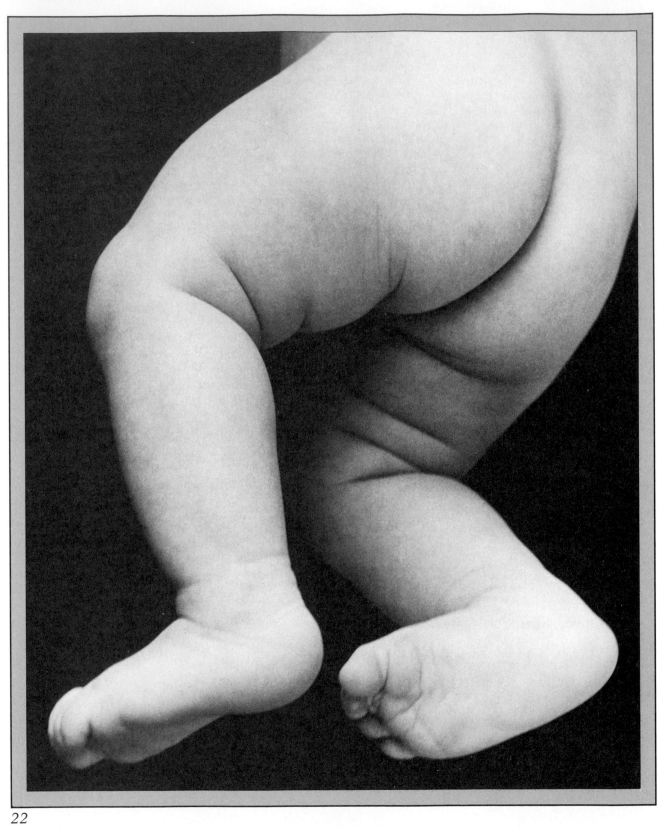

2

BIOLOGICAL FOUNDATIONS

The human brain is an awe-inspiring organ (see Figure 2-1). Your brain, along with the rest of your nervous system, controls everything that you sense, think, feel, and do. As you read these words, the activity of nerve cells in your brain interprets and gives meaning to the patterns of light that make up the letters on the page. As you think about what you have just read, the activity of your nerve cells is the basis of your thoughts and conclusions. As you feel emotions—love, hate, aggression, kindness—your feelings all are controlled by the brain. When you make a decision or carry out an action, it is your brain that determines what you do.

Even so, is it really necessary to know how the brain works to understand human thought and behavior? Some psychologists believe that the answer is no. They argue that a person (or other organism) can be considered a sealed "black box." By formulating appropriate psychological laws, psychologists should be able to predict what comes out of the black box (thought and behavior) on the basis of what goes in (past experiences, the present environment, and so forth). They argue that psychologists needn't be concerned with what happens inside.

But today most psychologists do not subscribe to this view of the organism as black box. They hold that to understand thought and behavior, they must know how the brain and nervous system work. For example, take the severe mental disorder known as schizophrenia. Schizophrenia is characterized by incoherent and illogical thought, delusions, hallucinations, and personality disturbances (see Chapter 13). Not long ago psychologists believed that schizophrenia had its roots in abnormal experiences, especially during childhood. For example, they believed that certain kinds of behavior by parents led to schizophrenia in children. But recent research has shown that schizophrenia is primarily a disease of the brain. Strong evidence suggests that some of the symptoms of schizophrenia arise from chemical imbalances in the brain (Snyder, 1982; Kornhuber, 1983). These imbalances lead to abnormal activity among nerve cells and, therefore, thought disorders. Other symptoms of schizophrenia appear to be due to brain damage (Seidman, 1983). Psychologists also know now that a tendency to acquire schizophrenia is transmitted genetically (Crowe, 1982; McGue, Gottesman, and Rao, 1986), a finding that tells them that the brain abnormalities are not caused exclusively by the environment. Past and present experiences do play a role in the development of schizophrenia, just as they do in normal thought and behavior. But we can fully understand normal and abnormal behavior only if we understand both biological and environmental influences.

In Chapter 1, you saw that the physiological bases of behavior offer psychologists an important perspective on human thought and action. In this chapter, you will get the biological foundation you need to understand phenomena such as sensation and perception, learning, memory, and psychopathology when they are discussed from a physiological perspective in the chapters that follow. We begin with a general overview of how the nervous system is organized.

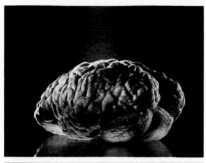

FIGURE 2-1 THE HUMAN BRAIN.
The front of the brain is to the left. The adult human brain is only 6 to 7.5 inches long and weighs only about 2.5 to 3 pounds (Blinkov and Glezer, 1968). But it and the rest of the nervous system control everything that people sense, think, feel, and do.

OVERVIEW OF THE NERVOUS SYSTEM

You can think of the nervous system as a complex integrating mechanism. On the basis of a person's past and present experience (inputs), the nervous system produces behavior (outputs). These outputs, or observable behaviors, are produced by **effectors** (see Table 2-1). Effectors are muscles and glands that make it possible for people to affect their world—to walk, talk, throw a ball, become excited or calm, and so on. The effectors with the most obvious effects are the *striated muscles.* These muscles make the skeleton move—arms lift, legs run, head turn, and so on. *Cardiac muscles,* another group of effectors, are the muscles of the heart and produce its rhythmic beating. *Smooth muscles* are the effectors that produce movement and contractions of a person's internal organs. They help the stomach and intestines digest food, make the blood vessels expand and contract, and so on. Closely coordinated with the effector muscles are the *glands,* effectors that release certain chemicals into the bloodstream and body. The most important of these are the *endocrine glands,* which secrete hormones into the bloodstream. By controlling effectors, the nervous system controls everything we do.

The nervous system gets its inputs from specialized **sensory receptors** that are inside the body and on its surface. As Table 2-1 shows, there are three broad classes of sensory receptors. You probably are most familiar with the receptors that make up your five major senses, the *exteroceptors.* These provide your nervous system with sensory information about the external world—about light, sound, touch, smell, and taste. *Propriocep-*

TABLE 2-1 THE NERVOUS SYSTEM INTEGRATES INPUTS AND PRODUCES BEHAVIOR

Receptors ⟶ (Information Input)	Integrative ⟶ Mechanisms	Effectors (Produce Observable Behavior)

1. Exteroceptors
  a. olfactory (smell)
  b. gustatory (taste)
  c. visual (sight)
  d. auditory (sound)
  e. somatic (skin senses)
2. Proprioceptors
  a. kinesthetic (muscles, tendons, and joints)
  b. vestibular (static position and movement of head)
3. Interoceptors (internal body organs)
	1. Nervous System
	  a. central nervous system
	  b. peripheral nervous system
		1. Striated muscle
		2. Cardiac muscle
		3. Smooth muscle
		4. Glands

Note: Sensory receptors provide information to the integrative mechanisms of the nervous system. The nervous system controls effectors, which produce observable behavior.

FIGURE 2-2 ORGANIZATION OF THE NERVOUS SYSTEM.

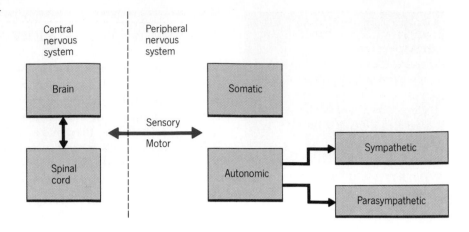

tors provide information to your nervous system about the actions of your body itself, such as the positions of your arms and legs, of your body in space, and of your head in relation to your body and surroundings. Finally, *interoceptors* provide your nervous system with information about internal body events, such as your blood pressure or the amounts of certain chemicals in your blood. In effect, receptors and their connections with the nervous system bring people all of their knowledge and experience of the world. The nervous system combines and integrates information about past and present inputs and, on the basis of this information, produces outward behavior. People's memories, thoughts, emotions, and many other mental events that cannot be outwardly observed are part of this process of integration.

The nervous system has two main parts (see Figure 2-2). The **central nervous system** consists of the brain and spinal cord—everything inside the bony protection of the skull and spine (vertebral column) (see Figure 2-3). The **peripheral nervous system** consists of the rest of the nervous system, distributed throughout the body. The peripheral nervous system forms the link between receptors, the central nervous system, and effectors. Thus, the peripheral nervous system contains *sensory neural pathways* that bring information from receptors to the spinal cord and brain and *motor neural pathways* that send information from the spinal cord and brain to effectors.

The peripheral nervous system itself has two main parts, the *somatic nervous system* and the *autonomic nervous system* (see Figure 2-2). Both the somatic and autonomic divisions have sensory and motor connections with the central nervous system. They differ in the organs that they contact and control in the body. The somatic system carries sensory information from exteroceptors and proprioceptors (for example, eyes, skin, muscles, and joints) and sends motor commands to the striated muscles. This system controls voluntary movements as well as involuntary adjustments of balance and posture. It controls the muscles that let you take notes in class, put on your coat, and stand without toppling over. In contrast, the autonomic system consists of sensory and motor pathways that connect primarily with internal organs of the body. This system

FIGURE 2-3   THE BRAIN INSIDE THE SKULL OF A LIVING HUMAN.
The picture was taken with magnetic resonance imaging, and shows the brain as if a slice were made down the middle from front to back. The top of the spinal cord inside the spine also is visible.

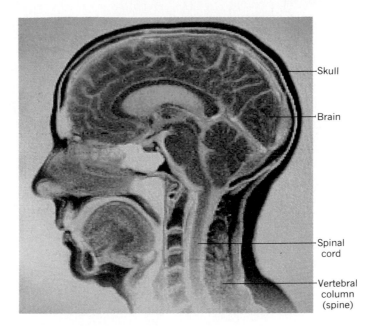

Skull

Brain

Spinal cord

Vertebral column (spine)

controls the movements of smooth and cardiac muscles as well as the release of chemicals from glands. It controls the digestion of food after lunch and the pounding of your heart if you are startled. The autonomic nervous system is further divided into the *sympathetic* and *parasympathetic* divisions. In general, the sympathetic division is active when you are expending energy. For example, it is active when you turn to fight an enemy or when you run away from that enemy, the so-called fight or flight response. The parasympathetic division helps your body to conserve energy, as, for example, when you are eating.

OF MAN AND BEAST

How Do They Compare?

We humans differ in thought and behavior from even our nearest relatives in the animal kingdom. We speak complex languages, we manipulate symbols, and we exert control over our environment far more profoundly than any other animal. The physiology of the brains of humans and other species helps to explain many of these differences. It also helps to explain many of the similarities in behavior—breathing, the sense of smell, the perception of light, the control of movement, and so on—that extend all along the evolutionary chain.

The brains of animals of different species differ in many ways. One difference is *size* (see Figure 2-4). The human brain is about 700 times larger than the rat brain, for example. But we humans should not feel too smug. Some species, including elephants, whales, and porpoises, have brains that are larger than ours (Blinkov and Glezer, 1968). The biological factor that is most clearly related to brain size is body size, especially the area of the body surface (Herschel, 1972). The larger the

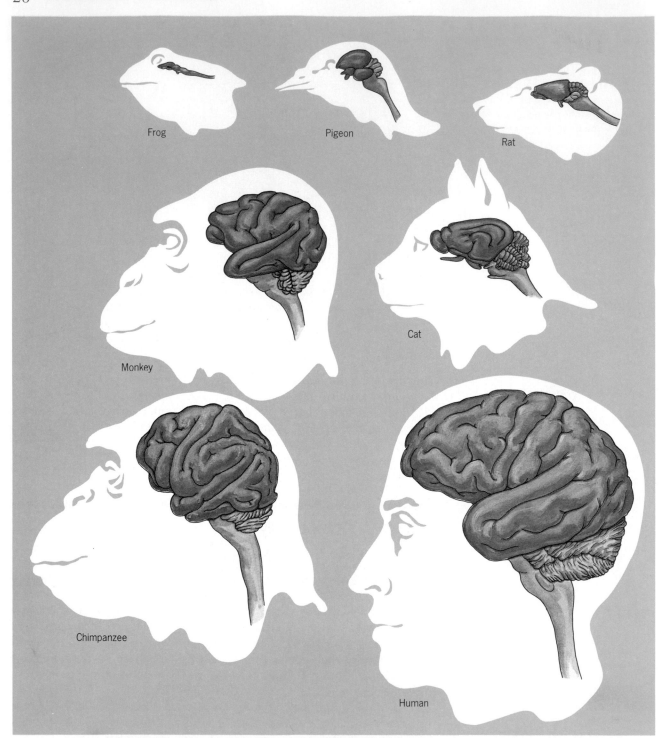

Frog

Pigeon

Rat

Monkey

Cat

Chimpanzee

Human

FIGURE 2-4   THE BRAINS OF SEVERAL VERTEBRATE SPECIES. All are drawn to the same scale. Notice that the brains of different species differ in size and in the extent to which the surface is wrinkled, or convoluted. However, the overall organization is very similar among species. (After Rosenzweig and Leiman, 1982.)

area of body (with all its receptors and effectors) to be controlled, the larger the brain to control it.

The *appearance* of the brain also differs among animal species. For instance, in humans and other primates, the brain is covered with grooves and wrinkles, called *convolutions*. But in animals such as rats and birds, the brain is essentially smooth (see Figure 2-4). As you will see a little later, a convoluted brain means that more surface area and, therefore, more brain cells, can fit into the skull.

Despite these and other differences among the brains of different species, animal brains also have marked similarities. For example, the overall organization of the brain is very similar in all vertebrates (animals with bony vertebral columns). Similarities to even very small subdivisions and structures of the human brain appear in the brains of other animals. The more closely species are related phylogenetically (that is, along the evolutionary chain), the more similar the organization of structures in their brains. Humans, monkeys, and apes are closely related species (all are primates), and their brains are more similar to each other than to the brains of dogs, cats, and rabbits. Another remarkable similarity among different species is in the anatomy and function of the cells that make up the nervous system. Indeed, the fundamental principles of cellular function have been found to be basically the same in the squid, the earthworm, and the human.

Why Study Other Animals?

Why would scientists want to study the brains of other animal species, if their ultimate goal is to learn about *human* thought and behavior? Scientists interested in how the nervous system controls behavior study other kinds of animals for three main reasons (Bullock, 1984). First, they do so to understand the evolutionary history, or phylogenetic roots, of the human brain. They trace what is old and what is new in the human brain—what evolution has brought about.

Second, they try to discover general rules or principles of brain function. Scientists who take this approach ask two different kinds of questions: (1) What in the nervous system correlates with known behavioral differences among animals? For example, if one species is aggressive and another is passive, what differences in their brains account for the difference? (2) What kinds of behavior correlate with known differences in the brains of animals? For example, if a certain brain structure is present in humans but not in other primates, or if a brain structure is larger in one species than another, how do these differences relate to behavior?

Third, scientists study the nervous systems of other animals to obtain information that is impossible to obtain from humans. Many studies that, for technical or ethical reasons, cannot be carried out in humans can be conducted in other animals. Animals provide scientists with "model systems" in which to address questions about how the human nervous system works because the nervous systems of humans and other animals are so much alike. Thus, much of what scientists know about how cells of the nervous system function originally has come from studies of the squid, leech, and frog. The basic findings then have been verified in mammals, including primates, and scientists have inferred that the cells work the same way in humans. Similarly, much of what they know about the functions of different areas of the brain comes from studies of rats, cats, and monkeys.

Without studies of other animals, scientists still would be in the Dark Ages in their understanding of how the nervous system controls both normal and abnormal behavior. They also would be in the dark about how to treat nervous systems that are functioning abnormally (see Gay, 1986). Let us turn now to some of what scientists have uncovered about the cells of the nervous system.

CELLS OF THE NERVOUS SYSTEM

The entire nervous system, with its incredible ability to govern thought and behavior, is made up of nerve cells (or neurons) and their supporting cells. All of the functions of the nervous system are the result of fine orchestration of these specialized cells.

Neurons

The **neurons** are the basic units of communication within the nervous system. They send information to and from the effectors and receptors and from place to place within the brain and spinal cord. Figure 2-5 shows a photograph of some neurons. The human brain contains an estimated 100 *billion* of these cells.

Although neurons come in many shapes and sizes, they all have the same basic structure (see Figure 2-6). The *cell body* contains a nucleus and many other tiny internal structures (or organelles) that regulate the life and chemical activities of the neuron. Cell bodies may range in size from 10 to 100 microns in diameter (one micron is one thousandth of a millimeter). Radiating from the cell body are many fine fibers called *dendrites* (from the Greek *dendron*, which means "tree"). The main function of dendrites is to receive information from other neurons. A fine fiber called an *axon*, also projects from the cell body. The axon carries information from the cell body to other neurons. The axons of some cells go only a short distance—a few microns or so—to a nearby neuron. Other axons are very long. For instance, some neurons in the human brain send their axons all the way to the end of the spinal cord—a distance of 3 feet (or more in a tall person)! Try imagining a fishing rod with a 4-inch diameter reel (the cell body) and a 2 mile long line (the axon), and you'll have an idea of the relative size of these long axons and their cell bodies. The axon is part of the neuron's communication system that transfers information outward; the dendrites are the parts of the neuron's communication system that mainly transfer information inward.

Many axons, especially the longer ones, are covered with fatty sheaths made up of a substance called *myelin*. Myelin is made of supporting cells

FIGURE 2-5 NEURONS OF THE BRAIN.

A thin slice of tissue was prepared so that only about 5 percent of the neurons actually present are visible. Then the tissue was photographed through a microscope.

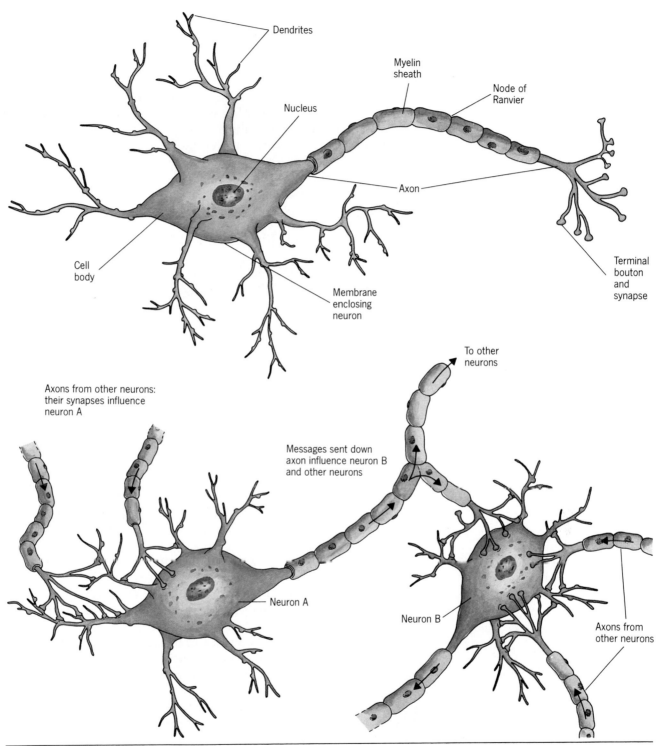

Dendrites

Myelin sheath

Node of Ranvier

Nucleus

Axon

Cell body

Membrane enclosing neuron

Terminal bouton and synapse

Axons from other neurons: their synapses influence neuron A

To other neurons

Messages sent down axon influence neuron B and other neurons

Neuron A

Neuron B

Axons from other neurons

FIGURE 2-6   NEURONS AND THEIR CONNECTIONS.
The top drawing shows a typical neuron. The bottom drawing shows how several neurons are connected to each other. Information from one or more neurons comes into the dendrites or cell body of neuron A, where processing and integration take place. Neuron A then sends the altered information down its axon to other neurons. (After Carlson, 1986.)

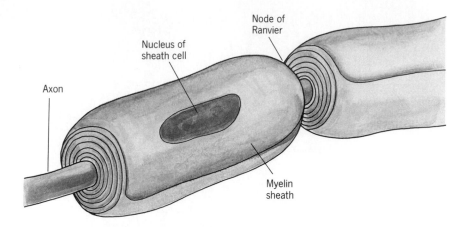

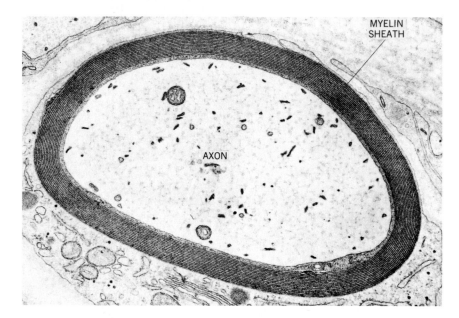

that wrap themselves around the axon (Morell and Norton, 1980) (see Figure 2-7). About every 1 to 2 millimeters along the axon, there is a bare, unmyelinated region called a *node of Ranvier.* The myelin sheaths and the nodes play an important role in the ability of axons to transmit information. We discuss this process later in the chapter.

The end of the axon usually branches many times into a treelike shape. Each branch ends in a *terminal bouton* (or terminal button). At this terminal bouton, one neuron contacts another. This point of contact is called a *synapse* (from the Greek *synapsis,* which means a conjunction or connection). A single neuron may be connected through over 100,000 synapses that come from other neurons and extend its own synaptic contacts to 1000 other neurons. The complexity of these connections— so vast that they are hard to fathom—is one reason that human nervous system function is itself so complex and richly various.

Supporting Cells

CENTRAL NERVOUS SYSTEM   The cells that support the billions of neurons of the central nervous system are called **glia**. There are about 10 times more glia than neurons (see Figure 2-8). The several types of glial cells serve several different functions (Watson, 1974; Stewart and Rosenberg, 1979). Glia provide physical support for neurons. They literally surround the neurons and help to hold them in place (whence the name *glia,* which is Greek for glue). Glia also nourish the neurons, supplying nutrients from the blood vessels and disposing of waste products. The glia also help regulate the chemical balance of the fluids that surround neurons.

Another important function of glia is to clean up the debris when neurons die. Many neurons die during the normal course of development and during aging (see Chapter 9). In addition some neurons are killed by head injuries and disease. Certain kinds of glia move into the area of brain damage, engulf debris from the dead neurons, and digest it. If the brain damage is large, the glia form a scar and wall off the area.

Certain kinds of glia also form the myelin in the central nervous system. These are the cells that wrap themselves around the axons to form the myelin sheath (see Figure 2-7). Thus glia are critical to central nervous system function.

PERIPHERAL NERVOUS SYSTEM   Just as the glia support the neurons of the central nervous system, the **satellite cells** support the neurons of the peripheral nervous system. The functions of the satellite cells are like those of glia (Peters, Palay, and Webster, 1976). For instance, one type of satellite cell, called the *Schwann cell,* forms myelin around axons in the peripheral nervous system. Like glia, Schwann cells also aid in the digestion of damaged axons.

Now that you've seen something of the cell structure of the nervous system, let's turn back to neurons and look at how they actually work.

FIGURE 2-8 GLIA AND NEURONS IN THE BRAIN.
This tissue was prepared so that all cells are visible, but only their cell bodies (not dendrites or axons) can be seen. The five large cells in the center are neurons. They are surrounded by many smaller cells, the glia (arrows). Glia constitute about 90 percent of the cells in the central nervous system and about half of the volume.

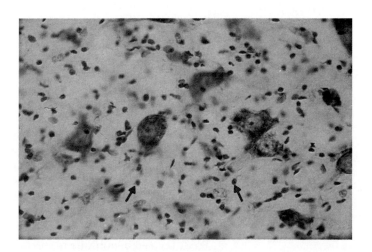

HOW NEURONS WORK

Neurons communicate with each other via electricity and chemicals. The cell body sends an electrical signal down the axon to the terminal boutons of the neuron. Then a chemical transmits information across the synaptic contact to the next neuron. In response to this chemical, the receiving neuron generates a new electrical signal and sends it down its axon, a chemical crosses the synapse to the next neuron, and so the process of communication continues millions and millions and millions of times. Many of the original discoveries about how neurons work were made by A. L. Hodgkin, A. F. Huxley, and their colleagues, who studied the giant neurons of the squid. Because some axons in the squid are as large as one millimeter in diameter, the scientists could carry out experiments that were impossible in the smaller neurons of vertebrates. In 1963, Hodgkin and Huxley received the Nobel Prize for their pioneering work. More recent research has shown that the principles they discovered hold true for the neurons of all species. Let's look in more detail at how neurons work.

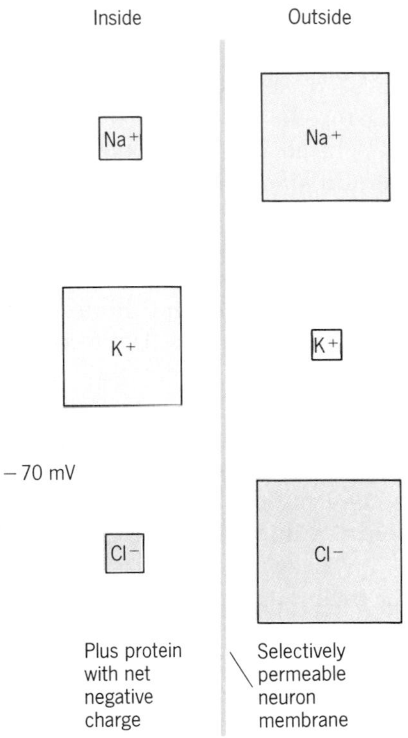

Electrical Potentials in Neurons

THE RESTING POTENTIAL   Let's begin by looking at a resting neuron—one that is not yet producing a signal. The cell body, dendrites, and axon all are enclosed within a membrane that keeps certain materials inside and keeps others out (see Figure 2-6). When scientists made measurements with tiny wires (called *microelectrodes*) placed inside and outside the neuron's membrane, they found that there is a small voltage difference, or electrical charge, across the membrane. (This voltage difference is much like that between the two terminals of a flashlight battery.) The voltage difference is referred to as an *electrical potential* because it is a potential (stored up) source of electrical energy. Because the neuron is at rest, this electrical potential is called a **resting potential**. The size of the resting potential is about -70 millivolts (a millivolt is one thousandth of a volt). In other words, the inside of the neuron is about 70 millivolts more negative than the outside. (This energy is much weaker than the 1.5 volt electrical potential present across the two terminals of a flashlight battery.)

Neurons have a resting potential because electrically charged molecules, called *ions,* are present in different concentrations inside and outside each neuron (see Figure 2-9). For example, inside the cell is a high concentration of negatively charged protein ions; outside is a high concentration of positively charged sodium ions (Na^+). The overall effect of such differences in concentrations of ions is to create a more negative charge inside the neuron than outside (the resting potential of -70 millivolts that shows in Figure 2-9).

The fluids inside and outside of the cell membrane have different concentrations of ions because of two properties of the cell membrane. First, the cell membrane is *selectively permeable*. In other words, some ions

FIGURE 2-9 IONS ARE PRESENT INSIDE AND OUTSIDE OF NEURONS.

Some of the ions are shown here: sodium (Na^+, with a positive charge), chloride (Cl^-, with a negative charge), and potassium (K^+). The size of each box represents the relative concentration (number of molecules in a standard volume of fluid) of each ion inside and outside the neuron. Also present inside the neuron are large protein molecules with a net negative charge. Because the concentrations of the ions are different inside and outside the neuron, an electrical potential is created and the neuron is about 70 millivolts more negative inside than outside.

FIGURE 2-10
CONCENTRATION AND
ELECTRICAL GRADIENTS.
(a) *The cell membrane is relatively impermeable to sodium, so sodium ions are held outside the neuron. The result is a concentration gradient for sodium across the cell membrane that pushes sodium ions into the cell. Potassium ions have a higher concentration inside the cell than outside, so these ions are pushed to the outside.* (b) *The positive charge on sodium ions attracts them into the cell (which is negatively charged). Because the membrane keeps the sodium ions out, there is an electrical gradient across the membrane. An electrical gradient pushes the positively charged potassium ions into the cell.*

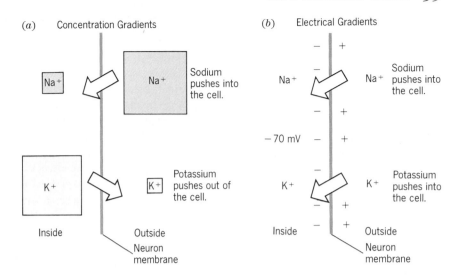

can pass through (*permeate*) it relatively freely, but others cannot. For example, the negatively charged protein and chloride (Cl^-) ions (in Figure 2-9) are stuck inside the cell; they cannot move out through the membrane. In contrast, the positively charged sodium ions move through the membrane, though with difficulty, and the potassium ions move through freely. Second, the membrane contains an active pump that continuously draws sodium ions across the membrane to outside the neuron as it draws potassium ions inside the neuron. This *sodium–potassium pump* helps regulate the concentrations of ions inside and outside the neuron.

All of these features of the neuron membrane and the ions inside and outside the neuron give rise to two gradients, or forces, across the membrane. The first is a *concentration gradient*. Ions in solution normally move from regions of high concentration to regions of low concentration, unless they meet with some barrier like a cell membrane. By analogy, imagine what happens when you squirt several drops of ink into a glass of water. The drops, with their high concentration of ink, disperse throughout the water into regions with no ink unless you prevent the dispersion with some barrier like a piece of plastic. Sodium ions around a neuron are like ink drops in that they push from their region of high concentration outside the neuron to the region of low concentration inside. But they meet a barrier, the cell membrane, which is relatively impermeable to sodium (see Figure 2-10a). The result is a relatively high concentration of sodium ions pushing into the cell under relatively strong force but being restrained from entering by the membrane. Potassium also has a concentration gradient, and it pushes out of the cell. The concentration gradient for each type of ion operates independently. The high concentration of sodium outside a cell and the force that pushes sodium in does not affect the concentration gradient for potassium that pushes it out of the cell.

The second force across the cell membrane is an *electrical gradient*. It operates on the principle that opposite electrical charges (+ and −) are attracted to each other, while similar charges (+ and +, or − and −) are repelled. Because the inside of the neuron has a negative charge of −70 millivolts, the positively charged sodium ions are attracted into the cell. But again the membrane retards this movement. The result is an electrical gradient for sodium ions across the cell membrane, and this gradient pushes sodium ions into the cell (see Figure 2-10*b*). The positively charged potassium ions also have an electrical gradient that pushes them into the cell.

You can see in Figure 2-10 that for potassium ions, the two gradients are pushing in opposite directions. The concentration gradient pushes potassium outside the cell while the electrical gradient pushes it in. These two opposing forces are almost exactly equal for potassium ions. In contrast, both the concentration and electrical gradients push sodium ions into the neuron. But sodium ions are held outside the neuron by its membrane. Sodium therefore is like a "cocked gun" ready to go off. If something should make the neuron's membrane suddenly permeable to sodium, these ions would rush into the cell. That is exactly what happens during an action potential.

THE ACTION POTENTIAL   The electrical signal that runs from the cell body down the axon of a neuron is called an **action potential**. It consists of a pulselike change in the electrical potential, or charge, across the cell membrane. The pulse lasts for only about a millisecond, a thousandth of a second.

During this thousandth of a second, the cell undergoes a sequence of two basic changes from the resting condition (see Figure 2-11). First, the cell membrane suddenly becomes permeable to sodium ions, as tiny "gates" open up and allow sodium ions to pass through channels in the membrane. As a result, the sodium ions are pushed into the cell by both the concentration and electrical gradients. This sudden influx of positively charged ions changes the voltage across the membrane from −70 millivolts (resting potential) to about +40 millivolts (action potential). After less than a millisecond, the membrane becomes relatively impermeable to sodium again: the gates close. Because the inside of the neuron now has a positive charge, the positively charged potassium ions are repelled, pushed outside the cell. This outflow of potassium ions helps to return the membrane to its normal resting potential. In fact, for a short period the electrical potential becomes slightly more negative (about −75 millivolts) than it is at rest. After several milliseconds, the membrane returns to its resting potential.

When the action potential is over, there is slightly too much sodium just inside the cell membrane and slightly too much potassium outside. These two ions return to their proper concentrations by the continuous action of the sodium–potassium pump that we mentioned earlier.

What triggers the "cocked gun"—action potential—to begin with? It is triggered whenever the voltage across the membrane is altered from −70 millivolts (resting potential) to about −60 millivolts. A smaller change in voltage won't work. The voltage across the membrane must reach a **threshold of excitation**, or the action potential won't start. When this threshold is reached, the membrane suddenly admits sodium

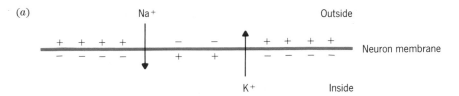

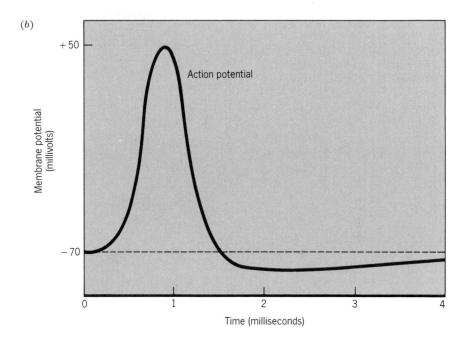

FIGURE 2-11 THE ACTION POTENTIAL.
During an action potential, the membrane's permeability to sodium increases, and sodium ions rush into the neuron (a). *As a result, the voltage in the neuron becomes positive* (b). *The positive charge repels the (positively charged) potassium ions* (a). *As the potassium ions leave the cell, the voltage inside the neuron becomes negative again* (b).

(the gates open) and the action potential is started. Once it starts, the entire sequence of events runs its course. Thus, the action potential is an *all-or-none* event. If threshold of excitation is reached, a full-blown action potential occurs. If threshold is not reached, no action potential occurs.

In their experiments, scientists trigger an action potential by applying voltages through fine wires placed near the neuron. As you will see, in nature other events bring the membrane to its threshold of excitation and start an action potential.

PROPAGATION OF THE ACTION POTENTIAL So far we have described the events that occur during an action potential at one place in a cell membrane. But what happens when one neuron communicates with another? In this case, the action potential reproduces itself over and over again—it propagates—along the length of the axon. The way this occurs differs somewhat for axons that are covered with a myelin sheath and axons that are not.

Unmyelinated Axons. Figure 2-12*a* shows how an action potential moves along an axon that lacks a myelin sheath. When the action potential occurs at one point on the membrane, as we have said, the electrical potential becomes positive just inside the membrane. This potential then

FIGURE 2-12 PROPAGATION OF AN ACTION POTENTIAL.
(a) *In an unmyelinated axon, an action potential occurring at one point causes a local spread of positive voltage to the next point along the axon (Time 1). When that point reaches threshold of excitation, the all-or-none action potential is regenerated (Time 2). This process continues from point to point along the length of the axon. (b) In a myelinated axon, an action potential occurring at one node causes an electrical potential that spreads passively all the way to the next node (Time 1). When the membrane potential at the next node reaches threshold, another all-or-none action potential is regenerated there (Time 2).*

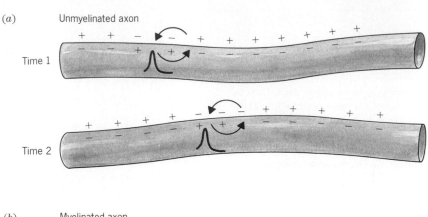

(a) Unmyelinated axon

Time 1

Time 2

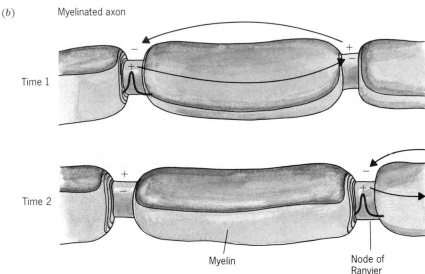

(b) Myelinated axon

Time 1

Time 2

Myelin

Node of Ranvier

spreads inside the axon. As a result, the neighboring point along the membrane becomes more positive, the threshold of excitation is reached, and an entirely new action potential is generated at that point. This process repeats itself from point to point down the axon, much as a lighted fuse ignites from point to point down its length. The beauty of this mechanism is that, because the action potential is an all-or-none event, the action potential at the end of the axon is the same size as the action potential at the beginning. The signal does not weaken as it is generated from point to point down the axon.

This mechanism may be elegant, but it is slow. The fastest that an action potential can propagate down an unmyelinated axon in a mammal is only about two meters in a second. An alternative is for the electrical potential to spread passively down the axon the way electricity is conducted down a wire. Passive electrical conduction is extremely fast. But the electrical potential gets smaller as it passively spreads. The signal is lost by the time it reaches the end of a long axon.

Myelinated Axons. The solution is the myelination of axons. The myelin sheath acts as an electrical insulator; an action potential cannot occur where there is myelin. An uninsulated node of Ranvier appears every millimeter or so along the axon, and the all-or-none action potential occurs at an uninsulated node (see Figure 2-12*b*). Then the electrical potential spreads passively down the axon and along the myelin at high speed. When the electrical potential reaches the next node, it still is large enough to reach the threshold of excitation and trigger a new, full-sized action potential. Then the renewed electrical potential spreads passively to the next node at high speed, and so on. Thus in a myelinated axon, the action potential essentially "jumps" from node to node down the length of the axon. Action potentials travel along a myelinated axon in a beautiful combination of high speed of passive electrical conduction and complete signal regeneration along the whole length of the axon. In myelinated axons, the action potential can propagate more than 100 meters in a second (225 miles per hour!) and remains as large at the end of the axon as it was at the beginning.

When an action potential has occurred at a point on the axon, the membrane potential is positive for nearly a millisecond (see Figure 2-11*b*). The membrane potential remains above the threshold for excitation for this length of time. Why isn't another action potential triggered immediately on the heels of the last one? The reason is that the membrane cannot produce another action potential for a millisecond or so. This **refractory period** keeps the neuron from firing action potentials indefinitely once it has started. The refractory period also limits the frequency at which the neuron can fire action potentials to about 800 to 1000 action potentials a second.

Synaptic Transmission

As you've seen, when the action potential has traveled the length of the axon, it reaches a terminal bouton that makes a synaptic contact with another neuron (see Figure 2-6). At this contact, **synaptic transmission** occurs. A signal passes from the axon of one neuron (the *presynaptic* neuron), across the synapse, to another neuron (the *postsynaptic* neuron). Figure 2-13 shows the structure of a single terminal bouton and its connection with another neuron. The bouton contains many tiny **synaptic vesicles** that are filled with a **chemical transmitter** (or **neurotransmitter**). When the action potential arrives, it causes the vesicles to empty the transmitter into the **synaptic cleft** that separates the terminal bouton from the postsynaptic neuron (see Figure 2-14). The transmitter then spreads across the synaptic cleft and makes contact with **receptor sites** in the postsynaptic membrane (Stevens, 1979).

When postsynaptic receptors are contacted by chemical transmitters, they change the permeability of the postsynaptic membrane to certain ions. That is, the receptors open gates for the ions to pass into the postsynaptic neuron. There are many different chemical transmitters and many different types of receptors in the nervous system. The particular transmitters and receptors determine which ions are allowed to pass into the next neuron (Stevens, 1979; Snyder, 1984). For example, some combinations of transmitters and receptors let sodium ions briefly pass through the postsynaptic membrane. When the positively charged sodium ions move into the neuron, the neuron briefly becomes slightly less negatively charged inside. That is, there is a slight shift in the resting

FIGURE 2-13 THE SYNAPSE.
(a) *Three-dimensional drawing of a synaptic connection between a terminal bouton and a dendrite of a neuron. The synaptic cleft is only about 200 nanometers across (a nanometer is one millionth of a millimeter). (After Stevens, 1979.)* (b) *An electron microscope photograph of a thin slice through two actual synaptic connections.*

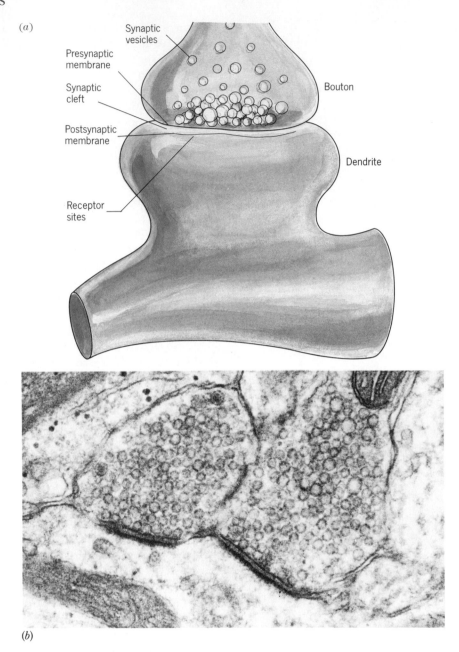

(a)

Synaptic vesicles

Presynaptic membrane

Synaptic cleft

Postsynaptic membrane

Receptor sites

Bouton

Dendrite

(b)

potential toward the threshold of excitation. Therefore, the effect of these kinds of transmitter–receptor combinations is *excitatory.* In other cases, the movement of ions makes the neuron more negatively charged inside. (Negatively charged chloride ions moving into the neuron have this effect, for example.) This effect is *inhibitory,* because the neuron's resting potential is shifted slightly away from the threshold of excitation. The entire process, from the arrival of an action potential at the terminal bouton of an axon to the production of an excitatory or inhibitory effect on the postsynaptic neuron, takes less than a millisecond.

Remember that a single neuron may receive thousands of synaptic contacts. At any given time, some of these contacts shift the postsynaptic

FIGURE 2-14   SYNAPTIC TRANSMISSION.
(a) *An action potential arriving at a terminal bouton causes synaptic vesicles (1) to fuse with the presynaptic membrane (2). Molecules of the chemical transmitter are emptied into the synaptic cleft and diffuse across the space to the postsynaptic membrane (3). The vesicle then closes (4) and will be resupplied with molecules of the transmitter. (From Stevens, 1979.) (b) An electron microscope photograph of synaptic vesicles fusing and emptying their transmitter into the synaptic cleft. (From Heuser, 1977.)*

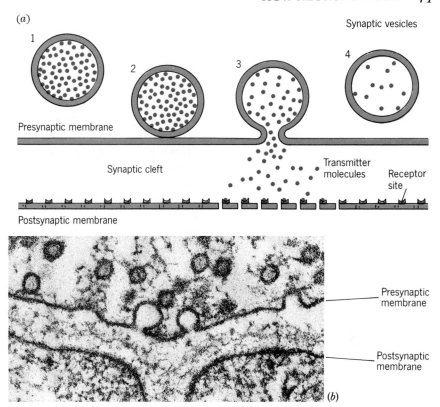

membrane potential away from the threshold of excitation and others shift the potential toward it. Whether or not the postsynaptic neuron reaches the threshold of excitation and fires an action potential depends upon the combination of all of these excitatory and inhibitory effects. This combination of effect is how neurons integrate incoming information and produce some output. If threshold is reached, an action potential is fired and propagated down the axon. The neuron has transmitted the result of the integration onward.

Not only do axons make synaptic contacts with other neurons, they also make synaptic contacts with the muscles and glands that produce observable behavior (look at Table 2-1 again). For example, long axons of neurons in the spinal cord have terminal boutons that make synaptic contact with striated muscles. In addition, axons of neurons in the autonomic nervous system make synaptic contact with the heart, with smooth muscles of internal organs and blood vessels, and with glands. When chemical transmitters are released from these terminal boutons, they excite or inhibit the target muscle or gland and cause it to increase or decrease its action.

NEUROTRANSMITTERS   The chemical transmitters of the nervous system are critical for cell-to-cell communication. They are essential to sensation and perception, movement, thinking, and so on. Too little or too much transmitter can lead to abnormal thought and behavior.

Perhaps the best studied of all the chemical transmitters is *acetylcholine* (ACh), which is found in many locations throughout the nervous system

(Kasa, 1986; Kelly and Rogawski, 1985). ACh is found at the synaptic connections between neurons and muscles. ACh excites muscles. When neurons release ACh to receptor sites on a muscle, the muscle contracts. (Curare, a chemical extracted from certain plants, blocks the action of ACh by taking over the receptor sites on muscles. Because curare prevents the muscles from contracting, it can paralyze and kill. Certain South American Indians have discovered this effect and hunt with arrows tipped with curare.) ACh also is a neurotransmitter in the brain, where its effects are primarily excitatory. In the autonomic nervous system, however, ACh may either excite or inhibit cells. The particular effect there depends on the nature of the receptor sites.

Another well-studied neurotransmitter is *norepinephrine* (NE, also know as *noradrenaline*). This chemical acts as a transmitter at synaptic contacts in many areas of the brain, spinal cord, and autonomic division of the peripheral nervous system (Moore and Bloom, 1979; Rogawski, 1985). Depending on the nature of the synaptic receptor sites, NE may either excite or inhibit. Neurons that use NE as a transmitter control wakefulness and arousal, learning and memory, and moods such as depression (Iversen and Iversen, 1981). It is known, for example, that drugs (such as imipramine) that increase the amount of NE at brain synapses reduce depression, whereas drugs (such as reserpine, once used to treat high blood pressure) that deplete the brain's store of NE cause serious depression in many people.

Dopamine (DA), another neurotransmitter, also is found in wide areas of the brain, and its action seems to be primarily inhibitory (Moore and Bloom, 1978; Grace and Bunney, 1985). At the beginning of the chapter, we mentioned that some symptoms of schizophrenia appear to stem from chemical imbalances in the brain. Dopamine has been implicated in this imbalance. The evidence suggests that in schizophrenics, either too much dopamine is released by the terminal boutons or too many post-synaptic receptor sites are present (Snyder, 1982). Drugs (such as chlorpromazine) that reduce the symptoms of schizophrenia act by blocking postsynaptic DA receptor sites. As you will see later in the chapter, DA also is used by neurons that are involved in the control of movement.

These three—acetylcholine, noradrenaline, and dopamine—are but a few of the many neurotransmitters that have now been identified. Understanding how neurotransmitters work and how they affect neurons and effectors is central to understanding of how the brain controls thought and behavior.

THE BRAIN'S MILIEU

The soft, vulnerable tissue of the brain and spinal cord are encased in a protective package. The outer part of this package is the hard, bony skull and vertebral column. The central nervous system also is covered by layers of tough connective tissue called the **meninges**. (This tissue becomes infected in the disease meningitis.) The space between the meninges and central nervous system is filled with **cerebrospinal fluid (CSF)**,

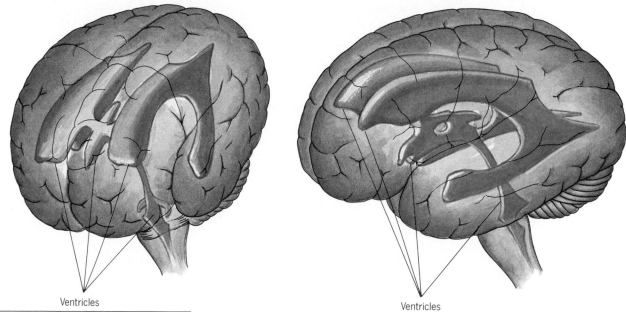

Ventricles

Ventricles

FIGURE 2-15   VENTRICLES.
The brain contains a series of
interconnected hollow chambers, called
ventricles. (From Rosenzweig and
Leiman, 1982.)

which offers another kind of protection to the brain. The soft, jellylike brain tissue floats in this liquid and is kept from pressing in on itself and crushing the base of the brain. The CSF also acts as a shock absorber. It reduces the force of shocks to the brain from sharp blows and even from ordinary movements of the head.

Inside the brain are a series of interconnected cavities, called **ventricles** (see Figure 2-15). CSF is produced in the ventricles. It fills and continuously flows out from the ventricles, into the space around the brain and spinal cord, and empties into the blood. You can see in Figure 2-15 that the tubes connecting the ventricles are quite narrow. If these tubes do not develop properly or become blocked, the outflow of CSF is blocked, and pressure builds up within the ventricles. The ventricles expand and press the overlying brain tissue against the skull, a condition called *hydrocephalus* (which means "water head" in Greek). Hydrocephalus can cause serious brain damage and mental retardation.

The brain is well supplied with blood. It receives 20 percent of the blood flow from the heart, even though it is only 2 percent of the body's weight. Because the brain cannot store its fuel (primarily glucose), it needs a continual flow of blood. When blood stops flowing to the brain, brain cells are damaged within a few minutes. Probably the greatest cause of brain damage in adults is *stroke,* the loss of blood flow to some region of the brain. Strokes happen because blood vessels get blocked or broken.

Throughout the brain, substances such as nutrients and wastes transfer between the blood and brain cells via fine capillaries that branch off from small arteries. Capillaries in the brain are quite different from those in other parts of the body. Cells of the brain's capillaries are bound together much more tightly and therefore prevent the passage of many substances between bloodstream and brain, substances that pass freely through capillaries in other parts of the body (Fenstermacher, 1985). Thus the capillaries form a **blood–brain barrier** that protects the brain from toxic substances in the blood. At the same time, capillaries in the brain speed up the transfer of nutrients such as glucose from the bloodstream.

STRUCTURE AND FUNCTION OF THE BRAIN

The 100 billion neurons of the human brain are organized into structures and systems that control all human biological and psychological functions. As you will see, individual areas of the brain are specialized into sensory, motor, and cognitive areas. But each area may contribute to many kinds of behavior and, conversely, particular behaviors arise from activity in many different brain structures. You also will see that *all* parts of the brain have some function. All of the neurons are busy carrying out their tasks as you go about your daily activities. The popular idea that people only use 10 percent of their brains is a misconception. The brain is an integrated and fully used system as it controls behavior: nothing is wasted. Let's turn now to the geography of the brain.

The main parts of the brain are mapped in Figures 2-16 and 2-17. At the top of the brain is the large **forebrain** (or **cerebrum**), which looks something like a cauliflower. The forebrain consists of the *cerebral cortex, thalamus,* and *hypothalamus* (shown in Figure 2-16, bottom) as well as the *basal ganglia* and *limbic system*. Beneath the forebrain is the **brain stem**, which consists of the *midbrain, pons, medulla,* and *cerebellum*.

The right and left halves of the brain are essentially mirror images of each other (look at Figure 2-17). Each half is referred to as a **cerebral hemisphere**. Almost every structure in the brain has a counterpart in the other cerebral hemisphere. You have a right and left cerebral cortex, a right and left thalamus, and so on.

In the next few pages, we discuss how the different parts of the brain are organized and what they do. For the sake of clarity, we treat each structure of the brain separately. But remember that the brain works as a whole. Virtually all of the structures communicate with each other and their functions are highly coordinated.

Forebrain: Cerebral Cortex

The **cerebral cortex** is a thin layer of tissue (about 3 millimeters thick) that covers the surface of the brain, just as bark covers the surface of a tree (*cortex* means "bark" in Latin) (see Figure 2-17). The cerebral cortex consists mostly of glial cells and the cell bodies and dendrites of neurons. Because the cortex looks grayish, it is referred to as *gray matter*. It is the cerebral cortex that contributes the wrinkled surface of the human brain that we described earlier (see Figure 2-4). You can appreciate the advantage of these convolutions with a simple demonstration. Take a sheet of notebook paper in your hand. The paper represents the cortex, and your fist is the skull. Obviously, the paper won't fit. But if you

FIGURE 2-16 STRUCTURES OF THE HUMAN BRAIN. (Above) *Left side of the brain.* (Below) *Brain in cross section between the two hemispheres as shown in the diagram. Shown is the inner wall of the right hemisphere.*

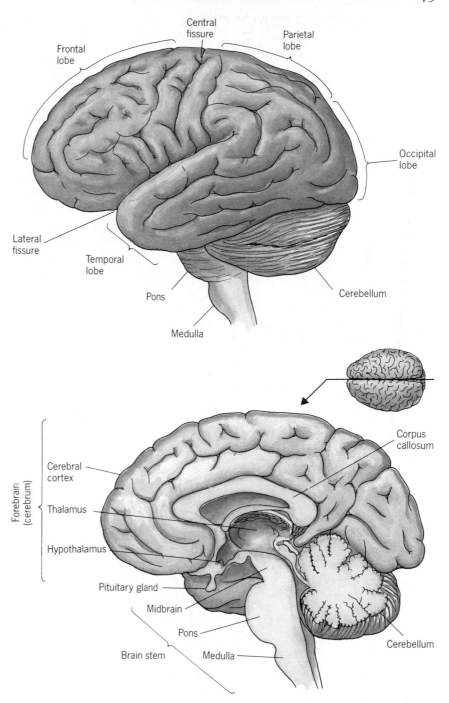

crumple the paper, it fits easily into your fist. You'll see that now the paper is wrinkled—just as the cerebral cortex is wrinkled. The wrinkles of the human cortex give it a surface area three times greater than if it were smooth. Other animals have much less cerebral cortex relative to their total brain volume because their cortex is less convoluted or, in some cases, completely smooth (see Figure 2-4).

FIGURE 2-17 A SECTION THROUGH A HUMAN BRAIN.
The cut was made through the center, from side to side as shown in the diagram.

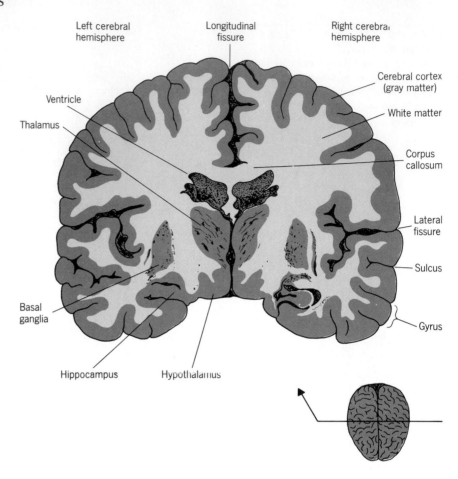

Each shallow indentation in the convoluted cortex is called a *sulcus* (which means "furrow" or "trench" in Latin) (see Figure 2-17). Each little mound of cortex between the sulci is called a *gyrus* (from the Greek *gyros,* which means "circle" or "dome"). Several identations are very deep; these are called *fissures*. The *longitudinal fissure* is the deep separation between the two cerebral hemispheres (see Figure 2-17). Two other fissures help divide the cerebral cortex into four different lobes, called the *frontal, parietal, temporal,* and *occipital* lobes (see Figure 2-16, top). The *central fissure* separates the frontal from the parietal lobe, and the *lateral fissure* separates the frontal and parietal lobes from the temporal lobe. As we describe later, each of these lobes has different functions.

Neurons in the different areas of the cerebral cortex communicate with each other by sending out long axons that loop under the cortex. Some neurons in the cortex also send long axons to, and receive long axons from, neurons in other areas of the brain and spinal cord. These axons travel together underneath the cerebral cortex and make up the *white matter* of the brain (see Figure 2-17). They look white because they are covered in white myelin sheaths.

Some areas of the cerebral cortex help control movement of the body, others receive and process sensory information, and still other areas have more complex integrative and cognitive functions. Let's look more closely at each of these three types of cortex.

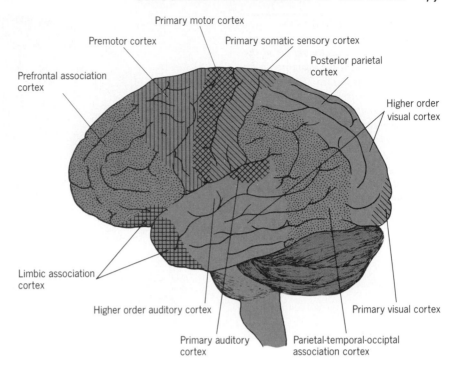

MOTOR CORTEX   The areas of the cerebral cortex that control body movements are located in the frontal lobes (see Figure 2-18). Neurons in the *primary motor cortex* send their axons into the spinal cord and control the actions of specific muscles. People with damage to their primary motor cortex feel muscle weakness and cannot control their fine movements (Ghez, 1985). They may find it difficult or impossible to button a button, wiggle their toes, or feed themselves.

Scientists have studied the organization of primary motor cortex by placing an electrode on the cortical surface and stimulating it with weak electrical current. The electrical current excites nearby neurons to fire action potentials, and specific body parts move. During experiments like these on patients undergoing brain surgery, researchers found that the primary motor cortex contains a *topographic map* of the body (Penfield and Rasmussen, 1952). Electrical stimulation of one part of the primary motor cortex produced movements in one part of the body, stimulation of another part produced movement in another part of the body, and so on (see Figure 2-19).

Two important principles emerged from the results of these studies. First, the primary motor cortex in each hemisphere controls movement of the *opposite* side of the body. Stimulation of the left motor cortex makes the right side of the body move, and vice versa. This opposition occurs because the axons of motor cortex neurons cross to the opposite side of the brain on their way to the spinal cord. The second principle is that muscles controlling very fine movements take up more space in the motor cortex than muscles controlling coarse movements. For example, notice that you have much finer control over moving your fingers than your toes (try writing with your toes!). You also have a much larger area

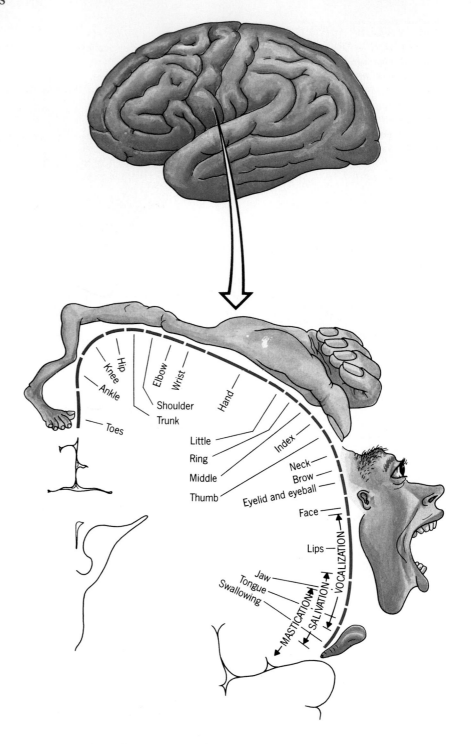

of motor cortex devoted to controlling your fingers than your toes (see Figure 2-19). In general, the finer the muscle control, the more cortical neurons devoted to it.

Just in front of the primary motor cortex is an area referred to as *premotor cortex* (see Figure 2-18). This region also is involved in the

FIGURE 2-20   ACTIVITY OF CORTEX DURING PLANS AND MOVEMENTS.

The drawings show the left hemisphere of the brain (front is to the left). Each colored square on the drawings indicates the amount of blood flow and therefore the amount of neural activity. Red and orange show more activity, blue and black less. (a) When the subject pushes his right thumb and index finger against a spring, the primary motor cortex becomes active. (b) When the subject rapidly touches each finger to his thumb in a complicated sequence, primary and premotor areas become active. (c) When the subject mentally rehearses the complex sequence of finger movements but does not actually move his fingers, only the premotor area becomes active. (From Roland, Larsen, Lassen, and Skinhoj, 1980, labels added.)

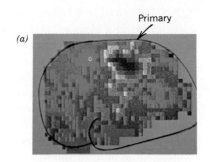

(a) Primary

Primary motor cortex active during a simple finger movement

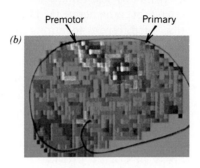

(b) Premotor   Primary

. . imary and premotor areas active during complex sequence of finger movements

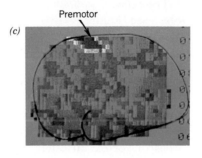

(c) Premotor

Premotor area active during mental rehearsal of complex sequence of finger movement

control of movement. But it is important for programming and planning complex sequences of movement (Freund, 1984; Goldberg, 1985; Ghez, 1985). Perhaps the most compelling evidence for this conclusion comes from studies of the brains of people who are awake—and thinking. When neurons become active, the blood flow near them increases. By measuring the blood flow in small areas of the cortex, researchers can measure the activity of the cortex. Studies using this method show that parts of the premotor cortex become active when people plan to make a complex movement (Roland, Larsen, Lassen, and Skinhoj, 1980) (see Figure 2-20). Neurons in the premotor cortex then relay these plans, or motor programs, to the primary motor cortex, which signals specific muscles to contract and carry out the plan. In the split second before you reach for a glass with your hand, or tie your shoe, or turn the pages of this book, your premotor cortex goes into high gear and relays the plan of action to your primary motor cortex.

SENSORY CORTEX How does your brain signal when your fingers have grasped a glass or tied a shoelace? In sensory areas of the cortex, neurons receive and process information about the environment. Sensory cortex helps people to sense and perceive the world.

Just behind the central fissure, in the parietal lobe, is the *primary somatic sensory cortex* (see Figure 2-18). This area receives and interprets information about the positions of body parts—fingers, arms, legs, and so on—and about touch and pressure to the skin. Like primary motor cortex, primary somatic sensory cortex in each hemisphere contains a topographic map of the opposite half of the body. When different parts of the body are touched, neurons in different parts of somatic sensory cortex become active (Mountcastle, 1984). Conversely, electrical stimulation of different locations in the somatic sensory map excites neurons there and produces in the patient a sensation of touch or tingling on the corresponding part of the body (Penfield and Rasmussen, 1952).

The *primary visual cortex,* in the occipital lobe, receives and interprets information from the eyes and helps people see. Surrounding the primary visual cortex are a number of *higher order visual areas.* These areas get input from the primary visual cortex and further process information from the visual world. Together, the primary and higher order visual areas of cortex provide people with their visual sensations and perceptions.

The *primary auditory cortex* lies along the lateral fissure in the temporal lobe (see Figure 2-18). Together with the surrounding *higher order auditory cortex,* this region is involved in people's ability to hear and interpret sounds. In chapters 3 and 4 we will discuss in more detail tactile, visual, and auditory perception and how the brain provides people with sensation and perception of the world.

ASSOCIATION CORTEX Association areas of the cortex link the sensory areas to one another, and they link the sensory areas with motor areas of cortex. In other words, they help to *associate* the sensory and motor functions of the cortex. These areas are involved in complex motor control, sensory perception, cognition, emotional behavior, memory, and language (Kupfermann, 1985). Without them, you might not be able to turn all the pages of this chapter to get to the end, remember the information on the pages, or feel happy when you score well on an exam on its contents. The size of the association cortex relative to sensory and motor cortex increases from lower to higher animals. Humans and other primates have much more association cortex than do other mammals.

There are three broad regions of association cortex in the human brain: prefrontal, limbic, and parietal-temporal-occipital (see Figure 2-18). The *prefrontal association cortex,* in the frontal lobes, has been the subject of thousands of studies, and yet its functions still are not fully understood. Patients with damage to the prefrontal cortex may perform normally on standard intelligence tests as well as on various tests of perception and memory. Nevertheless, they seem unable to organize their everyday activities and are inflexible in their approach to new problems (Milner and Petrides, 1984). Studies of cortical activity, using measures of blood flow, show that the prefrontal cortex becomes active

FIGURE 2-21 EFFECTS OF PARIETAL-TEMPORAL-OCCIPITAL CORTEX DAMAGE.

Damage to the right parietal-temporal-occipital association cortex produces neglect of stimuli in the left half of the environment. One patient, asked to draw a clock face, placed the numbers and clock hands on the right. Another patient also omitted parts of the left side of the body in his drawing. Another patient, a German artist, drew a self-portrait (a) before the damage, a second (b) two months, and a third (c) five months after the damage.

during many different types of thinking. For example, your prefrontal cortex becomes active if you start with 50 and successively subtract 3, or if you imagine walking alternately left and right as you encounter street corners (Roland and Friberg, 1985). Findings such as these have led one prominent researcher to conclude that "The frontal lobes are essential for synthetic reasoning, abstract thought, and the organization of independent behaviors in time and space toward future goals" (Goldman-Rakic, 1984).

The *limbic association cortex,* which includes part of the frontal and temporal lobes (see Figure 2-18), helps control emotions (Kupfermann, 1985). For example, electrical stimulation of this cortex in humans produces feelings such as fear (Penfield, 1958a). People with epilepsy of the temporal lobe are likely to have emotional disorders (Post, 1986). **Epilepsy** is a disease in which the neurons in a particular region of the brain are too active. During an epileptic seizure, there is synchronized or sustained firing of the neurons. People with epilepsy in the temporal lobe often feel especially sad, angry, aggressive, or guilty (Bear, 1979). In contrast, people with epilepsy in an area of cortex outside the limbic association area typically do not have emotional disorders.

The *parietal-temporal-occipital* association cortex is a large area with a variety of functions. One part of this area, found in the left hemisphere of most people, is important for the use of language. (More will be said about this later in the chapter and in Chapter 8.) Other parts of parietal-temporal-occipital association cortex, especially in the right hemisphere, are involved in people's perception of their body (or body image) and its relation to its surroundings (Heilman, 1979; Lynch, 1980). When this region is damaged, a remarkable set of symptoms arises. For instance, damage to one side of the brain may make a person ignore visual and auditory stimuli from the half of the environment opposite to the damage (see Figure 2-21). They also may neglect the opposite half of their own body and fail to wash or dress it. They may deny that the arm or leg on the opposite side even belongs to them! This area of cortex seems to be involved in people's recognition of and attention to spatial aspects of sensory information and their relation to the body. Many other sensory and motor functions also have been ascribed to parietal-temporal-occipital association cortex (Hyvärinen, 1982).

(a)

(b)

(c)

Other Structures of the Forebrain

THALAMUS   Deep in the center of the brain is the "inner chamber," or *thalamus* (see Figures 2-16 and 2-17). The thalamus is an essential link between the cerebral cortex and other parts of the brain. The thalamus is divided into groups of neurons that have common functions. Each group is called a **nucleus** (not to be confused with the nucleus inside an individual cell). Some nuclei in the thalamus have sensory functions. They receive information from sensory receptors, integrate it with information from other areas of the brain, and send the altered information along axons in the white matter to sensory cortex. For instance, neurons in one thalamic nucleus receive input directly from the eyes and send information to the primary visual area of cortex. Other thalamic nuclei have motor functions. They transmit information between motor areas of cortex and other structures of the brain involved in the control of movement. Still other thalamic nuclei communicate with association areas of cortex. Thus in many ways the thalamus is a way-station between the cerebral cortex, other areas of the brain, and the external environment.

BASAL GANGLIA   The *basal ganglia* are an important part of the motor control system of the brain. They consist of several nuclei (groups of neurons) situated between the thalamus and cerebral cortex (see Figure 2-17). The basal ganglia receive inputs from large areas of cerebral cortex and send information through the thalamus to premotor and frontal association cortex.

You can see how important the basal ganglia are for motor control by the problems that plague people with disorders of the basal ganglia (Côté and Crutcher, 1985). Perhaps the best known of these disorders is *Parkinson's disease,* which afflicts about 500,000 people in the United States. People with Parkinson's disease move very slowly. They have increased muscle tone, which makes their limbs and body rigid. When they are at rest, their arms and hands tend to tremble rhythmically. Many of these symptoms appear when pathways in the brain that carry the neurotransmitter dopamine to the basal ganglia are lost. Drugs that replace dopamine relieve some of the symptoms (Iversen, 1984). Another basal ganglia disorder is *Huntington's disease,* an inherited disease that affects about 10,000 people in the United States. People with Huntington's disease have uncontrollably jerky movements of their arms, legs, head, and tongue. These abnormal movements are caused by the death of neurons in certain nuclei of the basal ganglia.

The kinds of movement disorders that people suffer after damage or disease of their basal ganglia suggest that the basal ganglia are important for both starting and controlling movements after they have started. Researchers have drawn the same conclusions from studies of single neurons in the basal ganglia of monkeys performing various movements (Evarts, Kimura, Wurtz, and Hikosaka, 1984).

HYPOTHALAMUS   The *hypothalamus* is a small structure with powerful effects on major psychological and biological functions. These functions include the so-called four F's: fighting, fleeing, feeding, and mating. The hypothalamus helps people to control aggression and emotions, hunger and eating, and sexual behavior. The hypothalamus also is involved in people's feelings of thirst—fluid regulation in the body—in regulating body temperature, and in timing biological rhythms. (We will discuss many of these behaviors further in Chapters 5 and 10).

One way that the hypothalamus controls all of these many body functions is by influencing the autonomic nervous system. In addition, the hypothalamus forms a critical link between the brain and endocrine glands (Reichlin, 1978). The hypothalamus is located at the base of the brain, just under the thalamus (whence the name *hypo*thalamus) and just above the pituitary gland (see Figure 2-16). Many structures of the brain send information to the hypothalamus, and on the basis of this information, cells in the hypothalamus release chemicals into the pituitary gland. These chemicals enter the bloodstream and influence other glands and cells throughout the body. Thus the hypothalamus has a wide-reaching influence on bodily functions and behavior.

LIMBIC SYSTEM   The limbic system is made up of several structures in the forebrain and is involved with a person's emotions, motivation, learning, and memory. You are already familiar with some parts of the limbic system: the limbic association cortex (see Figure 2-18) and nuclei of the thalamus that are connected with limbic cortex. Another part of the limbic system is the large *hippocampus,* which lies deep in the temporal lobe (see Figure 2-17). The *amygdala,* located under the cortex of the temporal lobe, and the *septal area,* located just in front of the thalamus, also form parts of the limbic system.

The limbic system, as we have said, is involved in motivation and emotion. Some parts of the limbic system seem to inhibit aggressive behavior (Albert and Walsh, 1984). If they are damaged, either in lower animals or in humans, aggression increases. Other parts of the limbic system support aggressive behavior. If they are damaged, aggression decreases; if they are electrically stimulated, an animal attacks and acts aggressively (Carlson, 1986).

Still other parts of the limbic system are important to more positive emotions. In a classic laboratory study, rats continuously pressed a lever to get electrical stimulation of the septal area of the limbic system (Olds and Milner, 1954). When people get electrical stimulation of this area, they report that it makes them "feel great" and eliminates "bad" thoughts. Sometimes they start to think pleasurable sexual thoughts and feel sexually aroused (Heath, 1963, 1964). Thus the limbic system seems to be part of a "reward system" of the brain that is involved in people's and lower animals' appreciation of pleasure (Routtenberg, 1978; Wise, 1983).

The limbic system also affects learning and memory. The hippocampus in particular is important to memory functions (Rawlins, 1985; Zola-Morgan, Squire, and Amaral, 1986). People with a damaged hippocampus find it difficult to form any new memories. One man, for example, could not find his way home or recognize close neighbors even though he had lived in the same house for 8 years, because he did not remember any new information. He remarked that "Every day is alone in itself, whatever enjoyment I've had, and whatever sorrow I've had." "It's like waking from a dream; I just don't remember." Yet he could recall most of what happened in his life before his hippocampus was damaged (Milner, 1970; Milner, Corkin, and Teuber, 1968).

In sum, the limbic system is involved in a variety of functions, including emotion, motivation, learning, and memory.

CEREBRAL COMMISSURES   You probably take for granted your ability to clap your hands together, to twiddle your thumbs, and to clasp your hands behind your head. But these abilities are really quite sophisticated. We noted earlier that the forebrain consists of two halves (hemispheres) that are almost mirror images of each other. How does the right half know what the left half is doing? When your right primary motor cortex makes your left hand move, how is it coordinated with movement of your right hand, which is controlled by the left hemisphere?

The two hemispheres are coordinated by the **cerebral commissures** (from the Latin *commissura,* which means "a joining together," or "seam"). The cerebral commissures are bundles of axons that carry information from neurons in one hemisphere to the other. The brain has several cerebral commissures. The largest and most important is the *corpus callosum,* a huge bundle of about 250 million axons that connects the cerebral cortex of the two hemispheres (see Figures 2-16 and 2-17).

When researchers wanted to find out what the cerebral commissures do, they experimented by cutting them in laboratory animals. They performed a "split brain" operation. Roger W. Sperry pioneered research on the effects of this operation and in 1981 won the Nobel Prize for his work. Sperry and his colleagues found that split-brain cats could learn things with each hemisphere independently and that neither hemisphere interfered with nor assisted the other (Sperry, Stamm, and Miner, 1956). These results suggest that the corpus callosum is important in transferring information from one cerebral hemisphere to the other.

Studies of people in whom the two hemispheres were surgically cut to control the spread of epileptic seizures told the researchers more about the corpus callosum. In one experiment with split-brain patients, Sperry (1968, 1974) used a special test that let him show pictures of hand positions to only one hemisphere at a time (see Figure 2-22). When the right hemisphere saw the picture, patients could mimic the position with their left hand (which is controlled by the right hemisphere) but not with their right hand (which is controlled by the left hemisphere). Conversely, when the left hemisphere saw the picture, the patients could mimic the position only with their right hand. In another test, Sperry put one of the patient's hands in a certain position and asked the patient to mimic it with his or her other hand (the patient could not see either hand). As you'll see if you try it yourself, people with an intact corpus callosum can do this easily. But the split-brain patients could not. The information about hand position was not transferred from one hemisphere to the other. The results of these and other experiments indicate that when the cerebral commissures are cut, the two hemispheres act independently.

FIGURE 2-22   THE CORPUS CALLOSUM AIDS COMMUNICATION BETWEEN THE HEMISPHERES.
Split-brain patients were asked to mimic these pictures. Each picture was shown only to the right or left hemisphere. Patients could mimic the hand position only with the hand that was controlled by the hemisphere that had seen the picture. The other hemisphere seemed ignorant of the picture, and the patients could not mimic the picture. (From Sperry, 1974.)

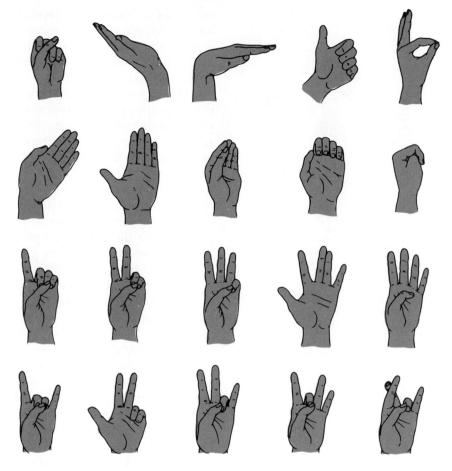

One hemisphere literally does not know what the other has experienced or is doing.

HEMISPHERIC ASYMMETRIES AND DOMINANCE The two hemispheres of the brain look *almost* exactly alike, but there are some important anatomical differences between them. For example, one part of the cortex in the temporal lobe is larger on the left side in 65 percent of all people, larger on the right side in 11 percent, and about equal in size in 24 percent (Geschwind and Levitsky, 1968). Similar asymmetries—differences between the two hemispheres—in size appear in the frontal lobes and thalamus (Galaburda, 1984).

Do these asymmetries have any practical effects on the way people act or think? Do the left and right hemispheres carry out any functions differently? One major difference between the functions of the two hemispheres is the ability to control fine movements of the hands (Hicks, 1978). About 90 percent of all people are right-handed. They have much better control of fine movements such as writing, turning screwdrivers, and dialing the phone with their right hand (controlled by the left hemisphere) than with their left hand (right hemisphere). The rest of us

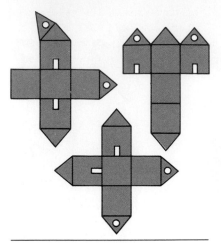

FIGURE 2-23   HEMISPHERIC DOMINANCE FOR NONVERBAL FUNCTIONS.
Split-brain patients blindly felt a solid three-dimensional form with one hand while viewing three (two-dimensional) drawings of solid forms that had been opened up such as those shown here. Patients had to choose which drawing would fold up into the shape in their hand. Split-brain patients were much more accurate when they felt with their left hand (right hemisphere) than when they felt with their right hand (left hemisphere). (From Nebes, 1974; after Levy-Agresti and Sperry, 1968.)

FIGURE 2-24   EFFECTS OF DAMAGE TO THE CEREBELLUM.
(a) *Told to move their arm at a "go" signal, people with damage to the cerebellum are slow to begin and move more irregularly than normal.* (b) *The patient can lower his arm to his nose only inaccurately and unsmoothly.* (c) *Asked to pat his thigh alternately with the palm and the back of his hand, the pattern is irregular.* (d) *The patient walks unsteadily, with a wide stance, and tends to fall. (Modified from Ghez and Fahn, 1985.)*

are either left-handed or control fine movement of both hands about equally (ambidextrous). Corresponding asymmetries in brain size occur in brain structures that control hand movements (Galaburda, 1984). But handedness is not the only asymmetry of brain function to affect so many basic, everyday activities.

Another well-established asymmetry is the ability of each hemisphere to process language. Researchers first discovered this asymmetry in people with brain damage. They found that over 95 percent of the speech disorders that result from brain damage follow damage to the left hemisphere (Geschwind, 1979). They inferred that the left hemisphere is more important than the right for controlling speech, and studies of split-brain patients have confirmed this hypothesis. For example, when split-brain patients see a picture only with the left hemisphere, they can describe the picture in words. Similarly, they can easily read material presented to their left hemisphere. But they have trouble reading or describing words or pictures presented only to their right hemisphere (Nebes, 1974; Sperry, 1974, 1982). The most marked asymmetries in brain size between the two halves of the brain are present in those parts of the brain (the temporal lobe especially) that are important for language (Galaburda, 1984).

The right hemisphere seems to be dominant for certain nonverbal functions, such as complex spatial abilities (Nebes, 1974). For example, in one experiment, split-brain patients were asked to identify the flattened, two-dimensional representations of three-dimensional objects (Levy-Agresti and Sperry, 1968). The patients were more accurate when they used their right hemisphere than their left (see Figure 2-23).

Some studies have suggested that the two hemispheres also differ in abilities such as mathematics and logical reasoning (both left dominant), and music and emotional expression (both right dominant) (Bradshaw and Nettleton, 1981; Silberman and Weingartner, 1986). Some researchers believe these findings mean that the left hemisphere specializes in analytic, sequential, and time-dependent functions whereas the right hemisphere specializes in dealing with integrated wholes, spatial, and emotional functions (Bradshaw and Nettleton, 1981). It has even been argued that the left and right hemispheres harbor two very different modes of thinking and that schools must be careful to educate both sides of the brain (Bogen, 1977).

Although studies show some functional differences between the two halves of the brain, it is simplistic to conclude that certain cognitive functions belong wholly to one hemisphere or the other. Many of the functional differences between the two hemispheres are small, and all represent a dominance of one hemisphere—not an all-or-none difference. Even the most striking hemispheric asymmetries—those for handedness and language—only represent dominances of one hemisphere over the other. You know, for example, that if you are right-handed (left hemisphere dominant), you still can do many things that require fine-motor coordination of your left hand (Hicks, 1978). What is more, even though the left hemisphere dominates language abilities, the right hemisphere has some language ability and is important in a person's understanding and production of language (Zaidel, 1976; Bradshaw and

Nettleton, 1981; Ross, 1984). Even if the functions of the two hemispheres were completely different, the cerebral commissures integrate the activities of the two sides of the brain. People's cognitive abilities are the product of an integrated brain, not two brains residing in one head.

The Brain Stem

Although the forebrain is critical for many of our sensory, motor, and cognitive abilities, the brain stem contributes to these and other critical functions.

MIDBRAIN   Part of the brain stem is the midbrain (see Figure 2-16) with its many structures and nuclei that contribute to people's sensory and motor abilities. For example, the *superior colliculus* gets input directly from the eyes and helps people to move their eyes and to see. It is especially important in signaling where in a person's surroundings a visual stimulus has come from, in orienting the person, and getting the person to attend to the stimulus (Schiller, 1984; Sparks, 1986). When you notice sudden movement to the side and turn your eyes to see where it comes from, your superior colliculi are doing their job. Closely related is the *inferior colliculus,* a part of the auditory system. The inferior colliculus relays information about sound to the forebrain and is involved in auditory reflexes and attention (Aitkin, Irvine, and Webster, 1984). If someone slams a door behind you, and you automatically turn your head, your inferior colliculi are working. Other midbrain nuclei communicate with the basal ganglia and help people control their body movements.

CEREBELLUM   You've probably seen baseball outfielders running, arms raised, to catch a ball curving through the air. These outfielders are depending in part on their cerebellum. *Cerebellum* means "little brain" in Latin, and if you look at Figure 2-16 you can see why it has this name. The cerebellum has a convoluted cortex, just like the forebrain. In addition, there are a number of nuclei under the cerebellar cortex, just as there are nuclei in the thalamus under the cerebral cortex.

The cerebellum helps control posture and movement (see Figure 2-24). One way it does this is by adjusting the muscles on the basis of sensory feedback about movements that already have occurred (Brooks and Thach, 1981; Ghez and Fahn, 1985). The cerebellum receives information about *plans* for movement from other brain structures and about *actual* motor performance from the sensory systems. On the basis of this information, the cerebellum seems to compare intention with performance and compensate for any errors. When you or the baseball outfielder reach out to catch a ball, the cerebellum is hard at work adjusting movements on the basis of sensory feedback.

People also use their cerebellum as they learn new motor skills and associations (Robinson, 1976; Ito, 1984; Thompson, 1986). Furthermore, once motor skills are well learned, the cerebellum helps to smooth people's performance by anticipating movements and any corrections that will be needed (Brooks and Thach, 1981). Thus the cerebellum is

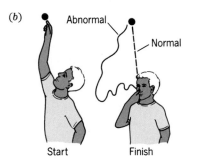

(*a*) Go

Normal

Abnormal

Delay

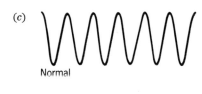

(*b*) Abnormal

Normal

Start   Finish

(*c*)

Normal

Abnormal

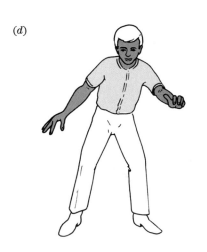

(*d*)

BOX 2-1
**THE PRIME MOVER:
WHAT STARTS
VOLUNTARY
BEHAVIOR?**

If you are sitting comfortably in your chair and suddenly decide to reach over and pick up your shoe, what started that behavior? How did neurons in your brain plan it and carry it out? Do neurons actually make the decision to act and begin firing *before* the action occurs? If so, what sort of decision do they make? How? You have seen that many parts of the brain are involved in starting and controlling movements. But how does "starting and controlling movement" translate into the activity of nerve cells in the brain?

One way to answer these questions would be to directly monitor the activity of single neurons before and during voluntary behaviors. Researchers could insert tiny electrodes into a person's brain and record the action-potential signals of neurons while the person, say, picked up her shoe. But for obvious ethical reasons, researchers cannot experiment like this on humans. They can, however, experiment on monkeys and other animals to find out how the brain starts and controls voluntary behavior.

In one of the first experiments of this kind, Edward Evarts (1966, 1973) trained monkeys to release a telegraph key when a light came on. Evarts used an electrode to record the activity of single neurons in the part of primary motor cortex that controls the monkey's arm movements. He found that the neurons started firing action potentials *before* the monkeys moved their arms (see Box Figure 1). The neurons also began firing action potentials just before the monkeys used their arms spontaneously to scratch, eat, and groom. Thus neurons in the primary motor cortex form part of a system that starts both learned and unlearned voluntary movements. These neurons cause specific muscles in the opposite arm to contract with a particular amount of force, and the result is a specific movement—a scratch, the release of a key, or the like (Evarts, 1981).

But what makes these neurons act? How do they "know" to command a muscle contraction? To answer these questions, scientists recorded from neurons in the premotor cortex of the frontal lobes (see Figure 2-18) while monkeys carried out various tasks (Tanji, 1984; Wise and Strick, 1984). For example, monkeys were instructed by one stimulus (patterns of lights) to bend or straighten their arms after another stimulus that came on several seconds later. The monkey's premotor cortex neurons became active during the interval between the two stimuli. What is more, the neurons became active only after one instruction (for example, bend arm) but not the other (straighten arm). Control experiments showed that the premotor neurons were not

BOX FIGURE 1 MOTOR CORTEX NEURONS AND VOLUNTARY MOVEMENT.
The primary motor cortex neuron (trace A) increases its action-potential activity before *the muscle contraction (trace B), which leads to release of the key (trace C). Thus, the neuron is part of the system that starts the voluntary act of releasing the key. (After Evarts, 1966, 1973.)*

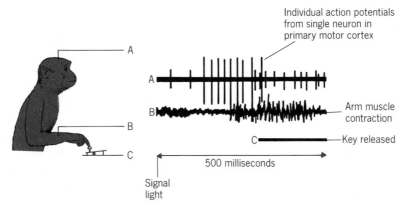

involved in learning skills and in their increasingly smooth, rapid performance with practice. If you play the piano better after a dozen lessons than one lesson, or if you do the newest dance better after an hour on the dance floor, your cerebellum has been doing its part.

PONS AND MEDULLA   The pons is the large bulge in the brain stem, just under the cerebellum (see Figure 2-16). The pons contains neurons simply responding to sensory cues and that they were not simply controlling specific muscle contractions. Rather, their activity reflected the *preparation* for particular movements (Wise and Strick, 1984). Premotor cortex neurons prepare for and plan intended movements. Once the plan is made, it goes to primary motor cortex to be carried out.

How does the premotor cortex prepare and plan movements? Part of the parietal-temporal-occipital association cortex appears to inform cells in premotor cortex about the location of objects in the immediate surroundings (Lynch, 1980; Ghez, 1985). The premotor cortex then uses this information to direct and guide movements. Other areas of the brain also help to plan and begin movement. Neurons in the basal ganglia appear to start voluntary movements in the absence of direct sensory guidance (Evarts, Kimura, Wurtz, and Hikosaka, 1984). For example, some basal ganglia neurons become active before

movements toward the *remembered* location of objects. The cerebellum also contains neurons that become active before movements, particularly practiced voluntary movements (Brooks and Thach, 1981). Thus, many brain structures are involved in various aspects of planning and initiating voluntary movements (see Box Figure 2).

But what about our original question: what *starts* voluntary behavior? In one sense, the answer is simple—all of the brain structures shown in Box Figure 2 do. But, you might ask, what makes neurons in *those* brain structures start the behavior? That

question may have no answer. Even if we could identify another area of the brain (call it area X) that starts activity in the areas shown in Box Figure 2, we still would ask what started the neural activity in area X, and so on indefinitely. In the end, we would arrive at the age-old questions of where volition comes from and whether there is free will. The only thing we can be sure of is that whatever the first (prime) mover is, it acts through nerve cells in the brain. There is no little man or woman in your head making decisions. The decisions are made by billions of neurons.

BOX FIGURE 2   HOW AREAS OF THE BRAIN START AND CONTROL VOLUNTARY MOVEMENT.
The arrows indicate the main direction of information flow from one structure to another. The basal ganglia, cerebellum, and parietal-temporal-occipital cortex receive information from still other areas of cortex and the sensory world. Thus voluntary movement is controlled by a complex and interconnected system.

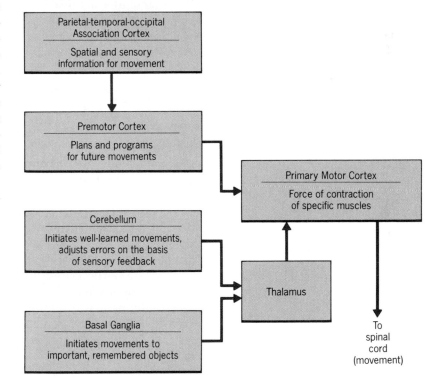

that receive information from the forebrain and send it on to the cerebellum. In addition, much of the pons consists of giant bundles of axons that carry information up to the cerebellum. The medulla oblongata (usually just called the medulla) is the long structure located between the pons and spinal cord. It contains nuclei that relay somatic sensory information (for example, about touch and pressure on the body surface) from the spinal cord to the thalamus.

Both the pons and medulla also contain nuclei that receive somatic sensory information from the head and face and nuclei that relay commands to control head and face movements. Large bundles of axons that carry sensory and motor information between the brain and spinal cord also pass through the pons and medulla.

RETICULAR FORMATION The reticular formation is a large, long structure that extends through the midbrain, pons, and medulla. It consists of over 90 different nuclei and an interconnecting network of dendrites and axons (*reticulum* means network in Latin). The reticular formation regulates general levels of activity, or arousal, of the brain. It does this by receiving sensory stimulation from the periphery and making widespread connections throughout the brain. If the connections between the reticular formation and the forebrain are cut in laboratory animals, the animals go to sleep permanently (Bremer, 1937). If the reticular formation is stimulated electrically, animals become aroused (Moruzzi and Magoun, 1949). These and many more recent experiments indicate that the reticular formation is important for controlling arousal, awareness, and attention (Kelly, 1985).

The reticular formation also modulates muscle tone in the limbs and controls breathing and heart rate. Thus the brain stem reticular formation is crucial to many basic biological functions (Kelly, 1985).

THE SPINAL CORD

The **spinal cord**, as you have seen, is the part of the central nervous system that extends down through the center of the bony vertebral column (spine) (see Figure 2-3). All somatic sensory information from the body and the back of the head—but not the face—enters the central nervous system at the spinal cord. In addition, all muscles of the body—except those of the head and throat—are controlled by neurons in the spinal cord.

Figure 2-25 shows a cross section through the spinal cord. The central butterfly-shaped portion consists mostly of cell bodies. Like the cerebral cortex, this area is referred to as *gray matter* because it too is grayish. Neurons in the part of this gray matter nearer a person's back receive sensory information; neurons nearer the front send out axons to control the muscles. Surrounding the spinal gray matter is spinal *white matter*, which consists of myelinated axons that transmit information up and down the spinal cord.

The spinal cord has two general functions. First, it acts as a kind of way station for information passing between the brain and the peripheral nervous system. When neurons in the motor cortex signal for a movement, action potentials travel down their axons in the white matter of the spinal cord. The axons make synaptic connections with neurons in the front part of the spinal gray matter, and these neurons in turn send their axons to various muscles of the body. Thus, as a result of commands from the brain, neurons in the spinal cord cause muscles to contract in

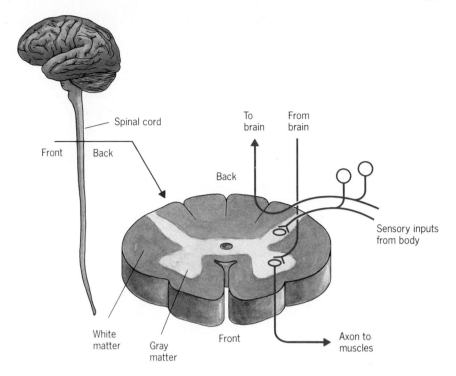

FIGURE 2-25   CROSS SECTION OF THE SPINAL CORD.
The sensory inputs and axons to the muscles are present on both sides of the spinal cord and serve the corresponding half of the body. Inputs and outputs are shown here for only one side of the spinal cord.

Spinal cord

Front   Back

To brain   From brain

Back

Sensory inputs from body

White matter   Gray matter   Front   Axon to muscles

particular sequences and with particular amounts of force, and coordinated movements occur. Axons carrying somatic sensory information from the body enter the back part of the spinal cord and either make synaptic connections with neurons in the spinal gray matter or go directly to the brain in the white matter (see Figure 2-25).

The spinal cord also controls certain reflexes. The **spinal reflexes** are automatic movements that result from direct sensory inputs to the spinal cord; they require no participation by the brain. The simplest spinal reflex is the *monosynaptic stretch reflex,* illustrated in Figure 2-26. Many muscles have a monosynaptic reflex, which is important in helping people to adjust quickly to changes in the loads on their muscles and to control their posture. For example, when you begin to lean forward while you are standing, the large calf muscle stretches and stimulates a monosynaptic reflex. In response, the calf muscle contracts, pushes down your toes, and prevents you from falling. The entire sequence takes only about 50 milliseconds and occurs without the participation of the brain (Greer, 1984), although the brain may be informed of the reflex.

When spinal reflexes involve two or more synaptic contacts, they are called *polysynaptic reflexes.* Some are quite simple and involve only two synapses in the sequence. For instance, when one muscle—say your biceps—stretches and contracts by its monosynaptic stretch reflex, a polysynaptic stretch reflex simultaneously inhibits motor neurons that control the opposing (triceps) muscle. The triceps relaxes, and your arm can move. If the triceps did not relax, it would pull in the opposite direction from your biceps at the same time, and you couldn't move your

FIGURE 2-26 EXAMPLE OF A MONOSYNAPTIC STRETCH REFLEX.
If a weight is dropped in a person's hand, the forearm moves down and stretches the biceps muscle. Receptors in the muscle sense the stretch and send action potentials along nerve fibers into the spinal cord. These fibers make synaptic contact directly onto motor neurons, which signal the muscle to contract. The arm pulls the weight up. This reflex is called monosynaptic *because only one neural synapse is encountered in the entire sequence.*

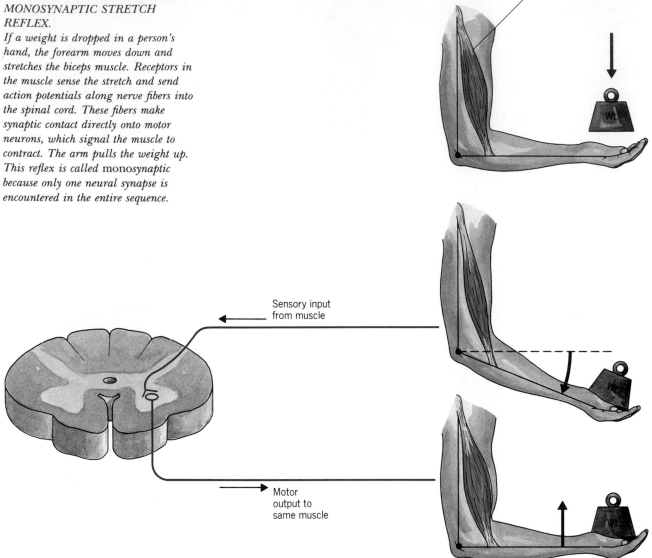

Biceps muscles

Sensory input from muscle

Motor output to same muscle

arm. Other polysynaptic reflexes are more complex and control more complex behaviors. For example, sexual stimulation of a man's penis causes penile erection and ejaculation through a polysynaptic reflex.

Although spinal reflexes can occur without the participation of the brain, the brain can influence them (Carew, 1985). For instance, when the doctor tests your "knee-jerk" stretch reflex by tapping the tendon in your knee (the tap stretches the muscle on the top of your thigh), you can make his or her day more interesting by preventing your leg from kicking upward. Your brain will have inhibited the monosynaptic knee-jerk reflex.

THE PERIPHERAL NERVOUS SYSTEM

As we noted at the beginning of the chapter, the peripheral nervous system links sensory receptors, central nervous system (brain and spinal cord), and effectors (muscles and glands) throughout the body. The **peripheral nerves** form these links. The peripheral nerves are collections of long axons and dendrites that carry information between the central nervous system and the periphery. Peripheral nerves are classified as *cranial nerves* or *spinal nerves,* depending where they enter or leave the central nervous system.

Cranial nerves enter or leave the central nervous system at the bottom surface of the brain. There are 12 pairs of cranial nerves; one member of each pair serves one side of the body. Most of the cranial nerves control senses and muscles in the head and neck. For example, the olfactory nerve serves the sense of smell, the optic nerve serves vision, and the auditory nerve serves hearing and the vestibular sense (position and movement of the head). Other cranial nerves tell you when your face has been touched. Still others control movement of the eyes, face, mouth, and tongue.

Spinal nerves enter or leave the central nervous system at the spinal cord. As with the cranial nerves, spinal nerves function in pairs that serve each half of the body. Spinal nerves that carry sensory information have their cell bodies just outside the spinal cord. Their axons enter the spinal cord and either continue up the white matter toward the brain or contact neurons in the spinal gray matter (see Figure 2-25). Spinal nerves that control movements are the axons of neurons located in the front part of the spinal gray matter. The spinal nerves pass through small openings between the bones of the vertebral column. If these bones press on the spinal nerves, the pinching or damage can cause severe pain or loss of sensation and motor control.

Recall that the peripheral nervous system is made up of somatic and autonomic divisions (see Figure 2-2). Both divisions connect with the central nervous system. They are distinguished by the body organs that they serve. The somatic division consists of cranial and spinal nerves that serve the striated muscles (motor) and the exteroceptors and proprioceptors (sensory). The autonomic division consists of cranial and spinal nerves that connect primarily with internal organs of the body. Let's look more closely at the autonomic nervous system.

Autonomic Nervous System

The autonomic nervous system once was thought to act relatively independently of the rest of the nervous system, and for that reason it was named *autonomic* (from *autonomous*, which means "self-governing"). But today we know that it is under the control of the central nervous system. The major function of the autonomic nervous system is to control the body's metabolism in response to demands from both the external world and the body's internal environment. Your autonomic nervous system helps to set the proper levels of activation when you become active or relaxed, excited or calm. Your autonomic nervous system is at work when your heart pounds with excitement at seeing someone you care about and when it pounds with fear at a horror movie. It's at work when you relax into an easy chair and when you munch on a snack. It does this

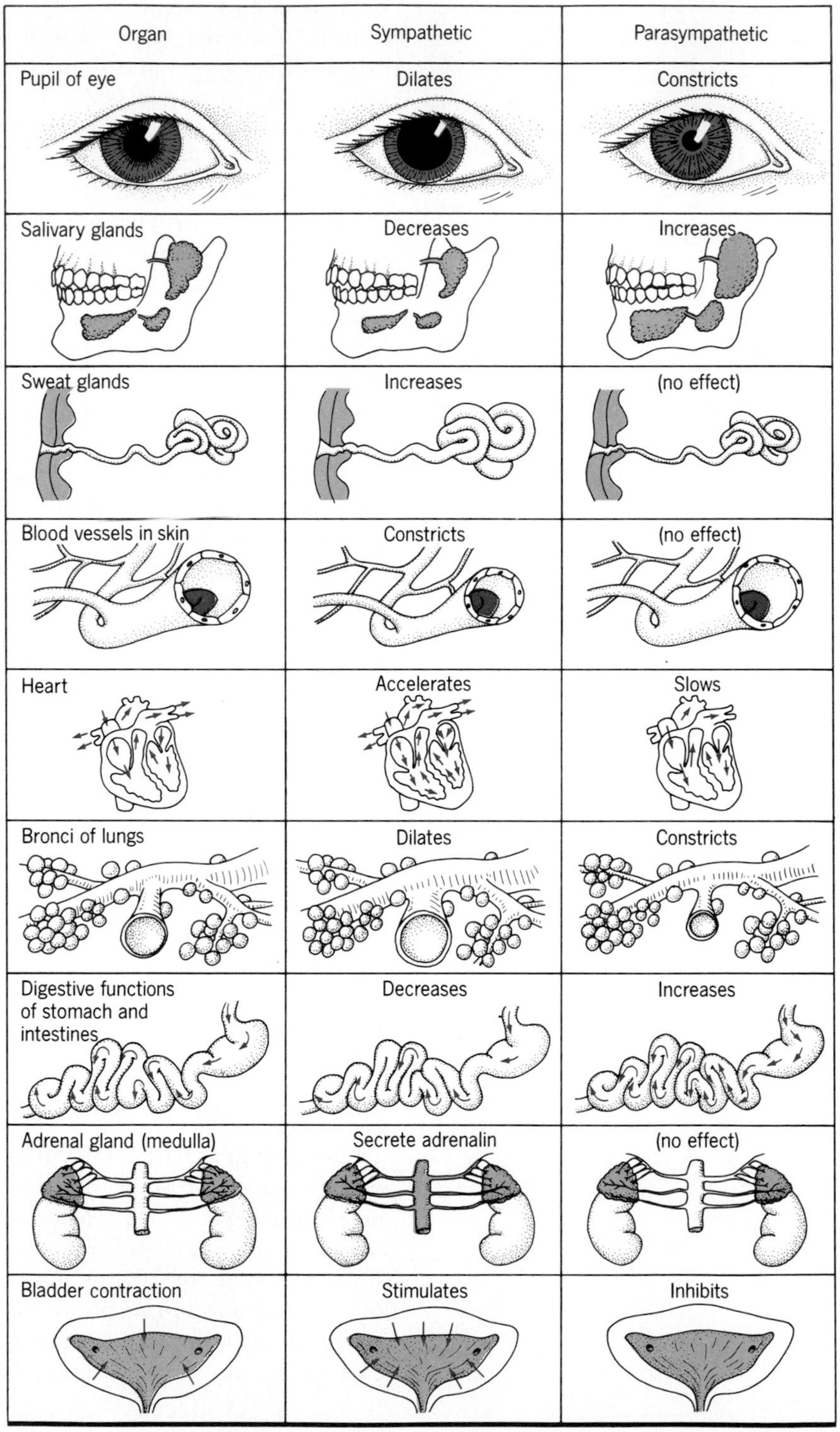

FIGURE 2-27 SOME FUNCTIONS OF THE AUTONOMIC NERVOUS SYSTEM.
Most organs influenced by the sympathetic division also are influenced by the parasympathetic division. The two divisions have opposite effects on the organs served by both.

Organ	Sympathetic	Parasympathetic
Pupil of eye	Dilates	Constricts
Salivary glands	Decreases	Increases
Sweat glands	Increases	(no effect)
Blood vessels in skin	Constricts	(no effect)
Heart	Accelerates	Slows
Bronci of lungs	Dilates	Constricts
Digestive functions of stomach and intestines	Decreases	Increases
Adrenal gland (medulla)	Secrete adrenalin	(no effect)
Bladder contraction	Stimulates	Inhibits

by controlling the contractions of your heart muscle and the smooth muscles throughout your body and by regulating the release of chemicals from glands.

The autonomic nervous system consists of two divisions—the sympathetic and parasympathetic. Many of the same body organs connect with both divisions. The two divisions tend to have opposite effects on the organs, for example, one division speeding up a reaction and the other slowing it down (see Figure 2-27). Usually both divisions are active to some extent, and they operate in a precisely controlled balance.

The *sympathetic division* is most active when you are expending energy from body stores. For instance, imagine that you are running a race. As you run, excitation of the sympathetic division increases your heart rate, increases sweating (to dissipate body heat), constricts blood vessels in the skin (to cool your body), opens the passages (bronchi) to the lungs (to increase respiration), and increases the secretion of adrenalin from the adrenal gland. At the same time, the sympathetic division decreases the activity of your stomach and intestines (to slow digestion) and reduces salivation and bladder contraction. In effect, the sympathetic division helps your body expend energy in an intense physical activity like running and reduces the bodily functions that are involved in storing and conserving energy. The sympathetic division also becomes more active when you are emotionally aroused. When you become excited (because you want to win that race), angry (because a competitor has cut in front of you), or frightened (because a large dog has run onto the race course), the sympathetic division again rapidly springs into action.

The *parasympathetic division* is most active when you are increasing the body's supply of stored energy. For example, imagine that after the race, you are hungry enough to eat an enormous lunch. As you eat, the parasympathetic system increases the activity of your stomach and intestines and increases salivation, all of which help you to digest. At the same time, the parasympathetic division decreases the activity of your organs involved in expending energy. It decreases your respiration (by constricting the passages to the lungs) and your heart rate.

GLANDS AND THE ENDOCRINE SYSTEM

As we noted earlier (see Table 2-1), glands are one of the effectors controlled by the nervous system. There are two types of glands, distinguished by how they release chemicals. **Exocrine glands** (from Greek words meaning "outside secreting") secrete chemicals through a duct. Examples are the lachrymal glands, which secrete tears onto the surface of the eye, and the sweat glands, which secrete sweat onto the surface of the skin. Similarly, the pancreas secretes digestive juices through ducts into the intestine. The autonomic nervous system controls the output of these glands.

The **endocrine glands** (from Greek words meaning "inside secreting") operate in a different way, and their effects generally are more wide-reaching than those of the exocrine glands. Endocrine glands have specialized cells that secrete chemicals into the fluids around capillaries.

These chemicals enter the bloodstream and are carried throughout the body. The chemicals secreted by the endocrine glands are called **hormones** (from the Greek *hormon,* which means "to excite or set in motion").

Figure 2-28 shows the locations of the major endocrine glands and some of the functions of the hormones they secrete. These hormones are critical to many behaviors and even to survival. Early in life, hormones help to determine the development of the body and the brain. For instance, growth hormone from the pituitary gland influences the growth of cells. Too little growth hormone can lead to dwarfism, and too much can lead to giantism. Hormones from the thyroid gland regulate metabolism and also influence growth. Too little thyroid hormone can lead to abnormal brain development and mental retardation, a condition known as *cretinism.* During adolescence, hormones control the development of physical sexual characteristics and of sexual behavior. For instance, the gonads (ovaries and testes) produce hormones that control the bodily changes that occur at puberty. Throughout life, hormones can modify people's moods and actions, their aggressiveness or submissiveness, and their desire to eat or drink.

As the hormones circulate in the bloodstream, they come into contact with cells throughout the body. But each hormone influences only those cells and organs with special receptors that recognize the specific hormone. When the hormone streams by, it binds to the cell membrane or enters the cell and binds to receptors inside. The hormone then modifies chemical reactions in the cell, which change the activity of the cell or cause it to produce certain proteins that alter growth or function.

Control of the Endocrine System

The nervous system controls the output of the endocrine glands in two important ways (Fink, 1985). One is through the connection from the autonomic nervous system to the adrenal gland, which we discussed earlier (see Figure 2-27). The other is through the hypothalamus, which regulates the output of hormones from the **pituitary gland**. The pituitary gland is located at the base of the brain, just under the hypothalamus (see the bottom of Figure 2-16 and Figure 2-28).

The hypothalamus contains specialized neurons called *neurosecretory cells,* which release hormones that affect the front of the pituitary gland (the **anterior pituitary**). In response, the anterior pituitary releases hormones into the bloodstream. These hormones control other endocrine glands in the body. For that reason, most hormones secreted by the anterior pituitary are called *tropic hormones* (tropic is pronounced with a long "o" as in "toe," and means "directed toward"). For example, one such hormone from the anterior pituitary (adrenocorticotropic hormone) stimulates the adrenal gland to secrete the hormone cortisone. The whole sequence of events is diagrammed in Figure 2-29*a*.

The hypothalamus also controls hormone secretion by the back of the pituitary gland (the **posterior pituitary**). In this case, neurosecretory cells in the hypothalamus send their axons into the posterior pituitary and release hormones directly into capillaries there. The hormones then enter the blood supply to the body (Figure 2-29*b*). Because the pituitary

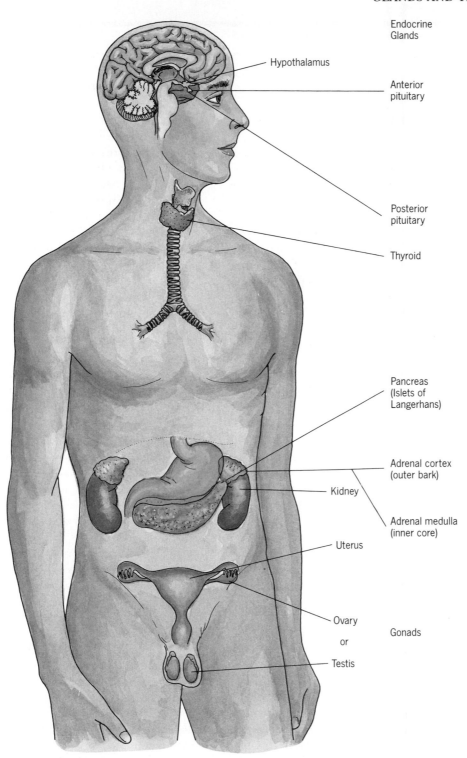

Endocrine
Glands

Hypothalamus

Anterior
pituitary

Posterior
pituitary

Thyroid

Pancreas
(Islets of
Langerhans)

Adrenal cortex
(outer bark)

Kidney

Adrenal medulla
(inner core)

Uterus

Ovary

or

Gonads

Testis

FIGURE 2-28 LOCATIONS AND FUNCTIONS OF THE MAJOR ENDOCRINE GLANDS.

There are many different endocrine glands throughout the body. Some of the glands secrete only one hormone whereas others secrete several. These hormones affect growth and behavior throughout our lives. (From Rosenzweig and Leiman, 1982.)

BOX 2-2
NERVOUS SYSTEM
PLASTICITY AND
RECOVERY FROM
DAMAGE

Every year, many people suffer damage to the nervous system. Their peripheral nerves are crushed or severed in accidents, and they lose sensation or movement in specific parts of their bodies. Spinal cords are injured in car and diving accidents, and people lose sensation and movement over large areas of the body. Brains are damaged by loss of blood supply (a stroke), by disease, and by head injury, and people lose sensory, motor, and cognitive abilities, depending on the brain regions affected.

Once neurons are damaged and die, they are never replaced. Nevertheless, many people recover many of their lost abilities after nervous system damage. One reason they recover is that *surviving* neurons show **plasticity**—they alter their anatomical connections and their function.

One type of plasticity is **regeneration**. When an axon is damaged, the neuron grows a new one. Regeneration occurs in the peripheral nervous system. When a peripheral nerve is cut or crushed, the damaged axons grow back to the peripheral targets and make new functional connections (Sunderland, 1978; Richardson, Aguayo, and McGuinness, 1983) (see Box Figure 1, top). This regeneration can lead to recovery of function after damage to a peripheral nerve.

But in the brain and spinal cord, damaged axons do not regenerate successfully. One reason is that glial cells, which remove debris from the damage, form a scar that blocks regeneration (Reier, Stensaas, and Guth, 1983) (see Box Figure 1, top). Scientists have tried to remedy this problem by reducing the scar formation or by implanting artificial guide tubes for regenerating axons to grow through. But so far, these methods have not promoted functional regeneration in the central nervous system. This failure suggests that there are other fundamental differences in the ability of the peripheral and central nervous systems to support regeneration (Bignami, Chi, and Dahl, 1986; Guth, Reier, Barrett, and Donati, 1983).

If axons in the central nervous system fail to regenerate, then how is behavioral recovery possible after brain damage? One mechanism is another type of plasticity, called **axon sprouting** (Cotman and Nieto-Sampedro, 1982). Undamaged axons sprout new terminals and make new synaptic connections onto other remaining neurons. The new connections replace those that have been lost (Box Figure 1, bottom). Neurons that receive the new connections may then change their physiological properties and partly take over functions that were lost following the damage (Spear, 1985; Tsukahara and Murakami, 1983).

Children with brain damage are likely to recover more completely than adults with similar brain damage (Teuber, 1975; Vargha-Khadem, O'Gorman, and Watters, 1985). This more complete recovery may occur because axons sprout and form new connections much more readily in an immature, developing nervous system than in an adult's (Goldberger and Murray, 1985; Marshall, 1985; Tsuka-hara and Murakami, 1983). For example, when the primary visual cortex is damaged, people and lower animals suffer a loss of vision. But when the damage occurs early in life, the loss of vision is not as great as when the damage occurs in adults. Studies of animals show that neurons in remaining areas of the immature brain sprout and physiologically reorganize more completely, and suggest that this reorganization leads to the improved vision (Spear, 1985).

Researchers have tried to increase plasticity of remaining neurons by giving drugs after brain damage. To some extent, they have succeeded. For instance, drugs that increase axon sprouting have been shown to reduce the behavioral deficits caused by brain damage in rats (Freed, de Medinaceli, and Wyatt, 1985; Sabel, Dunbar, Fass, and Stein, 1985).

One fascinating development in the attempt to treat brain damage is the brain transplant. This sounds like the stuff of science-fiction movies, in which the implanted brain of a donor takes over the behavior and thought of the host. The reality is less fantastic and potentially much more useful. Because the immature nervous system is more plastic than the adult, researchers have implanted embryonic or fetal brain tissue into the damaged brains of adult animals (Björklund and Stenevi, 1984; Fine, 1986; Freed et al., 1985). The transplanted tissue can serve several functions. It can act as a physical bridge along which regenerating axons can grow, and it can release chemicals that promote axon regeneration or sprouting. Transplanted neurons may connect with the host brain and partly replace damaged tissue. Transplanted cells also

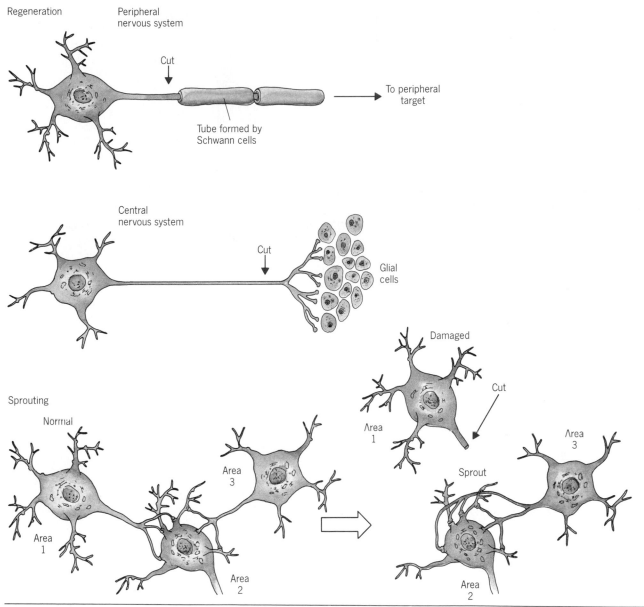

BOX FIGURE 1
REGENERATION AND SPROUTING IN THE NERVOUS SYSTEM.
(Top) *If a peripheral nerve axon is cut, the part connected to the surviving cell body begins to regenerate. The regeneration is aided by Schwann cells, which form a tube that guides the axon* to its peripheral target. Cut axons in the central nervous system also begin to regenerate, but regeneration fails, partly because the growing axon runs into scar formed by glial cells. (Bottom) If neurons in one area of the brain (Area 1) have their axons cut, or if the neurons themselves are damaged, their connections with neurons in other areas of the brain (Area 2) are lost. In response, undamaged neurons in a third area of the brain (Area 3) may sprout new axon terminals and replace lost synaptic connections.

BOX 2-2   *(continued)*

can release transmitters and replace those lost by disease or damage. For example, transplants of cells that release dopamine may help with Parkinson's disease (Gage, Björklund, Isacson, and Brundin, 1986; Olson, 1985). The outlook for brain transplants is promising. Some transplants have partly restored behavior (see Box Figure 2). The hope is that some day they will fully restore behavior lost by damage to brain and spinal cord.

BOX FIGURE 2 EFFECTS OF BRAIN TRANSPLANTS IN RECOVERY OF BEHAVIOR AFTER BRAIN DAMAGE.

Three groups of rats received damage to their primary visual cortex; a control group was not damaged. Two of the brain-damaged groups later got transplanted cortex from either the frontal lobe or occipital lobe of rat fetuses in the damaged area. All the rats later were tested for their ability to learn visual discriminations. Rats that had received a frontal lobe transplant learned to disciminate between light and dark stimuli nearly as well as controls; other brain-damaged rats were severely impaired. The findings suggest that some transplants can improve behavioral recovery after brain damage. (From Stein, Labbe, Attella, and Rakowsky, 1985.)

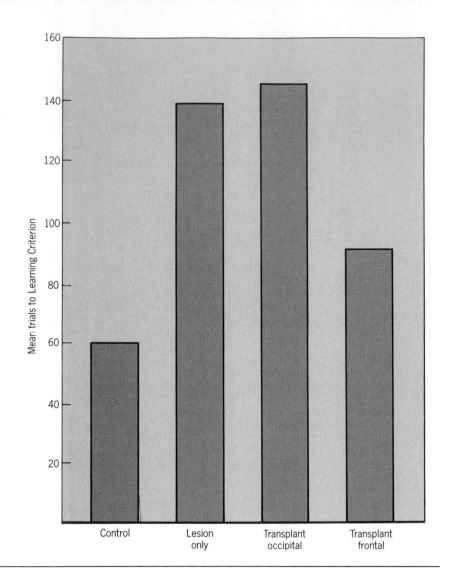

gland, particularly the anterior pituitary, is so important in controlling hormone secretion by other glands, it sometimes is referred to as the "master gland."

Neural and Hormonal Communication

The hormones secreted by the endocrine glands influence many organs throughout people's bodies. The endocrine system is actually a system of communication, sending hormonal messages throughout the body. These hormonal messages act together with messages from neurons to control behavior.

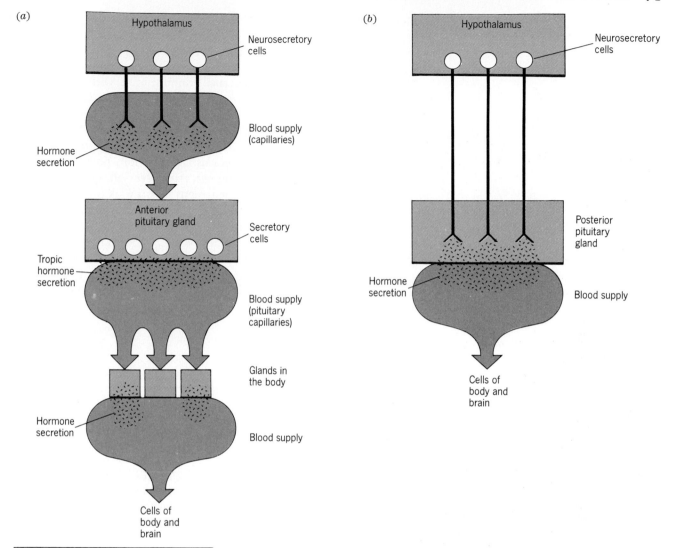

FIGURE 2-29 HYPOTHALAMUS CONTROL OF THE ENDOCRINE SYSTEM.
(a) *Hormones released by the hypothalamus reach the anterior pituitary and cause it to release tropic hormones into the blood. The tropic hormones reach and cause endocrine glands throughout the body to release other hormones into the blood.* (b) *Other cells in the hypothalamus release hormones directly into the blood supply of the posterior pituitary gland.*

Hormonal and neural messages work in tandem, but they operate somewhat differently. One major difference between the two is their speed of action. The nervous system performs very rapidly. Action potentials travel down axons in milliseconds. An entire reflex can occur in less than 50 milliseconds, and even complex perceptions and behavior take well under a second. In contrast, the endocrine system performs much more slowly. Hormonal messages make take minutes to reach their targets and exert their effects.

Neural and hormonal communications also differ in their forms of distribution. The nervous system sends messages over fixed lines of communication to precise locations. In this way, it is like a telephone system. In contrast, hormonal messages are diffuse; they enter the bloodstream and flow throughout the body. Hormonal messages are like radio programs broadcast over a wide area. Just as there are many different radio stations (each using a different wavelength), there are many different endocrine glands (each using different hormones). And just as a particular radio broadcast is received only by radio receivers tuned to the appropriate wavelength, a particular hormone is received only by cells with the appropriate receptors.

The neural and endocrine systems communicate with each other. Many areas of the brain influence the autonomic nervous system and hypothalamus, which, as we have seen, exert control over endocrine function. The endocrine system in turn influences neural activity. For instance, the levels of circulating hormones signal the hypothalamus to increase or decrease pituitary secretions. In addition, hormones in the blood reach neurons in the brain and can affect everything from sensory sensitivity to moods. Consider what happens if you walk into a store and find a robbery in progress: Your visual system perceives what is going on and signals the rest of your brain. Your hypothalamus and autonomic system spring into action and hormones mobilize you to choose between "fight and flight." Other areas of your brain determine the actions you take, and these actions are controlled by the neural motor system. In sum, neural and endocrine systems work in concert to produce coordinated, integrated behavior and thought.

SUMMARY

OVERVIEW OF THE NERVOUS SYSTEM

1. *The Biological Perspective.* The brain, along with the rest of the nervous system, controls everything that people sense, think, feel, and do. Although there are important species differences, the basic organization of the nervous system is similar for all mammals. Studies of lower animals have greatly contributed to our knowledge of the nervous system.

2. *Basic Organization of the Nervous System.* The nervous system is an integrative mechanism that produces behavior (outputs) on the basis of past and present experience (inputs). The inputs (sights, sounds, touch, and so on) are provided by specialized sensory receptors that are inside the body and on its surface. The outputs, or observable behaviors, are produced by muscles and glands that are controlled by the nervous system. The nervous system is di-

vided into two components. The first is the central nervous system, which consists of the brain and spinal cord. The second is the peripheral nervous system, which links the central nervous system to the receptors and effectors throughout the body.

CELLS AND HOW THEY WORK

3. *Cells of the Nervous System.* The basic units of communication in the nervous system are nerve cells (or neurons). These cells have dendrites that receive information from other neurons and an axon that sends information to other neurons. Each axon usually branches many times, and each branch ends in a terminal bouton that contacts another neuron at a synapse. Neurons are surrounded by supporting cells called glia (in the central nervous system) or

satellite cells (in the peripheral nervous system). The supporting cells give neurons physical and nutritional support, they help regulate the chemical balance around neurons, and they help clean up debris from dying neurons. Supporting cells also wrap themselves around axons to form an electrically insulating sheath called myelin.

4. *Electrical Potentials in Neurons.* When a neuron is at rest, different concentrations of electrically charged molecules (called ions) are present inside and outside the cell membrane. These ions produce a small voltage difference (called the resting electrical potential) across the membrane. When a neuron becomes active, certain ions flow rapidly through the membrane and a brief electrical signal, called an action potential, results. Neurons com-

municate by propagating action potentials along their axons. Myelin considerably speeds action potential propagation.

5. *Synaptic Transmission.* At the terminal bouton, an action potential causes a chemical neurotransmitter to be released into the space between the bouton and the next neuron. The transmitter interacts with receptor sites in the membrane of the receiving neuron and causes ions to flow through the membrane. Certain ions make the receiving neuron less likely to fire an action potential, and others make it more likely to fire. Each neuron typically receives thousands of synaptic contacts. Whether it fires an action potential and how it continues the communication depends upon the combined inhibitory and excitatory effects of all of these inputs.

STRUCTURE AND FUNCTION OF CENTRAL NERVOUS SYSTEM

6. *The Cerebral Cortex.* Neurons in the brain are organized into structures and functional systems. Part of the forebrain, the cerebral cortex, is divided into four lobes (frontal, parietal, temporal, and occipital) that serve sensory, motor, and associative functions. Sensory areas of cortex receive and process information about the environment— sights, sounds, touch, and so on. Motor areas plan and control movements of the body. Association areas interconnect sensory and motor areas and are involved in perception, complex motor control, cognition, emotion, memory, and language.

7. *Other Structures of the Forebrain.* The forebrain also consists of the thalamus, hypothalamus, basal ganglia, and limbic system. The thalamus consists mainly of groups of neurons (called nuclei) that have sensory, motor, and associative functions in concert with the cerebral cortex and other parts of the nervous system. The basal ganglia communicate with the thalamus and cortex in the control of movement. The hypothalamus helps control aggression and emotion, motivation (for example, hunger and thirst), and sexual behavior. The limbic system includes a number of interconnected brain structures and also is involved in motivation and emotion. The entire forebrain works as a whole in controlling behavior and thought.

8. *Cerebral Commissures and Hemispheric Dominance.* The forebrain has two hemispheres that are approximate mirror images of each other. The cerebral commissures, the most prominent of which is the corpus callosum, connect and coordinate the two hemispheres. Studies of people with brain damage and split brains indicate that some abilities depend more on one hemisphere than the other. But separate cognitive functions do not reside wholly in one hemisphere or the other.

9. *The Brain Stem.* The brain stem consists of the midbrain, cerebellum, pons, and medulla. These structures also contribute to sensory and motor abilities. The midbrain plays a role in vision, hearing, and attending to visual and auditory stimuli. The cerebellum helps control posture and movement on the basis of sensory feedback and is involved in learning new motor skills. The reticular formation extends through the midbrain, pons, and medulla. The reticular formation has widespread connections throughout the brain and is important in regulating general levels of arousal and activity of the brain.

10. *The Spinal Cord.* The spinal cord is the part of the central nervous system that extends down through the center of the bony vertebral column (spine). It controls certain reflexes—automatic motor responses that result from direct sensory inputs to the spinal cord and to not require participation by the brain. The spinal cord also acts as a kind of way station for sensory and motor information passing between the brain and the peripheral nervous system.

PERIPHERAL NERVOUS SYSTEM AND ENDOCRINE SYSTEM

11. *Peripheral Nervous System.* The peripheral nervous system consists of nerves (collections of long axons and dendrites) that connect the brain and spinal cord to sensory receptors, muscles, and glands throughout the body. The peripheral nervous system is divided into two subsystems. The somatic division carries sensory information from exteroceptors and proprioceptors (for example, eyes, skin, muscles, and joints) and sends motor commands to the striated muscles. It controls voluntary movements and involuntary adjustments of balance and posture. The autonomic division connects primarily with internal organs of the body and is further divided into two components. The sympathetic component is most active when people expend energy, and the parasympathetic component helps the body to conserve energy.

12. *Glands and the Endocrine System.* Like the nervous system, the endocrine system acts as a system of communication throughout the body. Its messages travel as hormones secreted into the bloodstream by glands. These hormones are critical to many

behaviors and even to survival. Early in life, hormones help to determine the development of the body and brain. During adolescence, they control development of physical sexual characteristics and of sexual behaviors. Throughout life, hormones can modify moods and actions. The output of endocrine glands is partly controlled by the brain, especially the hypothalamus. Hormones secreted by the glands in turn affect brain function. Thus, the endocrine and nervous systems work in concert to determine behavior and thought.

FURTHER READINGS

There are a number of excellent undergraduate-level textbooks available that provide an overview of nervous system function and its control of behavior. Two of the best are *Physiology of Behavior* by Carlson (1986) and *Physiological Psychology* by Rosenzweig and Leiman (1982). A somewhat more advanced general textbook is *From Neuron to Brain,* by Kuffler, Nicholls, and Martin (1984). This book provides more detail about neural function than do the first two books mentioned, yet it still is easy to read and is intended for the beginning student.

For a more encyclopedic overview of nervous system function, *Principles of Neural Science,* edited by Kandel and Schwartz (1985), includes over 60 chapters written by experts in the field and covers topics ranging from basic cellular structure and function to clinical disorders of the nervous system.

Another excellent source of information is the September 1979 issue of *Scientific American,* devoted entirely to articles about the brain by eminent researchers. It includes general theoretical articles that stimulate thinking about how the brain works as well as reviews of topics such as the brain mechanisms of vision, movement, and hemispheric dominance. The articles are well written and intended for the nonspecialist.

For futher reading about the frontal lobes, the November 1984 issue of *Trends in NeuroSciences* is an excellent source of material. Students interested in learning more about the functions of the corpus callosum and about the functions of the two cerebral hemispheres are referred to *Two Hemispheres—One Brain: Functions of the Corpus Callosum,* edited by Lepore, Ptito, and Jasper (1986). Further information about plasticity in the nervous system can be found in *Synaptic Plasticity,* edited by Cotman (1985), with chapters on neural plasticity during learning, development, and recovery from nervous system injury, all written by scientists in the field.

Students interested in the ethical issues surrounding brain research are referred to *Brain Control* by Valenstein (1973). This book contains a critical evaluation of the effects of brain stimulation and the use of brain surgery to control behavior in humans. Excellent discussions of the use of animals in research on nervous system function, and in health research in general, can be found in *Health Benefits of Animal Research,* edited by Gay (1986).

3

SENSATION AND PERCEPTION: VISION

Look around the room for a moment. Look at the patterns and shapes of objects and the vivid and varied colors of clothes, furniture, books, walls, windows, and lights. Now listen to the sounds in the room. Are people talking? Is music playing in the background? Now pick up a pencil or this textbook, and feel its shape, texture, and weight. All of this information about sights, sounds, and touch is coming to you through your senses. Indeed, everything you know about the world is a result of information that you get through your senses. Right now you are using your sense of vision to read these words. While you were growing up, you first learned about the world by seeing, hearing, touching, smelling, and tasting things. Today you are no different. This process of sensing continues throughout life.

How does all of this sensing occur? How do we receive and interpret sensory information? What is the relationship between things that are "out there" in the external world ("reality") and our experience of them? These are some of the questions that we will address in this and the following chapter. In the present chapter, we discuss **vision**—the sensation and perception of light. Vision is the most thoroughly studied and the best understood of all our senses, and therefore it can serve to illustrate general principles of sensation and perception. In the following chapter, we discuss how the other senses work and how many of the same principles apply to them.

Before we begin our discussion of vision, we set forth some basic concepts and describe briefly how sensation and perception are studied.

SOME BASIC CONCEPTS

Sensation versus Perception

Historically, philosophers and psychologists have drawn a distinction between sensation and perception. **Sensation** generally refers to the process by which we receive and experience relatively simple events in the external world. Sensation refers to our initial contact with the environment and the ways in which sensory receptors in the eye, ear, nose, and other sensory organs respond to stimuli and provide us with simple sensory experience. **Perception** usually refers to our experience of relatively complex events and the influence of factors such as attention and prior learning on our sensory experience. Perception has to do with how we interpret the sensory environment.

The more psychologists learn about how the sensory systems work and how people experience the world, the clearer it becomes that the distinction between sensation and perception is not so sharp as was once thought. For example, complex experiences that seem to be due to interpretation of the world often are based on simple events in the sensory receptors. Because of events that occur within the eye, a person's perceptions of patterns of light in a visual scene do not correspond precisely to the physical patterns of light. Psychologists now know that sensation inevitably changes the experience of external "reality" and that the changes begin as soon as external stimuli contact receptors. Because the distinction between sensation and perception has become blurred, many psychologists now use the terms interchangeably. The important thing is to understand how people experience stimulation of their senses.

Measuring Sensory Abilities

To understand how people receive and interpret sensory information, psychologists must measure the relationship between external stimuli and people's experience of them. A **stimulus** is any kind of physical event or energy that can produce a response. For example, electromagnetic energy (light) is a physical stimulus that produces a response that we experience as a visual sensation. Psychologists who study the relationships between physical stimuli and people's experience of them are engaged in the study of **psychophysics** (from the Greek roots *psyche*, "mind," and *physike*, "physical phenomena"). Many of the methods for studying these relationships have been in use since the mid 1800s, although new ones have been devised since then. These psychophysical methods are now used in many areas of psychology, including social and clinical psychology.

We turn now to a discussion of how these methods are used to measure people's basic abilities to detect, discriminate, and judge the intensity of sensory stimuli.

DETECTION   What is the softest sound you can hear? The faintest odor you can smell? The gentlest touch you can feel? At what intensity of light do you first perceive dawn? One question that people ask about your senses is how well they can detect very weak stimuli. That is, what is the **absolute threshold**, or minimum amount of energy that can produce a sensation? As you can see in Table 3-1, we humans are incredibly sensitive to very weak stimuli in our environment!

How do psychologists go about measuring absolute thresholds? To measure the threshold for light, we can ask a person to look at a screen and tell us when a spot of light appears. On each trial we project a spot of a particular intensity and ask the person to say "yes" if she sees it and

TABLE 3-1   APPROXIMATE VALUES OF ABSOLUTE THRESHOLDS EXPRESSED IN EVERYDAY TERMS

Sense	Threshold
Vision	A candle flame seen at 30 miles on a dark, clear night
Hearing	The tick of a watch under quiet conditions at 20 feet
Taste	One teaspoon of sugar in two gallons of water
Smell	One drop of perfume diffused into the entire volume of a three-room apartment
Touch	The wing of a bee falling on your cheek from a distance of one centimeter

Source: From Galanter, 1962.
Note: These values apply under ideal conditions and will vary from individual to individual and from time to time for the same individual.

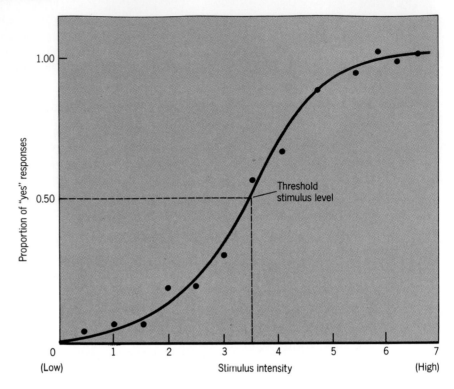

Stimulus intensity is plotted in arbitrary units on the horizontal axis, and the proportion of trials on which the person says that he or she saw it (yes responses) is plotted on the vertical axis. This is a psychometric function. The absolute threshold is defined as the stimulus intensity that was detected on 50 percent of the trials.

"no" if she doesn't. We repeat this procedure for a range of intensities, and each intensity is presented many times to ensure a reliable measure. The results are plotted in a **psychometric function**, such as the one shown in Figure 3-1.

Early psychologists were surprised to find that the psychometric function for absolute threshold is so gradual. They expected that there would be one intensity that is never seen (or heard, or felt, etc.) and another, of slightly higher intensity, that is always seen. But as Figure 3-1 shows, there is a *range* of stimulus intensities over which the observer sometimes reports detecting the stimulus (a "yes" response) and sometimes not. As the intensity is increased within this range, the proportion of trials on which the observer reports seeing the spot of light gradually increases. Thus there is not an all-or-none absolute threshold; the same intensity sometimes is detected and sometimes not. You may have experienced this phenomenon yourself. Have you ever been in the shower and thought you heard the telephone ring, but then, as you listened for it, decided that you hadn't heard it after all? First you think you heard it, and then you think you didn't. The ring of the telephone was near your absolute threshold for hearing.

Signal Detection Theory. Why does our ability to detect a weak stimulus vary in this way? **Signal detection theory** (Green and Swets, 1966) provides a widely accepted explanation. When an external stimulus occurs, it strikes sensory receptors and changes the activity of sensory neurons in the brain. This change is the *signal* that an external stimulus such as a flash of light or a sound has occurred. Neurons in the brain

FIGURE 3-2 SIGNAL DETECTION THEORY ANALYSIS OF ABSOLUTE THRESHOLDS.
(a) *This frequency distribution shows the level of neural activity in a sensory system when no external stimulus is present. It represents the noise in the sensory system. The horizontal axis shows different levels of neural activity (for example, number of action potentials per second discharged by sensory neurons). The vertical axis shows the relative frequencies with which the levels occur.* (b) *This shows the level of neural activity that occurs when effects of an external stimulus are added to the noise.* (c) *The two distributions are shown together in the same graph.* (d) *Illustrated is the process by which people decide whether a particular level of neural activity is due to noise alone or to signal plus noise.*

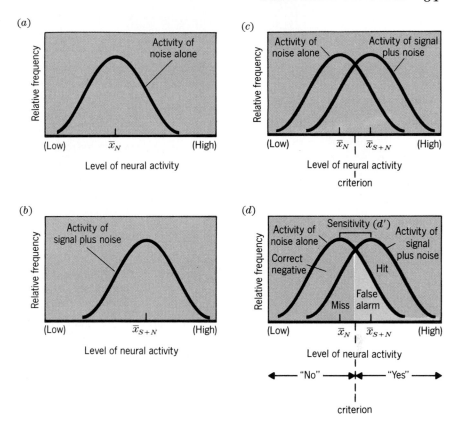

also have their own intrinsic activity, even in the absence of external stimulation. For example, the neurons that carry information from the eyes to the brain are active—they fire action potentials—even in total darkness (Barlow and Levick, 1969). This activity is the *noise* in the sensory system. Signal detection theory suggests that a major influence on a person's sensory threshold is the presence of noise in the sensory systems and the ability to detect a weak signal in this noise.

The effects of sensory system noise on a person's ability to detect very weak external stimuli are illustrated in Figure 3-2. As shown in Figure 3-2*a*, the level of intrinsic neural activity (noise) in the sensory system varies from moment to moment. Sometimes the noise level is high, and sometimes it is low, but usually it hovers around some mean level (symbolized $\bar{X}_N$; see Appendix for discussion of the mean, or average). When an external stimulus strikes a receptor, it produces neural activity (a signal) that is added to the noise, as shown in Figure 3-2*b*. Again, sometimes the signal-plus-noise level is high, and sometimes it is low, but usually it hovers around a mean level ($\bar{X}_{S+N}$) that is higher than the mean level for noise alone. As you can see in Figure 3-2*c*, the distributions of neural activity for noise alone and for signal-plus-noise overlap. When detecting a weak stimulus, a person must decide whether a particular level of sensory neural activity is due to noise alone or to signal-plus-noise. According to signal detection theory, we have some internal **criterion** for making this decision. (One possible criterion level is labeled in

Figure 3-2c.) Sometimes the level of signal-plus-noise neural activity is great enough to meet our criterion, in which case we perceive the external stimulus (flash of light, sound, touch, or the like). However, sometimes the exact same signal is added to a lower level of noise and does not reach the criterion level of activity. In this case, we do not perceive the external stimulus even though one actually did occur. Thus, according to signal detection theory, one reason that a person's ability to detect a weak stimulus varies from moment to moment is that the level of noise in the sensory system varies from moment to moment.

There is a second reason that measurements of sensory thresholds vary from time to time. Psychologists can only measure thresholds by asking people whether they have detected a stimulus, and their answers depend in part on people's motivations and expectations. Imagine, for example, that you are an air traffic controller. Your job is to report when aircraft are in the vicinity of your airport. You must watch a radar screen and report when a faint blip first appears on it. The blip is an aircraft. But you don't always know whether what you're seeing is a blip or not. If you think you see a blip but are not sure, whether you report it will depend in part on your expectations. If it is late at night and no incoming aircraft are expected, you might well pass it off as some noise in the radar system (or in your brain!). However, if an arriving flight is expected, you are more likely to say that you saw a blip and to report it as the expected flight. Your report also is likely to depend on the consequences you can expect your report to meet with. If there are many planes in the area and failing to report an arriving plane might lead to an accident, you are more likely to report the uncertain signal on your radar screen as a plane. However, if you may lose your job for reporting a plane that is not really there, you are less likely to report the signal as a plane. Thus, even something as seemingly basic as measuring the detectability of a simple stimulus varies according to complex psychological factors such as motivation and decision making.

In Figure 3-2c, a person's expectations and the consequences of reporting the presence of a weak stimulus determine the criterion level of neural activity at which a stimulus is reported. In a psychology experiment, just as in daily life, people can respond only yes or no to whether a stimulus is present. If the level of sensory neural activity is below a person's criterion, he or she will respond, "No, a stimulus is not present." If the level of activity is above a person's criterion, he or she will respond, "Yes, a stimulus is present." These responses result in one of four outcomes, as shown in Figure 3-2d. If a person reports that a stimulus is present ("yes" response) when it is not really there (when only noise is present), he has made a *false alarm*. If he correctly reports the presence of a stimulus (also a "yes" response), he has made a *hit*. If he reports correctly that a stimulus is not present ("no" response), he has made a *correct negative*, and if he reports that a stimulus is absent ("no" response) when it really is there, he has made a *miss*.

According to signal detection theory, whether a person responds yes or no and whether the response is correct depend on a person's criterion and sensitivity to the stimulus. Let's look first at some of the effects of changing a criterion. If the observer increases the criterion (shifts it to the right in Figure 3-2*d*), he will require a higher level of activity to indicate that an external stimulus is present. The air traffic controller who doesn't want to report a nonexistent flight may shift to a more cautious criterion of what is and what is not a blip on the radar screen. This shift will result in fewer false alarms, although it also will result in fewer hits. In contrast, if the observer decreases the criterion (shifts it to the left), a lower level of activity will be interpreted as a stimulus. The air traffic controller who doesn't want to miss any incoming flights and who shifts to a more liberal criterion will produce fewer misses and fewer correct negatives.

Of course, people's decisions about the stimuli they have or have not detected also are affected by their **sensitivity** to the stimulus. According to signal detection theory, sensitivity to a stimulus is reflected in the difference between the mean activity produced by noise in the sensory system ($\bar{X}_N$) and the mean activity produced by the signal plus noise ($\bar{X}_{S+N}$). (This difference is labeled d' in Figure 3-2*d*.) Sensitivity can be increased. For example, if a person is presented with a stronger stimulus that produces a larger signal, sensitivity increases (the distribution of signal-plus-noise moves to the right in Figure 3-2*d*), and the same criterion level results in more hits. The person more accurately detects the stimulus. If sensitivity is increased because the distribution of noise is moved to the left, the same criterion level results in fewer false alarms and more correct negatives. Again, the person more accurately detects the stimulus.

Thus, according to signal detection theory, we cannot measure absolute threshold. We can only get an index of someone's sensitivity to a stimulus independent of his or her criterion. How do we do this? In a signal detection experiment, psychologists determine the effects of criterion by varying it systematically while holding stimulus intensity constant at a particular value. They can vary the criterion by changing the *payoff* to a person for responding that yes, a stimulus is present or that no, it is not. For instance, on one set of trials the subject may get 50 cents for each yes response (no matter whether it is a hit or a false alarm) and lose 25 cents for each no response (no matter whether it is a miss or a correct negative). On another set of trials the subject may get 75 cents for each yes response and lose 10 cents for each no response. As a result, the subject will adopt a more liberal criterion (a shift to the left in Figure 3-2*d*) and will increase the tendency to respond yes. By charting the proportions of hits and false alarms for many different criterion levels, psychologists can measure the relative positions of the noise and signal-plus-noise distributions. This measure shows them a person's sensitivity to a stimulus that is independent of criterion.

Look back at Table 3-1. If you tested your ability to detect some of these weak stimuli and found that you could not, now you can understand why. Although human senses are incredibly sensitive, this sensitivity varies from person to person and from time to time in the same person depending on such factors as neural noise in the sensory system, expectations, and decision-making strategies.

DISCRIMINATION Have you ever tried to match up all the correct pairs of brown, black, and gray socks in your laundry? Have you ever lifted two suitcases to check which was heavier? Have you ever bit into two cherries to taste which was sweeter? If you have, then you have engaged in a process that psychologists call discriminating. A **discrimination** is a judgment about whether·two stimuli are different. If the two suitcases are very similar in weight and difficult to tell apart, their weights are near your **difference threshold**. Thus, a difference threshold is the least difference between two stimuli that is necessary for a person to be able to discriminate between them.

To precisely measure a difference threshold in a psychophysical experiment, we can present a *standard stimulus* and a *comparison stimulus* and ask the observer to judge whether the two stimuli differ from each other. For example, we can present a 100 gram weight (the standard) and a 90 gram weight (the comparison stimulus) and ask whether the comparison stimulus is heavier or lighter than the standard. We repeat this procedure a number of times for a series of comparison stimuli that are more or less similar to the standard. The most commonly used measure of the difference threshold is a physical difference between standard and comparison stimuli that can be discriminated 50 percent of the time. This measure is called the **just noticeable difference** (or **jnd**).

The size of the jnd depends upon the size of the standard stimulus. This relationship makes sense. If you are holding 50 pennies, adding one penny will make a just noticeable difference in weight. But if you are holding 500 pennies, adding a penny will not make a noticeable difference in weight; it will be necessary to add 10 pennies for you to feel the difference. Having observed this phenomenon, Ernst Weber (1834) proposed that the size of a jnd is a constant proportion of the size of the standard stimulus. This relationship is called **Weber's law** and is written as

$$\Delta I = KI \qquad \text{or} \qquad K = \frac{\Delta I}{I}$$

where ΔI is the jnd, I is the intensity of the standard stimulus, and K is the constant. Thus, K is a fraction that represents the amount (proportion) by which a stimulus must be changed to be just noticeably different. According to Weber's law, this fraction—called the **Weber fraction**—is constant for any given dimension of stimulus such as weight, brightness, loudness, and so forth. For example, if the Weber fraction is 2/100 for the dimension of weight, then 2 grams must be added to a 100-gram weight to be noticeable, and 20 grams must be added to a 1000-gram weight to be noticeable. Table 3-2 shows the Weber fractions for a number of sensory dimensions. The size of the fraction provides a measure of overall sensitivity to changes in intensity along a particular dimension. The smaller the Weber fraction, the greater the sensitivity. For example, among the dimensions shown in the table, people are most sensitive to changes in shock intensity—they can detect a 1.3 percent change—and least sensitive to changes in brightness—they can detect a 7.9 percent change. Experiments have shown that the Weber fraction is in fact constant for a wide range of stimulus intensities; the fraction changes only at extremely high or low standard stimulus intensities.

TABLE 3-2 TYPICAL WEBER FRACTIONS ($\Delta I / I$) FOR VARIOUS SENSORY DIMENSIONS

Dimension	Weber Fraction
Brightness	0.079
Loudness	0.048
Finger span	0.022
Heaviness	0.020
Line length	0.029
Taste (salt)	0.083
Electric shock	0.013
Vibration (fingertip)	
60 Hz	0.036
125 Hz	0.046
250 Hz	0.046

Source: From Teghtsoonian (1971).
Note: The smaller the number, the smaller the change in intensity necessary to produce a just noticeable difference.

*FIGURE 3-3 STIMULUS
INTENSITY AND ITS PERCEIVED
MAGNITUDE.*

*FIGURE 3-3 STIMULUS
INTENSITY AND ITS PERCEIVED
MAGNITUDE.*
*The curves show the relationship between
perceived magnitude (S) and the
physical magnitude or intensity (I) of
an electric shock, line length, and
brightness. (From Stevens, 1962.)*

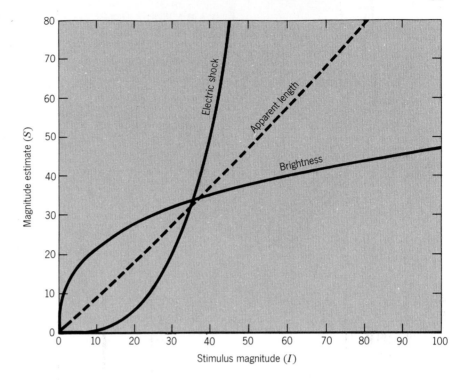

SCALING INTENSITY   Suppose you are in charge of lighting a theater
and are asked to double the brightness of the stage. Should you double
the number of lights that are turned on? If you want to make some
brownies taste twice as sweet, should you double the amount of sugar in
the recipe? Psychologists call the measurements involved in answering
questions like these **psychophysical scaling**: what is the relationship
between changes in the intensity of a stimulus and people's perception of
its intensity?

An ingenious method for measuring this relationship is called *magnitude estimation*. With this method, an observer is presented a standard
stimulus that is assigned some value. For example, a moderately intense
light might be presented and assigned a value of 10. Then another
intensity of stimulus is presented, and the observer is asked to assign it a
value that indicates its magnitude relative to the standard. For example,
if the observer sees a light that appears half as bright as the standard, she
assigns it a value of 5. If the light appears twice as bright as the standard,
she assigns it a value of 20. Measurements obtained in an experiment
such as this are shown in Figure 3-3 (the line labeled *brightness*). A low-
intensity light needs to be increased by a smaller absolute amount than a
high-intensity light for a person to notice the same increase in brightness
(magnitude). But an experiment with electric shock produces a different
result. It is necessary to increase a low-intensity shock by a *larger* amount
than a high-intensity shock to produce the same psychological increase in
sensation magnitude. Experiments with line lengths produce a still different result. When subjects estimate the apparent length of lines, there

TABLE 3-3 EXPONENTS OF THE POWER FUNCTIONS RELATING PERCEIVED MAGNITUDE (*S*) AND PHYSICAL STIMULUS INTENSITY (*I*) FOR A VARIETY OF STIMULUS DIMENSIONS

Dimension	Exponent	Stimulus Conditions
Loudness	0.6	Both ears
Brightness	0.33	5° target—dark
Brightness	0.5	Point source—dark
Lightness	1.2	Gray papers
Smell	0.55	Coffee odor
Taste	0.8	Saccharine
Taste	1.3	Sucrose
Taste	1.3	Salt
Temperature	1.0	Cold—on arm
Temperature	1.6	Warmth—on arm
Vibration	0.95	60 Hz—on finger
Duration	1.1	White noise stimulus
Finger span	1.3	Thickness of wood blocks
Pressure on palm	1.1	Static force on skin
Heaviness	1.45	Lifted weights
Force of handgrip	1.7	Precision hand dynamometer
Electric shock	3.5	60 Hz—through fingers

Source: From Stevens, 1961.

Note: For each dimension, $S = KI^n$, and only the exponent, *n*, differs among dimensions.

is nearly a one-to-one linear relationship between apparent length and actual length.

Thus, the relationships between physical intensity and psychological magnitude at first seem to differ according to the sensory dimensions illustrated in Figure 3-3: brightness, electric shock, and apparent length. But these relationships may not be so different after all. For all three dimensions, sensation magnitude (*S*) is proportional to stimulus magnitude or intensity (*I*) raised to some power (*n*) (Stevens, 1961, 1962). This is written as

$$S = kI^n$$

where *k* is a constant that depends on the unit of measurement. This relationship is called **Stevens' power law**. In Figure 3-3, the curves for all three dimensions follow the same power law, with an exponent *n* of 0.33 for brightness, 1.1 for line length, and 3.5 for electric shock. Indeed, the power law applies to many different stimulus dimensions; only the exponent differs among dimensions (see Table 3-3).

From the Stimulus to Experience

There is an old philosophical question that asks, "If a tree falls in the forest, but no one is there, has the tree made a noise?" This philosophical question points us squarely to an important point about sensation and perception. The stimulus is not the same as a person's experience of that stimulus. How *are* physical stimuli in the world translated into hu-

*FIGURE 3-4 GENERALIZED
SCHEME OF HOW SENSE ORGANS
PRODUCE NEURAL ACTIVITY
FROM ENVIRONMENTAL STIMULI.*
*The diagram at the top shows the
various structures that are involved in
transduction. The flow chart below shows
the events that take place at each
structure. Although there are some
exceptions to this scheme, most of our
sense organs operate in this way. (From
Thompson, 1967; after Davis, 1961.)*

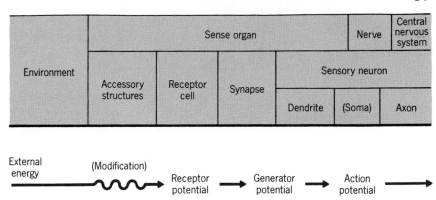

man experience? Psychologists put that question in this form: how do stimuli influence neurons in the brain, and how does the activity of neurons represent these stimuli?

The first step in the transformation of stimulus into experience is a transformation of external energy into the electrochemical activity of nerve cells, a process called **transduction**. For each of our senses a specialized **sense organ** carries out the transduction.

SENSE ORGANS Each sense organ is specialized to handle certain kinds of external energy. Eyes deal with light, ears deal with sound waves, the tongue deals with chemicals, and so on. Most sense organs have an **accessory structure**, which serves to focus, amplify, or alter particular environmental stimuli. The stimulus or the accessory structure itself then activates a **receptor cell**. For example, the eyeball is an accessory structure that focuses light onto receptor cells at the back of the eye. Similarly, most of the ear is an accessory structure that gathers sound waves from the air, amplifies them, and changes them into a form that affects receptor cells deep in the skull.

When a receptor cell is activated by a stimulus, it produces graded electrical activity called a **receptor potential** (see Figure 3-4). Each receptor cell makes a synaptic contact with a dendrite of a **sensory neuron**. When a receptor potential occurs in the receptor cell, it increases or decreases the amount of chemical transmitter released and sent to the sensory neuron. The transmitter produces graded electrical activity (called a **generator potential**) in the dendrite of the sensory neuron. If the electrical activity is large enough, it produces an action potential in the sensory neuron. The action potential then travels from the axon of the sensory neuron and into the central nervous system. For example, when auditory receptors deep in the skull are activated by sound stimuli, they release a chemical transmitter that activates the dendrites of auditory sensory neurons. The axons of these auditory sensory neurons then carry action potentials into the brain. Although the details of the scheme differ, the general principles are the same for all the senses.

NEURAL CODING OF STIMULI The axons of many sensory neurons make up each of a person's sensory nerves—optic nerves, auditory nerves, and so on. The action potentials transmitted along these nerves provide people with their sensory experience. In the final analysis, it doesn't really matter how these nerves are stimulated to produce action potentials. It is the activity in the nerve that signals the presence of a particular kind of sensory stimulus. For example, the sensation of light can be produced by light in the eye, by pressure on the eyeball, or by electric shock to the optic nerve. This fact was first recognized by Johannes Müller (1840), who proposed the **law of specific nerve energies**. This law states that gross sensory quality such as light, sound, touch, and so on depends on *which* nerve is stimulated, not on how it is stimulated. It is not the stimulus that determines the nature of the sensation, but rather the receptors and nerves that are activated by the stimulus.

Each sensory nerve connects to specific areas of the brain and activates neurons in those areas. Therefore, an extension of the law of specific nerve energies would hold that the area of the brain that is activated will determine a person's sensory experience. For example, if we completely bypass your eyes and optic nerves and *electrically* activate neurons in areas of your brain that get their inputs from the optic nerves, you will see lights. If we directly activate neurons in areas of your brain that get inputs from the auditory nerves, you will hear sounds. *Thus, sensory experience is nothing more than the activity of neurons in the brain.*

Sensory stimuli can vary in quality, quantity, location, and duration. Lights may be red or green, odors may be weak or strong, sounds may come from left or right, pain may be lingering or fleeting. How do neurons, which can only fire all-or-none action potentials, signal these properties? How do neurons represent, or **code**, information about the world?

One way in which some attribute of an external stimulus can be coded is by the particular *place* where neurons are activated. We have already seen that the gross quality of the stimulus (light, sound, and the like) activates a particular area of the brain. In addition, the activation of specific neurons within an area can signal specific attributes of stimulus quality. For example, a high-pitched tone might activate neurons in one place within the auditory cortex, and a low-pitched tone might activate neurons in another place within the auditory cortex. The particular neurons that are activated also can code the location of the stimulus. For example, when neurons in one area within the somatic sensory cortex (the part of the cerebral cortex devoted to the sense of touch) are activated, it signals that a person's hand has been touched, but when neurons in another area within the somatic sensory cortex are activated, it signals that the person's leg has been touched.

The *frequency* or *rate* at which a neuron fires action potentials also can code certain stimulus attributes. For example, a neuron firing five action potentials per second might signal a low-intensity stimulus whereas the same neuron firing 100 action potentials per second might signal that the same stimulus has a higher intensity.

Not surprisingly, the *duration,* or length of time, that a neuron fires action potentials can signal such properties as the duration of a sensory stimulus. For example, a visual neuron might fire action potentials for half a second in response to a beam of light that shines for half a second, or it might fire for five seconds in response to a light that shines for five seconds.

There are other ways for neurons in the brain to represent or code specific attributes of sensory stimuli (Uttal, 1973; Erickson, 1984). The central point is that although neurons can only fire all-or-none action potentials, they do so in a wide variety of ways to code a wide variety of stimulus attributes. A person's complex sensory experience consists of millions of such neurons discharging in many different ways as they represent the nature of stimuli in the world.

VISION

Visual Stimuli

Perhaps the richest and most beautiful array of sensory experiences reaches us through our sense of vision. Without the information that our eyes provide to us about color and shape, form and movement, we instantly become handicapped. As we have seen, the human visual system is attuned to detecting light—be that light from a magnificent sunset, a brilliant color, or the words on this page.

The light that we see is a form of electromagnetic radiation. Under certain physical conditions, electromagnetic radiation behaves as if it travels in waves through the atmosphere. Electromagnetic radiation includes not only the light that humans can see but also X rays and radio waves (see Figure 3-5). X rays and radio waves differ from light in their

FIGURE 3-5 THE RADIANT ENERGY (ELECTROMAGNETIC) SPECTRUM.

Radiation with very short wavelengths is on the left, and radiation with very long wavelengths is on the right. X rays, radar, and radio waves are electromagnetic radiation with different wavelengths. The portion of the spectrum that humans can see has been expanded below.

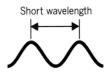
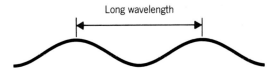
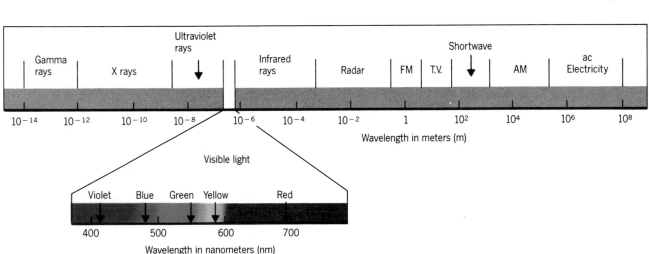

wavelengths (the distance between the peaks of the waves). The wavelength of light generally corresponds to its color, or hue. Human beings can see light in the wavelength range of from only about 400 nanometers to 700 nanometers (a nanometer is one billionth of a meter). The sensory systems of other living creatures are adapted to detecting light at other wavelengths.

Not only does electromagnetic radiation behave as if it travels in waves, it also behaves as if it travels in streams of particles, called *quanta*. A quantum of light (visible radiation) is called a **photon**, which is the energy released from a single electron. The intensity of light often is measured in terms of the number of photons that reach the visual receptors at the back of the eye. The intensity of light generally corresponds to people's experience of its brightness.

The Visual System

THE EYE The human visual system, which responds to light, is made up of eyes and all of their structures and the pathways between eyes and brain.

Look at your own eye in a mirror. The white part that you see is called the **sclera**, which is a strong elastic membrane that forms the eyeball (see Figure 3-6). At the front of the eye, the sclera becomes transparent and bulges forward to form the **cornea**. The space behind the cornea is filled with a watery fluid called the **aqueous humor**, which provides nutrients

FIGURE 3-6   THE HUMAN EYE. The top of the figure shows a horizontal section through the human eye, which is very similar to the eye of all vertebrates. A cross-section through a camera also is shown for comparison. (After Wald, 1950.)

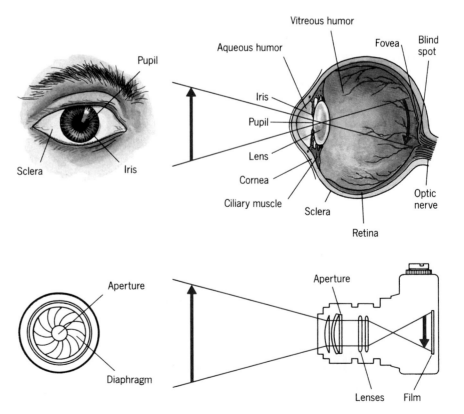

to the cornea and lens and also helps to maintain the shape of the cornea. Light entering the eyeball passes through the cornea. The cornea bends (refracts) the light and thus begins the process of focusing. In fact, the cornea provides about 70 percent of the eye's focusing power.

If you look through the cornea, you will see a colored disc (the **iris**) surrounding a central opening (the **pupil**). The iris opens and closes, much as the diaphragm of a camera does, to regulate the amount of light that enters the eye. In bright light the iris constricts, and the pupil becomes smaller; in a dim light, the iris dilates and the pupil becomes larger. A second function of the iris is to help focus the light. A smaller pupil gives you greater depth of focus. In other words, both near and far objects are in focus, not just objects at one distance, just as a smaller camera aperture provides a greater depth of focus for the photographer.

Just behind your iris is the **lens** of your eye. The lens can change the focus of an image that enters the eyes. Your lens changes focus by actually changing its shape; this process is called **accommodation**. The shape of the lens is controlled by the ciliary muscles. After light passes through the lens, it goes through a chamber that is filled with a jellylike substance, called the **vitreous humor**. The vitreous humor helps to keep the eyeball's shape, which is critical for good vision.

The Retina.   The **retina** is a delicate sheet of cells that covers most of the inner surface of the eyeball. The arrangement of these cells is shown in Figure 3-7. The retina's *receptor cells* are at the back of the eye, farthest from the source of light. The receptors make synaptic connections with the *bipolar cells,* and the bipolar cells in turn make synaptic connections with the *ganglion cells.* The axons of the ganglion cells course across the front surface of the retina and exit to become the optic nerve. Between the receptor cells and bipolar cells are the *horizontal cells,* which process information from side to side across the retina. For example, the horizontal cells can receive signals from many receptors and transmit them to a number of bipolar cells. Similarly, *amacrine cells* process information from side to side at the point of connection between the bipolar and ganglion cells. Finally, the recently discovered *interplexiform cells* receive signals from amacrine cells and send fibers back out to the point of contact between the receptors and bipolar cells (Dowling and Ehinger, 1975; Linberg and Fisher, 1986). The interplexiform cells may provide feedback such that incoming signals from the receptors are modified on the basis of activity that already is going on within the retina. Thus the cells of the retina integrate a great deal of information about the visual world before they transmit it to the brain.

The retina's receptor cells contain layers of a light-sensitive pigment (see Figure 3-7). When light strikes this pigment, a chemical reaction occurs (O'Brien, 1982) and the receptor cell membrane allows the passage of certain electrically charged molecules (ions). As these ions flow through the cell membrane, the electrical voltage inside the receptor cell changes. This is the receptor potential (see Figure 3-4). Light has been changed into the electrochemical activity of neurons.

You may have noticed that the darker it is, the harder it is to see the colors of things. This property of the visual system is a function of

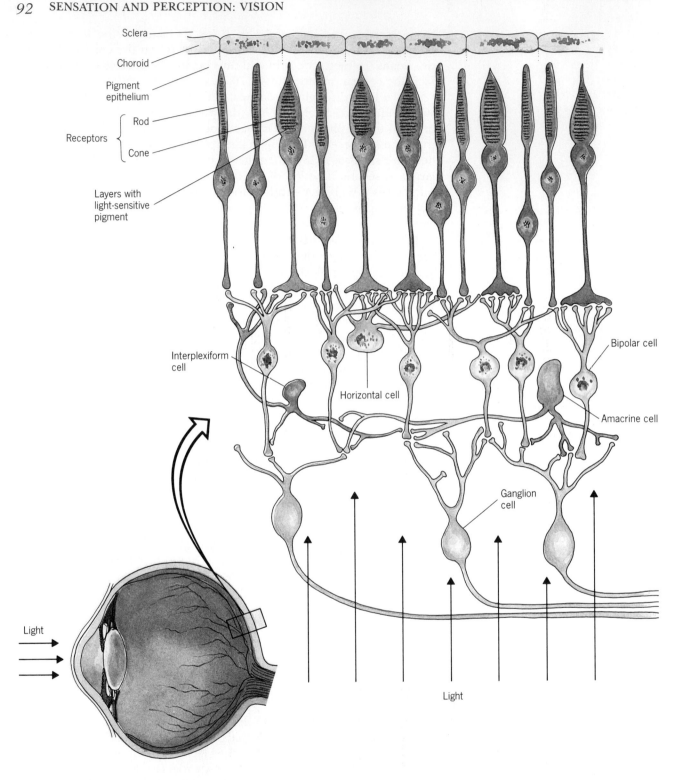

Sclera

Choroid

Pigment epithelium

Receptors {
  Rod
  Cone
}

Layers with light-sensitive pigment

Interplexiform cell

Horizontal cell

Bipolar cell

Amacrine cell

Ganglion cell

Light

Light

◀

FIGURE 3-7 CELLS OF THE RETINA.

The large drawing shows a cross section through the retina taken from the location indicated in the inset. This simplified drawing shows fewer cells and connections than actually exist in an area of retina this size. Information is processed and transmitted in sequence from the receptor cells, to bipolar cells, to ganglion cells. The axons of the ganglion cells project to the brain as the optic nerve. Signals also are transmitted from side to side across the retina by the horizontal and amacrine cells. In addition, the interplexiform cells may feed information from the amacrine cells back to the point of connection between the receptors and bipolar cells. (After Coren, Porac, and Ward, 1984, and Linberg and Fisher, 1986.)

the light receptors in the retina. There are two types of light receptors in the retina. Called **rods** and **cones** (see Figure 3-8), these two types of cells differ in important ways. Rods contain the light-sensitive pigment *rhodopsin*, which is sensitive to low light levels over a wide range of wavelengths. Cones contain one of three light-sensitive pigments, each of which is most sensitive to a different range of light wavelengths. In addition, the cone pigments require higher intensity light than rod pigments to undergo their chemical reaction. Because of their properties, cones are primarily responsible for people's ability to see colors and to see daylight or other high levels of light. Rods are responsible for vision in low light and play little role in the color vision.

At the center of the retina is the **fovea**. This specialized region forms a small depression (about .33 millimeter in diameter) where much of the neural tissue (ganglion cells, amacrine cells, interplexiform cells, and bipolar cells) is pushed aside (see Figure 3-6). When you look at something, you move your eyes so that the image is centered on the fovea of each eye. In bright light you can see more detail with your fovea than with more peripheral parts of your retina. There are several reasons for this. One is that the incoming light passes through less neural tissue at the fovea, and so less light scatters on the way to the receptor cells. Another reason is that the cones, which provide your daylight vision, are most densely packed in the fovea (see Figure 3-9). A third reason is that

FIGURE 3-8 RODS AND CONES OF THE RETINA.

This photograph was taken through a scanning electron microscope. The rods are cylindrical, whereas cones have more pointed tips. Rods vary between 1 and 2.5 micrometers in diameter (a micrometer is one millionth of a meter), whereas cones range from 1 to 8 micrometers in diameter. Both types of receptors are 60 to 70 micrometers in total length (the bottoms are not shown). Compare this photograph with the drawings of rods and cones in Figure 3-7.

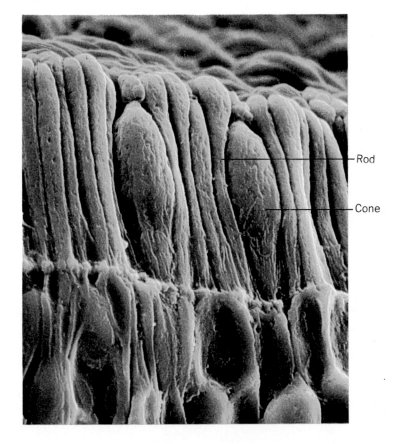
Rod
Cone

FIGURE 3-9 THE DISTRIBUTION OF RODS AND CONES IN THE HUMAN RETINA. Distance on the retina is expressed in terms of the angle relative to the central area, or fovea (0 degrees). The locations of different angles on the retina are shown in the horizontal section through an eye. There are 6 to 8 million cones in each retina, most of which are in the fovea. Therefore, the cones are packed more densely (there are more per square millimeter) in the fovea that elsewhere in the retina. There are 100 to 120 million rods, most of which are in the peripheral retina. Therefore, the rods are packed more densely in the peripheral retina. In fact, there are no rods in the fovea. (Data from Osterberg, 1935; figure modified from Pirenne, 1967.)

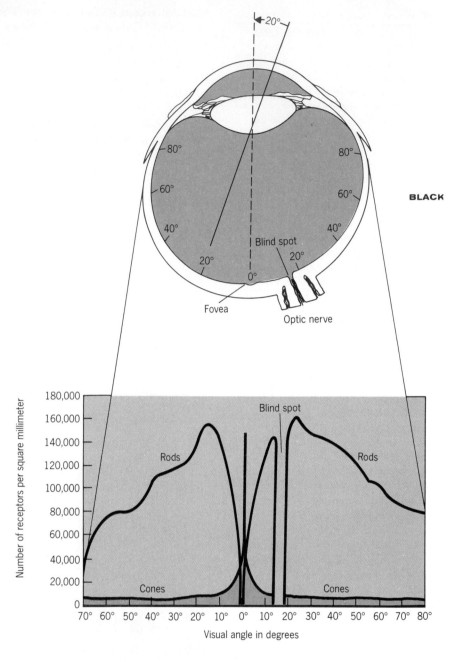

there is less combination of connections from foveal cones to bipolar and ganglion cells than from cones in the peripheral retina to bipolar and ganglion cells.

On a dark night, you may see a dim object (such as a shooting star) in your peripheral vision only to have it disappear when you look directly at it. It seems to disappear because when you look directly at it, you are using your fovea, which is not sensitive to the dim light. You can make the object reappear if you move your eyes again so that your peripheral retina is directed at it. Your peripheral retina has the highest density of

BOX 3-1
THE EYE AND
VISUAL
IMPAIRMENT

Over 110 million people in the United States have some sort of visual impairment that is caused by an abnormality in the eye. Luckily, most of these impairments can be corrected with glasses or contact lenses. But not all can be corrected. Over 10 million adults have some noncorrectable loss of sight, and over half a million people in the United States are legally blind. Now that you understand how the eye works, you can understand the causes of these abnormalities of the eye.

The most common visual problem is nearsightedness (technically called *myopia*), usually caused when the eye is too long and therefore visual images focus not directly on but in front of the retina (see Box Figure 1). Nearsighted people can focus properly only on nearby objects. The opposite problem, farsightedness (*hypermetropia*), occurs when the eye is too short, and the point of focus is behind the retina. Farsighted people can focus properly only on objects far away. Another abnormality in focusing, *astigmatism*, happens when the cornea is elliptical rather than round and so objects along one axis (perhaps the vertical) are out of focus when objects along another axis (perhaps the horizontal) are in focus. As people near the age of 40, many of them begin to notice the effects of *presbyopia* ("old eye"), a decreased ability to focus at close distances. Presbyopia is due to a progressive hardening of the lens and weakening of the ciliary muscles.

Other vision problems are caused when the amount of light that travels through the eyeball to the retina is inadequate. Disease or injury to the cornea can cut down light to the retina. In addition, the lens can become cloudy, a condition called a *cataract*. The most common cause of cataract is old age; 75 percent of people over 65 years of age have a cataract.

Damage to the retina also interferes with normal vision. For example, the retina may *detach*, perhaps after a blow to the eye. When the retina no longer lies smoothly on the back of the eyeball, images cannot be focused on it properly. In addition, receptors that lose contact with their source of nutrients can die, and blindness can result. People with diabetes also may suffer retinal damage, called *diabetic retinopathy*. In this condition, abnormal blood vessels, which do not supply the retina with adequate oxygen, form over the surface of the retina. If these blood vessels rupture and bleed into the vitreous humor, the passage of light to the retina is reduced and the retina may detach. *Retinitis pigmentosa* is an inherited condition in which the retina degenerates. At first, the rod receptors degenerate, and night vision deteriorates.

The leading cause of blindness among adults in the United States is *glaucoma*. A person with glaucoma has too much pressure within the eyeball. This pressure decreases blood flow in the vessels that provide oxygen to the retina, and it pushes on the optic disc. The ganglion cell axons degenerate, action potentials are not transmitted to the brain, and blindness occurs. Fortunately, caught early enough, glaucoma can be treated with drugs or surgery.

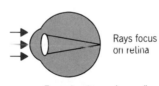

Emmetropic eye (normal)

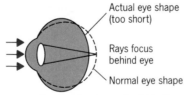

Hypermetropic eye (farsighted)

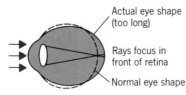

Myopic eye (nearsighted)

BOX FIGURE 1   THE FARSIGHTED AND NEARSIGHTED EYE. In the normal eye, light is precisely focused on the retina (top). If the eyeball is too short, light is focused behind the retina, and a person is farsighted (middle). If the eyeball is too long, light is focused in front of the retina, and a person is nearsighted (bottom). (After Coren, Porac, and Ward, 1984.)

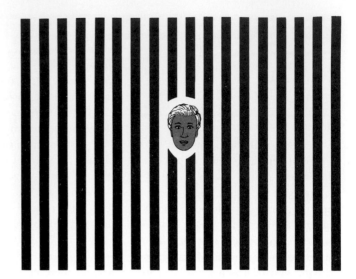

FIGURE 3-10
DEMONSTRATION OF THE BLIND
SPOT AND THE WAY IN WHICH
THE BRAIN FILLS IN MISSING
INFORMATION.
*Close your left eye and look at the X
with your right eye. If you slowly move
the book back and forth in front of you,
you will find a position at which the
picture of the face disappears. It
disappears when the face falls on the
blind spot in your retina. Notice that the
vertical stripes will appear to run
continuously from top to bottom. Your
brain fills in the hole with information
that is similar to the surrounding
stripes.*

rods (see Figure 3-9), and these, as we have seen, are most sensitive to dim light. Although the fovea offers the most detailed vision in bright light, it is blind in dim light. The cones that the fovea has in abundance are not sensitive to low light, and the fovea has no rods.

One region of the retina has no rods or cones (see Figure 3-9). This region is called the **blind spot**, or **optic disc**, and it is where axons of the ganglion cells leave the eye and become the **optic nerve**. Close one eye and look around. Why don't you see a hole in your picture of the world, corresponding to the hole that contains no receptor cells in your retina? The reason is that your brain automatically fills in the missing information in a way that is consistent with visual information that surrounds the blind spot. This phenomenon is demonstrated in Figure 3-10.

Another interesting aspect of the visual system is that the image that is projected onto the retina is upside down and backwards (see Figure 3-6). Yet people do not see things upside down or backwards because the retina and brain are designed to process sensory information about light and dark. They do signal an exact or "photographic" reproduction of an image.

VISUAL PATHWAYS IN THE BRAIN Information travels from the retina to the brain along the two optic nerves. Each nerve contains about 1 million ganglion cell axons (see Figure 3-11). As the two optic nerves enter the brain, they meet at the **optic chiasm**. At this point, axons from the half retina of each eye that looks at the right visual field go to the left hemisphere of the brain, and axons from each half retina that looks at the left visual field go to the right hemisphere of the brain. Thus each hemisphere of the brain receives information about the opposite side of the visual world. In albinos (people and other animals that lack pigment in the eyes, skin, and hair), this orderly crossing of half the optic nerve axons does not occur (Guillery, 1986). As a result, albinos have a number of vision abnormalities.

FIGURE 3-11   THE VISUAL PATHWAYS OF THE BRAIN.
(a) *A side view of the brain's visual apparatus seen as if the skull and brain were partly transparent.* (b) *This shows a horizontal section of the human brain viewed from the top. Because the optics of the eye reverse the visual image (see Figure 3-6), each half retina looks at the opposite half of the visual world (or visual field).* (c) *This is a side view of the rhesus monkey brain (front is to the left) to show many of the extrastriate visual areas of cortex. The primary visual cortex, or striated cortex, is shown in red. Extrastriate visual areas are shown in different colors. Two of these extrastriate areas, referred to as the fourth visual area (V4) and inferotemporal cortex (IT), are labeled. Recent research indicates that humans (indeed, most mammals) have similar multiple visual areas of cortex.* [(a) *and* (b) *after Coren, Porac, and Ward, 1984;* (c) *from Van Essen and Maunsell, 1983.*]

(a)

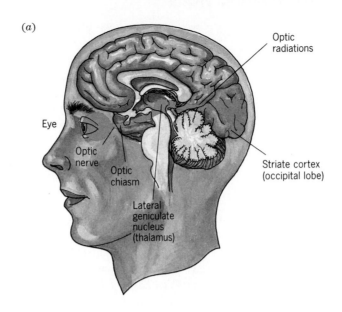

(b)

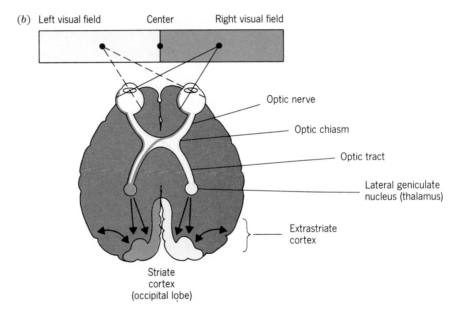

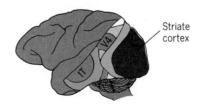

Beyond the optic chiasm, the ganglion cell axons enter the brain, where they are called the **optic tracts**. Axons project into many areas of the brain and form many visual pathways. The main projection of the optic tracts is to the **lateral geniculate nucleus**, which is located in the thalamus (see Chapter 2). The ganglion cell axons make synaptic connections with lateral geniculate neurons, and these neurons send their axons to the **primary visual cortex** (also called the **striate cortex** because it has a striped appearance in the human brain) in the occipital lobe. Because of the crossing of axons in the optic chiasm, the striate cortex of each hemisphere receives information from both eyes. This information relates only to events going on in the opposite half of the visual world (see Figure 3-11*b*). Thus someone who has damage in the left striate cortex will have difficulty seeing things in the right visual field, and this difficulty will be present for both eyes.

Research in humans and other animals indicates that there are many areas of cortex in addition to striate cortex that are involved in the ability to see (Van Essen and Maunsell, 1983). In fact, about half of the cerebral cortex in humans is devoted to vision. Areas of the cortex that lie beyond striate cortex are referred to collectively as **higher order visual areas**, or **extrastriate visual cortex**. The location of some of these areas is shown in Figure 3-11*c*. Neurons in striate cortex send axons to many of these extrastriate visual areas of cortex, and there also are many connections among the extrastriate areas.

The visual system is an elegant and complex network of specialized neurons that functions to provide people with visual information about the world. People perceive this information as unified forms or objects, not as quanta or wavelengths of light. Furthermore, people perceive that these objects exist in space, have particular locations, and can move from location to location. In the sections that follow, we discuss the nature and mechanisms of this perception of the visual world. We discuss how people see simple brightness and contrast changes and the way in which these changes are combined to produce patterns and forms. Then we consider how these forms are seen to move and how people recognize their location in space. Finally, we talk about color.

Brightness and Contrast

Brightness is the experience of a light's intensity. As you have already seen, people can detect very low intensities of light (see Table 3-1). To register a visual sensation, the human retina needs to absorb only one photon in each of 5 to 8 out of its 100 to 120 million rod receptors (Hecht, Shlaer, and Pirenne, 1942). As light intensity increases, the sensation of its brightness increases gradually according to Stevens' power law (look back at Figure 3-3). One of the most remarkable aspects of the human sense of vision is the enormous range of light intensities that people can see. The average light intensity of a sunny afternoon differs from that at dusk by more than a million to one. Yet people can see throughout this range without difficulty. One way in which the visual system adjusts to changes in light intensity, as we have seen, is by changing the size of the pupil. However, the pupil can change light intensity on the retina only by a factor of 16. A much more important mechanism is adaptation.

ADAPTATION   When you have been outside on a sunny day and then enter a dimly lit room, at first you can see almost nothing clearly. In a few minutes, however, you begin to see fairly well. This improvement is **dark adaptation**. After about 20 minutes in the dark, visual sensitivity is at its maximum (Hecht and Shlaer, 1938). Figure 3-12 shows how sensitivity to light changes during dark adaptation.

Your eyes also have to adjust after you have spent time in the dark and then enter daylight. At first, everything appears extremely bright and washed out. But after a few minutes, your eyes adjust, a process called **light adaptation**. Light adaptation takes about half the time that dark adaptation takes (Cornsweet, 1970).

You can demonstrate the large difference in sensitivity between a dark-adapted and a light-adapted eye in the following way. After spending 10 to 15 minutes in a darkened room, close one eye tightly and turn on the lights. Then, after several minutes, turn the lights off again. Now alternately open and close each eye. You can see quite well with the eye that was closed, because it remains relatively dark adapted. However, it is difficult to see with the eye that was opened and became light adapted. Knowing about this difference may come in handy if you ever have to get up in the middle of the night and turn on the room lights. Just close one eye to keep it dark adapted while the lights are on, and then use that eye to get back to bed after the lights are turned off.

The function of adaptation is to adjust the sensitivity of our visual system so that it can operate over the huge range of light intensities that we encounter in our environment. Light and dark adaptation result in

FIGURE 3-12 LIGHT SENSITIVITY DURING DARK ADAPTATION.

The solid line is the dark-adaptation curve. It shows the dimmest light that a person can detect (left-hand scale) after spending increasing amounts of time in the dark. Another way of saying this is that the curve shows how sensitivity *to light increases (right-hand scale) during time spent in the dark. The dashed curve represents the contribution made by cone receptors. They are sensitive only to relatively intense levels of light. The dotted curve represents the contribution made by rod receptors, which are sensitive to low light. The point at which the cones are no longer sensitive to light and rods dominate is called the rod–cone break. (After Goldstein, 1984.)*

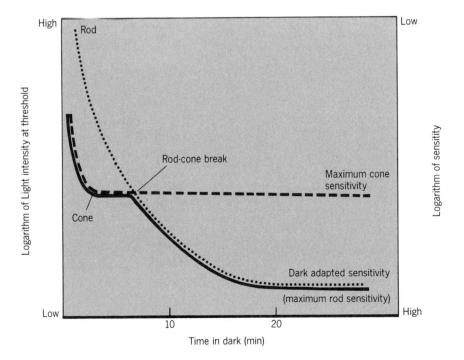

FIGURE 3-13 SIMULTANEOUS BRIGHTNESS CONTRAST.
The pattern at the top illustrates that areas of identical intensity can differ in brightness. The actual intensity distribution in the stripes is plotted at the bottom. Although light intensity is uniform across each of the stripes, the left edge of each stripe appears brighter than the right edge. You can verify that intensity actually is constant by covering the stripes to either side with plain paper so that a single stripe is bordered by two areas of equal light intensity. (From Cornsweet, 1970.)

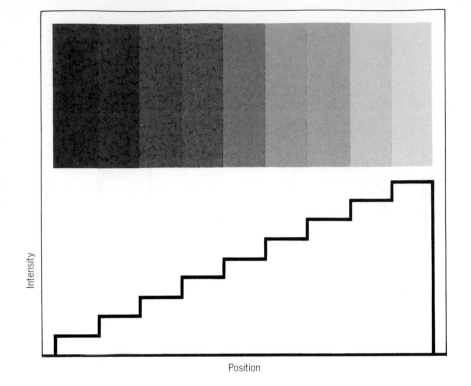

part from chemical changes in the rod and cone light-sensitive pigments and in part from neural changes in the retina (Green and Powers, 1982; Rushton, 1962).

BRIGHTNESS CONTRAST Put a gray plate on a black tablecloth, and then put the same plate on a white tablecloth. On the black background, the gray looks much brighter than on a white background. Many factors in addition to simple light intensity affect your perception of brightness. In fact, brightness often depends more on the intensity of nearby objects than on the intensity of the object you are looking at. This phenomenon, called **simultaneous brightness contrast**, is demonstrated in Figure 3-13. Light of a given intensity appears brighter when seen against a less intense area (the left border of each stripe) than when seen against a more intense area (the right border of each stripe).

Simultaneous brightness contrast is the result of neural events, called **lateral inhibition**, that go on within the retina itself (see Figure 3-14). The mechanism of lateral inhibition was first demonstrated in the eye of the horseshoe crab (Hartline and Ratliff, 1957). Later research showed that retinal cells in the eyes of mammals are subject to the same principles. Lateral inhibition enhances perception of differences in intensity.

Simultaneous brightness contrast and lateral inhibition illustrate three important points. First, a great deal of neural processing of the visual world occurs within the retina itself, before any message is sent out of the brain (there is more to the retina than meets the eye!). Second, much perceptual experience, which seems to involve interpretation of the environment, can be accounted for by events in the retina. Third,

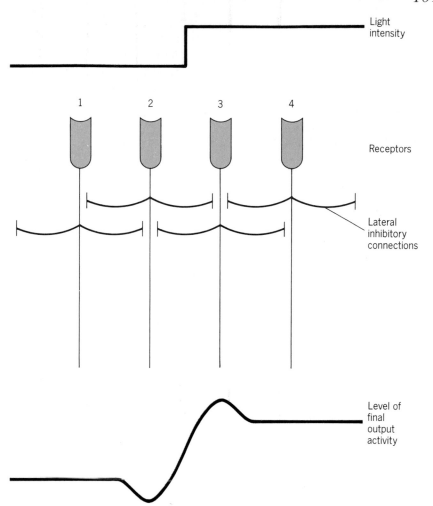

Light intensity

1 2 3 4

Receptors

Lateral inhibitory connections

Level of final output activity

FIGURE 3-14 A SCHEMATIC DIAGRAM TO ILLUSTRATE THE MECHANISM OF LATERAL INHIBITION.

Each of the receptors, numbered 1–4, is activated in proportion to the intensity of light falling on it. In addition, each receptor inhibits its two neighbors in proportion to the light intensity falling on it. For example, receptors 1 and 2 are initially activated by the same amount because they are stimulated by the same light intensity. But receptor 2 is inhibited more than receptor 1 because of its input from receptor 3. As a result, the final output activity from receptor 2 is less than that from receptor 1. Similarly, receptors 3 and 4 are initially activated by the same amount, but receptor 3 is inhibited less than receptor 4. As a result, the final output activity from receptor 3 is greater than that from receptor 4. The total pattern of final output activity shown at the bottom corresponds with the perception of the pattern of brightness at one of the dark–light borders in Figure 3-13. A mechanism of this kind occurs in the mammalian retina, where the connections that produce lateral inhibition are made by the horizontal cells (see Figure 3-7).

sensory systems respond primarily to abrupt changes in the environment. This last point is illustrated in another way by Figure 3-15. The visual system responds to the abrupt changes in light intensity and ignores the gradual changes.

BRIGHTNESS CONSTANCY If you walk with this book from a room lit by light bulbs outdoors into the sunlight, the *intensity* of light reflected from the pages increases dramatically. But the *brightness* of the paper, type, and figures appears about the same. This phenomenon of **brightness constancy** is related to brightness contrast. When you take the book outdoors, the intensities of light from the paper, type, and figures all increase together, and the ratios of their intensities remain about the same as when the book was indoors. Not only does your visual system respond primarily to changes in light and dark (resulting in brightness contrast), it also responds to the relative sizes of those changes. When the relative changes in the intensity of neighboring objects remain constant, the overall brightness remains constant. Brightness constancy is an extremely useful phenomenon. Without it, the page of this book would appear white outdoors and gray or even black indoors.

We pointed out earlier that brightness increases gradually as a function of light intensity. That is true as long as brightness is judged against a constant, dark background. But the natural visual environment is complex and includes many different surfaces and objects. The phenomena of brightness contrast and brightness constancy show that under

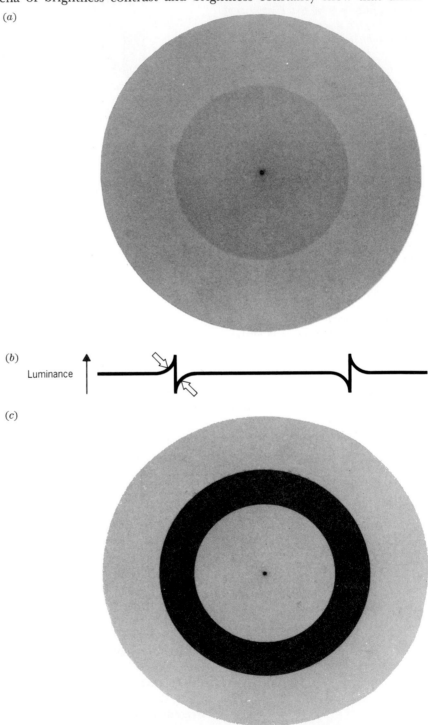

FIGURE 3-15 THE VISUAL SYSTEM RESPONDS PRIMARILY TO ABRUPT CHANGES IN LIGHT INTENSITY.
(a) *In the disc at the top, the center appears darker than the surround.*
(b) *The diagram shows the actual variation in light intensity from the center to the edge of the disc. The light intensity is the same at the center and at the edge. In between, there are two slow changes in intensity (indicated by open arrows), which are ignored by the visual system. Between the slow changes there is a single abrupt upward step in light intensity, to which the visual system responds. As a result, the surround of the disc appears brighter than the center.*
(c) *The disc at the bottom has a black band that obscures the changes in intensity. Now the center and surround have equal brightness, corresponding to their equal light intensity. (From Cornsweet, 1970, and Daw, 1984.)*

these natural conditions, the perception of brightness depends as much on the differences in intensity among nearby objects as it does on the physical intensity of light.

Pattern Vision

VISUAL ACUITY   Changes in brightness and contrast in the visual world produce patterns such as trees, faces, or the printed words on a page. A person's ability to see fine detail in these patterns is called **visual acuity**. The eye doctor who asks you to read letters on an eye chart is measuring your visual acuity. An acuity of 20/20 means that you are able to read a row of letters 20 feet away that is the same size as the letters that people with normal acuity can read at a distance of 20 feet. An acuity of 20/60 is less than normal: it means that you are able to read a row of letters 20 feet away that people with normal acuity can read from a distance of 60 feet.

A more precise way to specify visual acuity is to determine the minimum separation between two stimuli (such as two spots or lines) that you can see. This separation can be expressed in terms of the **visual angle** between two stimuli (see Figure 3-16). A person with normal visual acuity can see stimuli that are separated by an angle of about one minute (1/60

FIGURE 3-16   THE VISUAL ANGLE BETWEEN TWO STIMULI. Visual angle (θ) is a measure of the separation between two stimuli in degrees of arc. There are 360 degrees of arc in the circle around a person's head, and the width of one's thumb at arm's length is about 2 degrees of arc. In (a) and (b), the dots are separated by a visual angle of 15 degrees of arc; in (c) and (d), the dots are separated by an angle of 5 degrees of arc. Notice that for each visual angle, the separation of the image on the retina is the same regardless of the distance of the dots from the eye.

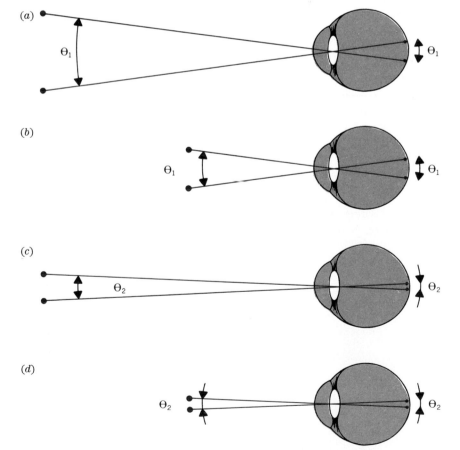

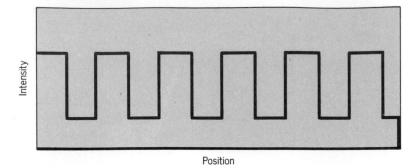

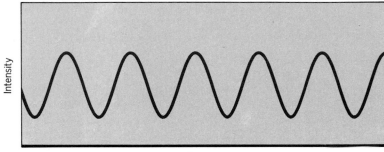

FIGURE 3-17 TWO KINDS OF GRATING PATTERNS.

*The top is a square-wave grating, in which intensity changes abruptly at the edges of the stripes. The bottom is a sine-wave grating, in which intensity increases and decreases gradually as a sine-wave function of location. The **spatial frequency** of a grating is the number of dark and light stripe pairs (called* cycles*) that are present across a specified distance. Thus, if there are three light and three dark stripes across one inch of the page, the spatial frequency is 3 cycles per inch. The **contrast** of a grating is the difference in light intensity between the darkest and lightest part of each stripe.*

of a degree) of arc. Visual acuity is determined by a number of factors, including optical quality of the eye, the spacing of retinal receptors, the connections between the receptor cells and neurons in the retina, and the connections between the retina and the brain (Wolbarsht, Wagner, and Ringo, 1985; Snyder, Bossomaier, and Hughes, 1986). In some animals, these factors combine to provide much better acuity than humans have. For example, the visual acuity of some species of falcons and eagles is about 2.5 times better than that of humans (Fox, Lehmkuhle, and Westendorf, 1976; Reymond, 1985). This sharpsightedness is extremely adaptive, because these birds must hunt for food from high in the air.

SPATIAL CONTRAST SENSITIVITY Your ability to see patterns depends on much more than your visual acuity. As you look around a room you see complex changes in light intensity across objects that vary in size and shape. Your visual system detects the difference between the pattern of threads in your clothing, the surface texture of the window glass, and the shadows cast by the sources of light. Although visual acuity determines the ability to see fine details in these patterns, your pattern vision also depends on your ability to detect the coarser changes in light and dark that make up the visual scene. To understand how people see patterns, it is necessary to understand how they detect these coarse changes.

Recent research on pattern vision has used special stimuli called **sine-wave gratings**. A grating is simply a repeating pattern of dark and light stripes (see Figure 3-17). Sine-wave gratings are particularly useful because they are simple, basic stimuli that form a kind of building block for all complex visual stimuli. The nineteenth-century French mathematician Jean Baptiste Fourier showed that any energy that increases and decreases in a complex function can be reproduced simply by summing appropriate simple sine-wave functions. Because a visual scene is a complex spatial function of changes in light energy, according to Fourier's theorem, any visual scene can be produced by adding the appropriate spatial sine-wave gratings. Conversely, any visual scene can be broken up into some set of sine-wave gratings. Therefore, if psychologists can understand how people see simple sine-wave gratings, they will have a better understanding of how people see complex scenes or patterns in general (Cornsweet, 1970; Shapley and Lennie, 1985).

With these principles in mind, psychologists have studied pattern vision by measuring the contrast (difference in intensity) that is necessary to detect sine-wave gratings that have different spatial frequencies—they measure **spatial contrast sensitivity**. As you might expect, very high contrasts (large differences in light intensity) are required to detect gratings with high spatial frequencies (fine stripes). As spatial frequency decreases (the stripes get broader), the contrast necessary to detect the grating progressively decreases—but only to a point. For very low spatial frequencies (very broad stripes), high contrast is again required. You can see this for yourself in Figure 3-18. The human visual system primarily detects changes in light and dark across space. If the changes are too coarse (occur over large distances), they are not readily detected.

NEURAL MECHANISMS OF PATTERN VISION   We saw earlier that neural processing of relative brightness and contrast begins in the retina. Signals from the retina are sent to the lateral geniculate nucleus of the

FIGURE 3-18   A DEMONSTRATION OF YOUR SPATIAL CONTRAST SENSITIVITY. This is a photograph of a sine-wave grating with spatial frequency that increases from left to right. The stripes actually go from the top of the photograph all the way to the bottom. However, the contrast decreases from top to bottom of the photograph. Notice that more contrast is required for a person to see the stripes on the left and right sides of the photograph than those in the middle. That is, a person is more sensitive to stripes of intermediate width than to very fine (high spatial frequency) or very broad (low spatial frequency) stripes.

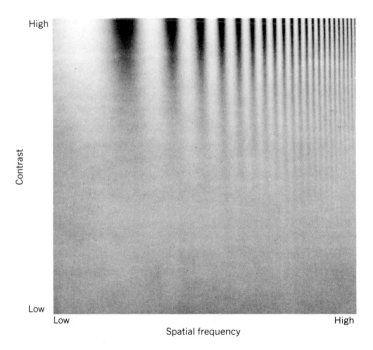

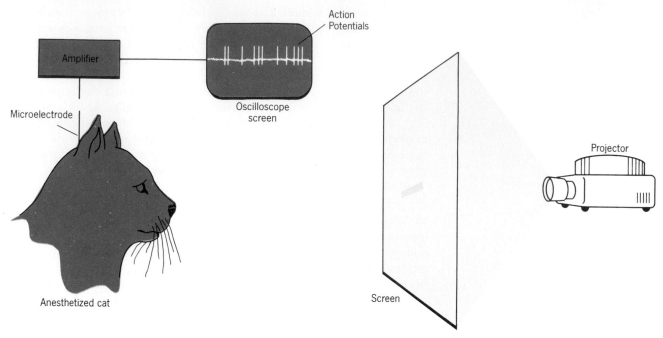

*F I G U R E 3-19 EXPERIMENTAL
SETUP TO DETERMINE HOW
NEURONS IN THE BRAIN
RESPOND TO VISUAL PATTERNS.
A microelectrode in the brain records the
action potentials that are produced by
a single neuron in a visual region,
such as striate cortex. This procedure is
called* **single-cell recording.** *After
amplification, the action potentials are
displayed on an oscilloscope. Light and
dark patterns are projected onto a screen,
and the response of the neuron (changes
in action potential activity) is monitored.*

thalamus (Figure 3-11*b*), which also receives inputs from nonvisual structures such as the reticular formation of the brain stem (described in Chapter 2). These nonvisual inputs can modify the neural transmission of visual information on the basis of arousal or attention (Singer, 1977). Thus, at the first synaptic connection in the brain, information from the eye can be altered by factors such as motivation and expectations. From the lateral geniculate nucleus, neural signals are sent to striate cortex (the primary visual cortex). The way in which neurons in striate cortex process these signals to provide spatial and pattern vision has been a topic of intense research over the past 25 years. Two researchers, David H. Hubel and Torsten N. Wiesel, received the Nobel Prize in 1981 for their pioneering research in this area.

To determine how neurons process visual pattern information, researchers place a microelectrode into striate cortex of an anesthetized cat or monkey to record the activity of single neurons. The animal faces a screen onto which various light and dark patterns are projected, as shown in Figure 3-19. The researchers vary the location, size, shape, and intensity of the visual patterns and determine which combinations cause changes in the neuron's discharge of action potentials. The changes in discharges of action potential are cell responses that signal the presence of certain visual patterns.

Figure 3-20 shows an example of what is found in experiments of this kind. The first thing that is found is that each neuron responds only to light that falls within a relatively small area of the visual field. This small area of the visual field is called the **receptive field** of the neuron. The second thing that is found is that even within the receptive field, only certain patterns of light and dark stimuli activate the neuron. In the example shown in Figure 3-20, the cell responds only to vertically

FIGURE 3-20   RESPONSES OF A STRIATE CORTEX NEURON TO VISUAL STIMULI.

(a) *A bar of light is turned on and off in an area that is outside the neuron's receptive field. The neuron discharges action potentials at a steady rate and does not change its activity.* (b) *A bar of light flashed on in a particular area of the receptive field increases the neuron's activity.* (c) *The same stimulus flashed on in another area of the receptive field produces inhibition and decreases the neuron's activity. The receptive field has both excitatory and inhibitory areas.* (d) *This shows that if a bar of light is oriented horizontally so that both the excitatory and inhibitory areas of the receptive field are stimulated, their opposite actions cancel each other, and the neuron does not respond. Thus this neuron responds only to bars of light that are vertically oriented and that appear in specific locations in the visual field.*

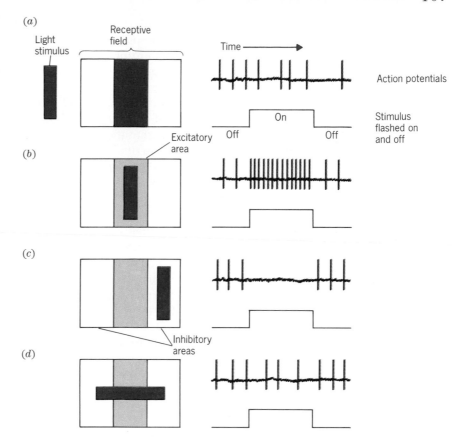

oriented bars of light that appear in particular locations in the receptive field.

Hubel and Wiesel (1962) found that different neurons in striate cortex have different kinds of receptive field properties. Many neurons are activated only by *light* bars of a certain orientation, like the one illustrated in Figure 3-20. Others are activated only by *dark* bars of a certain orientation. For some neurons, the length of the bar is critical whereas for others it is not. Some neurons have only one excitatory and one inhibitory area within the receptive field, so that only a dark–light contour of a particular orientation elicits a response. In addition, many neurons are activated when a stimulus is of a particular size and orientation but at any location within the receptive field. Thus neurons in striate cortex respond to particular *features* in visual patterns; they abstract information from patterns. Later we will consider how neurons that respond to simple features of patterns might indicate the presence of complex forms.

Form Vision

When you look around you, you tend to integrate the patterns of light and dark into meaningful forms that have shape and size. You distinguish your pencil and paper from the desk on which they lie and you distinguish the desk from the floors and walls of the room. You make distinctions of this kind almost automatically, without thinking about them. When you do this, you are actually carrying out two operations: you are organizing patterns into perceptual wholes, or forms, and you are separating these forms from the background.

PERCEPTUAL GROUPING Before 1900, most psychologists believed that unified perceptions of objects were made of a simple addition of elementary sensations, such as simple lines, levels of light intensity, colors, and so on. Then, around 1915, a group of psychologists rejected this idea and proposed that to understand how people perceive objects, the overall stimulus pattern, including interactions among elements in the pattern, must be considered. In essence, they said that perceived forms have a unity that is greater than the sum of the elementary stimulus elements that make up the form. These psychologists formed the **Gestalt school of psychology** (*Gestalt* is German for "whole form"), which was mentioned in Chapter 1. The Gestalt psychologists formulated a number of principles, or **laws of organization**, that explain why we perceive certain stimulus patterns as a unified group or form (Wertheimer, 1923/1958). The major laws of organization are illustrated in Figure 3-21.

According to the law of *simplicity* (also called the law of good figure), stimulus patterns are seen in a way that results in structure that is as simple as possible. This principle explains why the pattern to the left of Figure 3-21*a* is seen as a square and an ellipse rather than the more complex forms shown to the right. In Figure 3-21*b*, the randomly spaced crosses and dots to the left are seen as a triangle on a background pattern of crosses. This figure illustrates the law of *similarity,* which

FIGURE 3-21 ILLUSTRATIONS OF SOME OF THE LAWS OF ORGANIZATION PROPOSED BY THE GESTALT PSYCHOLOGISTS.
(a) *This illustrates the law of simplicity. (From Goldstein, 1984.)* (b) *This shows grouping by similarity. (From Coren, Porac, and Ward, 1984.)* (c) *This is an example of the law of good continuation. (From Goldstein, 1984.)* (d) *This demonstrates the principle of proximity.*

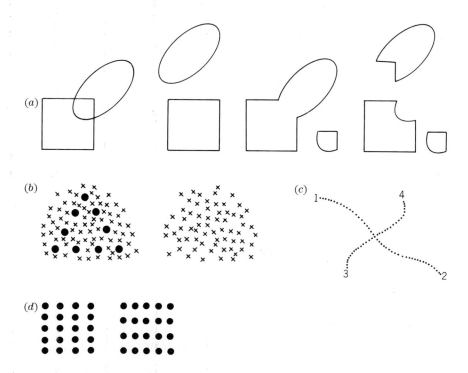

states that similar things tend to be grouped together. Color also plays a role in determining similarity, as shown by the pattern to the right of Figure 3-21*b*.

Figure 3-21*c* appears to be a smooth line of dots going from 1 to 2 and crossing over a smooth line of dots going from 3 to 4. People do not see this pattern as paths going from 1 to 4 or 3 to 2, because those paths involve making sharp turns. This figure illustrates the law of *good continuation,* which states that points connected together tend to be seen in a way that follows the smoothest continuing path. The law of *proximity* (or nearness) states that things that are near each other tend to be grouped together. As a result, the pattern on the left of Figure 3-21*d* is seen as vertical columns of dots whereas the pattern on the right is seen as horizontal rows.

Finally, components of a stimulus pattern that are moving together in the same direction tend to be grouped together. This is the law of *common fate.* An animal in the desert tends to blend into the background and is difficult to distinguish from the rocks and brush—as long as the animal remains stationary. However, as soon as the animal begins to move, it is readily perceived as a unified form.

FIGURE–GROUND SEPARATION   Another feature that the human visual system detects is the relation of people and things to their surroundings. Without this ability, life would be an endless series of crashes, bangs, and accidents. People not only perceive certain patterns as unified forms or figures, they also perceive these figures as separate from their background. For example, look at Figure 3-22. Is this a picture of a white vase on a black background, or the silhouettes of two faces on a white background? What determines how a person perceives which part of a pattern is the figure and which is the ground? Some properties of figure and ground are obvious. For example, forms that are in front of or cover other forms or textures are clearly seen as figures on a textured background—the woodpecker on a tree trunk, the airplane flying in front of the clouds, the car parked in front of the house.

Even without three-dimensional cues such as overlap, people organize what they see into figure and ground. Several principles determine how we do this. The *area* of an enclosed region helps determine whether it is seen as figure or ground. As the area becomes smaller it is more likely to be seen as figure. This is illustrated in Figure 3-23*a,* which is usually seen as a "plus-figure" rather than a "cross-figure." In addition, *orientation* of the stimulus relative to the main axes of space helps determine whether it is seen as figure or ground. As shown in Figure 3-23*b,* vertical and horizontal orientations are more likely than others to be seen as figure. Stimuli that have *symmetry* also tend to be seen as figure. In Figure 3-23*c,* the symmetrical white areas on the left appear to be the figures on a black background, while the symmetrical black areas on the right are the figures on a white background. Finally, according to the principle of *closure,* stimuli that are enclosed tend to be seen as figures against the background, as illustrated in Figure 3-23*d.* The pattern on the left is seen as a diamond between two vertical lines, rather than the letter *W* on top of the letter *M,* because the diamond is enclosed by a contour.

FIGURE 3-22   A REVERSIBLE FIGURE.
Which is the figure, and which is the background?

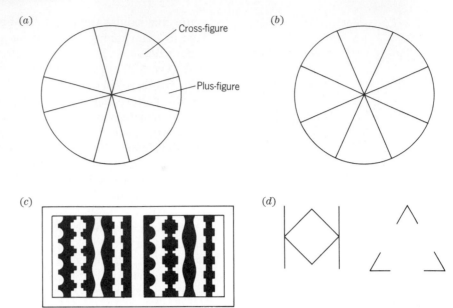

FIGURE 3-23 FACTORS THAT HELP DETERMINE WHICH PARTS OF STIMULI ARE SEEN AS FIGURE AND WHICH AS GROUND. (a) *This shows the role of stimulus area. (From Goldstein, 1984.)* (b) *This shows the effects of stimulus orientation. (From Goldstein, 1984.)* (c) *This shows the role of symmetry (compare the left and right halves of the pattern). (From Hochberg, 1971.)* (d) *This shows how closure separates figure from ground (left) and how people use closure to group patterns into unified forms (right). (From Coren, Porac, and Ward, 1984.)*

The factors that determine figure–ground separation are closely related to those that determine perceptual grouping. For example, the law of common fate not only tends to group patterns into a unified form, it also helps to separate that form from the background pattern (for example, it separates the animal from the background rocks and brush of the desert). In addition, areas that have partial closure tend to be grouped together. Because of this, we tend to see the pattern on the right of Figure 3-23*d* as a triangle rather than three unrelated acute angles.

Knowing these principles helps us to understand why there is ambiguity about whether the faces or the vase are figure or ground in Figure 3-22. The cues for figure and ground are relatively balanced in this picture, so the faces and the vase tend to alternate in appearing as figure and ground.

The factors that determine the perception of forms and the separation of figure from ground are powerful, and they can lead to the perception of forms that are not really present. Two examples are shown in Figure 3-24. These subjective, or illusory, forms seem to be produced by our tendency to transform incomplete elements of a pattern into simpler, stable, and regular figures (Kanizsa, 1976).

SHAPE CONSTANCY   Stand in front of a door. Its outline is a rectangle. As the door opens, its outline (and its image on your retina) becomes a trapezoid and then a line (see Figure 3-25). Nevertheless, you continue to perceive its shape as that of a rectangle. People perceive most forms or objects as keeping the same apparent shape despite changes in their orientation, a phenomenon called **shape constancy**. The same phenomenon also applies to much more complex shapes and forms, such as the car or the person seen from different vantage points. People make these adjustments for changes in position almost automatically. Shape con-

FIGURE 3-24 SUBJECTIVE FORMS.

On the left, there appear to be contours that outline a white triangle that is brighter than the background. However, the contours and white triangle are an illusion, as you can demonstrate by covering the three black circles with white paper. Similarly, the contours that outline the pear-shaped form on the right are an illusion. (From Kanizsa, 1976.)

stancy depends on two factors: familiarity with the object and knowledge of its position in space relative to the viewer. Shape constancy shows again that the perception of forms depends on the overall context in which forms are seen and not just on their retinal image.

NEURAL MECHANISMS OF FORM VISION   Earlier we described the way in which single neurons in striate cortex respond to features of simple visual patterns, such as oriented bars of light. Studies of the effects of brain lesions indicate that these neurons are responsible for the ability to see fine detail (Berkley, 1978; Miller, Pasik, and Pasik, 1980). But what about complex visual forms?

In an effort to understand the neural mechanisms of complex form vision, scientists have recorded from single neurons in extrastriate areas of the monkey's visual cortex. An area that has been studied in considerable detail is the inferotemporal cortex (see Figure 3-11), because damage to this area impairs the ability to identify and later remember visual forms (Gross, 1973; Mishkin, Ungerleider, and Macko, 1983). Like striate cortex neurons, many neurons in inferotemporal cortex respond best to simple patterns such as light or dark bars or contours of a particular orientation (Gross, Rocha-Miranda, and Bender, 1972). The major dif-

FIGURE 3-25 AN EXAMPLE OF SHAPE CONSTANCY.

As a door opens, the shape of its image on the retina changes. Yet you continue to perceive it as a rectangular door.

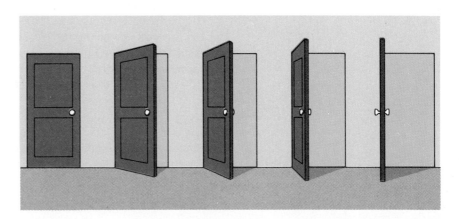

FIGURE 3-26 NEURONS THAT RESPOND TO FACES.
Shown are responses of a neuron in monkey inferotemporal cortex that responds better to profiles of monkey faces than to any other stimulus tested. The responses of the neuron are shown by the graphs, which give the number of action potentials discharged by the neuron (vertical axis) over time (horizontal axis). The time during which each stimulus was presented is indicated by the line under each graph. The neuron responded to the profile of a monkey face and not to front or rear views of a monkey face or to other stimuli such as a bottle brush (top row). In addition, removing or altering any of the components of the profile eliminated the response (bottom row). (Modified from Desimone, Albright, Gross, and Bruce, 1984.)

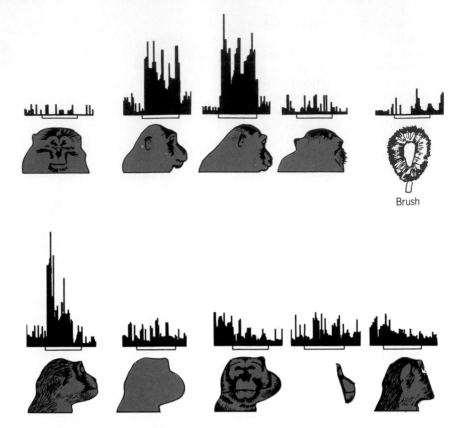

ference between the two cortical areas is that many neurons in inferotemporal cortex respond to the visual patterns wherever they appear over a wide area of visual space. Thus many of these neurons seem to show shape constancy (Schwartz, Desimone, Albright, and Gross, 1983).

A small proportion of inferotemporal cortex neurons have very different properties. These neurons change their activity only when certain complex forms are shown to a monkey (Desimone, Albright, Gross, and Bruce, 1984). For example, some neurons respond to a picture of a monkey's hand but not to a spot or bar of light, and they respond regardless of the location or the orientation of the hand. Other neurons respond only to faces. An example is shown in Figure 3-26.

Results such as these raise the possibility that form vision is a result of the activity of certain neurons in the brain that "recognize"—respond to—specific visual forms. Another possibility is that form vision is a result of the combined activity of many neurons that individually respond only to certain features of the form. Research on which of these theories is correct is very lively today (see Box 3-2).

Perception of Movement

Forms in the visual world are continuously moving. People walk by, balls arc through the air, wind blows the branches of a tree. Psychologists call this actual movement of stimuli **real movement**.

REAL MOVEMENT   A simple kind of real movement is the movement of a spot of light against a solid dark background. The human eye can detect that the spot is moving when it crawls along at about two-tenths of a degree of visual angle per second; in other words, at a rate of about 10 seconds to travel across your thumb held at arm's length (Aubert, 1886). If a stationary background is added, such as a square frame to surround the spot, then people can detect movement that is 10 times slower! As in other kinds of visual perception, the surroundings play an important role in the detection of movement.

Not only do visual stimuli move, but people's sensory apparatus—head and eyes—are constantly moving as well. Despite all of this movement, the visual system detects the difference between a stationary object seen in a sweeping glance and a moving object seen in an unmoving gaze. As you, for example, watch a moving car and see other cars that are parked or moving in other directions, you have no trouble perceiving the relative movements of all the objects in this complex visual scene. How does a person make these distinctions?

Usually three factors affect a person's perception of movement: movement of the figure, movement of the background, and movement of your eyes and head. Let us illustrate how these factors affect the movement of stimuli across your retina (see Figure 3-27). Imagine that you are sitting on a park bench with your eyes steady, looking across the street. A woman jogs by from left to right (Figure 3-27a). In this case, the image of the woman moves on your retina while the background remains stationary. Now imagine that you are sitting on a park bench when a woman jogs from left to right, and you follow her with your eyes (Figure 3-27b). Now the woman's image remains stationary on your retina while the image of the background sweeps across your retina in the opposite direction. Even so, you perceive the person to be moving and the background to be steady. Finally, imagine that the woman is standing still in

FIGURE 3-27   SOME FACTORS THAT AFFECT MOVEMENT PERCEPTION.

Shown are examples of how movement of the figure (a person), the background, and your eyes affect the movement of stimuli across your retina. In each case, the arrows show the direction in which different components of the scene move across your retina. (a) The figure moves while your eyes are steady. (b) The figure moves and you follow it with your eyes. The background therefore moves across your retina. (c) You move your eyes and the figure and background are steady. This causes both the figure and the background to move across your retina. (After Goldstein, 1984.)

(a)

(b)

(c)

One theory of the neural mechanisms of form vision is that specific neurons in the brain respond only to particular objects or forms, and therefore the recognition of objects depends on which of these neurons are active. Cells that respond to specific forms are often referred to jokingly as "grandma cells," because one extension of this theory is that all people have specific brain cells that respond only to the image of their grandmother's face. Results like those shown in Figure 3-26 seem to lend support to this theory.

One criticism of this theory is that form-specific neurons have not been found often even though recordings have been made from many different visual cortical areas. But it is possible that scientists have not yet studied the right area of the brain or have not used the correct stimuli in studying it. For example, neurons in inferotemporal cortex that seem to respond best to simple stimuli such as bars or contours may have to be tested for their response to images of a monkey's characteristic food, a tree in the forest, or the monkey's mate. Critics also say that if there are form-specific neurons, individuals would have to have at least one separate neuron for recognizing every object and person they encounter. The number of neurons required would be enormous, far more than are present in visual areas of even the human brain. Still others criticize the theory's ability to explain how people see and recognize new shapes and forms or how, for example, when you meet a new person, you can distinguish her from other people and recognize her when you see her again. It is unlikely that you already have a specific neuron for recognizing that person or that you rapidly develop one when you meet her.

An alternative theory is that form recognition involves the pattern of activity of thousands or even millions of neurons, each of which responds to a small component or simple feature of the overall form. As we discussed earlier, striate cortex neurons are excited or inhibited by just such simple features (see Figure 3-20). When you look at a face, some of these neurons are excited by the patterns of light and dark that play across the face, some are inhibited, and some do not respond at all (see Box Figure 1). The overall distribution, or pattern, of excited and inhibited neurons in striate cortex thus corresponds to that face. When you look at a different face, a different pattern of neurons is excited and inhibited. Many scientists theorize that these varying patterns of activity among thousands of neurons are the neural code for visual forms. The activity of such neurons in striate cortex may represent the first step in this coding. Most inferotemporal cortex neurons also respond only to simple features of forms, but they do so over a large area of the visual field. Perhaps the distribution of activity among these inferotemporal cortex neurons provides the identification of

the park, and you move your head and eyes from left to right (Figure 3-27c). In this case, the images of both the woman and the background sweep across your retina. Even so, you perceive the entire scene as stationary.

Two main theories try to account for the human ability to distinguish whether it is the figure, the background, or the viewer's eyes that are moving.

THEORIES OF MOVEMENT PERCEPTION

Information in the Scene. J. J. Gibson (1966) proposed that information within the visual scene itself is sufficient to provide a person with unambiguous cues about what is moving and what is not. A person need only consider the movement of objects relative to the background. In the first two examples above (Figures 3-27a and 3-27b), the viewer knows that the woman is moving because she covers and then uncovers parts of the background as she walks by. The viewer discounts the fact that in one

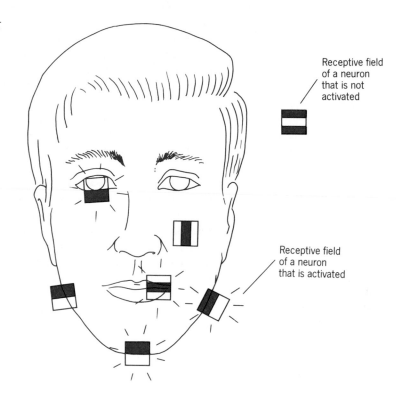

BOX FIGURE 1 HOW STRIATE CORTEX NEURONS MIGHT RESPOND TO A COMPLEX FORM, SUCH AS A FACE.

Neurons that have receptive fields that fall on lines or contours of the appropriate orientation change their activity. If the receptive field does not fall on a line or contour, or if the contour is of the wrong orientation for that neuron, there will be no response. The distribution of active neurons in striate cortex is thus relatively specific to this particular form. A different visual form will activate a different distribution of striate cortex neurons.

Receptive field of a neuron that is not activated

Receptive field of a neuron that is activated

visual objects independent of their location in space (Mishkin, Ungerleider, and Macko, 1983).

Which theory is correct? It may turn out that the recognition of form works in more than one way. Recognition of biologically significant forms and objects such as a monkey's hand or face may depend on form-specific neurons, whereas recognition and identification of other forms may depend on the pattern of activity among thousands of neurons responding to simple components of the stimulus.

case the woman's image moves across the retina and in the other case does not. In the third example (Figure 3-27*c*), the viewer knows that his or her eyes are moving because the woman and the background do not move relative to one another.

This is a compelling theory that works well in most situations. However, it cannot explain certain phenomena, such as how we can see the movement of a spot against a solid dark background. There must be additional information that is not in the visual scene. A second theory suggests what that information is.

Corollary Discharge.   When you start to move your eyes, your brain sends a command to the eye muscles to make them contract. According to **corollary discharge theory**, the motor areas of the brain send out an additional (corollary) signal (discharge) to other areas of the brain at the same time (von Holst, 1954). This signals to visual areas of the brain that an eye movement of a certain size and direction is about to occur. The visual areas of the brain then compare the expected eye movement to the movement of the visual stimulus on the retina. If the two movements match, then you know that your eyes moved, not the visual stimulus. If they do not match, then you know that the visual stimulus moved.

Two types of experiments support this theory. The first was described by Descartes (1664/1972) more than 300 years ago, and you can try it on yourself. Close one eye, and put your finger on the side of your other eyelid. Gently push the eyeball as you look at the edge of this book. Doesn't it seem as though the book has moved? The pressure moves your eye even though there has been no eye movement command from your brain and, therefore, no corollary discharge. Corollary discharge theory predicts that because the visual areas of the brain have not been signaled that an eye movement is about to occur, they will interpret the movement of your book across the retina as a movement of the book and not a movement of the eye (see Stark and Bridgeman, 1983; Bridgeman and Fishman, 1985). Movement of the book is, in fact, what you perceive.

The second type of experiment is the reverse of the first. If your brain commands your eyes to move but they do not, corollary discharge theory predicts that the world will appear to move anyway because your brain has been signaled to expect an eye movement. Because no movement occurs, the mismatch between the corollary discharge signal and the visual signal on the retina is interpreted as a movement. An experimenter tested the theory by using a drug to paralyze his eye movements, and when he tried to move his eyes but could not, the visual scene appeared to move, as the theory predicted (Stevens, Emerson, Gertstein, Kallos, Neufeld, Nichols, and Rosenquist, 1976).

It is likely that corollary discharges and information in the visual scene both play a role in the perception of movement. Both mechanisms probably work in concert to help people perceive movement.

APPARENT MOTION   When you watch cars pass by outside your window, the cars have actually moved. But when you go to the movies and watch a car move by on the screen, the movement on the screen is not real, but apparent. **Apparent motion** describes instances in which stationary stimuli appear to move.

Stroboscopic Movement.   One instance of apparent motion is **stroboscopic movement**. Stroboscopic movement is used to produce commercial signs in which the letters appear to move across the display. These signs take advantage of a simple kind of stroboscopic movement, the **phi phenomenon** (Wertheimer, 1912). Two lights are placed near each other and then flashed on and off in sequence. When the time between the two flashes is more than about 200 milliseconds, we see the two lights flashing in sequence. With intervals less than about 30 milliseconds, the two lights appear to flash simultaneously. But when the interval between the two light flashes is about 60 milliseconds, people see a single light moving smoothly back and forth between two points—this is the phi phenomenon. The phi phenomenon shows that the timing of stationary flashes of light can trigger the perception of movement. The spacing between the flashes also affects the perception of movement. The closer the flashes are to each other, the more likely they will be perceived as a single moving stimulus. In addition, stimuli with higher contrasts (brightness relative to the background) produce greater apparent movement than low-contrast stimuli (Anstis, Giaschi, and Cogan, 1985).

Motion pictures also depend on the phenomenon of stroboscopic movement. Motion picture film is a series of still photographs, each of which is similar to the last. In each successive photograph, the moving objects are slightly displaced. Twenty-four pictures are flashed on the screen each second, with a period of dark between each picture. The effect is a smooth apparent movement of the displaced objects.

The perception of stroboscopic movement probably involves neurons in certain visual areas of cortex. Some of these neurons respond to stimuli moving through their receptive fields more readily than they respond to stationary stimuli flashing on and off. Thus these neurons signal the presence of moving objects in the visual field. If two adjacent stimuli are flashed on and off with an appropriate interval between flashes, the neurons respond as if there were a single moving stimulus (Cremieux, Orban, and Duysens, 1984). As far as the neurons (and therefore you) are concerned, the sequentially flashed stimuli are real movement of a single stimulus.

Autokinetic Effect. Another instance in which you can get apparent motion is to look at a dim point of light in a very dark room. The light will appear to move, a phenomenon called **autokinesis** (self-movement). You can demonstrate autokinesis by looking steadily at a lit cigarette placed on a table about 2 yards away from you in a completely dark room. After a few minutes, the cigarette will appear to drift slowly. The movement, of course, is an illusion.

Autokinesis appears to be caused by slow eye drift (Matin and MacKinnon, 1964) plus corollary discharge. When you stare at a target for a time, your eyes actually drift slightly. This drifting is involuntary; no command to move the eyes has been sent from the brain. Therefore, no corollary discharge signal that the eyes are about to move is sent to visual areas of the brain. As a result, the movement of the image on the retina is interpreted as movement of the light rather than as movement of the eyes.

Depth Perception

To get some idea of how important a person's sense of depth perception is, close one eye and try to catch a ball that is thrown to you. Because we live in a three-dimensional world, we continuously make judgments about the depth of objects in space. We make these judgments despite the fact that the retina is essentially a flat sheet of cells and the images projected on the retina are two-dimensional. Our perception of depth in three-dimensional space is based on three major classes of cues, called static monocular, dynamic monocular, and binocular cues.

STATIC MONOCULAR CUES **Static monocular cues** for depth are based on features of stationary ("static") objects and require only one eye ("monocular") to produce the impression of depth. These cues can

be represented in flat two-dimensional pictures and for that reason are sometimes called **pictorial cues.** They are the cues that artists use to give the impression of depth in paintings or drawings.

Figure 3-28 illustrates some of the static monocular cues for depth. When one object overlaps another it is perceived as being the closer of the two; this cue is called *interposition.* The larger of two similar objects appears to be closer; this is the cue of *relative size.* The *relative height* of an object in the field of view also influences its perceived depth. Higher objects are seen as being more distant. *Linear perspective* refers to the tendency of parallel lines to converge as their distance from the eye increases, and this provides a cue for depth. If we look at a textured surface, the density of the texture elements increases with increasing distance. This depth cue is referred to as *texture gradient.*

An additional static monocular cue for depth is *shadowing,* which is produced by the way light interacts with objects. For example, when

FIGURE 3-30 AERIAL PERSPECTIVE AND DEPTH PERCEPTION.
In this painting by Caspar David Friedrich, the artist used aerial perspective to give the appearance of distance.

turned upside down, the photograph of a crater in Figure 3-29 appears to be a bump because raised areas intercept light and are brighter than lower areas that are in shadow. Another powerful monocular cue is *aerial perspective*. We look at objects through particles suspended in the air, and the more distant the object the more particles we look through. As a result, faraway objects look fuzzier than nearby objects. This aerial perspective provides a cue for depth, as shown in Figure 3-30.

Many of the static monocular cues for depth depend on past experience and learning. For example, the cue of relative size depends on a person's familiarity with the actual size of the objects in question. Similarly, the shadowing cue appears to depend on a person's experience that light generally comes from overhead. You can demonstrate this by turning the book upside down and looking again at Figure 3-29. Now the photograph appears to be a series of depressions rather than bumps because light coming from above would produce shadows on the top and bright areas on the bottom of depressions.

DYNAMIC MONOCULAR CUES As people or objects move through the world, they produce **dynamic** (moving) **monocular cues** for depth. For example, head and body movements cause the relative positions of objects in the environment to change. You can demonstrate this by closing one eye, holding up one finger, and then focusing on it with your open eye. When you move your head back and forth, the image of your finger moves relative to the background. This relative movement, called *motion parallax*, is a cue for depth.

Motion perspective provides another dynamic molecular cue for depth. As you move through a scene, objects close to you flow by more rapidly

FIGURE 3-31 ILLUSTRATION OF THE MOTION PERSPECTIVE CUE FOR DEPTH.
The photograph shows the flow of the environment as a car speeds across a bridge toward point A.

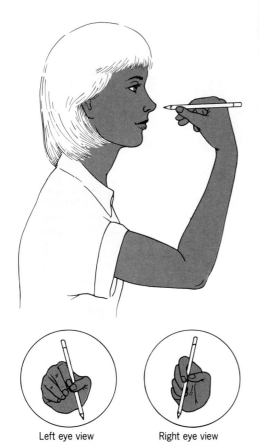

Left eye view   Right eye view

FIGURE 3-32
DEMONSTRATION THAT THE TWO EYES HAVE SOMEWHAT DIFFERENT VIEWS.
Hold a pencil near your nose as shown in the drawing. The tip of the pencil should be angled downward slightly. As you alternately open and close each eye, the pencil appears to swing back and forth as shown in the insets because the image on either retina is different. (After Coren, Porac, and Ward, 1984.)

than distant objects (see Figure 3-31). This pattern of streaming of the retinal image is a strong cue for depth (Gibson, 1950).

BINOCULAR CUES **Binocular cues** depend on the use of both eyes for the perception of depth. These powerful cues give very precise depth information. The most important binocular depth cue is *stereopsis,* the ability to see depth on the basis of differences between the retinal images in each eye. In humans, the two eyes are two to three inches apart. Because of this, the two eyes have slightly different angles of view and, therefore, slightly different retinal images of the same object. You can see this difference in retinal images by carrying out the demonstration in Figure 3-32.

Figure 3-33 illustrates why objects at different distances produce slightly different retinal images. When you fixate on (stare at) one object, the image of a more distant object falls on a somewhat different location on the right eye's retina than on the left eye's retina. That is, there is a *disparity* between the two eyes in the location of the retinal images of the second object. The same is true for objects that are closer than the one you are fixating on. This *retinal disparity* is the binocular depth cue in stereopsis. People are not conscious of the actual differences in the retinal images, but the retinal disparities are detected automatically by visual areas of the brain and lead to the perception of depth.

People have many cues for depth perception available to them. No single one of these cues is crucial for depth perception, because people can still perceive depth if any one of them is eliminated. However, the more cues that are available, the more accurately people can detect depth.

SIZE CONSTANCY As a car drives away from you, why doesn't it seem to get smaller? As a car drives away, its image on your retina does

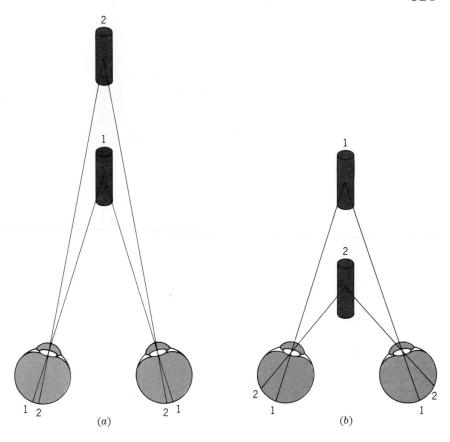

FIGURE 3-33   WHY OBJECTS AT DIFFERENT DISTANCES PRODUCE IMAGES THAT ARE DIFFERENT FOR EITHER RETINA.
(a) *The two eyes are fixating on (staring at) object 1, and its image is on the fovea of each eye. The image of a more distant object (object 2) is to the right of the fovea in the left eye and to the left of the fovea in the right eye because the two eyes view object 2 from different angles.* (b) *Object 2 is closer than the object on which the two eyes are fixating. In this case, the image of object 2 is to the left of the fovea in the left eye and to the right of the fovea in the right eye.*

become smaller. But the car seems to remain the same size because of the phenomenon of **size constancy**. Thus as people look at objects that are at varying distances, their perception of the objects' sizes remain constant. Size constancy occurs because as people look at objects in the world, they adjust their perception of the size according to their perception of how far away they are.

When depth cues are removed, size constancy breaks down. For example, if you look at something with one eye through a peephole, the object does appear to become smaller as it moves farther away (Holway and Boring, 1941). Size constancy also breaks down when people look at objects from a great distance. For example, cars do appear to be very small when people look at them from the top of a tall building or from an airplane, because few of the usual cues to distance are available in these situations (Day, Stuart, and Dickinson, 1980).

ILLUSIONS OF SIZE AND DEPTH   Sometimes people really should *not* believe their eyes, because in some instances depth cues and size constancy lead to errors in perception. One example of such an error is the *Ponzo illusion,* shown in Figure 3-34. The photograph includes a number of static monocular depth cues, especially the linear perspective cue provided by the receding road. Because these cues make the upper black bar

FIGURE 3-34   THE PONZO
ILLUSION.
The two black bars superimposed on the
photograph are exactly the same length.
However, the top bar appears larger
because it appears to be farther away.

appear farther away, the viewer expects its retinal image to be smaller
(size constancy). Because the retinal image of the top bar is not smaller
than that of the bottom bar, we perceive the top bar to be larger (Gregory, 1963).

Figure 3-35 shows another example of how depth cues can lead to
perceptual illusion. Each corner of the triangle (Figure 3-35a) has interposition cues that make the corner seem three-dimensional. But because
each corner has been drawn as if viewed from a different position, the
triangle is an illusory, *impossible object*—it cannot exist (Penrose and Penrose, 1958). M. C. Escher, a Viennese artist who worked early in this century, drew impossible objects in a number of his etchings (see Figure
3-35b). Notice that Escher also used linear perspective and additional
interposition cues (such as the pillars of the towers) to increase the perception of depth. He has created an illusion of continuously flowing
water.

These illusions demonstrate the power of two-dimensional cues in
producing the perception of three-dimensional depth. Usually depth
cues give accurate information about the distances of objects in three-
dimensional space. But sometimes they lead to perceptions that do not
correspond to external reality.

Color Vision

The perception of color immeasurably enriches human life. Color alerts
people to danger, helps them to remember, and arouses the emotions. In
many animal species, color aids in locating food, sends individuals into
battle, and triggers mating. All of this beauty and power can be measured in the laboratory and broken down into particular attributes.

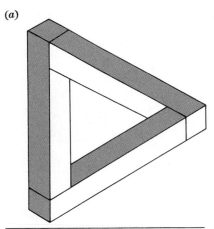

(a)

FIGURE 3-35 AN IMPOSSIBLE OBJECT.
(a) *The triangle on the left is a physical impossibility that has been created artistically by using interposition cues at each of the corners.* (b) *The engraving on the right is by the artist M. C. Escher. The channels and waterfall are produced by combining two impossible triangles like the one on the left. Compare the shaded surfaces of the impossible triangle to the flow of the water.* (Waterfall, *1961.)*

(b)

THE STIMULUS FOR COLOR Color is determined by three physical attributes of light: wavelength, purity, and intensity. The perception of **hue** corresponds principally to the wavelength of light. For example, red and blue are hues that correspond to light of long or short wavelengths. The *color circle* shown in Figure 3-36 shows the relationship between hue and wavelength. Psychophysical studies show that humans can discriminate about 200 different hues.

White light contains all wavelengths in the visible spectrum. If we add white light to light of a single wavelength, we reduce the purity of the single-wavelength light. The effect is to make the hue of the original light appear washed out. We refer to this result as a decrease in **saturation**, which is the sensation that corresponds to the purity of light. For example, if we add white light to red, we obtain pink, which is simply a less saturated red hue. Saturation is represented on the color circle by the distance between the edge of the circle and its center. The center of the circle represents the least saturated hue (white or gray) and the edge represents the purest or most saturated hue possible.

FIGURE 3-36 THE COLOR CIRCLE.
Each hue around the perimeter of the color circle is produced by light of a single wavelength. The only exception is that certain hues, such as purple, can be produced only by mixing two wavelengths of light. These are called **nonspectral colors** because they do not correspond to a single wavelength on the visible spectrum.

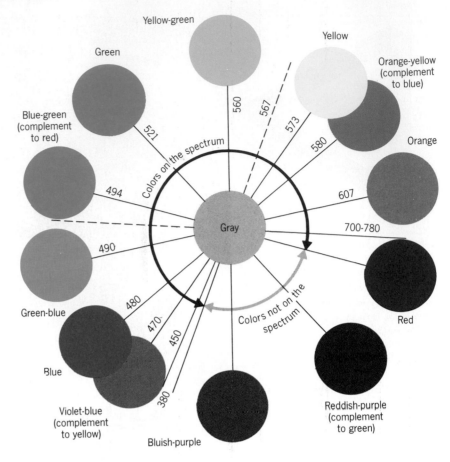

Finally, as we saw earlier, light can vary in intensity. The sensation of **brightness** corresponds principally to the intensity of light. The intensity of a light affects its color. For example, intense and dim blues appear different in color even though they have the same wavelength and purity. To represent brightness in the color circle, we must add a third dimension. This produces the *color solid* shown in Figure 3-37.

COLOR MIXING   Give a child a set of poster paints, and soon she has mixed red and blue into a brilliant purple, yellow and blue into a vivid green. She has unwittingly demonstrated that most colors are actually mixtures of many wavelengths. Color mixing is said to be *synthetic* because when people combine two or more wavelengths of light, they are synthesized into an entirely new color—the person can no longer perceive the individual wavelengths that make up the mixture. For example, if someone mixes a green light (wavelength of 500 nanometers) and a red light (650 nanometers), the combination will look exactly the same as a pure yellow light (570 nanometers). The red and green that went into the mixture will no longer be visible.

There are two ways to mix colors. One is called **subtractive color mixture**. Subtractive mixtures occur when people mix pigments, such as

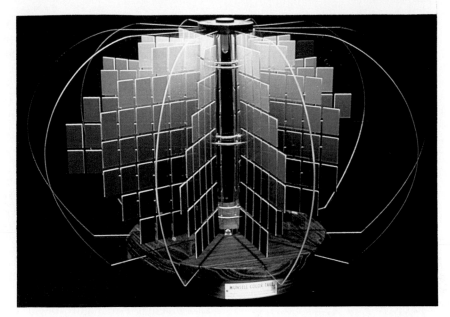

FIGURE 3-37   THE COLOR SOLID.

All three dimensions of colors are represented in the color solid, as shown in the inset. Hue (wavelength) is represented around the perimeter, as in the color circle. Saturation (purity) is represented by the distance between the edge and the center of the solid. Brightness (intensity) is represented by the vertical height of the solid. It has been estimated (Goldstein, 1984) that people can discriminate over 7 million colors produced by variations in hue, saturation, and brightness.

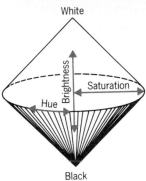

paints. The pigments absorb (subtract) certain wavelengths from the white light and reflect others. The wavelengths that are reflected to your eye give the pigment its color. Subtractive color mixture is illustrated in Figure 3-38.

The other way to mix colors is called **additive color mixture**. It happens when different wavelengths of light are added together, such as when two lights of different wavelengths are shined into the eye. Because white light contains all visible wavelengths, you would expect that an additive mixture of all wavelengths would produce white, and it does. Mixing two wavelengths together gives a color that corresponds to the wavelength between the two on the color circle. For example, mixing red and green lights produces yellow (see Figure 3-39), which is between red and green on the color circle. If two hues that are opposite to each other on the color circle are mixed together, the result is white (or a colorless gray). Such hues are called **complementary colors**. For example, yellow and violet-blue are complementary colors (see Figure 3-36).

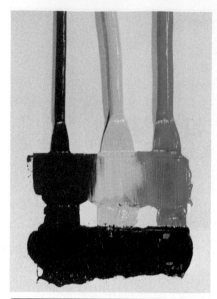

FIGURE 3-38   SUBTRACTIVE COLOR MIXTURE.
Greenish-blue paint reflects middle (green) and short (blue) wavelength light and absorbs—or subtracts—all the others from white light. Yellow paint reflects middle (green and yellow) wavelength light and absorbs all the other wavelengths. When greenish-blue and yellow paints are mixed, all wavelengths are absorbed except the middle (green) wavelength that the pigments both reflect; the result is green paint. Red paint absorbs all but the long (red) wavelengths. Therefore, when red, yellow, and greenish-blue paints are mixed, all wavelengths are absorbed and we get no color—black if the absorption of all the pigments were perfect.

FIGURE 3-39   ADDITIVE COLOR MIXTURE.
Combining lights of different hues is an example of additive color mixture. Additive mixture of three primary hues, such as red, green, and blue, yields white.

An important feature of additive color mixing is that by combining various amounts of three hues, it is possible to produce any other hue. These three hues are called **primary colors**. Generally they are red, green, and blue. However, almost any three hues can be used, so long as they are fairly far apart on the color circle and so long as two of the hues do not mix to produce the third. When the three primary colors are mixed together in equal amounts, they produce white light (see Figure 3-39).

EFFECTS OF CONTEXT ON COLOR   Although the hue of a stimulus generally corresponds to its wavelength, under some conditions identical stimuli can have different hues. For example, a color first seen alone changes appearance when it is surrounded by another color, a phenomenon called **simultaneous color contrast**. Generally, the surrounded color takes on the complementary color of the area surrounding it. For example, the cross in Figure 3-40 appears yellow when it is surrounded by violet-blue, and it appears slightly violet when surrounded by yellow.

When a person looks at a color for a long time, the perception of hue also changes (see Figure 3-41). After staring at a particular color for awhile, a person undergoes **chromatic adaptation**. The result is a **negative color afterimage** of the stimulus that was stared at, and the afterimage has the complementary colors of the stimulus stared at. A similar phenomenon occurs when you wear tinted sunglasses or ski goggles. When you take them off, the world takes on the complementary color of the tint of the glasses. The aftereffect of looking at the world through rose-colored glasses, then, is to see a world tinted green.

As you've seen, color contrast and chromatic adaptation can make the same wavelength have different hues. Under some conditions the opposite can happen: different wavelengths have the same hue. This phenom-

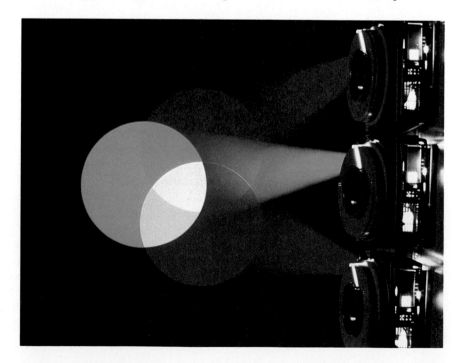

The cross at the top appears yellow; the
cross at the bottom appears gray or
violet. However, both crosses are printed
with exactly the same color ink. (You can
verify this by comparing the crosses
where they join on the left.) They look
different because of simultaneous color
contrast. (From Albers, 1975.)

On the left are four colored squares.
Stare at the X in the middle of the
squares for a minute or two. Then look
at the X in the white area to the right.
You should see a pattern of squares with
colors that are complementary to those on
the left. For example, you should see a
green square where the red square was, a
blue square where the yellow square was,
and so on. These are negative color
afterimages.

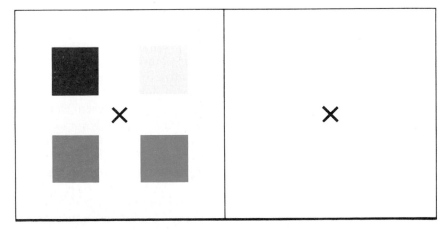

enon—called **color constancy**—occurs every time you walk from sunlight into an artificially lighted room. When objects such as your clothing are viewed in sunlight, their pigments reflect different wavelengths in different amounts from those they reflect in artificial indoor light. (The reason is that sunlight contains about equal intensities of all wavelengths; most artificial light contains more long than short wavelengths. As a result, objects reflect relatively more long wavelength [yellow and red] under artificial light than in sunlight.) Despite this difference, people perceive the colors of the objects to be about the same in the two situations.

How does color constancy work? One possible explanation is that the visual system adapts to the long-wavelength light that predominates in artificial light. People therefore become less sensitive to the yellows and reds in artificial light (Goldstein, 1984). Another possible explanation is that the visual system in some way calculates the relative changes in wavelength that occur over large areas of the visual field. Although the actual wavelengths of light reflected from objects differ in sunlight and artificial light, the relative changes in wavelength are similar under the two conditions. As a result, the perception of color remains constant (Land, 1983).

RETINAL AND NEURAL MECHANISMS OF COLOR VISION   How does the human visual system actually perceive color? As you might expect from explanations of other types of visual perception, the perception of color depends on activity in the retina and areas of the brain. Theories to explain the mechanisms of color vision have been intriguing scientists for hundreds of years, as you will see in the following sections.

Three Types of Cones.   For many years there were two competing theories of the retinal and neural mechanisms of color vision. The first was proposed by Thomas Young in 1801 and refined by Hermann von Helmholtz in 1878. Their theory is called the **trichromatic theory**; it states that the sensation of color results from the relative activity of three receptors, each of which is most sensitive to one of three primary colors. Young and Helmholtz based this theory on the observation that any hue can be produced by mixing three primary hues in proper proportions.

Earlier in the chapter, we noted that color vision depends on the activity of the cone photoreceptors in the retina. In 1964, two papers were published showing that there are three types of cones that do have the properties predicted by the trichromatic theory (Brown and Wald, 1964; Marks, Dobelle, and MacNichol, 1964). One cone type is most sensitive to short wavelength (blue) light, another to medium wavelength (green) light, and another to long wavelength (yellow-green) light (see Figure 3-42). Different wavelengths of light activate each type of cone to different extents. For example, a 500 nanometer (green) light activates the three cone types in different relative amounts than a 600 nanometer (orange) light. Thus, the relative activity of the three types of cones can signal the wavelength of light.

Opponent-process Retinal Neurons.   In 1878, Ewald Hering proposed a theory of color vision mechanism that is very different from the trichro-

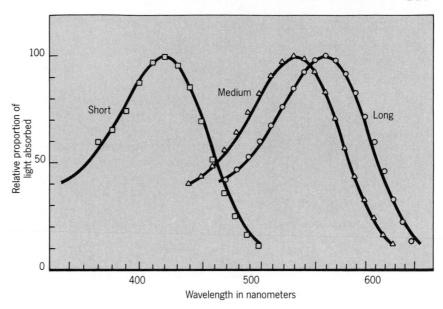

FIGURE 3-42   THREE TYPES OF CONE RECEPTORS.
The curves show the relative amount of light of different wavelengths that is absorbed by the three types of cones in the retina. Notice that each type is most sensitive to short (blue), medium (green), or long (yellow-green) wavelengths of light but that all three types absorb light over a wide range of wavelengths. As a result, light of a single wavelength activates each type of cone in different proportions. You can see this by drawing a vertical line from a point on the horizontal axis up through the three curves. (Adapted from Dartnall, Bowmaker, and Mollon, 1983.)

matic theory. Hering's theory is called the **opponent-process theory**. It states that the perception of color is based on two retinal processes that respond in opposite ways to the complementary hue pairs red–green and blue–yellow. Recent experiments have shown that the opponent-process theory also is correct: the trichromatic retinal cones combine their outputs to produce retinal mechanisms that operate in an opponent-process manner. The evidence has come from single-cell recordings in the optic nerves and brain of rhesus monkeys, whose color vision is nearly identical to that of humans (DeValois and Jacobs, 1968; Gouras and Zrenner, 1981). It was found that retinal ganglion cell axons are divided into two groups on the basis of their responses to color. One group is red–green opponent: they are excited by red light and inhibited by green light (R+/G− cells), or vice versa (R−/G+ cells). The other group is blue–yellow opponent: they are excited by blue light and inhibited by yellow light (B+/Y−), or vice versa (B−/Y+). The way in which the three cone types can combine to produce these opponent-process retinal outputs to the brain is shown in Figure 3-43.

As Hering recognized, the presence of opponent-process neurons explains several things about color perception. For example, mixing the complementary colors red and green produces a colorless gray because the red–green opponent cells are excited by one color of light and inhibited by the other. The excitation and inhibition cancel each other, and the result is no response: no color. For another example, seeing negative afterimages after having stared at a color can be explained by an imbalance in the opponent-process system. Thus, when you look at the yellow square in Figure 3-41, you fatigue the yellow half of the blue–yellow mechanism. Because the yellow half is fatigued, it counteracts the blue half of the mechanism less and the blue half becomes more active. When you then look at white paper (which reflects all wavelengths), the more active blue half of the mechanism makes you see a blue square.

(a)

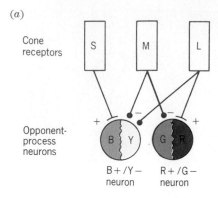

(b)

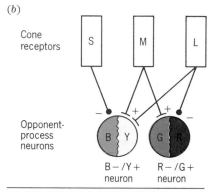

FIGURE 3-43 OPPONENT COLOR PROCESSING IN THE RETINA.

The three types of cones that respond most strongly to different wavelengths of light can combine to produce an opponent-process mechanism. (a) A red–green opponent neuron is excited by long wavelength cones and inhibited by medium wavelength cones; as a result, the neuron is excited by red and inhibited by green light (R+/G−). A blue–yellow opponent neuron is excited by short wavelength cones and inhibited by both medium and long wavelength cones; as a result, the neuron is excited by blue and inhibited by yellow light (B+/Y−). (b) This shows how the opposite arrangement of inputs can produce opponent-process neurons that are inhibited by red and excited by green (R−/G+) or inhibited by blue and excited by yellow (B−/Y+).

Thus the two theories of color vision that once seemed incompatible turn out both to be correct. The trichromatic theory describes the cone receptor mechanisms, and the opponent-process theory describes the neural mechanisms of color in the retina.

Color Processing by the Brain.   Of course, the neural processing of color is not complete in the retina. Recent research has shown that opponent-processing is combined with spatial information in the brain to provide the perception of color in patterns and forms. The combination of simple spatial and color information actually begins in the retina itself and continues to some extent in the lateral geniculate nucleus of the thalamus (Gouras, 1984). But the first detailed analysis of colored patterns occurs in striate cortex. As we saw earlier, neurons in striate cortex respond best to lines and edges of certain orientations. Many of these neurons also respond best when the lines and edges are of certain hues (Michael, 1978a, 1978b). For example, some striate cortex neurons are excited by a properly oriented red bar of light and inhibited by a green bar. Furthermore, these cells are inhibited if the area surrounding the red bar also is red and excited if the surrounding area is green. Thus the best stimulus for exciting a neuron of this kind is a properly oriented red bar on a green background. These mechanisms form a kind of pattern-specific opponent process. Figure 3-44 demonstrates a color aftereffect that depends on the close relationship between the orientation of a pattern and its hue.

Some evidence suggests that neural processing of color continues beyond striate cortex. For example, under conditions in which color constancy occurs for humans, some neurons in the fourth visual area of cortex (V4 in Figure 3-11) respond to the *color* people perceive rather than to the specific wavelengths that are present (Zeki, 1983). That is, these cells seem to show color constancy as humans experience it. Furthermore, if the fourth visual area is damaged, monkeys show deficits in color constancy even though their ability to discriminate wavelengths of light is normal (Wild, Butler, Carden, and Kulikowski, 1985). Thus, different aspects of color vision may be carried out by different visual areas of the brain.

COLOR DEFICIENCY   If your blind date shows up wearing a red shirt, violent orange jacket, green pants, brown shoes, one yellow sock and one white sock, you may suspect that your date also may be color-blind. About 8 percent of males and 0.05 percent of females have some form of color vision deficiency. The reason for this sex difference is that most forms of color vision deficiencies are hereditary and sex-linked. Women carry the gene for these color deficiencies usually without having the deficiency themselves, but when they pass the gene to their male children, the sons do have the deficiency.

People with normal color vision are called **trichromats** because, as we have seen, they have three types of cones and can match any hue with a mixture of three primary hues. **Dichromats** are partially color-blind because they are missing one type of cone (Rushton, 1975; Bowmaker, 1983). There are three kinds of dichromatic color deficiencies. In *protanopia* the long-wavelength cones are missing; in *deuteranopia* the medium-

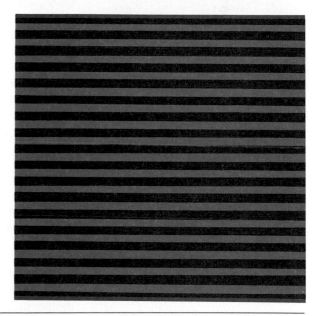

FIGURE 3-44 A DEMONSTRATION OF THE RELATIONSHIP BETWEEN COLOR AND PATTERN ORIENTATION.
First notice that the pattern at the left is made up of black and white horizontal and vertical lines. Now look at the vertical green grating for about 5 seconds, then at the horizontal red grating for about 5 seconds, and continue shifting your gaze between the two gratings for 2 or 3 minutes. Then
look back at the black and white pattern. Notice that the vertical white lines in the pattern now appear reddish and the horizontal white lines appear greenish. If you turn the book 90 degrees, the color of the lines will change so that vertical continues to appear reddish and horizontal continues to appear greenish. Thus this is a color aftereffect that is specific for lines of a certain orientation. When you adapt to lines of one hue and orientation, only white lines of the same
orientation take on the complementary hue (McCollough, 1965). One explanation of this phenomenon is that your cortical cells that respond best to lines of a particular orientation and hue are fatigued by the repeated exposure to that stimulus. Because of opponent-process mechanisms, the cortical cells that respond best to the same orientation and the complementary hue come to dominate.

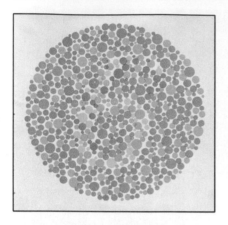

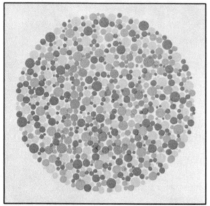

FIGURE 3-45 EXAMPLES OF PLATES USED TO TEST FOR RED–GREEN COLOR BLINDNESS. In plate 1, the red dots form a "6" pattern on the green dots. Dots that differ in brightness or saturation form no particular pattern. Therefore, people with normal color vision see a red 6 on a green background, but people with red–green color deficiency cannot distinguish these differences in hue and see only a random pattern of dots. Similarly, people with normal color vision see a green 15 on a red background in plate 2, but red–green color deficient people do not.

wavelength cones are missing. Both protanopes and deuteranopes perceive blue and yellow relatively normally, but they confuse red and green. For this reason, they are sometimes called red–green color-blind. As you can see from Figure 3-43, loss of either the long- or medium-wavelength cones would produce a loss of the red–green opponent color system, which explains why these people cannot distinguish between red and green hues. The blue–yellow opponent color system continues to operate relatively normally (Friedman, Thornton, and Pugh, 1985). The third kind of dichromatic deficiency is *tritanopia,* a loss of the short-wavelength cones, and is extremely rare. Tritanopes see red and green relatively normally, but they cannot distinguish blue and yellow. Their blue–yellow color blindness can be explained by a loss of the blue–yellow opponent system. **Monochromats** are completely color-blind. They have only one type of cone or, in some cases, no functioning cones. These individuals see the world as if on black and white film. Figure 3-45 can help you test whether you have a color vision deficiency.

Many dichromats do not know that they are color-blind. Although dichromats confuse some hues, they still can distinguish stimuli by their brightness and saturation. They have learned to apply common color names to what they see without realizing that what they see differs from what people with normal color vision see. Thus, a dichromat and a normal trichromat may both point at an object and call it "red," but what the dichromat sees is not the same as what the person with normal color vision sees (Graham and Hsia, 1958). This fact raises the intriguing possibility that sensation and perception of the world also differ among normal observers. Perhaps what you see is not the same as what a friend sees, even though you both call it the same thing.

Visual Development

What does the newborn infant see? How does visual perception change as people grow up? Does what people see as they grow up influence what they can see later on? These questions have interested philosophers and psychologists for centuries. Since the 1960s, research in animals and humans has provided some surprising answers.

NORMAL VISUAL DEVELOPMENT Many parents believe that their newborn babies cannot see. But psychologists have recently been able to show empirically that human infants can see at birth. For example, if newborns are shown a picture of a triangle or a square, their eyes scan the edges of the form, and they stare at the corners (Salapatek and Kessen, 1966). But the vision of infants in their first months is not as good as it will be after their first few months of development. Young infants are not very good at following a moving object with their eyes or at changing focus (accommodating) as an object is moved closer or farther away from them. Both accommodation and the ability to follow moving objects improve rapidly after birth and are fully mature by 3 to 5 months of age (Banks and Salapatek, 1983).

Given that newborn infants can see, how can psychologists find out what and how well they see? A particularly clever method involves showing infants two pictures at the same time and measuring the relative

FIGURE 3-46   THE PREFERENTIAL LOOKING METHOD FOR TESTING VISUAL ACUITY IN INFANTS.
The procedure takes advantage of the infant's preference for looking at patterns rather than at a plain gray area. The infant is held in the parent's lap facing a visual display, which contains a gray circle and a circle filled with a black and white striped grating pattern. The positions of the two stimuli are alternated randomly from trial to trial. An adult observer, who cannot see the stimuli, uses a television monitor to watch where the infant looks. If the infant consistently looks at the patterned stimulus from trial to trial, we conclude that she can see it. The width of the stripes can be changed and the finest grating that the infant consistently looks at provides an estimate of the finest detail she can see—her visual acuity. The child can be rewarded for looking at the patterned stimulus with a view of a toy animal that dances and beats a drum. (After Mayer and Dobson, 1980.)

amount of time spent looking at each one (Fantz, 1961). By using this *preferential looking method,* Fantz found that infants look at some patterns, such as black and white stripes, more than at others, such as a bull's-eye. The difference shows that newborn infants can discriminate among different forms and patterns.

More recently, investigators have used an elaboration of the preferential looking method to learn a great deal about the visual abilities of infants. For example, the procedure shown in Figure 3-46 has been used to determine how well young infants can see fine details (their visual acuity). Tests of this kind have found that 2-week-old infants have very poor visual acuity. They can see stripes only when the stripes are about ½ degree or wider, an acuity that corresponds to about 20/600 vision. By comparison, adults can see stripes that are about ¹⁄₆₀ degree wide. Visual acuity progressively improves during early childhood and reaches adult levels at about 5 years of age (see Figure 3-47).

Color vision also is not adultlike at birth (Banks and Salapatek, 1983; Werner and Wooten, 1985). Two-month-old infants can discriminate some hues, such as green and red. But their color vision is similar to adult tritanopes, who cannot discriminate blue and yellow. That is, 2-month-old infants have functioning long- and medium-wavelength cones but the short-wavelength cones seem to be absent or relatively insensitive. By 3 months of age, all three types of cones appear to be functional. However, 3-month-olds still may not have adultlike color vision (Werner and Wooten, 1985). Indeed, the age at which color vision becomes fully mature has not yet been determined.

Psychologists have studied extensively the ability of infants to perceive depth. In one classic study, Gibson and Walk (1960) demonstrated that infants could perceive depth by 6 months of age. They placed the infants on the centerboard of a visual cliff like the one shown in Figure 3-48.

Acuity was measured using the procedures shown in Figure 3-46. (Adapted from Teller, 1981.)

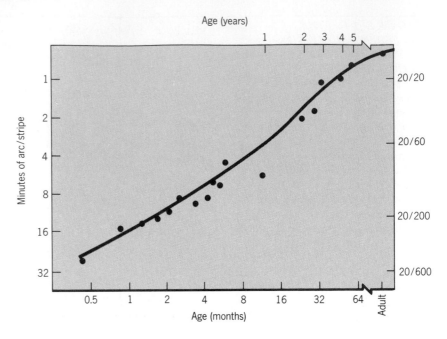

FIGURE 3-48   THE VISUAL CLIFF USED BY GIBSON AND WALK (1960).
The cliff consists of a deep and a shallow side, each covered with the same checked pattern. A glass top prevents the baby from falling into the deep side. Even so, the baby will not cross over the deep side to the mother.

The infants refused to crawl across the deep side of the cliff to reach their mothers, but they readily crawled across the shallow side. Thus the experimenters concluded that the infants perceived that the cliff had depth.

More recent experiments have been focused on when monocular depth perception first develops and which cues infants use. They show that sensitivity to static monocular cues, such as shadowing and relative size, develops between 5 and 7 months of age (Yonas, Granrud, and Pettersen, 1985; Granrud, Yonas, and Opland, 1985). Sensitivity to dynamic monocular cues develops even earlier. For example, 3- to 4-month-old infants blink at or withdraw their heads more from an object that seems to be looming toward them (a geometrically expanding display) than to an object that seems to be moving away (a geometrically contracting display) (Yonas, 1981). Thus, by the age of 3 or 4 months, infants respond to dynamic depth cues that indicate an impending collision.

To perceive binocular depth cues, an infant has to be able to look at, or fixate, objects with both eyes. This capacity is not present at birth. Newborn infants often look with one eye in one direction and with the other eye in another direction, a habit that may startle new parents. Babies do not develop the ability to point both eyes reliably at the same target until about 3 months of age (Aslin, 1977). Babies also begin to use stereoscopic depth cues at this age, and by 6 to 7 months of age, nearly all infants can use stereoscopic depth cues (Teller, 1982). But infants still cannot judge the depth of objects from binocular cues as precisely as adults can. By 3 to 5 years of age, stereoscopic depth perception is nearly as precise as in adults (Fox, Patterson, and Francis, 1986).

The main reason that infants' visual abilities are immature is that their eyes and brains are not fully developed. The retina itself (particularly the fovea) is immature at birth and does not take on the distant appearance of an adult's until sometime between 15 and 45 months of age (Hendrickson and Youdelis, 1984). Furthermore, although infants are born with a full complement of neurons in the brain, many are immature at birth. They are small, and their dendrites are not as large or complex as an adult's. In addition, infants have only about half as many synaptic connections onto striate cortex neurons as adults (Huttenlocher, de Courten, Garey, and van der Loos, 1982; Michel and Garey, 1984). During the first eight months after birth, there is rapid growth in the dendrites and synaptic connections among striate cortex neurons. In fact, the brain so exuberantly produces synaptic connections that the 8-month-old has some 40 percent *more* connections than he or she will have in adulthood. These excess connections are lost during childhood, and the striate cortex reaches maturity sometime between 3 and 11 years of age (ages between these have not been studied) (Huttenlocher et al., 1982).

Mature visual abilities thus seem to depend in large part on the maturation of the retina and brain. Only when the biological systems are mature does a person have the chance to have all of the visual abilities we have discussed. But as we explain in the following section, learning and experience contribute to normal biological development of the visual system. In this aspect of human development, as in so many others, nature and nurture interact.

ROLE OF THE ENVIRONMENT What role does a person's actual visual experience—what that person sees or cannot see—play in the development of the ability to see? The answer to this question has come from studies of people deprived of normal visual experience during development. For example, people who have cataracts or damaged corneas on both eyes early in life experience severe visual deprivation. Although diffuse light reaches the retina, these people do not have normal experience with visual patterns or forms. Some of these people later have had their vision corrected surgically (von Senden, 1960; Ackroyd, Humphrey, and Warrington, 1974; Apkarian, 1983). Immediately after their surgery, the patients could distinguish objects from background, could scan, and could follow moving objects with their eyes. But they could not recognize forms such as circles and squares by sight, even though they could easily recognize the same forms by touch and could make a circle or square with their fingers. With training and experience, their vision improved until most could recognize patterns, shapes, and objects. But vision of forms and visual acuity never became fully normal.

The permanent visual problems of these patients show that visual experience during development is necessary for normal vision. Experimenters have investigated how such abnormal visual experience affects the development of the brain in cats and monkeys. Like humans, animals that have had no experience with visual patterns during development can see when they grow up, but their vision is abnormal (Mitchell and Timney, 1984). Study of their brains shows that visual areas do not function normally (Sherman and Spear, 1982). For example, many neurons in striate cortex do not respond normally to the shape or orientation of visual stimuli, and many other neurons fail to respond to light at all (Wiesel and Hubel, 1965).

Less serious forms of visual deprivation than a complete lack of pattern vision also can affect how well we see. As we noted in Box 3-1, many people's eyes are shaped such that images focus abnormally on the retina. These people are near- or farsighted, astigmatic, or suffer other problems in vision. If these problems occur early in life and go uncorrected, they ultimately can result in **amblyopia**. Amblyopia, commonly called "lazy eye," is poor visual acuity caused by abnormalities in the brain. It arises because continuously blurred images on the retina do not provide neurons in the brain with normal visual stimulation during development. As a result, the neurons develop abnormally and do not respond well to fine details in the visual environment (Boothe, Dobson, and Teller, 1985). Even if the blurred image on the retina is corrected with eyeglasses when these people are adults, the neurons cannot respond to fine details and therefore poor visual acuity remains.

Early visual experience affects the development of neural connections and therefore visual perception in two ways. First, visual experience maintains innately specified connections in the brain. Connections that are adequately stimulated are maintained and develop normally, while those that are not wither away, or atrophy. Second, the early environment shapes, or "instructs," the formation of neural connections. That is, exposure to visual patterns and forms seems to guide the development of connections among neurons in the brain and therefore people's ultimate perceptual abilities.

CRITICAL PERIODS OF DEVELOPMENT Why can't people deprived of certain kinds of visual experience early in life acquire normal vision once they have surgery or are fitted with glasses as adults? Even if the deprivation produced abnormalities in the brain, why can't the abnormalities be reversed by later normal experience? The reason is that the visual system is susceptible to environmental influence only during a limited period of development, called the **critical period**. The existence of a critical period during which the environment can influence visual development was first demonstrated in experiments on cats (Hubel and Wiesel, 1970). Then researchers looked for a similar phenomenon in the visual development of humans. The clearest demonstration came out of studies of people with **strabismus**.

Strabismus is a condition in which the two eyes do not point in the same direction. People whose eyes turn inward toward the nose have *esotropia* (commonly called cross eyes) and those whose eyes turn outward have *exotropia* (commonly called wall eyes). Strabismus is a form of visual deprivation because the two eyes rarely see the same thing at the same time, and so a person is deprived of normal simultaneous stimulation of the two eyes. If strabismus occurs early in life and is not corrected, a person suffers from visual abnormalities in adulthood such as no binocular vision. Most people with early uncorrected strabismus lack stereoscopic depth perception.

One group of researchers (Banks, Aslin, and Letson, 1975) tested binocular vision in people whose strabismus appeared within a few months after birth and was surgically corrected at various ages (see

BOX 3-3
AMBLYOPIA AND CRITICAL PERIODS OF DEVELOPMENT

When Jane Freeman was a junior in college, majoring in psychology, she found that she could not keep up with the required reading. An eye exam revealed that she had amblyopia, or "lazy eye," in one eye. Her poor visual acuity in the lazy eye made printed lines appear blurry, and eyeglasses did not help. The eye doctor prescribed daily exercises and a patch over the normal eye to improve vision in the lazy eye. But Jane's vision never would be normal. Only when amblyopia is treated in childhood can normal vision return.

It has been estimated that about 4 percent of the people in the United States have amblyopia. As we discussed earlier, amblyopia results from abnormal visual experience during childhood, which causes abnormal brain development. A variety of conditions can lead to abnormal visual experience during development. Children who have improperly shaped eyes (who are nearsighted, farsighted, or astigmatic) experience almost continuously blurred images, which can result in amblyopia. Amblyopia also can be caused by early strabismus, because the child often uses only one eye and suppresses or ignores images from the other eye. The amblyopia develops in the eye that was suppressed (Birch and Stager, 1985). Amblyopia in one eye also can be caused if an eye doctor puts a patch over one of a child's eyes following an operation on the eyelid. Patching for only one week in a young child can lead to a long-lasting loss of visual acuity (Awaya, Miyake, Imayuni Shiose, Kanda, and Komuro, 1973).

Many studies have shown that there is a critical period of life during which abnormal visual experience can lead to amblyopia, just as there is a critical period during which strabismus can lead to poor binocular vision (Mitchell and Timney, 1984). In general, children are most susceptible to the effects of abnormal visual experience during their first 2 to 3 years. If their problems in vision are corrected during this time, their vision may develop normally. Past about 8 years of age, correction produces little or no improvement. For instance, eyeglasses or contact lenses will do little to improve the vision of adults who had uncorrected vision problems when they were children, because their brains no longer process the visual information normally. The only cure for amblyopia is treatment during childhood.

Because critical periods in visual development do exist, it is important that adults watch for and treat vision problems in infants and young children. One way vision can be tested in infants is with the preferential looking method (see Figure 3-46). This method, which was developed for basic research on vision in young infants, also can be used in the doctor's office or clinic. By using such early testing methods, permanent impairment of vision can be prevented.

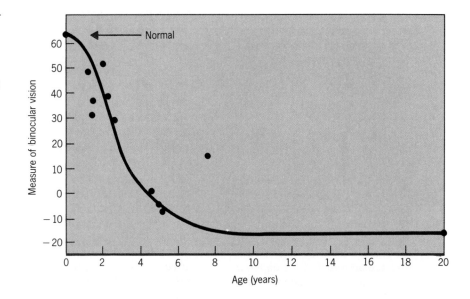

FIGURE 3-49   THE CRITICAL PERIOD FOR DEVELOPMENT OF BINOCULAR VISION.

A measure of binocular vision is plotted as a function of the age at which surgery was performed to correct strabismus that occurred within a few months of birth. Normal individuals have a score of about 60 on the test, whereas most individuals with corrective surgery after 4 years of age score around 0. (Adapted from Banks, Aslin, and Letson, 1975.)

Figure 3-49). They found that people whose eye alignment was corrected before 3 years of age developed good (though not quite normal) binocular vision; those corrected after 4 years of age developed poor binocular vision. They also found that strabismus *beginning* after 6 to 8 years of age has very little effect on binocular vision. They concluded, therefore, that there is a critical period of development, which ends by 4 to 8 years of age, during which visual experience influences binocular vision. Not only did the discovery of a critical period during which the environment influences visual development have important theoretical applications, it had important practical applications as well (see Box 3-3).

SUMMARY

SOME BASIC CONCEPTS

1. *Measuring Sensory Abilities.* Psychophysics is the study of the relationships between physical stimuli and people's experience of them. Such studies show that the detection of very weak stimuli depends both on sensitivity to the stimuli and on expectations and motivations to detect them. When people discriminate between two stimuli, their difference threshold is a function of the magnitude of the standard stimulus. According to Weber's law, the size of a just noticeable difference is a constant proportion of the size of the standard stimulus. For stimuli that are above threshold, the sensation of stimulus magnitude is proportional to the intensity of the stimulus raised to some power (Stevens' power law). These psychophysical laws apply to many different types of stimuli for each sense.

2. *From the Stimulus to Experience.* Each sense has a specialized sense organ that transforms external energy into the electrochemical activity of nerve cells. Sensory stimuli can vary in quality, quantity, location, and duration. These attributes can be coded by the place in the brain where neurons are activated, the frequency or rate at which a neuron fires action potentials, and the length of time that a neuron fires action potentials. Our complex sensory experience thus consists of millions of neurons discharging in many different ways to represent the nature of the external stimuli.

VISUAL STIMULI, THE EYE, AND THE BRAIN

3. *Visual Stimuli and the Eye.* Visible light is a form of electromagnetic radiation. The eyeball is an accessory structure that is specialized to focus the light onto receptor cells in the retina. There are two types of light receptors, called rods and cones. Rods are responsible for vision under low light. Cones are primarily responsible for color vision and for vision in bright light. The fovea is a specialized region of the retina that contains only cones and that provides vision of fine details.

4. *The Visual System.* The rods and cones connect with retinal neurons, which carry out a great deal of neural information processing before signals are transmitted to the brain. These signals are sent to the lateral geniculate nucleus of the thalamus and from there to striate cortex (primary visual cortex). From striate cortex, the signals are distributed to many extrastriate visual cortical areas. Thus, large areas of the brain are involved in processing visual information and providing visual experience.

FROM BRIGHTNESS TO COMPLEX FORMS

5. *Brightness and Contrast.* Brightness refers to the experience of light intensity. People can see over more than a millionfold range of intensities, largely because of dark and light adaptation, which adjust the sensitivity of the visual system under different levels of light. Perception of brightness depends on the differences in intensity among nearby objects as well as on the physical intensity of light. For example, light of a given intensity appears brighter when seen against a less intense area than when seen against a more intense area (the phenomenon of brightness contrast). In addition, objects often appear to have the same brightness when viewed under very different levels of illumination (the phenomenon of brightness constancy).

6. *Pattern Vision.* Pattern vision is the ability to see changes in light

and dark. In part, pattern vision depends on visual acuity, which is the ability to see fine details. In part, pattern vision depends on the ability to detect the coarser changes in light and dark that make up the visual scene. Studies of spatial contrast sensitivity indicate that people cannot readily detect changes in light and dark that occur over large distances. Thus, the visual system is specialized to detect relatively frequent changes in light and dark across space. This conclusion is confirmed by studies of the neural mechanisms of pattern vision. Such studies also indicate that neurons in striate cortex respond to particular features in visual patterns—they carry out a process of abstraction.

7. *Form Vision.* People tend to integrate patterns of light and dark into meaningful forms that have shape and size. To do this, people organize patterns into perceptual wholes, or forms, and we separate these forms from the background. The Gestalt psychologists formulated a number of principles, or laws of organization, that explain why people perceive certain stimulus patterns as a unified group or form. People recognize these forms (or objects) despite changes in their orientation in space (the phenomenon of shape constancy); this ability depends on familiarity with common objects and their positions in space. Thus, the perception of forms depends on the overall context in which they are seen and not just on their retinal image. There is controversy over the brain mechanisms of form vision. Some researchers believe that form vision is carried out by specific neurons that respond only to particular objects. Others believe that form recognition involves the pattern of activity of millions of neurons, each of which responds to a simple feature of the overall form.

MOVEMENT AND DEPTH

8. *Perception of Movement.* Objects in the world are constantly moving and people constantly move their eyes and heads as well. Thus, the perception of movement involves movement of objects, movement of backgrounds, and movement of viewers' eyes. One theory suggests that information within the visual scene is sufficient to provide cues about what is moving and what is not. An alternative theory holds that people distinguish between their own and objects' movements on the basis of neural (corollary discharge) information about expected eye movements. The evidence suggests that both mechanisms probably work in concert.

9. *Depth Perception.* The ability to judge the depth of objects in space (their position and distance relative to ourselves and to each other) depends on three types of cues. Static monocular cues are based on features of stationary objects and require only one eye. Dynamic monocular cues also require only one eye but are based on the relative movement of stimuli in the world. Binocular cues depend on the use of both eyes for the perception of depth. Cues for depth help people to perceive that an object viewed at different distances does not really change in size (the phenomenon of size constancy). These cues also are responsible for certain illusions of size and shape.

COLOR

10. *Color Vision.* Color is determined by three physical attributes of light: wavelength, purity, and intensity. The sensation of hue generally corresponds to wavelength, the sensation of saturation to purity, and the sensation of brightness to intensity. Most colors are actually mixtures of many wavelengths. Like other visual attributes, the color of a stimulus depends on the context in which the stimulus occurs. For instance, a color changes appearance when it is surrounded by another color (the phenomenon of simultaneous color contrast) and prolonged exposure to colored stimuli (chromatic adaptation) changes the perception of color. Thus, in some situations, the same wavelengths of light can produce different color sensations, and different wavelengths can produce the same perceived color.

11. *Mechanisms of Color Vision.* In the earliest stages of retinal processing, the sensation of color is produced by the relative activity of three cone receptors, as predicted by the Young–Helmholtz trichromatic theory. The outputs of these receptors are combined into a opponent-process mechanism, as predicted by Hering's theory. Thus, neurons in the brain respond in opposite ways to the complementary hue pairs red–green and blue–yellow. Different types of color deficiency result from a loss of one or more of the cone types, which produces abnormalities in the opponent-process neural mechanisms.

VISUAL DEVELOPMENT

12. *Development and the Environment.* Human infants can see a great deal at birth but not as much as adults. For instance, newborns can discriminate different forms and patterns, but their visual acuity is relatively poor, and depth perception is absent. Their color vision also is not mature. The maturation of visual abilities depends largely on the maturation of the retina and brain. The early visual environment plays an important role in visual development. Abnormal experience early in life can permanently alter the

development of visual areas of the brain and result in abnormal vision. There is a critical period of visual development. The human visual system is most susceptible to environmental influences during approximately the first 2 to 3 years of life.

FURTHER READINGS

Good general textbooks on sensation and perception include *Sensation and Perception* (2nd Ed.) by Coren, Porac, and Ward (1984), *Sensation and Perception* (2nd Ed.) by Goldstein (1984), and *Perception* by Sekuler and Blake (1985). These are scholarly and well-written books that are highly recommended to students who wish to learn more about the subjects covered in the present chapter.

The Psychobiology of Sensory Coding by Uttal (1973) contains excellent discussions of issues that confront psychologists who are interested in understanding how neurons code sensory information. Although it is over a decade old, this book continues to be timely in its consideration of fundamental principles of sensory coding.

Visual Perception by Cornsweet (1970) has become a classic in the field. This book is well written and contains excellent discussions of research and fundamental principles of visual perception. It also contains many excellent illustrations of certain perceptual phenomena.

Seeing: Illusion, Brain and Mind by Frisby (1980) is a well-illustrated book about visual perception, illusions, and brain mechanisms of vision. *Perception* by Rock (1984) also includes excellent illustrations of many perceptual phenomena. Both books include discussions and excellent demonstrations of a wide range of visual phenomena from brightness vision to complex visual perception.

Eye and Brain: The Psychology of Seeing (3rd Ed.) by Gregory (1977) describes the basics of visual sensation and perception in clearly understandable language. It is recommended to the beginning student. Also recommended is *The Intelligent Eye* by Gregory (1970), which focuses on illusions and the use of perceptual phenomena in visual art.

For those interested in further reading on the topic of visual development, *Development of Perception: Psychobiological Perspectives. Volume 2, The Visual System* is a good source. This book is edited by Aslin, Alberts, and Petersen (1981) and includes chapters on animal and human visual development that are written by scientists working in the field.

4

SENSATION AND PERCEPTION: AUDITORY, CHEMICAL, AND BODY SENSES

It is dinnertime, and you are incredibly hungry. As you walk across campus to the dining hall, you hear the hum of the exhaust fans and the clank of heavy stainless steel kitchen equipment. You hear other students talking on their way to dinner. As you open the heavy glass doors, the warm air hits you. You smell spices, tomatoes, and you know that tonight you'll be having spaghetti. You unbutton your jacket and move your smooth plastic tray along the cafeteria-style line, gathering the elements of your meal. You look around for a table, settle yourself, and look at the food you've bought. Looks okay, smells good. Too hot? You check carefully with your lips and then take your first tasty bite. In going for dinner at the dining hall as in an endless variety of other everyday actions, you rely on your senses.

You are in contact with your environment through a variety of senses in addition to vision (discussed in Chapter 3). Your sense of **hearing** (also called **audition**) allows you to detect and interpret sounds. Your chemical senses allow you to **taste** and **smell**. Your body senses give you information about touch, pressure, pain, and temperature on your skin (the **skin senses**), about the positions of your limbs and joints (**kinesthesis**), and about the orientation of your head and body in space (the **vestibular sense**). Many of the same basic principles of sensation and perception that apply to vision also apply to these senses. However, the auditory, chemical, and body senses also represent unique adaptations to the environment.

HEARING

The Stimulus for Sound

Sound comes from vibrations, or pressure changes, in a medium such as air, water, or even the walls of your room. For instance, the loudspeaker of a stereo produces sound by vibrating in and out and causing alternate compression and decompression (or rarefaction) of the air molecules next to the speaker cone. The speaker cone pushes on the air—causing compression—and then pulls away from it—causing rarefaction. These pressure changes are called **sound waves**. They travel outward from the speaker and ultimately reach your ear (see Figure 4-1*a*).

The simplest type of sound wave, a **pure tone**, is one that has the form of a sine wave (see Figure 4-1*b*). A sine wave sound stimulus is especially useful for studying hearing because the right combination of sine waves can produce any complex sound, such as music or speech. By knowing how the ear and brain respond to sine waves, you can deduce how they respond to any complex sound.

Two defining characteristics of sine waves are their frequency and amplitude. **Frequency** is the number of complete cycles of a sound wave in a period of time and is expressed as cycles per second. A **Hertz (Hz)** equals one cycle per second. You can hear differences in a sound's frequency when you hear a flute play two different notes. **Amplitude** is the greatest pressure of a sound wave. Amplitude usually is measured relative to some baseline, or standard sound pressure. The most com-

FIGURE 4-1   SOUND WAVES.
(a) *The cone of a stereo speaker vibrates in and out, causing increases (compression) and decreases (decompression, or rarefaction) in the pressure of air. These air pressure changes travel in a wave to the ear. You can actually feel air pressure changes by turning up the volume of the stereo and placing your hand near the speaker cone. You can see them by dangling a thread near the speaker cone and watching the thread move back and forth. These pressure changes are called sound waves.*
(b) *A simple sound wave is a sine wave, in which the air pressure increases and decreases sinusoidally over time, as shown here. Sound waves can vary in frequency (the number of pressure changes in a period of time) and in amplitude (the magnitude of the air pressure changes).*

(a)

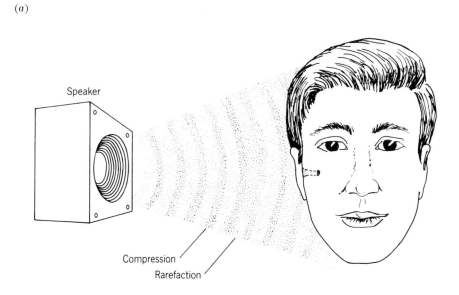

(b)

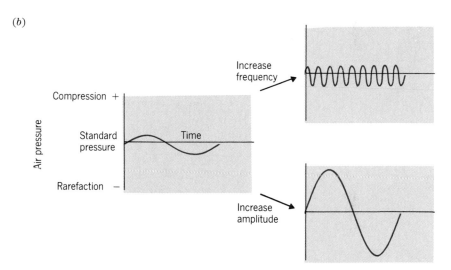

mon unit of sound amplitude is the **decibel (dB) sound pressure level (SPL)**. A dB SPL is the amplitude of sound pressure relative to the pressure of the weakest 1000-Hz tone that people can hear. Human conversation takes place at about 50 to 60 dB SPL, and rock concerts may blare forth at a painful 120 dB SPL or more. The decibel scale of sound amplitude is logarithmic; for example, a sound pressure of 80 dB SPL is 100 times greater than a sound pressure of 40 dB SPL.

The Auditory System

Just as the eye converts the light from green leaves and flashes of lightning into the electrochemical activity of brain cells, so does the ear convert the sound waves from the rustle of leaves and the crack of thunder

FIGURE 4-2   THE HUMAN EAR.
The ear consists of three main parts: the outer, middle, and inner ear. (Modified from Lindsay and Norman, 1977.)

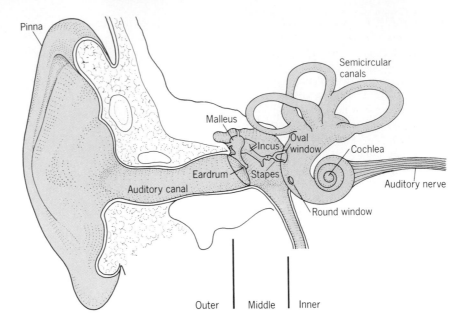

into the electrochemical activity of neurons. Most of the ear is an accessory structure that focuses, amplifies, and modifies the sound waves so that receptor cells deep in the skull can be activated. Figures 4-2 and 4-3 show how the human ear is constructed. Let's see how it works.

The process of hearing begins with the **pinna**, the fleshy outer part of the ear (Figure 4-2). Sometimes when you listen, you cock your head to one side or another so the pinnae catch the sounds better. Some animals (such as cats) can raise, lower, and swivel their pinnae to catch sounds from the right direction. The pinna funnels sound waves into the **auditory canal**. When sound waves reach the end of the auditory canal, they produce pressure against the **eardrum**. The eardrum is a thin membrane (like any drum skin) that vibrates to the sound waves. The vibration of the eardrum in turn causes three tiny bones in the middle part of the ear to vibrate. These bones, called the **ossicles**, form an efficient lever system that transfers the pressure from the vibrating eardrum to a smaller membrane, the **oval window** (Figure 4-3a). The movement of the lever system plus the smaller size of the oval window relative to the eardrum increase the pressure against the oval window 25 to 30 times. The oval window then has enough force to create pressure changes in the fluid that fills the spiral-shaped **cochlea** of the inner ear (fluid is more resistent to compression than air). Within the cochlea, these pressure changes in the fluid cause the **basilar membrane** to vibrate. When the basilar membrane vibrates, the **receptor cells** (also called **hair cells**) that rest on it move. These cells also are attached by tiny hairs to the **tectorial membrane** that arches over them (Figure 4-3b and 4-3c). Movement of the receptor cells relative to the tectorial membrane makes the tiny hairs bend, and as they do so, the receptor cells' membranes are more easily penetrated by certain nearby ions (electrically charged molecules). As the ions move through the receptor cell membrane, an electrical receptor

FIGURE 4-3 STRUCTURES WITHIN THE EAR.
(a) *An enlargement of the middle and inner ear shown in Figure 4-2. The* **ossicles** *are three tiny bones, named the malleus (hammer), incus (anvil), and stapes (stirrup). These bones form a lever system that connects the* **eardrum** *with the much smaller* **oval window**. *The oval window is the entrance to a spiral tube, called the* **cochlea**, *which is filled with fluid. (b) A cross section through the cochlea, and (c) an enlargement of part of the cross section. The* **receptor cells** *sit on the* **basilar membrane** *and have tiny hairs (hence the name* **hair cells**) *that make contact with the overhanging* **tectorial membrane**. *Together, these structures are called the* **organ of Corti**, *which runs the entire length of the cochlea. Auditory nerve fibers make synaptic contact with the receptor cells. (After Coren, Porac, and Ward, 1984.)*

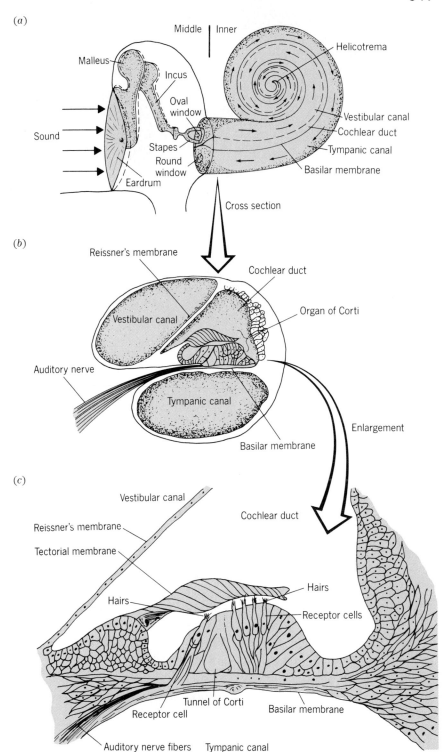

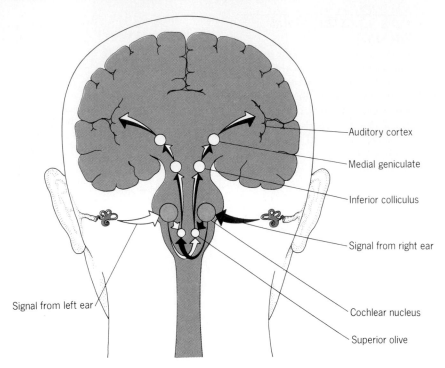

Information from the left ear is shown in
white, and information from the right
ear is shown in black. Auditory nerve
fibers from each ear carry signals to
the cochlear nucleus in the medulla,
where synaptic connections are made.
Neurons in each cochlear nucleus send
information to the superior olive nuclei
of both hemispheres. Thus, auditory
information from both ears reaches both
sides of the brain. From the superior
olive, auditory pathways ascend to the
midbrain (inferior colliculus), thalamus
(medial geniculate nucleus), and cortex.
(After Lindsay and Norman, 1977.)

Auditory cortex

Medial geniculate

Inferior colliculus

Signal from right ear

Cochlear nucleus

Superior olive

Signal from left ear

potential is created in the receptor cell (Hudspeth, 1985). The receptor cell then releases a chemical neurotransmitter, and this substance produces action potentials in the auditory nerve fibers that project to the brain. Thus, through an elegant sequence of events, waves of sound pressure in the air have been transduced into action potentials of neurons in the brain.

The brain has many auditory structures devoted to processing sounds, and these structures have many complex interconnections (see Figure 4-4). One result of these connections is that both ears send information to both sides of the brain. This information ultimately reaches the cerebral cortex, which has many areas that are involved in processing auditory stimuli. Cats, the species that has been studied most thoroughly, have at least six different areas of cortex that receive information from the ears (Woolsey, 1961). Not only does sensory information travel from ear to brain, but the brain sends projections directly back to the receptor cells. Thus the brain can modify what we hear before the information even leaves the receptors!

Perception of Pitch and Loudness

In everyday terms, people describe the sounds they hear as a rich variety: "sudden," "sharp," "piercing"; "low," "sweet," "soft"; "deafening," "rumbling," "frightening"; "bright," "tinkling," "joyous." But all the sounds people hear consist mainly of two perceptual qualities: pitch and loudness.

*FIGURE 4-5   THE HIGHEST
SOUND FREQUENCY THAT
PEOPLE CAN HEAR AT
VARIOUS AGES.*
*(From Hinchcliffe, 1962; after Schober,
1952.)*

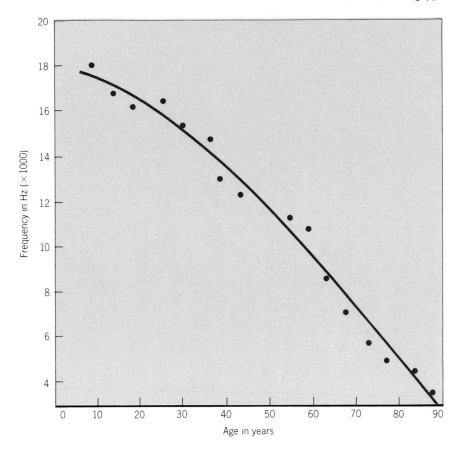

*FIGURE 4-5   THE HIGHEST
SOUND FREQUENCY THAT
PEOPLE CAN HEAR AT
VARIOUS AGES.*
*(From Hinchcliffe, 1962; after Schober,
1952.)*

PITCH   The **pitch** that people perceive is determined primarily by the frequency of the sound wave. For example, the lowest pitched note on a piano is approximately 28 Hz, a deep, resonant bass note. The highest pitched note on a piano is 4186 Hz, a high, pinging treble note. Under ideal conditions—no background noise, no partial hearing loss from too much loud music or advancing age—humans can hear frequencies ranging from 20 to 20,000 Hz. As people get older, the range of sound frequencies that they can hear gradually shrinks (see Figure 4-5).

Although the pitch that you perceive is determined mainly by frequency, the pitch of a sound also depends on other factors (Wightman and Green, 1974). For example, two sounds that consist of very different combinations of frequencies may be perceived by listeners to have the same pitch. Thus two different musical instruments, such as a clarinet and a piano, may both play a note pitched at middle C, but the frequencies produced by each instrument will differ. Also, some sources of sound (such as bells) produce in listeners a clear perception of pitch even though bells do not vibrate at a single dominant frequency. Although these examples show clearly that factors other than stimulus frequency influence the perception of pitch, psychologists do not yet understand the nature of these factors.

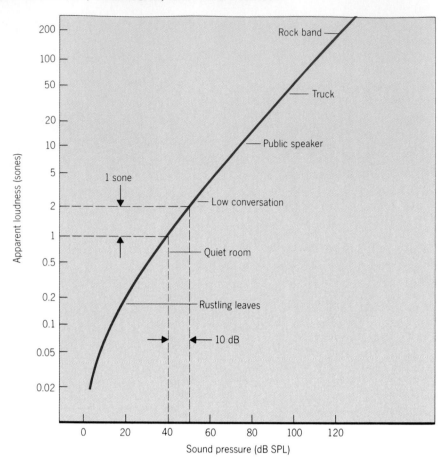

FIGURE 4-6 SOUND INTENSITY AND LOUDNESS.
The curve shows the relationship between sound intensity (sound pressure) and the perception of loudness for a stimulus with a frequency of 1000 Hz. Subjective loudness is measured in a unit called a **sone** *and is plotted in a logarithmic scale on the vertical axis. Intensity is measured in dB SPL, another logarithmic scale. Notice that over most of the intensity range, a 10 dB SPL increase in sound pressure doubles the perceived loudness of the stimulus. The intensity and loudness of some common sounds is indicated. (From Coren, Porac, and Ward, 1984; after Stevens, 1956.)*

LOUDNESS What makes you perceive a difference between the soft rustling of those green leaves and the loud rumble of an 18-wheeled truck by your bedroom window? Perception of the **loudness** of a sound is determined primarily by the amplitude of the sound wave. People are extremely sensitive to low-intensity sounds. At the threshold for hearing, a sound wave vibrates the eardrum only about 0.0000000001 centimeter, or about one-tenth the diameter of a hydrogen molecule! As sound intensity increases, your perception of its loudness increases exponentially (according to Stevens' power law; see Table 3-3). This relationship between sound intensity and perceived loudness is shown in Figure 4-6. People can hear over approximately a one millionfold range of sound pressure intensity, from a threshold of about 0 dB SPL to a painful 120 dB SPL.

The perceived loudness of a sound also depends on factors other than intensity. For example, the loudness of a sound also depends on its frequency. As Figure 4-7 shows, the lowest intensity necessary for a sound to be just loud enough to hear (the absolute threshold) differs for different sound frequencies. We humans are most sensitive to sounds between 2000 and 4000 Hz; sounds of lower or higher frequencies require much higher intensities for us to hear them. Even above threshold, for a person to perceive different frequencies to have the same

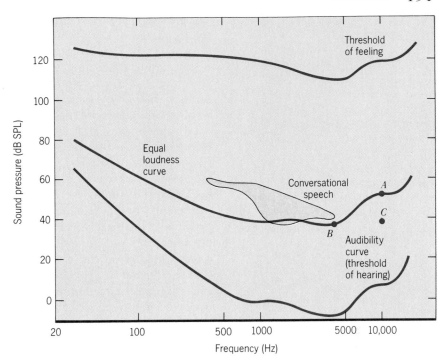

*FIGURE 4-7   SOUND
FREQUENCY AND LOUDNESS.*
*The bottom curve shows the lowest
intensity (sound pressure) at which
sounds of different frequencies can be
heard. The top curve shows the intensity
at which sounds of different frequencies
can be felt; higher intensity sounds are
painful and damage the receptor cells.
The middle curve is an example of an
equal loudness curve. It shows
intensities at which sounds of different
frequencies have the same perceived
loudness. Thus, a 10,000 Hz stimulus
of 55 dB SPL intensity (point A on the
equal loudness curve) has the same
perceived loudness as a 4000 Hz
stimulus of 40 dB SPL (point B on the
equal loudness curve). Furthermore, a
4000 Hz stimulus of 40 dB SPL
intensity (point B) is louder than
a 10,000 Hz stimulus of the same
physical intensity (point C below the
equal loudness curve). Notice that the
frequencies used in conversational speech
(shaded area) are primarily those to
which people are most sensitive.
(Adapted from Goldstein, 1984; after
Fletcher and Munson, 1933.)*

loudness, the sounds must be at different intensities. Thus the bass player in a country music band may have to play a low-pitched note (such as C_1, with frequencies around 50 Hz) with a higher intensity to sound as loud as the fiddler who is playing a high-pitched note (such as C_7, with frequencies around 2000 Hz). Another factor that affects loudness is how long the sound lasts. For example, we hear very brief sounds (those that last 200 milliseconds or less) as softer than long-lasting sounds of the same intensity (see Green, 1985).

Hearing Sound Frequency

Two main theories have been proposed to explain how people hear sounds of different frequencies. According to the **frequency theory**, sounds of a particular frequency cause the basilar membrane (Figure 4-3) to vibrate at that frequency. This vibration in turn stimulates receptor cells at the same frequency and causes the auditory nerve fibers to discharge action potentials at that frequency. For example, a note played at 500 Hz would cause auditory nerve fibers to discharge 500 action potentials per second, and these would signal the presence of the 500 Hz stimulus.

But the frequency theory runs into a big problem. Auditory nerve fibers can discharge at most about 1000 action potentials a second (because of their refractory period, the time when an axon cannot fire a second action potential). Therefore the frequency theory cannot explain how people hear sounds between 1000 Hz and 20,000 Hz—the range within which most of the sounds we hear actually fall. This problem is partly addressed by the **volley principle** (Wever, 1949). According to

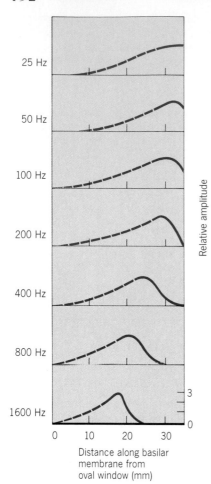

Relative amplitude

Distance along basilar
membrane from
oval window (mm)

*FIGURE 4-8 TRAVELING
WAVES ON THE BASILAR
MEMBRANE.*
*The distribution of the peak displacement
of the basilar membrane is shown for
different stimulus frequencies. The
higher the stimulus frequency, the closer
the peak displacement is to the oval
window. (From Békésy, 1960.)*

this principle, although individual nerve fibers may not be able to follow the frequency of stimuli, successive waves of individual fibers can follow the stimuli. Imagine four riflemen, each of whom can fire his gun only once every four seconds. But if each rifleman fires his gun one second after the last, successive shots in the volley will fire once a second. Auditory nerve fibers may fire in succession, too, and together discharge a volley of action potentials much faster than any fiber alone could do.

Another theory to account for how people hear sounds of different frequencies is called the **place theory**. It states that different sound frequencies stimulate receptor cells at different *locations* along the basilar membrane. Consequently, only certain auditory nerve fibers (those connected to the stimulated receptors) are activated to signal the presence of specific stimulus frequencies. Substantial evidence for this theory was provided by George von Békésy, who in 1961 won the Nobel Prize for his work. Békésy showed that vibration of the oval window produces *traveling waves* on the basilar membrane within the cochlea, much as shaking the end of a rope produces waves that travel down its length. Because the basilar membrane is stiffer and narrower at one end (nearest the oval window) than the other, the traveling waves produced by different sound frequencies peak at different places along its length (see Figure 4-8). Therefore, different receptor cells are activated by different frequencies. But place theory also has its limitations. For very low stimulus frequencies, such as those 100 Hz and below, nearly all of the basilar membrane is displaced, not just a narrow section of it. Place theory does not completely explain how people hear sounds at low frequencies.

The current thinking is that *both* frequency and place theories accurately describe part of the mechanisms of hearing sound frequencies (Evans, 1978). The frequency theory and volley principle probably account for how people hear frequencies up to 5000 Hz. The place theory probably accounts for how people hear frequencies throughout the audible range, from 20 Hz to 20,000 Hz. Thus both theories together account for the perception of frequencies between 20 and 5000 Hz, and the place theory alone accounts for the perception of frequencies above 5000 Hz.

Beyond the auditory nerve, in auditory areas of the brain, the frequency of a stimulus is signaled primarily by the activation of specific neurons (Aitkin, Irvine, and Webster, 1984). For example, within auditory cortex, some neurons respond primarily to high-frequency stimuli, and other neurons respond primarily to low frequencies. Thus, when you listen to music, different neurons are activated to signal the presence of each of the many frequencies that you hear.

Sound Localization

"Hey, wait for me," your friend calls to you. You turn automatically to the source of the sound. The ability to determine the source of sounds around you is called **sound localization**. Under ideal conditions, a person can locate the position of a sound in space with an accuracy of about 2 degrees of arc (that is about the width of your thumb held at arm's length; Oldfield and Parker, 1984a). People can discriminate between the locations of two sources of sound that are only about 1 degree of arc apart (Mills, 1958). Just as visual depth perception depends primarily on having two eyes that receive slightly different images, sound localization depends primarily on having two ears that receive slightly different sounds.

CUES FOR SOUND LOCALIZATION   Sounds can differ at the two ears in three main ways, and these provide three cues that people rely on for locating sound. One cue is **interaural time differences** in the arrival of a sound. When the source of a sound is to one side of your head, the sound waves from it reach one ear before the other (see Figure 4-9). Sound travels through the air at 1100 feet a second, and the two ears are about 9 inches apart. Therefore, sound coming directly from the left arrives at the left ear about 0.7 milliseconds before it arrives at the right ear. If the sound source is just slightly to the left, the difference in time of arrival to the two ears is even smaller. People can detect differences in arrival time at the two ears as small as 0.01 millisecond (Mills, 1958).

Another cue for sound localization is **interaural intensity differences**. When sound comes from the left, it reaches the left ear directly but must bend around the head to reach the right ear. Thus, the head casts a *sound shadow* that reduces the intensity of the sound at the farther ear (see Figure 4-9). The effect of this shadow depends on the frequency of the sound. Low-frequency sounds have long wavelengths (long distances between the peaks of the sound waves) that easily curve around the head; high-frequency sounds are more effectively blocked. Thus a note played at 200 Hz and coming from the side of the head has equal intensity at the two ears, while a whistle blown at 6000 Hz can be 20 dB SPL less intense at one ear than the other.

A third cue for sound localization is **interaural distortion differences**. Both the fleshy pinnae and the auditory canals (see Figure 4-2) reflect and distort sound waves. The amplitude and frequency of the sound waves are changed as the waves strike the folds of the pinnae and the walls of the auditory canals. This distortion differs for sounds that come from different directions. In addition, the distortion differs for the two ears because the sound waves strike each ear from a different angle. Experiments have shown that differences in distortion between the two ears can be an important cue for signaling the direction of a sound source (Wightman, Kistler, and Perkins, 1987). In fact, if cues produced by the pinnae are removed (for example, if the folds of the pinnae are filled with putty), the ability to localize the source of a sound deteriorates (Gardner and Gardner, 1973; Oldfield and Parker, 1984b).

People may be very good at determining the sources of sounds that come from the side, but we are very poor at discriminating whether a sound comes from directly in front or in back. The reason is that we have few cues to rely on, for there is little difference between sounds in front and back in the time, intensity, or distortion of the sound at the two ears. People tend to compensate for the lack of cues: when they have trouble telling where a sound comes from, they tend to turn their heads so that the sound source comes from the side and they can rely on the differences between what their two ears hear.

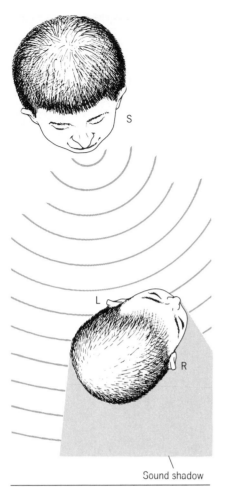

Sound shadow

FIGURE 4-9   ILLUSTRATION OF TWO CUES FOR SOUND LOCALIZATION.
When the source of the sound (S) is to the left, the sound reaches the left ear (L) before the right ear (R) because the distance is shorter. In addition, the head casts a sound shadow that reduces the intensity of the sound at the right ear relative to the left ear.

BOX 4-1
LISTENING TO
YOUR STEREO

The people who design and manufacture stereophonic records, tapes, and compact discs and the equipment for playing them have a vested interest in knowing the principles of sound localization, pitch, and loudness perception. And the people—like you—who listen to music and buy stereo equipment can save money and buy more wisely by knowing about these perceptual principles.

Manufacturers of stereo equipment often tout the enormous range of sound frequencies that their equipment can reproduce. They also charge much more money for systems that can reproduce high-frequency sounds (up to 20,000 Hz) than systems that have lower frequency limits (for example, 15,000 Hz). But most people around 20 years old cannot hear frequencies above 16,000 Hz, and by age 40 most people cannot hear above 13,000 Hz (see Figure 4-5). It doesn't make much sense to purchase equipment that reproduces sounds you cannot hear. It is much wiser to spend the money for equipment that reproduces sounds with a minimum of distortion, such as digital and laser sound-reproduction systems.

You might also consider buying equipment with a "loudness" switch. This switch allows you to compensate for your insensitivity to high- and low-frequency sounds. Remember that when sound intensity is low, people cannot hear high or low frequencies, only frequencies in the middle range (1000 to 5000 Hz) (see Figure 4-7). The loudness switch on a stereo system selectively makes the high- and low-frequency sounds intense enough to hear along with the middle frequencies when the volume of the system is turned down.

Most people purchase stereophonic, rather than monophonic, record, tape, and compact disc systems because stereophonic systems reproduce sound more realistically. The performers sound as if they're separated in space and the music sounds as if it comes from different locations, as it does in a live concert.

Stereophonic effects are achieved with interaural time and intensity cues for sound localization. Each stereo speaker reproduces sounds at a slightly different time and intensity from the other. When you sit midway between the two speakers or put on stereo headphones, you are in the best position to pick up these differences. You may have noticed, however, that when you wear stereo headphones the music appears to be located in different positions *within your head,* not in different positions in external space. The reason is that the headphones play the sound directly into your auditory canals and thus eliminate the interaural distortion cues that are introduced by the fleshy ridges of your pinnae. It's possible that someday recordings will be made with two microphones with artificial pinnae that introduce interaural distortion cues onto the recording itself. Then music heard through headphones would sound as real as if it were coming from external space. Maybe that will be the technological advance you'll see advertised as "Coming *soon* to a store near you."

NEURAL MECHANISMS OF SOUND LOCALIZATION Remember that if someone whispers in your left ear, information goes to both sides of your brain. Information from both ears, as we have said, goes to both sides of the brain. Neurons in the brain then can "compare" the sounds that arrive at the two ears. Studies of the activity of single neurons in animals while sounds were presented to each ear have shown how neurons make this comparison. These studies show that neurons in structures such as the superior olive and inferior colliculus (see Figure 4-4) are extremely sensitive to time and intensity differences in the sounds to each ear (Phillips and Brugge, 1985). For example, a particular neuron may increase its activity when a stimulus arrives at one ear 0.5 millisecond before the other but not when the two ears are stimulated simultaneously. Other neurons may discharge action potentials only when the time difference between the ears is longer (perhaps 0.7 millisecond) or shorter (0.1 millisecond). Similarly, some neurons discharge only when the intensity of the sounds at the two ears differs by specific amounts. The effect is that certain groups of neurons can signal the presence of sounds at different locations in space.

These physiological studies as well as behavioral studies of animals and humans with brain damage show that the left side of the brain is used for localizing sounds to the right of the head and the right side of the brain is used for localizing sounds to the left. Thus, even though both ears send information to both hemispheres of the brain there is a hemispheric specialization for localizing sounds on the *opposite side of auditory space* (Phillips and Brugge, 1985).

Perceiving Auditory Patterns: Speech

Think of the sounds that swirl around you every day—music, speech, the sounds of traffic and nature—and you will realize that most are complex sound patterns—complex changes in stimulus frequency and intensity over time. The way that you understand what other people say is an example of how you perceive auditory patterns. By some marvel of human development, you effortlessly perceive thousands upon thousands of complex spoken sound patterns every day. You recognize that some of these sound patterns combine to form words, such as "love," "beauty," or "psychology," and that even longer strings of sound patterns combine to form sentences. To see how people perceive the sound patterns of speech, we begin by considering relatively simple spoken sounds.

RECOGNITION OF PHONEMES The basic unit of speech is the **phoneme**—the shortest segment of sound that distinguishes one word from another. For example, in Figure 4-10, the /i/ in the word "spike" is a phoneme because if it were changed to /o/—"spoke"—the meaning of the word would change. (Single phonemes and pairs of phonemes are indicated by slashes: /). There are about 40 phonemes in North American English. These include vowel sounds such as the /a/ in "bat," the /i/ in "bit," and the /ai/ in "bait." Consonant sounds such as the /n/ in "neat," the /g/ in "good," and the /ng/ in "sing" also are individual phonemes. Phonemes are not the same as letters of the alphabet. Notice that a phoneme may be made of more than a single letter of the alphabet—/ng/, /ai/.

How do people recognize particular phonemes in speech? How do you know that your friend asked to borrow your "notes" and not your "oats" or your "nose"? One hypothesis is that the auditory system simply processes the particular stimulus frequencies and intensities (the **acoustic signals**) associated with each phoneme. For example, in Figure 4-10 the phoneme /s/ consists mainly of stimulus frequencies between about 4000 Hz and 8000 Hz. When you say /s/, neurons that respond to these frequencies discharge, and their response might signal the presence of that phoneme. The difficulty with this hypothesis is that sounds that are perceived as the same phoneme may have very different acoustic signals. For example, consider the word "dot," which contains three phonemes: /d/, /o/, and /t/. The stimulus frequencies present in all three phonemes differ when "dot" is spoken by people with high- or low-pitched

FIGURE 4-10 ILLUSTRATION OF THE PATTERNS OF SOUND FREQUENCY AND INTENSITY IN SPEECH.
(a) *The increases and decreases in sound intensity over time that occur when the word "SPIKE" is spoken into a microphone. Notice the complex changes in stimulus-waveform frequency and intensity.* (b) *A* **sound spectrogram** *of the same stimulus. Here, stimulus frequency is plotted on the vertical axis, time on the horizontal axis, and the amount of sound energy is indicated by the degree of darkness. Thus, when the letter "S" is spoken, there is a lot of sound energy between frequencies of about 4000 Hz and 8000 Hz and less energy at other frequencies. The entire word, with all of its variations in frequency and intensity, takes about 0.7 seconds to complete. (Modified from Evans, 1974.)*

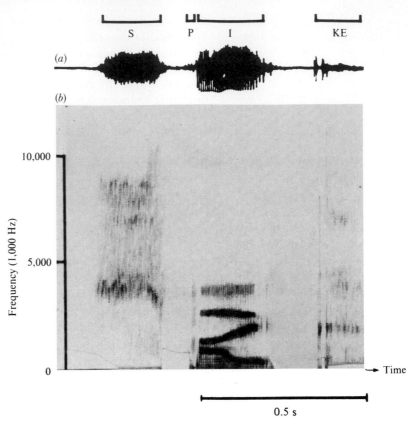

voices, yet people perceive the same phonemes and word in each case. Even for the same speaker, the acoustic signal can change according to the context in which a phoneme is used. For example, the phoneme /d/ contains different sound frequencies when it is part of the word "dig" from when it is part of the word "dug," yet people recognize the phoneme as /d/ in both cases. These are examples of the phenomenon of **invariance** in the perception of phonemes.

The phenomenon of invariance, as well as other experimental observations, has led researchers to conclude that we recognize different phonemes by carrying out a *feature analysis* of speech sounds (Abbs and Sussman, 1971; Eimas and Corbit, 1973). That is, we appear to recognize phonemes by the presence of distinctive features such as the *patterns of changes* in stimulus frequency and intensity rather than the particular stimulus frequencies and intensities that are present. For example, /o/ spoken by two different people might contain similar patterns of increases and decreases in stimulus frequency even though the specific frequencies that are present differ. People seem to recognize phonemes by these distinctive patterns. Many researchers believe that humans have **auditory feature detectors** in the brain that respond to the particular features of speech, just as we have neurons that respond to particular features of a visual stimulus.

Physiological studies in animals have provided direct evidence for the existence of auditory feature detectors in the brain (Evans, 1974). For

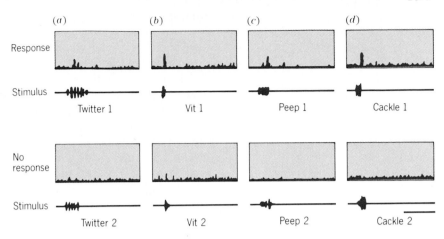

FIGURE 4-11 RESPONSES OF NEURONS IN SQUIRREL MONKEY AUDITORY CORTEX TO MONKEY VOCALIZATIONS.

The responses of four neurons (a–d) are shown by the graphs. Each graph gives the number of action potentials discharged by the neuron (vertical axis) over time (horizontal axis). The horizontal line to the lower right is a time scale 0.5 second long. A record showing the sound frequency and intensity pattern of each cell is shown under each histogram (stimulus). Each neuron changed its activity in response to one squirrel monkey call (top row) but not to another, only slightly different call (bottom row). The calls were two different kinds of "twitter," "vit," "peep," and "cackle" vocalizations. (Modified from Newman and Wollberg, 1973.)

example, single-cell recording studies in cats and monkeys have shown the existence of neurons that are unresponsive to steady tones but respond well to *changes* in tone frequency. Furthermore, many of these neurons are sensitive to the direction of change of stimulus frequency: some neurons respond only to increases in stimulus frequency and some only to decreases. Especially fascinating results have been found in auditory cortex of squirrel monkeys—tree-dwelling monkeys of South America that have a large repertoire of cries and calls that convey specific meanings. Many cortical neurons in these monkeys respond to certain calls but not to others or produce a different pattern of response to different vocalizations (Newman and Wollberg, 1973; Newman, 1978; see Figure 4-11). Results like these suggest that feature detectors in the brain can be used in the perception of complex sound patterns such as those present in phonemes.

Although psychologists now generally agree that humans carry out a feature analysis in the perception of phonemes, there is a great deal of disagreement about whether the features are *acoustic* or *linguistic*. Those who hold to the first view, that sound features in phonemes are acoustic, maintain that there are feature detectors for many different kinds of sound patterns, and speech sounds are only one example of these patterns. Those who hold to the second view, that sound features in phonemes are linguistic, maintain that the feature detectors are tuned specifically to respond to speech sounds. They argue, in other words, that speech forms a special class of sounds and that, at least in humans, feature detectors are specialized *speech* processors. So far, experiments have provided evidence to support both theories, and the controversy continues to simmer.

PERCEPTION OF CONTINUOUS SPEECH So far we have discussed perception of simple units of speech, such as phonemes. But how do people perceive continuous speech, which is made of long strings of sound patterns? How do you perceive that your friend wants to "borrow your psychology notes from last week when I had the flu"? One possibility is that you simply recognize the sound features in the phonemes and then combine the phonemes into syllables, words, phrases, and so on into the longer and more complex sequences that make continuous speech. This explanation is referred to as the **bottom-up theory** of speech perception.

The problem with bottom-up theory is that it does not account for the fact that the perception of continuous speech depends heavily upon *context*. For example, it does not account for the fact that you somehow know that your friend has asked to "see" your notes, not to "sea" them. Recognizing which word someone has used clearly requires more than simply recognizing the sound pattern. What is more, studies have shown that people's pronunciation of most words as they speak in a conversation is so sloppy that listeners cannot recognize about half the words when they are presented alone but recognize the same words perfectly well when they are bolstered by the context of continuous speech (Pollack and Pickett, 1964). These findings suggest that speech recognition is *conceptually driven,* and people's past experiences and knowledge guide their perception of the sound patterns in continuous speech. This explanation is referred to as the **top-down theory** of speech perception. It states that people's knowledge of the context and the meanings of phrases and sentences determines their perception of the sound patterns that make up speech.

A number of studies suggest that both the bottom-up and the top-down theories are correct. For example, Warren (1970) had subjects listen to a tape recording of the passage "The state governors met with their respective legislatures convening in the capital city," in which the first /s/ in "legislatures" was replaced with noise (the sound of a cough). None of the subjects even noticed that the /s/ was missing; they filled in the sound that should have occurred in the context. The context influenced their perception of the phoneme and the word. A more recent study showed that the more different the sound pattern of the noise is from the phoneme it replaces, the more likely subjects are to notice the missing phoneme (Samuels, 1981). In other words, acoustic information also influences perception of phonemes and words; context alone is not sufficient. Thus, as you perceive sound patterns in continuous speech, you take into account acoustic information in the signal—bottom-up processing—and also take into account the context, or meaning, of the words and sentences—top-down processing.

THE SKIN SENSES

Imagine picking up a lemon in your hand. How does it feel to your skin? Smooth and cool, firm and rounded, light and solid? Now imagine picking up a piece of sand paper, a cactus spine, a pile of books, a snowball. When you pick up something, you feel its texture, shape, and weight. Some things feel pleasurable and some painful, some hot and some cold, heavy and light, prickly and silken. Through your **skin senses**, you sense and perceive these qualities of people and things in the world. Specifically, the skin senses provide you with information about *touch, pressure, temperature,* and *pain.*

The Skin and Its Connections to the Brain

Your skin is a large sheet of cells with an area of about 21 square feet in the average adult. Skin keeps dirt and moisture out of the body, helps to regulate body temperature, and contains many nerve endings and a variety of sensory receptors (see Figure 4-12).

The variety of sensory receptors in human skin is quite remarkable. One kind of receptor, the Pacinian corpuscle, responds to changes in mechanical pressure, such as vibration. Others seem to respond to touch: Merkle discs, Meissner corpuscles, and Ruffini endings. The free nerve endings respond to pain (Iggo, 1985; Darian-Smith, 1984a). But these specialized receptors do not seem to be *necessary* to signal a particular type of stimulus. The cornea of the eye, for example, contains only free nerve endings but is very sensitive to touch, pressure, temperature, and pain.

The nerve fibers in the skin are long dendrites of sensory neurons that lie just outside the spinal cord or brain (see Figure 4-13). Bundles of these dendrites form the sensory nerves. When the skin receptors or nerve fibers are stimulated, action potentials are generated in the dendrites and transmitted toward the spinal cord and brain.

Information from the skin to the brain is carried in two different systems. One of these, called the **lemniscal system**, carries information primarily about touch and pressure. Figure 4-13 shows the pathways that make up the lemniscal system. Notice that pathways from each side of the body and head cross to the *opposite* side of the brain and end in **somatic sensory cortex** in the parietal lobe. Thus somatic sensory cortex receives information about touch or pressure on the opposite side of the body. Pathways that carry information primarily about pain or temperature are called the **spinothalamic system**. These pathways are more complex and tend to go to both sides of the brain.

FIGURE 4-12 A BLOCK OF SKIN.

Skin is made up of two layers, the outer **epidermis** *and the underlying* **dermis.** *The epidermis is a protective layer of tough dead cells. The dermis consists of live cells that are constantly dividing to produce the epidermis. A layer of fat cells usually is present beneath the dermis. Within the skin are small muscles, blood vessels, sweat glands and ducts, free nerve endings, and many types of receptors with nerve fibers that contact them. In addition, hairs may be associated with nerve endings. The sensory receptors in the skin include structures called Merkle discs, Meissner corpuscles, Krause end bulbs, Ruffini endings, and Pacinian corpuscles. (From Goldstein, 1984.)*

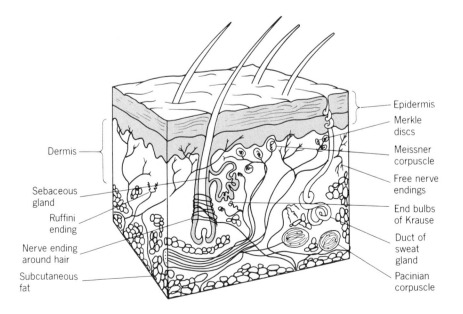

*FIGURE 4-13 CONNECTIONS FROM THE SKIN TO THE BRAIN. This is a simplified diagram of the pathways that carry information about touch and pressure from the skin to the spinal cord and brain. Thirty pairs of spinal sensory nerves carry information from various areas of skin on each side of the body to the spinal cord. In addition, pairs of cranial nerves carry information from the skin on each side of the head. Only one spinal nerve and one cranial nerve are shown in the diagram. Each nerve is made up of bundles of dendrites (nerve fibers) from sensory neurons near the spinal cord or brain. For the spinal nerves serving the body, axons of the sensory neurons enter the spinal cord. Some axons contact neurons in the spinal cord, and some axons run up the spinal cord to contact neurons in the medulla. From the medulla, neurons send their axons to the opposite side of the brain, where connections are made in the thalamus and then the cortex. For the cranial nerves serving the head, axons of the sensory neurons enter the brain, where they form pathways that also end in the opposite cortex. The area of cortex that receives inputs from the skin is called the **somatic sensory cortex**. (Modified from Thompson, 1967.)*

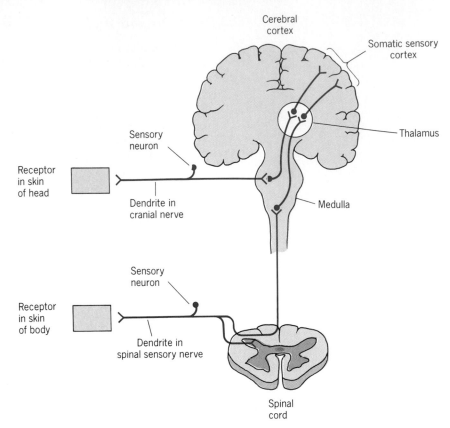

Perception of Touch and Pressure

SENSITIVITY AND DISCRIMINATION   We human beings are extremely sensitive to light touch or pressure on the skin. We feel soft breezes, an ant crawling along a shoulder, and a snowflake that falls on a cheek. As you probably know, some areas of the skin are more sensitive than others. It takes much more pressure for us to feel something on the feet than on the face (see Figure 4-14a). But sensations of touch show **adaptation**, just as other sensations do. Thus, if a stimulus is steadily applied to the skin, the sensation will gradually fade and disappear.

We also are extremely good at discriminating *where* a stimulus has touched the skin. One measure of this ability is the **two-point discrimination threshold**, which is the least distance between two stimuli that people require to tell that there are two separate touches rather than one. To demonstrate what this means, close your eyes and have a friend hold two pencils next to each other and touch them simultaneously to your thumb. You'll find that the pencil tips have to be about 3/16 inch (5 millimeters) apart for you to tell that there are two rather than one. Now do the same thing on the underside of your forearm. In this case, the pencil tips have to be about 1 5/8 inch (40 millimeters) apart for you to tell that there are two separate stimuli. Two-point discrimination thresholds for the entire body are shown in Figure 4-14b.

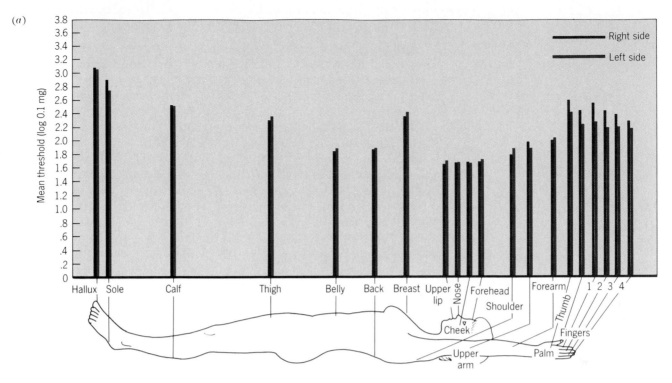

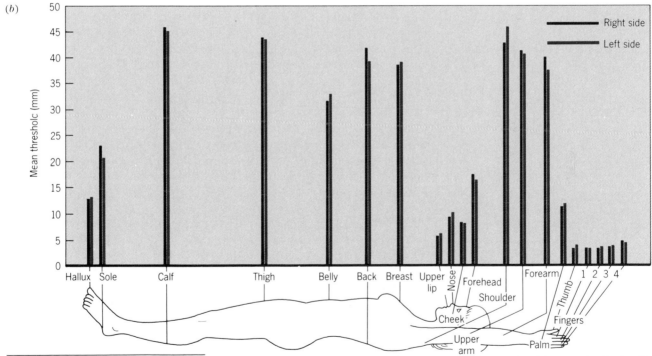

FIGURE 4-14 TOUCH SENSITIVITY AND DISCRIMINATION.

(a) *Pressure sensitivity thresholds for the body surface. These thresholds were determined by applying a fine nylon hair to the body surface and determining how much pressure was required for the stimulus to be felt. The higher the bar, the more pressure was needed. Males are somewhat less sensitive to pressure than females, but the relative sensitivities of body parts are similar for both sexes.* (b) *Two-point discrimination thresholds for the body surface. These were determined by touching the skin simultaneously with two pointed stimuli and finding how far apart the stimuli had to be for them to be felt as two separate touches rather than one. The higher the bar, the farther apart the stimuli. Results for males and females were similar. (From Weinstein, 1968.)*

How does the nervous system signal the presence and nature of stimuli that touch the skin? Electrical recordings from single peripheral nerve fibers in humans and other animals have shown that individual fibers respond best to specific types of sensory stimuli. For example, some fibers respond only to bending of a hair, some only to indentation of the skin, some only to light touch on the skin, and so forth (Iggo, 1985; Johansson and Vallbo, 1983). In addition, individual fibers respond to stimulation over only a limited area of skin. This area is called the **receptive field** of the fiber (visual neurons also have receptive fields; see Chapter 3). For example, the receptive field of one fiber may include a small area on the fingertip, and if the same finger is stimulated a knuckle away, the fiber does not respond. Individual neurons in somatic sensory cortex also respond only to particular *types* of sensory stimulation on particular *locations* on the skin (Mountcastle, 1984). Thus, where on the body surface a stimulus has been felt, as well as the type of stimulus it is, both are signaled by *which* neurons are activated.

The ability to discriminate that two touches on the skin are in separate places appears to depend largely on how many sensory neurons the nervous system devotes to particular parts of the body. This principle is seen most clearly in somatic sensory cortex, which contains a **topographic map** of the body surface (see Figure 4-15). A distinctive characteristic of the topographic map is that it is extremely distorted. For example, as much cortical tissue is devoted to processing signals from the lips or hand as to the entire back. If you compare this distortion to the two-point discrimination thresholds for the body surface shown in Figure 4-14*b*, you can see that they correspond closely. The cortex provides more cells for processing fine details with the fingertips and fewer cells for areas such as the back, which are relatively insensitive to stimulus location and detail. Species such as rabbits, which have very sensitive whiskers on the snout and do not use their forepaws for fine touch, have a very large portion of somatic sensory cortex devoted to the snout and a small portion for the paws (Woolsey, 1958). The more cortical tissue devoted to an area of skin, the more sensitive that area is to stimulus location and detail.

TEXTURE AND SHAPE   Touch your fingertip to a piece of textured fabric, such as corduroy or heavy knit, and hold it there without moving. You can sense that you are touching something but you probably cannot identify *what* you are touching. Now move your finger over the fabric. Now you can tell much more about the texture. Perception of the shape of objects works in a similar way. If you simply hold an object, such as a block of wood, you may not be able to identify its shape. But if you turn and move the object in your hand, you can identify it easily. These examples demonstrate a principle that you already have encountered in other senses, such as vision. People are much more sensitive to *changes* in sensory stimulation than to steady stimulation. The skin senses do not simply respond to the presence of a stimulus, they respond best to stimuli that change over time and space along the surface of the skin.

We mentioned earlier that neurons in somatic sensory cortex respond only to particular types of stimuli, such as touch or pressure, on the skin.

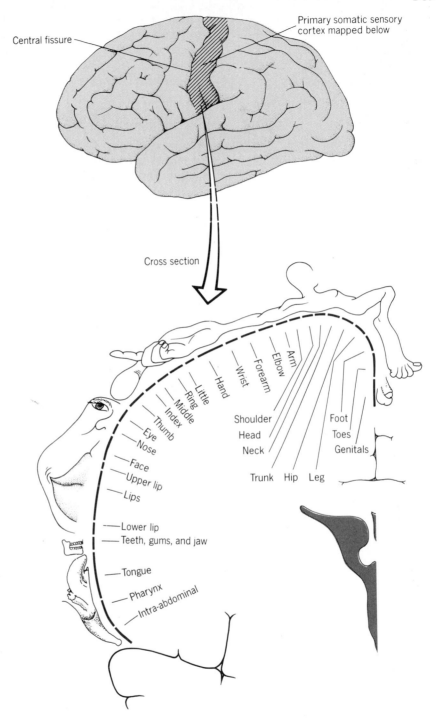

FIGURE 4-15 TOPOGRAPHIC MAP OF THE BODY SURFACE IN HUMAN SOMATIC SENSORY CORTEX.

The top drawing shows the region of the parietal lobe in which the map is located (front is to the left). The bottom drawing shows a section through somatic sensory cortex with the map superimposed. Each region of the map contains neurons that respond to touch on the particular location of the body indicated. Electrical stimulation of each region of the map produces the sensation of tingling on the corresponding body part. This particular map was charted using electrical stimulation of the cortex of human surgical patients. Notice that the map represents the opposite side of the body. (From Penfield and Rasmussen, 1952.)

Furthermore, like visual and auditory cortex neurons, neurons in somatic sensory cortex respond best to particular *features* of a stimulus (Whitsel, Dreyer, and Hollins, 1978). For example, some neurons are excited more by moving than by stationary stimuli on the skin, and some respond only to particular directions of movement. Experiments with monkeys also show that some somatic sensory cortex neurons respond best when the monkey actively touches and manipulates certain objects (Iwamura, Tanaka, Sakamoto, and Hikosaka, 1985). Neurons of this kind appear to be the basis of the perception of texture and shape, which is far better for moving than for stationary stimuli.

Perception of Temperature

Humans and other animals live in a wide range of climates, from very warm ones (the tropics) to very cold ones (Wisconsin!). Survival in these climates depends on an ability to sense the temperature and to act in ways to maintain a normal body temperature. ("I'm cold, I'll put on a sweater.") The ability to sense hot and cold also is extremely important for avoiding injury. If you had no feelings of temperature in your fingertips, you would always be burning yourself and only the signs of your injuries would alert you to danger.

The sensation of warmth or cold occurs when a stimulus causes the skin temperature to *change* from a reference skin temperature, called **physiological zero**. For most of the body, the physiological zero skin temperature usually is about 32°C (90°F), which maintains the internal body temperature at about 37°C (98.6°F). When something feels cold, it is because it has caused the skin temperature to fall below this temperature. Something that is warm has caused the skin temperature to rise above physiological zero. There is a **neutral zone** around physiological zero, however, within which changes in skin temperature cannot be felt. The neutral zone usually is 2° to 4°C to either side of physiological zero. This means, for example, that a stimulus 2° above physiological zero will not feel different in temperature, but a stimulus 6° above physiological zero (outside the neutral zone) will feel warm.

If you've ever noticed that when you first walk into a cold or hot room, your skin feels the shock of the temperature, but that gradually you seem to get used to the temperature, then you've noticed the phenomenon of adaptation. Like other senses, the sensation of skin temperature shows adaptation (Kenshalo, 1976). One effect of adaptation is to raise or lower the reference skin temperature. Perception of a temperature then depends on the new physiological zero. You can demonstrate this in the following way. For about five minutes, place your left hand in a bowl of water that is 30°C (86°F) and your right hand in a bowl of water that is 40°C (104°F). Then place both hands in a bowl of water that is 35°C (95°F). The 35° water will feel warm to your left hand and cold to your right hand because the adaptation has set a lower physiological zero for one hand and a higher physiological zero for the other.

Another effect of adaptation is that the adapting stimulus itself no longer produces a sensation. For example, if you place your hand in a bowl of 36°C water, at first it will feel warm, but after 10 to 20 minutes it will come to feel neutral in temperature. There are, however, limits to the range of temperatures to which people can adapt completely (Kenshalo and Scott, 1966; Darian-Smith, 1984b). Temperatures higher than about 37°C continue to feel warm or hot even after long periods of adaptation. Similarly, temperatures lower than about 28°C feel cold regardless of adaptation. These limits make sense from the point of view of survival. Very high or low temperatures can be dangerous to the body, and it is important that people be able to perceive them as hot or cold under any circumstances.

Pain

THE PERCEPTION OF PAIN   Pain is a complex sensory experience: it can be produced by a wide variety of stimuli, it can cause sensory as well as strong emotional responses, and its perception can be influenced by many different physiological and psychological factors. From an evolutionary standpoint, pain probably serves two functions. The first is to signal the possibility or fact of injury and tissue damage. In these cases the stimulus for pain is an external event such as burning heat, a sharp blow, or a cut to the skin, and the pain makes people withdraw or avoid the source of danger. The second function of pain may be to promote healing (Wall, 1979). When someone has been injured, pain often continues long after the external source of injury has been removed. The pain comes from the tissue damage itself—the burn, abrasion, cut, or the like—and its function may be to force the person to remain still and quiet so that the body can recover.

Have you ever noticed that sometimes a cut or bruise causes you much more pain than at other times? Perhaps the most remarkable aspect of pain perception is its extremely variable relation to the stimulus that evokes it. The relationship between pain and injury extends from injury with no pain to pain with no injury (Wall, 1978). Several factors seem to affect this variability in people's perception of pain. One factor that affects the perception of pain is a person's emotional state or level of stress. For example, there are many reports of soldiers with severe wounds who do not feel pain and go on to perform heroic deeds. So great is the stress of battle that they feel pain only after the battle is over. In fact, one study showed that although 83 percent of civilians about to undergo major surgery asked for painkillers, only 32 percent of seriously wounded soldiers did so (Beecher, 1956). **Stress-induced analgesia** is this reduction in pain (analgesia) that results when people are under stress.

Certain cognitive and social psychological factors also affect the perception of pain. In one experiment volunteer subjects got a series of increasingly intense shocks while they were in the presence of confederates of the experimenters who seemed to be getting the same intensity of electric shocks (Craig and Weiss, 1971). Some of the confederates—who were actually social models—reacted tolerantly to the shocks. Others reacted intolerantly. The subjects reported less pain and accepted more intense shocks when they were in the presence of a tolerant model than when they were in the presence of an intolerant model. These results did not arise simply from differences in the subjects' willingness to complain. When people are with a tolerant social model, measures of the autonomic reactions, such as skin potential and heart rate, decrease (Craig and Prkachin, 1978). What is more, when people are with a tolerant social model, psychophysical studies using signal detection methods show that their sensitivity to differences in shock intensity decreases, and when

FIGURE 4-16   WHAT IS PAINFUL?
Many cognitive factors can influence the perception of pain, including cultural attitudes, concentration of attention, and social modeling. This person feels little or no pain.

they are with an intolerant model, their sensitivity increases (Craig, 1978). Thus how people respond to others can affect their actual sensation of painful stimuli. This phenomenon, in fact, may explain cultural differences in response to painful stimuli and how, for instance, people may tolerate the sensation of lying on a bed of nails or walking across hot coals (see Figure 4-16).

MECHANISMS OF PAIN PERCEPTION   Although the perception of pain varies according to a person's social interactions and amount of stress, among other factors, the perception of pain is a very real and intriguing physiological process. There are several components to this process.

Specific Pain Pathways.   The free nerve endings in the skin (see Figure 4-12) appear to be the receptors for harmful stimulation (Willis, 1985). Fibers connected to these receptors respond almost exclusively to stimuli such as pinpricks, crushing, and very high or low skin temperature, but they do not respond to light touch or pressure. Similarly, neurons that respond selectively to harmful stimuli are found in the spinal cord, thalamus, and cerebral cortex (Perl, 1984; Willis, 1985). Thus, there are specific pathways in the brain that signal pain.

Why don't we *always* feel pain when these pain pathways are stimulated—that is, why is pain perception so variable? This question has puzzled scientists for years. An answer was suggested by Melzak and Wall in 1965, when they proposed the gate-control theory of pain perception.

Gate-control Theory.   The basic idea of the gate-control theory is that there is a neural "gate" that can be opened or closed to allow information about painful stimulation to be transmitted from spinal cord to brain along the specific pain pathways (Melzak and Wall, 1965; Wall, 1978). Three factors control the opening and closing of the gate (see Figure 4-17). First, when the pain-sensitive nerve fibers in the skin are active, transmission (T) cells in the spinal cord that signal the presence of painful stimulation also become active. Thus activity of the pain fibers opens the gate and increases the sensation of pain. Second, when nerve fibers that carry information about harmless stimulation on the skin— light touch and pressure, for example—are active, the pain-sensing fibers are inhibited and activity of the T cells decreases. Thus activity of touch- and pressure-sensitive fibers closes the gate and decreases the sensation of pain. This explains why gently rubbing the skin around an injury helps reduce the pain: the touch-sensitive fibers are activated and the gate is partly closed.

A third factor that affects the gate-control system is central control from the brain. Neurons in the brain have pathways back to the spinal cord and can influence the activity of the T cells. Because input from the brain also can open or close the gate, learning, attention, stress, and other cognitive factors can affect pain sensation. Strong evidence for such a central control mechanism came from the discovery that when certain areas of the brain were electrically stimulated, certain areas of the spinal cord were inhibited, and the sensation of pain was reduced (Reynolds, 1969; Perl, 1984).

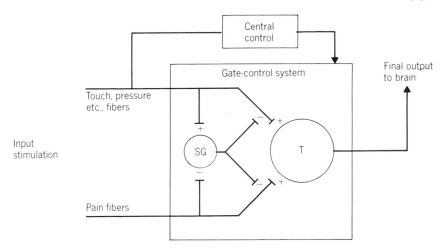

*FIGURE 4-17   DIAGRAM OF
THE GATE-CONTROL THEORY
OF PAIN.*

*Specific pain fibers enter the gate-control
system of the spinal cord and excite (+)
transmission (T) cells there. If the T cells
reach threshold, they discharge action
potentials that signal the brain that
painful stimulation has occurred. The
pain-fiber inputs can be inhibited (−) by
interneurons in a region of the spinal
cord called the substantia gelatinosa
(SG). This inhibition is increased by
activity of fibers that signal innocuous
stimulation (such as touch and pressure)
and decreased by activity of the pain
fibers themselves. Thus whether or not
the T cells are sufficiently activated
to signal the presence of painful
stimulation (that is, whether or not the
"gate" is opened or closed) depends on
the balance of activity between the pain
fibers and fibers carrying information
about touch and pressure on the skin.
Activity of the T cells (opening and
closing of the gate) also is affected by
descending influences from the brain
(central control). (Modified from Melzak
and Wall, 1965.)*

Although certain details of the gate-control theory, such as exactly
where inputs from pain fibers are inhibited, are still being investigated,
the main ideas of the theory can explain many aspects of pain perception
and have been widely accepted.

Endogenous Opiates.   The most recent (though certainly not the last)
piece to the puzzle of pain is the discovery of opiatelike substances that
occur naturally in the nervous system. While studying how opium-based
drugs such as morphine relieve pain, researchers discovered that neurons in brain regions involved in pain processing actually have receptors
for opiates (Kuhar, Pert, and Snyder, 1973). Then came the discovery
that the brain produces its own (endogenous) opiates (called **endorphins**) for pain control.

The picture that has emerged is that some neurons release endorphins, and these in turn inhibit neurons from sending pain information
to the spinal cord and brain. These endogenous opiates appear to contribute to the central control system (see Figure 4-17) by which the brain
affects pain transmission and perception. Thus the central control system can act in at least two different ways: by the release of opiates from
one neuron to inhibit another and by neural inhibition that does not
involve endogenous opiates (Watkins and Mayer, 1982; Mayer and Watkins, 1984).

The mechanisms that we have discussed have taken us a long way
toward an understanding of pain perception. They also help us to understand the mechanisms of pain relief (see Box 4-2).

BODY ORIENTATION AND POSITION

The simple act of walking down the street is actually an elegant feat of
sensory (and motor) processing. With each step, you lift one foot off the
ground, swing it alongside your body, and balance on the other foot.
Your arms swing by your side; your body and head bounce up and down
with each step. When you reach a corner, you rapidly turn your head to

BOX 4-2
RELIEF FROM PAIN

We inventive human beings have devised many ways to relieve ourselves from pain. Each method for relieving pain works on one or more of the physiological mechanisms by which parts of the body signal pain.

LOCAL ANESTHETICS

Because most people feel pain when their teeth are drilled or pulled by a dentist, they may ask for a local anesthetic to relieve the pain. Their dentist injects a drug such as Lidocaine directly into the gum or other tissue inside their mouth. Local anesthetics act by blocking the conduction of action potentials along nerve fibers near the injection. When the pain-sensing fibers no longer fire action potentials, the presence of painful stimuli is not signaled to the brain, and the relieved patient does not have a sensation of pain.

NARCOTICS

In contrast to locally acting drugs, narcotic drugs such as morphine enter the bloodstream. They are either injected directly into a blood vessel or enter the bloodstream through the stomach wall after the drugs have been swallowed. Once the narcotics reach the nervous system from the blood, they act on the opiate receptors of neurons that normally are influenced by the endogenous opiates. The pain transmission pathways of the central nervous system are inhibited and the perception of pain is dulled.

PLACEBOS

When researchers are testing how well drugs reduce pain, they usually include a control group of subjects who receive only a **placebo**—an inactive substance such as a sugar pill that the subjects *believe* reduces pain. Many people actually report a reduction in pain after taking a placebo. As you might expect, these *placebo effects* at first produced a great deal of controversy about the effectiveness of drugs and the adequacy of methods that were being used in pain research. But studies have shown that placebos can reliably produce relief from pain in about a third of the people tested (Beecher, 1955). An explanation is that a person's expectation of pain relief triggers the release of endogenous opiates, and these inhibit the pain transmission pathways (Fields and Levine, 1984; Mayer and Watkins, 1984). The placebo effect is a striking example of how expectations and learning can affect pain perception.

ACUPUNCTURE

Acupuncture originated in China before 2000 B.C. The Chinese inserted fine needles into the skin at certain "acupuncture points" (see Figure 1 for Box 4-2) and then twirled or, in more recent practice, stimulated them electrically. The Chinese reported that stimulation of the acupuncture points can relieve pain in parts of the body far from the acupuncture point. For example, a needle in the hand may reduce the pain of toothache. But Western scientists greeted these reports with deep skepticism, largely because they could not understand how acupuncture worked. The phenomenon did not fit with existing physiological knowledge. Many scientists concluded that acupuncture worked by the placebo effect.

The controversy surrounding acupuncture began to subside in the 1970s when diplomatic and scientific visits to China increased in frequency. Demonstrations of major surgery carried out on animals given only

look for oncoming cars and at the same time balance on the ball of your foot as you step off the curb. You do all of this almost automatically, without thought. Yet walking, as well as virtually every other physical activity you engage in, requires that you process a wealth of sensory information about the positions of your limbs and your body in space.

You draw on four different types of sensory information in your perception of limb and body position. Perhaps the most obvious is vision: you can see your limbs and body as they move. The skin senses also provide important information about the positions of your limbs. For instance, when you bend your arm, the skin stretches, producing changes in patterns of touch and pressure sensations that provide information about the position of the arm. Two additional sources of information about limb and body position involve senses that we have not yet discussed: kinesthesis and the vestibular sense.

acupuncture and no drugs convinced many scientists that the phenomenon was real. (Presumably, animals have no expectations that acupuncture will relieve pain.) Carefully controlled studies in humans and other animals have shown that acupuncture does produce analgesia and that it cannot be explained by the placebo effect (Wei, 1979; Richardson and Vincent, 1986).

Research suggests that acupuncture produces analgesia in two ways (Wall, 1978; Pomeranz, 1982; Mayer and Watkins, 1984). First, the needles appear to stimulate the skin's fibers for touch and pressure and to inhibit the pain-sensitive fibers; that is, they close the gate of the gate-control system (see Figure 4-17). Second, stimulation of skin or muscles with acupuncture needles signals the brain to release endogenous opiates that inhibit the pain transmission pathways. This effect explains how needles inserted in one part of the body can reduce pain at a distant part.

BOX FIGURE 1 AN ACUPUNCTURE CHART SHOWING SOME OF THE ACUPUNCTURE POINTS.
(From Coren, Porac, and Ward, 1984.)

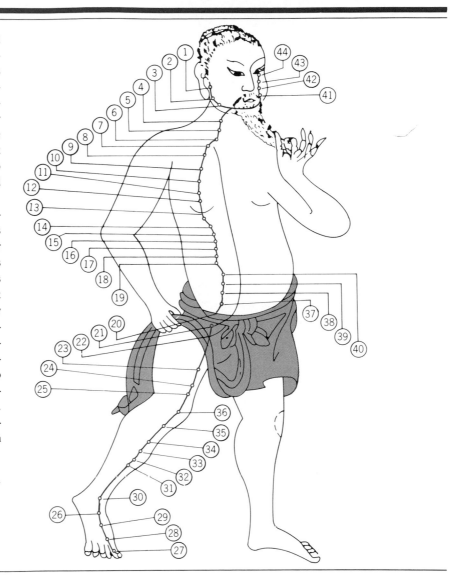

Kinesthesis

Without kinesthesis, you would have trouble lifting this book in your hands, combing your hair, or feeding yourself. **Kinesthesis** refers to sensations that come directly from the joints and muscles. There are two types of kinesthetic receptors in the tissues around the joints. One type of receptor is stimulated by movement of the joint. Another type is stimulated by tension on the joint, especially when the joint is held at an extreme position, such as when it is fully flexed or extended (Darian-Smith, 1984a).

The most important kinesthetic receptors provide information about the state of contraction of the muscles (Burgess, Wei, Clark, and Simon, 1982). Two types of these receptors are located directly on the muscle fibers and are stimulated when the muscle is stretched; hence they are

(a)

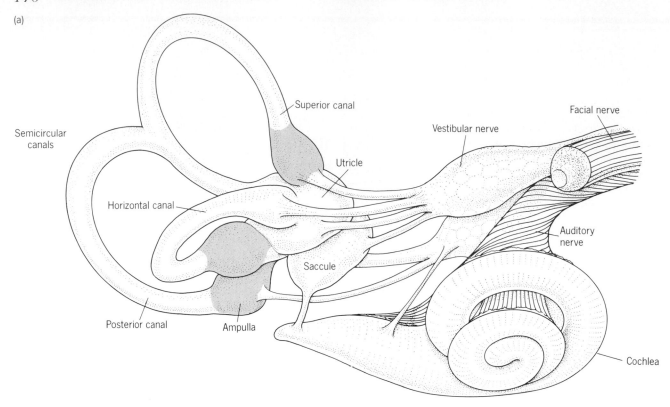

called **stretch receptors**. For example, when someone places a heavy pile of books in your hands, the biceps muscles in your arm are stretched, and the stretch receptors are stimulated. When the muscles contract, as you lift the pile of books, activity in these receptors stops. A third type of receptor is located on the tendon, where the muscles are connected to the bone. These receptors, called **Golgi tendon organs**, are stimulated both by stretch and by contraction of the muscles.

The nerve fibers connected to the muscle and joint receptors project to the spinal cord and brain in the same way as fibers connected to the skin receptors do (see Figure 4-13). Thus, just as there are neurons in somatic sensory cortex that respond to touch and pressure, there are neurons that respond to joint movement and the state of muscle contraction. These neurons signal the position of the limbs and body and the position of the neck and head relative to the body.

Vestibular Sense

The **vestibular sense** provides information about the position and movement of the head in space. Spin yourself around, and you'll have activated your vestibular sense. The sensory apparatus for doing this is attached to the cochlea, in your inner ear. If you look back at Figure 4-2, you will see three loops called the **semicircular canals**. These are shown in more detail in Figure 4-18. At the base of the semicircular canals are two additional structures, called the **utricle** and **saccule**. Together, the

FIGURE 4-18   THE SENSORY APPARATUS FOR THE VESTIBULAR SENSE.

◀ (a) *The vestibular apparatus of the right inner ear (compare with Figure 4-2). The three semicircular canals are called the superior, horizontal, and posterior canals. Each has a bulge at one end (shaded), called the* **ampulla**. *Receptor cells are located in the ampulla. The utricle and saccule are located at the base of the semicircular canals. (From Parker, 1980.)* ▶ (b) *The orientation of the semicircular canals in the head. Each canal is optimally stimulated by rotation of the head in a plane parallel to the canal. For example, the arrow indicates the direction of head rotation that optimally stimulates the left superior canal (labeled with an *). (From Miles, 1984.)*

(b)

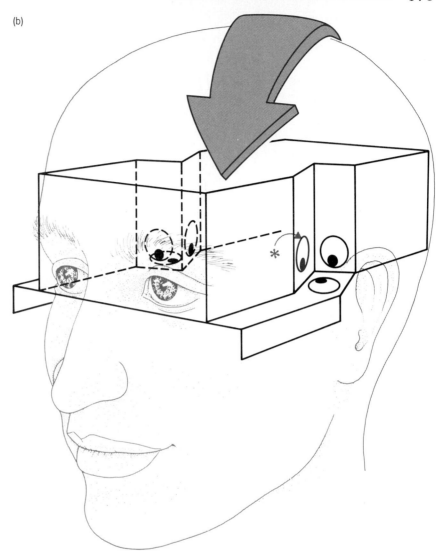

semicircular canals, the utricle, and the saccule make up the vestibular apparatus.

The utricle and saccule signal the direction of gravity; in a very real sense they tell you which way is up. They also signal *linear acceleration* of the head—changes in movement (acceleration) up and down, forward and backward, or side to side. They do this in an extremely clever way. Inside the utricle is a bed of receptor cells with small hairs protruding from their tops (Figure 4-19*a*). The hairs are embedded in a jellylike (gelatinous) substance that is covered with small calcium stones called otoliths. The saccule contains a similar bed of receptor cells, only there the bed is vertical and the hairs stick out to the side. When you stand still with your head upright, gravity pulls down on the otoliths. When you start to move your head (linear acceleration), the mass of the otoliths makes them lag behind. This lag makes the gelatinous substance bend the

FIGURE 4-19 RECEPTORS FOR THE VESTIBULAR SENSE.
(a) *Diagram of the receptor apparatus in the utricle. The receptor cells have small hairs and thus are called hair cells.*
(b) *The drawing on the left shows a view into the ampulla at the end of a semicircular canal. The drawing on the right is a section through the ampulla and shows how hairs on the receptor cells (hair cells) protrude into the gelatinous flap that blocks the flow of fluid through the ampulla and semicircular canal. (From Parker, 1980.)*

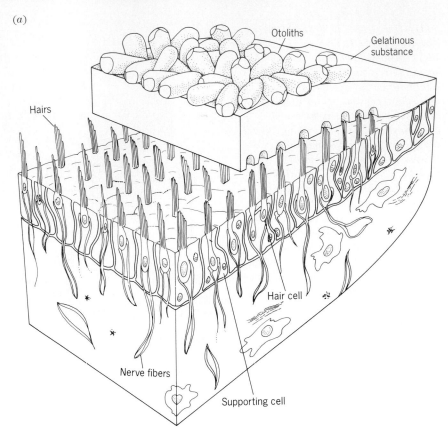

(a)

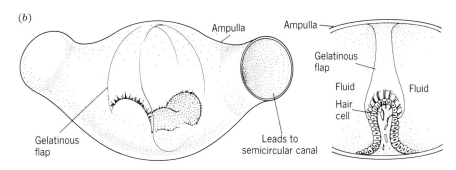

(b)

hairs and creates an electrical receptor potential in the receptor cells (Hudspeth, 1985). Thus, the utricle and saccule are accessory structures that allow gravity and changes in head movement to stimulate receptor cells. Because each ear contains a horizontal utricle and vertical saccule, the pattern of activation of the hair cells and nerve fibers connected to them can signal all possible directions of linear changes in movement of the head.

The semicircular canals are an accessory structure that stimulate receptor cells when there is *angular acceleration* of the head, that is, *changes in head rotation*. The receptor cells are located in a bulge (called the **ampulla**) at the end of each canal (see Figure 4-18*a*). These receptors also have small hairs, but they are embedded in a gelatinous flap that blocks the ampulla (see Figure 4-19*b*). Each ampulla and semicircular canal is filled with a fluid. When the head begins to rotate parallel to one of the canals (as in Figure 4-18*b*), the fluid lags behind because of inertia. (You can demonstrate how this occurs by floating a small object in a cup of water and then rotating the cup. The water and the floating object do not initially rotate with the cup; they lag behind.) Because the fluid in the semicircular canal lags behind the rotating canal, the fluid pushes against the gelatinous flap in the ampulla. This motion bends the hairs of the receptors and produces an electrical receptor potential. The receptor potential activates nerve fibers, which signal to the brain that the head has begun to rotate. Notice that on each side of the head the three semicircular canals are oriented in three different planes (see Figure 4-18*b*). Therefore, among the six canals, all possible directions of head rotation can be signaled.

As the head continues to turn, the fluid in the semicircular canal begins to turn with the canal and no longer pushes against the gelatinous substance. Thus, the semicircular canals only signal *changes* in head rotation. When rotation suddenly stops, the fluid continues to move for a time and again pushes against the gelatinous substance, but in the *opposite* direction (try this with the rotating cup of water). The receptor cells are again stimulated and produce the illusion that you are turning in the opposite direction. You can demonstrate this by closing your eyes (to remove visual information) and spinning like a dancer in one direction for 15 to 20 seconds. When you stop spinning, you will have the sensation of turning in the opposite direction. One way dancers avoid this sensation is by looking at a distant object (using visual information) when they stop spinning.

Perceptual Phenomena and Effects of Movement

PERCEPTION OF VERTICAL   We human beings have keen perception of vertical relative to gravity. We are very accurate in sensing whether we are standing or sitting on a tilted surface. Experiments in which subjects were placed on a tilting seat indicate that we can detect a tilt angle of less than 1 degree from true (gravitational) vertical (Benson, 1982). Much of this sensitivity depends on information from the visual and skin senses. However, kinesthesis—such as the sensation of muscle contraction—and vestibular information from the utricle and saccule also play a role. Thus a major function of kinesthesis and the vestibular sense is to help us to stay upright.

VESTIBULO-OCULAR REFLEX   A second major function of the vestibular sense is to coordinate eye and head position as we turn to look at something. It makes it possible for you to turn your head back and forth to look for cars as you cross the street or to look around a classroom for the best seat. As the head turns, the eyes move more rapidly in the same direction to fix on the visual stimulus. Then, as the turning head catches up, the eyes move slowly in the opposite direction so that they stay fixed on the stimulus. This automatic combination of eye movements helps to keep visual images stable on the retina as the head turns—a function called the **vestibulo-ocular reflex**. The reflex is controlled by neural connections between the semicircular canals and areas of the brain that control eye movements.

MOTION SICKNESS   Unfortunately, a number of unpleasant sensations also can be produced by stimulation of the vestibular sense. One of these is motion sickness. People may suffer nausea and dizziness from the motions made by vehicles such as ships, cars, airplanes, and spacecraft. Motion sickness does not occur with natural head movements. The most widely held theory of how motion sickness is caused is the **conflict hypothesis**. According to this theory, motion sickness is the result of a conflict between two sources of information about spatial orientation of the head and body (Young, 1984). For example, when you are in a car that is making many turns, your vestibular sense signals the turning while your eyes looking inside the car signal a stable environment. This conflict produces motion sickness, which can be relieved if you look outside the car so that your visual sense also signals turning. The conflict that produces motion sickness also can be between actual and *expected* sensory signals based on past experience. For example, you might feel nausea when an elevator begins to move in a direction opposite to the one you expect.

Fortunately, with time people tend to get over their motion sickness even though the conflicting stimuli still are present. Motion sickness disappears when people learn to predict the pattern of conflicting stimuli. For example, sea sickness decreases when people learn to predict the rolling motion of a ship. Yet a kind of reverse motion sickness actually can occur when the stimuli change again. For example, some people have *land* sickness after extensive time at sea. Their walk is unsteady, they are disoriented, and they feel motion sickness symptoms when they walk on steady ground. This land sickness appears to be due to a new conflict between an internal model (expectation) of a rolling ship and the visual-vestibular stimulation that is actually occurring on solid ground (Young, 1984).

EFFECTS OF ALCOHOL   Not a few people have complained that drinking alcohol makes them dizzy. The room spins, they complain. The dizziness that people feel after drinking alcohol is a result of direct effects on the vestibular apparatus (Money and Myles, 1975). When alcohol enters the bloodstream, it reaches all parts of the body, including the vestibular apparatus. Within the semicircular canals, the alcohol diffuses into the gelatinous flap of the ampulla before it enters the fluid that fills the ampulla and canal (see Figure 4-19*b*). Because alcohol is less dense than water, it makes the gelatinous flap less dense than the surrounding fluid. As a result, the gelatinous flap responds abnormally when the head is turned, which produces a conflict between expected and actual sensations. In addition, the receptor cells may be stimulated even when the head is not turned, and this stimulation produces abnormal eye movements (due to the vestibulo-ocular reflex). These effects cause dizziness, which disappears only when the alcohol enters the fluid of the semicircular canals and adjusts the relative densities of the fluid and the gelatinous flap. Later, when a person has stopped drinking, the alcohol leaves the gelatinous flap before it leaves the fluid in the semicircular canal. This effect can cause a recurrence of dizziness hours after the last drink—the reason why people who have had too much to drink may wake up the next morning to a room that seems to spin.

SMELL

The sense of smell, technically called **olfaction**, may be less central to the experience of most humans than to most dogs, but humans depend on the sense of smell to warn against dangers like fire and spoiled food. Smell also adds a pleasurable dimension to the human experience of the world—the scent of roses, fresh air, or delicious food. Perhaps the best testimony to the pleasures we derive from smell is the multimillion-dollar perfume and cologne industry that thrives only because we care about what and how we smell.

Smell Stimuli and Receptors

The sense of smell depends on the presence of gaseous molecules in the air. These molecules are carried into the nose, where they reach receptor cells located in the upper nasal passages (see Figure 4-20). Stimulation probably occurs when the odor molecules interact with small cilia on the receptor cells (Getchell, Margolis, and Getchell, 1985). The permeability of the receptor cell membrane then changes to produce action potentials that travel along the receptor cell axon to the olfactory bulb at the base of the brain.

We know very little about which properties of gaseous molecules determine what they smell like or about how the molecules actually stimulate the receptor cells. One theory, called the **stereochemical theory**, proposes that there are a small number of primary odor qualities such as musky, floral, minty, and putrid that are determined by the shape of the odor molecules (Amoore, 1970). According to this theory, similarly shaped molecules have similar odors, and differently shaped molecules have different primary odor qualities. This theory also postulates that each different shape of molecule stimulates the receptor cells by fitting into special sites on the receptor membrane, as a key fits into a lock. When a molecule fits into a receptor site, it changes the permeability of the membrane and stimulates the receptor cell. An alternative theory, called the **chromatographic theory**, proposes that different odors are caused by different patterns of flow of odor molecules across the mucous layer covering the receptor cells (Mozell, 1970). Because different molecules adhere in different patterns to the mucous layer, they stimulate different groups of receptor cells and produce different odors.

Experiments have provided evidence for and against both the stereochemical and chromatographic theories as well as other theories of smell that have been proposed. At present, there is no general agreement about the physical properties that determine what a substance smells like nor about how it stimulates receptor cells. But whatever the

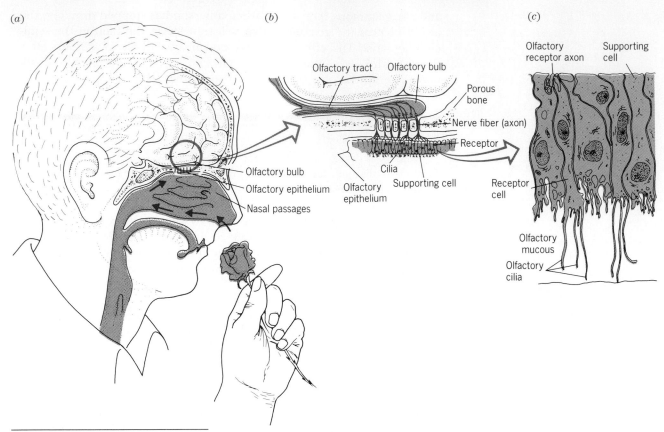

(a)   *(b)*   *(c)*

FIGURE 4-20 INSIDE THE NOSE.

(a) *When you sniff an odor stimulus (a rose), gaseous molecules in the air are drawn into the nasal passages and flow over the* **olfactory epithelium** *(smell skin). (b) and (c) The olfactory epithelium consists of receptor cells and adjacent supporting cells. The receptor cells have small cilia (hairlike structures) that protrude into a layer of mucous. The axons of the receptor cells pass through small pores in the bone at the top of the nasal passages and enter the* **olfactory bulb** *at the base of the brain. [(a) and (b) after Amoore, Johnston, and Rubin, 1964; (c) from Keverne, 1982a.]*

answers to these questions turn out to be, it is clear that each receptor cell responds to a number of different odor stimuli (Keverne, 1982a). Individual neurons in the olfactory pathways of the brain also respond to a broad range of odor stimuli (Tanabe, Iino, and Takagi, 1975). It seems that there are not specific receptors or neurons for specific odors. Instead, the neural code for the odor of a stimulus appears to be the *pattern* of activity among many neurons in olfactory centers of the brain (see Figure 4-21).

Sensation and Perception of Smells

ODOR QUALITY As we've said, we do not yet know the particular physical properties that make a thing smell one way or another. But certain things do smell alike, and there have been a number of attempts to classify odors on the basis of the similarities and differences of their smells. For example, Henning (in Woodworth, 1938) proposed that there are six basic odor qualities—fragrant, putrid, ethereal, resinous, spicy, and burned—and that all other odors can be classified by their similarity to these six primary qualities.

A more recent scheme for classifying odors is based on the observation that some people have a **specific anosmia**, an inability to smell specific odors (Amoore, 1977). For example, about one person in three cannot smell the chemical isobutyraldehyde (which has a malty odor), and

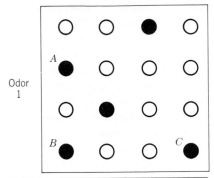

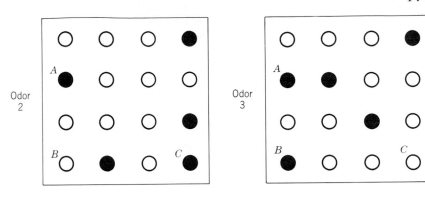

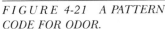

FIGURE 4-21 A PATTERN CODE FOR ODOR.

The simplified diagram shows how the odors of three different stimuli can be signaled by the pattern of activity among neurons in an olfactory structure of the brain. Each dot represents one of 16 neurons in an olfactory structure; filled dots are neurons that are activated by a particular odor stimulus. Notice that neuron A is activated by all three odors, neuron B by odors 1 and 3, and neuron C by odors 1 and 2. Thus, individual neurons may be activated by several different odors and therefore cannot signal the specific odor that is present. However, each odor activates a unique pattern of neurons. Therefore, the specific pattern of activated neurons can accurately signal, or code, the odor that occurred.

about one in 20 cannot smell trimethylamine (which has a fishy odor). Amoore (1977) used such specific anosmias to make inferences about the presence of primary odors, just as vision scientists have used specific types of color blindness to make inferences about the nature of primary colors. On the basis of these specific anosmias, Amoore suggested that there are at least 32 different primary classes of odors. Although these attempts at classifying odors have provided useful information about the sense of smell, there still is no general agreement about how many perceptual classes of odor qualities actually exist.

SENSITIVITY The human olfactory system is incredibly sensitive. Calculations based on absolute threshold measurements indicate that fewer than eight molecules of some substances (such as butyl mercaptan, which has a putrid odor) are required to produce a response in a receptor cell. What is more, people can smell as few as 40 molecules of these substances (De Vries and Stuiver, 1961). Even so, we humans are much less sensitive to odors than some other species. For example, dogs are 100 times more sensitive to some substances than we are (Moulton, 1977). The reason is that dogs have more olfactory receptors than humans do, about one billion compared to our 10 million.

ADAPTATION You have probably had the experience of entering a room with a strong odor (Uncle Harry's cigar) only to find that the odor seemed to disappear after a while. Here is another example of adaptation, the process by which continued exposure to a stimulus decreases sensitivity to it. Studies have shown that smell adaptation is not complete, however. Very intense odor stimuli continue to produce a sensation regardless of the state of adaptation (Cain and Engen, 1969).

Not only do we humans adapt to certain smells, but we also **cross-adapt**. In other words, exposure to one odor stimulus may decrease sensitivity to a different stimulus. Stimuli with similar smells produce the greatest degree of cross-adaptation (which is why you probably don't notice Uncle Fred's Tiparillo after Uncle Harry's been smoking his cigar for a while). But cross-adaptation also operates with stimuli that smell quite different (Moncrieff, 1956). These tendencies are consistent with the observation that we made earlier about individual olfactory receptors and neurons in the brain generally responding to a relatively large number of odor stimuli.

PHEROMONES AND OLFACTORY COMMUNICATION **Pheromones** (from the Greek *pherin*, "to transfer," and *hormon*, "to excite") are odorous chemicals that are released by animals and cause specific reactions in other animals of the species. Pheromones are a kind of olfactory communication among animals. Pheromones were first discovered and studied in insects, but they are now known to be important in many species.

There are two main types of pheromones. **Primers** produce physiological (usually hormonal) changes in the receiving animal that then alter the animal's behavior. For example, the odor of a strange male mouse causes hormonal changes in a female mouse that has just mated that prevent her from becoming pregnant (Bruce, 1959). The second type of pheromone, **releasers**, automatically trigger an immediate behavioral response from the receiving animal. For example, some releasers are powerful sexual stimulants that attract sexual partners. Female dogs in heat attract mates by giving off pheromones. Some pheromones also elicit or inhibit aggression, and some are used to mark scent trails and territorial boundaries. The male cat that sprays around the borders of the family living room is marking his territory.

Some evidence suggests that humans emit and respond to pheromones (Doty, 1981). For instance, newborn babies can discriminate the odor of their own mother's breast and prefer that odor to that of a strange mother (MacFarlane, 1975; Russell, 1976). Other studies have shown that college women who spend a lot of time together, either close friends or roommates, tend to have menstrual cycles that synchronize (McClintock, 1971). Over a period of 4 to 7 months, these women menstruated significantly closer together in time than they did at the beginning of the academic year. More recent studies have provided evidence that olfactory cues produce the menstrual synchrony (Russell, Switz, and Thompson, 1980).

It is clear that the effects of pheromones found in humans are quite subtle compared to those in lower mammals and insects (Rogel, 1978; Doty, 1981). Although odors may be able to influence our behavior toward each other, it is unlikely that there are releaser pheromones that produce immediate and automatic responses in us. Social and cognitive factors seem to play a greater role in our responses to olfactory stimuli than they do in other species. Nevertheless, perfume and cologne companies continue to spend millions in search of the perfect releaser.

TASTE

The sense of taste, technically called **gustation**, is extremely important to survival. For example, poisonous substances tend to be bitter, and nutritive substances tend to be sweet. Thus the ability to sense bitter and sweet has obvious survival value. Over and above the sensation of taste is something called **flavor**. When you eat a fine meal or sip a full-bodied cup of coffee, you are experiencing flavor, not just taste. The flavor of a substance is influenced by factors such as its temperature, its texture, and, especially, its smell. To see how important smell is, hold your nose while you eat. You'll find it difficult to distinguish between an apple and a raw potato, and the flavor of meat, fruit, and most other foods will be lost. As anyone with a stuffy nose from a head cold or an allergy can attest, the same loss of flavor happens then, too.

Taste Stimuli and Receptors

The physical stimuli for taste are chemicals that are dissolved in water, including the water in saliva. Classically, there are considered to be four basic tastes: sweet, bitter, salty, and sour. Each of these tastes is associated with a different chemical structure. For example, sourness generally corresponds to acids that release a hydrogen ion in solution. Molecules made up of carbon, hydrogen, and oxygen generally taste sweet. However, there are exceptions to these relationships, and the physical properties that produce different tastes are not fully understood. Indeed, as you will see, there is growing controversy about whether there are only four basic tastes.

Receptors for taste are, of course, located on the tongue. The surface of the tongue is covered with ridges and valleys, called **papillae** (see Figure 4-22a). There are about 10,000 **taste buds** lining the walls of the papillae, and each taste bud contains up to 30 **receptor cells** (see Figures 4-22b and 4-22c). Receptor cells live an average of only about 10 days and are constantly replaced (Beidler and Smallman, 1965). That is why when you burn the receptors on your tongue (the pizza is too hot!), taste returns in a few days. New receptor cells have been produced.

Different regions of the tongue are most sensitive to different taste stimuli (see Figure 4-23). For example, the front of the tongue is most sensitive to sweet tastes, and the back of the tongue is most sensitive to sour (Collings, 1974). However, all areas of the tongue (except the center, where there are no receptors) respond to all of the tastes tested. Indeed, experiments in which sweet, bitter, sour, and salty stimuli were applied to individual taste buds indicate that single taste buds can respond to two or more tastes (Arvidson and Friberg, 1980).

It is believed that taste stimuli produce an electrical potential in the receptor cell by interacting with specialized areas of membrane on the tips of the receptors (Keverne, 1982b). Nerve fibers that contact the taste receptor cells travel toward the brain in the cranial nerves and make connections first in the medulla and then in the thalamus and cortex (Norgren, 1984). Electrophysiological recordings from taste nerve fibers in animals indicate that individual fibers can respond to several or even all four taste stimuli tested (sweet, sour, bitter, and salty), although the fibers may respond better to one taste stimulus than the others (Pfaffmann, Frank, Bartoshuk, and Snell, 1979). Similar results have been found among neurons in the brain (Yamamoto, 1984; Smith, 1985). Thus, like odor, the taste of a stimulus does not appear to be signaled by the activity of neurons sensitive to only a single stimulus. Instead, different tastes seem to be signaled by the *pattern* of activity across many neurons.

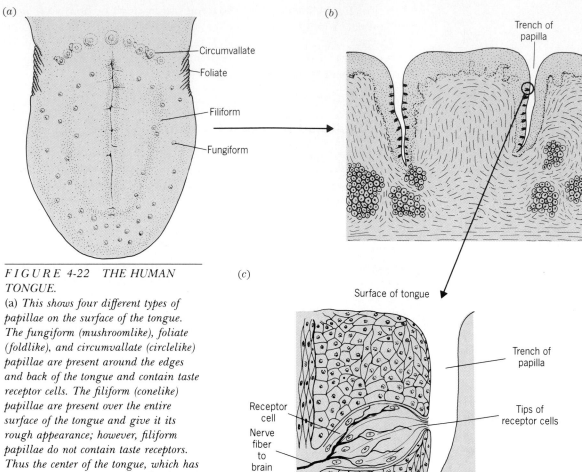

FIGURE 4-22   THE HUMAN TONGUE.
(a) *This shows four different types of papillae on the surface of the tongue. The fungiform (mushroomlike), foliate (foldlike), and circumvallate (circlelike) papillae are present around the edges and back of the tongue and contain taste receptor cells. The filiform (conelike) papillae are present over the entire surface of the tongue and give it its rough appearance; however, filiform papillae do not contain taste receptors. Thus the center of the tongue, which has only filiform papillae, is not sensitive to taste. (From Goldstein, 1984.) (b) A cross section through a papilla, and (c) an enlargement of a taste bud in the papilla. Each taste bud contains a number of receptor cells, which have fine tips that protrude into an opening in the trench of the papilla. There also are taste receptors on the roof of the mouth (on the palate) and the upper part of the throat (on the epiglottis and upper third of the esophagus). [(b) from Wyburn, Pickford, and Hirst, 1964; (c) from Woodworth, 1940.]*

Taste Qualities and Mixtures

TASTE QUALITIES   There is currently a great deal of controversy about the qualities of tastes. The classic view, originally based on introspection, is that all tastes (in absence of odor) can be characterized as sweet, sour, bitter, or salty and that there are no transitional qualities between them. A variety of recent psychophysical evidence has been interpreted as supporting this view (McBurney and Gent, 1979). The alternative view is that different tastes form a continuum of qualities. Different chemicals produce this continuum, with sweet, sour, bitter, and salty only the four most familiar tastes within it (Schiffman and Erickson, 1980). This view is analogous to the view of color vision as a continuum of hues produced by different wavelengths of light, with red, green, and blue the three primary colors along this continuum.

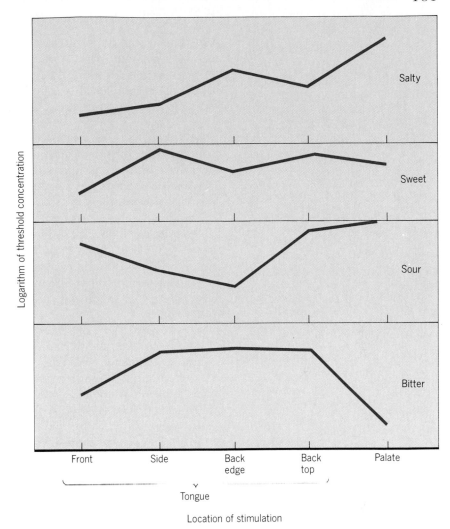

*FIGURE 4-23 TASTE
SENSITIVITY ON DIFFERENT
PARTS OF THE TONGUE.*
*The graphs show absolute thresholds for
four different taste stimuli at different
locations on the tongue and soft palate.
(Modified from Collings, 1974.)*

At present, this controversy is not resolved. Nevertheless, whether sweet, sour, bitter, and salty are unique taste qualities or simply points on a continuum of tastes, they have proved very useful in helping scientists to describe and understand how the taste system works.

TASTE MIXTURES An interesting property of taste stimuli is that when they are mixed they generally do not fuse to form a new taste but remain independent taste sensations (McBurney, 1984). For example, when sweet sugar (sucrose) and sour hydrochloric acid are mixed, they result in a sweet–sour solution and not one that tastes bitter, salty, or something else. People play on this independence of tastes when they prepare foods such as sweet-and-sour pork or lemonade. Although there are some instances in which mixed tastes do combine to produce a single new taste, these seem to be the exceptions (Schiffman and Erickson, 1980).

Factors That Influence How Things Taste

Why does a vinegary salad dressing spoil the taste of wine? Why do some people crave salt? Why do others avoid formerly favorite foods like the plague? As you will see in the following sections, the way that things taste to people is influenced by nutritional needs, adaptation, and aversions that grow out of past experiences and learning.

ADAPTATION Like other sensory systems, the taste system adapts to continued stimulation. The result is an increased threshold and a lower perceived intensity of the stimulus to which the system was adapted. Adaptation explains why some people repeatedly salt their food during a meal. As they adapt to the salt, they need more to taste the same degree of saltiness.

Adaptation to one taste stimulus also can affect the taste of another. A good example of this is the effect of certain substances on the taste of water. If you swish a bitter substance (such as strong caffeinated coffee) in your mouth for about 30 seconds, tap water will taste sweet. However, if you rinse your mouth with a salty solution, the same tap water will taste bitter-sour.

TASTE MODIFIERS Certain substances alter taste in other ways. For example, gymnemic acid (from the leaves of the plant *Gymnema sylvestre*) selectively suppresses sweet tastes. Sugar crystals taste like grains of sand after applying gymnemic acid to the tongue. Miracle fruit (a berry from an African shrub, *Synsepalum dulcificum*) makes normally sour substances taste sweet. After eating miracle fruit, a lemon tastes as sweet as an orange. These **taste modifiers** appear to have their effects by altering how substances interact with the membrane of taste receptor cells (Kurichara, Kurichara, and Beidler, 1969).

SPECIFIC HUNGERS A number of factors affect the pleasantness or unpleasantness of tastes and therefore people's preferences in food. One such factor is human biological and nutritional needs. For example, people and other animals deprived of salts tend to select foods high in salts and thereby increase the amount of salt in their bodies. This taste preference for substances that meet a biological need is referred to as a **specific hunger**. In one sad clinical case, a child who had survived with an abnormality of the adrenal glands, which causes a salt deficiency, by consuming large amounts of salt was hospitalized so that doctors could determine what caused his craving for salt. When the child was placed on a standard diet that did not satisfy his need for salt, he died. A specific hunger for sweet-tasting substances also can occur in individuals who are deprived of sugars.

Specific hungers are regulated by both taste and learning. This is shown by an experiment with rats that had a glucose (a type of sugar) deficit caused by treatment with insulin (Jacobs, 1967). The glucose-deficient rats were given a choice of drinking water, a glucose solution, and a much sweeter but less nutritious fructose (fruit sugar) solution. The rats initially drank the sweeter fructose solution even though it was less effective than glucose in relieving their biological need. This initial preference shows the importance of taste: the need for sugar increased the preference for sweeter tastes. After a day, however, the rats switched their preference to the more nutritive, less sweet glucose solution. This switch shows effects of learning: the rats associated the taste of glucose with relief of the glucose deficit.

CONDITIONED TASTE AVERSION Have you ever found yourself in the unpleasant situation of having eaten a food you liked only to be struck with nausea soon afterward from some illness *unrelated* to the food—perhaps a bout of the flu—and then couldn't stomach the very thought of that food again? This phenomenon is called **conditioned taste aversion** (and is of considerable interest to psychologists who study learning because it represents a very strong association that is formed after only a single pairing of a stimulus and a response; see Chapter 6). People with a conditioned taste aversion avoid the offending food not because they think that sickness will follow but because the food actually takes on an unpleasant taste to them (Garcia, Hankins, and Rusiniak, 1974). Clearly, experience and learning can alter how people perceive pleasantness and unpleasantness of tastes (see Logue, 1985).

OTHER WORLDS

Because people's experience of the world is determined by the properties of their sensory and perceptual systems, there is not always a one-to-one relationship between things that are out there—what we like to think of as "reality"—and the internal experience of them. This discrepancy between "reality" and experience becomes all the clearer when we consider the sensory worlds of other species. Ethologists and psychologists who study animal behavior have found that animals of different species live in their own sensory worlds, and in many cases, these are worlds that we humans can never experience. To study these other sensory worlds gives us a compelling view of sensation and perception and provides important insight into how sensory and perceptual systems work.

Same Senses, Different Ranges

VISION Members of certain other species respond to broader or different ranges of stimuli than people do. For instance, people literally do not see the world the same way as honeybees do. Recall from Chapter 3 that humans can see a range of wavelengths of light from about 400 nanometers—violet—to 700 nanometers—red (look back at Figure 3-5). But we are blind to shorter (ultraviolet) and longer (infrared) wavelengths. Honeybees can see wavelengths as short as about 300 nanometers; they can see ultraviolet light, in other words. As a result, objects that reflect ultraviolet light—for example, flowers, which are pretty important objects in a bee's universe—look very different to bees and humans (see Figure 4-24). Like humans, bees have three receptors for

FIGURE 4-24   FLOWERS LOOK DIFFERENT TO HONEYBEES AND HUMANS.
The photographs show the appearance of flowers under visible (to humans) and visible plus ultraviolet light. The flowers have different patterns of coloration when ultraviolet light is included. Honeybees can see these patterns whereas humans cannot. The ultraviolet patterns on the flowers are thought to serve as targets or guides for foraging bees.

color vision, but bees' receptors are most sensitive to ultraviolet, blue, and green whereas humans' receptors are most sensitive to blue, green, and yellow-green. Similar mechanisms in two different species have evolved into different ranges of vision.

HEARING   Although we humans can hear sound waves in the air that have remarkably high frequencies—as high as 20,000 Hz—there are many species that hear sound frequencies that are much higher (Hess, 1973). For example, dogs hear frequencies up to about 50,000 Hz. Dog whistles emit these high frequencies, which are inaudible to humans. Mice and bats hear sounds of 95,000 to 120,000 Hz, and seals hear up to 180,000 Hz! There is a world of sounds out there that we are missing. The ears of animals that can hear very high frequencies are built much like ours, but they respond to air vibrations of much higher frequencies.

Although humans can locate the source of sounds in space quite well, our ability is primitive compared to that of some animals. The bats that seem to "see" in the dark actually operate on extremely acute sound localization. To localize objects, they use a process called **echolocation** (Griffin, 1958; Simmons, Howell, and Suga, 1975). The bat emits a very-high-frequency sound (inaudible to humans), which echoes off objects such as the flying insects that the bat hunts. By determining the time it takes for the echo to return and comparing the stimulus frequencies present in the echo and the emitted sound, the bat can judge precisely the distance, speed, traveling direction, size, and even the texture of the target. By using echolocation—nature's sonar—a bat that is flying in the dark can zero in on and capture flying insects in less than a second. Physiological studies have shown that a large proportion of the bat's brain is devoted to auditory processing for echolocation (Suga, 1984). These studies also have provided a wealth of information that has helped us to understand how all brains, including those of humans, process sounds.

Different Senses

ELECTRIC SENSE   Many species possess senses that are completely alien to humans. One of these is the **electric sense**. It allows some water-dwelling animals to detect electric fields. Sharks, for example, can detect electric currents emitted from the skins of prey, even if the prey is hidden or camouflaged (Bullock, 1982). Sharks have specialized electric organs that are extremely sensitive to these electric currents.

Some fish produce their own electric currents, which they use for social communication and for sensing changes in the watery world around them (Lissmann, 1963; Bullock, 1982). For instance, a small Amazonian fish, *Eigenmannia,* generates an electric field along its body. This field is continually sensed by thousands of tiny receptors that measure the flow of electrical current along the fish's body. When an animal such as predator or prey with an electrical conductivity that is different from the water's enters the electric field, the field is distorted (see Figure 4-25). This distortion casts a kind of electric shadow on the body of the fish and changes the current flow to the receptors. Thus, the electric sense, like the senses to which we are more accustomed, responds to stimulus *change.*

FIGURE 4-25   THE ELECTRIC SENSE.
Certain fish generate an electric field along their bodies. A smaller fish, which has electrical conductivity different from the water, distorts the electric field. This distortion is sensed by electroreceptors along the body of the electric fish. The pattern of electric field distortion can provide information about the size, shape, distance, and the direction and velocity of movement of the smaller fish. (From Gould, 1982.)

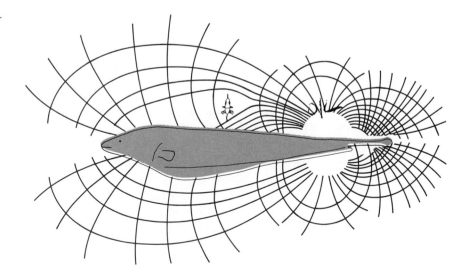

BOX 4-3
EXTRASENSORY PERCEPTION

Over the years there has been heated controversy about the existence of **extrasensory perception (ESP)**, perceptual abilities that do not depend on known sensory systems. ESP includes three different phenomena. *Clairvoyance* is the perception of objects or events that do not stimulate one of the known senses (for example, "sensing" the contents of a closed container). *Precognition* is the perception of future events, or "seeing" into the future. *Telepathy* is the communication of thoughts from one person to another (one form of which is mind reading). ESP is studied within the field known as **parapsychology**. Another topic of parapsychology is **psychokinesis**, the ability to manipulate or move objects mentally, for example, willing a certain number to come up when dice are thrown.

As with other phenomena, proof of the existence of ESP must rest on the results of controlled scientific studies. Some studies have, in fact, provided evidence for ESP. For example, in one well-known experiment, a woman thought to have telepathy was required to name which of five cards the experimenter was looking at on each test trial. Thirteen sessions of 200 trials each were given over a 5-year period. Because there were five possible cards, the laws of chance were that a subject could name the

target card correctly 20 percent of the time simply by guessing. But the woman in question was correct 27 percent of the time over the 2600 trials that were given, a result that is significantly greater than chance performance (Soal and Bateman, 1954).

Despite such demonstrations, most scientists doubt the existence of ESP. One reason is that even when evidence for ESP is found, it often is very weak and found only inconsistently. For example, even though the result just described was statistically significant, the woman performed only slightly better than chance (27 percent vs. 20 percent correct). Furthermore, in several of the testing sessions she performed at or below chance levels (for example, 13.5 percent and 19.5 percent correct out of 200 trials in two different sessions). Another cause for doubt is that it often has not been possible for other investigators to replicate ESP experiments. This difficulty is serious because experimental findings in science cannot be considered established fact unless they can be replicated by different investigators using similar methods.

Flaws also have been found in the methods of many ESP experiments (Diaconis, 1978; Gardner, 1981). Many times adequate experimental controls or safeguards against inadvertent cues have been lacking. In addition, it is difficult or impossible to determine what is chance performance for many phenomena (Diaconis, 1978). For instance, if a supposed

clairvoyant says that a murderer hid the gun in a particular location, what is the probability that it was a chance guess and what is the probability that it was based on available information (such as that the murderer was known to go to that location)? Furthermore, often it is not known when a clairvoyant has been wrong. Publicity tends to surround only successful cases, not the unsuccessful ones.

Another cause for skepticism is that many apparent examples of ESP and psychokinesis have been shown to be fraudulent (Randi, 1978; Hansel, 1980). For instance, one renowned "psychic" who claimed to possess telepathy and psychokinesis was filmed and found to be using magicians' tricks of deception, distraction, and illusion.

The controversy about the existence of parapsychological phenomena continues. Scientists must keep an open mind at the same time they demand the kind of repeatable and carefully controlled studies they demand before accepting any other phenomenon. Claims that acupuncture can relieve pain and that birds can sense the earth's magnetic field also were met with skepticism until repeated controlled studies showed them to be reliable phenomena. Some day perhaps ESP will no longer raise doubts. But despite many years of research, there still is insufficient evidence to convince most scientists that ESP exists, even in "sensitive" individuals.

MAGNETIC SENSE Another amazing sense possessed by other species is the ability to detect the earth's magnetic field. When it was first suggested that some animals could detect magnetic fields, many people were skeptical, because a magnetic sense is so foreign to human experience and because there was no explanation of the mechanisms involved. But it

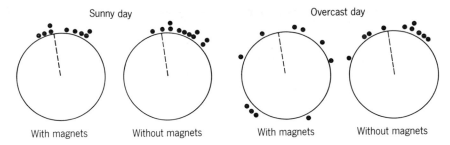

Sunny day   Overcast day

With magnets   Without magnets   With magnets   Without magnets

FIGURE 4-26   THE MAGNETIC SENSE.

Shown are results of an experiment that demonstrates that, on cloudy days, pigeons determine the direction of home on the basis of the earth's magnetic field. The pigeons had either magnets or brass bars mounted on their heads. When they were released on a sunny day, both groups of pigeons used the sun to determine direction and flew toward home. However, when they were released on an overcast day, the pigeons with magnets were disoriented, but those without magnets still flew toward home. The magnets produced a local magnetic field that disturbed the birds' ability to sense the earth's magnetic field, causing them to fly in random directions. The dashed line indicates the direction of home. Each dot shows the direction flown by an individual pigeon. (Modified from Gould, 1982; after Keeton, 1971.)

now has been demonstrated convincingly that bacteria, bees, fish, and some birds have this sensory capacity. On sunny days pigeons, for instance, primarily use the sun to navigate the direction of their homes. But on cloudy days, they navigate by the earth's magnetic field (Walcott, 1974) (see Figure 4-26). There is now evidence that homing pigeons have tiny magnetic particles in their heads (Walcott, Gould, and Kirschvink, 1979). These particles might function by aligning with the earth's magnetic field and changing the electrical properties of receptors that contain them (Kirschvink, 1982).

The fact that members of other species have senses different from our own can give us perspective on our environment and our place in it. We humans tend to assume that our sensory and perceptual systems are superior to those of other animals, but in fact they are only different, not necessarily better. Each species has evolved elegant sensory mechanisms to provide it with information about its world and to allow it to function adaptively in that world.

SUMMARY

HEARING

1. *Sound and the Auditory System.* Sound comes from vibrations, or pressure changes, in a medium such as air. These pressure changes, called sound waves, can be characterized by their frequency (in cycles per second, or Hertz) and amplitude (in decibels). Most of the ear is an accessory structure that focuses, amplifies, and modifies the sound waves so that receptor cells in the inner ear can be activated. The receptor activation causes auditory nerve fibers to transmit action potentials to the brain. Both ears send information to many auditory structures in both cerebral hemispheres. When neurons in these structures change their activity, they provide humans with the experience of sound.

2. *Perception of Pitch and Loudness.* The two principal subjective dimensions of sound stimuli are their pitch and loudness. Pitch is determined primarily by the frequency of the sound wave, though other factors also influence pitch perception. Loudness is determined primarily by the amplitude of the sound wave, though sound-wave frequency also affects perceived loudness. Under ideal conditions, humans can hear frequencies from 20 to 20,000 Hertz (Hz), and they can hear about a millionfold range of sound pressure intensity.

3. *Mechanisms of Hearing Stimulus Frequency.* Two mechanisms explain how people hear sounds of different frequencies. (a) For frequencies up to about 5000 Hz, auditory nerve fibers (singly or in groups) fire action potentials at the same frequency as the sound stimulus (frequency theory and the volley principle). (b) Throughout the audible range (20 to 20,000 Hz), different auditory nerve fibers are activated more by certain stimulus frequencies than by others (place theory). In auditory areas of the brain, the frequency of a stimulus is signaled primarily by which neurons are activated.

4. *Sound Localization.* Humans are very accurate at locating the source of a sound stimulus and at discriminating between the locations of two separate sounds. Sound localization depends primarily on having two ears that receive slightly different sounds. The cues that are used are differences between the two ears in the time of arrival, the intensity, and the distortions of sounds as they strike the two ears from different directions. Neurons in the brain are very sensitive to these interaural sound differences. Each side of the brain is used primarily for localizing sounds in the opposite side of auditory space.

5. *Auditory Pattern Perception.* Most sounds that people hear are complex auditory patterns—changes in stimulus frequency and intensity over time. Understanding speech is an important example of auditory pattern perception. Studies suggest that people distinguish basic units of speech (phonemes) by recognizing distinctive patterns of changes in frequency and intensity (feature analysis) rather than by recognizing the specific frequencies and intensities that are present. When people perceive continuous speech (long sequences of auditory patterns), people seem to carry out two operations. One is to recognize the sound features in basic elements of the pattern and then to combine these into the longer sequences that make up continuous speech (bottom-up theory). The second is to use past experience and cognition to guide perception of the sound patterns that make up speech (top-down theory).

THE BODY SENSES

6. *The Skin and Its Connections to the Brain.* The skin is a large sheet of cells that contains many nerve endings and a variety of sensory receptors. These receptors respond to touch, pressure, temperature changes, or painful stimulation of the skin. The receptors are contacted by nerve fibers that generate action potentials that are sent to the spinal cord and brain. Individual fibers carry information about (respond to) specific types of sensory stimuli. Pathways that carry information about touch and pressure cross to the opposite side of the brain and end in somatic sensory cortex. Within cortex, neurons code information about complex features of touch and pressure at particular locations on the body surface. Pathways that carry information about pain and temperature are more diffuse than those carrying information about touch and pressure, and they tend to go to both sides of the brain.

7. *Perception of Touch, Pressure, and Temperature.* People's sensitivity to touch and pressure and their ability to discriminate where stimuli have been applied to the skin differ for different parts of the body surface. For instance, sensitivity is greatest for the lips and fingers. As in other sensory systems, people are much more sensitive to changes in skin stimulation than to steady skin stimulation. Thus people are best at identifying complex textures and shapes when they are moving over the surface of the hands. Likewise, the sensation of warmth or cold occurs when a stimulus causes the skin temperature to change. Steady stimulation at a particular temperature leads to adaptation, and the stimulus no longer feels warm or cold.

8. *Pain.* Pain is a complex sensory experience: it can be produced by a wide variety of stimuli, it can cause sensory as well as strong emotional responses, and its perception can be influenced by many different physiological and psychological factors. Specific neural pathways for pain sensation arise from the free nerve endings in the skin. According to Melzak and Wall's gate-control theory, whether activation of these pathways leads to the perception of pain depends on whether other skin senses, such as touch and pressure, also are stimulated, and it depends on central control from the brain. The release of naturally occurring opiatelike substances (endorphins) in the nervous system also influences pain perception. Understanding these mechanisms helps people understand how local anesthetics, narcotics, placebos, and acupuncture relieve pain.

9. *Body Orientation and Position.* Information about the positions of a person's limbs and body in space comes partly from kinesthetic receptors in the joints and muscles. In addition, the vestibular sense relies on specialized receptors in the inner ear to provide information about the position and movement of the head. Kinesthesis and the vestibular sense help people to stay upright. The vestibular sense also coordinates eye and head position as people move their heads to look at something (the vestibulo-ocular reflex). If there is a conflict between two sources of information—vestibular and visual, for example—about the orientation of the head and body, motion sickness can result. In addition, abnormal stimulation of the vestibular apparatus produces the dizziness a person feels after drinking alcohol.

THE CHEMICAL SENSES

10. *Smell.* The sensation of smell (technically, olfaction) is produced by gaseous molecules in the air that stimulate receptor

cells in the upper nasal passages. For some stimuli, only 40 molecules need to reach the receptors to produce an odor sensation. There is no general agreement about which properties of gaseous molecules determine how they smell or how the molecules actually stimulate the receptor cells. Like other senses, smell shows adaptation and many odors seem to disappear with continuous stimulation. Many species release odorous chemicals, called pheromones, as a method of olfactory communication with other members of the species. The pheromones can prime a recipient animal to behave in a particular way or actually trigger in the recipient certain behaviors, such as sexual or aggressive responses.

11. *Taste.* The stimuli for taste (technically, gustation) are chemicals dissolved in water, including the water in saliva. These stimuli interact with specialized areas of membrane on receptor cells on the tongue. Different regions of the tongue are most sensitive to different taste stimuli; however, all areas of the tongue (except the center, where there are no receptors) respond to all tastes. Classically, there are considered to be four basic tastes: sweet, sour, bitter, and salty. However, recent research suggests that these may be just four familiar tastes on a continuum of taste qualities. Many factors can affect how a stimulus tastes. For instance, continued exposure (adaptation) to one stimulus can affect the taste of that stimulus as well as of other stimuli. Nutritional needs can affect the pleasantness of tastes and, consequently, people's food preferences (the phenomenon of specific hungers). Learning also is important, and even a single experience with a taste that was followed by illness can lead to a strong aversion to that stimulus (conditioned taste aversion).

SENSES OF OTHER SPECIES

12. *Other Worlds.* The sensory abilities of other species often differ from those of humans. Some species are sensitive to broader or different ranges of stimulation. For instance, bees can see wavelengths of light that are invisible to humans. In addition, dogs, mice, seals, and other animals can hear sound frequencies that are inaudible to humans. A second difference is that many species possess senses that are completely alien to humans. For instance, some fish generate and sense changes in electric currents in the water, and some birds are able to detect the earth's magnetic field. These examples make it clear that there is not always a one-to-one relationship between things that are out there ("reality") and our experience of them. In addition, they emphasize that our own sensory and perceptual systems are different from, but not necessarily better than, those of other animals.

FURTHER READINGS

Good general textbooks on sensation and perception include *Sensation and Perception* (2nd Ed.) by Coren, Porac, and Ward (1984), *Sensation and Perception* (2nd Ed.) by Goldstein (1984), and *Perception* by Sekuler and Blake (1985). These are scholarly and well-written books that are highly recommended to students who wish to learn more about the subjects covered in the present chapter.

The Senses, edited by Barlow and Mollon (1982), includes a number of excellent chapters written by experts in the field. The chapters are generally quite readable and understandable to the beginning student.

A classic in the field of sensation and perception is *The Human Senses* (2nd Ed.) by Geldard (1972). Although this book is somewhat outdated, it includes a scholarly and detailed discussion of fundamental principles of sensory processing.

For the more advanced student, the *Handbook of Physiology, Section I: The Nervous System; Volume III. Sensory Processes, Part 2* is an excellent source of detailed information about the sensory systems discussed in the present chapter. This volume is edited by Darian-Smith (1984b) and includes comprehensive and critical reviews of material by experts in the field.

A good source of information on the topic of pain perception is *Psychological Control of Pain* by Elton, Stanley, and Burrows (1983). This book contains material on topics ranging from the basic neural mechanisms of pain to complex cognitive, social, and cultural influences on pain perception.

Two good books on ethology and animal behavior, including discussions of the sensory worlds of other species, are *Ethology: the Mechanisms and Evolution of Behavior* by Gould (1982) and *Biology of Animal Behavior* by Grier (1984). Both books are clear and easy to read.

Several books can be recommended for further information about extrasensory perception and parapsychology. The *Handbook of Parapsychology,* edited by Wolman, Dale, Schmeidler, and Ullman (1977), contains chapters on history, research methods, and various topics of current interest in parapsychology. The chapters are written by people who work in the field. *Science: Good, Bad, and Bogus* by Gardner (1981) contains essays and articles that are critical of parapsychology and point out many of the reasons that most scientists have remained skeptical about it. *ESP and Parapsychology: a Critical Evaluation* by Hansel (1980) provides detailed descriptions and assessments of many of the classic studies of parapsychology.

5

CONSCIOUSNESS AND ATTENTION

Are you conscious? Of course I am, you say. But how do you know? How do you know if someone else is conscious? Are lower animals—your pet dog, say—conscious? Are "smart" machines, such as computers, conscious? All of these questions, which have long engaged philosophers and psychologists, lead inevitably to the central question: what is consciousness?

THE NATURE OF CONSCIOUSNESS

Not surprisingly, there is no single definition of consciousness that is accepted by all psychologists, although nearly all psychologists agree that the central aspect of consciousness is the sense of "I" or "self." As William James (1890) put it: "The only states of consciousness that we naturally deal with are found in personal consciousnesses, minds, selves, concrete particular I's and you's." **Consciousness** implies an awareness of personal identity and an awareness of the relationship between the external world and self (Natsoulas, 1978, 1983). Even though a person regularly enters the altered consciousness of sleep or even drug-induced insensibility, the person always perceives himself or herself to be the same person—"me" (Oakley and Eames, 1985).

Functions of Consciousness

Why do we humans have consciousness? Does it contribute anything essential to human thought and actions? The answers to those questions represent a wide range of opinion within the ranks of psychologists. Some psychologists believe that consciousness is simply an uninteresting by-product of experience and behavior and that it has no real functional importance (Skinner, 1964). Others, while acknowledging that consciousness is an important and real phenomenon, believe that it plays a passive role in information flow. For example, they suggest that consciousness is a *result* of thinking and processing information (Miller, 1962). Still other psychologists believe that consciousness plays an *active* role in mental life and in the control of behavior.

Psychologists who believe that consciousness plays an active role in mental life suggest that it has two broad functions (Kihlstrom, 1984; Mandler, 1983). The first function of consciousness is to *monitor* the self and environment. For example, people are conscious when they direct their attention to some stimuli rather than others. In addition, people generally are conscious when they acquire new information and behavior and integrate it with what they already know. The second function of consciousness is to *control* the self and environment. Thus, people are conscious when they solve problems and exercise choices and judgments. Consciousness allows people to organize their priorities, to engage in long-term planning, and to voluntarily begin and end behavioral and cognitive activities.

Consciousness in Relation to Other Mental States

THE UNCONSCIOUS   In addition to consciousness, most psychologists recognize the existence of an **unconscious** mental state. The unconscious is generally considered to consist of memories, knowledge, and thought processes that are not readily available to consciousness—that is, that a person is not aware of directly—but that nevertheless influence thought and action (Bowers, 1984; Kihlstrom, 1984). Thus, whereas consciousness consists of a state of awareness, unconsciousness consists of a state of unawareness of certain information and thoughts.

There are different views of the nature and contents of the unconscious. According to the psychoanalytic theories of Sigmund Freud and his followers, the unconscious consists mainly of primal sexual or aggressive desires and the thoughts and memories associated with them. Certain memories or intentions are pushed into the unconscious because they are unpleasant or threatening; they are said to be **repressed** (Breuer and Freud, 1893–1895/1974) (see Chapter 13). Although repressed material is not available to consciousness, it may affect behavior in the form of dreams, slips of the tongue, or even mental illness.

More recent cognitive-behavioral theories present a somewhat different view of the unconscious (Bowers, 1984; Kihlstrom, 1984). One such theory is diagrammed in Figure 5-1. In this view, the unconscious is made up of two parts. The first part consists of the workings of the early stages of sensation and perception. These workings include the initial reception and analysis of external sensory stimuli (see Chapters 3 and 4), which go on automatically and to which a person has no conscious access. The second component of the unconscious consists of **procedural knowledge**. This knowledge is the set of procedures, or cognitive skills, that people use to manipulate or transform information about the world. For example, highly practiced motor skills such as walking, drink-

FIGURE 5-1   A COGNITIVE THEORY OF CONSCIOUS AND UNCONSCIOUS MENTAL PROCESSES AND CONTENTS. Arrows indicate the possible flow of information among unconscious, preconscious, and conscious mental states. Information within the preconscious forms an interconnected network, indicated by the many dashed lines. (Modified from Kihlstrom, 1984.)

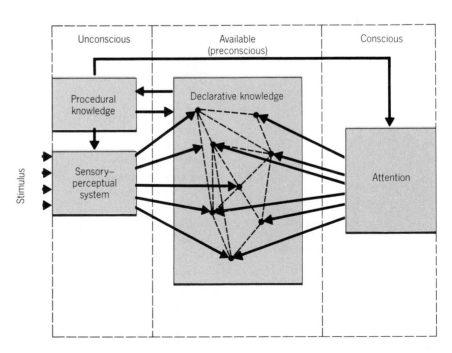

ing from a cup, or (for some people) touch-typing are procedures that are carried out unconsciously. The rules of grammar is another example of unconscious procedural knowledge. Although people use these rules in everyday speech, many are not aware of the grammatical rules that underlie their every utterance and could not state any of the rules of grammar if they tried. Notice that some kinds of procedural knowledge, such as the motor skills of walking or drinking from a cup, can be brought into conscious awareness if people direct their attention to them. But some procedural knowledge leads people to behave in certain ways or to make certain decisions without being aware of why they did so and can*not* be brought into conscious awareness.

THE PRECONSCIOUS   In addition to the conscious and unconscious, many psychologists recognize a mental state called the **preconscious** (see Figure 5-1). Like the unconscious, the preconscious contains information that a person is not presently aware of. But unlike unconscious information, information in the preconscious has been processed and is readily available to consciousness. Information of this kind is called **declarative knowledge** and consists of ideas, propositions, and declarations about the nature of the physical and social world. For example, you might have entertained the proposition that behaving in a certain way—learning psychology, for example, or smiling a lot—will make people like you. These sorts of propositions are preconscious declarative knowledge. Sensory information that is perceived and potentially available to consciousness but which a person does not notice at the moment also can be considered to be preconscious (Bowers, 1984). This kind of sensory information is sometimes referred to as **subliminal perception** (Dixon, 1981). For example, you suddenly realize that your roommate has just said something to you. "What did you say?" you ask, only to discover that you already know.

Preconscious knowledge can be viewed as a network of interconnected information (dashed lines in Figure 5-1). The information remains outside of consciousness until it is activated by some stimulus in the environment (the sensory-perceptual system) or by conscious attention. When the preconscious information is activated enough, it enters consciousness.

The Brain and Consciousness

One of the most intriguing questions to face scientists and philosophers is how consciousness and the brain are related to each other. Many early philosophers believed that the conscious mind is separate and distinct from brain function. For example, the great philosopher Descartes (1596–1650) believed that the mind—which he referred to as the rational soul—resides outside the body and uses the pineal gland of the brain as a point of contact and interaction with the body. Theoretical positions such as these are referred to as mind–brain dualism. Some modern philosophers continue to propose modified theories of a separation, or dualism, between the mind and brain (Puccetti and Dykes, 1978). However, modern research has made it clear that the conscious mind is the result of neural activity and has provided clues about the neural bases of consciousness.

ELECTRICAL STIMULATION One type of research that has shed light on the neural bases of consciousness has been based on the effects of electrical stimulation of the brain in people who were awake. Penfield and colleagues (Penfield and Rasmussen, 1952; Penfield, 1958b) applied electrical stimulation to the brains of patients about to undergo surgery for epilepsy, because the stimulation helped the surgeons to locate abnormal cortical tissue. Because the patients were awake at the time of surgery, they could report the effects of the brain stimulation. They reported that when sensory areas of cortex were stimulated, they had simple conscious sensory experiences such as flashes of light or buzzing sounds. When regions in the temporal lobe were stimulated, more complex experiences were evoked. The patients often recalled dreams or detailed memories of events that had occurred many years before. In some cases the experiences seemed so vivid and real that the patients felt as if they were reliving them. Thus, simply stimulating the cerebral cortex can produce conscious experience and evoke memories.

THE DIVIDED BRAIN Studies of "split-brain" patients also have shed light on the nature of consciousness and its relationship to brain function (Sperry, 1968, 1982, 1984). Recall from Chapter 2 that Sperry and colleagues studied patients whose connections between the two halves of the brain had been surgically cut to control the spread of epileptic seizures. As a result of this surgery, communication between the left and right cerebral cortex was disrupted, and certain sensory and motor functions were confined to each hemisphere (see Figure 5-2). By using a carefully controlled testing situation, it is possible for an investigator to communicate with each side of a patient's brain separately and to inquire about the abilities of each hemisphere (see Figure 5-3). Research of this kind has provided important information about the specialized functions of the two cerebral hemispheres and the brain mechanisms of consciousness.

Experiments of the kind shown in Figure 5-3 indicate that each hemisphere can independently associate information derived from two different sensory modes, such as visual and tactile information. For example, each hemisphere can associate a picture of a pear with the feel of a pear. In addition, each hemisphere can independently carry out cognitive tasks such as simple mathematical problems. Furthermore, when shown pictures of people, either hemisphere can recognize a patient's friends, relatives, and self. Either hemisphere also can identify a patient's own face in photographs, generate appropriate emotional reactions to the pictures, and display a sense of humor. Either hemisphere shows a sense of time and a concern for the future. For instance, each is cognizant of the patient's weekly schedule and the need for planning ahead. In split-brain patients, all of these functions can be carried out separately and in parallel by the two hemispheres. In fact, in certain situations the two hemispheres conflict with each other. As one patient noted (speaking with her dominant left hemisphere), "Sometimes I go to get something with my right hand, the left hand grabs it and stops it— for some reason. It seems to have a mind of its own" (Diamond, 1979).

What, then, can we say about the relationship between the brain and consciousness, given what we know about the functioning of split-brain

FIGURE 5-2 THE SPLIT-BRAIN OPERATION.
The diagram shows certain functions that are confined to each cortical hemisphere when the connections between the two cerebral hemispheres are surgically cut. As a result of this operation, visual information from the right visual field goes principally to visual cortical areas in the left hemisphere, and information from the left visual field goes principally to the right hemisphere when the patient looks straight ahead. Similarly, each hemisphere receives touch information from, and controls the movement of, the opposite hand. The main language centers in the left hemisphere also are separated from the right hemisphere, which has only relatively rudimentary speech comprehension and production. (Modified from Sperry, 1984.)

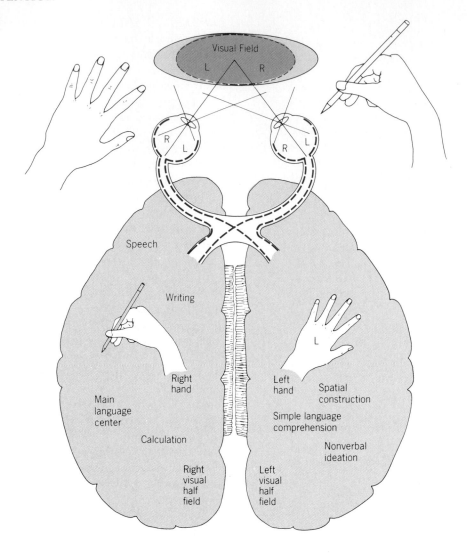

patients? Sperry (1984) has concluded that "These people live with two largely separate left and right domains of inner conscious awareness." In other words, the activity of each hemisphere can produce its own separate conscious experience. This is true both for the verbal hemisphere and for the hemisphere that has only rudimentary language function. The results also suggest that much of consciousness is a function of cortex, because a divided consciousness is produced by disrupting communication between the right and left cortex.

Finally, what does the evidence from split-brain research say about consciousness in those of us whose brains remain integrated wholes? Do we have one conscious mind—or two? Some theorists have taken results of split-brain studies to mean that we *normally* have two conscious selves, one in each hemisphere (e.g., Bogen, 1969, 1986; Puccetti, 1981; Oakley and Eames, 1985). They argue that the surgery simply reveals what is already there. But Sperry (1984) himself concludes, "The conscious mind is normally single and unified, mediated by brain activity that spans and involves both hemispheres."

FIGURE 5-3 TESTING SPLIT-BRAIN PATIENTS.
(a) *The testing situation for studying the mental abilities of each hemisphere in patients who have had the connections between the hemispheres cut. When the patient stares at the spot in the center of the screen, visual stimuli projected onto the screen can be presented separately to each hemisphere (see Figure 5-2). In addition, each hemisphere can touch and pick up objects (that are hidden from view) with the opposite hand. (b) This illustrates the results of a simple experiment carried out with this setup. When a visual stimulus (a pear) is projected in the left visual field (seen by the right hemisphere), the patients say that they did not see it and cannot identify it by touch with the right hand (sensed by the left hemisphere). But the patients correctly identify the pear by touch with the left hand (right hemisphere). Thus the right hemisphere has good perception and comprehension of the test stimuli whereas the left (more verbal) hemisphere is unaware of them. Conversely, when visual stimuli are presented in the right visual field, only the left hemisphere is aware of them. (After Sperry, 1984.)*

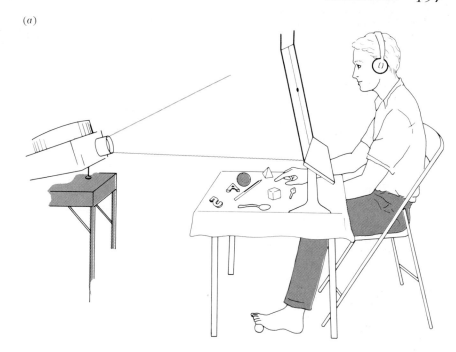

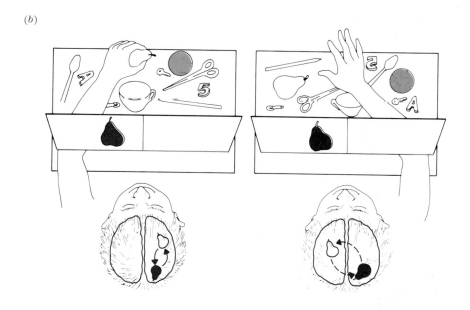

ATTENTION

"Class, I'd like you to direct your attention to this figure." "Wake up, you're not paying attention." "Turn your attention to this paragraph." "That movie just couldn't capture my attention." The way that people talk about attention in everyday speech suggests that it is a mental function located within the conscious mind, not the preconscious or unconscious. Psychologists also suggest that attention is a part of consciousness (see Figure 5-1). **Attention** has two important functions—to bring certain information *into* conscious awareness and to keep other information *out.*

People's external environments and their internal worlds continuously bombard them with a multitude of stimuli and events. At this moment, your radio may be playing, your clothes are touching various parts of your body, someone may walk through your field of vision, all while you are reading the words on this page. You also may have important matters on your mind, perhaps an exam coming up tomorrow or an argument that you had with a friend. All of these stimuli might be overwhelming if it were not for your ability to process some of the stimuli while ignoring others. When you focus your attention on a single task or set of stimuli, you are paying **selective attention.**

Selective Attention

RECEPTOR ORIENTATION One way by which people select certain external stimuli from among many is by physically orienting their sensory systems. They hear a crash or a siren and turn their heads toward it. They

FIGURE 5-1 LOOKING AT OBJECTS.
(a) *The pattern of eye movements recorded when a subject looked at a picture of a face for three minutes.* (b) *The eye movements during 10 minutes of looking at a picture of a man in the woods. Notice that most of the time was spent looking at particular areas of the pictures. Subjects did not haphazardly scan the pictures nor even spend the most time looking at elements with the most brightness contrast or detail. Rather, they spent time looking at features that give the most information about the meaning of the pictures. (From Yarbus, 1967.)*

(a)

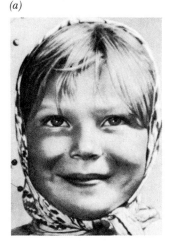

(b)

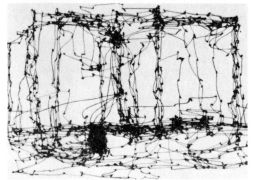

reach out their hands to touch things. If something appears in their peripheral field of vision, they turn their eyes to direct the foveas (the most sensitive part of each retina) at it for further analysis. Even when people look at a specific object or scene, they tend to selectively scan and attend to its most informative aspects (see Figure 5-4).

Although orienting responses are important to selective attention, they do not guarantee attention. Everyone has had the experience of looking at something without really seeing it—orienting to it without attending to it. Attention is more than a simple sensory process of orienting receptors. It is a psychological process.

PSYCHOLOGICAL SELECTION   Some important psychological aspects of selective attention can be illustrated by what is known as the *cocktail party phenomenon.* When you are at a party, there may be a virtual din: music is playing, the doorbell is ringing, ice cubes are clinking, and many small groups of people are standing around talking and laughing. Even though all of these sounds reach your receptors, you are able to selectively attend to sounds that are important to you and to tune out others. For example, you can carry on a conversation with an interesting new acquaintance and ignore other conversations that are going on around you even though the other conversations may be louder. You are engaging in auditory selective attention. You also may pay selective visual attention. In the laboratory, when shown two videotaped visual scenes that are superimposed on each other, subjects can monitor details of events in one scene while they ignore the other scene (Neisser and Becklen, 1975) (see Figure 5-5).

What factors affect our ability to selectively attend in situations such as these? To answer this question experimenters have studied auditory selective attention with a technique called *shadowing* (Cherry, 1953). In this technique the subject receives a separate message in each ear and must attend to and repeat (shadow) one message while ignoring the other (see Figure 5-6). Shadowing experiments have shown that the ability to attend selectively to an auditory message depends in part on a person's ability to distinguish the voice characteristics, such as pitch, intonation, and speed, of one speaker from another. When both messages are spoken by the same person or by people whose voices sound

FIGURE 5-5   STUDYING VISUAL SELECTIVE ATTENTION.
Videotapes were made of people playing a hand-slapping game (a) and a ball-throwing game (b). The two videotapes were then shown simultaneously on a television screen (c). Subjects were required to attend to one of the games and press a key whenever a particular event occurred (for example, whenever the ball was thrown). (After Neisser and Becklen, 1975.)

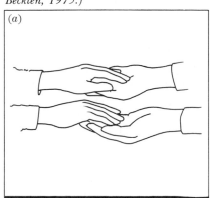

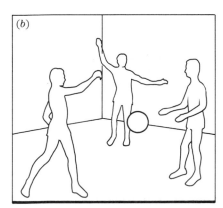

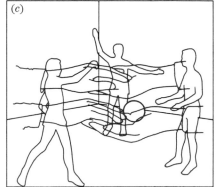

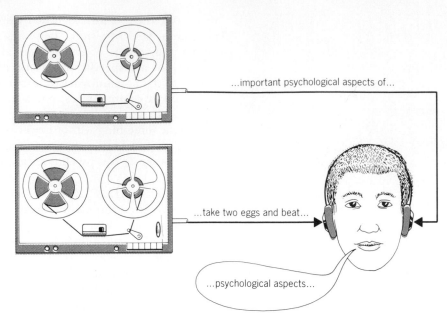

FIGURE 5-6 A SHADOWING EXPERIMENT ON AUDITORY SELECTIVE ATTENTION.
The subject wears headphones so that separate messages can be presented to each ear. For example, the subject may receive a message about psychology in the left ear and a message about cooking in the right. The subject's task in this dichotic listening *situation is to attend to and repeat (shadow) one of the messages while ignoring the other. This experimental situation is like a cocktail party with its many simultaneous conversations, but it has the advantage of being under experimental control.*

alike, the task of tuning out one message and attending to the other becomes much more difficult. When a message is meaningful and coherent grammatically, it also is easier for someone to attend to it in the face of a competing message. In addition, a person's ability to locate the source of the message is extremely important in selective attention. You can demonstrate this at a cocktail party by stepping out of the room. Because you've eliminated cues for localizing the source of conversations, your ability to selectively attend to one conversation out of several is reduced dramatically.

What about the rejected or ignored stimuli, those that a person selects out? In his original shadowing experiments, Cherry (1953) found that subjects could report very little about the ignored message when asked about it later. The subjects recognized that the other message was speech and could tell if there had been a change in voice from male to female. But they could not report the words or meaning of the unattended message and did not even know if the speaker had switched to a foreign language. One interpretation of these findings is that the verbal content of the unattended message was somehow blocked from perceptual processing. Another interpretation is that the meaning of the rejected message may have been perceived but not remembered. To test this hypothesis, Glucksberg and Cowen (1970) interrupted the shadowing with a signal for the subjects to note what had just occurred in the unattended message. The results of this experiment showed that the subjects could recall information in the competing message immediately after it occurred, but that the information was lost in less than five seconds (see Figure 5-7). These results indicate that some unattended material is perceived and briefly remembered but that it is not stored in long-term memory. That you do actually perceive some unattended verbal information can be demonstrated back at the cocktail party. If your name is mentioned in a conversation that you are not attending

FIGURE 5-7 DO PEOPLE REMEMBER INFORMATION IN AN UNATTENDED MESSAGE?
The graph shows results of an experiment to answer this question. The subjects took part in a shadowing experiment such as that illustrated in Figure 5-6. Single digits, from zero to nine, were embedded in the unattended message. In one condition, the subjects were told to report any digit they thought they heard during the messages (spontaneous detection rate). The subjects reported hearing only about 6 percent of the digits that were embedded in the unattended message (open triangle). In another condition, a light was flashed after a digit occurred in the unattended message and the subjects had to think back and remember if any digits had occurred (cued detection rate). The results in this condition are shown by the solid line in the graph. When the light flashed immediately after the digit had occurred in the unattended message, the subjects recalled hearing the digit about 26 percent of the time. However, if the cue was delayed by only 5 seconds after the digit occurred, the subjects' performance was the same as if there had been no cue. They could recall hearing a digit only about 5 percent of the time. (From Glucksberg and Cowen, 1970.)

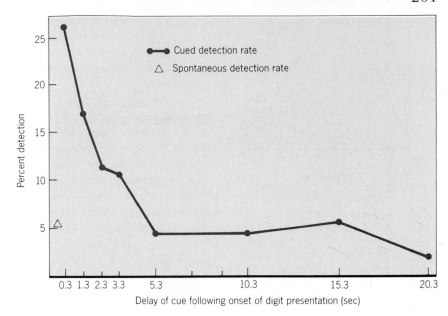

to, you are very likely to hear it and to shift your attention to that conversation.

WHICH STIMULI ARE SELECTED?   In the experiments we have described, the experimenter instructed the subject which stimuli to selectively attend to. In day-to-day life, however, many stimuli compete for attention, and usually no one tells people which to attend to. A variety of factors determine which of these stimuli will be selected. First of all, the nature of stimuli themselves influence the degree of attention they elicit (Broadbent, 1958). For instance, people tend to attend to visual stimuli that have more contrast or intensity than others and to stimuli that are moving rather than stationary. They also tend to attend more to high-pitched than to low-pitched auditory stimuli. Novel or unexpected stimuli also catch people's attention. Radio and television advertisers are aware of these factors and use them to draw people's attention to their messages.

Internal factors, such as people's interests and motives, also determine which stimuli are selected for attention. For example, the delectable chocolate pastry in a baker's window may catch your attention if you are a chocolate lover or if you are hungry, but you may not pay it any attention if you have just had a large meal.

VIGILANCE   A question of practical as well as theoretical importance is how well people can sustain selective attention for long periods of time. Many tasks require sustained attention, or **vigilance**, including looking for defects on an assembly line, watching for blips on a radar screen, monitoring the indicator dials of a nuclear reactor, or driving long distances. At all these tasks, the observer must remain attentive and alert for long periods to the possible occurrence of a signal or target. In one of the first controlled studies of vigilance, Mackworth (1950) had sub-

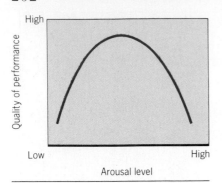

FIGURE 5-8 AROUSAL AND PERFORMANCE.

Performance on some vigilance tasks is best at intermediate levels of arousal and deteriorates if arousal is very low or very high. This deterioration occurs especially if the task is very difficult. (From Coren, Porac, and Ward, 1984.)

jects watch a clock hand move in small steps around a blank clock face. The subjects' task was to detect the occurrence of a double-size step in the movement of the clock hand. After only 30 minutes of paying attention, the subjects' error rate nearly doubled, from 15 percent to over 25 percent.

A variety of factors affect how well people perform on vigilance tasks such as this one (Warm and Jerison, 1984). First, the nature of the target affects vigilance. The more intense the stimulus and the more often it happens, the less people's performance deteriorates over time (Loeb and Binford, 1963; Smith, Warm, and Alluisi, 1966). Second, the rate at which background events occur affects vigilance. The more often there are background events—the single steps of the clock hand—the more subjects' performance falls off (Jerison and Pickett, 1964). Third, the subjects' level of arousal affects their performance. Moderate arousal generally is conducive to the best performance. Very low levels of arousal lead people to perform poorly on sustained attention tasks, an effect that you may have felt if you've ever dozed off during a long drive. In general, as arousal increases, the level of vigilance and, therefore, performance increase (Parasuraman, 1984). But in some situations, especially on difficult tasks, very high levels of arousal can reduce performance (Duffy, 1962) (see Figure 5-8). For example, if you become extremely excited while driving a car or extremely nervous on an exam, you may make more mistakes and perform worse than if you were moderately alert.

Why do people tend to become less vigilant over time on tasks such as these? Is it that people become less sensitive to the target over time, or do people become less willing to report sighting the target? Experiments that have used signal detection methods (see Chapter 3) generally have shown that sensitivity to these stimuli does not change over time; there is little or no fatiguing of the sensory system. Rather, the criterion for responding to the target changes (Swets, 1977; Parasuraman, 1984). The longer a person pays attention to a target, the more cautious he or she becomes about responding to it.

Divided Attention

We have said that during selective attention, people retain very little information about stimuli that are ignored. What if the task is changed and people are asked to attend to two or more stimuli at the same time? Experiments indicate that people are very poor at such tasks of **divided attention** if the stimuli are in the same sensory system—if the stimuli are all visual or all auditory, for example. Subjects can recall a string of six numbers (for example, 7, 3, 4, 2, 1, 5) with 93 percent accuracy if the numbers are presented at the same time to both ears because they can pay *selective* attention to either ear. But their accuracy drops to 20 percent if at the same time they hear half the numbers in one ear—7,3,4 in the left ear—they hear half the numbers in the other ear—2,1,5 in the right ear—and have to keep track of the order of the numbers in their two ears (Broadbent, 1954). The decrease in accuracy arises because the subjects must *divide* their attention between their two ears.

You've probably had the problem of dividing your attention between two auditory messages. If you've ever been talking on the telephone and someone in the room started talking to you, you probably found it extremely difficult to divide your attention and process information from both messages.

But there are times when people *can* divide their attention fairly well. One is when the information is in different sensory systems. For example, people can divide their attention between auditory and visual stimuli more effectively than between two auditory stimuli (Treisman and Davis, 1973). They may have little difficulty watching (but not listening to) a television show while they talk on the telephone.

Another time when people can divide their attention is when they have had so much practice that what they are doing becomes *automatic* (Schneider, Dumais, and Shiffrin, 1984). For example, if you are a practiced driver you can drive a car, chew gum, fiddle with the radio, and carry on a conversation at the same time. But when you were first learning to drive, you probably found it difficult to drive and talk to someone at the same time. As a task becomes more automatic, it requires less mental effort for a person to carry it out, and the person therefore can more readily divide attention between that task and other mental activities. In fact, it can be argued that highly practiced, automatic activities no longer require conscious attention. The highly practiced task becomes part of the unconscious store of procedural knowledge.

Theories of Attention

If people were open to every sight, sound, touch, and other stimuli in the environment, they would not be able to function. They would be so distracted and distractible that carrying on a conversation, getting dressed in the morning, and finding their way to school or work would be impossible. But at what point in mental processing do people select out certain information as irrelevant to their central task? How does the selection happen?

EARLY SELECTION (FILTER) THEORY   One early theory of how attention works proposed that irrelevant information is filtered out early in sensory processing (Broadbent, 1958). According to this theory, many bits of information strike a person's peripheral sensory systems and this information is retained only very briefly. An early filter selects certain of this information for further perceptual processing and analysis (see Figure 5-9a). Information not allowed through the filter is lost. The theory also suggests that the attentional filter samples different kinds of information from time to time, making it possible for people to switch processing among them.

A problem with this theory is that, as we have said, some information that people do not selectively attend to does get through—the sound of your name in a background conversation at the cocktail party. This objection can be met if we think of the filter as reducing, or *attenuating,* rather than completely blocking out incoming information (Treisman,

FIGURE 5-9 SIMPLIFIED FLOW DIAGRAMS OF THREE MAJOR THEORIES OF ATTENTION.
(a) *Early selection (filter) theory.*
(b) *Late selection theory. Both of these theories assume that there is an active attentional mechanism that filters or selects information to be processed. They differ in terms of whether the selection is assumed to occur early or late in the flow of information processing.*
(c) *Resource allocation (capacity) theory assumes that attention and information processing are limited by the mental capacity available and not by an active filter. Incoming information will be processed to the extent that mental capacity is not already allocated to carrying out other tasks. Furthermore, the amount of capacity allocated to each task (for example, tasks 1, 2, and 3 in the diagram) depends on the amount of mental effort that each demands.*

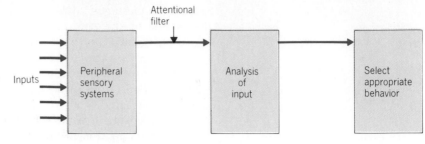

(*a*)   Early Selection (Filter) Theory

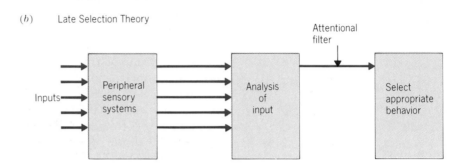

(*b*)   Late Selection Theory

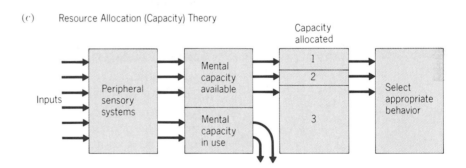

(*c*)   Resource Allocation (Capacity) Theory

1964). Then, if the information is important or salient enough, it is allowed through the filter for further processing.

LATE SELECTION THEORY   Another theory, the late selection theory, suggests that a substantial amount of information processing goes on before filtering or selection takes place (Norman, 1968; see Figure 5-9*b*). According to this theory, all stimuli that strike the peripheral sensory systems are monitored and processed to some extent. This processing goes on unconsciously, and the information is not stored permanently in memory. Then the attentional filter selects certain of this information for further conscious processing and storage in long-term memory.

RESOURCE ALLOCATION (CAPACITY) THEORY   Both early and late selection theories of attention assume that some mechanism actively filters or selects incoming information. However, some theorists reject the notion that there is an active selection mechanism in attention (Neisser, 1976). They suggest that people have only a limited mental capacity that can be applied to various tasks and that people's attentional abilities are determined by the requirements of the tasks and by how these resources are allocated (Kahneman, 1973) (see Figure 5-9c). Thus, if you are an expert chess player in a game with a novice, you probably can perform several other tasks at the same time, perhaps listen to music and think about a movie you just saw. You can do this because all of these tasks require relatively little mental effort from you—you have enough mental capacity for all of them. But if you are playing chess with an expert, you must devote more mental effort, or capacity, to the game. You must allocate much more of your attentional resources to this task and stop thinking about other things. According to this theory, people's information-processing capacities are relatively fixed. People may be able temporarily to increase this capacity by exerting more mental effort. However, for the most part, the number of tasks they can attend to at the same time will depend on how much mental effort (what proportion of their finite capacity) each task requires.

These theories of how people select and distribute attention are not mutually exclusive. It may be that some incoming information is filtered out early, just beyond the peripheral sensory systems, and other information is filtered out later, after some initial perceptual processing. Then people might allocate their finite mental resources among the information that has cleared both filters as well as among internally generated tasks that arise from memory and thinking, depending on the mental effort that each task requires.

DAILY RHYTHMS

Nature and Causes

Once people have directed their attention to incoming information or to performing some task, how well they perform depends on a variety of factors—including the time of day. You may have noticed that you are more alert and perform many tasks better at certain times of the day than at others. For instance, you may study better during the afternoon than early in the morning. What takes you half an hour to learn at 9 A.M. takes you an hour to learn at 9 P.M. Variations such as these are a result of rhythmic changes in many human biological functions over the course of the day. Indeed, the vast majority of bodily functions—from chemicals in the blood, to body temperature, to wakefulness—show marked daily rhythms. Some examples are shown in Figure 5-10. Before looking more closely at how daily rhythms affect behavior, let's examine the nature of daily rhythms themselves.

What causes daily biological and behavioral rhythms? One possibility is that they are simply passive responses to changes in the environment, such as sunrise and sunset or temperature variations over the day. However, most of the rhythms persist under constant environmental conditions (Aschoff, 1969; Wever, 1979). Experiments have been con-

FIGURE 5-10 DAILY RHYTHMS.
These are examples of some bodily functions that show marked rhythmic changes over the course of each day.
(a) Rhythms in sleep and waking. A on the scale is waking, and stages 1–4 represent increasingly deep sleep.
(b) Body temperature rhythms. Body temperature is highest during the day and lowest just before morning awakening. (c) Rhythmic changes in urinary potassium excretion, which reflects certain aspects of body chemistry.
(d) Levels of certain hormones in the blood (in this case, plasma cortisol level) also show daily rhythms. Shading in the figure shows changes in environmental dark and light over a period of 36 hours (0 is midnight; 12 is noon). Notice that all of the bodily rhythms are synchronized with each other and with the light–dark cycle. (From Groos, 1983.)

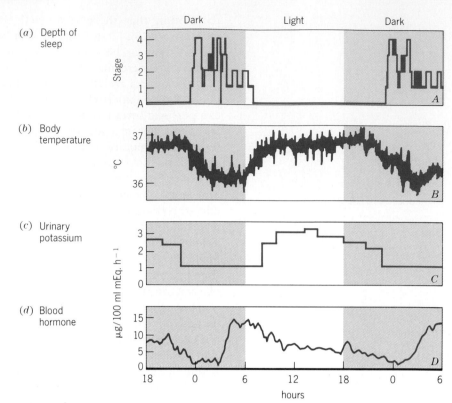

ducted in which volunteers spent many days and nights in a cave or underground bunker that gave them no environmental cues about when it was day or night. The ambient temperature was kept constant, the volunteers controlled the lighting, and they decided on their own when to eat and sleep. Despite the absence of environmental cues, the regular daily behavioral and biological rhythms continue—they *free run*—on their own (see Figure 5-11).

Although the volunteers' biological rhythms continued, two interesting changes took place. First, the rhythms did not keep to exactly a 24-hour cycle. For most people, natural free-running rhythms are slightly longer than 24 hours, they range between 24.5 and 25.5 hours. Second, the normal synchrony between different rhythms broke down. For instance, the body temperature rhythm normally was at its lowest point near the end of sleep and started to rise just before awakening. However, during free run, the relationship between body temperature and sleep–wakefulness cycles shifted. These results show that many human biological rhythms are generated from within the body—they are *endogenous*—and that the endogenous rhythms have a complete cycle of about 25 hours. Such endogenous rhythms are referred to as **circadian rhythms** (from the Latin *circa,* "about," and *diem,* "day") because their cycle is about a day long.

When volunteers who have been isolated from environmental cues return to a normal light–dark cycle, their body's rhythms return to a 24-hour cycle and become synchronized again (see Figure 5-11). This return

FIGURE 5-11   EFFECTS OF THE ENVIRONMENT ON DAILY RHYTHMS.

This is a day-to-day plot of an individual's sleep–wakefulness and body-temperature rhythms before, during, and after isolation from environmental cues. The solid lines indicate sleep, the dotted lines indicate wakefulness, and the triangles indicate the low point of body temperature during successive 24-hour periods. The upper nine periods show the rhythms during nine days in a normal environment (days 4 and 5 occurred on the weekend). Notice that the low point of the temperature cycle occurs near the end of the sleep period. From days 10 to 34, the individual was placed in an isolated environment that lacked daily variations in light–dark, temperature, noise, and so on. The rhythms continued in this situation, but they free ran in a cycle somewhat longer than 24 hours. As a result, the time at which the individual went to sleep became later each day. In addition, the cycle lengths for sleep–wakefulness and body temperature were slightly different, so that the low point of the temperature cycle shifted to the beginning of the sleep period. During the last 11 days, the subject reentered a natural environment. Both rhythms returned to a 24-hour cycle and again became synchronized. (From Dement, 1974.)

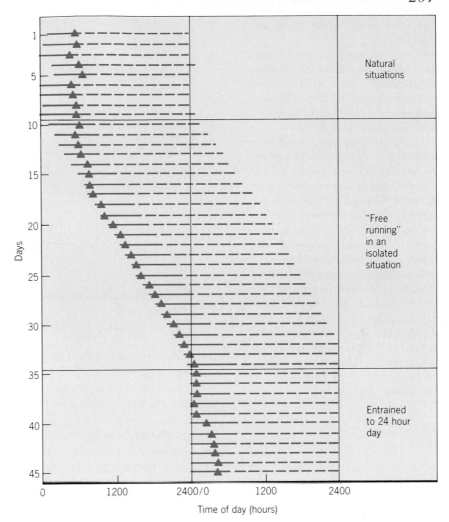

demonstrates another important point: although the circadian rhythms are endogenous, their cycle can be set *(entrained)* by environmental time cues such as temperature variations and the light–dark cycle, which are caused by the earth's rotation.

Circadian rhythms and their entrainment by the environment are highly adaptive mechanisms. They make it possible for a wide range of bodily functions to be synchronized with each other and with the daily alternation between daylight and darkness. This allows humans and other animals to respond efficiently to predictable rhythmic changes in the environment (Groos, 1983).

Internal Clocks

Circadian rhythms imply that people have an internal clock that sets our biological time and keeps us on schedule. In fact, we probably have at least two such internal clocks (Wever, 1975), an inference scientists have drawn because certain rhythms, such as sleep–wakefulness and body

FIGURE 5-12   CLOCKS IN THE BRAIN.

Results of an experiment demonstrating that the suprachiasmatic nucleus of the hypothalamus contains a clock for timing circadian rhythms. (a) These records show results of electrical recordings made from neurons in the suprachiasmatic nucleus of rats housed in complete darkness. Even though the nucleus was surgically isolated from the rest of the brain, the neural activity of the nucleus showed rhythmic increases and decreases over the course of each day. (b) Another region of the brain, the reticular formation, also normally shows rhythmic circadian activity; however, this was abolished when connections from the suprachiasmatic nucleus were cut. (c) Likewise, disconnecting the suprachiasmatic nucleus from the rest of the brain abolished normal circadian rhythms in the rat's motor activity. The horizontal axis shows hours over 5 successive days. (From Turek, 1985; after Inouye, unpublished.)

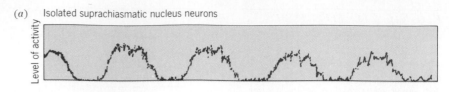

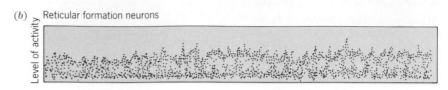

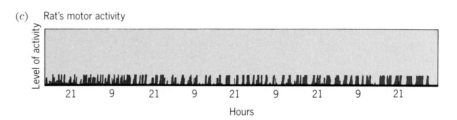

temperature, have different cycle times when they are allowed to free run (see Figure 5-11).

At least one of the clocks has been identified in research on laboratory animals (Jacklet, 1985; Turek, 1985). It resides within a group of neurons, called the suprachiasmatic nucleus, which is part of the hypothalamus at the base of the brain (see Chapter 2 for a description of the hypothalamus). Electrical recordings from the suprachiasmatic nucleus of rats housed in complete darkness have shown circadian rhythms in the activity of the neurons. These rhythms persisted even after the nucleus was surgically isolated from the rest of the brain (see Figure 5-12). This surgical isolation of the nucleus also stopped circadian activity of neurons in many other parts of the brain and stopped the circadian rhythm of many kinds of behavior, including sleep–wakefulness, motor activity, and feeding.

Researchers do not yet know how neurons in the suprachiasmatic nucleus generate circadian rhythms even in the absence of environmental stimulation (Johnson and Hastings, 1986). But they do know that these neurons have connections to many other areas of the brain, which allow them to regulate circadian variations in behavior. In addition, because the suprachiasmatic nucleus is part of the hypothalamus, which controls the release of hormones into the bloodstream, this neural clock is in a position to affect many basic physiological functions.

Circadian Rhythms in Human Performance

As we suggested earlier, circadian rhythms affect people's abilities to perform many tasks, including complex cognitive skills. Some kinds of tasks are done most efficiently at one time of the day, and others are done best at other times (Folkard and Monk, 1983). For example, people usually are best able to remember information they have just read in the

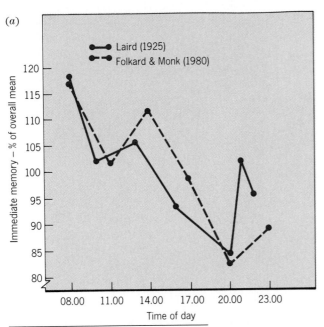

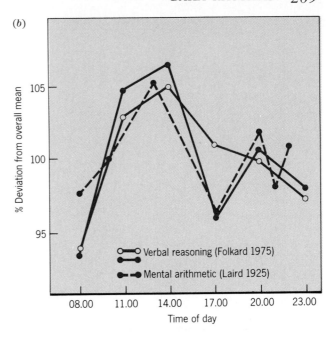

*FIGURE 5-13   DAILY RHYTHMS
AND PERFORMANCE.*

*People have circadian rhythms for
performing cognitive tasks, and different
tasks are performed best at different
times of the day. (a) This shows the
results of two different studies of
immediate memory of information read
in a passage of prose. (From Folkard
and Monk, 1980.) (b) This shows the
results of three experiments on
performance of verbal reasoning and
mental arithmetic tasks. (From Folkard,
1982.)*

morning, and the ability steadily declines over the course of the day. In
contrast, people usually perform best on mental arithmetic and verbal
reasoning tasks at about midday (see Figure 5-13).

People differ in their performance rhythms over the course of the day
(Kerkhof, 1985). You probably know people who are alert and ready to
go early in the morning—"larks"—and others who don't hit their stride
until the evening—"owls." By using a questionnaire that asked people
about the times of day they preferred to do various activities and felt
more or less alert, researchers could classify about 45 percent of adults
as moderate to extreme evening or morning types (Horne, Brass, and
Pettitt, 1980). Controlled studies of performance show that morning
types in fact perform best on some, though not all, tasks before noon,
and evening types perform best after noon (see Figure 5-14a). Morning
types and evening types also differ in their biological rhythms. In general, the biological rhythms peak an hour or two earlier for morning
types than for evening types (Kerkhof, 1985) (see Figure 5-14b). Thus the
difference in biological rhythms is more subtle than some of the performance differences between the two types of people (compare a and b
in Figure 5-14).

Because circadian rhythms affect the quality of people's performance
over the course of the day and night, disruptions of circadian rhythms
can interfere with performance. Disruptions of circadian rhythms is a
problem for workers who frequently change between day and night
shifts—some factory workers, doctors, nurses, airline crews, and so on
(Moore-Ede, Czeisler, and Richardson, 1983). Jet lag, which can bother
long-distance airline passengers, also is caused by disruptions of circadian rhythms. For example, when you fly from the United States to
Europe, there is a 6-hour or longer shift in time zones and the light–dark
cycle. As a result, your endogenous clock may say that it is 6 A.M. when

(a)

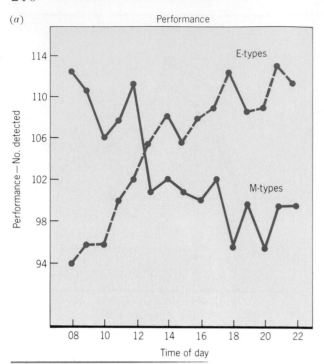

(b)

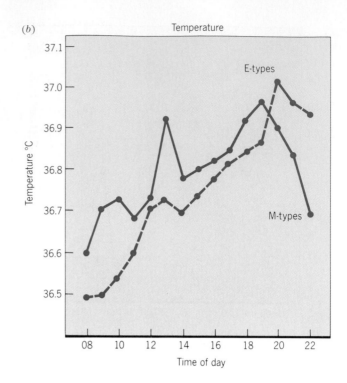

FIGURE 5-14 EARLY BIRDS AND NIGHT OWLS.

(a) *This shows the differences between morning types (M-types) and evening types (E-types) on a detection task. The subjects were required to detect errors in playing cards that passed them on a conveyor belt. Subjects who were classified as moderate to extreme morning types on the basis of responses to a questionnaire made fewer errors in the morning than in the evening. Subjects classified as moderate to extreme evening types showed the opposite pattern. (b) Morning and evening types also differed in their body-temperature circadian rhythms; the temperature rhythm was shallower and peaked earlier for the morning types. However, the differences in performance rhythms were much larger than the differences in body-temperature rhythms. (From Folkard and Monk, 1983; after Horne, Brass, and Pettitt, 1980.)*

the environment around you and the local clocks say that it is noon. Consequently, your performance on many tasks suffers, and it may be hard for you to adjust your appetite for sleep and meals to the new time zone. These problems come from a disruption in circadian rhythm rather than loss of sleep (Webb, Agnew, and Williams, 1971). It may take a week or more for the circadian rhythm to be entrained to the new light–dark cycle and for performance to return to normal. These adjustments take several days longer for west-to-east flights, which delay the circadian rhythm relative to time of day (your body clock says it is noon, but local clocks say it is late in the afternoon), than for east-to-west flights, which advance the circadian rhythm (your body clock says it is noon, but local clocks say it is early morning) (Klein, Wegman, and Hunt, 1972; Wever, 1979).

The most influential theory of why performance varies over the course of the day is the *arousal theory.* According to this theory, a circadian rhythm in physiological arousal level produces variations in performance (Kleitman, 1963; Colquhoun, 1971). For most people, arousal is thought to be lowest at about midnight, to increase fairly rapidly until about 7:00 A.M., and then to increase more gradually to a peak at around 5:00 P.M. For these people, tasks best done at relatively low levels of arousal are performed best early in the day and tasks best done at high levels of arousal are performed best later. Presumably, extreme evening and morning types have their highest levels of arousal at different times of the day. The arousal theory can account for much (though not all) of the data concerning circadian rhythms in performance (Folkard and Monk, 1983).

SLEEP AND DREAMING

So far in this chapter we have been talking about consciousness, attention, and some of the factors that affect them. But, of course, people do not spend their days in an unbroken state of conscious, alert, and wakeful attention. People spend a large part of each day unconscious—asleep. What is more, during sleep people frequently enter into an altered state of consciousness—dreaming. We spend about a third of our lives in these two mental states, almost completely out of touch with the external environment—the brain, our senses, and our cognitive process turned away from our surroundings. Let's look at what is going on during these states and consider why we sleep and dream.

The Nature of Sleep

Before the 1950s, there had been relatively little scientific study of either sleep or dreaming, primarily because of the practical problems involved in identifying and studying objectively these mental states. But the development of equipment to record brain waves, the **electroencephalogram**, or **EEG**, changed all that (see Figure 5-15). EEG recordings revealed that sleep consists of a number of distinct stages (Dement and Kleitman, 1957a) and provided an objective way to measure them.

STAGES OF SLEEP In a night of normal sleep, you actually proceed through a kind of journey from light to deep sleep, from dreams to dreamlessness. The characteristic journey is revealed by a pattern of brain waves such as appear in Figure 5-16. This figure shows what the EEG looks like during various stages of sleep. When first you are lying in bed, relaxed but still awake, EEG recordings show low-voltage brain-wave activity with many rhythmic fluctuations at a frequency of about 10 cycles per second. These oscillations are called alpha waves and are

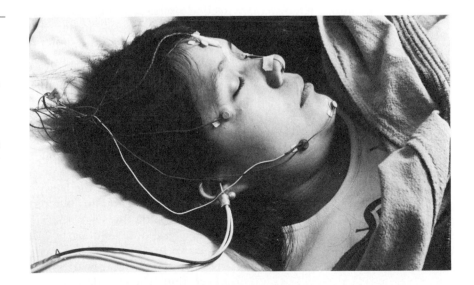

FIGURE 5-15 RECORDING BRAIN WAVES.
Wires have been attached to this woman's scalp to allow scientists to record her brain waves (EEG) while she is asleep. The EEG represents the electrical activity of many cells in the brain and is recorded through large electrodes such as these wires. The wires near the woman's eyes are for recording eye movements, and the wires on her chin give a measure of facial muscle activity.

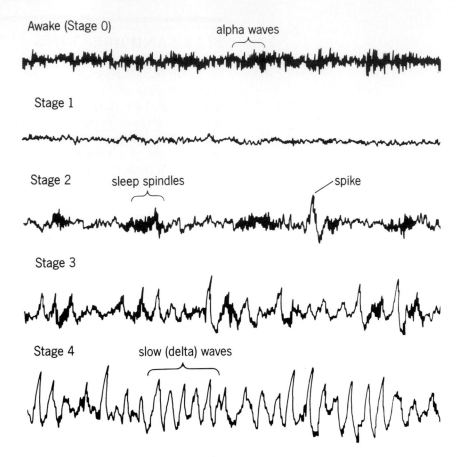

**FIGURE 5-16   EEG
RECORDINGS DURING DIFFERENT
STAGES OF SLEEP.**
*The top tracing shows the EEG during
relaxed wakefulness, often referred to as
stage 0 sleep. Each of stages 1–4,
increasingly deep sleep, is characterized
by unique EEG patterns and wave
forms. (From Dement, 1974.)*

characteristic of quiet, relaxed wakefulness. When you first fall asleep, the EEG shows your brain waves becoming flatter and containing a mixture of frequencies. Now you are in *stage 1* sleep. After a few minutes in stage 1, you enter *stage 2* sleep. Your EEG now is more irregular. It contains occasional spikes of activity and periodic 12 to 14 cycles per second oscillations called sleep spindles. In *stage 3*, essentially a transition between stages 2 and 4, your EEG is even more irregular. Finally, deep in *stage 4* sleep, your EEG has slow, rhythmic, high-voltage waves. These waves oscillate at a rate of between $\frac{1}{2}$ to 2 cycles per second and are referred to as delta waves. Because of these slow waves in the EEG, stage 4 sleep often is referred to as *slow-wave sleep.* Stages 1 to 4 represent increasingly deep sleep. It is easier to rouse a sleeper from stage 1 or 2 sleep than from stage 3 or 4 sleep.

During all of these four stages of sleep, the sleeper looks quiet and restful. The body is quite still and moves generally only to change positions. The eyes show only a few slow movements. Breathing is regular and deep, and the heart beats regularly and slowly. But people also go through another quite different and extremely interesting stage of sleep. During this stage, the EEG has the appearance of stage 1 sleep, but sleepers look anything but restful. Body and facial muscles twitch and move restlessly; sleepers may smile or grimace. Breathing becomes irregular and shallow, heart rate increases. Males nearly invariably have an erection. The eyes dart back and forth under closed eyelids. Because

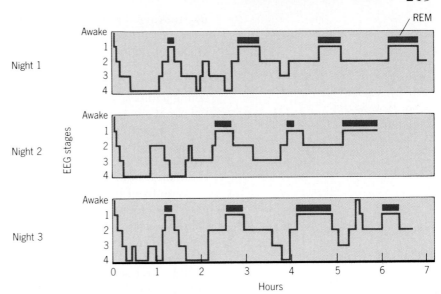

of these characteristic eye movements, this stage of sleep is called **rapid eye movement (REM)** sleep. By distinction, stages 1 to 4 usually are collectively called **non-REM** sleep.

Needless to say, researchers wondered what was going on during all the activity of REM sleep. To find out, they awakened sleepers in the middle of an episode of REM sleep and asked "What was going through your mind just before I woke you?" About 80 percent of the time the sleepers reported that they had been *dreaming*. When awakened and asked the same question during non-REM sleep stages, subjects reported that they had been dreaming only about 20 percent of the time (Dement and Kleitman, 1957b; Berger, 1969). Thus REM sleep is much more often associated with dreaming than non-REM sleep. The dreams that occur during REM sleep also tend to be vivid visual affairs with an hallucinatory quality, whereas those during non-REM sleep tend to lack sensory imagery and seem closer to wakeful thinking.

A TYPICAL NIGHT   During the course of a typical night's sleep, people cycle through the different stages of sleep several times (see Figure 5-17). Overall, most of our deep, stage 4 sleep occurs during the first third of the night. Periods of REM sleep occur 4 or 5 times during the night at about 90-minute intervals. During the second half of the night, the REM periods become longer, and they are separated by periods of lighter, stage 2 sleep. On average, people of college age spend nearly half the night in stage 2 sleep, 15 percent in stage 4 sleep, and about 25 percent of each night in REM sleep (Webb, 1975).

The Need for Sleep

Is sleep necessary, and if so, how much? If you go without sleep for long, you may feel tired and groggy, but will you suffer any more serious ill effects? The answers to these questions are critical for understanding *why* organisms sleep. Scientists have attempted to answer these questions by studying differences in sleep among individuals, changes in sleep patterns with age, the patterns of sleep among different species, and the effects of depriving people of sleep.

INDIVIDUAL DIFFERENCES   Although we can generalize and say that young adults sleep an average of 7.5 hours each night, there is substantial variability from person to person. For example, in one study of 4000 entering college students, 7 percent reported sleeping less than 6.5 hours a night, and 3 percent reported sleeping more than 9.5 hours (Webb, 1975). Some individuals have been studied who consistently sleep less than 3 hours a night, but they are very unusual.

Aside from the length of time that they sleep, no consistent psychological or physiological differences have been found between people who naturally sleep for very short or long stretches each night (Webb, 1979). For instance, there are no significant differences in personality measures—such as aggressive versus passive, introverted versus extroverted—between people who normally sleep 5.5 hours or less and people who sleep 9.5 hours or more each night. There also are no consistent differences in sleep time between males and females nor between people of high or low intelligence. In short, no one knows why some people sleep very little while others sleep much longer.

CHANGES WITH AGE   As any parent knows, newborn infants sleep more during every 24-hour period than do adults. The average newborn sleeps 16 hours a day, although the sleep time for young infants shows wide individual variations (Parmelee, Wenner, and Schulz, 1964). The timing of sleep periods also differs for infants and adults. Adults have nearly all of their sleep in a single nightly session, whereas newborns tend to sleep in 3- to 4-hour periods distributed over the day and night. About half of a newborn infant's sleep is spent in REM sleep. Thus, newborns have about 8 hours of REM sleep each day compared to about 2 hours for adults. As children age, their total amount of sleep each day decreases. As shown in Figure 5-18, this decrease comes at the expense of time spent in REM sleep; there is relatively little change in the amount of time in non-REM sleep from birth to early adolescence (Roffwarg, Muzio, and Dement, 1966).

From early adulthood on, there is only a small decrease in the total amount of time that people sleep. Individuals 60 years old or older sleep an average of 6.5 hours each night, only about an hour less than young adults. But older people do show changes in the pattern of their sleep (Webb, 1975). For instance, the number of awakenings during the night increases dramatically, from about one a night in young adults to about six a night in older people. In addition, older people have less deep, stage 4 sleep and more light, stage 1 sleep. Together, these changes account for the complaint of many elderly people that they do not sleep as well as they used to.

PHYLOGENETIC DIFFERENCES   How does the sleep of animals compare to that of humans? Studies of phylogenetic (interspecies) differences in sleep also have provided scientists with information about the

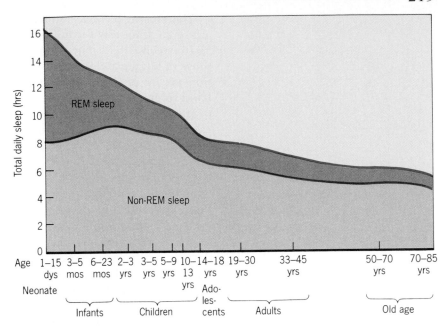

FIGURE 5-18   SLEEP OVER THE LIFE SPAN.

The amount of time spent in REM and non-REM sleep changes from infancy to old age. Until 10–13 years of age, time spent in non-REM sleep changes little, but time spent in REM sleep decreases dramatically. From early adolescence on, there is a small but steady decrease in the amount of time spent in both REM and non-REM sleep. (After Roffwarg, Muzio, and Dement, 1966.)

need for and nature of sleep. Such studies indicate that there is an enormous variability in sleep characteristics among different species (Campbell and Tobler, 1984; Zepelin and Rechtschaffen, 1974).

Some animals do not appear to sleep at all: for example, bullfrogs, tortoises, alligators, and the Dall porpoise. But it is possible that the usual behavioral and brain-wave measures of sleep are not appropriate with these animals. In any case, these animals are the exceptions. Virtually all of the 170 species that have been studied do show signs of sleep, although there is substantial variability in animals' total amount of sleep, even among mammals. For instance, horses, cows, and elephants sleep only 2 to 4 hours a day, whereas bats and opossums sleep 19 to 20 hours a day. Furthermore, some animals sleep in brief sessions that are spread out over the day and night, whereas others sleep in a single period at night. The percentage of time spent in REM sleep also varies substantially among species. At one extreme is a mammal, the echidna, that lacks REM sleep altogether. At the other extreme are elephants, which spend more than 45 percent of their sleep time in the REM stage.

If you have ever watched your pet dog sleep, you have probably witnessed periods of REM sleep. Just as in humans, a dog's legs and face twitch and the eyes dart rapidly back and forth under the closed eyelids. Is Fido dreaming? Because animals cannot talk to us, there is no way to find out directly. But because all of their other behavior is similar to that of humans during dreaming, it seems reasonable to infer that dogs and other nonhuman mammals dream.

SLEEP DEPRIVATION   After you have stayed up all night, you've felt the fatigue and need for sleep the next day. But how real is the need? What happens if you stay awake continuously for very long periods of time?

There have been a number of studies of people who have stayed awake continuously for more than 200 hours—about 8.5 days! (Naitoh, 1976; Webb, 1975). The major effect of this herculean feat is a pervasive sense of fatigue and sleepiness. Beyond that, the effects of sleep deprivation are surprisingly mild. Sleep-deprived people may develop a fine hand tremor, difficulty in focusing their eyes, double vision, a drooping of the eyelids, and an increased sensitivity to pain. However, neurological tests of reflexes, sensation, and body orientation remain normal. In addition, a variety of other physiological and biochemical measures of bodily function also remain relatively normal. Circadian variations in body temperature and other functions also continue despite the lack of sleep. Thus, although prolonged sleep deprivation does have some effects on bodily functions, the effects certainly are not debilitating (Horne, 1978, 1985).

What about psychological and behavioral changes? After about three days without sleep, a person may feel generally apathetic, irritable, inattentive, confused, and "spacy." But these effects may just reflect a very strong inclination to go to sleep, not psychopathology (Webb, 1975). For instance, as the sleep-deprived individual drifts off into borderline sleep, he or she loses touch with the environment and becomes inattentive and a bit confused. There have been reports of individuals who have had vivid hallucinations or emotional changes (such as a feeling that people are plotting against them) during prolonged sleep deprivation. However, these individuals may have been predisposed to some emotional breakdown in the face of any stressful situation, not just a lack of sleep. In general, there is very little evidence that lack of sleep by itself causes any real psychological disorder or pathology.

How deeply sleep deprivation affects a person's performance of cognitive tasks depends on the nature of the tasks. Sleep-deprived people show the greatest deterioration on tasks that are simple, dull, or prolonged. For example, their ability to detect a signal or target in a vigilance task declines markedly. Offering to pay tired people for performing well can stave off the effects of sleep deprivation for awhile, but after two nights without sleep, even highly motivated subjects make fewer correct detections than when they are well rested (Horne and Pettitt, 1985). Thus, tasks such as watching monitoring devices (such as a radar screen or the dials of a nuclear reactor) or driving long distances are very susceptible to effects of sleep deprivation.

Sleep-deprived people show less deterioration in performance of tasks that are inherently interesting and varied or that involve perceptual and motor skills (for example, working in a hospital emergency room) (Wilkinson, 1965; Horne, 1985). Furthermore, although their performance tends to get slower, it is not less accurate. For instance, after more than 50 hours without sleep, subjects carry out tests of logical reasoning at about 40 percent of the normal rate but show no increase in the number of errors committed (Angus and Heslegrave, 1985). So, should you ever put in an "all-nighter" or two to study for final exams? All in all, you may finish the exams more slowly but, as long as the exam questions are varied and interesting, you should not make more errors than if you had gotten enough sleep.

What causes sleep-deprived people to perform poorly? Webb (1975) has suggested that they perform poorly because they lapse into periods when they do not pay attention or do not want to continue. This suggestion would explain why performance is worst on long and tedious tasks that require sustained attention and why the major effect on inherently interesting tasks is just a slowing of performance. Thus, performance may fall off simply because of sleepiness rather than a deterioration in cognitive ability.

When people go without sleep, of course, they also go without periods of physical rest. Are effects of sleep deprivation due to *energy* loss—lack of physical rest—or *sleep* loss? To answer this question, researchers had subjects either rest quietly or engage in regular sessions of physical exercise during two days of sleep deprivation (Webb and Agnew, 1973; Angus, Heslegrave, and Myles, 1985). They found that performance deficits were similar for subjects in the two conditions. In addition, subjects who had rested got just as sleepy and slept just as much when they were allowed to as those who had exercised. These findings corroborate the common observation that people who are confined to bed 24 hours a day sleep normal amounts (Ryback and Lewis, 1971). Simple physical rest does not substitute for sleep.

Not surprisingly, people rapidly fall asleep at the end of a long period of sleep deprivation. But they do not make up all of their hours of lost sleep. One high school student stayed awake for 264 hours as part of a science project and as an attempt to break the world record for sleeplessness (Dement, 1974). At the end of the 11 days without sleep, the boy slept for 15 hours and he awoke essentially recovered. He next fell asleep about 24 hours later and slept a normal 8 hours. Observations such as this suggest that only part of each night's sleep is obligatory and must be made up if lost; the remainder may not be absolutely necessary (Horne, 1985).

Why People Sleep

It is clear from the studies we have just described that there is no simple answer to the question "How much sleep does a person need?" The need for and pattern of sleep differ from person to person and during the course of a person's life. There also are substantial differences in sleep among different animal species. And although people deprived of sleep for long periods get very sleepy, they do not suffer any major ill effects. Any theory of the function of sleep must be able to account for these observations.

The intuitive, commonsense theory is that the function of sleep is to provide *restoration* from fatigue. According to this theory, as the body uses energy, it wears down over the course of the day, and sleep allows it to recover (e.g., Hyman, 1979; Adam, 1980). A difficulty with this theory is that, as we have shown, there is little relation between physical exertion and how much a person sleeps. In addition, deprivation studies indicate that people can do quite well for long periods of time without the benefits of whatever restorative function sleep might serve. Some theorists have recognized these limitations of the restoration theory and have modified it by suggesting that sleep restores brain, especially cerebral cortex, biochemistry and function rather than the general physical function of the body (Horne, 1979, 1985).

An alternative to the restoration theory is that the function of sleep is to *keep organisms inactive* during times of the day when their behavior would be less effective in their environment or when that environment might prove dangerous (Webb, 1975). Proponents of this theory believe that when and how much members of a particular species sleep evolved as an adaptive, innate response that increases the survival of the species in its particular ecological niche. Thus members of species are awake during times when they can most effectively obtain food, and they sleep or remain inactive during times when they are in greatest danger from predators. In addition, the amount and pattern of sleep within a species depends on the safety of its sleeping place. Thus, grazing animals (such as cattle) sleep but little and intermittently because they have no safe sleeping place in the open fields. Furthermore, they sleep during either the day or night because the grasses they eat are available at any time. Humans evolved a single, long period of sleep at night because they had safe places to sleep, such as caves, and sleeping at night forced them to stay out of harm's way when nocturnal predators were about. Furthermore, humans forage and hunt for food best during daylight, so they sleep primarily at night.

These are but two of several theories of why we sleep. At present, no single theory of sleep has gained general acceptance. What can be said is that sleep is a compelling biological function that has evolved for an essential purpose but precisely what that is remains a mystery.

Sleep Disorders

Almost everyone has trouble sleeping on occasion, and up to 15 percent of adults have frequent and persistent complaints about the quality and amount of sleep they get (Weitzman, 1981). The most common complaint is **insomnia**: a difficulty in getting to sleep or in staying asleep (Dement, Seidel, and Carskadon, 1984). Many people who complain of insomnia actually sleep for the normal number of hours but their sleep falls short of their expectations. For instance, natural short sleepers may expect to sleep 8 hours each night "like everyone else." When they awaken after only 5 or 6 hours of sleep, they think that something is wrong with them. The best cure for this type of insomnia is to teach people that there are individual differences in normal sleep time.

Some people have insomnia because they take their waking concerns to bed with them. You've probably had the experience of occasionally lying awake worrying about a boy- or girlfriend, an upcoming exam, or a critically important decision about your life. This kind of sleeplessness is referred to as a *situational insomnia,* and it usually goes away with the situation that causes it (Webb, 1975). Other causes of insomnia may be more long-lasting, however. For example, some people have a chronic inability to fall asleep early enough at night to get enough sleep for their work or school schedule (Weitzman, 1981). They may not be able to fall asleep until 4 or 5 A.M., regardless of when they go to bed, and then they have to wake up at 7 or 8 A.M. to go to work or class! It is thought that these people have an unusual circadian sleep–wakefulness rhythm. They may be extreme "owls," the evening-type people described earlier.

Some psychological disorders, such as depression, are associated with insomnia (Cartwright, 1978; Weitzman, 1981). People who are severely depressed often have little or no stage 4 sleep, awaken many times during the night, and awaken early in the morning. In some cases, these sleep disturbances are a result of depression. In other cases, the sleep disturbances cause the depression. When the latter occurs, the depression is treated by adjusting the timing of sleep within the individual's circadian cycle.

A different kind of sleep disorder is **sleep apnea**, a breathing impairment that occurs during sleep (Weitzman, 1981). An apnea is a normal interruption in breathing, and everyone has apneas. But people who suffer from a problem with sleep apnea do not automatically start breathing again unless they wake themselves up. In severe cases, breathing may stop for a minute or two, hundreds of times each night, and each time, the person wakes up, takes a few breaths, and then goes back to sleep. People with sleep apnea may not be aware of their disturbed sleep and may not complain of insomnia. But because they wake up so many times, they go through the day severely sleepy and often fall asleep during the day. One cause of sleep apnea is an obstruction of the air passages in the throat. In these cases, the person almost always snores loudly for a series of breaths, then gasps and snorts, and then stops breathing. In other cases, however, sleep apnea occurs because areas of the brain that control breathing do not function normally during sleep. There is some evidence that Sudden Infant Death Syndrome, in which infants die in their sleep for no apparent reason, is due to sleep apnea (Kelly and Shannon, 1979).

A relatively rare sleep disorder is the **narcolepsy–cataplexy syndrome**, in which a person suddenly falls asleep at inappropriate times. People with this disorder have brief periods of muscle weakness or paralysis (cataplexy) and may collapse if they are standing. The cataplexy often is associated with a sudden onset of sleep (narcolepsy). The narcoleptic sleep begins immediately with REM sleep and dreaming. In fact, it is believed that this disorder is caused by abnormal timing of REM sleep (Weitzman, 1981).

In other kinds of sleep disorders, sleeping and waking themselves are normal, but people exhibit certain undesirable behaviors as they sleep. These forms of behavior are referred to as **parasomnia** (associated with sleep) disorders. Several are fairly common in children and adolescents but are rare in adults. For instance, about 15 percent of all children and adolescents have one or more episodes of *sleepwalking*. The child may sit up in bed or actually get up and walk around, open and close doors, walk up stairs, get dressed, and so forth, and then return to bed or go to sleep somewhere else. *Bed-wetting* is another relatively common parasomnia disorder, occurring at least once in about 30 percent of children between 4 and 14 years old. Bed-wetting has been ascribed to a variety of causes, including psychological and neurological problems, delayed maturation, poor toilet training, and urinary disorders. A third parasomnia disorder is *night terrors,* which occur in up to 4 percent of children (Carlson, White, and Turkat, 1982). When they have night terrors, children suddenly sit up in bed and let out a loud, high-pitched scream. Their pupils are dilated, their breathing and heart-rate are rapid, and they may be sweating. They seem agitated and panicky. Night terrors are not the same as bad dreams or nightmares. The children are not dreaming and, when they awaken, recall little of the episode.

Sleepwalking, bed-wetting, and night terrors have a number of features in common (Weitzman, 1981). None of them is associated with dreams; they all occur during non-REM sleep, usually in stages 3 and 4 during the first third of the night. In each case, it is difficult to wake the child during the disturbance, and afterward the child has little memory of what occurred. Perhaps most comforting for parents, all of these disorders tend to disappear on their own as the child gets older. Only in the rare instances in which the disorders persist into late adolescence is there real cause for concern.

Dreams

THE NATURE OF DREAMS   You probably can recall snippets of your dreams. But even people who never remember their dreams or who absolutely insist that they *never* dream do, in fact, dream regularly each night. Dreaming is the mental activity of sleepers, most of it, as we have seen, occurring during REM sleep. Studies indicate that sleepers may have two or more dreams during each REM sleep period (Snyder, 1970). Because people have three or more nightly REM periods (see Figure 5-17), they have six or more dreams each night. But by the time people awaken in the morning, their memories of the past night's dreams tend to be very poor. People remember best the last dream of the night, and their memories of interesting and exciting dreams are better than their memories of humdrum ones (Goodenough, 1978).

Individual dreams are not simply instantaneous mental images; they may continue for 15 minutes or more (Dement and Kleitman, 1957b). Most dreams consist of coherent stories that take place in familiar settings and are populated by real people, almost always including the dreamer (Snyder, 1970). Bizarre creatures and monsters are rare. Dreams about failure and misfortune occur about three times more often than dreams about success and good fortune. However, strong emotional feelings are uncommon. Overt sexual activity also is rare and occurs in only about 1 percent of the dreams studied. In short, the subject matter of most dreams is fairly mundane. Of course, physical laws of time and space do not apply in the dream world. In dreams, people can instantaneously change settings and move forward and backward in time. The suspension of laws of physical reality undoubtedly contributes to the common belief that dreams are fantastic and surrealistic.

What determines the content of dreams? To some extent, external events during sleep can influence dream content. For example, one study showed that a spray of cold water in the dreamer's face sometimes was incorporated into the imagery of an ongoing dream (Dement and Wolpert, 1958). But a much more potent determinant of dream content is common daily events. After reviewing the literature on the dream content of people with various personality characteristics and of people from different cultures, Webb and Cartwright (1978) concluded that people's dreams reflect their waking emotional concerns and styles.

EFFECTS OF DEPRIVATION   Do people need to dream? In a classic study of this question, Dement (1960) deprived subjects of most of their dreams by awakening them each time they entered a REM sleep period. The subjects were kept awake for a few minutes and then allowed to go back to sleep until they began another REM sleep period. Dement found that as the experiment progressed over several nights, he had to awaken the subjects more and more frequently to prevent REM sleep. When the subjects finally were allowed a night of uninterrupted sleep, they spent up to twice as much time as normal in REM sleep, a phenomenon referred to as *REM rebound.* To control for any effects of simple sleep loss or interruption, Dement later awakened the same subjects the same number of times as before but this time only during non-REM periods. The second series of interruptions did not produce a significant REM rebound. These results suggest that people need REM sleep, and because dreaming is closely associated with REM sleep, presumably people also need to dream.

What are the psychological effects of REM-sleep deprivation? In his original study, Dement (1960) reported that subjects were anxious, irritable, and had trouble concentrating after several nights of REM deprivation. But later studies (Dement, 1974) of volunteers deprived of REM sleep for up to 16 consecutive nights showed that they suffered no serious psychological disruption. Many other studies have led to the same conclusion (Webb, 1975; Cartwright, 1978). Loss of REM sleep also has little effect on a person's cognitive abilities or performance on tasks when awake (Webb, 1975; Vogel, 1975). For example, a person can remember material learned before the REM deprivation and can learn new material normally after REM deprivation. The most marked effect of REM deprivation is a somewhat greater variability in performance. Perhaps we should not be too surprised at the relatively mild effects of REM deprivation. After all, as we said earlier, people can be deprived of *all* sleep for many days without major effects. Nevertheless, it does seem strange that people seem to need REM sleep and dreaming but suffer few consequences if they are deprived of them.

THE MEANING AND FUNCTION OF DREAMS   Many theorists have tried to explain the function of dreams. Perhaps the best known is the psychoanalytic theory of Sigmund Freud (1900/1955). According to Freud, dreams allow people to express and fulfill certain unconscious wishes. Freud believed that unacceptable thoughts are repressed—pushed into the unconscious mind—and that these repressed thoughts form the underlying, or *latent content,* of dreams. Through a process that Freud called "dream work," the latent content is transformed into an acceptable symbolic form, called the *manifest content* of the dream. Thus the people and events in a person's dream—the manifest content—are the safe expression of repressed, unconscious thoughts. Freud also believed that by analyzing the symbolic content of people's dreams, an analyst might indirectly glimpse the underlying unconscious concerns.

Freud's theory has been revised and elaborated over the years, but the idea that dreams provide a safe expression or working through of a person's psychological concerns has remained (Miller, 1975; Fosshage, 1983).

Other theorists have approached dreams from the perspective of information processing and learning. For example, it has been suggested that REM sleep improves the long-term memory storage of material learned during the day (McGrath and Cohen, 1978; Smith, 1985). Still other theorists noted the large amounts of REM sleep that infants go through and have suggested that the REM state and dreams are necessary activators for central nervous system development (Roffwarg, Muzio, and Dement, 1966). Other theorists, noting the greater physiological activity of REM sleep compared to non-REM sleep, suggest that REM sleep restores the balance of activity in the nervous system or maintains the levels of certain chemicals in the brain (Stern and Margane, 1974).

No one yet knows for certain which of these theories is correct. Although REM sleep and dreaming seem to have a compelling biological function, no one yet has unraveled the mystery of that function.

HYPNOSIS

Modern hypnosis began in the late 1700s with Franz Anton Mesmer, who unwittingly developed a way of hypnotizing people while treating patients with various disorders. Mesmer's treatment—called mesmerism—had some success, perhaps because his patients' disorders were psychologically generated. Mesmer believed that the mesmerism came from a flow of "animal magnetism" from himself to the patient. In 1784 this claim was discredited (by a commission that included Benjamin Franklin), and hypnosis fell into disrepute for many years. But careful investigations by modern scientists restored the study of hypnosis to respectability.

Under **hypnosis**, a person experiences changes in perception, memory, and behavior in response to suggestions made by the hypnotist. The hypnotist usually induces hypnosis by asking a person to concentrate on some object while relaxing and staying open to suggestions. Hypnosis requires a person's cooperation; no one can be hypnotized unwillingly. What is more, not everyone can be hypnotized. About 10 percent of adults are very susceptible to hypnosis and about 10 percent cannot be hypnotized at all. Others fall somewhere between these two extremes (Hilgard, 1965).

Hypnotic Phenomena

Many people tend to misunderstand what it is like to be hypnotized. Although hypnotized people usually are relaxed, they are not sleeping. The EEG of a hypnotized person resembles the normal waking pattern more than the pattern during sleep (Tebecis, Provins, Farnbach, and

Pentony, 1975). In addition, people can exercise vigorously while they are hypnotized (Banyai and Hilgard, 1976). They do not turn into automata that respond irresistibly to suggestions made by the hypnotist, and they cannot be made to perform antisocial or self-destructive acts that they would not normally carry out (Orne, 1972). But hypnotic suggestion can change people's perceptions and behavior in ways that they report to be real and compelling (Bowers, 1976).

EFFECTS ON PERCEPTION   While under hypnosis, people may have *positive hallucinations,* in which they perceive objects and events that are not really there. For example, they might see someone sitting in a chair that actually is empty. They also may have *negative hallucinations,* in which they do not perceive something that they normally would. In one study, volunteers told under hypnosis that they were deaf had clear changes in tests of their auditory thresholds (Crawford, MacDonald, and Hilgard, 1979). In addition, when hypnotized people were told that they could not see a visual stimulus, brain activity produced by that stimulus actually decreased (Spiegel, Cutcomb, Ren, and Pribram, 1985).

Perhaps the best studied perceptual change during hypnosis is analgesia—relief from pain. Before chemical anesthetics were introduced in the 1800s, hypnosis was widely used to control pain during surgery. Its effectiveness since has been confirmed in modern laboratory studies (Hilgard and Hilgard, 1983). One study even showed that hypnosis was more effective in alleviating experimentally induced pain than morphine, a tranquilizer (Valium), aspirin, acupuncture, or a placebo (Stern, Brown, Ulett, and Sletten, 1977).

Studies of the perceptual effects of hypnosis have uncovered an extremely interesting phenomenon called the **hidden observer** effect. For example, although hypnotized subjects may *report* feeling no pain from a stimulus that is normally painful, they may show normal physiological responses to the pain stimulus. In addition, when an experimenter asks the subjects if some "hidden part of you" feels pain, they may report feeling pain (see Figure 5-19). The hypnotized person acts as if there were an internal "hidden observer" who is aware of external reality (Knox, Morgan, and Hilgard, 1974).

EFFECTS ON MEMORY   Sometimes people are given a suggestion during hypnosis so that when the hypnosis ends, they forget what happened while they were hypnotized, a phenomenon called **posthypnotic amnesia**. But on a prearranged cue, these people can once again remember clearly what happened during the hypnosis (Kihlstrom and Evans, 1979). Because the information later can be remembered, it no doubt was stored all along in the subjects' memories during hypnosis. The hypnotic suggestion seems to have interfered with their ability to retrieve the information from memory (Kihlstrom, 1985).

You've probably read newspaper stories about people who were hypnotized into remembering details of crimes that they had witnessed but later could not recall. Recently, the popular media have given a great deal of attention to cases in which people's memories seem to have been

FIGURE 5-19   HYPNOSIS, PAIN, AND THE "HIDDEN OBSERVER." The graphs show results of an experiment on hypnotic analgesia (pain reduction) in eight highly hypnotizable subjects. The subjects placed one hand and forearm in ice water, which rapidly produces severe pain. The upper curve shows the subjects' ratings of the degree of pain over a 45-second period. The subjects were then hypnotized and told that they would not feel pain. As shown by the bottom curve, the overt, consciously reported pain was greatly reduced by the hypnotic suggestion. At the same time, the subjects were asked if there was any other part of them that could feel the pain at a covert level. This pain was reported by "automatic key pressing" with the other hand, a response that seems to occur without the awareness of the subject. As shown by the middle curve, the covert key pressing reported a level of pain that was closer to that in normal waking. One interpretation of this result is that there is a covert "hidden observer" within each subject who feels much more pain than that reported verbally. (From Hilgard and Hilgard, 1983.)

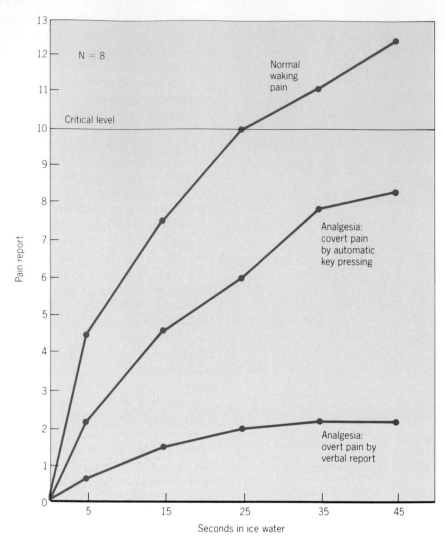

improved by hypnosis. This phenomenon, **hypermnesia**, is the subject of much current research and debate (see Box 5-1).

POSTHYPNOTIC SUGGESTION   As you've seen, there are several significant connections between the states of hypnosis and normal attention and awareness. Suggestions given during hypnosis are another such connection, for they may carry over to the normal waking state. For example, in one study a hypnotist suggested that every time in the following two days that the subjects heard the word "experiment," their hands would rise and touch their foreheads. After the hypnosis was ended, highly hypnotizable subjects did touch their foreheads about 70 percent of the time when they heard the word "experiment" (Orne, Sheehan, and Evans, 1968). People under hypnotic suggestion often carry out such behaviors without being aware that they are doing anything unusual and say that the behavior just seemed irresistible.

BOX 5-1
IS MEMORY
IMPROVED DURING
HYPNOSIS?

In 1976, 26 California schoolchildren and their bus driver were abducted at gunpoint and sealed inside an underground tomb. After his escape, the driver could not remember details about his captors, even though he had tried to memorize the license plates of their two vans. Under hypnosis, however, the driver suddenly could remember two license plate numbers, one of which was correct but for a single digit. His information led to the capture of the kidnappers.

This rewarding story and others like it suggest that hypnosis can improve memory. But most laboratory studies have failed to provide evidence for memory improvement under hypnosis (see Box Table 1). Instead, they show that the memory of unhypnotized control subjects tested in the same way is just as good as the memory of subjects tested under hypnosis.

Critics of the laboratory studies say that they differ in too many ways from real-life situations and therefore are irrelevant to the usefulness of hypnosis to solve crimes. For instance, they point out that in the laboratory, people are asked to remember lists of words or short prose passages whereas after a crime, people must remember a dynamic event that has sights and sounds. What is more, the consequences of remembering (or forgetting) a crime are far greater than the consequences of remembering a set of words in the laboratory. Perhaps factors such as these make hypnosis more effective for improving recall in real-life situations than in the laboratory. But recent research indicates that, even for very realistic situations, there is little or no difference in recall between hypnotized and awake subjects (Smith, 1983).

How, then, do we account for reports such as that of the kidnapped bus driver? One explanation is that hypnosis is invariably used after repeated attempts to remember in the waking state have failed, and repeated testing is known to improve recall whether or not the subjects are hypnotized (see Box Table 1 and Chapter 8). Another explanation is that subjects are more willing to guess when they are hypnotized than when they are not, and their freer guessing results in more correct answers. But freer guessing also results in more *errors* (Dywan and Bowers, 1983). Perhaps that was why one of the license plates that the bus driver remembered under hypnosis was totally wrong.

All in all, should hypnosis be used to help witnesses to remember? Yes and no. The research shows that material recalled under hypnosis may give police new leads to follow. But because it also may be full of errors, it should not be used as actual testimony in trials (Orne, 1979; Smith, 1983). Further, repeated questioning and encouragement of witnesses' guessing may help people to remember just as much information without hypnosis as with it (Smith, 1983).

BOX TABLE 1   MEMORY SCORES AND HYPNOSIS

Order	n	Condition	
		Hypnotized	*Waking*
High-susceptible group			
Hypnosis first	15	9.20	**9.80**
Waking first	15	**10.00**	8.60
Low-susceptible group			
Hypnosis first	11	7.64	**7.91**
Waking first	11	**9.09**	8.64
Overall mean scores		8.98	8.76

Results of an experiment to assess the effects of hypnosis on memory. Subjects were given an article about chemistry to read. Two weeks later, recall was tested by asking the subjects 33 short-answer questions. Two groups of subjects were used: one had high susceptibility to hypnosis and the other had low susceptibility. Half the subjects in each group were tested first while awake and then again while under hypnosis; the other half were tested in the reverse order. For both susceptible and unsusceptible subjects, there was no significant difference in memory scores between the waking and hypnotized conditions. However, notice that for both groups, memory was slightly better on the second test (bolded numbers in the table), regardless of whether it was given in the waking or hypnotized condition. (From Cooper and London, 1973.)

Theories of Hypnotic Behavior

Psychologists have offered two types of theories to account for the fascinating behavior of people who have been hypnotized (see McCabe, Collins, and Burns, 1978, 1979). One type of theory suggests that hypnotized people enter an *altered state of consciousness*. There are many ideas about the nature of the altered state. One prominent theorist suggests that hypnosis represents a *dissociation* of parallel streams of mental activity (Hilgard, 1977). During hypnosis one stream of mental activity governs thought and behavior separately from the normal stream of conscious awareness and voluntary control. Evidence for this idea has come from phenomena such as hypnotic pain relief, the hidden observer, and posthypnotic amnesia and suggestibility, in which there seems to be a division in a person's consciousness and little communication between parallel streams of perceptual and cognitive mental activity (Kihlstrom, 1984, 1985).

In contrast, *social psychological theories* suggest that hypnotized people act as they do because they are motivated to conform to the social demands of the situation. The hypnotized subject may be like the stage actor who convincingly takes on the role of the character he is playing. In the process, he succeeds in convincing himself as well as the audience (the hypnotist) that he is hypnotized, just as an actor temporarily and convincingly "becomes" the character he is playing (Coe and Sarbin, 1977; Spanos, 1982a, 1982b). Another way to look at it is that the hypnotized subject is a receptive member of the audience who becomes engrossed enough in the play (the hypnosis situation) to vividly imagine the effects suggested by the hypnotist (Barber, 1979). Social psychological theorists are *not* suggesting that hypnotized subjects are necessarily faking. Rather, they maintain that the interaction between hypnotist and subject is like any other social interaction and that responsive subjects have the attitudes, motivation, expectations, cognitive, and imaginative processes that lead them to behave appropriately during hypnosis. Evidence for this view has come from studies in which people who simply had been told to act *as if* they had been hypnotized and to follow the suggestions of a hypnotist were found to behave indistinguishably from hypnotized people.

A full account of hypnosis probably requires both sets of theories, the social psychological and the altered state of consciousness. It seems unlikely that all instances of hypnosis are simply social role-playing or responsiveness. In many instances hypnotized subjects behave quite differently from those who are acting *as if* hypnotized. The subjective experience of the two groups also seems to differ. People acting as if hypnotized experience themselves as trying to make the suggested behavior happen; hypnotized people experience the behavior as somehow happening to them involuntarily (Bowers, 1976). Although it is quite possible and even likely that social-psychological factors influence how hypnotized subjects act, many responses, particularly of highly hypnotizable subjects, are best understood in terms of changes in consciousness (Kihlstrom, 1985). Thus, both theories may be correct for different subjects and under different circumstances.

MEDITATION

Meditation is a practice that people engage in to alter consciousness by restricting their awareness to a single process. The meditator attempts to turn off perception of the external world and to achieve a "clear" state of awareness or a "unity" and "oneness" with the world (Naranjo and Ornstein, 1971; Delmonte and Kenny, 1985). Meditation is practiced according to many different techniques in many different cultures. Perhaps the most common type of meditation involves concentrating or focusing awareness on a single object, a practice called *concentrative meditation* (see Figure 5-20). Even in concentrative meditation, many techniques have evolved. For instance, Zen meditation involves concentration on one's own breathing. Some forms of Yoga meditation involve concentration on a visual object (the mandala), or a special sound (the mantra). One mantra well known in the West is the "Hare Krishna," which is chanted by meditating group members. Transcendental Meditation, which has become popular in the United States, uses a silent mantra that is the secret possession of the meditator. Sufi meditators make use of repetitive movements; the best known are the Mevlevi—whirling dervishes—of Turkey. In all of these meditative techniques, people restrict their attention and turn off their awareness of the external environment (Naranjo and Ornstein, 1971).

In the West, many people have turned to meditation to reduce arousal, anxiety, and stress. Meditation has been used to treat a variety of stress-related disorders, including various psychiatric disorders, high blood pressure, asthma, drug and alcohol abuse, insomnia, and stuttering (Holmes, 1984). Meditation also has been used to reduce stress on the job and to improve productivity (Delmonte, 1984). Clinical meditation techniques use the basic principles of meditation but have no religious trappings (Carrington, 1978; Benson, 1975).

Despite the claimed benefits, carefully controlled experiments cast doubt on meditation's special effectiveness at lowering general arousal, anxiety, or responses to stress. In any discussion of the effectiveness of meditation, it has to be recognized that assessing the effects of meditation creates many problems for researchers (Holmes, 1984). One problem is that meditators may be a self-selected group. If experienced meditators are found to have less stress or anxiety than nonmeditators, it may be simply that people who are less susceptible to stress or anxiety have chosen to practice meditation. Another problem is that meditators who are found to have less stress during meditation may be showing the benefits of meditation—or of simply sitting quietly and resting. Studies that report a reduction of arousal and stress during meditation generally have failed to take these problems in method into account (see Holmes, 1984).

But many studies of meditation have avoided these pitfalls. Most of these studies have examined the effects of Transcendental Meditation or similar methods and generally indicate that meditation can reduce measures of physiological arousal. However, virtually all of the studies indicate that meditation is no more effective than simple resting (Shapiro,

FIGURE 5-20   A PERSON PRACTICING CONCENTRATIVE MEDITATION.

Most meditators sit alone or in a group, isolated from sources of stimulation in the external environment. The individual sits in the lotus position (shown here) to reduce bodily movements and keep them out of awareness. The back is kept stiff to decrease drowsiness. In most forms of Yoga and Zen, the meditator focuses attention continuously on a meditation "object," such as a visual object, a sound, or his or her own breathing.

1982; Holmes, 1984, 1985a,b; Delmonte, 1985b). For instance, meditating subjects and resting subjects have similar heart rate, galvanic skin response, breathing rate, oxygen consumption, blood pressure, and muscle activity. Subjects' reports about their states of anxiety also are similar for groups who used meditation or other methods to rest or relax (Delmonte, 1985a).

Other well-controlled experiments have examined whether people who practice meditation could better control their response to a threatening or stressful situation than people who did not practice meditation. The results again showed no significant differences between the two groups (Holmes, 1984). In short, although meditation may well be effective in reducing anxiety, arousal, and responses to stress, there is no evidence that it is any better than simply sitting and resting.

What about other psychological effects of meditation? People who practice meditation report a general feeling of well-being and an altered awareness (Forem, 1973; Shapiro, 1980, 1985). There is no reason to doubt such feelings. But because people may report similar feelings after intense physical exercise, after a fine meal, or after sex, it is difficult to know whether meditation really produces a unique state of consciousness and, if it does, whether it is unique in doing so.

CONSCIOUSNESS AND DRUGS

TABLE 5-1
CLASSIFICATION OF COMMONLY ABUSED DRUGS ACCORDING TO THEIR PRINCIPAL EFFECTS

Sedative-Depressants
  Alcohol
  Barbiturates

Narcotic Analgesics
  Opioids:
    Opium
    Morphine
    Heroin
    Hydromorphone (Dilaudid)

Stimulants
  Amphetamines
  Caffeine
  Cocaine
  Nicotine

Hallucinogens
  Lysergic acid diethylamide (LSD)
  Marijuana
  Mescaline
  Peyote
  Phencyclidine (PCP)

Virtually any chemical substance can affect your consciousness. You become unconscious if you breathe air, a gaseous chemical, too rapidly, and you can become comatose and die if you drink too much water. But we are interested here in the way that certain chemicals affect consciousness so that they are attractive to people and lead people to abuse them. Otherwise sane people take the most extraordinary risks to get these chemicals. Every day thousands of people lose their jobs, their families, their health, and their lives because of their overwhelming desire to consume these alluring chemicals. What is it about drugs such as alcohol, opiates, and nicotine that makes them so seductive?

Technically, **drugs of abuse** are natural or synthetic chemicals that are habitually used by significant numbers of people for nonmedical purposes. Drugs of abuse interfere with a user's physical or psychological health, job, or social status. Table 5-1 classifies some of the more commonly abused drugs according to the most prominent effects of each drug. But this simple classification is only a part of the picture of the effects of particular drugs.

Drugs also can be classified according to whether they produce **physical dependence**, a physiological condition produced by prolonged exposure to particular drugs. Physical dependence cannot be observed directly; it is *inferred* when a **withdrawal syndrome** occurs after a drug is discontinued. For instance, if a 170-pound man drinks 30 ounces of 80-proof alcohol a day, at the end of 3 to 4 weeks he will be physically dependent on alcohol (Isbell, Fraser, Wikler, Belleville, and Eisenman, 1955). His physical dependence would be inferred from the way the man acts whenever his drinking slows and the level of alcohol in his blood falls. If the man is physically dependent, he shows signs of withdrawal. The main signs of withdrawal from alcohol are tremulousness ("the shakes"), restlessness, agitation, weakness, auditory hallucinations, disorientation, convulsions, visual hallucinations, and (rarely) death. These withdrawal signs and symptoms (a *symptom* is what the patient tells the doctor about, a *sign* is what the doctor can see) are listed in the order in which they usually appear. In mild cases of withdrawal, a person experiences only the first few symptoms.

Withdrawal from opiates such as heroin and morphine includes flu-like symptoms—a runny nose, fatigue, sweating, chills, depression, and psychological discomfort (Mansky, 1978). Two symptoms of opiate withdrawal have given us expressions now in everyday use. The chills of opiate withdrawal make the hairs on the body stand up—and the skin looks like a plucked turkey's ("goose bumps"). The expression that has come from this, used by opiate addicts who quit opiates suddenly, is to say that they are quitting "cold turkey." Because another symptom is jerking arm and leg muscles, addicts say that they are "kicking" their habit.

Drugs vary greatly in the degree, if any, of physical dependence they induce. Some drugs, like opiates, alcohol, and barbiturates, inevitably produce marked physical dependence in heavy users, as indicated by serious withdrawal syndromes. Other drugs, like nicotine and caffeine, are intermediate and produce milder withdrawal syndromes. Hallucinogens tend not to produce physical dependence at all. But physical dependence is not the same as **psychological dependence**, which refers to a drug user's obsessive concern with getting and using a (nonmedical) drug. Psychological dependence can exist independent of physical dependence, and vice versa.

Effects of Drugs on Consciousness

Drugs affect consciousness in a variety of ways. First, they have **acute effects**: immediate, direct effects on physiological systems. For example, alcohol drinkers have trouble pronouncing words clearly and keeping their balance, morphine reduces sensitivity to pain, and LSD and mescaline produce hallucinations. Virtually all drugs produce some acute effects. (We discuss the acute effects of alcohol, opiates, and nicotine in more detail in the following section.) Second, drugs that produce physical dependence affect consciousness during withdrawal. For instance, nicotine withdrawal produces irritability, caffeine withdrawal produces headaches, and alcohol withdrawal produces visual hallucinations (see Figure 5-21).

Drugs also affect consciousness through their chronic effects on the body, some of which are toxic, or poisonous. The leading cause of malignant brain tumors is cigarette smoking. But alcohol abuse produces more chronic diseases that affect consciousness. One condition produced by years of heavy drinking is **Korsakoff's psychosis**. In this disease, the alcohol-damaged brain does not function properly, and people lose the ability to store new information in long-term memory.

*FIGURE 5-21 ALCOHOL
WITHDRAWAL.*
*One of the symptoms of chronic
alcoholism and alcohol withdrawal is
delirium tremens, a state in which the
individual becomes confused and has
hallucinations.*

Because Korsakoff's psychosis often is incurable, afflicted people may go through life unable to remember anything that happened after the disease began.

Drugs also affect consciousness through Pavlovian conditioning—learning that occurs when two stimuli are presented together. Every time a smoker has a cigarette or a drinker has a glass of beer, the drug exerts a variety of physiological effects. After repeated use of the drug—the average pack-a-day smoker takes 50,000 to 70,000 puffs a year!—the drug user associates the drug's physical effects with all sorts of environmental stimuli that are present. The cigarette smoker pairs the drug, nicotine, with the sight, taste, and smell of cigarette smoke, with seeing other smokers lighting up, with talking on the phone, with sipping a cocktail—in short, with any stimuli or activities associated with smoking. Eventually, any of these stimuli can change the user's feelings and behavior, independent of the drug itself. So strong are these paired associations that when a formerly heavy drug user is exposed to a stimulus associated with the earlier drug use, the stimulus makes the person crave the drug. Thus, ex-smokers crave a cigarette when they see "their brand," alcoholics crave a drink when they see a bottle of liquor or beer, and heroin users crave heroin when they get near where they bought drugs in the past (O'Brien, 1976) (see Table 5-2).

Acute Effects of Drugs of Abuse

A drug does not have *an* effect. Rather, a drug has many effects, and these vary with the size of the drug dose, and with the user's expectations, previous drug experience, psychological and physical condition, and the situation in which the drug is taken. Here we look more closely at the acute effects of two drugs that are widely used: alcohol and nicotine, and we discuss the effects of opiates because they have been more thoroughly researched than most other drugs.

ALCOHOL Alcohol is a good example of how remarkably different are the effects of a single drug at different dosages. At low doses, alcohol

TABLE 5-2 STIMULI THAT PRODUCE FEELINGS OF CRAVING OR WITHDRAWAL IN DRUG-FREE HEROIN ADDICTS

1. Being offered a "taste" by an old "copping" buddy (fellow drug user).
2. Seeing a friend in the act of "shooting up."
3. Talking about drugs on "copping corner."
4. Standing on copping corner.
5. Seeing a successful pusher—making lots of money, envy.
6. Socially awkward situations: job interview, family criticism, feeling like an outsider at a party.
7. Talking about drugs in group therapy.
8. Seeing a few bags of heroin.
9. Seeing someone's "works" (drug paraphernalia).
10. Seeing pictures of drugs and "works."
11. Seeing antidrug poster with "good veins" and somebody "shooting up."

Note: Stimuli or events that elicited feelings of craving for heroin and heroin withdrawal reactions (tearing, runny nose, nausea) in heroin addicts interviewed by O'Brien (1976). The reactions were elicited months after the addict had last had heroin. They appear to be conditioned responses elicited by events previously associated with drug effects or with withdrawal.

tends to increase physical activity, enhance behavioral performance, and improve mood (Pohorecky, 1977). But at high doses, alcohol acts as a sedative and depressant of performance and mood (Mello and Mendelson, 1978).

One of the most powerful effects of high doses of alcohol is disruption of the storage of new material in long-term memory. People who have consumed a great deal of alcohol may enter a *blackout,* a condition in which they are conscious and functioning, but later remember virtually nothing that happened while they were intoxicated. In contrast, at low doses alcohol actually can improve memory (Mueller, Lisman, Spear, 1983). (This effect is small, however, so we do not recommend drinking as a study aid.)

Another important point to be made about drug effects is that the drug user often is unaware of the nature of the effect. For instance, many alcohol users believe that alcohol is a sexual stimulant that increases both sexual desire and performance. The truth is that at relatively high doses, alcohol increases drinkers' reports of sexual excitement but interferes with physiological mechanisms governing arousal in men (erection) and women (vaginal pulse pressure) (Briddell and Wilson, 1976; Wilson and Lawson, 1976). What is more, alcohol interferes with actual sexual performance, at least in males (Masters and Johnson, 1970). Many people also believe that alcohol helps them sleep better. But three to five 1-ounce drinks of 80-proof liquor significantly reduces the proportion of REM sleep (Mello and Mendelson, 1978) and increases the number of times a person awakens during the night. Alcohol also has the deadly tendency to make people believe that they can drive competently when, in fact, their abilities to respond accurately are impaired (Cohen, Dearnaley, and Hansel, 1958). Figure 5-22 shows the relation between a person's level of blood alcohol and the likelihood of having an accident if he or she drives.

*FIGURE 5-22   DON'T DRINK
AND DRIVE!*
*The graph charts the relative probability
of being in an accident as a function of
blood alcohol level. Blood alcohol levels
were determined for thousands of drivers
who were stopped at sites where accidents
occurred. Some of the drivers had been
in the accidents; others had not. The
higher the blood alcohol level, the
greater the probability of an accident.
(A 150-pound person who had drunk
3 to 4 ounces of 80-proof liquor fairly
steadily would have a blood alcohol level
of 0.10 percent). (From Zylman, 1968.)*

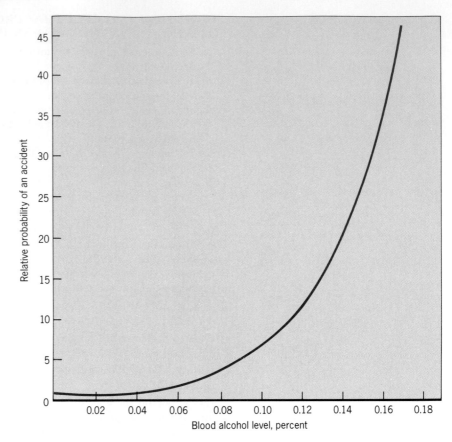

Recent research has shown that what people think about a drug, or what they expect it to do, can be a more important determinant of behavior than the drug's actual effects. For example, many people believe that alcohol releases repressed aggression and so they behave accordingly. This was shown by an ingenious study that disentangled the actual effects of alcohol from the effects of people's expectations about it (Lang, Goeckner, Adesso, and Marlatt, 1975). Some subjects were told that they would be given alcohol, and others were told that they would receive a nonalcoholic tonic. Then half from each group was actually given alcohol while the other half was actually given tonic (see Figure 5-23). After they had drunk, the subjects took part in a staged teaching exercise in which they were to deliver "shocks" to learners. The subjects were allowed to set the intensity of the shocks (which were not really delivered), and shock intensity was used as a measure of aggression. The results showed that the subjects' expectations were more important determinants of their aggression than alcohol itself. These results do not mean that alcohol cannot directly affect aggression. They simply suggest that our expectations about what a drug will do, at least at low doses, can be at least as important as the drug's direct chemical effects.

OPIATES   Natural opiates, such as opium, morphine, and heroin, are derived from the opium poppy. Synthetic opioids, such as methadone,

Subjects believed they drank:

	Alcohol	Tonic
Alcohol	4.6	2.9
Tonic	4.8	2.7

Subjects actually drank:

FIGURE 5-23   DRUGS AND EXPECTATIONS.

Results of an experiment designed to separate the effects of alcohol from the effects of expectations. Subjects were told that they would receive either alcohol or a nonalcoholic tonic. However, half of the subjects receiving each message actually received tonic; the other half received alcohol. The taste of alcohol was disguised so that subjects could not detect it. The subjects then delivered "shocks" in a "teaching" exercise. They could choose shocks (which were not actually delivered) that varied in intensity between 1 and 10 on an arbitrary scale. The number in each box is the average shock intensity set by subjects in each condition. Subjects who believed that they had drunk alcohol set the shock intensity significantly higher than those who believed they had drunk tonic— regardless of what they actually had drunk. (From Lang, Goeckner, Adesso, and Marlatt, 1975.)

also are classified as opiates because they have many of the same effects and appear to stimulate the same receptors on cells of the nervous system (see Box 5-2). In humans opiates change the body temperature, create euphoria (a "high"), increase activity, dull pain, and create constipation (Mansky, 1978).

As in the case of alcohol, opiates may affect consciousness and behavior in so many—sometimes contradictory—ways that no one can offer a simple description of their effects. For example, in one study (Lasagna, Von Felsinger, and Beecher, 1955) morphine was administered both to opiate addicts who were off the drug and to college students (who, presumably, also were not users). Morphine sedated the students but aroused and activated the addicts. The effects were opposite in naive and experienced users. Similarly, the activating effects of opiates increase with drug experience (Stewart, de Wit, and Eikelboom, 1984), but experience produces **tolerance** (less response) to other effects. For example, opiates often produce extreme nausea and low body temperature in inexperienced but not in experienced users.

Tolerance can be a problem in the medical use of opiates. Perhaps the most important medical use of opiates is to produce analgesia. There are two major components of pain: the perceptive and the reactive, or emotional. There is substantial evidence that opiates affect primarily the emotional component (Mansky, 1978). People given opiates perceive that they are in pain, but they just don't care! Unfortunately, because people quickly become tolerant to this effect, opiates are most effective against short-term pain.

NICOTINE (TOBACCO)   Tobacco and tobacco smoke contain many chemicals. But it is safe to say that a single one—nicotine—is the main reason that tobacco is so widely used. Nicotine is certainly necessary for the habitual use of tobacco; tobacco from which nicotine has been removed is soon ignored by smokers. Not only is nicotine responsible for the physical addiction to tobacco, but there is accumulating evidence that it is responsible for most of the direct actions of tobacco as well.

Of all drugs of abuse, nicotine may be the most chameleonlike; it behaves very differently in different situations. For example, its effects vary dramatically with dosage. At high doses, nicotine is deadly. A single drop of pure nicotine on the tongue or skin can kill a person (it used to be an active ingredient in insecticides) (Ashton and Stepney, 1982). Because nicotine is so potent, smokers learn to dose themselves very carefully. They know that smoking slightly too fast can make them dizzy and nauseated instead of pleasantly stimulated.

The effects of nicotine also vary dramatically with the smoker's situation. This characteristic is so striking that, soon after it was introduced to Europe, King James I of England noted about tobacco that: "Being taken when they goe to bed, it makes one sleepe soundly, and yet being taken when a man is sleepie and drowsie, it will, as they say, awake his braine, and quicken his understanding." These variable effects were clearly demonstrated in research (Mangan and Golding, 1978). Volunteers smoked in either a stressful or a boring environment while the experimenters recorded the smokers' brain waves. In the stressful envi-

BOX 5-2
HOW DRUGS
PRODUCE THEIR
EFFECTS

Although alcohol and nicotine both affect consciousness, they do so in very different ways. Alcohol is ingested as a fluid, which passes into the stomach and from there into the intestines. Very little alcohol is absorbed through the mucous lining of the mouth or through the stomach. Instead, most is absorbed by the small intestine. Therefore, anything that keeps alcohol in the stomach instead of allowing it to pass quickly into the small intestine will delay, and often reduce, the effects of alcohol. For instance, if a person eats before drinking, the opening between the stomach and the small intestine is closed (to permit food digestion in the stomach), and alcohol absorption is delayed.

After absorption in the intestines, alcohol goes to the liver, where it is metabolized (chemically broken down). Metabolism allows the body to convert alcohol into inert chemicals that can be cleared easily from the body. If you drink alcohol slowly enough (at less than the rate of metabolism, or about 1 ounce of 80-proof liquor every 1.5 to 2 hours), you will not feel the effects of the alcohol. But if you drink alcohol more quickly than it can be metabolized, it builds up in your bloodstream and affects your nervous system—and therefore your behavior.

Although we do not yet know exactly how alcohol causes its effects, recent research suggests that it alters the structure and function of cell membranes. Cell membranes contain lipids (molecules that make up fats) and proteins. The lipids provide the main physical structure of the cell membrane, and one of their functions is to form a barrier to keep certain substances out of the cell. However, when the cell membrane is exposed to alcohol, a "fluidizing" effect casts the lipids into disorder, and this effect can interfere with cell functioning (Goldstein, 1983b). Because this disordering can influence cell membranes all over the body, including the brain, it may explain why alcohol affects so many biological and cognitive functions.

Nicotine is usually ingested from tobacco, either inhaled as smoke or absorbed through the mucous lining of the mouth from chewing-tobacco or powdered tobacco. In tobacco smoke, nicotine is suspended in tiny particles of "tar" (the name given to a variety of substances other than nicotine that are present in tobacco smoke). The smoke goes quickly to the lungs, where nicotine is absorbed into the bloodstream and rapidly into the brain, heart, adrenal glands, and other organs. Nicotine spreads through the body extraordinarily rapidly; it enters the brain about 7 seconds after inhalation (Ashton and Stepney, 1982). Nicotine also leaves the brain very rapidly. Most is gone from the brain 5 to 10 minutes after it enters, and this rapid exit may explain why many smokers need to smoke almost constantly throughout the day.

After entering the brain, nicotine appears to exert its effects by stimulating particular synaptic receptors in the membranes of neurons (see Chapter 2). The receptor into which the nicotine molecule fits is normally stimulated by the neurotransmitter acetylcholine. Because the structure of nicotine is so similar to the structure of acetylcholine, nicotine fits very well into the receptor—so well that the receptor has been named a *nicotinic* receptor. When this receptor is stimulated it allows ions to pass through the cell membrane and changes the cell's activity (Feldman and Quenzer, 1984). Nicotine increases the number of action potentials discharged by many neurons in the brain. It is no wonder that nicotine alters perception, thinking, and consciousness.

ronment, smoking increased alpha-wave activity, indicating that it decreased arousal. In the boring environment, smoking decreased alpha-wave EEG activity; it increased arousal. Results such as these suggest that nicotine allows smokers to "normalize" or neutralize their emotional reactions in diverse environments. The smoker who says "I need a cigarette to calm down" and 10 minutes later says, "I need a cigarette to pick myself up" knows what he or she is talking about.

In addition to its arousal-modulating actions, nicotine has been shown to result in greater vigilance, shorter reaction times, and improved performance on memory tasks. Thus, tobacco can have useful effects. One drawback, of course, is that it can kill you.

Why Do People Abuse Drugs?

One reason that we examined the effects of drugs of abuse was to discover whether such drugs have any particular characteristics that make them so appealing. Now we can draw several conclusions about the nature of these drugs. First, most exert a wide variety of effects, and sometimes these effects are opposite to one another. Second, drug effects vary as a function of environment, an individual's previous drug experience, drug dose, and an individual's expectations about drug effects. Third, if someone consumes enough of a drug to become dependent, the withdrawal syndrome invariably is unpleasant.

These conclusions suggest that drug abuse cannot be attributed to any single drug action. In fact, drug users frequently abuse a wide variety of drugs (Bourne, 1975). It is likely that an important reason for using a drug is not to experience a *particular* drug effect, but rather to experience *any* drug effect, so long as it's not too unpleasant. Indeed, addicts have attributed their drug use to their desire to "get off the normal"—to change their level of consciousness as quickly and efficiently as possible (Wikler and Pescor, 1953). If so, perhaps the most basic question to ask about drug abuse is not why drugs are so attractive, but why sobriety is not.

SUMMARY

CONSCIOUSNESS AND ATTENTION

1. *The Nature of Consciousness.* Consciousness refers to the sense of "I" or "self"; it implies an awareness of personal identity and of the relationship between the external world and self. Some psychologists believe that consciousness is an uninteresting byproduct of experience and behavior or that it plays only a passive role in information flow. Others believe that consciousness plays an active part in monitoring and controlling oneself and the environment. Most psychologists also recognize the existence of unconscious and preconscious mental states, which consist of knowledge and thought processes that people are unaware of but that influence their actions.

2. *The Brain and Consciousness.* Many early philosophers believed that the conscious mind is separate and distinct from brain function. However, modern research has made it clear that the conscious mind is the result of neural activity. For instance, electrical stimulation of some regions of cerebral cortex in awake patients results in conscious sensations or even vivid memories and complex conscious experiences. In addition, studies of "split-brain" patients (people who have had the connections between the two cerebral hemispheres surgically cut) indicate that the activity of each hemisphere can produce its own separate conscious experience.

3. *Attention.* Attention functions to bring certain information into conscious awareness and to keep other information out. When people focus attention on a single task or set of stimuli, it is referred to as selective attention. In part, people select certain external stimuli by physically orienting their sensory systems. In addition, they mentally select certain information to be processed. What they select depends on physical characteristics of the stimuli as well as on their own expectations, interests, and motives. When people selectively attend to something, unattended information may be briefly perceived, but it is not permanently stored in memory. It is generally very difficult to divide attention—to attend to two or more stimuli at the same time. However, divided attention can be carried out fairly readily if the information to be processed appeals to different sensory systems (for example, auditory and visual) or if one of the tasks is well practiced or automatic. Several major theories have been proposed to account for the mechanisms of attention, including early selection (filter) theory, late selection theory, and resource allocation (capacity) theory.

DAILY RHYTHMS AND SLEEP

4. *Daily Rhythms.* The ability to attend to and perform many tasks is better at certain times of day than at others. Indeed, many physiological and psychological functions show marked daily cycles, called circadian rhythms. Although these rhythms can be set (entrained) by environmental time cues, they are generated from within the body. In fact, the brain seems to contain at least two internal clocks, one of which has been located within a group of neurons in the hypothalamus. These internal clocks control the daily fluctuations in many functions, including the ability to perform complex cognitive skills. Individual differences in circadian rhythms contribute to performance differences among people who are morning types and evening types. Circadian rhythms also are responsible for the disruption in performance that occurs with jet-lag and among workers who frequently change between day and night shifts.

5. *The Nature of Sleep.* In addition to the conscious mental state, people spend a large part of each day unconscious—asleep. Different stages of sleep are distinguished by physiological measures, especially measures of brain waves (via the electroencephalogram, or EEG). Stages 1–4 represent progressively deeper sleep, and people cycle through these stages several times each night. From stage 1 sleep, we often enter an additional stage of sleep in which muscles begin to twitch, breathing becomes irregular, and the eyes move rapidly back and forth. This rapid eye movement (REM) sleep is when most dreams occur. By distinction, stages 1–4 are collectively called non-REM sleep.

6. *The Need for Sleep.* Normal young adults sleep an average of 7.5 hours each night, but the amount varies substantially from person to person. The amount of time people sleep, and the timing of sleep over the course of the day and night, also varies substantially with age. There also is great variation in the amount of time different animals sleep, ranging from 2 to 20 hours a day for different species. When humans are deprived of sleep for long periods, certain physiological changes occur, but they are not debilitating. In addition, while sleep-deprived people show performance decrements on tasks that are simple, dull, or prolonged, there is much less deterioration in performance of tasks that are inherently interesting and varied. At the end of a period of sleep deprivation, only a small part of the lost sleep is made up. Theories of why people sleep must account for all of these observations, and at present no single theory has gained general acceptance.

7. *Sleep Disorders.* The most common sleep disorder is insomnia— difficulty in getting to sleep or in staying asleep. In some cases, insomnia occurs because people are trying to cope with daily concerns when they go to bed, and the insomnia usually goes away with the situation that causes it. In other cases, insomnia is longer lasting and may be due to an abnormally timed circadian rhythm of sleep–wakefulness. Insomnia also may be associated with psychological disorders, such as severe depression. A different kind of disorder is sleep apnea, in which breathing may stop during sleep. In another disorder, an individual may suddenly fall asleep at inappropriate times (narcolepsy–cataplexy syndrome). In certain parasomnia disorders (such as sleepwalking, bed-wetting, and night terrors), sleep–waking mechanisms are normal but certain undesirable behaviors occur during sleep. These disorders generally occur during childhood and disappear by late adolescence.

8. *Dreams.* Dreaming is mental activity that goes on during sleep, and about 80 percent of all dreams occur during REM sleep. Everyone dreams each night, usually six or more times. Individual dreams last 15 minutes or more and usually consist of coherent stories that take place in familiar settings and are populated by real people. The most potent determinant of dream content is common daily events. People who are deprived of dreams (by awakening during REM-sleep periods) usually show little or no psychological disturbance or disruption in task performance or cognitive abilities when awake. Nevertheless, when allowed an uninterrupted night of sleep, REM-deprived people make up much of the lost time in REM sleep, which suggests that people have a need for REM sleep and dreaming. There are many theories of the meaning and function of dreams, but none has yet gained wide acceptance. Thus, like sleep in general, REM sleep and dreaming seem to have a compelling biological function, but what that function is remains a mystery.

OTHER STATES OF CONSCIOUSNESS

9. *Hypnosis.* Under hypnosis, an individual experiences changes in perception, memory, and behavior in response to suggestions made by another person (the hypnotist). Perceptual effects of hypnosis may include perceiving things that are not really there or not perceiving things that are there. Hypnotized subjects may be made to forget things that happened during hypnosis (posthypnotic amnesia); however, there is little compelling evidence

that hypnosis enhances memory of past events. Some theorists believe that hypnosis produces an altered state of consciousness. Others argue that hypnotized individuals behave as they do in order to fulfill the expectations of the hypnotist—that they are enacting an expected role. Both theories may be correct for different subjects and under different circumstances.

10. *Meditation.* During meditation, a person alters consciousness by restricting awareness to a single process and achieves a "oneness" with the world. In the West, many people have turned to the use of meditation to reduce arousal, anxiety, and stress. Carefully controlled studies indicate that meditation can, in fact, have these effects. However, the studies also indicate that meditation is no more effective in reducing anxiety and stress than simply sitting and resting.

11. *Consciousness and Drugs.* Drugs can affect consciousness by their immediate, direct effects on physiological systems, by their long-term poisonous effects on the body, and by learned behaviors and feelings associated with drug use. In addition, drugs that produce physical dependence affect consciousness through withdrawal symptoms. The specific effects of any drug depend on drug dose, expectations of the user, previous drug experience, the situation in which the drug is used, and the psychological and physical status of the user. In many cases, the drug user is unaware of the actual effects of the drug.

Many drugs are widely abused— they are habitually used for nonmedical purposes and interfere with the physical health or the psychological, occupational, or social status of those who use them. Common drugs of abuse include alcohol, nicotine (tobacco), and opiates. People who chronically abuse drugs (addicts) seem to do so to change their level of consciousness as quickly and efficiently as possible.

FURTHER READINGS

A number of scholarly works on the nature of consciousness are available. A classic is William James' textbook on psychology: *The Principles of Psychology,* which was published in 1890 (current reprintings are available). In this text, James presents many ideas about the nature of consciousness that still have a major influence on contemporary thinkers. A more recent source of information is *The Unconscious Reconsidered,* edited by Bowers and Meichenbaum (1984). This book contains scholarly papers by many current thinkers and researchers.

For more information on attention, *Varieties of Attention,* edited by Parasuraman and Davies (1984), is recommended. Its chapters have been contributed by major investigators of attention. It may be somewhat difficult for the beginner.

Several excellent and readable books are available on sleep and dreams. These include *Some Must Watch While Some Must Sleep* by Dement (1974), *Sleep: the Gentle Tyrant* by Webb (1975), and *A Primer of Sleep and Dreaming* by Cartwright (1978). All three are by prominent researchers in the field and are very suitable for beginners.

Equally suitable for beginners who are seriously curious about hypnosis is Bowers' (1976) *Hypnosis for the Seriously Curious.* The author, a major researcher on hypnosis, presents a balanced description of the phenomenon.

A good source of information about meditation is *On the Psychology of Meditation* by Naranjo and Ornstein (1971). This well-written book discusses meditation from the perspective of Eastern practitioners and Western psychology. It describes the types and techniques of meditation and its purported effects. *The Varieties of the Meditative Experience* by Goleman (1977) also provides readable background on meditation. It is written by an American who went East to learn and practice meditation. An excellent review of the experimental evidence on meditation is Holmes' (1984) article on "Meditation and Somatic Arousal Reduction: A Review of the Experimental Evidence," published in *American Psychologist.* Commentaries on Holmes' analysis can be found in *American Psychologist* (1985, 40, 717–731).

Is Alcoholism Hereditary? by Goodwin (1978b) provides information about alcohol abuse and covers a broader range of topics than the title suggests. *Smoking: Psychology and Pharmacology* by Ashton and Stepney (1982) is a good source of information about smoking. A broad survey of drugs and information about drug abuse can be found in *A Handbook on Drug and Alcohol Abuse* by Hofmann (1983).

6

LEARNING

WHAT IS LEARNING?

Infants learn to talk and college students learn to pass tests. People of all ages learn to drive cars, count their change, and look forward to the smell of a holiday turkey roasting. Even animals learn—to come when called, to feel excited when their master comes home, to follow a scent. What *is* learning? Learning is the more or less permanent change in behavior, or behavioral potential, that results from a person's (or animal's) experience. Learning is "more or less permanent" because, as you surely know from studying for tests, people sometimes forget things that they once knew quite well. Learning is different from behavior that changes because of short-lived influences like fatigue. Learning does not affect actual behavior in every case, hence the phrase "behavioral potential." For instance, when the prisoner in an old Western movie sees his jailer put a wad of money in the desk drawer, the prisoner behaves no differently while he is behind bars. But he definitely has learned something, and if he ever escapes, his behavior may well change—and draw him straight to that drawer.

Finally, learning must result from a person's experience. Learning is not mainly a function of physical change such as maturation. For example, certain basic reflexes change as individuals get older: babies lose the rooting reflex in which they turn their head if one of their cheeks is stroked. This change in behavior is not considered learning, because the reflex disappears regardless of the baby's experiences. It is an invariant change that occurs in every healthy baby. Learning, unlike maturation, tends to produce diversity in behavior.

In this chapter, you will see some of the strategies that psychologists have used to determine exactly how people and animals learn. How does a pet learn to beg for food? How did you learn to drive, talk, use a computer, or use the right fork in company? As with other questions in psychology, psychologists have addressed questions about learning from several different perspectives. They have asked about the environmental conditions that are necessary for learning to occur and about the physiological changes that occur during learning. We turn now to these questions.

EARLY APPROACHES TO LEARNING

René Descartes, a seventeenth-century philosopher, proposed that all animal behavior, and much human behavior, was reflexive. Descartes conceived of a reflex as an automatic reaction to an external stimulus, such as a person's rapid withdrawal of his hand when he touches a flame (see Figure 6-1). Descartes' conception of a reflex was similar to the modern conception, although his ideas about physiology were consistent with those of his time. Descartes believed that much of human behavior is due to reflexes or inborn ideas and that little behavior is to be ac-

FIGURE 6-1 REFLEX OF DESCARTES.

In the 1600s, René Descartes proposed that an intense stimulus moved waves of animal spirits up hollow tubes to the brain. If the movement were strong enough, the brain would release "animal spirits" and move the muscles, causing a reflex. Here the fire (a) is the intense stimulus, the foot (b) is the part of the body that is stimulated, and (d), (e), and (f) are parts of the brain that Descartes thought were involved in reflexive behavior.

counted for by learning. (For instance, he believed that all people have an inborn idea of God.)

A very different view was held by British philosophers, the *Associationists* such as Thomas Hobbes (1588–1679). Hobbes held that human behavior is a product of mental acts, which are similar to reflexes in that they occur automatically and mechanistically. Later British Associationists such as John Locke (1632–1704) emphasized that virtually all ideas are learned. Locke proposed that humans are born without ideas or knowledge of how to behave. They are blank slates, *tabulae rasae,* upon which experience writes its story. The Associationists also speculated that all learning is produced as people sense—see, hear, and so on—two or more items or events together. That is, learning is produced by the *association* of events in time. Thus people learn that books contain printed pages because they have seen book covers together with printed pages so many times. People feel a pleasant sensation that they learn to call "love" when they see their mother, who has supported, nurtured, and caressed them. As you shall see, modern researchers have conducted studies expressly designed to evaluate the role of simple associations in learning.

Although the Associationists were influential philosophers, they did not test their ideas scientifically. In the late 1800s, when psychology ceased to be a branch of philosophy and became a science, the ideas of the Associationists began to be tested in the laboratory. Psychologists began to investigate how people and animals associate events with one another—how they learn.

PAVLOVIAN CONDITIONING

Ivan Pavlov (1849–1936) was a Russian physiologist who was interested initially in the study of digestion. He discovered a method of producing learning essentially by accident. While studying digestion in dogs, Pavlov discovered that, after repeated feedings, the dogs began salivating for food in response to cues (stimuli) that ordinarily preceded food. For instance, after repeated feedings, dogs began salivating at the sight of a food dish, or even the sight of the person who usually brought the food. Because the dogs had not always salivated under these circumstances, Pavlov realized that he not only had evidence that dogs learn, but also that a simple response (salivation) could serve as a measure of learning. In effect, he had a vista from which to view associations made in the mind.

In his laboratory, Pavlov discovered that if he regularly preceded the delivery of powdered meat to a dog by another stimulus, such as a tone, the dog eventually began to salivate in response to the tone (see Figure 6-2). The dog's behavior had changed due to experience. It had *learned.* Pavlov himself learned the principles that governed this kind of learning. First, an organism must be exposed to two stimuli that are regularly presented close together in time. In Pavlov's original research, one of

FIGURE 6-2 IVAN PAVLOV.
(a) *Ivan Pavlov with his aides and observers in his laboratory in St. Petersburg.* (b) *Pavlov had dogs held in harness and inserted a tube into their mouths to collect saliva. A screen in front of the dogs allowed Pavlov to present food without the dogs' prior awareness. Equipment recorded the dogs' salivary responses.*

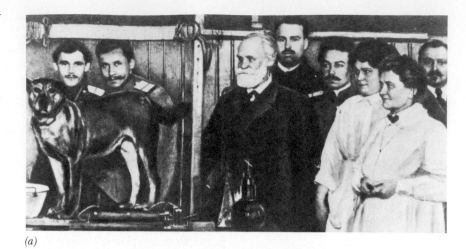

(a)

(b)

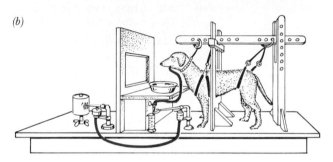

these stimuli was meat powder and the other was a bell or light. One of the two paired stimuli must elicit a reflex in the organism; the other must produce little behavioral response. The first type of stimulus is an **unconditioned stimulus (US)**. It produces a behavioral response (such as salivation) in the absence of conditioning. The response produced by the US is an **unconditioned response (UR)**. The second stimulus, the **conditioned or conditional stimulus (CS)**, produces little behavioral effect until it is paired with the US. Response to the CS is *conditional* upon being paired with the US.

In **Pavlovian conditioning** or **classical conditioning** the CS and the US are repeatedly paired until the CS eventually elicits a response that is similar to that elicited by the US (see Figure 6-3). This response is the **conditioned response (CR)**. For example, if the US (a puff of air delivered to the eye) originally elicited an eye blink (the UR), after many pairings with the US, the CS would also elicit an eye blink (the CR). The CR is usually much like the UR, although they may differ slightly in size or force. Thus in Pavlovian conditioning, the power to elicit a response is transferred from one stimulus to another. The experimenter *conditions* the animal, and the animal learns. Therefore, *conditioning* refers to a set of procedures that produces learning. Pavlovian learning occurs not only in dogs but in species ranging from flatworms to humans. It occurs in newborns as well as adults. Virtually every reflex can be conditioned. The modern definition of reflex is remarkably similar to that proposed by Descartes. A **reflex** occurs when a stimulus has a high likelihood of producing a particular response. Someone taps the tendon under your

FIGURE 6-3
PAVLOVIAN CONDITIONING.
In this example, a person learns to blink her eye in response to a 1-second tone (the CS) after the tone has been paired many times with a .25-second puff of air (the US) to her eye. (a) Before conditioning, the CS produced little behavioral effect. The US, however, produced a strong eye blink, the UR (measured by electrodes over the eye muscles). (b) During conditioning, the CS is delivered immediately before the air puff. The subject did not blink when she heard the tone, only in response to the air puff. Thus, this eye blink is still a UR, not a CR. (c) After many pairings of the CS and US, she begins to blink as soon as she hears the tone CS. Thus, the early part of this blink, the part before the air puff, is a CR. Evidence for this is presented in (d), in which it can be seen that after conditioning, the subject blinks to the CS presented by itself. Notice that the CR is not quite as large as the UR.

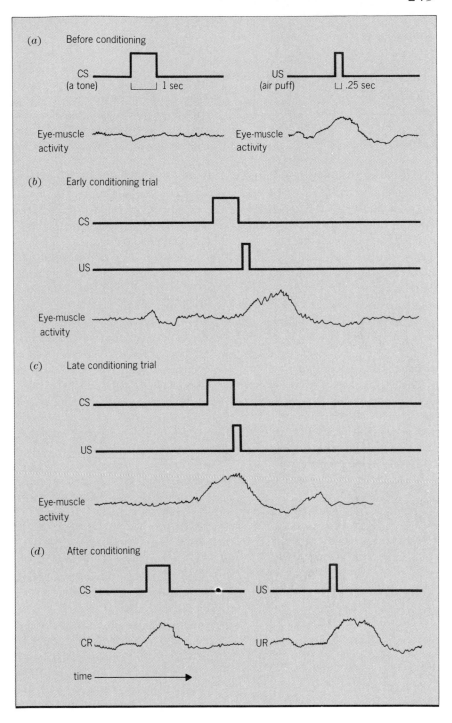

kneecap, and your knee jerks. That is a reflex. Someone pounds on your door in the middle of the night. You are startled: your muscles contract and your heart races. Those are reflexes. Some reflexes are more complex and can be influenced by thought or intention. For instance, one's response to sexual stimulation can be altered markedly by its context and the attitude of the participants. People who are worried about their work

BOX 6-1
THE RANGE OF
PAVLOVIAN
LEARNING

Pavlovian learning has a deep effect on human emotion. By it, for instance, people can learn to be afraid. Sometimes fear is adaptive and valuable. People's URs to touching a flame are a racing heart and the rapid withdrawal of their hands. This is, of course, exactly what we do when we discover we are inadvertently about to touch a flame. But some fears are irrational and interfere inordinately with people's lives. Psychologists call such fears *phobias*. Common phobias are fears of snakes, dogs, heights, enclosed places, and insects.

One major way in which phobias arise appears to be Pavlovian learning. In one study, for example, about half of phobics interviewed reported that their fear of animals had started with an early traumatic episode (Ost and Hugdahl, 1981). One woman

seen by one of the authors said that her fear of flying insects started when she was a little girl being driven in an open vehicle through a desert. Suddenly, toward evening, the vehicle was enveloped by a huge swarm of large moths. The moths flew wildly, getting caught in the girl's hair and beating their wings against her face. Now, whenever the woman sees a moth, even in a picture or a movie, she panics. Her heart races, she feels tremulous, and tries to escape.

Not only is overt behavior affected by Pavlovian learning, but so are basic physiological reactions to events. Often people are not even aware that they have produced a conditioned response. One of the most intriguing instances of conditioning involves the immune system, which manufactures antibodies that attack and destroy foreign substances, such as bacteria and virus. Allergies are caused by inappropriate or excessive immune responses to ordinarily harmless substances such as pollen or cat dander. Recently, researchers showed that the immune–

antibody reactions of animals can be conditioned (Ader and Cohen, 1981; see Chapter 11). What is the importance of learning that immune reactions might be conditioned? It is well established that stress, whether in the form of tension, worry, or exhaustion, reduces antibodies and makes people susceptible to disease (see Chapter 11). Through conditioning, cues paired with stress may themselves reduce antibodies and increase susceptibility to disease. This process also helps explain why allergies can so disrupt people's lives. People who are allergic to pollens sometimes sneeze when they see a *picture* of a rose because the appearance of a rose is a CS that has been paired with their allergic attacks in the past. People may react allergically both to allergens—pollens, cat dander, and so forth—and to things associated with allergens—a picture of grass, the owner of a cat.

People may not be aware of their conditioned responses, but they occur nevertheless.

are likely to show a very different intensity of reflexive response to sexual stimulation from those who are happily and passionately in love.

People don't often think of themselves as acting reflexively. Therefore, it is difficult to appreciate how much people's behavior is influenced by Pavlovian learning. But just think of how you would feel if someone called you an insulting name. "You *idiot!*" Probably you would flush, get tense, and feel angry or fearful. You certainly were not born with an instinctive reaction to the word *idiot*. You reacted this way, at least in part, because the insult previously has been paired with unconditioned stimuli—raised voices, physical pain, and so on. Your present reaction to the insult (the CS) is a CR similar to your initial response to these unconditioned stimuli. Box 6-1 presents research findings on some widely divergent examples of Pavlovian learning.

One reason that Pavlovian learning may be so wide-ranging is that people and animals need not experience the unconditioned stimulus for learning to occur. Take, for example, the case in which a dog has learned to cower when its master raises his voice because the master has always raised his voice when he has hit the dog. If the master wanted to condition another fear in the dog, he would not have to strike the dog again. Instead, he would only have to pair repeatedly his raised voice with a neutral stimulus, perhaps the new living room couch. Soon the dog would show fear in the presence of the couch. (Actually, many dogs learn not to fear the couch but their masters when they, the dogs, are near or on the couch. The couch becomes a **discriminative stimulus** that signals the dog when to fear its master.) This type of conditioning, in which an already conditioned CS replaces a US, is called **second-order conditioning**. It greatly increases the range of Pavlovian learning, because every CS can give rise to additional CSs and associated CRs. CRs acquired through second-order conditioning tend to be weaker than those acquired through first-order Pavlovian conditioning.

In addition to being struck with the ubiquity of Pavlovian learning, researchers were struck with the fact that it appeared to occur among all species in pretty much the same way. This encouraged them to search for and articulate "general laws" or "laws of learning." While researchers never universally agreed to these laws or principles, the great uniformity of conditioning data led to considerable agreement about the important characteristics of Pavlovian learning.

Major Features of Pavlovian Conditioning

One of the first things that researchers noted about Pavlovian learning is that animals do not learn associations between a CS and US if the two stimuli are presented far apart in time. Pavlov recognized the importance of a short **interstimulus interval** and consistently had the US follow the CS within 5 seconds (see Figure 6-4). What is more, if the US precedes the CS, a procedure known as **backwards conditioning**, an animal learns very little.

Researchers also argued that CS–US relations were characterized by **equipotentiality**. In other words, if a stimulus served effectively as a CS for one type of US, it could serve as an effective CS for any type of US. Likewise, if a US produced a CR to one type of CS, it would be an effective US for any type of CS. Thus pairing a tone (CS) with a shock (US) should make an animal learn to fear the tone, and pairing a light (CS) with a shock should make an animal fear the light. Conversely, pairing a tone (CS) with an air puff (US) makes an animal blink (CR) at the tone. To a great extent, the equipotentiality premise has been borne out by research. But, as you will see, there are certain exceptions to this rule.

STRENGTHENING LEARNING Certain procedures strengthen Pavlovian learning. The strength of learning, or **associative strength**, refers to the capacity of the CS to elicit the CR. Associative strength is usually measured in terms of the size of the CR, the rate at which the CR is learned, the proportion of times that the CS elicits the CR, and the resistance of the CR to extinction (we will discuss extinction shortly). In general, associative strength is increased when the size of the US is increased, when the number of CS–US pairings is increased, and when a

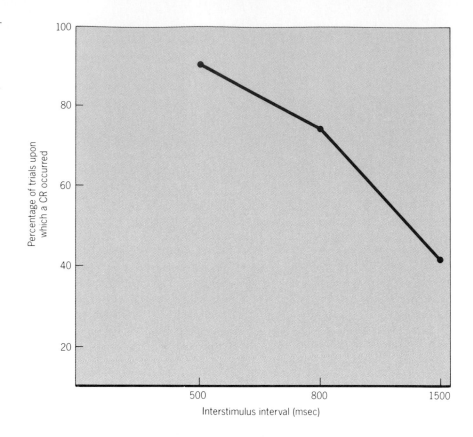

FIGURE 6-4 INTERSTIMULUS INTERVAL AND CONDITIONING. A blue light was the CS, and an air puff to the right eye was the US. The CS–US interstimulus interval was either 500, 800, or 1500 milliseconds, and the longer the interval, the poorer the conditioning. That is, the CS was less likely to elicit a CR. (Kimble, Mann, and Dufort, 1955, pp. 407–417.)

novel, distinctive CS is used. There are, of course, limits on the magnitude of an effective US, and after a certain point, additional conditioning trials do not seem to strengthen conditioning. In fact, most learning seems to occur early in Pavlovian conditioning (see Figure 6-5). It is easy to understand why a distinctive CS increases learning. The animal about to be conditioned is introduced into a new environment, full of sounds, smells, and objects. How is the animal to know that it is the tiny, blinking red light that predicts when it will receive the US? The more distinctive the CS, the more likely the animal will notice it and associate it with the US.

WEAKENING A LEARNED ASSOCIATION: EXTINCTION AND INHIBITION   Once a person or animal has made an association between a CS and US so that the CS reliably elicits a CR, the most effective procedure for reducing associative strength is extinction. The CS will elicit a smaller CR or will elicit the CR a smaller percentage of time. **Extinction** consists of presenting the CS by itself, unpaired with the US.

If a rabbit had always received a puff of air delivered to its eye after hearing a bell CS, it would have learned to blink its eye upon hearing the bell. There are a number of ways we could try to break up the CS–US association. We could simply not present the CS for many days and hope that the rabbit forgets the association. This strategy is ineffective because learned associations can be retained in memory for very long periods of

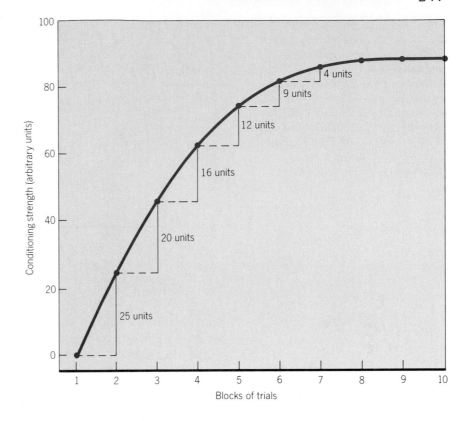

FIGURE 6-5a   LEARNING AND NUMBER OF CONDITIONING TRIALS.

This hypothetical curve shows that as the number of conditioning trials increases, an animal learns less on each trial. (From Schwartz, 1978.)

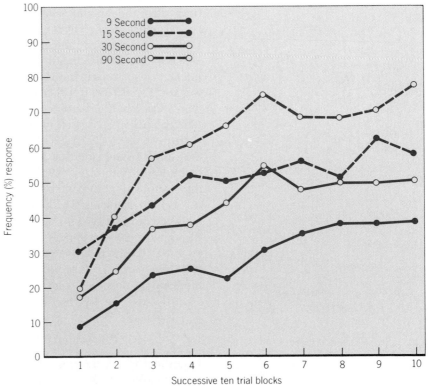

FIGURE 6-5b   TIME BETWEEN TRIALS.

The percentage of trials in which conditioned responses occurred increased steeply in early trials but flattened in later trials. The greatest amount of Pavlovian learning occurs when the interval between trials is long. The 90-second interval between CS–US pairings produced CRs on more learning trials than the shorter intervals did. Thus whereas long periods between stimuli (CS and US) reduce learning, spacing each pairing of stimuli far from other such pairings (the intertrial interval) increases learning. (From Spence and Norris, 1950.)

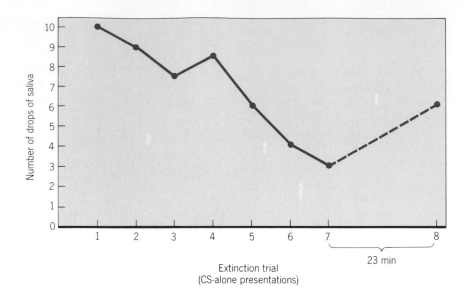

FIGURE 6-6 EXTINCTION.
Over seven extinction trials in which
a CS was presented by itself, the
conditioned response (salivation)
diminished. If the CS is withheld for a
time, in this case 23 minutes (extinction
trials occurred every minute), and then
presented again later, it elicits a larger
CR (e.g., more salivation) than it did
at the end of extinction; there is
spontaneous recovery of the CR.

time—months and even years. Extinction, on the other hand, almost always results in a rapid reduction in responding to a CS. Here we would simply ring the bell numerous times without delivering the air puff. In general, the more times we present the bell unpaired with air puff, the more associative strength is weakened. However, if on one occasion we present the CS a sufficient number of times to eliminate completely responding to the CS, when we present the CS at a later time (say, the next day) the animal will once again produce the CR (blink). This reemergence of the CR is called **spontaneous recovery** (see Figure 6-6). If the experimenter then continues to present the CS by itself, the CR will once again disappear. The CR may continue to emerge on subsequent tests of spontaneous recovery, but each time it will be smaller and weaker. Eventually, it will cease to emerge at all. Does this mean that the CS–US association has been completely abolished? No. If we once again pair the CS with the air puff, a blink CR will be acquired more quickly than if we use a CS that had never been paired with the US. This is one exception to the rule that a novel CS tends to produce better learning.

Pavlov hypothesized (1927) that two different learning processes produce acquisition and extinction. In acquisition, **excitation** causes the CS to become associated with the US. In extinction, however, **inhibition** overrides excitation and causes the animal not to produce a CR, even though the CS–US link is intact. To prove the existence of inhibition Pavlov (1927) gave a dog conditioning trials in which a "rotating object" (CS1) was paired with food (US) on some trials and with the clicks of a metronome on other trials:

$$CS1 \text{ (object)} \rightarrow US \text{ (food)}$$
or
$$CS1 \text{ (object)} + \text{metronome} \rightarrow \text{no US (food)}$$

In a short while, the dog salivated to the CS1, but *only* when it was not accompanied by the metronome clicks. Now, why did the metronome eliminate the salivary CR to CS1? One theory is that the dog had learned to break the CS1–US association when the metronome clicks were presented. In contrast, Pavlov's theory is that the metronome had become a **conditioned inhibitor** that could suppress a CR even though the CS–US link was intact. To test the theory Pavlov gave the dog a second CS, CS2—a tone of C sharp—and paired it with food. The dog quickly learned a salivary CR to CS2.

$$CS2 \text{ (tone)} \rightarrow US \text{ (food)}$$

Now, what happened when Pavlov presented the CS2 along with the metronome? The dog did not salivate. Because the CS2 elicited a CR reliably it is clear that the excitatory CS–US association was intact. It is also clear that the dog never learned to weaken the CS2–US link in response to the metronome—CS2 and the metronome had never previously been paired. This shows that the metronome had gained inhibitory power that could suppress conditioned responding despite a strong CS–US association. Pavlov believed that extinction does not break a CS–US association; the animal merely learns to inhibit the CR.

SPECIFICITY OF PAVLOVIAN LEARNING   If you have learned to salivate in response to chocolate cake, you are also quite likely to do so when you see chocolate brownies. Pavlov noticed that conditioned animals would salivate not only in response to the CS, but also to stimuli that were similar to the CS. That is, they showed **generalization** of conditioned responses (see Figure 6-7).

In a study of generalization of responses in people, a researcher used a conditioning procedure in which people ate while they were exposed to particular words: *style, urn, freeze,* and *surf* (the CSs) (Razrin, 1939/1971). After only a few conditioning trials, the words made the

FIGURE 6-7   GENERALIZATION OF PAVLOVIAN RESPONDING.
If a 600-nanometer light, which looks yellow, were used as a CS, an animal would be most likely to produce a conditioned response to a light of similar intensity. The further the wavelength of light becomes from the CS wavelength (the more dissimilar the stimuli), the less likely would be the animal to respond. Thus the animal would respond little to a green, 560-nanometer light or a red, 640-nanometer light.

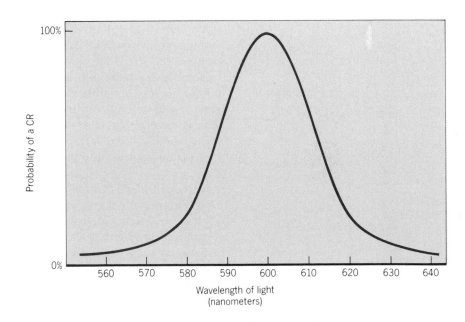

people salivate, just as the food had done. In testing for stimulus generalization, the researcher also tested to see whether people would generalize more on the basis of the sounds of the words or their meaning. Therefore he measured the amount people salivated in response to synonyms (*fashion, vase, chill, wave*) and in response to homonyms (*stile, earn, frieze, serf*). The people responded more to the synonyms, a finding that suggests that Pavlovian associations are made, and can generalize, from ideas and meanings as well as from physical features. This finding explains why, for example, if you are attacked by someone you may later become fearful or angry both at people who look like him and at people whom you link to him by the idea of a shared feature such as race, religion, or nationality.

Although people may generalize their conditioned responses from one object to another that is similar to it, they also can **discriminate**, or withhold their conditioned responses to objects that are dissimilar to the stimulus. In *discrimination training,* animals can be trained to produce CRs that are highly discriminated on the CS. They can learn, for example, to discriminate the CS of an 80 dB tone from tones of 70, 75, 85, and 90 dB. In later tests of generalization, these animals respond to the CS, but show little generalized response to other tones. Pavlov would say that discrimination involves learning to inhibit responding to stimuli similar to but not the same as the CS.

What Is Learned in Pavlovian Learning?

Answering the question of what is learned in Pavlovian learning may, at first, seem simple. A ready answer is that the CR is learned. Organisms learn to produce a behavior that is similar to the UR, in response to a cue that previously had little or no effect. But Pavlov as well as other researchers have been dissatisfied with this answer. Psychologists have wanted to know the kinds of mental or neural connections made during Pavlovian learning. Pavlov, for instance, speculated that the brain has many centers that control various responses. If one of these centers was stimulated, Pavlov believed, the behavior controlled by that center would be executed. He believed that these neural centers usually are stimulated by sensory information relayed from the outside world. For example, the neural center for salivation might be stimulated by sensory nerves that carry visual or olfactory information about food. These nerves excite a neural center that is sensitive to the sensory qualities of food (a US center), and it, in turn, excites a motor (or efferent) center (a UR center) that produces salivation (see Figure 6-8).

STIMULUS SUBSTITUTION Pavlov believed that the neural connections between the *unconditioned* stimulus and response centers are innate. He believed that a neural center also exists for a CS. A CS activates a neural center and that allows an animal to see a light (CS) or hear a bell (CS) (see Figure 6-8*a*). Pavlov believed that during excitatory conditioning, neural connections between the CS and US centers develop (see Figure 6-8*b*). Pavlov's theory has come to be called **stimulus substitution** theory because he thought that the CS becomes a substitute for the US.

FIGURE 6-8 PAVLOV'S THEORY OF NEURAL CONNECTIONS.
(a) *The neural centers that Pavlov believed were stimulated by external stimuli. If a stimulus were strong or biologically significant (e.g., food), stimulation of its neural center would elicit a reflex (e.g., salivation). A weak stimulus of little biological significance, such as a bell, would elicit no consistent behavioral response.* (b) *During conditioning, many pairings of CS and US (bell and food) cause an animal to connect the CS and US neural centers. Eventually, the bell alone first activates the CS neural center, then the US neural center, then the UR neural center, producing a behavioral response.*

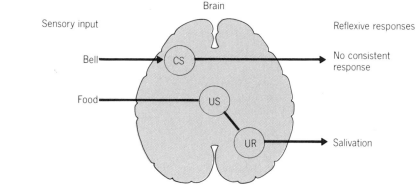

(*a*) Before conditioning

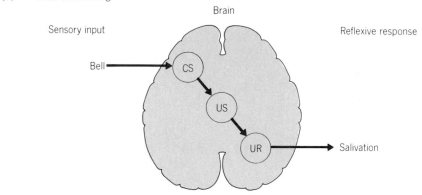

(*b*) After conditioning

Research since Pavlov's time suggests that his theory is incomplete and possibly wrong. First of all, the stimulus substitution theory demands that the CR and the UR be similar, if not the same, because both responses are supposedly produced by the same neural center. But many studies have shown that conditioned and unconditioned responses can differ markedly. For example, when animals are conditioned with a shock US, the UR is usually a faster heart rate. The CR, however, is usually a slower heart rate.

CONTIGUITY   Research also has shown a problem with another of Pavlov's ideas about learning, **contiguity theory.** Pavlov believed that CS–US associations occur merely because the two stimuli repeatedly occur close together in time. This theory is consistent with the views of the British Associationists and with the fact that long interstimulus intervals retard learning. But data now suggest that acquisition is determined by the informativeness of the CS (its signal value), not just the number of times that the CS and US are paired (Rescorla, 1968). When a researcher compared the amount of learning shown by groups of animals that had equal numbers of CS–US pairings but differed on the basis of the number of times that the CS or the US had been presented by itself, it became clear that the CS or US presented by itself interfered with learning (see Figure 6-9*a*). Learning depends upon something

FIGURE 6-9 SIGNAL VALUE OF THE CS.

This figure portrays two types of experiments that show that learning reflects better the signaling properties of the CS rather than simple CS–US pairing. (a) Both Groups 1 and 2 have an equal number of CS–US pairings. However, Group 2, on the average, will tend not to learn as strong a CR as Group 1 because for Group 2, the US is signaled by the CS on only half the occasions that it is presented. For Group 1 the US is signaled on 75 percent of its presentations. This suggests that learning is sensitive to the probability that the US will occur after the CS and not at other times (Rescorla, 1968). (b) This figure presents the basic procedures used in a blocking experiment (Kamin, 1969). Group 1 received 20 presentations of the shock US. Shock tends to produce "freezing" among rats. The first 10 US presentations were signaled by a tone CS. The second 10 were signaled by both the tone and a light CS. Group 2 received only 10 US presentations and all of these were signaled by the light alone. The test, consisting of the presentation of the light by itself, revealed that Group 1 showed less of a CR (freezing) than did Group 2. Group 1 showed evidence of less learning than Group 2 despite the fact that Group 1 had twice as many US exposures. Apparently, the light was an ineffective CS for Group 1 because it provided no new information about shock occurrence that was not already provided by the tone CS.

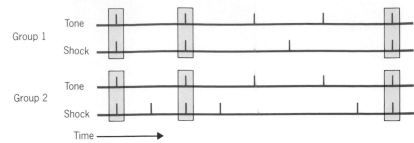

(a) CS–US (Tone–Shock) pairing

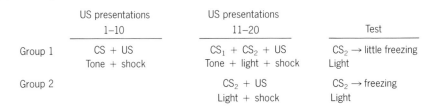

(b) Blocking

	US presentations 1–10	US presentations 11–20	Test
Group 1	CS + US Tone + shock	CS$_1$ + CS$_2$ + US Tone + light + shock	CS$_2$ → little freezing Light
Group 2		CS$_2$ + US Light + shock	CS$_2$ → freezing Light

besides the simple nearness of the CS and US in time (temporal contiguity).

Blocking experiments show that stimuli that occur close together in time do not necessarily become learned substitutes (see Figure 6-9b). For example, one group of animals is exposed to reliable CS–US pairings, such as the pairing of a tone with shock. The UR to shock is freezing or other fearful behavior. After pairings of tone and shock, the tone itself will make an animal freeze. Now the experimenter pairs a second stimulus, a light, with the tone. A **compound stimulus** now precedes the shock. But the animal learns little about the light. Even after many trials, the light itself hardly frightens the animal at all, despite the fact that light and shock have been paired many times. Why? The animal had already learned that the tone, the first CS, meant that a shock was coming by the time that the light was introduced into the conditioning procedure. Thus the light gave the animal no new information, and the association of the tone and shock *blocked* the association of the light and shock (Kamin, 1969).

SIGNAL VALUE According to *expectancy theory*, Pavlovian learning occurs when a previously unimportant stimulus (CS) gives an animal new information that allows it to predict or *expect* a biologically significant event (US) (Tolman, 1932). But this expectation does not necessarily lead the organism to respond just as it would respond to the US. Instead, the CR may prepare the organism for the US. For instance, when a dog owner opens a can of food for his dog, the dog does not react to the can opener in the same way that it reacts to food. It does not begin to chew its food bowl. Rather, it waits expectantly and looks for its first chance to eat the food.

The expectancy model can account quite nicely for the general characteristics of Pavlovian learning. For example, it explains why reliable

CS–US pairing and short interstimulus intervals produce rapid learning. Both of these characteristics permit accurate predictions regarding US occurrence. It also explains why conditioned inhibitors block CRs. An animal learns not to expect the US when the conditioned inhibitor is presented. Therefore it does not produce a CR. Thus associations are strongest when the CS is an informative *signal* of the US. The stronger the probability that the US will follow the CS and not occur at other times, the stronger the learned association between them. The association is strongest when the CS, and only the CS, lets the animal predict and prepare for every occurrence of the US. Thus, when the US is not paired with the CS [as in the Rescorla's (1968) study in Figure 6-9a], or when the US is already signaled by a stimulus (blocking effect), learning is less intense because the CS is not an accurate and unique signal of the US.

Although the expectancy theory improves on the stimulus substitution and contiguity theories, it is not without problems of its own. For instance, although backwards conditioning only slowly produces learning, and only weak CRs are acquired, learning nevertheless can occur (Wagner and Terry, 1975). How can expectancy theory account for learning an expectation of the US when the US *precedes* the CS? The current view of learning theories is that no one theory can adequately explain all learning phenomena. Components of different learning theories can account only for particular types of learning in particular situations.

In sum, in Pavlovian learning, the CR is not acquired through stimulus pairings or association alone. Rather, the acquisition of the CR is based upon the signal value of the CS: the relative probability that the US will occur only after the CS.

Adaptive Significance of Pavlovian Learning

Learned responses tend to be adaptive, to have survival value for the organism. Think about fears for a moment. We humans are born with few fears; we must learn most of them. We learn to avoid the many dangers that face us every day—speeding cars, hot burners, sharp knives, and the like—in part, because of Pavlovian learning. We also learn to feel excitement and pleasure in anticipation of a sumptuous dinner or meeting a loved one, and this learning makes it more likely that we will pursue the dinner, an attractive sexual partner, and so on. In short, conditioned reactions allow us to react to the signals of significant events rather than having to wait for the events themselves.

While it makes a good deal of sense that the ability to anticipate biologically significant events would confer a survival advantage, until recently there have been few data that directly support this notion. One recent example comes from research on the mating behavior of a fish— the male blue gouramie (Hollis, 1984). Male blue gouramies must defend their territory against other males. The researcher discovered that gouramies that were conditioned to expect a rival male after seeing a light conditioned stimulus were much better at defending their territory than were unconditioned males.

Looking at Pavlovian learning in light of its adaptive value helps to explain some of the findings in conditioning research. As you read earlier, sometimes a conditioned response is quite different from the unconditioned response. The heart rate (UR) of a frightened animal may speed up in one instance but slow down (CR) in another instance. An animal's reactions in nature help to explain this. When a rat, for example, is actually attacked (US) by a rival or a predator, it strenuously tries to flee or fight. Its heart races. But if a rat is still undetected when it sees a rival or a predator (CS), it freezes, probably to avoid detection. The heart rate slows. In short, there is a survival advantage to the rat's (or human's) heart rate slowing in one situation and racing in another.

OPERANT LEARNING

At around the same time that Pavlov was investigating how to elicit reflexes from his animals, Edward Thorndike (1874–1949;) was examining how cats learn to escape from small wooden boxes (**puzzle boxes**) to get food (see Figure 6-10). Thorndike was interested in finding out how animals learn to perform familiar acts like sitting on command or coming when called. These are not instinctive reflexes, but voluntary acts directed at an identifiable goal. Thorndike put a hungry cat in the puzzle box, put food in plain sight of the cat, and observed. First the cat groomed or sat. Then it paced, pawed at the bars of the box, or bit. Finally, it chanced to press a pedal on the floor of the box, opened the door, and found food and temporary freedom.

After they had pressed the pedal and won their rewards once, the cats invariably took less and less time to solve the puzzle on successive trials.

FIGURE 6-10   THORNDIKE'S PUZZLE BOX.

A puzzle box like that used by Thorndike (1911). The cat steps on the pedal, which is attached to a rope on pulleys (invisible to the cat), which unlatches the door to the box.

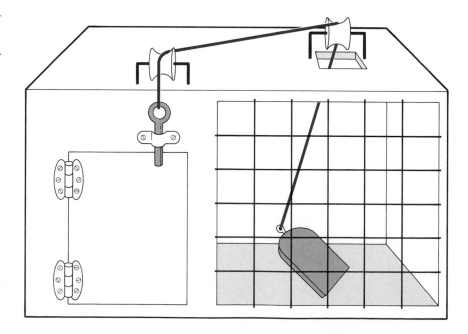

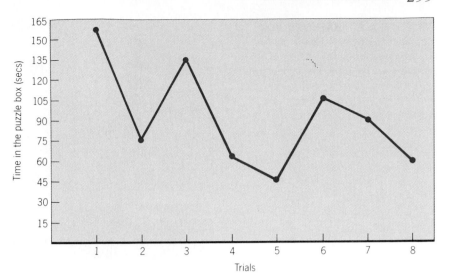

FIGURE 6-11   PUZZLE BOX
PERFORMANCE.
*One of Thorndike's cats in a puzzle box
took less time to escape from the box the
more often it was put inside it. But the
cat did not learn to escape in one fell
swoop. It learned gradually and in
piecemeal fashion.*

Notice that the decline of the **learning curve** in Figure 6-11 is uneven and gradual. The cats did not seem to learn suddenly a well-conceived strategy for escape, but instead learned to escape in a piecemeal and gradual fashion.

Like Pavlov, Thorndike developed a theory to explain the learning he observed. Thorndike assumed that when animals are placed in any new environment they engage in numerous seemingly random behaviors. For instance, in the puzzle box cats sniffed, paced, bit, and pawed. Over time, the cats came to pair some of these forms of behavior with desirable consequences. Stepping on the pedal was paired with escape. Sniffing and biting were not. In his **law of effect**, Thorndike proposed that behavior that is paired with (precedes) desirable consequences is strengthened—becomes more likely to recur. Conversely, behavior that does not lead to desirable consequences becomes less likely to recur. Thorndike called this form of learning **instrumental learning** because through it animals learned to act in ways that were *instrumental* to their becoming satisfied.

Although Thorndike believed that pleasant or unpleasant consequences are necessary for learning to occur, he believed that the animal actually learns to associate the environment and the particular act that precedes a pleasant or unpleasant consequence. Thorndike believed that learning strengthened the connection between the eliciting stimulus—in his experiments, the puzzle box—and the motor response. For instance, a cat put in a puzzle box might have responded at first by pacing. But once it had learned that stepping on a foot pedal opened the door, it was more likely to step on the foot pedal than to pace.

While Thorndike's observations were critical to the discovery of operant learning, it was left to later researchers to discover research methods that characterized the nature of instrumental learning. Principal among these was B. F. Skinner, one of the most eminent psychologists of this century. Skinner made technological and methodological advances that

FIGURE 6-12   SKINNER BOX.
A Skinner box typical of those used in the operant conditioning of rats. When animals press the lever, they receive food (reinforcement) from the pellet dispenser and food hopper. A signal light and speaker can serve as discriminative stimuli.

yielded a vast amount of research on how the environment influences instrumental behavior (see Figure 6-12). Skinner also clarified the differences between operant and Pavlovian learning.

Skinner (1937) concluded that Pavlovian and instrumental learning involve two very different procedures. In Pavlovian learning a biologically significant event (US) follows a neutral *stimulus* (CS). In instrumental learning a biologically significant event follows a *response* (which Skinner termed an **operant**). Accordingly, Skinner also held that Pavlovian and instrumental learning involve quite different behavioral, physiological, and cognitive processes, a view that is still debated today (MacKintosh, 1983). Because Skinner recognized that instrumental acts are not reflexes, he recognized that they can vary from one occasion to another. When the doctor taps your knee, your knee-jerk *reflex* is invariably the same. But when you, say, scratch your itchy knee, you may use one hand or the other and whichever fingers you please. Similarly, a cat in Thorndike's puzzle box might press the pedal with its hind paw on one occasion and with its front paw on another. Because both acts *operate* on the environment in the same way, Skinner would consider both to be examples of the same *operant* behavior; pedal pressing. Skinner's insights into this type of learning were so important that most psychologists now speak of *operant* rather than of *instrumental* learning.

Skinner also abandoned Thorndike's *law of effect.* Thorndike's law leads to circular reasoning: A cat presses a lever to get fish. Why? Because fish is satisfying. How do we know fish is satisfying? Because cats will press levers to get it. Skinner simply said that operant behavior is determined by its consequences. A **reinforcer** increases the probability that an animal will repeat the behavior that immediately precedes it; a **punisher** decreases the probability. For example, if a student smiled at his professor every time the professor looked his way, and the professor then looked at the student more and more, Skinner would call smiling a reinforcer. Notice that Skinner did not explain *why* events are reinforcing or punishing. He proposed a simple definition that avoided, to him, the unnecessary concept of satisfaction.

Not only did Skinner change how psychologists conceptualize learning, but he also designed technology that helped psychologists discover the major features of instrumental or operant learning (see Figure 6-12).

Major Features of Operant Learning and Performance

In a typical operant conditioning study, a rat, pigeon, or human is reinforced for emitting a particular *target* behavior selected by the experimenter. The relation between the target behavior and its consequence is called the operant **contingency**. One of Skinner's most important contributions to psychology was to pioneer research into how various operant contingencies influence behavior (Ferster and Skinner, 1957).

SCHEDULES OF REINFORCEMENT Almost no behavior is consistently reinforced. Although turning on a faucet is reinforced at a very high rate, most people have had the mildly startling experience of turning a faucet and having nothing happen. Other forms of behavior are even less consistently reinforced. Every time you call someone on the phone, ring a doorbell, or argue your point of view, you are uncertain of the consequences of your actions. How does the **schedule of reinforcement** influence learning? ("Reinforcement" refers to the process of pairing a consequence with a behavior; a "reinforcer" *is* a consequence—one that increases the rate of operant behavior.)

Perhaps the simplest schedule is the **continuous reinforcement** schedule, in which an animal is reinforced every time it emits the target behavior. The pigeon is given grain every time it pecks a key or a dog patted every time he bites the mailman. Continuous reinforcement schedules do result in operant responding, at least for a time, but they are not as powerful as other types of schedules. By *powerful* we mean that the schedule can produce a great many responses per unit of reinforcement. The continuous schedule is, by definition, a weak schedule because every target behavior earns reinforcement. There is also a pause after each reinforcement of the response, and so the animal does not respond continuously. Finally, these schedules are less powerful than others because animals become satiated. The pigeon eats so much grain that food is no longer reinforcing, and the dog gets tired of being patted.

Even so, continuous schedules are important in operant conditioning, especially when an animal is first being trained. During **shaping**, animals are reinforced every time they act in a way that is like the behavior that the conditioner is looking for. For example, if the conditioner wants a rat to press a lever, first the rat is reinforced (fed) for turning toward the lever, then for approaching it, then for touching it, and finally for pressing it. Reinforcing such **successive approximations** results in the rapid learning of operant behavior. (Not only do rats learn to press levers but humans learn to play tennis and make omelets because their teachers reinforce each tiny improvement in technique.)

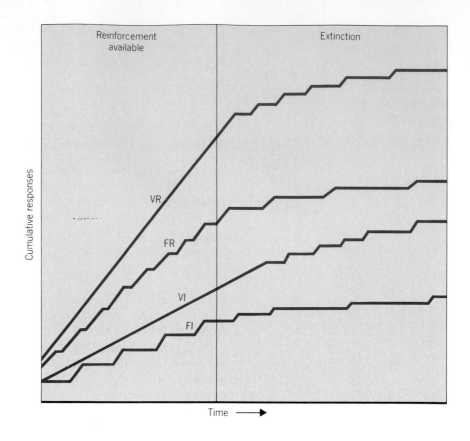

FIGURE 6-13 BEHAVIORAL EFFECTS OF SCHEDULES OF REINFORCEMENT.

In this figure, which shows the effects of four schedules of reinforcement on response rates, the steeper the slope, the faster the rate of responding. Variable ratio (VR) schedules produce high rates of responding, and responding slows gradually during extinction. Fixed ratio (FR) schedules also produce high rates of responding, but post-reinforcement pauses occur in which animals wait before starting to respond for another reinforcer. This doesn't occur with VR schedules because animals sometimes get reinforced for their first few responses after reinforcement. Notice that responding drops off abruptly when the FR schedule is changed to extinction. Both variable (VI) and fixed (FI) interval schedules produce less rapid responding than ratio schedules. FI schedules produce a scalloped response pattern because animals respond only when the interval of reinforcement unavailability is nearly over. Because this interval varies unpredictably for VI animals, this schedule produces low, steady rates of response. When extinction procedures begin, animals trained on a VI schedule are more resistant to extinction than FI animals. Because VI animals don't know when to expect reinforcement, extinction procedures do not alert them as quickly that there has been a change in the response contingency.

RATIO SCHEDULES Operant performance is usually stronger when animals are reinforced for some, not all, responses. In ratio schedules, animals are reinforced for a certain number of their responses. In a **fixed-ratio schedule**, animals must respond a set of times—say ten times—to get reinforcement. In a **variable-ratio schedule**, the reinforcement varies from trial to trial but averages, say, one in ten responses. Ratio schedules tend to produce high rates of responding, which is consistent with the fact that the amount of reinforcement is clearly related to the amount of responding: the more responding, the greater the reinforcement. It is relatively easy to "thin out" ratio schedules. One might start with a continuous reinforcement schedule, then reinforce every second response (a fixed ratio "2," FR 2), and then switch to an FR 5, FR 10, FR 25, and so on. Are there limits to the amount of responding that animals will make while on an FR schedule? Undoubtedly, but they are hard to find. In one instance, a monkey produced 120,000 responses in order to get a single food reinforcer (Findley and Brady, 1965)! Although both fixed- and variable-ratio schedules produce high rates of responding, fixed-ratio schedules tend to produce discontinuous or uneven rate response patterns, whereas variable-ratio schedules produce high, steady rates (see Figure 6-13).

INTERVAL SCHEDULES In interval schedules animals are reinforced when they respond after a period of time has passed following their previous reinforcement. For instance, in a **fixed-interval schedule** an animal might be reinforced for its first response after 2 minutes have passed since its previous reinforcement (an FI-2 minute schedule). In a **variable-interval schedule** animals are reinforced after intervals that vary around some average length of time. For example, in a VI-5 minute schedule an animal first might receive food for responding after 7 minutes have passed, and then it might be able to get food for any response that occurs after 30 seconds have passed. Over time, food will be available, on the average, 5 minutes after the previous food reinforcement. Compared to ratio schedules, interval schedules produce lower rates of responding, because in interval schedules the amount of reinforcement is not necessarily related to the rate of responding (see Figure 6-13). Variable-interval schedules produce low rates of fairly steady responding. Response rates are steady because the animal never knows when each interval will be over and reinforcement will once again be available. Like ratio schedules, variable-interval schedules produce behavior that is slower to be extinguished than do fixed schedules.

In all of these schedules, the same overriding principle obtains: animals respond to get the greatest amount of reinforcement for each response. Animals respond more on ratio schedules because they need to respond a lot if they are to obtain maximum reinforcement. Animals learn to respond only after 2 minutes have passed on an FI-2 schedule because they learn that earlier responses do not increase the likelihood of reinforcement.

Many of the effects of these schedules have been discovered in research with rats and pigeons. Is there any reason to believe that these effects are relevant to human behavior? Yes. Not only have many of these effects been replicated in experiments with humans, but they have been found in human behavior outside the learning laboratory. For instance, a fixed-ratio schedule is similar to *piecework* payment systems in which workers get paid only for producing a certain number of products, say for ten wooden toys. Although this payment schedule may seem fair—workers get paid exactly in proportion to their productivity—it was one of the first things that labor unions attempted to eliminate. This schedule leads to very high response rates that exhaust workers and create constant strain. Why don't workers simply work more slowly and decrease their fatigue? The answer may lie in Skinner's controversial suggestion about "voluntary" operant behavior: the effort that people expend is not really under their control. Instead, control resides in the environmental consequences of their actions: in this case, the pay schedule set by management.

If you think of human behavior that is extraordinarily persistent despite infrequent reward—fishing, gambling—usually that behavior is rewarded on a variable-ratio or variable-interval schedule. Gambling, for example, is rewarded on a variable-ratio schedule and gamblers will pull a slot machine endlessly or bet the farm on a horse race despite little reinforcement (see Figure 6-14). Just like animals on variable-ratio schedules, gamblers tend to continue placing bets even after long periods with no reinforcement. After all, they think the next bet may be the one that hits the jackpot!

FIGURE 6-14
REINFORCEMENT SCHEDULES
OUTSIDE THE LABORATORY.
(a) Slot machines offer a variable ratio schedule in which reinforcement—money—is produced by two operant behaviors: inserting coins into the machine and pulling the handle. People may play slot machines for hours without reinforcement, probably because they believe that they will win on the very next trial. (b) A recent newspaper article recounts the story of a man who developed a pattern of compulsive gambling. Common accounts of the origins of obsessive gambling tend to emphasize personality flaws or that it is a "sickness like alcoholism." Notice, however, that this unfortunate

individual clearly identifies the start of his serious gambling to a single instance in which he received tremendous reinforcement for horse betting. While

his preexisting personality may have been important in the development of his gambling problem, it would be a mistake to overlook the effect of operant learning.

(a)

(b)

His $15 bets became $25,000 habit

By Thomas M. Waller
Of The State Journal

The Super Bowl may be the top sports betting event, but this year a Madison man with a gambling problem is going to be on the sidelines.

"I went from a nickel-and-dime habit to $25,000 lost in the last three years," said John, a compulsive gambler who recently joined Gamblers Anonymous. "It wiped out most of our savings, and we're barely making ends meet."

A family man, John's life has been shaken by something he doesn't fully understand, something that began as recreational gambling and eventually cost him his job as a corporate manager. This is his story.

John began gambling in his youth, winning more than he lost at cards and in sports betting.

"I was pretty good at it," he said. "Over the years my $15 and $20 bets with friends became $50 and $100 bets through bookies, but it was still recreation. I had a good job, and I could afford it."

Six years ago, however, he began betting much larger sums, a change he attributes to his good luck during his second visit to Arlington Race Track.

"When I went there I didn't even know how to (bet on horses)," he said. "But I won $4,300 for picking the top three in a race. Within days my betting style changed."

To try to perfect his betting prowess, he answered an advertisement in USA Today by a Las Vegas sports betting information service.

Soon friends and acquaintances who knew he was doing well betting through four bookies (three in Dane County and one in Dubuque, Iowa) asked to get in on the action.

"Some of the bigger players asked me to place bets for them, so I did," he said. "I was a semi-bookie myself, but I made no money on it by placing bets for others."

(Wisconsin law forbids gambling and making book for a profit, with the exception of bingo on Indian reservations.)

Recreation became aggravation about three years ago, John said, when some of the people who asked him to bet for them didn't pay their gambling debts.

"Some of the guys didn't come through," he said. "I had $5,500 dumped on me and had to borrow from the bank."

John regrets he didn't stop his big-time betting then, but he felt compelled to "get even" and increased the

frequency and size of his bets. In football season, for example, he placed 30 to 40 bets per week and bet as much as $900 on one game.

Instead of quitting after taking in $900 on that Bears' game, the next week he bet $800 on the Vikings and $600 on Pittsburgh and lost both.

An avid Wisconsin Badgers fan, John said by 1982 gambling was dominating his life. He found himself cheering after a UCLA touchdown against Wisconsin.

"I didn't care who won," he said. "I just wanted to cover the point spread."

It was not unusual for John to get up at 5:30 a.m. Sundays to check his newspaper for, scores of Saturday night college games. The outcome of the games determined how much he would be able to bet on Sunday's pro games.

"One day I picked 10 pro games and lost nine of them because it was a day of upsets," he said. "I lost over $3,000 that day."

John said his wife could tell when he had bet on a game on whether he won because of his reaction afterward. When he lost and was silently despondent, she might ask how much he lost and he would lie, understating the loss.

Losing streaks were financed by

borrowing from banks and individuals.

With gambling debts weighing heavily, John said he had trouble sleeping and performing job duties. He kept betting, however, hoping his luck would change, and borrowing even more when it didn't.

John said he reached the bottom of the hole he was digging for himself recently when his employer learned he had been check-floating, using payroll checks provided willingly by some fellow employees.

(Check-floating involves legal cashing and writing of checks in such a way that interest-income can be doubled during the day or two it takes a check to clear.)

"The company said I was breaking its policy of borrowing from employees and fired me," he said. "It never occurred to me at the time that I shouldn't be borrowing from people who wanted to help. But now I can understand that it might look like they were being pressured, especially since I hired some of them."

Still unemployed and in debt, John has decided to seek help for his problem.

"In the past I'd bet my normal (a $200 to $300 bet) on the Super Bowl," he said. "Not any more. I've made a commitment to Gamblers Anonymous."

REINFORCEMENT PARADIGMS Suppose you have a 4-year-old child who screams at the dinner table. How might you help the child to act in a new way? You might yell at the child each time she yells, delay her getting her dessert, praise her when she doesn't yell, and so on. These strategies represent different **reinforcement paradigms**: different relations between operant behavior and reinforcers or punishers. Some paradigms involve **positive reinforcement**, in which a stimulus or consequence is presented when an animal performs an operant or target behavior and the reinforcement increases the likelihood of the target behavior. In **negative reinforcement** paradigms, on the other hand, operant behavior increases when a stimulus is removed or delayed. Perhaps the two most familiar reinforcement paradigms are reward and punishment training (see Figure 6-15), in which someone (or some animal) is punished or rewarded for a particular behavior. In *reward* training the consequence is a reinforcer that increases operant responding. In *punishment* training the consequence is aversive and decreases operant responding. Reinforcement paradigms influence people's lives every day. The young girl who is paid to do yard work is influenced by reward. The person who is singed by a hot stove burner is punished; reaching for the burner is the operant response, and being burned is the punisher. Both reward and punishment produce dramatic behavior change. Research has shown, however, that unless punishment is delivered wisely it can be ineffective or have negative effects (Azrin and Holz, 1966). For instance, research shows that the effects of punishment often exist only while punishment is imminent (only when the small boy is about to be scolded) and may be

FIGURE 6-15
REINFORCEMENT PARADIGMS.
Common reinforcement paradigms. Reinforcement paradigms are determined by two factors, the type of consequence and the relationship between the target behavior and the consequence (the contingency). Consequences are either reinforcing or punishing, and they may either be presented, removed, or delayed by the occurrence of the target behavior. These schedules have characteristic effects on the future occurrence of operant behavior. Reward, escape, and avoidance contingencies all increase rates of the target behavior, while punishment, withdrawal, and omission contingencies all reduce the future probability of the target behavior.

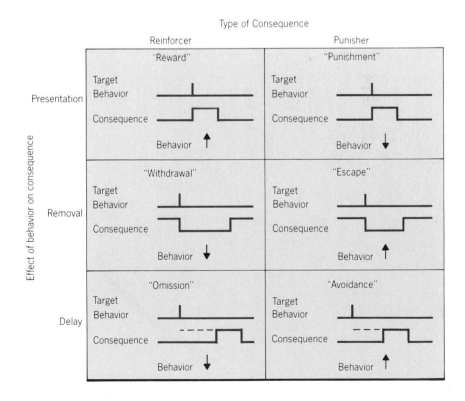

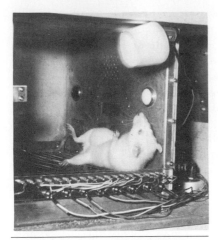

FIGURE 6-16   UNINTENDED EFFECTS OF PUNISHMENT.
The hungry rat in this picture learned that pressing the lever produced both food and a shock through the grid floor. The rat learned to get the food by pressing the lever with its hind foot and lying on its back so that its fur insulated it against the shock. This strategy subverted the experimenter's goals but shows that punishment can produce unanticipated operant behaviors.

accompanied by highly disruptive emotional behavior (crying, tantrums). For example, punishment may make people fearful and angry. An angry person might be aggressive and a fearful person may be too frightened to learn or perform. People (and animals) who strongly wish to avoid punishment may also avoid it in ways not intended by the operant conditioner (see Figure 6-16). Children may avoid punishment by lying, and felons may avoid punishment by forfeiting their bail.

Research shows (Schwartz, 1984) that in order for punishment to be maximally effective, punishment should be delivered so that

1. Punishment is as intense as possible or as intense as ethics permit. Joan is more likely to stop talking in class if her teacher punishes her with a 500-word essay than with a 100-word essay.
2. Punishment is delivered as soon after the target behavior as possible. Punishment that occurs a week after a boy breaks a neighbor's window is unlikely to be effective.
3. Punishment is introduced in an intense form in its initial application. The intensity of punishers should not be gradually escalated. A mother might want to use only the most mild form of punishment necessary; thus, she first shakes her head at her daughter, then scolds her, and finally spanks her. If the mother had scolded the daughter in the first place she may never have had to spank her.
4. Punishment should be certain—unavoidable.
5. Make sure that the punished response is not rewarded in any way while it is being punished. If a young boy is rewarded by his classmates' laughter for taunting his teacher, the teacher's punishment of him may never be effective.
6. Presumably, the punished behavior was rewarded in some way. Make sure the punished person or animal can gain access to this reward in some way other than through the punished behavior. If a child misbehaves in class to get attention, make sure that he or she can get attention in an acceptable way.

The four other reinforcement paradigms may be less familiar to you than reward or punishment, but nevertheless they are quite common. **Withdrawal** training is as familiar as a father's confiscating his daughter's car keys because she has broken a family rule. Withdrawal consists of taking away a reinforcer because of the occurrence of an operant. **Omission** training involves delaying access to a reinforcer. An example is a teacher's delaying children from going to recess because they talked too much in class. **Avoidance** training consists of delaying a punishment. An example is requesting and receiving an extension from the IRS on the deadline for submitting your taxes; the request is the operant, and tax payment is the punisher that is delayed. In **escape** training punishment stops once the operant response is made. This training is used by the bully who holds down a smaller child until the child says "uncle." Saying "uncle" is the operant response that ends the punishment. In most cases people use combinations of these paradigms. Putting people in prison, for example, involves *punishment*—rough treatment from guards and other prisoners—*withdrawal* from reinforcers like movies, the freedom to travel, and good food, and *omission* because prisoners must wait months or years before they can gain access to reinforcers.

OPERANT GENERALIZATION AND DISCRIMINATION Discrimination is a universal feature of learning. When a pigeon learns to peck a key for food, it has learned to direct its attention to the key instead of to any other environmental stimulus. It also has learned *how* to respond (keypecking) and *when* to respond (during training sessions). Researchers have been particularly interested in how animals learn when to make operant responses. Animals seem to learn that particular environmental stimuli signal that reinforcement is available. These are **discriminative stimuli**. Why do people work harder when the boss is watching? Why do children behave affectionately and obediently when a Christmas tree and presents are in the house? It may sound cynical to attribute children's affection to signals that rewards are available, but signals of reward and punishment do powerfully affect behavior.

Although people and animals must discriminate to learn, their discrimination is not perfect. For example, a young man may have learned to act suggestively when he hears a woman speak seductively. But he may be quite embarrassed if he makes a suggestive remark (emits the operant behavior) when the young woman is merely being courteous and has no romantic interest in him whatsoever. He has been trapped by **generalization**, a failure to discriminate between a stimulus signaling reinforcement and a similar, but essentially different, stimuli.

People and animals generalize widely from their learning unless they learn that certain stimuli are *uniquely* associated with reinforcement. The degree of generalization is called the **gradient of generalization**. For example, pigeons learned to peck a key for food while a 1000-Hz tone sounded constantly. After the pigeons learned to peck the key, they were given a generalization test in which tones of other frequencies were presented. They responded at every tone frequency, although they responded slightly more to the 1000-Hz tone, a result that reflects broad generalization (see Figure 6-17*a*). Instead of being tested right away, a second group of animals was trained further. They heard the 1000-Hz tone periodically, and food was available only when the tone was present. The tone began to serve as a discriminative stimulus. These pigeons produced the **generalization gradient** (degree of generalization) shown in Figure 6-17*b*. The extra training decreased their generalization dramatically. Pigeons that were trained still further and reinforced for responding only when they heard either a 450- or a 2500-Hz tone learned not only that hearing a tone predicted reinforcement, but also that particular tones predicted reinforcement (Figure 6-17*c*). Only when particular environmental cues, and not others, predict reinforcement do animals learn to discriminate. The pigeons did not know that the tone signaled a reward until the tone was presented periodically and the reward was available only then. The suggestive young man would never learn to discriminate if every woman reinforced his advances no matter how inappropriate or unwelcome they were. The ability to discriminate has tremendous survival benefit, for animals need to be able to learn when their behavior may lead to reinforcement.

FIGURE 6-17
GENERALIZATION AND
DISCRIMINATION OF OPERANT
RESPONDING.
(a) *This figure shows the keypeck responses of pigeons to a variety of tones after the pigeons had been reinforced for pecking while a 1000-Hz tone was continuously played. Each number refers to a different bird. (b) This graph shows the responses of pigeons after they had been reinforced for responding in the presence of a 1000-Hz tone but also had been given trials in which no tone was present, and responses were not reinforced. (c) This graph shows the responses of pigeons after they had been reinforced for responding only to a 450-and a 2500-Hz tone. Notice that as pigeons get more information about the response–reinforcement contingency, their responding becomes more highly discriminated. In (a) pigeons responded as much when tones were not presented as when they were. In (b) and (c) pigeons showed little responding when no tone was present. (From Jenkins and Harrison, 1960.)*

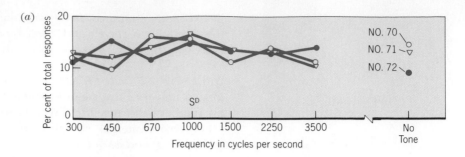

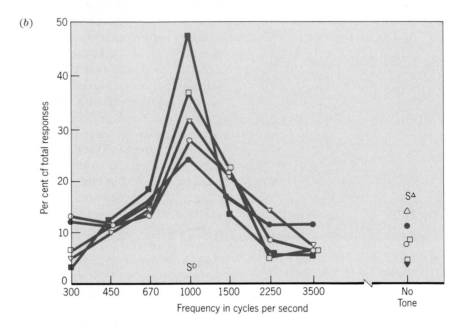

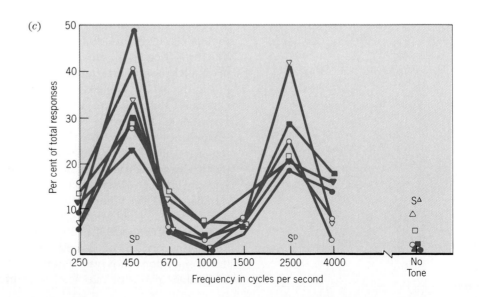

STRENGTHENING AND WEAKENING OPERANT LEARNING   Many of the principles discussed with respect to strengthening and weakening Pavlovian learning are relevant here. For instance, operant learning is strengthened by increasing the number of conditioning trials and by increasing the size of the reinforcer. However, the former statement is true only if one equates strengthening learning with the magnitude of the operant response (size or number of operant responses). If conditioning strength is equated with resistance to extinction, a different pattern emerges. As is the case with Pavlovian learning, extinction is the most effective way to weaken a learned operant response; responding declines if reinforcement does not follow an operant. While spontaneous recovery can occur, this too can be extinguished.

Two seemingly incongruous findings have been reported with respect to the rate of extinction. First, the larger the reinforcer (e.g., the more food), the more rapid the rate of extinction (Wagner, 1961). Second, if operant training is carried out for a great many trials, animals will often extinguish more rapidly than if fewer trials are used (Theios and Brelsford, 1964). It has been suggested that these effects occur because the larger the reinforcer and the greater the conditioning trials, the more an animal notices the beginning of extinction (Mowrer and Jones, 1945). When extinction begins, the highly trained or highly reinforced animal's expectations about reinforcement are dashed more quickly than are other animals'.

SECONDARY REINFORCEMENT   *Secondary reinforcement* in operant learning refers to a situation in which a previously neutral stimulus becomes reinforcing or punishing because it has been paired with another reinforcer or punisher. A ubiquitous example of this is money. People will work, scheme, and gamble to get money—even though there is nothing intrinsically appealing about it. It is reinforcing only because it has been associated previously with all sorts of desirable commodities that are **primary reinforcers**. A primary reinforcer is effective without its being paired with any other reinforcer: for example, food and drink are primary reinforcers. Secondary reinforcement, of course, extends the range of operant learning because it results in previously neutral stimuli becoming effective reinforcers or punishers. If secondary reinforcers are not regularly paired with a primary reinforcer, they will eventually lose their reinforcing effect.

What Is Learned in Operant Learning?

In Skinner's view, an organism learns to perform an operant because the operant is associated, or paired, with reinforcement. This then is really a contiguity theory of learning similar to Pavlov's theory of learning. But as with Pavlovian learning, contiguity alone does not adequately explain operant learning. Take, for example, the phenomenon of **learned helplessness**, which is induced when an animal is exposed to uncontrollable stress. An animal might be exposed to a series of shocks that it cannot control or avoid (Seligman and Maier, 1967). A person might be exposed to unrelenting criticism. Exposure to an uncontrollable stressor makes animals passive and unable to learn. A dog exposed to a series of intense

BOX 6-2
USES OF OPERANT
CONDITIONING

Whenever human behavior is followed by pleasant or unpleasant consequences, operant learning occurs. Scientists and educators have put this principle to work in many different operant conditioning programs for achieving important goals. Psychologists, for instance, have developed punishment programs in which psychotic children are shocked for banging their heads against walls. Shocks sound cruel, but they can reduce head-banging, a common form of self-mutilation among psychotic children. In many schools, children are reinforced for achieving academic goals: for learning to read or to count, for sitting still in class, for staying out of fights, and so forth. In clinics, patients are rewarded for changing the levels of their blood pressure or tension in their muscles (which may cause headaches).

Psychologists also have used operant techniques to increase the caloric intake and weight of anorexic patients. Anorexics, most of whom are women, starve themselves, sometimes to death (Isager, Brinch, Kreiner, & Tolstrup, 1985). The cause of anorexia nervosa, as this condition is called, is unknown. Most anorexics resist mightily any attempts to get them to eat. For years therapists were at a loss as to how to get anorexics to gain weight. But in the last 10 years, operant conditioning has been quite successful. The program involves a reward paradigm in which young women are reinforced for eating and gaining weight (Agras and Werne, 1977). One young woman, for example, entered treatment weighing about 90 pounds. She was put in the hospital for a week-long baseline period, during which time she was encouraged to eat but was not given any additional treatment (see Box Figure 1). Then she was reinforced for eating and gaining weight. Reinforcement consisted of attention and praise, freedom to leave her room, and eventually freedom to go on short trips outside the hospital. Her calorie intake and weight increased greatly under the reinforcement contingency. To prove that her weight gain during this period was due to the contingency between weight gain and reinforcement, a noncontingent reinforcement period was instituted in which she received the reinforcers, but they did not systematically follow her eating or weight gain. She ate much less once reinforcement was made noncontingent, and her weight began to level off. These results provide powerful evidence that simple, everyday events can exert powerful effects on behavior, if the events are made contingent.

BOX FIGURE 1 OPERANT CONDITIONING FOR ANOREXIA NERVOSA.
This figure shows the weight gain and caloric intake of a young woman who was treated for anorexia nervosa. (From Agras and Werne, 1977.)

and inescapable shocks will not be able to learn to escape the shocks if escape is later made possible. One theory of learned helplessness is that a dog will struggle when it is first shocked, but as it discovers that shock is unavoidable, it struggles for briefer periods. A second theory of learned helplessness is that the organism learns that it has *no control* over shock and becomes passive not because it is rewarded for passivity, but because it has learned that shock is uncontrollable.

Maier (1970), ingeniously, discovered a way to test the two theories of helplessness. He compared the learning performance of two different groups of dogs. One group had been exposed to inescapable shocks that produced helplessness; the second group also received intense shocks but for this group, shock was escapable if a dog remained absolutely still and passive when getting shocked. The results showed that only the first

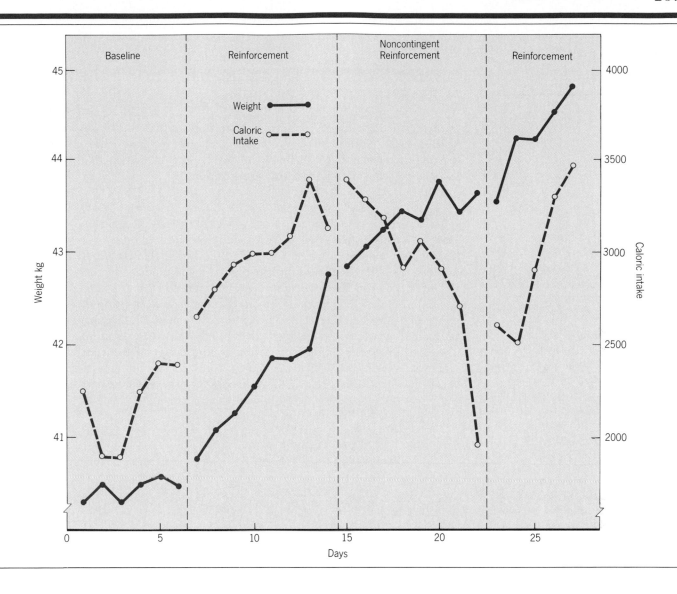

group became helpless; the second group later learned to avoid shocks just as shock-naive dogs would. How are these results relevant to understanding "what is learned"? Because of the way the experiment was designed, both groups of dogs had exactly the same shock experience, and both groups showed less and less activity over successive shocks. The only difference between the groups is that for one group shock was controllable (escapable) through inactivity, while for the other group it was not. The results showed that the contingency between shock offset and inactive behavior was not enough to produce similar learning in the two groups. One group learned to become inactive, while the other group learned that shock was uncontrollable. This suggests that animals can clearly discriminate when they do and do not have control over important environmental events and that an important factor in other operant conditioning phenomena is the organism's belief that it is controlling its environment. (See Chapter 13 for more information on learned helplessness.)

NONASSOCIATIVE LEARNING

In associative forms of learning, people and animals make associative links between stimuli or between stimuli and responses and thereby learn. But two kinds of learning do not appear to be based on these associative links: habituation and sensitization.

Habituation

Have you ever noticed that when you first put on a bandage you notice it, but after a period of time you forget it completely? **Habituation** is a decrease in behavioral response to repeated stimulation. In the case of the bandage, you learn to ignore, not attend to, the repeated tactile (touch) stimulation produced by the bandage. (Habituation does not cause all instances of decreased behavioral response. Both sensory adaptation and muscle fatigue produce decreased behavioral response as well. The key difference is that habituation occurs either in the central nervous system or in major nerve ganglia; it is not due to changes in sensory receptors or muscles.) Habituation clearly is of great evolutionary impor-

FIGURE 6-18 HABITUATION IN THE APLYSIA.
(a) *The* Aplysia *retracts its gill whenever its siphon is touched. (b) This response habituates rapidly with repeated stimulation. The diagram shows the response of a motor neuron that activates a gill-withdrawal muscle. When sensory siphon neurons are stimulated repeatedly, the responses of the motor neuron and the gill muscles get smaller and smaller. (From Castellucci and Kandel, 1976.) (c) A diagram of the neural circuit responsible for the gill-withdrawal reflex. Sensory neurons relay information from the siphon and make neural connections with motor neurons that activate gill muscles. Thus, only a single neural connection between sensory and motor neurons is involved in the reflex. During habituation the sensory neurons release less and less neurotransmitter to the motor neurons. (From Kandel, 1979.)*

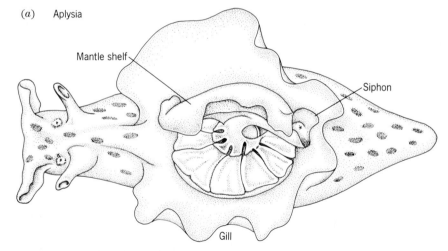

(a) Aplysia

Mantle shelf

Siphon

Gill

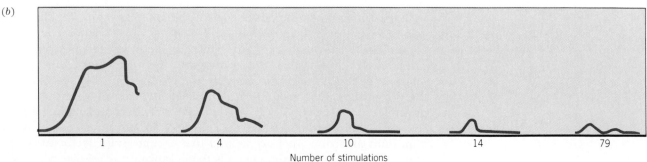

(b)

1   4   10   14   79

Number of stimulations

tance. Neither humans nor other animals could continually attend to every trivial stimulus in their environments and survive.

According to one cognitive theory of habituation proposed by the Yale psychologist Allan Wagner, every time an animal encounters a new stimulus, it must process information about that stimulus to determine whether the stimulus is safe, dangerous, tasty, insignificant, and so on (Wagner, 1976). Responses that habituate are themselves produced by the cognitive processing of attributes of the new stimulus, a process labeled **rehearsal**. Therefore, many of the behavioral responses that an animal makes to a new stimulus are produced by the animal's attempts to rehearse, or process, information about it. Habituation thus occurs because a stimulus stops being new. With repeated presentations and rehearsal, the animal builds up a memory of the stimulus, and once the animal recognizes the stimulus, it no longer responds to the stimulus by processing extensively information about it. Habituation is the retention of the stimulus in memory.

Researchers also have investigated the physiological basis of habituation (Castellucci, Pinsker, Kupfermann, and Kandel, 1970; Kandel, 1977). One animal known to show habituation is the *aplysia* (see Figure 6-18*a*), a simple invertebrate that lives in the ocean. This creature has a relatively simple nervous system and so is a good candidate for study.

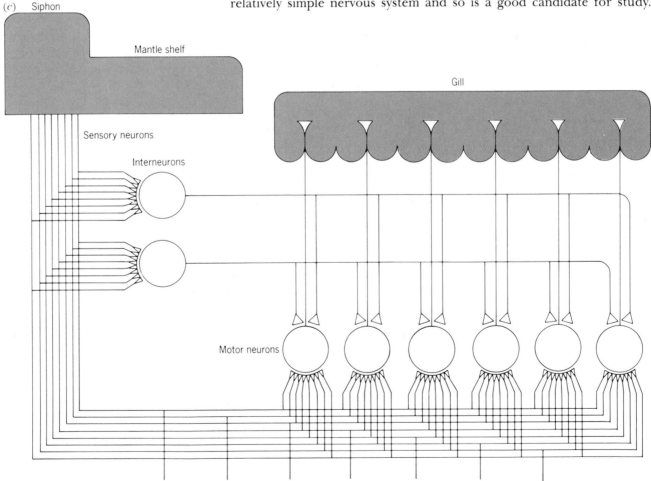

The human brain alone contains approximately 10 billion neurons; there are only about 15,000 neurons in an entire aplysia.

The aplysia has gills that it can withdraw reflexively when a particular area, such as its siphon, is touched or stimulated. Figure 6-18*b* shows the gradual decline in this reflex after repeated stimulation. To pinpoint the source of this habituation, the researchers first identified the specific sensory and motor nerves that are involved in the withdrawal reflex (Figure 6-18*c*). They found that sensory adaptation and muscle fatigue were not involved in the habituation. Then they inserted a microelectrode into a motor neuron and stimulated a single sensory neuron that communicated with that motor neuron. By recording the size of the **postsynaptic potentials** (see Chapter 2) after repeated stimulation, they saw that the *size* of postsynaptic potentials never decreased. But the *probability* that a postsynaptic potential would occur decreased as the number of stimulations increased. The sensitivity of the motor neuron had not changed, because when a potential occurred it was the same size at the beginning as at the end of habituation. The critical physiological change behind habituation was the release by sensory neurons of increasingly less neurotransmitter, and hence, the probability of a motor response became smaller and smaller.

This research shows the value of studying simple animals. But one potential drawback to this kind of study is that the issue under study— habituation—may be different in simple and more complex animals. Habituation in humans may occur quite differently from the way it does in the aplysia. In general, though, much research suggests that more complex animals usually do not wholly lose the abilities or processes of simpler forms. Instead, higher animals add to the capabilities that they have in common with more primitive forms. Thus, the aplysia probably does not answer all the questions about habituation in humans, but it probably sheds light on basic processes of habituation that occur in all species.

Sensitization

When people or other animals are repeatedly stimulated, not only do they habituate to the stimulus, but parts of their nervous systems become sensitized so that they react strongly to any *change* in stimulation. This phenomenon is called **sensitization**. For example, if the aplysia is habituated to stimulation of its siphon, and then its head is suddenly stimulated, the next time its siphon is stimulated, its gill-withdrawal response is much stronger. Any stimulus that disrupts habituation is a **dishabituator**. A dishabituator does not produce sensitization; it reveals it.

Although psychologists still must guess about the importance of sensitization, they are beginning to understand its physiological basis. Recent research suggests that two types of processes may produce dishabituation and sensitization. In the case of the aplysia, it appears that while head stimulation does not directly affect gill-withdrawal motor neurons, such stimulation does excite interneurons (neurons between sensory and motor neurons) that synapse on sensory neurons from the siphon (see Figure 6-19). This excitation results in increased neurotransmitter release from siphon sensory neurons, and thus, greater gill-withdrawal

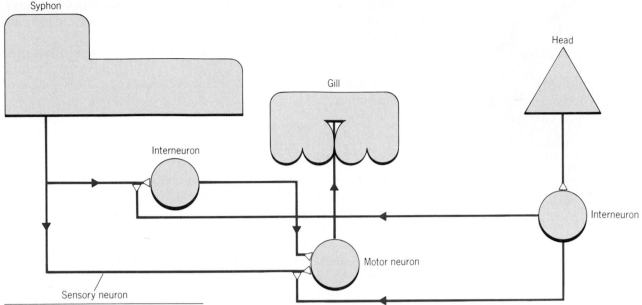

FIGURE 6-19   NEURAL CIRCUIT IN SENSITIZATION.
The arrows indicate the direction of neuronal impulses in the Aplysia. *(From Kandel, 1979.)*

response. In addition, recent research suggests that sensitization and habituation processes may occur within the same sensory-motor system, such as the auditory or visual system. Researchers have found that repeated stimulation of a sensory auditory structure produced habituation, while stimulation of an efferent auditory structure produced sensitization (Davis, Parisi, Gendelman, Tischler, and Kehne, 1982).

How, if at all, does sensitization allow animals to adapt to their environments? To answer this, remember that the habituated animal becomes increasingly less responsive to its environment. But this unresponsiveness can be dangerous. Just as continual orienting and responding would be maladaptive, so would too little alertness. Sensitization may be adaptive because it counteracts the tendency for an animal to pay less attention and respond less to harmless, familiar stimuli. Imagine that you have been driving down a monotonous stretch of road for several hours. You hardly notice the other cars or the traffic signs. However, if a police siren bursts in your ears, you would probably jump and pay tremendous attention to everything around you. Sensitization refers to the fact that responding to an habituated stimulus can be completely reinstated through the presentation of a second stimulus.

MODERN DEVELOPMENTS IN LEARNING THEORY AND RESEARCH

At this point, you may be feeling unsettled. You can probably appreciate the fact that Pavlovian and operant learning occur and even that they are relevant to your life. But you may also be thinking that they are not much like what you think of when you think of learning. You also may be

FIGURE 6-20   WOLFGANG KÖHLER. (1887–1968).

Köhler was stranded on the island of Tenerife, near Africa, during World War I. He took advantage of the opportunity by initiating the first studies of complex learning by primates.

wondering whether the theories that you have seen so far can explain how you learned to drive, how you learned the difference between right and wrong, and how you learned algebra. Isn't there something more to learning than conditioned reflexes and operant conditioning? Does the operant and Pavlovian learning of pigeons pecking and dogs salivating really account for how humans learn? We will now try to answer some of these questions.

Insight Learning

One question that we want to answer is: What is the relation between principles of operant learning and the kind of illuminating flashes of understanding that people (and, yes, lower animals) have in solving problems? You probably have had the experience of laboring to solve a problem, taking a break, and, then, when you are near sleep, on vacation, or relaxed in front of a warm fire, suddenly seeing the solution. Not only do insights occur suddenly, but they may occur when the learner has actually stopped working on a problem! This is far different from the gradual learning that occurs as animals struggle to master operant conditioning schedules. The German psychologist Wolfgang Köhler (Figure 6-20) argued that insight learning is very different from the piece-meal sort of learning that goes on in operant and Pavlovian learning, and that it is not unique to humans.

Köhler (1925) examined the learning of chimpanzees, our close cousins, in situations that permitted the animal to figure out how to solve problems (and get reinforced). For instance, in one experiment, Köhler nailed a banana to the ceiling of a room, too high for the chimpanzees to reach. The only other object in the room was a wooden box in the middle of the floor. As soon as the banana was nailed to the ceiling, all of the chimpanzees tried to jump up and get it. One chimpanzee, a male named Sultan, soon quit this futile effort and began to pace restlessly around the room. Suddenly, Sultan stood still in front of the box, then seized it and pushed it across the floor under the fruit. He then jumped on the box, sprang upward, and tore down the fruit (see also Figure 6-21). Perhaps the most striking display of insight (as well as of cheek), was Sultan's strategy for reaching a banana high above his head, when no movable furniture was nearby. Sultan calmly took the researcher by the arm, positioned him under the fruit, and climbed him until he could reach the fruit!

This type of learning is neither operant nor Pavlovian. The animals did not gradually learn how to secure reinforcement through successive approximations to the correct strategy. They seemed to wrestle with the problem for a long time and then suddenly hit upon the correct solution. Köhler argued that the animals make mental images of the elements of a problem and then figure out the consequences of various actions. Notice what a tremendous break this is from Thorndike's or Skinner's approach to explaining animal learning. Instead of explaining the chimps' learning on the basis of the pairing of stimuli and responses, Köhler attributed animals' learning to particular types of cognitive events—to particular

FIGURE 6-21   INSIGHT LEARNING IN THE CHIMP.
These pictures show the different strategies chimpanzees used to get a banana nailed to the ceiling, far out of their reach. The chimpanzees either stacked boxes (a,b), or stood on boxes and swung a long pole (c). The chimpanzee who solved the problem (d) joined two short poles into a pole long enough to reach the ceiling. The chimp shown in (d) is the inimitable Sultan. (From Köhler, 1925.)

(a)

(b)

(c)

(d)

thought processes. For many behavioral psychologists, speculation about mental processes was forbidden territory. They argued that if one cannot actually observe cognitive events, then it is dangerous speculation to infer such events and include them in a theory. But Wolfgang Köhler was one of the researchers who crossed into this forbidden territory and opened the way for other psychologists to study the role of cognition in learning.

FIGURE 6-22 TOLMAN'S MAZE.
A maze used to show that rats make
cognitive maps of important
environmental features.

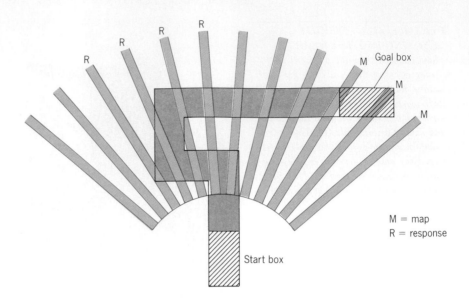

Cognitive Maps

Like Köhler, Edward Tolman (1886–1959) believed that animals make mental representations of events and objects and use these representations to guide behavior. To prove this, Tolman conducted an experiment in which he trained rats to run in a maze (Tolman, Richie, and Kalish, 1946; see Figure 6-22). First the rats were trained to run through a simple alley (the shaded alley in the figure) for a reward of food. Then this simple alley was replaced with multiple alleys (the red paths in the figure). If the rats had learned merely to execute certain motor responses to get food (as behaviorists like Thorndike had suggested), then they would turn left out of the start box and go into the alleys labeled *R* (for "response"). But if the rats had made a mental representation or **cognitive map** of where the food had been located in the past (in the goal box), they would turn right out of the start box, in the direction of the food's previous location (the alleys marked *M* for "map"). In fact, the rats regularly chose the *M* alleys, suggesting that animals form mental representations of their environments and that these mental representations guide their behavior.

Set or Concept Learning

Psychologists now know that animals can develop sophisticated representations of abstract relationships among stimuli. They can learn **sets** or **concepts**.

Harry Harlow (1949) was the first to show that animals can learn to respond to stimuli in terms of a learned, abstract concept. Harlow gave rhesus monkeys discrimination trials in which a tray containing two objects was placed outside of the bars of their cages. The objects were such things as a small blue ball, a pink triangle, a black circle, and a white cube. On each trial, one of the two objects covered a small piece of fruit.

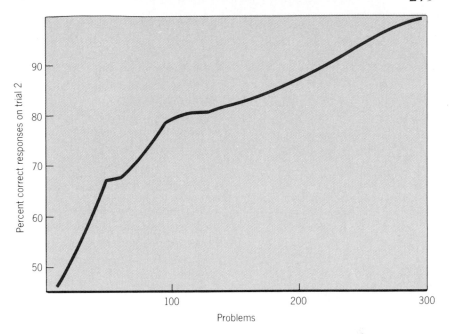

The monkey was allowed to pick up one of the objects and eat the fruit if it was under the selected object. But if the monkey selected the wrong object, it got no fruit. Over the next five trials, the monkey saw the same objects as on the first trial. The location of the objects was randomly changed across trials, but the fruit always remained under the same object. After six trials, the monkeys were given two new objects from which to choose, and so on through some 300 sets of objects.

How did the monkeys do on this task? Figure 6-23 shows the performance of monkeys on the *second* trial with each new pair of stimulus objects. The monkeys quickly learned which object hid the fruit and by the 300th problem were performing almost perfectly on the second trial. How did they learn?

What faced the monkey at the beginning of each new problem? Let's assume that the monkey had been reinforced for selecting the white cube on its previous problem set, and now it is faced with a pink triangle and a black circle on its next problem set. Which does it choose? How can it generalize information learned in its previous problems to this new problem? Our monkey might choose objects based upon their locations (e.g., to the monkey's right or left) or shape. Actually, neither of these features provided information about the location of the food. In each problem set, one of the stimuli was arbitrarily designated as always being correct, and the fruit was always hidden under it. Thus, in the problem described above, if the black circle was correct, the fruit would always be under it.

What guided the monkeys' selections was not any physical feature of the object, but instead, an abstract concept or rule. This concept was something like, "If I find fruit under an object on the first trial, that object will always have fruit under it for the rest of this problem set. If there is no fruit under the object I select, then the fruit must be under the other object, and I will try that one on the next trial." In effect, the animals learned the concept of "If I win, I'll stay with this object. If I lose, I'll shift." There is no other way to explain the monkeys' excellent performance in this learning task.

Harlow's research is important because it shows that animals can learn and use abstract concepts, and because it provides a method for investigating such concepts. In Chapter 8 we review research on how humans learn and use complex concepts to solve problems.

Observational Learning

The importance of mental representations to learning is probably clearest in the case of **observational learning**. Much human learning is produced not through operant or Pavlovian conditioning but through simple observation (Bandura and Walters, 1963). How else could one explain how children learn to "shave" like daddy or "read" the newspaper (upside down), or how adults so quickly develop the skills to perform complex activities like driving a car or selecting a wardrobe? Certainly, people need some step-by-step training, but much of these repertoires are acquired merely by observing others. Neither Pavlovian nor operant conditioning is able to account for such learning, for usually there is no period of gradual acquisition or trial-and-error learning that would be expected if operant or Pavlovian learning were involved. Moreover, in observational learning, people need not directly experience any reinforcer or consequence; they must merely observe what goes on around them.

FIGURE 6-24 IMITATION LEARNING.
Children learn early in life to imitate patterns of behavior that they see in their parents.

DETERMINANTS OF OBSERVATIONAL LEARNING   What determines whether an observed behavior will be learned? What determines whether a boy will try to shave like his father (Figure 6-24) or try to comfort a classmate who is crying? One basic determinant of observational learning is whether the observer actually *attends* to (watches intently) a behavior. People are especially likely to attend to modeled behavior when they think that the model seems competent when they identify with the model (Rosenbaum and Tucker, 1952; Rosenkrans, 1967). Also, people attend when there is a powerful *incentive* for learning modeled behavior. This probably explains why most teenagers seem incapable of learning that the verb "to be" takes the nominative case but learn to negotiate their parents' car through hairpin turns at 40 miles per hour. When teenagers observe the two classes of behavior, good grammar and driving skills, their level of interest and attention are determined by their expectations of reward for learning the two different skills.

Besides attention, a second factor that influences observation learning is remembering and *rehearsing* an observed behavior. Rehearsal can be verbal—rehearsing the lines of a poem—behavioral—practicing a dance step—or cognitive—imagining that you are distributing your weight correctly through a ski turn. Not only does rehearsal enhance the memory of modeled behavior, but it also improves the skill with which people perform the behavior.

For observational learning to occur, a person or an animal must

1. Attend closely to the behavior of another organism, even though the observing organism is not rewarded directly for observing.
2. See the relevance of the modeled behavior to its own situation.
3. Recall the modeled behavior when the observer is subsequently in a situation where the behavior is appropriate.

These requirements naturally limit the number of species in which observational learning can occur. Rats and pigeons do not have the cognitive sophistication to appreciate the relevance of modeled behavior. Observational learning does occur in monkeys and apes, however (Box 6-3).

RANGE OF OBSERVATIONAL LEARNING   What kinds of behavior, skills, and information can be acquired through observational learning? Although people certainly can acquire motor skills such as golf swings, crocheting, and dance steps, the range of observational learning is much more extensive. At the simplest level, people can acquire Pavlovian conditioned responses—a conditioned eye blink—through observation alone (Bernal and Berger, 1976). At the most complex level, observation can lead to the development of broad attitudes and behavioral dispositions such as altruism (Gelfand and Hartmann, 1980).

The broad range of behavior that can be learned through observation has led many theorists to suggest that observational learning is one of the most important influences on children's development. Anyone who has observed children knows that children do not need to be directly reinforced for imitating their parents: for dressing like them, talking like them, or adopting their moral and political convictions. They do this naturally, through observation. It has been shown that when children are exposed to adult models who consistently display nurturant behavior, the children are more likely to display concern for and help others in need (Gelfand and Hartmann, 1980). When they watch television programs in which giving help is a central feature, they help and share more (Friedrich and Stein, 1975). Likewise, when they watch violent programs, children are likely to act aggressively themselves (Gelfand and Hartmann, 1980; see Chapter 17).

NATURE OF OBSERVATIONAL LEARNING   We have seen that an important element in Pavlovian learning is learning when to expect the US. In operant learning the animal or the person apparently learns that it can control its environment. What is the nature of observational learning?

Some critics suggested that observational learning is really just operant conditioning. According to this view, what people learn in observational learning is not a particular response, but rather the general response of imitating modeled behavior. Is observational learning merely learning to imitate?

It would be very difficult to attribute observational learning to imitation alone. For instance, how does one account for the learning that

BOX 6-3
MONKEYS WHO ARE AFRAID OF SNAKES

Psychologists have been interested in monkeys' fear of snakes because the monkeys' fears may be a good model of human phobias. About 80 percent of wild monkeys fear snakes, but few of those reared in the laboratory do (Joslin, Fletcher, and Emlen, 1964). This suggests that snake fear is not genetically determined, but is learned. But how? Although some fears are probably produced by Pavlovian conditioning, it is unlikely that 80 percent of monkeys in the wild have had traumatic contacts with snakes (Joslin et al., 1964; Mineka, Keir, and Price, 1980). Perhaps the monkeys acquire their intense fear through observational learning.

To determine whether monkeys can learn a fear of snakes through observation, researchers exposed laboratory-reared monkeys to the reactions of wild-reared monkeys that were viewing a real snake or other stimuli (a toy snake, a model snake, and neutral objects such as blocks) (Cook, Mineka, Wolkenstein, and Laitsch, 1985). They measured the frequency of fearful behavior in the animals as they were exposed to the various objects. Fear behavior included flapping the ears, withdrawing, and grimacing (see Box Figure 1). At first monkeys reared in the wild displayed many fearful behaviors, whereas laboratory-reared monkeys showed virtually none. Then, for 3 weeks, monkeys who did not seem fearful watched fearful monkeys react to both the snake and neutral objects. Not only did the observers learn to fear snakes (Box Figure 2), but 3 months later they were still fearful.

Observational learning offers real survival advantages. Animals need not suffer the attack of a predator to learn to fear it. Observational learning would allow many monkeys to learn to fear snakes at the expense of

BOX FIGURE 1 FEAR GRIMACE.
A characteristic fear grimace in a young rhesus monkey.

---

occurs in which one learns *not* to imitate a model? In one well-known study (Bandura, Ross, and Ross, 1961), children watched an adult strike a bobbing plastic doll. When the adult then left the room, children usually imitated what the adult had done. But if they saw the adult being punished for striking the doll, they were unlikely to copy the aggressive acts (Bandura, 1965). It was not that the children had not learned the modeled behavior. They had decided not to *perform* it. In other words, humans do not just learn to imitate whatever they see. They learn through observation and then decide, based upon the prevailing incentives, whether to enact what they have observed.

Bandura, a Stanford psychologist who pioneered observational learning research, believes that observational learning depends upon the observer developing an imagined **schema** or representation of a sequence of motor acts. In executing this schema, learners actively compare their performance against what they remember about the modeled act. If you ever see young dancers trying to master a new dance movement or step, you can almost see them struggle to recall what it looked like when it was demonstrated and then they try to enact what they remember.

the few poor individuals who first showed their fellows that snakes are worthy of fear. The implications for human behavior are far-reaching. Parents who react fearfully to spiders, dogs, or heights may be conditioning the same fears in their children. Sometimes observational learning can lead to undesirable outcomes. Parents who react fearfully to other humans—those who are of a different race or religion—may be conditioning the same fear in their children, too. Therefore, it may be good for parents to act bravely and humanely, if not for their own good, then for the good of their children.

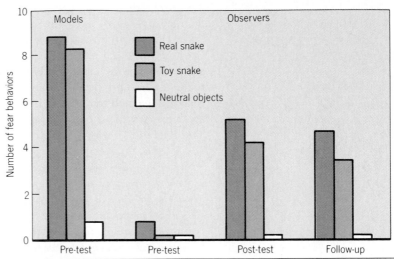

BOX FIGURE 2   EFFECTS OF MODELED FEAR IN MONKEYS. The number of fear behaviors such as fear grimaces (Box Figure 1) shown by model and observer monkeys. The pretest occurred prior to the six observational learning sessions, while the post-test and follow-up occurred 1–3 days and 3 months, respectively, after the final observational learning session. Notice that the observers' learned fear behavior was parallel to that of the model monkeys; observers showed the greatest fear to the real snake, slightly less fear to the toy snake, and virtually no fear to the neutral objects. The lack of fear to the neutral objects shows that observers did not learn a general fear of the experimental context or procedure, but rather they learned specifically to show fear responses to snake-like stimuli. *(From Cook et al., 1985.)*

BIOLOGICAL INFLUENCES ON LEARNING

All of the following have one important thing in common:

1. Training a pig to drop wooden coins in a piggy bank to get food reward.
2. Training a pigeon to peck a button to escape shock.
3. Using shocks to train a rat to avoid a flavored fluid.

What do they have in common? They won't work. You can come to understand why they won't work by examining the evolutionary pressures on each of these animals in its natural environment. For, although psychologists often study animals in laboratories, each animal's genetic endowment and its instinctive behavior patterns accompany it into the laboratory.

The Misbehavior of Organisms

The Brelands were a husband and wife team of learning researchers who trained animals to perform for zoos, businesses, and television commercials (Figure 6-25). Usually their operant conditioning procedures worked very well. But their failures are more illuminating than their successes. In one case, the Brelands trained a raccoon to pick up small metal coins and deposit them in a metal box to get food. After the raccoon learned to do this, the Brelands rewarded the raccoon with food after every second coin deposit so that he wouldn't get full too quickly. The Breland's report:

> *Now the raccoon really had problems (and so did we). Not only could he not let go of the coins, but he spent seconds, even minutes, rubbing them together (in a most miserly fashion), and dipping them into the container. He carried on this behavior to such an extent that the practical application we had in mind—a display featuring a raccoon putting money in a piggy bank—simply was not feasible. The rubbing behavior became worse and worse as time went on, in spite of nonreinforcement.*

> *(Breland and Breland, 1972, p. 183)*

The Brelands ran into a similar problem when they attempted to train pigs to pick up wooden coins and drop them into a piggy bank. At first the pigs learned to do this flawlessly (pigs, like raccoons, are fast learners, especially when food is the reinforcer). However, as the pigs continued to perform, they began to drop the wooden disks and root at them with their noses. Eventually it took the pigs 10 minutes to carry four coins six feet! Pig after pig interminably rooted at the coins.

FIGURE 6-25 AN OPERANT CONDITIONING SUCCESS.
Here, the Brelands were successful in operantly conditioning this little piggy to go to market.

What can explain the fact that these animals engaged in repetitive, seemingly pointless, behaviors even though these behaviors cost them considerable reinforcement? In each case the food reward appeared to trigger or elicit consummatory behaviors, even though the animal was not rewarded for such behaviors. These behaviors were so common in each species, and so persistent, that the Brelands were forced to conclude that the behaviors were instinctive. Apparently, evolutionary pressures had favored raccoons that washed their food and pigs that rooted when searching for food. In essence what was happening was that food, or the anticipation of food, was eliciting consummatory unconditioned responses (URs) in animals. The connection between food and these responses was so strong that it overcame the operant contingencies, a phenomenon labeled by the Brelands as **instinctive drift**. In a sense, the animals were trapped by their own instincts.

This finding was important because it provided clear evidence that John Locke was wrong: animals are not *tabulae rasae*. They do not enter the world ready to learn and perform any behavior that might be rewarded. Rather, animals bring with them into any learning situation tendencies and biases indelibly stamped into them through millions of years of evolution.

Species-specific Defense Reactions

For many years psychologists believed that one of the most important types of operant learning was avoidance learning, because it was so important to the survival of animals in their natural environments. Consider the case of the mouse scurrying home after a busy night eating grain in a farmer's nearby field. As the mouse runs along it suddenly hears a whooshing noise and then feels a sharp scratch on its back. The mouse looks to see a large owl sail past, having just missed making the mouse its appetizer. The relevance of avoidance learning? The mouse will immediately begin making defensive maneuvers the next time it hears a whooshing noise.

To study avoidance learning, psychologists have had rats jump over barriers, run in running wheels, and dart down alleys to avoid electric shock. Rats certainly learned these responses quickly and well, suggesting that animals can learn a wide variety of behaviors to avoid painful or dangerous stimuli. However, psychologists ran into trouble when they tried to train rats to produce other sorts of behaviors to avoid shock. For instance, psychologists discovered that rats had great difficulty learning to avoid shock by pressing a lever. Yet rats readily learned to press a lever for food. What was happening here?

Robert Bolles (1972b) suggested that whenever an animal is exposed to a painful or stressful event, it automatically engages in **species-specific defense reactions**. These defense reactions are innate behavior patterns that become part of the genetic endowment of a particular species because they increase the likelihood of surviving and reproducing. For example, when rats are threatened in their natural environments, they either freeze, flee, or fight. Bolles proposed that rats will learn avoidance behaviors to the extent that they are compatible with one of these defense reactions.

Bolles noted that rats learn the following shock-avoidance behaviors in a descending order of rate (the fastest learned behaviors first): jumping out of a box where shock is expected, running out of a box and down an alley, running in a running wheel, and turning a wheel or pressing a lever to avoid shock. Whereas rats can learn to jump out of a box to avoid shock in one or two trials, many rats never learn to avoid shock by pressing a lever. Rats can learn to jump out of a box because it involves an instinctive defensive reaction: fleeing. But pressing a lever to avoid shock resembles none of the rat's instinctive reactions to danger.

If you think again about the mouse that learned to flee when it heard the whoosh of an owl's wings, you may notice that something is wrong with this tale. Owls fly silently; their wings make no whooshing noise. If they did, all owls would have died from hunger long ago. This is not a trivial point. In most cases, animals have no opportunity to *learn* to avoid predators in the wild. Predators do not signal their attacks so that prey have a convenient CS.

> *The mouse does not scamper away from the owl because it has learned to escape the painful claws of the enemy; it scampers away from anything happening in its environment, and it does so merely because it is a mouse. The gazelle does not flee from an approaching lion because it has been bitten by lions; it runs away from any large object that approaches it, and it does so because this is one of its species-specific defense reactions. Neither the mouse nor the gazelle can afford to* learn *to avoid; survival is too urgent, the opportunity to learn is too limited, and the parameters of the situation make the necessary learning impossible.*

> (Bolles, 1972b, p. 190)

Thus, species-specific defense reactions reveal another instance in which animals seem to be programmed with particular behavior patterns that impose limits on what they can learn. In the case of the Brelands' work and species-specific defense reactions, limits are imposed on operant learning. In the case of avoiding a particular taste, you will see that nature has imposed limits on Pavlovian associations as well.

Learning Taste Aversion

When a psychologist named John Garcia was performing research on the effects of radiation, he observed that rats stopped eating their food and began to lose weight after they had been made nauseated by the radiation. Either the rats didn't eat simply because sick animals don't like to eat or because they associated their food with the radiation illness. The latter hypothesis seemed unlikely, because the taste of the animals' food and the illness were separated by many minutes. You'll recall that Pavlovian conditioning research showed that a conditioned stimulus and an unconditioned stimulus (here, the food and illness) must be presented close together in time for an animal to learn. However, Garcia speculated that associations between food and illness might be a special case.

An experiment comparing the associability of shock and poison with audiovisual (lights and noise) and flavor stimuli. As rats drank salty water, they heard clicks and saw flashes of light. One group of rats was shocked after drinking the water; the other was poisoned after drinking. Later, half of each group was given water accompanied by clicks and light flashes while the other half was given salty water. Rats that had been shocked drank the salty water freely but not water when it was paired with the lights and clicks. Rats that had been poisoned drank little of the salty water but readily drank water when it was paired with lights and clicks. (From Garcia and Koelling, 1966.)

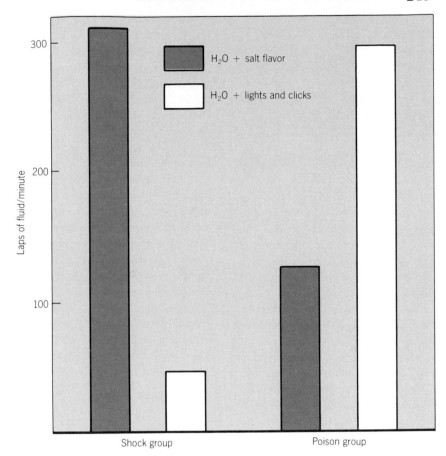

If rats are genetically *prepared* to associate the flavor of food with illness, they could associate the two even though they were separated by a long period of time.

In his experiments, Garcia showed that most animals quickly learn associations between flavors and internal consequences, such as illness, but learn associations between flavors and external consequences, such as shock or loud noises very slowly, if at all (see Figure 6-26). Conversely, most animals learn to associate external stimuli—lights, sounds, and tactile stimuli—with external consequences, but not with internal consequences.

Other research has shown that animals are not only likely to associate illness with certain tastes but are also likely to make these associations over long delays in time (Smith and Roll, 1967). Rats, for example, learned aversions to a sweet fluid when they were irradiated 12 hours after drinking it. In addition, and also consistent with Garcia's hypothesis, researchers have gathered evidence that suggests that this preparedness to associate flavors with illness is genetically programmed. Five-day-old rats formed taste–illness associations quite readily, but did not learn taste–shock associations (Gemberling, Domjan, and Amsel, 1980). Such an early behavioral tendency is probably genetically transmitted and not learned. Taste aversions are learned very rapidly, some-

One of the earliest recorded applications of taste-aversion conditioning occurred when the Roman philosopher, Pliny the Elder, dropped a poisonous spider into a friend's wine cup. The spider made the friend ill, and thereafter he stopped his excessive drinking. In a more recent application, American researchers in the 1930s began using aversion therapy to treat alcoholism. Some used aversion therapy in which an alcoholic was shocked repeatedly while tasting alcohol. Others injected the alcoholic with a drug that produced nausea and vomiting and asked the alcoholic to drink alcohol immediately after the injection. Both types of techniques had supporters, and it was difficult to determine which was superior because research on the techniques was usually done without adequate experimental controls (e.g., frequently there was no control group).

Once psychologists learned that rats were biologically prepared to associate tastes with illness, they decided to see if a similar preparation might help humans learn aversions to alcohol. To test this notion, researchers compared the effectiveness of

group therapy plus chemical aversion therapy, and group therapy plus shock aversion therapy (Cannon and Baker, 1981; Cannon, Baker, and Wehl, 1981). Alcoholic subjects were compared on how much alcohol they drank after treatment, on whether they showed signs of an alcohol aversion after treatment, and on whether the aversion was related to how much they drank. To measure conditioned aversion, Cannon used the subjects' heart rates in response to the taste of alcohol, the subjects' ratings of the flavor of alcohol, and the subjects' consumption of alcohol in a taste test. (They measured heart rate because people's hearts tend to speed up when they are frightened or repelled.) The people who had undergone

chemical aversion drank on significantly fewer days in the first 6 months after treatment than shock subjects did (see Box Figure 1). Moreover, only the chemical aversion treatment produced all of the following: heart rate accelerations to the taste of alcohol, less consumption of alcohol in taste tests, and negative taste ratings of alcohol. The aversion also was related to the success of the treatment: the faster the subject's heart rate on tasting alcohol, the longer the subject stayed abstinent. Researchers have produced similar results by using taste-aversion conditioning with other groups of alcoholics and with smokers (Cannon, Baker, Gino, and Nathan, 1986; Tiffany, Martin, and Baker, 1986).

BOX FIGURE 1 DRINKING FOLLOWING CHEMICAL AND SHOCK AVERSION THERAPY.
The mean number of days of abstinence that shock and chemical aversion subjects accumulated in the 6 months before and the 6 months after treatment. (From Cannon et al., 1981.)

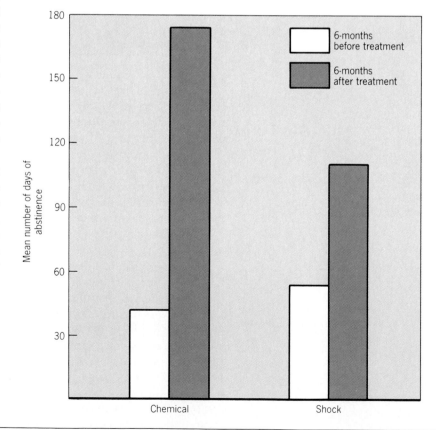

times after only a single pairing of a taste and an illness, and they are very resistant to extinction. These characteristics have led people to use taste-aversion conditioning for problems ranging from alcoholism to sheep predation (see Box 6-4). They also have led people to pay more attention to genetic contributions to learning. In particular, psychologists have come to realize that it is the rule, rather than an exception, that species are genetically *prepared* to learn certain types of associations better than others.

Preparedness

People apparently are biologically prepared to associate certain tastes with feelings of illness, and rats are apparently prepared to learn to jump out of boxes to avoid shocks. **Preparedness** describes the fact that particular species learn some types of associations much more readily than they learn others, apparently because of genetic programming (Seligman, 1970). In theory, because of adaptive pressures, such as predators or competition to mate, animals that easily learned particular types of associations were especially likely to survive and pass on their genes to later generations (Seligman and Hager, 1972).

CHARACTERISTICS OF PREPARED BEHAVIOR   Prepared learning is not the same thing as instinctive behavior in the form of, say, **fixed action patterns (FAPs)**. FAPs are stereotyped invariant patterns of behavior that occur in all members of a particular species, in response to a particular **releasing stimulus**. For instance, when the greylag goose sees an egg, or any similarly shaped object, lying just outside of its nest, it executes highly stereotyped retrieval behaviors (see Figure 6-27). Every greylag goose retrieves eggs with the same set of fixed movements.

FAPs differ from prepared behavior in that FAPs require no learning. Also, a FAP is always basically the same (i.e., stereotyped) across all members of a species. In contrast, some rats will learn to freeze in response to a shock cue, while some will learn to jump and run. Moreover, only prepared, learned behavior (not FAPs) can be strengthened or weakened through additional conditioning or through extinction.

Prepared learning depends on the special *relation* among certain stimuli or among certain stimuli and responses. Thus tastes do not always strengthen learning, but they do when they are followed by illness. Rats do not always learn to run faster than they learn other types of operant behaviors—but they do learn to run quickly (referring to both the learning and the running) when they are presented a cue previously paired with shock! Although it used to be thought that genetically transmitted dispositions to learn were rare, it now appears that they are fairly common in nature (Tinbergen, 1972).

Preparedness does not seem to be restricted to lower species. We humans apparently are prepared to learn certain things. One of the most dramatic examples of this is human language learning. Virtually all children learn language, and they learn it very rapidly at about the same stage of physical maturation, despite living in cultures or families in

FIGURE 6-27   FIXED ACTION PATTERN.
A greylag goose retrieves an egg with the same stereotyped movements, no matter the size of the egg. (After Lorenz and Tinbergen, 1938.)

FIGURE 6-28   PREPARED STIMULI.

Today many thousands of people are shocked, burned, or hurt in auto accidents—yet hardly anyone is phobic about electric wall outlets, stoves, or cars. Instead, people complain of fears of spiders and snakes, things that were threats to humans as they evolved.

which language use differs tremendously (Lenneberg, 1969). Chapter 8 presents other evidence that suggests that a special capacity to learn language is genetically programmed in us.

PHOBIAS: AN EXAMPLE OF PREPARED LEARNING?   If phobias are prepared, what characteristics should they have? First, as opposed to other sorts of fears, phobias should be learned quickly. Second, phobias should be extremely persistent, showing great resistance to extinction. Finally, people and animals should become phobic primarily to objects that have had adaptive or survival significance for many generations.

A comparison of phobias with nonphobic human fears supports the hypothesis that phobias represent prepared learning. Snakes, insects, heights, and exposed spaces, common objects of phobias, posed a survival threat to early generations of humans. People do not commonly become phobic about automobiles or electrical outlets, despite the fact that they are now a much more pervasive danger than snakes.

Phobics also often report that their fear was acquired in a single instance, while the conditioning of fears to nonprepared stimuli in the laboratory usually requires many stimulus–consequence pairings (Seligman, 1971). In a series of experiments, researchers tested the speed with which people acquire autonomic nervous system signs of a fear response: increased skin conductance of the hand (produced by sweating) and increased heart rate (Öhman, Dimberg, and Öst, 1984). In a typical study (e.g., Öhman, Eriksson, and Olofsson, 1975), nonprepared stimuli like slides of houses, or prepared stimuli like slides of snakes and insects (Figure 6-28) were paired with painful electric shocks. Subjects acquired both greater heart rate and skin conductance responses when prepared, as opposed to neutral, stimuli were paired with shocks (Öhman et al., 1984; see Figure 6-29). In fact, subjects showed autonomic responses after a single snake–shock pairing, and these were slow to extinguish. Finally, people do not even need direct experience with pain to show autonomic signs of fear in response to prepared objects. Merely telling people that they might be shocked is enough to produce greater autonomic responses to *pictures* of snakes or spiders but not to flower or mushroom pictures (Hugdahl and Öhman, 1977). Although a great deal of data has been gathered to support preparedness theory, it remains a theory and not a proven fact. It is always difficult to prove conclusively that some tendency or trait has a genetic origin (Delprato, 1980). Only with more research will psychologists know that the theory provides a valid account of the selective associations in phobias and other kinds of rapid and persistent learning.

Finally, if it is indeed the case that species are genetically prepared to learn particular associations, the general learning principles discussed earlier in this chapter are not invalidated. Although recent research has modified some of these principles (for example, the length of the CS–US interval over which learning can occur), most of these principles hold even for prepared associations. For instance, the strength of taste aversions increases with the number of conditioning trials, taste aversions generalize across similar flavors, and taste aversions can be extinguished. To a great extent, prepared associations differ from other associations only quantitatively—in how quickly they are acquired, how slowly they

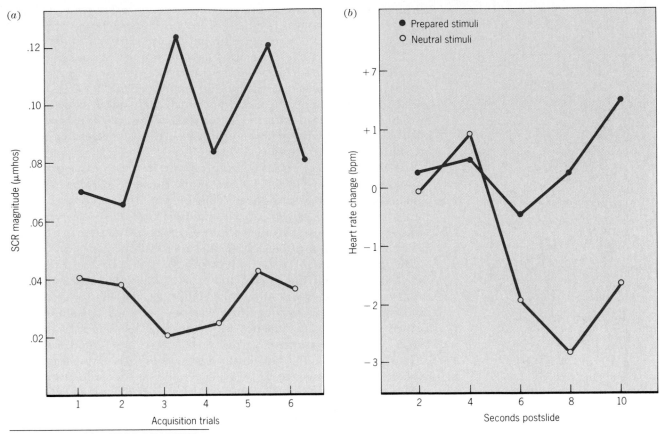

FIGURE 6-29   FEAR LEARNED TO PREPARED STIMULI.

The conditioned skin conductance (a) *and heart rate* (b) *responses elicited by prepared and neutral stimuli. Both types of stimuli had previously been paired with electric shock. You can readily see that subjects sweated more and showed greater heart rate responses when prepared stimuli had been paired with shock (From Öhman et al., 1984.)*

extinguish, and so forth. Only the principle of equipotentiality seems irrevocably violated in the case of prepared associations. Classes of stimuli are not interchangeable; a rose may be a rose by any other name, but it is not a snake.

LEARNING: AN INTEGRATION

Pavlovian, operant, insight, observational learning, habituation and sensitization—these topics comprise a great many phenomena that differ tremendously in nature and scope. But these types of learning do not exist in isolation. They interact to produce behavior.

What can account for the diversity of human learning? An analysis of learning from an evolutionary perspective reveals that the simplest organisms are capable of sensitization, habituation, and the acquisition of simple Pavlovian responses such as moving toward a light. Such learning appears to occur in a fairly automatic way, shows great consistency from animal to animal, and does not require conscious thought. Higher on the phylogenetic scale, more advanced animals are capable of nonassociative and Pavlovian learning as well as operant learning. Thus, mammals, birds, and fish are capable of operant learning (Thomas, 1980). Finally, the most advanced species, monkeys, apes, and humans, are capable of observational and insight learning, as well as the more basic forms of learning. Although there is not perfect congruence between phylogenetic level and learning capability (Griffin, 1978; Schrier, 1984), in general, phylogenetically primitive organisms are capable of only primitive forms of learning (for example, habituation) and advanced organisms are capable of both primitive and advanced forms of learning. Brain development is also associated with learning capability. Whereas primitive types of learning can occur in animals with quite modest brain capacities, more advanced forms of learning occur only in animals with relatively large, sophisticated brains (for example, a relatively large cortex [Bitterman, 1965; Jerison, 1973]).

The more advanced forms of learning have not just been stacked on top of more primitive forms. Rather, all the forms of learning of which humans are capable are *integrated*. This integration is, no doubt, determined both by humans' genetic endowment and also by experience. By "integration" we mean that the various forms of learning work together to permit the pursuit of biologically and socially important goals.

The various types, or levels, of learning (Razrin, 1965) are integrated and facilitate the pursuit of common goals (food, water, social acclaim) because the various types of learning influence one another—there is communication between them. For example, language, a sophisticated learned response, can influence the learning of simple Pavlovian responses. Once humans have learned a Pavlovian conditioned response, such as an eye blink, the rate at which the eye blink is extinguished can be influenced by language. If people are told that they will never again receive the US (for example, an air puff) after the CS (a tone), extinction will be more rapid than if they are not so instructed. People also can acquire what appear to be autonomic CRs if they are merely told that they might be shocked (Hugdahl and Öhman, 1977). Thus, phylogenetically older forms of learning have come under partial control of more recent forms. Pavlov recognized that Pavlovian learning could be influenced by language, and he labeled language the **second signal system**, meaning that it constituted one source of CSs and USs just as exteroceptive stimuli (bells, lights) constituted another source.

Even though primitive learning systems can be influenced by more phylogenetically recent forms of learning, this influence is certainly incomplete. Research shows that in particular conditioning paradigms, humans are conditioned despite what they know or what they try to do. For instance, in eye blink or skin conductance conditioning paradigms, people become conditioned even if they try to fight the conditioning. They can reduce, but not block, such learning (Dawson and Reardon, 1969). Also, as you saw in the section on taste aversion, alcoholics learn aversions to alcohol despite the fact that they know that their nausea is produced by drugs, not by alcohol.

In fact, it may be that in certain types of psychopathology such as phobias and addictions, primitive types of learning that are difficult to control make an item exceedingly attractive (in the case of addiction) or frightening (in the case of phobia). Because such learning is not under conscious control, people feel unable to understand or change their strong motivation to use drugs or avoid spiders. Many approaches to therapy appear to involve training the victim to gain control over primitive, automatic responses through complex types of learning such as insight (see Chapter 15).

SUMMARY

LEARNING

Learning is the more or less permanent change in behavior, or behavioral potential, that results from experience.

1. Early theories of learning introduced the idea that human behavior can be explained by natural laws. In particular, Descartes' use of the *reflex* as a basic unit of behavior and the concept of *association* have had lasting influence.

2. Ivan Pavlov discovered a procedure, *Pavlovian* conditioning, that produces learning. It involves pairing a stimulus that produces a reflex *(unconditioned stimulus, US)* with one that produces no reflexive behavior *(conditioned stimulus, CS)*. After such pairing the conditioned stimulus elicits a response *(conditioned response, CR)* that is similar to that elicited by the *unconditioned stimulus (unconditioned response, UR)*. Pavlovian learning is strengthened by increasing the number of CS–US pairings, and using a novel CS. *Extinction*, presenting the CS without the US, is the most effective way to weaken a learned Pavlovian response.

   Pavlov proposed a *stimulus substitution* theory of Pavlovian learning, that learning causes the CS to become a substitute for the US, and he proposed that co-occurrence of the CS and US in time was responsible for learning. Subsequent research suggests that the CS does not substitute for the US but rather allows the animal to predict or expect the US. Moreover, optimal learning is not determined by simple co-occurrence of the CS and US in time, but rather is determined by the CS being a reliable and unique signal of the US. Finally, Pavlovian learning is adaptive because it allows organisms to predict and prepare for significant events.

3. Operant learning is determined by the consequence of responses. Reinforcers are consequences that increase the future probability of the behaviors that precede them. Punishers decrease the future probability of the behaviors that precede them.

   Consequences can be delivered according to different *schedules of reinforcement*. In *ratio* schedules animals are reinforced as a function of the number of responses they make. In *interval* schedules animals are reinforced for responding after an interval has passed. In either type of schedule the response requirement (the ratio or interval) may be *fixed* or *variable*.

   There are six major types of *reinforcement paradigms: reward, punishment, omission, withdrawal, avoidance,* and *escape* training. These paradigms differ in whether operant behavior produces, removes, or delays a reinforcer or punisher. Reward, escape, and avoidance paradigms produce increased operant behavior; punishment, withdrawal, and omission training produce decreases.

   Operant behavior may be reinforced by both *primary* and *secondary reinforcers.* Primary reinforcers (e.g., food) are intrinsically reinforcing. Secondary reinforcers (e.g., a gold star) become reinforcers by being paired with primary reinforcers. Finally, animals appear to learn at least two things in operant conditioning: that responses have certain consequences, and that they (the animals) can control their environments.

4. In *habituation* repeated presentations of the same stimulus decrease responding. In *sensitization* presentation of one stimulus increases responding to an habituated stimulus.

5. Four concerns of modern learning research are insight learning, cognitive maps, concept learning, and observational learning. Insight learning comes suddenly, and may require that animals make mental images of the problem involved. Animals' maze learning suggests that they do not simply learn to execute particular motor responses. Rather, they appear to learn a mental map of a goal in space and then are able to use different behaviors to achieve that goal. Monkeys are able to learn abstract concepts and apply such concepts to new problems. Harlow's monkeys learned a win-stay/lose-shift strategy—to always stay with a successful response but immediately shift from an unsuccessful one. In observational learning, animals appear to make a mental representation of an observed behavior and then match their own performance to features of the representation. Although observational learning does not depend upon incentives or reinforcement, performance of learned behaviors is greatly influenced by incentives.

6. Animals appear to be instinctively *prepared* to make certain kinds of learned associations and not oth-

ers. Instinctively prepared associations are learned in few trials, are exceptionally persistent, and are made instead of other possible associations. Prepared associations differ from instinctive behaviors such as *fixed action patterns* (FAPs) in the FAPs require no learning, are stereotyped across all members of a species, and are not strengthened or weakened by learning contingencies.

7. Simple organisms are capable only of simple sorts of learning such as habituation, sensitization, and Pavlovian learning. Monkeys, apes, and humans are capable of complex as well as simple sorts of learning. Both types of learning have been integrated during the course of evolution so that they permit the pursuit and accomplishment of biologically significant goals.

FURTHER READINGS

It is always instructive to read a classic, and Pavlov's *Conditioned Reflexes* (Oxford: Oxford University Press, 1927) is just that. For a thorough and readable review of the general area of learning, we recommend *Psychology of Learning and Behavior* (2nd Ed.) by Barry Schwartz (New York: W. W. Norton, 1984). A more challenging review of concepts in learning is *Conditioning and Associative Learning* by N. J. MacKintosh (1983).

For in-depth treatments of particular topics in learning, we recommend *Biological Boundaries of Learning* by M. E. P. Seligman and J. L. Hager (Eds., New York: Appleton-Century-Crofts, 1972). Wolfgang Köhler's *The Mentality of Apes* (New York: Harcourt, Brace and World, 1925) is an older but still important record regarding Köhler's insights into insight learning. Also recommended is a classic on operant conditioning, B. F. Skinner's *Behavior of Organisms* (New York: Appleton-Century-Crofts, 1938). For a relatively recent treatment of observational learning and social learning theory, see Albert Bandura's *Social Learning Theory* (1977).

Several recent articles on new developments in learning include "The Conditioning of Drug-induced Physiological Responses" by R. Eikelboom and J. Stewart (*Psychological Review, 89*, 507–528) and Allan Wagner's paper "SOP: A Model of Automatic Memory Processing in Animal Behavior" (in N. E. Spear and R. R. Miller, Eds., *Information Processing in Animals: Memory Mechanisms*. Hilldale, N.J.: Erlbaum, 1981). Finally, for recent information on the neurophysiological basis of learning, see Richard Thompson's paper, "The Neurobiology of Learning and Memory" (1986).

292

7

MEMORY

How good is your memory? How good *can* a person's memory be? Do you remember your birthday? (Of course!) Do you remember the birthdays of everyone in your family, including your grandparents, aunts and uncles, and first cousins? (Memory shaky on a few of those?) How good are you at memorizing telephone numbers, or addresses, or Zip codes, or your own Social Security number? What were you doing on November second of last year, and on which day of the week did November second fall?

If you're like most people, you can't remember what you did last November second, and you need a calendar to find out which day of the week it was on. But a few remarkable people can almost instantly tell the day of the week on which any date falls. One of the first accounts of such a person came from William James (1890), who, in his *Principles of Psychology*, reported about "an almost blind Pennsylvania farmer who could remember the day of the week on which any date had fallen for 42 years past, and also the kind of weather it was, and what he was doing on each of more than 15,000 days" (James, 1890, pp. 660–661).

Now try to memorize the following numbers by reading through them once slowly and after one minute, write down as many as you can remember.

1–4–3–5–2–9–6–8–7–3–2–0–6–8–5–4–1

As you will see later in this chapter, most adults, when briefly presented with a series of numbers, can remember about seven of them. But some people can remember many more numbers than seven. A. R. Luria (1968), a well-known psychologist, studied a man with a remarkable memory who could remember large arrays of letters and numbers. For example, after briefly studying the array of numbers in Table 7-1, the man could recite from memory any column, row, or diagonal that Luria asked for.

Those few, rare people with remarkable memories have memories that function much like everyone else's, only much more efficiently. We ordinary mortals can, however, practice to the point that we can perform remarkable feats of memory. For example, one ordinary student who practiced memorizing numbers ultimately learned to recall over 80 of them (Chase and Ericsson, 1981). In this chapter, we show you how human memory, both ordinary and extraordinary, operates. By the time you have finished the chapter, you will understand how your memory is structured, how it operates, how information goes into and out of it, its limits, and how you can improve your own memory (see Box 7-3, p. 332 "Mnemonic Devices").

TABLE 7-1 TRY TO MEMORIZE THIS TABLE OF NUMBERS

6	6	8	0
5	4	3	2
1	6	8	4
7	9	3	5
4	2	3	7
3	8	9	1
1	0	0	2
3	4	5	1
2	7	6	8
1	9	2	6
2	9	6	7
5	5	2	0
x	0	1	x

Note: If you spend a few minutes trying to memorize this table of numbers, you may find that it is rather difficult. However, some people can remember such arrays fairly easily. Luria (1968) reported that one of his subjects quickly memorized the array and could later easily recite numbers from any column, row, or diagonal.

APPROACHES TO THE STUDY OF MEMORY

Although human memory has been a topic of speculation among philosophers for over 2000 years—both Plato and Aristotle discussed the nature and operation of memory—the scientific study of human memory has more recent origins. How is memory studied scientifically?

Introspection

If you were assigned the task of figuring out how memory operates, what research strategies would *you* employ? Much of what psychologists know today about memory actually comes from the study of people's performance on memory tests: of numbers, nonsense syllables, written passages, mental rotation of geometric forms, and other materials. Though it may surprise you, it turns out that the scientific study of memory began only a little more than a century ago. The German psychologist Wilhelm Wundt (see Chapter 1) undertook carefully controlled studies of people's mental responses to simple stimuli such as sounds and colors. Wundt's subjects were called upon to report the sensations, feelings, and images produced by these stimuli. Although Wundt was instrumental in beginning research on memory and related processes, his method, **introspection**, provided only limited information on the operation of memory. Fortunately, F. C. Donders, Hermann Ebbinghaus, and F. C. Bartlett developed alternatives to introspection, and their methods still play an important role in the study of memory.

Reaction Time and Memory

F. C. Donders (1818–1889), a Dutch physiologist of the nineteenth century, developed a method called **mental chronometry** to study the structure and nature of mental events. With this method, Donders measured the amount of time various mental events took, or more specifically, people's reaction times to stimuli. For example, Donders (1969/1869) measured the difference in reaction time between a person's response to a single stimulus, such as *ba,* and the person's reaction time in discriminating among several stimuli, such as *ba, bi,* and *bu.* Psychologists have used reaction times to examine mental events such as discrimination, association, choice and judgment, and memory.

Memory for Nonsense

Hermann Ebbinghaus' contribution to the study of memory was somewhat different. Ebbinghaus (1850–1909), a German psychologist, was interested in how associations are formed among mental elements and devised experimental techniques that dominated the study of human memory for more than half a century. In order to study memory in a way that would be uninfluenced by people's previous learning, Ebbinghaus devised thousands of nonsense syllables—which sounded like words but had no meaning. For example: DAZ–YIL–POF–WIC–SIG–TOL–MAJ–FAK–BOC–HAR–LAT–KEB–JIS–COL. With himself as a subject, between 1879 and 1885, Ebbinghaus carried out five experiments in memory. He used a method in which he assessed his memory for the **serial order** of syllables. After memorizing a list of nonsense syllables, he presented himself with the first syllable as a cue to the second syllable. After trying to remember the second syllable, he presented himself with the correct second syllable and tried to remember the third, and so on.

In one study, Ebbinghaus learned lists of 13 syllables so that he could repeat them twice without errors. He tabulated how long it took him to

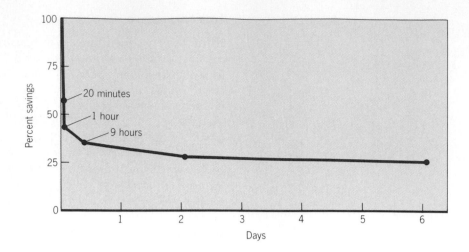

FIGURE 7-1   THE FORGETTING CURVE.

Ebbinghaus' curve shows that previously learned material, such as a list of nonsense syllables, disappears from memory systematically over time. When savings are 100 percent, no additional study is necessary to relearn the list. When savings are 0 percent, just as many trials are required to relearn the list as were required to learn the list initially. (After Ebbinghaus, 1885.)

do this. Later (sometimes the same day, and sometimes many days later) he relearned the same lists to see how much more quickly he could learn them and computed his time "savings." Thus, if it took him 1000 seconds to learn the list at first and only 400 seconds to relearn the list, he had saved (1000 − 400 =) 600 seconds. Six hundred seconds is 60 percent of the time it took him to learn the list originally. Figure 7-1 plots the savings that Ebbinghaus measured in one study.

Ebbinghaus' contributions to memory research have been enduring. Contemporary memory researchers not only use nonsense stimuli, but many of Ebbinghaus' findings are still an important part of our basic knowledge about human memory. For example, Ebbinghaus demonstrated that as the number of syllables to be learned increased, so did the difficulty of learning. He demonstrated that recall of syllables drops off rapidly at first and then much more slowly (also shown in Figure 7-1). He found that learning of nonsense syllables is more efficient when study is spaced over short periods rather than condensed into a single long period. He also found that even though he was testing himself on his associations between adjacent syllables, he also learned associations between nonadjacent syllables.

Although Ebbinghaus successfully demonstrated that memory could be studied objectively, his method was criticized because it did not allow researchers to examine memory in its natural context. After all, few people are called upon to memorize lists of nonsense words in their everyday lives. Some researchers have thought it important to study people's memory for meaningful material—the kinds of things that people encounter in their everyday lives.

Memory for Meaning

Sir Frederick Bartlett was a twentieth-century British psychologist who, in contrast to Ebbinghaus, was interested in people's "search after meaning." He studied how people remember meaningful material such as written passages, pictures, and stories like "The War of the Ghosts" (Part 1 of Figure 7-2). Bartlett (1932) had his students read stories or study pictures and then reproduce them after varying amounts of time:

15 minutes, a few hours, several weeks. Some students were asked to reproduce the information several times—**repeated reproduction**. Some were asked to convey the information to another student, who then conveyed it to another student, and so on—**serial reproduction**.

In Part 2 of Figure 7-2, you can see the reproduction of a story 20 hours after a student read the original story. The characteristics of the remembered version typify those that Bartlett commonly observed. Parts of the story, especially the ambiguous parts, are left out entirely. Many facts are changed, new information is supplied, and the story is more concrete than the original. The language is more modern than the original. (The student changed "hunting seals" to "fishing.") One of Bartlett's major contributions to research on memory for meaning is that people's knowledge of the world profoundly influences what and how they remember.

Like Donders and Ebbinghaus, Bartlett devised research methods and theories that still influence research on human memory. Later in this chapter, we examine many studies of memory for meaningful material.

STAGES OF MEMORY

By studying how people remember and forget, psychologists have found that the *process* of remembering is rather like a gigantic warehousing operation. Information is taken into the memory "warehouse," carried to the appropriate storage area, and eventually called back out for use. The memory process can be broken down into three different stages: acquisition or formulation, storage, and retrieval. Each stage poses a separate set of questions for researchers.

Acquisition of Information

The first of the three stages of memory, the **acquisition stage**, describes the point at which information is placed into memory. You see a face and remember it, you hear a tune and remember it, you write a telephone number down and remember it. But *how* do these kinds of information enter your memory? After all, your skull is not filled with old photographs, musical notes, or penciled phone numbers. Researchers have been interested in the mechanisms by which information is **encoded** for memory. How, if at all, is information acted upon or interpreted to prepare it for memory? In what form is the information stored?

Some people have proposed that information is encoded for memory much as a photograph registers an image on a thin film of light-sensitive chemicals. The information recorded in a photograph can be a fairly faithful representation of the object a person sees. Other people have proposed that information is encoded for memory more in the way a videotape recording captures a scene on a movie set as magnetic information that must be electronically transformed before people can recognize it. Human memory operates more like a videotape recording than a photograph. Just as a videotaping system requires a camera and electrical systems to encode and decode information, human memory is based

FIGURE 7-2 BARTLETT'S
STORIES
Bartlett employed stories such as "The War of the Ghosts" in his study of memory for meaningful information. The original story is shown in Part 1 of the figure. The story as recalled by a student 20 hours after reading the original is shown in Part 2. Part 3 shows the story as recalled by a man with an extraordinary memory called VP over a period of 1 year. (Parts 1 and 2 from Bartlett, 1932; Part 3 from Hunt and Love, 1972.)

"THE WAR OF THE GHOSTS"
Part 1   Original Story

One night two young men from Egulac went down to the river to hunt seals, and while they were there it became foggy and calm. Then they heard war-cries, and they thought: "Maybe this is a war-party." They escaped to the shore, and hid behind a log. Now canoes came up, and they heard the noise of paddles, and saw one canoe coming up to them. There were five men in the canoe, and they said:

"What do you think? We wish to take you along. We are going up the river to make war on the people."

One of the young men said: "I have no arrows."

"Arrows are in the canoe," they said.

"I will not go along. I might be killed. My relatives do not know where I have gone. But you," he said, turning to the other, "may go with them."

So one of the young men went, but the other returned home.

And the warriors went on up the river to a town on the other side of Kalama. The people came down to the water, and they began to fight, and many were killed. But presently the young man heard one of the warriors say: "Quick, let us go home; that Indian has been hit." Now he thought: "Oh, they are ghosts." He did not feel sick, but they said he had been shot.

So the canoes went back to Egulac, and the young man went ashore to his house, and made a fire. And he told everybody and said: "Behold I accompanied the ghosts, and we went to fight. Many of our fellows were killed, and many of those who attacked us were killed. They said I was hit, and I did not feel sick."

He told it all, and then he became quiet. When the sun rose he fell down. Something black came out of his mouth. His face became contorted. The people jumped up and cried.

He was dead.

Part 2

Two men from Edulac went fishing. While thus occupied by the river they heard a noise in the distance.

"It sounds like a cry," said one, and presently there appeared some in canoes who invited them to join the party on their adventure. One of the young men refused to go, on the ground of family ties, but the other offered to go.

on an elaborate neural system that processes and encodes sensory information into a lasting neural record that can be retrieved and decoded. The information that you remember—the faces, the tunes, the phone numbers—is stored in your memory in the form of verbal, visual, and other codes (we discuss these more thoroughly later in the chapter).

Storage of Information

The second stage of memory is the **storage stage**—the "warehousing" of the information that has been acquired. In some cases, people's storage

"But there are no arrows," he said.

"The arrows are in the boat," was the reply.

He thereupon took his place, while his friend returned home. The party paddled up the river to Kaloma, and began to land on the banks of the river. The enemy came rushing upon them, and some sharp fighting ensued. Presently someone was injured, and the cry was raised that the enemy were ghosts.

The party returned down the stream, and the young man arrived home feeling none the worse for his experience. The next morning at dawn he endeavored to recount his adventures. While he was talking something black issued from his mouth. Suddenly he uttered a cry and fell down. His friends gathered around him.

But he was dead.

Part 3

One day two young men from Egliac went down to the river to hunt seals. While there, it suddenly became very foggy and quiet, and they became scared and rowed ashore and hid behind a log. Soon they heard the sound of paddles in the water and canoes approaching. One of the canoes, with five men in it, paddled ashore and one of the men said: "What do you think? Let us go up-river and make war against the people."

"I cannot go with you," said one of the young men. "My relatives do not know where I have gone. Besides, I might get killed. But he," said he, turning to the other young man, "will go with you." So one of the young men returned to his village, and the other went up-river with the war-party.

They went to a point beyond Kalama, and the people came down to the river to fight them, and they fought. Soon, the young man heard someone say: "This Indian has been wounded."—"Maybe they are ghosts," he thought, because he felt perfectly OK. The war party suggested leaving, and they left, and the young man went back to his village.

There he lit a fire in front of his abode, sat down to await the sunrise, and told his story to the villagers. "I went with a war-party to make war with the people. There was fierce fighting and many were killed, and many were wounded. They said I was wounded, but I did not feel a thing. Maybe they were ghosts."

He had told it all, and when the sun came up, he gave a little cry. Something black came out of his mouth. He fell over. He was dead.

of information is successful. That is, when they try to recall that information later on, they not only can do so, but the information is not distorted or, worse, not lost to them. Their storage system has worked efficiently and accurately. But storage isn't always efficient or accurate, as anyone can attest who could have sworn that Columbus discovered America in 1493 and that the nation's Capitol is in the District of Colombia.

Though we all know from everyday experience that much information is successfully stored in memory, we know that there's often a difference between the quantity and quality of information that is placed into memory and the quantity and quality of information we later recall. Research on storage processes addresses questions such as: How is information registered in the nervous system? Are there different types of memory for different types of information? How is information organized in memory? What happens to information while it is apparently lying dormant? Is information lost from memory storage and if so, why and how is it lost or altered?

Although it is tempting to think that all those instances in which we cannot recover the information we placed into memory are failures of the storage system, failures in the retrieval system are at least as problematic.

Retrieval of Information

The final stage of memory, the **retrieval stage**, refers to the process of bringing information out of memory. People retrieve information under two different kinds of circumstances. When information is directly in front of them, people retrieve it from memory through **recognition**. When the information is not present, they must retrieve it through **recall**. Thus you recognize your psychology professor when you see him or her in the classroom, but you must try to recall what he or she looks like when you are at home. Although both recognition and recall make use of the same information from memory, psychologists have still not determined whether they are the same or different memory processes. We discuss recognition and recall more thoroughly later in the chapter.

In short, any successful information recording system, which is what memory is, must be able to faithfully encode, store, and retrieve information for later use. By understanding the stages of remembering, you understand the process. But what about the structure of the memory system itself? We turn to that now.

A MODEL OF MEMORY

How is the memory warehouse actually arranged into component parts? One influential answer to this question (but not the *only* answer) is a model developed by Richard Atkinson and Richard Shiffrin (1968, 1971; see Figure 7-3). The model identifies three major memory systems: sensory memory, short-term memory (sometimes referred to as working memory), and long-term memory.

A dog barks, the sun rises, smoke fills a room. According to Atkinson and Shiffrin's model, information from the environment first enters a sensory memory system. Each sense probably has its own place in the system. These sensory stores have a moderately large capacity but hold information for only a brief period of time. In the sensory store, some of the information is recoded and transferred into short-term memory. Its capacity for information is limited and retains information for only brief periods. Some of the information in short-term memory in turn can be

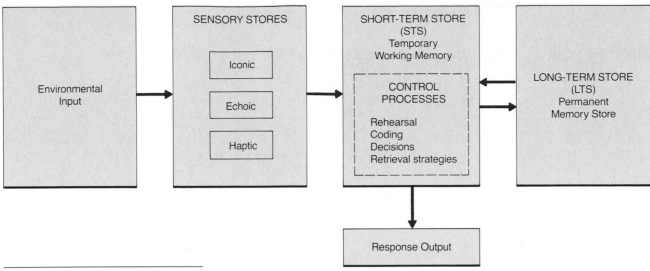

FIGURE 7-3   A MODEL
OF MEMORY.

Here you see the connections among the
sensory stores of memory, the short-term
store, and the long-term store. Each sense
probably has a sensory store. (Haptic
refers to the sense of touch.) The short-
term store controls the transfer to and
retrieval of information from long-term
store. The long-term store holds
permanent memories. (After Atkinson
and Shiffrin, 1971.)

recoded and transferred into long-term memory. There it can be held relatively permanently and eventually retrieved into short-term memory.

Researchers have tried to answer several questions about these memory systems.

1. How much information can the memory systems hold, and for how long can that information be retained?
2. How is the information placed into memory, how is it maintained in memory, and in what form is the information stored?
3. What is the structure of the stored information? How, if at all, are various pieces of information related to one another in memory?
4. How is information retrieved from memory, how is information searched for in memory, and what factors improve or impede the retrieval of information?

We turn now to some of the research into these questions.

Sensory Memory

What do people see or hear when they have only a brief exposure to a sight or a sound? In one study, a researcher briefly flashed cards that had pictures on them and asked people to draw exactly what was on the cards (Brigden, 1933). A few of the people said that although they felt they had seen all the pictures, they could not remember all of them when they tried to draw them. Findings such as these raise the question of whether people can see a large amount of information on a brief exposure and then rapidly lose that information or whether people see only a limited amount of information but remember much of it.

In an ingenious experiment, George Sperling (1960) devised a method to try and answer that question. Sperling showed people a display of 3 rows of 4 letters for 50 milliseconds (1/20 of a second; see Figure 7-4). You can try a rough approximation to the experiments we are about to

Stimuli

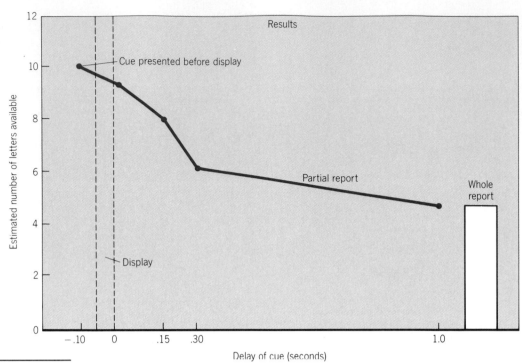

FIGURE 7-4   THE SPERLING EXPERIMENT.

When people were briefly shown a block of letters and then cued to report the letters from one row, the number of letters they could remember was a function of the number of seconds the cued report was delayed. (After Sperling, 1960.)

describe by preparing flash cards with block letters. Place the cards in front of a friend, uncover and cover them again very quickly, and ask your friend to recall as many letters as possible. When Sperling asked the people to report as many of the letters as they could (a *whole report* on the letters), they averaged 4.5 out of the 12. But then, Sperling varied the procedure. Rather than ask people to recall all the letters they had seen he asked them to recall only some of the letters (make a *partial report*). He presented them with a tone either shortly before the display was turned off or at delay periods up to 1 second. The people heard a high-pitched tone when they were to remember the top row, a medium-pitched tone for the middle row, and a low-pitched tone for the bottom row.

Sperling found that when the tone was presented immediately after the display was turned off, the people remembered an average of 3.3 letters from the row they had been cued to recall. Sperling argued that because the people did not know which row they would be asked to recall as they looked at the display, they must have had available to them in memory almost 10 letters (an average of 3.3 letters per row × 3 rows). Sperling believed that the people could report some of these letters because they retained a vivid mental image of the entire display. This mental image has been called an **icon** (Neisser, 1967). This iconic memory is short-lived. If the tone was not sounded until a full second after Sperling had turned off the visual display, the person recalled no more letters than would have been expected from the whole-report method Brigden used (see Figure 7-4).

Just where in the nervous system does the icon exist? At first, researchers suggested that the icon was an afterimage on the retina that involved the rods much as a spot of light stays in your vision when someone takes your picture with a flashbulb (Sakitt, 1976; Sakitt and

Long, 1979; Long and Sakitt, 1980). But whereas the longevity of afterimages—like those made by flashbulbs—are influenced by the intensity of a stimulus, memory for icons is not (Adelson, 1978; Adelson and Jonides, 1980). The icon probably is stored at a more central location of the nervous system than the retina.

The other senses also have similar memory systems. The sense of hearing, for example, seems to have **echoic memory** (Darwin, Turvey, and Crowder, 1972). In one study of echoic memory, subjects heard three lists of numbers and letters on a stereo tape recorder and headphones. One list sounded as if it came from the left of the listener, a second list from the right of the listener, and the third list from the middle. Immediately after the lists were presented, the listener saw a visual cue to recall one of the three lists. As in Sperling's study, this partial-report procedure yielded better performance than a comparable whole-list procedure. Iconic memories last about 1 second, but echoic memories last for as long as 4 seconds.

Short-term Memory

Short-term memory is the part of the memory structure in which we temporarily store information such as an unfamiliar telephone number. When you look up a number in the telephone book, dial it, but get a busy signal, you probably know from experience that you should repeat it to yourself or keep on dialing it. Unless you keep the phone number in your short-term memory with one of these tricks, you are likely to forget it and have to look it up all over again.

Short-term memory is the working memory that contains information currently in use, being acted upon, and in "consciousness" (Anderson, 1985; Baddeley, 1983; Baddeley and Hitch, 1974). Short-term memory consists in part of buffers, or memory stores, that hold verbal or visual information (Atkinson and Shiffrin, 1968, 1971; Baddeley, 1983, 1986). This buffer has a relatively limited capacity and can hold information for only a limited time. Information enters the buffer one item at a time. Once the buffer is filled, new items displace the older items. While items are in the short-term buffer, information about them may be transferred into long-term memory. The longer an item remains in the short-term buffer, the more information about it enters long-term memory.

As early as 1885, Ebbinghaus had reported that the longest list of nonsense syllables that he could recall correctly after having studied them only once—and therefore having taken them into short-term memory—was 6 or 7 (Ebbinghaus, 1885/1964). Similarly, most students can repeat accurately strings of 6 or 7 numbers (Jacobs, 1887). In 1956, George Miller published a now classic paper, "The Magical Number 7, plus or minus two: Some limits on our capacity for processing information" in which he concluded that the capacity of short-term memory is between 5 and 9 items. These items may be letters, numbers, nonsense syllables, or words. Items may be **chunked** together in short-term memory to increase its capacity. For example, you may find it difficult to remember all 17 of the following letters after only brief study:

I–B–M–U–C–L–A–J–F–K–I–R–S–O–P–E–C

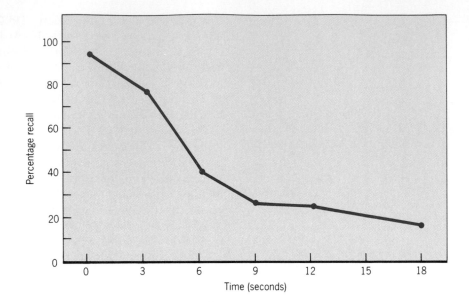

FIGURE 7-5 THE EFFECTS OF DISTRACTION ON SHORT-TERM MEMORY.
When people are distracted from rehearsing information, they rapidly lose information from short-term memory. (After Murdock, 1961.)

But if you see that these letters are made of chunks—acronyms for a major computer company (IBM), a college (UCLA), a president (JFK), a federal agency (IRS), and an oil cartel (OPEC)—you have only to remember five items.

Although information stays in short-term memory only briefly, it can be made to stay longer through the process of **rehearsal** (see Figure 7-3). When you silently repeat a telephone number to yourself, for example, you rehearse it. If someone then interrupts your rehearsal, the number may disappear from your short-term memory. In one study, subjects heard three consonants and were asked to remember them for up to 18 seconds (Peterson and Peterson, 1959). But they were also asked to count backwards by 3s immediately after they heard the consonants. The counting distracted them from rehearsing and interfered with their recall of the consonants. As Figure 7-5 shows, the loss of information from memory is rapid and largely complete in about 9 seconds. After 18 seconds, the subjects could recall less than 20 percent of the consonants.

What are the functions of rehearsal? Rehearsal both maintains information in short-term memory and helps transfer information from short-term to long-term memory (Atkinson and Shiffrin, 1968). **Maintenance rehearsal**, which involves repeating completed cognitive activities—repeating the telephone number you just looked up in the telephone book—holds information in short-term memory. **Elaborative rehearsal**, which involves a deeper and more thorough analysis of information—noting that the first three numbers of a telephone number are the same as your own and that the last four numbers correspond to the year of your birth—enhances the retention of information in long-term memory (Craik and Lockhart, 1972).

Long-term Memory

There is no reason to think that long-term memory has a limited capacity. No one has ever gotten so learned or so old that he or she awoke one morning and said, "That's it! My memory is full. I simply cannot ever remember another thing." The brain has a huge capacity judging from the fact the number of neurons has been estimated at about 100 billion. Once remembered, information in long-term memory can stay there for extremely long periods, sometimes even permanently. Even very old people continue to learn new information. These facts suggest that it must be extremely difficult to reach the full capacity of long-term memory.

Ordinary people can retain extraordinarily large amounts of information in long-term memory. For instance, in one study, people studied 540 different words (Shepard, 1967). When they were later presented pairs of old and new words, they correctly recognized 88 percent of the words they had studied. Other people were equally accurate at recognizing which of between 600 and 1200 sentences they had studied. People were 97 percent accurate at recognizing 600 color advertisements they had studied. In a study in which people saw 10,000 different pictures, they correctly recognized 73 percent of them (Standing, 1973).

People's long-term memory also has been tested under more natural circumstances. For example, 392 subjects were presented with the pictures and names of their high school classmates (Bahrick, Bahrick, and Wittlinger, 1975). The subjects in this study were people between 17 and 74 years old, who had graduated from high school between 2 weeks and 57 years earlier. Even after nearly 50 years, people who saw a classmate's picture mixed in with other pictures could correctly recognize the former classmates over 70 percent of the time (see Figure 7-6). When a classmate's name was mixed with four other names, recognition of the classmate's name was equally good. But people had much more trouble when they were asked to think of the name of the person in a picture. Thus, recognition proved easier than recall.

In a more recent study of long-term memory (Bahrick, 1984), 600 people who had taken one or more Spanish courses in high school or college were tested for reading comprehension, vocabulary, and so on. Although these former students forgot a good deal during the first three years after their Spanish courses, after that their memories were relatively stable.

FIGURE 7-6 LOSS OF INFORMATION FROM LONG-TERM MEMORY.
High school graduates were asked to identify the pictures and names of students from their yearbooks. Recognition of pictures and names was quite good, but recall of names was less good. (After Bahrick, Bahrick, and Wittlinger, 1975.)

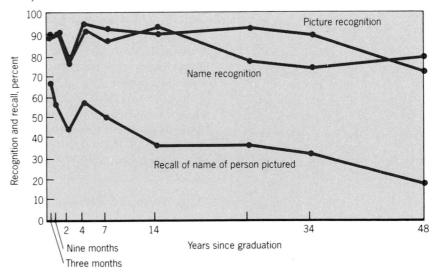

ENCODING OF INFORMATION

Now that you have been introduced to the basic systems of memory, we present research on some of the more difficult questions about memory. In this section, we examine the forms in which information is encoded and stored and how information is processed before it is placed in memory.

Short-term Memory Codes

What kind of information is stored in short-term memory? At least some of the information in short-term memory is in the form of acoustic (sound) codes. In one study that demonstrated the role of acoustic codes in memory, Conrad (1964) had subjects look at a series of consonants, one every .75 seconds, and then recall the consonants in sequence. The errors in recall were not random. As Table 7-2 shows, people tended to confuse letters that sounded alike—*n* with *m,* but not *n* with *v.* Even though people had *seen* the consonants, they must have at least partially represented them to memory as sounds.

But sounds are not the only types of codes that people use for encoding information in short-term memory. People who are deaf, for example, make more mistakes in remembering letters that look alike than sound alike. In one study, both deaf and hearing people were presented lists of letters that either sounded alike—DVPC—or that looked alike—KYXZ (Conrad, 1972). People who could hear made more mistakes on letters that sounded alike, and people who could not hear made more mistakes on letters that looked alike. In another study, this one of deaf people who were adept at sign language, the people were shown words that either sounded alike or that were signed alike (Shand, 1982). The subjects made more mistakes in recalling words for similar signs, an indication that their short-term memory codes included visual information.

The type of code used to represent information in short-term memory influences the amount of information that can be stored. As we have seen, short-term memory can store approximately seven chunks of information if the information is pronounced and encoded acoustically. But if the information takes a long time to pronounce, short-term capacity will be reduced (Schweickert and Boruff, 1986) and if the information is encoded semantically (in terms of meaning) or visually, capacity may be reduced to around three chunks (Zhang and Simon, 1985). One explanation for these differences in capacities is that the information placed into short-term memory must be placed there within a period of between 1.5 and 3 seconds (Baddeley, 1986; Yu et al., 1985) and it may take longer to encode information in semantic or visual form.

Maintenance Rehearsal and Short-term Memory

Most people probably rely on sounds for encoding information in short-term memory because these codes help them to rehearse and maintain information in memory. Maintenance rehearsal helps to encode informa-

TABLE 7-2   CONFUSION PRODUCED BY SIMILARITIES IN SOUND AND APPEARANCE OF LETTERS

Auditory Confusions
Stimulus Letter

		B	C	P	T	V	F	M	N	S	X
Response Letter	B	.	171	75	84	168	2	11	10	2	2
	C	32	.	35	42	20	4	4	5	2	5
	P	162	350	.	505	91	11	31	23	5	5
	T	143	232	281	.	50	14	12	11	8	5
	V	122	61	34	22	.	1	8	11	1	0
	F	6	4	2	4	3	.	13	8	336	238
	M	10	14	2	3	4	22	.	334	21	9
	N	13	21	6	9	20	32	512	.	38	14
	S	2	18	2	7	3	488	23	11	.	391
	X	1	6	2	2	1	245	2	1	184	.

Visual Confusions
Stimulus Letter

		B	C	P	T	V	F	M	N	S	X
Response Letter	B	.	18	62	5	83	12	9	3	2	0
	C	13	.	27	18	55	15	3	12	35	7
	P	102	18	.	24	40	15	8	8	7	7
	T	30	46	79	.	38	18	14	14	8	10
	V	56	32	30	14	.	21	15	11	11	5
	F	6	8	14	5	31	.	12	13	131	16
	M	12	6	8	5	20	16	.	146	15	5
	N	11	7	5	1	19	28	167	.	24	5
	S	7	21	11	2	9	37	4	12	.	16
	X	3	7	2	2	11	30	10	11	59	.

Source: R. Conrad, "Acoustic confusions in immediate memory." *British Journal of Psychology*, 1964, *55*, 75–84. Copyright 1964 by Cambridge University Press. Reprinted by permission.
Note: When people are presented a series of letters in rapid succession and then asked to recall the letters in order, their errors are clearly influenced by the similarity of the erroneous letter to the letter they are trying to remember. For example, if the letters were presented aurally, *b* and *t* were likely to be confused but this confusion was less likely when the letters were presented visually.

tion in long-term memory. In a study conducted by Glanzer and Cunitz (1966), subjects were presented with a series of words and asked to recall as many as possible, in any order. Some people were asked to recall the words immediately, some after 10 seconds of counting backwards by 3s, and some after 30 seconds of counting backwards by 3s. As this study of **free recall** (subjects did not have to recall the words in any particular order) shows (Figure 7-7), when subjects recall words immediately, they display what are called **serial position effects**. That is, they recall words from early in the list—the **primacy effect**—and those at the end—the **recency effect**—better than those in the middle.

It is not surprising that people remember better those items that they have most recently heard. They report them first and may even draw them from sensory memory (although other explanations have been

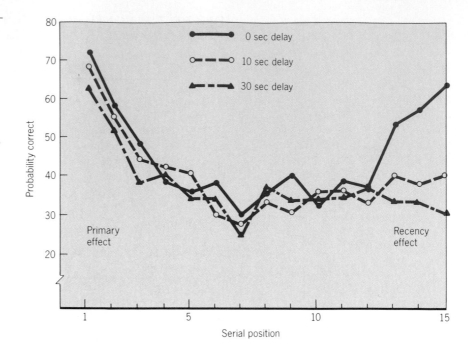

FIGURE 7-7 THE EFFECTS OF SERIAL POSITION ON RECALL.
When people were presented a series of words and then asked to recall as many of the words as possible, the number of words was affected by the length of time the people had to engage in a distractor task (counting backwards by 3s), and whether the words have been presented to the people early in the list (which can produce a primacy effect) or the words were presented late in the list (which, when there is no distractor task, can produce a recency effect). (From Glanzer and Cunitz, 1966.)

offered; Glenberg, 1984; Greene, 1986a, 1986b). Furthermore, while the most recent items are being reported, earlier items from the list may be lost from memory. In fact, when the delay period between the presentation of words and recall was extended, the recency effect disappeared (Figure 7-7). Because people could no longer rehearse the items, they disappeared from short-term memory. But their memory for items that had appeared early on the lists—the primacy effect—was largely unaffected by the delay. Why should delay not influence the primacy effect?

Several explanations for the primacy effect have been offered. One of the most compelling is that the early items are rehearsed most and subjects retrieve early items from long-term memory. In fact, people sometimes rehearse early items more often than later items. In one study, when subjects repeated items out loud as they were presented and had five seconds to repeat any item they wished, they rehearsed the early items most often, perhaps because fewer items competed for rehearsal during the early stages (Rundus, 1971; Rundus and Atkinson, 1970). When Waugh and Norman (1965) asked subjects to rehearse only the most recent item presented, the primacy effect was eliminated. In addition, the primacy effect diminishes the faster people are presented items to remember (Murdock, 1962). When people have less time to rehearse information, the information is less likely to be transferred into long-term memory (see Figure 7-8). These findings are consistent with Atkinson and Shiffrin's notion that items frequently rehearsed in short-term memory are most likely to be transferred to long-term memory. Although maintenance rehearsal can facilitate the transfer of information into long-term memory, it is not a very effective way to form long-term memories (Glenberg, Smith, and Green, 1977).

FIGURE 7-8   THE PRIMARY EFFECT AS A FUNCTION OF THE RATE AT WHICH INFORMATION IS PRESENTED.
This graph shows differences between recall of items that have been quickly (1 second per item) and slowly (2 seconds per item) presented. When items are freely recalled after having been presented slowly, the primacy effect is enhanced and the recency effect unchanged. The extra second per item may allow more time for rehearsal and, therefore, long-term storage. (After Murdock, 1962.)

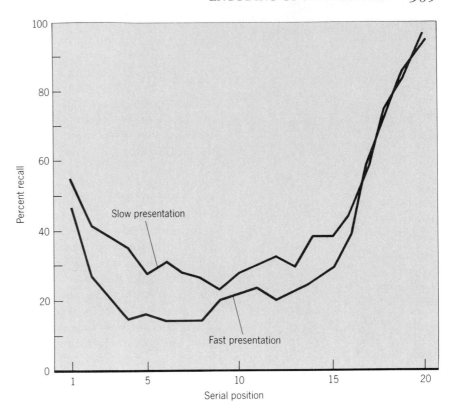

Encoding for Long-term Memory

Do you remember where you were when you learned that the space shuttle *Challenger* had exploded and all seven astronauts aboard killed? When Americans were asked about their memories for dramatic historical events, such as John F. Kennedy's assassination, most people clearly remembered the circumstances under which they had learned about these events (Brown and Kulik, 1977). These "flashbulb memories," as the researchers called them, show that people remember some information intentionally (e.g., the assassination) and some incidentally or unintentionally (the circumstances).

INTENTIONAL AND INCIDENTAL LEARNING   Have you ever found yourself singing or humming the theme song for a television program? There's a good chance that you never intentionally set out to learn the song, but instead, your learning of the song was incidental to watching the television program. Incidental learning can sometimes be as effective as intentional learning. For example, Hyde and Jenkins (1969) had people in four different groups recall a list of words they had heard. The first three groups were not told that their memory for the words would be tested. Subjects in the first of these three groups were asked to indicate whether the words they were presented contained the letter *e*. The second group was asked to estimate the number of letters in the words. The third group was asked to rate the words for their "pleasantness." A fourth group was told that they would be tested on their memory for the words but were not given other special instructions. Subjects in the fourth group—who had learned intentionally—recalled an average of 16.1 words, and those in the "pleasantness" group recalled 16.3 words—presumably through incidental learning. People in the other two groups recalled an average of fewer than 10 words. Why did the "pleasantness" group do so well? One popular answer is that they encoded the words more deeply than the subjects in the second and third groups.

LEVELS OF PROCESSING Although most memory researchers believe that research evidence supports Atkinson and Shiffrin's **dual process** distinction between short-term and long-term memory systems or stages, a memory model developed by Craik and Lockhart (1972) offers an alternative **single process** account of the findings that are used to support the distinction between short-term and long-term memory. At the same time, the model provides an explanation of the results from incidental learning studies.

Craik and Lockhart argued that both the rate of forgetting and the strength of memory depend on the depth or level to which information is processed while a memory is being formed. Instead of two separate memory systems, Craik and Lockhart (1972) proposed the existence of a single central processor with a limited capacity. This central processor may process information either shallowly, in a way that deals only with the superficial aspects of information, or it may process information more deeply, in a way that extracts more meaning. The more deeply information is processed, the better the memory for the material should be.

To test this theory, Craik and Tulving (1975) designed a study like the one conducted by Hyde and Jenkins in which people would have to process words at one of three different levels. Some subjects were asked whether words were in upper- or lowercase letters. Their answers required only shallow processing. A second group of subjects were asked whether words rhymed with other words. Their answers required deeper processing, because they had to think of the sound of the whole word and then compare it to the sound of another word. A third group of subjects was asked about the meaning of words, a task that required the deepest level of processing. They had to retrieve possible definitions from memory, compare the word to those possible definitions, and judge the adequacy of the possible definitions. The subjects were not told they would later be tested on their memory for the words.

Later, the subjects saw a list of 180 words and were asked to circle the 60 words they had seen before. Guessing would have produced a recognition rate of 33 percent. Those subjects who had processed the words shallowly remembered 42 percent, those who had processed them moderately remembered 65 percent, and those who had processed them deeply remembered 90 percent. These findings fit precisely with the theory.

Similarly, the depth at which people process pictures and other visual stimuli also affects how well they remember them. Subjects in one study (Bower and Karlin, 1974) saw pictures of people and were asked to judge either the sex of the person (a shallow judgment) or how much they thought they would like the person (a judgment thought to involve a deeper level of processing). Those who had judged how well they would like the people in the pictures remembered them better than those who had judged the people's sex. Deep encoding has even been shown to enhance memory for odors—subjects who tried to generate a name for an unknown odor or tried to describe a life event brought to mind by the odor were more likely to recognize the odor a week later (Lyman and McDaniel, 1986).

The depth of processing model shows that people's encoding strategies and reasons for learning affect the quality of the memories they form. This point is well illustrated in Box 7-3, "Mnemonic Devices to Improve Memory."

CONSTRUCTION AT ENCODING   Not only do strategies and reasons for learning affect memory, but what people already know affects it as well. Earlier in the chapter we noted that Bartlett's research with meaningful material such as the "War of the Ghosts" revealed systematic changes in the material when it was recalled. Bartlett thought that the changes in the reproductions occurred at the time of retrieval and were influenced by the subjects' cultural experiences. He believed that the subjects actually remembered only a few of the critical facts and central themes of the story and used these to reconstruct the story. Bartlett referred to memory for central facts and themes as the **schema**: "an active organisation of past reactions, or of past experience." Subsequent research (e.g., Dooling and Christiaansen, 1977; Hasher and Griffin, 1978; Snyder and Uranowitz, 1978) has shown that, in fact, errors are introduced into memory both at encoding (when memory is "constructed") and at retrieval (when information retrieved from memory is "reconstructed" to make a report).

Not only can prior knowledge affect the encoding of new information and later memory performance but so can the goals that people use when they are learning new information. This happens because the prior knowledge and goals influence the interpretation of new information and the way in which new information is represented in memory (Findahl and Hoijer, 1985; Summers, Horton, and Diehl, 1985; Wyer and Bodenhausen, 1985).

For example, when people were asked to read the following passage without knowing beforehand what the passage was about, they remembered many fewer of the ideas than those who had been told what the passage was about (Bransford and Johnson, 1972). Read the following passage and then, without looking at the passage again, write down all the ideas expressed in the passage that you can remember.

> *The procedure is actually quite simple. First you arrange items into different groups. Of course one pile may be sufficient depending on how much there is to do. If you have to go somewhere else due to lack of facilities that is the next step; otherwise, you are pretty well set. It is important not to overdo things. That is, it is better to do too few things at once than too many. In the short run this may not seem important but complications can easily arise. A mistake can be expensive as well. At first, the whole procedure will seem complicated. Soon, however, it will become just another facet of life. It is difficult to foresee any end*

to the necessity for this task in the immediate future, but then one can never tell. After the procedure is completed one arranges the materials into different groups again. Then they can be put into their appropriate places. Eventually they will be used once more and the whole cycle will then have to be repeated. However, this is a part of life.

(Bransford and Johnson, 1972, p. 722)

People who read this passage without knowing what it was about remembered only 2.82 ideas out of 18. Another group of subjects was told that the passage was about washing clothes *after* reading the passage but before they tried to recall ideas from the passage. These subjects rated the passage as no more comprehensible than the other group had and could recall no more information than the others. But a third group of subjects, who were told *before* they read the passage that it referred to clothes washing considered it quite comprehensible and remembered twice as many ideas from it.

Long-term Memory Codes

We have seen that acoustic codes are important in encoding information into short-term memory. What about the codes used for long-term memory? There is strong evidence that people use at least three different types of codes in long-term memory.

SEMANTIC CODES　One way that people encode long-term memories is according to **semantic encoding**. Information is stored in a form that reflects its meaning. For example, subjects saw a list of 41 words (Grossman and Eagle, 1970). After 5 minutes, they saw a second list of words and were asked which words they had seen previously. On the average, they incorrectly thought they had just seen 1.8 of 9 words that were synonyms of words on the first list. In contrast, they incorrectly thought they had seen 1.1 of 9 words that were unrelated to any of the words on the first list. Their memories had been affected by the semantic relationships between the words.

Similarly, in another study people saw 15 animal names, 15 vegetable names, 15 names of people, and 15 names of professions in random order (Bousfield, 1953). When the subjects were asked to write down as many as they could recall, there was a pattern to the order in which they recalled the words. They recalled the words in semantically related clusters—groups of farm animals, groups of domestic animals, groups of wild animals, and the like—which suggests that the words were stored or coded in a way that preserved their meanings.

VISUAL CODES　When you try to remember the face of someone you haven't seen in a long while, or to recall where you parked your car, or to recall where you misplaced your sweater (glasses, keys, books, wallet . . .), you probably look into your "mind's eye" to summon up an image of your memory.

We seem to code information in long-term memory according to the way it looks (Paivio, 1971; Paivio and Csapo, 1973). We are much more likely to confuse a (familiar) Oreo cookie with an (unfamiliar) Hydrox

(*a*)   Visual stimuli

NUMBER OF TIMES AN OBJECT WAS RECOGNIZED AS A FUNCTION OF THE SIMILARITY OF THE OLD AND NEW OBJECT.

Magnitude of Difference Between Original and New Stimuli

Retention Interval	*0*	*1*	*2*	*3*	*4*	*5*
0	77	39	28	6	5	5
2 hours	48	39	30	16	14	13
2 days	47	34	31	19	21	8
2 weeks	41	47	35	21	8	8

Bahrick, H. P., Clark, S., and Bahrick, P. (1967). Generalization gradients as indicants of learning and retention of a recognition task. *Journal of Experimental Psychology, 75,* p. 465.

FIGURE 7-9 SIMILARITY AND RECOGNITION.
This is an example of items on a recognition test. The original stimulus is labeled 0. The 10 new stimuli are labeled in degree of similarity to the old stimulus from 1 (most similar) to 5 (least similar). As shown in the table, people tended to recognize objects that most closely resembled the original stimulus. (After Bahrick, Clark, and Bahrick, 1967.)

cookie than with an (unfamiliar) granola bar, because Oreos and Hydrox cookies look so much alike. In a scientific demonstration that long-term memory uses visual coding, people saw drawings of 16 everyday objects for 2 seconds each (Bahrick, Clark, and Bahrick, 1967). Later, they were asked whether they could recognize the drawings they had seen. Each drawing was shown along with 10 other drawings that looked much like it (see Figure 7-9). As the table in Figure 7-9 shows, when subjects made mistakes, they tended to recognize objects that looked most like those they had seen before.

ACOUSTIC CODES   For most of us who are not musicians and who live in a culture that relies heavily on visual forms of communication—books, television, computer screens, and so on—acoustic coding is less effective than semantic or visual encoding as a basis for storing long-term information (Craik and Tulving, 1975). But we do store some information in long-term memory according to its sound. People who learn foreign languages, for example, constantly rely on acoustic codes to help them remember that if it's *me* in English, it's *moi* in French and *mi* in Spanish. In one experiment, subjects memorized pairs of numbers and words (**paired associates**) such as "27-tacks" (Nelson and Rothbart, 1972). One month later, they returned to the laboratory and tried to learn other pairs of numbers and words. Some of these pairs were identical to those they had learned at first, some of them consisted of pairs that sounded like pairs in the first list ("27-tacks" and "27-tax"), and some were entirely new. The subjects found it easiest to learn identical pairs, next easiest to learn pairs that sounded like those on the original list (thus they must have retained some acoustic information about the original pairs), and least easy to learn the entirely new pairs.

THE STORAGE OF INFORMATION

In that enormous warehouse where you store information in memory, you organize that information or risk losing it forever. But how do you organize it?

Episodic and Semantic Memory

Endel Tulving (1972) distinguished between knowledge about oneself—where you had dinner last night and how many brothers and sisters you have—and general knowledge about the world—that the Mississippi is the longest river in the United States. He distinguished between **semantic** and **episodic** memories in the following way:

How do people represent geometric shapes in their memory? People in the **propositional** camp argue that visual information is represented in memory by a set of rules—propositions—that can generate images. People in the **analog** camp argue that visual information is represented in memory in a form with physical features analogous to the images perceived. In other words, the mind's eye sees images that are analogous to what the visual system sees.

The analog camp offers studies of the manipulation of mental images to support their position (Corballis, 1986; Jolicoeur, 1985; Jolicoeur and Landau, 1984). For example, in one

BOX FIGURE 1 MENTAL ROTATION OF OBJECTS.
Mentally rotate the objects to determine whether the pairs are identical but viewed from a different angle. (After Shepard and Metzler, 1971.)

classic study subjects saw pairs of geometric figures and had to determine as quickly as possible whether the rotated figures were the same (Shepard and Metzler, 1971, see Box Figure 1). It was found that the difficulty of this task—measured as the time the subjects took to answer—correlated almost perfectly with the number of degrees that the second figure had to rotate to match the first (see Box Figure 2).

In another study, subjects were given one of the following tasks: imagine a rabbit sitting next to an elephant or imagine a fly sitting next to a rabbit (Kosslyn, 1975). Then the subjects answered true or false to statements such as "A rabbit has ears." It took the subjects longer to answer that question when they had paired the rabbit with an elephant than when they had paired the rabbit with a fly. These results suggest that there are physical limitations on the mental image space and when a rabbit is imagined next to an elephant the ears on the rabbit are very small and relatively difficult to "see." But when the rabbit is paired with a fly, the ears are much larger and therefore easier to "see." Finally, people studied a map of an imaginary island that showed seven objects (Kosslyn, Ball, and Reiser, 1978; see Box Figure 3). Then the people visualized the map, focused on one object, mentally scanned to a second object, and pressed a button once they reached it. The scanning times were directly proportional to the distances between the locations.

The strongest critiques of the analog theory have been made by Zenon Pylyshyn (1979, 1981, 1984). He has argued that studies such as the imaginary island study "may represent a discovery about what subjects believe and what they take the goal of the

BOX FIGURE 2   TIMING MENTAL ROTATIONS.

The amount of time required to mentally rotate objects for comparison (as in Box Figure 1) is systematically related to the number of degrees the object must be rotated. This is true whether the object is rotated on the plane of the picture (Part A) or rotated through the third or depth dimension (Part B). (After Shepard and Metzler, 1971.)

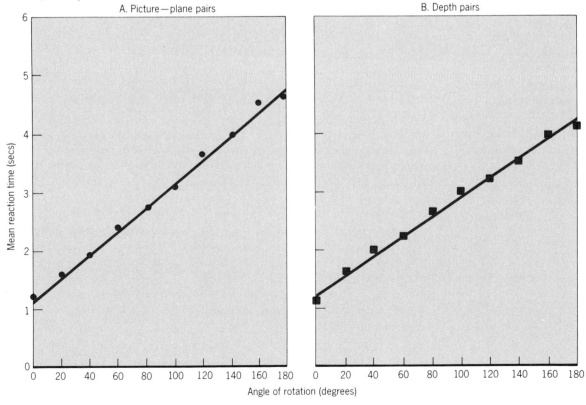

(continued)

(Box 7-1, continued)

experiment to be rather than a discovery about what underlying mechanisms of image processing are" (1981, p. 23). In fact, subjects' beliefs about imagery can influence scanning times (Goldston, Hinrichs, and Richman, 1985). What is more, Pylyshyn argues that imagery is a product of symbolically encoded propositions. Imagery makes use of these symbolic propositions to construct what people subjectively experience as images. These symbolic codes, he argues, are not analogous and do not look like what people see.

One example of visual information stored as propositions is a computerized graphics system. At the simplest level, the graphics information is represented as 1s and 0s. To see the image graphically, one must see the image constructed from the 1s and 0s according to a complex set of propositions in a computer program. Although researchers have demonstrated that visual images can be successfully represented in propositional form (computer graphics packages are an example), psychologists do not yet know whether images are stored as analogs or as propositions— or as some combination of these.

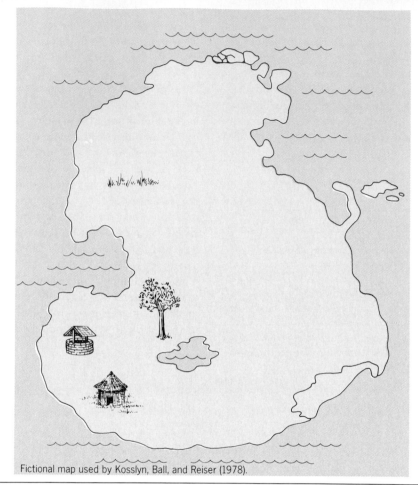

Fictional map used by Kosslyn, Ball, and Reiser (1978).

BOX FIGURE 3 SCANNING MENTAL MAPS.
When people were asked to memorize this fictional map and then mentally scan from one location to another, their scanning times were directly proportional to the distances between the locations. (After Kosslyn, Ball, and Reiser, 1978.)

> *Episodic memory receives and stores information about temporally dated episodes or events, and temporal-spatial relations among these events. . . . Semantic memory is the memory necessary for the use of language. It is a mental thesaurus, organized knowledge a person possesses about words and other verbal symbols, their meaning and referents, about relations among them, and about rules, formulas, and algorithms for the manipulation of these symbols, concepts and relations (pp. 385–386).*

It is sometimes difficult to distinguish between semantic and episodic information because people acquire their semantic knowledge during "dated episodes or events." Some have argued that there are separate memory stores for semantic and episodic information (Olton, 1984;

Shoben, Westcourt, and Smith, 1978; Tulving, 1985). Others disagree (McKoon and Ratcliff, 1979; McKoon, Ratcliff, and Dell, 1986; Mandler, 1985; Roediger, 1984). Even so, episodic and semantic information do seem to be retrieved with different cues (Stern, 1985). For example, when people were asked to think aloud while remembering the names of people they had attended school with between four and 19 years earlier (Williams, 1976), they reported using cues drawn from their personal, episodic memory. Said one

> *I guess it's almost easier for me to think of my home town, and think of people . . . that . . . I've still run into on occasion, when I go back there. And then sort of check to see if they meet the requirements. Like were they in high school with me. And I can think of people like Buddy Collendar, and John Tremble who still both live in my . . . Ah . . . home town . . . It's clear that I have to think of some other situations. It's like I want to think of, sort of prototypical situations and then sort of examine the people that were involved in those. And things like P.E. class, where there was . . . Ah . . . Gary Booth. Umm, and Karl Brist, were sort of, we always ended up in the same P.E. classes, for some reason. Umm, . . . I can think of things like dances. And I guess then I usually think of . . . girls (chuckle). Like Cindy Shup, Jody Foss, and Ah . . . Sharon Ellis (pp.1–2).*

In contrast, when people tried to remember the names of celebrities—people they did *not* personally know—they tended to rely on noncontextual cues (Read and Bruce, 1982). These people were first given cues such as: "On Broadway he created the role of Charley in *Charley's Aunt* but is perhaps best remembered as the scarecrow in the Judy Garland movie, *The Wizard of Oz*" (Read and Bruce, 1982, p. 282). (The answer, by the way, is actor Ray Bolger). The subjects successfully recalled the names when they could generate information associated with it. One subject recalled the name of the actor who played Maxwell Smart in the television series "Get Smart" by imagining the actor (Don Adams) falling down in a telephone booth. Another subject recalled the name of the actor who played Fred Mertz on "I Love Lucy" by first saying "Fred Williams," which led to the correct answer, William Frawley. In short, when people tried to recall episodic and semantic memories, they used different kinds of cues.

Network Models of Semantic Memory

Psychologists have proposed two major types of models by which the semantic meanings of memories are organized. In network models of semantic memory, people are assumed to remember networks of interconnected concepts. In some network models, concepts are organized hierarchically (see Figure 7-10) (Quillian, 1967; Collins and Quillian, 1969; Cooke, Durso, and Schvaneveldt, 1986). People might remember the superordinate *animal*, its subordinate, *bird*, and then its subordinate, *canary*. (These connections are sometimes referred to as "isa" relations, as in "a canary *is a* bird.") At each concept node, there are paths to information about the concept—a canary can sing and is yellow.

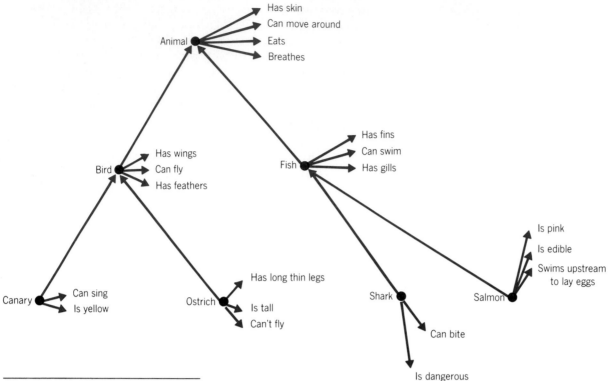

FIGURE 7-10 A NETWORK MODEL OF SEMANTIC MEMORY.
One way that semantic information may be stored in memory is in the form of hierarchical networks in which superordinate categories such as animal *are divided into subordinate categories such as* bird *and* fish—*which may be further divided into subordinate categories. (After Collins and Quillian, 1969.)*

This information is organized efficiently. Thus information about all types of animals—eat, breathe, have skin—is stored only at the superordinate level; information about birds—fly, have feathers—is stored only at the middle level; and information necessary to distinguish among types of birds—canaries sing and are yellow—is stored only at the lowest level.

If memory is organized in such networks, people ought to be able to recall certain types of information from a network more rapidly than other types. People ought to be able to say whether a canary can sing more rapidly than they can say whether a canary has skin. The information needed to answer the first statement is recorded at the same level of the hierarchy, whereas the information needed for the second statement is recorded at two different levels. As Figure 7-11 shows, the number of levels separating the information relates systematically to people's reaction times when verifying statements about information in the network (Collins and Quillian, 1969). Furthermore, network relationships among words are also systematically related to the speed and order of recall of the words (Cooke, Durso, and Schvaneveldt, 1986).

Critics, however, have challenged the network model. One study, for example, showed that people could verify a statement such as "a collie is an animal" faster than the statement "a collie is a mammal" (Rips, Shoben, and Smith, 1973). The network model would predict that *mammal* (a type of animal and therefore a mid-level category) should be

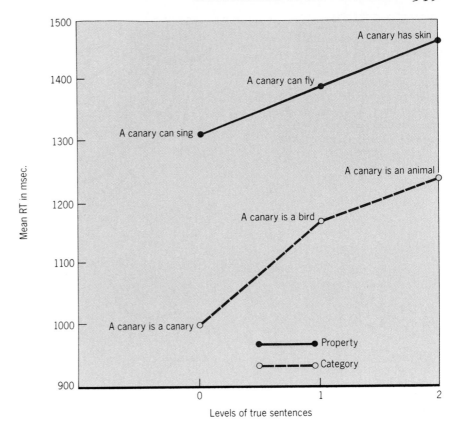

FIGURE 7-11   VERIFICATION TIMES FOR QUESTIONS ABOUT PROPERTIES AND CATEGORY MEMBERSHIPS.
People's reaction times to answer questions about various properties and their category membership are related to the number of levels separating information. (After Collins and Quillian, 1969.)

closer to *collie* (a lower level, specific instance of a mammal) than *animal* (the most general, highest level category).

Critics have said that the model does not index how typical the instances within a category are—*robin*, for example, is a more typical bird than a *penguin* (Rosch, 1973)—even though typicality influences how well people learn and understand what they read (Hupp and Mervis, 1982; Roth and Shoben, 1983). The model also has been criticized for not reflecting differences between semantic and episodic memory, not taking into account how retrieval strategies affect performance, and not explaining how statements are disconfirmed.

Network theories and models have been refined over the years. Thus, network models have been proposed in which the strength of the associations between concepts is taken into consideration and the process of retrieval is conceived in terms of one concept activating another concept (Collins and Loftus, 1975). For example, in Figure 7-12 *red* is more closely associated with *fire engines* than with *sunrises*. When one of the concepts in the network is activated (for example *red*), the process of **spreading activation** to other concepts makes them easier to retrieve. Those concepts that are already most strongly associated with the original concept will be retrieved earliest (*fire engines*). As time passes, activation spreads, and less closely associated concepts (*sunrises*) are retrieved.

FIGURE 7-12   A NETWORK
MODEL OF SEMANTIC MEMORY
IN WHICH LINE LENGTHS
REFLECT THE RELATEDNESS
OF CONCEPTS.

*FIGURE 7-12   A NETWORK
MODEL OF SEMANTIC MEMORY
IN WHICH LINE LENGTHS
REFLECT THE RELATEDNESS
OF CONCEPTS.*
In this network model of memory the
length of lines connecting concepts
represents the degree of relatedness
between the concepts. (After Collins
and Loftus, 1975.)

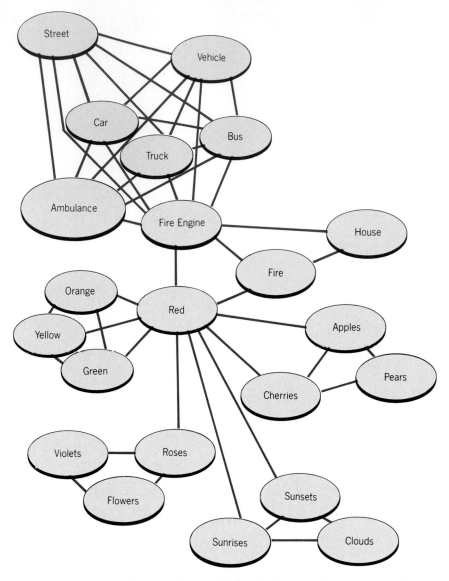

This may explain why you always think of that word you were trying to
remember in the middle of the night.

Feature Comparison Models of Semantic Memory

A second model of semantic memory depicts features specifying a concept hierarchically. The location of a feature in this hierarchy reflects the
degree to which the feature is necessary to the definition of the concept
(Smith, Shoben, and Rips, 1974). **Defining features** are essential,
whereas **characteristic features** describe properties of the concept that
are not essential. For example, Figure 7-13 shows the defining features
of the concept *robin* include "is living," "has feathers," and "has red
breast"—features without which a bird cannot be a robin. The characteristic features of *robin,* such as "flies," "perches in trees," and so on are

FIGURE 7-13 A FEATURE COMPARISON MODEL OF SEMANTIC MEMORY.

In the feature comparison model of semantic memory the meaning of a concept is defined by semantic features. The higher a feature is in the list, the more essential it is for defining the concept. (After Smith, Shoben, and Rips, 1974.)

		Concepts	
		Robin	Bird
Defining features		Is living	Is living
		Has feathers	Has features
		Has a red breast	—
		—	—
		—	—
		—	—
Characteristic features		Flies	Flies
		Perches in trees	—
		Is undomesticated	—
		Is smallish	—
		—	—
		—	—

common to robins, but also to many other species of birds. In this model, too, broader superordinate categories—such as *bird*—are more abstract and contain fewer defining characteristics than narrower, subordinate categories—such as *robin*.

To verify a statement such as "a robin is a bird" a person goes through two steps. First the person quickly compares the defining and characteristic features of the specific example *(robin)* with the broader category *(bird)*. If there is little overlap, the person says that the statement is false; if there is substantial overlap, the person says true. If there is a moderate level of overlap, the person then compares only the defining features and only if there is a perfect match between them does the person answer true. People tend to confirm statements about typical instances of a category more quickly than atypical instances. It takes less time to recall the typical defining characteristics of *robins,* birds that do "fly" and "perch in trees," than to recall the typical defining characteristics of *penguins,* which also are birds but neither fly nor perch in trees.

The model explains why people recall more quickly that "a canary is a bird" than that "a canary is an animal." Because the features of *canary* overlap more with *bird* than with *animal,* people need only compare their characteristic features—the first-stage comparison. It is likely that people retrieve information from their memories in the ways that both network models suggest. Human memory, in fact, probably is organized in a way that combines aspects of both hierarchical and feature-comparison models (Glass and Holyoak, 1986; Lorch, 1981; Stern, 1985).

RETRIEVAL PROCESSES

As you saw earlier in the chapter, people retrieve information from their memories in two basically different ways. They **recognize** information that they are presented with and must confirm in memory, and they **recall** information that has been presented to them in the past. If you

FIGURE 7-14a A RECOGNITION TASK.
Here are 15 drawings of a penny from which subjects were asked to recognize the most faithful reproduction.

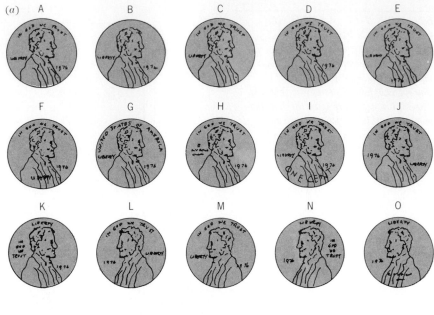

(a)

FIGURE 7-14b A RECALL TASK.
These drawings show subjects' attempts to draw a penny as they recalled it from memory. (After Nickerson and Adams, 1979.)

(b)

look at Figure 7-14, you can see the difference between recognition and recall. When people were asked which of 15 drawings most faithfully represented a penny (Figure 7-14*a*), they had to recognize it. When people were asked to draw a penny from memory (Figure 7-14*b*), they had to recall it (Nickerson and Adams, 1979).

When people have to recognize something or someone—the notes of a familiar tune, the features of a familiar face, the details of a familiar penny—they must retrieve the necessary information from their memory. But when people have to recall something—who was the president before Eisenhower?—they must retrieve the information from memory and then decide whether it matches the information or task before them. Recognition involves a one-process search, whereas recall involves a two-process search and comparison (Anderson and Bower, 1972).

The distinction between recall and recognition is not perfect. For example, multiple choice examination questions contain information that must be identified, but students usually have to recall other information to decide which alternative is correct. Psychologists, therefore, distinguish recognition and recall by several other criteria. We turn to these now.

Recognition

What happens during the recognition process? When you recognize something, you have made a comparison between information provided to you and the information you find in your memory. The comparison can yield an **identification** or a sense of **familiarity**. To illustrate the difference, sometimes you can identify (recognize) an old friend even though her appearance has changed and she no longer looks familiar, but sometimes you cannot identify someone even though her face does seem familiar (Mandler, 1980; Glass and Holyoak, 1986). You identify a person or an object when there is a match between the information you are given and critical features of the information stored in your memory. But the degree of familiarity you experience depends upon the number of features that match. "That sure looks like David," you say to yourself. "But his hair is too curly."

People easily recognize things that are familiar—pennies, nickels, dimes, quarters, and dollar bills; the face of your watch; a telephone dial. These are objects that you have seen and used thousands of times. By accessing just a few critical features of these objects from your memory and comparing them to the objects before you, you readily make accurate identifications. But if the recognition task is changed slightly—as in Figure 7-14a—so that you must recognize one of many similar objects by comparing them to features retrieved from memory, you recognize it less accurately and swiftly. Furthermore, if you try to draw these objects from memory (recall their features) you will soon discover that your memory for them is quite poor. This fact is evident in the Figure 7-14b drawings of pennies produced from memory (Nickerson and Adams, 1979).

As Figure 7-14a illustrates, not only the familiarity, but the **similarity** of objects influences how well people recognize them. Suppose Jack witnessed a crime committed by a white man, about 30 years old, who had brown hair and a mustache. The police ask Jack to look at a lineup of possible suspects consisting of three white women, two black men, one elderly white man, and one 30-year-old man with brown hair and a mustache. Jack picks the last suspect. Would you be very confident that Jack really recognized the right man? In fact, the quality of recognition memory in this sort of task can best be tested when targets (the perpetrator—if he really has been apprehended) and distractors (other lineup members) are similar.

This point is illustrated in a study in which the researcher (Tulving, 1981) took photographs of complex scenes and cut them in half (Figure 7-15). The subjects studied one half of the pictures and then were shown new pairs of pictures. These included the other halves of the pictures. Some of the pairs were highly similar, and some were highly dissimilar. The subjects had to determine which of the two pictures they had seen before. People were best at recognizing when the pairs were similar in

FIGURE 7-15   TARGET AND DISTRACTOR SIMILARITY.
Here we see pairs of targets and distractors in which the distractor is extremely similar to the target.
(a) Matched pairs; (b) mismatched pairs.
(From Tulving, 1981.)

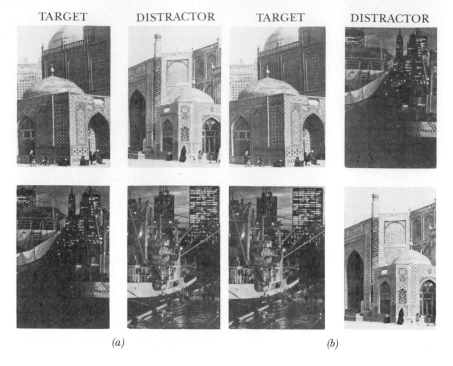

TARGET   DISTRACTOR   TARGET   DISTRACTOR

(a)   *(b)*

FIGURE 7-16a   IS THIS A DRAWING OF A MAN OR A RAT?

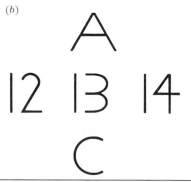

FIGURE 7-16b   IS THE CENTRAL FIGURE A B OR A 13?

appearance—probably because they could ignore features that were shared by the similar pictures and more easily detect distinctive features that could be matched to the features in their memory.

If you've ever tried to figure out *who* that woman is at a party, dressed most attractively, only to realize that she's the receptionist at your doctor's office whom you usually see in her white uniform, you'll understand that the **context** within which people try to recognize other people or things also influences recognition. If you look at the drawing in Figure 7-16*a*, it looks like a rat if you are looking for a small mammal, but it looks like a man if you are looking for a person (Bugelski and Alampay, 1961). Similarly, you will interpret what you see in Figure 7-16*b* according to your expectations. When people were shown scenes like those in Figure 7-17 for 150 milliseconds and were asked if they had seen objects like a fire hydrant or a sofa, they missed the object less than 30 percent of the time when it had been in its normal context (Biederman, Mezzanotte, and Rabinowitz, 1982). But they missed the object 40 percent of the time when it had been either in the wrong position or the wrong size. When the object was both the wrong size and in the wrong position, they missed it more than 50 percent of the time.

Availability versus Accessibility

Every student dreads it. There you sit, exam question in front of you, and you simply cannot think of the answer. You studied, you prepared, you *know* you know the answer. But for the life of you, you cannot summon it up. Psychologists distinguish between information that is **available** in memory and information that is **accessible**. You may have

(a)

(b)

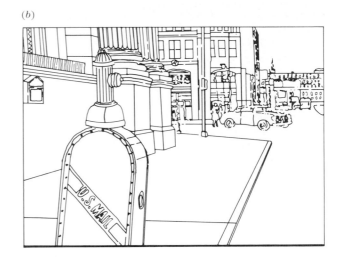

FIGURE 7-17   THE EFFECTS OF CONTEXT ON SCENE RECOGNITION.
(a) *The hydrant in appropriate context but the sofa both out of position and the wrong size.* (b) *The hydrant out of position. When people see these scenes for 150 milliseconds, their ability to recognize objects depends on the appropriateness of its context—both size and position. (After Biederman, Mezzanotte, and Rabinowitz, 1982.)*

studied, and the information may be available in your memory, but you may not be able to make it accessible during the exam.

In a study to demonstrate this difference, people learned words organized into categories such as "furniture" and "animals." Each set of words was identified by category before the subjects saw it. They were told, for example, that the words "chair," "sofa," and "table" belonged to the category "furniture." During the recall phase, the subjects were divided into two groups. One group again heard the category names and was asked to recall as many words as they could. The other group did not hear the category names. The first group recalled about twice as many words as the second. Those in the first group recalled about the same number of words per category, but recalled about twice as many categories. Although those in the second group initially could not recall—"access"—as many categories, a second test of their recall showed that the words not originally recalled were nonetheless available in their memories. In the second test, both groups heard the category names, and their recall levels were similar. One reason that hearing the category names may have improved the people's memories is that they served as the kinds of memory prompts known as retrieval cues.

Recall and Retrieval Cues

Retrieval cues prompt people to remember by specifying the goal of the memory search and by directing their generation and evaluation of possible answers. "Who," asks the professor, "was the president before Franklin Delano Roosevelt?" The retrieval cues are *president, Roosevelt,* and *before.* Figure 7-18 shows one way in which information about presidents might be organized in memory. This representation shows the associative links among the concept *president* and a number of specific presidents and which presidents were in office before others. Given the cue *president,* how might the generation and identification process work? The generation process is sometimes characterized as activating information and bringing it into short-term working memory, which, as we have

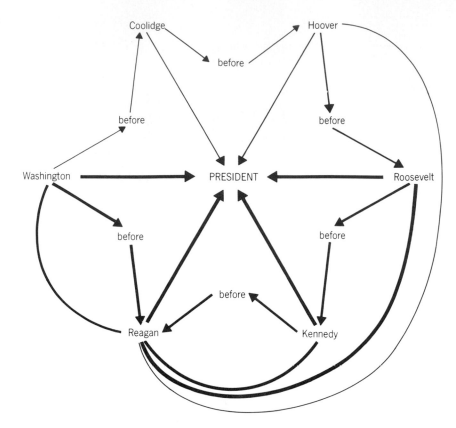

FIGURE 7-18 ASSOCIATIVE LINKS FOR PRESIDENTS.
This diagram shows the associative links among the concept president, *several specific presidents, and their succession in office. The strength of the link is reflected in the width of the lines between concepts. These links act as cues to retrieving information from memory to answer the question, "Who was president before Franklin Delano Roosevelt?"*

said, can hold only a limited amount of information (Glass and Holyoak, 1986; Graesser and Mandler, 1978). Cues activate associated concepts, and when activation reaches a certain threshold, a concept enters memory. In Figure 7-18 the strength of the associative links is reflected in their length. If the initial cue is *president,* associates of *president* will be activated and the presidential names with high levels of activation will enter working memory (these might include *Washington, Reagan,* and *Kennedy*).

Retrieval Inhibition

Retrieval cues generally bring the right information into consciousness, but sometimes they actually prevent people from getting at the information they want. Once you have used *president* as a retrieval cue, you are likely to activate the same paths and generate the same three names of presidents every time you use the cue again. This inhibition of retrieval, or **blocking** effect (Stern, 1985), has been demonstrated in many studies.

In one study people were asked to recall the names of the 50 states (Karchmer and Winograd, 1971). Half were given a list of 25 states to study before they tried to recall all the states. The other half did not get a list. Karchmer and Winograd then determined how many of the 25 states *not* included on the first group's study list were recalled by the two groups (this compares both groups on the same, unstudied states). The researchers found that those who had studied the "blocking" list recalled 18 of the states not on the list, but those who had not seen the list recalled even *more,* nearly 21 states.

Secondary Retrieval Cues

When people cannot retrieve information from their memories because of blocking or cue overload, they may resort to generating **secondary retrieval cues**. When the professor asks, "Who was the president before Franklin Delano Roosevelt?" you might run through the list of presidents you memorized in high school, or perhaps you can remember that Roosevelt took office early in the Depression and can recall who was president when the Depression began.

In a study of secondary retrieval cues, people were asked to come up with as many names of animals as they could in 30 minutes (see Figure 7-19*a*) (Gruenewald and Lockhead, 1980). People thought of fewer names as time went by. They also came up with most names in clusters. In a few cases as many as ten related animals were recalled in a brief period (see Figure 7-19*b*). These results are consistent with subjects generating secondary retrieval cues—farm animals, household pets, carnivores, flying animals. Although they may have thought of these secondary cues at a constant rate, as their number of animal names increased, they were less likely to think of new names from new secondary cues.

Encoding Specificity

When you have misplaced your keys, your wallet, or your textbook, you probably try to recall where it is by mentally replaying the events of the past hour or day. Then you recall that you went to the refrigerator for a soft drink and carried your textbook with you. Sure enough, when you go to the kitchen, you find your book in the refrigerator. A survey of a large group of people showed that nearly all used this strategy more than once a week (Harris, 1980). The strategy works because it generates secondary retrieval cues and matches the cues to the desired information. It works because whenever you experience an event, a number of specific aspects of the event are encoded in your memory—the time, the location, features of the setting, the people involved, the actions taken during the event, and so on. Retrieval cues that match these encodings are more effective than those that do not match.

The importance of the matching of cue to the information desired from memory is underscored in what is termed the **encoding specificity hypothesis** (Tulving and Thompson, 1973). The idea behind encoding specificity is that whenever a person experiences an event, a number of aspects of the event are encoded (e.g., the time, the location, features of the setting, the people involved, the actions taken during the event, and so on). Retrieval cues will be more effective if they match these encodings. Two separate bodies of research demonstrate how memory is improved when matches are made between retrieval cues and the information in memory.

Research on **state-dependency** indicates that recall (even more than recognition [Eich, 1980]) improves when people try to recall information while they are in the same physiological state as they were when they

*FIGURE 7-19a SECONDARY
RETRIEVAL CUES.*
*The number of names of animals that
subjects recalled in 30 minutes rose
steadily, but names were recalled faster
at first and more slowly as time passed.
(From Gruenewald and Lockhead,
1980.)*

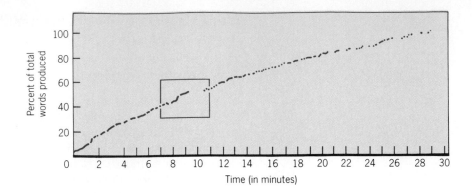

FIGURE 7-19b
*These are the names of animals that the
subject recalled in the four minutes
enclosed within the box in* (a).

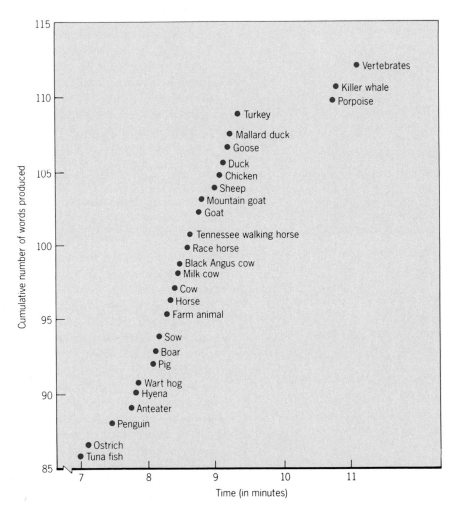

first learned the information. Although intoxication generally impairs
recall from long-term memory (Nelson, McSpadden, Fromme, and
Marlatt, 1986), what people learn when they are intoxicated is better
remembered when intoxicated (Goodwin et al., 1969), information
learned while under the influence of marijuana is best remembered
when on marijuana (Eich, 1980), information learned standing or lying

BOX 7-2
TIP-OF-THE-TONGUE
PHENOMENON

"The actor who played the captain in *Star Trek*? Oh, his name is on the tip of my tongue!" A number of researchers have examined this **tip-of-the-tongue (TOT) phenomenon.** When people were given dictionary definitions such as "an instrument used by navigators for measuring angular distances between the horizon and a heavenly body" and asked to recall the defined word, many could not immediately recall the words, but were certain that they knew them (Brown and McNeil, 1966). As they tried to recall the words, they answered questions about how many syllables the word had and what its first letter was. Most people thought of words that sounded like the target word—*secant* or *sextet,* instead of *sextant*—and some were similar in meaning. Furthermore, over 60 percent of the incorrect words had the same number of syllables as the correct word. Subjects generally knew when they had the wrong word but were close to retrieving the right one.

These findings show first of all that people can retrieve some information about a word before they recall the entire word itself. Second, the findings say something about the organization of memory. People remember by the meaning, length, and sound of words (see Table 7-3).

TABLE 7-3   CUING RECALL

	Country	First Letter of Capital City
1	Norway	O
2	Turkey	A
3	Kenya	N
4	Uruguay	M
5	Tibet	L
6	Australia	C
7	Portugal	L
8	Romania	B
9	Burma	R
10	Bulgaria	S
11	South Korea	S
12	Iraq	B
13	Cyprus	N
14	Philippines	M
15	Nicaragua	M
16	Yugoslavia	B
17	Colombia	B
18	Canada	O
19	Thailand	B
20	Venezuela	C

Source: After Baddeley, 1983.

Note: Cover the second column of letters and then try to generate the capital city for each of the countries. If you have difficulty, uncover the first letter of the city in the second column. Did this letter help you? How? When researchers supply subjects with the first letter of words (Gruneberg and Monk, 1974) or with rhyming words (Kozlowski, 1977), these cues aid recall.

Answers
1 Oslo   2 Ankara   3 Nairobi   4 Montevideo
5 Lhasa   6 Canberra   7 Lisbon   8 Bucharest
9 Rangoon   10 Sofia   11 Seoul   12 Baghdad
13 Nicosia   14 Manila   15 Managua
16 Belgrade   17 Bogota   18 Ottawa   19 Bangkok
20 Caracas

down is best remembered standing or lying down (Rand and Wapner, 1967), and information learned in a sad or happy mood is best remembered in the same mood (Blaney, 1986; Bower, 1981; Clark and Teasdale, 1985).

Another body of research indicated that memory is also influenced by contextual cues from the environment. This **context dependency** was demonstrated in an experiment in which 16 members of a university diving club learned lists of words while on land or underwater (Godden and Baddeley, 1975). Their recall was then tested on land or underwater (with writing tablets that worked underwater). They recalled better when they were in the same context as they had originally learned in. Researchers have gotten similar results in studies of memory for words (using music as the contextual cue; Smith, 1986), and memory for faces (Cutler and Penrod, 1987; Krafka and Penrod, 1985), though not all efforts to improve memory with contextual cues are effective (Fernandez and Glenberg, 1985). Thus, because people encode specifics about their internal body states and external environmental conditions along with other information, they can use the body state and environmental information as cues to retrieve additional material from memory.

Serial versus Parallel Searches

How do we find information in memory? What sorts of search strategies do we employ? Some researchers have compared memory searches and dictionary searches for a word. There are several ways to find a word in the dictionary. The most laborious, of course, is to start at the beginning of the dictionary and check every word in serial order until you find the word you want. A faster way is to check the first letter of a word—"love"—recall the alphabet, turn to the middle of the dictionary, find the *l* section, and search through the *l* words. Perhaps the ideal arrangement would be one in which all words could be examined at one time—a "parallel" search—and the correct one located very quickly.

In a now classic series of studies of short-term recognition memory, Sternberg (1966) presented subjects sets of randomly ordered numbers—9, 5, 4, 2. They saw each number for 1.2 seconds, and the sets varied from 1 to 6 digits. Then they saw one number and had to determine whether they had just seen it. Sternberg measured how long it took subjects to answer (see Figure 7-20). He concluded that the memory search was serial (all the numbers in the memory set are examined) because the larger the set of numbers people had seen, the longer it took them to answer. The subjects serially searched their memories at the remarkable rate of 26 numbers a second.

Sternberg also concluded that their search was **exhaustive** rather than **self-terminating**. That is, people seemed to search all the numbers in their memories and then responded, rather than examining each number individually and responding as soon as a match was made. Response times for numbers previously seen were the same as those for numbers not previously seen, and there was no evidence that the serial position of numbers previously seen had any effect on response times, as one would expect if the search were self-terminating.

Other researchers have found that people do respond faster when items are repeated in the memory set, a result that would not be expected if the search process were purely exhaustive (Baddeley and Ecob, 1973). Therefore some theorists have proposed that response times are partially determined by the strength or familiarity of the information stored in memory (Atkinson and Joula, 1974).

FIGURE 7-20   SERIAL SEARCH OF MEMORY.
The more numbers people have studied, the longer it takes them to recognize a number. The straight line represents the linear function that best fits the data. (After Sternberg, 1969.)

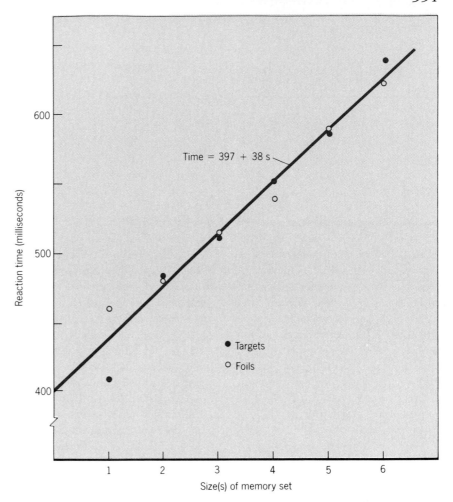

In addition, recall and recognition also seem to affect the way that people search their memories for information. When people were shown a set of numbers—5, 7, 2, 8, 3—and then asked which number came before the 8, they responded more rapidly when the numbers had earlier positions in the series—evidence for a self-terminating search (Sternberg, 1967). When they searched their memories to recall numbers, they took much longer than when they searched to recognize numbers. This finding suggests that during recall, people were making a separate decision about each number, whereas during recognition, they scanned all the numbers and then made a single decision. In short, the process for searching and deciding about information stored in memory varies with the kind of task people face.

Retrieval Failure: Forgetting

Everyone forgets things. But where does forgotten information go? Is it really gone from memory, or is it just unavailable? Psychologists have proposed several theories of forgetting.

BOX 7-3
MNEMONIC
DEVICES

People with remarkable memories, who can carry out complex mental calculations and remember vast quantities of material, probably use sophisticated encoding and storage strategies that may be within the grasp of the average person (Ericsson and Chase, 1982; Chase and Ericsson, 1982; Ericsson, 1985). Students have learned to increase the amount of numbers they can memorize from an ordinary seven to an extraordinary 82 by chunking the numbers and linking them to information already in their long-term memories. If you have ever doubted that "practice makes perfect," examine the improvement in two students' performance over a period of more than 250 practice sessions (Box Figure 1).

How is such performance possible? Chunking was one strategy the students employed. For example, one chunked 3–5–1 as the "old world record for the mile" (3 minutes, 51 seconds). They also developed strategies for stringing together small chunks

into larger chunks so that they could recall information at any point in the sequence rather than having to start at the beginning each time. Furthermore, the practice made them faster at recalling the information. All of us employ techniques such as note taking and reminders from friends to aid our memory (Intons-Peterson and Fournier, 1986), but you may not realize there are memory strategies you can employ when you cannot rely on notes or other people.

Another **mnemonic device** (*mnemonic* is derived from the Greek word for memory) or strategy to improve memory is the **method of loci**. The Latin poet Cicero described how the Greek poet Simonides used this method. Simonides was supposedly called away from a banquet hall in which he had delivered a poem. While he was outside, the roof of the hall collapsed and killed everyone inside. They were mutilated beyond recognition. But Simonides could identify the bodies because he remembered where everyone had sat. You can use this mnemonic device by identifying a natural sequence of locations, such as those in your room. Now, if you want to remember a shopping list, convert

each item on the list—socks, belt, batteries, compact disc—into an image, and place each image at one of the successive locations on your mental route around your room. By imagining socks on your door handle, belts on the floor inside your door, batteries hanging from your coat hook, and so on, you form a connection between information about the location (which is readily available from your long-term memory) and the new information you wish to remember. The locations serve as retrieval cues. When you get to the store, you mentally walk through your apartment to determine what you have placed at each mental location.

The **link method** also relies on mental images. With this method, you try to form mental images that link the items you are trying to remember. For the shopping list, you might imagine a living sock, wearing a belt, walking down the street, listening to a portable compact disc player, in which the batteries are dead. With this method, each part of the image serves as a retrieval cue for other parts. Although some people claim that bizarre images are the most effective (Lorayne and Lucas, 1974), others

---

DECAY Although many theorists, from Ebbinghaus to some more recent (Wickelgren, 1974), have proposed that forgetting arises from a decline in the strength of a memory, experimental and physiological evidence for such a theory has proved difficult to find. Some experimental findings contradict the idea of forgetting as the **decay** of information from long-term memory. As early as 1913, 12-year-old schoolchildren were found to recall a nearly learned poem better after 2 days than after being tested immediately, an effect called **reminiscence** (Ballard, 1913; Payne, 1987). Subjects repeatedly tested on the same material may also recall material on later tests that they did not recall before (Tulving, 1967; Erdelyi and Becker, 1974). Thus, over time, they remember more information—an effect called **hypermnesia** (Payne, 1987).

have shown you do not need to form bizarre images to make this technique work (Kroll, Schepler, and Angin, 1986), nor will bizarre images always improve memory (McDaniel and Einstein, 1986).

In the **pegword** method, you memorize a series of number-word rhymes. First you memorize a series such as this one, from a childhood song: one–thumb, two–shoe, three–tree, four–door, five–hive, and so on. Then you form a visual image that links an object to be memorized with each of the numbered objects. You might imagine for *1,* a sock on a thumb, for *2,* a belt wrapped around a shoe, for *3,* a tree with batteries as "fruit," and so on. The idea is that as you list the numbers, the words pegged to each will jog your memory and remind you of the object you're looking for.

One memory device you probably should not use is the storing of objects in unusual locations. Although people seem inclined to hide valuables and secret information in unusual locations (e.g., hide your jewelry in the freezer), it turns out that objects placed in unusual locations are more likely to be forgotten than ob-

jects placed in usual locations. Although the unusual location may be distinctive and therefore seem memorable, it may, in fact, be very difficult to remember the location when the object is needed (Winograd and Soloway, 1986).

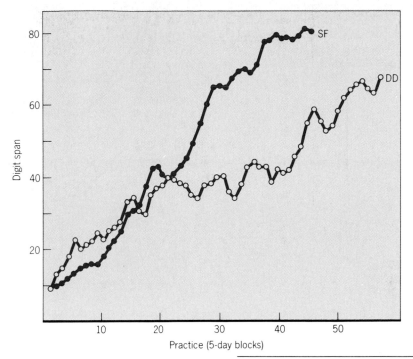

BOX FIGURE 1   THE EFFECT OF PRACTICE ON DIGIT SPAN. This figure illustrates the growth in digit span of two students, SF and DD, as a function of practicing encoding strategies that can improve memory. (After Chase and Ericsson, 1982.)

INTERFERENCE   If forgetting is not the result of decay of information, perhaps it is a result of some kind of **interference**. In a classic study, two subjects learned lists of 10 nonsense syllables either in the morning, after a night's sleep, or in the evening, just before going to sleep (Jenkins and Dallenbach, 1924). The subjects were then tested after 1, 2, 4, or 8 hours of sleep or after their normal daily routine (see Figure 7-21). The subjects remembered best after they had slept between learning and recall. The researchers concluded that when a subject was awake between learning and recall, other learning interfered with recall. But sleep prevented this interference.

There are two types of interference: **retroactive interference**, in which learning new material impairs the recall of previously learned

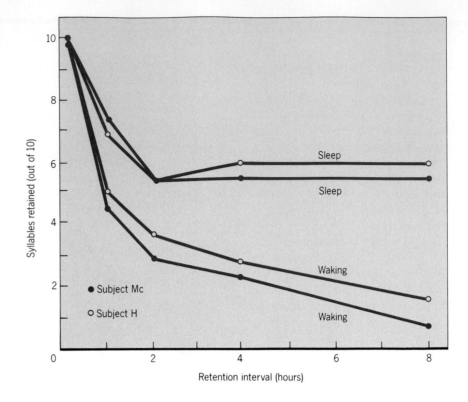

FIGURE 7-21   INTERFACE WITH MEMORY.
These lines show the number of nonsense syllables people remembered after sleeping and staying awake between learning and recall. When subjects sleep after learning, they recall more. (After Jenkins and Dallenbach, 1924.)

material, and **proactive interference**, in which previously learned material impairs the recall of newly learned material. Figure 7-22 illustrates the research designs used in studies of proactive and retroactive interference.

In one study of retroactive interference (Briggs, 1957), some of the subjects first learned a list of adjective pairs and then were given a second list of adjective pairs to learn. They were tested on this second (interfering) list 2, 4, 10, or 20 times before being tested on the original list. The degree of retroactive interference produced by the second list was strongly related to the number of times subjects had been tested.

Although researchers first thought that retroactive interference was the primary source of memory loss, they since have found that proactive

FIGURE 7-22   PROACTIVE AND RETROACTIVE INTERFERENCE RESEARCH.
This figure illustrates the research designs used in the study of proactive and retroactive interference.

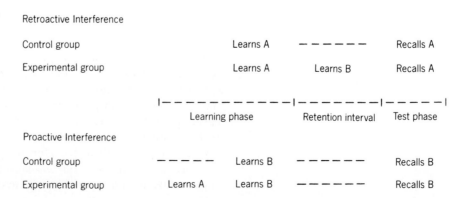

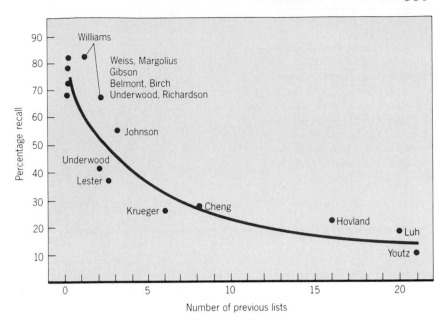

FIGURE 7-23 IMPAIRMENT OF MEMORY AS A RESULT OF PRIOR LEARNING.
Each point in the figure represents the results of experiments in which people studied lists of nonsense syllables and attempted to recall the list 24 hours later. The percentage of nonsense syllables recalled from a single list was a function of the number of lists previously studied. (After Underwood, 1957.)

interference, too, is an important source of loss. Researchers had been puzzled for years about Ebbinghaus' work on recall of nonsense syllables. Ebbinghaus reported that he could recall only 35 percent of newly learned nonsense syllables after one day, yet undergraduates some years later recalled 80 percent of the nonsense syllables when they were tested a day later (Underwood, 1948a, 1948b, 1949). It seemed unlikely that the students were actually better at the task than Ebbinghaus. But Ebbinghaus had learned hundreds of nonsense syllable lists, whereas the undergraduate subjects had learned only a single list. As shown in Figure 7-23, when the results from a number of memory studies were compiled, it was clear that after only 20 previous memory trials subjects' typical performance was around 20 percent compared to Ebbinghaus' 35 percent. Thus, prior learning experiences can influence later learning experiences.

How does proactive interference operate? In one study of proactive interference, for example, on each of four trials, people were presented the names of 3 kinds of fruit, a total of 12 different fruit. On each trial, they tried to recall the 3 kinds of fruit presented on that trial. As Figure 7-24 shows, the subjects accurately recalled fewer kinds of fruit with each trial, even though they had to remember the same number of fruit on each trial. They became bogged down because the retrieval cue *fruit* got overloaded as trials proceeded. On the first trial, the category included 3 names such as banana, apple, and pear, but on the second trial the category included not only the 3 new to-be-remembered fruits—orange, plum, and cherry—but the 3 fruits presented on the first trial. One or more of the fruit from the earlier trial might be recalled even before the 3 new fruits. By the fourth trial the "fruit" category had 12 possible associates, some of which may have been activated and recalled as many as three times on previous trials, and it was difficult for the subjects to retrieve the new names.

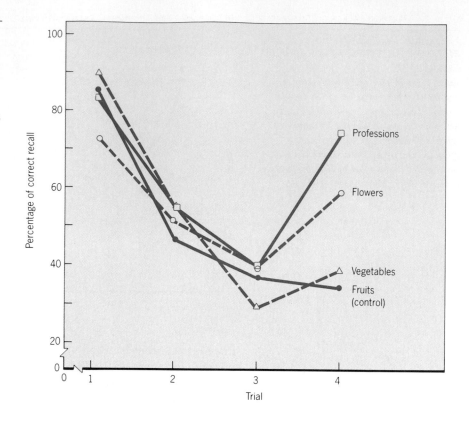

FIGURE 7-24 PROACTIVE INTERFERENCE.

Recall of new names from a particular category drops off as additional names are learned—the effect of proactive interference. However, if the category is shifted there is an increase in recall—an effect known as release from proactive interference. The increase in recall after a category shift is greater when the new category is dissimilar to the first category. (From Wickens, 1972.)

However, when people could learn a different category of items on their fourth trial—professions, flowers, or vegetables—they experienced **release from proactive interference** and recalled them well (Figure 7-24). The more unlike the category *fruit* was the new category, the greater the improvement in recall: "professions" were recalled better than "vegetables." The new retrieval cue was less likely to produce associations with the fruit studied on the earlier trials. Interference seems to arise when possible responses to retrieval cues compete (McGeoch, 1942; Postman, Stark, and Fraser, 1968).

Pathological Forgetting

Korsakoff's syndrome is a pattern of systematic loss of past memories (**retrograde amnesia**) and the failure to form new memories (**anterograde amnesia**). Korsakoff's syndrome usually is caused by severe alcoholism, which produces progressive brain damage, aggravated by poor nutrition (Ryan and Butters, 1984). A major part of the damage is to cells that produce the neurotransmitter norepinephrine. If the damage is to only one hemisphere (unilateral damage), there may be a loss in retention of visual inputs (a result of damage to the right hemisphere) or auditory inputs (a result of damage to the left hemisphere), but when people suffer damage to both hemispheres, they may have anterograde amnesia. Research with amnesia patients supports the distinctions between short- and long-term memory and between recall and recognition

Oliver Sacks (1985), a clinical neurologist, has reported the case of Jimmie G., a patient Sacks has treated since 1975. Jimmie, a healthy, happy, and handsome 49-year-old man, was first hospitalized in 1975. Jimmie knows when and where he was born, can report many details about his youth, speaks enthusiastically about his service as a submarine radio operator during the Second World War, recalls his shipmates and the ship's missions, and says he still remembers Morse code and touch typing. But his memories seem to stop at 1945. When Sacks asked him his age Jimmie replied 19, when asked the year, he responded: "Forty-five, man. What do you mean?

We've won the war, FDR's dead, Truman's at the helm. There are great times ahead" (p. 23). During their first meeting Sacks left the examining room and returned a few minutes later. Jimmie did not recognize him and even when reminded about their earlier conversation, could not recall it. Once, Sacks placed his watch, tie, and glasses on the table, asked Jimmie to remember them, and covered them while they continued conversing. When asked, several minutes later, what was under the cover, Jimmie could not remember. Jimmie tests above normal on intelligence tests, he is a "cunning and aggressive" checkers player and can solve complex puzzles and problems easily—providing they can be solved quickly. However, on tasks that tax memory, such as chess, Jimmie has difficulty for he forgets what he is doing.

Although Jimmie expresses consternation when confronted with objects or information that are, for him, anachronistic (he found it difficult to believe there was an aircraft carrier named after his contemporary, Admiral Nimitz, and could not understand how it would be possible to take a picture of the earth from the moon), even this consternation does not last long. Jimmie has a sense that he has a memory problem: "I do find myself forgetting things, once in a while—things that have just happened. The past is clear though" (p. 25). However, he does not appear to appreciate that he essentially can remember nothing that has happened since 1945.

What is wrong with Jimmie? Sacks' diagnosis is that Jimmie suffers from Korsakoff's syndrome—the loss of memory due to severe alcoholism.

memory. For instance, bilateral damage to the hippocampus interferes with the formation of long-term memories, while damage to the diencephalon interferes with short-term memory, attention, and encoding (Glass and Holyoak, 1986; Squire, 1986). In addition, Korsakoff patients can experience poor recall even though their recognition memory may be normal (Hirst et al., 1986; Kim et al., 1986).

People (like Jimmie, Box 7-4) with anterograde amnesia can retain verbal information and acquire new motor skills such as tracing an image while looking at it in a mirror, or learn the correct paths through mazes, and their skills may improve with practice, but they insist that they have never done the task before (Cermak, O'Connor, and Talbot, 1986; Martone, Butters, Payne, Becker, and Sax, 1984; Squire, 1986; Squire and Cohen, 1984). These findings have led a number of researchers, including Tulving (Alper, 1986; Mishkin and Petri, 1984; Squire, 1986; Tulving, 1985; Warrington, 1986), to extend the distinction between episodic and semantic memory to include a third type: **procedural memory**. A major justification for the distinction is that even though knowledge of events in episodic memory may be disrupted by damage to the hippocampus and amygdala, procedural knowledge—knowledge of motor skills, such as bicycle riding, that are acquired through practice—is not necessarily disrupted by such brain damage.

How *does* memory in Korsakoff patients function? First, they seem not to encode or retrieve information in a normal way. They may perform like normal patients in learning meaningless and unrelated information, but unlike normal subjects, Korsakoff patients do not improve when they learn familiar or meaningful material (Butters and Cermak, 1980). Although Korsakoff patients can use rhyming cues, they have trouble producing or using semantic retrieval cues (McDowell, 1979; Winocur, Kinsbourne, and Moscovitch, 1981). They also have trouble judging temporal order and monitoring and predicting how well they remember (Squire, 1982; Shimura and Squire, 1986).

Although most efforts to treat Korsakoff patients have been quite disappointing, recent research with the drug clonidine indicates that the drug may partially restore memory, possibly by providing a substitute for the norepinephrine that damaged brain cells cannot produce themselves (Arnsten and Goldman-Rakic, 1985). Fortunately, most people go through life with their memories intact, but research on memory disorders such as Korsakoff's syndrome sheds light on the normal processes of remembering and forgetting.

WHERE MEMORY IS LOCATED: THE PHYSIOLOGY OF MEMORY

Although research with animals and with brain-damaged patients such as those suffering from Korsakoff's syndrome has shed light on the functioning of the normal brain and the relation between the brain and memory, scientists still do not completely understand the role of the brain in memory. Indeed, although there is widespread agreement that the brain is unquestionably the principal site of memory, there is evidence from studies of both animals and humans that conditioned responses involving the spinal cord can be formed with no involvement of the brain (Shurrager and Culler, 1940; Ince, Brucker, and Alba, 1978).

As early as 1824, Pierre Flourens' studies of the brains of birds had established that the brain is divided into several different regions, each region serving different functions. In 1912, the physiologists Graham-Brown and Sherrington demonstrated that electrical stimulation of the cortex could produce enduring changes in responses to stimuli. Later researchers have tried to narrow the location of memory. The noted neuropsychologist Karl Lashley spent several decades carefully removing sections of the brains of trained rats in an effort to find what he called the **engram**—the site where learning takes place and a memory "trace" remains. To his surprise, Lashley found that removing parts of a rat's brain produced diffuse effects on its behavior but did not eliminate specific memories. In his *In Search of the Engram* (1950), Lashley reported that although he had determined many locations where engrams did not exist, he had been unable to determine where they did exist. He was therefore led to two conclusions. The first (a tongue in cheek conclusion): "I sometimes feel, in reviewing the evidence on localization of the memory trace, that the necessary conclusion is that learning just is not possible" (Lashley, 1950, p. 501). The second: the brain operates according to a principle of equipotentiality, and individual memories are not located at any specific location in the brain, but are somehow distributed throughout the brain.

But later, Wilder Penfield (1952) found that electrical stimulation of specific parts of the brain can evoke specific memories. A partial resolution to the localization dispute was offered in *The Organization of Behavior* (1949) by Canadian neuropsychologist Donald O. Hebb. Hebb argued that behavioral, perceptual, and memory patterns are built up gradually through the connection of sets of cells called **cell assemblies** and that very complex behaviors were formed through the action of sets of cell assemblies. Hebb's theory suggests that memory is localized, but not within one or even a small number of cells. This idea is consistent with Lashley's finding that it is difficult to eliminate specific memories through the destruction of small areas of brain tissue.

Recently, research by neuropsychologists has helped to narrow the search for the sites of memories. Some of these researchers have permanently implanted electrodes in the brains of rats and rabbits. The animals then are conditioned to perform particular acts, and their brain activity is monitored as they learn. In one common type of study, rabbits or cats are classically conditioned to blink in response to a tone. The procedure involves the pairing of the tone with a tiny and harmless puff of air blown into the eye. The air puff elicits a blink from the nictitating membrane (a second eyelid that is found in many animals). Conditioned responses such as an eye-blink response to a tone can be retained and acquired even when an animal's motor cortex or pyramidal tract is damaged or when its entire cerebral cortex or diencephalon is removed (Woody, 1986).

But despite the fact the conditioned response *can* survive the destruction or removal of large portions of the brain, researchers have found that by making a small cut or lesion in a specific area of the cerebellum, they can eliminate the learned eye-blink response (McCormick and Thompson, 1984; Thompson, 1986; Yeo, Hardiman, and Glickstein, 1984). Although it is tempting to conclude that this research has located the engram for the conditioned eye blink, other researchers have demonstrated that several other parts of the brain are also involved in the conditioned eye-blink response (Desmond and Moore, 1982, 1983). The conservative interpretation of the results is that they support the distributed engram notion advanced by Lashley. Memory appears to involve sets of neurons in several parts of the brain, including the cerebellum, hippocampus, amygdala, and cerebral cortex (Mishkin and Appenzeller, 1987; Thompson, 1986; Woody, 1985; Zola-Morgan & Squire, 1986).

SUMMARY

1. *Approaches to the Study of Memory.* Memory researchers have used a variety of methods including introspection, reaction times, and memory for nonsense and meaningful information. Three stages of memory are examined by researchers: the encoding, storage, and retrieval of information.

A MODEL OF MEMORY

2. *Sensory Memory.* One of the most influential models of human memory was proposed by Atkinson and Shiffrin. This model distinguishes among sensory memory, short-term or working memory, and long-term memory. There are separate memory systems for each of the senses.

Iconic memory is the memory for visual images. It has a fairly small capacity (about ten letters) and lasts about one second. Echoic memory (memory for sounds) also has a small capacity but lasts about four seconds.

3. *Short-term and Long-term Memory.* Short-term memory is used to temporarily store information that is currently in use—such as a telephone number that has just been looked up in a telephone book. Short-term memory for information such as words and numbers has a small capacity (7 ± 2 chunks), and information will be lost from short-term memory if it is not rehearsed. Maintenance rehearsal or simple repetition of information is sufficient to maintain information in short-term memory, but a more thorough analysis—elaborative rehearsal—helps assure that the information will be transferred to long-term memory. Long-term memory appears to have a nearly unlimited capacity, and information placed into long-term memory can remain available for decades.

ENCODING OF INFORMATION

4. *Short-term Memory Codes.* Some information is encoded into short-term memory in acoustic codes that reflect the sound of the information. Other information is encoded semantically or visually in terms of its meaning or appearance. It appears that acoustic encoding is more rapid than semantic or visual encoding. When retrieved from short-term memory, information that was placed into memory first (and probably rehearsed most often) is better remembered than later information—a primacy effect. In addition, information most recently placed into memory is also better remembered—in part, because the information is retrieved

first and may even be drawn from sensory memory.

5. *Encoding for Long-term Memory.* Some information is encoded into long-term memory intentionally, while other information is encoded unintentionally. Craik and Lockhart's depth-of-processing model holds that the strength of a memory and the rate at which information is lost from memory is a function of the depth to which the information was encoded. For example, thinking about the meaning of words will produce a stronger memory for the words than will studying the length of words. The encoding of information is sometimes referred to as a constructive process. When encoding information, the interpretations of the information made at encoding will influence what is encoded. If a meaningful interpretation is not possible, very little of the information is encoded into memory.

6. *Long-term Memory Codes.* Information is encoded into long-term memory in various forms. Semantic codes reflect the meaning of information, whereas visual codes reflect the appearance of the information, and acoustic codes the sounds of the information. Researchers are not entirely certain how visual information is encoded. Some use the results from mental rotation and mental scanning studies to argue that visual encoding preserves the physical features of the encoded information and is therefore analogous to images perceived by the visual system. Opponents of this analog view argue that visual information is stored in the form of rules or propositions that can be used to generate images.

THE STORAGE OF INFORMATION

7. *Episodic and Semantic Memory Models.* A distinction can be

made between a person's general knowledge or semantic memory and memory for the personal events of one's life—episodic memory. Two major models of semantic memory have been proposed. In network models people are assumed to remember networks of interconnected concepts. Some of these models are hierarchical with superordinate concepts (e.g., plants), subordinate concepts (e.g., fruit), and further subordinate levels (e.g., banana). Some network models assume that the strength of the associations between concepts varies, and when an effort is made to retrieve information, the links between concepts are activated (spreading activation) in such a way that more strongly associated concepts are recalled first.

An alternative model of semantic memory depicts concepts in terms of defining features that are essential to the concept ("has a red breast" is essential to the concept *robin*) and nonessential but are characteristic features (e.g., "flies" is a feature characteristic of many bird species). Studies of reaction times and order of word recall offer support for such network models.

RETRIEVAL PROCESSES

8. *Recognition.* When something or someone is recognized, a comparison is made between the information available (e.g., what the person looks like) and information retrieved from memory (any information that might be associated with the person). When critical features match, an identification may be made (you identify the person). If only some features match, this may produce a sense of familiarity but not identification. If a number of people, objects, or scenes are shown to a person, their similarity

will affect recognition accuracy. Higher degrees of similarity can help a person identify distinctive features that can be matched to features in memory. The context within which people attempt to recognize other people and things also influences recognition accuracy.

9. *Recall and Retrieval Cues.* Information may be available in memory even though it is not accessible. The accessibility of information is affected by the quality of the retrieval cues used to retrieve the information. Retrieval cues are used to activate information and bring it into short-term or working memory. The repeated activation of information can inhibit or block the retrieval of related information. If a person cannot retrieve the information he seeks, he may rely upon secondary retrieval cues.

10. *Encoding Specificity.* According to the encoding specificity hypothesis, whenever information is encoded, aspects of the situation (information about the location, about the encoder, about the other people present, and so on) may also be encoded. This additional information facilitates retrieval. People who are in the same physiological state at both encoding and retrieval remember better than people whose encoding and retrieval states do not match—memory is state dependent. Similarly, when environmental cues match at encoding and retrieval, memory performance is enhanced—memory is context dependent.

11. *Memory Searches.* The search for information in memory proceeds in a systematic manner. Some searches are exhaustive—all possible memory alternatives are considered before an answer is given. Other memory searches are self-terminating and answers are reported as soon as the sought-after information is encountered.

12. *Mnemonic Devices.* Mnemonic devices can serve as useful aids to memory. Chunking information together can reduce the amount of information that must be encoded. Other methods rely on making associations between new and old information. In the method of loci, to-be-remembered material is associated with familiar locations such as rooms in a house, and retrieval is facilitated by mentally walking through the rooms. Linking mental images of the information that is to be remembered also facilitates memory. The pegword method associates to-be-remembered information with previously memorized material such as childhood rhymes. The rhyme can then be used to retrieve the newly remembered information.

13. *Retrieval Failure.* Although there is little evidence that memory decays, it is clear that memories can be interfered with. Retroactive interference occurs when new information impairs the recall of previously learned material. In proactive interference, previously learned material interferes with the learning of new material. Release from proactive interference is obtained when new material is drawn from a different category than the previously learned material.

14. *Pathological Forgetting.* Korsakoff's syndrome is the result of brain damage induced by alcoholism and poor nutrition. Thus brain damage can result in the loss of incoming visual and auditory information and the inability to form new memories (anterograde amnesia). Damage to the hippocampus can disrupt long-term memory formation, while damage to the diencephalon can interfere with short-term memory, attention, and encoding.

Though people with anterograde amnesia can retain some verbal information and can learn new motor skills (procedural memory), they commonly will insist they have never seen the verbal materials or practiced the motor tasks before.

WHERE MEMORY IS LOCATED

15. *The Physiology of Memory.* Though it has been known that different parts of the brain serve different functions, progress in efforts to locate the sites of memory has been slow. After decades of research, Lashley, in the 1950s, concluded that memories are located throughout the brain. Penfield's research on electrical stimulation of the brain suggested that memories might be somewhat localized. More recent research indicates that damage to small regions of the brain can disrupt specific memories. However, neurons in several parts of the brain, including the cerebellum, hippocampus, amygdala, and cerebral cortex may be involved in any specific memory.

FURTHER READINGS

Research in cognitive psychology—research on memory and on language and problem solving (the topics covered in the next chapter)—has been growing rapidly in the past 20 years. There are now several interesting overviews of the developments that have taken place in cognitive research. One of the most readable is *The Mind's New Science* by psychologist Howard Gardner (1985). Gardner discusses the people and the ideas that have made cognitive psychology flourish. Along the way he discusses the interrelationships of psychology, computer science, the neurosciences, anthropology, and linguistics. A much shorter but more advanced overview of developments in cognitive psychology can be found in *Cognitive Psychology* by George Mandler (1985).

Introductory textbooks on human memory that cover in much greater detail the topics examined in this chapter include *Introduction to Human Memory* by Vernon H. Gregg (1986) and *The Structures and Strategies of Human Memory* by Leonard Stern (1985). Several textbooks that examine cognitive psychology more broadly but include excellent sections on memory include *Cognitive Processes* (2nd Ed.) by Lyle E. Bourne, Roger L. Dominowski, Elizabeth F. Loftus, and Alice F. Healy (1986); and *Cognition and Cognitive Psychology* by Anthony J. Sanford (1985). A less detailed but amusing introduction to memory can be found in *Your Memory: A User's Guide* by Alan Baddeley (1982).

More advanced treatments of memory research can be found in *Working Memory* by Alan Baddeley (1986). Baddeley emphasizes his own research

on short-term memory and offers a much broader and deeper picture than is possible in a single chapter. Readers who are interested in the neural mechanisms of memory may want to examine *Memory, Imprinting, and the Brain* by Gabriel Horn (1986). The relationships between memory and reasoning are explored in a series of chapters in *Experience, Memory, and Reasoning* edited by Janet L. Kolodner and Christopher K. Riebeck (1986) and *Knowledge Structures* edited by James A. Galambos, Robert P. Abelson, and John B. Black (1986).

Interesting accounts of memory in action can be found in several volumes on eyewitness memory. These include the very readable *Eyewitness Testimony* by Elizabeth F. Loftus (1979). A volume with chapters written by a number of research experts addresses many of the same issues in much greater detail: *Eyewitness Testimony: Psychological Perspectives*, edited by

Gary L. Wells and Elizabeth F. Loftus (1984). Recent research on children as eyewitnesses can be found in *Children's Eyewitness Memory* edited by Stephen J. Ceci, Michael P. Toglia, and David F. Ross (1987).

Somewhat different perspectives on memory and memory research are taken in *Memory Observed: Remembering in Natural Contexts* edited by Ulric Neisser (1982). The volume contains informative and often entertaining accounts of memory studies conducted in nonlaboratory settings including Neisser's own study of the memory of John Dean, whose testimony about President Nixon played a critical role during the Watergate scandal, and reports on the memory of people with very unusual memory abilities. A very interesting account of a man with unusual memory abilities can be found in *The Mind of the Mnemonist* by Russian neurologist A. R. Luria.

8

LANGUAGE AND THOUGHT

During the late 1960s and early 1970s, computer scientists were enthusiastic about the possibility that computers could be programmed to simulate even the most complex forms of human thinking. During this period, Allen Newell and Herbert Simon (1978 Nobel Prize winner in Economics) developed a program called the General Problem Solver (GPS) that could mimic human problem solving in such diverse areas as playing chess and proving theorems (1972). Others devised programs to solve visual analogies (Evans, 1968) and algebra problems (Bobrow, 1968), to identify organic compounds (Feigenbaum, Buchanan, and Lederberg, 1971), and even to act like a psychotherapist (Weizenbaum, 1966).

Computer programmers have proven adept at reducing many forms of expert knowledge to computer programs, but they have not been able to program some basic human capabilities. Programs may be able to control complex machines such as the space shuttle and beat chess masters, but no one has yet developed a computer program that combines the worldly knowledge, language and problem-solving abilities, and common sense of the average 6-year-old child.

It might be argued that the two crowning achievements of humankind are language and logical problem solving, and thus we should not be dismayed that we humans have yet to confer these on computers. In this chapter, we explore the complexities of language and thinking that have stymied computer programmers. First we explore scientific research on language—the simple components and structure of language, how language develops in children, how human and animal communication differ, and the relation between language and the brain. Then we examine the question of just how rational human thinking is. We shall look at logical thinking, problem solving, and decision making.

GRAMMAR AND THE STRUCTURE OF LANGUAGE

Why should it prove so difficult for computer programmers to develop programs as sophisticated in language and thought as a 6-year-old? One answer is that language is more complex than the other "systems" that programmers have simulated. For example, chess is relatively complex, with vast numbers of possible moves. But the body of knowledge required for chess is finite (all the action takes place on 64 squares on a board and involves 32 pieces of just six types), and the rules and procedures of the game are well-defined. Some aspects of language, as of chess, also are finite. Spoken language is based on a relatively small set of sounds, there are a limited number of word types, such as nouns and verbs, and a limited number of rules given how these word types can be combined to form meaningful utterances. Furthermore, everyday conversation uses relatively few words. Ninety-six percent of all telephone conversations are made up of just 737 words (French, Carter, and

Koenig, 1930). But in important ways, language also is relatively unlimited. For example, a typical college student may recognize 150,000 words, and a large dictionary may contain 400,000 English words, many of which are related to one another (as synonyms and antonyms, plurals and past tenses, rhymes, and so on). Furthermore, these hundreds of thousands of words can be combined into an infinite number of sentences, each one of which makes sense.

Although people can generate an infinite number of sentences, these sentences follow a systematic and finite set of rules called a **grammar**. A grammar tells how such things as verbs, nouns, and their modifiers relate to one another. A grammar provides rules for linking words into meaningful sequences. The typical native speaker of any language knows most of his or her language's grammar—at least implicitly. Even though the speaker may not be able to specify the implicit rules that govern speech, he or she nonetheless easily generates speech that conforms to the implicit rules. As you will see, these implicit rules of grammar are different from the explicit rules for correct speech and composition that were drilled into you in high school. A language can be examined at three levels: the **phonological** or sound level, the **morphemic** or meaning level, and the **syntactic** level, which concerns the rules for combining words. We begin our analysis at the phonological level.

Phonology of Language

Speech is, of course, based upon sounds—more particularly, sounds that vary in frequency and in overtones. The human voice is capable of generating sounds across a wide range of frequencies, from 65 to 900 Hz and with overtones (these are harmonics or multiples of the fundamental frequency) up to approximately 6500 Hz. Yet all the human languages on earth use a total of only 200 distinct sounds, and most languages get by with only 25 to 30.

PHONEMES   As you saw in Chapter 4, the sound components of speech are called **phonemes**. Phonemes are not uniquely linked to letters of the alphabet. Phonemes are the minimal units of speech in a language that distinguish meanings. The phonemes used in a language are identified by examining **minimal pairs** of words: words that are identical except for one sound. For example, "hat" and "bat" share the "at" sound, but /b/ and the /h/ change the meanings. Similarly, in "bat" and "bet," the /a/ and /e/ change the meanings.

Although our alphabet contains 26 letters, English actually uses about 40 phonemes. The /a/ sounds in "hat" and "hate" demonstrate that two phonemes are associated with the letter *a*. Because English uses a relatively large number of phonemes, it is quite difficult to learn as a second language. Hawaiian, for instance, makes do with only 12 different sounds. Young children can generate about 200 different phonemes, but as they learn their native language, they use only a small portion of these sounds. But once children become accustomed to the phonemes of their native language, they often find it extremely difficult to generate the sounds used in other languages—one of the reasons that people have foreign accents.

Because languages use different subsets of all possible phonemes, speakers of some languages have difficulty detecting the differences between phonemes used in other languages. For example, native speakers of Japanese, who do not have separate /r/ and /l/ phonemes, have difficulty mastering these phonemes when learning English. But native speakers of English have trouble hearing the Arabic languages' distinction between the /k/ in "key" and the /c/ in "coo." (However, if you pronounce the words carefully you can probably detect the different placement of your tongue for the two words.) Even native speakers of a language sometimes have trouble detecting and generating phonemic differences that matter to other native speakers. A Midwesterner, for example, may have trouble distinguishing the different /a/ and /e/ phonemes in "Mary," "merry," and "marry."

Morphemes

Although phonemes are the smallest units of distinctive sounds in language, the smallest units of language that carry meaning are **morphemes**. Morphemes may be words or part of words. A **free morpheme** is a word that stands on its own: dog, love, car, and so on. A **bound morpheme** is attached to and modifies the meaning of other morphemes. Bound morphemes include prefixes such as the *in* in *in*competent, the *s* in dog*s*, and the *blue* and *berry* in *blueberry*. Morphemes are combined according to systematic **morphophonemic rules** within a language. For example, English speakers know that see*ing* makes sense but *ing*see does not. The average English speaker knows approximately 50,000 morphemes and hundreds of thousands of combinations for them.

For psychologists who study language, the critical question is how people know what morphemes, the words formed from morphemes, and the sentences formed from words mean. What about words and sentences allows people to communicate meaning? The study of **semantics**—the field concerned with the meaning of language—has not yet yielded a conclusive answer. However, a number of theories of meaning have been advanced, each of which emphasizes a different aspect of meaning.

STRUCTURAL THEORIES OF MEANING Several researchers have focused on the interrelationships among words to try and learn about their meanings and concepts. In Chapter 7, you read about the associative network model (Quillian, 1967; Collins and Quillian, 1969) and the feature comparison model (Smith, Shoben, and Rips, 1974) of memory and meaning. These models attempt to describe the structure of the concepts and meanings stored in memory (in what has been termed the **internal lexicon**, or dictionary). The network proposes that concepts are organized hierarchically into superordinate and subordinate categories, and

The prototype

FIGURE 8-1   THE SMITH BROTHERS.

The prototypical Smith brother is shown at the top of the figure. He has more of the typical Smith brother features— a large nose, full beard and mustache, eyeglasses, and so on—than does any other brother. (After Armstrong, Gleitman and Gleitman, 1983.)

TABLE 8-1   TAXONOMY OF PLANTS AND ANIMALS

Hierarchy	Examples
Kingdom	Plant, animal
Life form	Tree, fish
(Intermediate)	Evergreen, freshwater fish
Generic	Pine, bass
Specific	White pine, black bass
Varietal	Western white pine, large-mouthed (black) bass

Source: Berlin, 1978, p. 12.

Note: A taxonomic hierarchy for plants and animals.

evidence suggests that people verify statements involving concepts at nearby levels in the hierarchy ("canaries have skin").

The associative network and feature models imply that a basic categorizing system may underlie the structure of word meanings. Do people organize their internal lexicons in hierarchical, taxonomic categories? Research provides strong evidence for this kind of taxonomy (Mervis and Rosch, 1981; Rosch, 1973, 1975; Rosch et al., 1976). Indeed, Berlin (1978), an anthropologist, has examined taxonomies in a wide variety of languages and cultures. He has found that animals and plants are commonly classified into hierarchical categories with between three and six levels. Berlin's names for these categories and a number of examples of the categories are shown in Table 8-1.

THE PROTOTYPE THEORY OF THE MEANING OF CONCEPTS   Although a hierarchical category model might suggest that there are clear and definite meanings for concepts found at various levels of the hierarchy, Eleanor Rosch and her colleagues have shown that natural categories (including such things as plants, animals, tools, vehicles, clothing, furniture) have "fuzzy" boundaries and that some instances fit people's notions of the concept better than others do. For example, people are likely to think that a robin fits the category of a bird better than a penguin does, that a German shepherd is more "doggy" than a dachshund, and a robbery is more crime-like than mail fraud.

When people judge how well a particular instance (*dachshund*) fits a category (*dog*), they judge the instance in light of a general **prototype** (the hypothetically most typical instance) that is not precisely defined (Rosch, 1973, 1975). For example, look at Figure 8-1, in which appear the many "Smith Brothers" and the prototype Smith brother, in the center of the group. As you can see, the prototype has more of the features of the Smith family—large nose, full beard and hair, large ears, and so on—than any other brother (Armstrong, Gleitman, and Gleitman, 1983). But none of the brothers has every Smith attribute, not even the prototype. Instead, the prototypical Smith brother, like other prototypes, consists of a set of attributes. Many of these attributes are shared by members of the category, and different members of the category possess different combinations of these attributes. Thus for the prototype *bird*, we expect feathers, wings, flying, egg laying, a beak, and two legs. Robins resemble the prototype quite well. But penguins do not fly,

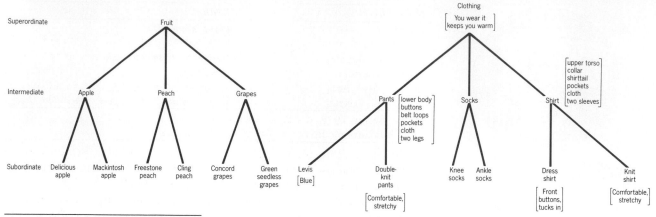

FIGURE 8-2   THREE LEVEL
TAXONOMIES FOR FRUIT AND
CLOTHING.
Sample attributes at each level of the
clothing taxonomy are shown in
parentheses. (After Rosch et al., 1976.)

and their feathers are more like fur. They are still birds, of course, but they do not fit the prototype as closely as robins do.

In their research, Rosch's group has worked with three-level hierarchies like those shown in Figure 8-2 (Rosch et al., 1983). Notice that at the subordinate level, objects share many characteristics and only a few distinguish among instances (Delicious and Macintosh apples differ slightly in skin color and texture). At the superordinate level, there are few shared attributes. The intermediate level captures most of the attributes that objects share and also many of their distinguishing features, too. The intermediate category names are those that people usually apply to objects (Anglin, 1977). In teaching language to young children, object names that correspond to intermediate categories—*grape, apple*—are used most often by parents, and children tend to learn these names first (Rosch et al., 1976). Only then do children learn and use the superordinate and subordinate names—*fruit, seedless grapes.* This progression explains why some infants call all adult males *daddy*, all small furry animals *doggy*, or, conversely, all dogs *Fido.* For a time, children overgeneralize or undergeneralize in their word usage, although they appear to use the same categories as adults (Huttenlocher and Smiley, 1987).

BEHAVIORAL THEORIES OF MEANING   A number of behaviorists have proposed that meaning arises from the classically and operantly learned associations between words or parts of language and other parts of language, and between language and sensation. Language is thought to stimulate responses. John Watson (1930/1970) thought that meaning resided in miniature motor responses stimulated by words. These motor responses supposedly mirror the large-scale motor responses people make to the referents. For example, can you feel your mouth move in response to the phrase "eat an ice cream cone"? Though you may not feel the movement, there is some evidence that your muscles discharge electricity when you think about eating ice cream.

In his analysis of language, the behaviorist B. F. Skinner (1957, 1974) equates meaning with the consequences of language. He prefers to call language *verbal behavior.* According to Skinner, the meaning of language depends on what has happened to the speaker when the speaker has used language in the past.

Critics of Skinner's position challenge the idea that the meaning of a word has very much to do with behavior associated with the word. For example, it is difficult to argue that the meaning of *dog* is "You pat it," "You walk it," "You play frisbee with it." A second problem with Skinner's theory is that it does not explain how people learn the underlying structure or syntax that is essential to the meaningful use of language.

None of these theories of meaning offer a complete explanation of meaning, but each has something to offer. The network, feature, and prototype models offer useful insights into the structure of the relationships among words and concepts and underscore that meaning arises from these relationships. The behavioral theories provide some insights into how word meanings are learned, but the theories have trouble accounting for the acquisition of syntax. Of course, words and concepts do not stand alone in language, for they are combined to form meaningful sentences and none of the theories of meaning explains how people assemble words into meaningful phrases. This aspect of language is essential.

Syntax

Although native speakers of a language prattle easily, generating an endless variety of sentences, never deliberating about the rules for combining words into meaningful utterances, without such rules, people would not be able to understand or generate new utterances. These rules for combining elements of language into meaningful utterances is called **syntax**. For example, the meaning of a sentence depends upon both the meanings of the words in the sentence *and* the patterns of relationships among the words: *dog bites man* means one thing, but the same words in a different pattern *man bites dog* mean something very different. How are such phrases assembled and understood?

PHRASE STRUCTURE   One of the first tasks of syntactic analysis is to specify the structure of sentences. One common approach is to break sentences into their smallest parts and devise rules for combining those parts (Chomsky, 1965; Tartter, 1986).

According to three simple **phrase-structure** rules, words can be built into phrases or **constituents**, and these constituents can then be combined into sentences. Simple Phrase Structure rules (PS) for assembling words into sentences include

PS 1: Sentences (S) consist of a noun phrase (NP) plus a verb phrase (VP).
PS 2: Noun phrases (NP) consist of an article (art), plus an optional adjective (adj), plus a noun (N).
PS 3: Verb phrases consist of a verb (V) plus a noun phrase (NP).

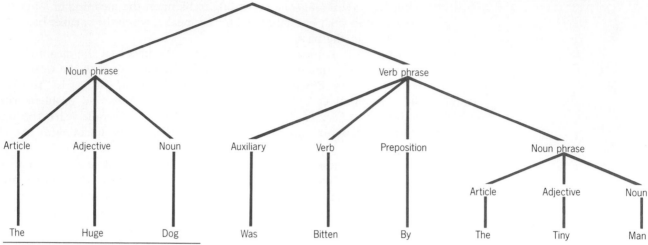

FIGURE 8-3   TREE DIAGRAMS OF SENTENCES.

Tree diagrams illustrating the construction of sentences from noun and verb phrases.

Simple multiplication says that with three nouns—*man, child,* and *dog;* three verbs—*kissed, bit,* and *saw;* four adjectives—*tiny, huge, ugly and no adjective;* and two articles—*the* and *a*—one can use these rules to generate 24 meaningful noun phrases (2 articles × 4 adjectives × 3 nouns) and 72 meaningful verb phrases (3 verbs × 2 articles × 4 adjectives × 3 nouns). Combining the verb phrases and noun phrases into sentences yields 1728 (24 × 72) syntactically correct sentences such as, "The tiny child kissed the huge man" and the sentence in the tree diagram in Figure 8-3.

By enlarging the rules to allow plural nouns, present tense verbs, and so forth, or by adding more words to the lexicon, we can dramatically increase the number of sentences the phrase structure rules will produce. We can also enlarge the phrase structure rules by adding other parts of speech (auxiliaries like *was, has been,* and prepositions like *by;* see the bottom sentence in Figure 8-3).

Phrase structure is clearly related to people's ability to generate and understand language. For example, studies have shown that when they speak, people pause between major constituent phrases and before the first content word of a constituent (Maclay and Osgood, 1959; Paccia-Cooper and Cooper, 1981). The pauses probably are necessary for planning the next constituent, not for breathing. Probably only part of sentences are in memory when people begin to speak (Lindsley, 1975). Although people may have a rough idea of what they are going to say, the pauses between constituents and before content words give them time to assemble their phrases and sentences.

Phrase structure is also important to people's comprehension of sentences (Fodor, Garrett, and Bever, 1968). In one study, for example, people could remember (and, therefore, presumably understand) sentences that were normal in meaning and syntax better than they could remember sentences with anomalous syntax (Miller and Isard, 1963). They remembered "Gadgets simplify work around the house" better than "Gadgets kill passengers from the eyes."

Syntax also can resolve ambiguities in sentences (Frazier and Rayner, 1982). In the case of the sentence: "Flying planes can be dangerous," the ambiguity arises because one cannot determine from the sentence alone whether piloting planes, or planes that crash from above, is dangerous.

THE REPRESENTATION OF SENTENCE MEANING   Although phrase structure influences comprehension, meaning may not be represented in a form that directly reflects the phrase structures we speak and hear. Read the following paragraph.

> *There is an interesting story about the telescope. In Holland, a man named Lippershey was an eyeglass maker. One day his children were playing with some lenses. They discovered that things seemed very close if two lenses were about a foot apart. Lippershey began experiments and his "spyglass" attracted much attention. He sent a letter about it to Galileo, the great Italian scientist. Galileo at once realized the importance of the discovery and set out to build an instrument of his own. He used an old organ pipe with one lens curved out and the other curved in. On the first clear night he pointed the glass towards the sky. He was amazed to find the empty dark spaces filled with brightly gleaming stars! Night after night Galileo climbed to a high tower, sweeping the sky with his telescope. One night he saw Jupiter, and to his great surprise discovered with it three bright stars, two to the east and later there were four little stars.*

Now, without rereading the paragraph, guess which of the following sentences appeared in the paragraph:

1. Galileo, the great Italian scientist, sent him a letter about it.
2. He sent Galileo, the great Italian scientist, a letter about it.
3. He sent a letter about it to Galileo, the great Italian scientist.
4. A letter about it was sent to Galileo, the great Italian scientist.

When a researcher tested people's memory for sentences like these, he found that if the sentences were similar in meaning to the original, people generally thought that they were the original (Sachs, 1967). Even though sentences 2, 3, and 4 have different phrase structure (sometimes referred to as their "surface structure"), they have a common meaning (or "deep structure"). Only when the sentence changed in meaning (as in sentence 1) did people more precisely identify which sentences were not in the original paragraph. These findings demonstrate that people tend to remember the *meaning* of speech rather than the exact wordings (Masson, 1984). It is clear that sentence generation and understanding are systematic. People are adept at taking the meanings of language and expressing them in sentences with a variety of surface structures. And people are equally adept at converting sentences with different surface structures but similar deep structures into their common meanings to understand what they hear and read. How might these meanings be represented?

The most popular current view is that the basic thoughts expressed in sentences are represented in propositional networks like the memory networks you saw in Chapter 7 (Anderson, 1985; Kintsch, 1974). Consider the sentence "Steve gave a beautiful necklace to Joan, who is the mother of Rachel." As shown in Figure 8-4 the sentence can be repre-

(a)

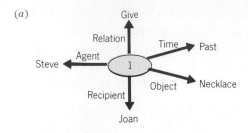

(b)

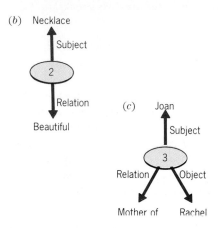

(d)

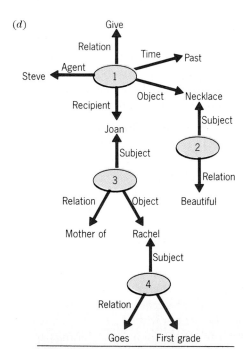

FIGURE 8-4 EXAMPLE OF A PROPOSITIONAL NETWORK.
Propositions are shown in parts (a), (b), and (c). Part (d) represents the propositions in (a), (b), and (c). (After Anderson, 1985; Kintsch, 1974.)

sented in three simple propositions (a), (b), and (c) akin to the phrases we discussed earlier. As Figure 8-4 shows, a proposition can include such things as *relations* (for example, the verb *gave*, the adjective *beautiful*, and the phrase *mother of*), agents (Steve), and *objects* (the *necklace* and *Rachel*).

The advantage of the network representation is that it can reflect the larger meaning relationships among propositions. Thus, propositions (a), (b), and (c) (Figure 8-4) can be assembled to form the upper portion of network (d) in Figure 8-4. This network represents the meanings expressed in the original sentence. Furthermore, additional propositions can be added to the network in a hierarchical manner—thus, the proposition that Rachel goes to first grade has been added to the original propositions in network (d).

Studies of propositions support the idea that people understand and remember the meanings of sentences rather than the exact wording of sentences. The time it takes people to read and understand a sentence, for example, is determined more by the number of propositions in the sentence (between 1 and 1.5 seconds per proposition) than by the number of words in it (Kintsch and Keenan, 1973; Kieras, 1981). Furthermore, people tend to better recall information that is close together in a propositional network. Thus, people who read that "Joan, who is the mother of Rachel, who goes to first grade, was given a beautiful necklace by Steve" are more likely to associate Steve and Joan in memory than they are to associate Steve and Rachel. Although Rachel is closer to Steve than Joan in the sentence, Joan and Steve are closer in the propositional network (Anderson, 1985).

LANGUAGE DEVELOPMENT

The following is a dialogue between a 3-year-old *Star Wars* fan and her father.

Rachel: I dreamed we were at the mountains and I saw a big spaceship.
Father: Really, what kind of spaceship?
Rachel: A big round spaceship.
Father: Who was in it?
Rachel: Luke, Han, and Lea. I was Lea and you were in there and you were Luke.
Father: What were we doing?
Rachel: Looking out the window to see Rachel.

This child, like others her age, has attained some remarkable milestones in language development. She is capable of understanding and producing the sounds of English. Her **semantic** development is well advanced. She has a vocabulary of several thousand words. She knows a great deal about how these words can be combined into meaningful phrases and sentences. She has acquired a sophisticated tacit understanding of English **syntax**. Most of her sentences are correct, and although she has not mastered some syntactic subtleties, such as irregular past tenses and plurals—she says *buyed* and *mouses*—she nonetheless can carry on a conversation and communicate her thoughts quite effectively. Her effectiveness at communicating indicates that she has also learned a great deal about the **pragmatics** of language, the social rules of language use, such as varying her language complexity to match the abilities of her listener.

Infants and children develop through a fairly orderly sequence of stages as they acquire language. In a few short years, they go from babbles to whole sentences. In the following section, we describe the early development of language.

The Prelinguistic Stage

Human babies appear to be predisposed to process the sounds of human speech. Newborns with 12 hours or less of contact with their mothers can discriminate their mother's voice from other voices and prefer to listen to their mother's voice rather than the voices of other women (DeCasper and Fifer, 1980; DeCasper and Spence, 1986). Young babies can localize the sources of sounds and watch the faces of people who are speaking. By the age of 4 months they can also detect the synchronization of speech and lip and mouth movements (Spelke and Cortelyou, 1981; Kuhl and Meltzoff, 1982).

While it was once believed that infants only gradually learned to discriminate speech sounds, more recent research clearly demonstrates that infants make most of the auditory discriminations of speech sounds that adults do—even between sounds that are almost identical (Aslin, 1981; Eilers and Oller, 1985; Eimas et al., 1971). Infants make these speech discriminations as early as they can be tested (at about the age of 1 month), which suggests that the ability may be present at birth. The test involves presenting a speech sound, such as a /p/, to a baby who is sucking on a nipple wired to record the baby's rate of sucking. The tester repeatedly presents a sound until the baby habituates to the sound and the sucking slows down. Once the baby is habituated, a similar sound is presented. If the baby hears a difference, the sucking rate increases. Although babies can discriminate most of the sounds in all languages, they acquire some discriminations as a result of experience with a language (deVilliers and deVilliers, 1978, 1979; Eilers, Gavin, and Wilson, 1979), and they lose other discriminations because they are not used in the specific language the baby acquires.

During the first few weeks after birth, infants communicate by crying—mainly out of hunger, anger, and pain. At about 3 to 5 weeks, infants generate new sounds called **coos**. These are vowel-like "ooooohs" and "aaaaaahs." At about their third or fourth month, babies begin to **babble**—to make sounds that resemble the vowel and consonant combinations of speech such as "pa" and "boo." Within a few weeks, these sounds may be repeated to form multisyllabic utterances such as "baba-babababa." The onset of babbling appears to be determined by maturational factors. Babies around the world start babbling at about the same age, even if they are themselves deaf (Lenneberg et al., 1965). The babblings of infants all around the world also are very similar, and so is the pattern in which phonemes make their appearance (Flavell, 1985; Oller and Eilers, 1982).

Developments during the babbling stage are related to later speech. As we have said, infants gradually restrict their babbling to the phonemes they will use in speech. In addition, babbling infants appear to learn about intonations. They babble in a higher pitch to their mothers than to their fathers, for instance (Lieberman, 1967). By 7 months, they have learned turn taking. Baby babbles, mother speaks, baby babbles, mother speaks, and so on. By 8 or 9 months, infants may be able to respond to verbal commands such as "Get the ball" (Benedict, 1979), although one can argue about how much the infant understands these words. By the end of their first year, infants do understand many words, even though they may not be able to speak them (Thomas et al., 1981; Oviatt, 1980). Furthermore, infants learn to communicate their desires through looking and pointing, often accompanied by insistent verbalizations—*dah! dah!* (Clark and Clark, 1977; Shatz, 1983).

One-Word Utterances

Between their tenth and thirteenth months of age most children have produced their first words. At first the child's vocabulary is limited to one or two words (often poorly pronounced). But by a year and a half, many children have vocabularies as large as 50 words, and by two years, 200 to 300 words (Corrigan, 1978, 1983; Lenneberg, 1967; Nelson, 1973). During the child's second year these words are generally used one at a time in what is called **holophrastic** speech (from the Greek *holos,* "whole," and *phrazein,* "to point out").

Nelson (1973) studied 18 infants and the first 50 words they learned. As Table 8-2 shows, half of these words consisted of names of general

TABLE 8-2 CHILDREN'S TWO-WORD UTTERANCES

Function of Sentence	Language				
	English	*Finnish*	*German*	*Russian*	*Samoan*
To locate or name	There book	Tuossa Rina (there Rina)	Buch da (book there)	Tosya tam (Tosya there)	Keith lea (Keith there)
To demand	More milk Give candy	Annu Rina (give Rina)	Mehr milch (more milk)	Yeshche moloko (more milk)	Mai pepe (give doll)
To negate	No wet Not hungry	Ei susi (not wolf)	Nicht blasen (not blow)	Vody nyet (water no)	Le 'ai (not eat)
To indicate possession	My shoe Mama dress	Täti auto (aunt's car)	Mein ball (my ball) Mama's hut (Mama's hat)	Mami chashka (Mama's cup)	Lole a'u (candy my)
To modify or qualify	Pretty dress Big boat	Rikki auto (broken car)	Armer wauwau (poor dog)	Papa bol'shoy (Papa big)	Fa'ali'i pepe (headstrong baby)
To question	Where ball	Missa pallo (where ball)	Wo ball (where ball)	Gde papa (where Papa)	Fea Punafu (where Punafu)

Source: After Slobin, 1971.
Note: Children's two-word utterances in several languages are quite similar.

objects that the *child* regularly used or encountered. The next most common categories of words referred to particular people and objects and were action words, that is, words that described or accompanied actions. Words that *parents* were likely to use, such as the names of articles of the child's clothing, were not among the child's first 50 words. This finding suggests that children do not merely imitate the language used by their parents but that a child's first words are those that the child is most likely to use.

Among the notable features of one-word language is the tendency for children to misuse words. Children often **overextend** the meaning of a word, and use it to refer to a much broader set of events and objects than an adult would. Thus, "dog" may be applied to any small four-legged animal with fur. Children also **underextend** words—thus, a child who has been given the label "sofa" for the soft piece of furniture she sees at a store may believe that the term applies only to sofas seen at stores. Over- and underextensions are clearly related to learning the exact meaning of terms. In order to learn the definition of a word, a child must learn the features that define and limit the application of a word. Once such features are learned the word will not be over- or underextended (Clark and Clark, 1977).

Most psychologists agree that when children speak in single words, they often mean more than the single word itself. The 15-month-old who commands *"milk"* and slams an empty glass on the dining room table means, "Give me some milk on the double!" The same child's "milk," accompanied by a knowing smile and pointing finger as her father pulls a cardboard carton from the grocery bag means, "Oh, I see some milk."

Telegraphic Language

Between 18 and 24 months of age, toddlers begin to combine words into simple but meaningful two-word utterances. These utterances—"give milk," "put bear"—are much like telegrams in which, because each word costs money, the nonessentials are left out. In their telegraphic speech, toddlers drop articles, auxiliary verbs, conjunctions, and prepositions (Brown, 1973). Not only does telegraphic speech appear at the same age all around the world, but the content of telegraphic speech is similar all around the world as well (Slobin, 1971; see Table 8-3).

Do two-word utterances indicate that children have mastered syntactic relationships, that is, that they know the proper ordering for words? Psychologists do not agree on the answer to this question. Although children at this stage of development *speak* telegraphically, they clearly *understand* complete sentences. They cannot repeat the complete sentences, but reduce them to telegraphic form. Why children speak telegraphically is not clear. It may be that children do not fully appreciate the syntactic functions of the deleted words. However, they do detect and use the important constituents of sentences—which suggests they are somewhat sensitive to syntax. It may also be that children do not have sufficient memory capacity to construct more complete sentences (deVilliers and deVilliers, 1978). In any event, children at this stage use simple rather than complex syntactic relationships.

PRAGMATIC DEVELOPMENT From the early months, in which infants learn to take turns babbling with their parents, they continue to learn the pragmatic, social uses of language (Shatz, 1983). The child also learns further pragmatics. For example, 4-year-olds will "talk down" to 2-year-olds (Shatz and Gelman, 1973) and take account of the knowledge of adults when talking with adults (Menig-Peterson, 1975). Four- and 5-year-olds also know how to ask for things politely and say "thank you" (Bates, 1976a; Becker, 1986; Becker and Smenner, 1986), though any parent will attest to the fact that they cannot be relied upon to do so. They know, for instance, that they need to stand close to communicate (Johnson et al., 1981). One- and 2-year-olds watch their speaking partners to determine whether their communications have been understood (Wilcox and Webster, 1980). Two-year-olds respond appropriately to one another, although their conversations may not be particularly complex (Garvey, 1975; Wellman and Lempers, 1977).

GRAMMATIC AND SEMANTIC DEVELOPMENT Children's sentences grow longer and more complex as they mature. In his study of language development in three children, Roger Brown (1973) examined the age and sequence in which the children mastered 14 **bound morphemes**, which are, as we said earlier, additions to words such as plurals and past tenses that change the words' meanings. The children acquired these morphemes in a generally fixed pattern (see Table 8-3) (deVilliers and deVilliers, 1973). This pattern of development could not be attributed to how often the children heard the morphemes. The pattern reflected the complexity or number of meanings to the morphemes (Slobin, 1982). For example, the morpheme *s* as in *he's* and *re* as in *we're* require mastery of number and the concept "ongoing process" (see Table 8-3).

Children typically overregularize morphemes (Slobin, 1982). "Look at the gooses" and "mommy buyed it at the store," they say. In the first case, the child has applied the regular morpheme for plurals (−*s*) to a noun with an irregular plural (*geese*), and in the second case, the child has applied the regular past tense morpheme (−*ed*) to an irregular verb (*bought*). Overregularization indicates that children have learned rules about such plurals and past tenses. In fact, children often first learn—in a rote way—a correct but irregular form such as *geese,* then learn the rule and overregularize to *gooses,* and only later return to *geese* as an exception to the rule (Slobin, 1973).

Later, children also learn **transformations** of simple declarative sentences into questions, negations, and compound sentences. These developments also proceed in a systematic fashion (Clark and Clark, 1977). For example, "who," "what," and "where" questions appear before "when," "how," and "why" questions (Bloom et al., 1982). At first, children tack these interrogatory words on the front of telegraphic declarative sentences: "What Mommy eating?" Gradually the sentence becomes more grammatical: the child adds auxiliary verbs: "What Mommy is eating?" Finally the sentence is reordered: "What is Mommy eating?" Likewise negations may start with head-shaking. Next, *no* is tacked on before or after a word or phrase: "No toothbrush." The *no* is later brought inside the sentence: "I no brush teeth," and much later in

TABLE 8-3 THE DEVELOPMENT OF GRAMMATICAL MARKERS

Semantic Relationship	*Examples*
Naming	That truck
Noticing	Hi truck
Nonexistence	Allgone truck
Recurrence	More truck
Possessor–Possession	Rachel truck
Agent–Action	Daddy push
Agent–Object	Daddy truck
Action–Object	Push truck
Action–Location	Sit chair
Entity–Location	Truck chair
Entity–Attribute	Truck big

Source: After Brown, 1973, pp. 358, 369; Shaffer, 1985.
Note: The development of 14 different grammatical markers in English. Morpheme number 1 is generally acquired first and number 14 last. Later acquired morphemes often build upon or are combinations of earlier acquired morphemes.

development appropriate auxiliary verbs are used: "I won't brush my teeth."

Between the ages of 2 and 6, children go through further semantic development and rapid growth in vocabulary. A child may learn an average of 10 new words a day and by age 6 possess a vocabulary of 14,000 words (Carey, 1977).

Theories of Language Development

The ancient Greek historian Herodotus reported that the Egyptian king Psammetichus had a shepherd, who could not speak, raise two children. After two years, the only word uttered by the children was *becos*—which sounded like the Phrygian word for "bread." Psammetichus concluded that Phrygian was a more ancient language than Egyptian. In the intervening 2500 years, several new theories of language development have been advanced by psychologists.

IMITATION   It may occur to you that children learn language through imitation. Clearly imitation plays some role in language learning or else children would not learn the language of their parents. Children often learn things—including the meaning of new words—by overhearing adults. But as a general theory of language learning, imitation has several problems. First, children only rarely directly imitate adult sentences. Instead, they generate their own, brand-new sentences. Second, as we have said, children clearly understand more complex speech than they can produce. The words that children first learn, as you saw earlier, are those for things and people they regularly meet, not the words their parents use (Nelson, 1977). Finally, the patterns of errors in children's speech are not those one would expect if children were imitating adult speech, because it is unlikely that children would hear adults make errors such as "feets" and "buyed." Fortunately, there are alternatives to the imitation theory.

REINFORCEMENT   In *Verbal Behavior* (1957), B. F. Skinner argued that children learn to speak in an adult manner because they are reinforced for speaking appropriately. In Skinner's view, parents shape children's speech through selective reinforcement—for example, by giving extra attention to those sounds in a baby's babbling that resemble phonemes. Once sounds have been shaped into words, parents selectively reinforce children's speech to encourage the formation of word phrases, then sentences, and then grammatically correct sentences.

Researchers Brown, Cazden, and Bellugi (1969) tested the shaping hypothesis by recording and analyzing conversations between mothers and their children. They found that mothers did give children approval and disapproval but not for correct and incorrect grammar. The mothers were far more likely to make their approval contingent on the truth of the children's speech. For instance, if a child made a mistake in naming an object, the mother would offer the correct name, but the mothers generally ignored grammatical errors. This is not to say that interactions with parents do not affect the quantity and quality of children's speech, for a number of researchers have shown that children whose parents talk with them a lot do master language more quickly. But the shaping process postulated by Skinner does not appear to be the primary mechanism for such learning (Clarke-Stewart, 1973; Norman-Jackson, 1982).

NATIVISM   One of the critical theoretical issues in children's language development is the question of the extent to which people have an innate propensity to learn language versus the extent to which language is learned through interaction with the environment. Some nativists argue that as a result of evolutionary pressures, humans are biologically predisposed to learn language and have a built-in set of perceptual and cognitive abilities specialized to facilitate language learning and production (Chomsky, 1968, 1975; Lieberman, 1984, 1985). To support the claim for such a **language acquisition device** (LAD), nativists have advanced several arguments.

First, the grammatical structure of language is extremely complex, but children somehow master it in only a few years. Second, the speech children hear contains few clues to correct adult grammar (it is full of false starts, incomplete sentences, and quite a few errors), and children hear too little speech to successfully generate the complete grammar on their own. Third, parents who possess only an implicit knowledge of grammar are not likely to be effective teachers of grammar. Fourth, if there is an LAD, one would expect to observe some **language universals**, such as patterns in speech development common to all environmental conditions.

As we have seen, there is good evidence for language universals: Infants are prewired to hear human speech, they babble even if they do not hear speech, and children of all cultures display similar patterns of phonological development, similar patterns in the development of phrase and sentence length, and similar patterns of syntactic and pragmatic development. The same patterns are even observed in children with learning disabilities; their rate of progress is merely slower (Lenneberg, 1967). In addition, nativists have sometimes supported their view with research that suggests there are **critical periods** in language learning (see Box 8-1), research on limitations in language acquisition in nonhumans, and research on the localization of language function in the human brain (we discuss the latter two topics later in the chapter).

INTERACTIONIST THEORY   Although most psychologists do agree that biological development influences language development, critics of the nativist position question whether it is necessary to postulate the existence of an LAD. Some theorists prefer to emphasize the interaction between biological development and the environment (Premack, 1985). They note that one reason that children show common patterns of language development is that they have very similar linguistic experiences. A babbling child evokes a different linguistic response from parents than the 2-year-old who is beginning to speak in brief utterances. As a child grows more sophisticated, the child's linguistic environment also grows more sophisticated and linguistic demands on the child also increase. We know that adults the world over use baby talk when talking to children.

BOX 8-1
THE CASE OF GENIE

The most thoroughly studied case of a deprived child is Genie (Curtiss, 1977, 1981; Curtiss, Fromkin, Krashen, Rigler, and Rigler, 1974). Genie, who was discovered in 1970 in Los Angeles, had been reared in extreme isolation from about 2 years of age until she was 13½ (past the age of puberty). Genie's father (who was probably psychotic) kept her in a small room with a window she could not see out of, tied her to a potty seat by day and caged her by night, fed her baby food by a spoon, and beat her if she made noises. Eight months after her rescue, Genie had learned 200 words and was speaking two-word sentences similar to those of normal children.

Three years after her rescue, Genie was administered a number of language tests. She scored well on word recognition, but her speech (phonology) was abnormal. She understood superlatives about 70 percent of the time, understood *in* quite well but not *under.* She understood verb tenses but had difficulty forming them herself.

In general, her progress resembled that of a normal child. Seven years after her rescue, Genie had acquired a wide variety of social skills and her verbal skills continued to improve. Her sentences were longer, but she had significant difficulty with grammar. She rarely used auxiliary verbs, had trouble with prepositions such as *over* and *under,* and found it difficult to understand compound sentences. In these ways, she was less sophisticated than a 5-year-old.

Interestingly, Genie does not display the normal pattern of left hemisphere language lateralization. On cognitive tests designed to differentiate left and right hemisphere brain damage Genie's responses resemble those of a person with left hemisphere damage, although there is no evidence of actual brain damage. Although she is right handed, when responding to language she shows greater electrical activity in her right hemisphere than her left. Genie otherwise excels in tasks that would normally be associated with the right hemisphere and shows deficits in

nonlinguistic left hemisphere functioning.

Unfortunately, Genie's case leaves many questions unresolved. It is impossible to determine whether there has been a shifting of Genie's language function to the right hemisphere as a result of her lack of normal early language experience (which would suggest that her language deficits result from inherent limitations in right hemisphere language processing), or whether, in any event, she would have been one of the unusual right-handers with right hemisphere language. Thus, it is unclear whether Genie's failure to achieve normal language results from an unusual pattern of brain lateralization unrelated to her deprivation, from late development because of her deprivation, or both. Genie's case is consistent with the view that a failure to acquire language before puberty may make it impossible to acquire sophisticated language skills, although it does not rule out the possibility of some language development even after any critical period has passed.

That is, they use short, simple, concrete and repetitive sentences (deVilliers and deVilliers, 1979). The interaction between the maturing child and the linguistic environment changes as the child's language abilities develop.

Is There a Critical Period in Language Development?

As we noted in Chapter 2, there is strong evidence for lateralization of language functions in the brain of adults. Indeed, over 95 percent of speech disorders produced by damage to the brain arise from damage to the left hemisphere. Such pronounced lateralization raises the question of whether the left hemisphere might be specially adapted for processing language. Research (some conducted in the 1860s) on the effects of brain lesions (damage to the brain) has indicated that if children sustained brain damage to the left hemisphere before they learned to speak, their speech often was delayed, but they eventually proceeded through the normal patterns of development (Basser, 1962; Restak, 1984). However, between the ages of 2 and 10 (after the onset of speech), the effects of brain lesions in the left hemisphere have more profound and enduring effects on speech than lesions in the right hemisphere.

Drawing on such research, Eric Lenneberg (1967) advanced the argument that there is a **critical period** for language development. He reasoned that during the first two years of life, the two hemispheres have equal potential for language. But the brain becomes increasingly lateralized between 2 years of age and puberty. Kinsbourne (1975) challenged this interpretation in two ways. First, he argued that the brains of young children are just as lateralized for language as adults. But he also argued that children's brains are more *plastic* or capable of adapting to injury. Thus, if a child sustains left hemisphere injury early in life, the right hemisphere can assume the functions of the left hemisphere. What is the evidence?

Even in newborn infants, speech sounds elicit stronger electrical responses from the left hemisphere than the right. In both adults and children, the portions of the brain associated with language are larger in the left hemisphere (Geschwind and Levitsky, 1968; Wada, Clarke, and Hamm, 1975). A study of three 9- and 10-year-old children who, because they suffered serious seizures, were given hemispherectomies (removal of one hemisphere of the brain) before they were 5 months old showed that although the children were somewhat physically disabled, they functioned normally in school (Dennis and Kohn, 1975; Dennis and Whitaker, 1976). Although Lenneberg would have predicted no differences between the children with right versus left hemispherectomies, the two children with left hemispherectomies had difficulty judging whether sentences were grammatically correct, whereas the child with the right hemispherectomy did not. Thus, it appears that there is significant brain lateralization for language early in life and that there are some limits to brain plasticity.

Research with so-called **feral children**—children who have been discovered living in the wild, sometimes in the company of animals such as wolves—and deprived children who have been raised in isolation and without benefit of significant human contact also provides evidence for a critical period of language acquisition. A review of the cases of 31 feral children who were rescued from the wild showed that only four learned to talk at all fluently, and no one knows which children might have heard language before living in the wild (Zingg, 1940). The case of one isolated child is described in Box 8-1.

LANGUAGE IN PRIMATES

People have known for a long time that animals can communicate in a crude way. Birds sing to one another, dogs bark at one another, cats howl and hiss at one another. Anyone who has ever had a pet dog or cat knows that these animals can learn sophisticated responses to human speech and can communicate to their masters their needs for food, drink, elimination, and others. If these animals can manage crude forms of communication, what about those more clever animals, the apes? Beginning in the 1930s, several teams of researchers (e.g., Hayes and Hayes, 1951; Kellogg and Kellogg, 1933) attempted to teach chimpanzees to talk. They all failed (Brown, 1958). The Kellogg's chimp, Gua, never managed any human speech, although Gua's playmate, the Kellogg's son Donald, rapidly learned to speak. After three years, the Hayeses' chimp, Viki, managed to say "papa," "mama," and "cup." We now know the chimps were not up to the task of speaking human language, for the chimpanzee and human vocal tracts are very different (Myers, 1976).

By the 1960s, notable language scholars were convinced that normal humans acquire language, but even its barest rudiments are beyond the capacities of an otherwise intelligent ape (Chomsky, 1968). Eric Lenneberg (1964) said that nonhuman animals could not acquire even the most primitive stages of language development. Despite such pessimism, researchers did not abandon hope. Instead, they tried new strategies with new animals. Although some research has been initiated with a gorilla named Koko (Patterson, 1978; Patterson and Linden, 1981), who has apparently attained a vocabulary of more than 600 words, most research has been conducted with chimpanzees. Rather than teaching these animals to speak, researchers have used other language channels.

Chimpanzee Studies

WASHOE In 1966 Allen and Beatrice Gardner "adopted" the 1-year-old chimpanzee, Washoe (Gardner and Gardner, 1975, 1978). Washoe lived with the Gardners for four years (in a trailer in their backyard). Rather than attempt to teach Washoe to speak, the Gardners taught Washoe American Sign Language (ASL), widely used by the deaf in North America. Although ASL is unrelated to spoken English and has a different grammar, it is a full language capable of communicating all nuances of English (Klima and Bellugi, 1979). Teaching sign language to a chimpanzee was a promising strategy because chimpanzees are adept at manipulating their hands.

Washoe learned signs one at a time. At first the teaching went slowly. Washoe learned 4 signs in the first 7 months of training. But after 22 months, she knew 34 signs, and after 4 years she knew 132 signs (compared to the 3000 words a 4-year-old child might know). More recently, Roger Fouts (who has trained Washoe and other chimps since Washoe left the Gardners in 1971) reported that by 1984 Washoe's vocabulary had reached 260 signs (*New York Times,* March 25, 1984). Washoe learned signs for objects (such as *banana* and *drink*), actions (*open* and *tickle*), and modifiers (*more* and *enough*). Washoe also generated many different two-sign combinations (294 over one 26-month period) that resembled the two-word combinations of 2-year-old children (Gardner and Gardner, 1971). In addition, she showed clear evidence of generalization. She could, for example, use the word *open* in conjunction with many objects, such as the doors on refrigerators, automobiles, houses, her trailer, and so on.

SARAH David and Ann Premack (Premack, 1971; Premack and Premack, 1972) raised their chimpanzee, Sarah, in a laboratory and used classical and operant conditioning to teach Sarah associations between variously shaped plastic tokens and words and relationships. To test her understanding of what a token represented, Sarah was presented an object (for example, an apple) and two tokens (for example, one for apple and one for banana) and had to select the correct token before she received the apple. Sarah did this correctly about 80 percent of the time—much better than chance, but certainly worse than the performance one might expect from a 3-year-old child.

Once Sarah learned individual words and relationships, she was reinforced for constructing and understanding sentences that combined many tokens. Thus, between 70 and 80 percent of the time Sarah was able to act correctly upon compound sentences such as "Sarah insert banana pail apple dish"—which, in English, is something like, "Sarah, place the banana in the pail and, Sarah, insert the apple in the dish."

LANA Researchers at the Yerkes Regional Primate Center in Georgia took still a different approach to teaching language (Rumbaugh, 1977; Savage-Rumbaugh, Rumbaugh, and Boysen, 1978; Savage-Rumbaugh et al., 1983). These researchers taught the chimpanzee Lana (and, later, chimpanzees Sherman and Austin) to use a wall-mounted computer keyboard. Each key on the keyboard is embossed with a different geometric symbol, and Lana was taught to associate these symbols with objects, actions, and relationships.

To make a request on a keyboard, Lana first had to press a key (the *please* key) that activated the computer. Then Lana had to name an agent, such as the machine or one of her attendants, followed by a verb key such as *give* or *make* (as in "make music"). Next came the name of the object requested and, finally, a terminal key akin to the "enter" key on a computer or the period in written language. Some of Lana's most common phrases are shown in Table 8-4.

More recently, Savage-Rumbaugh has been working with another chimpanzee, Kanzi, and using a computer system with a less formal method of training. Kanzi has apparently exceeded the performance of earlier chimpanzees, who had trouble understanding messages sent to them on the computer. Kanzi not only answers questions posed on the computer but also understands some spoken speech. Kanzi's performance resembles that of a 1- to 2-year-old child.

NIM CHIMPSKY Nim Chimpsky is the name of a chimpanzee (and an obvious play on the name of Noam Chomsky). During the late 1970s, a group of researchers at Columbia University, led by Herbert Terrace, trained Nim in American Sign Language (Terrace et al., 1979). Soon they reported that Nim had acquired an extensive vocabulary. Studies of Nim's use of language and his interactions with his trainers have led the research team to a set of conclusions very different from those of other animal language researchers (Sanders, 1985; see Table 8-5). They have questioned whether Nim has displayed *any* creative use of language, de-

TABLE 8-4 STOCK PHRASES PRODUCED BY LANA

Format					Total Occurrences
question	pronoun or noun	give	object name, food name, or proper name	to Lana in room	630

(?you give bread to Lana in room)

please machine give piece of	food name		310

(please machine give piece of bread)

question	proper name or pronoun	tickle or groom	proper name or pronoun	116

(?you tickle Lana)

common or proper name	name this	color	1181

(shoe name this red)

spite his large vocabulary. Can chimpanzees use language creatively? One way to address this question is to examine chimpanzees' mastery of syntax.

What Are the Linguistic Abilities of Chimps?

Roger Brown (1986) has questioned whether chimpanzees possess **syntactic capacities**, which he defines as the ability to compose symbols in such a way as to express meanings that are different from the sum of the meanings of the individual symbols: "A simple paradigm for English is

TABLE 8-5 EXAMPLES OF TWO- AND THREE-SIGN PHRASES PRODUCED BY NIM

Two-sign Combinations		Frequency	Three-sign Combinations			Frequency
play	me	375	play	me	Nim	81
me	Nim	328	eat	me	Nim	48
tickle	me	316	eat	Nim	eat	46
eat	Nim	302	tickle	me	Nim	44
more	eat	287	grape	eat	Nim	37
me	eat	237	banana	Nim	eat	33
Nim	eat	209	Nim	me	eat	27
finish	hug	187	banana	eat	Nim	26
drink	Nim	143	eat	me	eat	22
more	tickle	136	me	Nim	eat	21
sorry	hug	123	hug	me	Nim	20
tickle	Nim	107	yogurt	Nim	eat	20

Source: After Terrace, Pettito, Sanders, and Bever, 1979.
Note: Common two- and three-sign phrases generated by the chimpanzee Nim.

the contrast between 'dog chase cat' and 'cat chase dog'; the sum of the meanings is the same in both sequences, but the constructions, differing in word order, have completely distinct meanings" (Brown, 1986, p. 440).

Young children do possess syntactic abilities, but chimps do not, Brown has concluded. For example, although the mean length of children's utterances continues to grow as they develop, Nim's utterances held steady, at between 1.1 and 1.6 morphemes. Nim's longest, and not very profound, string consisted of 16 signs: "Give orange me give eat orange me eat orange give me eat orange give me you." Second, although word order is one of children's earliest syntactic devices, Nim (and other chimpanzees studied) do not systematically rely on symbol or word order (examine Table 8-5). Third, Nim rarely initiated signing, and 39 percent of Nim's signs were imitations or simplifications of the signs his teachers had just used (Terrace, 1979; Terrace et al., 1979).

Although Brown doubts that chimpanzees possess syntactic abilities, he concedes that they possess symbolic abilities. That is, they understand what symbols stand for. One study showed, for example, that chimpanzees could remember the names of objects that were out of sight.

Some linguists remain unconvinced that primates possess language abilities. Said Noam Chomsky: "It is about as likely that an ape will prove to have language ability as that there is an island somewhere with a species of flightless birds waiting for humans to teach them to fly" (*Are Those Apes Really Talking?*, 1980, p. 57). But the research to date does establish that chimps have some of the abilities or skills that are required for language. They can acquire and make limited use of fairly large vocabularies and can use words symbolically, but they have not shown an ability to use syntax. Of course, the case is not closed, for it is difficult to tell what new research and new research strategies may reveal about primates' language abilities.

LANGUAGE AND THE BRAIN

Imagine waking up in a hospital bed. You open your eyes and see that you are surrounded by your family. You wonder why you are in the hospital and cannot remember any reason you should be. You are about to ask what is going on when your sister begins to speak to you. Your happiness at seeing your sister gives way to concern and then panic as you realize that she is speaking to you in a language you cannot understand. When you interrupt her to speak, you discover that you cannot understand the very words you are speaking! What has happened to your mind? Although such events may seem like a nightmare, certain forms of brain damage can produce experiences just like them.

In fact, some of the most informative research on language and the brain has been conducted with people who have sustained various forms of damage to their brains—generally as a result of a stroke (brain hemorrhage) or accidental injuries.

Broca, Wernicke, and the Aphasias

During the 1850s and 1860s, the French surgeon Paul Broca (1861, 1865) observed that patients who had suffered strokes or injuries to their brains often could not express themselves normally. Their speech was halting and telegraphic, punctuated by many pauses, and full of slips of the tongue. The patients often could not retrieve the words they sought, and even when they were able to use nouns and verbs correctly, they often failed to use function words such as articles, pronouns, and auxiliary verbs. These disruptions of both spoken and written language are termed **aphasia** (from the Greek for "unuttered"). For example:

Patient: Cookie jar . . . fall over . . . chair . . . water . . . empty . . . ov . . . ov . . .
Examiner: "overflow?"
Patient: Yeah. (After Blumstein, 1982, pp. 204–205.)

and

E: Were you in the Coast Guard?
P: No, er, yes . . . ship . . . Massachu . . . chusetts . . . Coastguard . . . years. [Raises hands twice indicating "19"]
E: Oh, you were in the Coast Guard for 19 years.
P: Oh . . . boy . . . right . . . right . . .
E: Why are you in the hospital?
P: [Points to paralyzed arm] Arm no good. [Points to mouth] Speech . . . can't say . . . talk, you see. (After Gardner, 1975, p. 61.)

Broca's aphasia is sometimes characterized as an **expressive disorder** because one of its main symptoms is that victims seem to know what they want to say but cannot find the words for it. They therefore substitute words—*car* becomes *drive around*. Broca's autopsies of these patients revealed that they had damage in the frontal regions of the left hemisphere (see Figure 8-5).

A few years after Broca's work, the German surgeon Carl Wernicke (1874) discovered a second form of aphasia. **Wernicke's aphasia** is sometimes referred to as **receptive aphasia** because people with it have problems with comprehension. In contrast to the halting speech of Broca's aphasics, Wernicke's aphasics produce fluent but unintelligible speech. Entire substantive words are missing, there are many slips of the tongue, and erroneous phonemes are substituted for the correct ones: for example, *Escobistokilican* for *Episcopalian* (Canter, Trost, and Burns, 1985) and the following:

> *But I figured that if I defective my talking see my talking itself I I get my tongue back again to where I can talk from what they say why then it's liable to what will straighten me out again and bring me back to where I can hear something see . . .*

> *(From DeVilliers, 1978, p. 131)*

FIGURE 8-5 THE LEFT HEMISPHERE.
This figure shows the left hemisphere of the brain viewed from the left side. Major structures are indicated including Broca's area, Wernicke's area, and the angular gyrus, all of which are involved in speech.

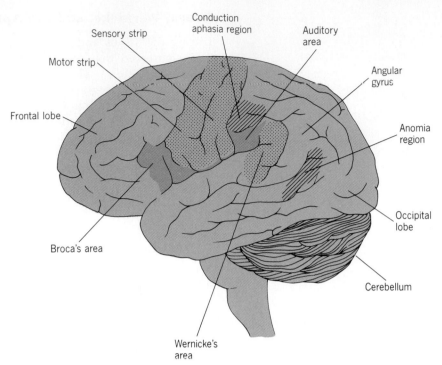

and

> Boy, I'm sweating, I'm awful nervous, you know, once in a while I get caught up, I can't mention the tarripoi, a month ago, quite a little, I've done a lot, well I impose a lot, while, on the other hand, you know what I mean . . .

(From Gardner, 1975, p. 68)

Patients with Wernicke's aphasia suffer damage to an area of the brain behind that implicated in Broca's aphasia (see Figure 8-5).

What do these speech failures say about normal language? First, the disruption of word-finding indicates that semantic and syntactic functioning are localized in the brain and that there may be separate semantic storage areas for word meanings and names of objects. Research indicates that Wernicke's aphasics suffer more severe semantic impairment than Broca's aphasics. Wernicke's aphasics produce less intelligible word substitutions, and they fail to use appropriate strategies when categorizing words. Furthermore, whereas Wernicke's aphasics can recognize the correct names for objects, they have more difficulty understanding words because they have trouble recognizing the semantic associations between words (Brownell, Bihrle, and Michelow, 1986; Caplan, Baker, and DeHaut, 1985; Goodglass and Baker, 1976; Grossman et al., 1986; Martin and Blossom-Stach, 1986; Payne and Cooper, 1985).

The research with aphasics also indicates that semantic and syntactic functioning are relatively independent. Whereas Wernicke's aphasics suffer the greater semantic impairment—"I can't mention the tarripoi"—Broca's aphasics suffer the greater syntactic impairment—"chair . . . water . . . empty. . . ." However, Broca's aphasics comprehend speech well and may be able to extract the meaning of speech without relying on syntactic cues to meaning. Broca's aphasics can extract most of the meaning from sentences even though they cannot use even simple syntactic information such as the subject-verb-object structure of sentences for clues to meaning (Caramazza and Zurif, 1976; Schwartz, Saffran, and Marin, 1980). Their comprehension appears to be based on the meaning of individual words (semantic information) and their understanding of what has been said before in the conversation (contextual information) but not on such things as word order.

Right Hemisphere Brain Damage

As we learned in Box 8-1, most people are left hemisphere dominant for language. For such people damage to the right hemisphere typically does not disturb language comprehension and production, although it may influence their language in other ways. For example, this kind of damage can affect their visual perception and interfere with their ability to recognize and name otherwise familiar faces and objects (Campbell, Landis, and Regard, 1986). These symptoms are well illustrated in the case of *The Man Who Mistook His Wife for a Hat* (1985), the title of a book by clinical neurologist Oliver Sacks. Right hemisphere damage also can make people ignore their left visual and tactile field, even to the point that they do not recognize or groom the left side of their body (Semenza and Goodglass, 1985).

Right hemisphere damage also can make people lose or exaggerate the emotional overtones of speech (Ross, 1981, Shapiro and Danly, 1985). Those whose central and anterior portions of the right hemisphere have been damaged may speak flatly and be unable to express their emotions in the usual intonations and inflections. In addition, they have difficulty understanding the emotional content of spoken and written language (Tompkins and Mateer, 1985). In contrast, patients with damage to posterior regions of the right hemisphere speak with exaggerated variations in pitch and intonation. They have trouble matching their pitch and intonation to the emotional content of sentences they are asked to speak (Shapiro and Danly, 1985). There is also evidence that the right hemisphere is involved in making inferences (Brownell, Potter, Bihrle, and Gardner, 1986). Thus, although the left hemisphere controls the most important aspects of language (the semantic and syntactic processing that are necessary for language production and comprehension), the left hemisphere does influence people's ability to process some of the more subtle aspects of language.

LOGICAL THINKING

Researchers on human thinking have been influenced strongly by philosophy, particularly by philosophical analyses of logic. For hundreds of years, thinking and logic were regarded as essentially the same thing. When the Irish mathematician George Boole wrote his highly influential volume on logical calculus, he entitled it *An Investigation into the Laws of*

Thought (1854) and believed he was investigating "the fundamental laws of those operations of the mind by which reasoning is performed." Boole unquestionably developed a sound "prescriptive" logic that specified how people *ought* to approach reasoning. However, much psychological research on reasoning has focused on the extent to which people think in the manner prescribed by logicians. In the second half of this chapter, we examine human rationality in three domains: deductive and inductive reasoning, problem solving, and decision making.

Deductive and Inductive Reasoning

You have undoubtedly encountered logical statements such as the following:

> Premise 1: All children are fun-loving.
> Premise 2: Rachel is a child.
> Conclusion: Therefore, Rachel is fun-loving.

These statements form a **syllogism**—an argument consisting of two premises (which are assumed to be true) and a conclusion. The object in syllogistic logic is to use the premises to determine whether the conclusion is valid. Rules of logic are applied when assessing the validity of a syllogism. One especially useful rule specifies that when presented the proposition *A implies B* and *given A,* we may *infer B* (logicians call this rule ***modus ponens***). Thus,

> If it snows (*A*), school will be canceled (*B*).
> It has snowed (*A*).
> Therefore, school is canceled (*B*).

A second useful rule specifies that when presented the proposition *A implies B* and given *B is false* we must infer that *A is also false* (logicians call this rule ***modus tollens***). Thus:

> If it snows (*A*), school will be cancelled (*B*).
> School is not cancelled (*not B*).
> Therefore, it has not snowed (*not A*).

These rules are part of **deductive logic**. In deductive logic, people can reason, *with certainty,* from premises to conclusions. In deductive logic, logically valid syllogisms need not be factually true:

> All cats are black.
> Tim's pet is calico.
> Therefore, Tim's pet is not a cat.

In **inductive logic**, however, we cannot reach conclusions with certainty. The difference between deductive and inductive reasoning can be illustrated with an example.

> In the past, all students who have studied this textbook carefully have attained great psychological understanding.
> Therefore, in the future, all students who study this textbook carefully will attain great psychological understanding.

Although it is very likely that the conclusion reached will prove true, it is impossible to know, *with certainty,* that the conclusion is true. There may be students who, even after careful study, do not attain great understanding.

Conditional Reasoning

Statements such as the following form what is called a **conditional syllogism**:

> If it is raining my car does not start.   (the first premise)
> It is raining.   (the second premise)
> Therefore, my car does not start.   (the conclusion)

A substantial body of research has demonstrated that people have trouble assessing the validity of certain types of conditional syllogisms (Clark and Chase, 1972; Marcus and Rips, 1979; Taplin and Staudenmayer, 1973). In one study, people were asked to evaluate syllogisms such as

> If the ball rolls left, the green lamp comes on. (if A then B)
> The green lamp comes on. (B)
> Therefore, the ball rolled left. (therefore A)

and

> If the ball rolls left, the green lamp comes on. (if A then B)
> The ball rolled right. (not A)
> Therefore, the green lamp did not come on. (therefore not B)

The people were asked to say whether the syllogism was always, sometimes, or never true (Rips and Marcus, 1977). The syllogisms appear in Table 8-6. The subjects had little difficulty with syllogisms 1 and 2, but had great difficulty with syllogisms 7 and 8. They failed to see that A is not true if B is not true. Two other types of errors were evident in the results. First, in syllogisms 3 and 4, many subjects denied the validity of the first term in the conditional and thought B was untrue if A was untrue. (They mistakenly thought that if the ball did not roll left, the light could not come on.) On syllogisms 5 and 6, many mistakenly believed that when A implies B, then A is necessarily true when B is true. (They mistakenly thought that the ball must have rolled left if the light came on.)

Why do people have trouble with these logical problems? People tended to treat some conditional syllogisms (syllogisms 5 and 8) as though they said that if A implies B, then B also implies A, but these syllogisms did not say this. In addition, the people are more likely to become confused when a premise or conclusion includes a negation (syllogisms 3 and 4). One classic demonstration of the difficulties people have with logical problems comes from a series of studies by Wason (1966, 1968; Wason and Shapiro, 1971; Wason and Johnson-Laird, 1972). In one experiment, people were asked to evaluate the following conditional statement:

If a card has a vowel on one side, then it has an even number on the other side.

TABLE 8-6 PERFORMANCE ON EIGHT CONDITIONAL SYLLOGISMS

Example	Form	True (Always)	Sometimes	False (Never)
1. If the card has an A on the left, it has a 7 on the right. The card has an A on the left. The card has a 7 on the right.	If A, then B A is true ∴ B is true	100%*	0%	0%
2. If the card has an A on the left, it has a 7 on the right. The card has an A on the left. The card does not have a 7 on the right.	If A, then B A is true ∴ B is not true	0%	0%	100%*
3. If the card has an A on the left, it has a 7 on the right. The card does not have an A on the left. The card has a 7 on the right.	If A, then B A is not true ∴ B is true	5%	79%*	16%
4. If the card has an A on the left, it has a 7 on the right. The card does not have an A on the left. The card does not have a 7 on the right.	If A, then B A is not true ∴ B is not true	21%	77%*	2%
5. If the card has an A on the left, it has a 7 on the right. The card has a 7 on the right. The card has an A on the left.	If A, then B B is true ∴ A is true	23%	77%*	0%
6. If the card has an A on the left, it has a 7 on the right. The card has a 7 on the right. The card does not have an A on the left.	If A, then B B is true ∴ A is not true	4%	82%*	14%
7. If the card has an A on the left, it has a 7 on the right. The card does not have a 7 on the right. The card has an A on the left.	If A, then B B is not true ∴ A is true	0%	23%	77%*
8. If the card has an A on the left, it has a 7 on the right. The card does not have a 7 on the right. The card does not have an A on the left.	If A, then B B is not true ∴ A is not true	57%*	39%	4%

Source: After Rips and Marcus, 1977.

Note: Asterisk denotes correct response. Rips and Marcus presented people with syllogisms like those in the first column and asked them to evaluate the conclusions by indicating whether the conclusion was always true, sometimes true, or never true.

Everyone was then shown the four cards in Figure 8-6a and asked which cards they would like to turn over. The most popular strategy (used by 46 percent of the subjects) was to turn over the first and third cards. This is not an optimal strategy, for no matter what appeared on the opposite side of the third card, the rule would not be falsified. Many subjects (33 percent) selected only the first card, but this is also less than optimal. The validity of the rule is optimally tested by turning over both the first card (which tests whether there is an even number when a vowel is shown—that is, given A, B should be true—*modus ponens*) and fourth card (which tests whether there is a vowel when an odd number is shown—that is, given not B, A should be not true—*modus tollens*). Only 7 percent of the subjects chose the first and fourth cards.

Do the results of studies such as these demonstrate that people are hopelessly illogical? Although people do have trouble solving abstract logical problems, most people find ways to cope successfully with real-world logical problems. When Johnson-Laird, Legrenzi, and Legrenzi (1972) and Cox and Griggs (1982) presented subjects with real-world rules to test, performance was much better than on the Wason task even though the logical structure of all the rules being tested are the same.

FIGURE 8-6a A LOGIC PROBLEM.
The subjects in the Wason (1966) study were presented the rule illustrated in this figure. The subjects were then allowed to turn over cards in order to determine whether the statement was valid. Which cards would you turn over?

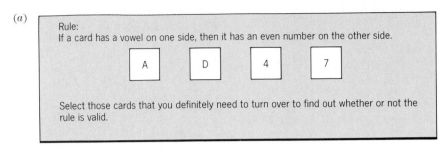

(a)

Rule:
If a card has a vowel on one side, then it has an even number on the other side.

| A | D | 4 | 7 |

Select those cards that you definitely need to turn over to find out whether or not the rule is valid.

FIGURE 8-6a A LOGIC PROBLEM.
The subjects in the Wason (1966) study were presented the rule illustrated in this figure. The subjects were then allowed to turn over cards in order to determine whether the statement was valid. Which cards would you turn over?

FIGURE 8-6b THE BARTENDER PROBLEM.
For these cards evaluate the rule shown in this figure. When Johnson-Laird, Legrenzi, and Legrenzi (1972) and Cox and Griggs (1982) presented subjects with these types of rules to test, performance was much better than on the Wason task, even though the logical structure of all the rules being tested are the same. In this instance, most subjects correctly chose to examine the "drinking" and "under 18" cards to test the drinking rule and the sealed envelope. Thus, there is good evidence that even if people have difficulty with abstract logical problems, they nonetheless can learn practical procedures that allow them to solve everyday "logical" problems.

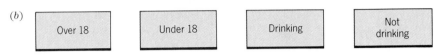

(b)

| Over 18 | Under 18 | Drinking | Not drinking |

Which cards should be turned over to test the rule:
"If a person is drinking, he is over 18."

[Correct answers: The Under 18 and the Drinking card]

For example, people were asked to evaluate the rule: "If a person is drinking, he is over 18" and presented the cards shown in Figure 8-6b. Most subjects correctly chose to examine the "drinking" and "under 18" cards to test the drinking rule. Thus, there is good evidence that even if people have difficulty with abstract logical problems, they nonetheless can learn practical procedures that allow them to solve everyday "logical" problems (Cheng, Holyoak, Nisbett, and Oliver, 1986).

Categorical Syllogisms

All psychologists are scuba divers.
All scuba divers drive Fords.
Therefore, all psychologists drive Fords.

These statements form a **categorical syllogism**. The premises in such syllogisms specify the relationships among categories (such as psychologists and Ford drivers) and yield logical conclusions. Notice that the premises need not be factually true. In forming categorical syllogisms, four kinds of statements can be used—*all, some, some not,* and *no.* For example, the first premise could read

All psychologists are scuba divers.
Some psychologists are scuba divers.
Some psychologists are not scuba divers.
No psychologists are scuba divers.

In Figure 8-7 diagrams represent the alternative meanings of these statements. Except in *no* statements, all the relationships are ambiguous, because they can be represented in different ways. You will note that unlike its use in ordinary language, in logic "some" can mean either "some" or "all." Table 8-7 shows 11 of the many pairs of premises that can be formed with these statements. For each premise, what can you

FIGURE 8-7 DIAGRAMS FOR FOUR TYPES OF CATEGORICAL PROPOSITIONS.

These diagrams illustrate four types of relationships in categorical propositions. The first diagram illustrates that all A are B can be represented in two ways: As can constitute a part of all Bs, or As and Bs can be identical.

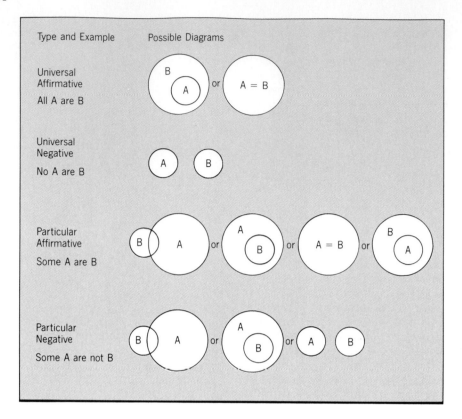

logically conclude about the relation between A and C? Among the possible answers are "All A are C," "Some A are C," "Some A are not C," "No A are C," and "No Valid Conclusion." For example in number 5 the premises might be

| Some A are B | Some used-car salespersons are honest people. |
| All B are C | All honest people are well-liked. |

and the correct logical conclusion is that

| Some A are C | Some used-car salespersons are well-liked. |

TABLE 8-7 EXAMPLES OF CATEGORICAL SYLLOGISMS AND THEIR LOGICAL CONCLUSIONS

Premises	Logical Conclusion	Premises	Logical Conclusion

(1) All A are B.
    All B are C.
	All A are C.	(7) Some A are B.
		    Some B are C.
			Can't say.

(2) All A are B.
    Some B are C.
	Can't say.*	(8) Some A are not B.
		    All B are C.
			Can't say.

(3) No A are B.
    All C are B.
	No A are C.	(9) Some A are not B.
		    Some B are not C.
			Can't say.

(4) All A are B.
    No C are B.
	No A are C.	(10) All A are B.
		    All C are B.
			Can't say.

(5) Some A are B.
    All B are C.
	Some A are C.	(11) All A are B.
		    No B are C.
			No A are C.

(6) No A are B. No B are C.	Can't say.		

*The conclusion "Can't say" means that no specific statement relating A to C necessarily follows from the premises.

Premise   Possible Meanings

All B are A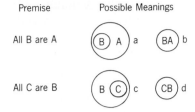

All C are B

Possible Combinations

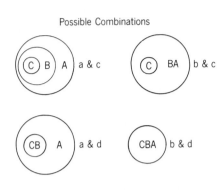

Conclusion: Some A are C (true no matter which
            combination is considered)

FIGURE 8-8
These diagrams illustrate the logical
combinations for the syllogism all A are
B and all C are B.

Most people have the greatest difficulty with invalid syllogisms such as

Some A are not B	Some men are not Republicans.
Some B are not C	Some Republicans are not wealthy.
Can't say	There are no logical conclusions.

(Ceraso and Provitera, 1971). Why are incorrect syllogisms so difficult? The terms used in the premises may create an *atmosphere* that predisposes people to accept conclusions with terms similar to those in the premises (Woodworth and Sells, 1935).

Positive premises may lead people to positive conclusions and negative premises to negative conclusions. For example, the negative premises in the following example would incline subjects to accept the conclusion even though it is not valid.

No A are B	No Martians are American citizens.
All B are C	All American citizens are taxpayers.
No A are C	No Martians are taxpayers.

The atmosphere hypothesis also suggests that when both premises are universal (both use "all" or "no"), people tend to accept a universal conclusion, and when both premises are particular (both use "some" or "some are not"), they tend to accept a particular conclusion. Thus, in the following example people are inclined to accept:

Some A are B	Some rock musicians are beer drinkers.
Some B are C	Some beer drinkers are ballet dancers.
Some A are C	Some rock musicians are ballet dancers.

Although the atmosphere hypothesis does a good job of accounting for people's errors on invalid syllogisms (Begg and Denny, 1969), other factors also introduce errors into syllogistic reasoning (Evans, 1982). People often *misinterpret premises* and may, for example, erroneously assume that "All A are B" also implies that "All B are A"—just because "all birds are egg-layers" does not mean that "all egg-layers are birds" (Chapman and Chapman, 1959). People also have *trouble generating all possible combinations* of premises (Fisher, 1981; Johnson-Laird, 1983; Johnson-Laird and Steedman, 1978). For example, the diagrams in Figure 8-8 show that the two premises "All A are B" and "All B are C" generate four possible combinations and yield the logical conclusion that "Some A are C." You might demonstrate for yourself how difficult it is to generate all eight combinations produced by "All A are B" and "Some B are C." If you can generate all eight diagrams, you will also encounter a final difficulty that most people have with categorical syllogisms—it is *difficult to evaluate* all the possible conclusions. In the case of "All A are B" and "Some B are C," there is no valid conclusion about A and C (Johnson-Laird, 1983; Johnson-Laird and Steedman, 1978).

Hypothesis Formation and Testing

We already have seen that hypothesis formation and testing are important components of the scientific method (Chapter 1), but all people form and test hypotheses, or tentative explanations about the events in their lives: If I stop smoking, I am likely to live longer. I think that if I telephone during dinnertime, I am likely to find that they are at home.

Drinking red wine seems to give some people headaches. A number of researchers have examined the strategies that people use to form and test hypotheses (Bower and Trabasso, 1964; Bruner, Goodnow, and Austin, 1956; Wason, 1960). As is the case with research on reasoning, the research on hypothesis formation and testing indicates that people typically make mistakes.

In one study people heard three numbers—2, 4, and 6 (Wason, 1960). They were told that the three numbers had been generated according to a rule. The subjects were to discover the rule by saying other sets of three numbers, and the experimenter would tell them whether their series conformed to the rule. When subjects thought that they had figured out the rule, they were to announce the rule to the experimenter. A transcript from one such session appears in Table 8-8. This person's performance was typical. It reveals a strong confirmation bias, or tendency to generate and test examples that are consistent with an hypothesis. But strategy leads people to generate many examples that are consistent with the correct rule for the wrong reasons (with examples that are inconsistent with the hypothesis). To **disconfirm** and rule out incorrect rules, people have to test a hypothesis. If the person in the experiment hypothesized that the middle number was the arithmetic mean of the other two, he or she could readily have disconfirmed the hypothesis by offering any sequence in which the middle number was not the arithmetic mean (2, 7, 10 rather than 2, 6, 10, for instance). Then he

TABLE 8-8 ONE SUBJECT'S PROBLEM SOLVING

Test Number			Reason Given for Test Numbers	Feedback
8	10	12	Two added each time.	yes
14	16	18	Even numbers in order of magnitude.	yes
20	22	24	Same reason.	yes
1	3	5	Two added to preceding number.	yes
Announcement: *The rule is that by starting with any number, 2 is added each time to form the next number.* (Incorrect)				
2	6	10	The middle number is the arithmetic mean of the other two.	yes
1	50	99	Same reason.	yes
Announcement: *The rule is that the middle number is the arithmetic mean of the other two.* (Incorrect)				
3	10	17	Same number, 7, added each time.	yes
0	3	6	Three added each time.	yes
Announcement: *The rule is that the difference between two numbers next to each other is the same.* (Incorrect)				
12	8	4	The same number is subtracted each time to form the next number.	no
Announcement: *The rule is adding a number, always the same one, to form the next number.* (Incorrect)				
1	4	9	Any three numbers in order of magnitude.	yes
Announcement: *The rule is any three numbers in order of magnitude.* (Correct)				

Source: Wason, 1960.

Note: Transcript from a subject attempting to discover the rule that generated the sequence 2, 4, 6.

or she would have avoided making a second wrong guess. The failure to use a disconfirming strategy reflects the general difficulty people have with *negative information* (Levine, 1966)—recall the problem people have with negative information when testing conditional syllogisms. It appears that part of the problem lies in the fact that in everyday life we are accustomed to looking for positive, confirming information. Thus, we may be especially insensitive to the value of negative information.

PROBLEM SOLVING

You are playing tic-tac-toe, and it is your move. You explore a number of alternative moves, your opponent's possible responses, your responses to your opponent's responses, and so on. You probably explore the alternatives to several moves ahead before your actual move. You are exploring what is called your **problem space**. The problem space consists of all the possible moves or problem "states" that you think are available and likely to take you from the beginning of a problem to its solution.

The Problem Space

One of the major difficulties with real world problems is that it can be very difficult for people to figure out just what the problem space is. For example, what is the problem space for achieving world peace? For some simple games, all the possible states of the problem can be represented fairly simply, and all possible paths to the goal can be represented with only a bit more complexity (see the Towers of Hanoi problem in Figure 8-9). A major task in problem solving is to find paths to a solution. If people could represent all problems schematically, their search for solutions might be greatly simplified.

Even though the version of the Towers of Hanoi problem shown in Figure 8-9 is quite simple (if there are just five disks, it would become extremely difficult), there are still many possible paths (e.g., a–b–c–g–i–h–f–d–e) that will ultimately reach the desired state "E"—see Figure 8-9). But searches of the problem space, even if the problem space can be successfully represented, become very difficult once a problem be-

FIGURE 8-9
Panel A: THE TWO-DISK TOWER OF HANOI PROBLEM. The objective is to stack the two disks shown on pole A on pole C using as few moves as possible. Only one disk may be moved at a time and the large disk may not be placed on top of the small disk. This game takes its name from a legend that a group of monks living near Hanoi is working on a 64 disk problem and it is prophesied that the world will end when they solve the problem (in about a trillion years; Raphael, 1976.)

Panel B: THE TOWER OF HANOI PROBLEM SPACE. All the possible states (the problem space) of the two-disk Tower of Hanoi problem. Arrows indicate permissible transitions. The optimal path is from the beginning state A through B and D to the end-state E. (After Sanford, 1985.)

Panel A

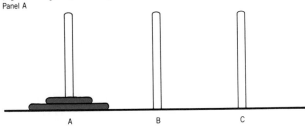

Panel B

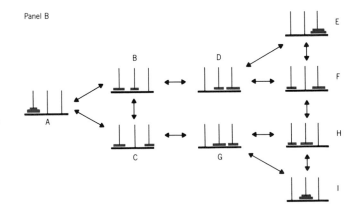

comes moderately complex. Even in a simple game like checkers where it is possible (though impractical) to specify the problem space, a problem solver has to decide how deeply to explore possible paths (Do you look 2, 5, 20, or 100 moves ahead?) and how many paths to explore before choosing a move. The alternatives can become mind boggling.

A very fast computer, looking at 35 paths to a depth of 100 moves, would require about 10^{138} years to explore all the alternatives (Winston, 1977)!

General Problem-solving Strategies

When solving a problem it is often helpful to apply some sort of **heuristic** or general rule of thumb to the problem. A heuristic can be contrasted with an **algorithm**, which is a set of procedures that guarantees a particular outcome. For example, you use your basic mathematical skills and apply an algorithm to get an exact answer to the product of 298×11. But to estimate the answer, you might use a heuristic and round 298 to 300 and 11 to 10 so that you can multiply it in your head. What kinds of heuristics are available to a problem solver?

GENERATE–TEST METHOD One straightforward problem-solving heuristic is to **generate** a possible solution to a problem and **test** it. For example, produce the name of a president whose name has an *e* as its fifth letter. You probably solve this problem by generating names of presidents and testing each. All well and good, but this method is not perfect (Newell and Simon, 1972). First, it may be difficult to continue generating alternatives. What do you do when none of the presidents names you recall works? Second, in some problems it may be difficult to test a possible solution. Determining whether a possible chess move is a good one can be extremely difficult. Third, the size of the search space may be very large, and it may take a long time to solve the problem. Imagine how long it would take to generate all the possible five-letter passwords someone might use to gain access to a computer. Finally, the correct solution may be low in the series of solutions you generate. Even if you remember the names of all the presidents, it may take you a long time to get to one that solves the problem.

THE MEANS–END METHOD Try to solve the following problem:

> *On one side of a river live five missionaries and five cannibals. All ten of them wish to get to the other side of the river and they have a boat that will hold as many as three people. As long as the cannibals never outnumber the missionaries, the missionaries are safe, but if the missionaries are ever outnumbered on either side of the river, they will be eaten. How can all ten get across the river?*
>
> *(Simon and Reed, 1976)*

You can apply the **means–end** heuristic to this problem. This heuristic strategy requires that problem solvers identify the ends they seek to achieve and find a sequence of operations (the means) to that end. One version of this strategy is called the **difference-reduction** method and is based on the idea that an operation should reduce the difference between the current state and the desired goal. Thus, in the missionary problem, preference should be given to operations that get as many missionaries and cannibals to the opposite river bank as possible (see Figure 8-10).

FIGURE 8-10
THE PROBLEM SPACE FOR THE MISSIONARIES AND CANNIBALS PROBLEM (Simon and Reed, 1976). Letters indicate the states of the problem. The numbers in the boxes—e.g., 54/01*—indicate the number of missionaries on each river bank (five on the left and none on the right) and the number of cannibals on each bank (four on the left and one on the right). The asterisk indicates the boat is located on the right bank. The numbers on the lines connecting boxes—e.g., 01—indicate the number of missionaries (none) and cannibals (one) that are moved to reach the next problem state. The beginning state is A and the end state is Z. (After Sanford, 1985.)

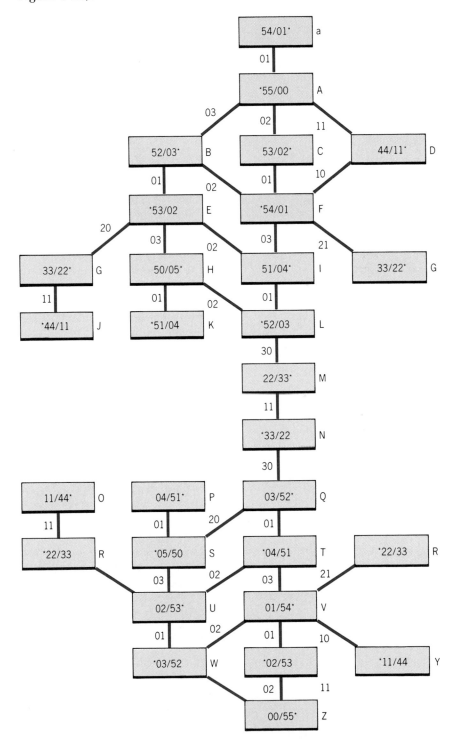

Unfortunately, even the difference-reduction strategy can lead a problem solver astray. For example, in the problem space for the missionary–cannibal problem, one way to get closer to the goal is to move as many people as possible across the river and return with just one (see Figure 8-10). However, this approach will create problems when the correct move is to return both a missionary and a cannibal rather than just one or the other. When people are given the missionary problem, they do seem to adhere to the means–end strategy even when it is not entirely satisfactory (Greeno, 1974; Jeffries et al., 1977).

Similarly, Atwood and Polson (1976) have shown that people are inclined to follow a difference-reduction strategy. Atwood and Polson used classic water-jug problems originally devised by Luchins (1942). Subjects were given the following problem:

> You have three jugs, which we will call A, B, and C. Jug A can hold exactly 8 cups of water, B can hold exactly 5 cups, and C can hold exactly 3 cups. A is filled to capacity with 8 cups of water. B and C are empty. We want you to find a way of dividing the contents of A equally between A and B so that both have 4 cups. You are allowed to pour water from jug to jug.

Two possible solution paths for this problem are shown in Figure 8-11. As the Figure indicates, people were, once again, sometimes led astray by the difference-reduction strategy.

ANALOGY METHOD   Arguments by analogy are quite common. Politicians frequently say that current foreign policy is similar to those of "Munich," in which efforts to appease Hitler before World War II backfired, or "Vietnam," where many believe the United States got bogged down in an unwinnable war. When people draw an *analogy*, they draw attention to the similarities in the structural features of two problems. Thus politicians invoke "Munich" when they fear that a foreign policy concession may actually whet the appetite of a hostile leader.

But reasoning is not always easy. Try solving the following problem:

> Suppose you are a doctor faced with a patient who has a malignant tumor in his stomach. It is impossible to operate on the patient, but unless the tumor is destroyed the patient will die. There is a kind of ray that can be used to destroy the tumor. If the rays reach the tumor all at once at a sufficiently high intensity, the tumor will be destroyed. Unfortunately, at this intensity the healthy tissue that the rays pass through on the way to the tumor will also be destroyed. At lower intensities the rays are harmless to healthy tissue, but they will not affect the tumor either. What type of procedure might be used to destroy the tumor with the rays, and at the same time avoid destroying the healthy tissue?

> (Adapted from Gick and Holyoak, 1980, pp. 307–308, from a problem originally devised by Duncker, 1945)

If you had trouble finding a solution, you are not alone. Only 5 percent of the subjects in the experiment found the correct solution (Duncker, 1945; Gick and Holyoak, 1980). Forty percent of subjects suggested an operation of some sort despite the fact that the problem ruled it out.

FIGURE 8-11 POSSIBLE SOLUTION PATHS FOR THE WATER JUG PROBLEM.
(Atwood and Polson, 1976.) Each state in the paths indicates the contents of the three water jugs (A, B, and C). The transitions between states are labeled to show which jug is poured into (arrow) which other jug. When asked whether they preferred to pour A into C (to get to state 2) or pour A into B (state 9), twice as many preferred state 9, which is more similar to the goal. Although this is generally a sound strategy, Atwood and Polson found that subjects most often deviated from the correct solution paths at points where optimal choices did not reduce differences between the current and goal state—more than 50 percent of subjects made mistakes at the transitions from states 5 and 11.

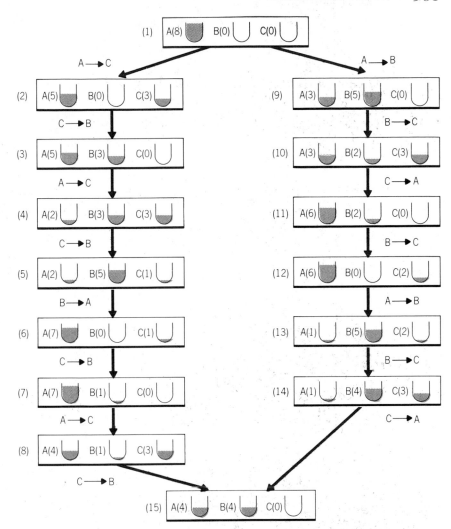

Twenty-nine percent suggested the delivery of X rays via the intestines or esophagus. The correct solution to Duncker's (1945) tumor/ ray problem is as follows: if several weak rays are sent from a number of points outside the patient, they can be arranged so they meet at the site of the tumor. Because the rays are individually weak, they will not harm healthy tissue, but because their summed strength will be great, they will destroy the tumor.

When researchers gave two other groups additional information, they found that more people found the right solution. Before reading the problem, subjects in both of these groups read three short stories, including the following:

A small country was ruled from a strong fortress by a dictator. The fortress was situated in the middle of the country, surrounded by farms and villages. Many roads led to the fortress through the countryside. A rebel general vowed to capture the fortress. The general knew that an attack by his entire army would capture the fortress. He gathered his army at the head of one of the roads, ready to launch a full-scale direct attack. However, the general then learned that the dictator had planted mines on each of the roads. The mines were set so that small bodies of men could pass over them safely, since the dictator needed to move his troops and workers to and from the fortress. However, any large force would detonate the mines. Not only would this blow up the road, but it would also destroy many neighboring villages. It therefore seemed impossible to capture the fortress. However, the general devised a simple plan. He divided his army into small groups, and dispatched each group to the head of a different road. When all was ready he gave the signal and each group marched down a different road. Each group continued down its road to the fortress so that the entire army arrived together at the fortress at the same time. In this way, the general captured the fortress and overthrew the dictator.

(Gick and Holyoak, 1980, p. 351)

When subjects were told that one of the three stories (the story presented here) was relevant to the radiation problem, 92 percent of them saw the correspondence and generated the correct solution to the radiation problem. But the important point is that people do not draw analogies automatically. People who read the military story but were not told about its relevance to the radiation problem performed about as well as those who had not read the story. Apparently the details of the military problems were too dissimilar for the people to detect the analogy. In short, when people do see that an analogy can be made, they often can successfully reason analogically (Gentner and Gentner, 1983). But people often respond to the surface features of problems and do not see possible analogies.

Furthermore, in some situations, even though people know there is an analogy between a problem they have solved in the past and a new problem, it may be difficult for them to make use of the information. For example, in a study in which students were provided the solutions to algebra problems, the students still have difficulty using the solutions to solve new problems (Reed, Dempster, and Ettinger, 1985).

Problem Representation

In discussing problem spaces and problem-solving strategies, we have emphasized the "operations" to a goal. But finding the steps to a goal is not the only task of a problem solver. The way in which a problem is represented also makes it easier or more difficult to solve:

Problem A: At sunrise a monk begins to climb a mountain. He reaches a temple at the summit at nightfall and spends the evening meditating and sleeping. At sunrise he begins descending the mountain, but since he is able to descend more rapidly than he climbed, he reaches bottom in the afternoon. When he reaches the bottom he observes: "There is a point along the trail that I passed at exactly the same time of day on my way up and my way down the mountain." Can you prove the monk is correct? Problem B: Two train stations are 50 miles apart. At 2 P.M. one Saturday afternoon, two trains start toward each other, one from each station. Just as the trains pull out of the stations, a bird springs into the air in front of the first train and flies ahead to the front of the second train.

When the bird reaches the second train it turns back and flies toward the first
train. The bird continues to do this until the trains meet. If both trains travel at
the rate of 25 miles per hour and the bird flies at 100 miles per hour, how
many miles will the bird have flown before the trains meet?

(Posner, 1973, pp. 150–151)

Most people have trouble finding an appropriate representation of
these problems, and they are difficult to solve unless they are appropriately represented. One useful representation appears in Figure 8-12*a*. As
the graph shows, no matter how rapidly the monk descends the mountain, his path has to cross his ascending path at some common time of day.

But graphic representation of the train problem is not helpful (Figure
8-12*b*). This problem requires a computation of how long the trains will
travel before meeting (one hour) and of how far the bird flies in one

FIGURE 8-12a   AN EFFECTIVE
REPRESENTATION OF THE MONK
PROBLEM.

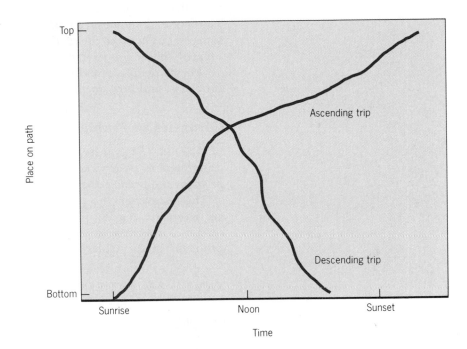

FIGURE 8-12b   AN
INEFFECTIVE REPRESENTATION
OF THE TRAIN AND BIRD
PROBLEM.

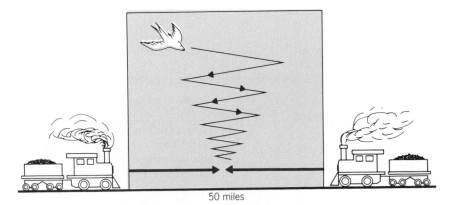

hour (100 miles). Some problems are best represented arithmetically, some algebraically, and some in other forms.

Another common difficulty in problem representation is that problem solvers sometimes think that a problem space is narrower than it actually is. For example, the matchstick problem in Figure 8-13 is impossible if one confines solutions to a two-dimensional desk top or piece of paper. In three dimensions, it is easy to assemble the matchsticks into a four-sided pyramid (see p. 388).

Similarly, the dots problem is impossible to solve if the solution is confined to the boundaries imposed by the square set of dots. Once the problem solver recognizes that lines can be drawn beyond these boundaries, the solution is much easier to find (Lung and Dominowski, 1985). By simply flipping the triangle in the circle, it becomes obvious that side t of the triangle is equal to the radius of the circle. Finally, the mutilated checkerboard problem is easily solved once the problem solver recognizes that each domino has to cover both a black and a white square. Thirty-one dominoes can be used to cover 31 black and 31 white squares, but because the mutilated board has 32 white and only 30 black squares, the dominoes cannot be used to cover all the squares.

Why do people have difficulty finding appropriate representations for problems, and how do they get around these difficulties?

Obstacles to Problem Solving

SET EFFECTS   You have three water jugs with specified capacities. By using them to pour water back and forth, how can you get the amounts of water required in the right-hand column in Table 8-9?

The researcher who presented these problems to subjects detected a **set effect** or regular mental orientation to the problems, which he termed a **mechanization of thought** (Luchins, 1939, 1942). All the problems in the table, except number 8, can be solved by filling B,

TABLE 8-9   SET EFFECTS

Problems	Capacity of Jug A	Capacity of Jug B	Capacity of Jug C	Desired Quantity
1	21	127	3	100
2	14	163	25	99
3	18	43	10	5
4	9	42	6	21
5	20	59	4	31
6	23	49	3	20
7	15	39	3	18
8	28	76	3	25
9	18	48	4	22
10	14	36	8	6

Source: Luchins, 1939.
Note: Using three jugs (A, B, and C) to pour water back and forth as necessary, how can you obtain a jug containing the desired quantity in the last column? All volumes are in cups.

Answers can be found on p. 388.

FIGURE 8-13 SOME BRAIN TEASERS.

Problem 1: Assemble six matches of equal length to form four equilateral triangles in which each side is equal to the length of one match.

Problem 2: Without lifting your pencil from the paper or retracing any path, connect all nine dots by drawing just four straight lines.

Problem 3: Determine the length of line t, *the side of a right triangle, given that the radius of the circle is 3 inches. (After Köhler, 1969.)*

Problem 4: Suppose you have a checkerboard from which opposite corners have been cut out so that 62 squares remain. If you have 31 dominoes, each of which will exactly cover two of the squares on the board, can you find a way to arrange the dominoes so they will cover all 62 remaining squares? Why or why not? (After Wickelgren, 1974.) The answer to Problem 4 is discussed on p. 384.

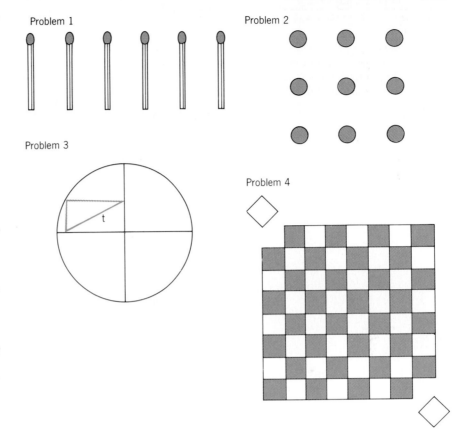

pouring B into C twice, and pouring B into A (B − 2C − A). The first five problems are most easily solved with this method, but problems 7 and 9 are more easily solved with A + C, and problems 6 and 10 are more easily solved with A − C.

Despite these easy alternatives, 83 percent of the subjects applied the formula B − 2C − A to problems 6 and 7, and 79 percent applied it to problems 9 and 10. Furthermore, 64 percent of these subjects failed to solve problem 8 (which is solved with A − C). They had become locked into a mental set of using B − 2C − A. Luchins tested another group of subjects, who were given only the last five problems, and therefore did not adopt the B − 2C − A set. Only 1 percent of these subjects used the B − 2C − A method, and 95 percent correctly solved problem 8.

FUNCTIONAL FIXEDNESS   Try your hand at the problems in Figures 8-14, 8-15, and 8-16. If you have difficulty with the problems, try to think of unusual ways objects in the problems might be used. Does this suggestion help? Why? If you have ever seen a baby use a cake pan for a hat, a skate, a hammer, and a drum, you have seen someone unhampered by **functional fixedness**—the tendency to recognize the customary functions of objects in a particular situation and miss other functions the object might serve.

FIGURE 8-14 THE CANDLE PROBLEM.

Your task is to support a candle on the wall. You are given only the objects shown in the figure: a box of tacks, the candle, and some matches. (After Duncker, 1945.)

If, like most of the subjects in Duncker's (1945) original study of the problem in Figure 8-14, you did not recognize that the matchbox can actually serve two *functions,* you will have difficulty with this problem. Although the matchbox is holding the thumbtacks, if the thumbtacks are dumped out and the matchbox is tacked to the wall, it will serve quite well as a candle holder! Interestingly, when Glucksberg and Weisberg (1966) presented this problem to subjects and labeled the box "a box," all the subjects solved the problem in less than a minute. Subjects who were merely given the box of tacks with the label "tacks" did not get the

FIGURE 8-15 THE STRING PROBLEM.

Two strings are suspended from the ceiling. You are to tie them together, but they are far enough apart that you cannot grab both strings at once. Using only the objects shown in the figure (a chair, pliers, tacks, and paper) can you tie the strings together? (After Maier, 1931.)

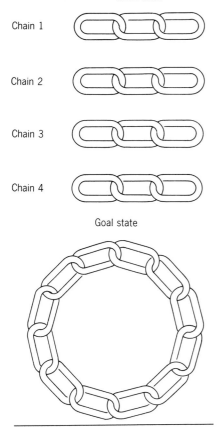

Given state

Chain 1

Chain 2

Chain 3

Chain 4

Goal state

FIGURE 8-16   THE CHAIN PROBLEM.
You are given four pieces of chain, each with three links. All the links in each chain are closed. Your goal is to join all 12 links into a single circular chain and spend no more than 36 cents. It will cost you 5 cents to open a link and 7 cents to close a link. (After Wickelgren, 1974.)

"hint"—they apparently did not recognize the box as a "box" but only as the container for the tacks.

In the two-string problem the solution is not obvious unless subjects recognize that the pliers can also serve at least two functions. In this case, the solution is to tie the pliers to the end of one string to serve as a weight, swing the "pendulum," and grab it while holding the other string. However, most subjects are "fixed" on the traditional function of the pliers—only 39 percent of Maier's (1931) subjects solved this problem in less than 10 minutes. The answer to the chain problem would be to open all the links in one chain and use those links to join the other three chains.

DECISION MAKING UNDER UNCERTAINTY

In the laboratory, researchers can devise problems with clear-cut solutions. But most of the everyday decisions that people make do not possess the logical certainty of syllogisms or the clear-cut answers of a laboratory exercise. Instead, people have to make most real decisions with sketchy and incomplete information: which used car is going to last longest? Will I enjoy my date with the person I met at the library? Should I get married now or wait? Which career should I choose? Decision making under these conditions of uncertainty is generally intuitive rather than strictly logical. In this section, we examine research that explores the **heuristics**, or rules of thumb, that people use to make intuitive judgments and some of the **biases** or imperfections of judgment that result when they rely on rules of thumb.

Over the past 15 years, led by the inspired work of Amos Tversky and Daniel Kahneman (1973, 1974, 1978; Kahneman and Tversky, 1972, 1973, 1982), researchers have begun to identify the heuristics used by decision makers in situations of uncertainty. In general, these heuristics let people make decisions quickly, efficiently, and fairly accurately. Unfortunately, they can lead people astray. These points are illustrated in research on two common heuristics—representativeness and availability.

The Representativeness Heuristic

People confronted tend to rely upon a **representativeness heuristic** and gauge the likelihood of an event according to its similarity to prototypes for the event (Kahneman and Tversky, 1973, 1982). For example, consider the following problem:

> *Linda is 31 years old, single, outspoken, and very bright. She majored in philosophy. As a student, she was deeply concerned with issues of discrimination and social justice, and also participated in antinuclear demonstrations (Kahneman and Tversky, 1982, p. 126). Which is more likely: that Linda is a bank teller, or that she is a bank teller who is an active feminist?*

When students saw this problem, over 80 percent chose the second alternative—a feminist bank teller. But this answer cannot be correct,

Answers: Problem 1

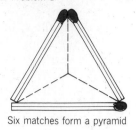

Six matches form a pyramid

Answer to Problem 2

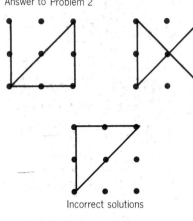

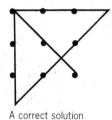

Incorrect solutions

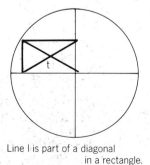

A correct solution

Answer to Problem 3   The easier diagram

Line l is part of a diagonal
in a rectangle.

because there are far more bank tellers than feminist bank tellers. But the students ignored this fact and apparently based their judgments on the fact that there was a better match between Linda and their notion of a feminist bank teller than between Linda and the more general category of bank teller.

People's assumptions about representative patterns also influence their judgments about processes that actually are random. For example, many people fall prey to the *gambler's fallacy*. According to this fallacy, for example, if someone tosses a coin several times, and heads has come up five times in a row, tails is "due." In fact, the coin has no memory for what has come up in the past, and heads is just as likely as tails on the next toss of the coin. Similarly, most sports fans believe that players sometimes have "hot hands" and therefore make a series of baskets in basketball, hits in baseball, and complete passes in football. However, when researchers examined the shooting sequences of basketball players, they found that the sequences closely approximated those one would expect when shots are independent of one another (Gilovich, Tversky, and Vallone, 1985). In other words, by chance alone there are going to be games in which a player hits a much higher percentage of shots than usual just as, by chance alone, there will be some games in which the same player will shoot well below average. People generally have difficulty understanding the influence on chance variations in such situations (Lopes, 1982, 1983; Wagenaar, 1970).

The Availability Heuristic

People also tend to use the **availability heuristic**. They tend to estimate the likelihood of events on the basis of the ease with which they can be brought to mind (Tversky and Kahneman, 1973). For example, tackle the following question:

> *In English words is the letter* R *more likely to appear in the first or third position?*

More than two-thirds of the people who answered the question said that *R* was more common as a first than a third letter. In fact, the reverse is true. Because words that begin with *R* are much more easily remembered than words that have an *R* in the third position (this fact tells us something about the organization of the internal dictionary), people conclude that words with *R* as a first letter are more common.

> *Imagine a group of ten people. Your task is to divide the people into committees so that no two committees have identical membership. Do you think you could form more unique eight-member committees or more unique two-member committees?*

> *(Tversky and Kahneman, 1973)*

If you said that more two-member committees can be formed, you have (fallen prey to) the availability heuristic and have reasoned that it is much easier to generate a large number of two-member committees with different membership than it is to generate eight-member committees. But in fact, equal numbers of different two- and eight-member commit-

BOX 8-2
BIASES IN DECISION MAKING

When you hear a weather forecast, the forecaster usually says that there is a particular chance of rain or sun: a 70 percent chance of light rain tomorrow afternoon or a 10 percent chance of clouds in the morning. Of course, weather forecasters are not the only people who make these types of confidence estimates about their predictions and judgments. All of us feel more or less confident about the decisions we make.

A number of researchers have investigated the question of whether people are appropriately confident. In one study people were asked to make choices on a large number of general knowledge questions (Fischhoff, Slovic, and Lichtenstein, 1977):

a: Aladdin is Persian.
b: Aladdin is Chinese.

The people also had to indicate their confidence in their judgments, on a scale ranging from guessing to certainty. The researchers discovered two things. First, they found that confidence and accuracy were moderately related. People tended to be correct when they felt most confident and least correct when they felt least confident. But the subjects had trouble matching their confidence judgments to their performance (perfectly calibrated judges would be accurate 60 percent of the time when they were 60 percent confident, 80 percent accurate when they were 80 percent confident and so on). The people did not calibrate well because they were generally overconfident. When people said that they were certain about their answers (100 percent confident), they were correct only 80 percent of the time. Similar results have been obtained in studies of other decision makers, including CIA analysts (Cambridge and Shreckengost, 1978), *Trivial Pursuit* players (Sharp, Cutler, and Penrod, in press), and even meteorologists (Lichtenstein, Fischhoff, and Phillips, 1982).

People are likely to be overconfident if they do not adequately analyze problems. In one experiment people responded to a set of fairly difficult questions and indicated their confidence levels (Koriat, Lichtenstein, and Fischhoff, 1980). The researchers tried to reduce the bias toward overconfidence, by making subjects consider arguments in favor of and against their choices. They asked one group of subjects to provide reasons in support of their choices, another group to provide reasons against their choices, and a third group to provide both types of reasons. Overconfidence diminished only in the group that provided reasons *against* their choices. These results, plus the fact that subjects generated more reasons for than against their choices lead to the possibility that overconfidence arises when people avoid evidence that disconfirms their hypotheses (Hoch, 1986; Skov and Sherman, 1986).

Although some decision makers are overconfident about their decisions, there are methods for reducing overconfidence. One method, as you have seen, is to force decision makers to argue against their choices. Other techniques that have been used successfully include providing people with detailed feedback about their performance (Cutler, Sharp, and Penrod, 1986) and increasing people's accountability for their decisions (Tetlock and Kim, 1987).

---

tees can be formed. (For every two-member committee, eight people are left over who can likewise be formed into a committee.)

Although the availability heuristic does not serve well in these *R* problems, it did provide people with quick and reliable estimates of the number of words they would be able to generate in a 2-minute period (Tversky and Kahneman, 1973). If you try this task yourself (have someone generate categories such as types of dogs, astronauts, presidents, and so forth for which you can make estimates and generate lists), you will probably find that those categories for which appropriate names come easily will also be the categories in which you are able to generate the greatest numbers of names in a 2-minute test period.

Earlier we asked whether people are rational decision makers. The answer is that people are not as rational as they could be. As you have seen, people have difficulty with logic, they are not very effective at testing hypotheses, they have difficulty reasoning by analogy, they often fail to represent problems effectively, they are prone to set effects and functional fixedness, and they rely on heuristics that sometimes lead them astray. However, even though there are clear limits to human rationality, most of us manage to solve most of our problems and make most of our decisions fairly effectively. We may not think as fast or as logically as a well-programmed, high-speed computer, but we do quite well given the constraints of time and the incomplete information with which we typically work.

SUMMARY

GRAMMAR AND THE STRUCTURE OF LANGUAGE

1. *Grammar.* A grammar is a set of rules that prescribes how the verbs, nouns, and modifiers of a language are linked together to form meaningful sequences. Knowledge of a grammar is largely implicit—people generally know how to speak correctly even if they cannot specify the rules they use when speaking.

2. *Phonology.* Spoken language is based upon phonemes that are the basic sound units of speech. Minimal pairs of words are used to determine the phonemes used in a language, as in the phonemes /b/ and /h/, which distinguish the words "bat" and "hat." Although people can generate about 200 phonemes, most languages use a much smaller number. English uses about 40 phonemes.

3. *Morphemes.* Phonemes are combined to produce morphemes—the smallest units of meaning in speech. Free morphemes are words that are meaningful by themselves: cat, dog, house, and so on. Bound morphemes combine with and modify the meaning of other morphemes. The morphemes are combined according to morphophonemic rules that, in English, for example, would accept jump*ing* but not *ing*jump. The average English speaker knows about 50,000 morphemes, and there are several theories that seek to explain how people learn and understand meaning.

4. *Theories of Meaning.* Structural theories of meaning attempt to describe the hierarchical organization of concepts in the internal lexicon or dictionary, while the prototype theory proposes that concepts consist of prototypes or typical instances that have fuzzy boundaries. Thus, some instances of a category fit a prototype better than others (a pigeon fits the prototype of *bird* better than an ostrich).

   Behavioral theories emphasize the learning of word meaning. Theorists such as Skinner argue that meanings arise from the consequences of speech.

5. *Syntax.* Syntax consists of the rules for combining words into meaningful utterances that are more than a mere stringing together of words. One simple but important set of syntactic rules concern phrase structures. These rules specify how words are combined to form such things as noun and verb phrases that can be further combined to form sentences. When speaking, people tend to pause between phrases and before the content words in phrases. This suggests that phrases play an important role in speech planning. Phrase structure also plays an important role in conveying meaning—proper phrasing makes speech much easier to understand.

   Although phrase structuring affects the communication of meaning, people do not necessarily remember language in terms of its surface structure, but instead remember the underlying deep structure of meaning in language. One theory about how the deep structure or meaning is represented in memory is in the form of propositional networks. These networks are based on propositions that consist of arguments (nouns) and relations (such as verbs and adjectives) that connect the arguments. Propositions can be linked together in many different ways to form networks that represent the meaning of sentences. The understanding of sentences is determined more by the number of propositions in the sentence than by the number of words in the sentence.

LANGUAGE DEVELOPMENT

6. *The Prelinguistic Stage.* In some ways humans appear predisposed to acquire and use language. Newborn infants with only a few hours of exposure to their mother's voice prefer their mother's voice to other voices. Infants can also make most of the auditory discriminations that adults make. Common patterns of language development are observed all around the world, indicating that early speech development is determined largely by maturational factors.

During the first few weeks after birth, infants mostly communicate by crying, but at 3 to 5 weeks they begin to coo and at 3 or 4 months to babble. Even phoneme development follows a common pattern. However, learning soon plays a role in language development. Infants gradually limit their babbling to the phonemes used in their native language, and they soon learn intonations and even turn taking. As early as 8 months, infants may show some understanding of verbal commands and at 1 year of age may be able to communicate their commands. First words may appear as early as 10 months.

7. *Telegraphic Language.* Between 18 and 24 months toddlers begin to combine words into simple telegraphic utterances. These utterances also follow a common syntactic pattern all around the world. Syntactic and semantic development also follow common patterns. Morphemes are acquired in a relatively fixed pattern, children commonly overregularize words, and sentence transformations all follow patterns. In addition, new words are added to the vocabulary at a rapid pace.

8. *Theories of Language Development.* Children do learn some language through imitation, and reinforcement can affect the rate of language development, but nativists argue that a major determinant of language development is a human predisposition to acquire language. They point, in particular, to the common patterns of language acquisition in children from language groups all around the world.

LANGUAGE IN PRIMATES

9. *Chimpanzee Studies.* Psychologists have made many efforts to teach language to chimpanzees. Early efforts to teach spoken language were largely unsuccessful. However, over the past 20 years several chimpanzees have been taught vocabularies of as many as several hundred words using sign language, tokens, and symbols. The most hotly contested research question concerns chimpanzees' syntactic abilities. Though chimpanzees appear to understand the meaning of symbols, they do not appear to combine symbols in a manner that allows them to systematically manipulate word order to communicate different thoughts using the same words.

LANGUAGE AND THE BRAIN

10. *The Aphasias.* Research with aphasic patients reveals that damage to particular brain structures can disrupt normal language. Damage to frontal regions of the left hemisphere can produce Broca's aphasia—a disruption of normal expression—whereas damage to posterior regions can produce Wernicke's aphasia, which disrupts language comprehension even though its victims produce fluid but unintelligible speech. Variations in the language problems of patients with different forms of aphasia suggest that there are separate areas for storing word meanings and object names, and that semantic and syntactic functioning rely on different brain areas.

Though the left hemisphere is usually dominant for language and damage to the right hemisphere may have little effect on language production and comprehension, the right hemisphere is involved in the processing of the emotional overtones of speech.

LOGICAL THINKING

11. *Syllogistic Reasoning.* Although people are generally very effective at governing their everyday lives and making everyday decisions, there are clear limits to human rationality. These limits are well documented in studies of logic, problem solving, and decision making. Conditional syllogisms are a part of deductive logic, which involves testing the validity of a conclusion from two premises. The conclusion of a particular syllogism must be *always true, sometimes true,* or *never true.* People have difficulty evaluating certain types of syllogisms. They are erroneously inclined to believe that if *A implies B,* then *B must imply A* and have difficulty when premises and conclusions are negative.

In categorical syllogisms, premises specify one of four types of relationships among categories: all, some, not, or some not. Among the problems people encounter when evaluating categorical syllogisms are difficulty with invalid syllogisms, a tendency to follow the atmosphere of the syllogism (e.g., negative premises tend to produce negative conclusions), and difficulty evaluating premises. When testing a hypothesis people tend not to seek disconfirmations of the hypothesis.

12. *Problem Solving.* When confronted with a problem, people often have difficulty generating the problem space, that is, all the possible states available from the beginning of the problem to its solution. If the problem space cannot be easily specified and a solution found, people often use a heuristic or rule of thumb such as trial and error, or they generate and test possible solutions. Alternatively people may use a means–end heuristic such as finding operations that reduce the difference between the present state and the goal. One heuristic that people do not readily use is drawing on analogies.

Sometimes people have difficulty solving a problem because they have not represented it effectively. Other times they may fail to see a solution because they have adopted a mental set that makes it difficult to generate alternative approaches or fail to see that objects or tools can serve more than their usual function.

13. *Decision Making Under Uncertainty.* In making real-world decisions people generally do not have complete information and may have to decide intuitively. Under such circumstances a heuristic such as representativeness may lead people to poor solutions. They may, for instance, choose alternatives that best fit their preconceptions. Or decision makers may choose alternatives that come to mind most readily—the availability heuristic. One other pitfall encountered by deci-

sion makers is a tendency to be unduly confident about their decisions.

Despite the fact that people may not perform perfectly on logical syllogisms, problem solving, and decision making, it is quite evident that almost all of us possess all the logical, problem-solving, and decision-making skills that are necessary to guide us through our everyday lives.

FURTHER READINGS

A number of general textbooks on language discuss topics examined in this chapter in detail. These texts include *Psychology of Language* by David Carroll (1986), which emphasizes language comprehension and production, language development, and language disorders in children. *Language Processes* by Vivien Tartter (1986) is a broad upper-level survey of research on language. *Psycholinguistics* by McNeill (1987) also offers a broad overview of research on language.

Language acquisition is considered in *Language Acquisition* by Jill deVilliers and Peter deVilliers (1978); *Child's Talk: Learning to Use Language* by Jerome Bruner (1983); *The Psychology of Language Development* by L. Riley (1986), and a recent and more technical volume *Mechanisms of Language Acquisition,* edited by Brian Mac-Whinney (1987). Those seeking a very readable account of language acquisition and the evolution of language will enjoy *Language and Speech* by George Miller (1981) and may be intrigued by a more technical treatment on language evolution in *The Biology and Evolution of Language* by Philip Lieberman (1984).

For a somewhat different perspective on language, a volume entitled *The Theory of A. R. Luria* by Donna Vocate (1986) presents the language theories of Luria—a leading Russian neurologist and psychologist. Luria is the author of *The Man with the Shattered Mind*—a fascinating account of his work with a man who suffered severe brain damage. Equally fascinating accounts of neurological disorders including aphasia can be found in *The Man Who Mistook His Wife for a Hat* by Oliver Sacks (1985). Recent research on aphasia is also reported in *The Cognitive Neuropsychology of Language,* edited by Max Coltheart, Remo Job, and Giuseppe Sartori (1986).

Those who are interested in primate language have several alternatives: *The Mind of an Ape* by David Premack and A. J. Premack (1983); an extensive article by David Premack entitled "'Gavagai!' on the future history of the animal language controversy" (1985); or *Nim: A Chimpanzee Who Learned Sign Language,* by Herbert Terrace (1979).

Among the best introductory accounts of research on thinking and problem solving are *Thinking, Problem Solving, Cognition* by Richard E. Mayer (1983); *Cognition* (2nd Ed.) by Arnold L. Glass and Keith J. Holyoak (1986); *Cognition and Cognitive Psychology* by Anthony J. Sanford (1985); *Cognitive Processes* (2nd Ed.) by Lyle E. Bourne, Roger L. Dominowski, Elizabeth F. Loftus, and Alice F. Healy (1986); *Cognitive Psychology and Its Implications* by John R. Anderson (1985); and *Judgment and Decision Making* edited by Kenneth R. Hammond and Harold Arkes (1986).

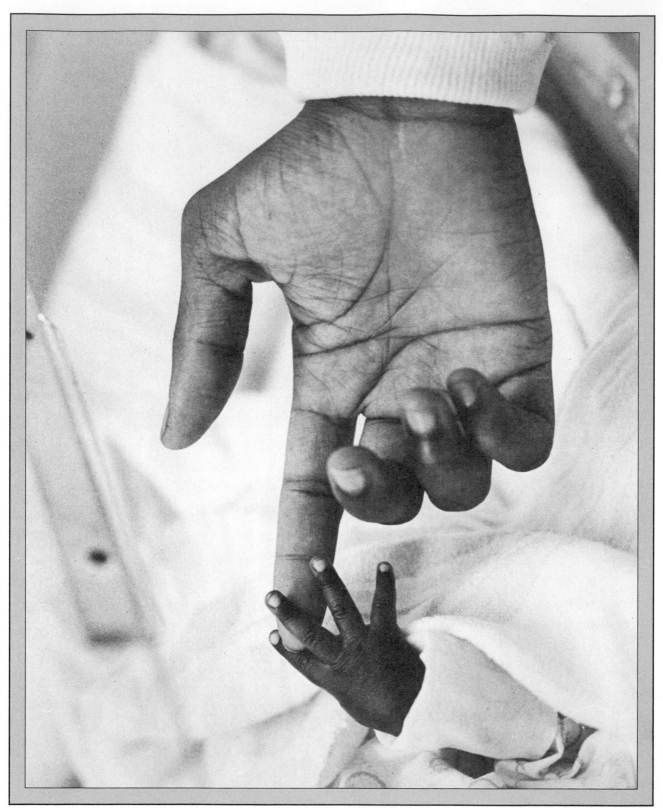

9

DEVELOPMENT: LIFE-SPAN CHANGES

Eli and Jessica are brother and sister, about a year apart in age. After each was born, each infant spent most of the time sleeping, eating, and eliminating waste. They were relatively helpless, unable even to roll over in their cribs. But from the moment of birth, both infants began to interact with their parents and to learn about the world around them. By the time each was 1 year of age, each could stand up on his or her own two legs and take the first shaky steps. Their social interactions had expanded to include young playmates as well as their parents. By the time each had reached the age of 2, Jessica and Eli had begun to talk. Along with their similarities in development, there were many differences between the two children. One child was more active physically and, by age 5, was climbing and swinging from the tops of swings and slides. The other was more verbal, enjoyed reading children's books, and put on stage productions with friends. In school, one excelled at mathematics (and as an adult would choose a career in architecture). The other excelled in reading and verbal skills (and by the age of 40 was a top-level corporate executive).

The most remarkable thing about Eli and Jessica is that they are fairly typical. Nearly all children progress from relatively helpless infants to active, competent individuals in only a few short years. Another fascinating thing about these and other children is that they quickly develop their own personal interests and activities. Developmental psychologists are interested in how such changes occur over the course of people's lives. One goal of developmental psychologists is to understand the changes that are universal, the changes that occur regardless of the individual's culture or experiences. Another goal is to understand why and how individual differences occur—why some children respond one way in a particular situation while others respond quite differently. To some extent, all psychologists share these two goals. But developmental psychologists are particularly concerned with the *processes* by which behavior changes during people's lifetimes. By studying behaviors from this dynamic point of view, developmental psychologists hope to better understand, predict, and modify behavior.

In Chapter 1 we pointed out that the study of development is one of many perspectives, or levels of analysis, that can be applied to understanding behavior. Any particular behavior, from sensation and perception to complex thinking, can be studied from a developmental point of view. You might well ask, therefore, why this book has a separate chapter on development. Why not just discuss the development of each behavior in its appropriate chapter? To a large extent we have done this. For example, you will find discussions on the development of visual sensation and perception in Chapter 3, of language in Chapter 8, and of personality in Chapter 12.

The present chapter has two main purposes. The first is to bring together three major threads in the development of the individual— physical development (changes in the body and brain), cognitive development (changes in knowledge about the world), and social development (changes in interactions with others). We consider each of these from the beginning of life through old age. Although each is discussed in a separate section, you will see that all three are interwoven in the development of the whole individual. The second purpose of the chapter is to

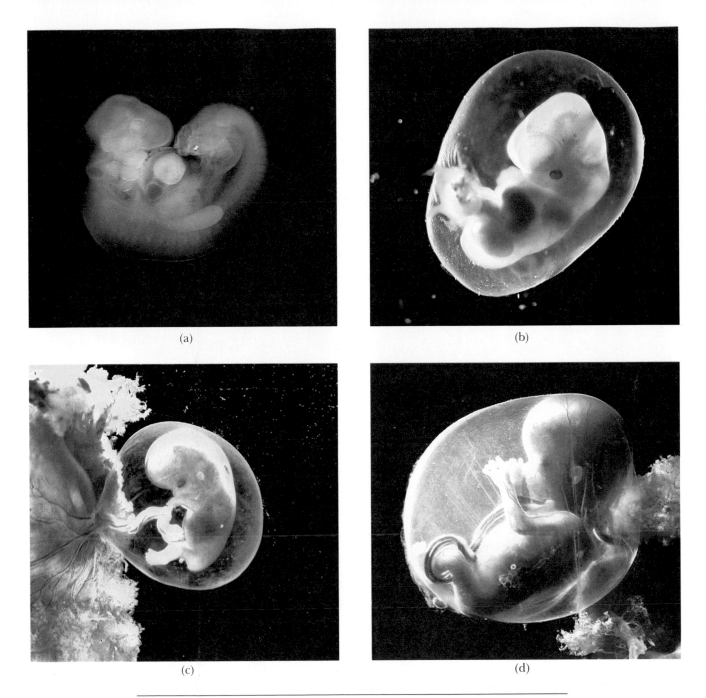

FIGURE 9-10 RAPID DEVELOPMENT OF THE EMBRYO AND FETUS.
(a) *At 4 weeks of gestational age, the embryo is $\frac{1}{4}$ inch long. It has a characteristic "C" shape, with a head and an elongated tail. The primitive skeleton is just visible. A tiny single-chambered heart can be seen in the center of the photograph. (b) At 6 weeks of age, the embryo is $\frac{3}{5}$ inch long. The heart is beating, and primitive arms and legs have formed. The eyes also have begun to take shape. The embryo floats within the fluid-filled* amniotic sac, *which absorbs vibration from the outside world. (c) At the end of the embryonic stage (8 weeks of gestational age), the embryo is a little more than 1 inch long. Fingers, toes, and primitive ears are visible. The* umbilical cord, *which carries the blood supply between the fetus and placenta on the wall of the uterus, also can be seen. (d) At 3 months of gestational age, the fetus is over 3 inches long and weighs about an ounce.*

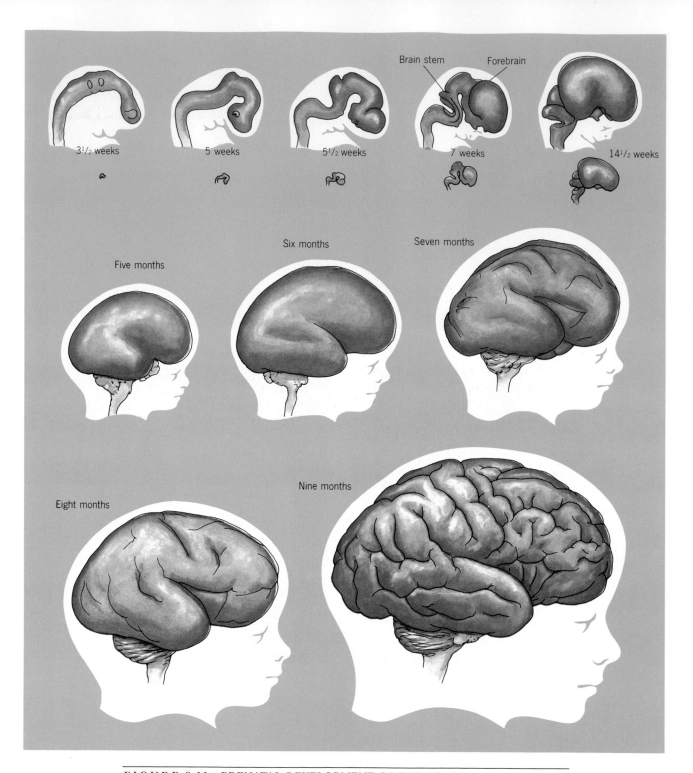

FIGURE 9-11 PRENATAL DEVELOPMENT OF THE BRAIN.
*The bottom sequence of drawings is to the same scale. The five drawings in the top row
have been enlarged to show more detail. Early in gestation, the two main divisions of the
brain (forebrain and brain stem) only appear as swellings. By 14 weeks' gestation, the
cortex has begun to grow over the brain stem. However, the convolutions of the cortex do
not begin to appear until between 6 and 7 months of gestational age. (After Cowan, 1979.)*

focus attention on certain conceptual issues in development. Let's begin by looking at two fundamental determinants of development: heredity and the environment.

DETERMINANTS OF DEVELOPMENT

For centuries, many scientists have maintained that virtually all human behavior is determined by inherited traits ("He's a born killer," or "She's a natural musician."). Other scientists have steadfastly maintained that virtually all human behavior is determined by the environment and learning. This is the age-old controversy over whether human behavior is a product of **nature** (heredity) or **nurture** (environment). As you will see, we now know that nature and nurture *interact* in producing who and what we are. Each of us is a product of both our genetic inheritance and our environment.

Genetics and Heredity

FIGURE 9-1 FATHER AND SON, MOTHER AND DAUGHTER. Physical appearance is strongly influenced by genetics.

Genetic inheritance certainly affects people's appearance (see Figure 9-1). Eye and hair color, for example, are genetically determined, and

FIGURE 9-3 CHROMOSOMES.
(a) *A photograph of the 46 chromosomes from a single human cell.* (b) *The chromosomes have been arranged in matching pairs. Half of each pair comes from either parent. The twenty-third pair consists of the sex chromosomes. The chromosomes here are from a male, so the twenty-third pair contains a large X and a smaller Y chromosome. If the individual were a female, the twenty-third pair would contain two X chromosomes.*

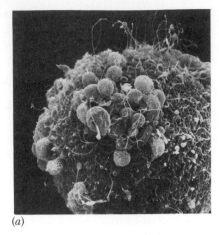
(a)

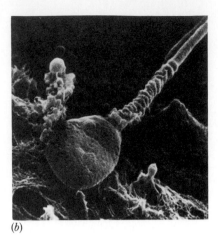
(b)

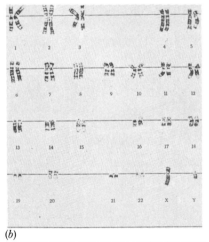
(a)

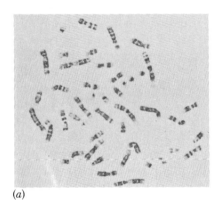
(b)

FIGURE 9-3 CHROMOSOMES.
(a) *A photograph of the 46 chromosomes from a single human cell.* (b) *The chromosomes have been arranged in matching pairs. Half of each pair comes from either parent. The twenty-third pair is the sex chromosomes. The chromosomes here are from a male, so the twenty-third pair contains a large X and a smaller Y chromosome. If the individual were a female, the twenty-third pair would contain two X chromosomes.*

features such as height and weight are strongly influenced by genetics. In addition, behavior is affected by the individual's makeup (Henderson, 1982; Scarr and Kidd, 1983; Wimer and Wimer, 1985). Before looking at how genes affect behavior, it is necessary to understand how genetic transmission works.

GENETIC TRANSMISSION The development of each individual begins at conception, when a sperm cell from a male merges with an ovum (or egg cell) from a female (see Figure 9-2). The genetic information from the male is carried by 23 **chromosomes** that are in the nucleus of the sperm cell. At conception, these chromosomes combine with 23 chromosomes in the ovum, which contain genetic information from the female. The resultant fertilized egg cell is called a **zygote**. It has 23 *pairs* of chromosomes, or 46 chromosomes in all—half from the mother and half from the father (see Figure 9-3). During development, the zygote divides in two, then each of these cells divides again, and so on through millions of cell divisions as the future infant is formed. With each division, the 46 original chromosomes are duplicated. Thus, every cell in the infant's body contains replicas of all the chromosomes that came from the mother and the father.

The unit of hereditary information in the chromosome is the **gene**. Each chromosome is made up of approximately 20,000 genes strung in a long chain. Thus, there are nearly one million genes in each cell of the body. Each gene consists of a complex molecule called *deoxyribonucleic acid (DNA)*. The structural details of the DNA molecule differ for each gene, and consequently the action of each gene is different. The actions of genes include control over the production of proteins and chemicals in each cell. In this way, the genes specify that some cells become nerve cells, some bone cells, some muscle cells, and so on. In addition, the genes specify details such as how nerve cells are connected. Through these actions, genes can influence many human functions, including the activity of the brain and behavior.

Each of the two chromosomes in a pair contains matched genes that influence the same traits. For example, the father's gene for eye color is present on one member of the chromosome pair and the mother's gene for eye color is on the other. When both genes specify the same trait—

for example, brown eyes—the genes are said to be **homozygous**. When the genes specify different traits—brown eyes from one parent and blue eyes from the other—the genes are **heterozygous**. When a gene pair is heterozygous, one of the genes may be dominant over the other. A **dominant gene** is one that determines the trait. A **recessive gene** determines the trait only when a dominant gene is not present (see Figure 9-4).

This simple pattern of dominant and recessive genetic inheritance operates for a number of traits, such as dark (dominant) and light (recessive) hair and the ability to taste a substance called phenylthiocarbamide (which is bitter to those who can taste it). However, genetic control of traits often is more complex than this simple either/or pattern, and in many cases both genes in a pair are expressed at the same time. For instance, people with one gene for normal red blood cells and one gene for abnormal red blood cells (sickle cells) have some normal and some abnormal cells, not just one or the other. Furthermore, most traits depend on the combined effects of many pairs of genes. For example, a person's height is influenced by genes that specify growth rate, bone formation, hormone production, and so on. Such traits are called **polygenic traits**. Genetic influences on behavior tend to be polygenic.

You should remember that a person's genes are not always outwardly expressed. You already have seen that this is so in the case of simple recessive genes. In addition, environmental factors can determine whether

FIGURE 9-4   AN EXAMPLE OF DOMINANT AND RECESSIVE GENE ACTION.

A pair of genes specifies the nature of pigments in the iris of the eye. A gene that specifies brown eyes (labeled B*) is dominant over a recessive gene that specifies blue eyes (labeled* b*). Therefore, parents that have one* B *gene and one* b *gene, as shown here, will have brown eyes. Half of the reproductive cells from either parent will have the* B *gene and half the* b *gene. At conception, these genes can combine in one of four ways: BB, bb, Bb, or bB. Three of these combinations result in a child with brown eyes, because the* B *gene is dominant. The* bb *combination results in a child with blue eyes. Thus, two brown-eyed parents can have a child with blue eyes. (After Fischer and Lazerson, 1984.)*

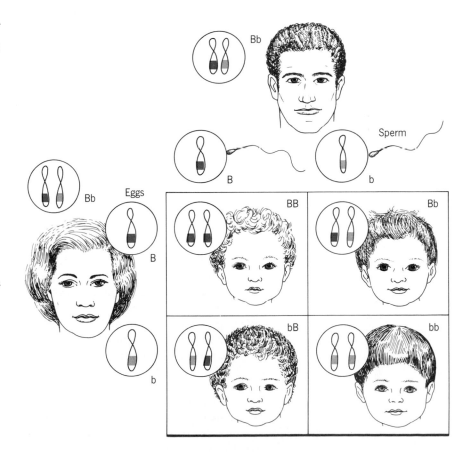

particular genes are expressed. For example, people with genes that normally would lead them to be tall do not grow tall if they do not have proper nutrition. The genes for a particular trait are referred to as the **genotype** for that trait. The actual physical characteristics that are displayed are referred to as the **phenotype**. Thus, the environment—for example, in the form of nutrition—can influence the phenotype—actual height—that will be expressed by a person's genotype—genes for hormone production, growth rate, and so on.

SEX-LINKED CHARACTERISTICS Of the 23 pairs of chromosomes we humans have, one pair is the sex chromosomes. (The other 22 pairs are called autosomes.) In males, one of these sex chromosomes is large and designated the X chromosome, and the other member of the pair is small and designated the Y chromosome (Figure 9-3). When sperm are formed, each sperm cell receives half (23) of the chromosomes—one member of each pair. Thus, half the sperm cells carry the X chromosome, and half carry the Y chromosome. In females, both members of the sex-chromosome pair are X chromosomes. As a result, all of the ova contain one X chromosome. At conception, only one sperm cell merges with the ovum. If the sperm carries an X chromosome, the fertilized egg cell will have two X chromosomes and develop into a female. If the sperm carries a Y chromosome, the fertilized egg cell will have a Y and an X chromosome and develop into a male. Thus the father's sperm determines the sex of the child.

Many characteristics, such as color blindness, certain types of baldness, and hemophilia (lack of a clotting factor in the blood) are determined by genes that are on the sex chromosomes. Such characteristics are referred to as **sex-linked traits**.

Behavior Genetics

Given the complexities of determining how genes affect behavior, scientists have had to devise ingenious methods for separating the effects of environment from heredity. In the study of genetic bases of behavior, **behavior genetics**, perhaps the best way to determine the influence of genes on behavior is to study individuals who have been raised in the same environment but who have different genotypes. Any differences in behavior can then be attributed to the different genetic makeups of the individuals. Behavior geneticists have used this strategy in studies of **inbred strains** of animals. Inbred strains are produced by mating brothers and sisters, and then mating brothers and sisters from the offspring, and so on. After about 20 generations of consecutive brother–sister matings, a relatively pure strain of individuals with nearly identical genotypes is attained. A number of such strains of mice now exist, and comparisons of their behavior have revealed genetically produced differences in behaviors such as activity level, learning ability, hoarding, sexual behavior, alcohol preference, and aggression (McClearn, 1970; Wimer and Wimer, 1985).

Behavior geneticists also have studied genetic bases of behavior by using **selective breeding**. In this procedure, they measure animals for some trait, such as learning ability. Individual animals that show an

FIGURE 9-5   INHERITANCE OF MAZE-LEARNING ABILITY IN RATS.

The rats were given 19 trials in a complex maze, and the number of blind-alley entrances was counted. Each graph shows the percentage of rats that made different numbers of blind-alley entrances. The top graph shows the performance of an unselected sample of 142 rats. Most rats made between 30 and 100 blind-alley entrances. But some made many fewer errors (they learned the maze very quickly) and some many more (they learned slowly). The "brightest" and "dullest" rats were then selectively bred, their offspring tested, and the brightest and dullest selectively bred again, and so on. The lower graphs show the performance of the first, third, and seventh generations from the selective breeding. By the seventh generation, there was almost no overlap in the maze-learning abilities of the bright and dull rats. (From Tryon, 1942.)

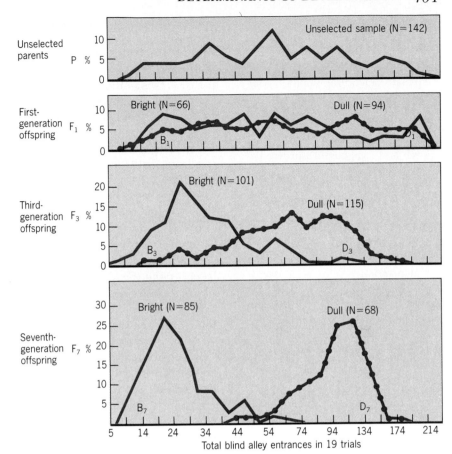

extreme of the trait—perhaps they are extremely rapid or extremely slow learners—then are selected and bred. Their offspring then are measured for the same trait, and the extreme individuals are again selected and bred. If there is a genetic contribution to the trait being studied, selective breeding will result in a systematic increase in that trait over successive generations. In the best-known study of selective breeding (Tryon, 1940), one group of rats was selected for superior performance in learning to run a complex maze, and another group was selected for poor performance in the same maze. After a few generations of selective breeding, "maze bright" and "maze dull" strains of rats were produced (see Figure 9-5). Other researchers have successfully bred animals for high and low degrees of emotional arousability, activity, aggressiveness, and alcohol preference (McClearn, 1970; Wimer and Wimer, 1985).

Ethics prevent researchers from carrying out selective breeding and inbreeding experiments to study the genetic bases of behavior in humans. But scientists have found other methods to study behavior genetics in humans. One of the most widely used is **twin comparisons**. The basic method is to compare the similarities in behavior of identical twins and fraternal twins. **Identical (monozygotic, or MZ) twins** arise from the same fertilized egg and therefore have identical genotypes. **Fraternal (dizygotic, or DZ) twins** arise from two separate fertilized eggs and are

TABLE 9-1 SOME BEHAVIORS INFLUENCED BY GENETICS

Visual Perception
   Spatial visualization ability
   Perceptual speed
Cognition
   Intelligence
   Mental retardation
Speech and Language Disorders
   Stuttering
   Reading disability (dyslexia)
Personality and Temperament
   Introversion-extroversion
   Anxiety/neuroticism
Psychopathology
   Affective disorders (mania and/or
     depression)
   Schizophrenia

Source: Compiled from Henderson, 1982, and Scarr and Kidd, 1983.
Note: These are examples of human behavioral characteristics for which there is evidence of genetic influence. In some cases, the genetic influence is known to be relatively weak, as in certain personality characteristics. In other cases, the genetic influence is quite strong, as in certain types of mental retardation.

no more alike genetically than any other siblings. If groups of MZ twins are more alike on some trait than are groups of DZ twins, a genetic basis for that trait is suggested. For instance, because studies have shown that intelligence test scores for MZ twins tend to be more similar than scores for DZ twins, the inference to be drawn is that there is a genetic contribution to intelligence (see Chapter 14). But twin comparisons have to be interpreted cautiously. It is possible that parents and other people treat identical twins more similarly than they treat fraternal twins. If so, the greater similarity of identical twins could be due to their upbringing (environment) rather than their identical genotypes. Nevertheless, carefully designed twin comparisons are valuable for suggesting genetic influences on behavior.

Behavior geneticists also study the influence of genetics on human behavior in **adoption studies**. The reasoning is that if adopted children resemble their biological parents and siblings (with whom they have some genes in common) on certain traits—intelligence, reading ability, activity level, or the like—more than they resemble their adopted parents and siblings (with whom they have no genes in common), it is likely that heredity influences the trait in question. Similarly, if children living with their biological parents resemble them more on certain traits than do adopted children living in the same household, it is again likely that heredity influences the trait in question. But adoption studies also must be interpreted cautiously, because adopted and biological children may be treated differently by parents and others.

GENES AND HUMAN BEHAVIOR Through their studies, behavior geneticists have provided evidence for genetic influences on a wide variety of human behavior, from visual perception, to speech disorders, to aspects of personality and temperament (see Table 9-1). A developmen-

FIGURE 9-6 A CHILD WITH DOWN SYNDROME.
These children tend to be short and stocky; to have a broad, short neck; and have large eyelid folds that make them look Oriental (the reason that the syndrome originally was called mongolism). Most of these children are severely mentally retarded, but the extent of retardation varies greatly from case to case.

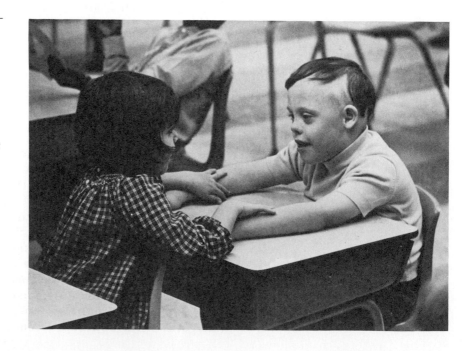

The environment in which a human fetus develops before birth can have profound and permanent effects on a child's physical and mental abilities. Among the environmental influences on the developing fetus are an expectant mother's diet, any drugs she may take, and even her emotional state.

NUTRITION

A developing fetus gets all nutrients for growth from the mother. Therefore the mother's diet must be adequate to nourish the fetus as well as herself. Babies born to mothers with nutritionally deficient diets tend to have lower birth weights, tend to be less resistant to illness, and are more likely to die during the first year of life than babies born to mothers with sound diets (Metcoff, 1978; Katz, Keusch, and Mata, 1975). Studies in animals indicate that a mother's malnutrition also can impair the brain development of her fetus (Dobbing, 1974; Patel, 1983). Although there is evidence that many of these effects can be reversed by proper nutrition after birth (Patel, 1983; Stein, Susser, Saenger, and Marolla, 1972), continued malnutrition after birth can lead to permanent impairments in neural and intellectual development (Dob-

bing, 1974, 1985; Cravioto and De-Licardie, 1978).

DRUGS

Because drugs that a pregnant woman takes enter her fetus's bloodstream, many drugs can produce birth defects. Such drugs are called **teratogens**. Perhaps the best-known example is the tranquilizer thalidomide. This drug prevents the normal development of the fetus's arms and legs if a pregnant woman takes it between a critical period of 27 to 40 days after conception. Before this effect was discovered and the drug was taken off the market, many children with abnormally formed limbs were born to mothers who had taken thalidomide (Taussig, 1962).

Cigarette smoking by a pregnant woman also affects the fetus because the nicotine, tar, and carbon monoxide that she inhales reduce the capacity of the blood to carry oxygen to the fetus. Many studies have shown that smoking during pregnancy lowers a baby's birth weight (Longo, 1982; United States Department of Health, Education, and Welfare, 1979). Smoking also increases fetal and newborn deaths by 20 to 35 percent (Meyer, Jonas, and Tonascia, 1976). Some studies suggest that the woman's smoking during pregnancy has no significant long-term effects on the physical, intellectual, or emotional development of children who survive the newborn period (Lefkowitz, 1981). However, others have shown that such children have problems paying atten-

tion later in life (Streissguth, Martin, Barr, Sandman, Kirchner, and Darby, 1984).

Women who drink alcohol during pregnancy also can have children with birth defects and other problems. Children born with *fetal alcohol syndrome,* for example, have physical problems such as low birth weight, an abnormally shaped head, and abnormal facial features (such as a flattened jaw and small eyes). They also are mentally retarded (Abel, 1984, 1985; DeLuca, 1981). Drinking as little as one drink a day increases the risk of miscarriage (Harlap and Shiono, 1980; Kline et al., 1980) and can lead to long-term problems in paying attention among surviving children (Streissguth et al., 1984).

MATERNAL STRESS

When a pregnant woman is under stress—whether from anxiety, grief, or fear—her autonomic nervous system becomes active, and various chemicals and hormones are released into her blood. These chemicals and hormones enter the fetus's blood. The fetus's physical activity increases dramatically—by up to several hundred percent (Sontag, 1941, 1944). If the stress persists, the baby is likely to be born underweight, to be hyperactive and irritable, and to have feeding difficulties. Fortunately, children subjected to prenatal stress can develop normally after birth if their later environment is normal (Werner and Smith, 1982).

tal disorder that provides a classic example of how genes can profoundly affect behavior is **Down syndrome**. Children with Down syndrome have moderate to severe mental retardation as well as a characteristic physical appearance (see Figure 9-6). About 95 percent of people with Down syndrome underwent a genetic error before birth in sperm-cell or (more commonly) egg-cell division. This error in cell division means that instead of the normal two chromosomes in the twenty-first position (see Figure 9-3*b*), there are three chromosomes. In ways that are not yet fully understood, genes on the extra chromosome produce nervous system abnormalities and mental retardation (Scott, Becker, and Petit, 1983; Smith and Warren, 1985). Thus Down syndrome is a genetic disorder that is not directly inherited from parents.

Down syndrome is only one of many genetic disorders that cause mental retardation, physical disabilities, and other problems in development. Although Down syndrome is not curable, the effects can be substantially alleviated through proper management—a prime example of environmental factors mitigating genetics. For example, cognitive stimulation and aggressive treatment of physical abnormalities can greatly improve the developmental outlook for affected individuals. Let's take a look at some of the ways in which environment interacts with genetic endowment.

Effects of the Environment

The environment can influence the development of individuals in a variety of ways. It can act through biological influences both before and after birth, it can act through a child's learning experiences, through the immediate social environment of family, friends, and teachers, or through the broader social and cultural environment in which a child grows up. Most scientists no longer argue about whether genes or environment is more important for the development of the individual. They recognize that development occurs through the joint action of genetic information and environmental influences that allow the genetic information to be expressed (Scarr and Kidd, 1983).

FIGURE 9-7 HOW GENOTYPE AND THE ENVIRONMENT MAY INTERACT IN THE DEVELOPMENT OF BEHAVIOR. Hypothetical data show how different genotypes (A, B, C, and D) *may have different reaction ranges (RR) of intellectual development (phenotypic IQ) that are possible under different environmental conditions. Notice that all four of the genotypes produce higher IQ with improved environment. Some genotypes respond more to environmental factors (have a larger reaction range) than others, and the same range of environmental conditions can improve on some genotypes more than others. (From Gottesman, 1963.)*

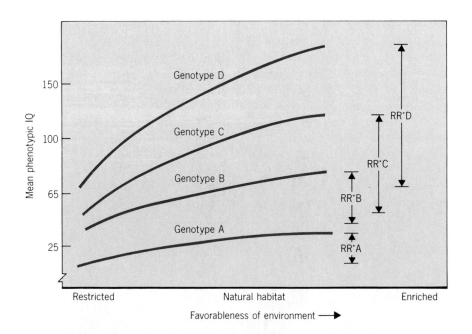

Genetic information and environmental influences do not simply add together to determine the development of behavior. Rather, they *interact* in complex ways. A particular genotype (genetic makeup) may produce a wide range of phenotypes (behavioral abilities), depending on the environmental conditions. The range of possible phenotypes for a given genotype is referred to as the **reaction range** of that genotype. The nature and size of the reaction range may differ for different genotypes (see Figure 9-7). As a result, different genotypes can result in the same phenotype—for example, IQ—and the same genotype can result in different phenotypes.

PHYSICAL DEVELOPMENT

People's behavior depends largely on their physical development throughout life. For example, sexual behavior depends on maturation of the sex organs, and cognitive abilities depend on development of the brain. In this section, we take a brief look at how the body and brain change from the moment of conception to old age.

Prenatal Development

BODY DEVELOPMENT   As we've described, human development begins when sperm and egg unite at conception. The first 266 days (38 weeks) of this process occur within the mother's body and are referred to technically as the **prenatal**, or **gestation**, **period**. During this time, the individual grows from a single fertilized egg cell (the zygote) to an infant with billions of specialized cells. The gestation period is divided into three stages: the germinal, embryonic, and fetal stages. The major events that occur during these stages are summarized in Figure 9-8.

The **germinal stage** lasts about 2 weeks from the time of fertilization. During this stage, the zygote is engaged primarily in cell division. By the end of the germinal stage, the zygote has become a small mass of cells, and it has moved through the mother's fallopian tube and attached itself to the wall of her uterus, the muscular organ in which it will continue to develop until birth (see Figure 9-9).

The **embryonic stage** lasts from the second to eighth week after conception. During this stage, the fetus's brain and heart begin to develop, and arms and legs appear (see color plate Figure 9-10*a* and *b*). It is during this period, when the limbs and critical internal organs are rapidly developing, that the embryo is most vulnerable to influences of the prenatal environment. By the end of the embryonic stage, the tiny embryo is recognizably human (see color plate Figure 9-10*c*).

The **fetal stage** lasts from the eighth week after conception until birth, which is usually 38 or so weeks after conception (see Figure 9-10*d*). By about 33 weeks after conception, the fetus's respiratory system has developed enough so that the fetus can breathe on its own and survive outside the uterus. At 38 weeks, most babies are ready for normal birth.

FIGURE 9-8   A SUMMARY OF THE PHYSICAL AND BEHAVIORAL CHANGES IN HUMAN PRENATAL DEVELOPMENT.

The entire process of gestation takes 38 weeks from fertilization. Because the precise date of fertilization usually is not known, physicians commonly calculate the age of the developing baby from the time of the mother's last menstruation, which occurs about 2 weeks before fertilization. They compute a 40-week (9-month) gestation period. However, it is more accurate to calculate gestational age from the time of fertilization, as has been done in this chart. (From Fischer and Lazerson, 1984.)

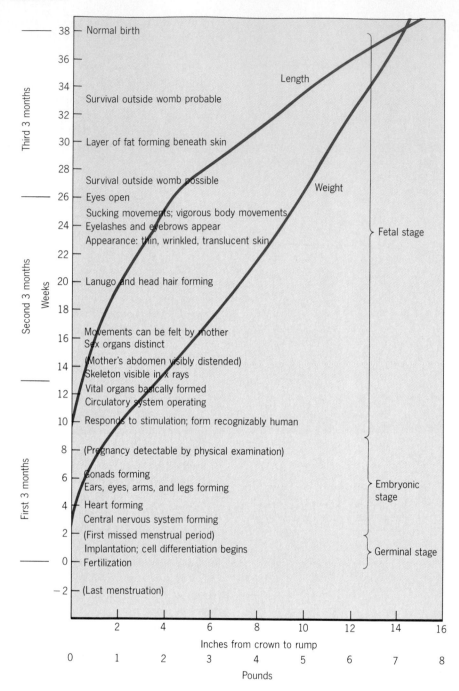

They have grown from a single cell into an amazingly complex individual who, on average, is about 20 inches long and weighs about $7\frac{1}{2}$ pounds.

DEVELOPMENT OF THE BRAIN   The brain begins to develop between the second and third week after fertilization, and by $3\frac{1}{2}$ weeks a primitive nervous system is present. As shown in Figure 9-11 (color plate), the brain develops rapidly throughout gestation. By the time of birth, virtu-

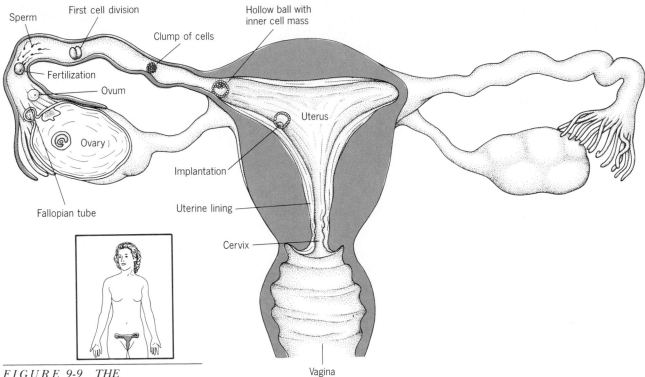

*FIGURE 9-9   THE
RELATIONSHIP BETWEEN THE
DEVELOPING ORGANISM AND
THE MOTHER'S BODY DURING
MOST OF THE 2-WEEK GERMINAL
STAGE.*
Fertilization takes place in the fallopian
tube, *which connects ovary to uterus.
The fertilized egg then begins a 3-day
trip to the uterus. After floating freely in
the uterus for 4 to 5 days, the zygote
becomes* implanted *in the wall of the
uterus, and a* placenta *begins to
develop. The placenta is an organ
attached to the wall of the uterus and
transmits nutrients and wastes between
the mother and the developing organism
by way of blood vessels in the umbilical
cord (see Figure 9-10c).*

ally all of the approximately 100 billion neurons in the human brain
already are present. That means that during prenatal development, the
brain generates an average of at least 250,000 new neurons per minute
(Cowan, 1979)!

But even this phenomenal rate of development may be an underestimate. Research in animals indicates that early in development, about
twice as many neurons are produced than will be present in the adult
brain. In addition, many neurons initially grow axons that connect to the
wrong targets. During the normal course of development, the excess
neurons die and the inappropriate connections degenerate, leaving the
appropriate connections in place (Cowan, Fawcett, O'Leary, and Stanfield, 1984; Clarke, 1985). Scientists believe that this overproduction
and, later, death of neurons and their connections is an important
mechanism for forming and fine-tuning the developing nervous system.

Infancy and Childhood

During the first 2 years after birth, the child is a virtual growing machine
(see Figure 9-12). By age 2, the average child is about 70 percent taller
than at birth (34 inches versus 20 inches) and nearly 400 percent heavier
($27\frac{1}{2}$ pounds versus $7\frac{1}{2}$ pounds) (Eichorn, 1979). A rule of thumb is that
girls grow to about half their adult height by 18 months of age and boys,
by age 2. Between the ages of 2 and 5 years, physical growth slows down
and then levels off at a relatively steady rate until adolescence.

Physical growth tends to proceed in two general directions. First,
early growth is more rapid in the head and upper body and later growth

FIGURE 9-12 GROWTH IN HEIGHT.

(a) *The solid lines show the growth curves for an average boy and girl. Some individuals mature early and some grow to be taller or shorter than average (dotted lines).* (b) *The average rate of height increase each year for boys and girls. The most rapid increase in height occurs during the first two years of life. Then growth rate levels off for several years. During adolescence, boys and girls have another rapid increase in height. This growth spurt generally occurs earlier for girls than for boys. (From Hall, Perlmutter, and Lamb, 1982; after Bayley, 1956.)*

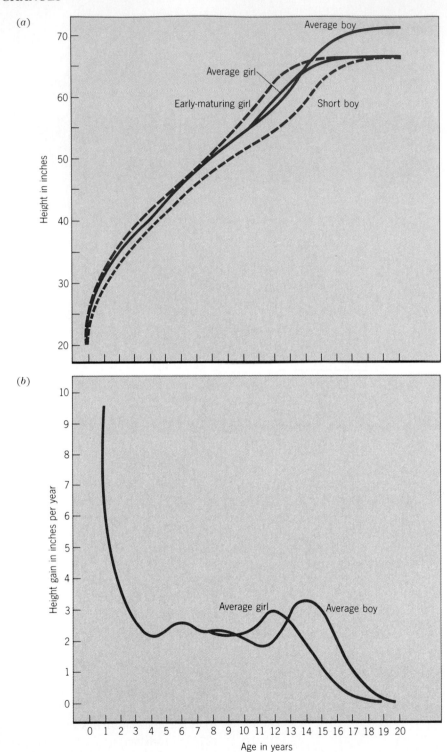

occurs more in the lower body; that is, growth proceeds in a **cephalocaudal (head-to-foot)** pattern. Second, the center of the body grows more early in life, and the arms and legs grow more later; a **proximodistal**

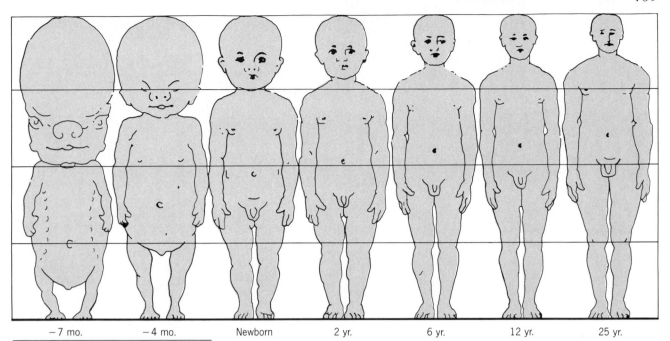

| −7 mo. | −4 mo. | Newborn | 2 yr. | 6 yr. | 12 yr. | 25 yr. |

FIGURE 9-13 RELATIVE GROWTH OF THE BODY FROM 2 MONTHS AFTER CONCEPTION TO ADULTHOOD.

At birth, the child's head is a quarter of the total body length. As the child grows, the trunk and legs become proportionally longer. The trunk also lengthens relative to body width. As a result, the adult's head is only one-eighth of total body length. (From Jackson, 1929.)

(**center-to-periphery**) pattern. As a result, the shape and proportions of the infant's body are very different from those of the adult (see Figure 9-13).

The brain also grows rapidly during the first two years after birth (Mann, 1984). At birth, the brain is about 25 percent of its adult weight and size. By 2 years of age, it has grown to about 75 percent of its adult weight. Although all of a person's neurons are present at birth, the number and complexity of the connections among neurons increase substantially after birth (see Parmelee and Sigman, 1983), and this increase is partly responsible for the growth in brain size. In addition, the brain grows as the number and size of glial cells increase. Remember that an important function of the glial cells is to form a sheath of myelin around the axons of neurons (see Chapter 2). This fatty substance aids in the proper conduction of impulses from one neuron to another. Thus, both the increased neural connections and the development of myelin after birth make possible more and more complex behavior and thought as the child grows. In some areas of the brain, these developmental changes continue until adolescence (Yakoviev and Lecours, 1967).

From Adolescent to Adult

The maturing brain signals the beginning of adolescence and the onset of **puberty**—the process of sexual maturation. Puberty begins when the hypothalamus, at the base of the brain, signals the pituitary gland to release certain hormones. In turn, the pituitary hormones cause other glands in the body to release hormones that stimulate growth and the development of adult sexual characteristics. The usual sequence of changes that occur during sexual maturation for girls and boys is shown in Figure 9-14. For girls, after breasts and pubic hair begin to develop,

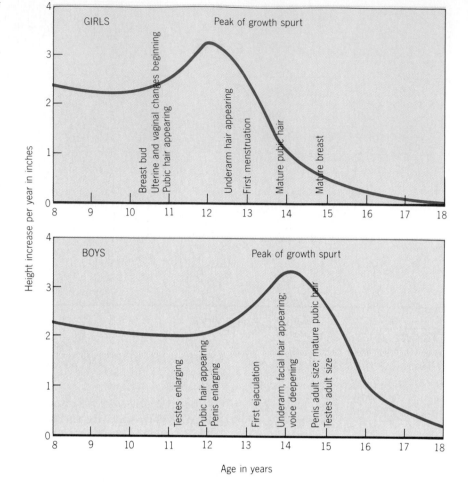

FIGURE 9-14 THE MAJOR PHYSICAL CHANGES DURING PUBERTY AND ADOLESCENCE. The curves show the rapid increase in height (the growth spurt) that occurs during this period (compare with Figure 9-12). Also shown are the average ages at which adult sexual characteristics appear. The order in which these changes occur is usually universal, but the ages at which they begin can vary widely among normal individuals. (From Fischer and Lazerson, 1984; after Tanner and Whitehouse, 1976, and Tanner, 1978.)

perhaps the most exciting change during puberty is **menarche**—the onset of menstruation. For boys, the first signs of puberty are the growth of penis and testes and the appearance of pubic hair. Soon afterwards, boys first ejaculate semen. Both boys and girls become fertile—able to reproduce sexually—by the end of puberty.

Many of the early signs of sexual maturation take place during a rapid increase in height, the adolescent's growth spurt (Tanner, 1978; see Figures 9-12 and 9-14). Not only do adolescents grow taller, but their muscle size and strength, especially boys', also increase. The growth of different parts of the body is not uniform during the growth spurt. For instance, hands and feet reach adult size before the rest of the body. Much to their embarrassment, young adolescents may feel that their bodies are gawky, awkward, and out of control.

Adolescents also may become self-conscious and concerned about the differences in the ages at which puberty begins for them. Although for boys the *average* peak of the growth spurt occurs at about 14 years of age, it occurs several years earlier or later in various individual boys. Likewise, the age at which sexual maturation begins differs by 4 to 6

FIGURE 9-15 DIFFERENT PEOPLE MATURE AT DIFFERENT AGES.
All of these boys are 13 years old, but some have begun their adolescent growth spurt and sexual maturation whereas others have not. These four girls also are all about the same age, but they, too, have begun to mature at different ages.

years in individual boys. As a result, one boy may still look like a child while his best friend has grown into a man (see Figure 9-15, top). These differences are perfectly normal, but they can lead to differences in athletic abilities and social acceptance that may distress the late-maturing boy (Clausen, 1975; Gross, 1984).

Girls generally have their peak growth spurt at about 12 years of age—2 years earlier than boys. For this reason, 12-year-old girls often are taller than boys their age. (However, eventually boys grow taller than girls on average.) Individual girls, too, reach sexual maturation at various ages (see Figure 9-15, bottom). For instance, although the *average* age of menarche among girls in the United States is 13 years, it is normal for girls to begin menstruating any time between the ages of 10 and 16. Because the beginning of menstruation often has symbolic, psychological significance for a girl, the age at which she begins menstruating can affect a girl's self-esteem. For instance, girls with very early or late onset of menarche may feel out of step with their peers (Greif and Ulman, 1982). In addition, how physically mature a girl looks can affect her prestige among her friends (Faust, 1960; Gross, 1984).

Puberty, a biological phenomenon, ends with sexual maturity—the ability to produce children. Adolescence, a social and cultural phenomenon, continues for some time longer, until the beginning of adulthood. Physical growth ceases, on average, at about 18 years of age in girls and 20 years of age in boys. However, development—physical change—does not stop until the end of life.

Adult Development and Aging

FIGURE 9-16   THE FACE CHANGES IN APPEARANCE DURING LATE MIDDLE AGE.
The tip of the nose becomes thicker, the eye openings appear smaller, and changes in bone structure reduce the length of the face.

THE BODY AND PHYSICAL PERFORMANCE   Most people reach their peak of physical strength and endurance between the ages of 20 and 30 (Hershey, 1974). By age 30, muscle strength, maximum output of the heart, and maximum breathing capacity have begun to decline. By the age of 40 or 45, body fat has begun to be redistributed, and most people put on weight—usually in the trunk area. As the comedian Bob Hope said, "Middle age is when your age begins to show around your middle." In addition, areas of skin that have been exposed to the environment become thinner and flatter (Selmanowitz, Rizer, and Orentreich, 1977). The face also begins to look different (see Figure 9-16). These physical changes of middle age can have important psychological consequences. For instance, many middle-aged women worry that they are losing what they have been taught to believe is their major asset—physical attractiveness—and their self-esteem may tumble (Sontag, 1977; Stevens-Long, 1984).

Physical changes progress into old age. Many elderly people actually become shorter, partly because they slump and partly because of a decrease in bone mass (see Figure 9-17). Muscle size and speed of contraction also decrease. Aging also takes its toll on internal body organs. The heart muscle becomes weaker, blood flow decreases, and breathing capacity continues to decline.

These bodily changes are paralleled by declines in physical performance with age (Stones and Kozma, 1985). Beginning at about age 30, a person's physical speed, strength, and endurance decline at an average rate of about 1.5 percent a year. For example, the handgrip strength of an average 70-year-old man or woman is only about 70 percent that of an average 30-year-old. People's day-to-day physical activity also slowly declines (at about 0.5 percent per year), and physical performance also tends to become slower as people age.

It is important to recognize that there is considerable individual variability in the extent to which physical changes occur during aging. Dimi-

FIGURE 9-17   PHYSICAL CHANGES PROGRESS INTO OLD AGE.
Many elderly people stoop because of muscle atrophy, decreased elasticity of the ligaments, shrinking and hardening of the tendons, and flattening of the discs in the spine.

trion Yordanidis was 98 years old when he completed a 26-mile marathon race in 7.5 hours (Stones and Kozma, 1985), and Hulda Crooks climbed 14,494-foot Mount Whitney at the age of 90 (see Figure 9-18). Different people age at different rates.

THE BRAIN   The brain also continues to change in the course of normal aging (Jones, 1983; Creasey and Rapoport, 1985). For instance, the size and weight of the brain decrease with age. These changes appear to be most marked after the age of 50, with an average decrease of 2 percent of brain volume every 10 years thereafter (Miller, Alston, and Corsellis, 1980). A major cause of the decrease in brain size is the loss of neurons, which disappear from various areas of the brain at different rates. For example, many cortical and subcortical areas show no loss of neurons with age, whereas other areas of the brain may lose 50 percent or more of their neurons by the time a person is 70 years old. Synaptic connections also decline with age, more severely in some areas of the brain than in others.

In view of these structural changes, it is not surprising that measures of brain function also change with aging. For instance, there are alterations in cortical electrical activity evoked by sensory stimulation and a slowing of the main frequencies in the brain waves of the elderly (Obrist, 1976). In addition, when sensory information is processed, the brain of an older adult uses energy more slowly than that of a young adult (Smith, 1984). Age also brings changes in the chemistry of the brain and a reduction in some neurotransmitters (McGeer and McGeer, 1981). These age-related changes in the brain undoubtedly contribute to deteriorations of sensory, motor, and cognitive function.

As with physical changes in the body, these age-related changes in the brain are averages—the actual amount of change varies considerably

FIGURE 9-18   MANY PEOPLE REMAIN PHYSICALLY ACTIVE INTO OLD AGE.
In 1986, 90-year-old Hulda Crooks begins her twenty-third climb up Mount Whitney, the tallest peak in the contiguous United States. Ms. Crooks took up mountain climbing at the age of 43 and made her first assault on Mount Whitney in 1962, at the age of 66.

from person to person. It also is important to distinguish between the normal aging process and the changes that occur with disease. For instance, conditions such as Alzheimer's disease and reduced blood flow to the brain produce much more severe brain atrophy and cognitive deficits than occur in the normal course of aging. Although the elderly are more susceptible to such diseases than are young adults, severe neural abnormalities and **senility**—severe intellectual impairment—are not necessary concomitants of aging.

COGNITIVE DEVELOPMENT

The newborn infant lies in her crib. She has a wide range of sensory capacities, although some still are not fully developed. She can move her head, eyes, arms, and legs, though not very well. As she lies there, she feels the warmth of her blanket. But how does she know that the blanket is separate from herself and not a part of her like her arms and legs? For that matter, how does she know that her arms and legs are part of her and not separate like her blanket? Where does self end and non-self begin? As she lies there thinking about this (can she think?) she becomes hungry. What can she do to bring food? How can she get her diaper cleaned?

These are but a few of the many problems the newborn infant faces upon entering the world. The task ahead is monumental—to learn about the world and to learn to manipulate it. **Cognitive development** refers to this process. It refers to the development of sensation and perception, of the ability to learn, to reason, and to solve problems. As you will see, cognitive development continues from birth through old age.

The World of the Newborn

As you saw in Chapter 5, newborn infants spend about 16 out of every 24 hours sleeping. The average newborn (and there are wide variations among individual infants) sleeps for 3 or 4 hours, wakes up hungry and eats, remains alert for less than a half hour, and then becomes drowsy and goes back to sleep. Thus, the average newborn is alert for only about 3 hours each day. Although babies may sleep for half the time during their first 2 to 3 years, their periods of sustained alertness rapidly lengthen over the first month or so. During these periods, babies gather information about the world and interact with it. How efficiently and effectively infants can do this information gathering and interacting depends on their sensory and motor abilities. These abilities form the foundation for later cognitive development.

SENSORY ABILITIES Newborn infants have all of the sensory capacities required to begin learning about their environment, but their sensory abilities generally are more rudimentary than those of adults. For instance, young infants can see objects and scan their eyes over them, and they can tell the differences among different shapes and patterns. But newborns see much less of the detail and color in objects than adults do. Furthermore, newborns cannot change the focus of their eyes very well. They focus best on objects between 8 and 20 inches away—about the distance of a mother's face when the infant nurses. Vision rapidly improves over the first six months to a year, although it may be several years until it is fully mature (development of vision was discussed in more detail in Chapter 3).

Infants also can hear at birth (Aslin, Pisoni, and Jusczyk, 1983). Psychologists study hearing in newborns by monitoring their heart rate, breathing, or sucking and charting whether these signs change when a sound is played. If the behavior does change, we can infer that the infant has heard the sound. Studies show that although newborn infants hear sounds, their threshold of hearing is higher than in adults. In other words, adults can hear fainter sounds than newborns. In addition, the newborn's ability to discriminate between sounds that differ in frequency or intensity is not as good as an adult's. Despite this, newborn infants can discriminate between the human voice and other sounds and can even detect differences in speech sounds. In addition, they can localize and turn their head toward the source of a sound. As with vision, an infant's

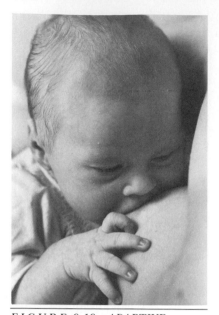

FIGURE 9-19 ADAPTIVE REFLEXES.
The rooting and sucking reflexes have clear adaptive value for newborn infants. When touched on the cheek, infants turn their head toward a nipple. When a nipple is placed in their mouth, they reflexively suck on it.

hearing improves rapidly over the first year, although it will be several years before it is fully mature.

Newborn infants have a well-developed sense of taste (Cowart, 1981; Steiner, 1977). They can discriminate among different tastes and prefer sweetness from the time of birth. This ability is adaptive, because human milk tastes sweet. Newborns also can smell, and they react differently to different odors (Steiner, 1977; Alberts, 1981). They grimace at unpleasant odors and smile and lick their lips at pleasant ones. The sense of touch is particularly well-developed in newborn infants. In fact, as we saw earlier, the fetus can react to touch only six weeks after conception. Researchers have used the infant's sensitivity to touch to learn about the development of its motor and sensorimotor behavior.

MOTOR ABILITIES   At birth, much of the infant's motor behavior consists of **reflexes**—automatic reactions to stimuli. Some of these reflexes are obviously adaptive for the infant. For example, in the *rooting reflex,* when an infant's cheek is lightly touched, he will turn his head toward the stimulus and open his mouth. When something is placed on an infant's lip or tongue, the *sucking reflex* is stimulated and the infant automatically sucks. Parents rely on their infant's rooting and sucking reflexes during feedings (see Figure 9-19). Other reflexes are not so obviously adaptive to humans and may harken back to our primate heritage. For instance, when an object is pressed against an infant's palm, the infant can grasp it tightly enough that he can be lifted off the ground (see Figure 9-20). This *grasping reflex* also is present in infant monkeys and helps them to hold onto their mothers' fur.

Reflexes represent some of the infant's first sensorimotor interactions with the world. As the infant's body and nervous system develop over the first year after birth, these reflex behaviors gradually disappear and are replaced by coordinated voluntary **actions** (Hay, 1984). The infant's

FIGURE 9-20 THE GRASPING REFLEX.
Infants reflexively grasp so tightly onto anything placed in their hands that they can support their own weight.

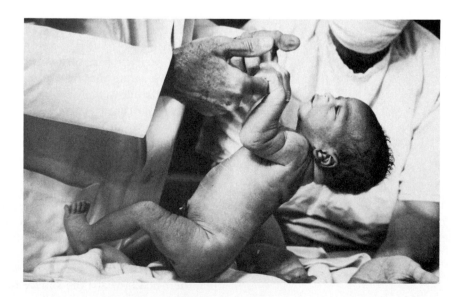

1 month — Chin up

2 months — Chest up

3 months — Reaches for object but usually misses

4 months — Sits with support

5 months — Grasps objects

6 months — Sits easily in high chair; grasps dangling objects

7 months — Sits alone

8 months — Gets self into sitting position

9 months — Stands holding furniture

9 months — Crawls on abdomen

10 months — Walks if both hands are held

10 months — Creeps on hands and knees

11 months — Stands alone

12 months — Walks when led by hand

13 months — Walks alone

18 months — Goes up and down stairs

FIGURE 9-21   THE SEQUENCE OF DEVELOPMENT OF VOLUNTARY CONTROL OF ACTIONS. The ages at which certain behaviors appear are averages; many normal children develop these behaviors several months earlier or later than the ages shown. However, the sequence of development is usually the same for all children. *(From Mussen, Conger, Kagen, and Huston, 1984.)*

voluntary control over his or her body generally follows the same cephalocaudal and proximodistal pattern that we described earlier for physical development. For instance, babies first gain control over the muscles of head and neck, then abdomen and arms, and, finally, legs. They can voluntarily control the movement of their arms before their hands and fingers (see Figure 9-21).

One true milestone in voluntary control that occurs at the end of the infant's first year is the development of walking (see Figure 9-21). At birth, the infant could not even lift his head up. By 2 months, he could lift up his head and chest. By 4 months, he could sit up. By 7 months, the baby could roll over and could sit alone. Between 9 and 13 months, the pace of physical development seemed to quicken. At 9 months, he could crawl around and could stand while supported. By 10 months, he could walk by holding onto something and "cruised" around by holding onto objects in his path. At 12 to 13 months, he is walking on his own.

Mastering this complex voluntary action called walking depends partly on genetically determined sequences of maturation of the body and nervous system. Cross-cultural studies show that children raised in different cultures, with widely different child-rearing practices, all learn to walk at about the same age. For instance, Hopi Indian children who spend much of their first year strapped to a cradle-board walk at about the same age as Hopi children who have never been tightly swaddled (Dennis and Dennis, 1940). Environmental stimulation also plays a role in motor development. The role of the environment is shown by a study of infants raised in a severely understaffed orphanage (Dennis, 1960). The infants spent most of their first year lying in their cribs, they had no toys, and they usually were fed from a bottle propped on the crib. The babies were rarely held by an attendant and were never placed in a sitting position. When they were between 2 and 3 years old, only 8 percent of these children could walk on their own. A follow-up study showed that only 15 hours of sensorimotor stimulation over a 1-month period greatly improved the motor abilities (including locomotion) of 7- to 8-month-old infants who had been raised in a similar setting (Sayegh and Dennis, 1965). Thus, the development of a sensorimotor ability as fundamental as walking is a product of the interplay between nature and nurture.

Early Development of Learning and Memory

LEARNING IN INFANTS Infants are able to learn—to modify their behavior or behavioral potential as a result of experience—right from birth. Newborn infants show habituation, a simple form of learning in which they stop responding to a repeated stimulus. In addition, newborn infants can learn through operant conditioning (in which making a particular response brings about either reward or punishment; see Chapter 6). For instance, newborn infants have been taught to turn their head in one direction to receive milk when they hear a bell (Papousek, 1967).

Although newborn infants can learn, they do not learn as readily as older children. For one thing, for a reward to reinforce their learning effectively, the reward must occur almost immediately—within 1 or 2

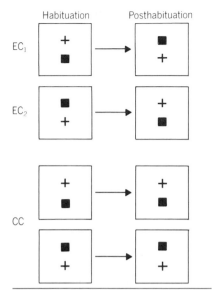

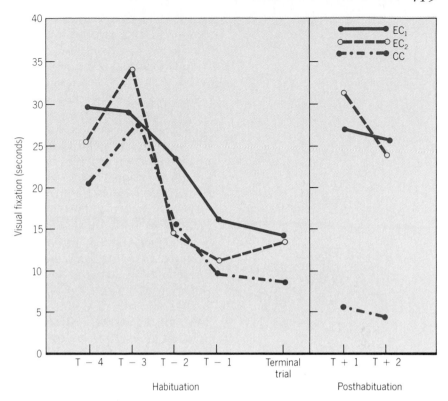

FIGURE 9-22   MEMORY IN INFANTS.

Two-day-old infants' responses to geometric forms indicate that they remember past events. The infants were shown the stimuli for 40-second periods separated by 5 to 10 seconds. During the habituation trials, both experimental (groups EC₁ and EC₂) and control (group CC) infants were shown a cross and a square. The left part of the graph shows the amount of time the infants spent looking at the stimuli during the last five 40-second trials. Initially, the infants spent most of the time looking at the forms. Then they habituated and spent less time looking—an indication that the infants remembered seeing the stimuli before. Then infants in the control group were shown the same stimuli, and habituation continued (right part of the graph). Infants in the experimental groups were shown a novel stimulus (the same forms with their relative positions reversed). These infants again spent most of the time looking at the stimuli. The inference is that the infants recognized that the novel stimulus was different from their memory of the standard stimulus and that the decrease in looking had not been due to fatigue. (From Antell and Caron, 1985.)

seconds of the infant's response (Millar, 1972), whereas older children can learn when there are longer delays between the response and the reward. In addition, newborn infants require many more learning trials than do older infants. For instance, to learn to turn their head to get milk after hearing a bell, newborn infants took an average of 177 trials spread out over 3 weeks, whereas 3-month-old infants learned the same response in an average of only 42 trials spread over a few days (Papousek, 1967). Thus, learning ability seems to improve rapidly over the first few months after birth.

DEVELOPMENT OF MEMORY   How well do newborn infants remember what they have learned? Do they remember seeing the mobile that hangs over the crib? Do they recognize their mother and father? The presence of memory in newborn infants can be tested with a simple habituation procedure. When infants are shown a new stimulus, such as a geometric form, they spend some time looking at it. But after being shown the stimulus repeatedly, the infant becomes habituated and spends less time looking at it (see Figure 9-22). The habituation suggests that newborn infants remember or, more specifically, *recognize* what they have seen.

However, the memory of infants is not as good as that of adults. The ability to recognize things and people seen before improves during early childhood. For instance, 2-year-old children are not as proficient as 4-year-olds at recognizing objects that they were shown earlier (Myers and Perlmutter, 1978), and 5-year-olds are not as proficient as adults (Nelson and Kosslyn, 1976).

Another way to measure memory is to test *recall*—the ability to remember material that is not present at the time retention is being tested. A 1-year-old demonstrates recall, for example, when her parent says "peekaboo" and the child puts her hands over her eyes. A child also might be asked to describe each of six pictures that he or she had been shown earlier to demonstrate recall. In both children and adults, recall memory is not as good as recognition memory. However, the difference in amount remembered between recall and recognition memory is greater for young children than for adults. The amount of information that can be recalled improves throughout childhood.

Why isn't the memory of young children as good as that of adults? What is the cause of the improvement with age? To answer those questions, remember that psychologists recognize three different stages of memory: encoding (or acquisition), storage, and retrieval (see Chapter 7). The *storage* stage is just what the name implies—the storage or retention of information to be remembered. *Encoding* is the process by which the information is put into a form that can be stored permanently, and *retrieval* is the process of getting the information back out of memory. Both the encoding and retrieval of information to be remembered can be enhanced when people use certain strategies. The main reason that memory improves with age seems to be that children learn to use these memory strategies as they grow older.

What are some of these strategies for encoding information in memory? Repeating or rehearsing material to be memorized, using mental imagery, and organizing information into categories or chunks (for example, organizing a long distance telephone number into several chunks: "1" for long distance access; the area code; the three digit exchange; and the final four digits). Young children generally do not use such encoding strategies when they are memorizing material, whereas older children do (Flavell, Beach, and Chinsky, 1966).

Strategies for retrieving information from memory generally involve the use of a cue. Some people cue their memories by tying a string around their finger to remember to call someone, or they try to remember someone's name by forming a mental image of their first meeting. With retrieval as with encoding strategies, children are not as proficient as adults (Ackerman, 1985).

As children grow older they also develop **metamemory**. That is, they come to understand the variables that affect their own memory performance and how their performance can be improved (Flavell, 1982). By 10 years of age, children know more about the workings of their memory system than they did when they were 5 or 6, and they are better at forming a goal to remember something and at planning strategies to attain the goal (Kreutzer, Leonard, and Flavell, 1975).

So far we have discussed the encoding and retrieval stages of memory. What about storage? Perhaps surprisingly, many studies suggest that actual storage capacity does not change very much with age (Werner and Perlmutter, 1979; Brainerd, 1985). For instance, if young infants are allowed to look at stimuli for long periods of time, their ability to later recognize the stimuli is as good as that of older children. Apparently, the young infants have only a limited ability to *encode* stimuli, but once the stimuli are encoded, their permanent memory storage is as good as that of older children.

Intellectual Development: Piaget's Theory

In addition to the question of how learning and memory develop, a central question in developmental psychology is how children acquire knowledge about the nature and workings of the world—how they think, reason, and solve problems. The most influential theory of intellectual development is that of Swiss biologist and psychologist Jean Piaget (1896–1980). Piaget's ideas have dominated the study of cognitive development for several decades. As you shall see, although some aspects of Piaget's theory have been challenged, modified, and expanded, the basic theory remains intact. It continues to guide many researchers, parents, and educators.

One of Piaget's basic ideas is that people acquire knowledge by *interacting* with the world. According to Piaget, an infant does not learn that a toy is different from a blanket by passively inspecting them. The infant learns that they are different by interacting with them—by grasping them, mouthing them, banging on them, as well as looking at them. Through these actions, the baby constructs **schemes** about the world. A scheme is a structured piece of knowledge, or concept, about a physical or mental interaction with the world. For an infant, a scheme may be all of the sensorimotor knowledge about a rattle. For an adult, a scheme may be all of the sensorimotor and mental knowledge about driving a car or adopting a particular social role.

Piaget (1936/1952) believed that two processes go on as schemes are constructed. These processes are **assimilation** and **accommodation**. Assimilation occurs when people incorporate a new object or event into an existing scheme. Accommodation occurs when people modify a scheme to include the new object or event. For example, suppose that an infant has an object scheme that involves all of her sensorimotor experience of grasping her blanket. When she is first presented with a ball, the baby tries to grasp it and assimilate the ball into the scheme of objects. But the ball feels different from a blanket, and her usual grasping movements do not work on the ball. Therefore, the baby accommodates her object scheme to include the sensorimotor experience of the ball. You can see that assimilation and accommodation are interactive; Piaget believed that both are involved in the acquisition of all new knowledge throughout life.

Piaget (1971, 1983) proposed that intellectual development progresses through a series of **developmental stages**. These stages have a number of important features: (1) Changes that occur from stage to stage are qualitative, not simply quantitative. According to Piaget, the whole way a child thinks during one stage of development is different from the way he or she thinks during another stage. Furthermore, the new thinking capacities apply to a wide range of activities. (2) The changes that occur from one stage to the next are relatively abrupt rather than gradual. (3) The order in which the stages occur is the same for all children. Different children may spend more or less time in a particular developmental stage, but all children progress through the same sequence.

Piaget believed that there are four stages of cognitive development. He referred to these as the sensorimotor, preoperational, concrete operational, and formal operational stages. Let's look at each of these stages and some of the ingenious observations that led Piaget to propose them.

SENSORIMOTOR STAGE (BIRTH TO 2 YEARS) Piaget (1936/1952) believed that young infants begin to learn about the world through their sensory and motor interactions with it. At first, newborn infants can carry out only simple reflex actions. Then they carry out simple voluntary actions, such as voluntary grasping and kicking. They often

FIGURE 9-23 DEVELOPMENT OF THE CONCEPT OF OBJECT PERMANENCE.
Six-month-old babies do not have a concept of object permanence. When the toy elephant is blocked from view, the baby seems to lose interest—as if the object has ceased to exist for him. Gradually, over the next few months, the baby will learn that objects continue to exist even when they are beyond the baby's direct sensorimotor range. Then a baby will push the paper aside to get at the hidden elephant.

engage in voluntary behaviors repetitiously. For instance, an infant may shake a rattle over and over, repeatedly experiencing the sensorimotor activity. Piaget called these **circular reactions**. Early in the sensorimotor period, these circular reactions seem to be produced for their own sake, simply for the sensorimotor experience. Later the infant seems to experiment, to vary the action in order to vary the result. For instance, Piaget noted that his 11-month-old son, Laurent, repeatedly dropped a piece of bread from different heights as if to see what the different effects would be (this game is more fun for the child than for the parent).

Piaget suggested that through these sensorimotor activities, infants learn that objects are separate from themselves. In addition, they learn the concept of **object permanence**—that objects continue to exist even when they are out of sight, hearing, or touch (see Figure 9-23). For infants less than about 6 months old, "out of sight, out of mind" literally seems to apply. However, by the end of the sensorimotor stage, infants will search for an object even if they did not see it being hidden. They would not search if they didn't know that the object still existed somewhere.

PREOPERATIONAL STAGE (2 TO 7 YEARS)   The infant's transition from the sensorimotor to the preoperational stage is marked by the ability to form mental representations of objects, people, and events. Now the young child shows that he can think about past and future events and can manipulate symbols, including words. These abilities show in pretend play and imitation of past events. For instance, the child who pretends that her doll is Mommy going off to work in the morning is manipulating a symbol of Mommy and thinking about the past. Children also begin to develop categories during the preoperational period. For example, they understand that the category "cars" includes many objects with a wide variety of characteristics, not just the blue object in the driveway.

Despite these advances, Piaget believed that the preoperational thinking of children is limited in several ways. For one, he believed that the child's preoperational thinking is **egocentric**. In other words, the child views everything only from his or her own perspective. This egocentrism was demonstrated by the clever "three mountains test" shown in Figure 9-24. Egocentrism also is demonstrated by the 4-year-old who assumes that everyone knows his friends and asks a complete stranger, "Do you like [my friend] Johnny?" Another limitation of preoperational thought is that it is not logical. The child cannot relate facts in the consistent and logical way that adults do.

CONCRETE OPERATIONAL STAGE (7 TO 11 YEARS)   According to Piaget, logical thought first appears in the concrete operational period, but even then the child can apply logic only to thought about concrete objects and situations (Inhelder and Piaget, 1959/1964). For Piaget, logical thought refers to **operations**—mental actions or representations that are reversible.

Perhaps the best example of a concrete operation that develops during this stage is **conservation**. Children who understand conservation re-

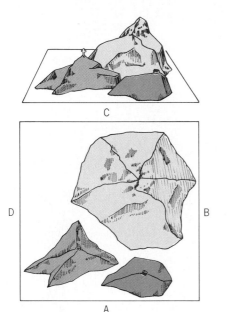

FIGURE 9-24   EGOCENTRISM IN CHILDREN.

This "three mountains test" was used by Piaget and Inhelder (1948/1967) to assess whether a child could take the point of view of another person. The child is shown a model of three mountains that differ in color and that have different objects at their peaks (a house, a cross, or snow). The child is allowed to look at the model from all four sides. Then the child is seated on one side of the model. The experimenter places a doll at another position around the table and asks the child to choose which of 10 photographs shows the scene as the doll would see it. Children in the preoperational stage of cognitive development choose the photograph that shows the scene from their own point of view rather than from the doll's. Piaget concluded that such children are egocentric and cannot think from the perspective of another individual. (From Piaget and Inhelder, 1948/1967.)

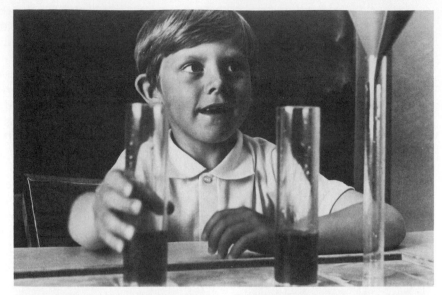

FIGURE 9-25   A TEST FOR CONSERVATION.
This well-known test was devised by Piaget. The child is shown two beakers that are filled to the same level with colored water. Then the water in one beaker is poured into a narrower beaker while the child watches. The child then is asked whether the short wide beaker and the tall narrow beaker both contain the same amount of water. A child in the preoperational period of cognitive development focuses on the height of the water and says that the tall narrow beaker has more. A child in the concrete operational period understands that there has been a reversible change in the appearance of the water and answers that both beakers contain the same amount of water. This child has demonstrated conservation.

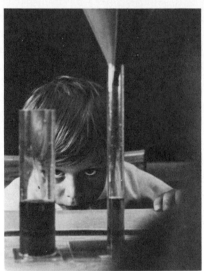

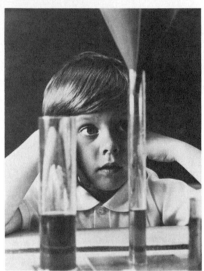

cognize that irrelevant changes in the external appearance of an object have no effect on the object's quantity (weight, length, volume, or the like). One test for conservation is illustrated in Figure 9-25. Parents often (perhaps unwittingly) use the child's lack of the conservation principle when doling out such goodies as soda.

Other concrete operations that develop during this period are transitivity and class inclusion. **Transitivity** refers to the ability to make logical inferences on the basis of separate relationships. For example, told that John is taller than Barbara and Barbara is taller than Frank, a concrete operational child will be able to infer that John is taller than Frank. **Class inclusion** refers to the ability to reason logically about the relationship between classes and subclasses. For instance, when shown eight orange candies and four green candies and asked whether there are more orange candies or more candies, a preoperational child will answer that there are more orange candies. A child in the concrete operational stage will know that there are more candies. This child understands that "candies" represents a class and "orange candies" is a smaller subclass.

FORMAL OPERATIONAL STAGE (11 YEARS AND OLDER) Fully adult thinking and logic appear in the stage of formal operations, which begins around the time of adolescence. Now the individual is able to carry out mental operations on abstract ideas and hypothetical statements as well as on concrete objects and situations. Now the individual can think abstractly.

The difference between concrete operational and formal operational individuals is illustrated by their understanding of situations such as the one shown in Figure 9-25. As we have said, a concrete operational child will know that both beakers contain the same amount of liquid. A formal operational adolescent or adult can go a step further. She can formulate the *abstract principle* that physical quantities stay the same even if they change in shape, and she can make *hypothetical inferences* about what will occur in situations that she has never actually observed.

Another aspect of intellectual thought by formal operational individuals is that they *systematically search for solutions* to problems. An example is shown in Figure 9-26. A child in the concrete operational period will haphazardly try various factors to determine which affects the speed of the pendulum's swing. Usually, the child gets the wrong answer or only a partial answer. In contrast, an adolescent or adult in the formal operational period will form hypotheses about which of the four possible factors is important and then will systematically test the hypotheses. Usually, he or she correctly discovers that only the length of the string affects the pendulum's speed once it has started moving. Note that although our examples have been of mechanical and scientific problems, formal operational reasoning can apply to any sphere of thought, including philosophy and politics.

Not everyone develops formal operational levels of thinking. For instance, in some non-Western cultures it has been very difficult to find evidence of the appearance of formal operations (Greenfield, 1976; Price-Williams, 1981). It is not clear whether this lack is due to differences in schooling, the structure of other languages, or to other cultural differences. Furthermore, even in the West, adolescents and adults of above average intelligence are more likely to achieve formal operational thought than are those of average intelligence. Formal operational thinking appears to represent a cognitive maturity that is fully attained only by some people (Dulit, 1972).

Challenges to Piaget's Theory

As with any theory that has had wide impact, Piaget's theory of cognitive development has been challenged from a number of fronts. One criticism that has been raised is that children do not seem to be completely consistent in their cognitive abilities. For instance, some researchers have noted that a child who fails a particular cognitive test in one

FIGURE 9-26 SYSTEMATIC SEARCH FOR SOLUTIONS.
This pendulum problem was used by Inhelder and Piaget (1955/1958) to test children for formal operational thought. The child is given a set of weights and a string that can be adjusted in length. The task is to determine what factors affect the speed of the pendulum's swing once it has been set in motion. Is it the length of the string, the amount of weight attached, the height from which the weight is released, or the force of the initial push?

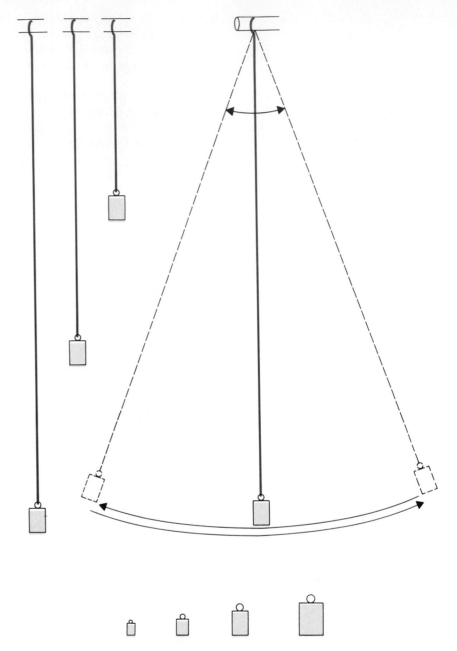

situation may pass the test if the situation is changed somewhat. For example, according to Piaget, children under about 7 years of age cannot take the perspective of another person on tasks such as the "three mountains test." But any parent who has seen his or her 3-year-old sympathize with an unhappy friend might argue that young children *can* take someone else's point of view. Recent laboratory studies, such as the one illustrated in Figure 9-27, also suggest that young children are not egocentric under certain conditions. When a situation is similar to a child's real-life experiences, is relatively simple, and is well understood

FIGURE 9-27 ANOTHER TEST FOR EGOCENTRISM.
This test shows that young children can take the point of view of another person in some situations. (a) Two walls are arranged in the form of a cross. As the child looks on, a policeman doll is placed at the end of one wall so that it can "see" only areas B and D (areas A and C are blocked from view by the wall). The child is then given a little boy doll and asked to hide it so that the policeman cannot see the doll. Nearly all children between 3½ and 5 years of age correctly hide the little boy doll in areas A or C. Once it is clear that the children understand this task, a more difficult one is introduced. Two policeman dolls are placed as shown in (b) and the child is asked to hide the little boy doll so that neither policeman can see it. Ninety percent of children between 3½ and 5 years of age correctly hide the little boy doll in area C. Note that children in this age range (Piaget's preoperational stage) routinely fail the "three mountains test" shown in Figure 9-24. But on this test they clearly can take the perspective of both policeman dolls into account (From Donaldson, 1978.)

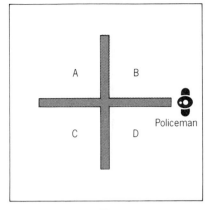
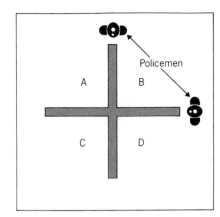

(a) (b)

by the child, he or she may show certain cognitive abilities that might not show up under different circumstances (Donaldson, 1978).

A related finding is that training or practice often can improve a child's performance on tests of cognitive ability. For instance, recall that Piaget believed that the concrete operation of transitivity appears only in children older than about 7 years of age. Given the premises that John is taller than Barbara and Barbara is taller than Frank, 4- or 5-year-old children generally cannot say whether John or Frank is taller. But is that because they do not have the logical abilities or because they cannot remember the premises? Studies have shown that if children are trained to memorize the premises, nearly all 4- and 5-year-olds make the correct inference that John is taller (Trabasso, 1975). Perhaps the training helps the young child encode and store the information so that it is better retrieved and applied to the solution of the transitivity task.

Observations such as these have raised questions about whether cognitive development is really "stagelike." In its purest form, a stage theory proposes that the child's mind acts consistently at any point in its development (Flavell, 1982). In other words, if cognitive abilities develop in stages, the abilities should be manifested in different situations relatively consistently. However, as you have just seen (and there are many other examples), children may show a degree of inconsistency in their cognitive abilities. They may show egocentrism or transitivity (or object permanence, conservation, and so forth) in one situation but not in another. What is more, they may show some characteristics of a stage of cognitive development but not others (Flavell, 1982; Fischer and Silvern, 1985). For instance, a child may show transitivity but not conservation, even though both abilities have been theorized to be present in the concrete operational stage of development. These findings have led some contemporary theorists to argue that cognitive development does not represent across-the-board changes in the *nature* of children's thinking, as suggested by Piaget. Rather, these theorists see cognitive development as a gradual process of learning, a progressive accumulation and organization of knowledge that is applied differently in different situations (for example, Chi and Rees, 1983; Carey, 1985).

In response to these challenges, Piagetian theorists argue that inconsistencies in children's cognition do not rule out the existence of stages of cognitive development. They recognize that the environment influences children and may produce inconsistencies in cognitive performance (Flavell, 1982; Case, 1985; Fischer and Silvern, 1985). For instance, they suggest that children's developmental stages place an upper limit on their cognitive abilities and that factors such as motivation, attention, simplicity of the situation, limitations of memory, and training all may influence how those abilities will be shown. In addition, they suggest that certain special human abilities, such as the ability to develop rules of grammar and speech, enjoy a special place in the cognitive scheme of things and therefore may not strictly follow stages of development followed by other abilities.

Although Piaget's theory has been challenged and modified, its basic tenets remain widely accepted. Most psychologists agree that cognitive development depends on maturation as well as on a child's interactions with the world. In addition, most psychologists agree with Piaget's basic descriptions of children's intellectual abilities (sensorimotor, preoperational, concrete operational, and formal operational) and the general sequence in which they develop. Whether all aspects of Piaget's theory ultimately prove to be correct can be determined only by further research. However, it already is clear that Piaget's insightful descriptions of children's behavior have had a profound influence on our understanding of intellectual development.

Changes in Cognitive Abilities During Aging

"You can't teach an old dog new tricks" and "He's getting old and his memory is failing him" are common sayings. But are these sayings true? Do learning and memory fail people as they get older? Although more work has been done on the changes in children's cognition than adults', researchers are beginning to understand better how adults progress and retrogress in learning, memory, and problem-solving abilities.

LEARNING   People are able to learn new information throughout their lives. However, there does seem to be a decline in learning skills as people get older (Botwinick, 1984). A sequential design study of verbal learning ability illustrated this tendency (Arenberg and Robertson-Tchabo, 1977). Men between 30 and 76 years of age were tested on their ability to learn lists of words (a serial-learning task) and word associations (a paired-associate task). There was little difference in performance among the men who were less than 60 years old. But men older than 60 made many more errors than the younger men. When the same subjects were retested 7 years later, those who had been in their 30s and 40s when first tested showed little change in learning performance. Men who had been in their 50s showed little change on some tests and moderate

BOX 9-2
STUDYING COGNITIVE ABILITIES DURING AGING

How would you go about studying whether learning (or problem solving, or social interactions, or any other behavior) changes as people get older? Perhaps you would study adults of different ages, say from 20 to 70 years old, and simply compare the abilities of each age-group. A **cross-sectional experimental design** like this has the advantage of allowing you to assess behavior over a wide range of ages relatively quickly and inexpensively. However, it also has problems. Perhaps the most serious is that it is difficult to be sure that any differences between age-groups are due to aging rather than to differences among groups of people who were born at different times and thus have different experiences (such groups are called **cohorts**). For instance, suppose that you find that 20-year-olds solve complex mechanical problems more readily than 70-year-olds. Is this result due to a decline in cognitive ability with age, or is it due to the fact that 20-year-olds are still in school or just recently out of

school and therefore are more used to solving complex problems and taking tests. Or is it because 70-year-olds were born and educated at a time (50 years earlier than the 20-year-olds) when society was less technologically advanced and there was little training with mechanical devices? Differences that are due to common experiences rather than to age itself are called **cohort effects**, and they can lead to errors in interpreting results of cross-sectional developmental studies. Another problem with cross-sectional studies is that they only allow you to make comparisons between groups of people and do not allow you to determine how individuals change with age.

Realizing these problems, perhaps you would take a group of young adults (say, 20 years old) and test their abilities every 10 years until they were very old. This method is referred to as a **longitudinal experimental design**. If you had the time, money, and patience (and if you lived long enough) to carry out such a study, you would have eliminated the problems of the cross-sectional design. But you would have introduced new problems. When you repeatedly test the same individuals, their scores may improve with practice. Such **practice effects** may cause you to underestimate declines in performance with age. In addition,

as subjects age, those in poor health will drop out of the study or die, and there is evidence that subjects who remain in longitudinal studies tend to be those who are most intelligent and perform best (Schaie, 1977). Therefore, by the end of your study you probably will be testing a select group of people with the highest scores and you again may underestimate the effects of aging. This problem is referred to as a **selective drop-out effect**.

These experimental designs—and many of their associated problems—apply to studies of infant and child development as well as to studies of aging. However, the problems are particularly troublesome in studies of aging because the time span of interest is so much longer than in studies of early development. What to do? The best solution is to use a **sequential experimental design**, which combines aspects of both cross-sectional and longitudinal designs. For instance, you might test problem-solving ability in five age groups (20, 30, 40, 50, and 60 years of age) and then retest the same subjects 10 years later (when they are 30 to 70 years old). Such a design provides many of the advantages of the cross-sectional and longitudinal designs and minimizes the problems of both.

---

declines on others. However, men who had been in their 60s or 70s when first tested consistently showed declines in learning ability when retested 7 years later.

Why does learning ability decline with age? One important factor is referred to as *pacing*. People become slower at processing information when they get older (Cerella, 1985). When older subjects are given more time to study material to be learned or more time to think about their response during testing, their performance improves (Canestrari, 1963).

Another factor that influences learning ability in the elderly is the *familiarity* or *meaningfulness* of the material to be learned. Laboratory studies of learning generally require that the subjects learn lists of nonsense syllables such as "tluk" and "grib." One investigator found that many elderly subjects considered such tasks to be so silly that they refused to try very hard to learn them and therefore tested very poorly. When the task was made more meaningful by asking the subjects to learn familiar words or names, the elderly adults readily learned them (Hulicka, 1967). Young adults also test better on learning more meaningful material, but the improvement usually is greater for the elderly.

Other factors also seem to contribute to the poorer performance of elderly subjects in studies of learning ability (Botwinick, 1984; Perlmutter and Hall, 1985). Older people may have a decreased ability to focus *attention* on the task and become distracted by irrelevant stimuli. They also may be more adversely affected by the *stress* inherent in many testing situations. In addition, the elderly seem to be more *cautious* about responding. If they are unsure of an answer, elderly subjects tend to say, "I don't know," or simply fail to respond. Young adults are more willing to guess when they are unsure and thus make many fewer such errors of omission. When the learning and testing situation minimizes these factors, elderly subjects test better on learning ability. However, even under apparently optimal conditions, their learning ability seems poorer than that of young adults.

MEMORY There is little doubt that the elderly often have more difficulty remembering things than do young adults. This is shown by both cross-sectional and longitudinal studies of memory. What is the source of this memory deficit? Is it due to a decline in encoding, permanent storage, or retrieval?

At least part of the deficit seems to occur at the encoding stage of memory (Craik and Byrd, 1982; Waugh and Barr, 1982). Older people do not use encoding strategies to the same extent as do young adults. For example, young adults tend to form mental images to help them memorize pairs of words. To memorize an association between "woman" and "banana," they might imagine a woman eating a banana. Elderly people generally do not form these mental images. However, when they are trained to use encoding techniques, elderly people's performance improves (see Figure 9-28).

But even when provided with encoding strategies, the elderly subjects do not perform as well as young adults (Figure 9-28). It is likely, therefore, that the memory deficit is not entirely at the encoding stage. Research suggests that elderly people also have a retrieval deficit, as is illustrated by differences in performance between tests of recognition and recall memory (Craik, 1977). On a test of recognition, subjects might be shown a list of words and then asked to state which of the original words appeared in a second list. The original words themselves serve as cues for memory. In a recall test, however, the subjects must remember previous items without external cues. Many studies have shown that although recognition ability shows some decline with age, recall ability declines much more. This finding suggests that older adults have trouble generating cues to retrieve information from storage.

Unlike encoding and retrieval stages of memory, storage itself appears to be relatively unaffected by the aging process (Walsh, 1983; Poon,

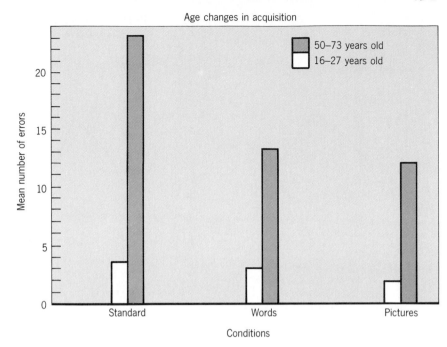

FIGURE 9-28   HELP WITH THE USE OF ENCODING TECHNIQUES IMPROVES THE MEMORY OF THE ELDERLY.

Young adult and elderly subjects were given lists of word pairs (such as loud-tie and red-heart) to memorize. During testing, the subject was shown the first word in each pair and had to remember the second. In the standard *condition, no help was given and elderly subjects made many more recall errors than did young adults. In the* words *condition, both groups were provided with a short phrase that included both words (for example, "a loud tie") to help encoding. The performance of the older subjects improved. In the* pictures *condition, both groups were shown a drawing that illustrated the word pair (for example, a picture of a red heart). This picture also improved the performance of the older subjects. Notice that help with encoding strategies produced very little improvement in the performance of young adults, perhaps because they already used such strategies. (From Canestrari, 1968.)*

1985). Of course, it is difficult for psychologists to be certain about this because any encoding or retrieval deficits make it difficult to assess exactly what is contained in long-term memory. However, because the elderly are nearly as good as young adults at remembering well-learned information when tested with simple recognition or when given cues to help retrieval, psychologists have inferred that memory storage is unaffected by aging. Furthermore, results such as those shown in Figure 9-29 indicate that older adults are as good as younger adults at remembering information that is contemporary *for them.*

We have noted that permanent memory storage in infants is as good as that of older children. Given that permanent storage also shows little or no decline in the elderly, it is logical to conclude that the permanent storage stage of memory is relatively constant throughout life. Developmental changes in memory do occur, but they seem to be primarily in the encoding and retrieval of information.

PROBLEM SOLVING   Not only do people of all ages learn and remember, they also solve problems in their daily lives. People engage in problem solving when they want to attain some goal but do not immediately know how to go about doing it.

To test the problem-solving abilities of people at various ages, researchers have resorted to games like the familiar "Twenty Questions." In this game, one player thinks of a person, place, or thing (the target), and the other player has 20 questions, which can be answered only by yes or no, with which to figure out the target. The player's task is to use as few questions as possible, and so the best strategy is to ask questions that eliminate as many alternatives as possible in a single stroke. For example, it is better to ask "Is it a person?" which eliminates many possibilities,

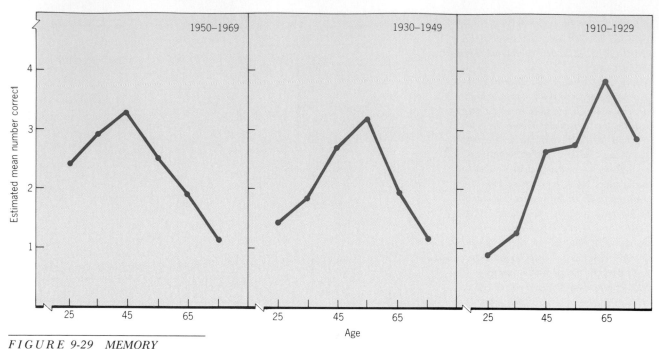

FIGURE 9-29   MEMORY
STORAGE IN THE ELDERLY.
*Long-term memory of past events is as
good for older adults as for young
adults when the information to be
remembered is appropriate to the age-
group. Storandt, Grant, and Gordon
(1978) gave subjects a questionnaire to
test their knowledge of people and events
in the world of entertainment. Young
adults knew more about recent people
and events (left panel) whereas older
adults knew more information that was
current when they were young (right
panel). Middle-aged adults knew more
about information from an intermediate
date (middle panel). Notice that the
long-term memory scores (number of
items correctly remembered) of people and
events* that occurred during their
youth *are about the same for each age-
group even though the period of time
over which the information had to be
remembered was longer for the older
subjects.*

than "Is it Jane?" which eliminates only one. Researchers have used tasks of this sort to study how concept formation and problem-solving ability change with age (Denney, 1985). They find that older people ask fewer questions that eliminate many possibilities at once and need to ask a larger total number of questions to solve the problem than do young adults (see Figure 9-30).

Other studies have shown similar deficits among the elderly on a variety of problem-solving tasks. For instance, the elderly perform more poorly than young adults on tests of concept formation, verbal reasoning, and Piagetian tests of formal operations (Rabbit, 1977; Denney, 1982; Reese and Rodeheaver, 1985). One reason for these deficits seems to be that older adults behave more rigidly than do young adults. For instance, once they have formed a hypothesis, the elderly do not seem to discard it in the face of new information as readily as young adults do. In addition, many older people repeatedly ask the same questions or fail to ask questions in a systematic way when trying to solve problems in laboratory tests (Botwinick, 1984). In part, these deficits may be results of decreases in memory. However, memory deficits cannot be the only reason for problem-solving deficits because they have been found even when older subjects are allowed to keep a record of previous answers (Brinley, Jovick, and McLaughlin, 1974; Arenberg, 1982).

Effects of Experience and Practice   Most of the problem-solving tasks studied in the laboratory do not involve the sorts of problems that people routinely must solve in their daily lives. It turns out that elderly people who have a great deal of experience or skill in solving particular kinds of problems may not show age-related declines in performance (Charness, 1985). For example, people who are highly experienced and skillful at

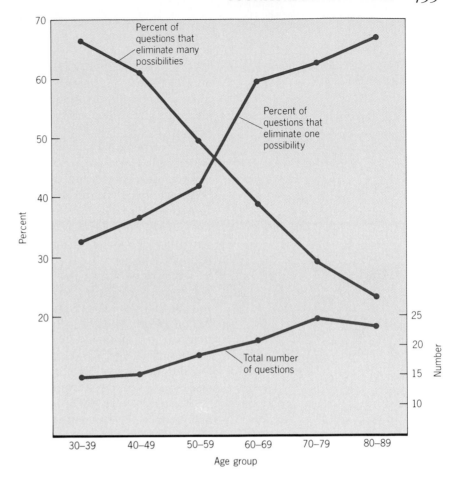

FIGURE 9-30 PROBLEM SOLVING IN THE ELDERLY.
Performance on many problem-solving tasks declines with old age. For instance, when playing the game "Twenty Questions," the number of broad questions that eliminate many possibilities declines with age while the number of narrow questions that eliminate only one possibility increases. As a result, the total number of questions required to solve the problem increases with age. (From Denney and Denney, 1982.)

the game of chess show little or no decline in chess-playing performance with age (Charness, 1981a, 1981b). But the same individuals showed the usual age-related declines in memory performance when given traditional laboratory memory tasks. Their store of experience and knowledge about solving chess problems compensated for any deficits they had in encoding and retrieving information about the problems.

Training and practice also have been shown to lead to marked improvements in problem-solving performance among the elderly (Giambra and Arenberg, 1980; Denney, 1982). For example, in a recent longitudinal study of the effects of training elderly people to solve problems of logical reasoning, the subjects, who were aged 64 to 95 years, got 5 hours of training (Schaie and Willis, 1986). The subjects previously had shown reliable declines in cognitive functioning over the previous 14 years. The training involved modeling, feedback, and practice in identifying the rules for solving the reasoning tests. When tested on new tasks that involved the same general rules, 60 percent of the subjects showed significant improvements in performance. Moreover, 45 percent of the subjects returned to the level of performance they had shown 14 years earlier, before any decline had set in. Results such as these indicate that for at least some of the elderly, declines in cognitive performance are due to disuse and can be partly or entirely reversed by appropriate training and practice.

WHAT IS THE OUTLOOK?   What, then, can psychologists conclude about changes in cognitive abilities during aging? Should people be gloomy or optimistic about their intellectual prospects in old age? The answers seem to depend on many different factors. The extent to which declines in cognitive ability affect actual performance depends on factors such as a person's familiarity and experience with the tasks at hand. Older adults have accumulated a lifetime of experience, knowledge, and wisdom that they bring to everyday tasks (Neimark, 1982), and this accumulation often offsets deficits that may occur in cognitive abilities. In addition, individuals who practice—who continue to use their cognitive abilities in their daily activities—generally show smaller declines in performance with age than individuals who do not exercise their abilities (Denney, 1982).

The quality of an older adult's physical health also may affect his or her cognitive abilities. *Severe* losses of learning, memory, or problem-solving ability are largely the result of reduced blood flow to the brain or of neurological disorders such as Alzheimer's disease. In fact, it may be that *time until death* is a better predictor of cognitive decline than actual chronological age (Riegel and Riegel, 1972). That is, the greatest cognitive decline in the elderly may occur within a few years of death, whether death occurs at age 70 or at age 90. Although some degree of cognitive decline does seem to be associated with normal aging, many people maintain excellent cognitive function well into old age (see Figure 9-31). The picture of inevitable senility that many people have of the elderly is a misconception. There is a wide degree of variation among older individuals in the decline in cognitive ability and performance that may occur.

FIGURE 9-31   MANY PEOPLE MAINTAIN EXCELLENT COGNITIVE FUNCTION INTO OLD AGE.
There is a long list of artists, scientists, legislators, business executives—and everyday people—who continue to process information and think clearly well past their 70s and 80s.

SOCIAL AND PERSONALITY DEVELOPMENT

In addition to the dramatic changes in intellectual and cognitive abilities that occur during the first few years of life, rapid changes take place in children's social interactions—in their relationships with parents, siblings, and peers. Furthermore, changes in social interactions continue into adulthood and old age. In this section, we follow the development of the individual's personality and social interactions.

Infancy

TEMPERAMENT Any parent who has had more than one child will tell you that no two infants are alike. Virtually from the moment of birth, infants seem to differ in **temperament**—the characteristic ways in which they respond to people and events. Thomas and Chess (1977, 1980) have carried out detailed longitudinal studies of children's temperamental qualities from the time of birth until early adolescence. They have found that infants tend to fall into three groups. *Easy infants* have regular patterns of eating and sleeping, react positively to new people or objects, adapt quickly to changes in the environment, and generally are cheerful. *Difficult infants* have irregular patterns of eating and sleeping, react negatively and tend to withdraw from new people and situations, adapt poorly to change, show intense expressions of mood, and generally are fussy. *Slow-to-warm-up infants* show negative responses to new situations but do adapt after repeated encounters, and both their positive and negative moods tend to be mild. Thomas and Chess (1977) found that about 40 percent of the infants in their sample had an easy temperament, about 10 percent were difficult, and about 15 percent were slow to warm up. The remaining 35 percent of the babies did not fall readily into one of these three categories.

As children grow up, some of their temperamental qualities persist, and some change substantially (Beckwith, 1979). For instance, in their longitudinal study, Thomas and Chess (1977, 1980) found that any individual child may show consistency over time in some traits, distortion in others, and complete change in still others. Both consistency and change are responses to influences in the child's environment and to parents' attempts to shape the child's behavior.

Just as the parents influence the child, the child influences the parents' behavior. As you might imagine, for example, parents often react very differently to difficult babies than to easy babies. Thus, a child's ultimate personality and social development are products of the interaction between his or her own temperamental qualities and responses and those of the parents.

ATTACHMENT The first social interaction between parent and child occurs immediately after birth. In recent years, a lot of attention has been given to the suggestion that the first few hours or days after birth are critical for the establishment of an emotional **bond** between infant

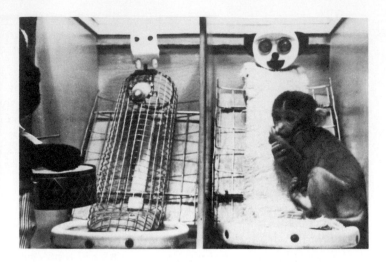

FIGURE 9-32 ATTACHMENT AND CONTACT COMFORT.

Infant monkeys raised with two surrogate mothers spent more time clinging to the warm, soft, terry cloth mother (which had no bottle for feeding) than a wire mother that provided food. They went to the wire mother only when they were hungry (left). In addition, when a frightening object was introduced (stuffed bear with a toy drum on the left), the infant monkeys ran to the cloth mother (right). Studies such as these indicate that contact comfort is more important than food in establishing an attachment between the infant monkey and the surrogate mother.

and mother (Klaus and Kennell, 1976). As a result, many hospitals now allow the mother and infant close contact right after birth rather than immediately removing the infant for bathing and tests. In addition, many hospitals have instituted practices such as "rooming in," in which the infant stays in the mother's room rather than in a nursery. Although these practices are emotionally satisfying for many parents, reviews of many studies of early contact and mother–infant bonding indicate that the presence or absence of early contact has no long-lasting effects on the formation of emotional attachments (Lamb, 1982; Goldberg, 1983; Myers, 1984). Similarly, father's attendance at the birth and extensive early contact with their infants have no long-lasting effects on the emotional relationships between fathers and infants (Palkovitz, 1985). Thus, adoptive parents and parents who are unavoidably separated from sick or premature infants immediately after birth needn't worry that they have missed out on a critical bonding opportunity. There are many different routes to strong parent–infant attachments.

Attachments form out of many repetitions of interactions between parents and infants. Many of the events that lead to strong parent–infant attachments take place during the first months and years after birth. In part, attachment forms because caregivers feed infants and satisfy their basic need for food. But classic studies with infant monkeys, carried out by Harry Harlow and his colleagues, indicate that there is much more to attachment than feeding (Harlow and Zimmermann, 1959; Harlow, 1971). Harlow raised infant monkeys with two surrogate mothers. One mother was made of hard wire mesh and had a bottle for feeding. The other was soft and warm but did not provide food. The infant monkeys became more attached to the warm, soft mother than to the mother that fed them (see Figure 9-32).

Harlow's experiments suggest that physical *contact comfort* is an important source of the attachment that forms between infant and parents. Another factor that influences the quality of attachment is a caregiver's responsiveness and sensitivity to an infant's signals—his or her smiles, vocalizations, and cries (Ainsworth, Blehar, Waters, and Wall, 1978). Parents who respond quickly and sensitively to the infant's needs foster a

FIGURE 9-33   ATTACHMENT TO FATHERS AND MOTHERS.
Fathers as well as mothers show sensitivity and affection when feeding and holding their babies, and infants may form attachments to both parents.

stronger, more secure attachment in the infant. Parents who are less responsive and affectionate tend to foster weaker, less secure attachments.

Most research on attachment has focused on the mother–infant relationship. But studies show that many fathers also are sensitive and nurturant with their infants and that deep attachments between fathers and infants also form (Parke and Tinsley, 1981; Lamb, Pleck, and Levine, 1985; see Figure 9-33).

FEAR OF STRANGERS AND SEPARATION   You may have had the experience of picking up a friend's 8-month-old infant only to have the infant burst into tears. Don't take it personally. Most infants show **stranger anxiety**—a fearful reaction to a stranger—between about 8 months and 1 year of age (Emde, Gaensbauer, and Harmon, 1976). A related phenomenon is **separation anxiety**, in which the infant becomes fearful and distressed when temporarily separated from the primary caregiver. For instance, when a 1-year-old infant sees his or her mother walk away or notices that she is gone, the infant may begin to cry. Separation anxiety is common among infants in many cultures, from the !Kung San of Africa to Guatemalan Indians. In all of these cultures, it begins at 6 to 8 months of age, peaks at about 15 months, and declines by 2 to 3 years (Kagan, Kearsley, and Zelazo, 1978).

These common anxieties are signs of attachment to parents. Indeed, the extent to which infants show stranger and separation anxiety has been used as a measure of the degree of parent–child attachment (Ainsworth et al., 1978). In addition, these anxieties seem to reflect cognitive developments in the child (Mussen, Conger, Kagen, and Huston, 1984). For instance, stranger anxiety may occur when infants acquire the ability to recognize that the face of an unfamiliar person is not the same as their memory of their parents' faces. Similarly, separation anxiety requires that infants be able to compare the memory of their parents' presence with the situation in which the parents are absent. These anxieties may disappear when infants develop the ability to anticipate future events, such as that mother will return.

Childhood through Adolescence

The period from the age of 2 or 3 through adolescence spans about 15 years, or only about 20 percent of a person's life. But during this period, enormous changes take place in the development of the person's social interactions and personality—changes that will affect the remaining 60 years or so of adult life. In this section, we discuss the changes associated with socialization, the development of a sense of morality, and the development of a sense of personal identity and self-concept.

SOCIALIZATION   **Socialization** is the process by which individuals acquire the attitudes, social skills, and behaviors that are expected by other members of their society. There are a number of influences on socialization, including parents, friends, and the media. Before discussing the nature of these influences, let's consider how they might operate.

The main theoretical approach to understanding how socialization takes place is **social-learning theory** (Bandura, 1977b). As the name implies, this theory suggests that socialization is learned as people inter-act with their environments. In part, socialization occurs through princi-ples of Pavlovian and operant conditioning (see Chapter 6). For instance, when a little girl shares her dolls with a friend, she may receive positive reinforcement for this social behavior by gaining a playmate or by receiving praise from her mother. In addition, socialization is thought to occur through observational learning. Children often attempt to imitate

FIGURE 9-34 OBSERVATIONAL LEARNING AND IMITATION.
According to social-learning theory, imitation is one way that children learn the values and behavior expected of members of their society. Children are more likely to imitate models who seem similar to them physically or psychologically, who appear to have status and power, and who are kind and loving (Bandura, 1969). Children also are more likely to imitate behavior if they see positive consequences for the model they are observing.

specific behaviors that they see other people—models—carry out (see Figure 9-34). Children also may observe other people's behavior and form general concepts that guide their own actions. For example, the little boy who notices that his mother does all of the family cooking and cleaning may learn that housekeeping tasks are reserved for women and may resist doing them himself.

What, then, are some of the environmental influences on socialization, and how do they affect people? *Parents* are the most important socializing influence during the childhood years. All parents have certain standards of what they want their children to be like. In attempting to impart these standards, parents use different strategies and techniques. Studies have shown that the techniques parents use can be important determinants of socialization. For instance, 5-year-old boys who have been physically punished for aggressive behavior tend to show *more* aggression at school than boys who have been less severely punished (Sears, Whiting, Nowlis, and Sears, 1953). One explanation for this result is that parents who use physical punishment serve as models for aggressive behavior.

Diane Baumrind (1973) has conducted a number of studies of parental child-rearing practices and how they affect the behavior of preschool children. She identified three main styles of rearing children. *Permissive* parents tend to be warm and nurturant toward their children but lax in disciplining and rewarding the children's behavior. These parents also make relatively few demands for mature intellectual, social, or emotional behavior. When they are 3 to 4 years old, the children of permissive parents tend to be more immature, less likely to explore, and less self-reliant than other children. Other studies suggest that as adolescents, children of permissive parents are the most likely to engage in drug abuse and other forms of socially unacceptable behavior, particularly if parents are permissive to the point of neglect (Conger, 1977).

A second parental style has been called *authoritarian*. These parents are less warm and affectionate toward their children than are permissive parents. In addition, they exert much more control over their children's behavior and tend to do so by resorting to their power. These parents simply dictate decisions and give their children little say or explanation. The young children of authoritarian parents tend to be more discontented, withdrawn, and distrustful than other children. They may follow the rules when their parents are around but disobey them when their parents are not there. When they reach adolescence, these children tend to be less mature in moral development and less able to think and act for themselves than are other adolescents (Elder, 1980). Perhaps these tendencies are results of not having been encouraged to take responsibility for their own actions while they were growing up.

Authoritative parents also exert firm control over their children. But they are loving, supportive, and involve their children in decisions. They are receptive to the children's feelings and opinions and explain the reasons for their decisions to get the children's compliance. The children of authoritative parents are the most likely to be competent and independent and to show self-control. In addition, they tend to be friendly and achievement oriented, characteristics that last during adolescence.

BOX 9-3
DIVORCE AND
SINGLE PARENTS

About 40 percent of all marriages in the United States end in divorce, and about 90 percent of the children of divorced families live with their mothers. In addition, about 3 percent of all children live with mothers who never married (United States Bureau of the Census, 1982). As a result of these trends, about 40 percent of children born in the 1970s will spend some part of their childhood living with a single parent (Clarke-Stewart, 1982), nearly always the mother. How do these family arrangements affect the socialization of the children?

For one thing, research shows that boys seem to be affected more adversely by the absence of a father than do girls. The boys tend to have some difficulty in achieving a masculine identification. For example, they are less interested in "masculine" toys and activities than are boys in two-parent homes (Huston, 1983). In addition, boys who live only with their mothers tend to be more anxious and aggressive and to show less self-control (Crouter, Belsky, and Spanier, 1984).

These effects are greatest if the father is absent during the child's preschool years. Although girls are less adversely affected by living only with their mother, their social development does show some effects. For instance, they are more likely to be sexually precocious and inappropriately assertive around males than are girls who live with both parents (Hetherington, 1972).

Much less is known about the effects on children of living only with their father. But studies do suggest that 6- to 11-year-old boys who live only with their fathers are better adjusted than those who live only with their mothers. They are less demanding and more mature, sociable, and independent. Conversely, girls who live only with their mothers are better adjusted than those who live with only their fathers (Santrock and Warshak, 1979; Warshak and Santrock, 1983).

Children who grow up in a single-parent family may continue to show effects as adults. For example, they are more likely to feel lonely and to have low self-esteem, less likely to report having a satisfying sex life, and more likely to have problems with their own marriages than people who

grew up in a two-parent family (Biller, 1976; Shaver and Rubenstein, 1980).

In view of the effects of living in a single-parent family, is it better for the parents to have stayed together "for the sake of the children"? Studies suggest that children fare better in a stable single-parent home than in a two-parent home that is full of conflict. Even the emotional upheaval that often occurs at the time of divorce has fewer long-term effects on the children than continuing family discord (Rutter, 1971; Emory, 1982). Furthermore, negative fallout from divorce and living in a single-parent family is not automatic. Many factors determine the outcome, including the age and temperament of the child, the custodial parent's child-rearing practices and style (warmth, authority, and so forth), the amount of contact the child continues to have with the non-custodial parent, the presence of other adult models such as step-parents, and the presence of conflict between the parents after the divorce (Biller, 1976; Crouter et al., 1984; Warshak and Santrock, 1983). Many children of single-parent families grow up to be happy, well-adjusted adults.

These children have been prepared to assume responsibility for their own lives. They seem to have internalized social rules, possibly because they feel they have had some say in setting and following rules as they were growing up (Lewis, 1981).

Peers (children of similar age) also are important in shaping a child's social behaviors (Hartup, 1983). By 5 to 6 years of age, children begin to display **conformity** to group norms. They tend to act in ways that are in accord with the behavior of others in their group. Clearly, the desire to conform to group norms can shape a child's social behaviors. Children also help to socialize each other through reinforcement and punishment. For instance, preschool children who are friendly and helpful tend to receive positive responses from their peers and are likely to act that way again.

As children enter adolescence and become more independent of their parents, peer groups take on even greater importance. Adolescent peer groups are a kind of training ground for adult relationships. They teach important social skills such as how to interact with others of one's own age and how to relate to a leader. The adolescent's understanding of many of these social skills may come more from peers than from parents.

Discord can occur when the values and behaviors that are reinforced by adolescents' peers differ from those of their parents. But the **generation gap**—yawning differences between parents' and peers' norms—has generally been exaggerated. Certainly there may be differences in taste between adolescents and adults—for instance, in clothes and music— and there may be disagreements about mundane domestic issues ("keep your room clean"). But ideas about the important moral and social modes of behavior usually are shared by adolescents' parents and peers (Coleman, 1980). There is little empirical support for the belief that juvenile delinquency occurs because adolescents throw over parents' standards in favor of peer values. Delinquent adolescents generally come from families in which the parents have been neglectful or themselves show antisocial behavior (Bachman, 1970; Ahlstrom and Havighurst, 1971). In general, parents and peers are part of a network of interrelated and concordant socializing influences.

A third influence on the socialization of children are the *media*, especially television. By the age of 18, the average child has spent 15,000 hours watching television (see Figure 9-35)! During these hours of TV watching, children may get a very distorted view of the world. For example, they see about three times as many males as females, and the male characters behave more competently and are more dominant than the female characters. Black and Hispanic characters usually are cast in situation comedies, and they are more likely than whites to be depicted as unemployed or to have low-prestige jobs (National Institutes of Mental Health, 1982). Children learn stereotypes about minorities from such shows, particularly if the children have had little real-life contact with the minority group portrayed (Greenberg, 1972).

FIGURE 9-35   THE INFLUENCE OF TELEVISION BEGINS EARLY.
At age 4, the average child spends more than 2 hours a day watching television. By age 12, about 4 hours a day is spent in front of the TV (Comstock, Chaffee, Katzman, McCombs, and Roberts, 1978).

Children who watch television also are exposed to a great deal of aggression and violence. Physical violence occurs an average of nearly five times a program during prime time evening shows and nearly six times a program during weekend daytime shows such as cartoons (Signorielli, Gross, and Morgan, 1982). Indeed, the National Coalition on Television Violence reported that in 1985 the average "war cartoon" depicted 41 acts of violence an hour! Many studies have shown that watching violent TV programs increases aggressive behavior among children, especially if the children are more aggressive than average to begin with. In addition, repeated exposure generally leads to increased aggression (Stein and Friedrich, 1975; National Institutes of Mental Health, 1982; Liebert, 1986). Whether or not watching TV violence increases aggression among adolescents and adults is a matter of some controversy, and no clear-cut answer is yet available (see Chapter 17). However, it seems clear that television contributes to the influence of parents and peers in socializing young children.

MORAL DEVELOPMENT   Moral development is closely related to socialization. How do people acquire moral standards and the ability to make moral judgments? Consider the two moral dilemmas that are posed in Table 9-2. Psychologists who study moral development are interested in how and why people arrive at their answers to dilemmas such as these, not in whether their answers correspond to an arbitrary standard of right or wrong.

T A B L E   9-2   MORAL DILEMMAS

DILEMMA 1:

A little boy who is called John is in his room. He is called to dinner. He goes into the dining room. But behind the door there was a chair, and on the chair there was a tray with fifteen cups on it. John couldn't have known that there was all this behind the door. He goes in, the door knocks against the tray, bang go the fifteen cups and they all get broken!

Once there was a little boy whose name was Henry. One day when his mother was out he tried to get some jam out of the cupboard. He climbed up onto a chair and stretched out his arm. But the jam was too high up and he couldn't reach it and have any. But while he was trying to get it, he knocked over a cup. The cup fell down and broke.

Was one boy naughtier than the other? Would you punish them the same?

DILEMMA 2:

In Europe, a woman was near death from cancer. One drug might save her, a form of radium that a druggist in the same town had recently discovered. The druggist was charging $2000, ten times what the drug cost him to make. The sick woman's husband, Heinz, went to everyone he knew to borrow the money, but he could only get together about half of what it cost. He told the druggist that his wife was dying and asked him to sell it cheaper or let him pay later. But the druggist said, "No." The husband got desperate and broke into the man's store to steal the drug for his wife. Should the husband have done that? Why?

Source: Dilemma 1 is from Piaget, 1932/1965. Dilemma 2 is from Kohlberg, 1969.

Note: These are two well-known moral dilemmas used to study moral development. How would you respond?

The most influential theory of how moral judgment develops was proposed by Lawrence Kohlberg (1969, 1976), whose work grew out of that of Piaget. On the basis of how individuals of different ages respond to dilemmas such as those in Table 9-2, Kohlberg proposed that people progress through a series of stages in the development of moral reasoning. At first, children make moral judgments strictly on the basis of direct physical consequences. Thus a young child might answer that John was naughtier than Henry because he broke more cups than Henry did. Only when they are older do children take into account the intention behind a behavior. An older child might say that Henry was naughtier because he should not have gone into the cupboard for jam when his mother was out, whereas John broke the cups by accident while he was obediently coming to dinner. To children at this stage of moral reasoning, following the rules and having good motives are the most important considerations.

Still later, people make moral judgments on the basis of principles that they consider to be intrinsically correct rather than simply because society has made particular rules or laws. Before reaching this stage, a person might answer dilemma 2 in Table 9-2 by saying that Heinz should not have stolen the drug because it was against the law. But a person in the most advanced stage of moral development might say that the principle of saving his wife's life supersedes Heinz's obligation to obey society's law against stealing. Martin Luther King, Jr., and his followers were making moral judgments at this level when they conducted illegal sit-ins in an effort to correct unjust racial laws.

In all, Kohlberg proposed that there are six stages of moral development, as shown in Table 9-3. Both cross-sectional and longitudinal studies indicate that people do progress sequentially through these stages (Colby, Kohlberg, Gibbs, and Lieberman, 1983; Rest, Davison, and Robbins, 1978). In fact, a similar overall sequence of moral development has been found among people in many cultures around the world (Edwards, 1982; Snarey, 1985). But not all people pass through all stages at the same ages. How quickly and how far people progress in moral development depend on a number of factors, including their degree of cognitive development. For instance, going through high school and college helps people to develop principled moral judgment (Rest et al., 1978). In addition, studies suggest that formal operational thinking is necessary (though not sufficient) for the development of more advanced moral judgment (Walker, 1986). In the United States, where the level of education is generally high, most 10-year-olds make moral judgments on the basis of stage 1, and to a lesser extent, on stage 2 and 3 reasoning. Only in early adolescence (12 to 14 years old) do significant numbers of people use stage 3 or 4 reasoning. Stages 5 and 6 rarely develop until late adolescence or early adulthood. In fact, some people never make moral judgments on the basis of stage 5 or 6 reasoning.

Does moral *judgment* predict moral *behavior*? Many studies have found that there is a significant relationship between the two. But the relationship is often weak, and sometimes absent (Blasi, 1980). For instance, many students cheat in school even though they are quite capable of judging cheating to be wrong. Clearly, many factors in addition to an ability to make moral judgments influence social behavior.

TABLE 9-3 KOHLBERG'S STAGES OF MORAL DEVELOPMENT

Level and Stage	What Is Considered to Be Right
Level I: Preconventional	
Stage 1: Obedience and punishment orientation	To avoid breaking rules backed by punishment, obedience for its own sake, avoiding physical damage to persons and property
Stage 2: Instrumental purpose and exchange	Following rules only when it is to someone's immediate personal interest; acting to meet one's own interests and letting others do the same; right is an equal exchange, a good deal
Level II: Conventional	
Stage 3: Interpersonal accord and conformity	Living up to what is expected by people close to you or what people generally expect of people in your role; being good is important
Stage 4: Social accord and system maintenance	Fulfilling the actual duties to which you have agreed; laws are always to be upheld except in extreme cases where they conflict with other fixed social duties; right is also contributing to society, the group, or institution
Level III: Postconventional, or Principled	
Stage 5: Social contract, utility, individual rights	Being aware that people hold a variety of values and opinions, that most values and rules are relative to your group but should usually be upheld because they are the social contract; some nonrelative values and rights like life and liberty, however, must be upheld in any society regardless of the majority opinion
Stage 6: Universal ethical principles	Following self-chosen ethical principles; particular laws or social agreements are usually valid because they rest on such principles; when laws violate these principles, one acts in accordance with the principle; principles are universal principles of justice: the equality of human rights and respect for the dignity of human beings as individual persons; the reason for doing right is the belief, as a rational person, in the validity of universal moral principles and a sense of personal commitment to them

Source: Snarey, 1985; after Kohlberg, 1981.
Note: Kohlberg's six stages of the development of moral judgment. These stages are divided into three levels, termed *Preconventional, Conventional,* and *Postconventional* (or *Principled*).

FIGURE 9-36   THE
BEGINNINGS OF A SELF-CONCEPT.
As early as 9 months of age, infants look
at themselves and smile in a mirror.
However, they do not seem to distinguish
that the image is self *as opposed to any*
particular infant. For instance, if the
infant's face is marked with tape or red
paint, she shows no recognition that the
marked face she sees in the mirror is
her own. By around 15 months of age,
children do begin to show evidence of
self-recognition. Now if her nose is
marked with red paint, the child may
touch her nose rather than the nose in
the mirror. By 18 to 20 months, nearly
all children touch their own (painted)
noses.

SELF-CONCEPT AND IDENTITY   A third major change in social and personality development during childhood is the emergence of a self-concept and a sense of identity. A **self-concept** is an understanding that one is a separate and independent person. The beginnings of a self-concept actually occur within the first year or two of life (see Figure 9-36). By 18 to 20 months of age, nearly all infants have developed at least a rudimentary concept of self. They show self-conscious behavior in front of a mirror and can recognize themselves in a picture or videotape (Brooks-Gunn and Lewis, 1984).

Initially, a child's self-concept is expressed primarily in concrete physical terms. Before age 7, children describe themselves by listing their physical attributes (such as hair color and height), age, favorite possessions, and activities. Gradually, after that age, the concept of self evolves into a more psychological characterization (Damon and Hart, 1982; Harter, 1983). By the time children are in their mid-teens, they more often describe themselves in terms of their inner thoughts, emotions, and attitudes than in terms of physical attributes. They also conceptualize themselves more in terms of interpersonal feelings and relationships and think of themselves in more abstract terms than do young children (Rosenberg, 1986; see Chapter 16). These changes in self-concept can be attributed to advances in cognitive development—to a shift from concrete to abstract modes of thought and to the developing ability to see the world, including the self, from the point of view of others (Rosenberg, 1986).

Adolescence marks a period of intense self-searching. The adolescent's task is no longer simply to be self-aware. Adolescents must begin to make choices about the kind of people they want to be and what their roles will be in society. They must achieve a sense of individual **identity**. In doing so, some consciously try out different forms of hairstyle, dress, and other external characteristics as well as social roles. They may go through a prolonged "identity crisis." Others seem to make the transition to an adult identity fairly smoothly (see Figure 9-37).

Erik Erikson's (1963, 1968) **theory of psychosocial development** has been particularly influential in stimulating thinking and research on how adolescents form an identity. Erikson proposed that there are eight stages of psychosocial development from birth to old age. Each stage is characterized by the need to resolve a *developmental crisis* that arises as the individual encounters the social environment (see Table 9-4). A pivotal stage occurs during the period of adolescence, when the young person must resolve the crisis of *identity versus role confusion*. During this stage, the adolescent rethinks and integrates the issues of all earlier developmental crises and forms an identity that will influence further development.

According to Erikson, the danger at this stage is role confusion, in which the individual is uncertain about his or her identity. In extreme cases, adolescents fail to resolve the identity crisis. They cannot "find" themselves and never form a firm sense of identity. Erikson (1968) referred to this state as **identity confusion**. He believed that identity confusion leads to delinquency—that it leads the individual to drop out of school, quit jobs, and perhaps suffer emotional problems.

FIGURE 9-37 IDENTITY FORMATION.
In an effort to find a personal identity, many adolescents actively experiment with different appearances and roles. Others undergo less "storm and stress" in the process of identity formation. Both kinds of adolescents may succeed in their quest and go on to a happy, productive adulthood.

TABLE 9-4 ERIKSON'S STAGES OF PSYCHOSOCIAL DEVELOPMENT

BASIC TRUST vs. MISTRUST (birth to 1 year): Infants learn that they can trust others to care for them and respond to their needs. If the infant's needs are not met consistently, he or she will mistrust the world.

AUTONOMY vs. SHAME AND DOUBT (1 to 3 years): Children develop a sense of self-control and freedom of self-expression—they establish themselves as autonomous individuals. Erikson believes that if the parent punishes attempts at autonomy, the child will develop shame (a feeling of being exposed, or self-conscious) and self-doubt.

INITIATIVE vs. GUILT (3 to 6 years): After they attain a sense of autonomy, children begin to take the initiative and plan their own activities. The initiative includes an active curiosity about sex and the child begins to identify with the same-sex parent. If the child's initiatives are punished, he or she may develop a sense of guilt over contemplating goals or initiating acts.

INDUSTRY vs. INFERIORITY (6 to 12 years): Children enter school and begin to acquire skills (industry) used by adults in society. The child must find an area of competence or mastery. Otherwise, he or she will develop a sense of inadequacy or inferiority.

IDENTITY vs. ROLE CONFUSION (12 to 18 years): During adolescence, young people reassess their solutions to all of the earlier crises in order to form a sense of identity—who they are and where they fit in society. The danger is role confusion, an uncertainty about sexual identity, potential occupation, and future role in society.

INTIMACY vs. ISOLATION (young adulthood): Once a sense of identity has been established, the individual is ready to form intimate relationships with others. Erikson believes that the most important of these is a trusting, sexual love relationship. The alternative to intimacy is a deep sense of isolation and consequent self-absorption.

GENERATIVITY vs. STAGNATION (middle adulthood): Now the adult's primary concern is to establish and guide the next generation (generativity). This is achieved primarily through having and caring for children, though it can include being productive and creative in other activities. Those who are not generative have a pervading sense of stagnation and personal impoverishment.

EGO INTEGRITY vs. DESPAIR (old age): In the final stage, people develop ego integrity—a sense that there is meaning to life, whatever its triumphs and disappointments. The individual comes to accept his or her life as something that had to be. The alternative is despair that time is too short to start another life or to try other roads to integrity. This person fears death.

Source: Erikson, 1963.
Note: Erikson's eight stages of psychosocial development, from infancy to old age. Erikson proposed that during each stage, the individual must successfully pass certain turning points, or developmental crises, to continue a normal pattern of development. Each crisis is described in terms of an alternative between two basic attitudes or values.

Sex Roles and Identity   In their search for personal identity, adolescents must adopt a sex-role identity. **Sex roles** are the personality characteristics and behavior that one's culture defines as appropriate for males and females. A **sex-role identity** is a person's inner belief that his or her interests and behavior conform to those norms.

Children begin to show differences in sex roles before the age of 2. For instance, by 20 months of age, boys and girls choose toys and

FIGURE 9-38 EARLY DEVELOPMENT OF SEX ROLES. Results of a longitudinal investigation in which the researchers studied the play of young children in a day-care center. Boys and girls were given free choice of traditionally masculine toys (a set of tools, a train, and a truck), feminine toys (a soft female doll and blanket, a tea set, and a play house), and neutral toys (a set of stacking rings, a toy hourglass, and a chiming toy). Until about 18 months of age, there was little difference in the percentage of time that boys and girls spent playing with masculine toys (top graph) or with feminine toys (bottom graph). But by 20 months of age, clear differences had appeared, and these differences persisted throughout the length of the study. (From O'Brien and Huston, 1985.)

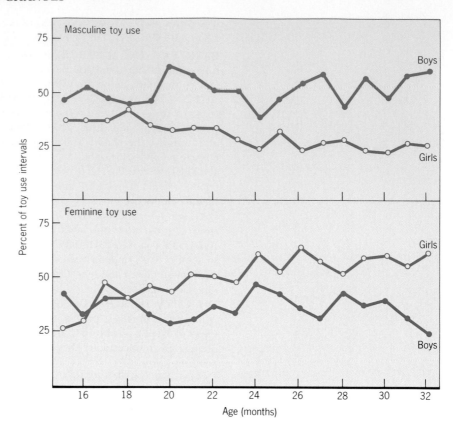

activities that fit the sex stereotypes of their culture (see Figure 9-38). Between ages 2 and 3, children learn to categorize themselves and others correctly as males and females, and by the time they are 4 or 5 years old, children know most of the sex stereotypes for adult occupations and social roles (Huston, 1983).

How do young children develop sex roles and sex-role identity? Social-learning theorists argue that these qualities are learned the same way as other socialization: boys and girls learn different behaviors through reinforcement and punishment and by observing and imitating others (Mischel, 1970). They maintain that parents, teachers, peers, and the media all contribute to this social learning of sex roles. For instance, research shows that most parents have different expectations for their daughters and sons and react more favorably when the children engage in "sex-appropriate" behavior than when they do not (Fagot, 1978). It is interesting to note that parents often are unaware that they treat boys and girls differently.

By early adolescence, most children have a firm concept of their sex-role identity. In the United States, the traditional male sex role involves acting independent, unemotional, logical, and competitive. The traditional female sex role involves acting tactful, gentle, emotionally expressive, and sensitive to the feelings of others (Broverman, Vogel, Broverman, Clarkson, and Rosenkrantz, 1972). But social and economic changes have produced changes in sex-role expectations in recent years, and it has become more acceptable for both males and females to behave in ways traditionally reserved for members of the other sex. The combination in the same person of certain traditional male *and* female sex-role characteristics and behavior is referred to as **androgyny** (Bem, 1974; Spence, Helmreich, and Stapp, 1975). For example, an androgynous man might be emotionally expressive, sensitive to others' feelings, independent, and logical. An androgynous woman might be tactful, gentle, competitive, and independent. As androgynous behavior becomes more widely acceptable by society, men and women may be able to embrace both the masculine and feminine within themselves while remaining comfortable with their sex-role identity. In addition, artificial sex-based constraints on behavior and choices of occupation may be eliminated (Bem, 1984).

Adulthood and Old Age

Where does adolescence—and its developmental tasks—end and adulthood begin? There really is no clear point of demarcation between these two stages of life, and many of the psychological issues of late adolescence continue in early adulthood.

INTIMATE RELATIONSHIPS AND MARRIAGE As people enter early adulthood, one of their major tasks is to form intimate relationships. Erikson theorized that young adults face the developmental crisis of *intimacy versus isolation* (Table 9-4). The adolescent who emerges from the search for identity is prepared to enter committed, close relationships with others, even though this may call for sacrifice and compromise. Those who fail to develop intimate relationships, Erikson maintains, face social and emotional isolation.

For most people, the central intimate relationship is a heterosexual, loving relationship that leads to marriage. About 95 percent of Americans get married, many in their early 20s. Married partners must learn to live well together, to coordinate their activities, carry out their duties—provide food, shelter, and clothing; shop, cook, and clean; give love and affection, and so on—and respect each other's rights. In most marriages, the husband takes the dominant role, and the wife acts as a complement to him (Scanzoni and Scanzoni, 1976). Less frequently the wife is dominant or husband and wife are equal partners. Because the adjustments that marriage requires can be difficult and stressful, many marriages eventually dissolve.

Nevertheless, marriage can be extremely satisfying. Two important characteristics of happily married couples are their affection and commitment to each other (Skolnick, 1981). Happily married couples have conflicts, but they are not deeply divisive. In contrast, unsatisfactory marriages are marked either by the avoidance of conflict or by conflicts that result in serious hostility and tension. Personality factors also contribute to the satisfaction and stability in people's marriages. For instance, husbands and wives who are similar in personality tend to be most satisfied with their marriages. High socioeconomic status and, especially for husbands, occupational status also correlate with satisfying

TABLE 9-5   CHARACTERISTICS OF HAPPY AND
UNHAPPY MARRIAGES

Happy Marriages	
Most Characteristic	*Least Characteristic*
1. Person likes spouse 2. Person admires and respects spouse 3. Person and spouse enjoy each other's company 4. Person would marry spouse again 5. Marriage has improved over time	1. Marriage is utilitarian living arrangement (as opposed to a close personal relationship) 2. Person has seriously considered leaving spouse 3. Serious conflicts and disagreements between the spouses 4. Person and spouse have discordant personality traits 5. Sexual adjustment is or has been a source of tension

Unhappy Marriages	
Most Characteristic	*Least Characteristic*
1. Person is critical of spouse 2. Serious conflicts and disagreements between the spouses 3. Spouses have discordant personalities 4. Person tries to avoid conflict with the spouse 5. Marriage is a utilitarian living arrangement (rather than a close personal relationship)	1. Marital relationship has improved over time 2. Person sees spouse very much like self in temperament 3. Spouses basically agree on child-rearing 4. Person is pleased with spouse's performance on daily tasks 5. Person feels loved by spouse

Source: Skolnick, 1981.
Note: Qualities that are most and least characteristic of satisfactory and unsatisfactory marriages. The results are based on responses to detailed questionnaires and interviews in a 20-year longitudinal study of 232 individuals.

marriages. Clearly, many factors contribute to the quality of any marriage (see Table 9-5).

PARENTHOOD   Most married couples eventually have children, and children introduce new stresses into a marriage (LeMasters, 1957; Miller and Sollie, 1980). There are more decisions to be made, new physical, emotional, and social demands to be met, and added economic burdens. Nevertheless, parenthood can be extremely satisfying, and it provides an opportunity for individual growth. Indeed, Erikson suggested that parenthood helps to resolve the major developmental crisis of middle adulthood—the crisis of *generativity versus stagnation.* Nurturing children can increase an adult's sense of helping to form and guide the next generation.

When the last child has grown up and left home, the parents are left with an **empty nest.** Popular belief has it that the empty nest produces stress, especially for mothers whose lives have revolved around home and children. But studies indicate that when the nest empties, parents' life satisfaction actually increases (Neugarten, 1970; Glenn, 1975). Parents then have fewer chores and responsibilities. A previously homebound mother has time and energy to devote to outside interests—community activities, her own education, or work. At the same time, parents' disposable income increases. The husband and wife also have more privacy and time together. Perhaps for all these reasons, wives' happiness with their marriages increases after the children leave home (Glenn, 1975). Nearly all mothers view the empty nest with a sense of relief (Rubin, 1979).

OCCUPATIONS Young adults not only must meet their needs for intimacy, they also must choose a line of work that will satisfy them both financially and personally. A variety of factors influence the choice of an occupation, including a person's sex, social class, and luck. For example, a person's social class affects the range of choices of occupations he or she is likely to have and also the amount of money available for education and job training. Although sex differences in occupations have decreased in recent years, many jobs—from fire fighter to top-level corporate executive—still are rarely held by women. This disparity is due partly to job discrimination by those who make hiring and promotion decisions. In addition, it is due partly to choices made by women themselves, who often have been socialized to select particular careers.

Retirement from work marks a major life transition for older adults. Some people view retirement as a negative change, others view it very positively. The most important factors in determining whether people adjust well to retirement are their health and income (Kimmel, Price, and Walker, 1978; McConnell, 1983). People who can maintain an adequate income and who remain healthy tend to find retirement to be pleasant. In addition, people who retire voluntarily at the expected age are more satisfied than those who retire involuntarily five or more years before they expected to. When people can plan ahead for retirement, they adjust more easily. All in all, most people adjust well to retirement and find it to be a satisfying experience.

SUMMARY

DETERMINANTS OF DEVELOPMENT

1. *Genetic Determinants of Development.* Each person is a product of both genetic inheritance and environment. Genetic information is carried by chromosomes, which are made up of genes—the units of hereditary information. Genetically influenced traits are specified by pairs of genes, one from each parent. Most traits depend on the combined effects of many such pairs of genes. All genes for a particular trait are the genotype for that trait. But not all genes are outwardly expressed. For instance, recessive genes are not expressed if they are paired with dominant genes that specify a different trait. The traits that are expressed are the phenotype.

2. *Behavior Genetics.* The study of genetic bases of behavior is called behavior genetics. Animal studies, using inbred strains or selective breeding, have revealed genetically produced differences in learning ability, aggressiveness, sexual behavior, alcohol preference, and a variety of other behaviors. Studies of human behavior genetics, based on studies of twins or adopted children, also have provided evidence for genetic influences on a wide variety of behaviors, including visual

perception, cognitive abilities, speech and language disorders, personality and temperament, and psychopathology.

3. *Environmental Determinants of Development.* The environment can influence development via biological effects before and after birth, learning experiences, the immediate social environment, and the broad social and cultural environment in which individuals live. Effects of the environment and heredity interact in complex ways. As a result, a particular genotype may produce a wide range of phenotypes, depending on environmental conditions. Conversely, different genotypes can produce the same phenotype.

PHYSICAL DEVELOPMENT

4. *Early Physical Development.* The 38 weeks of prenatal development take place within the mother's body. During this time, the organism grows from a single cell to a fully developed newborn baby. Growth of the body continues at a rapid pace during the first 2 years after birth. The brain also develops rapidly; it is 25 percent of adult size at birth and 75 percent of adult size by age 2. Physical growth then slows until adolescence, which is marked by a growth spurt and the beginning of sexual maturation. By 18 to 20 years of age, physical growth ceases.

5. *Adult Physical Development.* A variety of physical changes takes place as people age, including redistribution of body fat, decrease in bone mass, and decrease in muscle size and speed of contraction. Physical performance also declines. People reach their peak of physical strength, speed, and endurance between the ages of 20 and 30, after which there is a slow decline. The brain also changes with age, especially after

the age of 50. It decreases in size and weight, and some areas of the brain lose 50 percent or more of their neurons. These figures represent averages, however. In the absence of disease, many people remain in excellent physical condition until old age.

COGNITIVE DEVELOPMENT

6. *Cognitive Abilities of the Newborn.* From the moment of birth, infants begin interacting with and gathering information about the world. Newborn infants have all of the sensory capacities necessary to do this, although early sensation and perception generally are more rudimentary than in adults. The motor behavior of newborn infants consists primarily of reflexes. Reflexes gradually give way to coordinated voluntary actions, such as grasping and walking. Development of these fundamental sensorimotor abilities depends on the interplay between genetically determined sequences of maturation (nature) and effects of the environment (nurture).

7. *Early Development of Learning and Memory.* Infants can learn from the moment of birth, although they do not learn as readily as older children. Newborn infants also can remember what they have learned, and their long-term memory storage seems to be as good as that of adults. But young children are not as proficient as adults in encoding information to be remembered or in retrieving it from memory storage. These abilities improve during childhood, as children increase their use of memory strategies and increase their understanding of variables that affect memory performance (metamemory).

8. *Piaget's Theory of Intellectual Development.* The most influential theory of how children develop

the ability to think, reason, and solve problems is that of Jean Piaget. Piaget believed that people acquire knowledge by interacting with the world and that they construct schemes (knowledge or concepts) through assimilation (incorporating new information) and accommodation (modifying old information). Piaget also proposed that intellectual development progresses through a series of developmental stages, referred to as the sensorimotor, preoperational, concrete-operational, and formal-operational stages. According to Piaget, these stages represent qualitatively different ways of thinking that occur relatively abruptly and in the same sequence for all children.

9. *Challenges to Piaget's Theory.* Piaget's theory has been criticized on the grounds that children are not completely consistent in their cognitive abilities. In addition, training and practice often improve a child's performance on cognitive tests. Thus, some theorists argue that cognitive development is not really stagelike, but rather that it represents a gradual process of learning and a progressive accumulation and organization of knowledge that is applied differently in different situations.

10. *Changes in Learning and Memory During Aging.* People can learn new information throughout their lives. But learning skills seem to decline with age. This decline is due to factors such as slow processing of information. The elderly also show declines in memory performance, partly because they use fewer encoding strategies for remembering information and partly because they use fewer cues to retrieve information from memory. Long-term storage itself appears to be relatively unaffected by aging and, under favorable conditions, the

elderly are nearly as good as young adults at remembering information.

11. *Problem Solving in the Elderly.* Laboratory studies indicate that performance on a variety of problem-solving tasks declines with age. But training and practice can markedly improve older adults' problem-solving performance. What is more, when tasks are familiar and the subjects have experience with them, they show little or no decline in performance with age. Older people have accumulated a lifetime of experience, knowledge, and wisdom that they bring to everyday tasks, and this can offset cognitive deficits that may occur. The picture of inevitable severe intellectual impairment that many people have of the elderly is a misconception.

SOCIAL AND PERSONALITY DEVELOPMENT

12. *Early Social and Personality Development.* As children's cognitive abilities improve early in life, dramatic changes in their social interactions also occur. Strong attachments are formed between the infant and both parents during the first months and years after birth. These attachments occur because parents meet the infant's basic physical needs and also because parents give love and comfort. Personality development also begins early, and even very young infants show differences in temperament. Some of these temperamental qualities persist; others change as children grow up.

13. *Socialization in Childhood and Adolescence.* Socialization is the process by which individuals acquire the attitudes, social skills, and behavior that are expected by members of their society. Parents are the most important socializing influence during the childhood

years, and whether parents are permissive, authoritarian, or authoritative can strongly shape children's behavior. Peers also are important in shaping children's social behavior, particularly as children enter adolescence and become more independent of their parents. A third socializing influence is the media, especially television. Children learn social stereotypes from the media, and the aggression and violence portrayed on television can increase aggressive behavior among children.

14. *Moral Development.* The acquisition of moral standards and the ability to make moral judgments are closely related to the process of socialization. According to Kohlberg, people progress through six stages in the development of moral reasoning. At first, children make moral judgments strictly on the basis of direct physical consequences. In the most advanced stages, moral judgments are based on the individual's view of what is intrinsically just. How quickly and how far people progress in moral development depends on a number of factors, including their degree of cognitive development.

15. *Self-concept and Identity.* Infants begin to form a self-concept within the first year or two of life. Young children express self-concepts in concrete physical terms, whereas adolescents express them in terms of their inner thoughts, emotions, and attitudes. Erikson proposed that people progress through eight stages of psychosocial development and that a pivotal stage is the formation of a personal identity during adolescence. One important aspect of identity formation is the adoption of a sex-role identity—a belief that one's interests and behaviors conform to the cultural norms for one's sex. By early adoles-

cence, most children have a firm concept of their sex-role identity.

16. *Social Development in Adulthood and Old Age.* As people enter early adulthood, a major task is to form intimate relationships. Erikson theorized that committed, close relationships are requisites for continued normal adult development. For most people, the most important intimate relationship is a heterosexual love relationship that leads to marriage. Most married couples eventually have children, and although parenthood introduces new demands, it also provides an opportunity for personal growth. Another important task of young adulthood is to choose an occupation. Retirement from work marks a major transition for older adults. Most people adjust well to retirement and find it satisfying.

FURTHER READINGS

There are many excellent undergraduate-level textbooks on the topics discussed in this chapter. Most cover either child development (from conception through adolescence) or adult development and aging (from late adolescence or early adulthood through old age), but not both. Good texts on child development include *Child Development and Personality* by Mussen, Conger, Kagan, and Huston (1984), *Human Development* by Fischer and Lazerson (1984), and *Child Psychology Today* by Hall, Lamb, and Perlmutter (1986). Good texts on adult development and aging include *Adult Life* by Stevens-Long (1984), *Aging and Behavior* by Botwinick (1984), and *Adult Development and Aging* by Perlmutter and Hall (1985).

More detailed descriptions and illustrations of physical development can be found in *A Child Is Born* by Nilsson, Furuhjelm, Ingelman-Sundberg, and Wirsen (1977), well known for its spectacular photographs of the developing embryo and fetus and its authoritative material on the basics of genetics, conception, and the process of intrauterine development. Tanner's (1978) *Foetus into Man: Physical Growth from Conception to Maturity* gives even more detail and covers physical development to maturity.

A good overview of early cognitive development can be found in Flavell's (1985) *Cognitive Development*. Further readings on Piaget's observations and theory of cognitive development are best obtained from Piaget's own writings. The most relevant are *The Origins of Intelligence in Children* by Piaget (1936/1952), *Early Growth of Logic in the Child* by Inhelder and Piaget (1959/1964), and *The Growth of Logical Thinking from Childhood to Adolescence* by Inhelder and Piaget (1955/1958). Alternative views of cognitive development can be found in *Intellectual Development: Birth to Adulthood* by Case (1985). In addition to proposing a new theory, this book provides good overviews of alternative theoretical approaches. *Mechanisms of Cognitive Development,* edited by Sternberg (1984), also provides alternative viewpoints by experts working in the field of cognitive development. Both *Aging and Human Performance,* edited by Charness (1985), and the *Handbook of the Psychology of Aging,* edited by Birren and Schaie (1985) contain excellent chapters by active investigators in the field of aging.

An excellent source of further information about social and personality development is the *Handbook of Child Psychology* (4th Ed., Vol. IV). *Socialization, Personality, and Social Development,* edited by Hetherington (1983). This volume contains thorough reviews of the literature on a variety of topics. A well-written overview of research and theory in social learning can be found in *Social Learning Theory* by Bandura (1977b).

Further readings about moral development can be found in Piaget's (1932/1965) *The Moral Judgement of the Child.* In addition, Kohlberg (1981, 1984) has published two volumes of *Essays on Moral Development.* Each volume contains essays written by Kohlberg and his colleagues.

For more on marriage and family relationships, *Men, Women, and Change: a Sociology of Marriage and Family,* by Scanzoni and Scanzoni (1976) is recommended. This text considers relationships between men and women before marriage, the structure and process of marriage, the effects of children, and so on.

10

BASIC MODELS OF MOTIVATION

Why does a pet cat sometimes eat its food and sometimes not? Why does one person pursue money and another, religious inspiration? Why does a baby cry for his mother one moment and act unconcerned about her the next? Because psychologists cannot explain behavior just by what they observe in a particular situation—the presence of cat plus food, and the like—we must consider that something changes *within* humans and other animals that can account for changes in their behavior. *Motivation* is the label for what changes; it is an internal process or state that presumably accounts for why people and other animals do or do not pursue particular goals on particular occasions. In this chapter, we discuss the goals that organisms pursue, and we present various theoretical or conceptual explanations for this pursuit. Whereas other chapters in this book are devoted to *how* people pursue goals—how we get information from our environments, how we engage in purposive movement, how we learn—Chapters 10 and 11 are concerned with *why* we pursue the goals we do.

If our pet cat were pawing at a kitchen cabinet, a person familiar with both the cat and the kitchen might realize that the cat was trying to get at her food. In one sense, the puzzle of the cat's motivation to paw at the cabinet should be solved: the cat was hungry. For the motivational psychologist, however, the puzzle would just be beginning. What does it mean to be hungry? Was the cat motivated to get food because she felt unpleasant hunger pangs? That is, did the cat pursue food because she felt bad, or did she feel fine and only get hungry when she smelled the faint odor of fish as she passed by the cabinet? That is, did the cat pursue the food because it smelled so good? If the smell had moved the cat to seek food, how had she known that the fishy odor meant that food was available? Had she learned the association between odor and food, or was the association innate? Lord Berkeley, the British philosopher, declared that only a mind "debauched by learning" would find such questions interesting (James, 1890). We hope that we can show you why these questions are not only interesting, but also important.

The study of motivation is an attempt to answer why the young man struggles to win his father's approval, why the dog cringes in response to the wrath of his master, and why people spend countless hours, days, and years working to attain political office. The study of motivation is the study of *what* we fear, dream of, strive for, and *why* we fear, dream, and strive. In short, the study of motivation is concerned with what gives life meaning.

MOTIVATION CONCEPTS AND THEORY

Instinct Theory

Two early American psychologists were highly influenced by Darwin's theory of natural selection. This theory posits that organisms survive and procreate to the extent that their behavior and physiology are appropriate for survival in their environment. If an organism survives and procreates, it passes its genes onto its offspring. The offspring inherit the genetically determined behavioral and physiological characteristics of their parents.

William James (1890) and William McDougall (1908), the two American psychologists, were greatly influenced by Darwin's ideas, and they proposed that much human and animal behavior is **instinctive**. That is, organisms inherit from their parents the disposition to pursue food, water, and sex because pursuing these goals helps a species to survive and reproduce.

James believed that all organisms share basic instincts such as those to eat and procreate, and that humans also possess instincts for sociability, sympathy, rivalry, and love. McDougall believed that there are ten major instincts including flight, repulsion, and gregariousness. McDougall and James believed that an instinct is a genetically determined tendency to act in a particular manner in the presence of certain stimuli. For instance, the tendency to flee might be triggered by stimuli such as a hulking beast, a loud noise, or a snake.

Why did early psychologists like James believe that much human behavior is instinctive? Before Darwin, philosophers attributed much of the behavior of humans and lower animals to reason. Plato, Aristotle, and Spinoza emphasized that motivation, especially human motivation, arises out of rational analysis and the exercise of will. But the early psychologists were dissatisfied with the theories of motivation based on reason because they saw lower animals brought little rational analysis to their acts. As James observed, *"Now, why do the various animals do what seem to us such strange things,* in the presence of such outlandish stimuli? Why does the hen, for example, submit herself to the tedium of incubating such a fearfully uninteresting set of objects as a nest full of eggs, unless she has some sort of a prophetic inkling of the result?"* (James, 1890, p. 386). According to James, the hen sits on the eggs merely because the appearance of the eggs elicits an instinctive brooding reflex: "To the broody hen the notion would probably seem monstrous that there should be a creature in the world to whom a nest full of eggs was not the utterly fascinating and precious and never-to-be-too-much-sat-upon object to which it is to her" (James, 1890, p. 387).

According to early instinct theorists, human behavior is just as instinctively determined as is animal behavior. The apparent complexity of human motivation stems from the fact that humans are affected by many more instincts than are lower animals. For instance, the sight of a fawn elicits the following instincts in the panther: to stalk, pursue, kill, eat. In the human the sight of the fawn might elicit those same instincts, and others—to protect and nurture out of a sympathy instinct, to acquire as property out of an acquisitiveness instinct, and to study out of a curiosity instinct. Such competing instincts, according to James, can influence one another and result in complex and often unpredictable human behavior. Although we humans may differ from lower animals in that we can reason about the consequences of our instinctive behaviors—the woman walks toward a fire knowing that she does so to get warm—this awareness does not change the fact that, for James, her approach to the fire on a cold night is still instinctive.

FIGURE 10-1   LEARNING AFFECTS WHAT WE LIKE!
A young man enjoys a snack of termites. People from some cultures recoil at the thought of eating insects but relish Roquefort cheese, mold-impregnated rancid animal's milk. Clearly, many motivational goals are learned.

You might ask how James and other instinct theorists account for the diversity of motivated behavior in humans. The stimulus of cold might elicit very different motivated behaviors among different people in different situations: huddling for warmth, striking matches, donning more clothing, or turning up a thermostat. How can all of these be instinctive? After all, humans evolved in the absence of matches and thermostats. Similarly, the sight of a termite might elicit disgust in people from one culture but hunger in people from a different culture (see Figure 10-1).

James and McDougall both acknowledged that instinctive tendencies can be modified by learning, especially learning associated with early occurrences of instinctive behavior. For example, James notes that a strange dog elicits two competing instincts in a child: impulses to "fear" or "fondle." If the child fondles the dog and the dog bites him, the child's fear instinct will be strengthened, and the child may fear dogs for many years. But if the dog is friendly, the child may acquire a resilient fondness for dogs. James describes this process as the inhibition of instinct by "habit." The child acquires a habit of either approach or avoidance of dog, and the habit inhibits the competing instinct. (You will notice that James was describing a process that we would now label *instrumental,* or *operant, learning.*)

PROBLEMS WITH INSTINCT THEORY   Today scientists still recognize that aspects of motivated behavior have genetic roots. But three telling criticisms of instinct theory have caused scientists to explore alternative models of motivation. One criticism is that no one has been able to identify the core instincts. James listed less than 50 human instincts, but by the 1920s authors had proposed the existence of almost 6000 instincts (Murray, 1964). In fact, the belief in the existence of many instincts was so common that writers humorously suggested that there must be an instinct to believe in instincts (Weiner, 1985b).

Instinct theory also has been criticized on the grounds that simply attributing each type of motivated behavior to a different instinct does not *explain* the behavior. For example, we could attribute eating to a hunger instinct, and we then could point to the fact that all creatures eat thereby arguing that hunger is instinctive and not learned or dependent upon environmental conditions. Thus, we attribute observed eating to instinct, and we infer instinct based on observation of eating. This reasoning is circular and leads us nowhere. A third criticism is that instinct theory does not reveal *how* instincts affect behavior. It does not reveal whether our pet cat felt hungry because she felt hunger pains or because she smelled fish.

One response to these criticisms is drive theory. We turn to it now.

Drive Theory

At the heart of drive theory is the concept of **need**. Needs arise from the biological requirements of an organism. When a certain need becomes strong, for instance, as occurs when an organism hasn't eaten for many hours, a **drive** is activated. Drive implies activation and arousal; it mobilizes the organism to seek a goal that will satisfy its need. Thus, drive theory differs from instinct theory in several important ways. First, drive

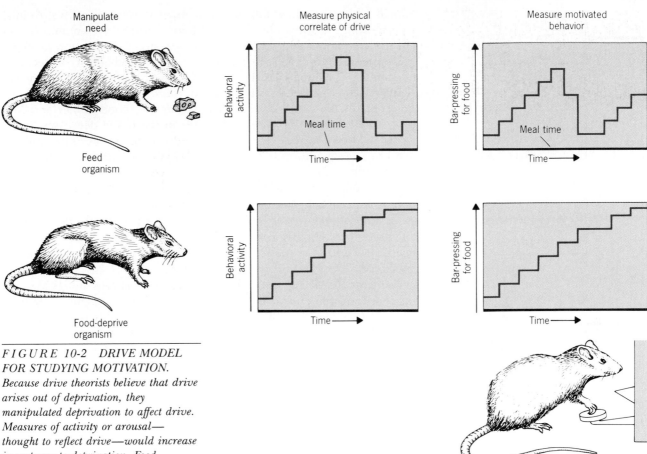

Manipulate
need

Feed
organism

Food-deprive
organism

Measure physical
correlate of drive

Behavioral
activity

Meal time

Time→

Measure motivated
behavior

Bar-pressing
for food

Meal time

Time→

Behavioral
activity

Time→

Bar-pressing
for food

Time→

*FIGURE 10-2   DRIVE MODEL
FOR STUDYING MOTIVATION.
Because drive theorists believe that drive
arises out of deprivation, they
manipulated deprivation to affect drive.
Measures of activity or arousal—
thought to reflect drive—would increase
in response to deprivation. Food
deprivation increased activity in this
hypothetical experiment and feeding
decreased it. Changes in activation or
arousal would parallel changes in
motivated behavior. For example,
increased activation would accompany
increased pursuit of a goal, as when a
rat presses a bar for food.*

theory posits drive, or physical arousal, as a mechanism that fuels behavior. Because drive was viewed as a real physical process, it was thought to have physiological correlates that could be measured and characterized. Drive theory suggested that scientists could study the process central to motivation—drive—and would no longer need to infer motivation from the observation of motivated behavior alone. Instead scientists could determine level of motivation by measuring drive.

Another advantage of drive theory was its identification of *need* as a crucial determinant of drive. Because need was largely a function of deprivation, scientists could manipulate drive by creating deprivation, then measure changes in drive, and then determine whether changes in drive level were accompanied by changes in motivated behavior (see Figure 10-2).

Not only did drive theorists offer drive as the mechanism that activates motivated behavior, but they also proposed a process that might result in specific sorts of drive. This process is called **homeostasis**.

HOMEOSTASIS   One of the most important concepts in the study of motivation is the concept of *homeostasis,* or "equal state." The French physiologist Claude Bernard (1813–1878) was the first to observe that

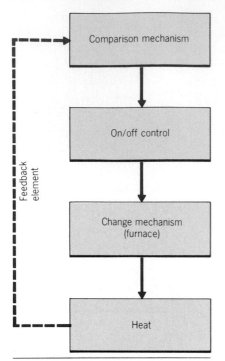

FIGURE 10-3   A THERMOSTATICALLY CONTROLLED TEMPERATURE-REGULATING SYSTEM.

In this system, the change mechanism is a furnace, the feedback mechanism is any heat-sensitive element such as air. The comparator mechanism compares the level of heat in the room, as indicated by air temperature, with a preset level. If the room temperature is below the preset level, an on/off mechanism is activated and the furnace is engaged. This produces the product, heat. When the room temperature reaches the preset level, the comparator detects this and the furnace is turned off.

animals must maintain a stable internal environment to survive. Animals must be able to control their internal temperatures, the amount of oxygen in their blood, and their level of blood sugar to function properly.

Homeostasis operates through a change mechanism, a feedback mechanism, a comparison mechanism, and an on/off mechanism (see Figure 10-3). One body system that operates homeostatically is the one that controls the concentration of water in the blood (Tafler and Kennedy, 1965). When the amount of water in the blood decreases, receptors in the hypothalamus are activated and stimulate cells in the pituitary gland to secrete a hormone called **vasopressin** or **antidiuretic hormone (ADH)**. When vasopressin is released, the kidneys do not filter water from the blood into the bladder. Rather, water returns to the blood. Here the feedback mechanism is the blood that carries information about water level to the hypothalamus. The hypothalamus receptors constitute the comparison mechanism. The pituitary cells are the on/off mechanism and turn the kidney reabsorption mechanisms—the change mechanisms—on and off (see Figure 10-3).

Homeostatic mechanisms not only affect internal physiological states, but they also influence overt behavior. An excellent example of this is thermoregulation (Satinoff and Henderson, 1977). When heat-sensitive neurons in a mammal's brain (in the hypothalamus and other structures) detect that the animal's body temperature has fallen too low, the animal's behavior and physiology change to generate and conserve heat. Metabolism increases, which produces more heat; veins and arteries near the body surface shrink, diverting blood to the internal organs; and body hairs stand erect as the body traps heat in a thicker fur coat. (Humans get "goosebumps.") The behavioral changes include shivering, huddling, and increased activity. In cold-blooded animals such as reptiles, behavior changes even more radically. Because these animals cannot heat themselves by producing heat internally, they must shuttle between sun and shade. By finding warm and cool spots, reptiles can maintain their body temperatures within a 3 to 4°C range.

Homeostasis may provide a good model of how organisms control their internal environments and how imbalance gives rise to drive, but it does not explain how drive affects human behavior. How does a fall in body temperature cause us to buy a winter coat, or how does a fall in blood sugar cause us to seek food? Three more general motivational theories have been offered to explain how drive produces motivated behavior. One of these theories, ethological drive theory, arose in the 1930s and 1940s out of observations of animals in their natural environments. Another, Freudian motivational theory, arose out of an attempt to apply homeostatic principles to human behavior observed in psychotherapy sessions. Finally Hullian drive theory arose out of basic research on animal behavior. The fact that three major motivational theories arose out of the homeostatic model illustrates the tremendous influence this model has had on psychology.

ETHOLOGICAL APPROACHES TO MOTIVATION   **Ethologists** are scientists who study animal behavior in the animals' natural environments. Ethological drive theory was proposed by such prominent ethologists as

Konrad Lorenz and Niko Tinbergen—both Nobel laureates. Ethological drive theory holds that drives are instinctive but that they can be influenced by experience.

Ethologists believe that there are two major determinants of motivated behavior: drive level and the presence of a **releasing stimulus**. According to ethological drive theorists, animals have innate (instinctive), specific patterns of behavior (such as the fixed action patterns discussed in Chapter 6). For example, cats groom themselves, dogs wag their tails, and people startle when they are frightened by loud noises. Ethologists such as Lorenz (1966) and Tinbergen (1952) believe that each behavior pattern has its own energy source or drive (Figure 10-4). If animals do not act in ways important to their survival, **action-specific energy** (drive) builds up to uncomfortable levels until the energy is expended. When the animal encounters an appropriate releasing stimulus, it expends the pent-up action-specific energy (Figure 10-5). Thus, a cat grooms when she feels something sticky on her face, a dog wags her tail when she sees her master, and a baby cries when a loud firecracker sounds close by.

Ethologists have inferred that such stimulus–response relationships are innate because they do not vary among animals within a species. All

FIGURE 10-4   ETHOLOGICAL MODEL OF DRIVE.
This schematic captures Lorenz's model of how energy and releasing stimuli interact to yield motivated behavior. The fluid collecting in the reservoir represents action-specific energy. The weight on the scale connected to the pulley represents a releasing stimulus. Both energy buildup and the releasing stimulus release energy. Both are connected by an animal's intrinsic inhibition of the motivated behavior. This inhibition, represented by the spring, keeps the animal from engaging in a motivated behavior unless the stored-up energy and the releasing stimulus together exceed the inhibitory force. The inhibitory force keeps the animal from endlessly eating, drinking, and so on. (Lorenz, 1966.)

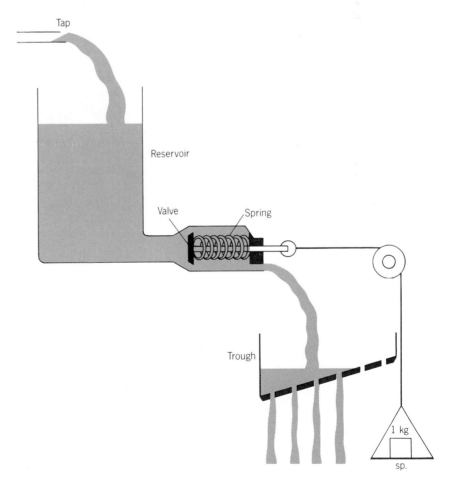

Tap

Reservoir

Valve   Spring

Trough

1 kg

sp.

FIGURE 10-5   HOW A BAT "RELEASES" A MOTH.
A moth flies in a zigzag pattern to escape a pursuing bat, which flies in the lighter, longer streaks of light. Because moths zigzag only after detecting the bat's high-frequency cries, ethologists consider the cries as releasing stimuli for the moth's evasive flight. Because the zigzagging helps the moth to survive, the instinctive pattern of behavior is genetically transmitted. (From Roeder, 1963.)

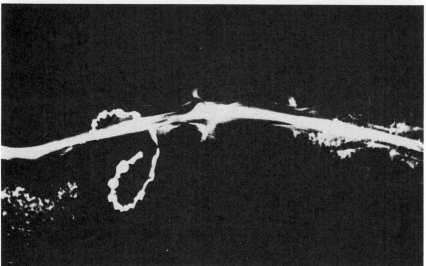

dogs wag their tails when they see their pack leader or their human masters. The *particular* releasing stimulus may vary, but the basic relationship between releasing stimulus and response does not.

What led ethologists to suggest that specific drives build over time? First, ethologists noted that specific behavior patterns sometimes occur in the absence of any releasing stimulus. Such **vacuum** behaviors (behaviors that occur in a vacuum) tend to occur only when an animal has not engaged in the behavior for a long time. Ethologists argued that if motivated behaviors are not elicited by releasing stimuli, energy must build up making the behavior occur spontaneously. They labeled this energy a drive.

Ethologists also noted that when an animal is prevented from engaging in one type of motivated behavior, it often engages in apparently unrelated, seemingly inappropriate behavior. For example, if a hungry rat can see food but is afraid to approach it (perhaps it had been shocked for eating), it may begin grooming itself (Bindra and Spinner, 1958). Ethologists call these apparently irrelevant behaviors **displacement activity** and believe that they occur when drive spills over into a different motivated activity.

Finally, when animals engage in a motivated behavior repeatedly (eating, drinking, grooming, sex), ethologists noted that it becomes more and more difficult to elicit the behavior. They interpreted this to mean that each occurrence of the motivated behavior reduced drive levels; the behavior became more difficult to elicit because there was no energy left to "fuel" it (see Figure 10-4).

Ethologists have argued that drive must be somewhat *specific* to particular motivated behaviors because depleting drive levels for one type of behavior does not deplete drive levels for other behaviors. The animal that has just eaten has less motivation to eat but not less motivation to engage in sexual behavior.

IMPRINTING AND COURTSHIP BEHAVIOR   Two phenomena of animal behavior—imprinting and courtship behavior—illustrate nicely the importance of releasing stimuli and drive to motivated behavior.

Imprinting describes learning in which infants form enduring attachments to objects in their environments. According to ethologists, young animals have a specific drive to remain close to an imprinted object or organism. The sight and sound of this organism releases in a young

FIGURE 10-6 MOTHER LORENZ.
Young geese follow Konrad Lorenz. The geese imprinted on Lorenz because they were exposed to him rather than their mother soon after birth. The period of greatest imprinting among ducklings is 13 to 16 hours after hatching. (Hess, 1958.)

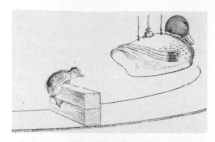

FIGURE 10-7   THE STRUGGLE TO IMPRINT.

A duckling will struggle to keep up with an object upon which it has imprinted. In fact, the more ducklings have to struggle to keep up with the imprinted object, the greater their later attachment to the object.

animal the drive to follow and remain close (see Figure 10-6). The strength of the imprinting drive shows in the fact that ducklings will struggle to follow the animal on which they have imprinted despite obstacles in their path (Figure 10-7).

Konrad Lorenz discovered that young animals pass through a **critical period** during which they imprint on almost any moving object they encounter. A critical period is a time during an animal's development when it must learn a particular kind of behavior. Beyond the critical period, it will not be able to learn the behavior. Lorenz discovered that ducklings imprint on moving objects within 24 hours after hatching (see Hess, 1958, 1972). If ducklings do not imprint during the 24-hour critical period, they do not imprint later on.

Because the first thing a newborn duckling is likely to see is its mother, the duckling is likely to imprint on the correct object—the mother duck. Because the critical period during which imprinting can occur is quite brief, ducklings do not imprint on dangerous objects that they might encounter later (e.g., predators). Apparently, ducklings begin imprinting on the sound of their mother's quacking even while they are in their shells. Once they hatch, ducklings exposed to quacking in the shell will follow a quacking object over one that says, for instance, the words "come, come, come" (Hess, 1972). Thus the drive to imprint is instinctive, but the object of imprinting depends on environmental influences.

The relationship between drive and releasing stimuli can be seen in the courtship behavior of male guppies (Baerends et al., 1955). The external markings of male guppies change gradually after courtship (Figure 10-8). The intensity of a male guppy's courtship behavior depends both on the length of time since his last courtship and on the size of a female model that is present. The less time since mating, the larger the female must be to elicit courting by the male. According to ethologists humans eat sweet foods at the end of a meal because only a potent releasing stimulus (a rich dessert) will elicit eating when the hunger drive is low.

Ethologists' drive theory seems quite capable of accounting for some characteristics of human motivation. For one thing, the level of our motivation increases as time passes since we have engaged in a behavior. Rutabaga may not be a person's favorite food, but it might elicit enthusi-

FIGURE 10-8   GUPPY MARKINGS REFLECT MOTIVATION.

The dark markings of the male guppy (lebistes reticulatus) *that are related to courtship behavior. Markings number 4, 5, and 6 are most highly related to courtship. The longer the time since courtship, the darker these markings are. Therefore, these markings are be thought of as reflecting sexual drive. (Baerends et al., 1955.)*

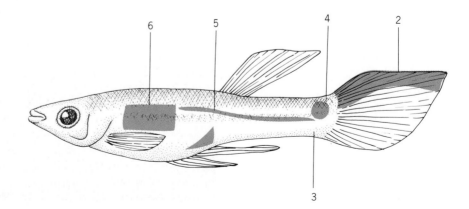

astic eating if a person were starving (had high hunger drive). Second, intense motivation often feels unpleasant and is associated with increased activity—both features consistent with increased energy levels or drive. Third, motivation seems to be action-specific: a person who is really hungry is not appeased by sexual activity. Also, particular stimuli powerfully affect people's motivation levels, and some of these "releasing stimuli" are learned. Hunger is released by food, aggression by a hurled insult, fear by a snarling dog. Finally, there is evidence that critical periods may occur in human development. Humans, for example, probably have a critical period for learning language. If humans do not learn language during their first 10 or 12 years of life, they are unlikely ever to speak normally (Kesner and Baker, 1980). Many people learn *second* languages later in life, but only if they first learned language before the age of 10 or 12.

PROBLEMS WITH ETHOLOGICAL DRIVE THEORY Despite the explanatory power of ethological drive theory, critics have pointed out inadequacies in its concepts and data. Some have argued that displacement activities are not the products of strong drives but of relatively weak cues. They suggest that most animals showing displacement activity are torn between two goals—for instance, between approaching and avoiding food. The two motivations cancel out one another, and the animals, in a fairly neutral motivational state, engage in behaviors with low survival priority: they groom, pace, or scratch. Let us suppose that a young girl would like to eat a piece of a hot, freshly baked pie. She is torn between eating the pie and avoiding burning her mouth, and so she picks up a magazine and begins reading. The ethologist could say that she reads out of her high, frustrated hunger drive. The critic would argue that she reads for the same reason as she reads when she is bored. Because biologically important approach–avoidance behaviors have canceled out one another, she engages in a less important behavior.

Another empirical problem for ethological drive theorists, and for all drive theorists for that matter, is that drive is nowhere to be found! Scientists never have found a physiological process or mechanism with the properties of "drive." As you will see, the physiological bases of motivated behaviors are quite complex. Finally, ethological drive theory does not account for the tremendous impact of cognition on motivation, nor does it account for the fact that organisms sometimes produce high levels of motivated behaviors when they should, theoretically, have low drive levels.

FREUDIAN THEORY Freudian theory of personality is another drive theory with a heavy emphasis on instincts (Brenner, 1957). Freud's ideas about motivation were based not on laboratory research but on his observations of patients undergoing a type of psychotherapy known as **psychoanalysis** (see Chapter 15). Freud believed that all humans are driven by two powerful, biologically based instincts: self-preservation/sexual procreation, and death/aggression. According to Freud, all instincts, or motivations, have a *source,* an *aim,* and an *object.* The source of human motivation is the workings of the body. Thus the source of a person's motivation to eat, reflecting the self-preservation instinct, is physical activity and metabolism, which deplete energy and create hunger. The source of sexual motivation is the operations of our sexual organs. These physiological processes produce tension or drive, which a person finds unpleasant.

The *aim* of all instincts is always the same: to reduce tension. People must find a suitable *object* by which to reduce tension or they become unhappy, fatigued, tense, and anxious. The *object* for Freud was similar to the releasing stimulus for the ethologists, but Freud made a very important assumption. Freud recognized that, as opposed to other animals, humans live in societies with elaborate social rules, laws, and moral codes that thwart individuals' instinctive drives. (Other animals certainly live in societies and must often defer to other animals, but Freud would say that they do so primarily out of instinct.) Humans are the only animals who must continually live without directly satisfying their instinctual drives. We cannot mate with all attractive members of the other sex. We cannot destroy all those who would stop or frustrate us. We cannot do so because as children, we learned moral laws so thoroughly that our consciences do not permit us to ignore them.

Freud's revolutionary contribution to the theory of motivation was his suggestion that people use substitute objects to satisfy their instinctive drives when a biologically appropriate object is unavailable or inappropriate. The baby sucks his thumb when a breast is unavailable; a man punches a wall when he cannot hit his boss; and a young boy develops a crush on his teacher because he is morally prohibited from acknowledging his sexual attraction to his mother. Finding a substitute object for instinctive drives is called **sublimating**. Freud thought that sublimation was vital to the development and survival of civilization and that much of human culture and institutions depend on sublimation. The poet writes poetry as a substitute for making love to an unobtainable, beautiful woman, and the politician defeats her opponent because she cannot in conscience drive a spear through the opponent's heart. Another revolutionary aspect of Freud's thinking was to suggest that people often are unaware of the true nature of their motivation. The politician is probably unaware that she is in politics to satisfy her aggressive needs. She probably would say that she is in politics for "the good of the people."

CRITICISMS OF FREUDIAN DRIVE THEORY   Freud's ideas on motivation have profoundly influenced views of human behavior. But despite countless research investigations, they do not enjoy strong experimental support. There is little doubt that some of Freud's basic ideas are valid, for example, that people are often unaware of their true motivation. But the very flexibility that makes Freudian theory so attractive also makes it difficult to test or confirm empirically.

Freudian theory also has been criticized on the grounds that it is unlikely that all motivated behavior can be traced to two basic instincts. For example, Freud said that young animals remained close to their parents to receive nourishment, reflecting the self-preservation instinct. However, we now know that among young monkeys touch and warmth are more important than nourishment in encouraging parental contact (Eagle, 1984; see Chapter 11).

HULLIAN DRIVE THEORY   Clark Hull, for many years a professor at Yale University, was one of the most influential psychologists of this century (Figure 10-9). Hull was instrumental in describing how motivational processes could be studied experimentally. Unlike Freud and the ethologists, Hull believed that a single type of drive—an undifferentiated activating force—could be channeled into a wide range of behaviors. Hull still had to explain why animals engage in different types of motivated behavior at different times. If the same drive is behind all motivation, why do you drink on one occasion and eat or work on another? What gives direction to a person's motivation?

For ethologists, drive exerts a directional influence. An animal is motivated to seek food by a hunger drive, to seek water by a thirst drive, and so on. But for Hull, drive pushes an organism but in no particular direction. According to Hull, two things happen when deprivation produces a state of need in an organism: (1) drive increases and (2) the organism detects the need state through internal receptors. For instance, if a need for food is produced by food deprivation, internal receptors would detect stomach contractions. These internal sensations are important because they serve as cues (or *discriminative stimuli*; see Chapter 6) for particular responses. For example, when you feel the need for food, you know that by buying food, cooking it, and eating it, you will stop feeling the internal sensations of need and your hunger drive will be reduced. In essence, internal sensations of hunger serve as signals so that operant responses that lead to eating will be reinforced through drive reduction (Figure 10-10). In short, Hull theorized that need automatically produces drive but that the behaviors that reduce drive are largely learned.

Hull originally proposed that motivation is a joint function of drive and learning, which he termed **habit**:

$$\text{Motivation} = \text{Drive} \times \text{Habit}$$

In theory, the more an animal has been rewarded for a particular motivated behavior (habit), and the greater its drive, the more likely the motivated behavior is to occur. For example, hungry rats were trained to press a bar for food (Perin, 1942; Williams, 1938). Bar-presses were reinforced from 5 to 90 times. Later these rats were allowed to press a bar after going hungry for 3 or 22 hours. During this test they were not reinforced for pressing the bar. In theory, the stronger a rat's motivation, the more times it should press the bar before stopping. Figure 10-11 shows that, consistent with Hull's theory, the greater a rat's drive (induced by food deprivation), and the stronger the rat's habit (the more it had been reinforced), the more times it pressed the bar without reinforcement.

While the foregoing model of motivation accounted nicely for the influence of drive and habit, Hull (1952) became convinced that his model was incomplete. Motivation, he said, is influenced not only by

FIGURE 10-9   CLARK HULL (1884–1952).

Hull was a Yale psychologist whose major contributions were in the fields of learning and motivation. Psychologists recently voted Hull the most important contributor to psychology of the mid-twentieth century.

FIGURE 10-10   HULLIAN MODEL OF MOTIVATED BEHAVIOR.
According to Hull, internal stimuli associated with particular needs signal the organism when to engage in motivated behavior and what type of motivated behavior to pursue. Thus, stomach contractions might lead a hawk to pursue a mouse—a dry throat, to pursue water. When a hungry hawk eats, the internal cues for hunger (stomach contractions) are reduced, and drive is reduced. Because drive is unpleasant for animals, the behaviors that led to drive reduction are reinforced.

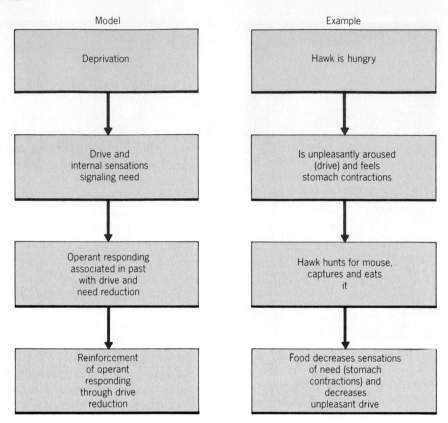

habit and deprivation, but also by the characteristics of the available goals. All other things being equal, for example, the motivation of the girl who is promised $10 for doing yard work is likely to be stronger than

FIGURE 10-11 MOTIVATION = HABIT × DRIVE.
Rats that had been reinforced many times or that had been hungry longer pressed the bar more than other rats. (Adapted from Pevin, 1942.)

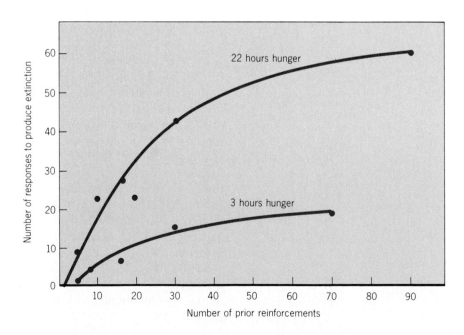

the motivation of the girl promised only $1. Hull and others labeled these goals **incentives,** and Hull redefined motivation as

$$\text{Motivation} = \text{Drive} \times \text{Habit} \times \text{Incentive}$$

The Incentive Model of Motivation

Have you ever eaten a dessert when you were so full that eating was actually painful? Why did you do it? Have you ever had trouble resisting eating peanuts after you had one or two? Clearly, your hunger drive is stronger *before* you eat the first peanut, but you probably have more trouble resisting peanut number 12 or 20 than peanut number 1. Many motivational theorists argue that people's behavior often is motivated by the quality and desirability of stimuli rather than by internal states produced by needs or homeostatic imbalance (e.g., Bindra, 1974; Bolles, 1972a; Klinger, 1975). They argue that motivated behavior depends strongly on the presence of powerful motivational stimuli or incentives—the smell of food, the sight of an attractive sexual partner, and the like.

A powerful method for getting animals to engage in motivated behavior is to expose them to a small amount of the incentive stimulus, a technique called **priming**. Priming stimulates the organism to pursue more of the incentive stimulus. For instance, if a rat is given a small bit of food, it will immediately begin working on an operant schedule to get more food, even though it had free access to food until it was primed (Eiserer, 1978)—the "peanut effect." Similarly, rats that had previously given themselves heroin or cocaine will quickly resume responding for the drug if they are injected with small amounts of it (Stewart, 1984). Notice that an animal need not be deprived or homeostatically imbalanced for priming to work. Priming stimuli are effective apparently because they *remind* an animal of the pleasant or unpleasant qualities of the incentive.

The concept of incentives lets psychologists explain, for example, why many monkeys trained to give themselves cocaine will do so until they kill themselves (Deneau, Yanagita, and Seevers, 1969). It seems unlikely that monkeys have an internal "need" for lethal doses of cocaine. Instead, the cocaine is a pleasurable incentive—to the point of death. Incentive theorists recognize that *needs* influence behavior (Bindra, 1974), but they place greater emphasis on incentive stimuli than on drives. It has been suggested that drive theorists view behavior as being *pushed* by drives, and incentive theorists see behavior as being *pulled* by incentives. Moreover, incentive theorists view drive as exerting its effects *through* incentives—by altering incentive value. If rats drink grape juice when they are thirsty, they later show a stronger preference for grape juice than if they had drunk it when they were not thirsty (Revusky, 1967). Deprivation or the resulting drive made the grape juice taste better. You eat more when you are hungry not because of the awfulness of hunger pangs or an aroused state, but because food tastes better.

Finally, incentives affect people's behavior even if they have not been primed with an incentive. Previous learning often creates *expectations* about goals, and such expectations can have powerful effects on motivated behaviors. What directs motivated behavior is not just how tasty a food is or how fascinating a play is, but expectations about the food or the play. People often undertake major projects because of their expectations about the results. They go to college not because each and every class is so enjoyable, but because they *expect* that their lives will be better—eventually—if they do go.

Incentive theory is still influential, but theorists have modified and added greatly to it. They recognize that motivation, especially human motivation, is influenced by complex cognitive processes and they have incorporated cognitive processes into motivational theory (see Chapter 11). Also, some researchers, dissatisfied with simply attributing motivation to pleasure or displeasure with stimuli, were led to study the physiological reasons that stimuli were either pleasant or unpleasant. This led motivation researchers to study the role of physiological arousal in motivation.

Arousal Theories

According to drive theorists, drive or arousal is always aversive. The basis of motivation is the animal's avoidance of unpleasant drives. According to arousal theorists, however, the pleasantness of drive or arousal depends on the type of stimulation. If an animal has had relatively little stimulation, stimuli that increase its arousal level will be rewarding. An animal that has been exposed to a lot of stimulation finds more stimulation punishing. According to this theory, organisms will work for stimulation if they have low levels of arousal. This hypothesis has a great deal of subjective appeal for anyone who has ever been bored. Moreover, it is supported by research on the effects of sensory deprivation.

In one study of sensory deprivation (Bexton, Heron, and Scott, 1954), undergraduates were placed in an environment of little sensory stimulation (Figure 10-12). The great Canadian neuropsychologist, D. O. Hebb, describes this experiment and its results.

Their subjects were paid handsomely to do nothing, see nothing, hear or touch very little for 24 hours a day. Primary needs were met, on the whole, very well. The subjects suffered no pain, and were fed on request. It is true that they could not copulate, but at the risk of impugning the virility of Canadian college students I point out that most of them would not have been copulating anyway and were quite used to such long stretches of three or four days without primary sexual satisfaction. The secondary reward, on the other hand, was high: $20 a day plus room and board is more than $7000 a year, far more than a student could earn by other means. The subjects then should be highly motivated to continue the experiment, cheerful and happy to be allowed to contribute to scientific knowledge so painlessly and profitably.

In fact, the subject was well motivated for perhaps four to eight hours, and then became increasingly unhappy. He developed a need for stimulation of almost any kind. In the first preliminary exploration, for example, he was allowed to listen to recorded material on request. Some subjects were given a talk for 6-year-old children on the dangers of alcohol. This might be requested, by a

*FIGURE 10-12   SENSORY
DEPRIVATION.*
*The subject in a sensory deprivation
experiment is isolated from tactile,
auditory, and visual stimulation.*

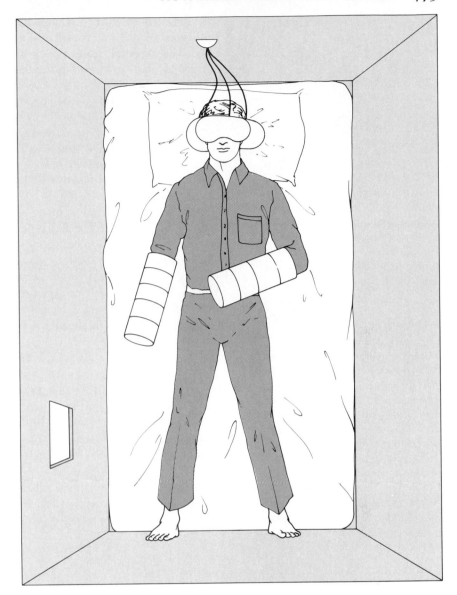

*FIGURE 10-12   SENSORY
DEPRIVATION.*
*The subject in a sensory deprivation
experiment is isolated from tactile,
auditory, and visual stimulation.*

*grown-up male college student, 15 to 20 times in a 30-hour period. Others
were offered, and asked for repeatedly, a recording of an old stock-market report.
The subjects looked forward to being tested, but paradoxically tended to find the
tests fatiguing when they did arrive. It is hardly necessary to say that the whole
situation was rather hard to take, and one subject, in spite of not being in a
special state of primary drive arousal in the experiment but in real need of
money outside it, gave up the secondary reward of $20 a day to take up a job at
hard labor paying $7 or $8 a day.*

(Hebb, 1966, pp. 68–69)

Clearly, people and other animals pursue stimulation and challenges.
People ride roller coasters, read murder mysteries, and listen to loud
music. Animals will work to gain access to puzzles (see Figure 10-13).

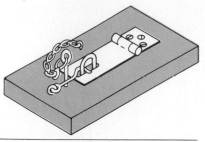

FIGURE 10-13 MECHANICAL PUZZLE APPARATUS.
A puzzle for which monkeys will work to gain access. The monkeys are not rewarded for solving the puzzle—trying to solve the puzzle is, itself rewarding. We won't insult you by telling you the solution. (From Harlow, Harlow, and Meyer, 1950.)

FIGURE 10-14 AROUSAL AND MOTIVATION.
(a) A curve that shows a frequently observed relationship between arousal and performance. Motivated behavior often is weak or disorganized at very low or very high levels of arousal. (From Hebb, 1966.) (b) The relationship of arousal and performance of motivated behavior according to drive theory. If the behavior has high habit strength, the greater the arousal (drive level), the stronger or more persistent should be the motivated behavior. Much research shows that the performance of organisms is best at moderate levels of arousal, as suggested by graph "a."

The drive theorist must acknowledge that organisms are not uniformly motivated to reduce arousal and attain a calm, physiologically quiescent state. Thus arousal can not only "drive" or push behavior, but it can also serve as a goal or incentive for behavior.

Arousal theorists (Bindra, 1959; Hebb, 1966) have used the **Yerkes–Dodson law** to support their assertion that there is an optimal level of arousal for motivated behavior. Yerkes and Dodson (1908), two early experimental psychologists, noted that animals often seemed to perform best at moderate, rather than high, levels of motivation. They found that high levels of motivation led to the best performance on easy tasks, whereas low levels of motivation led to the best performance of difficult tasks.

A simple interpretation of drive theory is that the higher the level of arousal, the stronger and more persistent should be motivated behavior. But imagine that you have to write an essay on an examination. Would you be able to write a better essay if you were moderately worried about your performance or if you were absolutely terrified? Consistent with the Yerkes–Dodson law, researchers have observed in a variety of situations that high levels of arousal are often associated with weak or disorganized motivated behavior (Malmo, 1966; see Figure 10-14*a,b*).

GRAY'S AROUSAL MODEL OF MOTIVATION   What exactly *is* arousal, and how should psychologists measure it? Arousal once meant faster brain waves (as recorded by EEG) and increases in heart rate, sweating (skin conductance), and behavior. But these measures of arousal often do not agree (Lacey, 1967). Although a stimulus (for example, a shock) might increase some measures of arousal (EEG frequency and sweating), it might decrease other measures (heart rate, behavior).

Recently, psychologists have proposed that there are different types of arousal, and these reflect different motivations. One of the most influential of the new arousal theories is that proposed by Jeffrey Gray (1982), a British psychologist. Gray suggests that both reward and pun-

(*a*)

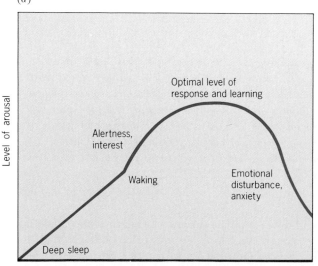

(*b*)

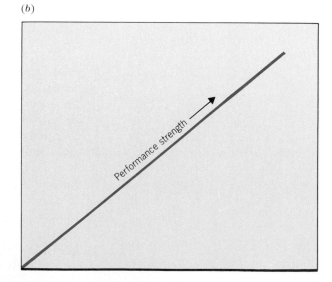

ishment increase arousal but that the arousal is very different in the two cases. Gray has labeled the arousal system activated by punishment the **Behavioral Inhibition System** or **BIS** and the system activated by reward the **Behavioral Activation System** or **BAS**.

THE BEHAVIORAL INHIBITION SYSTEM   Gray (1982a, 1982b) has hypothesized that the BIS is likely to become active in several types of situations. The first is direct punishment such as shocking a rat or harshly criticizing a person. Second is the failure to receive an expected reward (called *frustrative nonreward*). Third is exposure to startling or novel stimuli as when a gun goes off close by. When the BIS is activated by any of these means, three things happen:

1. Ongoing behavior is inhibited. If a gun went off while you were walking down the street, you would stop walking.
2. Arousal increases. You would become very alert and perhaps start to sweat.
3. Attention increases. You would immediately scan your environment to find where the shot came from and whether you would be the next victim.

An activated BIS causes people and other animals to stop what they are doing and to appraise their situation. BIS arousal is unpleasant—in everyday language we would label it *anxiety* or *fear*—and appraising the situation often helps animals avoid stimuli that increase BIS activity.

One important aspect of Gray's theory is that he has linked particular motivational processes to particular brain structures. Gray has noted that BIS activation stems from activation of neurons in the septal and hippocampal areas of the brain (Gray, 1982a; see Figure 10-15).

THE BEHAVIORAL ACTIVATION SYSTEM   In contrast to the BIS, the BAS is activated by rewards or by the *absence* of expected punishment (Gray, 1975). When the BAS is activated, behavior increases, especially approach behavior. Thus, when people encounter a reward—a tasty food, money—or discover that they will not receive an expected punish-

FIGURE 10-15   RAT SEPTUM AND HIPPOCAMPUS.
The septal and hippocampal regions dissected from the rat brain. These regions are thought by Gray to be critically involved in mammals' reactions to punishers, absence of expected rewards, and startling, novel stimuli. These structures are both part of a larger system of brain structures, the limbic system, *long thought to play a role in emotional reaction (e.g., rage, anger). (From Gray, 1982.)*

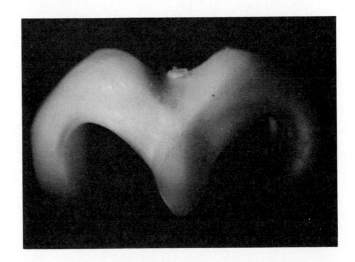

ment, they become aroused and pursue additional rewards. The BAS explains priming quite nicely: a little taste of peanuts activates the BAS and leads people to eat more. In a sense, the BAS is an inborn motivational system that tells people when they have found a biologically

(a)

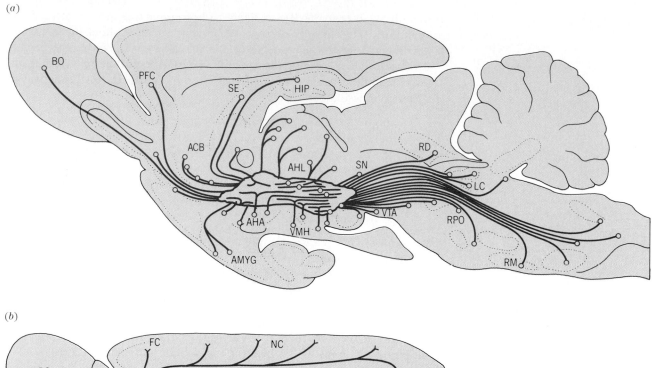

(b)

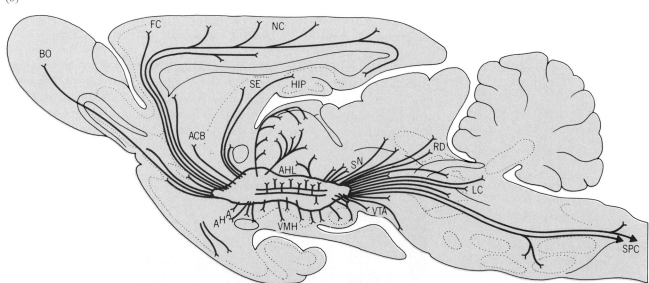

F I G U R E 10-16 MEDIAN FOREBRAIN BUNDLE IN THE RAT BRAIN.
(a) *Fibers that lead into the median forebrain bundle (colored).* (b) *Fiber tracts that lead out of this area. This area is rich in neural connections with other areas of the brain. To help you*

locate where this area is we have identified some important brain regions: ACB = nucleus accumbens, AHA = anterior hypothalamic area, AHL = lateral hypothalamic area, AMYG = amygdala, BO = olfactory bulb, FC = frontal cortex, HIP = hippocampus, LC = locus coeruleus, NC = neocortex,

PFC = prefrontal cortex, RD = dorsal raphe nucleus, RM = nucleus raphe magnus, RPO = nucleus raphe pontis, SE = septum, SN = substantia nigra, SPC = spinal cord, VMH = ventral medial hypothalamus, VTA = ventral tegmental area. (From Stellar and Stellar, 1985.)

important and desirable substance and induces them to pursue it. The BAS is responsible for a rat's rapid progress down a maze that has previously led to a reward. It is also responsible, in theory, for the excitement and frenzied searching young children show on an Easter egg hunt.

Gray has not yet identified the BAS with a particular brain region. But research (Stellar and Stellar, 1985) suggests that the **medial forebrain bundle** and its connections may be involved. This area is activated by food, sexual stimuli, and pleasurable drugs (opiates, cocaine, amphetamines). Electrical stimulation of this area seems to prime animals to pursue pleasurable incentives. The median forebrain bundle is part of an extensive neural system in which dopamine is the principal neurotransmitter (Figure 10-16).

Gray's model also helps to explain why a stimulus might increase one kind of arousal but not another. Rewards or the expectation of rewards usually increases heart rate, whereas punishers or the expectation of pun-

FIGURE 10-17   PITTER-PATTER OF PLEASURE.

Human subjects were given either 0, 2, or 5 cents per trial for pushing a button. Some subjects got paid after all five trials (/5), some after two (/2). Subjects paid the most showed the largest heart rate increases. Moreover, only subjects who got paid after all five trials showed heart rate increases across all five trials. Because these heart rate increases cannot be attributed to body movement of the subject, they probably are due to an internal arousal mechanism—possibly the BAS. (From Tranel, 1982.)

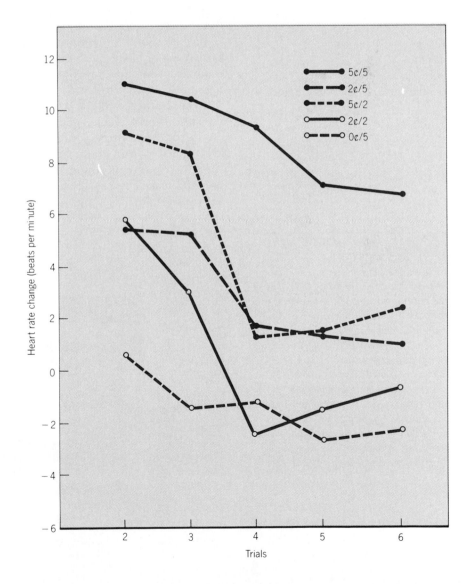

ishment usually increase sweating. Researchers have argued that BAS arousal increases heart rate, and BIS arousal increases sweating (Fowles, 1980). In support of this, incentives increase people's heart rates, and the size of the increase is determined by the magnitude of the incentive (Figure 10-17). Punishers and frustrative nonreward increase sweating (Fowles, 1980, 1982).

GRAY'S AROUSAL THEORY: AN APPRAISAL   A theory's value depends, in part, on its ability to explain existing experimental data and observations. Here Gray's theory shines. First, Gray notes that anxiety (see Chapter 13) has many features in common with BIS effects. The anxious person scans the environment frequently, as if searching for danger. The anxious person is likely to be quite aroused—to sweat copiously and have difficulty sleeping or relaxing—and last, anxious people are likely to stop what they are doing if they are startled or frightened. Thus, features that Gray attributes to the BIS seem to "go together"—as if they are influenced by the same system. In addition, drugs have been found that reduce anxiety markedly. These drugs reduce arousal and help anxious people sleep better and relax (Figure 10-18). Gray has argued that if anxiety is due to BIS activation, then these drugs should affect the septal-hippocampal region. Indeed, there is now evidence that this is the case (Gray, 1982a).

Gray also noted that if antianxiety drugs really reduce BIS activation, they also should block some of the effects of punishers. Punishment or the threat of punishment often causes rats to freeze. For example, if rats are trained to run down an alley for food but are later shocked for running if a tone is sounded, theoretically the tone should activate the BIS and make the rat freeze. But rats on antianxiety drugs run despite the tone (Stein, Wise, and Belluzzi, 1977; also see Fowles, 1980). More-

FIGURE 10-18   DRUGS THAT REDUCE ANXIETY.

Pictured are some drugs that reduce anxiety. Alcohol is probably the oldest of the antianxiety agents. Both alcohol and the later discovered barbiturates *have antianxiety actions, but neither is medically prescribed because of their intoxicating effects and the risk of addiction. Today the most commonly prescribed antianxiety agents are* benzodiazepines *like* Librium *and* Valium *(see Chapter 15). Gray notes that all of these antianxiety agents have one thing in common; they exert strong effects on the septal-hippocampal area of the brain.*

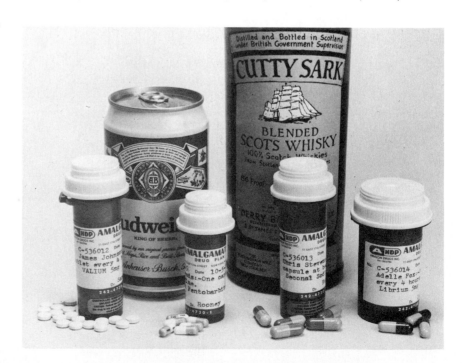

over, Gray reasoned that if an animal were trained to *escape* an electric shock through some active response like running, then antianxiety drugs would have no effect on learning because the running would not have depended upon the BIS (remember, the BIS produces motor *inhibition*). Again, this is what the data show.

While less research has been conducted on the BAS than on the BIS, Joseph Newman, a University of Wisconsin psychologist, has recently gathered data that suggest that psychopaths and other disinhibited people—risk takers—perform on experimental tasks as if their BASes were dominant over their BISes. **Psychopaths** impulsively engage in pleasurable activities despite the likelihood that they will eventually suffer punishment or pain (see Chapter 13). Psychopaths and other disinhibited individuals have been found to respond to punishment by increasing, not decreasing, their activity. They could not slow their activity even to obtain a reward and were difficult to distract from a rewarding activity even with punishment (Kosson and Newman, 1986; Newman and Kosson, 1986; Newman, Widom, and Nathan, 1985). All these findings suggest that disinhibited individuals have a low threshold of BAS activation or that their BASes resist interruption by the BIS.

As you can see, Gray's theory can account for many phenomena: why animals freeze in response to signals of punishment, why anxious people act as they do, and why antianxiety drugs are effective. Gray's ideas about the BAS help us understand why we pursue goals, why priming enhances our pursuit of incentives, and it may shed light on the nature of psychopaths. Gray's theory is attracting considerable research attention and will be investigated thoroughly in years to come.

GENERAL MOTIVATIONAL THEORY: ACQUIRED MOTIVATION

A man looks at a calendar, realizes that winter is on the way, and sets out to buy a winter coat. A young girl is straining to see a classmate's answers to an exam question when her teacher's voice causes her to jump with alarm. A 16-year-old boy takes a cigarette out of his father's cigarette pack and smokes it. After the first few puffs, he is overcome by nausea and feels intensely ill. Yet 6 months later he is smoking frequently and enjoys smoking. Each of these people is showing **acquired motivation**. How does a once neutral stimulus like a calendar page or a teacher's voice acquire such significance that it causes a man to rush out and spend his money or a girl to startle? What causes a once-repugnant item like a cigarette to become so desirable?

DRIVE THEORY   Drive theory would suggest that the man who rushes out to buy a winter coat after he notices a calendar is showing the power of an acquired drive. Hull and other drive theorists hypothesized that, in addition to **primary drives** produced either by deprivation (hunger) or by powerful stimuli (pain), behavior is influenced by **secondary drives**. A secondary drive is produced or activated by a previously neutral stimulus that has been paired with a primary drive.

Neal Miller, a prominent experimental psychologist, provided some of the earliest evidence of how secondary drives are acquired. In a classic experiment, Miller (1948) shocked rats in the white side of a long, narrow compartment (Figure 10-19). The rats quickly learned to run from the white to the black compartment through a small door. Presumably, the shocks activated a fear drive, and rats reduced this drive by escaping from the white compartment. To prove that the white compartment had itself acquired the ability to elicit a fear drive, Miller changed the nature of the experimental task. The rats were put back in the white compartment, but the linking doorway was closed and their escape blocked. The rats could open the door only by turning a small wheel in the white compartment. Eventually the rats learned to turn the wheel and did so repeatedly to escape to the black compartment. The white compartment, a previously neutral stimulus, supported the acquisition of wheel turning. Shock escape could not have reinforced wheel turning because rats were not shocked in the second part of the experiment. The white compartment had acquired the ability to produce fear by having been paired with the shocks, and the rats learned to reduce this learned, secondary drive by turning the wheel.

Thus, according to drive theorists a man might buy a winter coat after looking at a calendar because he had associated "November" with the coldness of winter; "November" elicited a secondary "coldness" drive. He also might have learned to turn up his heater, run in place, and vacation in Florida to reduce his secondary "coldness" drive.

FIGURE 10-19   MILLER'S PREFERENCE COMPARTMENT.
The white and black compartments used by Miller to study acquired drives in rats. Notice that the flooring and colors let the rats discriminate easily between the two sides of the alley. (From Miller, 1948.)

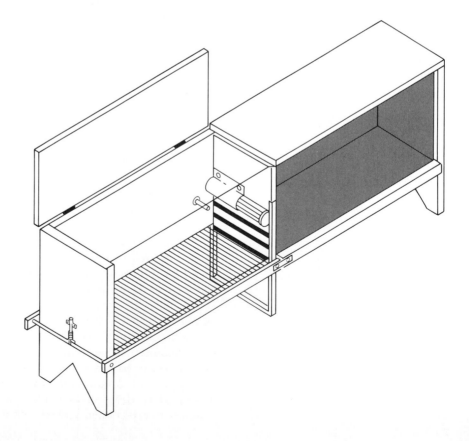

INCENTIVE THEORY   As we noted earlier, incentive theory holds that an important determinant of motivation is an animal's *expectation* that a stimulus will be pleasant or unpleasant. Because expectations are learned (people don't expect something to be pleasant or unpleasant unless they have some experience with it), learning plays a major role in incentive motivation.

Recent research has shed light on how incentive motivation is learned. Donna Capaldi and her colleagues at Purdue University have shown that animals can learn about the desirability of an incentive even when their motivation or drive for the incentive is low. For example, hungry rats (that were not thirsty) readily learned the location of water, information that they used later when they were thirsty (Capaldi, Hovancik, and Davidson, 1979). Drive reduction was not necessary for learning. In later research, rats learned to prefer stimuli paired with saccharin solutions and to prefer the sweetest of the saccharin solutions (Davidson, Capaldi, and Campbell, 1985). Because saccharin has no caloric value and therefore cannot reduce hunger, the rats learned to prefer it for its pleasurable sweetness and not because it reduced their hunger drive. But rats that were very hungry preferred weaker saccharin solutions than rats that were less hungry. Apparently, the very hungry rats associated the unpleasant sensations they felt with saccharin. A drive theorist would say that saccharin elicited a secondary hunger drive. Thus, Capaldi's research reveals that animals can learn about the incentive value of stimuli and also that these stimuli can acquire secondary drive properties. Whether a neutral stimuli becomes associated with a pleasurable incentive or an unpleasant drive depends in part on how deprived the organism is.

OPPONENT-PROCESS THEORY   Drive and incentive theories of acquired motivation address how a neutral stimulus can increase motivation after being paired with drives or incentives. In contrast, the **opponent-process theory** addresses why the effects of powerful motivators change when people are exposed to them repeatedly.

Consider this vignette: A college student takes a tough final exam. She worries constantly about how well she did and becomes convinced that she has failed the exam. She believes that she will get a poor grade in the class, her overall grade average will suffer, she will fail to get into medical school, and she will die in ignorance and poverty. After three days of agony, she discovers that she has got a B on the exam. She is relieved, even euphoric. She had received Bs on other exams, but they had disappointed her. Why did this B make her so happy?

When she got a B before, she had not expected to get a much lower grade and therefore the B didn't provide the same sense of relief. However, this account doesn't reveal what process resulted in her euphoria.

Solomon's opponent-process theory holds that the central nervous systems (CNSs) of mammals are organized so that they automatically *oppose* strong emotional reactions. These opposing reactions (produced by **opponent processes**) get stronger with every repetition of the strong emotion. The student who had worried so terribly about her grade was overjoyed at her B because of an opponent process. Every time she had worried about her grade, her CNS tried to reduce the worry by produc-

Child first
sees dog

"Thump
thump"

Fifth time
child sees dog

Tenth time
child sees dog

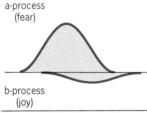

a-process
(fear)

b-process
(joy)

*FIGURE 10-20 OPPONENT
PROCESSES.*
*The first time the boy meets a dog his
initial responses (a-processes) produce a
feeling of fear. The a-processes might
include a pounding heart and trembling
limbs. However, even in this first
encounter the body begins to oppose
the initial emotional reaction with
b-processes. These grow in size, occur
sooner after the a-processes begin, and
last longer each time the boy meets the
dog. Eventually, the b-processes
overwhelm the a-processes and the boy
experiences joy upon meeting the dog.*

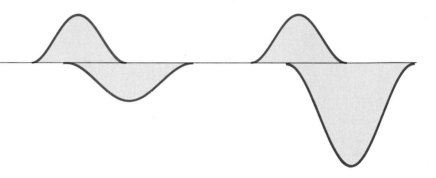

ing opposite emotional responses (joy, relief). She didn't notice these
opposite emotional reactions because her worry was so severe. At most
they might have reduced her worry over time. But once she got her B,
her worry departed, and her joy and relief were unmasked.

Solomon has labeled organisms' initial responses to emotional events
a-processes. For example, if a person is slapped the a-processes elicited by
the slapping would probably produce fear or anger. According to Solomon as long as an emotional event remains the same (e.g., does not get
larger or smaller) our initial emotional responses to the event (our a-
processes) will not change no matter how many times we experience the
event. You have all noticed that you often react less to an event after its
first occurrence; the first roller coaster ride is the scariest, and the first
kiss the sweetest (see "habituation," Chapter 6). According to Solomon,
we feel different after an event occurs repeatedly because the body's
opponent processes (**b-processes**) grow with every occurrence of the
event (Figure 10-20).

When our emotional feeling after an event is produced by a-processes
we are in an A-State. When b-processes have grown so large that they
overwhelm the a-processes, we are in a B-State. Thus, the boy's initial
fear of the dog in Figure 10-20 is an A-State; his later joy is a B-State.
Sometimes b-processes never grow sufficiently large to overwhelm the a-
processes. Thus, while a spouse's kiss may become less exciting over

many years of marriage, it often retains some appeal. Table 10-1 lists major features of a- and b-processes.

TABLE 10-1 CHARACTERISTICS OF OPPONENT PROCESSES

A-Processes

1. Produce initial emotional reactions to emotionally significant stimuli or events.
2. Size and duration determined by intensity of the instigating stimulus.
3. Maintain their size and duration across repeated elicitations.

B-Processes

1. Produce secondary responses (or after-reactions) to emotionally significant stimuli or events.
2. Increase in size and duration each time they are elicited.
3. Maximum size and duration determined by the size of the initial emotional reaction to a stimulus (the a-process).
4. Tend to remain large once they have grown large even if they are dormant for long periods.

Let's look at whether opponent-process theory is consistent with observations of motivational processes. When dogs are administered shocks in Pavlovian conditioning trials (e.g., Katcher et al., 1969), their initial response to shock is terror. The dogs screech, their hair stands on end, and they tremble. When the dogs are released from shock harnesses, they appear subdued, hesitant, and cautious. But after the dogs have been given many shocks over many days, they appear anxious and afraid when they get the shocks. But they no longer seem terrified. When the dogs are released from their shock harnesses, they seem euphoric, frisky, and playful.

Now let's examine the case of people learning how to parachute (Epstein, 1967). When people are learning how to parachute, they are terrified during the first few jumps. Immediately afterwards, they seem stunned, stony faced with shock. But after several jumps, they are no longer terrified during the jump. They seem merely tense or anxious, sometimes even eager. Immediately after these jumps (given safe landings), the jumpers are jubilant, exhilarated, and happy.

Do these two examples fit the opponent-process model? The initial terror produced by the shocks or jumps represents the influence of a-processes. Notice that in both examples, the A-State (terror) diminishes as the subjects repeatedly encounter the frightening stimuli. As the A-State diminishes, the relief and happiness—the B-State—increases.

It is likely that people parachute for sport not because they want to feel terror and shock (the A-State) but because they enjoy the opponent-process. Skydiving is an example of *acquired* motivation because people only begin to enjoy it fully after repeated skydives—their enjoyment depends upon repeated experiences with it—growth of the b-process.

The opponent-process theory also explains aspects of drug addiction. People first take a drug because it feels pleasant: the A-State. But the pleasant effects decrease with repeated drug use and give way to unpleasant after-effects, withdrawal symptoms: the B-State. They fall into the vicious circle that is drug addiction because every dose only temporarily replaces the B-State with the A-State, and when the B-State returns it is larger than ever (Solomon, 1977).

Why should the CNS be organized to oppose strong emotional reactions? Opponent processes serve as natural homeostatic brakes that prevent people from pursuing significant motivational goals indefinitely: from listening to a particularly beautiful piece of music for a week and not eating, sleeping, or working or eating chocolates until we fall over. Solomon would say that all intense emotional reactions weaken upon repetition, and so people are freed from chocolate, or music, or whatever, allowing us to pursue other experiences. Unfortunately, in a few cases, like drug addiction, homeostatic reactions trap people in a vicious cycle of a- and b-processes.

THEORIES OF BASIC MOTIVATION: AN APPRAISAL

Research arising from general theories of motivation has abated since the 1950s. As you have seen, each theory of motivation tells part of the story of motivated behavior, but none tells the whole story. Drive theories can account for the effects of deprivation on motivated behavior, yet they do a poor job of accounting for motivated behavior that occurs in the absence of physiological need. Incentive models can account for the powerful effects of goals, but they do not explain fully *how* incentives exert their effects. Arousal theories fall victim to ambiguity about defining and measuring arousal. Gray's arousal theory provides insight into how arousal differs in pleasurable versus unpleasant motivational states, but it does not account for the role of complex cognitive processes in motivation.

Many investigators today are investigating particular types of motivated behavior and have abandoned the attempt to account for all motivated behaviors in terms of a general motivational model (Locke, Shaw, Saari, and Latham, 1981).

We now turn to research findings on two specific types of motivated behavior: eating and sexual behavior. These are both considered basic motivations in that they occur in even the most simple animals, and they are less influenced by learning and sophisticated cognitive processes than complex types of motivation (see Chapter 11).

HUNGER, EATING, AND BODY WEIGHT

All living beings need food to survive. It is no wonder that food is such a powerful motivator. Food, of course, supplies the body's energy. Although people's need for this energy is continuous, they feel hungry and eat only a few times a day. What determines when people feel hungry and when they feel sated and stop eating?

Patterns and Size of Daily Meals

BEGINNING A MEAL   One factor that determines when people feel hungry is *learning* (Weingarten, 1985). Most Americans eat three meals a day; most ancient Romans ate twice a day. These were the patterns established by their societies. When mealtime comes people feel hungry. You probably have had the experience of missing lunch only to find that you feel less hungry by mid-afternoon. Then, at dinner time, you feel hungry again. Your hunger can increase and decrease on a learned schedule. *Social factors* also can affect hunger. For example, we are more likely to feel hungry and to eat more in the company of others who are eating than when we are alone (Edelman, Engell, Bronstein, and Hirsch, 1986).

Physiological factors make people feel hungry. The stomach contracts as muscles in its lining produce hunger pangs. But even people who have had to have their stomach surgically removed continue to have feelings

FIGURE 10-21   GLUCOSE, THE LIVER, THE VAGUS NERVE AND EATING.
Rabbits got injections of a substance (2DG) that blocks glucose use by cells. When 2DG was injected into the portal vein, which goes from the intestines to the liver, the rabbits began to eat within about 10 minutes. When 2DG was injected into the jugular vein, and therefore reached the liver slowly, eating began in over an hour. When the vagus nerve, from the liver to the brain, was cut, injecting 2DG into the blood supply to the liver did not make the rabbits begin eating rapidly. Thus, the vagus nerve signals glucose use in the liver to the brain. When glucose use is low, or blocked, the animals become hungry and begin eating. (From Novin, VanderWeele, and Rezek, 1973.)

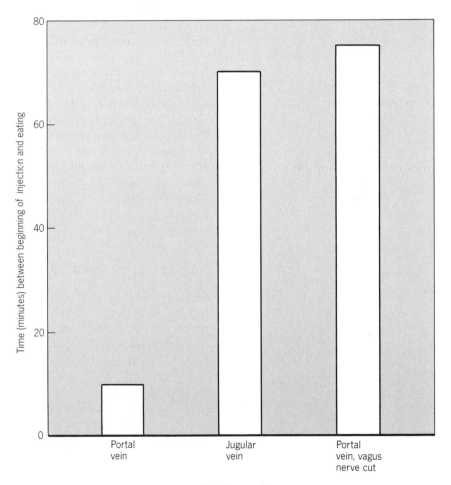

of hunger (Pack and McNeer, 1943). Besides stomach contractions, a principal physiological cause of hunger is the *availability of glucose* (a simple sugar) in the blood (Mayer, 1955). Glucose provides energy for the body and brain. The body stores excess glucose primarily as glycogen (a carbohydrate) and between meals, breaks down these stores into glucose for energy. When glucose in the blood falls, people feel hungry. Note that it is not simply the amount of glucose in the blood that determines whether people feel hungry; it is whether cells in the body can use the glucose. [Diabetics, for example, lack the hormone (insulin) required for glucose to enter the cells of the body. Thus, although their blood is full of glucose, their cells cannot use it. As a result, diabetics feel hungry unless they are treated with insulin.]

The body has sensors (called **glucostats**) that measure the use of blood glucose. These sensors are located in the liver, which absorbs nutrients from the bloodstream. Nerves from the liver send the signal from the glucostats to the brain, and the results are hunger and eating (Novin and VanderWeele, 1977; Russeck, 1971; see Figure 10-21).

ENDING A MEAL What makes people feel sated and stop eating? It is unlikely that satiation is signaled by the level of nutrients (such as glucose) in the blood, because usually people feel sated long before nutrients are absorbed from the intestines into the bloodstream.

Neural signals from the stomach itself seem to contribute to the feeling of satiation from a meal (Deutsch, 1978). As the stomach fills, pressure sensors in the stomach lining are stimulated and send information to the brain. But stomach volume alone does not signal satiation. If you are hungry and drink lots of water, you still feel hungry. Neural sensors apparently also signal the nutritive value of your stomach contents.

Hormones released during eating also contribute to satiety (Baile, McLaughlin, and Della-Fera, 1986; Smith, 1984). For instance, when food contacts the surface of the mouth, stomach, or small intestine, the intestine releases a hormone called **cholecystokinin** (**CCK**) into the blood. CCK then stimulates the vagus nerve, which signals the brain to inhibit eating.

Long-term Control of Eating and Body Weight

The factors we have discussed so far determine people's daily patterns of hunger and satiety. Several psychological and physiological factors also influence long-term eating habits—why some people consistently eat more than do other people. As we shall see, some of these factors are related to whether people are fat or thin, but many are not.

RESPONSIVENESS TO FOOD CUES One obvious determinant of how much we eat at a meal is the sight, smell, and taste of the food. People differ in the extent to which their eating is influenced by these food cues. Some people are stimulated to eat by seeing food and eat as much as they can, whereas other people stop eating when they are full even if they see more food. Some people also eat much more good-tasting food than poor-tasting food, whereas others eat only slightly more good than poor food (Schachter, 1971). Results such as these suggest that for some people, eating is controlled largely by *external* cues such as taste and the amount available. For other people, eating is controlled largely by *internal* cues for hunger and satiety.

At first researchers thought that overweight people tended to be guided by external cues and normal-weight people by internal cues (Schachter, 1971). However, more recent studies indicate that responsiveness to external or internal cues is not clearly related to body weight (Rodin, 1981). Whether people respond more to external or internal cues may be due to a variety of factors, such as learning or even genetic inheritance.

RESTRAINED AND UNRESTRAINED EATERS   You may know people who constantly diet; they are always trying to restrain their eating. Other people eat as much as they want at each meal; they are unrestrained eaters. Studies show that restrained and unrestrained eaters differ in other ways as well. For instance, if unrestrained eaters are induced to eat more than they should, their control seems to break down completely and they go on to eat still more. Unrestrained eaters stop eating sooner after first overeating (see Figure 10-22). Underweight, normal, and over-

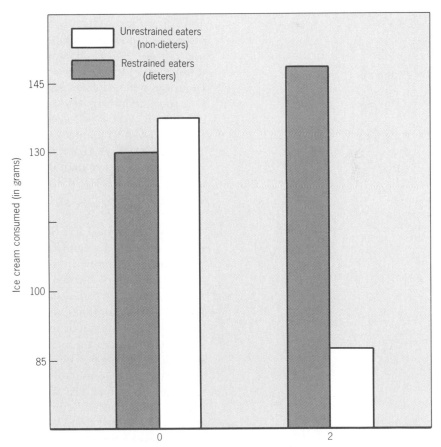

FIGURE 10-22 "NOW THAT I'VE BLOWN MY DIET . . ."
One group of dieters drank two milkshakes; another group did not. Both then were encouraged to eat as much ice cream as they wanted. The dieters who first had milkshakes ate more ice cream than the others. But among nondieters, those who had had milkshakes ate less ice cream than those who had not. (From Hibscher and Herman, 1977.)

weight people all behave in these ways. They eat according to whether they are restrained or unrestrained, not according to their weight (Hibscher and Herman, 1977).

STRESS AND AROUSAL Stress also affects how much people eat. Laboratory studies with rats indicate that stress produced by a mild tail-pinch can increase daily food intake by over 100 percent (Rowland and Antelman, 1976). Similarly, some people respond to anxiety and stress by overeating (McKenna, 1972; Schachter, Goldman, and Gordon, 1968). Stress and arousal may make people more sensitive to environmental cues, including food cues, and as a result they eat more. Eating also may serve to reduce anxiety and stress for some people. Evidence suggests that obese people eat more under high than low anxiety and people of normal weight eat less when they are anxious than when they are not (McKenna, 1972).

FAT CELLS Body fat is stored in fat cells, called **adipocytes**. The fat cells of overweight people are larger than those of normal-weight people and contain up to twice as much fat (lipid). In addition, very obese people have about three times more fat cells than people of normal weight (Hirsch and Knittle, 1970). The number of fat cells people have is partly determined by genetic factors. In addition, experiments with animals indicate that diet affects the number of fat cells. Rats fed fattening foods grow more fat cells than rats on a normal diet (Knittle and Hirsch, 1968). The number of fat cells can increase at any age, from infancy to old age. Once the fat cells are present, dieting can reduce their size but not their number (Hirsch and Knittle, 1970).

Experiments suggest that substances in the bloodstream signal the amounts of lipids in fat cells (Harris and Martin, 1984) and that size of fat cells (or their lipid content) is regulated by the body (Faust, Johnson, and Hirsch, 1977). Interestingly once people are overweight, they do not necessarily eat more than people of normal weight (Thompson, Billewicz, and Passmore, 1961). Rather, overweight people tend to stay overweight by expending less energy (Faust, 1984; Keesey and Powley, 1986).

METABOLISM AND EXERCISE Body weight is determined not only by energy intake (what and how much people eat) but also by energy expenditure. The more energy people use, the less is stored as fat. In the average person of normal weight, about 75 percent of the energy they take in maintains resting bodily functions, referred to as **basal metabolism**. The rest supports active physical behavior.

The body's metabolism of energy is not constant. The rate of basal metabolism differs among individuals and from time to time in the same individual. When people eat less, their basal metabolism decreases. In fact, when people diet, their basal metabolism falls disproportionately, and they lose much less weight than their reduced energy intake might suggest. This is why dieters often find it so difficult to lose weight even though they are eating less. Conversely, overeating raises basal metabolism disproportionately, and the weight gain is less than the increase in calories might suggest (Keesey and Powley, 1986). Thus, variations in basal metabolism are important determinants of body weight.

People can increase the amount of energy they expend by engaging in physical exercise. Not only does metabolism increase during exercise, it remains high for some hours afterward. Furthermore, when people exercise, they do not tend to eat more to compensate for the increased energy use, and therefore lose weight (Thompson, Jarvie, Lahey, and Cureton, 1982). This weight loss does not decrease basal metabolism. Thus, the amount of exercise people get influences both body weight and eating (Stern, 1984).

GENETIC INFLUENCE   Obesity tends to run in the family. Is that because of environmental factors such as eating or exercise habits or because of genetic influence? Studies comparing monozygotic (MZ)—identical—and dizygotic (DZ)—fraternal—twins (see Chapter 9 for a discussion of this method) suggest that heredity influences the development of obesity. For instance, if one identical twin is overweight, the other is likely to be overweight also (Borjeson, 1976). In contrast, fraternal twins are much less likely to be equally fat (these measures correct for differences in height) (see Figure 10-23). Studies comparing adopted individuals with their adoptive and biological parents also point to a genetic influence on body weight. These studies show no relationship between the body weight of relatives by adoption but a strong relationship between biological relatives (especially the mother's weight, but both biological parents' weights were statistically significant). This correlation applies for people of all weights, suggesting that it is body weight and not just obesity that is genetically influenced (Stunkard et al., 1986).

The nature of the genetic influence on body weight is not fully understood. As we have seen, there are a number of factors that affect body weight, any of which could be genetically influenced. Indeed, research indicated that the number of fat cells and the rate of basal metabolism (Bogardus, Lillioja, Ravussin, Abbott, Zawadzki, Young, Knowler, Jacobowitz, and Moll, 1986) both are inherited to some extent. The presence of a genetic influence on body weight does not mean that body weight is genetically *determined*. Body weight is a result of the balance between energy intake (eating behavior) and energy expenditure (due to basal metabolism and activity), both of which can be modified by the individual.

Theories of Eating and Regulation of Body Weight

Clearly many factors, both cognitive and physiological, produce long-term differences among individuals in eating behavior and body weight. Two types of theories have emerged to explain these differences. One type emphasizes the cognitive factors, and the other emphasizes the physiological.

Cognitive theories suggest that food intake is the primary determinant of body weight. Although these theories allow that physiological factors

FIGURE 10-23   GENETICS OF BODY WEIGHT.
In each pair of twins, one is overweight. In the MZ twins, the other member also tends to be overweight. But in the DZ twins, the other member is not necessarily overweight. (From Borjeson, 1976.)

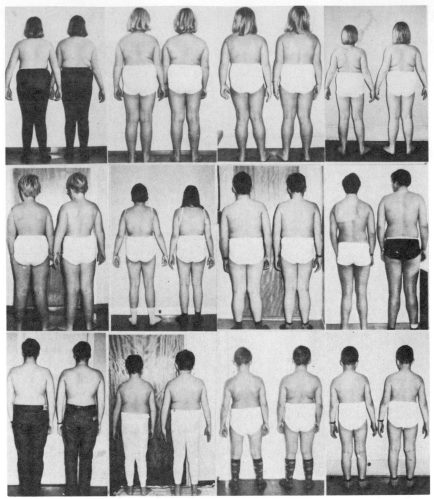

IDENTICAL (MZ)

influence eating, they hold that what and how much people eat is largely controlled by learning and social influences (Herman and Polivy, 1984). According to this view, overweight results from abnormally learned eating habits. Cognitive theories are basically incentive-motivation models of hunger, eating, and weight regulation.

An alternative theory is that people have physiological **set points** for particular body weights, and their long-term eating and energy use are adjusted to maintain body weight near this set point (Keesey and Powley, 1986). People have sensors that monitor fat-cell size or levels of insulin (which controls energy storage). When these signals exceed certain limits (the set point), changes in energy input (eating) or output (metabolism) occur to return people to their set body weight. This theory allows that cognitive factors can influence eating but that metabolism changes to compensate for changes in food intake. According to this theory, obese people have high set points, and their eating, metabolism, and activity levels maintain their weight near this set point (Keesey and Powley,

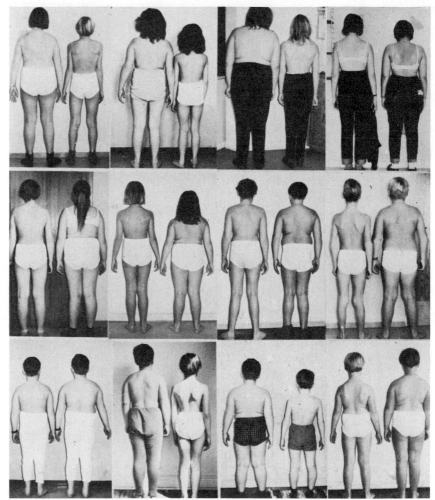

FRATERNAL (DZ)

1986). Thus, the set point theory is a homeostatic (drive) model of hunger, eating, and weight regulation. At present, there is no general agreement about which theory is correct.

BRAIN MECHANISMS OF EATING   Research on the brain mechanisms behind eating has centered on two nuclei (groups of neurons) within the hypothalamus (this structure is described in Chapter 2). One pivotal discovery was that damage to the ventromedial hypothalamus (VMH, see Figure 10-16) produced animals that overeat dramatically and eventually become very obese (Heatherington and Ranson, 1940; see Figure 10-24). Paradoxically, these animals are finicky eaters. Given only unpalatable foods, they do not overeat or gain weight. Damage to the lateral hypothalamus (LH, see Figure 10-16) produces almost the opposite effect: the animals stop eating (Anand and Brobeck, 1951). They rapidly lose weight and may starve to death unless they are force-fed. Over time, however, animals with LH lesions resume eating, but they

BOX 10-1
BULIMIA AND ANOREXIA NERVOSA

Throughout our discussion of hunger, eating, and weight regulation we have considered the problem of obesity. Two other eating disorders have received a great deal of attention in recent years: bulimia and anorexia nervosa (Bemis, 1978; Crisp, 1984; Fairburn, 1984; Pirke and Ploog, 1986 are excellent reviews). **Bulimia** refers to recurrent eating binges. A bulimic person eats a large amount of food in an hour or two and feels as if the eating is out of his or her control. In some cases, bulimics then induce vomiting or use laxatives to purge themselves of the food they have eaten. Bulimics tend to be overly concerned with body weight and shape and fear becoming fat. Although bulimics overestimate their body size (Willmuth, Leitenberg, Rosen, Fondacaro, and Gross, 1985), they actually maintain their body weight within normal range. Some people with bulimia know that their pattern of eating is abnormal; however, some bulimics do not consider themselves to have an eating problem. Most bulimics are young women, and it is estimated that about 10 percent or more college women have some bulimic symptoms, such as binge eating at least once a month (Gray and Ford, 1985; Nevo, 1985).

Anorexia nervosa is a more serious eating disorder that results in substantial weight loss (Box Figure 1). People with anorexia nervosa severely reduce their food intake and may stop eating for long periods. About half of anorectics alternate starvation with bulimia. Anorectics tend to be preoccupied with food and often hoard it. They stop or reduce eating not because they have lost a desire for food, but because of a desperate desire to be thin. However, anorectics almost always have a very distorted body image and often insist that they are overweight even though they have become emaciated. Women with anorexia nervosa stop menstruating. In addition, anorectics have many symptoms of starvation and malnutrition, including low body temperature, low basal metabolism, abnormal circadian rhythms, and sleep disturbances. About 1 person in 100,000 has anorexia nervosa, though mild forms of anorectic behavior may be much more widespread, and the incidence seems to be increasing. About 95 percent of anorectics are women, and their symptoms usually appear when they are 17 to 18 years old. In about 10 percent of the cases, anorexia nervosa is fatal.

There is much controversy about the causes of anorexia nervosa (Be-

FIGURE 10-24
VENTROMEDIAL HYPOTHALAMUS LESIONS AND BODY WEIGHT.
The rat on the left is a normal adult. The rat on the right, from the same litter, received a lesion of ventromedial hypothalamus, overate, and became obese. It weighs 65 percent more than the other rat. (From Hetherington and Ranson, 1940.)

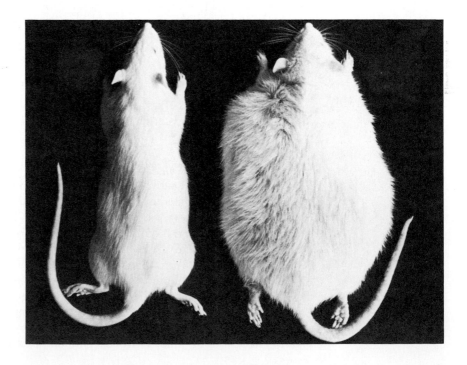

mis, 1978; Crisp, 1984; Pirke and Ploog, 1986). One hypothesis is that it is a by-product of our culture's preoccupation with thinness. Nearly all anorectics begin by routine dieting after they hear comments that they are "filling out" or "getting plump." Once they begin to diet, they seem unable to stop. A related hypothesis is that anorexia nervosa is the result of a learned fear, or phobia, of becoming fat. It also has been proposed that anorexia nervosa stems from abnormal family interactions. Perhaps it serves to get the attention from family members or to avoid interpersonal conflicts. Another possibility is that anorexia nervosa is due to abnormal hypothalamic control of eating. For instance, the body-weight set point may be abnormally lowered. There also is evidence of a genetic predisposition for anorexia nervosa (Crisp, Hall, and Holland, 1985; Scott, 1986). Of course, anorexia nervosa

may have many cognitive and physiological causes (Pirke and Ploog, 1986), just as many cognitive and physiological factors influence normal eating.

BOX FIGURE 1   ANOREXIA NERVOSA.
This woman suffers from anorexia nervosa. A defining characteristic of anorexia nervosa is a loss of at least 25 percent of original body weight.

maintain their weight below normal. Humans with VMH or LH damage due to tumors in the hypothalamus show similar syndromes.

One interpretation of these findings is that the LH is a "feeding center" in the brain. It monitors the levels of nutrients in the blood and the other signs of hunger we have discussed, and it controls the onset of eating. When the LH is damaged, these functions are lost and people do not eat. Conversely, the VMH is viewed as a "satiety center." It monitors satiation after a meal and inhibits eating, perhaps by inhibiting the activity of the nearby LH. When the VMH is damaged, this inhibition is lost, and an individual overeats (Grossman, 1984; Stricker, 1983).

An alternative explanation of these findings has been proposed (Keesey and Powley, 1975, 1986). The hypothalamus may be involved in regulating weight, and its influence on eating is secondary to this role. Animals with LH damage do not always stop eating. Under some conditions (for example, if their body weight is low before the LH is damaged), they actually increase their food intake (see Figure 10-25). The hypothesis is that the LH functions to establish a set point for body weight. Damage to the LH lowers the set point, and animals eat less to regulate their body at the new set point. The VMH, on the other hand, may control the body's energy stores. For example, the VMH may normally activate basal metabolism so that energy expenditure matches

FIGURE 10-25 DO LATERAL HYPOTHALAMIC LESIONS LOWER BODY WEIGHT SET POINT?
Effects of lateral hypothalamus (LH) damage on eating and body weight. The top curve shows the weight gain of normal rats. A second group of rats got lesions of the LH, stopped eating, and lost weight. A few days later, they began eating again and maintained lower than normal body weight (middle curve). A third group of rats was starved to 80 percent of normal body weight before getting LH lesions (bottom curve). They ate more than normal immediately after the operation and until their body weights matched those of the other group of LH-damaged rats. (From Powley and Keesey, 1970.)

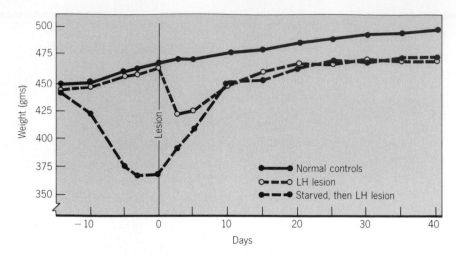

energy intake. This idea receives support from recent studies showing that electrical stimulation of the VMH produces rapid and large increases in energy use (Atrens, 1985) and that VMH damage reduces energy use (Vilberg and Keesey, 1984). Thus, according to this view, animals gain weight after damage to the VMH because the damage leads to lower than normal energy expenditure (Keescy and Powley, 1986).

SEXUAL MOTIVATION

Motivation for sex differs in important ways from motivation for food. Food reduces a physiological need for energy, which is required for the organism to survive. Although sex is necessary for the survival of the species, it is not needed for the survival of the individual. Nor does an individual have to engage in sexual behavior to feel healthy, happy, or successful.

Sexual motivation and behavior are influenced by many different factors. Sexual developmental and sexual behavior are influenced both by physiological changes (hormone effects on the body and brain) and by learning. We will consider the hormonal and neural bases of sexual behavior first.

Hormonal Mechanisms

ORGANIZATIONAL EFFECTS AND SEXUAL DIFFERENTIATION All fetuses have the potential for developing into either a male or a female. Hormones determine the path of development. If the fetus is exposed to hormones called **androgens** (the most important of which is *testosterone*), it will develop into a male. If the fetus is not exposed to androgens, it will develop into a female. Normally, whether androgens are present depends on the genetic makeup of the fetus. If the fetus is genetically female (XX chromosomes), its gonads develop into ovaries that do not

Normal Sexual Differentiation

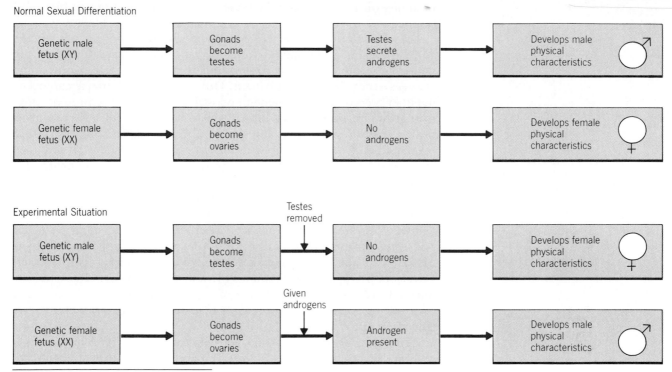

Experimental Situation

FIGURE 10-26
ORGANIZATIONAL EFFECTS OF
ANDROGEN HORMONES.
The normal developmental situation is
shown at the top. Experimental
situations in which a genetic male fetus
is deprived of androgens and a genetic
female fetus is given androgens are
shown at the bottom. Experiments such
as these are carried out in animals.
However, hormonal abnormalities can
produce similar effects in humans.
Notice that in the absence of the
necessary hormonal effects, nature creates
a female. The presence of androgens
changes this basic female blueprint into
a male.

secrete androgens or secrete them in insufficient amounts to produce the male pattern of development. However, if a genetically female fetus is exposed to enough androgens, it will develop male physical characteristics (except for its gonads, which remain ovaries). Conversely, if a genetically male fetus is deprived of androgens (for example, by removal of the testes), it will develop female physical characteristics (Jost, 1985; Figure 10-26).

These **organizational effects** of hormones produce permanent changes in the organization of sexual characteristics. For the organizational effects to occur, the hormones must be present during a **critical period** in prenatal development. For instance, if androgens are absent during the critical period, the fetus will develop female characteristics, and administration of androgens later will not reverse these effects.

ACTIVATIONAL EFFECTS Another effect of sex hormones is to activate latent sex characteristics or behaviors. These are referred to as **activational effects.** Many of the sexual changes that occur at puberty represent the activational effects of hormones. At about 12 to 14 years of age, the brain causes the testes or ovaries to secrete sex hormones into the bloodstream. In boys, the primary sex hormone is the androgen testosterone. It produces many of the physical changes at puberty such as maturation of a boy's genitals, growth of his muscles and beard, and deepening of his voice (because the larynx enlarges). In girls, the primary sex hormone is **estradiol,** which is an **estrogen.** It produces physical changes at puberty such as maturation of a girl's genitals and breasts, widening of her pelvis, and increased fat deposits on breasts, hips, and buttocks.

Some of these activational effects of the sex hormones are sex-specific and permanent. For example, testosterone can cause maturation of the penis and scrotum only in a boy (obviously), and once these maturational changes occur they are permanent. Other activational effects can occur in either boys or girls and depend on which hormones are present. Boys may grow breasts or wider hips if given estrogen, and girls can grow beards if given androgen. But many of these activational effects are reversible; they last only as long as the necessary hormone is present. For example, if a man's testes stop secreting testosterone, his beard disappears.

Hormones also have activational effects on sexual behavior. For example, androgens affect men's sex drive and sexual performance. Men who are castrated (their testes have been removed) or whose testes do not secrete normal amounts of testosterone usually lose their sex drive as well as their ability to ejaculate and to have an erection (Bermant and Davidson, 1974; Davidson, Camargo, and Smith, 1979). Replacement injections of testosterone increase the sexual activity of these men, and controlled studies show that these changes are not due to placebo effects (Davidson et al., 1979).

Androgens also affect sexual behavior in women. Normally, androgens are secreted by women's adrenal glands. If the adrenal glands are removed (because of cancer), sexual desire and activity decrease (Waxenberg, Drellich, and Sutherland, 1959). Conversely, administration of androgens to women increases their sexual desire (Money and Ehrhardt, 1972).

Neural Mechanisms

Many of the reflexes behind sexual behavior are controlled by the spinal cord. Many men who have had their spinal cord severed in an accident still can have an erection and ejaculate when their penis is stimulated directly (Comarr, 1970). Because the connections between the spinal cord and brain have been cut, these reflexes are controlled by the spinal cord alone. But the brain profoundly influences sexual behavior. When men and women become sexually aroused while looking at erotic pictures, their sexual arousal is a result of brain influences.

Some of the most important brain structures for the control of sexual behavior are located in and around the hypothalamus. In males, an important region is the preoptic area (so named because it is located near the optic nerves at the base of the brain). Destruction of the preoptic area reduces copulation in rats and primates (Larsson and Heimer, 1964; Slimp, Hart, and Goy, 1978). Conversely, electrical stimulation of the preoptic area produces mating behavior in males (Perachio, Marr, and Alexander, 1979; Van Dis and Larsson, 1971). Furthermore, if testosterone is implanted in the preoptic area of a castrated rat (which normally is not sexually active), the rat engages in sexual behavior (Johnston and Davidson, 1972). Presumably, one of the normal actions of testosterone is to influence male sexual behavior by altering the activity of neurons in the preoptic area.

In females, the anterior and ventromedial hypothalamus (see Figure 10-16) seem to be most important in controlling sexual behavior. Damage to these areas disrupts sexual behavior in female rats (Kalra and Sawyer, 1970; Mathews and Edwards, 1977). When estradiol is implanted in the ventromedial hypothalamus of female rats, their sexual behavior increases (Pfaff, 1980).

The neural and hormonal mechanisms of sexual motivation and behavior are closely linked. The hypothalamus controls the pituitary gland (located at the base of the brain; see Chapter 2), which releases many hormones that are important in sexual development and behavior. Hormones in turn affect the structure and function of the hypothalamus. For instance, male humans' and animals' preoptic areas are larger and contain more neurons than females' (Gorski, Gordon, Shryne, and Southam, 1978; Swaab and Fliers, 1985). This and other sex differences in brain structure and function are organized by the presence of certain hormones early in life (Goy and McEwen, 1980). In addition, as we have seen, hormones administered into the hypothalamus produce sexual behavior in both adult males and females. Thus, the hypothalamus is an important point of communication between hormonal and neural factors that control sexual behavior and motivation.

Characteristics of Sexual Behavior

Sexual behavior is absolutely necessary to the survival of the human species, and this necessity suggests that sexual behavior might be instinctive. Perhaps learning is too unreliable, too hit and miss, to ensure the survival of the species. If so, we should find that sexual behaviors are fairly similar across diverse cultures. Is sexual behavior really stereotyped and instinctive?

Research with castrated guinea pigs has shown that sexual behavior does not occur unless males are given testosterone (Grunt and Young, 1952). Moreover, among females of most mammalian species, sexual behavior will not occur unless estrogen levels are high. Thus, a minimal level of hormones is necessary for sexual behavior to occur. However, considerable evidence suggests that much variation in sexual behavior, and especially human sexual behavior, can best be understood as a product of learning rather than of hormonal control. For instance, some men continue to engage in sexual behavior for years after being castrated—despite low levels of testosterone (Money and Erhardt, 1972). After castration, some men lose their sexual motivation almost immediately, whereas others show a gradual decline over many years. Research shows that the amount of sexual experience before castration determines the rate of decline (Beach, 1969; also see Hart, 1968), an indication that learning is involved in the maintenance of sexual behavior.

If learning contributes to sexual behavior, we should observe variations in sexual practices from culture to culture. Indeed, this is the case. For example, people in some cultures kiss (Hopi of Arizona, the Truckese of the Carolina Islands) but not in others (the Manus of New Guinea). The frequency of sexual behavior also varies across cultures. The typical American couple has intercourse about two to three times a week, whereas the Aranda of Australia report having intercourse three

FIGURE 10-27 BEAUTY IS IN THE EYE OF THE BEHOLDER.
In modern Western society slimness is considered attractive. In other societies and at other periods in history, plumpness has been preferred.

FIGURE 10-28 THE ODALISQUE BY INGRES.
A preference for the plump human form has occurred off-and-on throughout human history. One of the oldest depictions of the human form is the "Venus of Wilendorf" dating from 20,000–30,000 years B.C. The statue is of a ponderously obese woman with a bulging abdomen and thighs. In 1911 a French clinician, Heckel, complained that fashion kept his patients obese, "It is beyond a doubt that in order to have an impressive décolleté each woman feels herself duty bound to be fat around the neck, over the clavicle and in her breasts. . . . As to treatment, one cannot obtain weight reduction of the abdomen without the woman sacrificing in her spirits the upper part of her body. To her it is a true sacrifice because she gives up what the world considers beautiful."
(Bruch, 1973.)

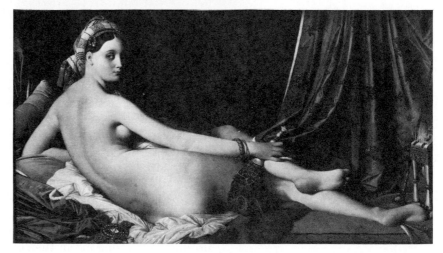

to five times a night (Ford and Beach, 1951)! Even the object of sexual desire appears to be determined, in part, by social influences and learning. Homosexual behavior is more common in cultures where it is condoned—for instance, among the Keraki of New Guinea and the Siwan of Africa—than in cultures where it is punished—for instance, among the Bedouin of Africa, where it is punished by execution (see Klein, 1982).

Experience and learning strongly shape people's evaluation of sexual attractiveness. Human cultures vary widely in the features considered attractive. For example, in America in the 1980s, to be attractive is to be quite slim (Figure 10-27), yet throughout much of history plumpness was considered attractive (Figure 10-28), and it remains attractive to a variety of societies in modern times (Ford and Beach, 1951).

Contribution of Learning to Sexual Behavior

How might learning affect sexual motivation or behavior? The most complete data on the role of learning and experience in sexual behavior comes from research on the development of heterosexual behavior among rhesus monkeys (see Goldfoot, 1977). For example, rhesus monkeys isolated shortly after birth and kept isolated for 6 months never develop appropriate or successful sexual behavior. They show *interest* in members of the opposite sex, but they cannot act on their interest. Monkeys allowed to stay with their mothers but no other monkeys during their early development have disturbed sexual behavior but somewhat less than more isolated monkeys. Less than 40 percent of the males, for example, learn to copulate in adulthood. When monkeys are allowed fairly consistent access to their mothers and peers during the first five years of life, almost all show normal sexual behavior. Research has shown that the effects of early isolation on sexual behavior are not due to changes in sex hormone levels.

What can explain the sexual inadequacies of rhesus monkeys raised in isolation? At one time it was thought that socially isolated male monkeys never learned the motor skills necessary for sexual acts because they never practiced appropriate sexual behaviors during early play (e.g., mounting postures; see Figure 10-29). But research later showed that previously isolated monkeys readily mounted "dummy" monkeys (Deotsch and Larsson, 1974). Isolated monkeys show not only sexual difficulties but lots of aggression and fearfulness and little mutual grooming (Figure 10-30). Researchers now believe that fear interferes with appropriate sexual behavior. In effect, these young monkeys never learned to trust other monkeys (Figure 10-31). Monkeys reared in isolation probably can mount a dummy monkey because the dummy makes

FIGURE 10-29 PRACTICE OF SEXUAL BEHAVIORS.
Young rhesus monkeys practice normal adult sexual behaviors. (From Goldfoot, 1977.)

FIGURE 10-30 SOCIAL ISOLATION PRODUCES FEAR.
An infant rhesus monkey grimaces in fear when approached by another infant. Fearful behavior is common in animals isolated from others when young. (From Goldfoot, 1977.)

FIGURE 10-31 TRUST IN THE MONKEY.
Young rhesus monkeys learn to trust one another through play and mutual grooming. (From Goldfoot, 1977.)

no menacing movements! Learning appropriate sexual behavior means learning to trust.

What Sexual Behavior Tells Us about Motivation

As we have seen in the foregoing sections, adequate sexual behavior depends on an adequately functioning physiological system and on learning, which can influence the choice of sexual objects as well as the frequency and competence of sexual behavior. Moreover, appropriate sexual behavior does not depend on learning about *sex* alone. Sexual behavior occurs as part of a human's or an animal's whole social repertoire. Those who have not learned to trust others are affected in the expression, and perhaps the level, of their sexual motivation. Thus, we can see that, at least in higher animals, sexual motivation is somewhat complex, not only because it has many determinants, but also because it is interdependent with other types of motivation and abilities.

What about the relationship between biological or hormonal influences and learning or experience in sexual motivation? In the face of different social rules and kinds of training for sexual behavior, biological sexual needs manifest themselves as societies permit or encourage. Perhaps a good analogy is to think of biological influence as a stream that must flow from high to low terrain, with social practices, norms, and attitudes forming the terrain through which the water must flow. The stream must flow in the face of great variation in the terrain, and therefore, the terrain influences the form and appearance of the stream. In this analogy, the influence of biological forces is very much like a "drive," but the drive is nonspecific and highly influenced by the environment. John Money, a prominent sex researcher, has remarked, "The sex drive appears from the hormonal point of view to be neither male nor female, but undifferentiated—an urge for warmth and sensation of close body contact and genital proximity" (Money, 1961, p. 246). Thus, when sexual drive increases, sexual behavior tends to be expressed through people's customary channels. If the male sex hormone androgen is administered to male heterosexuals, they report a greater desire for heterosexual activity; yet, testosterone produces greater homosexual motivation among male homosexuals (Kinsey, Pomeroy, and Martin, 1948). Incentive theorists would argue that what is crucial in determining the characteristics of people's sexual behavior is their learning about incentives in the environment that signal the opportunity for pleasurable sexual activity. A minimal level of drive appears necessary for sexual behavior to occur, but given this minimal level, incentives can powerfully influence sexual behavior.

Homosexuality

Does the study of motivation provide insight into the causes of homosexuality? The causes of homosexuality have been debated for many years—with hypotheses ranging from demonic possession to genetic influence. Moreover, as we have seen, cultures have varied widely in their stance toward homosexual behavior. Yet despite frequent persecution and discouragement, homosexual behavior has occurred in many cultures throughout history. Why?

Before we can consider the possible causes of homosexuality, we must define it. Are homosexuals people who engage in sexual acts with members of their own sex or fantasize doing so? If we adopt the latter definition, as many as half the males in the United States would be considered homosexual (Kinsey, Pomeroy, and Martin, 1948). Perhaps homosexuals are those who not only engage in sexual activity with members of their own sex, but also have adopted a **gender role** of the opposite sex. That is, they have adopted the mannerisms, interests, and perspectives of persons of the opposite sex. One problem with such a definition is that it eliminates from consideration all those people who engage exclusively in sex with same-sexed individuals, yet have adopted gender roles appropriate for their sex. Any adequate definition of homosexuality must take into account the fact that homosexual behavior extends along a continuum. At one end of this continuum are heterosexual individuals who have virtually no fantasies about homosexuality and have no homosexual experiences. At the other end are individuals who are "exclusive" homosexuals, those who have virtually no heterosexual fantasies or experiences. Between these extremes of sexual orientation are all possible gradations: people who are bisexual; people who some-times, mainly, or nearly always engage in homosexual or heterosexual fantasy or behavior.

Isolated or aperiodic homosexual acts frequently occur in humans or animals when they are denied access to the other sex. Prisons and single-sex schools are places where situational homosexuality may flourish. However, we are interested in why a decided homosexual orientation occurs when heterosexual partners are available. This kind of exclusive homosexuality appears to be uniquely human.

One of the earliest psychological theories of homosexuality was that of Freud. Freud proposed that homosexuality reflected the inadequate resolution of the Oedipal conflict (see Chapter 12). Males became homosexual because they are sexually attracted to their mothers yet fear punishment from their fathers. To reduce their fear of their father's punishment, young boys unconsciously reject their desire for their mothers. In fact, they *identify* with their mothers and so develop a homosexual orientation. Freud theorized that female homosexuality developed out of a similar process. Because girls fear competing with their mother for their beloved father, they identify with their father and develop homosexual interests. In essence, Freud considered that for both males and females, homosexuality is a *defense* that removes the individual from competition with the same-sex parent.

Freudian theory has been influential, but some of its predictions have not been supported by research. One common characterization of homosexuals, based in part on Freudian theory, is that they avoid heterosexual activity because they find women frightening or repugnant (because sexual relations would, at an unconscious level, constitute incest). Such characterizations of homosexuals as *heterophobics* certainly seem incorrect. The great majority of homosexuals report having been sexually aroused by heterosexual stimuli at some point in their lives (Bell and Weinbert, 1979). Homosexuals merely find homosexual activity *more* pleasurable and arousing.

Another psychological theory of homosexuality is that homosexual girls and boys are sexually precocious and therefore tend to have early sexual experiences with members of their own sex. In this way, early sexual arousal comes to be associated, through Pavlovian learning, with others of their sex (Feldman and McCulloch, 1971; Green, 1974). Data do show that homosexuals generally report having been sexually aroused earlier in life than is true of most heterosexuals (Saghir and Robins, 1973). Moreover, the data also show that homosexuals, especially males, often have their *first* sexual encounter with someone of their own sex. Thus, it is possible that early learning *stamps in* a homosexual orientation. Although such early sexual experiences may contribute to homosexuality, they are not necessary or sufficient to produce homosexuality. Many individuals have had early homosexual experiences and yet have not become homosexuals (e.g., Kinsey et al., 1948).

Biological theories of homosexuality include genetic and hormonal theories. One early genetic study yielded compelling support for a genetic basis of homosexuality. Kallman (1952) studied the sibling of mono- and dizygotic twins. Kallman found that less than half of dizygotic twins were concordant for homosexuality, but 100 percent of monozygotic twins were concordant. However, several subsequent studies failed to replicate Kallman's result. Therefore, a genetic basis of homosexuality remains to be proven.

Finally, many researchers have investigated the hypothesis that homosexuality is caused by prenatal or later exposure to abnormal hormone levels. One early and intuitively appealing theory of homosexuality was that it was caused by abnormally low androgen (testosterone) levels in homosexual males, and by abnormally high androgen levels in homosexual females. Indeed, several studies have found low androgen levels in male homosexuals (for example, Margolese and Janiger, 1973). However, the meaning of this finding is unclear. Stress reduces androgen levels. Given that homosexuals are subject to stress from the social disapproval they encounter, stress could account for their reduced androgen levels. That is, low androgen is a result not a cause of homosexuality.

Some theorists have reasoned that because exposure to postnatal androgen causes adult male homosexuals to report even greater sexual interest in males, it is the organizational effects of androgens, rather than their activating effects, that affect homosexual orientation. Perhaps some male fetuses are exposed to low levels of androgen and do not undergo the hypothalamic changes that correlate with a heterosexual orientation. Likewise, some female fetuses may be exposed to high levels of androgens. Studies show that male rat fetuses exposed to low androgen levels are more likely than other males to assume the female's posture of sexual receptiveness when exposed to normal males (Dorner, 1968). But some data conflict with this theory. For instance, in the disease *congenital adrenal hyperplasia,* human female fetuses are exposed to abnormally high androgen levels. Even so, most of them develop into heterosexual women (Ehrhardt, Evers, and Moncy, 1968). Thus, although exposure to prenatal androgen may influence sexual orientation, it is not the sole influence.

Psychologists do not know *the cause* of homosexuality, and perhaps there is no single cause. Homosexuality may be related to hormonal factors, family relationships, or a combination of factors. We believe that our analysis of homosexuality provides a lesson, however. Whatever the cause(s) of homosexuality, we can see that it appears to involve some disturbance of a *natural* process important to the development of sexual orientation. Realizing that the cause of homosexuality may merely be an abnormally high level of androgen during gestation or a defense against a hostile family environment helps us see homosexuality as a natural phenomenon rather than as a moral problem. It's nice to know that heterosexuals need not go through life (carrying the burden of) feeling morally superior to Oscar Wilde, Henry James, W. H. Auden, Somerset Maugham, Walt Whitman, Herman Melville, Tchaikovsky, Isaac Newton, Michelangelo, or Leonardo da Vinci—all homosexuals. Freud eloquently described the relationship of homosexuality to normal sexual development processes when he wrote to the concerned mother of a homosexual (see Box 10-2).

BOX 10-2
A LETTER FROM FREUD

Dear Mrs. X:

I gather from your letter that your son is a homosexual. I am most impressed by the fact that you do not mention this term yourself in your information about him. May I question you, why do you avoid it? Homosexuality is assuredly no advantage, but it is nothing to be ashamed of, no vice, no degradation, it cannot be classified as an illness; we consider it to be a variation of the sexual function produced by a certain arrest of sexual development. Many highly respectable individuals of ancient and modern times have been homosexuals, several of the greatest men among them (Plato, Michelangelo, Leonardo da Vinci, etc.). It is a great injustice to persecute homosexuality as a crime, and cruelty too. If you do not believe me, read the books of Havelock Ellis.

By asking me if I can help you, you mean, I suppose, if I can abolish homosexuality and make normal heterosexuality take its place. The answer is, in a general way, we cannot promise to achieve it. In a certain number of cases we succeed in developing the heterosexual tendencies which are present in every homosexual, in the majority of cases it is no more possible. It is a question of the quality and the age of the individual. The result of the treatment cannot be predicted.

What analysis can do for your son runs in a different line. If he is unhappy, neurotic, torn by conflicts, inhibited in his social life, analysis may bring him harmony, peace of mind, full efficiency, whether he remains a homosexual or gets changed. If you make up your mind he should have analysis with me!! I don't expect you will!! He has to come over to Vienna. I have no intention of leaving here. However, don't neglect to give me your answer.

Sincerely yours with kind wishes,

Freud

P.S. I did not find it difficult to read your handwriting. Hope you will not find my writing and my English a harder task.

(From Freud, 1935, the *American Journal of Psychiatry;* from Geer, Heiman, and Leitenberg, 1984, p. 297.)

SUMMARY

BASIC MODELS OF MOTIVATION

1. *Motivational Concepts and Theory.* A variety of theories have been forwarded to explain motivated behavior—instinct, drive, incentive, and arousal theories. Each of these theories accounts well for particular aspects of motivated behavior. Instinct theories explain why the same motivated behaviors occur in both humans and animals—the behaviors are evolutionarily adaptive. Drive theory and the principle of homeostasis explain the effects of deprivation on motivation, and so on. However, no single theory of motivation provides a complete account of motivation.

2. *Acquired Motivation.* Acquired motivation describes the process by which experience converts a neutral stimulus into a potent motivator, or changes the nature or magnitude of a stimulus's motivational effects. According to Hullian drive theory, neutral stimuli become motivators by being paired with basic, or primary drives. Research shows that neutral stimuli also gain motivational value by being paired with incentives. Opponent-process theory explains why repeated exposure to stimuli alters their motivational impact. The elicitation of an emotional response by a stimulus automatically produces an opposite emotional reaction in humans and animals. The development of such opponent processes can have significant motivational effects. For instance, humans may take drugs to avoid drug withdrawal symptoms, which may reflect opponent processes to pleasurable drug effects.

HUNGER, EATING, AND BODY WEIGHT

3. *Hunger and Satiety.* Physical events like stomach contractions and a fall in blood glucose level produce feelings of hunger, while satiety is associated with stomach pressure, and detection of nutrients in the blood. Some of these physical responses are affected by learning. For example, humans experience stomach contractions at times they normally eat.

4. *Long-term Control of Eating and Body Weight.* Food cues, stress, number of fat cells, metabolic rate,

and exercise all can influence eating patterns or body weight. Food cues may stimulate people to eat more but these people do not necessarily gain weight because their metabolism increases to burn off excess calories and keep them at set point. On the other hand, people with a large number of fat cells tend to weigh more than other people, but they do not necessarily eat more. Twin studies have shown that genes influence body weight, possibly by helping to determine the number of fat cells or basal metabolism.

5. *Theories of Eating and Weight Regulation.* Eating and weight regulation have been attributed to both learning and social influences and to maintenance of body weight set point. The former theories emphasize that our body weight is determined by our food intake and that our food intake is affected by social influences and learned habits. According to set-point theory, organisms homeostatically defend a body weight set point. If an organism is below its set point, it eats more and its metabolism slows down. If it is above its set point, it eats less and its metabolism increases.

SEXUAL MOTIVATION

6. *Hormonal Mechanisms.* Hormones may influence sex and sexual behavior through their organizational or activational effects. In the former, hormones exert a developmental influence and create permanent changes. In the latter, hormones activate behaviors or characteristics already present, but latent, in the organism.

7. *Neural Mechanisms of Sexual Behavior.* Sexual behavior is influenced at different levels of the nervous system. For example, the spinal cord has all that is necessary to produce erection and ejaculation if the penis is manually stimulated. However, the brain, and especially the hypothalamus, also influence sexual behavior. In fact, one of the organizational effects of sex hormones is to produce differences in hypothalamic structure.

8. *Sexual Behavior.* As with hunger and eating, sexual behavior is influenced by learning as well as by physiological structure. This accounts for the diversity in sexual behavior seen in people of different cultures. Moreover, castrated males with previous sexual experiences may engage in sexual activity long after their androgen levels have dropped. Monkeys do not learn to mate successfully if they have not learned as youngsters to affiliate with and trust other monkeys.

9. *Homosexuality.* Finally, an analysis of the causes of homosexuality suggests that sexual orientation may be determined by early experiences, prenatal hormone exposure, social and family interactions, genetic influences, or combinations of those factors. What is clear is that to understand the development of a homosexual orientation, one must understand the determinants of a heterosexual orientation.

FURTHER READINGS

An edited book that contains classic readings on motivation is *Motivation* by Dalbir Bindra and Jane Stewart (Penguin, 1966). Though dated, many of the papers in this volume had profound effects on conceptualizations of motivational processes. A text by Robert Bolles, *Theory of Motivation* (Harper and Row, 1975), also provides a thorough and valuable account of the classic theories of motivation. A recent review of motivational theory that is quite readable and informative is Frederick Toates' *Motivational Systems* (1986).

If you would like to obtain additional information on particular types of motivation, or on particular motivational theories, some of the following are appropriate: Richard Solomon's "An opponent-process theory of motivation: 1. Temporal dynamics of affect." *Psychological Review,* 1974, *81,* 119–145; Jeffrey Gray's *The Neuropsychology of Anxiety: An Enquiry in the Functions of the Septo-hippocampal System* (1982); and John Garcia's paper "Behavioral regulation of the *milieu interne* in man and rat." *Science,* 1974, *185,* 823–831.

11

COMPLEX MOTIVATIONAL PROCESSES, EMOTION, STRESS, AND COPING

Over the past 20 years psychologists have become increasingly convinced that human motivation cannot be explained by the basic motivational theories discussed in Chapter 10. Psychologists discovered that they could only account for human motivation if they considered the roles that cognitions and complex forms of learning play in motivation. They realized that the same event, say, failing a test, will have very different motivational effects depending upon the student's causal attributions, how the student views himself, the student's plans and goals, and the student's expectations. Complex motivational theories address how such cognitive factors as views of self, or attributions of cause, influence motivated behavior.

THEORIES OF COMPLEX MOTIVES

In Chapter 10, you read about several theories of basic motivation. In this chapter, you will read about theories of complex motivation. These theories tend to be narrower in focus and tend to be directed at particular motivated behaviors, for example, achievement motivation. There are numerous theories of complex motivation (Sorrentino and Higgins, 1986) and many are directed at specific motivational phenomena. However, some general theories of complex motivation have been proposed that appear to have wide applicability. We present two of these.

An Attribution Theory of Motivation

Let us suppose that you are a runner who has been training diligently for a marathon. You and your running partners are aiming to run the marathon in under 3 hours 30 minutes. You have run several marathons in the past, but you have never broken this barrier. On the day of the race, you run the entire 26-mile marathon smoothly and without stopping. As you cross the finish line, the timer calls out, "Three hours 28 minutes and 15 seconds." You feel ecstatic. You have joined the ranks of "serious" runners. You contemplate a spot in the Olympics, congratulate yourself on your superb physical condition and your diligence in training so hard.

But 15 minutes later you hear that your running partners all run faster than you. One of them even says "Of course, it was an easy run. The course was mostly downhill, the temperature was in the 50s, and there was a 15 mph wind at our backs most of the way. We couldn't have had an easier course." You are ecstatic no more. You tell yourself that you're just an average runner after all, and you stop thinking about an Olympic career. You decide that you will stop running for a while.

How does motivation theory account for your dramatic shift in mood and motivation level? Although there are several approaches to **attribution theory** (e.g., Heides, 1958; Kelley, 1967), all attribution theories hold that the causes to which people attribute their behavior strongly determine their level of motivation and the type of motivated behavior they engage in. Thus as a marathon runner, your motivational level was high as long as you thought that your performance was caused by your characteristics or *internal* attributes such as athletic skill or diligence. However, once you attributed your good performance to an *external* characteristic such as the easy course, you had little further motivation to run.

Theorists have identified four major types of causes to which people attribute their successes and failures (although these attributions may differ from one culture to another; Weiner, 1985a,b): The attributions are ability, effort, task difficulty, and luck. Attribution theorists also are interested in the sorts of information that people use to attribute causes and in the actions they take upon attributing causes. How might people arrive at the causal attributions listed above? What sorts of information might people use to make a causal attribution regarding a successful outcome?

> *Ability:* If a person has a past history of success at similar tasks, he might infer that a success is due to high ability.
> *Effort:* If a person struggled so hard he became fatigued, he might attribute success to the effort he expended.
> *Task difficulty:* If the task is one mastered by most people, his success might be due to low task difficulty.
> *Luck:* If a person notices that ability and effort don't seem to influence outcome, he might conclude that any success in the task is due to luck.

For example, if a person has a history of succeeding at a task—*ability*—if many others have failed at that task—*task difficulty*—and if the person works at the task with little *effort,* the person would attribute any success to great skill or ability. However, if the person failed at the task, he or she might attribute the failure to low effort, great task difficulty, bad *luck,* or a combination of these.

Research by E. L. Deci and his colleagues provides an example of how causal attributions can affect people's motivation. Although one of the most tried and true findings in psychology is that reward increases the probability that the rewarded behavior will recur, Deci and others have found that the effects of reward, at least in humans, depend on what people attribute the reward to. For instance, Deci (1972, 1975) had people work on challenging block puzzles. One group was told that they would be paid for each puzzle completed (the reward-informed condition), a second group was paid for each puzzle completed but was not told beforehand that they would be paid (reward-uninformed), and a third group was given neither payment nor information about payment (no reward). After the puzzle-working session was over, individuals were left alone for a short time when they could simply sit, read magazines, or go back to working on the puzzles. An experimenter observed what individuals did during this waiting period. Subjects who had gotten no reward and those not told ahead of time that they would be rewarded (reward-uninformed) spent more time solving puzzles during the waiting period than the subjects who had been told that they would be paid for each puzzle they completed. What is more, subjects tended to rate working on puzzles as more enjoyable if they had *not* been paid for working on them (Calder and Staw, 1975). These differences among the groups arise, according to Deci, because people who were not rewarded or who did not expect to be rewarded, attributed their task involvement to the pleasure they experienced in the puzzles, but those who expected a reward attributed their task involvement to the external factor of payment. During the waiting period, when the monetary incentive was absent, reward-informed persons had no reason to continue performing the task. Other subjects, though, stayed interested in puzzle solving because their attribution was internal—they solved the puzzles because of *their* capacity to enjoy such mental challenges. This capacity would remain whether or not they were paid.

Obviously people do not spend their days making causal attributions. People tend to search for causes of events that are surprising, disappointing, or important (Weiner, 1986). Thus, a student asks why she failed a test, why her dormitory blew up, or why she was not accepted to law school. She is less likely to ask herself why she passed a test, why her dorm remained intact, and why she was accepted to law school.

Exactly how do attributions influence motivated behavior? According to Bernard Weiner, a leading attribution theorist, making attributions leads to specific emotions, and the emotions, in turn influence our behavior.

$$\text{Causal Attribution} \longrightarrow \text{Specific Emotion} \longrightarrow \text{Action}$$

Assume that you fail a class. You first feel just plain bad. This bad feeling is caused by your failure, and is not dependent upon your making an attribution. However, you then ask yourself why you failed. If the answer is that you didn't study (an effort attribution), you feel guilty. However, if you decide that you failed because of low ability (lack intelligence), you feel shame. These specific emotional states then lead directly to motivated behavior. Guilty feelings might lead you to study harder, shame might lead you to switch to an easier major or leave school. In general, humans work to avoid unpleasant emotional experiences and they pursue pleasant emotional experiences.

Weiner's attributional model of motivation is important, not only because it shows how cognitions influence motivation, but also because it emphasizes the clear relationship between emotion and motivation.

Attribution theory may have important implications for society. Does the parent who rewards a child's good report card with a special treat undermine the child's pleasure in learning? Would people enjoy their work more if the link between their pay and their productivity were less obvious? In general, attribution research suggests that the motivation to perform tasks is enhanced if people attribute their successful performance to their own ability or effort. If also suggests that when people attribute their failures to lack of ability, they are least likely to keep trying. Finally, when people attribute their successes or failures to luck—to factors beyond their control—their motivation is likely to falter, no matter what the outcome. We shall analyze the motivational effects of attributions further when we discuss achievement motivation.

Self-efficacy Theory

Every single day, people must cope with countless challenges. We must remember appointments, perform complex mechanical operations (like driving a car), write and read complex material, face an angry boss or friend, start conversations, give directions. Each of these challenges demands that we determine a goal, identify the behavioral and cognitive responses critical to reaching that goal, and execute those responses. But even as we plan all of these steps, we also evaluate our ability to carry out our plan of action or coping plan. In other words, we evaluate our personal effectiveness or **self-efficacy**. These evaluations, according to Stanford psychologist Albert Bandura (1977a, 1982), determine our course of action, our persistence on that course, and our emotional response to challenges.

How do people's evaluations of their personal effectiveness affect their motivation? For one thing, people avoid tasks at which they judge themselves likely to fail. Failure can have very disturbing or even harmful consequences: students tend to avoid classes that they believe are too difficult for them. Novice mountaineers tend not to start climbs that demand great skill. People's evaluations of their personal effectiveness operate in a second way. When people think that they are likely to be effective in a task, they are more likely to try it and to do well at it. For example, suppose that two people are playing tennis when one starts to win a succession of points. According to self-efficacy theory, the losing player will strive harder and longer to reverse the course of the game *if* she is confident of her abilities: "I know I can beat this bum. I should be playing better than this." People who believe that they are equal to a challenge are likely to face each challenge with equanimity, if not with enthusiasm. However, *over*confidence can interfere with a person's performance. Overconfidence may lead a person to overestimate his or her ability, to underestimate a challenge, and to prepare insufficiently. The less confident tennis player, though, might accept an impending loss with less struggle. She might also worry about her ability to perform and belittle herself for losing. But she also might plan and prepare well for the next challenge.

Four general sources of information influence people's evaluations of their efficacy (Bandura, 1982).

1. *Performance attainments:* Perhaps the strongest determinant of estimates of self-efficacy is a person's success or failure in meeting a similar challenge in the past.

2. *Vicarious experiences:* Observing others succeeding or failing at a task provides people with valuable information about their likelihood of success. For example, seeing an accomplished gymnast *fail* at a daunting maneuver might keep the beginner from even attempting the maneuver. However, seeing Olympic gymnasts like Olga Korbut and Mary Lou Retton *succeed* at daring tumbling maneuvers on TV might encourage otherwise cautious [but arrogant] 50-year-old business executives to attempt handstands on a coffee table. Watching others perform tasks provides information about task difficulty.

3. *Verbal persuasions:* The football coach who urges his team on: "You can do it! You can beat these guys!" is using verbal persuasion to bolster his team's estimate of their ability or efficacy. The faith healer who exhorts a crippled woman "Walk, walk! I can feel power flowing into you! Walk!" is, if nothing else, increasing the woman's appraisal of her ability to stand up and walk. In contrast, verbal persuasion may also lower a person's sense of efficacy. For example, in 1986 a promising rookie trying out for the Green Bay Packers football team was told by a veteran player (who was competing with the rookie for his position) that he had little chance of making the team. The rookie accepted defeat and left the training camp. The team coaches eventually persuaded him to return (*The Capital Times,* 1986).

4. *Physiological state:* Frequently, people appraise their likely effectiveness on a task by feedback from their bodies. For example, a person unused to public speaking would probably have a low sense of efficacy if he noticed as he approached a speaker's dais that his heart was pounding and his legs felt weak. A tennis player would probably discount her chances of winning a match if she sensed fatigue and soreness in her muscles before the match.

It is important to remember that efficacy is not the same as skill, ability, or learning. Thus, no matter how much verbal persuasion he uses, a coach cannot make his players win if they are unskilled. Although high estimates of one's self-efficacy cannot themselves produce great skill, they can influence learning. When people are confident that they can learn something—a computer language, an athletic skill, a dance step—they will spend more time and effort trying to learn it. Thus, a high estimate of one's self-efficacy may influence, not only a person's motivation to perform, but also the motivation to learn.

What evidence is there that estimates of self-efficacy are important for motivation? For instance, Bandura claims that past successes ("performance attainments") make a person confident of success and that this confidence, or high self-efficacy appraisal, leads the person to perform better. However, a critic of self-efficacy theory might argue that those who have performed well in the past will perform well in the future, and it is unnecessary to assume that self-efficacy estimates have anything to do with the improved performance (see Figure 11-1). One of the strongest sources of evidence for the way that people's estimates of their self-efficacy motivate their behavior is the close relationship between the two. For instance, Bandura and his associates treated people who were abnormally afraid of harmless snakes (Bandura and Adams, 1977; Bandura, Adams, and Beyer, 1975; Bandura, Adams, Hardy, and Howells, 1980). They used four different procedures to strengthen these people's beliefs that they could encounter snakes without being harmed. The four treatments were:

Enactive: People were encouraged to approach and touch the snakes.
Vicarious: People observed others approach and handle the snakes.

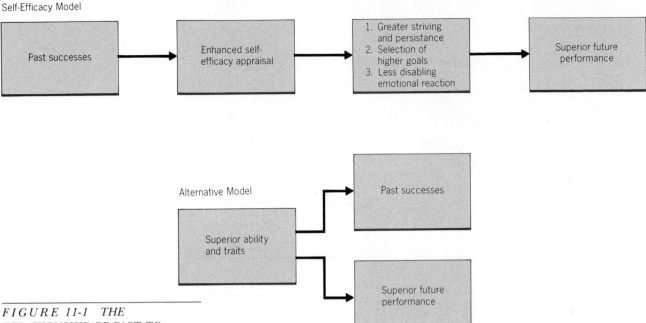

FIGURE 11-1 THE RELATIONSHIP OF PAST TO FUTURE PERFORMANCE: TWO MODELS.

According to one model of motivated behavior, information about past successes and verbal persuasion influence people's appraisals of their efficacy and, therefore, their performance. An alternative model is one that does not involve self-efficacy appraisal at all; people with the greatest skills and abilities performed the best in the past and will continue to perform the best in the future.

Cognitive: People imagined various people approaching and handling snakes successfully.

Emotive-oriented: People imagined the snakes while they were deeply relaxed.

All of these treatments had been shown in previous research to help people reduce their fears. But did the treatments also increase the people's belief in their own self-efficacy, and would the level of their self-efficacy predict how well they coped with snakes? The results are displayed in Figure 11-2. As this figure shows, all of the treatments made the fearful people feel more efficacious than the control procedure did. Moreover, all four treatments also increased the people's coping *behavior.* The most successful treatment in both measures was the enactive treatment.

An impressive feature of these data is that subjects showed parallel increases in self-efficacy and coping behavior even when the treatment they received did not require them to confront directly the feared object. For example, in the cognitive treatment subjects never actually had to try to touch snakes or cope with them. This suggests that the behavior change is not due to prior successful performance (see Figure 11-1). Rather, the treatments apparently directly affected the people's confidence in their ability to deal with snakes and their confidence then improved their ability to cope.

Other evidence also supports the theory that people's estimates of their self-efficacy determine their motivated behavior. For example, many studies have shown that the best predictor of how long smokers can abstain from cigarettes following treatment for smoking is their confidence in their ability to remain abstinent (Condiotte and Lichten-

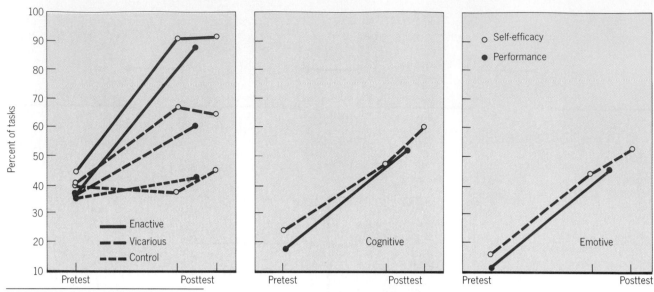

FIGURE 11-2   RELATION OF SELF-EFFICACY ESTIMATES TO PERFORMANCE.

The coping behavior (coping tasks completed) and estimates of self-efficacy of people with abnormal fears of snakes before and after they received one of four kinds of treatment or a control procedure. People showed parallel increases in both their self-efficacy estimates and their performance after any of the four types of treatment (inactive, vicarious, cognitive, or emotive). Notice that untreated controls showed no increases in self-efficacy estimates or performance.

stein, 1981; Erickson, Tiffany, Martin and Baker, 1983; Tiffany et al., 1986). The smokers generally predict their relapses weeks or months before they actually relapse. Their predictions are quite accurate because they are, in effect, self-fulfilling prophecies. According to self-efficacy theory, smokers who have little confidence in their ability to abstain relapse for two major reasons. First, the very real difficulties in quitting smoking undermine their already low confidence (Erickson et al., 1983; Tiffany et al., 1986). Second, unconfident smokers make fewer attempts to cope with their urge to smoke, are less careful to avoid cigarettes, and so forth. Their lack of confidence not only reflects their vulnerability, it actually intensifies it.

Theories of Complex Motivational Processes: Important Themes

The models of basic motivation like drive and arousal models, which we described in Chapter 10, do not adequately account for why we humans may derive more enjoyment from winning when the competition is tough rather than weak (because it provides more information about our efficacy level) or why losers prefer to attribute their losses to bad luck. Psychologists have found that it is necessary to consider a person's cognitions, his knowledge and thought processes, in order to explain much human motivation.

The two theories of complex motivation we reviewed—attribution and efficacy theories—illustrate the central role of complex cognitive processes in complex human motivations. They show that people cannot understand the effects of motivators, such as money or other rewards or punishments, without taking into account cognitive factors such as a person's goals, a person's attributions and resultant emotional reactions, and a person's self-concept (e.g., estimate of personal competence).

Indeed, goals, emotions, and self-concepts have been identified as central themes of theories of complex motivational processes (Sorrentino and Higgins, 1986).

We will now discuss three different types of motivated behavior, aggression, affiliation, and achievement, in order to acquaint you with research on these important behaviors, and to show you how basic and complex motivational processes are relevant to each. We consider these to be complex motivations in that they are highly varied in their expression and highly influenced by learning and complex cognitive processes.

THE MOTIVATION BEHIND AGGRESSION

After reading a newspaper story about a particularly grisly murder, probably every single one of us has asked what could possibly make a person show such callous disregard for human life? Granted, murder is an extreme act, but even so, it introduces the question that is at the heart of the present section: What motivates aggression?

First, we must define aggression. Aggression is often defined as behavior executed with the *intent* of causing harm, either physical, material, or psychological harm. However, this neat definition raises several other questions. Does aggression demand that the victim not want the pain or harm? Is a threat or coercion aggression even though no significant harm is done? For instance, when a bully threatens to punch another child unless the child obeys him, is the threat aggression? A major reason that aggression is difficult to define is that the term seems to refer to many different types of behavior.

Types of Aggression

Consider these two cases of aggression: a young man carves initials into a picnic table, and a gang of teenagers assaults a lone, obviously destitute man late at night. Most psychologists would place these cases of aggression into two different categories. They would label the first **instrumental** aggression, and the second, **hostile** aggression (Berkowitz, 1984). Hostile aggression occurs for the sole purpose of causing injury or harm. The teenagers attacked the man to hurt him. Instrumental aggression, on the other hand, may serve many purposes. The young man might have carved initials for any of several reasons. He might have been romantically motivated, he might have been grasping at some semblance of immortality, and so on.

Not only are the goals of hostile and instrumental aggression different, but they affect people's (and other animals') bodies very differently as well. For instance, when a predator stalks its prey—a type of instrumental aggression—the aggression occurs with relatively little autonomic nervous system arousal (see Figure 11-3). However, in the case of hostile aggression (Figure 11-4), there is generally a great deal of autonomic arousal—the heart races, there is copious sweating, and the extremities

FIGURE 11-3   PREDATORY AGGRESSION.
A barn owl approaches a mouse. In predatory aggression such as this, there is little vocalization, or behavioral display.

FIGURE 11-4 HOSTILE AGGRESSION.

A male baboon engages in an aggressive display, an example of hostile aggression. Much of the aggression between males of the same species is hostile, characterized by great arousal of the autonomic nervous system, vocalization, and display.

tremble as arousal increases (Eichelman, Elliott, and Barchas, 1981). Because of these differences in the degree of autonomic arousal, some writers have come to refer to hostile aggression as "hot" and instrumental aggression as "cool."

Hostile and instrumental aggression are only two of the ways that aggressive behaviors can be classified. Kenneth Moyer (1976) has listed eight types of aggression that he believes have different motivational bases and involve different physiological systems (see Table 11-1). There is now evidence that Moyer was at least partly correct; different types of aggression do indeed appear to have different motivational bases. Thus types of aggression may be linked more closely on a conceptual or linguistic basis than on their psychological and biological origins.

TABLE 11-1   TYPES OF ANIMAL AGGRESSION

Type	Example
Predatory	An animal stalks, catches, and kills its natural prey
Intermale	A male attacks a strange male of the same species
Maternal	A female dog attacks a male dog that has approached her young
Sex-related	Two male elk charge each other in competition for available female elk
Fear-induced	An animal, cornered and unable to escape, becomes aggressive
Irritable	A bear with painfully diseased teeth attacks another bear
Instrumental	Wild dogs nip at each other to get better positions for eating a fresh kill
Territorial	One robin drives another robin away from its territory

Source: Moyer, 1976.

Physiological Processes in Aggression

Psychologists today are working to identify and understand more about the physiological bases of aggression. Considerable research now suggests that the neurotransmitter **norepinephrine** is involved in at least some types of aggression. For instance, researchers have found that high levels of *norepinephrine* in the brain are associated with high levels of hostile aggression in male rats (for example, intermale aggression) but are associated with low levels of predatory aggression (for example, mouse killing; Eichelman et al., 1981). The link between aggression and norepinephrine also has been borne out in a study of humans. Among a group of military men, investigators discovered a significant correlation between aggression rating scales and levels of *MHPG*, a major metabolite of norepinephrine (Brown, Ballenger, Minichiello, and Goodwin, 1979; Goodwin, 1978a).

Some studies also show links between laboratory animals' aggression and the class of hormones known as androgens. For example, if females of a variety of species, including humans, are given androgen before their birth, they are more likely than other females eventually to show aggressive behaviors such as rough and tumble play (Hays, 1981). Second, the males of most species tend to be more aggressive than females, and males generally have higher androgen levels. Finally, castrating males, which removes their bodies' main source of androgens, tends to reduce their aggressiveness, and administering replacement androgens tends to restore their former levels of aggressiveness (Hawke, 1950).

Does the link between androgen level and aggression suggest that androgen may produce an aggression "drive" that can only be lowered through aggressive acts?

In one study (Schuurman, 1981), the researcher sampled the androgen levels in the blood of male rats before and after they met other male rats. He found that the rats with the highest androgen levels *before* the meetings were most likely to act aggressively when they met another male. But when he measured androgen levels *after* the encounters, he found that the aggressive rats that had won their fights tended to have even higher levels of androgen than before the fight. The losers' androgen levels had gone down. Winning fights apparently boosted the level of the aggression-related hormone. Therefore, if androgen is somehow responsible for a "drive" to aggress, it doesn't behave as traditional drive theory would predict. Instead of going down after an animal aggresses and wins—as drive theory would predict (see Chapter 10)—androgen levels actually increase. This kind of increase in aggressive behavior is consistent with incentive theory and suggests that aggression may actually beget aggression. Researchers also have found that once a child successfully aggresses against another child, he is much likelier to act aggressively again (Patterson, Littman, and Bricker, 1967).

Psychological Processes in Aggression

From a psychological perspective, what motivates organisms to aggress? In the case of instrumental aggression, it is sometimes easy to understand the underlying motivation. The predator hunts prey to get food. The boy carves initials in a picnic table to declare his love for his girlfriend. People often aggress because they are reinforced for doing so: aggression pays off! The likelihood that a child will aggress in the future has been found to depend on whether he had been rewarded for getting

TABLE 11-2 PEOPLE'S PERCEPTIONS OF LONG-TERM CONSEQUENCES OF AN ANGRY EPISODE

Consequence	Episodes in Which Change Occurred "Somewhat" or "Very Much" (%)
You realized your own faults	76
You realized your own strengths	50
Your relationship with the angry person was strengthened	48
You gained respect for the angry person	44
You did something that was good for the angry person	39
You did something that was for your own good	38
Your relationship with the angry person became more distant	35
You lost respect for the angry person	29

Source: Averill, 1983.
This table displays the percentages of angry episodes that resulted in the consequences listed on the left side of this table.

his way in the past (Patterson et al., 1967). In a study of the effects of anger and aggression, one researcher (Averill, 1983) administered questionnaires to large groups of people who had been either the recent targets of anger or aggression or the aggressors. The great majority of the aggressors—those who had expressed anger or aggression— reported that the experience had benefited them personally. That may not be surprising, but the majority of people who had been *targets* of aggression also reported that the experience had been beneficial (see Table 11-2). Like so many other types of behavior, aggressive behavior is influenced by its consequences. Instrumental aggression may be reinforced by feelings of satisfaction or by the receipt of food, money, or sexual privileges.

How about hostile, or "hot," aggression, aggression that occurs only to cause harm? Does it offer the aggressor any kind of reinforcement other than the aggression itself? Hostile aggression apparently is reinforced by the pain of its victim. Under what circumstances is this type of aggression likely to occur? One way of producing hot aggression in the laboratory is to provoke and anger people by either criticizing them harshly and unfairly or by inflicting mild pain on them. People angered in these ways are likely to act aggressively, and they are especially likely to do so if they think that their aggression will hurt someone else (Baron, 1977).

In one study (Berkowitz, Cochran, and Embree, 1981), young women were asked to push buttons either to subject a woman in an adjoining room to unpleasant blasts of noise or to reward her with nickels. The women pushed the buttons while one of their hands was immersed in either cool or very cold water. Half of the women were told that the noise would hurt the woman; the other half were told that the noise would help the woman do better on the task that she was performing. The results revealed two clear effects. First, women in pain from the cold water were especially likely to punish the woman, and they were especially unlikely to reward her. Second, among these subjects, those who had been told that the blasts were hurtful were the most likely to punish and the least likely to reward.

Under these circumstances then, pain or discomfort motivates its victims to aggress in turn—even if they cannot aggress against the person who hurt them (Swart and Berkowitz, 1976). The urban riots that occurred in several cities in the United States between 1967 and 1971 tended to occur on the hottest days of the year. Did the discomfort of that heat stimulate people's aggression (Berkowitz, 1984)? This effect has a striking correlate in animal research: an animal that suffers pain may attack a second animal even though the second animal was not acting aggressively (Figure 11-5). Monkeys caused pain, for example, will attack other monkeys, rats, or even stuffed animals (Plotnick, Mir, and Delgado, 1971). Thus, the poet W. H. Auden was correct when he observed

FIGURE 11-5   PAIN-ELICITED AGGRESSION.
A raccoon and rat coexist peacefully until the floor under them is electrified. Then the raccoon attacks the rat. Shock- or pain-elicited aggression has been demonstrated in a variety of species. (From Azrin, "Pain and aggression," Psychology Today, *1967, 1.)*

I and the public know
What all school children learn
Those to whom evil is done
Do evil in return.

If one effective way to increase aggression is to inflict pain, a second way is to *frustrate* an organism. Frustration occurs when an organism is prevented from securing or enjoying a goal or reward. For example, pigeons become aggressive if they do not get a food reward they have expected (Azrin, Hutchinson, and Hake, 1966). The effects of frustration can also be seen in the effects of competition. Competition can be frustrating because two or more individuals strive for the same goal. After boys and girls competed in a bowling game, they played more aggressively than others who had not competed (Nelson, Gelfand, and Hartman, 1969).

While inflicting pain or frustration may produce reflexive aggression in both humans and other animals, the provocation of aggression in humans frequently involves more complex cognitive processes. For example, Pastore (1952) found that frustration was much more likely to produce aggression when the victim of frustration viewed the cause of frustration as arbitrary and avoidable. Thus, you are more likely to get angry and aggressive if your date abruptly cancels your plans for no particular reason than if he or she cancels them due to illness. Averill (1983) similarly noted that anger and aggression typically involve a judgement and attribution. "Over 85 percent of the episodes described by angry persons involved either an act that they considered voluntary or unjustified (59 percent) or else a potentially avoidable accident (for example, due to negligence or lack of foresight, 28 percent). . . . More than anything else, anger is an attribution of blame" (Averill, 1983, p. 1150). Therefore, among humans, anger and aggression typically involve causal attributions about the behavior of others. "Did she mean to miss the appointment?" "Did he intend to mispronounce my name?" . . . and so on.

Finally, the *observation* of aggression or cues for aggression also influence the likelihood of aggression. As we discussed in Chapter 6, merely observing people acting aggressively tends to increase the likelihood of further aggressive acts. Even cues associated with aggression, such as the presence of a gun, can increase aggressive behavior (Berkowitz and LePage, 1967). This finding suggests that the presence of handguns in American society may not only increase the consequences of aggression (serious gunshot wounds) but also may increase the likelihood of aggression. What can we conclude, then, about the nature of the complex motivation behind aggression? First, any attempt to account for the motivational basis of aggression must acknowledge that aggression takes many different forms and that animals engage in these different forms for very different reasons. This diversity is typical of complex motivations. The Freudian and ethological theories of aggression, as you saw in Chapter 10, hold that aggressive behavior stems from a drive that builds and eventually requires expression. Although some data support this notion, most data do not. The data show that there are many types of aggression that are elicited under varying conditions and that do not reflect the influence of a central aggression drive or force. In addition, expression of aggression seems to produce more aggression, not less.

Second, it is helpful to view many acts of aggression as *strategies* to desirable outcomes. People and other animals learn these strategies through operant conditioning and observation, just as they learn many other kinds of behavior. Learning is another central characteristic of a complex motivation. Not only does aggressive behavior have a learned component, it may also have an instinctive component. For example, the aggressive response of the animal in pain is probably instinctive (Ulrich and Azrin, 1962).

Third, cues or signals of aggression—such as the presence of a gun— also tend to elicit aggression, perhaps because they serve as reminders of the pleasing consequences of aggression. This tendency for cues to stimulate aggression is consistent with an incentive model of motivation in that the expectation of reward determines the behavior of the organism. Finally, complex cognitive processes are involved in the provocation of aggression in humans. Aggression is frequently the product of the attribution of blame.

THE MOTIVATION TO AFFILIATE

The world is filled with countless examples of the motivation to unite or attach, connect or associate with another. Psychologists infer the motivation to **affiliate** when a person or other animal takes pleasure from the mere presence of or contact with another, or feels displeasure by being separated from another. The motivation to affiliate reflects a need or desire for physical and emotional closeness and is similar to what people call love. Our first inclination might be to think of affiliation as being uniquely human. However, observation of ducklings remaining close to their mother or an imprinted object (Figure 11-6), or a mother robin flying repeatedly to her nest to care for her fledglings, reminds us of the ubiquity of this motivation.

Theories of Affiliation

Freud advanced one of the first theories of affiliation. He proposed that infants' love for and attachment to their parents begin in the infants'

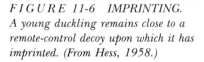

FIGURE 11-6 IMPRINTING. A young duckling remains close to a remote-control decoy upon which it has imprinted. (From Hess, 1958.)

dependence on the parents to satisfy their basic biological needs for food, warmth, and the like. However, as the infant grows older, the basis of this affiliation changes. For example, Freud proposed that a young boy eventually affiliates with his father because he has *identified* with his father in order to allay his fear of his father (see Chapter 12). This theory has two features in common with many other theories of affiliation—that the affiliation between infant and parent depends upon the satisfaction of the infant's biological needs and that the basis of affiliation changes over the course of development.

In contrast to Freud's emphasis on the satisfaction of biological needs, later psychoanalytic theories emphasized the power of affiliation to satisfy *social* needs. For example, several psychoanalytic theorists have emphasized that people derive a sense of strength and security from attachments and close relationships with others. John Bowlby (1969) proposed that one of the most important jobs of the mother is to provide her infant with a base of security. Alfred Adler held that the need for social contact and support is innate. In contrast, Harry Stack Sullivan held that the need for social contact is learned. As people learn that others provide protection and security, they feel anxious and unhappy when they are cut off from this support.

Another perspective on affiliation was provided by two learning theorists, John Dollard and Neal Miller (1950), who saw the motivation to affiliate in terms of Pavlovian conditioning. Like Freud, they assumed that the infant's affiliation with his or her parents was based on the satisfaction of basic biological needs or drives. But unlike Freud, they thought that through Pavlovian conditioning, the child comes to associate certain stimuli with aversive drives such as hunger and fear such that these stimuli themselves eventually elicit the conditioned drives. The child also comes to associate the stimuli with reductions in the aversive drives, for example through eating or being soothed. (This model is essentially the same as Hull's model of conditioned drives, which we discussed in Chapter 10).

Learning theorists suggest that the stimuli that become associated with aversive drives and the pleasurable satisfaction of these drives are principally associated with the child's parent or other caregiver. It is this parent who comes when the infant cries from hunger or fear—the aversive drives—and it is also this parent who feeds and reassures the infant—the satisfaction of the drives. Therefore, a stimulus such as your mother's face may cause you to feel sad and lonely when you are far from home—because it elicits primitive feelings of need. Her face also can make you feel tremendously glad and fulfilled when you see her after a long separation—because her face elicits feelings of satisfaction and fulfillment.

The Development of Attachment and Affiliation

Harry Harlow (1905–1981), a University of Wisconsin psychologist, spent much of his life studying the development of affiliation and attachment. However, Harlow preferred not to use these rather staid, academic terms; Harlow said that he studied love. Harlow believed that love could be subdivided into five types.

FIGURE 11-7 MATERNAL LOVE: CARE AND COMFORT. The earliest stage of maternal love, according to Harlow is care and comfort, *in which the mother (or other caregiver) stays close to the infant and satisfies its biological needs.*

1. Maternal love.
2. Infant love.
3. Peer, age-mate love.
4. Heterosexual love.
5. Paternal love.

In the following sections, we will concentrate on Harlow's research into the affiliation behavior, and specifically the maternal and infant love, of rhesus monkeys. Not everything uncovered by this research is relevant to human behavior. But as you will see, there are some striking parallels to the love between human and monkey infants and mothers.

MATERNAL LOVE   Harlow believed that the love of a rhesus mother unfolds in three stages: *care and comfort, maternal ambivalence,* and *relative separation.* During the care and comfort stage, the mother physically protects, holds, and nurtures the infant (see Figure 11-7). Indeed, she seems to *need* close, steady contact with her infant to keep on nurturing it. If the infant is taken away from her for several hours, she may nurture it less or even reject it altogether (Harlow, 1971). At first, the mother who has just given birth will hold and cuddle not only her own infant but any small, furry, clinging object. If she is separated from her infant in the first week after its birth, she will cry and become upset, but will quiet if she has another infant to hold and care for. At first, in fact, the mother will quiet and care for a kitten, although eventually she will reject it, probably because the kitten cannot cling to her as her own infant would. Several weeks after she has given birth, the rhesus mother will be appeased by and take care of only her own infant. Thus, Harlow's research shows that at first the mother's behavior can be accounted for by an instinctual need or drive to nurture a small, furry, clinging object. But her later behavior seems to depend on her having learned the characteristics of her own infant.

In the next stage of love, *maternal ambivalence,* the mother lets the infant cling less and nurse less and lets the infant wander farther away from her. Human mothers, too, gradually let their infants venture farther away (Rheingold and Eckierman, 1971; Figure 11-8).

Finally, during the stage of *relative separation,* about a year after the infant's birth, the young monkey can be separated from its mother for long periods of time without causing either the mother or the infant great distress. When they are together, the youngster makes relatively few demands on its mother, and she therefore is unlikely to punish it for approaching her. Mother and child have begun to live somewhat independent lives.

INFANT LOVE   What determines the infant monkey's attachment to its mother? Harlow noted that infant monkeys' affiliation with their mothers began in the infants' needs for food and warmth. The infants cried, for example, when they were hungry or cold. When the infants were older, however, they seemed motivated by a desire for security and protection. In this interpretation, Harlow seems to agree with John Bowlby, who proposed that the basis of the attachment between human

FIGURE 11-8 MATERNAL AMBIVALENCE.
During the maternal ambivalence *stage of maternal love, mothers allow their children to wander from them. But they remain watchful and concerned about their children's welfare.*

FIGURE 11-9 SEPARATION DESPAIR.
The despair of a young rhesus monkey after its mother has been taken away.

infants and mothers is security for the infant. Thus although they venture farther and farther from their mothers, when they are disturbed or frightened, their first response is to hurry back to their mother's protection.

What is it about a rhesus mother that sustains her infant's attachment? In classic experiments, Harlow and his colleagues discovered that when infant monkeys were separated from their real mothers, they developed close attachments to surrogate mothers that were soft, warm, moved, and gave milk (see Chapter 9). The tactile features of the surrogate mothers—the **contact comfort** they afforded—were most important in sustaining the infants' attachment. The infants spent most of their time clinging to the soft terrycloth surrogate even if they got milk from a hard, wire surrogate. Young monkeys formed attachments on the basis of contact comfort and the satisfaction of basic biological needs.

As the infant matures, it develops a close emotional bond with its mother, a bond that seems to be related to infant's developing ability to experience fear. During this stage, the mother's provision of protection and security becomes especially important to the infant. The infant now shows signs of having become attached to its mother as a specific individual. When they are separated, the infant protests (crying, scrambling around its cage) and acts *despairing* (sitting immobile and inactive, withdrawn, Figure 11-9). But the same infant responds far less when a less familar member of its troop is removed. The infant's protest increases in proportion to its fear of being separated from its mother. Taking the infant away from its mother and putting it in a strange place or exposing it to strange monkeys increases the level of its protest (Mineka and Suomi, 1978). Losing physical contact with its mother intensifies the infant's fear and touching her calms the infant. If the mother and infant are separated only by a wire mesh so that they can

Jaak Panksepp and his coworkers at Bowling Green University believe that they have begun to answer one of the fascinating riddles in human behavior. At first, they were puzzled by the similarities in the ways that people behaved under two quite different sets of circumstances: Withdrawal from the class of addictive drugs known as opiates and separation from someone to whom they were attached. Opiates, as we discussed in Chapter 5, occur in drugs and are produced by the body. The body's own opiates have biological effects that are similar to those of opiate drugs derived from the opium poppy. In both withdrawal and separation, people feel heightened sensitivity to pain, negative moods, tearfulness, and feelings of worthlessness and hopelessness. Might drug withdrawal and the pain of separation be characterized by similar physiological processes—decreased opiate activity in the brain?

Panksepp and his colleagues hypothesized that animals suffering from separation distress have abnormally low levels of endogenous opiates. Their research produced substantial support for the hypothesis. First, they discovered that tiny amounts of the opiate morphine dramatically reduced the crying that animals from several species did when they were separated (Panksepp, Siviy, and Normansell, 1985). Conversely, an **opiate antagonist,** which blocks opiate receptors in the nervous system, greatly increased the distress of young animals separated from the parent or from one another (Panksepp, Meeker, and Bean, 1980; see Box Figure 1).

Finally, if opiates really are involved in feelings of affiliation, there should be some evidence that opiates are involved in the learning of social bonds. In an intriguing study, Panksepp and DeEskinazi (1980) trained very young rat pups to run down a maze to get to their homes. All the rats learned this quite quickly. Then the researchers started extinction; when a pup ran down the maze, it no longer led to home. Most pups very quickly learned to stop running down the maze. However, pups never stopped running the maze if they were given small doses of morphine when they reached the place where their homes previously had been located. The morphine had no such effect *unless* the rats first had been trained to expect to find their home. An opiate antagonist *increased* the rate of extinction (Panksepp et al., 1985). Panksepp concluded that the morphine gave the rats the same reward as they had experienced when they had found their homes.

The implications for humans? These results suggest that increases in opiates in certain areas of our brains might be the physiological mechanism that makes us feel good when we meet loved ones or arrive home. Is this why "there's no place like home?"

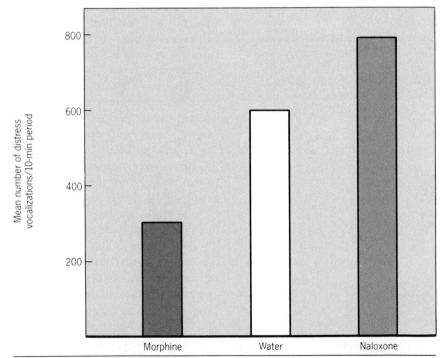

BOX FIGURE 1 EFFECTS OF OPIATE AND OPIATE ANTAGONIST ON SEPARATION DISTRESS.
The mean number of cries of distress from chicks given either morphine, water, or the opiate antagonist naloxone just before being separated from other chicks. The morphine greatly reduced their crying. The opiate antagonist increased it greatly—to about 80 cries a minute. (From Panskepp et al., 1985, p. 9.)

touch somewhat, they are less distressed than if they are separated by a glass shield that lets them see and hear each other but not touch (Suomi, Collins, Harlow, and Ruppenthal, 1976).

Evidence from experiments on monkeys suggests, then, that the complex motivation to affiliate between mother and infant is based on both inborn, biological factors and on learning. Like aggression and hunger, the motivation to affiliate also has a physiological basis. Recent research points to the importance of *endogenous opioids* in affiliation motivation (Box 11-1).

While affiliation motivation seems similar in human and animal infants, decided differences emerge as humans mature and become capable of complex information processing. An example of this is college students' decisions about where to live when they attend college. For many students this decision is based on affiliative needs rather than financial or educational concerns (Niedenthal, Cantor, and Kihlstrom, 1985). The beginning college student has just left her family and must now have her day-to-day affiliative needs met by college acquaintances. Thus, in choosing a residence, affiliative concerns are often paramount: "What types of people will live there?" "Will they like me?" "Will I be happy there?" (Cantor, Markus, Niedenthal, and Nurius, 1986). How does a student attempt to satisfy her need for affiliation (love, social support, friends) in this situation? It turns out that students' self-concepts are critical. Research by Nancy Cantor and John Kihlstrom (Cantor et al., 1986) revealed that students often have clear ideas about their own personality characteristics (e.g., quiet, studious, spontaneous), and those of students who live in various types of college residences (e.g., coed dormitory, single-sex dorm, fraternity, sorority, rented house, apartment house, cooperative, room in a private residence). Students appear to make residence decisions by choosing a residence that they think will house people with personalities similar to their own. Thus, students attempted to "match" their own personalities with a personality model of a "typical" resident. If a student saw herself as happy-go-lucky, outgoing, and liberal, she chose a residence where she thought others would be happy-go-lucky, outgoing, and liberal.

THE IMPORTANCE OF SATISFYING AFFILIATION NEEDS Studies of infants and young children who have been separated from their mothers strongly suggest they also keenly feel the effects of these separations. Just like the rhesus infant, the human infant at first does not know his or her mother as a distinct individual. But within about 3 months after birth, the human infant, like the infant monkey, comes to know his or her mother (and other regular care-givers) and develops a specific attachment to her, a process termed **bonding** (see Chapter 9). Human infants protest and despair when they are separated from their mother or a care-giver to whom they have bonded. Only her return can soothe the infants' despair. In the second half of the infant's first year, the mother's presence provides the infant with a secure base from which to explore the environment (Bowlby, 1969).

Not only are there similarities between the ways that monkey and human infants act out their attachments, but they may suffer similar consequences when their needs for attachment are not met. John Bowlby (1969) has argued that infants who are physically separated from their mothers may later become "anxiously attached" children. Anxious attachment is characterized by excessive dependency and insecurity. In humans, too, emotional separation may have effects similar to those of physical separation. In one study (Blehar, Lieberman, and Ainsworth, 1977), for example, the investigators watched mothers feeding their newborn babies. Some of the mothers were responsive and affectionate, and others were indifferent and rather neglectful. When the babies were observed again when they were a year old, the babies of indifferent mothers acted frightened and distressed when they were placed in a new, strange environment without their mothers, but they were not comforted when their mothers returned to them. These were *insecurely attached* babies. Some of the babies actually avoided contact with their mothers. These were *avoidant* babies. In contrast, the babies of the more responsive mothers, who also protested when their mothers left them in the strange situation, sought the comfort and attention of their mothers when they returned and, once comforted, began to explore the novel environment. These were *securely attached* babies.

This research, by itself, does not prove that a mother's unresponsiveness makes baby insecurely attached. Perhaps the mothers of insecurely attached infants are relatively unresponsive *because* their infants are anxious and unaffectionate? This is doubtful because maternal indifference seems to precede signs of insecure attachment rather than vice versa (Bell and Ainsworth, 1972). This is consistent with Harlow's research showing that maternal separation causes anxious infants.

The different kinds of attachment observed in children are related to the caregiving styles of their mothers. For instance, in one study, the mothers of securely attached infants reacted more readily to the crying of their infants than did the mothers of other infants (Ainsworth, Blehar, Waters, and Wall, 1978). Thus, insecurely attached or avoidant infants may suffer from *emotional separation* from their mothers. If you think for a minute about the evolution of humans and other species, you will understand why children experience great pleasure in being close to their parents and great anxiety and depression if they are separated. Separation quite literally threatens a child's survival. Only the nearness of a caring parent can ensure the dependent child of the food, shelter, and emotional sustenance it needs to survive, reproduce, and continue the species. Thus it seems that we humans, like other animals, have evolved with built-in motivational systems that severely punish separation and richly reward affiliation.

To sum up what we know about the motivation to affiliate with others, early personality theorists stressed that infants are drawn to others for the satisfaction of basic biological needs for food, warmth, and the like. However, more recent research shows that the complex motivation to affiliate with others appears to be a distinct influence, not one that is secondary to the motivation for food or warmth. In particular, mother and infant appear to need close contact comfort in order to have their affiliation motivation satisfied. Research on the physiological (opiate) basis of affiliation and separation suggests that they may entail both incentives and drives. Affiliation may produce feelings of pleasure that are intrinsically enjoyable—they don't depend upon the existence of any preexisting unsatisfied drive. However, separation, especially separation to a strange or unfamiliar environment, may set up a powerful drive similar to opiate withdrawal.

Other research findings show that the attachment between infant and mother develops in stages. Depending on the stage of affiliation, theories that stress the innate (Adler) and learned (Sullivan) aspects of affiliation motives are both correct. Cantor and Kihlstrom's research showed that complex information processing—the matching of self-concept with a concept of others—is important to affiliation behavior in adults. Finally, as we discuss further in Chapter 12, if an infant's needs for affiliation are not met, the infant's attachment or affiliation behavior may be disrupted, with harmful consequences for later development.

THE MOTIVATION TO ACHIEVE

Why do some of your classmates work diligently to get good grades and do well in school while others seem not to care much? Why do some of the people who work for good grades also work hard on a variety of other tasks, sometimes even when there is no apparent payoff for striving? Why do they try so hard to win word games, or to solve puzzles, or to run a 7-minute mile? What is it that drives these individuals to struggle so hard (Figure 11-10)? What, in short, separates high achievers from others?

Over the past 40 years psychologists have studied **achievement motivation**, the motivation that induces people to strive to complete moder-

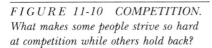

FIGURE 11-10 COMPETITION. What makes some people strive so hard at competition while others hold back?

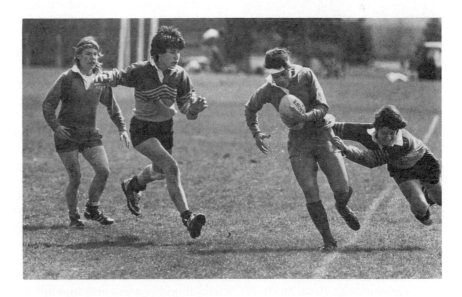

ately difficult tasks. As psychologists have viewed it, achievement motivation cannot be inferred from hard work alone nor from measures of a person's success such as income, artistic creativity, or inventions. Measures of success are not always good measures of achievement motivation, because there are many reasons for success—luck and genius, for instance. The person high in achievement motivation tends to work unusually hard, but mostly at moderately difficult and significant tasks. Achievement motivation is unlikely to determine how long you rake leaves (a fairly simple task), but it is likely to determine how hard you work to succeed in your chosen occupation.

Measures of the Need to Achieve and the Fear of Failure

Psychologists measure people's need to achieve and fear of failure with a variety of methods (Nicholls, 1984). The classic method, which was developed by the pioneer researchers into achievement motivation, John Atkinson and David McClelland (McClelland, Atkinson, Clark, and Lowell, 1953), is a projective personality test called the **Thematic Apperception Test** or **TAT** (see Chapter 14). On this test, a person looks at a series of ambiguous pictures of everyday life and then writes a brief story about what he or she thinks is occurring in the picture. The psychologist then rates the story with respect to its achievement themes (see Figure 11-11). Research has shown the TAT to be a moderately reliable measure of the need to achieve (Haber and Albert, 1958; McClelland et al., 1953; Sorentino and Higgins, 1986). Finally, how a person scores on the need to achieve on the TAT does relate to how he or she behaves in other areas of life. The test, in other words, is valid (Figure 11-12*a,b*).

Psychologists also have used the TAT to measure a person's fear of failure. Researchers have found that people who strongly fear failing tend to respond to the TAT with themes that reflect criticism and failure and to set low, conservative goals for themselves (Heckhausen, Schmalt, and Schneider, 1985).

Outside the world of the TAT—in the everyday world, that is—people act in many ways that reflect their need for achievement. People with a strong need to achieve tend to choose occupational goals that are more appropriate to their abilities than do those with little need to achieve (Morris, 1966). People with a strong need to achieve tend to prefer competitive business careers in which they are likely to get tangible evidence of their success or failure such as profits (McClelland, 1961, 1965). People with a strong need to achieve can delay gratification longer than others, tend to get better grades in courses relevant to their chosen careers, and are more successful in business (McClelland, 1961, 1965; Mischel, 1961; Raynor, 1970). One fascinating piece of research has shown a connection between the stress on achievement in children's grade school readers and the number of patents issued to the general population (see Figure 11-13; deCharms and Moeller, 1962). A cultural emphasis on achievement manifested itself both in terms of themes in childhood readers and in adult achievement (patents issued).

FIGURE 11-11 THEMATIC APPERCEPTION TEST.
This picture from the Thematic Apperception Test (TAT) may elicit from people information about their need to achieve. The person who says, for example, "The young woman has just been encouraged by her mother to accomplish as much as she can in life." shows concern about success and accomplishment (McClelland, 1953).

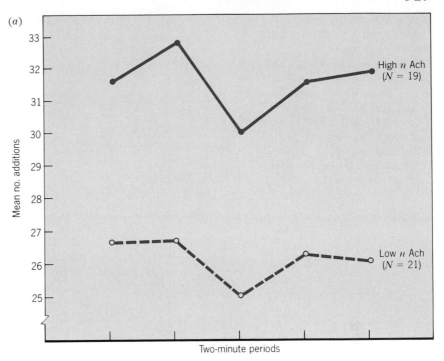

FIGURE 11-12   NEED FOR
ACHIEVEMENT AND
PERFORMANCE.
People with high and low needs for
achievement respond differently to tasks.
When people with a high need for
achievement are asked to solve simple,
repetitive addition problems, (a) they
complete more of them than do people
with a low need for achievement. On a
scrambled word task, (b) those with a
strong need to achieve show greater
improvement over the course of the
task. (From Lowell, 1952.)

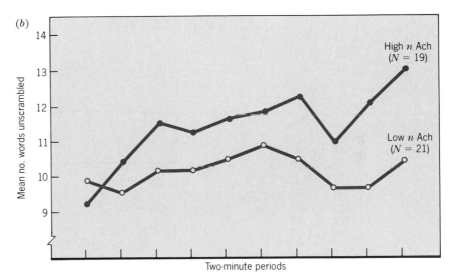

Theoretical Models of Achievement Motivation

Why do some people have a strong motivation to achieve and others a weak motivation? According to John Atkinson and David McClelland, two underlying motives contribute to achievement motivation. One is the *need to achieve*; the other is *fear of failure*. The person with both a strong need for achievement and little fear of failure has a strong motivation to achieve. Conversely, the person with both little need for achievement and a strong fear of failure has a weak motivation to achieve.

FIGURE 11-13 THE ACHIEVEMENT MOTIVE AND PATENTS ISSUED.
The figure shows the relation between the number of pages in schoolchildren's readers that contained achievement images and the number of patents issued in the United States, between 1800 and 1950. The number of patents is consistent with the emphasis on achievement in the readers. (From de Charms and Moellar, 1962.)

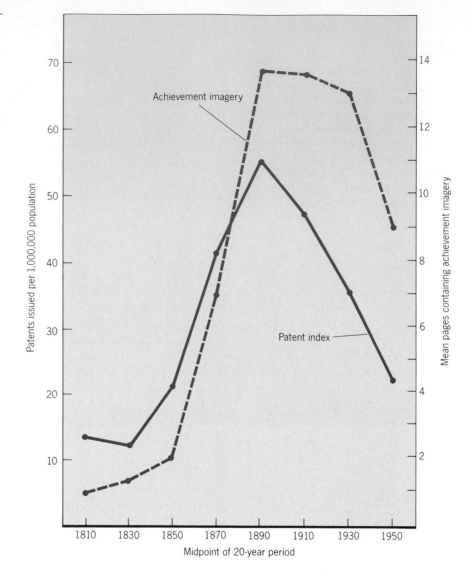

The stronger a person's need for achievement, the greater the probability of success, and the greater the incentive value of success, the greater that person's motivation to achieve. One wrinkle in this formula is that the greater the probability of success, the lower its incentive value and vice versa. In other words, those goals that are easy to achieve have a low incentive value. They are less likely to make a person feel proud of achieving them than are goals that are harder to achieve. As Groucho Marx said, he wouldn't join any club that would have him as a member.

People avoid tasks when they are strongly afraid of failing at them. Just as people need (more or less intensely) to achieve, they need to avoid failing. We are driven, then, in part by our desire to feel pride in our achievements and in part by our desire to avoid shaming ourselves by failing (Atkinson and Raynor, 1974). We are likelier to feel shame if we fail at an easy task than a hard one. We are likely to feel we have tried our best if we miss naming the capital of Outer Mongolia or don't come in first in the New York Marathon. But we are likely to feel foolish if we miss naming the capital of the United States or run out of energy to finish our usual 1-mile jog.

John Nicholls (1984) has recently suggested that the goal of achievement motivation is to demonstrate to oneself or others one's competence or ability. People are particularly likely to be motivated to achieve when they want to demonstrate their ability compared to that of others (rather than simply demonstrating their own ability). For instance, research has shown that if people perform a task that does *not* lead them to compare themselves with others, people with high and low motivation to achieve perform alike. But if the task does lead them to compete with and compare themselves with others, then highly and less motivated people perform very differently. When people perform tasks that do not reflect their abilities, they choose moderately challenging goals to engage their attention and hold their interest. But when a task supposedly reveals information about a person's abilities, then performing the task becomes risky. People high in achievement motivation select tasks that provide a reasonable chance of success; such tasks allow them to demonstrate their ability. People with little achievement motivation avoid tests of their ability and choose either a ridiculously easy task they know they can do or one so hard that their failure is meaningless.

Atkinson's model of achievement motivation is also consistent with the relationship between achievement motivation and task difficulty. For Atkinson, however, task selection is determined by a person's expectation that a task will produce pride versus shame. Nicholls emphasizes the informational consequences of task selection, whereas Atkinson emphasizes the emotional consequences.

The Origins of Achievement Motivation: Life Experiences and Attributional Styles

Highly motivated people believe that they are good achievers—have "lots of ability"—and are eager to prove it to themselves and others (Kukla, 1972). Less motivated people tend to believe that they are not very competent and avoid tests of their abilities (Arkin, Detchon, and Maruyama, 1982). Where do these differences in confidence come from? Virtually all of us are born with the desire to prove our mastery and competence. Yet some of us seem to lose it. Certainly, part of the explanation lies in the level of success people experience in their lives. People who are generally successful at competitive tasks are more likely to test themselves in the future than those who generally fail. Another part of the explanation lies in the *attributions* that people make about the *causes* of their success and failure (Weiner, 1985). The attributions about success that are most likely to lead to future achievement hold that the causes of success are internal, stable, and controllable (see Table 11-3). For example, the student who gets an A on a test is more likely to keep striving if she attributes her A to her intelligence and hard work: intelligence is internal and stable, and hard work is under her control. What is more, she is not likely to be deterred if she attributes a failing grade to an external, unstable, and uncontrollable cause: "I failed the test because I was kept from studying by illness." Conversely, when people attribute success to external, unstable, and uncontrollable factors—luck—or failure to internal and stable characteristics (controllability may not be important here), they are likely to stop trying hard to achieve.

TABLE 11-3 ATTRIBUTIONS ABOUT CAUSES OF SUCCESS AND FAILURE

People attribute outcomes of their actions to factors that differ according to:

Locus (location)

Internal—caused by some feature within a person:
  "I failed because I had a headache."
External—caused by some feature outside a person:
  "I missed the putt because the green was too bumpy."

Stability

Stable—caused by something enduring and fairly constant:
  "I got an A because classes in this subject are always easy."
Unstable—caused by something that changes fairly frequently:
  "I did well on the exam because I was not as tired as usual."

Controllability

Controllable—caused by something within a person's control:
  "I caught ten fish because I know how to cast my line correctly."
Uncontrollable—caused by something beyond a person's control:
  "The meal turned out poorly because the oven isn't working right."

In support of the attributional model of achievement motivation is one study showing that people's success at quitting smoking (which presumably reflects striving to achieve a significant goal) was positively related to their stable and internal positive self-attributions—"I was able to quit because I have great self-control" (Eiser and Sutton, 1977). Training people to change their attributional styles can increase their striving to achieve. For instance, people tend to strive longer if they are taught to reattribute the reasons for failure from internal and stable causes ("I'm not good at this") to external or unstable causes ("I didn't try very hard at this") (Anderson, 1983; Weiner, 1985).

To sum up, then, theories of achievement motivation illustrate themes of complex motivational theories. First, according to Nicholls, self-concept is important in that beliefs about personal abilities are thought to guide the selection of achievement tasks. Moreover, for Nicholls an important goal of achievement motivation is to demonstrate personal competence. This is similar to Bandura's notion that people are motivated to display self-efficacy. Atkinson's model of achievement motivation emphasizes the emotional goals of achievement behaviors; people strive to feel pride and avoid shame. Finally, Weiner's theory emphasizes that the attributions people make about successes and failures influence later achievement behavior. According to attribution theory, people strive longer to achieve if they attribute their failure to external causes because then failure does not reflect badly on their efficacy. People's

motivation and performance on tasks are enhanced if they attribute successes to internal, stable factors such as their intelligence or skill.

Finally, it is important to note that complex cognitive processes such as making attributions and appraising one's abilities rest on more basic motivational processes. Thus the motivation to achieve is influenced by the size of the reward one expects (the incentive), by level of deprivation, and by strength of habit (someone may be more likely to undertake well-learned tasks). Complex motivational models do not replace models of basic motivation. They do, however, complement them and increase the scope of motivational theory. They explain why a composer like Schubert might struggle to write gorgeous music for many years despite poverty and obscurity, and they may explain why you find some classes challenging and fascinating and others threatening and onerous.

EMOTIONS

What is emotion, and why should it be discussed in the context of motivation? Emotion is a feeling or mood, but it also refers to how people act and how their bodies react. We discuss emotion in the context of motivation because, as we discuss later in this section, emotions reflect, support, and reinforce motivation. In the following sections, we examine how people express emotion and then we consider theories of the origins of emotions and the functions of emotions.

Expression and Recognition of Emotion

One of the first questions that researchers asked about emotional expression was whether it is learned or innate. Charles Darwin (1809–1882) argued that the expression of certain emotions is innate. Armed with video recorders and photographs, modern researchers have expanded on Darwin's position and have offered four compelling arguments that some emotional expressions are innate:

FIGURE 11-15   THE INFANT'S INBORN EMOTIONAL EXPRESSIONS.
An infant who is less than 2 days old can perceive and imitate an adult's emotional expressions of happiness, sadness, and surprise. (From Field, Woodson, Greenberg, and Cohen, 1982.)

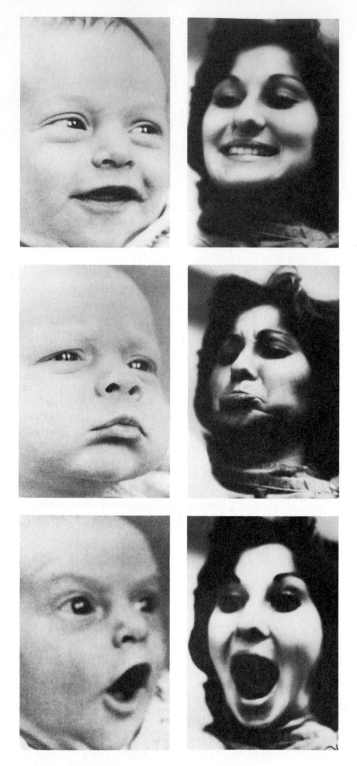

1. Similar emotional expressions are seen in a variety of species, suggesting that humans have inherited some of their emotional expressions from lower species (see Figure 11-14).

2. The smiles, cries, and certain other emotional expressions of infants are the same as those seen in adults and occur so early in life that they are unlikely to have been learned. In one study, 36-hour-old infants were found to imitate emotional facial expressions of adults (see Figure 11-15, Field, Woodson, Greenberg, and Cohen, 1982), indicating that infants are prepared at birth to execute coordinated emotional facial expressions.

3. Blind and deaf children develop emotional expressions that are virtually identical to those of sighted and hearing children (see also Eibl-Eibesfeldt, 1973; Goodenough, 1932).

4. Finally, human facial expressions communicate the same information across a wide variety of cultures. For example, people from a wide variety of cultures accurately identify facial expressions of a range of emotions (Ekman, 1973). To ensure that the ability to identify facial expressions was not simply a consequence of people's exposure to mass communications, New Guineans who had had limited contact with mass media also were asked to portray basic emotions (Ekman and Friesen, 1971). They were excellent at it (see Figure 11-16). Although

FIGURE 11-16 EMOTIONAL FACIAL EXPRESSIONS ARE SIMILAR ACROSS CULTURES.
A Caucasian woman living in a Western country and a native New Guinean man were asked to display different emotional expressions: happiness, anger, disgust. As you can see, the two individuals use the same expressions despite coming from quite different cultures.

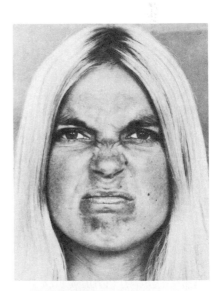

the recognition of emotion of facial expressions seems to be a universal ability, people do vary in the ability to produce communicative facial expressions. In general, women are better at this than men. It is not known whether this difference is due to societal influences or genetic factors. (Wagner, MacDonald, and Manstead, 1986).

Not only do there seem to be universal facial expressions of emotion, but humans from different cultures seem to agree on the emotional significance of nonverbal features of speech such as pitch, loudness, and rate (Frick, 1985). Indeed, people can almost perfectly identify joy, sadness, anger, and fear by these features of speech alone (Johnson, Emele, Scherer, and Klinnert, 1986). Thus nonverbal features of speech as well as facial expressions may be innately determined routes of emotional expression.

Of course, it is not the case that all forms of emotional expression are invariant across cultures. The fact that learning plays a role in emotional expression can be seen in the case of striking, culture-specific forms of expression such as the practice of the Nez Perce American Indian women who severed their fingers to demonstrate their grief (DeVoto, 1947). Each society superimposes its own forms of emotional expression on the innate bedrock of universal expressions.

Neural Processing of Emotion

Some of the most fascinating recent work in the study of emotion concerns the neural processing of emotional information. Although the brain does work as an integrated whole, research has shown that the right hemisphere is especially important for processing emotional information. For instance, people who have suffered injuries to the right hemisphere have great difficulty recognizing the mood of a speaker from the speaker's tone of voice (Leventhal and Tomarken, 1985). People generally can recognize the emotions in tones of voice more readily if the voice is presented to the right, as opposed to the left, hemisphere (that is, to the left ear, Safer and Leventhal, 1977). The two hemispheres of the brain differ in their sensitivities to emotions in general and to types of emotion as well. The right hemisphere is important for processing negative (dysphoric) emotions such as depression and sadness. The left hemisphere is important for processing positive emotions such as pleasure and happiness (see Figure 11-17). The EEG analysis has shown that people experiencing positive moods as they watched television had greater brain-wave activity in the frontal lobe of their left than their right hemisphere. When the people rated their moods as more negative, they showed greater amounts of right frontal than left frontal brain activity (Davidson et al., 1979). People who are chronically depressed also show more EEG activity in their right hemispheres than do nondepressed people (Schaffer et al., 1983). When the influence of the left hemisphere is reduced, by either surgery or injury, people generally show excessive worry, guilt, pessimism, and crying. However, when the influence of the right hemisphere is reduced, people tend to laugh, to be euphoric, and to show lack of concern (Sackeim et al., 1982).

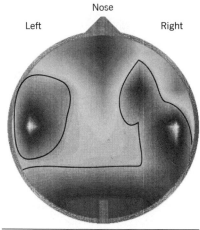

FIGURE 11-17
PHYSIOLOGICAL EVIDENCE OF LATERALIZED EMOTIONAL PROCESSING.
This photograph shows a representation of electroencephalographic (EEG) activity in the cortices of people exposed to a film that produced disgust. The dark areas outlined in color represent the area of greatest cortical activity. This figure shows that when people experience powerful negative emotions, their right hemispheres are more active than their left hemispheres. (Figure supplied by Richie Davidson, University of Wisconsin.)

Not only are positive and negative emotions processed differently by the brain, but strongly positive emotions preclude the processing (or experiencing) of strongly negative emotions. We humans simply cannot feel very happy and very sad at the same time (Diener and Iran-Nejad, 1986). This antagonism may correspond to the contradictory responses of approach and avoidance. As we discuss later in this chapter, one important, adaptive consequence of emotions is their ability to signal to an animal when to approach and when to avoid a stimulus (e.g., Schneirla, 1959; Young, 1961). The animal that feels intense pleasure and wants to mate or that feels intense displeasure and wants to flee is at an extraordinary disadvantage if he or she wavers ambivalently. Perhaps the antagonism of strong emotions and their corresponding lateralization promotes survival in both love and war.

In humans, the lateralization of emotions begins during the first year of life. When 10-month-old infants saw a happy, smiling face, they showed more left hemisphere EEG activity (Davidson and Fox, 1982). Infants start out processing simple emotions such as interest and disgust in both hemispheres. However, by 1 year of age, when infants start to show the more complex emotions of fear and sadness, their processing of emotions has become lateralized (Fox and Davidson, 1984).

Theories of Emotion

Psychologists and others who have studied the origins of emotional expression have been interested in a variant on the old chicken and egg question: which comes first, the emotion or its physical expression? They have offered several intriguing theories to try and answer this question.

PERIPHERAL ORIGINS OF EMOTIONS   One of the earliest concepts of emotion was proposed independently by the American psychologist

FIGURE 11-18 PERIPHERAL ORIGINS OF EMOTION.

One theory of emotion is that people's peripheral reactions to events determine their emotional reactions. The boy who sees a lion approaching finds his heart pounding and this feedback from his body causes his fear.

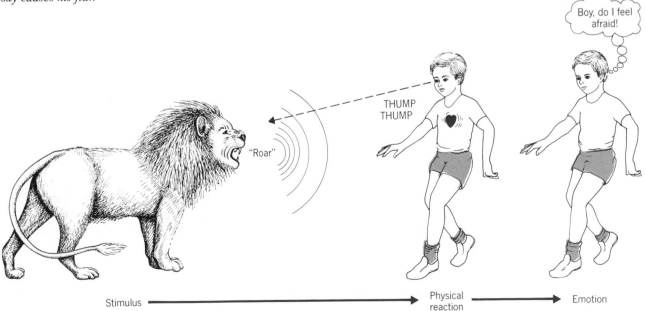

William James (1890) and the Danish physiologist Carl Lange (1895/ 1967).They said that people's awareness of their emotions comes from their bodily reactions to emotionally significant events: you see a lion, your heart pounds, your muscles tense, your hands tremble, your mouth goes dry, and from all this feedback, you feel fear. They held that you feel fear *because* your heart pounds, not that your heart pounds because you feel fear (see Figure 11-18). According to this theory, your feeling of fear comes from your sensing the combination of reflexive physical reactions.

James believed that the difference between thoughts and emotions was that only with emotions do people have strong peripheral, bodily responses (peripheral, outside the CNS). Many theorists of emotion since James also have recognized that emotions are associated with responding of peripheral organ systems. In particular, the autonomic nervous system (ANS) has been implicated in emotions, the sympathetic branch with fear and anger, the parasympathetic branch with disgust and sexual excitement (see Chapter 2 for a discussion of the ANS). Fear has been found to be associated with a pattern of high sympathetic activation but little parasympathetic activity, rage with equal activity of the two divisions, and disgust primarily with parasympathetic activity (Wenger, Jones, and Jones, 1956).

Despite the fact that the autonomic nervous system is aroused during emotional states, modern theories of emotion no longer hold that bodily responses *initiate* or determine a person's emotional responses. An American physiologist named Walter Cannon (1927) criticized the James–Lange theory on the following grounds:

1. Roughly similar physiological changes occur in different emotions such as fear and rage, yet people perceive the two emotions as being quite different.
2. If peripheral organs are stimulated by a drug injection so that the heart beats faster, sweating occurs, and so on, people feel aroused but do not experience any strong emotion.
3. Some emotional reactions occur *before* the peripheral organs have time to react.
4. If nerves to peripheral organs are separated from the brain, emotions still occur.

Even though data conflict with the James–Lange theory, theories of the peripheral origins of emotions keep reappearing. A recent revival of a peripheral theory is Zajonc's restatement of Waynbaum's theory. Waynbaum, a nineteenth-century French physician, hypothesized that people's emotions are greatly influenced by the contraction of the facial muscles. Robert Zajonc (1985) has taken this idea and proposed that the contraction and relaxation of the facial muscles affects the blood supply to the brain and the temperature of particular regions of the brain. These changes give rise to the states that people call emotions (see Figure 11-19). In support of his theory, Zajonc points to results such as those produced by Paul Ekman (Ekman et al., 1983), who had people mold their faces into one of six expressions. For example, he said, "Raise your eyebrows and pull them together. Now raise your upper eyelids,"

*FIGURE 11-19   DO FACIAL
MUSCLES CONTROL EMOTIONS?
The circulatory system and muscles of
the head and neck. Waynbaum's theory
was that contracting the muscles of the
face associated with various emotions
altered the blood supply to the brain.
The resulting changes in the brain
created various emotions. Zajonc has
hypothesized that muscle contractions of
the face affect the blood supply to and
temperature of the brain, thereby
determining emotions. (From Sappey,
in* Traite d'Anatomie Descriptive. *Delalgaye Lecrosnier, Paris,
1888–1889; Zajonc, 1985.)*

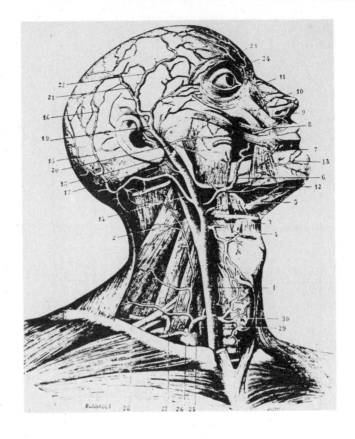

*FIGURE 11-20   DO FACIAL
EXPRESSIONS INFLUENCE
EMOTIONS?
When subjects were coached to mold their
faces into certain emotional expressions,
they actually felt the emotions. For
instance, in these photos the man was
first asked to (a) "raise your brows and
pull them together," (b) "now raise your
upper eyelids," (c) "now also stretch
your lips horizontally, back toward your
ears." What emotion do you think the
young man felt? (From Ekman et al.,
1983.)*

and so forth. By following the instructions, a person had molded his face
into an expression of fear (see Figure 11-20). The people in the study
actually showed physiological changes consistent with their facial expressions. Figure 11-21 shows how the people's heart rates and skin temperature reflected their different emotional expressions. Moreover, the importance of facial expression was revealed by the fact that the facial
coaching technique actually resulted in greater physiological responding
than did the instructions to "relive" an emotional experience.

Zajonc's theory has not yet been adequately tested. It seems that some
of the criticisms of the James–Lange theory could also be lodged against

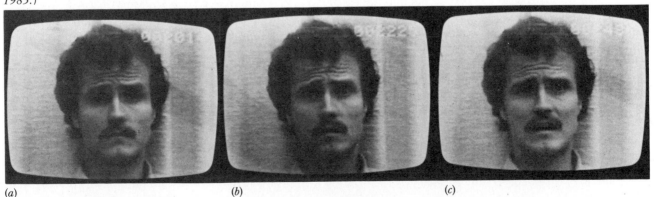

(a)   (b)   (c)

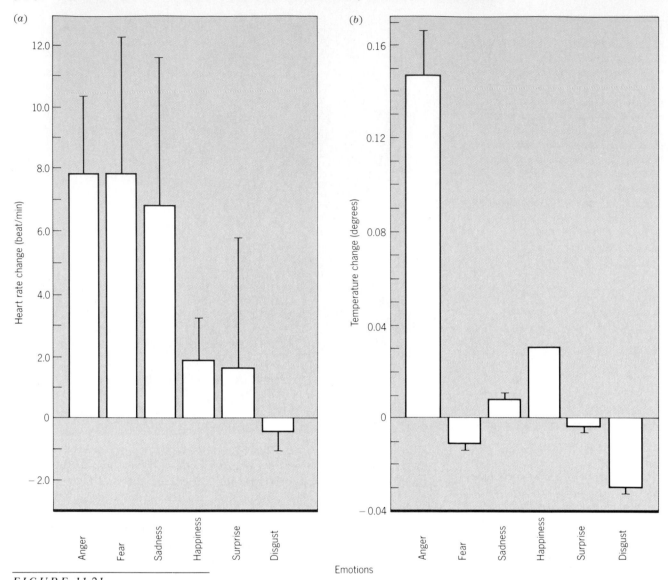

(a)

(b)

Emotions

FIGURE 11-21
PHYSIOLOGICAL CHANGES
ASSOCIATED WITH EMOTIONS.
If subjects were coached to make a happy,
disgusted, or surprised expression, their
heart rates changed little. If subjects
were coached to make an angry, fearful,
or sad expression, their heart rates went
up. These emotions also produced
characteristic changes in the skin
temperature measure. (From Ekman
et al., 1983.)

it—for example, could the facial muscles affect brain functioning quickly enough to explain rapid emotional changes? However, this theory is attractive because it accounts for the strikingly consistent link between facial expression and emotion.

THE ATTRIBUTION THEORY OF EMOTION In a classic experiment in social psychology, Stanley Schachter and Jerome Singer (1962) gathered evidence for a very influential theory of emotion that holds that people's labels—a cognitive function—strongly determine the nature of their emotional experiences. According to this theory, emotions are produced when, first, some stimulus or event increases their arousal, and, second, when they make an attribution about the cause of the increased arousal. For instance, when our young man sees a running

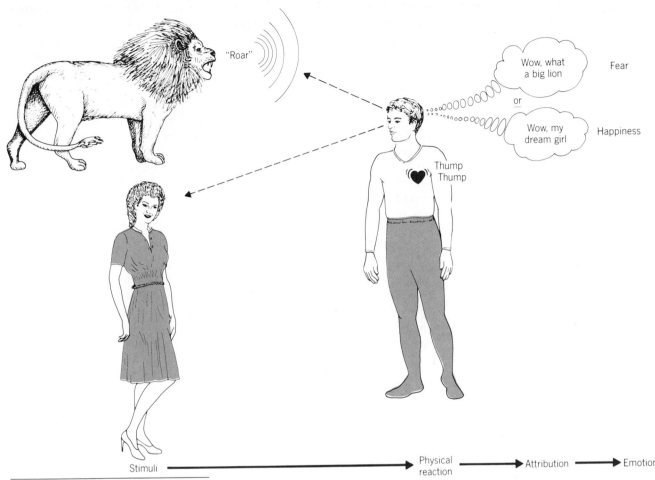

"Roar"

Wow, what a big lion — Fear

or

Wow, my dream girl — Happiness

Thump Thump

Stimuli ———————————————→ Physical reaction ——→ Attribution ——→ Emotion

FIGURE 11-22 ATTRIBUTION THEORY OF EMOTION.

In the attribution theory of emotion, the same physiological reaction can lead to different emotional experiences, depending on how a person interprets the reaction. The young man who sees a lion and a young lady at the same time and whose heart then races feels either fear or eager anticipation, depending on his causal attribution.

lion, he experiences a reflexive heart rate increase and then interprets or decides—cognitive functions—what has caused his heart to race before he experiences an emotion (see Figure 11-22).

Schachter and Singer performed experiments in which some individuals were injected with the drug epinephrine, which increases heart rate and respiration and causes trembling. But Schachter and Singer told subjects that they were participating in an experiment on the effects of a vitamin on vision. Half the subjects got a placebo injection, the other half, epinephrine. Then some of the subjects in each group got either accurate information—that the injection would produce arousal—or inaccurate information—that the injection would produce itching. The subjects then waited in an adjacent waiting room where there was another "subject" who had received similar treatment. This person was really a confederate of the experimenters. The confederate acted euphorically—flew paper airplanes, played basketball with the wastepaper basket—or angrily—complained, left the waiting room in a huff.

What did the results of this experiment show? First, the subjects given placebo injections did not report strong emotions no matter what they had been told or how the confederate behaved. This result is consistent with Schachter's hypothesis that people must be aroused before they can feel emotion. Of the subjects who received epinephrine, those who had been told that it would produce itching *were* influenced by the confederate's behavior. If a subject had been exposed to a euphoric confederate, the subject reported feeling euphoria. If a subject had been exposed to an angry confederate, the subject reported feeling angry. But those subjects who had been told that the injection would increase arousal were not influenced by the confederate. They attributed their arousal to the drug.

In another demonstration of how people's attributions influence their emotional experiences, people who felt little fear were told that they would be given a drug that would increase their arousal, whereas other low-fear subjects were not given this information (Nisbett and Schachter, 1966). Then all of the subjects were asked to tolerate degrees of electric shocks. Actually no subject had been given any drug, but those who *believed* that they had been given the drug tolerated more intense shocks and rated the shocks as less painful than those who had not been so fortified. Apparently, people judge pain by how much they react physiologically to a painful stimulus. If people believe that a drug has aroused them, they attribute less of their pain—a form of arousal—to an external stimulus like an electric shock and therefore judge it as less painful.

Experimental results like these help to explain certain aspects of everyday behavior. For instance, take two students who are trying to quit smoking. People who quit smoking usually go through a period of withdrawal from the drugs in cigarettes that can last days or weeks (see Chapter 5). One student has read about the physical sensations she can expect after quitting, so she is prepared when she starts feeling physically aroused and agitated. She correctly attributes her arousal to quitting smoking, and therefore does not have any significant emotional reaction to it. But the other student does not know much about withdrawal. When he becomes aroused several days after quitting, he attributes his arousal to stressful events happening around him—therefore he gets very angry at someone who bothers him, very anxious about an upcoming test, and so on. This greater emotional response probably places him in greater danger of relapsing.

As impressive as Schachter's data are, subsequent research shows that attribution effects are fairly weak in many circumstances. For instance, in the Nisbett and Singer study reported before, if high-fear subjects were used instead of low-fear subjects, the attribution effect would not have occurred (Leventhal and Tomarken, 1985). Strongly fearful people probably would have assumed that the painful shocks were causing their physical sensations. Whenever people are fairly certain about why they are feeling something, information that contradicts their beliefs usually has little effect. This does not mean that Schachter's theory is wrong, only that in most instances of emotional reaction, his theory provides no better explanation of the emotion than many competing theories.

According to the attribution model, emotions are differentiated by people on the basis of causal attributions, not on the basis of different patterns of physiological arousal. However, a number of researchers have shown that different emotions *are* associated with different patterns of physiological arousal. When people were asked to think intently about experiences from their past that had produced happiness, sadness, anger, fear, or relaxation, they reported that they felt the appropriate emotion again. Each emotion was found to be associated with a different pattern of cardiovascular activity (Schwartz et al., 1981). Similarly, researchers have found that different kinds of fear are associated with different patterns of physiological activity (Lang et al., 1983). Thus, modern psychophysiological recording techniques have shown that Cannon was wrong when he argued that emotions all are associated with the same type of physiological arousal. However, his other criticisms of the James–Lange theory are still considered to be valid.

EMOTIONS AS MOTIVATIONAL SUPPORT SYSTEMS   Many early theories emphasized that emotions arise from frustration, from an interruption in the pursuit of a goal or the conduct of an activity (e.g., Freud, 1926; Young, 1961). Frustration theorists held that emotions involve disorganized physiological activity and have a disorganizing or disruptive effect on behavior. The deer browsing on grass stops in fear when it senses the presence of a hunter, for example.

More recently, theorists have come to consider emotions as support systems for, rather than disruptors of, motivated behavior (e.g., Buck, 1985; Izard, 1978; Lang, 1984; Leeper, 1948; Plutchik, 1980). These theorists all consider emotions not merely as feelings but also as complex physiological, behavioral, and attitudinal states. When a vicious-looking dog lunges and barks at a small boy, the boy not only experiences strong feelings, but he also shows characteristic physiological and behavioral responses. He not only feels fear, he also has a racing heart, tense muscles, a grimace of fear, and he flees. "Fear" comprises all of these responses.

When we look at emotions as this complex mixture, we can understand their *functional* significance. Emotions are functionally significant in three ways:

1. Emotions *reflect* or *signal* the nature and level of an individual's motivation (Figure 11-23). Darwin recognized that animals that can recognize another's emotional state have a survival advantage. Thus, a young monkey approaches a calm, adult male but flees from an enraged adult.
2. Emotions serve as *support* systems for motivated behavior. They physiologically prepare an individual to pursue goals appropriate to particular motivational states: to mate, to eat, to flee.
3. Emotions *reinforce* motivated behavior. The pleasure one feels from eating rewards one's pursuit of food. The fear felt by the infant separated from his mother punishes him for straying.

Research on the nonverbal communication of emotions by political candidates and television newscasters suggests such communication to be powerful indeed (Lanzetta, Sullivan, Masters, and McHugo, 1985). Researchers analyzed videotapes of the facial expressions of newscasters before the 1984 presidential election (Mullen et al., 1986). They catego-

FIGURE 11-23   ADAPTIVENESS OF A CAT'S EMOTIONAL EXPRESSIONS.

Darwin's depiction of a cat threatened by a dog. Notice that the emotionally expressive behaviors of the cat are functional or useful. The cat arches its back and raises its fur, both of which make it appear larger. Its visible fangs look frightening. Its flattened ears are difficult for a foe to bite or grasp. We humans have inherited some of these fear expressions—our body hair stands up when we are frightened. (From Darwin, 1872.)

rized anchormen's facial expressions as positive (smiling) and negative (frowning or scowling) as the men said a candidate's name. Results showed that two anchormen showed no bias for either candidate. (None of the anchormen showed a bias based on what they said on their newscasts.) But one anchorman smiled more when he said one candidate's name. Telephone surveys indicated that in four communities, voters who had watched this newscaster were more likely to have voted for the candidate toward whom he had shown his bias. (Of course, people vote for reasons besides the look on a newscaster's face!) More research is needed to unravel the interesting, and potentially important, communication values of emotional expression.

How are emotions support systems for motivation? Emotional responses promote and permit motivated behavior. For example, when you feel afraid, your autonomic nervous system responds by raising your heart rate and respiration, muscle tension, and by releasing the sugar glycogen. All of these responses help you to escape from or struggle with what has frightened you. Likewise, when people are sexually motivated, they feel emotions called *sexual pleasure* or *lust,* and the associated physical responses—sexual arousal, orgasm, resolution—allow them to engage in and enjoy sexual activity. Information about motivation and emotions actually may be coded or contained in the same networks in the brain. Thus, it has been suggested that emotional responses—sweating, trembling, blushing, smiling, and so forth—may serve as "read-outs" or progress reports on the activation of motivational networks in the brain (Buck, 1985; Lang, 1984).

Classifying Emotions

Another relatively recent concern of motivational theorists has been to classify all the *basic emotions.* Basic emotions are those that are highly evolutionarily adaptive and, therefore, appear in many species. Basic emotions also are not mixtures of other, more elementary, emotions (Izard, 1972; Plutchik, 1980). Carroll Izard (1972) has listed the following as basic emotions: interest, joy, surprise, distress, anger, disgust, contempt, shame, and fear. Robert Plutchik (1980) has listed the following: joy, sadness, acceptance, disgust, fear, anger, expectation, and surprise.

One current perspective on emotions does not attempt to list basic emotions, but instead categorizes emotions with respect to how people describe or label their emotional experiences. In general, people categorize their emotional experiences along three primary dimensions: pleasantness/unpleasantness, arousal, and controllability. Thus, people view fear as being unpleasant, highly arousing, and characterized by feelings of loss of control. Anger is unpleasant, highly arousing, but rated higher on the control dimension (Mehrabian and Russell, 1974).

In sum, then, a complete view of emotions requires that psychologists study, not only how people say they feel, but also how they respond physically and behaviorally. The basic emotions not only feel different but are accompanied by different expressions and other physiological changes. Some theorists emphasize that the bodily changes people experience in reaction to environmental events determine their emotions.

Others emphasize that attributions of causes and other cognitive processes determine the nature of emotional responses. Regardless of the origins of emotions it is clear that they are functional and adaptive. They signal motivational states, prepare individuals for motivated behavior, and reinforce motivated behavior.

STRESS AND COPING

Why follow a discussion of motivation and emotion with a discussion of stress? Because stress really represents a challenge to ordinarily adaptive motivational and emotional response systems. In fact, severe stress reflects a breakdown of normal motivational and emotional processes.

Stress is a broad term that describes an environmental challenge, a **stressor**, that leads an organism to try to cope, adapt, or escape. People's and other animals' emotional and behavioral responses usually let them adapt or cope adequately with stressors. In fact, as we noted in our discussion of arousal theories of motivation in Chapter 10, animals actually seem to require and prefer a moderate level of environmental challenge. As Goethe noted, "Nothing is harder to bear than a succession of fair days." But stress describes environmental challenges severe enough to threaten psychological or physiological well-being.

Stressors and Their Effects

Precisely what sort of environmental event any individual finds stressful depends, of course, on the species of animal involved, the capabilities of the individual organism, and the features of the organism's environment. Rattlesnakes can go for weeks without drinking water, but most humans would die. Surgeons work quite contentedly on open body cavities of living people, but most other people would be overcome by the sight. Although stressors vary widely, Thomas Holmes and Richard Rahe (1967) listed events that most people find stressful. On the Social Readjustment Rating Scale (for selected items see Table 11-4), events are listed in order of Holmes and Rahe's evaluation of their stressfulness. Some of the events—an outstanding personal achievement, for example—actually are positive. But stress describes attempts to cope with environmental changes, be they positive or negative. Negative events, it is true, usually arouse greater stress than positive events (Thoits, 1986).

For many people, a string of day-to-day problems may be more stressful than a single cataclysm (Kanner, Coyne, Schaefer, and Lazarus, 1981). People find day-to-day events that involve conflict—arguments, for example—or frustration—delays, inability to attain resources, losses, failures, and feelings that one's life and efforts are meaningless (Coleman and Hammen, 1974)—especially stressful.

Stressors have both short- and long-term effects, and these effects differ as a function of the type of stressor, its duration, and so on (Watkins and Mayer, 1982). Hans Selye (1956) discovered that many

TABLE 11-4 SOCIAL READJUSTMENT RATING SCALE

Life Event	Life-change Units
Death of spouse	100
Divorce	73
Marital separation	65
Jail term	63
Death of close family member	63
Personal injury or illness	53
Marriage	50
Fired at work	47
Marital reconciliation	45
Retirement	45
Change in health of family member	44
Pregnancy	40
Sex difficulties	39
Gain of new family member	39
Business readjustment	39
Change in financial state	38
Death of close friend	37
Change to different line of work	36
Change in number of arguments with spouse	35
Foreclosure of mortgage or loan	30
Change in responsibilities at work	29
Son or daughter leaving home	29
Trouble with in-laws	29
Outstanding personal achievement	28

Source: Adapted from Holmes and Rahe, 1969.

intense physical stressors produce a three-stage pattern of effects, the **general adaptation syndrome** (**GAS**).

The first stage of the *GAS,* the *alarm reaction,* is itself divided into two stages (Selye, 1950). In the *shock phase,* the animal's body temperature and blood pressure drop, the stomach and intestinal lining are irritated, and steroid hormones pour out of the **adrenal cortex**. Among the steroids released by the adrenal cortex are **cortisol** and **corticosterone**, compounds that reduce inflammation and allergic reactions (Turner, 1960). If a stressor is severe enough, characteristic tissue damage results (Figure 11-24). In *countershock phase* of the alarm reaction, the animal begins to adjust to the initial effects of shock, and some of these effects are reversed. Blood pressure and temperature both increase, for example.

If the stress continues, the animal enters the state of *resistance.* The responses that began in the countershock phase are sustained and made more efficient. Most or all of the immediate effects of the stressor seen in the shock stage are neutralized or reversed. For example, the body replaces the steroids that were released from the adrenals during the shock phase.

Finally, if the animal cannot adapt to or escape from the stress, its physical resources become depleted, and it enters the third stage of the GAS, *exhaustion.* Now the animal stops trying to adapt physically or

FIGURE 11-24 PHYSICAL
EFFECTS OF STRESS.
*Intense stress may (a) enlarge the
adrenal cortex, (b) shrink the thymus
gland, (c) shrink the lymph structures,
and (d) ulcerate the stomach and upper
intestine (Selye, 1976). This figure
shows the adrenal glands, thymus
glands, lymph nodes, and stomachs of
two rats. The tissues on the right come
from a rat that had been under stress.
(From Selye, 1952.)*

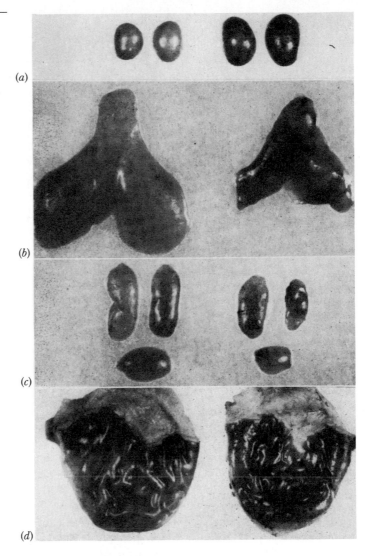

(a)

(b)

(c)

(d)

behaviorally. With its resources exhausted the animal is susceptible to disease and death.

Each stage of the GAS has different consequences for an organisms's ability to adapt. This is illustrated by some of Selye's research using the stressor of extreme cold (see Figure 11-25). Selye (1976) placed rats in a refrigerator that was maintained at a near-freezing temperature. Two days later, when rats were in the alarm reaction stage, he removed some of the rats and placed them in an even colder environment. These rats were less able to adapt to this extreme cold than were control rats not previously exposed to cold. However, when Selye removed a second group of rats from the refrigerator 5 weeks later, these animals showed exceptional resistance to extreme cold. Evidently, these animals were in the resistance stage of the GAS and had adjusted behaviorally and physiologically to cold. Finally, Selye removed a third group of rats from

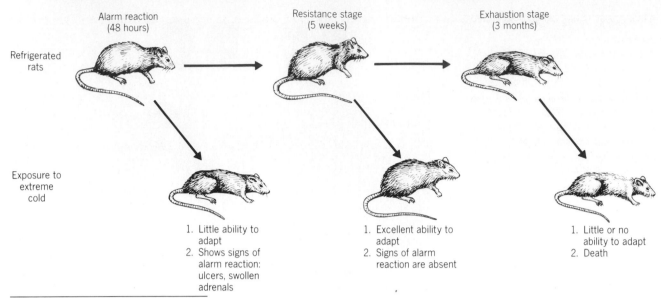

Alarm reaction
(48 hours)

Resistance stage
(5 weeks)

Exhaustion stage
(3 months)

Refrigerated
rats

Exposure to
extreme
cold

1. Little ability to
   adapt
2. Shows signs of
   alarm reaction:
   ulcers, swollen
   adrenals

1. Excellent ability to
   adapt
2. Signs of alarm
   reaction are absent

1. Little or no
   ability to adapt
2. Death

*FIGURE 11-25   GENERAL
ADAPTATION SYNDROME.*

*A rat exposed to chronic cold due to
refrigeration shows different abilities to
adapt to an extreme cold challenge that
depend upon the length of time that the
rat was exposed to the chronic cold. If a
rat is exposed to the extreme cold while
in the alarm reaction stage, it shows
little ability to adapt and shows physical
signs of the alarm reaction. If a rat is
exposed to the extreme cold after 5 weeks
of refrigeration, the rat adapts well to
the cold, showing few physical signs of
disease (e.g., ulceration). Finally, when
rats are exposed to extreme cold after 3
months of refrigeration, they have little
ability to adapt and sometimes die. This
shows how the ability to adapt changes
from the alarm reaction stage, to the
resistance stage, to the exhaustion stage.*

the refrigerator—several months after they were placed there. When
these animals were exposed to extreme cold they died rapidly. Selye
hypothesized that these animals were in the exhaustion stage and had
lost their ability to adapt to additional stress.

In his pioneering research, Selye principally used physical stressors to
produce the GAS. He subjected rats to cold and injected others with a
variety of compounds. Selye's research is broadly relevant, however,
because the GAS can be elicited by psychological stressors like conflict,
as well as by physical stressors (Lazarus, 1977; Selye, 1956). Although we
human beings evolved to cope primarily with physical challenges—
predators, human enemies and rivals, and so on—today we typically
must cope with psychological challenges. An elevated heart rate, high
blood pressure, and sweating may do us more harm than good against
these psychological challenges. "If millions of years ago animals and
humans were primarily faced with physical stressors of survival, then,
when subjected to an acute stressor, the most adaptive coping mechanism would have been mobilization of all defenses to escape from or
subdue the threatening stimulus. . . . Because present-day humans primarily face psychological stressors of a chronic, intermittent nature, the
physiological alterations, when occurring for a prolonged period of time,
are no longer adaptive" (Burchfield, 1985, p. 387). We may be poorly
equipped to cope with the psychological stressors of our crowded,
complex, technologically dense environments.

The Link Between Stress and Disease

Although the mechanisms are still being uncovered, scientists know that
stress makes humans and others more susceptible to disease. Have you
ever noticed that you are likely to catch a cold during exam period or
soon after you've made it through a stressful interview or confrontation?

BOX 11-2
TYPE A BEHAVIOR PATTERN

Rosenman and Friedman developed an interview assessment to identify persons susceptible to stress-related heart disease. In this interview individuals are asked questions such as the following:

1. Does your job carry heavy responsibility?
   a. Is there any time when you feel particularly rushed or under pressure?
   b. When you are under pressure does it bother you?
2. Would you describe yourself as a hard-driving ambitious type of man in accomplishing the things you want, or would you describe yourself as a relatively relaxed and easygoing person?

Rosenman and Friedman were able to distinguish between two types of indi- viduals using this interview. One type, **Type B** individuals tend to be rela- tively calm, easygoing, not to struggle against time pressures, and not to be easily angered. But **Type A** individ- uals often feel pressured, and are am- bitious, impatient, competitive, walk and talked rapidly, and are easily an- noyed by delays. Not only did Type A individuals admit to these traits dur- ing the interviews, but their very in- terview behavior gave them away. As opposed to Type Bs, Type As would impatiently interrupt the interviewer, express their annoyance that the in- terview took as long as it did, and so on.

Why did Rosenman and Friedman link Type A behavior pattern with cor- onary disease? First, they realized that many cases of heart disease could not be attributed to other cardiac risk fac- tors: for example, smoking or dietary habits. Second, a variety of experi- ences with their patients planted the idea in their minds that stress might be the responsible factor. For exam- ple, businessmen told them that their colleagues who had heart disease appeared to seek out pressure and worked under a greal deal of stress. In another incident, "We had called in an upholsterer to fix the seats of the chairs in our reception room. After inspecting our chairs, he asked what sort of practice we had. We said we were cardiologists and asked why he had wanted to know. 'Well,' he replied, 'I was just wondering, be- cause it's so peculiar that only the front edge of your chair seats are worn out" (Friedman and Rosenman, 1974, p. 71). Thus, Rosenman and Friedman had an important insight— the people most likely to suffer from stress-related disease are those whose personalities cause them to seek out stress or put pressure on themselves. They are aggressive, ambitious, impa- tient (sitting on the edge of their seats!), and hard-driving—in other words, Type As.

In laboratory mice, stress increases the incidence of mammary tumors, and protection from stress decreases the incidence (Riley and Spackman, 1974; Solomon, Amkraut, and Rubin, 1985). Stress in humans has been linked to diseases such as stomach ulcers (Weiss, 1971) and hyperten- sion (Henry, Stephens, and Santisteban, 1975). These diseases are **psy- chosomatic**: they have a psychological cause and a *somatic* (physical) consequence.

For many years, heart disease also has been attributed to stress, yet it has been difficult for researchers to identify all the mechanisms involved. Two physicians, Ray Rosenman and Meyer Friedman, hypothesized that stress can damage the heart and that a particular type of individual is most likely to experience repeated stress reactions (Friedman and Rosen- man, 1974). Box 11-2 describes how Type A behavior pattern is assessed and how Rosenman and Friedman discovered a link between this pattern and heart disease.

Research over the past 10 to 15 years supports Rosenman and Fried- man's contention that Type A behavior places a person at risk for cardiac disease. In one study (Friedman and Rosenman, 1974) 3500 men were studied for a decade. Men classified as Type A were three times more likely than Type B to develop heart disease. Although this finding has not been replicated in every study to attempt it, the replication has been frequent enough (with both men and women) to affirm the validity of Rosenman and Friedman's hypothesis (See Baker, Dearborn, Hastings, and Hamburger, 1984).

How does Type A behavior increase the risk of heart disease? High serum cholesterol levels increase the risk of heart disease, and there is copious evidence that stressors—especially difficult to control stressors—elevate serum cholesterol levels (Pare, Rothfeld, Isom, and Varady, 1973; Rahe, Rubin, and Arthur, 1974). These high levels may result from the release of cortisol from the adrenal cortex during stress (Glass, 1977). In addition, there is evidence that Type A individuals have a lower threshold for elicitation of a cardiac stress response than Type Bs. In one study, short vignettes were read to both Type A and B coronary patients. Some of the vignettes described situations thought to elicit responses to stress, and other vignettes were neutral (see Table 11-5). The Type A subjects showed greater cardiac acceleration in response to the stressful vignettes than the Type B subjects did (Baker, Hastings, and Hart, 1984; see Figure 11-26).

TABLE 11-5   TYPE A AND NEUTRAL VIGNETTES

Type A Scenes	*Neutral Scenes*
1. You are standing in a slowly moving line at the store. Although the sign says "10 items, cash only," the person in front of you has 15 items and wants to write a check.	1. You are walking along the beach. You notice the sand as you walk and watch the gulls flying about the pier and the fishing boats.
2. You are driving and are almost late for an important appointment. Another car cuts you off and slows down. You miss the traffic light and cars behind you honk their horns.	2. You are watching the sun as it sets. The sky is streaked with many different colors and the clouds appear to be edged with a brilliant light.
3. You are supervising and training a new employee who doesn't seem to "catch on" quickly. Training him and fixing his mistakes cuts into your own work until you find you're behind schedule.	3. You are relaxing in your favorite chair at the end of a long day. It's snowing outside and there is a fire burning in the fireplace. The warmth of the fire is soothing.
4. You are recovering from your heart attack and the doctors have told you to limit your activities. You feel restless and bored with nothing to do. Time is passing very slowly.	4. You are strolling through the park on a summer afternoon. The air feels fresh because it rained the night before. It feels good to get out and stretch your legs.
5. You have a difficult job assignment. There are others who think they could do the job more quickly and better. Many interruptions and thoughts of other work responsibilities keep slowing you up.	5. You are walking in the country near a farm. You notice the different farm buildings and the animals. Beyond the farm you see rows of corn growing in the fields.

Source: Baker et al., 1984.

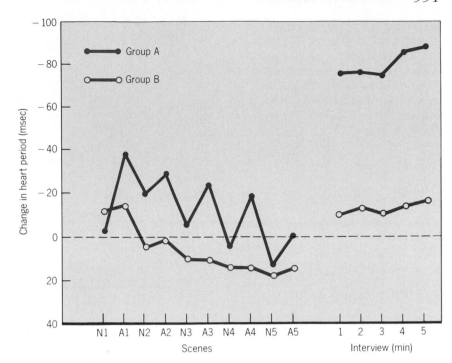

FIGURE 11-26   HEART RATE RESPONSES OF TYPE A AND TYPE B CARDIAC PATIENTS. Group A patients were Type A individuals who had had a heart attack. Group B patients also had had a heart attack but were not assessed as Type As. The Type A patients showed greater heart rate responses to Type A vignettes (A) than to neutral ones (N). They also showed higher heart rates during the Type A assessment interview (see Box 11-2). (From Baker et al., 1984.)

THE IMMUNE SYSTEM   Cells in the **immune system** are responsible for recognizing and attacking foreign cells or material (**antigens**) that enter the body (see Chapter 5). The immune system is not located in any single place: its cells are distributed throughout the body. However, major types of immune system cells do have a single origin. Both **B** and **T cells, lymphocytes** (or white blood cells), develop in bone marrow. The T cell (see Figure 11-27) is then processed further in the thymus gland. These cells are circulated in the blood and lymph fluids and are concentrated in lymphatic organs: the lymph nodes and spleen (Marvack and

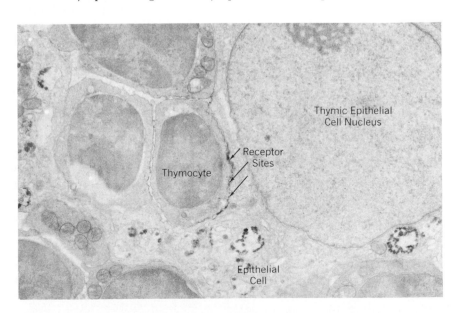

FIGURE 11-27   IMMUNE SYSTEM ANTIBODY: THE T CELL. The dark body at the center of this photomicrograph is a thymocyte or an immature T cell. The dark areas on the border of the T cell are receptor sites that allow the cell to identify its target. The receptors detect two things in their identification of a target. First, the receptors detect proteins on another cell's surface that identify the target as a living cell. Second, the receptors identify antigens (foreign material). The T cell initiates attack only if it has identified a foreign (infected), living cell. The thymocyte pictured here is bound to an epithelial cell that makes up part of the lining of the thymus gland. (From Marrack and Kappler, 1986.)

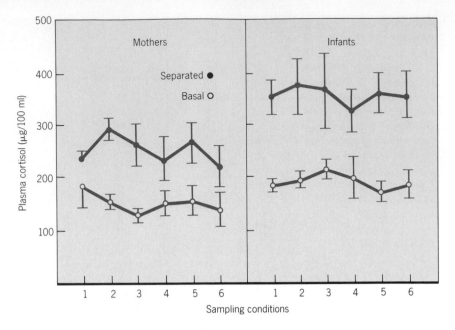

Kappler, 1986). While B cells bind with and destroy foreign cells or material in the body, T cells attack the body's own cells that have been altered. They are aided by a host of other immune system cells: for example, monocytes, mast cells, and natural killer cells (whose main function appears to be tumor suppression).

Stress makes people vulnerable to infection because it reduces the efficiency of the immune system. Steroids like cortisol released into the blood during times of stress suppress cells in the immune system (see Figure 11-28). There is also evidence that the central nervous system may directly affect immune system functioning. Fibers from the CNS connect via synapses to organs of the immune system (bone marrow, spleen, etc.) and probably influence immune response through these pathways (Felten, Overhage, Felten, and Schmedtje, 1981).

The immune-suppressant effects of stress have been demonstrated in both humans and animals. In animals, stressors such as overcrowding, starvation, electric shock, and noise have been shown to reduce the activity or efficiency of components of the immune system (Solomon et al., 1985). As you saw in the discussion of affiliation earlier in this chapter, when infants are separated from their mothers, they protest and despair. Does this separation compromise infants' immune responses? Christopher Coe and his colleagues recently have found that infant squirrel monkeys separated from their mothers show clear signs of immune suppression (reduced antibody response) (Coe, Weiner, Rosenberg, and Levine, 1985; see Figure 11-29). In one study of humans, researchers compared the immune systems (lymphocyte production) of husbands before and after the deaths of their wives (Schliefer, Keller, Camerino, Thornton, and Stein, 1983). Their immune responses were signficantly weaker after the wife's death. Other studies suggest that such stressors as space travel, examinations, and surgery also can suppress

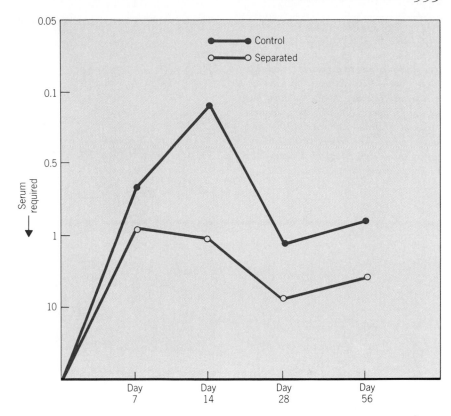

FIGURE 11-29   MATERNAL SEPARATION AND IMMUNE RESPONSE.
This figure shows the amount of serum required to neutralize antibodies to which infant squirrel monkeys had been exposed. One group of infants was separated from their mothers before antigen injection and remained separated throughout the experiment, while the other group remained with their mothers continuously (controls). Then blood samples were drawn from both groups 7, 14, 28, and 56 days after the antigen injection. As the figure shows, more serum was required from separated infants (higher values on the ordinate reflect less blood serum) to neutralize the antigen than was required from control infants. Therefore, antibodies were more efficient or plentiful in the blood of controls. (From Coe et al., 1985.)

immune responses (Dorian et al., 1983; Goodwin et al., 1981; Kimzey, 1975).

Some cautions about the effects of stress on immune responses: the immune system is complex. A stressor may depress one immune component but enhance another (Solomon et al., 1985). A stressor may have different effects over time, and brief stress may enhance immune response whereas prolonged stress may depress it (Manyon and Collector, 1977). Finally, immune response fluctuates spontaneously over time, regardless of stress level (Hall, 1985). Even so, most of the evidence indicates that prolonged physical and psychological stressors compromise the immune system and render people susceptible to disease.

Combating Stress

Much of the response to stress is genetically programmed and automatic. When subjected to intense stressors our heart races, we sweat, our pituitary releases ACTH, we grow tense, and so on. Are we helpless victims of our genetic endowment? No. We are helpless victims only if we *believe* that we are.

THE IMPORTANCE OF CONTROL: CAN WE COPE?   Research now suggests that the harmful effects of stress diminish greatly when people have some control over stressors or believe that they have control. When

*FIGURE 11-30   ULCER
PRODUCED BY UNCONTROLLABLE
STRESS.*
*The arrow points to a gastric (stomach)
ulcer such as those found in rats that
had no control over shock. Rats that had
no control over shock had approximately
twice the ulceration as animals that had
shock control. The bottom part of this
figure shows a histological section of the
ulcerated tissue. (From Weiss, 1971.)*

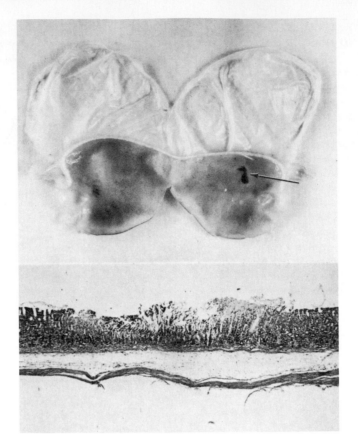

humans and animals are given ways to *cope* with stress, they usually suffer
little harm. For example, in one study two groups of mice were exposed
to painful electric shocks (Skalr and Anisman, 1979). Only one group
could control their escape from the shocks, although rats in both groups
escaped when rats in this "in control" group escaped. The helpless mice
had faster tumor growth than the other "in control" mice. In similar
studies, researchers found that rats that had control over shocks had
stronger immune responses and fewer gastric ulcers than helpless rats
(Laudenslager, Ryan, Drugan, Hyson, and Maier, 1983; Weiss, 1971; see
Figure 11-30).

In one study with humans, researchers compared the natural immune
response (killer cell activity) of "good copers" with "poor copers" (Locke
et al., 1984). Good copers were undergraduates who had recently experienced high levels of stress—the death of a loved one, for example—but
who had reported few psychological symptoms like depression in response. Poor copers had experienced both high levels of stress and
psychological symptoms. The blood of the good copers had more killer
cell activity than the blood of the poor copers.

Richard Lazarus and his colleagues discovered that people cope with
the stress of everyday life in a variety of ways (Folman, Lazarus, Dunkel-
Schetter, DeLongis, and Gruen, 1986):

1. *Confrontive coping.*

   "I stood my ground and fought for what I wanted."
   "I tried to get the person responsible to change her mind."

2. *Distancing.*

   "I made light of the situation; I refused to get too serious about it."
   "I went on as if nothing had happened."

3. *Self-control.*
   "I tried to keep my feelings to myself."
   "I tried not to act too hastily or follow my first hunch."

4. *Seeking Social Support.*

   "I talked to someone to find out more about the situation."
   "I talked to someone about how I was feeling."

5. *Accepting Responsibility.*

   "I criticized or lectured myself."
   "I realized that I brought the problem on myself."

6. *Escape-Avoidance.*

   "I just wished the situation would go away."
   "I tried to make myself feel better by eating, drinking, smoking, using drugs, or medication, and so forth."

7. *Planful Problem Solving.*

   "I knew what had to be done so I redoubled my efforts to make things work."
   "I made a plan of action and followed it."

8. *Positive Reappraisal.*

   "I decided that the experience had allowed me to grow as a person."
   "I decided that the experience had shown me what was important in life."

People used different coping responses with different types of stressors. In the face of controllable stress, people resorted to accepting responsibility, confrontive coping, planful problem solving, and positive reappraisal. In the face of uncontrollable stress, people used distancing and escape-avoidance. Which types of coping worked best? According to subjects' ratings, planful problem solving, self-control, and seeking social support were most successful.

SOCIAL SUPPORT   Seeking social support is a generally effective way to cope with stress (Cohen and Wills, 1985). People with lots of social support—many warm friendships, a happy marriage, and the like—are less likely to have physical and psychological problems than those with less social support. Those who are more socially isolated are likely to die younger, relapse to smoking more quickly, and suffer more depression (Coyne and Syme, 1985; Mermelstein, Cohen, Lichtenstein, Baer, and Kamarck, 1986).

Social support probably helps people to cope with stress because it increases their feelings of efficacy. Peggy Thoits (1986) recently has suggested that one important component of social support is other people's help in coping with problems. Moreover, people's evaluations of their overall worth, lovability, importance, and competence depend partly on the perceived appraisals of those with whom they regularly interact (Thoits, 1985). In other words, people infer that they are competent, they make a positive *attribution* about their efficacy, if others prize and value them.

A recent study by Camille Wortman and her associates has provided some initial insights into the types of social support that are most helpful to highly stressed individuals (Lehman, Ellard, and Wortman, 1986). These researchers interviewed 94 people who had lost a spouse or a child in an automobile accident. Respondents were asked to describe support attempts made by others (friends, family) and to indicate whether they felt that such attempts were helpful or unhelpful. Table 11-6 shows that the supportive responses that were *least* helpful were those that either invalidated the mourners' feelings (e.g., minimization) or those that placed a demand that the mourner change his or her behavior (i.e., to "snap out of it," or follow specific advice).

TABLE 11-6 SUPPORT ATTEMPTS THAT BEREAVED PARENTS AND SPOUSES FOUND HELPFUL AND UNHELPFUL

Helpful Responses	Unhelpful Responses
1. Contact with others who were similar	1. Encourage recovery
2. Provide opportunity to express feelings	2. Give advice
3. Express concern	3. Rude remark or behavior
4. Simply be available	4. Minimization and forced cheerfulness
5. Provide a philosophical perspective	5. Identification with feelings ("I know how you feel")
6. Compliment the deceased	

Source: Lehman et al., 1986.

Our review of stress effects reveals that stressors have two different sorts of harmful effects. One sort occurs regardless of the organism's ability to cope with the stressor. The second sort occurs only when the organism finds itself unable to cope. For example, controllable shock produces ulceration in animals, but the same amount of shock produces much greater ulceration if it is uncontrollable (Weiss, 1971). The research on humans that we have just reviewed also shows that coping, and by implication feelings of control or competence, reduces the harmful effects of stress.

FIGURE 11-31 RELATIONSHIP BETWEEN COPING AND CATECHOLAMINE RELEASE.
The researchers measured two catecholamines (neurotransmitters) that are released into the blood when people are stressed: epinephrine and norepinephrine. Women with tremendous fears of spiders were asked to perform tasks about which they felt strong, moderate, or little competence: viewing a spider, touching a spider with a short stick, or touching the spider with their hand. The women showed much stronger stress responses when their feelings of efficacy were moderate as opposed to strong. Thus, the greater the feelings of competence or self-efficacy, the less was the stress response. You may wonder why the women showed low stress responses for tasks for which they had the weakest self-efficacy (touching the spider). This task was not stressful because all women refused to do it! (Adopted from Bandura et al., 1985.)

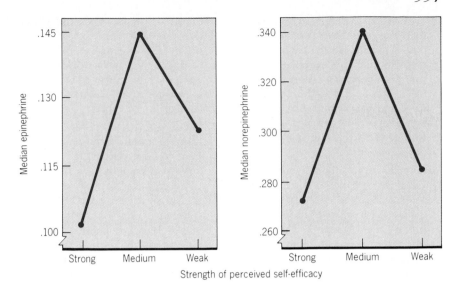

Motivational theory suggests the importance of feelings of control or competence. Indeed, according to Albert Bandura's self-efficacy theory and Nicholls' view of achievement motivation, the desire to demonstrate competence is a central goal of human motivation. Bandura, in fact, has gathered evidence that it is precisely those stimuli or events that threaten people's sense of their own competence or control that are most stressful (see Figure 11-31; Bandura et al., 1985). Thus, it appears that an inherent feature of severe stressors is that they threaten people's sense of control and people respond by trying to gain control. Successful coping increases feelings of competence and control and results in feelings of pride and satisfaction. However, failure, or inability to cope, is harshly punished with feelings of shame and depression. Feelings of impotence, lack of control, are so threatening that humans and other animals will deplete all their psychological and physical resources in efforts to cope.

SUMMARY

1. Complex and basic emotions differ in that complex motivations are more varied and more highly influenced by learning and complex cognitive operations. Although most theories of complex motivations are specific to particular motivational phenomena, some theories are of more general relevance.

2. To the extent that people attribute successful performance to their own ability or effort, their motiva-

tion to perform a task often is enhanced, especially when a task is at least moderately difficult. But if success is attributed to luck or to an external factor such as payment, task motivation is often reduced.

3. According to efficacy theory, people find it rewarding to demonstrate their competence. In general, people choose tasks that let them demonstrate competence

and avoid tasks that demonstrate incompetence because the latter lower their appraisals of their self-efficacy. Appraisals of efficacy influence how hard people try to accomplish goals. When they are sure that they can accomplish a task, they do not give up easily.

4. Hostile aggression has infliction of pain as its primary goal. In instrumental aggression, inflicting pain is a subservient goal. Types of ag-

gression also differ according to their targets, their physiological bases, and the particular behavior through which the aggression is expressed. Research suggests that there is not an undifferentiated drive to aggress, but that aggressive acts are learned and are used to the extent that they have pleasing consequences.

5. Humans and other animals develop through stages of affiliation. The newborn is motivated to remain close to any warm, soft, nurturing object. Later, the infant is motivated to remain close only to the particular adult who has cared for it, usually the mother. Instinct is important in affiliation of early infancy, whereas learning is more important later on. Evidence suggests that the pleasant feelings associated with affiliation are produced by the body's own opiates. If affiliation needs are not met in childhood, it can have long-lasting effects on behavior.

6. Achievement behavior is influenced by the motives of the need to achieve and the fear of failure. People tend to attempt tasks if they have a strong need to achieve, if they believe that they are likely to succeed in the task, and if the task has high incentive value. People avoid tasks when they strongly need to avoid failure, when they are likely to fail, and when the incentive value of failure is high. The incentive value of failure is great-

est on easy tasks. When the incentive value of failure of a task is high, failure produces a feeling of shame. Achievement motivation has also been attributed to a desire to demonstrate competence in comparison to others.

7. Some emotional expressions are learned; others are innate. The James–Lange theory of emotion holds that emotions are subjective states produced by the body's reaction to significant stimuli. The attribution theory of emotion holds that different emotions are produced by different attributions about the cause of arousal. According to modern theories, emotions help animals to carry out motivated behaviors, permit communication about motivational states, and reinforce motivated behavior. The two cerebral hemispheres process emotional information differently.

8. When people's abilities to cope or adapt to environmental events are challenged, they are under stress. Chronic or extreme stress may overwhelm people's ability to cope, exhaust their physical and psychological resources, and make them susceptible to disease. Stress interferes with the cardiovascular system and with the body's immune system. The effects of stress can be reduced if an individual can influence either the stressor or how he or she responds to the stressor.

FURTHER READINGS

An excellent general review of complex motivational theories is Bernard Weiner's *Human Motivation* (1985). One recent edited book that deals with complex human motivations in general, and with achievement motivation in particular, is Douglas Kleiber's and Martin Maehr's *Advances in Motivation and Achievement* (1985). An excellent book on emotion, that groups theories of emotions according to overarching themes, is Robert Plutchik's *Emotion: A Psychoevolutionary Synthesis* (1980).

Two additional very recent reviews of emotion are the edited volume by Robert Plutchik and Henry Kellerman, *Emotion: Theory, Research, and Experience: Biological Foundations of Emotion* (1986), and the work *The Emotions* by Nico Frijda (1986). Be warned, the former volume contains chapters that only the biologically sophisticated reader will understand.

For the reader who is interested in readings on specific topics covered in Chapter 11 we can recommend Hans Selye's classic book *The Stress of Life*, the book by Richard Lazarus and Susan Folkman, *Stress, Appraisal and Coping* (1984), Paul Ekman's *Emotion in the Human Face* (1982), John Bowlby's book *Loss: Saddness and Depression* (1980), and a recent book devoted to achievement motivation, *Achievement Motivation in Perspective*, by Heinz Heckhausen, Heinz-Dieter Schmalt, and Klaus Schneider (1985).

12

PERSONALITY PSYCHOLOGY

f a friend of yours asked you to describe your personality, that probably would seem like a simple thing to do. You'd probably describe yourself with a list of attributes: "I'm outgoing, energetic, happy, persistent, and thoughtful," or perhaps you'd say, "I'm shy, quiet, intelligent, and sometimes moody." If your friend asked you to describe your professor, you might offer, "Oh you know the type. Lots of reading. No extensions on papers. A real slave driver," or "He's the laid-back type. Doesn't care if you come to class as long as you hand in the assignments." Describing personality types is a time-honored tradition. Indeed, the ancient Greek philosopher Theophrastus (c. 372–287 B.C.) wrote a series of 30 character sketches in which he described a variety of personality types such as "The Flatterer," "The Surly Man," and "The Tasteless Man" (Anderson, 1970).

Greek physicians such as Hippocrates (c. 460–370 B.C.) and Galen (c. 130–200 A.D.) believed that all people could be classified into a few basic temperament types, that were determined by the proportion of various substances in the blood. Each temperament, or *humour,* was thought to be the product of a particular physical type. Galen suggested that people fall into one of four basic types (see Figure 12-1). These types were the *melancholic* (from the Greek words for "black"—*melas*—"bile"—*chole*), which described people who were sad, anxious, and gloomy; *choleric* (from the Greek word for "yellow bile"), which described

FIGURE 12-1 CLASSIC PERSONALITY TYPES.
In this diagram, the inner circle shows the four personality types proposed by the ancient Greek physicians Hippocrates and Galen. The outer circle shows the traits that Eysenck and others have associated with the four classic personality types. (After Eysenck and Rachman, 1965.)

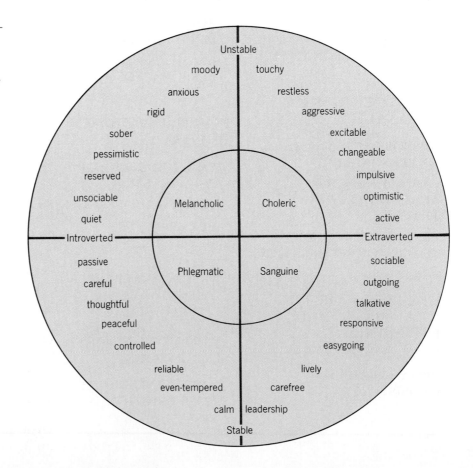

FIGURE 12-2   A MEDIEVAL REPRESENTATION OF FOUR BASIC PERSONALITY TYPES.
In this instance each type is also linked to one of the four basic elements of matter. From left to right these are: the sanguine man (air) with excess blood, the melancholy man (earth) with excess black bile, the choleric man (fire) with excess yellow bile, and the phlegmatic man (water) with excess phlegm.

people who were irritable and readily angered; *sanguine* (from the Latin word for "blood"—*sanguis*), which described cheerful, easygoing people; and *phlegmatic* (from the Greek word *phlegma*, for "inflammation"), the "clammy" humour of the body produced by inflammation and thought to characterize sluggish, dull, calm, and controlled people. These descriptions are of more than historical interest. We still use them today. We still use the word *sanguine* for people who are ever optimistic, and we label perennial sadsacks as *melancholy*. We describe people who are irascible and cranky as *choleric* and those who are hard to rouse to action as *phlegmatic*.

As you read this chapter on the psychology of human personality, you will see that "type" theories are still popular and command substantial attention from researchers. But type theories are only one of several varieties of personality theories. Like most psychological phenomena, personality can be examined from a number of theoretical perspectives. In this chapter, you will also read about the exploration of personality from a Freudian or psychodynamic perspective, a biological perspective, a learning perspective, and what has been termed the "phenomenological" perspective. None of these perspectives has a corner on the truth, and each has contributed important insights.

WHAT IS THE PSYCHOLOGY OF PERSONALITY?

Scientific theories of personality are relative youngsters. Although Galen and other ancients produced systematic theories of human personality more than 2000 years ago, the modern scientific study of personality dates from about 1900. Around that time the French psychologist Alfred Binet and the American psychologist James McKeen Cattell began measuring and recording specifics of people's intelligence, motor skills, and reaction times. They brought a *psychometric* approach to the study of human behavior, and before long, psychologists began to test and measure the differences in people's "personalities." As early as World War I, military recruits took tests that were designed to determine whether they were especially nervous, fearful, or self-doubting—traits that were thought to make a recruit unfit for the rigors of military training and combat. These early personality tests, which have been refined enormously, laid the groundwork for research on important characteristics of personality.

Around 1900, a second set of events important to personality psychology emerged in Vienna. Their prime mover was the physician Sigmund Freud, who developed *psychoanalysis,* a personality theory and a clinical method of treating emotionally disturbed patients (see Chapter 1). Psychoanalysis profoundly changed perceptions of human development and behavior both within the scientific community and among the general public. Although Freud's theories always have provoked controversy, there is no doubt that he was one of the most influential theorists in personality psychology.

From these two sets of events—psychometrics and psychoanalysis—the study of personality quickly developed. By the 1920s, psychologists were conducting experimental research on personality. The first textbooks in personality psychology appeared in 1937.

What is personality? The word *personality* has roots in the Latin *persona* (a character in a play or a person) and in the Etruscan word, *phersu* (a mask worn by actors). Thus it is fair to say that personality originally referred to outward appearances. But over the years people have assigned the word many meanings. In 1937 Gordon Allport collected 50 different definitions of *personality,* and classified them according to whether they were derived from etymology, theology, law, philosophy, sociology, external appearance, or psychology. Allport himself offered the following definition of personality:

> *the dynamic organization within the individual of those psychophysical systems that determine his or her unique adjustment to his or her environment (1937, p. 48).*

Other theorists have offered other good definitions of personality, as Table 12-1 shows. Although it would be convenient if psychologists agreed on one definition of personality, each seems to emphasize a slightly different aspect of personality. The theories vary in the extent to which they attempt to account for all the differences and similarities in human behavior, they vary in what they regard as the essential aspects of personality and human experience, and they vary in the factors they use to explain behavior.

TABLE 12-1 DEFINITIONS OF PERSONALITY

Linton	"Personality is the organized aggregate of psychological processes and states pertaining to the individual" (1945, p. 84).
Cattell	"That which permits a prediction of what a person will do in a given situation" (1950, p. 2).
McClelland	"The most adequate conceptualization of a person's behavior in all its detail that a scientist can give at a moment in time" (1951, p. 69).
Guilford	"A person's unique pattern of traits" (1959, p. 5).
Pervin	"Personality represents those characteristics of the person or of people generally that account for consistent patterns of behavior" (1984, p. 4).

Basic Issues in the Study of Personality

Psychologists do agree that any comprehensive theory of personality must address certain basic issues: What is the structure and content of personality? Which processes explain how personality functions? How does personality develop? One way to evaluate and compare personality theories is to assess how well they answer these questions.

THE BUILDING BLOCKS OF PERSONALITY Most personality theorists try to identify the enduring and stable aspects of personality. They have suggested various of these stable building blocks for personality. *Type,* for example, as you have seen already, has been considered a stable structure of personality. Other theorists have proposed that personality is built from stable structures such as *traits, instincts,* and *habits.* As we describe later, personality theorists also differ in how complex they perceive personality to be—in how few or many building blocks they hypothesize and the complexity of the connections among them.

Personality theorists may be interested in the building blocks, it is true, but they also must stand back and assess the whole structure of personality, how all the components combine to form a whole person. Personality theorists try to account for how people's learning, perceptions, social experiences, emotions, and motivations all work together to shape their individual personalities and influence their behavior. What you have learned and felt, perceived, strived for, and endured all have shaped the (often unique) things that you do.

WELLSPRINGS OF PERSONALITY In the previous two chapters, you read about the simple and the complex *motivations* behind human behavior. The concept of motivation has been important in the study of personality as well. As you read about various theories of personality, you will see that they subscribe to various ideas of motivation. Some theorists, such as Freud, place special emphasis on drives that are thought to activate behavior and shape personality development. Other theorists subscribe to the idea of homeostasis, or equilibrium, as an important factor in personality, and still others speak of self-fulfillment and growth or of a person's search for competence and mastery. All of these theorists have tried to specify the wellsprings of behavior and how these merge into an individual's personality.

Some theories, such as Freud's, give heavy emphasis to the internal (though often unconscious) factors that influence personality and behavior. Freud saw people as acting upon their environment and playing important roles in determining their own behavior. In stark contrast, learning theorists, such as B. F. Skinner (whom we discuss later in the chapter), give heavy emphasis to the influence of environmental contingencies of reinforcement on human behavior. Whereas Freud would have us look inside the individual to understand behavior, Skinner would have us look to the outside world. Other theorists typically have found a middle position. The dispute over internal versus external determinants of behavior is long-standing and still lively today.

UNIQUE AND BROADLY SHARED CHARACTERISTICS   You and every other person on this earth are unique, and yet there are many similarities among people. Part of the personality theorist's task is to identify the similarities and differences in personalities: why some people are highly motivated to achieve and others are not, why some people are intelligent, or adaptable, aggressive, emotional, stable, unconventional, and so on, whereas others are not. By understanding individual personalities, they (and you) can understand why people respond so differently in similar situations.

Theories of personality can be differentiated by their relative emphasis on individual versus broadly shared or universal aspects of personality. Allport used the term *idiographic* for personality theories, based on intensive studies of individuals, that describe the unique characteristics of those individuals. He used the term *nomothetic* for theories, based on studies of groups and broadly shared characteristics, that describe the general and universal laws of personality.

PERSONALITY DEVELOPMENT   Most comprehensive theories of personality take into account the fact that adult personality is a product of the complex interplay of the biological endowments of **nature** (those characteristics and abilities people are born with) and the environmental influences of **nurture** (the influence of all the experiences people have during a lifetime). Specifying how nature and nurture interact—in particular, specifying the extent, the form, and the importance of parents, peers, and cultural influences on personality development—is an important task for any personality theorist.

We turn now to these many specific theories of human personality—to the many ideas about what makes us human beings "tick."

TRAIT THEORIES OF PERSONALITY

As you have seen, as long as 2000 years ago, the Greeks had theories to describe basic personality **types**. People were described as *either* melancholic *or* choleric *or* phlegmatic *or* sanguine. Later theorists described personality in terms of a larger number of basic characteristics, or **traits**. Instead of being thought to possess exclusively one or another trait, people were thought to possess varying degrees of traits. For the most part, these early descriptive systems were based on casual observation and were strongly influenced by prevailing philosophies of human nature—as inherently good or evil, freely willed or predetermined and the like. Not until the twentieth century were trait and type theories based on systematic, scientific methods of inquiry.

Trait theories all possess certain features that distinguish them from other theories of personality. First, they agree that people are generally predisposed to behave in particular ways—that is, people possess traits, and these traits are the basic building blocks of personality. Second, they agree that these traits and behaviors are organized systematically. Many, for example, focus on the relationship between traits and behavior. A theorist might note that one student acts in a certain way: she spends a lot of time with her friends, goes to lots of social events such as parties, concerts, and movies, and belongs to a hiking club and the track team. When these various acts are considered together, the theorist might conclude that the student has a *trait* of sociability—a general predisposition to behave sociably. If the student also acts in other ways—she is president of the hiking club and the campus film society and influential in her dormitory—the theorist might conclude that she also has a trait of leadership. In sum, trait theories emphasize behavioral predispositions and the organization of traits. We turn now to three basic trait approaches to personality: Allport's trait theory, Cattell's factor-analytic theory of traits, and Eysenck's trait-type theory.

Allport's Trait Theory of Personality

Gordon Allport's (see Figure 12-3) major role in trait theory was as a scientific commentator who helped to define trait theory and identify critical issues for trait theorists. Allport recognized that traits cannot be directly observed or measured, but must be inferred from behavior. He suggested that through systematic observation, psychologists should be able to assess the *frequency* with which a particular pattern of behavior is displayed, the *range* of situations in which the behavior is displayed, and the *intensity* of the behavior. He stressed that such observations must be made *reliably*. In other words, either several observers would have to infer the same findings from observations, or a test must produce the same pattern of results if administered repeatedly.

THE NATURE OF TRAITS   In his personality text, Allport defined a *trait* as

> *a generalized and focalized neuropsychic system (peculiar to the individual),
> with the capacity to render many stimuli functionally equivalent, and to initiate
> and guide consistent (equivalent) forms of adaptive and expressive behavior
> (1937, p. 295).*

Although this definition sounds obscure, it implies that a trait is the readiness to respond in a similar way to a variety of stimuli. For example, look at Figure 12-4. It is a model of the stimuli and responses associated with "Communist phobia," as Allport described it in 1961. The trait of "Communist phobia" acts like a filter that makes people see somewhat different stimuli—people from Russia, books by Karl Marx, and Fidel Castro—as more alike than they actually are. Furthermore, once filtered through the trait, the different stimuli can produce a variety of behaviors, all of which serve the same function—to express the trait.

Allport was interested in determining the number of traits a person might possess and used a variety of methods to find out. When he and one of his graduate students (Allport and Odbert, 1936) combed an unabridged dictionary for trait labels, they found 17,953 candidates—though after eliminating synonyms, they reduced the list to a mere (!) 4504 terms. At the other extreme, though, he found that when his Harvard undergraduate students were asked to describe their classmates'

FIGURE 12-3   GORDON ALLPORT (1897–1967).
Allport was one of the first personality theorists and, for more than 40 years, one of the most prominent. His most influential work was his 1937 textbook, Personality: A Psychological Interpretation, *revised in 1961 and published as* Pattern and Growth in Personality.

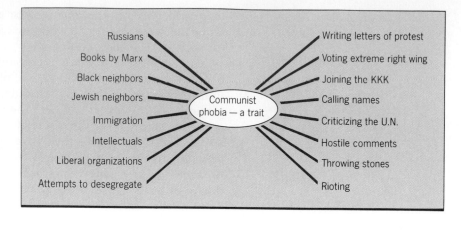

FIGURE 12-4 ALLPORT'S TRAIT CONCEPTION.
This shows a "Communist-phobia trait." According to Allport, traits operate like filters, which make various stimuli look more alike to a person than they would otherwise be. Because the person interprets the stimuli as similar, the person's behavior toward them also is interrelated. The stimuli for "Communist phobia" appear on the left. The responses appear on the right. (After Allport, 1961.)

traits, the average description contained only 7.2 traits. That number may suggest that the number of personality traits can be reduced to a handful (or that Harvard undergraduates were then of few words), but Allport's theory of traits does not lend itself to such easy simplification.

Allport (1961) distinguished among several categories of traits and arranged them hierarchically. At the top of the hierarchy, he placed **cardinal traits**, the master motives or passions that pervade every aspect of life. Few people have cardinal traits, but those who do are obsessed by them. For example, the woman who possesses an overwhelming desire for power angles for power in all spheres of life: at work, in friendships, in her marriage, and so on. Allport observed that certain cardinal traits have been named after prominent people who exemplified the trait. *Machiavellian* describes a cynical and cunning fifteenth-century Italian political philosopher. *Chauvinism* was named after an excessively patriotic French soldier.

In contrast, everyone has **central traits** like neatness (or its opposite), thriftiness, industriousness, trustworthiness, competitiveness, and the like. These represent a relatively small number of dispositions that have a broad influence on an individual's behavior. Central traits can become cardinal traits if they dominate behavior. Finally, Allport identified a category of **secondary traits** that do not have a broad or consistent influence on behavior. These traits take the form of preferences and aversions. You may prefer Tina Turner to Cyndi Lauper, cookies to cake, and sports cars to station wagons, but your preferences tell only a limited amount about your basic personality.

Cattell's Factor-Analytic Theory of Traits

If Allport personified the idiographic approach to trait theory, Raymond B. Cattell (see Figure 12-5) personifies the nomothetic approach. Cattell's theory of personality also is built around traits, and Cattell also distinguishes among types of traits. Perhaps his most important distinction was between **surface** and **source traits**.

SURFACE TRAITS You have observed surface traits in the fellow who, for instance, is rude to the clerk in the bookstore, curt and unfriendly

FIGURE 12-5 RAYMOND B. CATTELL (b. 1905).
Cattell was born in England and in 1937 moved to the United States. He has proposed an influential trait theory of personality.

with his lab partner, and argumentative with his roommate. From your observations, you may have concluded that this fellow possesses the trait of hostility. According to Cattell, **surface traits** are those traits that, to a casual observer, seem to "go together." Cattell (1957) attempted to determine how many different surface traits people commonly use to describe themselves and others. He reduced Allport and Odbert's 4504 traits to 171 relatively different traits and had observers rate people on these traits. He was able to reduce further the observations to 36 different clusters—to which he later added another 10 surface traits detected through other methods—for a grand total of 46 surface traits (Cattell and Kline, 1977). Table 12-2 illustrates one surface trait, sociability, together with some of its component dimensions.

TABLE 12-2   CATTELL'S CONCEPTION OF TRAITS

Surface Trait		
Sociability, sentimentalism	vs.	Independence, hostility, aloofness
Responsive	vs.	Aloof
Affectionate	vs.	Cold
Social interests	vs.	Lacking social interests
Dependent	vs.	Independent
Friendly	vs.	Hostile
Frank	vs.	Secretive
Even-tempered	vs.	Sensitive
Source Trait		
Dominance		Submission
Self-assertive, confident	vs.	Submissive, unsure
Boastful, conceited	vs.	Modest, retiring
Aggressive, pugnacious	vs.	Complaisant
Willful, egotistic	vs.	Obedient

Source: After Cattell, 1950, 1965.
Note: This table illustrates one of Cattell's surface traits (sociability versus independence) and a source trait (dominance versus submission), together with examples of their underlying components.

SOURCE TRAITS   Surface traits say more about perceptions of behavior than about behavior itself. **Source traits** are the basic, underlying structures that provide coherence to personality and that explain behavior. According to Cattell, source traits are independent dimensions of personality that can be detected only through sophisticated methods such as factor analysis (examined more closely in Chapter 14). Factor analysis is a technique that allows the researcher to reduce many variables to a much smaller set of "factors." These factors group those variables that measure essentially the same thing.

Cattell and his coworkers began their research on source traits by constructing a large questionnaire out of the 46 surface traits and administering it to large numbers of subjects. They analyzed the responses to the questionnaires by factor analysis and identified 15 source traits of personality. One source trait, dominance versus submissiveness, is illustrated in Table 12-2 (Cattell, 1965). They also identified one factor for intelligence. With these results, Cattell developed his *Sixteen Personality*

16 PF TEST PROFILE

LOW SCORE DESCRIPTION	STANDARD TEN SCORE (STEN) → Average ←	HIGH SCORE DESCRIPTION
	1 2 3 4 5 6 7 8 9 10	
Reserved, Detached, Critical, Aloof, Stiff (Sizothymia)	A	**Outgoing**, Warmhearted, Easygoing, Participating (Affectothymia)
Less Intelligent, Concrete-Thinking (Lower scholastic mental capacity)	B	**More Intelligent**, Abstract-Thinking, Bright (Higher scholastic mental capacity)
Affected by Feelings, Emotionally Less Stable, Easily Upset, Changeable (Lower ego strength)	C	**Emotionally Stable**, Mature, Faces Reality, Calm (Higher ego strength)
Humble, Mild, Easily Led, Docile, Accommodating (Submissiveness)	E	**Assertive**, Aggressive, Stubborn, Competitive (Dominance)
Sober, Taciturn, Serious (Desurgency)	F	**Happy-go-lucky**, Enthusiastic (Surgency)
Expedient, Disregards Rules (Weaker superego strength)	G	**Conscientious**, Persistent, Moralistic, Staid (Stronger superego strength)
Shy, Timid, Threat-Sensitive (Threctia)	H	**Venturesome**, Uninhibited, Socially Bold (Parmia)
Tough-Minded, Self-Reliant, Realistic (Harria)	I	**Tender-minded**, Sensitive, Clinging, Overprotected (Premsia)
Trusting, Accepting Conditions (Alaxia)	L	**Suspicious**, Hard to Fool (Protension)
Practical, "Down-to-Earth" Concerns (Praxernia)	M	**Imaginative**, Bohemian, Absent-minded (Autia)
Forthright, Unpretentious, Genuine But Socially Clumsy (Artlessness)	N	**Astute**, Polished, Socially Aware (Shrewdness)
Self-assured, Placid, Secure, Complacent, Serene (Untroubled adequacy)	O	**Apprehensive**, Self-reproaching, Insecure, Worrying, Troubled (Guilt proneness)
Conservative, Respecting Traditional Ideas (Conservatism of temperament)	Q₁	**Experimenting**, Liberal, Free-thinking (Radicalism)
Group-dependent, A "Joiner" and Sound Follower (Group adherence)	Q₂	**Self-sufficient**, Resourceful, Prefers Own Decisions (Self-sufficiency)
Undisciplined Self-conflict, Lax, Follows Own Urges, Careless of Social Rules (Low integration)	Q₃	**Controlled**, Exacting Will Power, Socially Precise, Compulsive (High strength of self-sentiment)
Relaxed, Tranquil, Unfrustrated, Composed (Low ergic tension)	Q₄	**Tense**, Frustrated, Driven, Overwrought (High ergic tension)

A sten of | 1 | 2 | 3 | 4 | 5 | 6 | 7 | 8 | 9 | 10 | is obtained
by about | 2.3% | 4.4% | 9.2% | 15.0% | 19.1% | 19.1% | 15.0% | 9.2% | 4.4% | 2.3% | of adults

FIGURE 12-6 CATTELL'S 16PF. Cattell's Sixteen Personality Factor Questionnaire (16PF) has been administered to many groups of people. This example shows the profiles of four different groups: Olympic athletes (shown in solid color), scientific researchers (shown in solid black), airline pilots (shown in dashed color), and general neurotics (shown in dashed black). Average scores on each of the scales are between 4.5 and 6.5. As the figure shows, athletes tend to be assertive, emotionally stable, and venturesome; the researchers intelligent and sober; the pilots emotionally stable, controlled, tough-minded, and relaxed; the general neurotics apprehensive, tense, and affected by feelings. (After Cattell, 1956, 1965, 1973.)

Factor Questionnaire or *16 PF* (Cattell, Eber, and Tatsuoka, 1970; Cattell and Krug, 1986; see Figure 12-6). The *16 PF* has been administered to many different types of people, in many different cultures, and reveals different patterns of responses on many of the scales. Cattell and his colleagues have used the *16 PF* in a wide variety of research settings to examine the relation between personality characteristics and behavior (Cattell, 1986). For example, when they compared the personality characteristics of husbands and wives, they found that those in stable marriages had more similar personalities than those in unstable marriages and that the personality characteristics associated with stable marriages seemed to foster greater warmth, trust, and self-sufficiency in those relationships (Cattell and Nesselroade, 1967).

Eysenck's Trait-Type Theory of Personality

You know a little bit about the person sitting next to you on a plane trip if you notice that he puts sugar and cream in his coffee. You know a bit more if you find out that he drinks half a dozen cups of coffee every morning. And you know a lot more if you deduce that he is friendly and outgoing. Hans J. Eysenck (see Figure 12-7) argues that personality is hierarchically organized. People have **specific responses** or individual acts that may or may not be characteristic of them. These are at the lowest level of the hierarchy. (Today the man put cream in his coffee.) People have **habitual responses** or characteristic patterns of behavior that are repeated in similar situations. These are at the second level of the hierarchy. (The man always puts cream in his six cups of coffee.) Finally, **traits** are interrelated sets of habitual responses. They are at the third level of the hierarchy. (The man likes to have a 10-minute chat with each cup of coffee. He has the trait of sociability.)

Eysenck further proposes that there is an even more general level of personality organization called the **type**, that is based on interrelationships among traits (Eysenck, 1967, 1984; Eysenck and Eysenck, 1969, 1985; see Figure 12-8). Thus, like Cattell, Eysenck believes there are a small number of basic dimensions of personality that serve to unify and direct behavior, but he further argues that a few basic types encom-

FIGURE 12-7 HANS J. EYSENCK (b. 1916).
Eysenck was born in Germany and fled to Britain after the Nazis came to power. His work on type theory represents a blend of theoretical approaches.

FIGURE 12-8 EYSENCK'S MODEL OF PERSONALITY.
Eysenck's personality model is hierarchically arranged with specific responses or behaviors at the lowest level of the hierarchy, habitual responses at the second level, traits at the third level, and types (of which there are three: Extraversion, Neuroticism, and Psychoticism) at the highest level. (After Eysenck, 1967.)

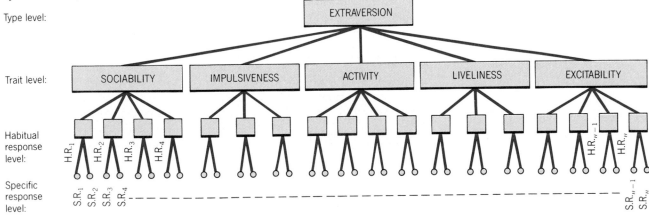

FIGURE 12-9 SAMPLE ITEMS USED BY EYSENCK.

FIGURE 12-9

	Yes	No
1. Do you usually take the initiative in making new friends?	_____	_____
2. Do ideas run through your head so that you cannot sleep?	_____	_____
3. Are you inclined to keep in the background on social occasions?	_____	_____
4. Do you sometimes laugh at a dirty joke?	_____	_____
5. Are you inclined to be moody?	_____	_____
6. Do you very much like good food?	_____	_____
7. When you get annoyed do you need someone friendly to talk to about it?	_____	_____
8. As a child did you always do as you were told immediately and without grumbling?	_____	_____
9. Do you usually keep "yourself to yourself" except with very close friends?	_____	_____
10. Do you often make up your mind too late?	_____	_____

Note: The above items would be scored in the following way: *Extraversion*—1 Yes, 3 No, 6 Yes, 9 No; *Neuroticism*—2 Yes, 5 Yes, 7 Yes, 10 Yes; *Lie Scale*—4 No, 8 Yes.

pass a wide variety of traits (Eysenck, 1984). Eysenck believes that people possess more or less of each type, with most people in the average range on each.

Like Cattell, Eysenck uses a questionnaire and factor analysis to identify personality dimensions. In his early research, Eysenck (1947) examined 700 neurotic soldiers on 39 personality variables. He detected two underlying personality dimensions, **introversion–extraversion** and **neuroticism**. Eysenck even was able to relate these two dimensions to the four major personality types identified by Hippocrates and Galen. More recently, Eysenck (1952, 1975; Eysenck and Eysenck, 1968) added a third personality dimension, **psychoticism**, that differentiates between normal and psychotic people.

What are these three personality types actually like? The typical **extravert** is sociable, exuberant, likes parties and craves excitement, and is frequently impulsive. In contrast, the typical **introvert** is shy, self-controlled, quiet, introspective, and inhibited rather than impulsive. People high in **neuroticism** tend to be emotionally unstable, easily aroused, worrisome, and frequently complain about anxieties and bodily aches. People low in neuroticism are emotionally stable, reliable, calm, and even-tempered. Eysenck has developed a number of questionnaires designed to measure people on these three dimensions. One of the most popular is the Eysenck Personality Questionnaire (EPQ), which contains 90 items (see Figure 12-9). After administering the EPQ to large numbers of people, Eysenck has concluded that types of people show characteristic differences. For example, he has found that neurotic patients are high on neuroticism and low on extraversion; criminals tend to score high on all three dimensions. Studies of the differences between intro-

TABLE 12-3 INTROVERSION–EXTRAVERSION DIFFERENCES

Introversion

Higher arousal levels in the morning	More reliable, conscientious, and
Better work alone than in groups	punctual
Better work under quiet conditions	Less absent from work
Prefer slower, more accurate work	Quicker reaction time
approach	Able to hold breath longer
Prefer theoretical and scientific jobs,	Higher academic achievement
including teaching math	Emphasize virginity and fidelity
More sustained vigilance under bor-	Report more frequent masturbation
ing conditions	More masochistic
	Oversocialized superego

Extraversion

Greater tolerance for pain	More talk and coffee breaks at work
Greater increase in arousal during	More characteristic of sociology and
the day	history majors
Higher arousal levels in the evening	More characteristic of sportsmen,
Better work in groups than alone	parachutists, and commandos
Better general adjustment	More characteristic of criminals
Prefer quicker, less accurate work	More tough-minded in attitudes
approach	More susceptible to alcohol
Less easily conditioned	Intercourse earlier in life, more
Less characteristic of university	often, and with more partners
students	Adjust more easily to time changes
Less tolerance for sensory deprivation	Undersocialized superego
Slightly more characteristic of men	Abnormal behavior more likely to be
More quickly learn how to swim	sociopathic
during childhood	

Source: After Potkay and Bern, 1986.
Note: Eysenck has distinguished between people who are introverted and extra-verted, and research with his Introversion–Extraversion scale has detected a number of differences between introverts and extraverts.

verted and extraverted individuals have revealed a large number of such differences (see Table 12-3).

Eysenck has also examined the physiological bases for extraversion and neuroticism. He has found, for example, that there is a strong genetic component to extraversion. Identical twins score much more similarly on tests of extraversion than do fraternal twins (Shields, 1976). Basic physiological differences interact with environmental factors, Eysenck maintains, to produce personality differences. For example, studies indicate that extraverts and introverts differ in their characteristic levels of arousal (Eysenck, 1970). Examination of levels of arousal in the reticular formation (see Chapter 2) indicates that extraverts have lower levels of arousal and tend to seek out stimulation, whereas introverts have higher levels of arousal and tend to avoid external stimulation. Furthermore, introverts are more readily aroused by external events and are more responsive to punishment. Therefore, they tend to learn social prohibitions more readily. In contrast, extraverts seem more responsive to rewards (Nichols and Newman, 1986). Eysenck has used these differ-

TABLE 12-4   FIVE COMMON PERSONALITY FACTORS

Factor 1
Surgency
Talkative–Silent
Sociable–Reclusive
Adventurous–Cautious
Sociable–Reclusive

Factor 2
Agreeableness
Good-natured–Irritable
Mild, Gentle–Headstrong
Cooperative–Negativistic
Not Jealous–Jealous

Factor 3
Conscientiousness
Responsible–Undependable
Persevering–Quitting, Fickle
Fussy, Tidy–Careless
Scrupulous–Unscrupulous

Factor 4
Emotional Stability
Calm–Anxious
Composed–Excitable
Not Hypochondriacal–
Hypochondriacal
Poised–Nervous, Tense

Factor 5
Culture
Imaginative–Simple, Direct
Artistically Sensitive–Insensitive
Intellectual–Nonreflective, Narrow
Polished, Refined–Boorish

Source: Digman and Inouye, 1986; after Norman, 1963.

Note: Five personality factors commonly found by researchers.

ences to explain why introverts and extraverts would learn different patterns of behavior.

In sum, then, trait and type theorists differ from other personality theorists in that they regard traits as stable, basic building blocks of personality and assume that personality can be described with a limited number of traits or dimensions. Type theorists assume that personality can be described in a small number of types. Although the exact number of types is a matter of heated dispute (Cattell, 1986; Eysenck, 1986), several researchers have found support for five basic personality factors (e.g., Digman and Inouye, 1986; Fiske, 1949; Norman, 1963; see Table 12-4). Of course, despite their similarities, trait and type theorists differ in their emphasis on unique versus shared personality traits and on the physiological bases of personality.

In addition, a trait theorist such as Allport favors an individualized, idiographic approach to personality whereas factor-analytically oriented theorists like Cattell and Eysenck emphasize a nomothetic approach. The theorists also differ in their emphasis on the physiological bases for personality differences. Although Allport, Cattell, and Eysenck all assume that personality has a physiological basis, only Eysenck has produced evidence for the physiological bases of his personality types.

THE PERSON OR THE SITUATION: WHICH DETERMINES BEHAVIOR?

One of the assumptions implicit in trait and type theories of personality is that the measured traits and types predict how a person will behave in a variety of situations—that is, it is presumed that across a wide variety of settings an individual who is high in aggressiveness will tend to be more aggressive than a person who is low in aggressiveness. However, early research findings cast some doubts on this assumption. For example, in a series of studies conducted in the 1920s, Hartshorne and May (1928, 1929, 1930) tested the honesty and altruism of 11,000 grade school and high school students. The students were given 33 different "behavioral" tests that provided them (unknowingly) with opportunities to lie, cheat, and steal at school, at home, in church, at play, and in athletic competitions. Hartshorne and May wanted to test whether the children's behavior was consistent across situations. Would honest children be honest in all or most situations, for example, or would honesty vary greatly according to the situation? Would some children be honest at home but not at school?

What Hartshorne and May found was that there was only a weak correlation (an average of $r = .23$) between honest behavior in one situation and another. But behavior within a particular situation, such as the classroom, was somewhat more consistent. The investigators concluded that the traits of honesty and dishonesty are not "unified character traits, but rather specific functions of life situations. Most children will deceive in certain situations and not others" (1928, p. 411). Later, more detailed reanalyses of the data produced similar conclusions (Burton, 1963). Although many personality theorists took these findings seriously, and a number developed "interactionist" theories that emphasized the importance of both traits and situations (Brunswick, 1943; Lewin, 1935; Murray, 1938), none of these theories produced measurement techniques that allowed researchers to determine the precise relation between personal characteristics and situations.

Behavioral Consistency

The controversy about behavioral consistency lay dormant until 1968, when Walter Mischel published a provocative book, *Personality and Assessment*. There he reviewed the evidence for behavioral consistency across situations. He found an average correlation of only .30, which led him to conclude that except for intelligence, consistencies in behavior had not been demonstrated, and the concept of personality traits as broad predispositions was untenable. Mischel further argued that when traits are assessed, the descriptions do not mirror actual behavior but reflect socially agreed-upon ways of describing behavior. Although Mischel's arguments had been made before, the coherence of his position and the quality of the research evidence he mustered to support his position created a storm of controversy among personality psychologists.

Trait theorists were quick to respond to Mischel's attacks. They devised new studies and techniques to address Mischel's criticisms. Some examined the **consistency in personal traits over time**. For example, one researcher tested students in junior and senior high school and retested them more than 10 years later (Block, 1971, 1977). Even though different judges made the ratings, Block found an average correlation on 114 personality variables of over .55. Others administered personality tests at 6- and 12-year intervals to 460 adult men between the ages of 17 and 85 and found correlations between .59 and .87 (Costa, McCrae, and Arenberg, 1980). More recently, a researcher examined the stability of personality characteristics over a 30-year period (1947–1977) by using a standard personality inventory (the Minnesota Multiphasic Personality Inventory, or MMPI) (Finn, 1986).

Block found correlations ranging as high as .97. Furthermore, he found greater stability among older men (average age 21 years in 1947; see Table 12-5). This pattern of results agrees with that predicted by personality theories (such as Freud's) that emphasize greater personality change early in life. Other researchers, too, have found evidence of substantial stability in personality measures over periods as long as 50 years (Conley, 1985; Mussen, Eichorn, Honzik, Bieher, and Meredith, 1980; Olweus, 1977).

Other researchers have sought to demonstrate there is **consistency in behavior across situations**. Seymour Epstein, for example, has argued (1979a, 1979b, 1980, 1983) that studies often have failed to produce findings of behavioral consistency across situations because their samples were too small. For example, when observations of behavior, self-ratings, and ratings by others have been collected in large numbers over a period of days, measures of sociability and impulsivity correlated only weakly (.30) from day to day, but correlations averaged over several days were as

TABLE 12-5 30-YEAR RETEST RELIABILITY
COEFFICIENTS BY AGE/COHORT GROUP

Scale	Older Cohort[a]	Younger Cohort[b]
Negative vs. Positive Affectivity[c]	.61	.59
Constraint[c]	.78	.47***
Neuroticism	.58	.47
Psychoticism	.85	.40***
Cynicism	.72	.56*
Denial of Somatic Problems	.14	.45*
Social Extraversion	.66	.58
Stereotypic Femininity	.81	.59**
Psychotic Paranoia	.52	.12**
Depression	.27	−.08*
Delinquency	.81	.81
Stereotypic Masculinity	.73	.69
Neurasthenic Somatization	.17	−.20
Phobias	.69	.42**
Family Attachment	.78	.48***
Intellectual Interests	.81	.46***
Religious Fundamentalism	.97	.74***

[a] $N = 78$.
[b] $N = 96$.
[c] Higher order factors.
* $p < .05$. ** $p < .01$. *** $p < .001$.
Note: Personality characteristics can be quite stable over periods on many years—as reflected in the reliability of tests administered 30 years apart. As shown here, older people tend to show even greater stability (as indicated by the significant differences in reliability coefficients denoted with asterisks).

high as .9 (Epstein, 1979a). When researchers used this method of aggregation on the original Hartshorne and May data, they found strong correlations (between .61 and .80) on the measures of honesty and altruism (Rushton, Jackson, and Paunonen, 1981). Findings like these—emotions and behavioral impulses are stable when measured in the aggregate—have been interpreted by some as strong evidence for the existence of broad dispositions, or traits (Epstein, 1983).

Are people's personalities consistent from one situation to another and from one time to another? The last word on the controversy has not yet been written. But the controversy has benefited psychologists who study personality. It has underscored weaknesses in theory and method and spurred these psychologists to come up with better ways to produce answers about human personality.

BIOLOGICAL THEORIES OF PERSONALITY

You may have heard at some time or another that redheads have fiery tempers, that fat people are jolly, and to never trust a man with a mustache. These snatches of folk wisdom are attempts at explaining

FIGURE 12-10 NINETEENTH-CENTURY ADVERTISEMENT FOR PHRENOLOGY.

As illustrated in this advertisement, phrenology has, at times, held much popular appeal.

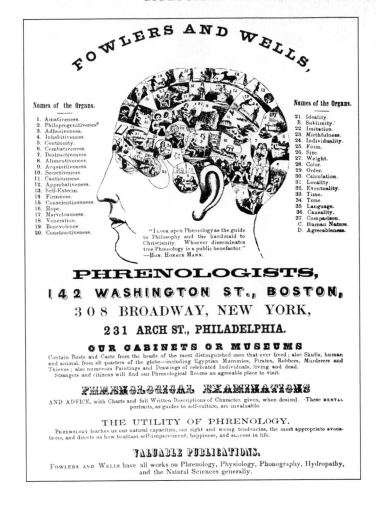

personality by biological traits. Psychologists have long been interested in the same goal. What more logical place than the human body, after all, to explain the mysteries of the human personality? As you saw earlier, the humours theory of body fluids was popular for centuries as a biological explanation of personality types. In the late eighteenth century, a German anatomist Franz Gall (1758–1828) argued that one could assess individual differences on 45 different "faculties" or traits such as self-esteem, secretiveness, combativeness, destructiveness, and hopefulness by studying the bumps on a person's skull. His theory of this practice, called **phrenology**, was that each faculty was associated with a different region of the brain, and the pattern of bumps reflected the degree of development of each faculty. Phrenology (see Figure 12-10) has been repudiated by the scientific community. However, other biological models of personality have been proposed more recently.

Body Types and Personality

In this century, probably the earliest and most influential biological explanation for personality came from William Sheldon, a psychologist

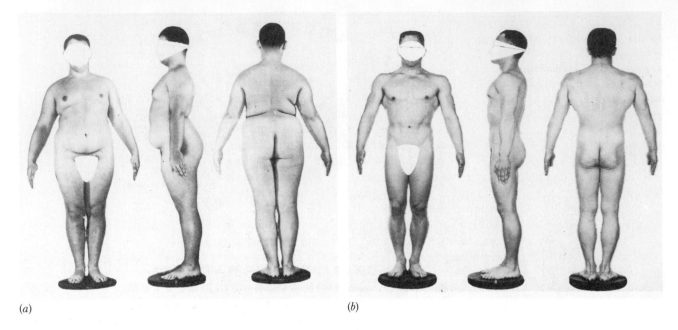

(a)   (b)

and physician. Sheldon took a **constitutional approach** to personality, arguing that a person's body type determines his or her personality and behavior. After studying body types in the photographs of 4000 men (see Figure 12-11), Sheldon concluded that men have three basic body types, or **somatotypes**. **Endomorphs** are rounded and have protruding stomachs, and are relaxed in posture and movement. **Mesomorphs** have a heavy, hard, rectangular shape; their muscles and bones dominate their frames. **Ectomorphs** are slender and fragile with a lot of skin relative to their body weight.

Then Sheldon tied these body types to personality types. Heavy, round endomorphs, he suggested, are sociable and love eating and comfort. Tall, thin ectomorphs have restrained movements, are overresponsive, secretive, love privacy, and fear social interaction. Mesomorphs stand and move assertively, love physical adventure, risk, and competition, and want dominance and power.

Although Sheldon's theory of body types never has been very popular among psychologists (see Humphreys, 1957), researchers have confirmed some of Sheldon's ideas about temperamental differences among somatotypes (Cortes and Gatti, 1965; Gascaly and Borges, 1979; Yates and Taylor, 1978). Several studies also link body types to criminality (Gibbens, 1963; Glueck and Glueck, 1956; Shasby and Kingsley, 1978). But, as some have noted, though body and personality characteristics may be related, that is a far cry from knowing that body type *determines* personality. Perhaps a man's body type influences the types of social experiences he has, and these social experiences determine his personality characteristics. Perhaps, for example, an overweight endomorph is less likely than the muscular mesomorph to be rewarded for his efforts to dominate others. He, therefore, may have to deflect his feelings of re-

FIGURE 12-11 SHELDON'S SOMATOTYPES.
These photographs illustrate three extreme examples of Sheldon's somatotypes—(a) *endomorph,* (b) *mesomorph, and* (c) *ectomorph.*

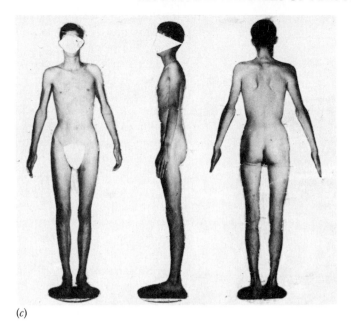

(c)

jection through humor and heightened sociability, in short, by acting jolly. Thus although his body type does not determine his personality— fatness doesn't *make* a man jolly—it may indirectly shape his personality through his social behavior.

Genetics and Personality

One offshoot of the search for a biological explanation to personality has been the search for the genetic basis—if any—of personality characteristics. As in other areas of inquiry, psychologists conduct twin studies to assess heritability. They compare the similarity in personality of monozygotic twins (identical twins, whose genes are identical) to the similarity of dizygotic twins (fraternal twins, whose genes are half identical). In such studies, the researchers seek to establish how much of the similarity in characteristics can be accounted for by genetic factors. As we discussed in Chapter 9, crudely speaking, one can argue that differences in monozygotic twins must be environmentally determined, whereas differences in dizygotic twins raised together must be genetically determined. (Few people would argue that dizygotic twins are raised in *identical* environments, just highly similar ones). From their findings about the twins' similarities, the researchers compute a **heritability coefficient**, which reflects the degree of genetic influence on personality or another characteristic. For instance, if large numbers of identical twins never resembled each other on a measure of personality, then the heritability coefficient would be zero. If they always resembled each other, the coefficient would be 1.00. Sandra Scarr (1966), for example, compared the activity levels of 61 identical and fraternal twins between the ages of 6 and 10. (Why activity level? A child's activity level may be related to other aspects

SOCIAL POTENCY	61%

A person high in this trait is masterful, a forceful leader who likes to be the center of attention.

TRADITIONALISM	60%

Follows rules and authority, endorses high moral standards and strict discipline.

STRESS REACTION	55%

Feels vulnerable and sensitive and is given to worries and easily upset.

ABSORPTION	55%

Has a vivid imagination readily captured by rich experience; relinquishes sense of reality.

ALIENATION	55%

Feels mistreated and used, that "the world is out to get me."

WELL-BEING	54%

Has a cheerful disposition, feels confident and optimistic.

HARM AVOIDANCE	51%

Shuns the excitement of risk and danger, prefers the safe route even if it is tedious.

AGGRESSION	48%

Is physically aggressive and vindictive, has taste for violence and is "out to get the world."

ACHIEVEMENT	46%

Works hard, strives for mastery and puts work and accomplishment ahead of other things.

CONTROL	43%

Is cautious and plodding, rational and sensible, likes carefully planned events.

SOCIAL CLOSENESS	33%

Prefers emotional intimacy and close ties, turns to others for comfort and help.

FIGURE 12-12   THE HERITABILITY OF TRAITS. According to twin studies, the estimated degree of heritability for 11 personality traits, as measured by the Multidimensional Personality Questionnaire. (Tellegen, 1982; after Goleman, 1986.)

of personality.) She found that identical twins were more similar than fraternal twins and got a heritability coefficient of .70 for the activity level of identical twins.

In Sweden nearly 13,000 pairs of twins took the Eysenck Personality Inventory (a forerunner of the EPQ, discussed earlier in the chapter) (Floderus-Myrhed, Pederson, and Rasmussen, 1980). The researchers found heritability coefficients of .50 (for men) and .58 (for women) for neuroticism, and .54 and .66, respectively, for extraversion. Correlations this high suggest that extraversion and neuroticism have some genetic base. They are not the only personality traits with a genetic base, though. A study of over 800 identical and fraternal twins showed that in a wide range of personality characteristics identical twins were generally twice as much alike as the fraternal twins (Loehlin and Nichols, 1976).

Most personality researchers see a need for more high-quality research before any firm conclusions can be reached about genetic influences on personality. Studies of identical twins who have been raised apart provide the strongest evidence of genetic influences on personality. One such study has been under way at the University of Minnesota since 1979 (Bouchard et al., 1981; Goleman, 1986; Lykken, 1982). Out of a total of 350 pairs of twins, the researchers have studied 44 pairs of identical twins and 21 pairs of fraternal twins who were separated at birth, usually because both were put up for adoption. The twins have been administered a host of standard personality measures. These measures indicate that about half the variability in traits can be accounted for by heredity (see Figure 12-12). Most interesting of all, the twins raised apart (see Figure 12-13) seem as similar in personality as identical twins raised together. In fact, some of the similarities in the lives of these twins are remarkable: they share distinctive interests, attitudes, mannerisms, and postures (see Holden, 1980). Psychologists who are investigating the biological and the sociobiological roots of human personality are producing some of the most exciting new research today. In a few years, we may have a cohesive biological theory of personality.

PSYCHOANALYTIC THEORY

Psychoanalytic theory originated with the study of individuals and ever since has most commonly been applied to individuals. The psychoanalytic theory of Sigmund Freud (see Figure 12-14) was a revolutionary milestone in psychology. Freud himself observed that his theory was a profound challenge to the human self-image. His discovery of the influence of unconscious and sometimes uncontrollable psychological forces on behavior deeply challenged existing theories of rational human behavior.

Freud's influence on psychology and society has been deep and enduring. In everyday speech, people talk about "Freudian slips," the "unconscious," "ego trips," the "Oedipus complex." All of these terms originated in Freud's theories of human personality. Although psychoanalytic theory is often criticized, its influence has remained strong because it seeks to explain and encompass so much of human behavior in an integrated and coherent way.

FIGURE 12-13   TWO PAIRS OF REUNITED TWINS FROM THE MINNESOTA TWIN STUDY.
The Minnesota twin study has uncovered some remarkable similarities in twins raised apart and reunited as adults. Jim Lewis and Jim Springer drove the same kind of car, smoked the same kind of cigarette, had the same hobby (woodworking), both had a nailbiting habit, and both developed migraines at the same age. Jerry Levey and Mark Newman were both fire captains, drank the same beer (and held their bottles in the same way), and were both bachelors.

The Structure of Personality

CONSCIOUSNESS   As a result of his clinical experiences, Freud came to place great emphasis on the distinction between conscious and unconscious experiences. In fact, Freud distinguished three levels of experience that can be represented in a kind of psychic map (see Figure 12-14). At the **conscious** level is everything that an individual is aware of at a given point in time, including perceptions, sensations, memories, and the like. At the **preconscious** level are thoughts not presently in consciousness but that *could* be called into consciousness. In your preconscious, for example, may be the quiet sounds around you as you have been

reading or the memory of what you had for dinner last night. At the third level of the psyche is the **unconscious**. According to Freud, the unconscious is the repository of the deep, inaccessible drives and urges that determine behavior. As Figure 12-15 suggests, the unconscious is the largest part of the psyche. Its unusual features are perhaps most apparent in dreams. The unconscious in dreams is not logical. Instead, it operates by symbols—snakes for penises, and an octopus for an over-

FIGURE 12-15   A MAP OF
FREUD'S STRUCTURE OF
THE MIND.
This map reflects Freud's ideas about
the structure of the mind, showing the
id, the ego, and the superego, and
their relationship to the conscious,
preconscious, and unconscious. (After
Healy, Bonner, and Bowers, 1930.)

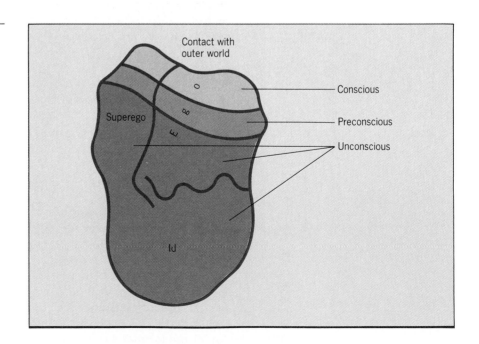

bearing mother, for example. The unconscious also can disregard time and space. Objects in dreams often are entirely out of proportion, and totally unconnected experiences and people often are drawn together.

The unconscious cannot be directly observed (which creates problems for researchers who wish to examine it scientifically), but Freud believed that the workings of the unconscious could be observed in dreams, through hypnosis, and through free association. According to Freud, one of the primary objectives of psychoanalytic theory is to demonstrate how unconscious processes and life events, particularly repressed memories and traumas, affect behavior and cause people psychological distress. As Freud put it: "our scientific work in psychology will consist in translating unconscious processes into conscious ones, and thus filling in the gaps in conscious perceptions" (1950, p. 382).

THE ID, EGO, AND SUPEREGO   In his book *The Ego and the Id* (1923), Freud suggested that the human psyche consists of three components that cut across the conscious, preconscious, and unconscious mind. The **id**, he said, represents the biological foundations of personality. It is the source of the energies for instinctual urges, such as aggression and sexuality, and as these energies build up the id seeks methods to release the accumulated tension (see Chapter 8). In seeking to release this tension, the id exercises no logic and no morals, is selfish and demanding, and seeks immediate and unrestrained gratification. As Freud put it, the id obeys the **pleasure principle**: it pursues pleasure and avoids pain.

The **ego**, on the other hand, is a kind of executive manager for the personality. The ego is rational and seeks to govern behavior in a manner that is consistent with social expectations. The ego operates according to the **reality principle**: it is practical and defers the gratification sought by the id until the person can achieve pleasure without incurring the costs of punishment or social reproach. The ego is oriented to the real world and is based on well-developed cognitive and perceptual skills. Its primary task is to find acceptable ways of satisfying the demands of the id.

Finally, the **superego**, Freud suggested, is the last portion of the personality system to develop. It usually appears somewhere between the ages of 3 and 6. The superego is the branch of personality concerned with morality. It is composed of two parts. The first is referred to as the **conscience**, and it is developed through punishments administered by parents. The conscience is primarily concerned with bad behavior, and it controls behavior by making a person feel worthless or bad. The second part of the superego is the **ego-ideal**, which is developed through the rewards given by parents. It steers behavior in the direction of the good and the self-sacrificing. When the ego-ideal prevails, the individual feels proud. The dynamics of the personality are such that the ego is pressured from several directions—from the instinctual urges of the id, from the moralistic demands of the superego, and from reality.

Personality Processes

INSTINCTS   Like scientists who came after him, Freud saw that infants are born with the instinctive urges to seek comfort and avoid discomfort by suckling, by eliminating body wastes, and by keeping close to the warm touch of another person's body. Out of such instinctive urges, Freud believed, the infant's body becomes excited and filled with an energy that must be expressed. In the early formulations of his theory, Freud suggested that there are two types of instincts: **ego instincts**, which are directed to self-preservation, and **sexual instincts**, which are directed to preservation of the species. For Freud, sexual instincts included not only sexual intercourse, but also affection for family, friends, and even community. Freud later subsumed the ego and sexual instincts into a single **life instinct** (**eros**) and its associated energy (**libido**). The life instinct contrasted with the **death instinct** (**thanatos**): the striving to return to an inorganic state. The death instinct is one of the more controversial aspects of Freud's theory, and many psychoanalysts today prefer to concentrate on the sexual and aggressive instincts, which they regard as part of the id.

According to Freud, humans instinctively seek to reduce the tension developed through the buildup of energies. People can achieve this release of gratification in many different ways. An almost infinite variety of objects and people serve as targets for aggression or sexual gratification. Freud called the expenditure of instinctual energies through an object, **cathexis**. One important feature of Freud's theory is that the instincts can be blocked, delayed, transformed, and even combined. For example, a young man who cannot find a sexual partner may substitute nonsexual affection for his friends to partially satisfy his sexual instinct. A young woman who falls out of love with her boyfriend may transfer her love to a more promising man. People often turn their aggression and sexual impulses on themselves in self-destructive acts, such as car accidents, drinking, quarreling, even suicide.

ANXIETY Anxiety is so common a psychological term today that it crops up on television talk shows, supermarket-rack bestsellers, and the conversations of grade-school children. It was psychoanalytic theory that contributed this concept to us. In some ways, Freud equated anxiety with fear. Anxiety, he saw, has the emotional and physiological qualities (the autonomic responses to fear) usually associated with responses to external threats, like a car speeding at you. But Freud emphasized that anxiety is not always a response to an external threat. Only **reality anxiety** is a response to an external threat. In contrast, **neurotic anxiety** arises out of the unconscious as a result of threats from the instincts. Neurotic anxiety can take the form of "free floating" or general anxiety such as a fear that an impulse like aggression or sexual feelings will get out of control; **phobias**, which are extreme and apparently irrational fears; and **panic attacks**. Freud thought that phobic people actually feared their instinctual desire for the feared object. A snake, for example, might represent an unconscious sexual wish, and the exaggerated fear of the snake might be a defense against acting on that sexual desire. A second form of internally generated anxiety is **moral anxiety**, which is based on the feelings of guilt and shame produced by the conscience as it tries to punish the immoral impulses of the id.

DEFENSE MECHANISMS Because anxiety is so painful, Freud suggested, people must find ways to defend themselves against it. People develop **defense mechanisms** against anxiety and these defense mechanisms distort and falsify reality and exclude feelings of anxiety from consciousness. Everyone, not just neurotic people, uses defense mechanisms. We use them unconsciously and in combination. Although our defense mechanisms may protect us from our anxieties, they do so at a cost: they prevent us from confronting our anxieties and learning successful methods for coping with them.

Perhaps the most basic defense mechanism is **denial**. Young children, whose personalities are still forming, are especially likely to use the mechanism of denial. "See?" says the 4-year-old whose face is covered in crumbs, "I didn't eat any cookies." Parents also may teach children to resort to denial. When a child gets hurt, for example, a parent may say "Don't cry, you're fine." The parent is actually teaching the child to deny the pain of the injury. As adults, people deny reality by not hearing bad news ("No, I didn't hear anything about an exam.") or by forgetting ("I thought you said I'd get $100, not $50."). Patients deny the problems in their illnesses, husbands and wives deny the problems in their marriages, parents deny the behavior problems of their children. Even entire societies can get caught up in denial, as when most Germans denied the evidence of the concentration camps during World War II.

Another very basic defense mechanism is **repression**, which is the forcing of unacceptable thoughts and wishes into the unconscious. The thoughts and wishes are not destroyed; they remain in existence, and a person must constantly expend energy to keep them out of consciousness. Freud believed that people repress certain memories because they are too painful to acknowledge. A major part of psychoanalytic therapy may involve a person's gradually revealing and coping with these repressed memories.

One of the most primitive defense mechanisms is **projection**. When we project, we (unconsciously) assume that thoughts and impulses come from outside of us. Thus, rather than see ourselves as hostile, unscrupulous, spiteful, miserly, unfaithful, dishonest, or the like, we project these characteristics onto the people around us. ("It's not me who is selfish," thinks the wife, "it's my husband." "I did badly on my report card because the teachers are stupid," complains the student.) Similarly, someone (Janet) who feels attracted to another person of the same sex (Mary), but who finds homosexuality objectionable, may project these feelings of attraction onto the other person—thus, Janet may believe it is Mary and not herself who is behaving seductively.

Displacement, discussed earlier, is a defense mechanism that arises when people remove their impulses from someone or something unsatisfying to someone or something that may be satisfying. The boy who cannot hit his father may try to hit his little brother. The baby who cannot suck a mother's breast uses a pacifier or a thumb.

One of the more elevated defense mechanisms (more elevated than hitting baby brother, at least) is to **sublimate** an impulse rather than the object of the impulse. Someone who feels a strong impulse to act aggressively might stop breaking windows or bones and turn destructive energies to other, socially accepted activities—perhaps by joining the military or becoming an aggressive football player. Someone with strong sexual impulses might channel them into creative activities. For example, Freud suggested that Leonardo da Vinci's desire to paint madonnas was a sublimated desire for his mother.

When people convert an undesirable impulse into its opposite, they may create **reaction formations**. The seething man who treats his wife with exaggerated kindness, the inveterate cheat who endlessly documents her scrupulousness, perhaps even the macho man who cannot accept any softness because it smacks of femininity—each may be in the throes of a reaction formation (Hall, 1954). But how does one know whether someone's behavior is a true reflection of feelings or a reaction formation? One clue is the degree of exaggeration or inappropriateness of the person's behavior. Even so, not every exaggerated behavior indicates a reaction formation. Diagnosing reaction formations can be a tricky business.

Finally, the defense mechanism **rationalization** intrudes when people try to justify their behavior through plausible but inaccurate explanations. Probably everyone has had the experience of doing unpleasant things and later trying to explain away or reinterpret them. ("I hit the child, but it was for her own good." "I didn't keep John's secret, but it was a silly thing to keep secret.") Most worrisome are those rationalizations that truly hurt large numbers of people—the thousands of "infidels" killed in the name of various gods and the murderous, destructive acts that are the "will of God."

Psychoanalysts have described many other defense mechanisms and have elaborated greatly on Freud's original ideas about the structure and workings of the personality. In the following section we turn to how Freud combined structure and process to account for what he termed the **psychosexual stages** of development and the personality types that he associated with each of those stages.

Personality Development

Freud believed that over the course of development, people's (libidinal) energies are devoted to different interests and objects and parts of the body, or **erogenous zones.** Each area and its associated drives (hunger, elimination, and sex) gives way to the next as the primary focus of a child's activities. However, if a child cannot solve the problems of development at any of these stages, or if progress is interrupted by childhood traumas, he or she may become **fixated** at a particular stage. Fixation can occur, Freud thought, if children are overly indulged or overly frustrated in their efforts to satisfy their libidinal urges.

THE ORAL STAGE The **oral stage** occurs during the period between birth and 18 months. According to Freud, infants of this age are almost entirely id: they cannot distinguish between themselves and the external world, their behavior is dictated by instinctual, biological impulses, and they are essentially selfish. At this stage, infants' activities focus on biting, holding food in their mouth, swallowing, spitting, and closing their mouth. Freud associated these five actions with particular personality traits. He suggested that children who derive great pleasure from taking things into their mouth (*oral-receptive*) or who are frustrated by being underfed may become generally acquisitive later in life and may, for example, hunger for power or knowledge. Similarly, children who take pleasure in biting (*oral-aggressive*) may develop into adults who are verbally aggressive.

THE ANAL STAGE   The child in the anal stage (between 2 and 3 years of age) focuses on anal activities such as the holding and elimination of feces. Freud thought that defecation gave children both relief from the tension of holding in waste and pleasurable stimulation of the anus. At this stage, he suggested, children's psyches struggle as the developing ego strives to control the id's impulsive pleasure in defecation. The demands of social reality (that one control one's impulses and become toilet trained) now come into conflict with instinctual demands. Children who do not control their bowel movements may be punished and may retaliate by, for instance, intentionally soiling their clothes. Generally the ego prevails because the child's increasing awareness of the external world gives him or her the motivation to control defecation and, thereby, to win parents' approval and avoid their displeasure.

If there are difficulties in toilet training and a child does not fully resolve the conflicts between social demands and anal impulses, Freud believed that the child might develop the reaction formation of an *anal personality*. For example, Freud thought that *anal-retentives* are interested in orderliness and cleanliness (a reaction to their interest in dirtiness and disorder) and are stingy, obstinate, and cannot "let go" (a reaction to social demands that they part with their feces). *Anal-expulsives,* in contrast, tend to be messy, highly emotional, and aggressively destructive.

THE PHALLIC STAGE   In the **phallic stage** (during the fourth and fifth years), children's libidinal tensions focus on their genitals. From infancy, boys and girls both derive pleasure from stimulating their genitals. By the time they are 4 or 5 years old, children know the anatomical differences between boys and girls. When boys realize that girls do not have a penis, they may become afraid that they may lose theirs. Around the same time, children also realize that there is a sexual relationship between their parents. A boy is likely to see his father as a rival for his mother's affection and may project hostility onto his father and fear retaliation from his father. Freud suggested that boys who worry that their fathers might retaliate by cutting off the boys' penis suffer from **castration anxiety**. Freud called this tangle of sexual wishes and fears the **Oedipus complex** (after the hero of Sophocles' tragedy, *Oedipus Rex,* who unknowingly killed his father and committed incest with his mother). Freud thought that the Oedipal conflict was a universal and biologically based fact of life in which the boy desires his mother, yet also fears punishment or retaliation from his father. The Oedipal conflict is successfully resolved, he thought, when the boy represses his hostile rivalry and identifies with his father, that is, models himself after his father and views the world from his father's perspective. This adjustment allows the boy to keep loving his mother and reduces his fear of punishment from his father.

According to Freud, the experiences of girls during the phallic stage are different from those of boys. Girls realize they do not have a penis and develop **penis envy**. They grow to dislike their mother because they blame her for their lack of a penis and turn their affections toward their father, who does have a penis. As she matures, a girl ultimately does come to identify with her mother, and this adjustment allows her to keep her father as a love object. Freud actually went further and argued that because girls fear their father less than boys do (because girls already have "lost" their penis), girls do not as fully resolve these sexual conflicts and develop weaker superegos. Not too surprisingly, Freud's analysis of female development during the phallic stage has come under vigorous attack from modern critics as muddled and, the idea of penis envy especially, chauvinistic.

THE LATENCY STAGE   Between the ages of 5 and 6, children enter the **latency period**, which lasts until the ages of about 12 or 13 (the age of puberty). Freud believed that during the latency period, the sexual instincts are dormant. The sexual instincts have not disappeared, but they are temporarily repressed. Girls and boys usually keep a studious distance from each other during this stage, and there are no new major sexual developments until puberty. Freud believed that a person's typical behavior patterns are established by the age of 5.

THE GENITAL STAGE   Puberty ushers in a host of hormonal and physiological changes (see Chapter 9) that signal the final stage of psychosexual development. The erotic impulses, which were primarily auto-erotic before latency, now surface with a new emphasis. Adolescents become interested in genital sexuality, particularly sexual intercourse, in the context of romantic *relationships*. Freud believed that the adolescents and young adults who could develop a fully mature, genital personality were ideal types. Having matured past latency, their sexual energies are no longer repressed and can be expressed with people who are appropriate love objects and channeled into creative work. These people know how to defer gratification and have learned the most difficult art of all: how to love.

Evaluating Psychoanalytic Theory

Even those psychologists who reject psychoanalytic theory acknowledge that Freud gave the world invaluable concepts—of the unconscious mind, the ego, and other mental structures, defense mechanisms such as anxiety, repression, and projection, and others. Although he did not originate these concepts, Freud enriched them and demonstrated their interconnections. His emphasis on the importance of childhood experiences influenced virtually all later theories, and his emphasis on the role of sexuality in development opened the door to a once-forbidden topic.

But psychoanalytic theory also has been the target of extensive criticism. As a theory, it is much more literary and descriptive than it is scientific. Because it is imprecise, it is very difficult to derive testable hypotheses from the theory. Furthermore, empirically minded scientists find the concepts behind the theory difficult to test and research. Because they cannot adequately measure ideas such as id, ego, and super-ego, they find it virtually impossible to assess the scientific validity of the theory. Critics point to the difficulties in determining the existence, much less the effects, of such things as libidinal energy. Some critics challenge the idea that personality development is essentially in place by middle childhood. Still other critics dismiss the theory as a product of the historical era in which Freud lived and challenge the idea that a theory based on clinical experiences with neurotic, middle-class, Viennese, Victorian women (for these were the types of patients Freud typically saw) can tell us much about general human development.

Of course, the major test of any theory of personality is empirical evidence, and in the 90 years since Freud first began publishing his theory, a considerable number of empirical studies have been conducted. Freud himself was not particularly concerned with empirical verification of his theory. When in 1934 the American psychologist Saul Rosenzweig wrote to tell Freud about his research on repression, Freud's response was

> I have reviewed with interest your experimental investigations for verifying psychoanalytic propositions. I cannot value these confirmations very highly since the abundance of reliable observations upon which these propositions rest makes them independent of experimental verification. Nevertheless [they] can do no harm.

> (Mackinnon and Dukes, 1962, p. 32)

Despite Freud's lack of enthusiasm for such research, other researchers have attempted to test Freudian theory. Interestingly, psychologists who have reviewed this research have not yet arrived at a consensus about the implications of the research, but some reviewers have found support for Freud's theories. For example, Kline (1981) reviewed over a thousand studies and concluded that they affirmed the validity of psychoanalytic theory. When others reviewed over 1900 publications, they concluded that there was general support for Freud's theory, even though not every single one of his ideas had been confirmed.

FREUD'S THEORETICAL SUCCESSORS

Over the 50-year period in which he was actively writing, Freud developed, refined, and sometimes changed his psychoanalytic theory. The theory also has been refined by Freud's successors. Nowadays it is virtually impossible to find psychoanalysts who subscribe to a psychoanalytic theory exactly as Freud proposed it, but untold numbers of psychologists and personality theorists can trace their intellectual lineage directly back to Freud and there are even larger numbers whose work has been profoundly influenced by Freud and his theories.

As is likely to happen when someone devises a rich, original, and provocative theory, Freud rapidly developed a very large following, first in Europe and later in America. Many of these followers themselves became very famous and influential psychoanalytic theorists. Some of

FIGURE 12-16   ALFRED ADLER (1870–1937).

Adler was an original member of the Vienna Psychoanalytic Society, who later broke relations with the members of the society.

them remained quite loyal to Freud and his intellectual legacy (and are often termed **neo-Freudians**), but a number of them found reasons to criticize and modify Freud's theory. These revisions sometimes produced dramatic clashes between the critic and Freud and his more devout followers. As a result, many of the critics left the ranks of Freudian orthodoxy and developed their own personality theories. These theories were clearly derived from Freud's psychoanalytic theory but had different emphases and new ideas. We discuss several of these in the following sections.

Adler: Inferiority and Compensation

Alfred Adler (see Figure 12-16) was the first major theorist to break with Freud. In 1907 Adler published a book in which he incorporated the concept of compensation into psychoanalytic theory. Adler drew an analogy between physical compensation (as when one arm or lung becomes stronger to compensate for infirmity in the other) and psychological compensation. In his theory of "Individual Psychology" Adler argued that someone who had psychological and social **inferiorities** might strive to overcome them. For example, the child who felt that an older brother or sister was intelligent might compensate by working especially hard in school. The man who feels weak and powerless might compensate by relentless weight lifting, and the person who was poor might compensate by striving to accumulate wealth. When Adler presented his views to the Vienna group, 40 other physicians requested that he leave the group. Adler resigned, broke with Freud, and went on to form his own psychoanalytic group.

Adler thought that we are all inclined to believe that we are inferior in some (even many) ways and that we all attempt to compensate for these perceived inferiorities. Indeed, in Adler's view, the basic motivation that we all share is the **striving for superiority**—not a striving to be better than the people around us, but a striving to improve ourselves. One of the important ways in which Adler differed from Freud was by emphasizing the social determinants of behavior whereas Freud emphasized the biological determinants (such as libido). Thus, Adler was interested in family dynamics and believed that birth order was an important influence on the development of personality. He thought, for instance, that the oldest child in a family could feel threatened by the birth of a new baby and might regress (become more babyish) to regain the attention lost to the new baby. Similarly, the younger child, never having been pampered like the older child, is unlikely to be sensitive to displacement by younger children in the family but may develop feelings of inferiority toward the older child.

Jung: The Collective Unconscious

Carl G. Jung's (see Figure 12-17) theories differed from Freud's in many ways. Like Adler, Jung thought that Freud placed too much emphasis on sexuality. Jung viewed libido as a general **life energy**, of which sexual

FIGURE 12-17   CARL G. JUNG (1875–1961).
A Swiss physician trained in psychiatry, Jung developed an interest in psychoanalysis. Freud regarded Jung as his successor and persuaded the International Psychoanalytic Association to elect Jung president during the years 1910–1914. However, Freud and Jung had a falling out and Jung resigned as president of the psychoanalytic group in 1914.

urges were just one aspect (Jung, 1969). He thought that personality was composed of three parts, which partially overlap with Freud's conception. To Jung the **ego** represented the conscious "I" of experience. It contains all thoughts, feelings, perceptions, and memories available to consciousness. Jung also believed that a **persona** or social self develops as a shell around the ego. The persona is the self as presented to others. Another personality component Jung called the **personal unconscious**. He believed that it contains experiences that were once conscious but since have been repressed or forgotten. (This concept is roughly analogous to Freud's preconscious.)

Jung also proposed the provocative and controversial concept of a **collective unconscious**, the "memory traces" of repeated human experiences that have accumulated over the millions of years of human development. Jung believed that since time immemorial, our ancestors have encountered "mother," "father," "self," "god," "evil," "heroes," "death," and the like. Accumulated human experiences with these **archetypes** have produced in us, Jung believed, inherited tendencies to respond to these objects in shared, often highly emotional ways. (Examples of Jung's archetypes appear in Table 12-6.) In other words, these inherited tendencies are present in the collective unconscious and are shared by all people. Thus, they represent a broad set of dispositions. Jung believed that deviations from these tendencies can produce abnormal personality development. Although some people have accused Jung of claiming that memories and ideas can be inherited, Jung made no such claim. He believed only that people share very broad inherited traits, including tendencies to think in certain ways.

TABLE 12-6   EXAMPLES OF JUNG'S ARCHETYPES

Archetypes	Definitions
Self	Organizing core of personality, as wholeness and unity
Persona	Public, conforming, artificial self
Shadow	Darker aspects of self, repressed animal instincts, inferiorities
Anima	Feminine component in men
Animus	Masculine component in women
Wise old man	Spiritual principle in men
Magna mater	Material principle in women, of nature and earth
God	A psychic reality, projected final realization on external reality
Quaternity	Natural fourfold division of ideal completeness

Horney: The Growth Principle

The major difference between the ideas of Karen Horney (see Figure 12-18) and Freud was her emphasis on the role of cultural influences (as opposed to Freud's emphasis on biological influences) on personality development. Horney had particular difficulty accepting Freud's views on women. For example, she felt that the notion of penis envy might simply reflect the fact that psychoanalysis was developed by *male* analysts treating neurotic females, and Freud had little to say about normal

FIGURE 12-18 KAREN HORNEY (1885–1952).

A German physician, Horney was one of the first women trained in psychoanalysis. During the 1930s she published a series of theoretical books that led, in 1941, to her rejection by traditional Freudians.

female development or female sexuality. Horney therefore assumed the task of developing a psychology of women. Much of her psychological analysis of women examines the influence of women's feelings of inferiority. Horney believed these feelings reflected social influences. She noted that women traditionally have had few opportunities for personal development and have had to accept roles secondary to males.

Horney also rejected Freud's view that most of the important matters in development are settled in childhood. She replaced his pleasure and death instincts with her **growth principle**. It was her belief that people are born with a capacity for growth and strive to achieve their full potential. She argued that human energy is directed toward this development and toward achieving an inner unity or sense of consistency. She also believed that people's personalities continue to develop throughout their lives.

Erikson: Ego Psychology

Erik Erikson (see Figure 12-19) and a number of other psychoanalysts argued against Freud's characterization of the ego as dependent on the id and insisted, instead, that the ego is largely autonomous (for which they are called **ego psychologists**).

Erikson's most notable contribution to personality theory is his eight-stage theory of psychosocial development, which was discussed in Chapter 9. He believed that each stage of life is associated with a crisis that arises from conflicts between physiological development and the demands of society. Each crisis must be resolved for the individual to continue with normal ego development, while a failure to resolve the conflicts can lead to characteristic problems of development.

LEARNING THEORIES OF PERSONALITY

As you have seen in earlier chapters, many psychologists have contributed to learning theory, including most notably Pavlov with his work on classical conditioning and Skinner with his work on operant conditioning. Even early behavioral theorists such as John Watson recognized that learning theories had something to say about personality development. For example, Watson at one point made the following claim:

> *Give me a dozen healthy infants, well-formed, and my own specified world to bring them up in, and I'll guarantee to take any one at random and train him to become any type of specialist I might select—doctor, lawyer, artist, merchant-chief, and, yes, even beggar-man and thief, regardless of his talents, penchants, tendencies, activities, vocations, and race of his ancestors.*
>
> *(Watson, 1930, p. 65)*

Unfortunately, Watson never developed a learning theory of personality development, nor did his research lay the groundwork for such a theory. These tasks fell to later investigators.

FIGURE 12-19 ERIK ERIKSON (b. 1902).
Erikson was born in Germany, but moved to the United States in 1933. He was trained in psychoanalysis by Anna Freud (Sigmund Freud's daughter and a noted psychoanalyst in her own right) and at the Vienna Psychoanalytic Society. His most influential work is Childhood and Society (1950) *but he has written extensively about development throughout the life span.*

The Marriage of Psychoanalysis and Learning Theories

As we saw earlier, psychoanalytic theories of personality can be criticized on the grounds that they are imprecise and cannot accurately predict behavior. In contrast, learning theories are both very precisely specified and seek accuracy of prediction. Thus, it was natural that someone would try to combine the strengths of psychoanalytic and learning theories. During the 1940s, sociologist John Dollard and psychologist Neal Miller took on this challenge.

The influence of psychoanalysis on Dollard and Miller's theory is evident in the aspects of personality that they try to explain. For example, they tried to find behavioral explanations for defense mechanisms, anxiety, neurotic behaviors, and so on. Miller and Dollard (using mostly animal subjects) built on research like Watson's study of Little Albert (in which the young Albert was made to fear furry objects by being frightened with a clanging bar when they were present) to demonstrate that an emotional response such as anxiety could be conditioned to previously neutral stimuli after one or a few pairings of the stimulus and the anxiety. Thus, a person who has an automobile accident on a bridge later may find it very frightening to drive across any bridge.

Although Dollard and Miller's work is no longer the leading behavioral theory of personality, their contributions were extremely important, for they demonstrated that it was possible to operationalize and conduct scientific research on psychoanalytic concepts. Their work thereby gave psychoanalysis a stamp of respectability in some academic circles. They also demonstrated that many of the phenomena identified by Freud could, in principle, be accounted for by learning theory, and they emphasized the role of imitative learning—an important aspect of current learning theories of personality.

Skinner and Personality

B. F. Skinner has consistently rejected the idea that internal psychological experiences are important or need to be accounted for (this position is called his "radical behaviorist" perspective). In his influential and provocative *About Behaviorism* (1974), Skinner has gone so far as to assert that

> *The exploration of the emotional and motivational life of the mind has been described as one of the great achievements in the history of human thought, but it is possible that it has been one of the great disasters. In its search for internal explanations supported by the false sense of cause associated with feelings and introspective observations, mentalism has obscured the environmental antecedents which would have led to a much more effective analysis (1974, p. 165).*

Despite his attack on inquiry into the mind's inner workings, Skinner has, nonetheless, applied his learning theories to the kinds of behaviors that interest personality psychologists. Where he differs from most personality theorists and even many learning theorists is in arguing that basic principles of learning are adequate to account for *all* the behaviors that interest personality researchers.

In Skinner's analysis, personality is nothing more or less than an individual's pattern of behavior, and it is unnecessary to resort to concepts like **traits**, the **unconscious**, or **defense mechanisms** to uncover the origins of behavior patterns. Thus, Skinner essentially rejects the idea that it is interesting or useful to inquire about the structure of personality. He focuses almost exclusively on the learning process through which the patterns of behavior that others call "personality" develop.

In Skinner's view, all the important aspects of personality development can be explained with basic learning principles. Thus, for instance, children learn socially desirable forms of behavior (which others might label traits) such as "self-reliance" through their parents' reinforcement (in the form of praise, food, and affection) of the desired behavior. Skinner notes that even well-intentioned parents can unwittingly produce undesirable kinds of behavior in their children by paying attention to them at the wrong times. Parents who ignore their children while they are well behaved but when they are naughty shower them with attention—even negative attention like a scolding—may reinforce the misbehavior and increase the chances that the children will misbehave again. As we saw in Chapter 6, it is difficult to extinguish forms of behavior that are on partial reinforcement schedules!

The Social Learning Approach

One of the common conceptual threads that can be found in Freudian and learning theories is the notion of **identification**. Freud talked about identification as a defense mechanism in which a person, say a child, internalizes or assumes the characteristics of another person who is thought to be very powerful or otherwise desirable. Thus, boys identify with their fathers to vicariously share in the father's relationship with the mother. Among learning theorists, John Watson (1925) believed that imitative responses could be classically conditioned. Skinner also has said that people can be reinforced to imitate behavior.

Social learning theory is not a theory of personality development, but rather a set of general principles that can be broadly applied to the learning of all sorts of behavior, including that associated with personality. As you saw in Chapter 6, imitative or observational learning is one type of learning process and is considered to complement classical and operant learning as bases for personality development. Unlike operant conditioning, the observational learning perspective does not suggest that the person who observes behavior must be directly reinforced in order to learn the behavior. Observers of behavior can be *vicariously* reinforced by observing the consequences of other people's behavior. However, in Albert Bandura's (1977, 1986; see Figure 12-20) view, direct reinforcement is important in determining whether behavior is actually performed. Bandura and other social learning theorists also have emphasized that social learning processes are a joint product of interactions between the organism and its environment—what Bandura

FIGURE 12-20   ALBERT BANDURA (b. 1925).
Bandura is probably the leading social learning theorist.

terms **reciprocal determinism**. Social learning theorists are interested in the ways the individual adapts to a changing environment. Thus, social learning theory rejects Freud's emphasis on internal and biological determinants of behavior and also rejects the radical behaviorists' emphasis on environmental contingencies.

SELF-REGULATION AND EFFICACY   Do you plan to give yourself a break after you finish reading this chapter? If you're like most people, suggests Bandura, anticipating rewards and regulating your behavior accordingly is for you an important part of social learning. Even radical behaviorists like Skinner have acknowledged that people use reinforcement to regulate their own behavior. According to Bandura, through the rewards and punishments administered by *others,* people develop a set of *internal standards* by which to govern their behavior. You probably have learned to establish goals and plans for accomplishing those goals, and you reward or punish yourself according to how well you realized your goals. Self-criticism is a common form of punishment. Thus, your behavior in pursuit of goals is governed by **expectancies**—your expectations of future rewards.

In recent years, Bandura (1977, 1982) has emphasized one important aspect of personality, which he terms **self-efficacy**. Self-efficacy, as you saw in Chapter 11, refers to one's belief that one can act successfully in certain ways and control events. People's beliefs about their own efficacy or the lack of it arise from their experiences in trying to realize goals. If they are generally successful, their sense of efficacy strengthens. If they are generally unsuccessful, their sense of efficacy weakens. People's feelings about their own efficacy are important for several reasons. First, these feelings will influence the difficulty of the goals that people establish for themselves. People who are confident that they can regulate their own behavior and successfully influence events are likely to set more difficult goals for themselves. Second, they are likely to prepare and or plan more thoroughly to attain goals. Third, they are likely to be more persistent than people who do not feel efficacious. If you are confident that you can accomplish the goal—read the chapter, write the paper, pass the exam, get a good grade in the course, graduate with honors, and live happily ever after—you will stay at it longer and try harder.

Bandura has applied learning principles to people's feelings about their own efficacy (Bandura, 1978, 1982). In sum, Bandura's view of personality development centers around the effects of observational learning on the formation and changes in an individual's goals and feelings of efficacy.

PHENOMENOLOGICAL APPROACHES TO PERSONALITY

During the 1960s, a "third force" appeared in American psychology. The *phenomenological* or *humanist tradition* has been termed the **third force** because it has been meant to serve as an alternative to psychoanalytic and behavioral theories. Whereas psychoanalytic theories tend to emphasize the internal determinants of behavior and behavioral theories emphasize the external determinants, the phenomenological approach emphasizes the conscious experiences of individuals and their subjective awareness of themselves and the world around them. According to this view, if one is to understand another person, one must understand how he or she experiences and understands the world. One must understand their individual **phenomenology**. People's experience of the world—including their experience of themselves—is seen to be the key to understanding the development and structure of their personality.

Phenomenological psychologists are also interested in human choice, creativity, and self-actualization. They have been influenced by the existentialist writings of people like philosopher Jean Paul Sartre, who believed that people have a responsibility to make choices that will determine the course of their lives, rather than simply letting life take its course. Existentialists have argued that *being* is the ultimate objective of life and that *being* implies an awareness of nonbeing and the inevitability of death. From this awareness comes, inevitably, **existential anxiety**. The existentialists and phenomenologists believe that living responsibly, being aware of the possibilities of growth, and taking steps to promote growth are the antidotes for existential anxiety.

As part of their effort to promote personal growth, the phenomenologists have sought to develop a psychology of healthy individuals. They reject psychodynamic approaches to personality as emphasizing what is unhealthy about people rather than what is healthy. The phenomenologists have sought ways to help people develop their potential, to encourage people to grow rather than merely adapt to their circumstances. They believe that psychologists should seek to understand humans rather than merely explain or predict their behavior.

A great many psychologists have endorsed the general aims of phenomenological psychology. We will examine two of the central figures of the phenomenological movement: Carl Rogers and Abraham Maslow.

Self Theory

The central figure in the phenomenological movement was probably Carl Rogers. The most important structural component of Rogers' theory is the **self**, which refers to the full set of an individual's experiences and perceptions and the meanings and values the individual attaches to those perceptions and experiences. It is, in essence, those perceptions and experiences we refer to when we think of the "I" or "me." The self is ever-changing but has an integrated, patterned quality. It is an interrelated set of experiences. Rogers was primarily concerned with the fit between two aspects of the self: the *actual self* and the *ideal self.* The actual self is the self-concept or self perceived by the individual and need not consist of objectively correct perceptions. The ideal self is the self-concept to which the individual aspires. When the fit between the two is good, a person has a positive self-concept and high self-esteem, but when the fit is poor, a person has low self-esteem and may be maladjusted.

SELF-ACTUALIZATION   Perhaps the most distinctive feature of Rogers' personality theory is its emphasis on personality change. Rogers (1951) said that people have a basic striving to actualize, maintain, and enhance their experience. Thus, whereas Freud emphasized drives, Rogers emphasized the human inclination toward what he called **self-actualization**. This inclination expresses itself, he suggested, at a variety of levels: satisfaction of basic needs such as hunger and thirst, development from a simple to a complex person who is an independent and efficacious adult, and self-expression and creativity.

CHILDHOOD AND DEVELOPMENT   Like Freud, Rogers was concerned about childhood development. He argues that the self-concept arises because we learn about ourselves through interactions with others. Furthermore, self-evaluations depend heavily on what others think of a person. Rogers (1951) emphasized the child's need for **positive regard** and what the child learns about **conditions of worth**. Rogers believes that we all have a need for sympathy, liking, warmth, acceptance, and respect from others and that children's experiences with their parents strongly determine how easy or difficult it will be for the child to achieve self-actualization. If parents provide children with **unconditional positive regard**, then they will be able to accept and grow with their own experiences, and this process will lead to greater self-acceptance and greater self-actualization. However, if the parents' attention and affection is made conditional and given to the child only when the child acts in certain ways, the child will learn that there are conditions of worth. Conditional regard is an important and necessary part of socialization, but Rogers was concerned about the danger that the child might be forced to deny experiences that otherwise feel appropriate. If this happens, the quest for social approval may take precedence over the child's own experiences. Children may come to rely on other people's interpretation of their experiences rather than their own interpretations. In Rogers' view, this conflict between the actual and ideal self poses a major threat to self-actualization.

Humanistic Personality Theory

Abraham Maslow was broadly trained in psychology—in behaviorism, in work with primates, and in psychoanalysis—but he found that established theories did not provide him with a satisfactory model of human development. In his own work, Maslow was a "humanist" who emphasized that people are basically good (or, at worst, neutral), and, like Rogers, that they strive for self-fulfillment. It was Maslow who coined the term "third force" to contrast his psychology of "human potential" with behaviorism and psychoanalysis. Two of Maslow's enduring contributions to personality psychology are his analyses of motivation and self-actualization.

THE HIERARCHY OF NEEDS   Maslow suggested that humans are motivated by a set of needs, some of which require satisfaction and some of which promote growth. These needs compete with one another for satis-

*FIGURE 12-21 MASLOW'S
HIERARCHY OF NEEDS.*
Maslow placed basic physiological needs
at the bottom of the needs hierarchy and
self-actualization at the top.

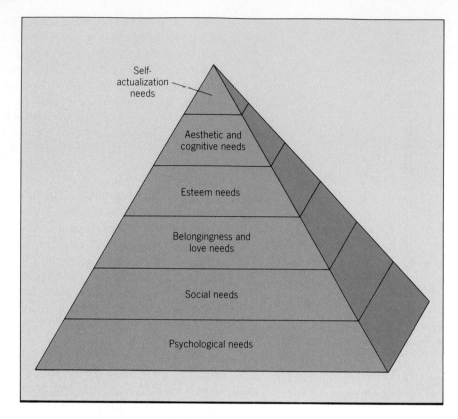

faction and can be arranged in a hierarchy (see Figure 12-21). At the lowest level are physiological and other **basic needs** that must be satisfied before needs at higher levels (**metaneeds**) can be addressed. At higher levels are psychological needs. The levels of need can be defined as follows:

1. *Physiological needs* include the need for such things as food, water, sleep, and sex.
2. *Safety needs* include the need for protection, security, order, freedom from pain, stability, and dependency. Safety needs are evident in such things as fear of the unknown and fear of losing control.
3. *Belongingness and love needs* include the need for love and affection in intimate relationships, and acceptance within the family and the broader social community.
4. *Esteem needs* encompass the need for respect from others and self-respect, a sense of worthiness, and self-esteem.
5. *Self-actualizing needs* are rather different from the other needs. They are unique to each person and involve the attainment of the individual's full potential. Satisfying needs for self-actualization can take place only once a person has generally satisfied lower level needs. Maslow believed that people who have not satisfied basic needs will not have the energy or time to satisfy the higher needs.

THE SELF-ACTUALIZED INDIVIDUAL   Who is self-actualized and what are these people like? Through a mixture of clinical and historical studies, Maslow sought to identify the characteristics of self-actualized individuals. He described self-actualization and self-actualized people in the following way

> *It may be loosely described as the full use and exploitation of talents, capacities, potentialities, and other factors. Such people seem to be fulfilling themselves and to be doing the best they are capable of doing, reminding us of Nietzsche's exhortation "Become what thou art." They are people who have developed or are developing to the full stature of what they are capable (1970, p. 150).*

Among the people Maslow identified as self-actualized were well-known historical and public figures such as Albert Einstein, Franklin and Eleanor Roosevelt, Abraham Lincoln, and William James. Some of the characteristics that Maslow thought distinguishes these people from those of us who are not fully actualized are shown in Table 12-7.

TABLE 12-7   CHARACTERISTICS OF SELF-ACTUALIZED INDIVIDUALS

1 Perceive reality accurately and fully
2 Show greater acceptance of themselves, others, and things generally
3 Are spontaneous and natural
4 Tend to focus on problems rather than on themselves
5 Prefer detachment and privacy
6 Are autonomous and thus tend to be independent of the physical and social environment
7 Have a fresh outlook; appreciate much of life
8 Have mystical or peak experiences
9 Enjoy a spirit of identity and unity with all people
10 Have deep interpersonal relations with only a few people, usually self-actualizers like themselves
11 Possess a character structure that emphasizes democratic ideals
12 Are quite ethical
13 Are creative
14 Have an excellent sense of humor that is philosophical rather than hostile
15 Resist enculturation; are not easily seduced by society

Source: Based on Maslow.

When all is said and done, all theories of human behavior, all theories of personality, make certain assumptions about human nature. Some assume that human nature is intrinsically good, some that it is bad, some that human behavior is rational, some that it is irrational. Some assume that we have free will and some that human behavior is fully determined by such factors as biological inheritance and environmental influences. Although no psychological theorist can authoritatively answer these philosophical questions, they are raised implicitly by the assumptions of each theory. As shown in Table 12-8, each of the theories we have examined can be characterized in terms of its basic concepts, the causes of behavior it posits, and its focus.

TABLE 12-8   A COMPARISON OF THE MAJOR
PERSONALITY THEORIES

Theory	Some Major Contributors	Focus	Main Concepts[a]
Trait	Allport, Cattell, Eysenck	Individual characteristics	Idiographic or nomothetic; surface vs. source; introversion–extraversion
Psychoanalytic	Freud	Sexual motivation and development	Energy, instinct, libido, cathexis, id, ego, superego
Psychoanalytic Successors	Jung, Adler, Horney, Erikson	Personal growth; social influences	Archetype, compensation, inferiority, neurotic trends, attachments
Biological	Sheldon	Genetic and biological factors	Body types, heritability
Social Learning	Skinner, Bandura, Mischel	Learning	Reinforcement, modeling, self-efficacy
Phenomenological	Rogers, Maslow	Subjective experiences	Unconditional regard, positive self-regard, self-expression

[a]Not descriptive of all theorists within a category.

SUMMARY

WHAT IS PERSONALITY?

1. *Ancient Conceptions of Personality.* The idea that there are systematic differences between people has early origins. Ancient Greek physicians proposed that differences in blood substances produced different types of people who could be characterized sad or *melancholic;* irritable or *choleric;* easygoing or *sanguine;* and sluggish or *phlegmatic.* Although these terms are still used to characterize people, over the past century scientific studies of individual characteristics of personality have provided the empirical basis for a number of theories of personality.

2. *Defining Personality.* Although psychologists have offered many different definitions of personality, a definition given by Allport a half century ago captures the most important aspects of personality: "the dynamic organization within the individual of those psychophysical systems that determine his or her unique adjustment to his or her environment" (1937, p. 48).

BASIC ISSUES IN THE STUDY OF PERSONALITY

3. *Building Blocks of Personality.* Personality researchers and theorists share a common body of interests. They are interested, first, in establishing the basic stable building blocks of personality. Some theorists emphasize types, while others emphasize traits, and yet others emphasize instincts or habits. Irrespective of the building blocks that are used, personality theorists also share a desire to establish how these building blocks are assembled together to form individual personalities.

4. *Wellsprings of Personality and Personality Development.* Personality theorists are also concerned with the forces that shape personality and activate behavior. Most theorists are therefore concerned with motivation and with the factors that bring about changes and development in personality. Theorists commonly confront the question of how the environment

and internal factors interact to produce behavior. Thus, personality theorists are very interested in the respective roles of nature and nurture.

5. *Unique versus Shared Characteristics.* Personality psychologists differ in the extent to which they emphasize unique characteristics of individuals (the idiographic approach) as opposed to characteristics shared by many individuals (the nomothetic approach).

TRAIT THEORIES OF PERSONALITY

6. *Allport's Trait Theory.* Allport built his personality theory around traits, which he regarded as a readiness to respond in a similar way to a variety of stimuli—as in a "Communist phobia." Allport was interested in establishing the number of traits people might possess. Though he was able to devise a list of more than 4500 trait terms, he found that most people describe acquaintances in a matter of a few traits. Allport did not regard all traits as equally important. He used the term *cardinal traits* to refer to passions or motives that pervade many aspects of a person's life. He referred to less pervasive traits that reflect preferences and aversions as *secondary traits.* Allport emphasized an idiographic approach to personality.

7. *Cattell's Factor-Analytic Trait Theory.* Cattell's theory is also built on traits, but Cattell's approach is nomothetic. He also makes a hierarchical distinction between different classes of traits. Cattell uses the term *surface traits* for traits that reflect the characteristics people believe go together. Through factor analyses of surface traits, Cattell has further identified 15 more basic, underlying *source traits* of personality. Cattell and others have examined

the relationships between these personality source traits and behavior.

8. *Eysenck's Trait-Type Theory.* Eysenck also argues that personality is hierarchically organized, with *specific* responses or behaviors that may not be characteristic of a person at the bottom of the hierarchy, *habitual responses* or characteristic behaviors at the second level, *traits* or interrelated sets of habitual behaviors at the third level, and *types* or interrelated sets of traits at the highest level. Eysenck has used factor analysis to identify three dimensions that underlie personality: *introversion-extraversion* (sociability), *neuroticism* (emotional stability), and *psychoticism* (normality versus psychosis). Research indicates that extraversion and neuroticism are related to individual differences in arousal levels and conditionability.

THE PERSON VERSUS THE SITUATION

9. *Behavioral Consistency.* One assumption of trait and type theories is that traits and types will predict a person's behavior in a variety of settings. However, early personality research indicated little consistency in behavior across situations. Walter Mischel has used this research to argue that theories that regard traits as indicators of broad behavioral dispositions are not tenable. However, other researchers have demonstrated a general consistency in traits over long periods of time. Others have combined multiple observations of behavior and personality ratings over periods of many days for many individuals and found evidence for broad consistency of behavior. At present the question of how consistent behavior is across situations is still open to debate.

BIOLOGICAL THEORIES OF PERSONALITY

10. *Body Types.* Some personality theorists have emphasized biological determinants of behavior. William Sheldon argued that body types (*somatotypes*) determined personality and behavior. His studies led him to conclude that tall, thin *ectomorphs* are overresponsive and fear social interaction; that heavy, round *endomorphs* are sociable and comfort seeking; and that hard, muscular *mesomorphs* are competitive and power-seeking. Although subsequent research indicates that body types are associated with such things as criminality, it is not clear whether body type predisposes individuals to certain types of behavior or whether people respond differently to people with different body types and thereby shape their behavior.

11. *Genetic Bases of Personality.* Studies of the heritability of individual characteristics indicate that characteristics such as activity levels, Eysenck's measures of neuroticism and extraversion, social potency, reactions to stress, alienation, and sense of well-being are all based, at least in part, on heritable, genetic factors.

PSYCHOANALYTIC THEORY

12. *The Structure of Personality.* Freud made a distinction among the conscious (those things of which we are aware at any point in time), the preconscious (those things that could be called into consciousness), and the unconscious (those contents of the psyche that cannot be called into consciousness). Freud further distinguished among three other components of the psyche that cut across the three levels of consciousness. Freud identified the *id* as the instinctual urges (such as

aggression and sexuality) that form the basis of personality. The id pursues pleasure and avoids pain. The *ego* is the executive manager of the personality. It is oriented to the social realities of the world. The *superego* is concerned with morality and consists of the conscience and ego-ideals. Personality dynamics reflect the interplay of pressures from the id and the superego on the ego.

13. *Personality Processes.* Freud believed that instincts such as self-preservation, sexual instinct, and even a death instinct partly govern behavior. He also believed that people instinctively seek relief from anxieties. Freud thought some anxieties arose from real threats, but that neurotic anxieties could arise from the fear of acting on instinctual impulses, from phobias and panic attacks, and from feelings of guilt. To protect themselves from anxieties Freud thought that people employ a variety of defense mechanisms: the most basic defense mechanism is denial of the threat; repression involves the forcing of the threat out of consciousness; projection involves the unconscious assumption that it is another person who is the source of the undesirable thoughts or impulses. Other defense mechanisms include displacement, sublimation, reaction formations, and rationalization.

14. *Personality Development.* Freud believed that over the course of development a person's libidinal energies are channeled to different parts of the body. This channeling gives rise to different problems of development that influence personality. At the oral stage children are almost entirely id: their behavior is largely instinctual. If a child derives too much pleasure from putting things in its mouth and becomes "fixated" at the oral stage, Freud

believed the child might be overly acquisitive in later life. Similarly, if a child becomes fixated at the anal stage, he or she may in later life be very interested in cleanliness and orderliness.

During the phallic stage Freud believed that children become aware of the sexual relationship between parents. Boys at this stage might become overly worried about competing with their father for their mother's affection and develop castration anxiety. Freud thought that girls at this stage might develop penis envy. Freud thought sexual instincts are dormant during the latency period between the ages of about 5 and 11, but reawaken during the genital stage—at which point adolescents become interested in romantic and sexual relationships with others.

FREUD'S THEORETICAL SUCCESSORS

15. *Alfred Adler.* Adler pioneered the notion of compensation for social and psychological inferiorities. Adler believed that people strive for superiority or self-improvement. He thought Freud placed too much emphasis on sexuality and preferred to emphasize the effects of social determinants of personality development including such factors as family dynamics and birth order.

16. *Carl Jung.* Jung also rejected Freud's heavy emphasis on sexuality. He largely accepted Freud's notion of the ego, but also emphasized the persona or social self that people present to others. Like Freud, Jung was interested in the unconscious side of the psyche and believed that much of human behavior is influenced by the collective unconscious, or traces of human experience that accumulated over the eons. Jung thought these experi-

ences were developed out of repeated encounters with archetypal experiences such as "mother," "evil," and "death" and that these experiences predisposed people to react to these objects in common, often emotional, ways.

17. *Karen Horney and Erik Erikson.* Horney challenged Freud's analysis of female development and sexuality. Her own analysis emphasized social influences on women's feelings of inferiority. She also rejected Freud's belief that most of the important matters of development are settled in childhood. Erikson's most notable contribution to personality theory is his eight-stage theory of development that emphasizes the resolution of life crises throughout the life span.

LEARNING THEORIES OF PERSONALITY

18. *Dollard and Miller and Skinner.* These theorists drew on learning research and psychoanalytic theory to develop a behavioral theory of personality. Skinner has made the most radical behavioral proposals concerning personality: he rejects the idea that it is informative to explore the inner workings of the mind and finds it unnecessary to use concepts such as traits, unconscious, or defense mechanisms. In Skinner's view all the important behaviors a person engages in can be adequately accounted for by principles of learning.

19. *Social Learning.* Social learning theorists such as Bandura are interested in the reciprocal effects of environments on people and people on environments. Social learning theories of personality give special attention to the mechanisms of observational learning. Bandura has been particularly interested in the devel-

opment of self-regulation and self-efficacy. He has applied learning principles to figure out how people develop and act on their goals.

PHENOMENOLOGICAL APPROACHES TO PERSONALITY

20. *Self Theory.* One of the central figures in the phenomenological movement was Carl Rogers, whose theoretical focus was on the full set of experiences (both the "I" and the "me") that make up the self. Rogers was concerned with the congruence between the actual self as perceived by an individual and the ideal self to which people aspire. He believed that self-esteem is high when these two are congruent. Rogers tried to identify elements of childhood and adult experience that would promote self-actualization. He emphasized that children benefit from unconditional positive regard that allows them to grow with their own experiences.

21. *Humanistic Personality Theory.* Like Rogers, Maslow emphasized the human striving for self-fulfillment. He distinguished among a hierarchical set of human needs ranging from basic physiological needs we all share to complex self-actualizing needs that are unique to individuals. To combat the traditional emphasis on the problems of personality development, Maslow studied self-actualized individuals in an effort to identify the characteristics that distinguish them from the rest of us.

FURTHER READINGS

Where should one begin to find additional information about the theories of personality reviewed in this chapter? One obvious source is the original writings of the theorists. The most important of these works are referenced in the text of the chapter, and the reader is encouraged to consult the text and the bibliography of this textbook to locate specific volumes.

At a more general level, the reader may be interested in any of a number of recent textbooks that devote entire chapters to topics that, due to limitations of space, are merely touched upon in a paragraph or two in this text. Among the more informative texts are *Personality* (2nd Ed.) by Seymour Feshbach and Bernard Weiner (1986); *Personality: Strategies and Issues* (5th Ed.) by Robert Liebert and Michael Spiegler (1987); *Paradigms of Personality* by Jane Loevinger (1987); *Personality* (4th Ed.) by Lawrence Pervin (1984) and a complementary set of readings in *Current Controversies and Issues in Personality* edited by Pervin (1984); *Introduction to Personality* by E. Jerry Phares (1984); *Personality: Theory, Research, and Applications* by Charles Potkay and Bem Allen (1986); *Theories of Personality* (3rd Ed.) by Duane Schultz (1986); and *The Human Personality* by Jerome Singer (1984).

Other overviews of research include "Personality: Current Controversies, Issues, and Directions" by Lawrence Pervin in *Annual Review of Psychology* edited by M. Rosenzweig and L. W. Porter (1985); and "Personality: Developments in the Study of Private Experience" by Jerome Singer and John Kollgian in *Annual Review of Psychology,* edited by M. Rosenzweig and L. W. Porter (1987). More specialized readings include *Personality and Individual Differences* by Hans Eysenck and Michael Eysenck (1985) and *Hans Eysenck: Consensus and Controversy* edited by Sohan Modgil and Celia Modgil (1986), both of which examine Eysenck's theory of personality in some detail. In *Consistency in Personality* (1986) Daniel Ozer considers a wide range of approaches to the problem of behavioral consistency and the person–situation interaction. *The Neuropsychology of Individual Differences,* edited by Lawrence Hartlage and Cathy Telzrow (1986) reviews neurological differences associated with individual differences in temperament and other characteristics. In *Personality and Social Intelligence* (1987) Nancy Cantor and John Kihlstrom examine individual differences in social knowledge, self-knowledge, and self-regulation.

604

13

PSYCHOPATHOLOGY

When you think of "abnormality," "craziness," "insanity," or "psychopathology" what comes to mind? Do you think of people who act bizarrely, people who are frightening, people who are ill, or even people who are trying to escape legal prosecution?

Psychopathology or abnormality is *socially defined.* It is frightening or repugnant behavior that violates social norms and codes. Behaviors by themselves are not intrinsically abnormal and even the most horrifying acts—suicide, murder, cannibalism, and eating feces—may be understandable and not considered insane under certain circumstances. In the case of suicide, consider the suicide of the noted author, Arthur Koestler (see Figure 13-1), who, along with his wife, committed suicide apparently because he decided that it would be too unpleasant to live with a painful, debilitating, terminal disease. In the case of murder, consider the recent case of a young boy who killed his father after the father repeatedly had beaten him and his younger sister (see Figure 13-2). Thus, murder may not be evidence of psychopathology. In the case of cannibalism, it has been a religious practice of whole societies. The Fore Islanders of New Guinea believed that Kuru, a fatal neurological disease, was caused by sorcery. Research revealed that it was caused by a "slow virus." Transmission of the slow virus was caused by the ritualistic consumption of brains of the deceased. In the context of the society in which it is practiced, such religious cannibalism cannot be considered a sign of madness. Finally, even a behavior as disgusting and as apparently "mad" as *coprophagia* (eating feces) is not necessarily evidence of madness. During the Civil War, for example, Union prisoners of war scavenged undigested food in feces to eat to stay alive. Because abnormality is socially defined, there are contexts in which all of these distressing forms of behavior can occur without their being viewed as signs of madness.

Not only is abnormality defined in terms of social norms and particular social contexts, but abnormality also generally has no clear motiva-

FIGURE 13-1   IS SUICIDE ABNORMAL BEHAVIOR?
Arthur Koestler and his wife Cynthia. Arthur Koestler killed himself by taking an overdose of barbituate when he was 77 years old and suffering terribly from leukemia and Parkinson's disease. He at one time commented that it is not the nature of humans to die "peacefully and without fuss" as animals do. Koestler decided to end his life when he no longer derived enjoyment from it. Does his suicide constitute abnormal behavior? Does the suicide of his wife Cynthia, who decided to join him in death even though she was 21 years younger than he and suffered from no illness?

*FIGURE 13-2 IS PATRICIDE
ABNORMAL?*
*Richard Jahnke killed his father after
the father had beaten him and sexually
assaulted Richard's sister for many
years. Although murder violates legal
codes, is it always* abnormal *behavior?
Here Jahnke arrives in court with his
attorney.*

tional basis, that is, it is hard for people to see what the "payoff" for abnormal behavior is. Finally, common ideas of abnormality emphasize that it is a *behavior,* rather than, say, a physical symptom, that earns a person the label of "abnormal." In fact, any sign of physical disease would reduce the likelihood of a person's being labeled as abnormal— physical disease sometimes is a good explanation of bizarre behavior that makes it more understandable and less frightening.

THE HISTORY OF ABNORMALITY

Throughout much of human history, the prevailing view of madness has been that it reflects the invasion of an individual by evil spirits. There is even evidence that prehistoric peoples held this view, as evidenced by **trephined** skulls (see Figure 13-3). Trephination is the practice of boring a hole in the skull so that the cause of illness may escape. During the 1600s and 1700s, madness was especially likely to be attributed to demonic possession or to the possession of the soul by evil animal spirits (Kemp, 1985; see Figure 13-4).

The attribution of madness to demonic possession had dire consequences for people suffering from mental disorders. Treatment usually was bizarre or barbaric and aimed at driving out the animal or evil spirits (see Figure 13-5). Madness often was attributed to conspiring with the devil, and people were tortured until they confessed to their crime. By one estimate, over 100,000 such "witches" were hanged or burned

FIGURE 13-3 TREPHINATION.
These Paleolithic skulls show evidence of trephining, the practice of chipping small holes in the skull, ostensibly to free the evil spirit trapped inside. The practice suggests that prehistoric peoples thought that the sufferer's disturbance was inside the head, not a trivial conclusion.

FIGURE 13-4 GIROLAMO DI BENVENUTO'S ST. CATHERINE EXORCISING A POSSESSED WOMAN.
A devil is exorcized from a woman in this fifteenth century work. Exorcism is still accepted by the Catholic Church as a way of removing evil spirits.

between the mid-1500s and the 1600s in Europe and America (Deutsch, 1949). Some of the people labeled witches were not suffering from mental disorders (Kemp, 1985), but many undoubtedly were. The link between madness and demon possession was no accident; both refer to behaviors that defy ordinary understanding. Why did the witch shout to the heavens? Why did he or she pace for hours? Abnormal behavior, or madness, is behavior in search of an explanation.

Not only has madness defied understanding but it has driven people to drastic attempts at solutions. Why? Because madness can be frightening and disturbing. Embedded in our culture are strong remnants of early, emotional reactions to abnormality and madness. As Michel Foucault, a French psychologist and historian noted, "From the fifteenth century on, the face of madness has haunted the imagination of Western man" (Foucault, 1965, p. 15).

Physiological Origins

Today, in many societies, demonic possession still is believed to be the cause of abnormal behavior. It remains one accepted explanation by the Catholic Church, for example (Kemp, 1985). But scientific views of ab-

FIGURE 13-5 EARLY TREATMENT OF "MADNESS."
A "distillation" treatment of madness. With purgatives and heat treatments, the demons or animals inhabiting the brains of madmen presumably were released. Notice the rodents leaving the cone placed over the head of a madman in the tub. One theory of madness was that it was caused by "rats of the brain."

normal behavior began to emerge in the late 1700s. These views typically emphasized the physiological **etiology**, or cause, of mental disorders. The Scottish physician William Cullen (1712–1790) attributed mental disorders to defects of the nervous system. Franz Joseph Gall (1758–1828) proposed that mental disorders, as well as all other personality and intellectual traits, arose from the structure of the brain (see Figures 13-6 and 13-7). Although Gall recognized that the skull might not accurately reflect underlying brain structure, many of his followers were much less cautious and developed the practice of **phrenology**, in which personality, temperament, and mental health were interpreted from the patterns of bumps and indentations in a person's skull because the skull was assumed to mirror the underlying parts of the brain and its particular psychological "faculties." Today we know that except in relatively rare types of mental retardation, there is no relation between skull configuration and personality traits or mental status.

Another theory of mental disorders that stressed physical causes was that of Anton Mesmer, an Austrian physician of the late 1700s who believed that many types of mental disorders arise from an obstruction, or inadequacy, in the flow of an invisible force or fluid (*animal magnetism*) necessary for proper mental functioning. Mesmer's ideas fell into disfavor once they were declared scientifically unsound by a special committee appointed by the French government (on which sat Benjamin Franklin).

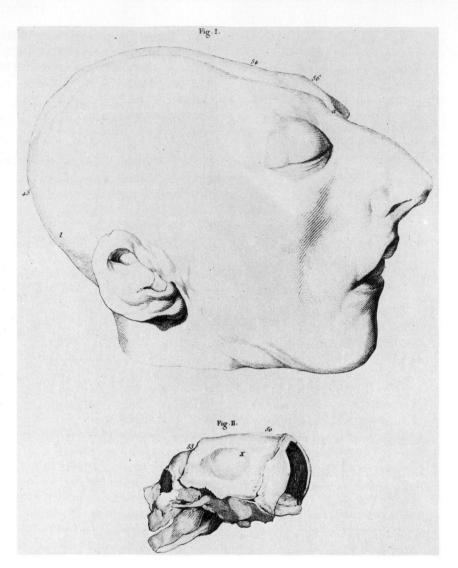

FIGURE 13-6 IS ABNORMALITY REFLECTED IN THE FACE?
This drawing appeared in Gall's 1819 Atlas of drawings of the face and skull. The face and skull are claimed to be those of a 25 year old "idiot." During the time of Gall, and much later, many thought, erroneously, that certain facial features indicated madness.

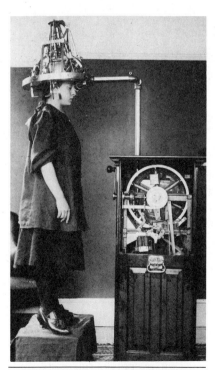

FIGURE 13-7 PHRENOLOGY DEVICE.
A young woman of 1907 inserts her head into the Lavery Electric Phrenometer, a device designed to measure accurately the configuration of the skull. Even during this century, many believed that a person's intellect and personality were related to the shape of the skull.

In the mid-1800s, physicians began to notice that many people hospitalized for mental disorders reported a history of syphilis. The physicians suggested that the germ that caused syphilis also caused mental disorders. **General paresis**, a mental disorder that was associated with syphilitic infections, accounted for one-third of all admissions to psychiatric hospitals (asylums). This disorder was characterized by delusions of grandeur in which people believed that they were capable of extraordinary feats or that they were extraordinary people like Christ or royalty, by **dementia** (decreased mental powers, poor memory, and poor reasoning abilities), and eventually by paralysis and death. Research by Richard von Krafft-Ebing (1840–1892), a German neurologist, and August von Wasserman (1866–1925), a German physician and bacteriologist, finally proved that one germ caused both syphilis and general paresis. Thus general paresis provided clear evidence that biological disturbances could produce classic symptoms of mental disorders.

European scientists examined biological factors in their search for the origins of mental disorders in part because they were influenced by the beliefs of ancient peoples that madness had biological origins. For example, both the ancient Egyptians and Greeks attributed **hysteria** to a loosely attached, "wandering" uterus. (In hysteria a patient, usually female, complains of disease but no disease can be found.) Scientists and physicians also may have examined biological factors because of the enormous strides being made in physics and medicine. The discovery of electric current, for example, inspired Mesmer to search for an "electric" force of animal magnetism. Similarly, Louis Pasteur's mid-nineteenth-century discovery that germs were associated with disease informed his contemporaries' search for a link between syphilitic infection and general paresis.

The search for physiological origins of mental disorders has resulted in very significant increases in our understanding of these conditions. However, this increased understanding has been complemented by insights into the psychological and social (psychosocial) origins of mental disorders.

Psychosocial Origins

Much current research on the etiology of mental disorders concerns the influence of psychosocial factors. It is difficult to trace clearly the historical origins of the concept that psychosocial factors contribute to mental disorders. Rather, this concept arises from diverse ideas and events.

Such historically prominent medical figures as the Greek physician Galen (130–200) and the English physician Thomas Sydenham (1624–1689) departed from the traditional explanation of hysteria—a wandering uterus—and attributed it to overwork, worry, or unrequited love. The eminent French neurologist Jean Charcot (1825–1893) made observations that suggested the psychosocial origins of mental disorders. While Charcot was chief of the medical service at Salpetrière Hospital in France, a group of hysteric patients was housed with epileptic patients while the hysterics' ward was being renovated. Before their move the hysterics complained of numerous disorders—abdominal pain, urinary/genital complaints, and so on. However, after being housed with the epileptics, Charcot noted that most hysterics had "developed" seizure disorders. Because epilepsy was known not to be contagious, Charcot realized that the hysterics had been influenced by their environments—by observing the seizures of the epileptics.

Reports that mental disorders could be helped by psychosocial treatments (those not intended to alter physical functioning directly) also encouraged belief in psychosocial etiologies. Reformers such as Phillipe Pinel in France and William Tuke in England worked in the late 1700s to reduce the then-prevalent inhumane treatment of the insane in hospitals and asylums. Making conditions more humane frequently resulted in dramatic improvements in the behavior of the insane. Finally, belief in psychosocial origins received a tremendous boost when, in the early 1900s, Freud and his followers reported that people with mental disorders improved dramatically when they were able to identify a deeply disturbing thought or event. This suggested that some types of disorders are due to repression of psychologically distressing or threatening information.

Biological or Psychosocial Origins?

Although historically there has been a great deal of controversy over whether mental disorders are caused by biological or psychological factors, and although many researchers today are trying to determine the etiologies of mental disorders, scientists are today much less inclined to separate or characterize disorders on the basis of a psychological versus biological origin.

One reason for this is that we now know that almost every disease or disorder can be affected or produced by both biological and psychological processes. For example, consider lung cancer. Clearly the symptoms of this disease are produced by a biological process, that is, malignant cells in the lungs. However, the single biggest risk factor for this disease is a "mental disorder"—addiction to tobacco smoking—which increases the risk of lung cancer 20 times. Thus, lung cancer, a physical illness, is most frequently caused by an environmental/behavioral factor. As Chapter 11 shows, there are many examples of how stress, another environmental/ behavioral influence, can affect the course of almost any disease or disorder. Moreover, physiological factors such as genetic inheritance can render a person more or less susceptible to the effects of stress and thereby alter the risk of stress-related disease. Biological and psychological effects sometimes are inseparably intertwined in mental disorders. As one researcher concluded "The fish is in the water and the water's in the fish" (Goodwin, 1976).

Despite their greater appreciation of the interaction of environmental and biological factors in the development of mental disorders, psychologists still do refer to some disorders as being environmental or biological in origin. They do so when a biological or psychological explanation provides the more direct and satisfying account of a disorder. For example, poor performance on an IQ test may result from physiological factors such as Down syndrome or from a lack of educational opportunity. When we try to explain or account for the low IQ of a Down syndrome child we attribute it to his or her congenital illness—even though educational factors conceivably could affect the child's IQ score. We do this because the congenital illness is the most direct, sufficient explanation. Thus, when clinicians label a disorder as biologically caused, they do not mean that the disorder is unaffected by environmental or behavioral factors, merely that biology provides the *more* satisfying single account.

CLASSIFICATION OF MENTAL DISORDERS
Syndromes

The first formal and detailed classification of mental disorders was produced in 1883 by Emil Kraeplin (1856–1926). Kraeplin, a physician, believed that all mental disorders were due to physical diseases, perhaps due to slow-acting germs as in the case of general paresis. He stressed a **syndromal** approach to classification.

A **syndrome** is a collection of signs and symptoms that occur together. (A **sign** is what an examiner can see or feel; a **symptom** is what the examiner must be told. For instance, sweating is a sign; a headache is a symptom.) In a case of the flu, the signs and symptoms that go together are feelings of weakness, sore throat, fever, headache, sinus congestion, and possibly nausea. Because these symptoms and signs seem to set in and go away together, physicians infer that they are aspects of the same disease. When clinicians believe that they know the cause of symptoms, they use the term *disease;* when they do not know the cause, they use the term *syndrome.*

Kraeplin proposed that there were two major types of mental disorders: dementia praecox, a disorder characterized by hallucinations and thought disorders, and manic-depressive psychosis, a disorder characterized by disturbed mood. Although Kraeplin's classification scheme has influenced more recent classification systems, it was found to be too restrictive. (For example, he did not categorize hysteria as a mental disorder.) At various national and international conferences, additional syndromes have been added to the list of disorders.

Diagnostic and Statistical Manual (**DSM**)

In 1952, the American Psychiatric Association published the first *Diagnostic and Statistical Manual* (DSM-I). This manual and the subsequent DSM-II (1968) were highly influenced by Freudian personality theory. For instance, disorders like dissociative reaction (where a person has multiple personalities) and phobias (irrational fears) were both categorized as neuroses because both, according to Freudian theory, are caused by the same thing—too much anxiety. The developers of DSM-III (1980) were dissatisfied with particular characteristics of DSM-I and II: there were no clear rules for diagnosis, it relied too heavily on Freudian theory, and research showed that clinicians could not use DSM-II reliably (two clinicians seeing the same person often arrived at different diagnoses). Perhaps the biggest fault of DSM-II was that new, effective treatments for mental disorders were developed after its publication, and its diagnostic categories did not predict who would respond best to which treatment (Klerman, 1986; Millon, 1986).

Whereas DSM-II was influenced by Freudian theory, DSM-III was influenced by a disease model of psychopathology whose origins can be traced back to Kraeplin (Klerman, 1986). In DSM-III and the revised version soon to be in use, DSM-IIIR, mental disorders are classified on the basis of observable symptoms, response to treatment, course/prognosis, and genetic evidence. To promote reliable use, DSM-III contains clear rules for making diagnoses. It permits more reliable diagnosis than DSM-II did, although some diagnostic categories (personality disorders, for example) still cannot be diagnosed reliably (Garfield, 1986).

The major diagnostic categories of DSM-IIIR appear in Table 13-1. In DSM-IIIR, disorders are evaluated along five dimensions or axes.

Axis I is major *clinical syndromes* that usually require the primary attention of the therapist or assessor.

Axis II is either ingrained, inflexible *personality traits* or *developmental (childhood) problems* that may be relevant to the treatment or assessment of the client.

Axis III is *physical disorders or illnesses*, other than mental disorders, that may be relevant to understanding or treating the client's problems.

Axis IV is the severity of *psychosocial stressors* that might influence the client's condition and affect response to treatment.

Axis V is the highest *level of adaptive functioning* achieved by the client over the past year in social relationships, work, and the use of leisure time.

TABLE 13-1   DSM-IIIR, 1986: SELECTED MENTAL DISORDERS

Axis I, CLINICAL SYNDROMES	*Psychoactive Substance Use Disorders*
Disorders Usually First Evident in Infancy, Childhood, or Adolescence	*Psychoactive Substance Dependence and Abuse Disorders*
Disruptive Behavior Disorders	Alcohol
Conduct disorder	Amphetamine
Attention deficit—hyperactivity disorder	Cannabis
Oppositional-defiant disorder	Cocaine, etc.
Anxiety Disorders of Childhood or Adolescence	*Schizophrenia*
Separation anxiety disorder	*Schizophrenia*
Avoidant disorder	Paranoid
Overanxious disorder	Catatonic
Eating Disorders	Disorganized
Anorexia nervosa	Undifferentiated
Bulimia nervosa	Residual
Pica	*Delusional (Paranoid) Disorder*
Rumination disorder of infancy	*Psychotic Disorders Not Elsewhere Classified*
Gender Identity Disorders	Schizophreniform disorder
Gender identity disorder of childhood	Schizoaffective disorder
Transsexualism	Brief reactive psychosis
Tic Disorders	Induced psychotic disorder
Tourette's disorder	*Mood (Affective) Disorders*
Organic Mental Syndromes and Disorders	*Bipolar Disorders*
	Depressive Disorders
Dementias Arising in the Senium and Presenium	*Anxiety Disorders (or Anxiety or Phobic Neuroses)*
Alzheimer's disease	Panic disorder
Multi-infarct dementia	Agoraphobia without history of panic disorder
Psychoactive Substance—Induced Organic Mental Disorders	Social phobia
	Simple phobia
Alcohol intoxication	Obsessive-compulsive disorder
Alcohol withdrawal	Post-traumatic stress disorder
Amphetamine intoxication	Generalized anxiety disorder
Amphetamine withdrawal, etc.	

Somatoform Disorders

Somatization Disorder

Dissociative Disorders
(or Hysterical neuroses, dissociative type)

Multiple Personality Disorder

Sexual Disorders

Paraphilias
Sexual Dysfunctions

Sleep Disorders

Factitious Disorders

Impulse Control Disorders Not Elsewhere Classified

Adjustment Disorder

Psychological Factors Affecting Physical Condition

Axis II, DEVELOPMENTAL DISORDERS

Mental Retardation

Mild mental retardation
Moderate mental retardation
Severe mental retardation
Profound mental retardation
Unspecified mental retardation

Pervasive Developmental Disorders

Autistic Disorder
Pervasive developmental disorder

Specific Developmental Disorders

Academic skills disorder

Language and speech disorders
Motor skills disorder

Other Developmental Disorders

Personality Disorders

Cluster A

Paranoid
Schizoid
Schizotypal

Cluster B

Histrionic
Narcissistic
Antisocial
Borderline

Cluster C

Avoidant
Dependent
Obsessive compulsive
Passive aggressive personality disorder

Axis III, PHYSICAL DISORDERS
AND CONDITIONS

Axis IV, SEVERITY OF
PSYCHOSOCIAL STRESSORS

None, minimal, mild, moderate, severe, extreme, catastrophic

Axis V, GLOBAL ASSESSMENT OF
FUNCTIONING

Source: Diagnostic and Statistical Manual of Mental Disorders (3rd Edition, IIIR).

Box 13-1 provides an example of how DSM-III might be used to classify someone with the symptoms or signs of a mental disorder.

In Chapter 14, we discuss some of the reasons for using a classification schema. For the present, we will say that most psychologists believe that if a client has the same symptoms as another client, both are probably suffering from the same disorder. The course, prognosis and response to treatment of one client should give the psychologist information about the other client. A classification scheme allows psychologists to make predictions about a mental disorder and treat it, even though its cause is unknown.

The classifications of mental disorders are not written in stone. Classifying mental disorders is a dynamic, changing *process* that reflects new scientific findings, new theories of psychopathology, changes in societal norms and attitudes, and changes in symptoms and signs themselves. Because behaviors are viewed as normal or abnormal based partly on their social context, it makes sense that as society changes, so will its view of what constitutes abnormal behavior. An excellent example of this is homosexuality. Homosexuality was once listed as a mental disorder by

Case History: Mrs. M. is a 26-year-old librarian who is intelligent and dedicated to her job. She is diabetic. Mrs. M. received a promotion 6 months ago and now has several older, more experienced employees working under her. Recently, her mother died suddenly, and Mrs. M. regrets that she and her mother never were close. In fact, she feels guilty because she and her mother argued the last time they were together. For the past several months, she has been having frightening experiences that she cannot explain. Out of the blue, she begins to feel tremendously worried but has no idea about what causes her fright. During these episodes, her hands tremble, she breaks into a sweat, and she feels faint. At the height of these episodes, she feels as if she can't breathe and that her heart is beating so furiously that it will burst.

Mrs. M. is performing satisfactorily at her job but she realizes that these episodes are beginning to interfere with her work.

According to DSM-IIIR Mrs. M. might be classified as follows:

DSM-III Axis Response	*Justification*
I—Probable diagnosis: anxiety disorder, panic disorder	The symptoms Mrs. M. reports (feelings of terror, pounding heart, faintness) are consistent with the syndrome of panic disorder
II—None	Nothing in Mrs. M.'s history shows that she had a personality or developmental disorder
III—Diabetes	This disorder and its treatment can produce symptoms similar to those reported by Mrs. M.

DSM-III Axis Response	*Justification*
IV—Stress level: extreme	The death of her mother plus her job responsibilities constitute an extreme level of stress
V—Global assessment of functioning: "8" = slight impairment of functioning	The client experiences only mild problems at work due to her problem. She has an active social life.

As you can see, DSM-III asks the diagnostician to evaluate a patient on a variety of dimensions—physical health, adaptive functioning, and stress level. Therefore, it provides a more complete picture of a person's functioning than did previous diagnostic systems.

---

the American Psychiatric Association. But at its convention in December 1973, the trustees voted to remove homosexuality from the list of mental disorders. (Only when a person is distressed by his or her homosexuality is it still considered a mental disorder.) This change—the removal of homosexuality from the list of mental disorders—was precipitated by scientific findings that many homosexuals are happy, well-adjusted members of their communities (Thompson, McCandless, and Strickland, 1971) as well as by changing social attitudes about homosexuality.

CHARACTERISTICS OF MENTAL DISORDERS

What features characterize mental disorders today? Like the behaviors historically labeled mad, some of the conditions labeled mental disorders in DSM-IIIR also cause people to react with disgust or fear. But in some conditions, only the victim of the mental disorder is aware that anything is wrong. This is often the case with people who suffer from panic attacks, for example.

Mental disorders share other characteristics as well. First, people with mental disorders often experience discomfort and suffering. In centuries past there was frequently little concern for the feelings of the afflicted person. Now we recognize that in many cases mental disorders are extremely painful for the victim. One of the characteristics of mental disorders that may make them so painful is that many victims feel helpless to predict or affect the course of their disorder. People with mental disorders thus may experience a sense of loss of control, and to others their behavior may appear erratic and unpredictable.

Another characteristic of mental disorders is that the principal symptoms and signs tend to be behavioral and phenomenological, not physiological. In other words, the main indicators tend to be unusual behaviors or a person's subjective (phenomenological) reports—"I'm constantly worried." The main indicators of a mental disorder tend *not* to be simple physical signs such as a high fever, a rash, or a biochemical test. Finally, mental disorders interfere with a person's ability to function or perform at peak efficiency.

Although many mental disorders share these characteristics, it is hard to list ironclad characteristics because disorders come to be considered *mental* disorders for a great variety of reasons: because physicians would not or could not treat the condition, because the disorder results in great behavioral or cognitive disturbance, or because the disorder is thought to be caused, at least in part, by psychological factors. Thus although mental disorders share some characteristics, they also differ greatly in terms of the evidence of their biological cause, their types of symptoms, and their responsiveness to treatment.

PERSPECTIVES ON MENTAL DISORDERS

In the following sections, we present information on certain mental disorders listed in DSM-IIIR. As you read, be aware that each disorder has been investigated by psychologists whose models or theories for conceptualizing mental disorders differ greatly. For instance, you have seen in earlier chapters that some psychologists believe that behavior—abnormal and otherwise—is learned according to principles of conditioning. These *behaviorally* oriented psychologists believe that the behaviors characteristic of mental disorders are acquired via observational, Pavlovian, and operant learning (see Chapter 6). In their research, these investigators typically try to determine whether the abnormal behaviors associated with mental disorders are associated with particular environmental events, are altered by changes in their consequences, or are due to poor coping skills. In addition, *cognitive-behaviorists* believe not only that learning but also peoples' attitudes and attributions play a causal role in mental disorders.

Other psychologists are guided by the ideas of Freud and his followers. These *psychodynamic* psychologists believe that personality structures are determined early in life by important events such as toilet training, the parents' administration of discipline, and the way affection is given (see Chapter 15). In theory, early childhood events influence personality structure, and personality structure renders individuals more or less susceptible to different mental disorders. Therefore, psychodynamically oriented researchers typically examine the relationship between measures of personality structure, or developmental events, and the types of mental disorders that people develop.

Biologically oriented researchers believe that the mental disorders they study are caused, at least in part, by physiological abnormalities (such as neurotransmitter imbalances). These researchers do not necessarily believe that physiological factors alone account for mental disorders, but they believe that investigating physiological variables is necessary to get a complete picture of mental disorders. Typically, biologically oriented researchers conduct studies in which they determine whether a mental disorder is associated with levels of a neurotransmitter, with a particular electrophysiological pattern (such as an EEG pattern), or with a particular genetic pattern.

According to a *sociological* perspective, mental disorders are greatly influenced by social, educational, and economic conditions. Investigators who endorse a sociological model of abnormality typically investigate the relationship among mental disorders and such variables as socioeconomic status, educational and cultural opportunities, and social and cultural norms.

Any researcher's theoretical model influences his or her research on, and conceptualizations of, mental disorders. It influences the particular questions researchers ask, the variables they measure, how they measure variables, and how they interpret results. Thus, the scientist with a biological orientation may investigate whether alcoholism is related to genotype. The scientist with sociological orientation may investigate whether alcoholism is associated with poverty and with the absence of strong social sanctions for heavy drinking. In fact, alcoholism does appear to be affected by genotype (Goodwin, 1976), *and* better educated, wealthier individuals tend to have fewer alcohol-related problems (Vaillant, 1983). Mental disorders are complex and almost certainly determined by many different causes. A thorough understanding of mental disorders relies on information gathered by people who take many different perspectives. As we review the major types of disorders, we attempt to show how different theoretical models yield *complementary* research findings.

Schizophrenia

Schizophrenia was one of the disorders included in Kraeplin's early classification system, and one of the most serious of all mental disorders—serious in terms of the behavioral disruption it produces, its cost to society, and the suffering it causes its victims and those who care about them.

Remember, too, that although we may refer to people as schizophrenic, they are *people* who *have* schizophrenia. Schizophrenia is not the sum total of a person. It is a disorder that affects someone's life.

INCIDENCE AND COURSE OF SCHIZOPHRENIA   Schizophrenia is not very common; perhaps only about 1 person in 100 suffers from it. However, because the disease can be so long-lasting and debilitating, it has been estimated that as many as 30 percent of all hospital beds in the United States are occupied by schizophrenics (Andreasen, 1984).

As you will see in the following sections, there are several different types of schizophrenic disorders, and these last from a whole lifetime (schizophrenia) to just 1 or 2 weeks (schizophreniform illness). About 10 to 25 percent of schizophrenics recovered in the days before the development of modern drug treatments (McHugh and Slavney, 1983). As you will see in Chapter 15, this figure is no doubt much higher with today's more effective drug and psychological treatments.

Two bits of caution are in order on the subject of schizophrenia. First, although we speak of schizophrenia as if it were a single disorder, there are subtypes of schizophrenia, and it is likely that different subtypes of schizophrenia have distinct etiologies (American Psychiatric Association, 1980). Second, as we review the major features of the schizophrenia syndrome, it is tempting to think that they invariably are seen in schizophrenics. But people with schizophrenia vary in their behavior just as anyone else does. The following characteristics are generally true of schizophrenics, but by no means are they universally so.

DESCRIPTION   According to DSM-IIIR, to be diagnosed schizophrenic, someone must show deterioration in functioning in areas such as work, social relations, and self-care; the person must show continuous signs of the illness for at least 6 months; and the person must show at least one specific symptom or sign such as those listed in Table 13-2. If deterioration lasts less than 6 months, a person is classified as having schizophreniform illness. Research has shown that schizophreniform

TABLE 13-2   SPECIFIC DIAGNOSTIC CRITERIA FOR SCHIZOPHRENIA

A. Characteristic psychotic symptoms. Either (1), (2), or (3) [for at least one week (or less if symptoms successfully treated)]:
  (1) two of the following:
    (a) delusions
    (b) prominent hallucinations (throughout the day for several days or several times a week for several weeks and each hallucinatory experience is not limited to a few brief moments)
    (c) incoherence or marked loosening of associations
    (d) catatonic behavior
    (e) flat or grossly inappropriate affect
  (2) bizarre delusions (i.e., involving a phenomenon that the individual's subculture would regard as totally implausible, e.g., thought broadcasting, being controlled by a dead person)
  (3) prominent hallucinations [as defined in (1)(b) above] of a voice with content having no apparent relation to depression or elation, or a voice keeping up a running commentary on the individual's behavior or thoughts, or two or more voices conversing with each other

Source: Diagnostic and Statistical Manual of Mental Disorders (3rd Edition, IIIR).

illness is characterized by greater emotionality than is schizophrenia and has a better anticipated outcome or prognosis (American Psychiatric Association, 1980; Garmezy, 1970; Langfeldt, 1937).

Thought Disorder   Disordered thinking is a hallmark of schizophrenia (Chapman and Chapman, 1973). The effects of disordered thought pervade all of the schizophrenic's activities and seize the attention of the listener or observer. Consider the following response to the question, "Why do you think people believe in God?"

> *Uh, let's, I don't know why, let's see, balloon travel. He holds it up for you, the balloon. He don't let you fall out, your little legs sticking down through the clouds. He's down to the smoke stack, looking through the smoke trying to get the balloon gassed up you know. Way they're flying on top that way, legs sticking out. I don't know, looking down on the ground, heck, that'd make you so dizzy you just stay and sleep you know, hold down and sleep there. I used to be sleep outdoors, you know, sleep out doors instead of going home.*

> *(Chapman and Chapman, 1973, p. 3)*

What is unusual about this response? You might say "everything." But that's not really true. The schizophrenic speaker generally used acceptable grammar and sentence construction. Also, individual sentences seem to make some sense ("I don't know, looking down on the ground, heck, that'd make you so dizzy"). Moreover, some aspects of the passage are relevant, even if only tangentially so, to the question. For example, God protects you ("don't let you fall out of the clouds").

Hundreds of papers have been written that attempt to describe characteristic deficits of schizophrenic thought processes. Some of these deficits involve the *form* in which schizophrenics attempt to communicate and some the actual information (the *content*) of the schizophrenics' communication.

In the passage just quoted, notice how the individual skips from thinking about God to balloon travel. This is a good example of the loose associations that are often apparent in schizophrenics' speech (see Table 13-2). Loose associations are those in which a thought or word triggers verbal production on a topic only tangentially related to an earlier train of thought. Other characteristics of the form of schizophrenic speech are that it is *illogical, incoherent* (incomprehensible), and has a *poverty of content* (it contains little useful information). Additional examples of schizophrenic speech appear in Box 13-2.

Delusions are a striking characteristic of the content of schizophrenic communication. A delusion is a belief that diverges from the views and beliefs of the rest of society and that cannot be supported with cogent argument or evidence. The presence of delusions is one reason that schizophrenia has traditionally been considered a psychosis, a disorder in which the individual loses touch with reality. Some of the more common types of delusions of schizophrenics follow:

Persecution delusions: beliefs that one is being punished or plotted against by powerful forces.

Thought broadcasting: A person's belief that his or her thoughts are being broadcast in some way so that others know what he or she is thinking.

Delusions of being controlled: a person's belief that his or her thoughts or behavior are being controlled magically by outside forces.

Some examples of delusional material appear in Box 13-2.

Perceptual/Attentional Deficits   As Kraeplin noted of schizophrenics, "It is quite common for them to lose both inclination and ability on their own initiative to keep their attention fixed for any length of time" (Kraeplin, 1919; from Chapman and Chapman, 1973, p. 8). Thus, many schizophrenics cannot concentrate on tasks or screen out irrelevant information in experimental tasks (Chapman and McGhie, 1962). They may claim that they feel "flooded" with irrelevant information (Freedman and Chapman, 1973).

The inability to attend effectively to the environment may start early in life, before some of the more dramatic symptoms of schizophrenia are present. It is known that children with one schizophrenic parent are 10 to 15 times more likely to develop schizophrenia than are children from the general population (Erlenmeyer-Kimling, 1968). Researchers recently have discovered that a much higher percentage of children between 7 and 12 years old whose parents are schizophrenic show deficits on attention and short-term memory tasks such as recalling a series of numbers than do the children of parents with no mental disorders (Cornblatt and Erlenmeyer-Kimling, 1985). Moreover, the children of schizophrenics who have attentional deficits are much more likely than other children to develop later problems in school with family or peers. Perhaps these children with behavioral and attentional problems will develop symptoms of schizophrenia in later life.

The most dramatic perceptual or attentional problem of schizophrenics is the occurrence of **hallucinations**. Hallucinations are illusory sensory experiences—the hearing of voices, the seeing of things that are not there. In other words, there are no eliciting external stimuli. Sometimes schizophrenics know that the voices they hear or their other hallucinations are not real, but at other times they believe that they are.

Emotions in Schizophrenia   Two basic types of emotional behavior are typically seen in schizophrenia. During acute psychotic episodes, sudden increases in schizophrenic symptoms, a person may show dramatic mood swings that are inappropriate to the situation. For example, one minute a schizophrenic may laugh and giggle uncontrollably in response to some unremarkable, ordinary event. The next minute she may dissolve into tears when she is asked why she is laughing.

But intense emotions of acute psychotic episodes usually are short-lived. The predominant emotional pattern of chronic schizophrenics—those who have had the disease for many years—is that of *flattened* emotions. Such schizophrenics do not express the emotional highs and lows that most people do. Rather, they tend to be fairly expressionless and

FIGURE 13-8 DISORGANIZED
SCHIZOPHRENIA.
This young man is displaying the
childlike giggling and mirth
characteristic of disorganized
schizophrenia.

seem not to care about things that motivate most of us. For example, some seem insensitive to pain, and many seem incapable of experiencing pleasure, a condition called **anhedonia** (which is also characteristic of the depressed). Perhaps the most distressing emotional consequence of schizophrenia for the family of the schizophrenic is the schizophrenic's apparent lack of pleasure in social relationships. Schizophrenics often seem not to enjoy people anymore.

TYPES OF SCHIZOPHRENIA   Although the foregoing symptoms are characteristic of schizophrenia, there is much variability in the behavior of schizophrenics and in the course of the disorder. This variability has given rise to the belief that schizophrenia is not one disorder, but rather a variety of disorders. For this reason, some writers even use the term "the schizophrenias." A variety of classification schemas has been used to categorize the subtypes of schizophrenia; some major subtypes are listed below.

DSM-IIIR SUBTYPES OF SCHIZOPHRENIA

Disorganized Type   Disorganized schizophrenics are those whose most striking symptoms are emotional. They tend either to be extremely emotional, giggling and laughing inappropriately (see Figure 13-8), or to be extremely withdrawn, with a flattened, emotionless expression. The giggling gave rise to an earlier name for this subtype, hebephrenic schizophrenia, which means "child mind" in Greek. The outlook for those with this subtype of schizophrenia is not good. The disorder starts early in life, produces great impairment, and tends to be chronic.

Catatonic Type   Although it was once common, this subtype of schizophrenia is now quite rare, perhaps because of the drugs now used to

FIGURE 13-9   CATATONIC
SCHIZOPHRENIA.
Some of these men display one of the
dramatic features of catatonia: waxen
flexibility. Notice their unusual postures.

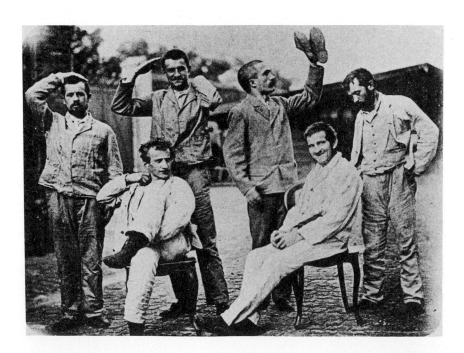

BOX 13-2
STATEMENTS OF SCHIZOPHRENICS

AWARENESS OF THOUGHT DISORDER

How—how—HOW? In the name of God—How does a person learn to think differently? I am crazy wild this minute—how can I learn to think straight?

> (*Jefferson, 1948; from Kaplan, 1964, p. 5*)

FEELINGS OF BEING CONTROLLED

So the monster was out and the ghost of some old berserker ancestor rose up within me and suggested that I could do something about it, and the fierce hatred exalted that it had possessed itself of a massive and powerful body. And the thing that was in me was not I at all—but another—and I knew that no power on earth but a strait-jacket could hold her.

> (*Jefferson, 1948; from Kaplan, 1964, p. 33*)

AUDITORY HALLUCINATIONS AND DELUSIONS OF PERSECUTION

Being a stranger I was surprised to hear someone exclaim twice: "Shoot him!", evidently meaning me, judging from the menacing talk which followed between the threatener and those with him. I tried to see who the threatener, and those with him were, but the street was so crowded, I could not. I guessed that they must be gangsters, who had mistaken me for another gangster, who I coincidentally happened to resemble. I thought one or more of them really intended to shoot me so I hastened from the scene as fast as I could walk. These unidentified persons who had threatened to shoot me, pursued me. I knew they were pursuing me because I still heard their voices as close as ever, no matter how fast I walked.

> (*White, in Kaplan, 1964, p. 133*)

DISORDERED VISUAL PERCEPTION

My head was frequently surrounded by a shimmer of light owing to the massive concentrations of rays, like the halo of Christ is pictured, but incomparably richer and brighter: the so-called "crown of rays." The reflection of this crown of rays was so strong that one day when Professor Flechsig appeared at my bed with his assistant Dr. Quentin, the latter disappeared from my seeing eyes.

> (*Schreber, 1955; from Kaplan, 1964, p. 130*)

These words all were written by people who at one time in their lives experienced the symptoms of schizophrenia. Some of the excerpts were written while the person was experiencing schizophrenic symptoms—for example, those of Lara Jefferson—and others were written after the person had recovered from the schizophrenic episode—those of Schreber and White.

treat schizophrenia. A prominent feature is stupor—a profound unresponsiveness to the environment. Unusual motor behavior also is a major feature of catatonia. It may include rigidity, posturing, and unusual mannerisms. One of the dramatic signs of catatonia is "waxen flexibility," a term that refers to the tendency of the schizophrenic to remain in whatever position he or she is placed (see Figure 13-9). Many catatonics are mute and sometimes appear stuporous.

Paranoid Type   The primary features of this subtype are delusions, especially delusions of grandiosity or persecution (see Box 13-2). The classical paranoid schizophrenic is the person who thinks that he or she is Napoleon or Christ. Paranoid schizophrenia often starts later in life than the other subtypes and seems to run in families.

Undifferentiated Type   This classification is used for people who have clear symptoms of schizophrenia—delusions, hallucinations, and affective disturbance—but who do not meet the criteria for other subtypes.

Residual Type People fitting this classification do not have prominent delusions or hallucinations but do show some of the following: social isolation, poor occupational or scholastic functioning, poor grooming/hygiene, odd speech, and inappropriate affect.

Psychologists try to place people in various diagnostic categories because different syndromes have different times of onset, different courses, different responses to treatment, and the like. Thus, if they can categorize a person, they can predict what to expect: that hebephrenia tends to be chronic or that the disorder may respond well to drugs.

Although the classification found in DSM-IIIR is widely used by clinicians, other classifications have been proposed. These also can be helpful in guiding predictions about prognosis, responses to treatment, and so on.

One classification that has been widely used for over 30 years is that of process versus reactive schizophrenia (see Bernheim and Lewine, 1979). **Process schizophrenia** arises gradually, early in life, is associated with severely flattened affect, and tends to be chronic. **Reactive schizophrenia** often becomes evident suddenly, when a person has an acute psychotic episode. Reactive schizophrenics often show fairly good adjustment both before and after acute psychotic episodes, and they may not experience an initial episode until they are in their 20s or 30s.

A fairly recent and controversial classification system is that of *positive- versus negative-symptom schizophrenia* (Strauss, Carpenter, and Bartko, 1974). Negative-symptom schizophrenia is characterized by an *absence* or insufficiency of normal functioning, such as flattened effect, social withdrawal, and muteness. Positive symptoms reflect the *presence* of abnormal functioning, such as hallucinations, delusions, and extreme emotionality. Positive and negative symptoms may represent the influences of *two independent processes* that are both common in schizophrenia. Thus, both may be present in the same person, and the two types of symptoms may be present at different times. However, when one type of

FIGURE 13-10 CAT SCANS: NORMAL BRAIN, SCHIZOPHRENIC'S BRAIN.
Computerized Axial Tomography (CAT) scanning involves an x-ray beam sent through a part of the body. Because x-rays are reduced by specific amounts by the different types of tissues through which they pass, detectors on the other side of the body can determine the amount and type of tissue through which the x-rays have passed. (a) The CAT scan of the brain of a normal individual. (b) The CAT scan of a person with schizophrenia. Notice the large ventricles, thought to be characteristic of negative-symptom schizophrenia.

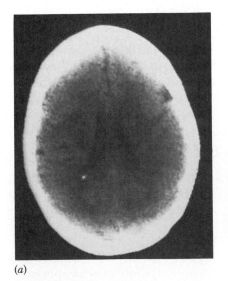
(a)

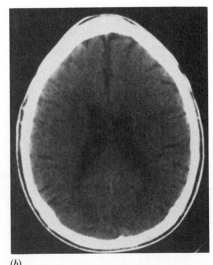
(b)

symptom consistently predominates, a person may be classified as either a negative- or positive-symptom schizophrenic.

The distinction between negative- and positive-symptom schizophrenias is attracting great research interest because evidence now suggests that they may have different etiologies. Negative symptoms have been associated with deficits in activity of the neurotransmitter **dopamine** (MacKay, 1980), and negative symptoms tend to be found more often in people with generalized brain pathology (see Figure 13-10*a,b*). Negative symptoms also respond more poorly to drug treatment (Crow, 1980). Positive symptoms have been associated with excess dopamine activity, tend to be short-lived, respond well to drug treatment, and tend to predominate in people who show little evidence of generalized brain disease (Andreasen, 1985; Crow, 1985; see Table 13-3).

TABLE 13-3 CHARACTERISTICS OF POSITIVE-
AND NEGATIVE-SYMPTOM SCHIZOPHRENIAS

Characteristics	Positive	Negative
Symptoms/signs	Hallucinations, delusions, thought disorder	Flattened affect, poverty of speech, anhedonia
Course	Acute episodes	Chronic
Response to drugs	Good	Poor
Neurotransmitter status	Increased dopamine receptors	Dopamine inactivity
Brain pathology	None	Enlarged ventricles, decreased cortex

The classifications of schizophrenia are somewhat *arbitrary*. Schizophrenia, or the "schizophrenias," is a puzzle. Scientists are still debating how many pieces there are to this puzzle and how the pieces fit together. There is still disagreement about how to classify people with this disorder.

CAUSES OF SCHIZOPHRENIA What causes schizophrenia? This single question has inspired thousands of research studies, and happily, this tremendous research effort is beginning to bear fruit.

One feature of schizophrenia that captured scientists' attention right away is that schizophrenia runs in families. Is schizophrenia then a genetic disorder? Can we inherit genes for schizophrenia from a parent? If a child is raised by a schizophrenic, is the experience so psychologically disturbing that the child is especially likely to develop schizophrenia?

In support of environmental causes of schizophrenia, observations of *psychodynamic* theorists led them to report that overprotective or rejecting mothers were present in a high proportion of the cases of schizophrenia (Kasanin, Knight, and Sage, 1934). Sociologically oriented researchers noted that schizophrenia did not occur in equal rates among all social classes. It occurred most frequently among the inner-city poor,

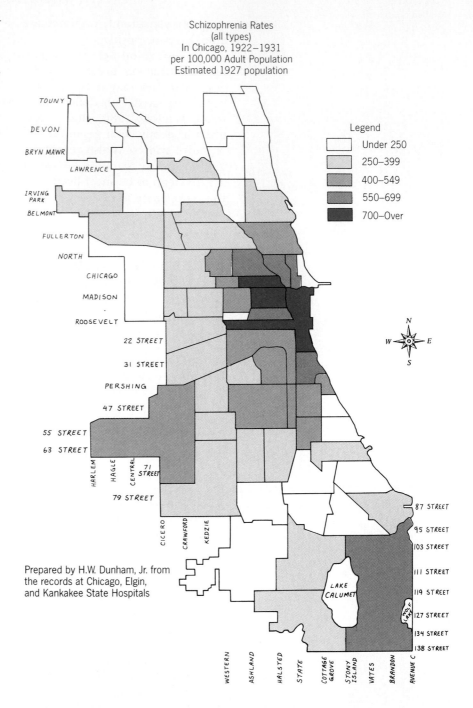

Schizophrenia Rates
(all types)
In Chicago, 1922–1931
per 100,000 Adult Population
Estimated 1927 population

Legend

	Under 250
	250–399
	400–549
	550–699
	700–Over

Prepared by H.W. Dunham, Jr. from
the records at Chicago, Elgin,
and Kankakee State Hospitals

suggesting that schizophrenia might be caused by poverty and environmental stressors (see Figure 13-11). In survey after survey, the highest
incidences of schizophrenia were found among the lowest socioeconomic
classes (Hollingshead and Redlich, 1958). Also, studies show that more
people are hospitalized for schizophrenia during periods of economic
decline (Neale and Oltmanns, 1980). However, biologically oriented researchers argue that schizophrenia is so debilitating to children that it

causes their mothers to act overprotectively and rejectingly, and *causes* its victims to occupy the lowest social classes, for example, because they can't hold jobs. Biologically oriented researchers point to genetics as a key to understanding this disorder.

TWIN STUDIES Many studies conducted in the 1930s and 1940s *suggested* a genetic basis to schizophrenia, but because of inadequacies in the designs of these studies, they did not yield conclusive results. Recent studies, however, have yielded very convincing evidence of a genetic basis to schizophrenia. One source of such evidence is twin studies. If schizophrenia is completely genetically determined, then if one monozygotic (identical) twin becomes schizophrenic, the other should as well.

In a major study of the concordance of twins for schizophrenia, Gottesman and Shields (1972) determined that the concordance rates for monozygotic twins was 42 percent (10 of 24 twin pairs were concordant), whereas the concordance rate for dizygotic twins was 9 percent (3 of 33 twin pairs were concordant). Thus, twins that were genetically similar were almost five times more likely to develop schizophrenia than were less similar twins. There also was strong evidence that the severity of schizophrenia was related to the likelihood of concordance; the greater the severity, the greater the concordance (see Table 13-4). Another impressive piece of evidence that genetic inheritance is important to schizophrenia is the fact that, in many cases, what is inherited is not just schizophrenia, but a particular *type* of schizophrenia (see Table 13-5).

Despite this evidence some scientists have argued that data on twins cannot prove the case for genetic transmission (see Neale and Oltmanns, 1980). They have argued that the higher concordance rates for monozygotic twins can be explained by the fact that schizophrenia is caused by the way one is treated, and monozygotic twins are treated more similarly than are dizygotic twins. Thus, their higher concordance is due to similar treatment, not similar genes. To answer this criticism, another type of study has been conducted.

Adoption Studies In adoption studies investigators find the children of schizophrenic and normal parents who have been adopted away at an

TABLE 13-4 CONCORDANCE OF SCHIZOPHRENIA AMONG MONOZYGOTIC TWINS

Criterion	Mild Cases	Severe Cases
Unemployed, or in hospital within past 6 months	27%	80%
In hospital more than 2 years	38%	77%
Classified as hebephrenic	33%	91%
Classified as "strict" schizophrenia	20%	81%

Source: Gottesman and Shields, 1972; reproduced in Neale and Oltmanns, 1980, p. 189.
Note: These data show that if a twin was labeled mildly schizophrenic, the co-twin had the same severity of schizophrenia or the same type of schizophrenia 20 to 38 percent of the time. If a twin was labeled severely schizophrenic, the other twin suffered equally 77 to 91 percent of the time.

TABLE 13-5 THE CONCORDANCE OF SCHIZOPHRENIA SUBTYPES AMONG MONOZYGOTIC TWIN SCHIZOPHRENICS

Diagnostic Label of Twin	*Diagnostic Label of Co-Twin*				
	Hebephrenic	*Catatonic*	*Paranoid*	*Catatonic-Paranoid*	*Mixed*
Hebephrenic	2	—	—	—	—
Catatonic	—	1	—	—	1
Paranoid	—	—	2	—	—
Catatonic-Paranoid	—	—	—	7	—
Mixed	—	—	—	—	1
				Total number of twin pairs = 14	

Source: Kringlen, 1967; reproduced in Neale and Oltmanns, 1980, p. 1986.
Note: In all cases but one, if one member of a schizophrenic, monozygotic twin pair was diagnosed as having one subtype, the co-twin received the same diagnosis.

early age. If schizophrenia is genetically determined, then the biological (genetic) children of schizophrenics should have a higher rate of schizophrenia than control children, even though the former were raised away from their biological parents. In this method researchers match the rearing conditions of the children of schizophrenics and nonschizophrenics. The results of such studies are quite clear. The biological children of schizophrenics are more likely to be schizophrenic than are the biological children of nonschizophrenics, if both are adopted. In one study (Heston, 1966), 5 of 47 (10.6 percent) schizophrenics' children were eventually diagnosed as having schizophrenia, but no child of nonschizophrenic parents was so diagnosed. These findings, along with those of twin studies, constitute compelling evidence of a genetic basis of schizophrenia.

But consider the data again for one moment. Gottesman and Shields found that the concordance rate for schizophrenia in monozygotic twins was 42 percent. What about the 58 percent of the schizophrenic monozygotic twins whose co-twin was *not* schizophrenic? Other twin studies show similar levels of discordance in schizophrenic, monozygotic twins (Fisher, 1973). Apparently, the same genetic makeup does *not necessarily* lead to concordance.

In a Finnish adoption study (Tienari et al., 1983), researchers evaluated the psychological status of both adopted children *and* adoptive parents as healthy or as mildly or severely psychologically disturbed. The researchers found that the biological children of schizophrenics had higher rates of psychosis than other children. But if the biological children of schizophrenics and nonschizophrenics were raised in relatively healthy adoptive families, the two groups of children did not differ in terms of mental disturbance. Family environment affects the development of schizophrenia in other ways, too. Schizophrenics who lived with a spouse or parents after they got out of the hospital were more likely to show disturbed behavior and to be rehospitalized than were those schizophrenics who lived alone (Brown, Carstairs, and Topping, 1958; Leff, 1976).

What is it about families that can be harmful to schizophrenics? Researchers have found that the level of **expressed emotion** in a family relates significantly to the likelihood that a schizophrenic person's symptoms will worsen (Brown, Birley, and Wing, 1972; Leff, 1976). Expressed emotion consists of communications about the schizophrenic family member that are hostile, critical, and reflect marked overinvolvement (extreme concern and anxiety about the schizophrenic). The researchers found that when schizophrenics were discharged to families high in expressed emotion, 58 percent required rehospitalization, but only 16 percent of those discharged to families low in expressed emotion required rehospitalization. Others have found that schizophrenics living in families characterized by high expressed emotion were three to four times more likely to relapse to schizophrenia than other schizophrenics (Leff, 1976; Vaughn et al., 1984; see Miklowitz et al., 1986). The researchers also tested to see whether the most disturbed schizophrenics might not produce the most disturbed families. They found that the expressed emotion in schizophrenic families related most to relapse, not the severity of schizophrenic symptoms. Although the hypothesis about the link between expressed emotion and schizophrenia has been borne out in some research, other research has not shown a link between them (MacMillan, Gold, Crow, Johnson, and Johnstone, 1986). Further research will reveal the conditions under which expressed emotion influences schizophrenia.

DIATHESIS–STRESS MODEL   Today, scientists realize that both genetic and environmental factors often play causal roles in the development of mental disorders. A currently popular way to think of the roles of genetic and environmental factors is in terms of susceptibility to stressors (environmental or physiological challenges to organisms). According to this view, schizophrenics are born with a genetic predisposition to develop the disease, but they will not do so unless they are exposed to certain types of environmental stressors.

Table 13-6 depicts a *hypothetical* diathesis–stress model of schizophrenia. In this model, Type 1 schizophrenia is a genetic disease that causes brain abnormalities and, therefore, schizophrenic symptoms. Substantial evidence suggests a high rate of brain abnormalities among schizophrenics. Type 2 schizophrenia is produced purely by nongenetic factors such as birth trauma and complications during pregnancy. Research does show that low birth weights (possible signs of complications during prenatal development) and birth trauma are associated with later schizophrenia (McNeil and Kaij, 1978; Silverton, Finello, Mednick, and Schulsinger, 1985). Moreover, birth trauma appears to be more common among those schizophrenics with little genetic background of schizophrenia (Kinney and Jacobsen, 1978). Finally, the third type of schizophrenia involves an interaction between genetic endowment and environmental stress.

In Table 13-6 the Type 3 diathesis is a genetically transmitted neurotransmitter (dopamine) abnormality of the sort found in positive-symptom schizophrenia. There is considerable evidence to implicate dopamine in schizophrenia (Karson, Kleinman, and Wyatt, 1986). One bit of evidence is that antipsychotic drugs reduce symptoms of schizophrenia in direct proportion to their blockage of dopamine receptors (Andrea-

TABLE 13-6   A HYPOTHETICAL DIATHESIS–STRESS MODEL OF SCHIZOPHRENIA: THREE ETIOLOGIES

Type 1	*Type 2*	*Type 3*
Genetic diathesis		
Generalized brain disease: e.g., enlarged ventricles	None	Neurochemical imbalance (e.g., excess dopamine receptors)
Stressors necessary for disease occurrence		
None	1. Birth trauma and intrauterine complications (viral infections) 2. Hostile/emotional family environment 3. Poverty	1. Hostile/emotional family environment 2. Poverty
Type of schizophrenia that results		
Negative symptoms	Negative or positive symptoms	Positive symptoms

sen, 1979; Creese, Burt, and Synder, 1976). Perhaps dopamine abnormalities make people more *sensitive* to external stressors. Thus, if a person with this diathesis is exposed to a high level of stress, he or she is likely to become schizophrenic. In a less stressful environment the individual remains largely symptom free.

As you have seen by now, scientists who adopt different approaches to a mental disorder contribute ideas that are complementary, rather than contradictory. Biologically oriented scientists have shown that schizophrenia has a genetic component. Other scientists have identified gestational and environmental factors that may cause or worsen schizophrenia: complications during prenatal development, birth trauma, poverty, and disturbed family environments.

The diathesis–stress model is an important etiological concept. According to the diathesis–stress model, schizophrenia is not inherited, but a predisposition to schizophrenia is. This predisposition becomes apparent only if a person encounters certain forms of environmental stress.

We turn now to disorders of mood.

Affective Disorders

Affect means mood. Therefore, *affective disorders* are mental disorders that have as their primary feature a disturbance in mood. There are several different types of affective disorders, or affective syndromes. In one type of affective disorder, **major depression**, a person experiences one or more major depressive episodes, episodes characterized by hopelessness, an inability to experience pleasure, and profound sadness. In a second type of affective disorder, **bipolar disorder**, a person experiences a manic episode and possibly depressive episodes as well. During a **manic episode** a person is excessively energetic, shifts rapidly from one idea to another, and has feelings of *grandiosity* (believes that he or she has extraordinary abilities).

INCIDENCE AND COURSE More people suffer from depression than schizophrenia. Depression has been called the common cold of mental disorders (Seligman, 1975). Estimates are that between 10 and 20 percent of all people become significantly depressed at some point in their lives. But only about 10 percent of these—about 1 percent of the general population—ever experiences a manic episode (Goodwin and Guze, 1979).

In many cultures, depression is two to three times more common in women than in men, and women are more likely to suffer repeated depressions (Amenson and Lewinsohn, 1981). No one knows the exact reason for this difference between the sexes, but the difference probably is due to both biological and cultural factors. For one thing, female sex hormones may have depressant effects, and the depressions that many women experience after giving birth—*postpartum* depressions—may be due to powerful hormonal changes (Parry and Rush, 1979). For another thing, as we describe later, differences in the ways that boys and girls are treated also may contribute to the greater depression of women.

Affective disorders can occur throughout the life span. Children sometimes become depressed. Although only about 1 percent of all children become depressed (Kashani and Simonds, 1979), as many as 60 percent of those children with severe educational and aggression problems may show signs of depression (see Petti, 1981). Childhood depression can be particularly difficult to detect because children are less likely than adults to admit to being sad or even to understand that they *are* sad (Poznanski, Mokkros, Grossman, and Freeman, 1985). But the most common age for an initial bout of depression is about 40, and for a manic episode, the early 30s (Goodwin and Guze, 1984).

Most bouts of depression are brief. One-quarter of them last less than 1 month, one-half last less than 3 months, and only 25 percent last a year or longer (Lewinsohn, Hoberman, Teri, and Hautzinger, 1985). Finally, someone who has been depressed before is two to three times more likely than others to become depressed again (Amenson and Lewinsohn, 1981).

DESCRIPTION We all experience mood swings, periods of great elation and periods when we feel sad. How do these normal mood swings differ from affective disorders?

Major Depression According to DSM-IIIR, to warrant a diagnosis of major depression a person must have experienced one or more major depressive episodes marked by at least five major features of depression (Table 13-7). A person who is depressed is chronically sad and doesn't enjoy or care about his or her usual activities anymore. Therefore he or she usually withdraws socially and avoids most recreational and social activities. Because even eating offers no pleasure, people who are severely depressed usually have poor appetites and lose weight. (Mild depression sometimes is associated with overeating.) The person's face looks fatigued or unhappy. He or she may cry easily. The depressed person also may have a limited attention span, slowed speech and thought processes, and disturbed sleep. Finally, people who are depressed feel hopeless about the future and contempt for themselves.

TABLE 13-7 PRINCIPAL CHARACTERISTICS
OF A MAJOR DEPRESSIVE EPISODE

(1) depressed mood most of the day, nearly every day (either by subjective account, e.g., feels "down" or "low," or is observed by others to look sad or depressed)

(2) loss of interest or pleasure in all or almost all activities nearly every day (either by subjective account or is observed by others to be apathetic)

(3) significant weight loss or weight gain when not dieting or binge-eating (e.g., more than 5% of body weight in a month), or decrease or increase in appetite nearly every day (in children, consider failure to make expected weight gains)

(4) insomnia or hypersomnia nearly every day

(5) psychomotor agitation or retardation nearly every day (observable by others, not merely subjective feelings of restlessness or being slowed down) (in children under six, hypoactivity)

(6) fatigue or loss of energy nearly every day

(7) feelings of worthlessness or excessive or inappropriate guilt (which may be delusional) nearly every day (not merely self-reproach or guilt about being sick)

(8) diminished ability to think or concentrate, or indecisiveness, nearly every day (either by subjective account or observed by others)

(9) thoughts that he or she would be better off dead, or suicidal ideation, nearly every day; a suicide attempt

Source: Diagnostic and Statistic Manual of Mental Disorders (3rd Edition, IIIR).

This description may capture the major features of depression, but it conveys little of the pain of severe depression. Price (1978) wrote of severely depressed people:

> *First, it is very unpleasant: depressive illness is probably more unpleasant than any disease except rabies. There is constant mental pain and often psychogenic physical pain too. . . . Secondly, the patient is isolated from family and friends, because the depression itself reduces his affection for others and he may well have ideas that he is unworthy of their love or even that his friendship may harm them. Thirdly, he is rejected by others because they cannot stand the sight of his suffering. There is a limit to sympathy. . . . Fourthly, and finally, the patient tends to do a great cover-up. Because of his outward depression he is socially unacceptable, and because of his inward depression he feels even more socially unacceptable than he really is. He does not, therefore, tell others how bad he feels. . . . Provided some minimal degree of social and vocational functioning is present, the world leaves the depressive alone and he battles on for the sake of his god or his children, or for some reason which makes his personal torment preferable to death.*

Bipolar Disorder   According to DSM-IIIR, to be diagnosed for bipolar disorder, a person must have had at least one manic episode and may also have had depressive episodes. Table 13-8 lists the principal features of manic episodes. Typically, people who are manic exude happiness and goodwill. They seem so happy and energetic that sometimes they are suspected of being on drugs. Moreover, their happiness may be infectious; it may amuse others. One book on diagnosis suggests that "experi-

TABLE 13-8 PRINCIPAL CHARACTERISTICS OF A MANIC EPISODE

A. One or more distinct periods lasting at least one week (or any duration if marked if impairment in occupational functioning or in usual social activities or relationships with others) when mood was abnormally and persistently elevated, expansive, or irritable.

B. During the period of mood disturbance, at least three of the following symptoms have persisted (four if the mood is only irritable) and have been present to a significant degree:
  (1) inflated self-esteem (grandiosity, which may be delusional)
  (2) decreased need for sleep, e.g., feels rested after only three hours of sleep
  (3) more talkative than usual or pressure to keep talking
  (4) flight of ideas or subjective experience that thoughts are racing
  (5) distractibility, i.e., attention too easily drawn to unimportant or irrelevant external stimuli
  (6) increase in activity (either socially, at work, or sexually) or physical restlessness
  (7) excessive involvement in activities that have a high potential for painful consequences, which is not recognized, e.g., buying sprees, sexual indiscretions, foolish business investments, reckless driving

Source: Diagnostic and Statistical Manual of Mental Disorders (3rd Edition, IIIR).

enced clinicians who find themselves amused by a patient immediately consider the possibility that the patient is manic or hypomanic (mildly manic)" (Goodwin and Guze, 1984, p. 17). People who are manic seem to be operating at high speed. They talk rapidly and dart from one subject to another. Although the primary manifestation of mania is euphoria, people may become outraged if their unrealistic plans are thwarted.

Mania might seem like a desirable state of mind if it were not typically marked by a profound lack of judgment. This lack of judgment, coupled with boundless energy, leads people suffering from mania to find themselves in risky business ventures, inappropriate and ill-fated sexual and romantic relationships, and ridiculous artistic or scholarly enterprises. For example, one person seen by one of the authors decided to write the "correct Bible of the Christians, Jews, and Huns."

> *One manic patient, who had been a successful salesman, decided to expand his business to Hawaii. He purchased a plane, hired four pilots to fly it, took all his employees with him to set up an office in Honolulu, wrote a series of bad checks, and ended up deeply in debt. Although he had no insight at the time of his illness, when asked afterwards if he really needed four pilots, he replied ruefully, "Heavens, no. I didn't need any pilots. I didn't need an office in Honolulu. I didn't even need an airplane ticket."*
>
> *(Andreasen, 1984, p. 50)*

Not only do people gripped by mania have boundless energy, but they can go days without sleep. Before modern drug treatments, about 15 percent of people suffering from mania died from exhaustion (Andreasen, 1984).

Causes of Depression   Why do people become depressed? As in the study of the causes of schizophrenia, clinicians and researchers have taken many different perspectives on the causes of depression. Some favor a biological model, others an environmental model. As their work supplies ever more information about depression's causes, course, and treatment, it becomes clear that a variety of factors may contribute to depression. Some of the factors associated with an increased risk of depression are low social and occupational class, stressors such as marital problems, work problems, death of a loved one, absence of social support, heredity, and being born female.

According to psychoanalytic theory, depression results from the real or symbolic death or loss of a loved one. Although the loss makes the survivor feel deserted or abandoned, he or she feels too guilty to direct anger at the loved one. After all, one is *not* supposed to feel angry at anyone for dying. Therefore, the emotionally abandoned person turns the anger *inward*. This inward-turning of anger is the wellspring of depression. Psychoanalytic theory accounts nicely for the fact that loss or death often provoke depression, and it accounts for the fact that people who are depressed often are filled with disgust or anger at themselves. But it accounts less well for those depressions that occur without any apparent loss.

Reinforcement Reduction   A theory of depression offered by certain behaviorally oriented psychologists is the *reinforcement reduction* hypothesis. According to this theory, depression occurs when people experience significant reductions in rewards or significant increases in aversive consequences (Lewinsohn et al., 1985). This theory holds that as people become more depressed, they also tend to become less active, and, therefore, they become withdrawn and less likely to engage in pleasant activities that might alleviate their depressions. Research has shown that compared to people who are not depressed, those who are depressed are less active, find pleasant activities to be less enjoyable, are extremely sensitive to aversive stimuli, and tend to be socially withdrawn (Lewinsohn et al., 1985). Finally, this theory explains how the loss of a job or a loved one provokes depression: these stressors reduce reinforcement and increase negative consequences. But this theory explains less well why some people can experience grievous tragedies and not become significantly depressed whereas others become seriously depressed in response to apparent trivialities or why some people become depressed repeatedly. These important individual differences suggest that some people have behavioral, cognitive, or physiological characteristics that make them especially susceptible to depression.

Attributional Style   One characteristic that might explain individual differences in the incidence of depression is *learned helplessness* (described in Chapter 6). Within the past 15 years, Martin Seligman, Lyn Abramson, and other cognitive-behavioral psychologists have described and researched the **learned helplessness model** of depression (Seligman, 1975). This model has its origins in the observation that if animals are repeatedly shocked, they develop many of the features of depression.

They become inactive, act helpless, and show cognitive (learning) deficits. Shock itself does not produce learned helplessness; shock must be *uncontrollable*. People generally are not subject to electric shocks, but they certainly are subject to other stressful events. As we have discussed, stressors provoke depression in humans. Evidence now suggests that the development of depression in response to stressors sometimes is related to a person's sense of control. Depression sometimes is related to a particular *attributional,* or explanatory, *style.* People who explain *bad* events on the basis of their own personal characteristics are likely to become depressed (Abramson, Metalsky, and Alloy, in submission; Abramson, Seligman, and Teasdale, 1978; Peterson and Seligman, 1984). In comparison to nondepressed people, depressed people attribute bad events to defects in themselves that are stable, general, and global (see Tables 13-9 and 13-10). They are likely to attribute events like a date going badly or losing a job to factors intrinsic to them, to factors always characteristic of them in virtually all situations, to factors out of their control, and to factors that doom them to suffer similar bad events again and again.

Depression has been found to be associated with this attributional style among children, depressed undergraduates, normal adults, and adults being treated for depression (Nolen-Hoeksema, Girgus, and

TABLE 13-9 ATTRIBUTIONAL STYLE QUESTIONNAIRE QUESTIONS

When people are asked the following questions, their responses reflect their attributional style:

You go on a date, and it goes badly.

1. Write down the one major cause of this event.

2. Is the cause of the date going badly due to something about you or something about other people or circumstances?

Due to other people (circle one number)	1	2	3	4	5	6	7 Due to me

3. In the future when dating will this cause again be present?

Never again present (circle one number)	1	2	3	4	5	6	7 Always be present

4. Is the cause something that just influences dating or does it also influence other areas of your life?

Just this situation (circle one number)	1	2	3	4	5	6	7 All situations

Source: Peterson and Seligman, 1984, p. 352.

Note: Question 2 asks whether the cause of the bad event is *internal* (due to the respondents' personal characteristics). Question 3 concerns *stability* (will it last over time?). The last question concerns *globality* (will the cause influence many areas of the respondents' life?).

TABLE 13-10 DEPRESSIVE AND NONDEPRESSIVE STYLES OF CAUSAL EXPLANATIONS

Event: Break-up with Boyfriend	
Depressive Explanation	*Nondepressive Explanation*
I guess it was really because I'm just so insecure—I always have been. I just can't let well enough alone. I keep needing more and more proof that a person really loves me.	We just didn't get along. I think he was looking for a mother or something, not a girlfriend. I got along a lot better with my other friends than I did with him—that's when you know something's not right with the relationship.

Event: Losing a Job	
Depressive Explanation	*Nondepressive Explanation*
I just wasn't smart enough to keep all the client's accounts straight, to remember the new changes in the tax codes, and to keep my boss abreast of new investment opportunities. Who am I kidding—I've never been able to keep up with my wife or with my brother and sister. It's why I had trouble all through school and it's why I never win those word games.	The job was impossible. If they had wanted me to work 70 hours a week they should have paid me to work 70 hours a week. I've got news for them, they're not going to find anyone, at least anyone good, who's going to put up with their demands.

Seligman, 1986; Peterson and Seligman, 1984). In one study (Raps, Peterson, Reinhard, Abramson, and Seligman, 1982), 30 people hospitalized for depression were compared with 15 nondepressed schizophrenic patients and 61 nondepressed medical and surgical patients (normals). Only those who were depressed had high scores on the Attributional Style Questionnaire (see Table 13-11). People's scores on the questionnaire also predicted the total amount of time that the people remained depressed. In another study (Persons and Rao, 1981), it was found that the extent to which depressed patients improved in response to treatment was related to changes in attributional style. As patients improved their attributional styles became less internal, stable, and global.

TABLE 13-11 SCORES ON THE ATTRIBUTIONAL STYLE QUESTIONNAIRE

Style Characteristic	*Depressives*	*Schizophrenics*	*Normals*
Internality	4.90	3.51	4.30
Stability	4.89	4.01	4.06
Globality	4.84	4.10	3.65
Composite	4.88	3.87	4.00

Source: Raps et al., 1982.
Note: Scores ranged from a high of 7 to a low of 1. High scores represent high levels of the attributional characteristic, and low scores mean low levels. The composite score represents all three of the basic attributional style characteristics.

Some researchers have found that a person's cognitive style precedes depression. For example, they have found that a depressive attributional style predicts which people develop the most depressive symptoms after being in prison and after receiving disappointing grades in college (Metalsky, Abramson, Seligman, Semmel, and Peterson, 1982; Peterson and Seligman, 1984). But other researchers believe that depression precedes and causes the attributional style (Brewin, 1985). In fact, the relation between them may be reciprocal: explanatory style may predispose a person to depression, and depression may, in turn, increase a depressive explanatory style (Nolen-Hoeksema et al., 1986).

People probably learn an attributional style from their parents. For example, explanatory styles and levels of depression were correlated in one group of children and their mothers (Seligman et al., 1984). Moreover, data on the origins of explanatory style suggest a reason that females suffer from depression more than males. Third-grade teachers in one study criticized boys and girls differently (Dweck and Licht, 1980). Whereas boys were criticized for specific misdeeds—"Don't talk so loud while I'm trying to teach."—girls were criticized for internal, global, and stable characteristics—"You're so lazy!" "Can't you ever stop talking?"

MULTIPLE CAUSES OF DEPRESSION   Although there is growing evidence that attributional style is related to depression, it alone does not cause depression. It probably is only one factor in a complex sequence of events that leads to depression.

Other factors implicated in depression are heredity, stress, and interpersonal relations or social support. Stress and social support are implicated in research showing that women are most likely to become depressed before or after giving birth if their lives are stressful (their baby has health problems, they cannot find good child care) *and* if they receive little support from their spouses (O'Hara, 1986). Research also suggests that people who are depressed respond to stress differently from those who are not depressed. The depressed feel as though they have more at stake when they are under stress; they feel more vulnerable. In addition, they tend to become more hostile under stress (Folkman and Lazarus, 1986).

Because depressed people's sadness or hostility often make those around them feel bad, they may become increasingly isolated, and their personal relationships increasingly strained (Coyne, 1976, 1985). As their isolation increases, their negative mood worsens—a vicious circle.

Finally, there is evidence that biological factors can influence the development of depression. First, there is strong evidence that bipolar depression has a genetic influence (Allen, 1976) and there is growing evidence that major depression has as well (Tongersen, 1986). Research also shows that deficits of neurotransmitters (e.g., norepinephrine) may cause depression. However, evidence suggests that the relationship between neurotransmitter levels and depression is complex. There appear to be different types of depression, and these different types are associated with different types of neurotransmitter abnormalities (excesses or deficits; Willner, 1985).

In sum, depression may not be a single "disease" or disorder. Rather, depression is a group of symptoms (sadness, insomnia) that can be triggered by different factors, or a combination of different factors: death of a loved one, job stress, giving birth, and so on. Moreover, people apparently differ with respect to susceptibility to depression. Some people have a cognitive diathesis for depression—they attribute bad events to internal, stable, global causes, while others have a genetic diathesis. These insights into the nature of depression are important because, as you will see in Chapter 15, some have led to new effective treatments for depression (e.g., cognitive therapy).

Anxiety Disorders

Anxiety disorders have great historical importance, because it was from working with people suffering from anxiety that Freud arrived at his revolutionary ideas about the nature of psychopathology. Anxiety disorders are also of great importance because they, like depression, are so widespread. Although clinicians do not agree whether anxiety disorders are variants of a single, basic disorder, they do agree that anxiety, which comes from an Old French word for painful, choking sensation (*anguisse*), is made up of both emotional suffering and accompanying physical sensations (see Table 13-12).

Anxious people may report feeling worry, tension, or dread. They usually report feeling fearful and look fearful, although they may not be aware of the source of their fear. Anxious people usually are acutely aware of their heightened state of physical arousal—their sweating,

TABLE 13-12   SIGNS AND SYMPTOMS OF ANXIETY

  I. Physical Signs
    1. rapid breathing
    2. sweating
    3. trembling, shaky voice
    4. pacing, repetitive purposeless movements
 II. Physical Symptoms (Complaints)
    1. difficulty breathing
    2. a choking sensation
    3. a racing heart
    4. frequent urination
    5. hot and cold flashes
    6. dizziness
    7. faintness
    8. chest pains
    9. gastrointestinal complaints (e.g., upset stomach)
III. Cognitive and Affective Complaints
    1. constant worry—inability to relax
    2. a lack of confidence
    3. extreme attentiveness—scanning the environment
    4. feelings of a lack of control

Source: After *Diagnostic and Statistical Manual of Mental Disorders* (3rd Edition, IIIR).

tremulousness, and pounding heart—and they feel unable to quiet their body. Indeed, the feeling of loss of control is a hallmark of anxiety.

According to DSM-IIIR, there are seven major types of anxiety disorders: panic disorders, agoraphobia, obsessive-compulsive disorder, generalized anxiety disorder, social phobia, simple phobia, and post-traumatic stress disorder. In the following sections, we will concentrate on all but post-traumatic stress disorder.

INCIDENCE AND COURSE Research suggests that generalized anxiety disorder, an anxiety state, is the most common anxiety disorder. Next in incidence are phobias and then panic disorder, another anxiety state. Women are diagnosed for anxiety disorder about three times more often than men (Hallam, 1985).

Anxiety disorders may be quite widespread, but because they are often not as painful, disturbing, or debilitating as affective disorders or schizophrenia, people with anxiety disorders are less likely to seek or to be referred for psychological treatment. "Anxiety" was found in two separate studies to be the fifth most common diagnosis made by general practitioners in the United States (Hallam, 1985). It is estimated that about 4 to 5 percent of the U.S. population is treated for anxiety disorders each year (Schweitzer and Adams, 1979). But because many people with anxiety disorders avoid psychological or psychiatric help, indirect measures may give a more accurate reflection of these disorders. For example, over 70 million prescriptions were written for just two of the many minor tranquilizers like Valium in the United States in 1972 (Rickels, 1979). One in every 10 men and 1 in every 5 women in Britain get tranquilizer (benzodiazepine) prescriptions in the course of a single year (Lader, 1981). These figures suggest that anxiety is a very common problem.

Whereas depression is likely to improve spontaneously with the passage of time, anxiety disorders may persist for years. Most anxiety disorders appear when people are in their late teens to early 20s and may persist until they are over 50 (Goodwin and Guze, 1979). In one survey people suffered from a phobia (agoraphobia, the fear of open spaces) for an average of 13 years (Marks and Herst, 1970). In another survey of people diagnosed between 1937 and 1940, only 1 of 19 was completely free of phobic symptoms 20 years after diagnosis (Errera and Coleman, 1963). Generalized anxiety disorder may last just as long (Hoges, Clancy, Hoenk, and Slymen, 1980).

PHOBIC DISORDERS **Phobic disorders** fall into three major subtypes: agoraphobia, social phobia, and simple phobia. All are characterized by high levels of anxiety. As you have seen in other chapters, the defining feature of a phobia is an extreme and irrational fear of a particular object, activity, or situation. The fear leads a person to avoid or flee from the feared object or activity. The phobic individual realizes that the fear is irrational but feels powerless to control or reduce the fear.

In **agoraphobia** (from the Greek meaning "fear of the marketplace"), people fear being in situations in which they feel vulnerable. Usually, agoraphobics fear leaving the house, being out-of-doors, being alone, or

A 28-year-old British woman who suffered from agoraphobia reported the following to her psychologist. Her words paint a portrait of the panic and other symptoms often associated with this form of anxiety disorder

The first day it hit me, really hit me, was the day I took my youngest child to the nursery. She was just 3, and when I dropped her off I thought "Oh God, at last I'm on my own; the last one's at school." So I set off for the shops, and I had not got very far, about a hundred yards up the road, when I started to feel sort of dizzy. I thought "What's happening?" You know, I always had the fear of a heart attack and experienced palpitations before, indoors and outdoors, but nothing to the extent of this. So I thought I'd keep walking and I'd be all right. I carried on walking but the further I got, the worse it got; my legs started to go; I felt in every part of me there was something wrong; I couldn't breathe; I was constantly swallowing; my throat seemed to close up and I felt like screaming out "Somebody help." . . . There was a small kiosk place there that sold tea, so I thought I'd have a cup of tea and see how I felt. I started to drink the tea but I couldn't swallow it. I was absolutely panic-stricken. I had tremors in my arms and legs.

I used to go short distances out of the house, but after getting these attacks in the shops I used to get them in the post office. Supermarkets used to terrify me. I'd go in like a bull in a china shop, grab everything off the shelves, things sometimes I didn't even need, and I'd get to the queue [line]; and if there were a couple of people standing there I used to drop the basket and just go out. I couldn't even wait those few minutes. I was, I was all right as long as I was rushing around—I wasn't looking at anything you know—just going mad picking up anything. As soon as I got outside I thought "Thank God that's over." But if I had to wait I'd feel dizzy, I thought I was going to be sick, I couldn't breathe and my chest, well, it seemed everyone could hear it. The palpitations made me think it was my heart.

I didn't think I was completely agoraphobic because I understood agoraphobics to be entirely housebound. I'd never actually talked to this relative in the family who's been housebound for 10 years because it's a disease you cannot talk about. I thought these fears about dying were not agoraphobia because I used to get attacks indoors. Also, I couldn't go in a lift [elevator], and that's claustrophobia. I thought you couldn't have the two, agoraphobia and claustrophobia, because you'd be in such a turmoil, which I was. Anyway, my husband was trying to jolt me, which didn't help because it made me draw back more. He was trying these drastic steps, and he'd not got the knowledge anyway. He never sort of sympathized with me. More often than not I did try for his sake and the kids' sake— get myself all built up and say "Today is the day I'm going out." And I'd get to the door—and then go back and make myself a cup of tea, still with my coat on. Then I'd try again, come back, and think "I just can't do it" and take my coat off. I must have put my coat on four or five times. This was going on for over 18 months when this other doctor said I should see a psychiatrist.

Anxiety: Psychological Perspectives on Panic and Agoraphobia, R. S. Hallam (1985).

having their movement restricted in any way (for example, waiting in line). Agoraphobia often is associated with panic attacks (see Box 13-3).

In **social phobias**, the individual is very afraid of being evaluated or scrutinized by others. People may be afraid of public speaking, of performing in public, or of using public restrooms. In **simple phobias**, people fear specific objects such as snakes, spiders, heights (*acrophobia*), or enclosed spaces (*claustrophobia;* see Figure 13-12).

Although simple phobias are probably the most common of all phobias, people with agoraphobia tend to seek treatment more often, because agoraphobia tends to create greater disruption in its victims' lives. People who are afraid of heights may be somewhat embarrassed and inconvenienced over their unwillingness to fly or to stand at the top of buildings, but these events are not central in the lives of most people.

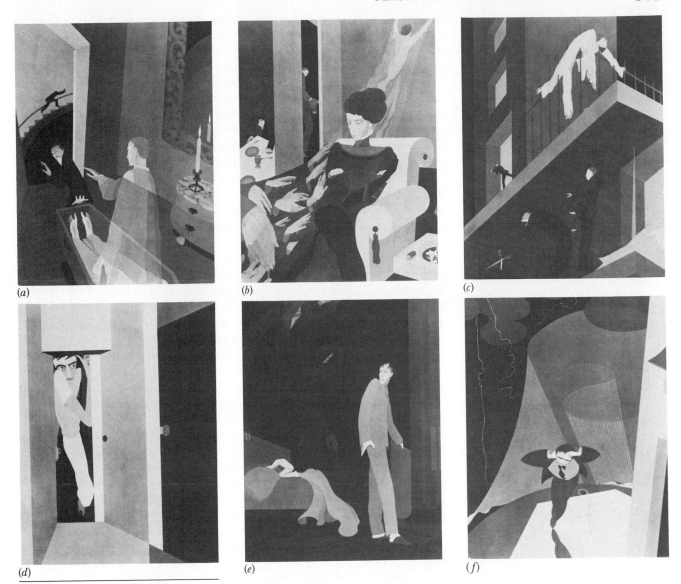

(a) *(b)* *(c)*

(d) *(e)* *(f)*

FIGURE 13-12   PHOBIAS.
Artist John Vassos's depictions
of different types of phobias:
(a) Necrophobia—fear of the dead.
(b) Mysophobia—fear of dirt
and contamination. (c) Aichmophobia—
fear of sharp, pointed objects.
(d) Claustrophobia—the fear of small,
enclosed spaces. (e) Hypnophobia—fear
of sleep. (f) Astrophobia—fear of storms.

Someone who fears going outside may remain housebound for years, and that is a crippling state of existence.

All phobias have in common the fact that their sufferers experience high levels of anxiety. It may be sporadic as in the case of simple phobias, or fairly constant in cases of agoraphobia. Consistent with this, agoraphobia disrupts life much more than simple phobias. Finally, simple phobias are much more easily treated (see Chapter 15).

ANXIETY STATES   The second major type of anxiety disorder is **anxiety states**, comprising panic disorder, generalized anxiety disorder, and obsessive-compulsive disorder. The prominent features of **panic disorder** are panic or anxiety attacks, isolated bouts of extreme anxiety, usually lasting minutes, but sometimes hours. These attacks are accompanied by characteristic thoughts and fears: "I'm going crazy!" "I'm dying!" "I'm losing control!" In addition to these frightening thoughts, people having a panic attack experience the physical symptoms of extreme anxiety such as racing heart, a fainting sensation, tremors, and nausea. These physical symptoms confirm victims' worst fears and convince them that they are going crazy, dying, or both. Panic attacks may be triggered by particular activities—driving, flying—or may occur seemingly out of nowhere.

In **obsessive-compulsive disorder** a person is plagued by recurrent thoughts or obsessions. People may obsess about violence, about dirt, germs, or disease, or about having done something wrong. A woman might fear that she has forgotten to turn off a burner on the stove. Obsessions tend to "pop" into someone's thoughts, persist, and to grow stronger until the person engages in some act, a *compulsion*, that somehow reduces the obsessional thoughts. A compulsion may be related to obsessions in perfectly rational ways. For instance, the person who obsesses about germs develops a handwashing compulsion. The person who worries that someone is under her bed at night develops a *checking* ritual in which she looks under her bed before going to sleep. But compulsions also may be linked to an obsession in a magical way. For example, one young woman who was a client of one of us had an obsessive fear of getting into a traffic accident. Whenever she entered a car, she began to multiply by sevens as a way to ward off the threat of an accident.

Everyone may engage in compulsive behavior at one time or another. But the true obsessive-compulsive is distinguished by the frequency of obsessional thoughts and the resulting compulsions. A person who obsesses about germs may wash her hands 100 times per day, sometimes with caustic cleansers like bleach. Some checkers search under their beds countless times every night, until they fall asleep from exhaustion. Compulsive behavior does not provide any long-lasting relief for the individual, and it is not pleasurable. It merely provides temporary relief from the nagging doubts that plague them.

The person with **generalized anxiety disorder** suffers from anxiety that has lasted for at least a month. The anxiety makes the person feel tense and worried, makes him or her perpetually monitor the environment—as if searching for danger, and he or she displays many of the physical symptoms associated with anxiety and panic attacks.

The various anxiety states and phobias differ in many ways. The person with a simple phobia fears only one type of object and otherwise seems quite normal. The person with generalized anxiety disorder fears no particular object greatly, yet seems to fear everything. What is more, there is evidence that the different types of anxiety disorders respond to different drugs (Andreasen, 1984). Panic disorder responds to antidepressants (such as imipramine); other anxiety disorders respond to antianxiety agents (such as Valium). Despite these differences panic, obsessive-compulsive, generalized anxiety, and phobic disorders all are characterized by anxiety.

CAUSES OF ANXIETY DISORDERS   In previous chapters, you read about learning theories of the causes of anxiety disorders. In Chapter 6, you read about how fears and phobias might develop through *observational* learning and about how biological *preparedness* may contribute to the learning of phobias. In Chapter 11, you read about how anxiety might be produced by activation of the Behavioral Inhibition System (Gray, 1982). Here we examine two other explanations of anxiety disorders: the psychoanalytic and biological approaches.

Psychoanalytic Theory   Freud was struck by one of the cardinal features of anxiety disorders—their irrationality. After all, there is no apparently rational reason for the phobic person to flee from an earthworm. There is no reason for the obsessive-compulsive person to wash his hands repeatedly. If humans are intelligent, rational creatures, what accounts for this victory of irrationality over rationality?

Freud argued that as humans evolved to be intelligent and rational, they maintained many *instincts* of more primitive species (see Chapter 10). According to Freud, these powerful instincts had to be maintained, because they motivated behavior responsible for survival: eating, drinking, sex, and aggression. But human societies forbid people from satisfying their instinctual needs whenever they arise. People learn that they cannot engage in sexual activity or kill whenever they wish, or they will be censured, isolated, or punished. This early experience with punishment makes a profound impression, and most people become fearful of breaking social codes or of violating taboos. Freud believed that instinctual behaviors were fueled by psychic energy that he called **libido**. This energy produces a *drive* to engage in instinctive behaviors, and this energy is expended or released whenever the instinctive behavior occurs. However, if instinctive behaviors are blocked and do not occur, this produces a buildup of libido. The result is that the individual appears highly energized due to the buildup of instinctual energies (the person may pace, wring his hands, appear nervous). According to Freud, the fright of the anxious person comes from one of two sources (Freud, 1926). It comes from an unconscious fear of punishment or from an unconscious fear that the instinctual drive may be so strong as to overwhelm one's rational self (the ego).

Freud suggested that the objects of phobias symbolize instinctive desires, and because the objects stimulate prohibited instinctive desires, they elicit fear. For Freud, at the heart of every phobia or obsessive fear lies a wish—a desire. For the hand-washing obsessive, the instinctive desire might be sexual. If as a child, someone learned that sex was taboo or dirty, the appropriate "cure" is to wash. For the person with a snake phobia, sexual desire may be aroused because the snake represents a penis to the unconscious mind. The phobic person fears the snake, not because the snake itself is so frightening, but because the snake elicits a powerful instinctive desire that the person knows is taboo. We all learn such taboos as children, and we have instinctive desires to violate these taboos. But people who are anxious have learned an especially strong fear and have not learned to satisfy their instinctual needs well *without* violating a social norm. The anxious person is trapped in conflict.

Freud's theory of the development of anxiety disorders still influences the way many psychologists think about anxiety disorders. The concepts of unconscious motivation and the stress on early learning remain highly influential today. But Freud's ideas about the importance of instincts are now regarded as too simplistic or just incorrect. Psychologists now know that motivations other than those for food, sex, and aggression influence behavior (see Chapter 10).

Object Relations It was in recognition of the importance of social needs—rather than basic biological needs—that modern psychoanalytic theorists have adopted a different view of anxiety. Such **object-relations** theorists as Heinz Kohut and Otto Kernberg (Eagle, 1984), believe that a crucial developmental milestone is a child's development of a sense of self. They believe that a secure sense of self is crucial to an individual's psychological well-being and to the ability to adapt to new or threatening situations. (The self is similar to Freud's concept of ego and directs expenditures of instinctual energy—as does the ego—but also constitutes the core of an individual's identity. Without a secure sense of self, the individual does not exist psychologically as a separate person.)

Object-relations theorists believe that anxiety arises from experiences in which the *self* is found lacking or wanting. For example, the anxious person may unconsciously fear being engulfed by someone else. Thus, a young woman may be anxious because her fragile sense of self is threatened by her husband, a powerful individual who makes her feel inadequate. Yet her very sense of inadequacy attracts her to her husband, whom she believes will nurture and protect her.

Object-relations theorists believe that people develop an insecure sense of self during early childhood, when their parents do not give them love and a feeling of security or the encouragement to explore and become independent. Although little experimental research has been done to test object-relations theory, it receives indirect support from research (reviewed in Chapter 11) such as that in which Harry Harlow found that young monkeys reared without adequate attention from the parents grew up to be fearful, disturbed adults and that in which Mary Ainsworth found that mothers who were not nurturant tended to have dependent children (Ainsworth, Bell, and Stayton, 1971). The views of analytic and object-relations theorists have had an unsurpassed impact on the practice of psychotherapy with anxiety disorders. Yet, even as Freud himself predicted, we are now beginning to understand the biology of anxiety states, and this will no doubt influence future treatment approaches.

Biological Theory In Chapter 10 we reviewed one biopsychological model of anxiety; Gray's Behavioral Inhibition System model in which anxiety has been traced to the septal-hippocampal region of the brain. Now we will briefly review evidence that supports a biological model of one type of anxiety disorder: panic. In the 1940s, it was noted that strenuous exercise sometimes causes panic attacks. Because exercise increases the lactic acid in the blood, it was suggested that lactic acid somehow triggers panic reactions. Direct evidence of this was obtained when researchers (Pitts and McClure, 1967) found that lactate injections produced immediate panic reactions in people with a history of panic disorder but had no effect on others. Although the exact mechanism through which lactic acid produces panic is unknown, recent evidence suggests that it may produce panic by increasing brain levels of carbon dioxide (Liebowitz et al., 1985). Indeed, if patients with panic disorder breathe carbon dioxide, it reliably causes panic. This may be why soldiers sometimes panic when wearing gas masks. The masks force them to rebreathe their carbon dioxide. Carbon dioxide may stimulate brainstem chemical receptors or a nucleus in the brain called the **locus ceruleus** (blue place). The chemoreceptors act as sensors that detect changes in blood chemicals. Panic may be a natural reaction when the brain detects that the body is receiving too much carbon dioxide and too little oxygen, in essence, that the person is suffocating! According to this explanation, people with panic disorder have more sensitive chemoreceptors than normal individuals.

The locus ceruleus may be involved in the production of other anxiety symptoms. If the locus ceruleus is stimulated artificially, animals show evidence of great fear and distress. There is now evidence that carbon dioxide stimulates the locus ceruleus (Elam, Yoa, Thoren, and Svensson, 1981). The drug clonidine suppresses locus ceruleus activity and blocks panic attacks (Liebowitz, Fyer, McGrath, and Klein, 1981). People who have panic attacks are more anxious and aroused than other individuals even *before* their panic attacks (Liebowitz et al., 1985). Perhaps their high levels of anxiety make the locus ceruleus especially sensitive to increases in carbon dioxide.

As was the case with schizophrenia and affective disorders, psychologists have studied anxiety disorders from a variety of perspectives—learning theory, psychoanalytic, and biological. Psychoanalytic theories hold that anxiety can be traced to strong, instinctive motivations of which we are often unaware. These motivations elicit fear (anxiety) because people fear punishment for acting on these motivations and they also fear that these motivations will gain control over their rational selves (egos). In Chapter 6 we described the learning theory explanation of phobias—that phobias arise from early traumatic experiences with the feared object, or through observation of others who display fear of an object. Moreover, many learning theorists believe that humans are genetically prepared to acquire fears of phobic objects (Chapter 6). Finally, researchers have found that anxiety states may be due to extreme sensitivity of physiological systems that are intended to signal when a person is in physical danger.

Other Mental Disorders

Humans are heir to many other mental disorders besides those of schizophrenia, affective, and anxiety disorders. You already have read about substance-abuse disorders (in Chapter 5) and about psychosexual and eating disorders (in Chapter 10).

SOMATOFORM DISORDER   Some people suffer from somatoform disorders, in which they develop symptoms that primarily involve complaints about their physical health. In one type of somatoform disorder, **somatization disorder**, people complain about back pain, heart palpitations, weakness or fatigue, breathing problems, and menstrual complaints. Because people with this disorder show no signs of any physical disease, it is thought that their physical symptoms have a primarily psychological origin. In general, all somatoform disorders involve many complaints about physical health in the absence of any physical lesion or abnormality.

ORGANIC MENTAL DISORDERS These are syndromes of disturbed cognitive functioning and behavior, the causes of which can be traced to diseases that cause damage to the brain. One organic mental disorder is **dementia**, a decline in mental status or abilities. Dementia usually occurs in people older than 50 or 60 years of age, and its prominent symptoms are memory problems, an inability to deal with abstract concepts, problems in recognizing familiar objects or people, and, eventually, extreme changes in personality. The most common cause of dementia is **Alzheimer's disease**, which strikes 10 to 15 percent of the population over age 65 (Andreasen, 1984). Its effects are so devastating that it and related disorders account for more than half of all patients in nursing homes and municipal hospitals (Lechtenberg, 1982). Researchers recently have found that Alzheimer's disease is transmitted genetically in some cases, and in other cases may be the result of genetic and environmental interaction (St. George-Hyslop et al., 1987). Moreover, researchers have found that Alzheimer's disease is associated with the deposition of a protein, an *amyloid* protein, in the brain (see Figure 13-13). It turns out that the gene that controls the production of this protein is located on chromosome 21 (Goldgaber, Lerman, McBride, Saffiotti, and Gujdusek, 1987) and this is indeed the location of the genetic defect in persons who develop familial Alzheimer's disease (St. George-Hyslop et al., 1987).

FIGURE 13-13 ALZHEIMER'S DISEASE: ABNORMAL PROTEIN DEPOSITS.
(a) *Shows an amyloid plaque of protein in brain neurons (arrow) and near a blood vessel in the cortex (asterisk) found in a person with Alzheimer's disease.*
(b) *Amyloid deposit in blood vessels surrounding the brain of a person with Alzheimer's disease. (From Selkoe, Bell, Podlisny, Price, and Cork, 1987.)*

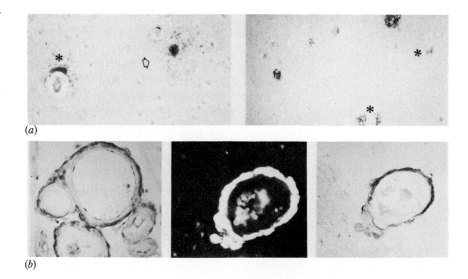

FIGURE 13-14   AUTISM.
Autistic children tend to be profoundly solitary.

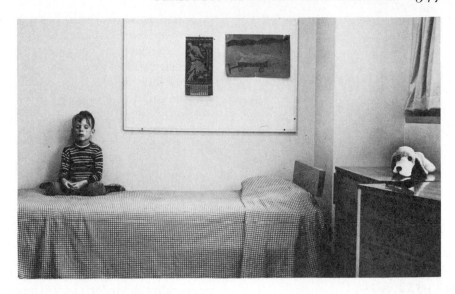

DEVELOPMENTAL DISORDERS   Some mental disorders first become evident in infancy, childhood, or adolescence. Disorders in this category include stereotyped movement disorders such as **Tourette's tic syndrome** and *pervasive developmental disorders* such as **infantile autism**. In Tourette's syndrome, a child is beset by involuntary motor and vocal tics. For example, the child may show recurrent jerking movements of the hands or face accompanied by odd staccato vocalizations: barks, expletives, shouts. Infantile *autism* is a devastating chronic disorder that is diagnosed in infancy or early childhood. The autistic child withdraws into a profound aloneness (see Figure 13-14). His or her ability to speak or communicate is severely impaired, and some autistic children show cognitive and perceptual deficits—hallucinations and delusional thinking—similar to those shown by schizophrenics. Most autistic children also are mentally retarded. One of the most pervasive of the disorders of infancy, childhood, or adolescence is **mental retardation**. Although there are many different kinds of mental retardation, all are characterized by subnormal intelligence and deficient adaptive behavior. Adaptive behavior is behavior that lets people live independently and productively. People who are mentally retarded may not be able to grasp important concepts—such as of time or money—or skills—work, grooming, and shopping—that are necessary for independent lives. People who are mildly mentally retarded (IQ 50–70) can live fairly independently and may be able to learn to support themselves. The severely or profoundly retarded cannot live independently. Many have such profound intellectual and physical problems that they require lifetime care.

One of the most common forms of retardation is **Down syndrome**, a genetic syndrome that results in retardation accompanied by physical abnormalities like a short, stocky stature, flattened nose, heart malformation, and eventually symptoms resembling Alzheimer's disease. Generally, people with Down syndrome have only moderate to mild retardation, and most can learn basic academic skills. Researchers know that Down syndrome is caused by the inheritance of an extra (third) twenty-first chromosome. (The same chromosome that has been implicated in inherited cases of Alzheimer's disease.) Other types of mental retardation are inherited through different genetic and biological mechanisms. But the cause of most cases of mental retardation (about 75 percent) is unknown. Some of these cases are apparently caused by subtle disease or brain damage, some by social and educational deprivation (Zigler and Seitz, 1985).

PERSONALITY DISORDERS   *Personality disorders* are lifelong personality styles or dispositions that are painful or unpleasant either for the sufferer or for those around him or her. They tend not to occur in bouts or to be as disabling as other mental disorders. For these reasons, personality disorders are listed separately in DSM (see Axis 2 in Table 13-1).

Each personality disorder is associated with a prominent personality style that may last for a person's entire lifetime. People with **paranoid personality disorder** may be perpetually suspicious and distrustful but not have the hallucinations, delusional thinking, or bizarre speech of the (psychotic) paranoid schizophrenic. People with **schizoid personality disorder** are cold, aloof, and find it extremely difficult to establish or maintain friendships. People with **histrionic personality disorder** behave dramatically and have outbursts that seem designed to capture attention. Their personal relationships are stormy because they tend to act selfishly but also crave affection and approval.

A sometimes dramatic personality disorder is **antisocial personality disorder** (**psychopathy**). Most psychopaths are males and from childhood violate social, legal, or moral rules (see Table 13-13). As adults, people with this disorder tend to be chronic liars, poor workers, and poor parents and to engage in unusual and promiscuous sexual activities. They generally fail to plan ahead, are impulsive, commit many illegal acts (often poorly planned—as if the psychopath were not worried about apprehension), and take drugs and alcohol. A pervasive feature of psychopathy is the inability to develop close relationships with others, relationships marked by loyalty and trust. One man first recognized his own psychopathic tendencies:

> *I can remember the first time in my life when I began to suspect I was a little different from most people. When I was in high school my best friend got leukemia and died and I went to his funeral. Everybody else was crying and feeling sorry for themselves and as they were praying to get him into heaven I suddenly realized that I wasn't feeling anything at all. He was a nice guy, but what the hell. That night I thought about it some more and found that I wouldn't miss my mother and father if they died and that I wasn't too nuts about my brothers and sisters for that matter. I figured there wasn't anybody I really cared for but, then, I didn't need any of them anyway so I rolled over and went to sleep.*
>
> *(McNeil, 1967; in Davison and Neale, 1982, p. 277)*

TABLE 13-13 ANTISOCIAL PERSONALITY DISORDER

1. Truancy
2. Expulsion or suspension from school
3. Arrests or referral to juvenile court
4. Running away from home
5. Persistent lying
6. Repeated sexual intercourse in casual relationships
7. Repeated drunkenness or substance abuse
8. Thefts
9. Vandalism
10. Poor grades relative to intelligence
11. Chronic violations of home or school rules
12. Initiation of fights

Source: Diagnostic and Statistical Manual of Mental Disorders (3rd Edition, IIIR).
Note: According to DSM-IIIR, to be diagnosed as an antisocial personality a person must have a history of three or more of the behaviors listed above.

There is evidence that both genetic and environmental influences contribute to psychopathy. Adoption studies have shown that the rate of criminality and psychopathy is highest in children when *both* the child's biological and adoptive fathers had criminal or psychopathic histories (Hutchings and Mednick, 1977; Schulsinger, 1977). Psychopaths also seem to react to punishment in an unusual manner. Whereas most people respond to punishment by slowing down their behavior and inspecting their environments, psychopaths actually speed up their behavior and seem not to attend to the punishment or what led up to it (Gorenstein and Newman, 1980; Nichols and Newman, 1985). This tendency may explain why psychopaths don't seem to learn from their mistakes.

We have reviewed a great many mental disorders in this chapter ranging from anxiety disorders to Alzheimer's disease. These disorders differ in many respects; for some like schizophrenia, bipolar affective disorder, and Alzheimer's disease there is a genetic predisposition, whereas for others like phobia there is relatively little evidence of a genetic influence. Some disorders may occur in short episodes like a bout of depression or a brief psychotic reaction, while others can be chronic, lasting many years—schizophrenia, generalized anxiety disorders, and antisocial personality disorders. Despite such differences these disorders all have in common the fact that they disrupt psychological functioning—personality and cognition. They also have in common the fact that they are gradually yielding up secrets about their causes. We now know that schizophrenia can be related to reduced size of the cerebral cortex, that a particular attributional pattern predisposes people to depression, and that some cases of Alzheimer's disease are linked to a genetic abnormality of chromosome 21. As you shall see in Chapter 15, some of these recent discoveries have led to new, effective treatments.

SUMMARY

Historically, behavior that was frightening and repugnant and violated social norms was considered abnormal. The discovery that general paresis was caused by syphilis inspired the view that abnormality was caused by physical disease. The work of Charcot and Freud suggested that psychopathology was influenced by social and environmental factors.

Kraeplin proposed the first classification scheme for mental disorders. In DSM-IIIR, the most recent classification system, disorders are classified by their symptoms, course and prognosis, response to treatment, and genetic origins.

Most mental disorders are characterized by discomfort and suffering, impairment of functioning, a sense of loss of control, erratic behavior, and symptoms and signs that are behavioral and phenomenological, not physical.

SCHIZOPHRENIA

1. *Incidence and Course.* Schizophrenia is a rare but potentially devastating illness characterized by thought disorder, delusions, perceptual and attentional deficits, and disturbed emotions. Schizophreniform illness is relatively short-lived; schizophrenia can last a lifetime.
2. *Description.* Schizophrenia has been divided into subtypes on the bases of symptoms and course. One traditional classification lists disorganized, catatonic, paranoid, and undifferentiated types. A recent classification divides schizophrenia into positive and negative types; the former is characterized by hallucinations, delusions, and emotionality, the latter by flat affect, withdrawal, and muteness.
3. *Etiology.* Genetic inheritance can predispose an individual to schizophrenia, but environmental factors also influence schizophrenia. One theory is that expressed emotion—communication patterns that are hostile, critical, and overinvolved—increases the risk of schizophrenia. Diathesis–stress theories hold that schizophrenia occurs when people with a preexisting psychological or genetic predisposition for schizophrenia encounter an environmental stressor.

AFFECTIVE DISORDERS

There are two major types of affective disorders: major depression and bipolar disorder. Major depression is characterized by major depressive episodes, bipolar disorder by manic episodes and possibly by depressive episodes.

1. *Incidence and Course.* Twenty percent of people may become depressed in their lives; bipolar disorder affects only about 1 percent of the population. Most depressive episodes are short, but about 25 percent last a year or longer.
2. *Description.* Major depression is characterized by sadness, social withdrawal, sleep disturbances, loss of appetite, and feelings of hopelessness. The manic seems energized, euphoric, and impetuous and often requires little sleep.
3. *Etiology.* Freudian theory emphasizes that real or symbolic loss triggers depression. Behaviorists emphasize loss of reinforcement. The learned helplessness theory holds that an attributional style in which bad events are attributed to internal, stable, and global causes predisposes people to depression. Bipolar disorder is influenced by genetic inheritance.

ANXIETY DISORDERS

Anxiety disorders are characterized by anxiety, emotional discomfort similar to fear, and characteristic physical sensations: pounding heart, tremulousness, dizziness, and so on.

1. *Incidence and Course.* Anxiety disorders are fairly common. Generalized anxiety disorder is the most common, followed by phobia and panic disorder. Anxiety disorders tend to be long-lasting—some persist for many years.
2. *Description.* Phobic disorders involve irrational fears. Panic disorder is characterized by anxiety attacks. Obsessive-compulsive disorder is characterized by irrational fears coupled with magical rituals to counter the fears. In generalized anxiety disorder, a person suffers from chronic anxiety.
3. *Etiology.* Freudian theory holds that anxiety is triggered by unconscious fear of punishment or a fear that instinctual forces may become so strong as to overwhelm the ego. Object-relations theory holds that anxiety is the result of an insecure sense of self. Panic disorder has been explained biochemically, as, for example, a response to elevated carbon dioxide levels in the brain.

OTHER MENTAL DISORDERS

Other mental disorders include addictive disorders, eating disorders, psychosexual disorders, somatoform disorders such as somatization disorder, organic mental disorders such as Alzheimer's disease, developmental disorders such as mental retardation, and personality disorders such as antisocial personality.

FURTHER READINGS

An outstanding general review of psychopathology can be found in *Abnormal Psychology* by Davison and Neale (1985). A review from a psychiatric-medical perspective is Goodwin and Guze's *Psychiatric Diagnosis* (1979). *The Broken Brain* by Andreasen (1984) is a readable review of the biological evidence for the causes and treatment of major mental disorders.

Contemporary Directions in Psychopathology, edited by Millon and Klerman (1986), contains several excellent, challenging chapters on the history and conceptual bases of the classification of mental disorders.

Recommended work on specific mental disorders include Neale and Oltmann's *Schizophrenia* (1980). Willner's *Depressions; A Psychobiological Synthesis* (1985) is thorough and challenging. Vaillant's *The Natural History of Alcoholism* (1983) is a valuable compendium. Eagle's *Recent Developments in Psychoanalysis: A Critical Evaluation* (1984) presents object-relations theory in a clear and interesting manner.

Finally, Kaplan's *The Inner World of Mental Illness* (1964) contains writings of people suffering from mental disorders, and Gilman's *Seeing the Insane* (1982) presents photographs and artwork depicting people considered "insane" throughout history.

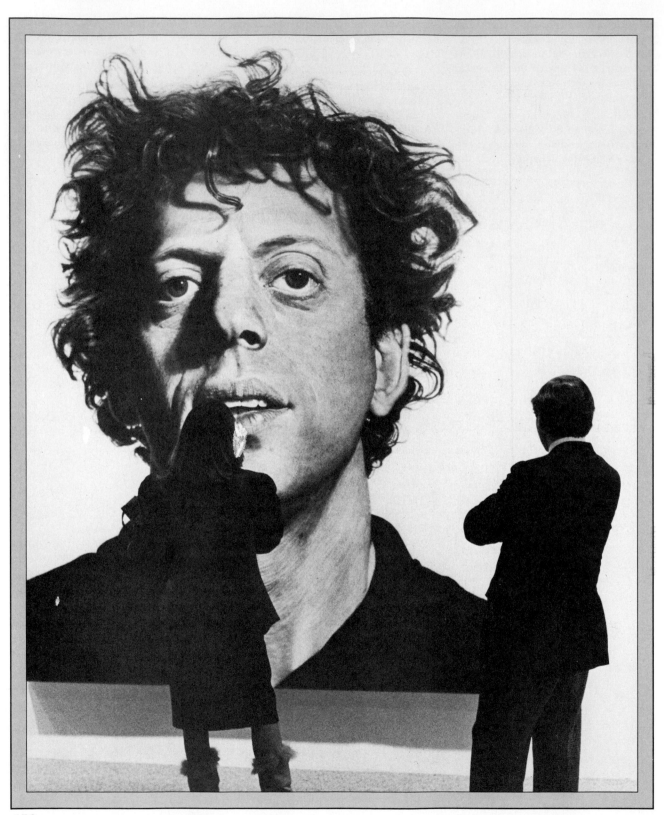

14

ASSESSMENT OF PERSONALITY, BEHAVIOR, AND INTELLIGENCE

A girl meets a boy at a small party at the beach. They spend all day together, and at the end of the day, he asks if he can drive her home. She says yes. Why has she accepted his offer? A man takes his car into a repair shop. He gets an estimate of the cost of repairs from the young shop manager, who also describes how his shop would perform the repair work. But the man decides to take his car to a different repair shop, even though the other shop gave him a higher estimate. Why does he take his business elsewhere? A mother is asked whether she will allow her young son to go on a camping trip with a man and his son who recently moved into the neighborhood. After several meetings with the neighbor, she agrees, and her son goes on the trip. Why does she agree?

In each situation described here, a person made an *interpersonal assessment* that played a major role in his or her decision. The girl at the beach concluded that the boy was attractive and trustworthy. The man needing automobile repairs decided that the shop manager was untrustworthy or incompetent. The mother decided that her neighbor was responsible and had good intentions. Each one of us makes assessments like these every day. Whom can we trust? Who is responsible? Who will be an excellent worker? We have to appraise others' psychological attributes, their intellectual, personality, and emotional characteristics.

The general goals of formal, psychological assessment are similar to those of informal, interpersonal assessment. People try to assess others psychologically to make sound decisions. But in formal psychological assessment, psychologists use specialized procedures and instruments to gather data and make decisions about people.

THE GOALS OF ASSESSMENT

Psychologists assess people to identify appropriate treatments, to establish their capabilities—their ability to cope with emotional stress, for example—to discover personality characteristics, and to predict behavior, such as the course of a problem or illness. In keeping with these goals, a psychologist assessing a psychologically disturbed person often first must arrive at a diagnosis, because a diagnosis usually suggests the best treatment, the course of a problem, and so on.

Both practical and social factors shape the particular goals of the assessor. Practical factors include the needs of the agency or individual for whom the assessor works. Some information is important to society as a whole (Wade and Baker, 1977). For example, to meet a practical need during World War II, the U.S. Office of Strategic Service (OSS) set out to identify people who could conduct espionage, sabotage, and subversion. The OSS staff used psychological tests, interviews, and behavioral tests (see Table 14-1) to identify people with the necessary qualifications (see Table 14-2). Another goal of assessment that is important to society is predicting who will commit suicide. Suicide seems so terrible and wasteful to society that psychologists often try to gauge who is at risk for suicide. Unfortunately, psychologists have not yet discovered an accurate means for doing so.

TABLE 14-1 PORTION OF OSS PLAN

Orientation Period
Briefing in Washington, D.C.
Arrival and orientation at Station S
Dinner
Otis Test of Mental Ability, sentence completion test, health questionnaire, work conditions survey, vocabulary test, personal history form
Belongings test
First Day
Breakfast
Instructions for terrain test
The Brook
The Wall
Construction; postconstruction interview
Personal history interview (X condition)
Lunch
Propaganda skills, map memory test, Bennett Mechanical Comprehension Test, Instructions for Manchuria Propaganda Assignment
Leaderless group discussion; sociometric assessment
Dinner
Instructions for interrogation test
Stress interview
Poststress interview
Test of ability to evaluate and to abstract intelligence information
Preparation for teaching test
Adapted from Wiggins, 1973.

Theoretical orientation and scientific considerations also influence assessment goals (Wade and Baker, 1977). For example, the psychologist who adheres to psychoanalytic personality theory usually wants to assess a person's personality structure (ego strength perhaps), whereas a behaviorally oriented psychologist usually wants to assess the actual behavior

TABLE 14-2 GENERAL AND SPECIAL QUALIFICATIONS FOR OSS OVERSEAS SERVICE

General Qualifications

1. *Motivation for assignment:* war morale, interest in proposed job.
2. *Energy and initiative:* activity level, zest, effort, initiative.
3. *Effective intelligence:* ability to select strategic goals and the most efficient means of attaining them; quick practical thought—resourcefulness, originality, good judgment—in dealing with things, people, or ideas.
4. *Emotional stability:* ability to govern disturbing emotions, steadiness and endurance under pressure, snafu tolerance, freedom from neurotic tendencies.
5. *Social relations:* ability to get along well with other people, good will, team play, tact, freedom from disturbing prejudices, freedom from annoying traits.
6. *Leadership:* social initiative, ability to evoke cooperation, organizing and administering ability, acceptance of responsibility.
7. *Security:* ability to keep secrets; caution, discretion, ability to bluff and to mislead.

(continued on next page)

Special Qualifications

8. *Physical ability:* agility, daring, ruggedness, stamina.
9. *Observing and reporting:* ability to observe and to remember accurately significant facts and their relations, to evaluate information, to report succinctly.
10. *Propaganda skills:* ability to apperceive the psychological vulnerabilities of the enemy; to devise subversive techniques of one sort or another; to speak, write, or draw persuasively.

From OSS, 1948, pp. 30–31.

of a client (perhaps to identify situations in which a client drinks too much). Among the scientific considerations that influence assessment goals are data on the accuracy of particular types of predictions. For example, psychologists would like to be able to predict whether someone is dangerous and likely to act violently. Although this kind of assessment is socially important, many assessors will not predict whether someone is dangerous because research shows that these predictions usually are not accurate (Shah, 1978).

After determining the goals of assessment, psychologists decide how to conduct the assessment.

PSYCHOMETRIC CRITERIA FOR THE EVALUATION OF ASSESSMENT DEVICES

Psychometric refers to the measurement (metric) of psychological factors. Since every psychological assessment strategy purports to measure some psychological attribute, psychometric criteria are relevant to the evaluation of all psychological assessment devices, even when they appear to be nonquantitative in nature. For instance, an assessor may use an interview to determine whether a young man is, or is not, schizophrenic. Here, the assessor is attempting to discover whether the young man shows enough signs of schizophrenia to warrant a schizophrenia diagnosis (see Chapter 13). No numbers are used in this assessment, but it still involves measurement. (The assignment of people or objects to types—for example, psychotic versus nonpsychotic—is a very crude sort of measurement, though. The English philosopher and mathematician Lord Alfred North Whitehead noted that the use of a typology was a "halfway house on the road to measurement.")

Reliability

Reliability means that a measure is repeatable. A reliable test or measure yields the same score if used repeatedly on the same individual. For example, an accurate scale is a reliable measure. A person weighed repeatedly over a short time span weighs the same at each weighing. In theory, there is a specific exact value, or **true score**, for any measurement. For example, a person's exact weight might be 143 pounds or his or her IQ might be 126. According to reliability theory (Nunnally, 1978), to the extent that a test is reliable, it should consistently produce scores close to the true score. We can never be sure of exactly what the true score is—it is hypothetical—but we can be sure that if a test or measure produces scores that vary greatly when the measured variable should not have changed, we know that the measure is unreliable.

One method psychologists use to determine if an assessment is reliable is checking whether its items agree with one another. In this **internal consistency** method psychologists check whether the items yield responses that are *positively correlated* with one another. When items are positively correlated, high scores on one item are associated with high scores on another. For instance, in people who are diagnosed as de-

TABLE 14-3 SELECTED ITEMS FROM THE BECK DEPRESSION INVENTORY

For each item, please circle the number by the answer which best describes you.

A.

1. I do not feel sad
2. I feel blue or sad
3. I am blue or sad all the time and I can't snap out of it
4. I am so sad or unhappy that it is quite painful
5. I am so sad or unhappy that I can't stand it

B.

1. I am not particularly pessimistic or discouraged about the future
2. I feel discouraged about the future
3. I feel I have nothing to look forward to
4. I feel that I won't ever get over my troubles
5. I feel that the future is hopeless and that things cannot improve

C.

1. I don't have any thoughts of harming myself
2. I have thoughts of harming myself but I would not carry them out
3. I feel I would be better off dead
4. I feel my family would be better off if I were dead
5. I have definite plans about committing suicide
6. I would kill myself if I could

D.

1. I make decisions about as well as ever
2. I try to put off making decisions
3. I have great difficulty in making decisions
4. I don't make any decisions at all any more

E.

1. I can sleep as well as usual
2. I wake up more tired in the morning than I used to
3. I wake up 1–2 hours earlier than usual and find it hard to get back to sleep
4. I wake up early every day and can't get more than 5 hours of sleep

Note: The options with higher numbers indicate greater depression. Because this test is reliable, a very depressed person would mostly select items numbered 4, 5, or 6.

pressed, disturbed sleep and feelings of sadness generally are positively correlated. Thus, if a depressed person took the Beck Depression Inventory (BDI, see Table 14-3), he should respond positively to many items on the test. This would yield a high positive correlation among the items. Since responses to the items would agree with one another and not vary greatly, the test is, by definition, reliable.

When two variables agree perfectly the correlation is 1.00 (r is the abbreviation for correlation). This means that for every 1-unit increase in one variable, there is a 1-unit increase in the second variable (assuming comparable units of measurement). Correlations above .60 generally are considered strong, correlations of .31 to .60 generally are considered moderate, and correlations of .30 and below generally are considered weak. These are just guidelines, however, and circumstances may cast a particular level of correlation in a very different light. Because the topic of correlation is so important to your understanding of assessment, we urge you to review the material on correlation in the Statistical Appendix.

When we measure a physical variable such as weight or height, we use only a single measure or item (a scale or ruler). The BDI, however, contains diverse items—items measuring sleep, mood, and self-concept. Depression is harder to measure accurately than is height or weight; it has many dimensions (sleep problems, mood, etc.) and it is internal (it cannot be directly seen or felt). Reliability theory indicates that the more items a test has, the more reliable (repeatable) its results (given that the items measure the same thing; Nunnally, 1978). Because most psychological variables have many facets or dimensions and are internal, most psychological tests have many items to ensure high reliability.

Sometimes psychologists use the **split-half** method to determine reliability. In this method psychologists divide the test in half and separately administer items from each half to the same group of subjects. If the test is reliable, subjects scoring high on one half should score high on the other half. Psychologists also determine reliability with the **test–retest** method. By administering a test twice, they check whether the test yields the same answers each time. The test–retest method is not a good method to use when the thing that you wish to measure changes quickly over time. For instance, a test of tiredness might show a person as tired at one testing (at night) but not at another (in the morning) even though the test was reliable and really did measure tiredness. Similarly, one problem with the split-half method is that half a test is not as good as a whole test. This is because half a test has fewer items than a whole and therefore lower reliability. In general, internal consistency measures are the best for establishing reliability.

Validity

A test is reliable when its items agree with one another. **Validity**, the second important standard for any assessment device, refers to the extent to which a test measures *the* particular psychological or physical dimension in which the assessor is interested. For example, a test developer who wishes to assess depression might construct a test with many questions about memory, because she knows that depression interferes with memory. She might ask, "Do you have trouble recalling people's names after you meet them?" "Do you have trouble remembering appointments?" Because all the questions concern memory, they are reliable. But are they a valid measure of depression? No. First, memory trouble is only one symptom of depression. Second, not all depressed people have memory problems. Third, conditions other than depression cause memory problems—for example, drugs and dementing illnesses. Although all the test items tapped memory, and did so reliably, they did not necessarily tap depression. The moral of the story? A test may be reliable but not valid.

Validity is concerned with whether the thing measured is useful and appropriate to our assessment goals. An example may make this clear. As we have already discussed, the assessor's memory test has poor validity for the purpose of measuring depression. However, suppose a researcher wished to determine whether a new drug helped people with poor memories. The first step would be to identify people with poor memories. The memory test might be quite valid for this purpose. This illustrates a very important concept regarding validity. Validity does not exist in a test or assessment strategy. Rather, validity must be evaluated with respect to a given assessment device, as it is used to address a specific assessment question, in a specific assessment context.

EVALUATING VALIDITY   How is validity evaluated? In the 1950s, psychologists generally thought that there were three distinct kinds of validity: **content**, **criterion**, and **construct**. Later, they realized that the first two are merely special cases of construct validity (Cronbach, 1984).

To check the **criterion validity** of an assessment, psychologists compare its results against a particular outcome or criterion. For example, they may check a personality test designed to detect schizophrenia and anxiety disorders against the criterion of a psychiatric diagnosis. If the test is a valid assessment device, then it should predict who does, and who does not, receive a particular psychiatric diagnosis.

In **content validation**, psychologists compare two things: the behavior and attitudes elicited by the assessment and the behavior and attitudes the assessor wishes to measure. An assessment with high content validity should elicit the same behaviors and attitudes that are of interest to the assessor. For instance, suppose that an assessor were interested in predicting which people might engage in criminal activity. Our assessor hypothesizes that criminals come from families where there are many children and little supervision by, or contact with, parents. Thus, his test consists of many questions about people's early home environment: "Did your father discipline you at least once a year?" "Did your parents generally meet and talk to your friends?" The test might have high *criterion* validity in that it might predict criminal behavior. However, it has little *content* validity, because it does not elicit any direct evidence of criminal behavior. A test with high content validity would ask people about any previous criminal activity or their likelihood of committing a crime in the future.

Psychologists don't always try to elicit and measure directly the behavior in which they are interested. Sometimes they try to develop **indirect** assessments (assessments without content validity), because they are interested in information that a person may wish to conceal or alter. For instance, a man about to be tried for murder might try to create the impression that he is, or was, mentally ill. A **direct** assessment probably would make him answer or act in ways that he believed suggested mental illness. In this situation, the psychologist may be better off using an indirect assessment. In addition, psychologists are often interested in assessing personality dimensions whose content cannot be directly sampled in a test. Subtle psychological dimensions like overcontrolled hostility (Megargee, 1966) or ego strength must be inferred: they cannot be sampled directly. But when psychologists use indirect assessments—those that do not have content validity—they have to be careful that the assessments have criterion validity (Bersoff, 1973).

CONSTRUCT VALIDITY Ideally, validity should be based on sound theory and on data that arise out of systematic tests of the theory. This standard describes **construct validation**.

Suppose that you wish to validate a test of anxiety. How do you prove that you are really measuring anxiety itself? First, you would characterize the nature of anxiety. Anxiety is a **hypothetical construct**—it cannot be seen or touched. Rather, you infer that anxiety exists because people's behavior suggests the existence of an enduring personality characteristic or trait with the properties of anxiety. Hypothetical constructs are forces or dispositions that are not directly observable, but the existence of which we infer based upon their hypothesized effects. (You will realize after some thought that almost all psychological variables are really hypothetical constructs. We cannot directly see, hear, or feel schizophrenia, intelligence, or learning. Rather we must *infer* the existence of these based on a variety of observations and measures.)

The existence of hypothesized variables or constructs is not peculiar to psychology. Scientists from all fields attempt to characterize not-directly-observable forces or processes to account for the state of nature. For instance, gravity is a hypothetical construct that is inferred to exist based upon observed effects—aspects of planetary motion and the tendency of bodies within earth's atmosphere to fall.

Before you can measure a hypothetical construct like anxiety, you must decide what its properties are and how these will influence your test or measures. For instance, clinical observations and theories of anxiety suggest that the anxious person will display more frequent bouts of autonomic nervous system arousal (heart rate increases, sweating, trembling), report more nausea, difficulty breathing, worry, specific and non-specific fears, should be less able to work efficiently under pressure, and should be less confident about mastering difficult tasks than a person who is not anxious. None of these is *the* essential feature of anxiety, and so you will compare your test against all of them. You see, you would use several **convergent measures** to determine whether the test was detecting something that has the properties that we attribute to anxiety. If your test has construct validity, high-anxious subjects will differ from low-anxious subjects on most of the convergent measures. Construct validation demands that the assessor (1) Characterize as specifically as possible the factor or construct that the assessment device is intended to measure. For instance, how should the construct affect behavior across diverse situations? (2) Devise multiple convergent measures of the construct. And (3) determine whether the results of the test agree with the results of other measures of the construct. For example, do people who score highly on the test also score highly on the other construct measures? Notice that at the same time that you are validating your test, you are also validating your construct! You can show that your test is valid only if your notions about the construct are also correct.

It is not always necessary to use a construct validation approach for a test or measure. For instance, if you wanted to predict a specific type of behavior, such as alcohol consumption by alcoholics, you could use criterion or content validation. However, the more abstract the target of your assessment, the more likely you would need construct validation. Later in this chapter, when we discuss the assessment of intelligence, we will discuss a specific example of construct validation.

STRATEGIES OF ASSESSMENT

Psychologists have several assessment strategies available to them. They choose among them according to their particular goals, their personality theory, and the practical needs with which they are faced.

Interviewing

Interviewing undoubtedly is the most frequently used assessment strategy. In fact, when clinicians work one-on-one with a client, it may be their only assessment strategy.

UNSTRUCTURED INTERVIEWS   There are two basic types of interviews: structured and unstructured. An **unstructured interview** often has several goals: to establish a good relationship with the client, to get to know as much as possible about the client's life in a brief period of time, and to pursue hypotheses about the nature of the client's problem. To accomplish the first goal, the psychologist might ask the client nonthreatening questions, express interest in the client's perception of his or her problem, and listen sensitively. To accomplish the second goal, the psychologist might ask about the client's education, family, and perceptions of his or her strengths and weaknesses. To accomplish the third goal, the psychologist zeroes in with questions on possible causes of the client's problem. These questions are often guided by the assessor's personality theory. For example, a Freudian clinician might ask a client about his or her childhood. A behaviorally oriented clinician would be much more interested in the stimuli that seem to worsen a client's problem and in how people in the client's environment respond to the problem (Kanfer and Saslow, 1969).

The psychologist also would observe closely *how* the client answered questions: worriedly, nervously, evasively? Did the client respond with appropriate emotion to nuances in the questions? Such observations can be extremely important. For instance, they might suggest why a client has difficulty getting along with others.

Psychologists often can gather a great deal of useful information in unstructured interviews, information that helps them make accurate predictions about behavior (Sawyer, 1966). But psychologists may do poorly in assessing someone when they must remember and integrate a great deal of information (Wiggins, 1973). It can be difficult to remember and to weigh it correctly (Arkes, 1981). If a psychologist on the admissions committee of a graduate school in clinical psychology were interviewing a young woman to see whether she would make a good psychotherapist, he might note that although her letters of recommendation from her undergraduate professors are excellent, she is extremely difficult to talk to and she cannot seem to speak her mind. Which type of information should he weigh more? Which is the more valid?

STRUCTURED INTERVIEWS   In **structured interviews**, psychologists address a specific goal, often that of making a correct diagnosis. The structured interview is given and interpreted consistently time after time. For many years, a formidable problem with psychiatric or psychological diagnosis was that it was unreliable. Two assessors interviewing the same patient might agree on a diagnosis only half the time or less (Beck, Ward, Mendelson, Mock, and Erbaugh, 1962; Hunt, Wittson, and Hunt, 1953). In one review, the authors concluded that only three diagnostic categories could be reliably detected by independent diagnosticians: alcoholism, mental retardation, and organic brain syndrome (dementia) (Spitzer and Fleiss, 1974). This lack of reliability in diagnosis has been corrected substantially by the introduction of clearer standards for making diagnoses and by the development of structured diagnostic interviews. Table 14-4 shows how a structured interview focuses an assessor's attention on criteria important for making diagnoses.

TABLE 14-4   STRUCTURED INTERVIEW QUESTIONS REGARDING MANIA: NIMH DIAGNOSTIC INTERVIEW SCHEDULE

1. Has there ever been a period of a week or more when you were so much more active than usual that you or your family or friends were concerned about it?
2. Has there ever been a period of a week or more when you went on spending sprees—so much money that it caused you or your family some financial trouble?
3. Have you ever had a period of a week or more when your interest in sex was so much stronger than is typical for you that you wanted to have sex a lot more frequently than is normal for you or with people you normally wouldn't be interested in?
4. Has there ever been a period of a week or more when you talked so fast that people said they couldn't understand you?
5. Have you ever had a period of a week or more when thoughts raced through your head so fast that you couldn't keep track of them?

Note: These are just a partial sample of the questions in the Diagnostic Interview Schedule that are targeted at eliciting symptoms of mania (see Chapter 13 for a description of mania).

TABLE 14-5 AGREEMENT BETWEEN DIAGNOSES OF PSYCHIATRISTS AND LAYPERSONS WHO USED A STRUCTURED INTERVIEW

Diagnostic Category	Percent of Agreement
Alcohol abuse or dependence	90%
Antisocial personality	94%
Panic	92%
Major depression	86%
Agoraphobia	91%
Simple phobia	86%
Obsessive-compulsive disorder	91%

Source: Helzer et al., 1985.

Note: Percent of agreement refers to how often both assessors agreed that a particular diagnosis was or was not appropriate.

Do structured interviews work? Do they allow assessors to diagnose reliably? The answer seems to be yes. In one study 101 people admitted to a psychiatric hospital were independently evaluated and diagnosed by two psychiatrists who used a structured interview (Helzer et al., 1977). The psychiatrists arrived at the same diagnosis 92 percent of the time. Another study showed that interviews allowed even lay interviewers to arrive at diagnoses that were highly consistent with those of psychiatrists (Helzer et al., 1985; Table 14-5).

The question of whether structured interviews are valid really asks whether diagnosis is valid, and valid for what purpose? Some diagnoses, including those arrived at through structured interviews, possess modest to moderate levels of validity, depending on the purpose to which the classification is put: for instance, prediction of response to treatment, prediction of future symptoms. For example, diagnostic labels are reasonably good at predicting who will complete a tour of duty in the army or navy, how long psychopathy will last, and the amount of social or work problems a person may have (Goodwin and Guze, 1984; McGlashan, 1986). However, diagnostic labels are not good at predicting specific types of pathological behavior such as suicide attempts or people's short-term responses to treatment (Endicott, Nee, Cohen, Fleiss, and Simon, 1986). One reason that diagnosis does not accurately predict specific types of behaviors is that, as we noted in Chapter 13, people given the same diagnostic label can behave in different ways and show different clusters of symptoms. Thus, while two individuals might both qualify for the same diagnostic label, say schizophrenia, one might do so by having persecutory delusions and blunted affect (emotional unresponsiveness), while another individual might qualify by having auditory hallucinations and by being catatonic (see Chapter 13; Endicott et al., 1986).

Projective Tests

In **projective tests**, people are exposed to ambiguous pictures, images, or other stimuli and are asked to report their thoughts and emotional reactions (see Figure 14-1). Projective test stimuli are intended to have little obvious meaning. Therefore, any interpretation or reaction that a client volunteers is attributed to his or her psychological characteristics. In other words, the client must *project* meaning onto the test stimuli.

Imagine that a salesclerk asks a customer, "How are you going to pay for that?" Some people respond, "cash," others, "check," and others "credit card." But one person says, "I've got money! Don't you think for one minute that I can't pay for what I want!" You probably can learn something about this man from his unusual response. Is he hostile? Is he worried that others look down on him? If you agree that psychologists can learn something meaningful about personality from responses to ambiguous stimuli, then you accept the basic premise behind projective tests: they are intended to yield information on basic personality structure (Wade and Baker, 1977). A hallmark of projective tests is that they are unstructured. People have great freedom in responding so that their projections are not overly influenced by the test situation.

Depending on their personality theory, psychologists do or do not use projective tests and, if they do, interpret the results differently. For

FIGURE 14-1 PROJECTIVE TEST STIMULI.
Pictured are inkblots similar to those used in the Rorschach test, a projective test.

example, many psychodynamically oriented psychologists believe that a person's true instinctual desires or conflicts are most directly communicated when he or she is least defensive. They believe that responses to ambiguous stimuli give them a glimpse of unconscious conflicts relatively unaltered by defenses. Thus, if a young man were asked directly whether he hated his father, he might defensively deny it. But if he were shown an inkblot that looked vaguely like male genitals, he might say that it looked like a sword with pools of blood around it. The Freudian might interpret the inkblot as representing the father and the response as representing aggression toward and fear of the father. Because the young man does not *consciously* recognize the inkblot as representing his father, so the argument goes, he projects his unconscious motives onto it. In contrast, behaviorally oriented psychologists attribute psychopathology to learning processes rather than to personality structure or unconscious motivations and therefore, rarely use projective tests (Wade, Baker, and Hartmann, 1979).

THE RORSCHACH TEST   The most frequently used projective test is the Rorschach inkblot test (Wade and Baker, 1977; see Table 14-6). The Rorschach test consists of ten cards, each containing an inkblot like those in Figure 14-1. Clients are shown each inkblot and asked to say what it might represent. The examiner writes down the client's statements and later interprets them. Although there are several interpretational systems, most score the same basic elements. For example, most systems attach special significance to the report of certain types of movement in the inkblots: "That looks like a train moving away from me." Also, most systems attach significance to *what* clients see and *where* they see it in the inkblot as well. Thus it is highly significant if a person sees a springing cat in part of an inkblot devoid of any catlike form. These rare types of responses are given special emphasis because years of clinical observation have shown that they are more likely than others to reflect psychopathology. Rarity alone is not always interpreted as reflecting pathology, though. Sometimes testers ascribe an unusual response to creativity or intelligence.

After examining all of a client's responses to the ten inkblots, the clinician attempts to arrive at an overall description of the client's personality and the client's strategy for dealing with the world such as

TABLE 14-6 TESTS THAT CLINICAL PSYCHOLOGISTS ADVISE CLINICAL PSYCHOLOGY STUDENTS TO LEARN

1. Rorschach Inkblot Test (P).
2. Thematic Apperception Test (P).
3. Wechsler Adult Intelligence Scale (O).
4. Minnesota Multiphasic Personality Inventory (O).
5. Bender–Gestalt Test (P).
6. Wechsler Intelligence Scale for Children (O).
7. Picture drawings (P).
8. Sentence Completion Test (P).
9. Stanford–Binet Intelligence Scale (O).
10. Halstead–Reitan Neuropsychological Battery (O).

Source: Wade and Baker, 1977.
Note: The Rorschach was recommended most often, the Halstead, least often.
P = projective test; O = objective test.

whether the person relies on inner resources to deal with stress or seeks help from others (Erdberg and Exner, 1984). Proponents of the Rorschach test also claim that it can help psychologists predict suicide and make psychiatric diagnoses (Exner and Weiner, 1982; Exner and Wylie, 1977).

RELIABILITY AND VALIDITY OF PROJECTIVE TESTS   Most studies of projective tests suggest that they are only modestly reliable (Nunnally, 1978). A person's response to a projective test is likely to change from one occasion to the next, suggesting that the test is not measuring the same thing on every occasion. Projective tests are not especially valid either. In one classic study, expert clinicians were allowed to use their favorite projective tests in arriving at diagnoses (Little and Schneidman, 1959). Results showed that their performance was little better than chance. In another study, five assessors rated the personality characteristics of 30 psychiatric patients on the basis of information yielded by a biographical data sheet, an interview, and an objective personality test (the Minnesota Multiphasic Personality Inventory), and the Rorschach (Sines, 1959). The assessors rated the patients' personality characteristics from the information yielded by each type of assessment, and the ratings were compared to those of expert clinicians who had seen the patients in psychotherapy. Table 14-7 shows the results. As you can see, a biography plus an interview and the MMPI generally improved accuracy. The Rorschach did just the opposite. One promising development in the usefulness of projective tests is a new scoring system for the Rorschach; evidence suggests that it improves diagnostic accuracy (Erdberg and Exner, 1984).

Despite a general lack of research support, many clinicians still rely on projective tests. They value their personal skill with the tests more than they value research results. Many report that they have found projective tests to be helpful (Wade and Baker, 1977). Although they consider them to be helpful, clinicians may not be good judges of tests' predictive accuracy (Chapman and Chapman, 1967; Arkes, 1981; see Figure 14-2). Like other people, they may remember evidence that confirms their beliefs and forget evidence that contradicts them (Snyder, 1981).

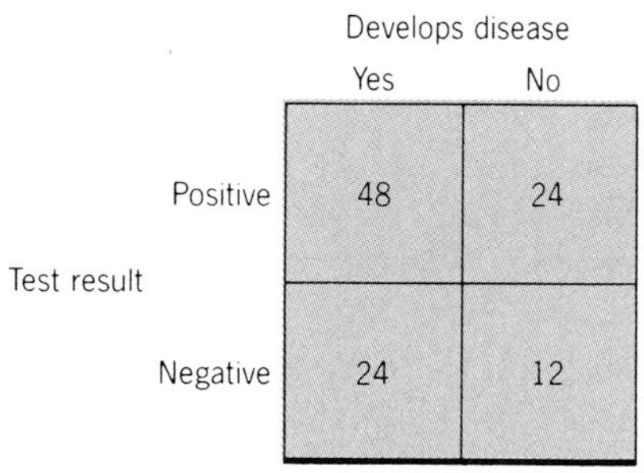

Develops disease

	Yes	No
Positive	48	24
Negative	24	12

Test result

FIGURE 14-2   CAN CLINICIANS JUDGE RELATIONSHIPS WELL? Clinicians, like all people, may make poor judgments because they are susceptible to cognitive distortions and biases. For example, examine the relationship between a test result and the development of a disease as portrayed in this figure. If the test result is positive, is the person more likely to have the disease? On a scale of 1 to 100 with 0 meaning no relationship and 100 meaning a perfect relationship, on average people rate the strength of the relationship at 54. Actually there is no relationship. The diseased will outnumber the disease-free by 2 to 1 no matter how they perform on the test. Such cognitive biases or errors may make clinicians poor judges of the worth of their assessment practices. (From Arkes, 1981.)

TABLE 14-7   VALIDITY OF PERSONALITY EVALUATIONS MADE FROM VARIOUS TYPES OF ASSESSMENTS

Assessments	Validity Coefficient
Biography + interview + MMPI	.595
Biography + interview	.566
Biography + interview + MMPI + Rorschach	.480
Biography + interview + Rorschach	.450
Biography + MMPI + Rorschach	.403
Biography	.396
Biography + MMPI	.378
Biography + Rorschach	.368

Source: Wiggins, 1972; after Sines, 1959.
Note: The validity coefficient is interpreted like a correlation coefficient. High values indicate greater agreement between the assessors' evaluations and those of the clinician-psychotherapists.

Objective Tests

As opposed to projective tests, **objective** tests are highly structured, or standardized. People have relatively few options when they respond to a question on an objective test. Objective tests frequently have a multiple-choice or true–false format, and to some extent the interpretation is built into objective tests.

OBJECTIVE TEST DEVELOPMENT STRATEGIES There are two major strategies for constructing objective tests. In the *empirical* approach, the test constructor chooses items for their actual relationship with the criterion trait. In the *theoretical* approach, the test constructor chooses items on the basis of his or her theories about the *criterion* target trait. Two examples will make this distinction clear.

The Minnesota Multiphasic Personality Inventory (MMPI) is an empirically constructed test (see Table 14-6). The developers of the MMPI wanted a test that would help them diagnose types of psychopathology, such as schizophrenia, mania, and depression. They gathered many miscellaneous test questions and administered them to normal controls (724 visitors to the University of Minnesota Hospitals) as well as to large groups of psychiatric patients. Then they identified those items that best distinguished the normal subjects from each of the diagnostic groups. A hypothetical example of this procedure is presented in Table 14-8. As you can see, theory contributes little to the selection of test items in the development of an empirically constructed test. Items are retained solely on the basis of their discrimination of the criterion (for example, schizophrenia, mania). In all, the MMPI contains 13 scales. Three of the scales (the L, F, K Scales) are *validity* scales that are designed to reveal whether a subject is answering questions randomly or untruthfully. The other 10, *clinical* scales are designed to detect evidence of psychopathology. Figure 14-3 displays the results of the administration of the MMPI to two different individuals. When people score high on a particular MMPI scale, they have answered the questions the same way as the criterion group did.

TABLE 14-8 SELECTING ITEMS FOR AN OBJECTIVE PSYCHIATRIC INVENTORY

Question	Controls True	Controls False	Schizophrenics True	Schizophrenics False	Scoring Key True	Scoring Key False
1. I subscribe to too many magazines.	42%	58%	35%	65%	0	0
2. I often hear things I am not suppose to.	27%	73%	55%	45%	1	0
3. I think that most people trust me.	67%	33%	31%	69%	0	1

Source: Wiggins, 1972
Note: Only the second and third questions discriminate the schizophrenic and normal groups. Schizophrenics are more likely to answer the second question as true and the third question as false. Therefore, on the "Schizophrenia Scale" of a test like the MMPI, question 2 would be keyed "true," question 3 would be keyed "false," and question 1 would be removed from the scale.

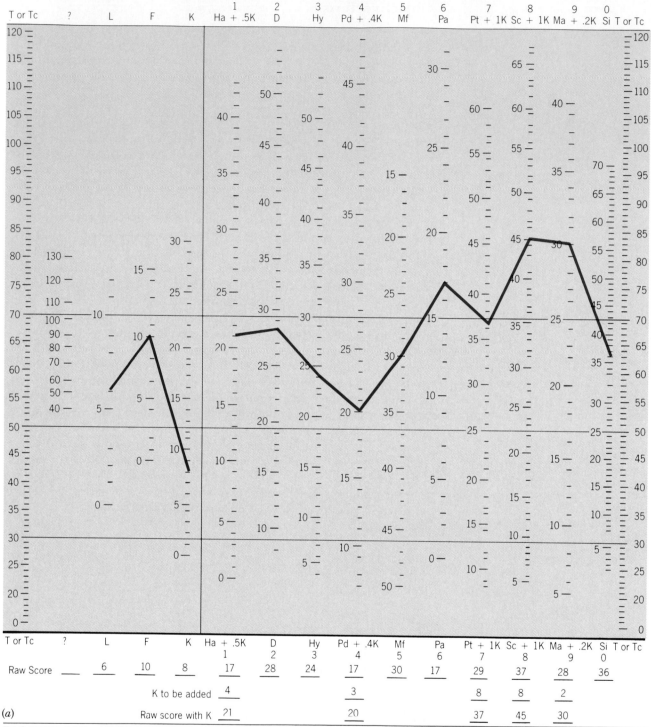

	?	L	F	K	Ha + .5K 1	D 2	Hy 3	Pd + .4K 4	Mf 5	Pa 6	Pt + 1K 7	Sc + 1K 8	Ma + .2K 9	Si 0
Raw Score	___	6	10	8	17	28	24	17	30	17	29	37	28	36
K to be added					4			3			8	8	2	
Raw score with K					21			20			37	45	30	

(a)

FIGURE 14-3 MMPI PROFILES.

(a) *Shows the results of the administration of an MMPI to a 38-year-old, white, married, female technician.* (b) *Shows the results of an MMPI given to a 40-year-old, married,* *white male business executive. The scales upon which the profiles are plotted are: Hs = hypochondriasis; D = depression; Hy = hysteria; Pd = psychopathic deviate; Mf = male/female (a scale* *intended to reflect homosexuality); Pa = paranoia; Pt = psychasthenia (similar to an anxiety state); Sc = schizophrenia; Ma = mania; Si = social introversion. The woman*

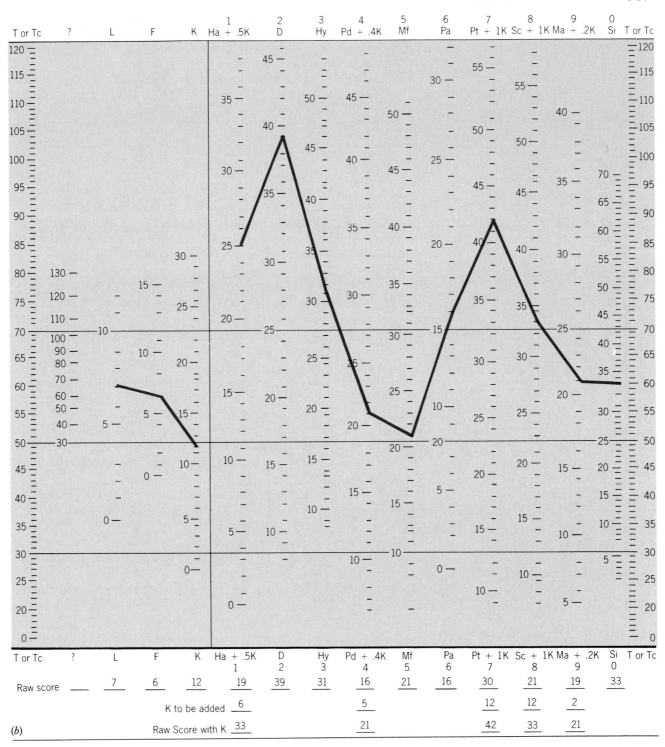

T or Tc	?	L	F	K	1 Ha + .5K	2 D	3 Hy	4 Pd + .4K	5 Mf	6 Pa	7 Pt + 1K	8 Sc + 1K	9 Ma + .2K	0 Si	T or Tc
Raw score		7	6	12	19	39	31	16	21	16	30	21	19	33	
K to be added					6			5			12	12	2		
Raw Score with K					33			21			42	33	21		

(b)

might receive a diagnosis of schizophrenia, the man a diagnosis of major depression or an anxiety disorder. In general, the highest scores on a scale, especially scores over 70, are considered to indicate a person's psychological problem. Psychologists often use the two highest scores to arrive at a diagnosis. (From J. D. Matarazzo, Wechsler's Measurement and Appraisal of Adult Intelligence. *Baltimore, MD: Williams and Wilkins, 1972.) Also, MMPI profile sheet copyright 1748 by the Psychological Corporation. Reproduced by permission granted in test catalog.*

For a theoretically constructed test, the testers begin by writing questions based on their *understanding* of the criterion. For instance, testers interested in devising a test of schizophrenia build on what they have learned from working with and doing research on schizophrenics. Because they know, say, that schizophrenics often have auditory hallucinations, they might include a question such as, "I sometimes hear too many voices." After writing the questions, the test developers administer the test to large groups of people to determine whether it actually measures schizophrenia (construct validation). Once the test has been validated, interpretation is built in and people who answer questions in the keyed direction are presumed to be schizophrenic.

Although both approaches have produced widely used tests—the empirical approach, the MMPI, the theoretical approach, the newer Millon Clinical Multiaxial Inventory, or MCMI—the theoretical approach is more popular today because it tends to yield tests that are more reliable and stable (Jackson, 1971; Wiggins, 1972).

RELIABILITY AND VALIDITY OF OBJECTIVE TESTS Some objective tests are more reliable than others. For instance, tests of intellectual or cognitive performance, such as IQ tests or neuropsychology tests, generally are quite reliable (Jensen, 1980). However, tests of personality traits or psychopathology, such as the MMPI, the MCMI, and the California Psychological Inventory, generally are less reliable (Dahlstrom, Welsh, and Dahlstrom, 1975). Similarly, some objective tests are more valid than others. In general, people's performance on tests of cognitive ability is a relatively good predictor of their other cognitive and intellectual activities; such as their performance in school and at work. But results from diagnostic and personality tests relate only modestly—about $r = .30$—to other measures of personality and diagnosis (Bem, 1972; Bem and Allen, 1974; Mischel, 1968).

Cognitive and intellectual objective tests are more reliable and valid than personality and diagnostic tests because of what they measure. Both types of tests measure **traits**, enduring personal characteristics that manifest themselves across time and place (see Chapter 12). However, there is evidence that cognitive-intellectual and personality-diagnostic traits differ.

Physical strength is a trait. It is a characteristic of a person that can be manifested in different ways (for example, arm wrestling, ability to do manual labor), at different times, and in different places. If someone is strong in one context, he also will tend to be strong in a different setting, using different measures of strength. Furthermore, he will tend to remain strong over considerable periods of time.

Intellectual ability is traitlike. It is manifested in a great many ways: in a person's memory abilities, reading comprehension, mathematical skill, vocabulary, and so on. Intelligence also is an enduring characteristic of behavior. People who perform best on mental tests at Time 1 tend to perform best on those tests at Time 2, even if the tests are separated by months or years. Neuropsychological tests also reveal traits. These tests detect brain damage that people have acquired by injuries and by disease, such as brain tumors, strokes, and dementing illnesses. Trauma and

FIGURE 14-4   THE TRAIL-
MAKING TEST.
*In this neuropsychological test, a person
must connect the letters and numbers in
alphabetical and numerical sequence.
Thus, a person might connect 1 to A,
A to 2, 2 to B, and so on. People with
particular types of brain damage (such
as lesions of the right parietal lobe)
cannot perform this task well. (From
Davison and Neale, 1985.)*

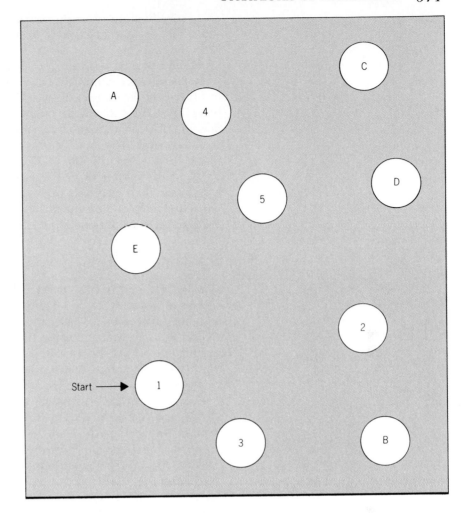

disease produce pathological cognitive traits such as poor memory or the inability to solve perceptual problems or puzzles (see Figure 14-4). Because neuropsychological traits are results of brain damage, they are fairly stable across time and place and can be measured reliably (Heaton, Nelson, Thompson, Burks, and Franklin, 1985).

Personality traits tend to be less stable—less traitlike—than cognitive or neuropsychological traits. Personality traits are susceptible to temporal and situational factors. For example, as we described in Chapter 12, researchers found that children showed very little consistency across situations in traits such as helpfulness, cooperativeness, deceptiveness, and persistence (Hartshorne and May, 1928, 1929). Thus, children may be perfectly honest with their friends but dishonest at home. Other studies, too, show that people's behavior varies greatly from one situation to another (Dudycha, 1936). It may seem odd that human behavior isn't more traitlike, that one person isn't *generally* sweet and demure or that another isn't *generally* clever and industrious. However, environmental and situational cues powerfully influence behavior and overwhelm the influence of individual differences in traits. Therefore, tests of personality traits often do not relate strongly to other measures of the same trait, because behavior indicative of the trait changes greatly across time and place.

We do not want to paint too bleak a picture of objective personality tests. For instance, although they are only moderately predictive of extra-test behavior, they *are* predictive. They also are better at predicting some types of traitlike behavior better than $r = .30$ (Hogan, Desoto, and Solano, 1977; Paunonen and Jackson, 1985). Psychopathological traits, such as mania, test more consistently than do nonpathological traits (Alker, 1972; Hogan et al., 1977).

In summary, some objective tests have impressive reliability and validity. Usually these are tests of cognitive or intellectual traits or abilities. Objective tests of personality traits tend to be less reliable and valid because personality traits change across time and place.

Direct and Behavioral Assessment

Some of the impetus for developing direct and behavioral assessment measures arose from a general dissatisfaction with traditional approaches to assessment, for example, projective and objective tests. Such dissatisfaction centered around the psychometric properties of the tests and the personality theories on which some of the tests were based (e.g., trait theory, Freudian theory). While behavioral assessment strategies arose out of a learning theory approach to psychopathology, direct assessment approaches arose because they are economical, easily administered and interpreted, and often surprisingly accurate (Kanfer and Saslow, 1965).

DIRECT MEASURES Suppose that you were a psychologist, and you were given the job of predicting how well students would perform academically in high school or college. How would you do it? Because you know that IQ and scholastic achievement tests predict later grades, you might decide to administer all your students the Scholastic Aptitude Test (SAT) or the American College Test (ACT). All well and good, but you should not ignore another strategy that probably would be as accurate as these tests—**self-predictions**: "What grades do *you* think you will get in your first year of college?" A considerable body of research shows that, on average, self-predictions predict grades as accurately as objective achievement tests (Shrauger and Osberg, 1981). You also might look at your students' past grades because they also predict later grades. Direct, simple behavioral measures do an equally good job at predicting people's vocations, their performance in the Peace Corps, and the outcome of psychotherapy (Mischel, 1972; Shrauger and Osberg, 1981). The best predictor of whether people who have quit smoking will stay off cigarettes is their own predictions of their success (Tiffany, Martin, and Baker, 1986).

In the context of direct assessment, psychologists have measured the size and rates at which alcoholics drink alcohol (Sobell, Schaeffer, and Mills, 1972), the frequency and severity of headaches among headache sufferers (Blanchard and Andrasik, 1985; see Figure 14-5), and how closely phobics will approach what they fear (Paul, 1966).

*FIGURE 14-5   HEADACHE
DIARY.*
*Clients rate the intensity of their
headaches from 0 to 5 throughout the
day. (From Blanchard and Andrasik,
1985.)*

Name _____
Date _____

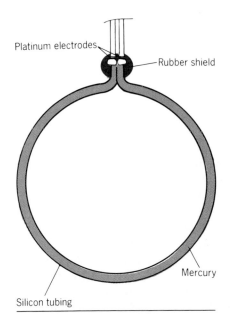

A mercury strain gauge

*FIGURE 14-6   DIRECT
MEASURE OF SEXUAL AROUSAL.*
*A mercury strain gauge can be placed
around a man's penis to measure his
sexual arousal. As the circumference
of the gauge increases, the electric
conductivity of the mercury decreases.
This is recorded on a polygraph.*

How might psychologists directly assess whether men might be rapists? They might ask each man whether he is aroused by forcible sexual intercourse or whether he might ever commit rape. They might take a more sophisticated direct approach and measure the men's sexual arousal in response to stories with themes of violent, forced sex. For example, researchers played audiotape stories of sexual activity to men who had been convicted of rape and other crimes (Quinsey, Chaplin, and Upfold, 1984). They also measured the men's sexual arousal (the size of their penile erections) as the convicts listened to the stories (see Figure 14-6). Compared to rapists, the other men were more sexually aroused by stories of women who consented to sex. Rapists were aroused by stories of rape, forced sex. Rapists also were aroused by other, nonsexual forms of violence directed at women (Figure 14-7).

In direct assessments, psychologists either measure the behavior that they are interested in—such as students' grade-point average—or simply ask clients to predict something about the behavior in question. Indirect approaches to assessment (such as projective and objective tests) are sometimes called *sign* approaches, in which test responses are signs of personality structures, and direct approaches are called *sample* approaches, in which psychologists gather a sample of the behavior in which they are interested. In direct assessments, they typically measure how someone performs or has performed in a particular situation. Thus, direct assessments have great content validity. As psychologists sometimes say, "The best predictor of future behavior is past behavior in a similar situation."

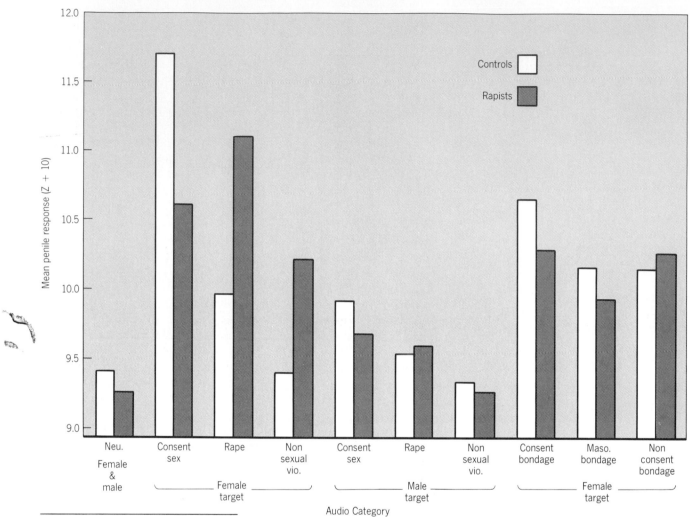

FIGURE 14-7 DIRECT RESPONSES TO STORIES OF VIOLENCE.

The penile responses of rapists and nonrapists (controls) who heard stories in which either a man or a woman was the target of violence or sexual activity. The stories also involved either rape, nonsexual violence, consenting sex, moderately violent nonconsenting sex, moderately violent consenting sex, or mildly violent consenting sex. Rapists became more sexually aroused than nonrapists only when sex was associated with extreme violence. (From Quinsey, Chaplin, and Upfold, 1984.)

BEHAVIORAL ASSESSMENT Because behaviorally oriented psychologists believe that much human behavior is learned, they are interested in directly measuring the intensity and frequency of behavior because these measures, they believe, reflect the strength of learning. Therefore behaviorists use direct assessments in a special way.

For example, take the case of people who often have headaches. Perhaps these people have learned to report headaches because, when they were young, one of their parents served as a model for them—dramatically reporting headaches. The behaviorist would take a thorough family history to determine whether, as a child or adolescent, the sufferer had known anyone with frequent headaches. Perhaps the headache sufferers were generously rewarded for reporting headaches. Relatives may have shown them sympathy or affection and freed them from some unpleasant chores: "Don't bother with that term paper if you have a headache, dear." To identify these sorts of rewards, the behaviorist would ask the headache sufferer's family, friends, and coworkers to report on how they react to the sufferer's complaints. Finally, the behaviorist tries to discover the stimuli that seem to trigger headache reports. Perhaps the headache sufferer leads a highly stressful life and stress brings on his headaches. Through numerous pairings a variety of stimuli (e.g., the boss's face, the office) have become associated with his stress responses (e.g., muscle clenching, increased heart rate). Because of Pavlovian learning these stimuli have become capable of eliciting both stress responses and, therefore, headaches. If the behaviorist can identify the environmental cues that elicit headaches, perhaps the association can be extinguished. As you can see, a behaviorally oriented psychologist primarily uses direct assessments to determine how learning contributes to either the *report* of a problem or to the problem itself.

DIRECT AND BEHAVIORAL ASSESSMENTS: STATUS   Direct and behavioral assessments are straightforward, economical, and often accurate, but they have limitations, too. First, self-reports have little value when people do not want to tell the truth. Ask someone in prison whether he will ever commit another crime, and he will say no. One of the authors of this book has interviewed numerous imprisoned felons in the context of making a decision about whether the felon should be released on parole. No felon ever predicted that he would engage in crime upon his release. Obviously, self-prediction in this circumstance was worthless. Second, direct assessments may be inadequate or incomplete measures of complex psychological constructs such as anxiety. You might ask a person how anxious she is, or observe whether or not her hands sweat and tremble. However, as we discussed earlier, anxiety has many components and these might be assessed best by an extensive objective test that taps many aspects of anxiety. Finally, direct approaches are inappropriate for measuring constructs of which someone is unaware or unconscious. For example, direct or behavioral assessments would be of little help in the assessment of unconscious motivations held to be important by Freudian personality theory.

The Science and Art of Assessment: Integrating Information

In practice, psychologists usually have to thread their way carefully through many kinds of information to assess the cause, course, and treatment of anyone's behavior. For a moment, suppose that you are a psychologist in the military. You have been asked to evaluate a young sailor who complains of headaches and therefore has asked to be relieved of various duties. His superior officers wonder whether his headaches are real or just excuses for avoiding unpleasant duties. Your task is to find out the source of the headaches and to provide information to the officers and to the sailor himself that will be helpful.

First you consider hypotheses about the source of the headaches. Perhaps the sailor is reporting headaches to escape his duties. Perhaps he actually has headaches but exaggerates their frequency or severity. Perhaps he is telling the truth. If he were purposely exaggerating his headache reports, you might expect to find that he is dissatisfied with certain elements of military life and is willing to go to great lengths to avoid them or that his personality makes it likely that he might lie and not worry about getting caught, that is, that he may be psychopathic (see Chapter 13). Direct assessment approaches are of little use to you here. You already have concerns about the young man's truthfulness, and he probably could not tell you if he were psychopathic, even if he wanted to. Psychopathy is a complex psychological construct, the meaning of which the young man could not intuit.

Therefore, you might interview the sailor to find out how happy he is in the military, to get as much information as possible about his headaches (frequency, type of pain, and so forth), and you ask about his family history of mental disorder and physical complaints. Then you inspect his service record. Are there any indications of dissatisfaction? Are there many transfer requests? Are there reports of disciplinary actions? Then you give him one or two personality diagnostic tests, such as the MMPI or the Eysenck Personality Inventory (EPI; see Chapter 12). Both tests can reflect psychopathy. The MMPI also reflects **hypochondriasis**, the tendency to report physical complaints in the absence of demonstrable physical lesions or damage.

You find that the sailor seems satisfied with the navy. You see no evidence of psychopathy or hypochondria. Therefore, you closely evaluate his description of his headaches. As a well-trained clinical psychologist, you know that there are headache **syndromes** (see Chapter 13), different types of headaches, each with different associated signs and symptoms. A rose may be a rose, but a headache is not necessarily a headache. There are classic migraines, common migraines, cluster headaches, muscle-contraction headaches, and tumor headaches. Now you, the assessor, will take advantage of one of the most important virtues of a syndromal, or diagnostic, approach to assessment; if the young man's headache is legitimate, his symptoms should "fit" one of the well-known headache syndromes. A syndrome provides a context or perspective for viewing or interpreting headache symptoms and signs.

The young man reported that his headaches started late in his adolescence. They may awaken him from sleep and are accompanied by nausea. Also, the pain is throbbing and restricted to one side of his head. He says that he sees unusual jagged lines and flashing lights prior to a headache. The age of onset, the frequency, and the associated symptomology all fit the headache syndrome of classic migraine. Because the headache symptoms fit those of a classic migraine syndrome, and because you see neither the motivational signs nor the personality type that would be associated with exaggerated or false headache reports, you inform his superiors that he probably suffers from genuine headaches. You also refer him to a neurologist for medical diagnosis and possible treatment.

Psychologists make assessments like these, integrating and evaluating evidence from many different sources. Each client whom the psychologist sees is a mystery to be solved.

We now turn to the assessment of one particular trait—intelligence—because it provides an ideal forum for discussing construct validity, because the assessment of intelligence is a currently controversial topic, and because it introduces ethical issues involved when people are the targets of assessment.

ASSESSING INTELLIGENCE

One of the first scientists to study thoroughly individual differences in mental abilities was Sir Francis Galton (1822–1911). Before Galton there was relatively little scientific interest in individual differences in mental ability (Carroll, 1985). Now social scientists and others often *first* compare people on their intelligence. In his book *Hereditary Genius* (1869), Galton proposed that mental abilities are genetically transmitted. In 1883, Galton coined the term **eugenics**, the practice of regulating marriages and family size according to the traits of the parents (Gould, 1981).

Galton, and later, Hermann Ebbinghaus (1897), developed simple tests of mental and sensory functions. However, these tests were only modestly related to other measures of intelligence, such as teachers' ratings of students' intelligence.

In the late nineteenth century, the French Ministry of Education was interested in identifying retarded children quickly so that special programs could be offered to them. This led French psychologist Alfred Binet (1857–1911) to develop a test of mental retardation. Binet felt that Galton's and Ebbinghaus' tests of mental ability were too simple to measure the sophisticated reasoning processes that he thought were central to intelligence. Therefore, Binet developed relatively sophisticated tests of reasoning and problem solving and administered these tests to French schoolchildren. Binet and his collaborator Theophile Simon (1873–1961) also thought that the mental abilities associated with intelligence increased with age, at least until adolescence. Binet reasoned that many skills and processes change at some point during childhood, but unless a measure reflected change and growth *throughout* childhood, it was probably not tapping intelligence.

The Binet–Simon test soon showed itself to be a fairly accurate predictor of which children would, and would not, develop learning problems. Binet used test scores to assign children to special classes in which, he believed, they received help with their learning problems (Gould, 1981). The reputation of the Binet test spread, and in 1916 the Stanford psychologist, Lewis M. Terman, revised and standardized the Binet–Simon test for use in America. The success of this test inspired the development of additional intelligence tests. Some, like the Binet test and the Wechsler Adult Intelligence Scale (WAIS), were individually administered. Others, like the Army Alpha Test (for literates) and the Army Beta Test (for illiterates) were administered to large groups.

Intelligence tests are remarkable in that scores on them are related to a wide range of other behavior, such as grades, vocational status, and years of schooling a person completes. Because of this and because IQ tests sensitively tap specific mental abilities, they have been of tremendous benefit in identifying students with learning problems, in helping vocational counselors, and in diagnosing neurological problems (Matarrazzo, 1972). However, as with other powerful tools, intelligence tests also have been used for purposes that are controversial, and possibly harmful.

One American psychologist who influenced the study of intelligence earlier in this century was H. H. Goddard. Goddard believed that intelligence was not only important for all sophisticated mental operations—mathematics, reasoning, judgment—but also for moral behavior, because he thought that moral behavior depended on the victory of intellect over emotion. Goddard believed that intelligence was genetically determined and one of his great concerns was that the retarded (or *morons*, as he called them, from the Greek for "foolish") would reproduce excessively and degrade the collective intelligence of the American population. Goddard therefore argued that morons be sterilized, confined, or otherwise prevented from breeding and that immigrants be screened so that no morons entered the United States. He succeeded in the latter after administering the Binet test to newly arrived immigrants in 1913 and "proving" that about 80 percent of them were morons. Of course, the cultural backgrounds of the immigrants rendered much of the test meaningless.

As Stephen Jay Gould, the evolutionary biologist, noted

> *Consider a group of frightened men and women who speak no English and who have just endured an oceanic voyage in steerage. Most are poor and have never gone to school; many have never held a pencil or pen in their hand. They march off the boat; one of Goddard's . . . women takes them aside shortly thereafter, sits them down, hands them a pencil, and asks them to reproduce on paper a figure shown them a moment ago, but now withdrawn from their sight. Could their failure be a result of testing conditions, of weakness, or confusion, rather than an innate stupidity? Goddard considered the possibility but rejected it.*
>
> *(Gould, 1981, p. 166)*

In an effort to buttress his claim that intelligence is wholly genetically determined, Goddard traced family members descended from a "feeble-

FIGURE 14-8 INHERITANCE OF INTELLIGENCE: FABRICATED DATA?

The descendants of the "feeble-minded tavern wench" described by Goddard. Do you notice anything odd about this photo? It was published in a 1912 book by Goddard that was intended to prove that feeble-mindedness, or retardation, runs in families. Apparently, Goddard or one of his collaborators colored the eyes and mouths of the pictured children, giving them a bizarre and diabolical appearance. One later intelligence researcher, the British psychologist Cyril Burt apparently misrepresented evidence to support his hypothesis that intelligence is entirely genetically determined (Lewontin, Rose, and Kamin, 1984.)

minded tavern wench" (Gould, 1981). If low intelligence is indeed genetically determined, he reasoned, then her descendants should also be feeble-minded. This is what Goddard reported that he found. But now it appears that Goddard may have altered the evidence to make a better case that the descendants were "feeble-minded" (see Figure 14-8). We also know today that similarity among family members may reflect environmental as well as genetic similarity.

Goddard was not the only scientist to misuse data to try and prove that intelligence is genetically determined and that various cultural and racial groups are genetically doomed to produce mental defectives (Gould, 1981; Lewontin, Ruse, and Kamin, 1984). An awareness of this history provides an illuminating perspective for the analysis of modern views of intelligence and intelligence testing. This history also serves as a reminder that personal prejudice, hunches, and fears all can compromise the ostensible objectivity of the scientist.

IQ Tests

The two most commonly used individually administered IQ tests in the United States today are the Stanford–Binet and the Wechsler Intelligence Scales. The Stanford–Binet (the Binet test modified by Terman) is used with people between 2 and 18 years of age. The Stanford–Binet contains items that assess a young child's eye–hand coordination, identification of common objects, drawing of geometric figures, and memory. Older children and adults take tests of reading and basic mathematics skills, vocabulary, and analogical reasoning. Table 14-9 shows items like those on the Stanford–Binet.

The Stanford–Binet test gave us the term **intelligence quotient (IQ)**. Binet originally characterized a child's intelligence by identifying the child's **mental age**: identifying the age at which most children could correctly answer a question. Thus, a child with a mental age of 6 could answer most of the questions answered by other children 6 and under, but not questions answered mostly by children older than 6. An 8-year-old-child with a mental age of 6 would be considered to have below-normal intelligence; an 8-year-old with a mental age of 10 would be

TABLE 14-9   STANFORD-BINET ITEMS

Age	Task
2–2$\frac{1}{2}$	Must insert geometric-shaped blocks into appropriate holes in formboard
	Must identify parts of the body of a paper doll
	Must remember and repeat digits 2 to 4
6	Must define words such as *envelope*
	Must identify what object is missing from a picture (e.g., a handle from a suitcase)
	Must answer "similarities" items: "An inch is short, a mile is . . . ."
Average Adult	Must define *disproportionate*
	Must explain how to measure 3 pints of water with a 5-pint and a 2-pint can
	Must explain a proverb

considered above average. Later Terman, William Stern, and others discovered how to reflect the relationship between a child's mental age and chronological age (age since birth) with a single number. This number is a quotient produced by dividing a child's mental age (MA) by the chronological age (CA) and multiplying by 100 (to eliminate decimals):

$$\frac{MA}{CA} \times 100$$

Thus, a child of 8 who passed items typically passed by 10-year-olds would have an IQ of 125 (10/8 × 100); an 8-year-old passing items typically passed by 6-year-olds would have an IQ of 75 (6/8 × 100).

Defining intelligence in terms of mental age creates problems. For example, once people become adults, intelligence does not change systematically with age. It makes no sense to say that someone had a mental age of 41 or 56. Therefore, modern IQ tests compare an individual's performance with that of others of the same age. Average performances by each age group is arbitrarily assigned a score of 100. To the extent that an individual scores better than those in his age-group, the IQ exceeds 100. To the extent that he or she scores worse than the average of the age-group, his or her IQ falls below 100.

TABLE 14-10 ITEMS LIKE THOSE ON THE WECHSLER ADULT INTELLIGENCE SCALE—REVISED

Item Type	Item or Item Type
Information	Why does mercury rise in a thermometer when it is heated?
	Who wrote *Les Pecheurs de Perle*?
Comprehension	Why does it cost more to mail a large package than a letter?
	What does this saying mean, "As the twig is bent, so the tree grows"?
Arithmetic	If a man spends $35.21 on a new pair of pants, how much change does he receive from a $50 bill?
	How much time will a man require to drive 400 miles if he is driving at a speed of 60 mph?
Similarities	In what ways are a piano and a violin alike?
Digit Span	Repeat a series of digits either forwards or backwards from memory
Vocabulary	What does *autumn* mean?
	What does *egregious* mean?
Digit Symbol	Match numerals (1, 8, 3) with arbitrary symbols (^, {, *) and draw the symbol every time you see the number in a timed test
Picture Completion	Identify what is missing from a picture of a fairly common object or scene (e.g., one windshield wiper might be missing from a car)
Block Design	Arrange blocks to match designs on cards
Picture Arrangement	Arrange a series of cartoon pictures so that they tell a logical story
Object Assembly	Put together jigsaw puzzles of familiar objects

Note: A number of these tasks are timed, and full credit is given only for rapid performance.

There are three Wechsler tests: the Wechsler Adult Intelligence Scale—Revised (WAIS-R) for adults; the Wechsler Intelligence Scale for Children—Revised (WISC-R) for children between 6 and 17; and the Wechsler Preschool and Primary Scale of Intelligence (WIPPSI) for children between 4 and $6\frac{1}{2}$. Table 14-10 shows items like those on the WAIS-R.

The Stanford–Binet and the Wechsler both yield IQ scores as a function of the number of questions answered correctly within alloted time limits. The mean, or average, IQ yielded by both types of tests is 100. IQs in excess of 140 generally are regarded as indicating giftedness (or genius); scores below 70 to 75 generally are regarded to reflect retardation.

RELIABILITY OF IQ TESTS   Intelligence tests are quite reliable. Correlations among these tests or among several administrations of the same test range from .80 to .95 (Jensen, 1980). IQ test scores are usually quite stable over time, once a person has passed early childhood. For instance, the correlation between the first and second administration of the Stanford–Binet is .87 if the interval is 10 months, and .70 if the interval is 5 years (Thorndike, 1933). The Stanford–Binet and the Wechsler tests also appear to measure the same thing. Scores on the two tests are highly correlated (in the .75 to .90 range [Wechsler, 1981]).

VALIDITY OF IQ TESTS   As we have said, IQ tests are valid in that they predict many kinds of behavior associated with intelligence. IQ tests certainly accomplish their original goal: they predict academic success. Arthur Jensen (1980), a University of California–Berkeley psychologist has observed, "No other single fact that we can determine about a child after the age of 5 better predicts his or her future educational progress and attainments than the IQ. Children with higher IQs generally acquire more scholastic knowledge more quickly and easily, get better marks, like school better, and stay in school longer" (pp. 316–317). But the correlation between IQ and academic achievement generally falls steadily from elementary school until graduate school. As students get older, they have greater freedom to select courses they wish to take. In grade school, where all students take the same courses, high IQ students generally get the highest grades, and low IQ students get the lowest grades. However, once students can select their courses, low IQ students generally select courses or majors for which they have greater aptitude or those with more lenient grading policies. Therefore, the strong relationship between grades and IQ disappears as one climbs the educational ladder (Goldman and Hewitt, 1976; Goldman and Slaughter, 1976).

People's IQ scores relate to the kinds of jobs they take as adults as well as to the amount of schooling they complete (McCall, 1977; see Figure 14-9). Low IQs virtually eliminate people from particular occupations. (Today, of course, this is at least partly due to the fact that tests similar to IQ tests are used to screen people entering certain professions.) Studies have shown that faculty members at Cambridge University in England had IQs ranging from 110 to 141 (see Jensen, 1980). The IQs of a class of medical students ranged from 111 to 147 (Matarazzo, 1972). The lowest IQ score among them, 111, still is superior to that of

FIGURE 14-9
IQ, INTELLIGENCE, AND
OCCUPATION.
These figures depict the correlations among IQ scores measured in youth (3 to 16 years of age), with IQ at age 40, level of education attained as an adult, and adult occupational status (where high-status occupations, such as doctor, judge, professor, are given high scores, and low-status occupations, such as manual laborer, are given low scores). Research shows that people in high status occupations have higher IQs than those in lower status occupations. This could occur because training for, or engaging in, a high-status profession increases IQ (e.g., due to reading books). However, research such as that shown in this figure suggests that people who end up in high-status occupations had higher IQs even as children. For example, the correlation between IQ at age 9 and adult occupation is about r = .50 *for both males and females. (From Jansen, 1980, originally in McCall, 1977.)*

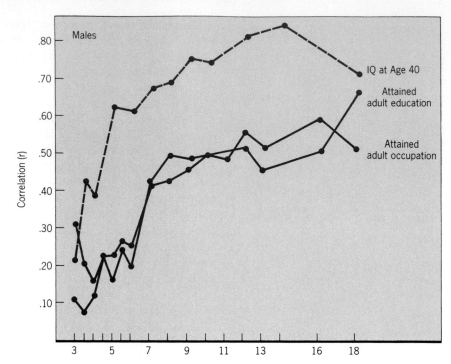

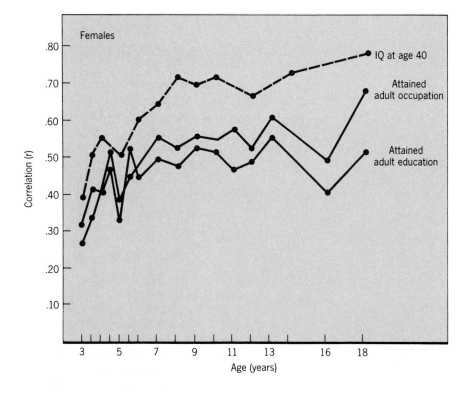

77 percent of the general population. Other correlates of IQ are teacher's ratings of students' brightness, the IQ of a person's spouse, and the level of performance *within* occupations (Jensen, 1980).

In sum, IQ scores tend to be fairly stable, different IQ tests appear to measure the same thing (at least their scores are highly intercorrelated), and what they measure is a common basis for many different scholastic and occupational pursuits. What, then, do IQ tests measure?

What IQ Tests Measure

Behavioral scientists disagree strongly about whether IQ tests accurately measure intelligence. One reason for this is that they do not agree about what intelligence is. Table 14-11 displays some of the many definitions that have been offered for intelligence. A statement by the British psychologist Cyril Burt provides a strong and unequivocal characterization of intelligence (and IQ, since Burt thought IQ was an accurate measure of intelligence). Cyril Burt told a radio audience in 1933

> *By intelligence the psychologist understands inborn, all-around intellectual ability. It is inherited, or at least innate, not due to teaching or training; it is intellectual, not emotional or moral, not specific, i.e., it is not limited to any particular kind of work, but enters into all we do or say or think. Of all our mental abilities, it is the most far-reaching.*
>
> *(Carroll, 1985, p. 90; original quotation from Simon, 1974, p. 241–242)*

This single quotation comprises most of the seminal assertions about intelligence that have inspired bitter and prolonged debate over the past 70 years, viz.:

1. Whether intelligence is an independent attribute, one relatively free of influence from other characteristics of people such as motivation level or personality.
2. Whether intelligence is a *unitary* "all-round" trait or disposition that affects every activity that can be characterized as being intellectual or cognitive in nature.
3. Whether intelligence is inborn and not influenced by teaching or training.

TABLE 14-11   DEFINITIONS OF INTELLIGENCE

Lewis M. Terman (1921)	"The power to think abstractly."
Alfred Binet (1910)	"Comprehension, invention, direction, and censorship; intelligence lies in these four words."
Edward G. Boring (1923)	"Measurable intelligence is simply what the tests of intelligence test, until further scientific observation allows us to extend the definition."
Lloyd G. Humphreys (1971)	"Intelligence is defined as the entire repertoire of acquired skills, knowledge, learning sets, and generalization tendencies considered intellectual in nature that are available at any one period of time."
Robert J. Sternberg (1985)	"Intelligence is goal-directed adaptive behavior."

Source: After Jensen, 1980.

Binet set out to detect retardation only. Gradually, however, it became evident that he was measuring something more. Binet was too successful. His test had predictive validity at all score levels; that is, it predicted school performance among high, as well as low, IQ scorers. The test clearly measures something other than retardation alone. Because IQ test scores are related to school performance and reflections of other cognitive abilities, most behavioral scientists concluded that the IQ test reflects general intelligence. Unfortunately, they also began to equate intelligence with IQ test results. For many, the test *became* the construct that it was designed to measure, almost as if a stopwatch became a racehorse's speed. We must always remember that our definition or characterization of intelligence need not be consistent with the results of IQ tests. Cyril Burt was defining intelligence for his audience solely on the basis of his appraisal of the IQ test research literature. Intelligence may be much more, or much less, than this.

IS IQ INDEPENDENT? Does the IQ test measure a pure, crystalline factor, independent of traits other than the ability to solve complex problems? No. People's motives and their personality traits both affect how well people do on the IQ test. One example of this is related by two clinicians who tested the IQ of an institutionalized child. "What is an orange?" they asked. The child professed not to know. The child apparently hoped that if he did not answer the question correctly, the test givers would stay longer. This lonely child was more interested in warm human contact than in answering questions about oranges (Zigler and Seitz, 1985).

DOES IQ REFLECT A SINGLE THING? For the past 80 years, scientists have debated whether the IQ score reflected a unitary and pervasive cognitive ability or a whole host of tendencies and abilities, including the effects of motivation and personality. Charles Spearman (1863–1945), one of the most influential intelligence researchers of this century, believed that the most important determinant of IQ is *g*. For Spearman, *g* (for *general* factor) was a characteristic of brain functioning that accounts for the human's ability to accomplish complex mental activities (Spearman, 1923). Spearman argued for the existence of *g* based upon the results of a statistical technique that he pioneered: **factor analysis** (see Box 14-1).

The factor analysis of mental test scores shows that one factor accounts for much of the variability in performance on different mental tests. If a person does well on one type of mental or cognitive test, he or she is likely to perform well on other types of cognitive tests (Hill, Reddon, and Jacobson, 1985; Jensen, 1980; Matarazzo and Matarazzo, 1984; McNemar, 1942). However, as Table 14-12 shows, factor analysis reveals more than one factor. Performance on IQ tests also is related to a *verbal comprehension factor* (often associated with good performance on the information, comprehension, similarities, and vocabulary subtests), a *performance* or *perceptual organization factor* (often associated with good performance on the picture completion, picture arrangement, block design, and object assembly subtests), and a *memory* or *freedom from*

TABLE 14-12   TYPICAL FACTOR LOADINGS
FOR THE WAIS—R

Subtest	Factors and Factor Loadings			
	G	*VC*	*PO*	*FD*
Information	.82	.75	.27	.30
Digit Span	.65	.30	.22	.64
Vocabulary	.86	.81	.26	.34
Arithmetic	.76	.44	.34	.55
Comprehension	.80	.71	.30	.27
Similarities	.81	.67	.36	.27
Picture Completion	.73	.44	.56	.17
Picture Arrangement	.68	.42	.42	.23
Block Design	.74	.27	.69	.33
Object Assembly	.64	.19	.73	.17
Digit Symbol	.64	.32	.38	.36

Source: Hill et al., 1985.

Note: G = general factor; VC = verbal comprehension; PO = perceptual organization; FD = freedom from distraction.

distraction factor (associated with good performance on the digit-span subtest). The existence of factors other than *g* led Spearman and others (Vernon, 1950) to propose the existence of a hierarchy of mental abilities that affect test performance.

Some critics have argued that *g* has been afforded too much attention. In fact, some scientists have argued that *g* doesn't exist. One, for example, charged that IQ performance (and "intellect") was really a product of some 150 fairly independent mental abilities (Guilford, 1982). However, research has shown that tests designed to measure these "independent" abilities, while not correlated highly with each other, do have significant *g* relations (Brody and Brody, 1976; McNemar, 1964).

It appears that Cyril Burt, Spearman, and others were at least partly correct. There does appear to be a mental disposition or ability that influences performance on a wide variety of cognitive tasks. These authors labeled this general mental ability "intelligence." In general, evidence suggests that *g* has properties usually associated with intelligence—for example, the ability to solve spatial or mathematical problems. But intelligence test scores do not predict perfectly school, work, or social functioning. Many people, for example, have observed that the principal determinant of good adjustment among the retarded is personality, not IQ (Weaver, 1946; Zigler and Seitz, 1985). Personality and motivational factors other than those tapped by the IQ test can strongly influence people's social adjustment, work performance, and success.

If we define intelligence as the totality of processes producing "goal-directed adaptive behavior," then a measure of *g* (IQ) is certainly a very incomplete measure of intelligence. However, if we define IQ as a cognitive ability associated with superior performance on a variety of *cognitive* tasks, superior academic performance, and the attainment of higher levels of occupational positions, then IQ constitutes a fairly good measure of intelligence. As you can see, much of the disagreement over

BOX 14-1
FACTOR ANALYSIS

You have seen that a correlation coefficient reveals the extent to which two variables are related. Scientists who wanted to understand relations among measures of mental abilities, however, were faced with a riddle that seemed too big for the correlation coefficient. IQ tests contain many subtests, of vocabulary, memory, reasoning, general information, and so forth, and it was almost impossible to determine how all the subtests related to one another based on correlations among them. (There would be 55 intercorrelations for the WAIS-R alone.) Factor analysis was developed by the English statistician Karl Pearson and by Spearman to help researchers chart the relations among many variables.

Instead of mental test scores, assume that we have physical test scores for each of several hundred people (Jensen, 1980). The physical tests include softball throw, hand grip, chinning, 50-yard dash, 100-yard dash, one-leg balance, mirror star tracing, pursuit rotor tracking, 1-mile run, and 5-mile run/walk. We are interested in the *nature* of athletic ability.

Is athletic ability unitary or are there different types of athletic ability?

In factor analysis, every variable is first correlated with every other variable. This produces a correlation matrix (Box Table 1). If performance on all of the tests were caused by the same thing, or factor (athletic ability), all scores would be highly correlated; a person who does poorly on one test should do poorly on the others and a person who does well on one should do well on the others. The correlation matrix shows that this is not the case. Let's see how factor analysis might help reveal the nature of the relationship between two of the tests, the 1-mile run and the 100-yard dash (Box Figure 1). As Box Figure 1 reveals, a correlation between these tests (variables) shows that high values on one variable are *generally* associated with high values on the second variable. However, this is not a perfect relationship. The correlation is only of moderate magnitude. Thus, some individuals ran quickly in the 1-mile run and slowly in the 100-yard dash (this negative relationship is captured in the second regression line). How do we interpret or make sense of these seemingly contradictory findings? We might assume that performance on

the two tests should be positively correlated because they are both caused, in part, by the same thing—a physiology that produces footspeed. But what could explain the instances in which the two variables are negatively related? Perhaps performance on one of the tests relates to a second *factor* that actually hurts performance on the other test. For example, heavy muscles may boost performance in the 100-yard dash but hurt performance in the 1-mile run. Thus, you can see that we identify each regression line with a different causal *factor* (e.g., footspeed, endurance).

Factor analysis clusters those measures that are highly related to one another and poorly related to other tests and measures. If all measures correlated highly, then we conclude that they all tap a single characteristic. But often, measures are influenced by different factors, and factor analysis groups them together by their correlations. The greater the variability in scores that is accounted for by a factor, the higher the correlation (*loading*) between the test and the factor. Box Table 2 shows the relation of four factors to various physical tests. Much of the variability is accounted for by the first factor, except in the

BOX TABLE 1 CORRELATION MATRIX FOR MEASURES OF PHYSICAL ABILITY

Variable	1	2	3	4	5	6	7	8	9	10
1. Softball throw		.76	.78	.32	.32	.29	.30	.44	.12	.16
2. Hand grip	.76		.93	.47	.47	.00	.00	.00	.14	.19
3. Chinning	.78	.93		.39	.39	.00	.00	.00	.15	.20
4. 50-yard dash	.32	.47	.39		.84	.00	.32	.32	.28	.22
5. 100-yard dash	.32	.47	.39	.84		.13	.28	.48	.65	.62
6. One-leg balance	.29	.00	.00	.00	.13		.00	.38	.27	.28
7. Mirror star tracing	.30	.00	.00	.32	.28	.00		.68	.09	.05
8. Pursuit rotor tracking	.44	.00	.00	.32	.48	.38	.68		.48	.47
9. 1-mile run	.12	.14	.15	.28	.65	.27	.09	.48		.93
10. 5-mile run/walk	.16	.19	.20	.22	.62	.28	.05	.47	.93	

Source: Jensen, 1980.

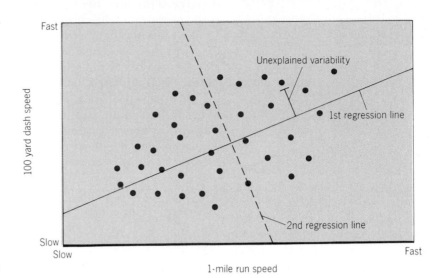

Scores on the 100-yard dash and the
1-mile run are plotted. This figure
shows that performance on the two tests
is fairly highly correlated (r = .65);
high scores on one variable are
associated with high scores on the second
variable. However, notice that the
relationship is not perfect. If it were
perfect, each data point (representing a
person's score on both tests) would lie
exactly on the dark regression line. The
distance between each data point and the
regression line may be considered
variation in performance on the two tests
or measures that cannot be accounted for
by the relationship between the two
variables (the two tests). Regression lines
are computed so that the variations
around the lines are as small as possible.
To the extent that scores on the two
measures lie on the regression line, we
say that the regression "accounts for"
variability in the two sets of scores.
Perhaps there is a second variable or
factor that can account for the
unexplained variability on the two
measures. Factor-analytic computations
produce a second regression line that is
designed to "account for" this previously
unexplained variability. Notice that
while the first regression line accounts
for why high scores on one test are
associated with high scores on the second
test, the second regression line shows
that, in some instances, high scores on
one measure are associated with low
scores on the other measure (for instance,
cases where the person ran the 100-yard
dash quickly, but the 5-mile run/walk
slowly). (From Jensen, 1980.)

BOX TABLE 2

Physical Test	Factors and Factor Loadings			
	I	*II*	*III*	*IV*
1. Softball throw	.70	−.45	.27	.42
2. Hand grip	.67	−.70	−.13	.04
3. Chinning	.65	−.70	−.13	.11
4. 50-yard dash	.70	−.11	.14	−.52
5. 100-yard dash	.86	.14	−.11	−.38
6. One-leg balance	.30	.31	−.03	.73
7. Mirror star tracing	.38	.26	.80	−.14
8. Pursuit rotor tracking	.63	.52	.47	.17
9. 1-mile run	.66	.53	−.45	−.02
10. 5-mile run/walk	.67	.48	−.48	.05

Source: Jensen, 1980.

one-leg balance and the mirror star tracing tests.

Jensen (1980), who developed this example, labeled the first factor "general athletic ability" since it accounts for so much variability in so many of the tests. Now, look at the pattern of loadings for factors 2 to 4. How would you label these factors? The labels that Arthur Jensen (1980) applied to these factors appear at the bottom of this page.

Answer. Factor 1 = general athletic ability; Factor 2 = hand and arm strength vs. resistance to fatigue of leg muscles; Factor 3 = hand–eye coordination/motor dexterity; Factor 4 = body balance.

IQ derives from disagreements about the nature of intelligence and not disagreements over the IQ tests per se. What do you think—does IQ really measure intelligence?

One criticism that many scientists (for example, Gould, 1981) level at the concept of any single measure of cognitive ability, such as g, is that it all too often has been used to argue that IQ has a genetic basis (as Burt stated, "It is inherited, or at least innate, not due to teaching or training"). Perhaps one reason that theories of both g and the genetic origins of intelligence go together (e.g., Burt, Jensen, Spearman) is that theorists who already believe that intelligence is genetically determined find it easier to imagine the inheritance of a single trait (g) than the conjoint inheritance of numerous, independent cognitive abilities. However, it is important to realize that the existence of a broad cognitive ability does not imply that the ability is genetically determined. It is entirely possible that g represents a learned, cognitive ability (Ferguson, 1956). Because g says little about whether measured IQ (or intelligence) is inherited, we must address that question directly.

Origins of Intelligence and Mental Test Performance

CULTURAL RELATIVITY OF INTELLIGENCE AND MENTAL TEST PERFORMANCE Does genetic inheritance affect people's performance on IQ tests? Some scientists have argued that IQ cannot be strongly genetically influenced because it is so socially and culturally determined. Consider the test items listed in Table 14-10. It is obvious that someone must be familiar with Western culture and education to answer them correctly. Others have argued that measures of intelligence must be *relevant* to the culture of the individual assessed, but the underlying disposition and ability that we measure remains the same across diverse cultures (Jensen, 1980). Suppose we are interested in footspeed. Footspeed itself would remain basically the same across diverse cultures, even though it might be measured (stopwatch versus a competitive race) and expressed (100-yard dash, 100-meter dash) in culturally specific ways.

If we change our focus and consider the cultural relativity of intelligence rather than IQ and adopt a broad definition of intelligence, or adaptive functioning, we see that what we would consider intelligent behavior varies from culture to culture. Intelligence in Silicon Valley would be associated with computer skills; intelligence among the Bushmen of Africa would be identified with hunting and tracking. However, some scientists still would argue that intelligent behavior is influenced by g. Cross-cultural studies suggest that people from diverse cultures associate the properties of g with intelligence. African Bushmen who scored well on tests of g were those whom other Bushmen considered intelligent (Reuning, 1972). The Bushmen's concept of practical intelligence did not differ essentially from the Western concept. Research also shows that to the extent that cognitive tests measure g, they are valid predictors of educational and occupational status in different ethnic groups: Americans of European ancestry and Americans of Japanese ancestry, all living in Hawaii (Nagoshi and Johnson, 1986). Intelligence tests also predict the competence in day-to-day skills, especially those involving verbal skills, and school performance, of Philippine children living in a rural barrio (Church, Katigbak, and Almario-Velazco, 1985).

GENETICS AND IQ   Let us assume that people can inherit a trait that boosts their intelligence. How would we prove that the trait is influenced by genes? We cannot merely determine whether children and parents have similar IQs. Strong similarities could be due to the fact that the parents and children share the same environment. A straightforward approach is to compare the resemblance of monozygotic and dizygotic twins (Scarr and Carter-Saltzmann, 1985; see discussion of behavioral genetics in Chapter 9). To the extent that monozygotic twin pairs are more similar in IQ than are dizygotic twin pairs, IQ is probably a function of genetic influence. As Table 14-13 shows, monozygotic twins are more similar in IQ than are dizygotic twins (Lewontin et al., 1984). There probably is a genetic component to IQ. However, it does not wholly determine IQ test performance. If it did, the correlation between IQs of monozygotic twins would be 1.00 (assuming our measure of IQ was perfectly valid). The difference in correlations between the two types of twins merely suggests that heredity has a large effect. Estimates are that around 30 to 50 percent of the variability in IQ in the U.S. population of white adolescents is due to genetic influence (Vanderberg and Vogler, 1985). This interpretation, however, rests on the assumption that the environments of monozygotic twins are no more similar than those of dizygotic twins.

TABLE 14-13   CORRELATIONS OF IQs IN IDENTICAL AND FRATERNAL TWIN PAIRS

Trait	Number of Studies	Mean of Correlations Identical Twins	Mean of Correlations Fraternal Twins	Mean Difference
General intelligence	30	.82	.59	.22
Verbal comprehension	27	.78	.59	.19
Numbers/mathematics	27	.78	.59	.19
Spatial visualization	31	.65	.41	.23
Memory	16	.52	.36	.16
Reasoning	16	.74	.50	.24
Clerical speed/accuracy	15	.70	.47	.22
Verbal fluency	12	.67	.52	.15
Divergent thinking	10	.61	.50	.11
Language achievement	28	.81	.58	.23
Social studies achievement	7	.85	.61	.24
Natural science achievement	14	.79	.64	.15
Total Means =	211	= .74	= .54	= .21

Source: Nichols, 1978; reproduced in Scarr and Carter-Saltzmann, 1985.

If the rearing environments of monozygotic twins were more similar than those of dizygotic twins, the greater similarity of monozygotic twins' IQs could be due to their greater environmental, rather than genetic, similarity. Monozygotic twins are more likely than dizygotic twins to dress alike and play and study together (Lewontin et al., 1984). But research suggests that monozygotic twins are treated similarly only to the extent that they *are* similar on the basis of behavior, personality, or intellect (Scarr and Carter-Saltzman, 1979; Lytton, 1977). Also, if environmental similarity produces high IQ correlations, then monozygotic twins who are treated most similarly should have the most similar IQs. But this is not the case (Plomin, Willerman, and Loehlin, 1976). Finally, Bailey and Horn (1986) have recently obtained evidence that IQ differences *between* monozygotic twins is due, in part, to environmental factors unique to monozygotic twins. Because these environmental factors (e.g., prenatal environment?) create differences only within monozygotic twin-pairs, Bailey and Horn argue that the concordance of IQs among monozygotic twins actually may underrepresent the contribution of heredity to IQ in the general population.

Adoption studies also provide evidence that genetic factors influence IQ. In these studies researchers examine the correlations between parents and children in both adoptive and nonadoptive families. Results generally show that there is a higher correlation between the IQs of biologically related (nonadoptive) parents and their children than between adoptive parents and their children. Researchers have concluded that the common genetic bond between biological parents and their children causes them to have more similar IQs.

As with twin studies, criticisms have been lodged against adoption studies. For example, adoptive families are uniformly better educated and have higher socioeconomic status than the average nonadoptive family (Kamin, 1974; Lewontin et al., 1984). The similarity of adoptive families may, therefore, reduce the correlations between parents' and adoptive children's IQs. Also, adoptive studies have shown that although environment influences IQ less than genetic factors, environmental differences among families exerted large effects on achievement in school (Scarr and Carter-Saltzman, 1985). This is additional evidence that IQ is not the sole determinant of academic achievement.

What can we say to sum up the results of studies on IQ performance? First, it is undoubtedly true that personality and motivation, and not just cognitive ability, influence performance on IQ tests. Second, although IQ performance has many determinants, factor analysis suggests that a broad cognitive factor or ability, labeled *g*, appears to be the principal determinant. Third, IQ performance is significantly related to academic and occupational performance, but it is by no means the sole, or even the most powerful, determinant of this performance. Parental example, encouragement, and socioeconomic status may be even more influential (Scarr and Carter-Saltzman, 1985; Lewontin et al., 1984). Fourth, considerable evidence suggests that the ability to perform well on IQ tests is determined, in part, by genetic inheritance. However, the research that supports this conclusion is extremely difficult to do, and some have offered alternative interpretations (Gould, 1981; Lewontin et al., 1984). Research consistently reveals environmental influence of IQ, but genetic influence appears the single most important influence identified (Vandenberg and Vogler, 1985). Finally, IQ does not necessarily reflect intelligence. IQ primarily taps the ability to solve mathematical, verbal, or spatial-constructive problems. If one defines intelligence (as many behavioral scientists do) as *goal-directed adaptive behavior,* then you might view mental problem solving as just one attribute of intelligent behavior. Other attributes might include high frustration tolerance, high achievement motivation, excellent interpersonal skills, and creativity.

Special Topics in Intelligence

RACIAL DIFFERENCES IN IQ   Black people in America typically score about 15 points lower on IQ tests than white Americans (Jensen, 1985). In 1969, Arthur Jensen suggested that genetic factors were significantly responsible for this difference. Jensen based his hypothesis on arguments such as these (Mackenzie, 1984; Scarr and Carter-Saltzman, 1985):

1. IQ tests are unbiased and just as accurate in assessing the IQs of blacks as of whites. Hence, the racial difference in IQ cannot be due to faults in the tests (Jensen, 1980).
2. Blacks do worse on IQ tests than other minority groups who are at least as socially and economically disadvantaged.
3. Research on IQ variation *within* races suggests that such variation is due to genetic factors. Therefore, it is reasonable that IQ variation *between* races also is due, to a significant degree, to genetic influence.
4. There is no indisputable evidence that environmental factors can account for the racial difference in IQ.
5. Blacks and whites differ most on those tests that tap *g* most directly. Evidence suggests that *g* reflects fundamental differences in information-processing by the brain that are unlikely to be influenced by cultural factors (Jensen, 1985). Hence, the black–white difference in IQ cannot by due to sociocultural factors.

Those who disagree with Jensen's arguments make their case as follows: First, blacks and whites are more similar than different on the basis of IQ (see Figure 14-10). Second, Jensen's arguments are indirect. For instance, it is quite possible that genetic factors may produce differences in IQ within, but not between, races. If two races are exposed to different environments, differences within and between them may stem from distinctly different causes (Lewontin, 1970; see Figure 14-11). Some studies conflict with Jensen's (1985) claim that *g* reflects basic information-processing mechanisms in the brain that are immune to cultural influence. In general, complex, rather than simple, information-processing tasks correlate best with *g* (Rushalla, Schalt, and Vogel, 1985; Sternberg, 1985). As information-processing tasks become more complex, they are likely to be influenced by cultural factors (Borkowski and Maxwell, 1985; Posner, 1985; Rabbitt, 1985).

Researchers have directly addressed the question of racial differences in IQ. In one study, blood markers were used to determine levels of

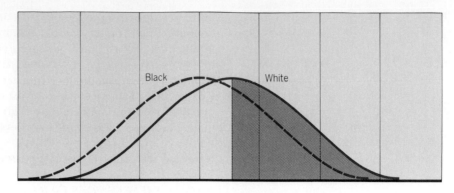

FIGURE 14-10 BLACK–WHITE IQ DISTRIBUTIONS IN THE UNITED STATES.
The two distributions substantially overlap. Some blacks score higher than most whites. Information about a person's race tells us relatively little about his or her IQ. We would be able to predict a person's IQ better from his or her educational achievements and occupational status. (Figure from A. Anastasi, Differential Psychology *(3rd Ed.), New York: Macmillan, 1958.)*

black and white ancestry (Scarr, Pakstis, Katz, and Baker, 1979). These markers of ancestry were then correlated with performance on four cognitive tests thought to tap *g*. Results showed little evidence that black

Population A   Population B

FIGURE 14-11 CAUSAL INFLUENCES WITHIN AND BETWEEN POPULATIONS.
The figure shows the heights of two populations of people. As you can see, the average height of Population A is greater than that of Population B. Within both populations, individual differences in height (variability) are determined by genetic inheritance. However, let us suppose that people in Population B live in an area that experiences severe food shortages. We know from other research that the reaction range of human height is

about 3 inches; i.e., environmental factors tend to influence height up to 3 inches (Tannes, 1978). This environmental factor would not influence height in Population A at all since all members of this population are adequately nourished. Variations in height within Population A are due almost entirely to genetic influences. However, malnutrition would regularly reduce the height of Population B individuals up to 3 inches. Thus, different causal factors may explain height differences within a population as opposed to differences between

populations. By best estimates, the reaction range of human IQ is 10 to 20 points (e.g., Zigler and Seitz, 1985). Hence, it is theoretically possible that if blacks and whites are characteristically exposed to different environments (differing, for instance, in poverty level, encouragement for study, role models for academic achievement), then environmental factors alone could account for black–white IQ differences, while IQ differences within each population are caused largely by genetic factors.

or African ancestry was associated with test performance. However, because blood markers are not completely reliable indicators of African ancestry (Mackenzie, 1984), these findings provide only modest support for an environmental interpretation.

In a second study, the researchers examined the IQs of mixed-race and white children, all of whom were raised in white environments (Eyferth, 1961). The mixed-race children had been born to white European mothers and black U.S. soldiers stationed in Europe after World War II. If genetic theories of intelligence are correct, mixed-race children should have had lower IQs than white children. But the two groups of children did not differ on IQ; the mean IQs of white and mixed-race children were 97.2 and 96.5, respectively.

In sum, no information conclusively supports either a genetic or an environmental hypothesis about the source of racial differences in IQ. The weight of recent, direct evidence favors the environmental interpretation, but studies in support of both hypotheses may be interpreted differently. In addition, we must remember that racial differences in IQ may have *both* environmental and genetic origins.

We have reviewed the question of black–white IQ differences thoroughly because it has received considerable attention in the popular press, because it illustrates how behavioral scientists can marshall evidence to support diametrically conflicting viewpoints, and finally, because some people may treat blacks and whites differently if they operate on incomplete information on this topic. Should society alter any social or political policy as a function of whether genes influence the black–white IQ difference?

Research clearly shows that environmental factors can influence IQ. Shouldn't society's goal be to develop *each* child's mental and intellectual development as fully as possible, regardless of race? There is good evidence, in fact, that this is being done. Recent research shows that black–white differences in academic achievement tests have declined over the past 15 years, perhaps because a higher percentage of blacks are remaining in school than in the past (Jones, 1984).

INTELLIGENCE ACROSS THE LIFE SPAN   What constitutes intelligent behavior changes over the life span (Sternberg, 1985). A young child may be judged intelligent because he can write his own name, but an adult earns little admiration for this skill. Intelligence is related to age in even more ways. In particular, aspects of intelligence change differently as people age.

Raymond Cattell (1963, 1971) labeled and characterized two factors in intelligence—fluid and crystallized intelligence. **Fluid intelligence** appears to be measured by tests that expose a person to somewhat novel problems without much verbal or informational content, such as the block design and digit symbol tests (Table 14-10). Tests of **crystallized intelligence**, in contrast, measure verbal-informational knowledge and previously acquired skills. Vocabulary, information, and arithmetic tests on the WAIS are examples. Thus, fluid intelligence allows us to acquire new knowledge and solve new problems; crystallized intelligence reflects the ability to apply and use previously acquired knowledge. In theory, crystallized intelligence results from the application of fluid intelligence.

When you solve a new problem or figure out the definition of a new vocabulary word, you add to your store of crystallized knowledge. A test item that would measure fluid intelligence is

lion is to jackal as cow is to _____ :

grass   wolf   sheep   camel

A question that would tap crystallized intelligence is

Jesus was to Peter as Joseph Smith was to _____ :

Brigham Young   William McKinley

Mary Eddy Baker   Horace Greeley

Notice that the first question is largely one of logic whereas the second requires greater prior acquisition of knowledge.

For many years, scientists have been interested in the effects of age on intelligence. Some studies have suggested that intelligence declines with age. Others suggest that intelligence either remains steady or actually increases (Horn and Donaldson, 1976; Baltes and Shaie, 1976). Fluid intelligence apparently begins to decline relatively early in life. But crystallized intelligence steadily increases until old age (see Figure 14-12). The relatively early decline in fluid intelligence can result in cases in which older people have remarkable vocabularies and an impressive storehouse of knowledge but have difficulty mastering new technologies or solving new problems. A decline in fluid intelligence may account, in part, for some older people's reluctance to move, to change occupations, or to pursue new experiences.

What can account for the early decline in fluid intelligence? No one is sure, but scientists have suggested that fluid intelligence is related to the biological growth or maturation of the brain (Horn and Donaldson, 1980). While the brain is growing, fluid intelligence increases, but when neurons begin decreasing in number, fluid intelligence declines (see Chapter 9).

FIGURE 14-12 INTELLIGENCE AND AGE.
Crystallized intelligence increases until a person reaches his or her 60s or 70s. Fluid intelligence begins declining as early as the early 30s. These rates of increase and decline are estimates, of course, and as with other personality and intellectual attributes or traits, variability and idiosyncratic patterns between individuals are the rule.

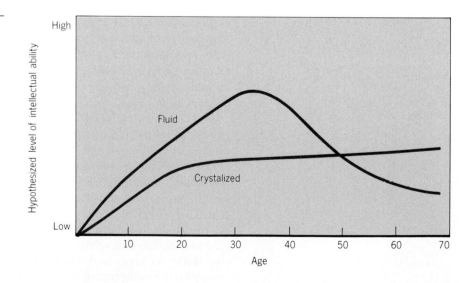

The age-dependent nature of intelligence gives rise to the names *fluid* and *crystallized*. During childhood and adolescence, fluid intelligence is "poured into" various intellectual activities or educational pursuits. Age, however, solidifies the products of these activities into "crystals" of skills and knowledge that persist well after fluid intelligence has declined. Therefore, the amount of crystallized intelligence of an older person may reflect the wisdom, or folly, of his youth.

INFORMATION PROCESSING AND INTELLIGENCE Finally, we turn to the relatively recent emphasis on an *information-processing* analysis of intelligence. This approach aims to find basic cognitive strategies or abilities that produce intelligent behavior and to discover the *basic cognitive* processes that constitute the building blocks of intelligence.

Advocates of this approach first try to identify the basic cognitive processes that underlie performance on an intellectual test. Thus, the information subtest on the WAIS requires that subjects perceive the letters and words that constitute a question, decode their syntax and meaning, determine the type of information necessary to answer the question, search long-term memory for the necessary information, and produce the information in words. Second, the researcher tries to determine which basic processes are most closely linked to the quality or speed of intellectual performance.

For example, Hunt, Lunneborg, and Lewis (1975) found that people high in verbal ability can find verbal memories faster than people lower in verbal ability. Perhaps this is one of the basic information processes that is tapped by tests of *g*.

Recently, Robert Sternberg (1985) at Yale University has proposed a model of intelligence that shows how information-processing abilities might interact with other factors to yield intelligent behavior. The first attribute of his three-part model is that intelligent behavior is *socioculturally defined*. Intelligent behavior can be defined as intelligent only within a given context. For example, certain South Pacific Islanders can navigate long distances by the stars or by the flow of oceanic currents (Berry, 1980). But this ability does not typify intelligence in modern America. Sternberg notes that not only can intelligent humans learn to behave optimally in particular contexts, but intelligent people also choose the contexts in which they perform. Sternberg notes that many of the "Quiz Kids," who were child prodigies on radio and television shows, led rather undistinguished lives. The ones who seemed to be most successful over the long haul were those who were able to find something they were both good at and interested in (see Box 14-2). Thus, for Sternberg, intelligence is more than just *g*, it also involves an optimal selection of environments and tasks in which to invest or use *g*.

The second attribute of intelligence, the *experiential* attribute in Sternberg's model, is the ability to learn and cope with new tasks or challenges and the ability to process information automatically. Although Sternberg views these two abilities as separate, he thinks that they interact. For instance, consider the cases of two students reading a particularly difficult passage in a psychology textbook. One student grasps the information quite well; the other student has to struggle.

BOX 14-2
THE FATE OF THE
QUIZ KIDS

The *Quiz Kids* began as a radio show on June 28, 1940, and ended its run as a television show in the mid-1950s. In the show, an adult quizmaster asked a small panel of precocious children questions on topics ranging from ornithology and mathematics to biblical history. The show instantly became a hit. The nation was delighted to see 7- and 8-year-old children answering questions that would stump most adults. At its peak the show elicited 20,000 letters per week from its loyal followers.

The contestants had IQs that ranged from about 135 to over 200. If the IQ test is indeed a valid predictor of academic and professional success, we should find that the contestants tended to become leaders in science, education, and literature. A recent follow-up of the Quiz Kids reveals that many did become highly successful (Feldman, 1982). They became professors, a diplomat, and even a Nobel laureate (James Watson, the co-discoverer of DNA). Yet in reading the biographical sketches of the Quiz Kids, one is struck more by the range of fates that awaited them rather than by their success.

Box Figure 1 shows the comedian Jack Benny greeting five of the Quiz Kids in Hollywood in 1941. The diverse fates awaiting the Quiz Kids are reflected in the histories of these young contestants. Richard Williams became the Director for China at the U.S. State Department, Gerard Darrow died fairly young and impoverished, having spent much of his life holding odd jobs (proofreader, greenhouse worker) and receiving welfare.

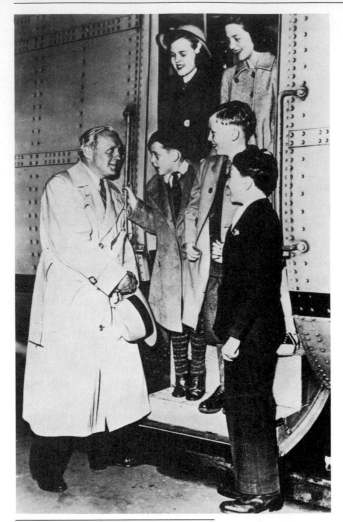

BOX FIGURE 1   JACK BENNY GREETS THE QUIZ KIDS.
Jack Benny and Quiz Kids Gerard Darrow, Richard Williams, Claude Brenner (in front, left to right) and Joan Bishop and Cynthia Clyne (in back, left to right). (From Feldman, 1982.)

Another, Claude Brenner, graduated from MIT as an engineer and was involved in the Gemini, Apollo, and Skylab U.S. space missions. Still another, Joan Bishop, has had a varied musical career, but her most consistent employment has been as a singer in a piano bar.

Clearly, a high IQ does not ensure professional success, scientific accomplishment, or notoriety. It is probably best to think of IQ, or *g,* as a necessary but not sufficient condition for certain types of intellectual and professional accomplishment. A high IQ is required to graduate from MIT in engineering, but having a high IQ does not guarantee success in engineering or any other field. Most related to success among the Quiz Kids was not IQ but rather a relentless pursuit of what they were good at and were interested in (Sternberg, 1985).

What accounts for this difference? The first student masters the new information more readily both because she is superior at mastering novelty per se and because she needs to allocate less attention and effort to the act of reading. Reading has become more automatic for her.

The third and final attribute of intelligence, a *componential* attribute, is superior or more efficient information processing. The information-processing components associated with intelligence may be quite basic, such as searching through memory for the names of letters, or they may be higher order processing skills—what Sternberg terms *metacomponents*. Metacomponent processing skills are more global; for example, they would involve decision-making processes such as deciding what problems require initial solutions, or selection or more basic information-processing skills necessary to solve a problem.

Sternberg's theory is quite broad. He has tried to characterize the essential features of all intelligent behavior, not just that displayed on IQ tests or in school. However, the breadth of Sternberg's theory may be a problem. According to Sternberg's theory, adaptive behaviors such as the appropriate use of social skills—knowing when to smile—might be considered to reflect intelligence. Other theorists (Jensen, 1980) identify intelligence much more closely with specific cognitive skills (those that contribute to performance on tests of *g*). Some behavioral scientists might argue that no matter how well a ditch digger fits into his sociocultural niche, he is not as intelligent as the scientist who is unhappy in his marriage and socially awkward, but who performs like a champ on IQ tests. Intelligence is, they argue, intrinsically, an intellectual-cognitive attribute. Who is right? That's up to you to decide.

SUMMARY

The principal steps in psychological assessment are to determine the goal of assessment, select the appropriate assessment strategy, and apply the selected assessment strategy or device in a manner consistent with assessment goals.

1. *The Goals of Assessment.* Frequent goals of psychological assessment are to identify an appropriate treatment, identify a person's abilities, discover personality characteristics, and make specific behavioral predictions.

2. *Psychometric Criteria for the Evaluation of Assessment Devices.* A reliable test or measure produces repeatable results. If all items of a test reliably measure the same variable, then the answers to different items should be highly correlated.

3. *Validity.* Validity is concerned with whether the thing we measure is useful and appropriate to our assessment goals. A test is not valid or invalid; rather it is valid for some purposes and not others. If a test or other assessment strategy is supposed to measure a hypothetical construct (e.g., anxiety, depression), *construct validation* is used to determine the validity of the test. In this procedure, the results of the test are compared with findings obtained on numerous other measures of the same construct.

4. *Strategies of Assessment.* The major assessment strategies are structured and unstructured interviewing, projective and objective testing, and behavioral or direct assessment strategies. The particular assessment strategy used depends upon theoretical, psychometric, and pragmatic factors.

THE ASSESSMENT OF INTELLIGENCE

The first successful intelligence test was developed by Alfred Binet, a French psychologist interested in identifying mentally retarded children. The Binet test soon proved itself useful in predicting the academic accomplishments of both high and low scorers; it identified geniuses as well as the retarded. Much of the controversy over IQ tests is not due to the tests themselves but rather the uses to which the tests have been put.

1. *IQ Tests.* IQ tests contain questions that tap a variety of intellec-

ASSESSMENT OF PERSONALITY, BEHAVIOR, AND INTELLIGENCE

tual and cognitive abilities. Subjects are asked to recall items from memory, explain the similarities between items, do mathematical problems, define words, and so on. Psychometric research has revealed that IQ tests are quite reliable and are moderately valid for predicting later academic and professional accomplishments. For instance, children with high IQs tend to acquire more scholastic knowledge, get higher grades, and stay in school longer.

2. *Intelligence and the IQ Test.* Considerable debate has traditionally surrounded three assertions regarding intelligence as it is assessed by IQ tests: (1) that intelligence is independent of personality and motivational influences, (2) that intelligence is unitary and pervasive, influencing all we say or do that is intellectual in nature, and (3) that intelligence is inborn and innate. Research now suggests that performance on IQ tests is not independent of motivational and personality factors. Also, factor analysis research suggests that IQ tests do tap a unitary cognitive ability or trait (called *g*) and that this ability appears to influence performance on a wide variety of cognitive tasks. Finally, considerable research suggests that *g* is genetically influenced.

3. *Is* g *Intelligence?* Disagreement with respect to this question seems to be produced largely by disagreements about what intelligence is. There is much evidence that high levels of *g* are associated with excellent mathematical performance, a prodigious vocabulary, excellent spatial/perceptual reasoning ability, school achievement, and pro-

fessional attainments. For some psychologists this is sufficient to view *g* as a good measure of intelligence. However, for other psychologists intelligence is a much broader concept. Some argue that intelligence is the collection of processes yielding goal-directed adaptive behavior. For these psychologists *g* would be only one contributor to intelligence.

4. *Racial Differences in IQ.* Blacks in the U.S. score on average about 15 points lower on IQ tests than do whites. Some have argued that this difference is due primarily to genetic differences between the races. It is now impossible to evaluate this claim with certainty. However, recent research suggests that a substantial portion of the IQ difference between blacks and whites is due to environmental influences.

5. *Intelligence Across the Life Span.* Some aspects of cognitive or intellectual performance decline as we grow old, while other aspects remain stable or grow. *Fluid* intelligence appears to be measured best by questions that confront the subject with a novel problem. *Crystallized* intelligence is best measured by tests that tap previously learned verbal/factual information. Research shows that while fluid intelligence increases quickly in youth, it begins to decline in middle age—sometimes by age 30. Crystallized intelligence, on the other hand, may grow across the life span.

6. *Information Processing and Intelligence.* A recent thrust of intelligence research is to break intelligence down into its basic elements. For example, Robert Sternberg has proposed that part of intelli-

gence is learning the skills we are good at. Other parts concern the ability to cope with novel challenges or tasks, automatizing information-processing steps, and more efficient basic information processing.

FURTHER READINGS

A number of books provide excellent general introductions to psychological assessment and psychometric theory. An eminently readable introduction is Arthur Jensen's *Bias in Mental Testing* (1980). A general introduction to assessment that is less tied to intelligence testing is Anne Anastasi's *Psychological Testing* (1982), or Lee Cronbach's *Essentials of Psychological Testing* (1984). If you are especially interested in psychometrics and are mathematically inclined, an excellent text is Jum Nunnally's *Psychometric Theory* (1978). A now somewhat dated text that gives the student an excellent perspective on the whole assessment enterprise is Jerry Wiggins' *Personality and Prediction* (1973).

If the student is interested in special topics in assessment, some recommended books are Stephen Gould's *The Mismeasure of Man* (1981), a book detailing how ideas about intelligence have been used to support, often inappropriately, social or political agendas or personal biases. Robert Sternberg's large *Handbook of Human Intelligence* (1985) provides an excellent compendium of papers on intelligence, and Ruth Feldman's *Whatever Happened to the Quiz Kids?* (1982) provides interesting examples of how much, and little, a high IQ can propel people toward personal and professional happiness and success.

700

15

PSYCHOPATHOLOGY: TREATMENT

SOMATIC TREATMENTS ———————

ELECTROCONVULSIVE THERAPY

PSYCHOSURGERY

DRUG TREATMENTS

PSYCHOLOGICAL TREATMENTS ———————

VERBAL PSYCHOTHERAPIES

BEHAVIOR THERAPY

EFFECTIVENESS OF PSYCHOLOGICAL TREATMENTS

There is a saying that "desperate times require desperate measures." History shows that desperate measures of every conceivable sort have been used in the treatment of mental disorders (see Chapter 13 for a full discussion of mental disorders). How can psychologists stop people who are depressed from feeling that they are evil, selfish, and worthless? How do they help anxious people not to worry incessantly about what someone else might consider trifles? If one hallmark of psychopathology is the helplessness or loss of control felt by sufferers, surely a similar sense of helplessness is felt by a victim's family and friends. Could anyone have stopped the comedian W. C. Fields from drowning in an endless series of martinis? Could anyone have stopped the poet Sylvia Plath from escaping an interminable depression through suicide? Could anyone have retrieved the great dancer, Nijinski, from his impenetrable schizophrenia (see Figure 15-1a–c)?

Even today a tremendous variety of treatments, some desperate, some not, are aimed at mental disorders. Some treatments are targeted at changing people's physiological functioning, some at increasing their

FIGURE 15-1   FIELDS, PLATH, AND NIJINSKI.

The comedian W. C. Fields, the poet Sylvia Plath, and the great ballet star Nijinski; Each succumbed to a mental disorder that could not be stayed. Fields tried to stop drinking many times but found he was not happy without alcohol. When asked at the end of his life what he would change if he had his life to live over, he replied wistfully, "You know, I'd like to see how I would have made out without liquor" (Taylor, 1949). After repeated bouts of severe depression, Plath killed herself. Nijinski gradually entered a psychosis from which he never recovered. Just before he was hospitalized, he wrote, "I am a simple man who has suffered a lot. I believe I suffered more than Christ. I love life and want to live, to cry but cannot—I feel such a pain in my soul—a pain which frightens me. My soul is sick. My soul, not my mind. The doctors do not understand my illness" (Nijinski, 1936; in Kaplan, 1964).

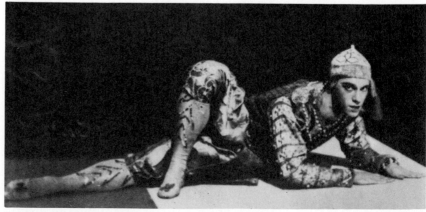

behavioral skills, and some at improving their ability to deal with strong emotions. In this chapter, we will explore the theoretical and experimental bases of diverse treatments of mental disorders, attempt to show how such treatments are carried out, and evaluate evidence of the effectiveness of these treatments.

SOMATIC TREATMENTS

Soma means "body" in Greek, and **somatic treatments** are those therapies the effectiveness of which can be understood best in terms of their direct effects on the body's structures or processes. In contrast, the effectiveness of **psychotherapies** can, in theory, be understood best on the basis of their effects on the mind (or *psyche* in Greek). That is, we cannot gain an appreciation of how or why psychotherapies work without considering their effects on psychological or mentalistic variables, for example, attitudes, beliefs, or expectations. But it is not enough to say that somatic therapies affect the body whereas psychotherapies affect the mind. When a patient or client is given a somatic treatment, it almost always affects the client's mental operations, attitudes, beliefs, and expectations. For instance, just anticipating a somatic treatment might cause a patient to become hopeful, fearful, or depressed. Although somatic treatments affect mental operations, their effects can best be understood by examining how they affect the body.

Electroconvulsive Therapy

Theoretically, somatic treatments should evolve in the following way: scientists should gather data on the nature of the physiological abnormality that produces a mental disorder and then develop treatments designed to correct the physiological abnormality. While this scenario seems eminently reasonable, it does not describe the development of many somatic treatments. The evolution of these treatments can often be attributed to wrong thinking, incorrect evidence, or luck.

Electroconvulsive therapy (**ECT**) arose out the belief of the Hungarian physician, Von Meduna, in the 1930s that epileptics were less likely than others to become schizophrenic. He hypothesized that epileptic seizures (convulsions) somehow cured or prevented schizophrenia (Valenstein, 1986). Therefore, he produced convulsions in his schizophrenic patients by administrating drugs. He and others (Cerletti, see Snyder, 1980) soon reported that their patients seemed to improve following drug- and electrically induced convulsions. But more recent research has shown that epileptics are not less likely to develop schizophrenia than others (Valenstein, 1986), and ECT is not especially effective against schizophrenia (Ottosson, 1985). Research has shown, however, that ECT is quite effective in alleviating severe depression.

ECT often has been portrayed in the popular press as a cruel and inhuman treatment, and in fact, years ago ECT could be painful and dangerous (Ottosson, 1985). Strong electrical charges were delivered

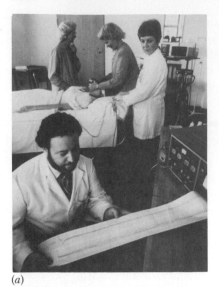

(a)

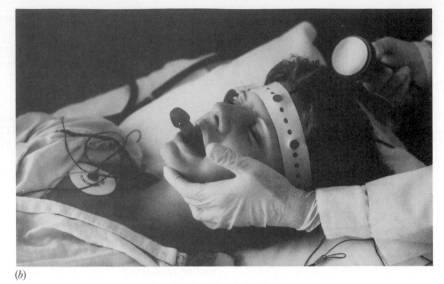

(b)

FIGURE 15-2
ELECTROCONVULSIVE THERAPY.
A patient about to receive ECT. (a) A
nurse, an anesthesiologist, and a
psychiatrist are in attendance. (b) Metal
electrodes are attached to one side of the
patient's head, and electricity is
introduced that produces a cortical
seizure for about 30 seconds. Patients
generally receive six to eight treatments
at 48 to 72 hour intervals. (From
Goldstein, Baker, and Jamison, 1986.)

across the entire brain, and the patient had muscular contractions that sometimes broke bones. But today, patients receive less electricity, it is delivered to only one cerebral hemisphere, and a drug prevents violent muscle contractions (see Figure 15-2).

ECT is stressful, requires anesthesia, and can produce unintended effects. Therefore, it is generally used only with severely depressed patients—those with physical signs of depression, such as weight loss and sleep disturbance, thoughts of suicide, and feelings of extreme hopelessness and sadness. ECT is also used in less severely depressed people who have not improved following other treatments (e.g., drug therapy). ECT often is used in combination with other treatments—usually psychotherapy.

What are the effects of ECT? Every somatic treatment has two types of effects: presumed **therapeutic effects** and **side effects**. Therapeutic effects are intended to improve the patient's mental disorder. Side effects are unintended, undesirable effects that do not improve the mental disorder. (Some side effects are sufficiently severe and long-lasting so as to produce disease; an **iatrogenic** illness is one produced by treatment.) Most research has shown ECT to be exceptionally effective against physical signs of depression and usually rapidly improves a patient's mood. Moreover, these effects are remarkably reliable. A review of ECT revealed it to be superior to antidepressant medication (see Figure 15-3).

PLACEBOS   About 30 percent of the patients who received sham ECT or placebo improved in the research depicted in Figure 15-3. Typical **placebo** treatments are ones that are intended to produce an expectation of, or hope for, improvement, but that have no other effects (see Chapter 4). Both sham ECT, which involves all aspects of real ECT except the electrical shock, and placebo treatment, an inert medication, are designed to make patients *expect* to improve. But neither contains the active ingredient of ECT—electric shock. A placebo, meaning "I shall

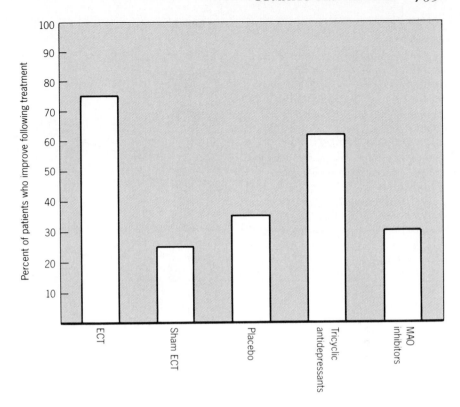

FIGURE 15-3 EFFECTIVENESS OF ECT.

The graph shows the mean percentages of depressed patients who improved following ECT, sham ECT (all aspects of ECT except the electric current), placebo, and two types of antidepressant medicine: tricyclic antidepressants and monoamine oxidase inhibitors. (From Janicek et al., 1985.)

please" in Latin, is a treatment that comprises a promise to please (produce therapeutic change), but *only* the promise.

Researchers use placebos to show that somatic treatments do something more than merely produce hope. Why do some patients improve following placebo treatments? Some patients might improve regardless of treatment (or no treatment!); they are recovering on their own when the placebo is given. Some patients improve because a placebo induces hope, and hope can chase away a variety of disorders, including depression. Hope is associated with biochemical changes in the brain that may have beneficial effects. Several studies have shown that placebo effects are eliminated or reduced if, along with a placebo, patients are given drugs that block opiate receptors in the brain (see Chapter 5; Levine, Gordon, and Fields, 1979). In other words, people apparently react to a placebo by manufacturing opiates in their own bodies, and these opiates may have a host of beneficial effects. To call a placebo *inert*, therefore, is inaccurate. A placebo is not inert, it merely does not contain a therapeutic ingredient in which the researcher or therapist is primarily interested.

Patients are not alone in being influenced by hopes. Therapists also may be affected by the hopes and expectations that accompany the use of a new treatment. For example, if a therapist believes that a new therapy will be successful, the therapist may pay more attention to patients who report that they are feeling better, or the therapist may appear more optimistic in dealing with patients, and this very optimism may benefit patients. In research, to reduce the likelihood that a thera-

F I G U R E 15-4 (a) *SINGLE-BLIND DESIGN.*
In a single-blind *experimental design, patients do not know the specific treatment they are receiving. They may know the types of treatments being evaluated, but not which one they will actually get.*
(b) *DOUBLE-BLIND DESIGN.*
In a double-blind *design, both therapist and patients are unaware of which patients receive the actual treatment and which receive the placebo. Some third party randomly assigns patients to treatment groups. Only after treatment does the third party reveal the treatment given each patient.*

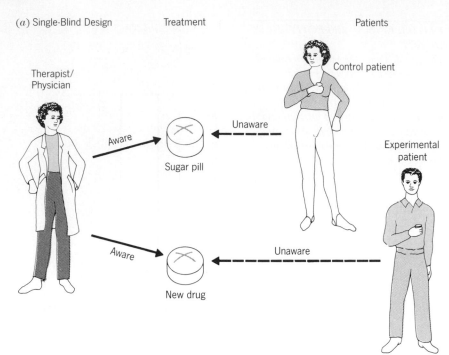

(*a*) Single-Blind Design

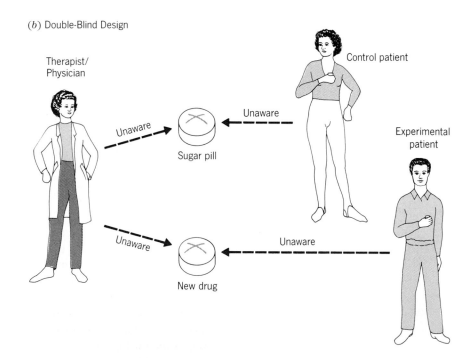

(*b*) Double-Blind Design

pist's psychological reactions will interfere with the evaluation of a new treatment, clinicians use a *double-blind* research design. In this design, neither the therapist nor the patient knows whether the patient is getting the experimental treatment or a placebo (see Figure 15-4).

Psychosurgery

Thousands of people receive surgery every day and we accept it as desirable and appropriate. Why then do so many people react with fear and distress to the idea of **psychosurgery**? Psychosurgery is the surgical destruction of part of the brain with no apparent neuropathology for the purpose of alleviating a mental disorder. Many critics have charged that psychosurgery is not only poor medicine, but unethical as well (Breggin, 1980; Kaimowitz, 1980).

Why is there such controversy over this form of treatment? New treatments are often controversial, at least until their benefits and risks are well understood. But psychosurgery is an old treatment that probably had its origins in trephining, between 1500 and 2000 B.C. (Lisowski, 1967). Controversy surrounds psychosurgery because the risk of political or social abuse is great when surgery is justified on the basis of a person's moods, beliefs, and "abnormal" behavior and where there is no *direct* evidence of brain damage.

The first published reports of the intentional destruction of brain tissue for the purpose of alleviating mental disorders began to appear in the late 1800s, and the first widely used technique was developed by the Portuguese neurologist, Egas Moniz, who was awarded the Nobel Prize in 1949 for pioneering this technique (Valenstein, 1980a). Moniz's procedure, later modified by the American physicians Walter Freeman and James Watts, involved destroying the prefrontal area of the brain and came to be called a **leucotomy** (from the Greek *leuco* meaning "white matter," referring to nerve fibers, and *tome,* meaning "knife") or **lobotomy**. These procedures were based on animal research showing that prefrontal lesions in monkeys had a calming effect. Originally, in prefrontal lobotomies, the skull was opened and a knife inserted into the brain between the frontal and prefrontal lobes. In **transorbital lobotomies** in the late 1940s a surgical instrument was inserted behind the eye and to sever fibers in the frontal lobes (Figure 15-5). This procedure could be performed during an office visit without general anesthetic. About 35,000 lobotomies were performed in the United States between 1935 and 1978, about 500 a year between 1945 and 1978 (Valenstein, 1980a). Today lobotomies and other types of psychosurgery involve the destruction of relatively small amounts of brain tissue by means of electrodes inserted into various areas of the brain (Figure 15-6). By one estimate, no more than 200 a year are now performed in the United States (Valenstein, 1986).

TARGETS OF PSYCHOSURGERY Psychosurgery has been used to treat a great variety of mental disorders, ranging from depression and schizophrenia to obsessive-compulsive anxiety disorder (conditions treated by psychosurgery in one recent study of 52 patients are listed in Table 15-1). Generally it has been used only with the most severely affected patients, those so severely agitated and disturbed that their lives have stopped having even a semblance of normality (Valenstein, 1980b). Most candidates for psychosurgery require calming and have not benefited from nonsurgical treatment (Mirsky and Orzack, 1980).

FIGURE 15-5 TRANSORBITAL LOBOTOMY.
A thin instrument was forced into the space between the eye and skull and then rotated to destroy frontal lobe tissue. (From Valenstein, 1968.)

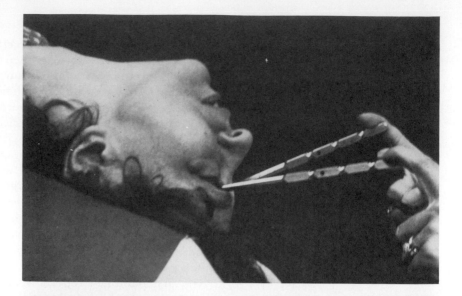

FIGURE 15-6 MODERN LOBOTOMY.
Electrodes are inserted through holes drilled in the skull, and brain tissue is destroyed by radiowaves or electric current. (From M. Hunter Brown reprinted in Valenstein, 1980a.)

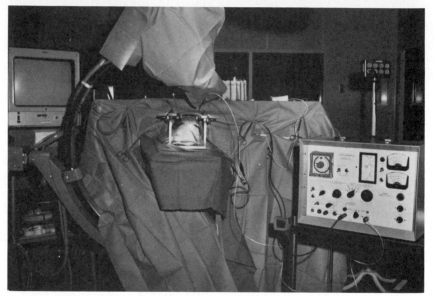

EFFECTIVENESS In evaluating whether psychosurgery works, psychologists must ask just what psychosurgery is effective at. They also must ask exactly what psychosurgery is supposed to do: calm patients or lead to broader beneficial effects?

In a recent evaluation of psychosurgery, researchers evaluated its effectiveness in relieving particular symptoms and in improving social and vocational functioning (Mirsky and Orzack, 1980). Results showed that about half of the psychosurgery patients benefited substantially from their operation in such areas as behavioral disturbance, impulse control, suicidal thoughts, obsessive-compulsive thoughts, hallucinations, and excessive anger. Moreover, by their own ratings and by ratings of people

TABLE 15-1 REASONS FOR PSYCHOSURGERY

Surgeon	Depression	Obsessive-Compulsive	Depression Obsessive	Schizophrenia	Affective Schizophrenia	Pain	Total
I	3	1		3	1		8
II	3	1		2	1		7
III	4				1	5	10
Other					1		2
IV	5	2	12	2	4	—	25
Total	15	4	13	7	8	5	52

Note: The diagnoses of patients evaluated in the Mirsky and Orzack study who received psychosurgery from different surgeons.

who knew them well, the psychosurgery patients' symptoms became less severe following surgery. There was little evidence of cognitive or intellectual impairment due to the surgery. Many of the patients who had been operated on worked in business or the professions. The positive results of this evaluation and others (e.g., Teuber, Corkin, and Twitchell, 1977) led the National Commission for the Protection of Human Subjects of Biomedical and Behavioral Research to conclude in 1977 that psychosurgery "can be of significant therapeutic value in the treatment of certain disorders or in the relief of certain symptoms" (Chorover, 1980, p. 246).

Despite the evidence that modern psychosurgery can help some patients with severe mental disorders, it is doubtful that it will ever again be widely used. The conditions that led to its initial popularity—large numbers of institutionalized and uncontrollable mental patients and the absence of any alternative effective treatments—no longer exist. The success of alternative therapies, especially pharmacological therapies, has left few candidates for such irreversible and extreme treatments. What is more, people remain concerned that the procedure may produce subtle cognitive and motivational deficits. Once brain neurons are destroyed they will never return—and neither will those aspects of personality that they subserve.

Drug Treatments

In the early 1950s about half of all the hospital beds in the United States were occupied by psychotic patients. Many of these were schizophrenics who remained hospitalized for months or years without improving despite a variety of treatments ranging from psychotherapy to ECT. However, by 1970 the number of patients in mental hospitals had fallen dramatically (see Figure 15-7). This decrease can be attributed largely to the discovery of antipsychotic drugs.

Histamine is a naturally occurring chemical in the brain that can produce declines in blood pressure. Because some surgical patients experience a dangerous, precipitous fall in blood pressure (a *hypotensive crisis*) following surgery, in the 1940s physicians began administering *anti*histamines to patients prior to surgery. In the 1940s a French physician, Henri Laborit, noticed that the antihistamine drug promethazine

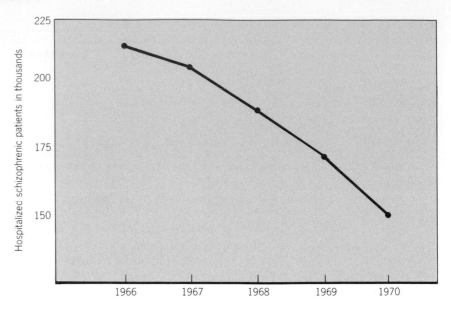

FIGURE 15-7 IMPACT OF ANTIPSYCHOTIC DRUGS. The relation between the number of patients in mental hospitals in the United States and the introduction of antipsychotic drugs. (From Freedman, 1985; modified from Davis and Cole, 1975.)

TABLE 15-2
ANTIPSYCHOTIC DRUGS

Generic Name	Trade Name
Butaperazine	Repoise
Chlorpromazine	Thorazine
Fluphenazine	Prolixin
Haloperidol	Haldol
Loxapine	Loxitane
Molindone	Moban
Perphenazine	Lidone
Trifluoperazine	Trilafon
Thioridazine	Stelazine
Thiothixene	Mellaril
	Navane

Source: Simpson and May, 1982.

not only protected surgical patients against low blood pressure after surgery but also appeared to calm patients before surgery. The calming effects of antihistamines led researchers to investigate whether these drugs might help psychiatric patients. In 1952, the French psychiatrists Jean Delaz and Pierre Deniker administered a new antihistamine, chlorpromazine (often referred to by its commercial or trade name, *Thorazine*) to a variety of psychiatric patients. They found that chlorpromazine was remarkably effective in calming agitated schizophrenic patients and virtually eliminated some of their symptoms (e.g., hallucinations). Over the past 30 years, many similar antipsychotic, or **neuroleptic**, drugs have been marketed (see Table 15-2).

Because antipsychotic drugs are so effective in helping schizophrenics, virtually every patient showing the symptoms of schizophrenia is prescribed such medication. Typically, a psychiatrist (a medical doctor trained to assess and treat mental disorders), administers a small test dose of one of the antipsychotic drugs (Simpson and May, 1982). If a patient is agitated or aggressive, the psychiatrist prescribes a sedating drug, such as chlorpromazine. If a patient is withdrawn and lethargic, the psychiatrist prescribes fluphenazine (Prolixin), a drug that has activating effects. If a patient responds well to the test dose (for example, does not become too drowsy or too active), the psychiatrist increases the dose. Too much drug can produce undesirable side effects; too little allows schizophrenic symptoms to reappear. The duration of drug treatment varies greatly. Patients with a first schizophrenic episode may be withdrawn from drugs after 6 months. Patients with chronic schizophrenia may be kept on antipsychotics for years. Even they, however, are withdrawn from drugs periodically to reduce the likelihood of serious side effects (to be discussed later).

EFFECTIVENESS   As we have said, antipsychotics have revolutionized the treatment of schizophrenia, allowing thousands of schizophrenics to leave hospitals and lead relatively independent lives. When antipsychotics were introduced, they were hailed by some as panaceas and reviled by others as "chemical straitjackets" that controlled patients by making them stuporous. The truth appears to lie somewhere between these two extremes. In evaluating the efficacy of antipsychotics it is important to note that not all schizophrenics respond favorably to these drugs, and some symptoms are more responsive than others. In general, the **positive symptoms** of schizophrenia (see Chapter 13) are most affected by antipsychotics. Symptoms like hallucinations and delusions are alleviated more than **negative symptoms** like social withdrawal and flattened affect. This difference may arise because negative symptoms are associated with structural brain pathology (such as enlarged ventricles due to neuron loss) whereas positive symptoms are associated with neurotransmitter imbalance (Andreasen, Olsen, Dennert, and Smith, 1982; see Chapter 13). Presumably, antipsychotics improve neurotransmitter imbalance but not structural abnormalities.

In Chapter 13 you saw that schizophrenia may be caused by excessive activity of neurons that are stimulated by the neurotransmitter **dopamine**. It is now well accepted that all drugs that reduce the symptoms of schizophrenia (Table 15-2) inhibit the activity of **cAMP (cyclic adenosine 3′,5′ monophosphate)**. Normally, when dopamine occupies the post- synaptic receptors of a neuron, this causes cAMP to change the nature of proteins in nerve cell membranes. When these membranes are changed sufficiently, ions begin to flow freely across the nerve membrane and an action potential can result (see Chapter 2). Antipsychotic drugs prevent dopamine from activating cAMP and so prevent action potentials and neuronal transmission in dopaminergic neurons. There is a direct correlation between the ability of an antipsychotic drug to reduce schizophrenia symptoms and its potency in blocking cAMP activity (Feldman and Quenzer, 1984).

Evidence of the clinical effectiveness of antipsychotic drugs comes from studies in which the performance of schizophrenics given antipsychotics is compared with the performance of schizophrenics who are given placebo. In many studies, schizophrenics are discharged from the hospital and kept track of for a period of time by researchers who see whether medicated and placebo-treated patients differ in the return of symptoms, problems in living, and rehospitalization. These follow-up studies consistently show that patients receiving antipsychotic drugs perform significantly better than patients given placebo (Davis, 1980). So many studies have found results favoring antipsychotics that the odds that these results are due to chance has been calculated at 1 in 1 billion. For example, in one study, the researchers randomly assigned 120 people hospitalized for a first schizophrenic episode to either a medication or a placebo group (Crow, MacMillan, Johnson, and Johnstone, 1986). The researchers followed these patients for 2 years after their hospital discharge. Results showed that 46 percent of patients on medication were rehospitalized, and 62 percent of patients receiving placebo were rehospitalized (see Figure 15-8).

Antipsychotic drugs do not cure schizophrenia in the way that penicillin cures a bacterial infection. Antipsychotics do not eradicate the root causes of schizophrenia—which might include a genetic predisposition,

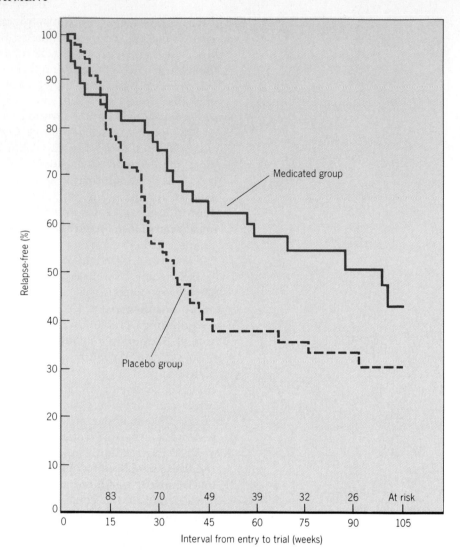

FIGURE 15-8
ANTIPSYCHOTICS REDUCE
RELAPSE.
A comparison of the relapse of placebo
patients and patients receiving
antipsychotic medication over a 2-year
period. (Crow et al., 1986.)

social stress, birth trauma, or a slow virus. But they do relieve the symptoms of schizophrenia—in many cases markedly.

Research suggests that schizophrenics may have dysfunctional frontal lobes. For example, schizophrenics perform poorly at psychological tests that assess frontal lobe performance, and they show less blood flow to—and therefore less activity in—the frontal lobes while taking such tests than normal subjects (Weinberger, Berman, and Zec, 1986). When schizophrenics are given antipsychotic drugs, the drugs do *not* increase frontal lobe activity or improve test performance (see Figure 15-9; Berman, Zec, and Weinberger, 1986). These results are consistent with the idea that medication does not reverse the information-processing or cognitive deficits of schizophrenia. Somehow, though, antipsychotic drugs allow schizophrenics to compensate in their daily lives for such deficits.

Antipsychotics have great benefits, but they also have costs. Side effects include symptoms associated with **Parkinson's disease**—a shuf-

FIGURE 15-9 FRONTAL LOBE FUNCTIONING IN SCHIZOPHRENIA.
"Maps" of blood flow to brain regions of schizophrenic and normal subjects during tests of frontal lobe functioning. The top maps represent cortical activity in the left and right hemispheres of nonschizophrenic controls; the bottom row represents cortical activity in the left and right hemispheres of schizophrenics. Light areas represent high brain activity, dark areas low activity. (From Berman et al., 1986.)

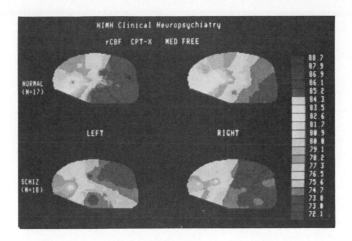

fling gait, tremor in the fingers, feelings of agitation or restlessness, an expressionless face, and others—symptoms that are unpleasant and painful. Parkinsonism is not an inevitable result of antipsychotic treatment, especially as low doses. But some patients must endure mild to moderate Parkinson's symptoms or face a return of schizophrenic symptoms.

The syndrome of **tardive dyskinesia** (*tardive* = prolonged, *dyskinesia* = abnormal movement) can be an even greater problem than Parkinsonism because unlike Parkinsonism, it may be permanent, persisting after the drug has been stopped. In tardive dyskinesia, a patient shows unusual body or facial movements. It is not life-threatening, but it can be embarrassing and cause patients to avoid others. Both Parkinsonism and tardive dyskinesia often can be prevented through the conservative use of medication, and new drugs are being developed that may eliminate these side effects. However, as with all treatments the benefits of any drug treatment must be weighed against the costs. A more human face can be put on this cost–benefit evaluation by considering a personal account of schizophrenia (see Box 15-1).

ANTIDEPRESSANT DRUGS   As happens so often in research on somatic treatments, the discovery of the most widely used drug for depression came about by chance. Researchers working with drugs against schizophrenia had produced a new drug that they labeled **imipramine**. They soon discovered that it had little effect on schizophrenia, but it seemed to alleviate depression among the patients tested (Andreasen, 1984).

Although most schizophrenics get antipsychotic drugs, many depressed patients do not get antidepressant drugs. Therapists often do not recommend antidepressants if a person is not suicidal, has no previous history of affective disorder, and has few physical signs of depression. In these cases, therapists rely on psychological therapies.

People considered right for antidepressant drugs usually are given a moderate dose that is increased gradually, until therapeutic effects are evident (see Table 15-3). It often takes 2 to 4 weeks before the full

BOX 15-1
SCHIZOPHRENIA
AND ITS
TREATMENT

The following is a personal account of schizophrenia by Mark Vonnegut, son of novelist Kurt Vonnegut. Mark Vonnegut describes prominent symptoms of schizophrenia: hearing voices (auditory hallucinations), an unusual focus of attention, and grandiosity—an exaggerated sense of importance.

By this time the voices had gotten very clear. At first I'd had to strain to hear or understand them. They were soft and working with some pretty tricky codes. Snap-crackle-pops, the sound of the wind with blinking lights and horns for punctuation. I broke the code and somehow was able to internalize it to the point where it was just like hearing words. In the beginning it seemed mostly nonsense, but as things went along they made more and more sense. Once you hear the voices, you realize they've always been there. It's just a matter of being tuned to them.

I didn't exactly lose contact with objective reality. There was just so much more going on.

Had someone asked me about what was going on, I would have had quite a bit of trouble taking the question seriously and even more trouble getting my voice and words to work right. I would have been much more interested in their clothes or face than the ques-

tions, and would have thought they were really asking something much deeper. I was on my way to Vancouver, and knew it most of the time, but if asked where I was, that would have been a long way down the line of answers that came to mind.

(1975, pp. 137–138)

Here are Mark's reactions to his treatment in a mental hospital.

One thing I noticed about the lag between being trustable and being trusted is that the doctors are always the last to catch on. The first to realize you've gotten better and start to treat you accordingly are the other patients. The realization flows up the hierarchy rather than down. After the patients catch on, then the maintenance staff and the lower orderlies realize you're OK, and so through the various orders of nurses until the news reaches the doctors. It works the same for relapses. Doctors and nurses continue to treat a briefly recovered patient as well days after the other patients realize the poor joker's completely out of his mind again.

(1975, pp. 172–173)

The reason that professionals are often the last to know in mental institutions is that they spend less time with patients than other staff and patients (Rosenhan, 1971).

About drugs, Vonnegut noted, "While I very likely owe my life to Thorazine, I doubt if I will ever develop much affection for it or similar

tranquilizers. They act very quickly and are invaluable in many situations, but have numerous unpleasant side effects" (1975, p. 272).

Taking Thorazine was part of doing things right. I hated Thorazine but tried not to talk about hating it. Hating Thorazine probably wasn't a healthy sign. But Thorazine has lots of unpleasant side effects. It makes you groggy, lowers your blood pressure, making you dizzy and faint when you stand up too quickly. If you go out in the sun your skin gets red and hurts like hell. It makes muscles rigid and twitchy.

The side effects were bad enough, but I liked what the drug was supposed to do even less. It's supposed to keep you calm, dull, uninterested, and uninteresting. . . . On Thorazine everything's a bore. Not a bore exactly. Boredom implies impatience. You can read comic books and Reader's Digest *forever. You can tolerate talking to jerks forever. Babble, babble, babble. The weather is dull, the flowers are dull, nothing's very impressive.*

(1975, pp. 252–253)

Thus, Mark Vonnegut, as a patient, appreciated the fact that psychiatric medication is a mixed blessing; he felt it saved his life, yet he hated some of its effects. Efforts are constantly under way to develop new drugs that have strong therapeutic effects, but few side effects.

antidepressant effects of the drug are felt. Commonly, the patients first report an increased appetite and better sleeping, and they look livelier. Later, as long as a month after treatment begins, the patient begins to report feeling better. Once people have recovered from depression, they may stay on antidepressants for a year or more, with periodic attempts to withdraw them gradually from the drug. Although antidepressants produce a wide variety of side effects (blurred vision, constipation, elevated heart rate), most are not particularly serious.

TABLE 15-3
ANTIDEPRESSANT DRUGS

Generic Name	Trade Name
Tricyclics	
Amitriptyline	Elavil
Imipramine	Tofranil
Doxepin	Sinequan
Amoxapine	Asendin
MAO Inhibitors	
Phenelzine	Nardil
Isocarboxazid	Marplan

Source: Jacobson and McKinney, 1982.

There are two major classes of antidepressant drugs: **tricyclics** and **monoamine oxidase inhibitors** (**MAOs**). Because MAOs can be more dangerous, physicians usually initially prescribe tricyclics and choose among them on the basis of how activating or sedating a particular drug is. Only after trying two or three tricyclics unsuccessfully do physicians ordinarily consider prescribing an MAO inhibitor (Jacobson and McKinney, 1982).

Effectiveness A large body of research indicates that antidepressants, especially tricyclic antidepressants, help many depressed patients to whom they are given. About 60 to 70 percent of depressed patients are helped by tricyclics—report better mood, become more active, and stop thinking about suicide—whereas only about 20 to 40 percent of patients improve on a placebo (Klerman and Cole, 1965). Even more patients improve if psychological therapies are combined with antidepressant medication (Simons, Murphy, Levine, and Wetzel, 1986).

At first glance, a 70 percent improvement rate seems strikingly effective. But about 30 percent of this 70 percent would respond positively to placebo, and 30 percent of depressed people do not respond to placebos or tricyclics. Thus about half of all depressed people are not helped by tricyclics. What accounts for the lack of consistent beneficial effects of tricyclics? Recent research suggests that, like schizophrenia, depression is heterogeneous, that is, there are subtypes of depression. For instance, in one recent study (Stewart et al., 1985) the authors found that depressed patients diagnosed as having Major Depression consistent with DSM-III criteria showed very different responses to antidepressants on the basis of whether or not they also experienced panic attacks (see Figure 15-10).

Antidepressants also help people with anxiety disorders. In one study, patients reported themselves and physicians rated the patients as less anxious after being treated with antidepressants than after being treated with placebo or with drugs that are usually used to treat anxiety (Kahn et al., 1986). Not only was a tricyclic drug more effective in reducing anxiety, in general, than was an antianxiety agent, but it was also extremely effective in reducing depression. However, it reduced depression only among those patients who also suffered from panic attacks. Finally, research has shown that depressed patients who also have panic disorder are more likely than other depressed patients to have a strong family history of both depression and anxiety (Leckman, Merikangas, Pauls, Prusoff, and Weissman, 1983). This research all suggests that Major Depression, as defined by DSM-IIIR (see Chapter 13) may actually comprise two separate disorders, one with and one without panic attacks, and that only the former responds to tricyclic antidepressants. Research is likely to reveal whether these two disorders differ as well in cause, in course if untreated, and the role of stress in their development.

How do tricyclic antidepressants produce their effects? In the 1950s, a drug called **reserpine** was used to treat hypertension. But it was soon noted that many patients on reserpine became depressed (Freedman, 1985). Reserpine depletes neurotransmitters such as serotonin, dopamine, and norepinephrine. Another discovery made in the 1950s was that the drug **iproniazid**, used for tuberculosis, produced euphoria

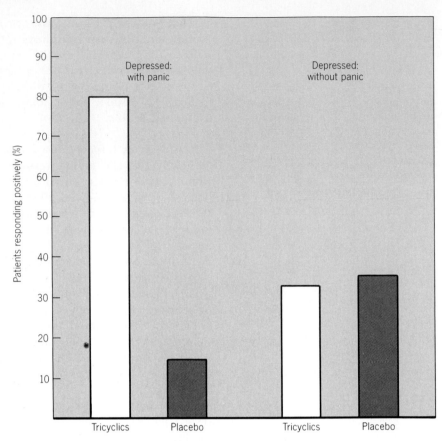

FIGURE 15-10   EFFECTIVENESS
OF ANTIDEPRESSANTS.
*When patients reported panic attacks in
addition to depression, they were much
more likely to benefit from antidepressant
(tricyclic) medication than from a
placebo. Depressed patients who did not
report panic attacks responded similarly
to tricyclics and placebo. This suggests
that depression with panic, and
depression without panic, may be distinct
disorders. (Stewart et al., 1985.)*

(Freedman, 1985). Later it was found that his drug inhibits *monoamine oxidase,* an enzyme that depletes the neurotransmitters just mentioned. Thus, one drug that depletes certain neurotransmitters produces depression, and one drug that prevents the depletion of these transmitters induces euphoria. This provided powerful evidence for the **biogenic amine** theory of depression. (Biogenic amines are neurotransmitters derived from amino acids that contain a carbon chain and a nitrogen–hydrogen group; norepinephrine, serotonin, and dopamine are all biogenic amines.) This theory received an additional boost when it was discovered that tricyclic antidepressants increase levels of biogenic amines by preventing their reuptake (that is, the neurotransmitters were not reabsorbed by neurons and remained in the synapse).

Although there is strong evidence that biogenic amines are involved in depression, the exact relationship is unknown. Some studies suggest that people who are depressed have low levels of neurotransmitters (Cooper, Prange, Whybrown, and Noguera, 1972). Other studies suggest that depressed and nondepressed people do not differ on the basis of neurotransmitter levels (Goodwin, Post, Dunner, and Gordon, 1973; Willner, 1985). It is possible that this inconsistency has arisen because the diagnosis of major depression has been used to label people with two different types of affective disorders—one related to low serotonin levels and the other not (Willner, 1985).

In one study, for example, the authors found that some depressed people had normal levels of serotonin but that others had low levels (Asberg, Thoren, Traskman, Bertilsson, and Eringberger, 1976). Among the latter, the lower their serotonin levels, the more depressed they were. These data are similar to those about the relationship between depression and panic attack in that both types of data suggest that there may be multiple types of depression, each with a different cause and response to treatment. Future research will no doubt reveal the many syndromes of depression.

ANTIANXIETY DRUGS   Antianxiety drugs, like antipsychotic and antidepressant drugs, were discovered in the 1950s. They met a very receptive audience because physicians wanted relaxant drugs and drugs that promoted sleep. Before 1950, the drugs available for these purposes were barbiturates, which are highly addicting, produce intoxication, and are dangerous at high doses. Physicians welcomed antianxiety drugs (notably the **benzodiazepines** chlordiazepoxide, *Librium*, and diazepam, *Valium*) as cures for the stresses and anxiety of modern life. Today 100 *million* prescriptions are filled every year for these drugs in the United States (Feldman and Quenzer, 1984). One type of antianxiety agent accounts for fully 53 percent of the 25 million sleeping pills prescribed every year (Smith, 1979)!

Usually antianxiety drugs are prescribed for people who complain of too much stress in their lives, people who have trouble sleeping, or people who complain often of physical problems yet show no physical evidence of disease. Most antianxiety agents probably are *not* given to people diagnosed for anxiety disorders. In general, antianxiety agents are targeted at a symptom—anxiety—rather than at a disease or syndrome.

In the past, doctors prescribed antianxiety drugs for extended periods of time. But today most physicians are aware that long-term, steady use can produce great psychological dependence; people come to believe that they cannot face life without the drug. Therefore physicians now prescribe these drugs only for a short period. Many physicians today also believe that if patients report chronic anxiety, the appropriate treatment is not an antianxiety agent but psychotherapy.

Effectiveness   It has been difficult to establish the effectiveness of antianxiety drugs. Because anxiety can fluctuate greatly from day to day, it is difficult to prove that reductions in anxiety are due to drugs. People complaining of anxiety are susceptible to placebo effects; as many as half respond positively to a placebo. Even so, it is now fairly well established that antianxiety agents reliably reduce symptoms and signs of anxiety more effectively than placebos (Greenblatt and Shader, 1978). (However, as we noted earlier, tricyclic antidepressants may be even more effective in reducing anxiety; Kahn et al., 1986; Stewart et al., 1985.)

OTHER DRUG THERAPIES   Physicians use a variety of other drugs to treat abnormal behavior. They use the mineral **lithium carbonate** to treat bipolar illness. Lithium has been shown to be remarkably effective in many patients with mania or bipolar affective disorder and sometimes

TABLE 15-4 DRUGS FOR MENTAL DISORDERS

Mental Disorder	Drug
Schizophrenia	Phenothiazines
	Butyrophenones
Major depression	Tricyclics
	MAO inhibitors
Anxiety disorder	Chlordiazepoxide
	Diazepam
	Tricyclics
Bipolar depression	Lithium chloride
Alcoholism	Disulfiram

completely eliminates the wild mood swings associated with these disorders.

Another widely used drug is **disulfiram (Antabuse)**, given to alcoholics. It interrupts the alcohol metabolism process and a poison (acetaldehyde) builds in the alcoholic's bloodstream when he or she drinks alcohol. The person feels flushed and nauseated. Some people lose consciousness. But many alcoholics report that taking Antabuse helps them to resist alcohol.

SOMATIC THERAPIES: SUMMARY Our review of somatic treatments revealed principles relevant to all treatments of mental disorders. First, treatment should be administered as a function of diagnosis (see Table 15-4). Second, some patients respond positively to the very promise or hope of a new treatment. If a treatment has a *specific* therapeutic action, it should show effects above and beyond those produced by a placebo. Third, patients' responses to treatment can tell us something about the nature of the disorder being treated, and this information should be used to refine concepts of mental disorders. Fourth, the costs of treatment must be weighed against the benefits. Sometimes these costs are obvious—great expense, dangerous side effects. However, sometimes these costs are subtle. A treatment can make a patient feel dependent on a physician or therapist, or it may delude patient and therapist into believing that the real cause of a patient's problems has been identified.

PSYCHOLOGICAL TREATMENTS

By one recent estimate, there are over 250 different types of psychological therapies (Herink, 1980). Here we will describe some of the major types of psychological therapies, their effectiveness, and the theories upon which they are based.

Verbal Psychotherapies

PSYCHOANALYTICALLY ORIENTED PSYCHOTHERAPY The first type of verbal psychotherapy to be widely used was that developed by Sigmund Freud. Freudian **psychoanalysis** is relatively rare today because it requires a tremendous commitment of time on the part of the therapist and a tremendous commitment of time and money on the part of the client. In traditional psychoanalysis, a client is seen by an analyst for 4 to 6 hours a week, for 2 to 10 years. Traditional psychoanalysis is appropriate for a restricted range of people, those who are highly motivated and have anxiety problems.

Although classic analysis no longer is widely used, Freud's ideas about psychopathology and about therapeutic change still influence many psychotherapists (Wade and Baker, 1977). Today, many therapists practice *psychoanalytically oriented psychotherapy*. Psychoanalytically oriented psychotherapy, often called **dynamic therapy**, involves one to two sessions a week for 10 weeks to 2 years and is appropriate for a greater variety of clients (Luborsky, 1984). Despite procedural changes, dynamic therapy retains an emphasis on Freudian theory.

From our previous discussions of Freud (Chapters 10, 12, and 13), recall that Freud believed that anxiety occurs for two reasons, both of which involve unusually strong instinctual drives. One source of anxiety is the panic of the ego when it is threatened with loss of control; the id is in revolt and threatens to dominate personality. Such loss of control is inherently frightening for the ego. It is also frightening because the ego anticipates punishment from others if antisocial instincts are directly expressed.

The ego is threatened with a rebellious id whenever instinctual needs are consistently thwarted. Instinctual needs are not met when **defense mechanisms** are inadequate. Remember, defense mechanisms allow people to disguise the true nature of their motivations. An ideal defense elicits praise and approval and lets people hide their true motivation, express libidinal energy, feel good about themselves. For example, a young man takes solicitous care of his mother. Even though his unconscious motivation is sexual desire for her, he feels no guilt over his solicitousness because he has fooled his superego, and he wins societal approval for caring so well for his mother. Most important, he partly gratifies his instinctual needs by remaining nonsexually intimate with his mother. In contrast, another young man relies on a defense involving **repression**. His sexual desire for the mother is too strong and threatening, and so he suppresses the unconscious wish and his instinctual needs are not gratified at all. This latter sort of inefficient defense allows instinctual energy to accumulate. Because the ego has not satisfied the young man's instinctive needs, the id threatens to overthrow the ego by seeking direct satisfaction of instinctive needs. This threat is felt as anxiety.

How do dynamic psychotherapies help people who suffer from anxiety? In most dynamic therapies

1. The therapist is accepting of the client.
2. The therapist encourages the client to review events of his or her early life and to report dreams.
3. The therapist makes an effort not to introduce his or her own personality into the psychotherapy session.
4. The therapist gently points out to the client how his or her present problems are not isolated events, but rather part of a pattern that started early in life. (A problematic pattern is often referred to as **repetition compulsion**.)
5. The therapist suggests how the client's problem pattern is manifested within the therapy itself.

These therapeutic ingredients are designed to let people lower their defenses gradually—in part because the therapist is so nonjudgmental. In addition, gathering information about the client's childhood may reveal information about the origins and nature of the client's repetition compulsion.

For instance, suppose that Richard is a young man who consistently disappoints those around him—especially his superiors at work—by not completing important assignments. Richard wants to do better, but he just doesn't seem able. Richard's therapist has several hypotheses about the origin of Richard's problem. Perhaps Richard procrastinates because he fears success. Perhaps he procrastinates because he fears harsh evaluation of the finished product. Richard's history reveals that he had a threatening, sarcastic father who humiliated him whenever Richard competed with him. Richard ended up wanting to humiliate and punish his father, yet he was frightened by the prospect of his father's retaliation. He therefore discovered a marvelously successful strategy for vanquishing his father in this competition: he failed at all competitions, even those not involving his father. He knew that his repeated failures hurt his father terribly; his father wanted Richard to be a "chip off the old block" and to fail only in competition against him (the father). Because defenses are unconscious, Richard could hide from himself his fear of and anger toward his father and avoid feeling guilty. Yet by failing, he also could express that anger toward his father. Although this defense system temporarily reduced his anxiety, it interfered with Richard's functioning. The unconscious strategy Richard learned in youth overgeneralized so that in later life he reacted to all authority figures as if they were his father, resulting in continued failure.

Once the therapist believes that he or she has spotted the client's problem pattern, he or she tactfully suggests the nature of the problem and how it might show up in the client's behavior. If the therapist merely tells the client about the problem pattern, the client does not profit from the information. The therapist must arrange for the client to discover for himself or herself the nature and origins of the repetition compulsion and to do so with emotion relevant to the compulsion. How does the therapist do this?

Crucial to dynamic psychotherapy is the process of **transference**. Transference refers to the process by which a client responds to the therapist and others in his or her current life as if they were important people from the past, especially a parent. The therapist's neutrality allows clients to project characteristics of their parents or other important figures onto the therapist. For example, Richard's therapist asks him if he has had any dreams lately—because Freudian therapists believe that dreams may symbolically reflect a person's unconscious motivations. After Richard reports a recent dream, his therapist asks if he can remember another dream. Richard angrily responds, "What's the matter, isn't one enough for you?" The following ensues:

Therapist   You sound as if you're angry at me.
Richard   No. Not really.
Therapist   It's OK if you are angry.
Richard   I know that. I know the rules.
Therapist   Again, I sense that you are angry. You first seemed to get angry at me when I asked you if you had had any more dreams.
Richard   I felt that I hadn't satisfied you with the one I told you about.
Therapist   Ah! You felt I was disappointed in you—disapproving. You felt that my asking about any additional dreams reflected criticism, not interest.

Richard   Yeah. I guess it did. I got angry automatically—but now I know that you didn't mean it so it's OK.

Therapist   I wonder why you got angry? Have you felt at other times in your life that people were being demanding of you, expecting too much? Are you in a sense prepared for this?

Richard   Well—everybody meets somebody like that sometime.

Therapist   I suppose so.

In this case, the therapist pointed out Richard's excessive emotional response and planted the seed of the idea that Richard might have acted as he had reacted to others in his life. The therapist did not explicitly connect Richard's reactions to his feelings toward his father. Richard will have to make this connection himself when he is once again feeling anger or fear of his father. Notice that Richard seemed reluctant to explore his anger or to speculate about its source. First he denied that he was angry (a denial defense mechanism), and then he said that "everybody" meets someone who is too demanding (a defense involving intellectualization). Both defenses keep Richard from recognizing the magnitude of his anger or its relationship to his father.

The goal of dynamic psychotherapy is to help people lead less anxiety-ridden, more productive lives. But it must achieve an intermediate goal in the meantime. It helps the patient substitute efficient defense mechanisms for inefficient ones. Freud characterized this goal with the statement: "Wo es war, soll ich verden." "Where id is, so shall ego be." This means that therapeutic improvement lies in the ego's becoming more able to satisfy id-based instinctual needs. Once the ego satisfies instinctual needs effectively, the id exerts less direct influence on personality and behavior. Richard, for instance, might discover that he harbors deep resentment against his father and need not feel guilty about this. If he feels the need to express his resentment against his father, he can learn to do so directly, and not through repeated failures. Once Richard understands the underlying reasons for his failures, this understanding automatically removes an important reason behind the failures—to hide from himself his anger at his father.

Insight into troubled behavior has another important function. It gives people hope. Often people enter therapy at a very low ebb. They are anxious, depressed, and mystified about why their lives have gone so wrong. They do not understand their problem, cannot control it, and have lost hope in their ability ever to control it. When people begin to understand and interpret their behavior, their universe suddenly changes. They see that, instead of being random and capricious, their behavior is understandable. What's more, if they can understand the reasons that they have behaved as they have, they may be able to change. Hope may be a necessary component of any successful therapy.

According to the Freudian model, the well-adjusted individual has achieved a stalemate between two competing factions of the personality: the **id**, representing personal, biological influences, and the **superego**, representing social, cultural, and moral influences. The **ego** is neutral in this conflict. It maintains control over psychic, libidinal energy as long as it satisfies id-based needs and avoids both social or physical punishment and feelings of guilt engendered by the superego. Some theorists have found this vision disturbing because it portrays the ego, or self, as striving to placate an insatiable id and a domineering superego. Moreover, many people are disturbed by the fact that, for Freud, the true motivations for one's actions are unknowable because they are unconscious (Maddi, 1980). **Humanistic**, *growth*, or *fulfillment* therapies arose in opposition to this view of human nature.

PERSON-CENTERED THERAPY   **Person-centered therapy** was developed by Carl Rogers and is based on the theories and beliefs of such humanistic psychologists as Abraham Maslow (1908–1970) and Rogers himself (1902–1987). For Freud, humans were essentially selfish, biological creatures whose altruistic attributes are acquired through the influence of society. But to humanists like Rogers, humans were essentially benign creatures whose good, generous, and gentle natures need not come in conflict with the goals of society. True, humans may act in cruel, callous, and selfish ways, but Rogers did not believe that such actions reflect basic human nature.

Rogers and other humanistic theorists believed that humans are born with a drive to achieve their full potentials—not only in growth and biological maturation, but also in emotional, cognitive, and personal development. This drive to achieve full human potential has been called an **actualizing** or **self-actualizing** drive. Given an ideal or healthy environment, each human is free to achieve his or her potential. However, in flawed environments actualizing drives are thwarted—and this leads to maladaptive behavior.

During development, children acquire a sense of *self*—an individual identity. Children's appraisals of themselves, their self-concepts, are greatly influenced by how others treat them, especially people like parents, who have a strong emotional relationship with the child. A child strives for approval and praise from others and generally strives to avoid criticism, blame, or censure. Rogers attributed this striving to a *need for positive regard*. As children grow older, they internalize this need into a *need for positive self-regard* (Rogers, 1959). Children learn standards for self-approval based on the standards others have applied. If parents have criticized a child for "showing off," a child will feel guilty or anxious about such behavior later in life because he or she will have incorporated the parents' standards. According to Rogers, striving for positive regard can be damaging when it thwarts self-actualization.

In Rogers' view, the source of much maladaptive behavior, anxiety, and unhappiness is a mismatch between a person's standards for positive self-regard and his actualization tendencies. This mismatch arises when children are given *conditional*, rather than unconditional, positive regard. For example, parents may show a child love and affection *only* if the child meets their expectations or standards. Let us assume that a young girl has inborn athletic skills and a very competitive nature. If her parents withdraw their love from her whenever she displays her competitive spirit, she will soon learn that this aspect of her personality is undesirable and unlovable, and thus, her actualization tendency in this area will be thwarted. She will become insecure and *defensive* about her competitiveness, and this defensiveness may produce anxiety, frustration, anger, and unhappiness. Her life will be a constant struggle between expressing her innate abilities and dispositions and striving to adhere to the standards for social and self-approval.

Rogers' ideas about defensiveness and anxiety may strike you as similar to those of Freud. According to both theories, there is a constant struggle between expressing inborn tendencies (actualizing drive, libidinal energy) and achieving self-approval (positive self-regard, satisfying the superego) that may result in defensiveness and anxiety. The major difference between the two models of personality is that to Rogers, there was *no need for defenses at all*. Because inborn human nature is not selfish and antisocial, Rogers believed that defenses are unnecessary and that all people should be encouraged to reach their full potentials.

As opposed to dynamic therapy, person-centered therapy is often quite brief—sometimes lasting just a few months. There are three main ingredients to person-centered therapy: *congruence, acceptance*, and *empathy* (Rogers and Stevens, 1967). Congruence means that a therapist is aware of his or her own feelings and attitudes and genuinely communicates these to a client. If someone feels that a therapist is genuine, he or she will believe that what the therapist says really reflects the therapist's beliefs and values. When the therapist then communicates acceptance and empathy for the client, it has great force. The client may think: "This person is not only listening to me but seems to accept me for what I am. More than that, he(she) seems to value me—maybe even love me—and I've been absolutely honest with him, he really knows me." Perhaps the most powerful tool of the person-centered therapist is the provision of the unconditional positive regard that the client did not receive as a child.

Here is a transcript of a therapy session reprinted in one of Rogers' books:

Therapist   That catches a little more of the flavor of the feeling, that is, it's almost as if you're really weeping for yourself.
Client   And then of course, I've come . . . to see and to feel that over this, see, I've covered it up. (Weepy.) But . . . and . . . I've covered it up with so much *bitterness,* which in turn I had to cover up. (Weeps.) That's what I want to get rid of! I almost don't *care* if I hurt.
Therapist   (Gently.) You feel that here at the basis of it, as you experienced it, is a feeling of real tears for yourself. But that you *can't* show, mustn't show, so that's been covered by bitterness that you don't like, that you'd like to be rid of. You almost feel you'd rather absorb the hurt than to . . . than to feel the bitterness. (Pause.) And what you seem to be saying quite strongly is "I do *hurt* and I've tried to cover it up."
Client   I didn't *know* it.
Therapist   M-hm. Like a new discovery really.
Client   (Speaking at the same time.) I never really did know. But it's . . . you know, it's almost a physical thing. It's . . . it's sort of as though I—I—I were looking within myself at all kinds of nerve endings and—and bits of, of . . . things that have been sort of mashed. (Weepy.)

Therapist As though some of the most delicate aspects of you—physically almost—have been crushed or hurt.
Client Yes, and you know, I do get the feeling, oh, you poor thing. (Pause.)
Therapist Just can't but feel very deeply sorry for the person that is you (Rogers and Dymond, 1954, pp. 326–327).

Notice that the therapist's responses to the client tend to acknowledge what the client has said to the therapist and indicate the therapist's understanding and acceptance of the client.

There is little or no teaching or interpretation in person-centered psychotherapy because the therapist believes that the capacity for growth and change resides within each client. The therapist's duty is to create an atmosphere in which the client begins to value and accept all aspects of him- or herself. Once this occurs, the client's actualization tendencies are unleashed, and the client becomes less anxious, more spontaneous, freer and less defensive, and more appreciative of others.

COGNITIVE THERAPY Epicetus, the Roman philosopher, noted, "It is not events, but what men make of them, that is important." This is not a bad explanation of **cognitive** or **cognitive-behavioral** psychotherapies. The various cognitive therapies are united by a set of core tenets. All cognitive therapies proceed from the idea that a prime factor in feelings—especially anxiety and depression—is *how* people think about events over and above the events themselves. Neither repressed information nor primitive drives cause anxieties. No, it is people's *conscious processing of information* that makes them suffer; they mislabel what happens to them, they misattribute events, or they simply dwell on particular types of events too much. Cognitive therapists hold that changing a person's thought patterns, or cognitions, about events helps alleviate anxiety and depression.

There is considerable support for the idea that patterns of cognition influence people's feelings. For example, learned helplessness research (Peterson and Seligman, 1984; see Chapter 13) indicates that a particular attributional style predisposes certain people to depression. As this research shows, if people attribute the bad things that happen to them to some characteristic of themselves that is stable and global, they are more likely to become depressed than if they attribute the bad things to some external factor or to an internal characteristic that is fleeting and circumscribed. Of two people fired from their jobs, one attributes the firing to his lack of intelligence, the second to her boss's irrationality. According to the learned helplessness theory, the first person is more likely to become depressed. Cognitive therapists suggest that if this person took into account all the factors that led to his firing—his boss's temper, a downturn in the economy, the fact that he had little seniority—he would feel less depressed. He might remain unhappy, but not seriously depressed.

Aaron Beck, a prominent cognitive therapist and theoretician, has proposed that depression is a consequence of "pervasive negative misconstructions of objective experiences" (Beck, 1967). Beck has proposed that depressed individuals

1. View *themselves* as deprived and disabled.
2. Believe that their *worlds* are full of obstacles to satisfaction and happiness.
3. Anticipate *futures* filled with disappointment and despair, devoid of gratification.

Beck believes that depressed people fall prey to cognitive distortions, failure of information processing (Hollon and Beck, 1979). They engage in

1. *Selective abstraction.* They form conclusions based on meager evidence, perhaps an isolated incident, and ignore contradictory, more relevant evidence. For example, a student is invited to a party and is greeted enthusiastically by the host and hostess. He takes part in several interesting conversations during the party, and everyone seems interested in what he has to say. Later, the host offers drinks to his guests but forgets to offer one to the student. He tells himself, "I knew they really didn't want me here. They were only being polite."

2. *Arbitrary inference.* They reach conclusions in the absence of evidence. For example, a young woman has applied for a job at a law firm. When she hasn't heard from the law firm in two days, she concludes, "That's it. I knew I wouldn't get the job. I stank in the interview, and this proves it."

3. *Overgeneralization.* They arrive at a belief on the basis of an isolated event and use the belief to predict what will happen in dissimilar situations. For example, a 68-year-old woman has been complaining to her harried physician about some of her aches and pains. After 2 or 3 minutes of this he snaps at her, "Well, what do you expect, you are close to 70 years old!" Later, as she talks to a neighbor and then to her daughter-in-law, she remains reticent because she is convinced that they find her boring and an imposition, just as her physician seemed to.

4. *Magnification.* They exaggerate the importance of negative events or consequences of their actions; they turn a mediocre or undesirable outcome into a catastrophe. For example, a young woman learns that she has failed a surprise quiz in a psychology course. She is distraught, convinced that it ends any future she might have had in psychology.

5. *All-or-none thinking.* They tend to think in absolute terms; an event is either good or bad, an action successful or an abysmal failure, and an acquaintance either an altruistically motivated saint or an unworthy scoundrel. For example, an insurance salesman gets mixed feedback from his boss in his quarterly evaluation. The boss notes his good points—his sales were increasing, he made several good suggestions for processing financial information. But his boss also notes that several other employees have complained that he is "pushy," and two clients called the office to complain that he had been too forceful in

his sales pitch. The salesman later tells his wife that his boss had "raked him over the coals" and had thoroughly criticized him.

Aaron Beck and his colleagues recently have extended their cognitive analysis to include anxiety disorders (Beck, Emery, and Greenberg, 1985). A brief case history of one of Beck's own clients reveals how cognitive distortions can result in an escalation from normal worry or fear to a panic attack. Beck's client recalled having a "flash" when he felt some chest pains while skiing. He thought, "This could be a heart attack just like my brother's" (Beck et al., 1985, p. 5). According to Beck, this misattribution was critical to the development of panic. Had the young man attributed his pain to exertion and altitude sickness, he would have weathered his symptoms, just as he had in the past. The crucial stimulus in anxiety disorders is a thought that "pops" into someone's mind shortly after, or during, an experience of anxiety or arousal.

How do cognitive therapists attempt to change their clients' thought processes, and thereby their anxiety and depression? Beck and his colleagues have listed ten principles that guide cognitive therapy (see Table 15-5). As these principles reveal, cognitive therapy requires that there be a good, working/learning relationship between the therapist and client. Therapists are quite directive. They tell clients what to do and even assign homework. Therapists assume that they have knowledge to impart to their clients. One of the first goals of cognitive therapy is to make clients aware of the thought processes that lead to their problems. Several techniques help clients discover their own thought processes. For example, for an agoraphobic (a person who has anxiety attacks when exposed to open spaces), the therapist might accompany the client outdoors while the client describes his or her thoughts.

Once clients are aware of their troublesome thought patterns, the therapist helps them correct these patterns. The therapist begins by asking about the client's beliefs, attitudes, and attributions. For example, suppose that a client has generalized anxiety disorder, and the client and therapist have learned that the anxiety is associated with the client's telling himself that he is inadequate. For example, the client tells himself that he cannot make love to his wife adequately.

TABLE 15-5 PRINCIPLES OF COGNITIVE THERAPY

1. Cognitive therapy is based on the cognitive model of emotional disorders.
2. Cognitive therapy is brief and time-limited.
3. A sound therapeutic relationship is a necessary condition for effective cognitive therapy.
4. Therapy is a collaborative effort between therapist and patient.
5. Cognitive therapy uses primarily the Socratic method.
6. Cognitive therapy is structured and directive.
7. Cognitive therapy is problem-oriented.
8. Cognitive therapy is based on an educational model.
9. The theory and techniques of cognitive therapy rely on an inductive method.
10. Homework is a central feature of cognitive therapy.

Therapist   How do you know this?

Client   Because she just doesn't seem to enjoy it. Sometimes she seems like she's not there.

Therapist   What is the evidence that she doesn't enjoy sex with you?

Client   Well, a couple of times she's told me that she doesn't like the way I do—you know, this or that.

Therapist   Are you saying that in order for you to feel that you're a good lover you have to do things right or especially well all the time?

Client   So you think I'm overreacting.

Therapist   It's a possibility isn't it?

Through questioning centered around clients' faulty thought processes, therapists try to lead clients to reexamine, and then change, their beliefs and attitudes.

Several types of therapy involve not individuals but groups of people, couples, and families. These therapies are based on the idea that psychological problems arise in part from relationships among people and that people's behavior and communication must be analyzed and changed if psychological problems are to be resolved.

FAMILY THERAPY   Many types of therapy are used with social groups. Here we describe a single type, a family therapy called **strategic therapy** (Stanton, 1981). Strategic therapy shares certain important features with other group therapies. For example, it holds that psychological disturbance can be traced to deeply ingrained communication patterns, and one principal goal of the therapist is to disrupt these patterns.

According to strategic therapists, psychologically disturbed individuals are produced by psychologically disturbed families with confused or disorganized family structures. For instance, in American culture fathers and mothers head the family and decide important issues involving their children. Parents are united by their physical intimacy, their age, their common experiences, and so on. Children generally see themselves as subservient to the parents and are taught to respect their parents. But in disturbed families allegiances within generations are weak, and boundaries between generations are blurred.

According to strategic therapists, the problems that family members complain of reflect the family's attempt to solve preexisting problems. For example, a family might seek therapy because an adolescent daughter develops an eating disorder and fights with her mother. The therapist discovers that the father is cold and distant from the mother, and the mother is overinvolved in her daughter's life. The daughter's hostility is designed to keep her mother at bay, but her refusal to eat gives her parents a common problem and makes them communicate more. In effect, the daughter's eating problem and hostility reflect her unconscious attempts to bring her mother and father closer together. In strategic therapy no one in the family is portrayed as "sick" or disturbed. Individual disturbance arises from family communication patterns and all family members are responsible for these.

One technique strategic therapists use to change a family's disturbed communication patterns is to "reframe" their symptom or problems. If a mother and father talked primarily about a "problem child," the therapist might reframe the problem differently. An excellent example of this reframing appears in a transcript of a therapy session led by Virginia Satir, a pioneer family therapist. The parents had sought therapy because of their schizophrenic son, Gary. Satir (S) asked the mother why she wanted therapy.

Mom   Well, I hope that we can work together to find a solution so that we can all become a real family again.

S   All right. So what you're talking about—you are aware that in some way Gary has been hurting, and you don't understand why, that there was a time when Gary didn't hurt and the family—

Gary   I don't understand. What do you mean by the word "hurt"?

S   Hurt. Hurt.

Gary   Pain? Physical, mental, anguish?

S   Mental, maybe physical. I don't know.

Gary   Are you saying that I am hurting?

S   This is what I am saying the family is saying. There was a time when you didn't hurt. I'm checking this out. And you want to now have a family in which things are again where people aren't hurting (Satir, 1967, pp. 104–105).

By reframing the problem from an individual with a mental disorder to a family that's hurting, Satir takes the family's focus off the "identified patient" and changes how they communicate.

Strategic therapists also use specific exercises to change family structure. For instance, in a family in which the father and mother are distant from one another, the therapist might tell them to go by themselves to the zoo for four days in a single week. Once the parents are trapped together at a zoo that has become too familiar, they might begin to communicate. Merely telling the parents to communicate more might not have worked because such direct instructions can sometimes produce resistance.

People often resist change if they feel threatened and defensive. One technique that strategic therapists use to reduce defensiveness is to ascribe positive motives to family members' actions. For instance, Gary's father had locked Gary in his room for 24 hours. Satir tries to find out whether the father had acted out of anger, frustration, or the desire to punish.

Gary   Let's say I (*inaudible phrase*). "May I go down to get a drink of water?" I would have come back, but you grabbed me like this.

Mom   We had water right in the room, Gary.

S   OK. Now just a minute. I'm trying to look at what the facts are. Now, the facts were, you were in a room and you couldn't get out. Now, my question was . . .

Gary (overlapping)   (*Inaudible phrase*) . . . in anyway. I couldn't get out. I can't remember exactly whether it was locked or not.

S   Now, the question was, "Why did Dad do it?" That's your question to him, so I'm asking him.

Dad   Well, the question, the reason at that time was, ah, ah, we couldn't trust Gary to, oh, be sure that he was doing what we thought was right.

S   Did you want to punish him?

Dad   No! No punishment.

Mom   No.

Dad   Oh, we felt that he was sick, that Gary was sick, and that he needed rest, terrifically.

S   So this was a way you wanted to protect him.

Dad   Right.

S   But Gary didn't feel that way about it, but nevertheless that was your intention.

Dad   Right. (Haley and Hoffman, 1967, pp. 137–139).

Satir guides the father from his original reason for locking up his son—that he might not do what was "right"—to wanting to protect him. Satir also endorses Gary's belief that being locked up felt like punishment, even though the father insists that hadn't been his intention. In theory, attributing benign motives to people makes them less defensive, less blaming, and more likely to change.

Another tactic of strategic therapists is the **paradoxical directive** (Stanton, 1981). Paradoxical directives are instructions that appear absurd because they seem intended to produce change that is contradictory to the family's goals. A common paradoxical technique is "prescribing the symptom." For example, suppose that a family has sought therapy because a teenage daughter is anorexic. The daughter may be using anorexia to punish her parents. But the therapist tells her not to give up her anorexia because it is so important in keeping the family together, because it keeps her parents concerned and involved with her. The therapist also tells the parents to concentrate on the anorexia because it represents the daughter's attempt to bring them close to her. These directives clearly undermine the intended function of the anorexia to hurt the parents.

Behavior Therapy

Behavior therapy has its origins in learning theory and research. As psychologists found that they could control animal behavior with Pavlovian and operant conditioning (see Chapter 6), they became interested in how they might condition human behavior. Thus, unlike some other therapeutic procedures, many behavior therapy treatments are not derived from a formal personality theory. Rather, their origins were pragmatic—they represent the application of behavior change techniques to the alleviation of human problems.

PAVLOVIAN-BASED TECHNIQUES

Fear-reduction Techniques   Perhaps the first widespread behavior therapy technique was **systematic desensitization**. This treatment was based on the Pavlovian conditioning procedure. In systematic desensitization, phobic clients first are taught to relax. Then they are asked to imagine gradually more frightening scenes or to encounter the objects of their fears. For example, someone afraid to receive injections might be asked to imagine a syringe and needle. Later, he would be asked to imagine the needle piercing his skin and then seeing his own blood fill the syringe. Eventually, he might be asked to touch a needle and syringe and actually receive an injection. In systematic desensitization, the phobic images can be thought of as conditioned stimuli (CSs) that are paired with relaxation instructions, the unconditioned stimulus (US).

According to learning theory, phobic stimuli become frightening because they are paired with unpleasant events or because someone observes others reacting fearfully to the stimuli (observational learning). In either case, presenting the fear stimulus (CS) by itself, not paired with an unpleasant event or with the expression of fear by others, should result in the *extinction* of the learned fear response. In addition, pairing the feared stimulus with relaxation (the US) is intended to produce a new learned response (conditioned response, CR)—relaxation. After many pairings, the phobic should feel calm and relaxed when exposed to phobic stimuli.

Since the introduction of systematic desensitization by Joseph Wolpe in the 1950s (Wolpe, 1958), other fear- or phobia-reduction treatments have been developed by behavior therapists. One is **flooding**, or **implosion** therapy, in which an individual is exposed right away to frightening stimuli. Flooding differs from systematic desensitization in that exposure is not gradual, and the client is not taught to relax before exposure. Another fear-reduction procedure involves modeling. In this procedure, the fearful person watches a nonfearful model go through the dreaded event. For instance, in one study, children who were very afraid of the dentist watched a film in which children coped successfully with their fears and anxieties about the dentist (Klingman, Melamed, Cuthbert, and Hermecz, 1984). Modeling is effective in reducing fear, especially when observers can practice coping with their fear, a treatment called *participant modeling* (Perry and Furukawa, 1986).

In all of these behavioral techniques—systematic desensitization, flooding, modeling—fearful subjects are *exposed* to what they fear. Exposure may be beneficial for several reasons. First, exposure to the feared stimulus (CS) may allow fear to extinguish. Second, people may gain confidence in their ability to cope with what they fear. As you saw in Chapter 11, *self-efficacy theory* suggests that an increase in confidence, or self-efficacy, leads people to strive harder and longer to achieve important goals (Bandura, 1977). Finally, exposure may help because it lets people *practice* coping with what they fear. The importance of practice is illustrated by studies showing that the benefits of exposure treatments are enhanced if clients are given the opportunity to rehearse newly acquired fear-coping strategies (e.g., Klingman et al., 1984). Fear-coping strategies might include self-directed relaxation or focusing of attention on a distracting thought (e.g., "I wonder what I'll have for dinner tonight," etc.).

BOX 15-2
A CASE OF
AVERSION
THERAPY

"Chronic ruminative vomiting" is a rare but dangerous condition in infants. The infants regurgitate food that they have eaten and keep it in their mouths, sometimes chewing it again (ruminating). This activity is not only unpleasant to observe, but it is also dangerous. Infants may breathe in the food and choke, or they may starve to death.

When chronic vomiting is related to disorders of the intestinal tract, the vomiting stops once the disorder is treated. But some cases of chronic vomiting are psychosomatic and cannot be traced to physical disease. One psychoanalytic theory is that psychosomatic chronic vomiting is caused by the infant's receiving insufficient love and nurturance from the mother. The infant seeks gratification from within and so regurgitates food, which gives a sense of physical if not emotional nurturance. In contrast, behavior therapists assume that psychosomatic chronic vomiting is a learned response. Vomiting due to a temporary physical illness may inadvertently be paired with stimuli so that these stimuli later elicit conditioned vomiting. Research with animals has shown that vomiting can be conditioned in this manner (Collins and Tatum, 1925).

Peter Lang and Barbara Melamed, two University of Wisconsin psychologists, were asked to help treat a 9-month-old infant who had suffered from chronic vomiting for about 4 months. The infant vomited 10 to 15 minutes after each meal and had gone

from 17 pounds at 6 months to 12 pounds at 9 months (see Box Figure 1). Although many treatments had been used and the infant had been hospitalized three times, the infant's physician wrote in hospital notes, "Therapy until now has been unsuccessful and the life of the child is threatened" (Lang and Melamed, 1969, p. 3).

Behavioral treatment involved delivering painful electric shocks to the infant whenever he seemed as if he were about to vomit. Electrodes on the infant's throat signaled the muscle contractions that preceded vomiting. The shocks quickly suppressed vomit-

ing, and the vomiting virtually stopped after the third session. Few shocks were required after the third day of treatment. (There was one conditioning session each day.) As Box Figure 1 shows, the infant's health improved, he gained weight quickly, and he left the hospital five days after the last of the eight conditioning sessions.

The costs and benefits of psychological treatments have to be evaluated no less than those of somatic treatments. Although shocking a baby sounds horrifying, this treatment must be gauged with respect to its benefits.

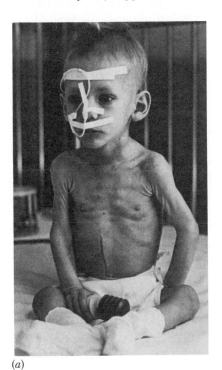

(a)

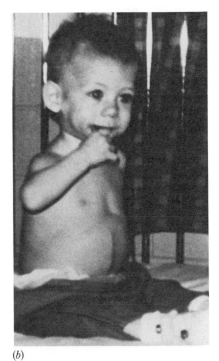

(b)

BOX FIGURE 1 BEHAVIOR THERAPY FOR CHRONIC VOMITING.
(a) *A 9-month-old infant just before treatment for chronic vomiting.* (b) *The infant 13 days later, 5 days after the* last treatment session. The researchers followed the infant and determined that the weight gain was sustained for many months following treatment. (From Lang and Melamed, 1969.)

Aversion Techniques   Among the first behavior therapy procedures used was **aversion therapy** (Voegtlin, 1940), and it remains widely used today. Pictures of young children have been paired with electric shock for child molesters, cigarettes have been paired with nausea for cigarette smokers, and a loud, startling bell has been paired with urination for children who wet their beds. In aversion therapy, a target stimulus (the CS in Pavlovian terms) is paired repeatedly with some unpleasant stimulus (US). According to Pavlovian theory, repeated pairings of the CS with the unpleasant US should eventually result in the CS eliciting a response (a CR) similar to that elicited by the US (the UR). Aversion therapy makes the target stimulus or activity less attractive to individuals. That is, it creates *aversions* to previously attractive activities or desirable stimuli (see Box 15-2).

Aversion therapy must be applied very carefully. Psychologists always must be careful to justify any treatment that causes pain or suffering or that is dangerous (Kattwinkel, 1949).

SKILL TRAINING TECHNIQUES   Some behavioral therapists use observational learning to teach people complex skills necessary to their healthy functioning. For example, therapists have trained shy and socially awkward people how to meet and interact with members of the other sex. First students are identified by their peers as being extremely socially appealing and effective, and then they use these socially skilled students as models. That is, they expose their socially unskilled clients to the models' behavior so that the clients can learn social skills.

Some behavior therapists also teach skills through direct instruction, demonstration, and other coaching techniques as well as through modeling. For example, in one study, alcoholics were taught and given the chance to practice skills for coping with strong urges to drink (Chaney, O'Leary, and Marlatt, 1978). They were taught how to cope in situations likely to elicit the urge to drink: situations of frustration or anger ("Your boss tells you that you are grossly incompetent because he blames you for someone else's mistake"), states of negative emotion ("You and your wife are separated, and you miss her terribly"), situations of great temptation by others ("Your drinking buddies urge you to have 'just one'"), and situations of great internal temptation ("You would really like the taste of beer and feel that you will be able to control your drinking"). Alcoholics given this kind of skill training spent fewer days drunk and consumed fewer drinks in the year following treatment than did people in a control group who either participated in a group discussion of alcoholism or who received no treatment (see Table 15-6).

TABLE 15-6   ALCOHOLICS' DRINKING BEHAVIOR AFTER SKILL TRAINING

	Treatment	
Follow-up Measure	*Skill Training*	*Controls*
Number of days drunk	11.1	64.0
Total drinks consumed	399.8	1592.8

Source: Chaney, O'Leary, and Marlatt, 1978.

Another behavior therapy technique that relies on operant conditioning is the *token economy* in which people are reinforced with tokens for desirable or appropriate behaviors (Ayllon and Azrin, 1968). They can exchange tokens for rewards (such as food, money), or other things that they like. Token systems have been used with children in classrooms to increase their time studying and with psychotic or retarded hospital patients to teach a variety of desirable behaviors such as dressing or toileting themselves (Lovaas, 1977). Researchers also have found that increasing the number of rewards in the social systems of married couples, families, and others can increase people's satisfaction and happiness. Couples are happier if they schedule time to give each other back scratches, if they prompt each other to express affection and the like (Patterson, 1971).

BEHAVIORAL MEDICINE **Behavioral medicine** is the application of behavioral techniques for maintaining or attaining good health. Behavioral medicine relies on techniques like relaxation training, biofeedback, operant conditioning, and cognitive behavior therapy. For example, researchers have found that training individuals to relax by systematically tensing and relaxing major muscle groups helps the individuals to control headache pain (Blanchard and Andrasik, 1985; see Table 15-7) and

TABLE 15-7 A THERAPIST'S SCRIPT IN RELAXATION TRAINING

Initial Steps in Relaxation: Relaxation of the Hands, Arms, and Shoulders

1. Take a deep breath and hold it (for about 10 seconds). Hold it. OK, let it out.
2. Raise both of your hands about halfway above the couch (or, arms of the chair), and breathe normally. Now, drop your hands to the couch (or, down).
3. Now hold your arms out and make a tight fist. Really tight. Feel the tension in your hands. I am going to count to three, and when I say "three," I want you to drop your hands. One . . . two . . . three.
4. Raise your arms again, and bend your fingers back the other way (toward your body). Now drop your hands and relax.
5. Raise your arms. Now drop them and relax.
6. Now raise your arms again, but this time "flap" your hands around. OK, relax again.
7. Raise your arms again. Now, relax.
8. Raise your arms above the couch (chair) again and tense your biceps until they shake. Breathe normally, and keep your hands loose. Relax your hands. (Notice how you have a warm feeling of relaxation.)
9. Now hold your arms out to your side and tense your biceps. Make sure that you breathe normally. Relax your arms.
10. Now arch your shoulders back. Hold it. Make sure that your arms are relaxed. Now relax.
11. Hunch your shoulders forward. Hold it, and make sure that you breathe normally and keep your arms relaxed. OK, relax. (Notice the feeling of relief from tensing and relaxing your muscles.)

Source: Adapted in part from Jacobson, 1938.
Note: Eventually clients are instructed to relax all major muscle groups.

FIGURE 15-11 RELAXATION LOWERS BLOOD PRESSURE.
This figure shows the drop in blood pressure among people who received relaxation training (compared with controls put on a waiting list for treatment). "Pre" measures were taken just before treatment began; "post" measures were taken 5 and 6 weeks after treatment ended. (From Hoelscher et al., 1986.)

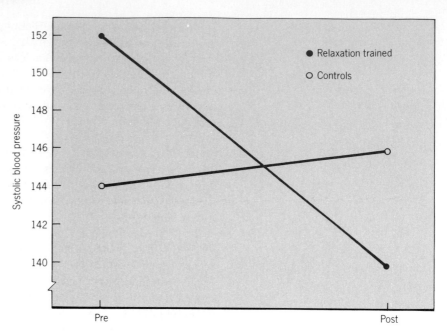

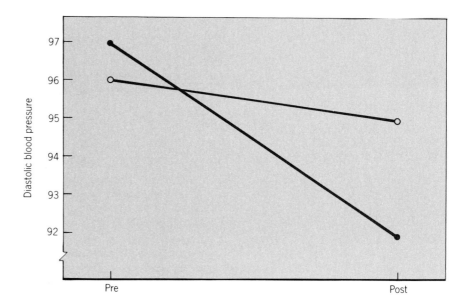

to reduce their blood pressure (Hoelscher, Lichstein, and Rosenthal, 1986; see Figure 15-11). Similar results have been obtained through a procedure in which people are given information about the functioning of particular physiological systems. For example, people with high blood pressure might be attached to a monitor that sounds a tone, that rises and falls with their blood pressure. Headache sufferers have been given biofeedback about the level of their muscle tension, and cardiac patients have been given feedback about their heart rates. In theory, the feedback lets people discover strategies to control the workings of their body.

Biofeedback yields results similar to those of relaxation training (Blanchard and Andrasik, 1985).

Finally, in the past 5 to 10 years, researchers have used cognitive therapy techniques in addition to behavior therapy to help medical patients. For example, they have used cognitive treatment to train people who have had heart attacks to identify and cope with the stress of their illness and to adopt new behavior patterns that reduce the risk of further heart disease. The treatment reduced symptoms of heart disease (Oldenberg, Perkins, and Andrews, 1985).

Effectiveness of Psychological Treatments

There is an old saying that "The proof of the pudding is in the eating." We should evaluate pudding on the basis of the use for which it is intended; does it taste good? In evaluating psychotherapies we must ask how well the therapies fulfill or perform their functions. Do psychotherapies reduce the symptoms of mental disorder and do they help people to live richer or happier lives? The answers to these questions appear to be yes, but these "yeses" rest shakily upon an ever-changing substrate of complex research findings.

THE COMPLEXITY OF PSYCHOTHERAPY RESEARCH   Psychotherapy research is very difficult to do. This is because it is extremely difficult to carry out treatments in a standardized manner. Thus, if one treatment produced better results than another, it might be that it was merely implemented better. It is always difficult to know whether therapeutic success or failure should be attributed to the type of therapy or to characteristics of the therapist. It is also difficult to choose a consistent measure of success in treatment. The behavior therapist insists that improvement be measured on the basis of a client's behavior whereas the person-centered therapist is usually more interested in how a client says he or she feels.

Finally, it is difficult to evaluate psychotherapies because people now seek psychotherapy for problems ranging from severe mental disorder to the pursuit of an "expanded consciousness." In 1957, only 13 percent of the United States population had sought psychotherapy. Today that figure has risen to 30 percent—80 million people—at an estimated cost in excess of $4 billion a year (Meredith, 1986). Naturally, it is difficult to compare the effects of various psychotherapies when they are used with very different types of people and problems. Despite all these problems, psychologists have made progress in evaluating the effectiveness of psychotherapy.

HANS EYSENCK CASTS DOWN THE GAUNTLET   In 1952 the noted British psychologist Hans Eysenck charged that research showed that about two-thirds of patients receiving psychotherapy improved, but so did two-thirds of patients who received no treatment! In other words, most patients with mental disorders improve spontaneously over time. In Eysenck's view, there is little evidence that psychotherapy is beneficial (Eysenck, 1983). Other evidence supports Eysenck's charges against psychotherapy. Hans Strupp (1984) a Vanderbilt psychologist, conducted research in which depressed or anxious male undergraduates received "therapy" from either professional psychotherapists or from nonpsychologist college professors selected on their ability to relate well to students. The therapy was fairly brief, with students receiving a maximum of 25 hours. Results showed that professional therapists and college professors produced comparable outcomes. Students who saw either type of "therapist" did better than those not receiving therapy, but it made little difference which type of therapist was seen (Strupp, 1984). Surely, critics of psychotherapy argued, if effective psychotherapy demands training, experience, and knowledge of a theory of psychotherapy, then professional therapists should outperform well-meaning but untrained college professors.

RECENT RESEARCH ON PSYCHOTHERAPY EFFECTIVENESS   Until the 1970s Eysenck was correct—there was little evidence that psychotherapy was effective (Hollon and Beck, 1979). Since 1970, however, many studies have been performed comparing the effects of psychotherapy with either no treatment or with a placebo condition. In a review of 475 controlled studies of psychotherapy involving thousands of clients, researchers found that people who received psychotherapy were better off in a variety of ways than those who received no therapy (Smith, Glass, and Miller, 1980). This conclusion has been confirmed in subsequent studies (Landman and Dawes, 1982).

But others reviewed the same studies as Smith and concluded that psychotherapy has little effect if it is compared with placebo treatments (Prioleau, Murdock, and Brody, 1983). Psychotherapy, according to these critics, is more beneficial than nothing at all (being placed on a waiting list), but is not consistently more effective than brief and simple placebo treatments (for instance, brief discussion group). In fact, most studies comparing different types of psychotherapies with each other and with placebos usually yield the same results: different types of therapy are equally effective, and they are superior to no treatment, but they are rarely more effective than a placebo treatment (Garfield, 1983; Sloane, Stapler, Cristol, Yorkston, and Whipple, 1970).

Defenders of psychotherapy have responded to these data by noting the inappropriateness of using placebo treatments in the evaluation of psychotherapy (e.g., Parloff, 1986). Parloff and others argue that it is not surprising that the effects of psychotherapy are often similar to those of placebos, because *both are psychological treatments.* Both produce hope, and both create the expectation of improvement.

The fact that most therapies yield comparable results is a testament to the powerful elements that they all share (Frank, 1974; Klein and Rabkin, 1984). All psychotherapies have elements such as these in common: suggestion, support, explanations, emotional release, practice, exposure to negative stimuli, encouragement, and reinforcement (Garfield, 1984). If all therapies have so many elements in common, perhaps we should feel comfortable with the fact that all therapies seem comparably effective? Every therapy is successful! But several authors have noted that this proclamation has an "Alice in Wonderland" quality to it (e.g.,

Luborsky, Singer, and Luborsky, 1975; Rachman and Wilson, 1980; Stiles, Shapiro, and Elliott, 1986). In *Alice's Adventures in Wonderland*, Alice and a motley crew of creatures participated in a race organized by a Dodo bird

> *First, it marked out a race-course, in a sort of circle ("the exact shape doesn't matter" it said) and then all the party were placed along the course, here and there. There was no "One, two, three and away," but they began running when they liked, and left off when they liked so it was not easy to know when the race was over. However, when they had been running a half hour or so . . . the Dodo suddenly called out, "The race is over!" and they all crowded round it, panting and asking, "But who has won?"*

The Dodo's reply?

> *"Everybody has won and all must have prizes!"*

> *(Carroll, 1865/1962, p. 45; quoted in Stiles*
> *et al., 1986, p. 165)*

In contrast to the arguments of some defenders of psychotherapy, we believe that a comparison between a psychotherapy and a well-chosen comparison treatment or placebo can be quite meaningful. We believe that it would be and should be disturbing if psychotherapy were no more beneficial than an intimate discussion with a plant pathologist (e.g., Strupp, 1984). Moreover, psychotherapies are very distinct, both in terms of their underlying theory and in terms of execution (e.g., Sloane et al., 1970). If the theories or practices associated with the various psychotherapies have any validity at all, surely different therapies should produce different outcomes and the best therapies should be better than placebos! Hans Eysenck recently observed that nothing about a placebo treatment

> *would justify us in regarding it as a substantive form of treatment when we judge it in terms of the psychoanalytic, cognitive, or other theories which have been advanced to legitimize the many different forms of psychotherapy. . . . None of the theories would have predicted placebo to be just about as effective as psychotherapy; it is hardly necessary to go beyond that.*

> *(Eysenck, 1983, p. 290)*

The concept of psychotherapy requires that you profit more from discussing your problems with a psychotherapist than with a pharmacist or a ditch digger. Moreover, psychotherapists should achieve better results if they are *well*-trained in at least one type of psychotherapy. If this is not the case, then training psychotherapists could be made considerably easier, and cheaper!

The most persuasive evidence of the value of psychotherapy is that an increasing number of recent studies are showing that (1) psychological therapies do produce results superior to those produced by placebos, and (2) different psychological therapies do yield different effects. Psychotherapy (either cognitive therapy or a therapy called interpersonal therapy) is consistently helpful in alleviating depression. For example,

*FIGURE 15-12 COGNITIVE
AND DRUG THERAPY FOR
DEPRESSION.*

*The proportion of patients remaining
well over a 12-month period following
four different types of treatment for
depression: CT is cognitive therapy;
CT + P is cognitive therapy + placebo;
CT + TCA is cognitive therapy +
tricyclic antidepressant; and TCA is
tricyclic antidepressant. Cognitive
therapy yielded the better outcomes,
antidepressant drugs worse outcomes.*

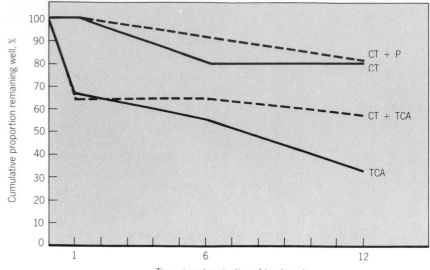

researchers compared the effects of cognitive therapy alone, antidepressant medication alone (pharmacotherapy), cognitive therapy plus pharmacotherapy, and cognitive therapy plus a placebo medication, in terms of their ability to alleviate the symptoms of depression (Simons, Murphy, Levine, and Wetzel, 1986). Results showed that depressed patients given cognitive therapy alone remained depression-free at a much higher rate than patients given pharmacotherapy alone (Figure 15-12). Cognitive therapy and antidepressant drugs produce comparable short-term improvement in depression, but cognitive therapy produces longer lasting benefits (Kovacs, Rush, Beck, and Hollon, 1981). Patients who received both cognitive therapy and antidepressant drugs did better than patients receiving either treatment by itself (Hollon et al., 1983).

Several studies also have shown that cognitive behavioral treatment (coping-response training) helps addicts more than comparison treatments or placebos (Chaney et al., 1978; Hall, Rugg, Tunstall, and Jones, 1984; Tiffany et al., 1986). Cognitive and behavior therapies also have been found superior to other treatments for specific outcomes such as people's ability to approach a feared object or people's ratings of their anxiety (Rachman and Wilson, 1980; Smith et al., 1980; Stiles et al., 1986).

NEW DIRECTIONS IN THERAPY AND THERAPY RESEARCH Researchers are becoming less interested in determining whether treatments are effective and more interested in *how* treatments work and with whom they work (Garfield, 1984; Parloff, 1986; Strupp, 1984; Vandcn Bos, 1986). For example, Lester Luborsky and his colleagues are developing measures of transference that can be used in evaluating the process of psychoanalytic or dynamic psychotherapy (Luborsky et al., 1985). In addition, new, sophisticated measures are being developed to assess the complex social interactions that go on in psychotherapy or that might be affected by psychotherapy (Benjamin, Foster, Giat-Roberto, and Estroff, in press; Humphrey, Apple, Kirschenbaum, 1986).

Another recent emphasis in psychological treatment is target populations. Certain people—of certain ages, of certain groups—have special problems. For example, data show that American blacks have a greater risk of hypertension than whites. Psychologists therefore have developed wide-scale programs to help blacks to prevent hypertension (decreasing salt intake, taking medicine even though they feel healthy, and so on). Smoking-prevention programs have been aimed at adolescents. The presumption behind these treatments is that it is easier to prevent people from starting to smoke than it is to get them to quit once they are addicted (Leventhal and Cleary, 1980).

Also, today treatments are more likely to be used in combinations than they were in the past. For example, a depressed alcoholic might take antidepressant drugs, might participate in family therapy if family problems contribute to his or her drinking or depression, might participate in individual psychotherapy aimed at both the drinking and depression, and finally go to Alcoholics Anonymous (AA), nonprofessional self-help groups of alcoholics who meet regularly.

In closing, we wish to observe that the quality of treatments for mental disorders has improved dramatically over the course of the lives of the authors. This is an exciting time for psychologists; we are at last beginning to unlock the secrets of psychopathology and its treatment.

SUMMARY

SOMATIC TREATMENTS

Somatic treatments are intended to produce benefits through their direct effects on the body.

1. Electroconvulsive therapy (ECT) involves the passage of electric current through the brain and is known to help depression. It improves symptoms of depression better than *placebo* treatments. Placebos are treatments that give a person hope or expectation of help but are intended to have no other effects.

2. Psychosurgery is the surgical destruction of a brain region with no evident neuropathology for the purpose of alleviating a mental disorder. These operations are rarely performed today. They have helped some people with obsessive-compulsive disorder or depression, but superior methods are available today.

3. Drugs have had a major impact on the treatment of mental disorders. Antipsychotic drugs such as phenothiazines were so helpful in reducing the symptoms of schizophrenia that the populations of mental hospitals declined dramatically after their introduction. These drugs reduce activity of dopamine neurons. Antipsychotics also may create harmful effects such as Parkinson's symptoms.

4. Antidepressant drugs reliably reduce the signs and symptoms of depression. About 60 to 70 percent of depressed patients improve with antidepressants; only 20 to 40 percent improve with placebos. Antidepressants appear to increase the activity of biogenic amines (e.g., norepinephrine) but this may not be the source of their beneficial effects.

VERBAL PSYCHOTHERAPIES

1. Psychoanalytically oriented psychotherapy, based on Freudian personality theory, remains influential. A major goal of this therapy is to help clients express instinctual drives in socially appropriate ways, to substitute adaptive defense mechanisms for maladaptive ones. Therapists help clients understand unconscious motivations of their actions, help them become more comfortable with their instinctive needs, and allow them to find new ways to express these needs.

2. For humanistic therapists such as Rogers, humans are essentially good, with inherent drives to self-actualize—achieve their full potential. Rogers said that psychological disturbance arises when society thwarts self-actualization. The client-centered therapist is congruent, accepting, and empathetic, thereby providing the client with an atmosphere in which he or she can develop and grow—self-actualize.

3. Cognitive psychotherapy is based on the notion that much psychological disturbance is produced by how people view or interpret events and not by the events themselves. Cognitive therapists help clients discover the irrational thinking that led to their psychological problems and help them adopt new views of themselves and the world.

4. Strategic family therapy is one of many types of family therapy. Strategic therapists believe that disturbed families have disorganized structures, that these sustain disturbed communication among family members, and that the family's acknowledged problems reflect attempts to deal with more basic problems. Strategic therapists attempt to break up disturbed communication patterns by reframing the identified problem, and they change family structure through specific exercises.

BEHAVIOR THERAPY

Behavior therapy has its origins in learning theory and research. Therapies based on Pavlovian conditioning principles include fear-reduction procedures such as systematic desensitization in which fear is extinguished through repeated exposure to the feared object. In aversion therapy, a behavior or stimulus is made unattractive by its pairing with a punisher. Other behavior therapy procedures are intended to increase the individual's skills.

EFFECTIVENESS AND EVALUATION OF PSYCHOLOGICAL TREATMENTS

Hans Eysenck has argued that psychotherapy is no more effective than no treatment in alleviating mental disorders. But studies now suggest that psychological treatments, especially behavioral and cognitive therapies, do consistently produce effects superior to those of placebos. Various types of psychotherapy produce similar effects, perhaps because most verbal psychotherapies contain powerful common elements: suggestions, support, explanation, and so on.

FURTHER READINGS

Abnormal psychology textbooks provide excellent introductions to the treatment of psychopathology. An excellent text is Michael Goldstein, Bruce Baker, and Kay Jamison's *Abnormal Psychology: Experiences, Origins, and Interventions* (1986). Another useful general resource that discusses the treatment of mental disorders is John Griest and John Jefferson's *Treatment of Mental Disorders* (1982).

Resources that deal with particular therapeutic approaches are *Techniques of Family Therapy* by Jay Haley and L. Hoffman (1967), which deals with family therapy; *Great and Desperate Cures* by Elliot Valenstein (1986), which describes the history of psychosurgery; *Principles of Psychoanalytic Psychotherapy* by Lestor Luborsky (1984); and Carl Rogers' *A Way of Being* (1980), a book that discusses issues relevant to humanistic therapy.

A book that deals with important themes relevant to treatment is Jerome Frank's *Persuasion and Healing* (1974), a classic discussion of core elements of psychotherapy. David Rosenhan's "On Being Sane in Insane Places" (1973) provides a fascinating, but now somewhat dated, glimpse into the practice of assessment and treatment in mental hospitals. Salvatore Maddi's *Personality Theories: A Comparative Analysis* (1980) provides a scholarly and interesting presentation of how personality theories can be translated into psychotherapies. Finally, Mark Vonnegut's book, *The Eden Express* (1975), provides a personal glimpse into the development of schizophrenia.

742

16

SOCIAL COGNITION: PERCEIVING SELF AND OTHERS

Social behavior comes in many forms. It may be as simple as people's unconscious adjustments as they walk down the sidewalk to avoid bumping into one another, or it may be as complex as the elaborate social efforts involved when a government seeks to alleviate the effects of a famine halfway around the world. Although humans are not the only social animals (even bees and ants live in fairly complex social systems), humans certainly live the most complex and varied social lives of all animals. In fact, it can be argued that one of the things that makes humans distinct from other animals is the very complexity of human social life. Social psychologists have long been interested in social behavior at all its levels of complexity. But they are not alone in these interests. Probably for as long as humans have reflected on social life, they have puzzled over questions such as Who am I? Why am I attracted to one person and not another? Why are people sometimes aggressive and hostile and at other times altruistic and caring? How do children acquire social graces (and why do some of them learn too few graces)? How do people learn their values and attitudes, and how can these change over time?

In part, people's interest in social behavior arises from the fact that all of us are almost constantly immersed in social experiences. In our personal lives we interact daily with large numbers of people. Some of these people are close, intimate friends and family members; others are perfect strangers. Some are coworkers and classmates; others supervise or are supervised by us. Some are people we have known for years; others have been newly introduced. No matter who the others are that people our daily lives, we must interact effectively with them in order to have our many physical and social needs met.

At another level, each of us is part of a larger social community that now extends worldwide. We need only pick up the daily newspaper or tune in to the evening television news to see that events all around the world can and do influence our lives. Whether these events pose direct threats to our existence (nuclear war and accidents or the cutoff of vital fuel supplies), arouse our sense of injustice (the exploitation and torture of political prisoners), or touch our emotions (the pictures of starving children in famine-stricken countries), most of us are increasingly aware that our social lives are influenced by people and events far away from us.

In this chapter and the next we will explore research on basic social psychological issues. In this chapter, we examine three fundamental aspects of social life—the influence of social experience on the ways we perceive ourselves, the ways we perceive others, and the relation between the social world and the formation and change of attitudes.

THE SELF

As we have said, humans are not the only animals that live in societies. Even insects such as termites, ants, and bees have social lives insofar as they live together cooperatively in large numbers. Insect societies possess some of the features of human societies. For example, just as humans specialize (some work as computer programmers, some as farmers, some as waiters, some as parents), insects do, too: various portions of the insect society carry out specialized tasks such as food gathering, soldiering, breeding, and caretaking. But unlike members of insect societies, humans possess a **self-awareness** that is more highly refined than the self-awareness of any other species.

You, for instance, can think *about* yourself. You can ask the simple question, "Who am I?" and generate a multitude of answers, about the many roles that you play (student, child, friend, employee, athlete), about your personal characteristics (gender, age, place of birth, special abilities, values and beliefs), and about the impression you want to make to others (the self you present to your parents, say, as opposed to your friends). Psychologists have long been aware of the many ways in which people can answer the question "Who am I?", and have given serious thought to developing researchable (that is, operational) definitions of self.

Defining the Self

William James, writing in 1890, clearly recognized the problem of developing an adequate psychological definition of self. James made a distinction between the *me* (which he thought of as the object or recipient of experience) and the *I* (which he thought of as the aspect of self that takes an active initiating role in the world). James further distinguished among three components of the *me:* (1) the material *me,* or the physical characteristics of a person; (2) a spiritual *me,* the inner core of identity, consisting of a person's enduring values, beliefs, and goals; and (3) the social *me,* the self that is known by other people.

All of us have a *self-concept* or theory about ourselves, a sense of who and what we are. Where does the self-concept come from? How does it develop? How does it change? In considering the self-concept, J. H. Cooley (1922) emphasized that it develops out of our interactions with other people. Cooley coined the phrase "the looking-glass self" to describe the notion that people's self-perceptions are reflections of how they think that others perceive them. In fact, Cooley thought that each person has many self "reflections": how one believes that one appears to others, how one thinks that others evaluate that appearance, and how one responds to or feels about that evaluation. In other words, a person's self-concept depends heavily on what one thinks and feels about other people's responses to oneself. As a later theorist, G. H. Mead (1934), emphasized, the self-concept develops only when people become aware that they are the objects of other people's perceptions—when they become aware of themselves to the extent that they can view themselves from someone else's perspective.

Measuring the Self

Theorists such as James, Mead, and Cooley have offered useful definitions of the self and interesting hypotheses about the development of the self-concept. But theories must be tested, and researchers have employed

TABLE 16-1   HOW CHILDREN DESCRIBE THEMSELVES

Category	Percent of Children	Category	Percent of Children
Own activities		School (excluding teachers)	71
Hobbies, amusements	48	Miscellaneous	5
Sports	43	Demographic	
Daily schedule	43	Age, birthdate	25
Places lived	5	Name	19
Skills	8	Residence	16
TV	10	Birthplace	11
Books	6	Health	11
Jobs	3	Sex	10
Miscellaneous		Race, ethnic	5
experience	6	Religion	3
Significant others		Self-evaluation	
Family	38	Moral	20
Friends	43	Physical	15
Pets	22	Intellectual	10
Teachers	16	Emotional	2
Public figures	0	Physical characteristics	
Attitudes		Hair color	13
Likes and dislikes	52	Weight	11
Vocational	18	Height	10
Hopes and desires	12	Eye color	11

Source: Adapted from McGuire and Padawer-Singer, 1976.
Note: Percentage column indicates percentage of the 252 children who gave at least one response in that category.

a variety of methods to assess the contents and development of self-concepts. For example, one researcher simply asked subjects to answer the question "Who am I?" 15 times over a period of a few minutes (Gordon, 1968). The first few answers that people gave tended to reflect social characteristics such as age, sex, ethnicity, and occupation, whereas their later responses were more likely to reflect personal attributes such as intelligence, personal interests, and sensitivity.

When 252 sixth graders were asked to "tell us about yourself" and complete a separate questionnaire about their personal appearance, demographic characteristics, and the composition of their families (McGuire and Padawer-Singer, 1976), they most often mentioned their schools and the things they liked and disliked (see Table 16-1). They gave little emphasis to evaluating their personal characteristics. The researchers were also interested in determining whether the sixth graders were more likely to spontaneously mention characteristics that distinguished them from their classmates, and found that they were. For example, a high proportion of foreign-born students (44 percent) mentioned their birthplace, whereas only a small proportion (6 percent) of native-born students mentioned it.

Self-schemas and Self-concept

Instead of asking what the contents of self-concepts are like, some researchers view the self as a process. For example, Seymour Epstein

(1973) has suggested that the self-concept is a theory about the self that people develop unconsciously as a way to interpret and understand their old and new life experiences.

Schemas are cognitive structures that contain organized knowledge and beliefs about a specific domain—such as the self—and serve to categorize and organize new information about that domain. **Self-schemas** are components of schemas. They contain people's knowledge and beliefs about the specific roles that they play, about the specific people with whom they interact, about their personal characteristics and values, about the specific situations they encounter, the specific behaviors in which they engage, and so on. The complexity of people's schemas for specific roles, behaviors, characteristics, and situations vary enormously. Among your own schemas, for instance, you probably have a fairly extensive and complex network for the role of student but a fairly simple and sparse network for the role of "President of the United States."

There is evidence that when people have a schema for a particular kind of behavior or characteristic, they pay more attention to information that is relevant to that schema. They also find it easier to judge and remember this relevant information (Bargh, 1982; Fiske and Taylor, 1984). In one interesting study to test this hypothesis, undergraduate women responded to a questionnaire, and their responses led researchers to form them into three groups, one of women who were relatively masculine (*masculine schematics*), one of women who were relatively feminine (*feminine schematics*), and one of women who were androgynous (a mixture of masculine and feminine) (Markus et al., 1982). Several weeks after completing the questionnaire, all the women were asked to select from among eight masculine, eight feminine, and eight neutral adjectives those that best described them, and they were to describe incidents from their past to illustrate their answer. The women who had been classified as having self-schemas for masculinity and femininity, it was found, could make their judgments more rapidly than aschematic subjects. Feminine schematics responded much faster to feminine words than masculine; the opposite held true for masculine schematics. In addition, the schematic subjects recalled, more than the other women, incidents from their lives to illustrate their self-schemas (see Figure 16-1).

Self-schemas also can influence judgments about the self and memory. For example, in one study, undergraduates expressed opinions in response to 60 different statements, such as "I would like to travel freely from country to country." The students then read 120 statements, some of which they had seen before, and were asked to identify those that they had seen before. Of the 30 students in the study, 18 said they had decided whether they had seen a statement before by determining whether it was relevant to them personally (Markus et al., 1982; Rogers, 1977, 1981). Research such as this demonstrates that people's self-concepts, such as reflected in the schemas they hold about themselves, can influence how they process and remember social information and even how they explain their own behavior (Kulik, Sledge, and Mahler, 1986).

Self-schemas may even be more important than other types of schemas (such as schemas for roles and situations), because people's

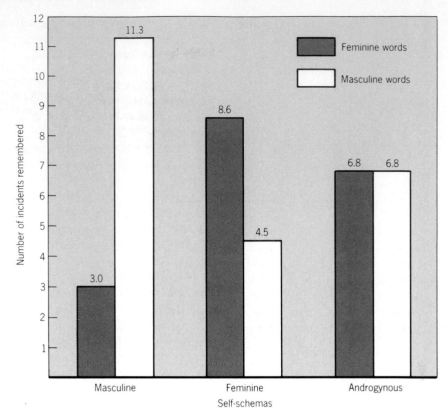

FIGURE 16-1 *SELF-SCHEMAS. Undergraduate women who had self-schemas for masculinity and femininity recalled more incidents from their own background that illustrated their self-schemas than women who had androgynous self-schemas. (After Markus et al., 1982.)*

information about themselves holds much greater emotional immediacy for them than other types of information (Greenwald and Pratkanis, 1985).

PERCEIVING THE SELF

Are you a kind and considerate person? Would you describe yourself as aggressive? Cheerful? Conscientious? Gregarious? Hard working? Articulate? Are you a leader? Are you a liberal? A conservative? More important, how do you know the answers to these questions? Why did you give the answers that you did?

Self-perception Theory

One answer to the question of how we know about ourselves comes from **self-perception theory** (Bem, 1965, 1972), which holds that we human beings learn about our own attitudes, feelings, and other inner states in the same way that other people learn about them: by inferring them from our own behavior. We do not have an advantage over others when it comes to understanding what we believe and feel, and we have to rely on the same external information that is available to other people to infer our beliefs and feelings. To explain our own behavior, according to this line of thought, we examine the environment for causes of our behavior. If we find no apparent cause, we examine our preexisting attitudes, and if we cannot find such an attitude, we infer one from our behavior.

In a study designed to illustrate the operation of self-perception, people were recruited to receive electrical shocks. Some of these people were told that the experimenter wanted them to escape the shock, whereas others were told that the experimenter wanted them to endure the shock. After each shock, the subjects rated its intensity. As predicted by self-perception theory, the subjects who escaped the shocks (and therefore perceived themselves as escaping an aversive stimulus) rated them as more intense—despite the fact that all shocks were equally intense (Bandler, Madaras, and Bem, 1968).

Judging Oneself in Light of Others

Although self-perception theory may have appeared, at first, to be a rather radical view of how we learn about ourselves, you will probably agree that much of what we know about ourselves derives from the comparisons we make between ourselves and others. How many times have you asked yourself questions such as How good a student am I? How good am I at racquetball? How attractive am I? How happy am I? Obviously, such assessments have to be made in light of what we know about others and ourselves.

Just how important is information supplied by others in these assessments? Probably the classic experiment on the influence of others on inferences about ourselves was the study conducted by Schachter and Singer in 1962 and discussed in Chapter 6. You will recall that Schachter and Singer were interested in determining how people judge their emotional states. They hypothesized that emotions are composed of two elements: physiological arousal combined with a cognitive label for that arousal. They further hypothesized, in a manner consistent with self-perception theory, that cognitive labels could be generated by or inferred from information or cues supplied by other people. When the subjects in that study entered the laboratory, they were told that the experiment was designed to examine the effects on vision of a new vitamin called Suproxin. Subjects were injected with the "vitamin" and taken to a separate room where they were asked to wait with another subject while the Suproxin took effect. Some subjects were in fact given a stimulant (epinephrine) that produced physiological arousal and other subjects were given an inert placebo. Some of the subjects who received the stimulant were informed about its actual effects, some were told nothing about its effects, and others were told that the "vitamin" might cause headaches or numb feet. Subjects in these various conditions were then exposed to the friendly or angry confederate and finally asked to complete a mood questionnaire, which assessed the impact of the physiological arousal and the behavior of the confederate.

Although the findings from the study were rather complex (see Figure 16-2), subjects who had received no information about the drug's effects

FIGURE 16-2 SELF-REPORT OF
EMOTIONAL STATE.
Social comparisons: Subjects' reports
of happiness as a function of the
information they received, the mood
of the confederate, and the drug
they received. (After Schachter and
Singer, 1962.)

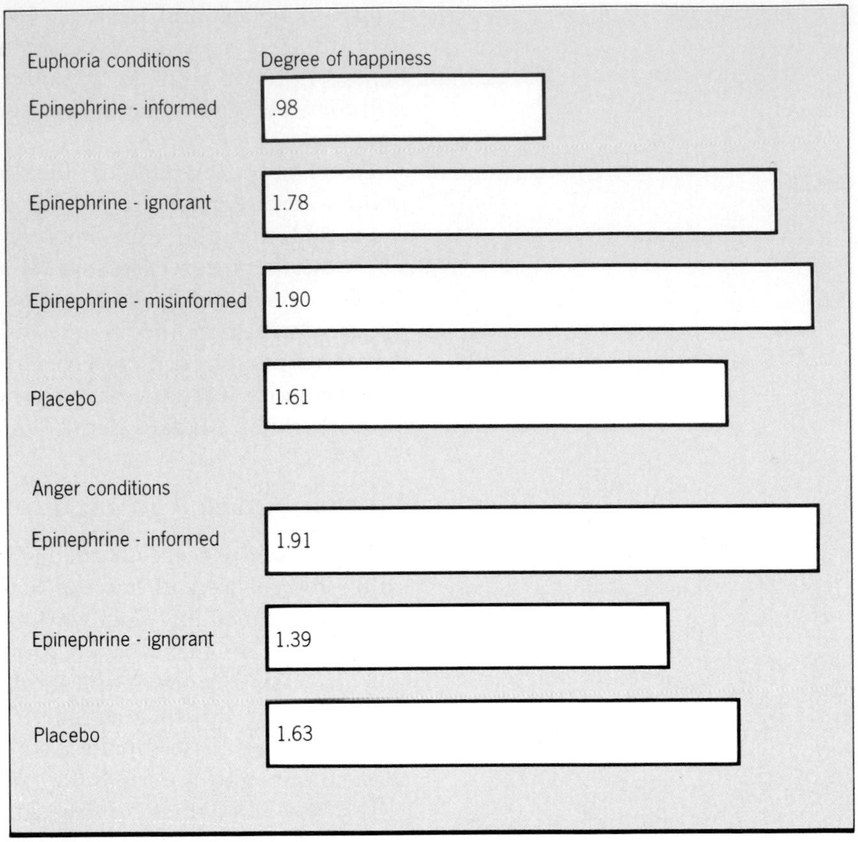

Euphoria conditions	Degree of happiness
Epinephrine - informed	.98
Epinephrine - ignorant	1.78
Epinephrine - misinformed	1.90
Placebo	1.61
Anger conditions	
Epinephrine - informed	1.91
Epinephrine - ignorant	1.39
Placebo	1.63

or were misinformed seemed to "absorb" the mood of the confederate
and expressed that mood on the final questionnaire. These results have
been replicated by many researchers (e.g., Erdman and Jahnke, 1978;
Schachter and Latane, 1964; Valins, 1972), although others have had
trouble replicating the results (e.g., Maslach, 1979). The underlying theory has been criticized—Leventhal (1974), for instance, noted that even
the placebo groups in the original study seemed to absorb the confederate's mood even in the absence of arousal. Nonetheless, a recent review
of the many studies fostered by the original Schachter and Singer experiment concludes that emotional arousal can be intensified by misattribu-
tions about the source of the arousal—precisely the process postulated
by Schachter and Singer.

Objective Self-awareness

You probably have found yourself in situations from time to time where
you felt incredibly awkward. Perhaps you were at a restaurant with an
important date and spilled water all over yourself. Perhaps you went to a
job interview and fell off your chair. Perhaps you have sat nervously in
class as the instructor went around the room asking all the students to
announce their names and explain their interest in the class. In each of
these situations, you probably felt *acutely* aware that you were the object
of other people's attention.

Self-consciousness may have made you want to cringe—or to break into a performance that would astound your audience. Researchers have been curious to find out how self-awareness influences behavior (Duval and Wicklund, 1972; Wicklund, 1975; Wicklund and Frey, 1980 and Carver and Scheier, 1981; Scheier and Carver, 1983). Robert Wicklund (1975) has distinguished between those situations in which a person's awareness is outwardly focused on the environment—a state of subjective self-awareness—and situations in which attention is focused on the self—**objective self-awareness**. People who are objectively self-aware focus intently on their own values, standards, and attitudes and critically evaluate the extent to which they meet their own expectations. Feeling self-conscious, in other words, makes people wonder whether they measure up.

In one study the researchers manipulated students' feelings of objective self-awareness in an interesting way (Ickes, Wicklund, and Ferris, 1973). First, the subjects were led to believe that they had scored high or low on a fictitious personality trait labeled *surgency*. Then they were asked to complete a questionnaire that assessed their self-esteem. Half the students completed the questionnaire while they were seated in a cubicle where they could see themselves in a mirror. Seeing themselves in the mirror presumably made them more self-aware. The other students had no mirrors in their cubicles. Although the students who had been told that they were high in surgency tested higher in self-esteem than those low in surgency, the mirrors also affected the students' self-esteem responses. Consistent with the theory of objective self-awareness, the subjects who had been able to see themselves in the mirror and who were therefore more self-conscious rated themselves lower in self-esteem than those not confronted with the mirrors.

Introspective Awareness

Just because we are aware of ourselves does not mean that we understand ourselves or the causes of our behavior. In fact, people sometimes have great difficulty determining the causes of their behavior. For example, in one study, randomly selected shoppers were asked to evaluate four identical nightgowns or pairs of stockings and to select the one of highest quality (Nisbett and Wilson, 1977). The shoppers chose the article on their extreme right most often. However, when asked to explain their choice, not a single shopper thought that the article's position had influenced them and when the experimenters suggested that it might have done so, the shoppers reacted as though there might be something seriously wrong with the experimenters! In another study people heard a human voice in one ear and tones in the other ear (Wilson, 1975). Afterwards, subjects said that they had not heard *any* tones, and they could not distinguish between new tones and those they had heard earlier. Nonetheless, the subjects *liked* the old tones better than the new tones.

Of course, studies like these do not mean that people never understand why they act as they do. They simply show that the subtle factors that do affect behavior can go undetected. In important matters, people are likely to seek out, pay close attention to, give great weight to, and

BOX 16-1
SELF-MONITORING

As you have been reading about self-presentation, you may have been thinking that you usually do—or don't—think about the impression you make in social situations. Mark Snyder has been investigating the differences among people in the extent to which they think about how their behavior appears to others (Snyder, 1974, 1979, 1986; Snyder and Gangestad, 1986). Some people are very concerned about social proprieties and social presentations. These **high self-monitors** use this information to carefully construct their own self-presentations. They are skillful at expressing or concealing their true feelings to behave in socially acceptable ways. **Low self-monitors**, on the other hand, are less concerned with the impressions they make on others, are less sensitive to social cues, are more likely to reveal their true feelings, and are less likely to shape their behavior to fit the social situation (see the Self-Monitoring Scale in Table 1 for Box 16-1; Snyder and Gangestad, 1986).

High self-monitors are more socially adept than low self-monitors (Danheiser and Graziano, 1982; Ickes and Barnes, 1977; Ludwig, Franco, and Malloy, 1986; Shaffer, Smith, and Tomarelli, 1982; Snyder and Gangestad, 1986). They are more socially adept because they pay more attention to social cues, learn appropriate social behaviors more rapidly, can imitate others more effectively, are better at communicating their emotions, are more relaxed and friendly in social situations, and disclose more about themselves than do low self-monitors.

Differences in self-monitoring have interesting connections to people's choices of social partners. For example, high self-monitors who are especially sensitive to social cues like to be with other people who enjoy doing what they like to *do* (Snyder, Gangestad, and Simpson, 1983). Low self-monitors like to *be* with people they like, regardless of the social activity. High self-monitors are also more willing than low self-monitors to break up with one date in favor of another if the other is skilled in doing things that the high self-monitor enjoys. High self-monitors also have more sexual partners than low self-monitors (Snyder and Simpson, 1984; Snyder, Simpson, and Gangestad, 1986). Snyder's work clearly underscores the fact that our self—and our attentiveness to our self-presentations—play an important role in our social behavior.

BOX TABLE 1 SELF-MONITORING SCALE

Item No.	Item
1.	I find it hard to imitate the behavior of other people. (F)
2.	At parties and social gatherings, I do not attempt to do or say things that others will like. (F)
3.	I can only argue for ideas which I already believe. (F)
4.	I can make impromptu speeches even on topics about which I have almost no information. (T)
5.	I guess I put on a show to impress or entertain others. (T)
6.	I would probably make a good actor. (T)
7.	In a group of people I am rarely the center of attention. (F)
8.	In different situations and with different people, I often act like very different persons. (T)
9.	I am not particularly good at making other people like me. (F)
10.	I'm not always the person I appear to be. (T)
11.	I would not change my opinions (or the way I do things) in order to please someone or win their favor. (F)
12.	I have considered being an entertainer. (T)
13.	I have never been good at games like charades or improvisational acting. (F)
14.	I have trouble changing my behavior to suit different people and different situations. (F)
15.	At a party I let others keep the jokes and stories going. (F)
16.	I feel a bit awkward in public and do not show up quite as well as I should. (F)
17.	I can look anyone in the eye and tell a lie with a straight face (if for a right end). (T)
18.	I may deceive people by being friendly when I really dislike them. (T)

Note: High self-monitors tend to give the answer indicated at the end of each question (T = true of me, F = not true of me). Low self-monitors tend to give the opposite answer.

remember the information that influences their behavior (Adair and Spinner, 1981; Kraut and Lewis, 1982).

Self-presentation

Because we humans are social animals, who crave human contact from the moment of birth, who feel profound distress from loneliness, not only do we form our self-concepts on the basis of how others respond to us, but we also actively seek to foster certain impressions about ourselves in others. Thus part of our self-concepts form out of the way we seem to others. As Goffman (1955, 1959, 1967, 1971) says, we become deeply involved in the **presentation of self in everyday life**. He described social interaction as a kind of theatrical ritual in which each participant acts out a role, consisting of carefully chosen nonverbal and verbal forms of behavior, each of which presents the person in a particular light.

There are a large number of experimental demonstrations of various self-presentation strategies. In one study people read "self-descriptions" of someone whom they thought they were going to meet. The descriptions actually had been prepared by the researchers. Then the people were asked to write descriptions of themselves (Gergen and Wishnov, 1965). The researcher found that the descriptions resembled those the people had read. People who had read a boastful description, for example, described themselves more positively than people who had read a self-effacing description. A similar finding emerged from another study (Newtson and Czerlinsky, 1974). Here, politically moderate students presented themselves as more conservative to conservative audiences and more liberal to liberal audiences. Still other researchers found that women dressed for interviews either to look conventional or liberal, according to the image they thought that the interviewers wanted (von Baeyer, Sherk, and Zanna, 1979). Perhaps the most startling findings come from studies that indicate we are sometimes actually persuaded by our own self-presentations (e.g., Jones, Gergen, and Davis, 1962; Rhodewalt and Agustsdottir, 1986).

PERCEIVING OTHERS

Have you been to a party or a meeting recently where you met someone for the first time? What happened during the initial interaction? What sticks out in your memory about the person? Can you remember your initial impressions of the person? Select a couple of people you know fairly well and think back to first interactions with them. Can you recall your first impressions of these people? Were they positive or negative? Have your first impressions changed? In what ways?

Impression Formation

It turns out that our first impressions of people are often difficult to change. Social psychologists have long been interested in how people form impressions, that is, the information and social cues they use—consciously or not—to form impressions about others.

FORMING FIRST IMPRESSIONS   Solomon Asch (1946) demonstrated the power of first impressions in a simple laboratory study. To half of his subjects, he described a person as intelligent, industrious, impulsive, critical, stubborn, and envious. To half he described the person in the reverse order (starting with *envious*). One group first heard positive traits, and one group first heard negative traits. Those who heard the negative traits first thought that the negative traits outweighed the positive and rated the person as significantly less sociable, humorous, and happy than those in the first group, who heard the positive traits first. Other researchers have also found such **primacy effects** (Luchins, 1957).

CENTRAL TRAITS   One of the early, influential researchers into how people form impressions was Asch (1946). He gave subjects in one group the following description of a hypothetical person:

> intelligent–skillful–industrious–*warm*–
> determined–practical–cautious

People in a second group received the following description:

> intelligent–skillful–industrious–*cold*–
> determined–practical–cautious

Although the difference in the original lists differed in only one adjective, the impressions that the people formed in the two groups were

TABLE 16-2   IMPRESSION FORMATION

	Stimulus Traits Person A	Stimulus Traits Person B	Stimulus Traits Person C	Stimulus Traits Person D	Stimulus Traits Person E
	intelligent	intelligent	intelligent	intelligent	intelligent
	skillful	skillful	skillful	skillful	skillful
	industrious	industrious	industrious	industrious	industrious
	warm	*cold*	*polite*	*blunt*	
	determined	determined	determined	determined	determined
	practical	practical	practical	practical	practical
	cautious	cautious	cautious	cautious	cautious
	Percentage of Subjects Indicating That Trait Is Characteristic of Person				
	A (warm)	B (cold)	C (polite)	D (blunt)	E (no key trait)
generous	91	8	56	58	55
wise	65	25	30	50	49
happy	90	34	75	65	71
good-natured	94	17	87	56	69
reliable	94	99	95	100	96
important	88	99	94	96	88

Note: Subjects saw sets of stimulus traits that varied by only one term and were asked to form an impression of the person described by those traits. Then subjects were asked whether a new set of traits (bottom half of the table) were characteristic of the person. The change of a single trait sometimes produced dramatic differences in the percentage of subjects who said that a new trait would characterize the person.

dramatically different. Those who had been told that the person was warm thought that he also was much more generous and humorous than did those who had been told that the person was cold. By contrast, when the original descriptions differed only in the adjectives *polite* and *blunt* instead of *warm* and *cold,* the people's impressions in the two groups did not differ significantly (Table 16-2).

These results suggest that certain traits are more important than others in creating impressions. Social psychologists call these **central traits**. Do central traits influence impressions in more naturalistic situations? In fact, the same results occur in less contrived situations (Kelley, 1950). Kelley led half the students in an introductory psychology class to believe that a guest lecturer was "a rather *cold* person, industrious, critical, practical, and determined." The other half the class was led to believe the guest was "a rather *warm* person, industrious, critical, practical, and determined." The students expecting a cold guest lecturer

FIGURE 16-3 A MULTIDIMENSIONAL REPRESENTATION OF TRAITS. (From Rosenberg et al., 1968.)

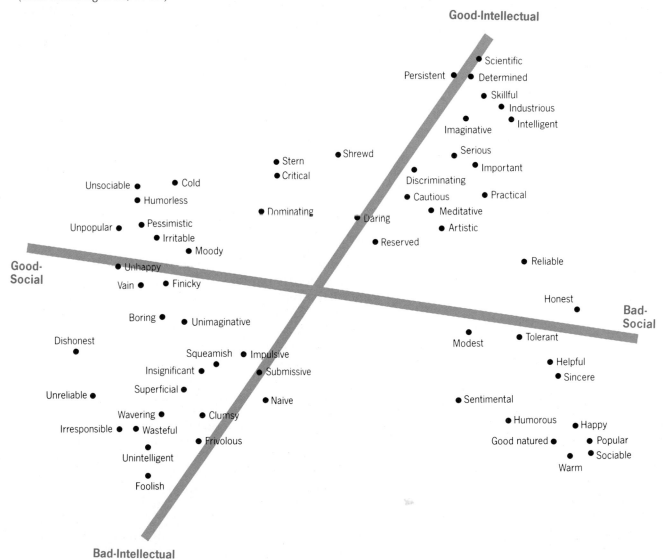

interacted with him less during class (thereby confirming their expectations with their *own* behavior) and gave him lower ratings after class than those who expected a warm person.

IMPLICIT PERSONALITY THEORIES   Implicit in the idea of central and, therefore, peripheral traits is the possibility that people carry around some sort of organized mental model of how traits fit together. People generally entertain certain expectations about how traits fit together and use these expectations both to evaluate other people and to infer characteristics and traits they have not actually observed—just as Asch's subjects inferred that a warm person would be generous but that a cold person would not. Several research methods have been used to assess the contents and organization of these **implicit personality theories**. To find out more about the structure, content, and origin of people's implicit theories of personality, social psychologists have asked people to rate the similarity of adjectives describing traits, such as *warm* and *generous,* to indicate how likely people are to have various traits (if a person is *warm,* how likely is he or she also to be *generous?*), and to sort lists of traits into groups that describe a separate whole people. Social psychologists also analyze ratings of traits through multidimensional scaling, a procedure that can be used to graphically represent the relationships among traits (see Figure 16-3).

For example, some people were asked to rate the character traits of other people whom they knew well. Then a group of university students were asked to rate the character traits of their classmates in the first class of the semester. Regardless of how long the subjects had known one another, they linked the same groups of traits in their descriptions. Clearly, people possess implicit personality theories, and these theories provide consistency in our judgments of others.

Attributions and Social Inferences

You now have seen that people's implicit theories about personality and social schemas contain coherent and organized knowledge about the social world and allow people to effectively attend to, understand, interpret, and remember the important social information with which they are almost constantly surrounded. In this section, we change our focus slightly and examine the ways in which people make judgments that help them to explain other peoples' behavior and to predict their behavior in the future.

THE NAIVE PSYCHOLOGIST   Fritz Heider (1944, 1958) is responsible for launching research on what he termed everyday or "naive psychology." In some of his early research, Heider (Heider and Simmel, 1944) presented student subjects with a short animated film in which several geometric shapes (a circle and large and small triangles) move about inside a rectangle and then leave it when one of its sides is opened. Nearly all the students interpreted the film in human terms. For example, some described the moving shapes as a fight between two men over a woman in which one man chases the other out of a house. The subjects had **attributed** human qualities to the objects in the film. Results like these led Heider to draw analogies between the processes involved when people perceive objects and people. First, he thought that people are motivated to detect the causal relationships in the world, both among objects and among people. Second, he thought that people's judgments about both objects and people must take into account information about the *observed* behavior, the *context* in which the behavior occurs, and the perceiver's *expectations* about the causes of behavior.

Of course, people, unlike objects, have *intentions* and *motivations,* can *cause* actions, and have *abilities.* Heider argued that people use these characteristics to infer the causes of others' behavior. For example, imagine that you are trying to determine why one student sat with another student for 3 hours at the library going over their calculus book, and gave the second student his class notes. Was the first student acting out of an internal or personal factor like kindheartedness, or was he acting out of a situational factor, like the promise of a return favor? If you decide that the helping student acted out of kindness, then you have made a **dispositional** attribution. But if you learn that the first student helped because the second student paid him to help, then you are more likely to make a **situational** attribution. If you are trying to assign responsibility for an outcome (a friend gets an A on an examination in the toughest organic chemistry course on campus), you will want to know whether the person in question had the ability to produce the outcome and how much effort he or she exerted to effect the outcome. If your friend, for example, has always struggled in chemistry courses and studied only moderately, you are likely to make a situational attribution: that the exam was unusually easy and not that your friend did well by dint of hard work and natural aptitude for chemistry (a dispositional attribution).

How systematic are people in making these attributions? Psychologists have suggested that the process of making attributions operates according to several principles. We turn to these now.

CORRESPONDENT INFERENCES Social psychologists have advanced several theories about how people make attributions about other people's intentions (Jones and Davis, 1965). People, it has been argued, make attributions so that they can conclude that an actor's behavior and the intention that produced the behavior correspond to a stable underlying disposition in the actor. That is, people seek to make **correspondent inferences**. Inferences are correspondent when a person can label both the behavior and the disposition of an actor with the same term: he is a hostile person and that is why he picked that fight; she is a kind person and that is why she shared her class notes. The more information that people have about a person and his or her behavior, the more accurate their inferences about intentions.

Several regularities influence people in the making of correspondent inferences (Jones and Davis, 1965). First, and perhaps most important, people make inferences about others' intentions from analyzing **noncommon effects**. They more easily and confidently make inferences when they can determine that a particular action has distinctive features

(Ajzen and Holmes, 1976; Newtson, 1974). Why, for example, did you choose to take introductory psychology? If you had several other introductory classes available to you (biology, calculus, American literature, and economics), we might infer that you are interested in human behavior, because none of the other introductory courses is primarily concerned with this topic. Your interest in human behavior is the noncommon feature. Second, people are less likely to assume that socially desirable behavior arises from someone's disposition because there are alternative explanations for that kind of behavior. Thus, they are less likely to assume that one student coached another in calculus out of the goodness of his heart than out of the expectation of an extrinsic reward such as tickets to a basketball game or the loan of a car on Saturday night. Conversely, people are more likely to attribute socially undesirable behavior to someone's disposition, because they believe that it seems more likely to reveal the person's true intentions (Jones and McGillis, 1976; Miller, 1976).

Together these two regularities—the analysis of noncommon effects and of socially desirable or undesirable behavior—add up to a **discounting principle** (Kelley, 1971). People discount the role of a given cause in producing an effect if other plausible causes are also present.

THE COVARIATION MODEL   People attribute the causes of others' behavior on the basis of the covariation or co-occurrence of events (Kelley, 1967, 1972). In other words, they analyze events that happen together and draw conclusions about their causes from their analysis. They may try to figure out why Steve tripped over Joan's feet while they were dancing, or, more important, they may try to figure out why the leader of one country has threatened to send troops into another country (Fiske and Taylor, 1984; McArthur, 1972). People formulate hypotheses and then test these hypotheses about social behavior along three major dimensions (Kelley, 1972).

1. **Distinctiveness**—has Steve tripped over other dance partners' feet in the past; has the national leader made belligerent threats in the past?
2. **Consistency**—does Steve almost always trip over his dance partner's feet when he dances with her; does the national leader almost always engage in sabre-rattling?
3. **Consensus**—do most people trip over Joan's feet when they dance with her?

As Table 16-3 shows, the attributions one makes about Steve's behavior depend on one's judgments about these factors of distinctiveness, consistency, and consensus. One is more likely to make a personal, or dispositional, attribution when one learns that Steve trips over lots of partners' feet, and almost always trips over Joan's feet, despite the fact that few of Joan's other partners trip over her feet.

Experimental tests of this model do, in fact, provide strong evidence that people's naive psychology for making attributions conforms pretty well to the model. When McArthur (1972) presented subjects with descriptions of a fictitious person and systematically manipulated infor-

TABLE 16-3 KELLEY'S ATTRIBUTION MODEL

	High Distinctiveness — Steve does not trip over almost any other partner's feet.				Low Distinctiveness — Steve trips over lots of partners' feet.			
Consistency	High Consistency — In the past, Steve has almost always tripped over Joan's feet.		Low Consistency — In the past, Steve has almost never tripped over Joan's feet.		High Consistency — In the past, Steve has almost always tripped over Joan's feet.		Low Consistency — In the past, Steve has almost never tripped over Joan's feet.	
	High Consensus	Low Consensus	High Consensus	Low Consensus	High Consensus	Low Consensus	High Consensus	Low Consensus
Consensus	Almost everyone else who dances with Joan trips over her feet.	Hardly anyone else who dances with Joan trips over her feet.	Almost everyone else who dances with Joan trips over her feet.	Hardly anyone else who dances with Joan trips over her feet.	Almost everyone else who dances with Joan trips over her feet.	Hardly anyone else who dances with Joan trips over her feet.	Almost everyone else who dances with Joan trips over her feet.	Hardly anyone else who dances with Joan trips over her feet.
Attribution	Joan is not coordinated. She is at fault. An *entity* attribution should be made.	Steve and Joan are jointly responsible. Both are *necessary* to produce the outcome. A *person–entity* attribution is warranted.	Usually Steve is able to overcome Joan's uncoordination, but not today. A *circumstance* attribution is warranted.	It's a bad day. A *circumstance* attribution is warranted.	Steve and Joan are jointly responsible. Either is *sufficient* to cause the outcome. A *person–entity* attribution is warranted.	Steve is uncoordinated and is at fault. A *person* attribution should be made.	Steve and Joan are both uncoordinated. Usually they overcome it. But not today. Attribution is ambiguous.	Steve is uncoordinated. Joan is usually able to overcome it. But not today. Attribution is ambiguous.
Common attributions	Joan 61%		Circumstances 49%		Circumstances 73%		Steve 86%	

Source: After McArthur, 1972.

Note: According to Kelley's attribution model, people use information about distinctiveness, consistency, and consensus as the basis for making attributions about social behavior. When people in one study were asked to account for behavior such as Steve's tripping over Joan's feet while dancing, their most common attributions were those that appear at the bottom of the table.

mation about distinctiveness, consistency, and consensus, the resulting attributions largely conformed to predictions. Nonetheless, the models require some qualifications. For example, when subjects are asked to make attributions about a behavior and are allowed to choose information freely, they tend to prefer information about consistency over information about distinctiveness, and they want information about consensus least of all (Alicke and Insko, 1984; Kruglanski, 1977; Major, 1980). Furthermore, people also seek and use other kinds of information entirely, including information about the actor and the setting in which the behavior occurs (Hilton and Slugoski, 1986; Ross and Fletcher, 1985; Trope, 1986). In addition, Kelley's model has been criticized for being too rationalistic—it assumes, for example, that people can make accurate assessments of covariation and make use of consensus information, but there is strong evidence that such judgments are difficult for people to make (Crocker, 1981; Borgida and Nisbett, 1977).

Attributional Biases

Just as people often receive more sensory information than they can effectively process, they also receive more social information than they can effectively process. Therefore people must rely on well organized, shorthand representations of their social knowledge—schemas and implicit personality theories—and on efficient procedures for applying that knowledge to new social information—such as attribution models. Unfortunately, one of the costs of relying on these quick and efficient procedures is that not all information gets processed, not all information gets stored, and not all judgments and inferences are as accurate as they might be under ideal circumstances. Such is the case with attributions: attributions are not always made in the best possible ways and in an optimal manner.

Two main problems have been detected in people's attributional judgments. The first type are *errors*. They are judgments that are not consistent with the information on which they are based: Steve did not give Joan his calculus notes; he gave her his phone number. The second type of problems are *biases*. As we shall see, they are judgments that are based on fundamentally reliable information but lead to slightly and systematically imprecise results. There are so many examples of attributional biases that we cannot consider them all here. Instead, we will first examine three **cognitive biases (and errors)**, so called because they seem to arise from the deficiencies in the collection and processing of social information. Then we turn to three types of **motivational biases**—so called because they seem to serve basic needs, such as for self-protection.

Probably the most common cognitive error that people make is to overattribute causation to a person's disposition and underattribute it to situational factors. This error has been termed the **fundamental attribution error**. When people make attributional judgments, they often are less sensitive to situational cues than is appropriate (Miller, Jones, and Hinkle, 1981; Ross, 1977; Ross, Amabile, and Steinmetz, 1977). In one early study on this fundamental attribution error, subjects evaluated essays which either supported or opposed Castro's programs in Cuba

(Jones and Harris, 1967). Although the subjects were told that the essay writers had been assigned a position on Castro—pro or con—the subjects thought that the writers who had been assigned to write pro-Castro essays were actually more pro-Castro than the writers who had been assigned to write anti-Castro essays. Some critics have challenged the appropriateness of the title "fundamental attribution error" (Harvey, Town, and Yarkin, 1981) on the ground that it is extremely difficult to accurately assess the true cause of behavior—in other words, they argue that the studies reveal a bias, but not necessarily an error.

Try the following test (Fiske and Taylor, 1984). Complete the ratings in Table 16-4, following the instructions carefully. After you have rated yourself and your friend, add up the ratings (ignore the pluses and minuses). If you are like most people, the score you have given your friend is greater than that you have given yourself. This difference reflects what has been termed the **actor–observer bias** (Anderson, 1985; Jones and Nisbett, 1972) and refers to people's general tendency to overestimate the effects of dispositions on other people's behavior (Kelley and Michela, 1980; Monson and Snyder, 1977; Ross, 1977). You probably rated yourself a 0 fairly often when you were working on Table 16-4. This tendency arises because you are sensitive to the ways in which your behavior *varies* across situations. However, when you rate a friend, you are more likely to make use of the $+2$ and -2 categories, because you are sensitive to the *consistency* in your friend's behavior across situations.

TABLE 16-4 RATING SCALE

First, rate a friend of yours on the following characteristics using the scale that follows. Then go back and do the same for yourself.

Rating Scale

-2	Definitely does not describe
-1	Usually does not describe
0	Sometimes describes, sometimes not
$+1$	Usually describes
$+2$	Definitely describes

	Friend	*Self*
Aggressive	_____	_____
Introverted	_____	_____
Thoughtful	_____	_____
Warm	_____	_____
Outgoing	_____	_____
Hard driving	_____	_____
Ambitious	_____	_____
Friendly	_____	_____
Total	_____	Total _____

Now, go back, ignore the pluses and minuses, and total up the two columns.

Why do people entertain these different biases about their own behavior and that of others? Two reasons may explain the difference (Jones and Nisbett, 1972). First, actors and observers have *different information* about behavior. As an actor, you have much more information available to you about your own past behavior than does any observer of your behavior (Eisen, 1979). Second, actors and observers view behavior from *different perspectives*. Actors are more alert to aspects of the situation (the presence and behavior of other people, the location, and so on) to which they are responding than to aspects of their disposition. These aspects of the situation are more influential when actors make inferences about the causes of their behavior than they are when observers make such inferences. For the observers, actors' dispositional qualities and their behavior are the more influential factors (Storma, 1973).

Interestingly enough, people's biases seem to operate according to other principles, too. For example, positive events and outcomes tend to be attributed to actors whereas negative events and outcomes tend to be attributed to the situation. Furthermore, differences in attributions about one's own behavior can be reduced if observers are instructed to take the role of or empathize with the actors they observe. The observers then become more sensitive to the situational factors that the actor is responding to (Regan and Totten, 1975).

As we noted earlier, people resort to consensus information (which reflects the beliefs or experiences of large numbers of people) less often in forming attributions than to information about distinctiveness or consistency. Even when it is available, people tend to underuse consensus information. In one study, for example, subjects saw a summary of the findings from earlier studies of altruism and obedience and then were asked to predict how someone new would behave under identical circumstances. Even though the people learned that practically no one had behaved altruistically in the earlier studies, they essentially ignored that information in making their predictions. In general, people are not very adept at using consensus (or "base-rate") information (Kahneman and Tversky, 1973). Part of the problem may be that people do not quite see how consensus information is relevant to them or their judgments, for there is some evidence that people use consensus information more effectively *if* the relevance of that information is made clear to them.

Several attributional biases involve people's projections of their own attitudes onto others. For example, we humans generally assume that others will act as we would act. This **self-based** bias is clearly evident in the results of a study in which students were asked whether they would be willing to walk around their campus for 30 minutes wearing a sandwich board bearing the advertisement, "Eat at Joe's" (Ross, Greene, and House, 1977). Some students agreed and others refused, but more important, students' estimates of how many other students would agree to wear the sign were sharply affected by the students' own attitudes about carrying the sign. Students in both groups estimated that about two-thirds of their fellow students would make the same choice they had made. Clearly, the students inferred that most people were like them. This tendency to use one's own behavior and preferences as the basis for predicting other people's responses may reflect a human need to see one's own behavior and beliefs as "normal" (Zuckerman, Mann, and Bernieri, 1982). Another possibility is that we tend to associate with people who are like us, and our projections about other people's beliefs and behavior reflect our biased sampling of our friends. At present, psychologists do not fully understand the sources of the self-based bias.

A related self-serving bias is evident in people's tendency to take credit for their successes and, to a lesser extent, deny responsibility for their failures (Miller and Ross, 1975; Zuckerman, 1979). For example, students have been found to regard examinations on which they have done well to be good indicators of their preparation and knowledge, but examinations on which they have done poorly are regarded as poor indicators (Arkin and Maruyama, 1979; Davis and Stephan, 1980). Even professors are more likely to claim credit for students' performance when the students have done well than when they have done poorly (Arkin, Cooper, and Kolditz, 1980; Tetlock, 1980). Some psychologists maintain that the self-serving bias is best explained by motivational factors (such as people's desire to see themselves in a favorable light), and others maintain that it is best explained by cognitive factors. According to the cognitive position, people accept credit for their successes because success fits their expectations and because they typically can see the relationship between their effort and success.

ATTITUDES AND BEHAVIOR

Do you regard yourself as a feminist, or do feminists make you uneasy? Would you describe yourself as a conservative or a liberal? Are you a Republican or a Democrat? A Protestant, Catholic, Jew, or perhaps an atheist? Do you prefer rock and roll, jazz, or classical music? Which toothpaste do you brush with? Do you prefer coffee or tea or Classic Coke? Do you kiss on first dates? What do you think of people who use drugs? What is your favorite television program? Why do you possess these attitudes and preferences? Where did they come from? Have you always held them? What would make them change?

We live in an age when some social attitudes and social behavior have changed fairly dramatically. Attitudes toward blacks and women are two good examples. Over the past 20 years attitudes of whites toward blacks have become considerably more positive and there have been substantial improvements in educational and career opportunities for some blacks. Over the past 20 years, people also have become far more accepting of women working outside the home and women—even those with young children—are entering the work force in increasing numbers (Shiels, 1983). Spurred, perhaps by the feminist movement, the work force has also changed. The number of women entering traditionally masculine professions has increased dramatically. For example, between 1975 and 1985 the proportion of women architects rose from 4 to 11 percent and the proportion of women lawyers and judges rose from 7 to 18 percent, although women still earn only about 68 percent as much as men in comparable work situations ("Job Market," 1987). Social psychologists have studied people's attitudes, the better to understand these and similar changes in social values and behavior. One question that has intrigued them is the relationship between changes in social attitudes and social behavior: which causes the other? To answer that question (if it can be answered at all!) requires us to take up the topic of attitudes themselves.

Defining Attitudes

"He's got an attitude," you say, meaning that he's got a chip on his shoulder. But social psychologists mean something different when they investigate people's attitudes. Social psychologists have been investigating attitudes for more than a half century (McGuire, 1985). Some early psychologists, such as the behaviorist John Watson (1925), even defined social psychology as the study of attitudes. Various social psychologists have tried to define **attitude**. Gordon Allport offered the following classic definition: "an attitude is a mental and neural state of readiness, organized through experience, exerting a directive or dynamic influence upon the individual's response to all objects and situations with which it is related" (1935, p. 810). Allport emphasized that an attitude is a preparation or readiness for a response, not behavior but the precondition of it. Others defined attitude as "an enduring organization of motivational, emotional, perceptual, and cognitive processes with respect to some aspect of the individual's world" (Krech and Crutchfield, 1948, p. 148). This definition emphasizes "organization" and the subjective experience of holding an attitude. A third definition worth noting is that an attitude is the intensity of positive or negative affect for or against a psychological object. A psychological object is any symbol, person, phrase, slogan, or idea toward which people can differ as regards positive or negative affect (Thurstone, 1946, p. 39).

When considered together, these definitions underscore the three components of attitudes that concern contemporary researchers. The **affective** component consists of a person's feelings and emotions (including physiological responses) toward an object. The **cognitive** component consists of the cognitions (knowledge, facts, belief, and opinions) a person holds about an object. Third, the **behavioral** component consists of the mental and physical processes that prepare a person to respond in a particular way to an object. For example, with regard to South African *apartheid,* you may know that it is a governmentally ordained form of racial segregation (cognition), you may feel a strong sense of revulsion about it (negative affect), and you may have written to your Congressional representative urging sanctions against South Africa (the behavioral component).

Learning Attitudes

You unquestionably have definite attitudes about many things, but where have these attitudes come from? How have they developed? Will

BOX 16-2
MEASURING ATTITUDES

Chances are good that you have been surveyed about your attitudes on some issue or other. A major problem for those who study attitudes is that they are abstract. They cannot directly observe attitudes, and so they find acceptable **operational definitions** of attitudes (recall our discussion in Chapter 1). Modern techniques for measuring attitudes have grown out of the work of a number of researchers.

The most common type of attitude scale is the **Semantic Differential** (Osgood, 1965; Osgood, Suci, and Tannenbaum, 1957). In this procedure, people are simply presented a statement and asked to rate that statement on a series of bipolar adjectives: good–bad, many–few, and so on (see Table 1). Responses represent three dimensions of people's attitudes: (1) an evaluative (good–bad) dimension, (2) a potency (weak–strong) dimension, and (3) an activity (fast–slow) dimension.

Recently, some social psychologists have sought to assess attitudes more

directly by measuring people's physiological responses to attitude objects (Cacioppo, Petty, and Morris, 1985; Petty and Cacioppo, 1981). These psychologists present people with attitude objects and measure such things as changes in skin conductance, dilation of the pupil of the eye, and facial muscles. Some measures (those of facial muscles, for example) do appear to reflect the direction and intensity of attitudes (Cacioppo, Petty, Losch, and Kim, 1986). Physiological approaches to attitude measurement have the advantage of not relying on people's verbal reports. This advantage was demonstrated in a study of people's reactions to emotional displays (McHugo et al., 1985). The subjects in the study were shown videotapes of speeches by Ronald Reagan in which he expressed happiness, evasiveness, or anger (see Box Figure 1). Although people with favorable attitudes toward Mr. Reagan *reported* more positive responses to the videotapes, the physiological measures indicated that the facial responses of *all* the viewers were essentially mirroring what was presented in the videotapes. In other words, the physiological measures showed a common pattern

of responses that was obscured by the verbal reports.

BOX FIGURE 1   EXPRESSING ATTITUDES.
Still frames from the videotapes of Ronald Reagan, displaying happiness (top), evasiveness (middle), and anger (bottom). (From McHugo et al., 1985.)

BOX TABLE 1

3. Semantic Differential Scale

Rate how you feel about the church on each of the scales below.

good	____ (+2)	____ (+1)	____ 0	____ (−1)	____ (−2)	bad
unfavorable	____ (−2)	____ (−1)	____ 0	____ (+1)	____ (+2)	favorable
pleasant	____ (+2)	____ (+1)	____ 0	____ (−1)	____ (−2)	unpleasant
negative	____ (−2)	____ (−1)	____ 0	____ (+1)	____ (+2)	positive

they change in the future? These are questions of critical importance to attitude researchers.

It probably comes as no surprise that most adolescents and young adults have attitudes very much like those of their parents and that parents are the most important sources of attitudes for young people (Tedin, 1974). Teachers and peers are also important sources of attitudes for adolescents and young adults. Parents serve as an important **reference group** for children. As children grow up and leave home, they are exposed to a broader set of reference groups, and changes in their attitudes become fairly common.

All three of the major learning theories we have considered in earlier chapters have been applied to attitude formation. You will recall that in **classical conditioning**, if a conditioned stimulus (a bell ring) is repeatedly paired with an unconditioned stimulus (food) that produces an unconditioned response (salivation), the conditioned stimulus will eventually elicit the unconditioned response even in the absence of the unconditioned stimulus. In **operant conditioning**, responses are more or less likely as a result of their positive and negative consequences, or reinforcements. In **observational learning**, responses are acquired through the observation of other people's behaviors and the consequences of those behaviors.

CLASSICAL CONDITIONING OF ATTITUDES   Can attitudes be classically conditioned? The answer is unquestionably yes. One early study by Razran (1940) illustrates the process. Razran first had subjects indicate how much they agreed with slogans such as "Workers of the world, unite." Later the subjects listened to some of these slogans while they were sitting in a neutral setting, listened to other statements while they were eating a free lunch, and listened to still others while they inhaled unpleasant odors. The subjects later rated the slogans they had heard during (paired with) the lunch more positively than they had at first, rated the slogans paired with the unpleasant odors lower than they had at first, but did not change their ratings of slogans paired with the neutral condition. Interestingly, subjects could not recall the conditions under which they heard the slogans. Other researchers since have replicated and extended these findings (Berkowitz and Knurek, 1969; Staats and Staats, 1957, 1958; Zanna, Kiesler, and Pilkonis, 1970).

OPERANT CONDITIONING OF ATTITUDES   Can attitudes be operantly conditioned? Again, the answer is unquestionably yes. When two researchers conducted a telephone survey of Harvard undergraduates' attitudes toward Harvard, they found that by saying "good" or "uh-huh" to the students' positive or negative comments, they could influence the students to make more positive or negative comments (Hildum and Brown, 1956). What is more, the operantly conditioned responses tend to have an enduring effect on attitudes. A researcher reinforced subjects over the telephone for positive or negative statements about a student "Spring Festival" (Insko, 1965). One week later, the researchers surveyed the students again and found that those reinforced for positive statements expressed more positive attitudes toward the festival than those reinforced for negative statements. These findings have also been replicated and extended by a number of researchers (Insko and Cialdini, 1969; Kerpelman and Himmelfarb, 1971).

OBSERVATIONAL LEARNING OF ATTITUDES People also seem to learn attitudes by observing others. Studies show that children will imitate the behavior (more than the words) of adults, particularly when the adult's behavior has been rewarded (Bryan, Redfield, and Mader, 1971; Bryan and Walbek, 1970; Rushton, 1975).

Although they offer powerful explanations of the processes of attitude formation (and change of attitudes), learning theory has not been dominant within social psychology. Some researchers have concentrated on the motivational aspects of attitude change, whereas others have explored the impact of the content of persuasive communications (and the characteristics of the senders and receivers of such messages) on attitude change.

Consistency Theories of Attitude Change

According to consistency theories of attitude change, if people hold a particular attitude that is inconsistent with their other attitudes or with their behavior, then they will be motivated to change their attitudes or behavior. The fundamental notion is that people are motivated to maintain an equilibrium, or consistency, between their attitudes and behaviors. They find inconsistency unpleasant. In the following section, we examine two theories built around the motivation to maintain consistency. Both of these theories are concerned with the conditions under which cognitive elements are in equilibrium and the means by which equilibrium can be restored.

BALANCE THEORY Fritz Heider (1946, 1958), whose work on attributions you saw earlier, formulated the basic tenets of **balance theory**. Heider examined attitudes and behavior from an individual's point of view. He analyzed the relationships among cognitive elements in models consisting of dyads (two elements) and triads (three elements). Figure 16-4 shows a number of triads that represent balanced and unbalanced relationships. In these relationships, a single individual (P) holds or changes his or her attitude about another individual (O) as a result of the similar or dissimilar attitudes that they both hold about another object, person, idea, event, and so on (X). A balanced cognitive state exists when P likes (denoted with a +) O, and they both agree about (either both like, +, or both dislike, −) X, or when P dislikes O and they disagree about X. An unbalanced state exists when P likes O but they disagree about X or when P dislikes O and they agree about X. In general, triads are in balance if the product of their relationship signs is positive and unbalanced if the product is negative. For example, if you like Sally (+) and you like football (+), but Sally detests football (−), then the product (+ × + × −) is negative, and there is cognitive imbalance in the triad.

When students were asked to rate the pleasantness of the eight kinds of relationships represented by the triads in Figure 16-4, they rated

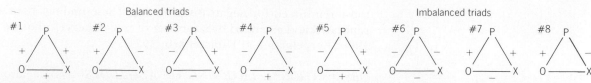

Perceived pleasantness of p-o-x triads							
				p-o-x Triad number			
1	2	3	4	5	6	7	8
Relation							
p-o	+	+	−	−	−	−	+	+
p-x	+	−	+	−	+	−	+	−
o-x	+	−	−	+	+	−	−	+
Pleasantness	26.2	39.5	62.4	55.3	58.4	54.8	57.0	58.2

FIGURE 16-4 RELATIONSHIP TRIADS.

In this figure, p = *you,* o = *other person, and* x = *an issue or an object. A positive sign indicates a positive relationship between two elements in the triad and a negative sign indicates a negative relationship. Figures in the bottom row represent students' ratings of the pleasantness of each triad. Lower numbers indicate greater feelings of pleasantness. (After Jordan, 1953.)*

balanced relationships by subjects as generally more pleasant (mean = 45.9; lower scores indicated greater pleasantness) than unbalanced relationships (mean = 57.1; Jordan, 1953). Heider postulated that imbalance fosters a state of unpleasant tension that motivates people to restore balance among cognitive elements. You can see that an unbalanced triad can be restored to balance if the sign of any of the relationships is changed. Thus, you might change your attitude toward either football or Sally. In general it is thought that the weakest or least well established relationship will change to establish balance.

COGNITIVE DISSONANCE THEORY Probably no social psychological theory has generated as much interest and research as Leon Festinger's (1957) theory of **cognitive dissonance**. As in balance theory, a major premise of Festinger's theory is that people are motivated to maintain consistency among the cognitive elements that make up their attitudes. But in contrast to balance theory, cognitive dissonance theory places less emphasis on logical consistency than on the psychological comfort and discomfort of the individual. According to Festinger, people experience **dissonance** (or discomfort) when their cognitions—beliefs, opinions, self-perceptions, and the like—do not fit together harmoniously. For dissonance to occur, two cognitive elements must be related and yet opposite to one another. The resulting discomfort produced by this conflict is thought to motivate people to attempt **dissonance reduction**. The strength of the efforts to reduce dissonance will depend on the proportion of cognitions that are dissonant and how important the cognitions are to the individual.

	Dependent Variable	
Condition	Enjoyment of task	Willingness to participate in similar experiments
$1 reward	+ 1.35	+ 1.20
$20 reward	− .05	− .25
Control	− .45	− .62

FIGURE 16-5 THE CLASSIC DISSONANCE EXPERIMENT.
In this experiment subjects were paid either $1 or $20 to deceive other "subjects." As predicted by dissonance theory, subjects paid $1 experienced more attitude change than those paid $20.

Festinger suggested three ways in which people could reduce dissonance. First, one of the dissonant elements could be changed (to take our case of Sally and football, we could change our attitude about one of them). Second, people can reduce the proportion of dissonant elements by adding consonant cognitions about all the other reasons we like Sally, such as the fact that she is fun to be with, the fact that she is a dependable friend, the fact that we both enjoy flower shows, and so on. Third, we could change the importance of the cognitions ("Football really is not that important to my life"). As you might imagine, one of the criticisms directed at dissonance theory is that it lacks some of the precision of balance theory (the triad method of analysis makes much clearer predictions than does Festinger's theory). Nonetheless, dissonance theory has served as a useful guide to a large body of research.

The classic dissonance experiment is one in which subjects spent an hour performing extremely dull tasks and then were paid either $1 or $20 (a lot of money at the time) to describe these tasks as pleasant and enjoyable to other "subjects" (Festinger and Carlsmith, 1959). Afterwards the $1 subjects rated the experiment as more positive than either the $20 subjects or control subjects who were not asked to mislead the waiting participants (Figure 16-5). The results confirmed the dissonance theory prediction that dissonance would be aroused by telling someone that a boring experiment was interesting. Since subjects could not deny having performed the attitude-discrepant behavior, they would have to either change other cognitive elements or change their attitude toward the experiment. Subjects paid $20 might easily explain their behavior as motivated by the money (change other cognitive elements), but those paid $1 had **insufficient justification** for their behavior, so they were likely to change their attitude toward the experiment.

Consider the following situation: researchers interview students just before or just after the students have registered for classes and ask the students how good they think their classes will be. Which students would give higher ratings to their classes? Rosenfeld, Giacalone, and Tedeschi (1983) conducted such a study and found that the students who had already registered rated their classes as more promising than the students who had not already registered. Similar findings have been obtained in studies of women who have selected household products as payment for participating in a study (Brehm, 1956) and bettors at the racetrack (Knox and Inkster, 1968). In general, people appear to reduce **postdecision dissonance** by rating their choices more favorably or by devaluing the alternatives they have not selected.

ALTERNATIVE INTERPRETATIONS OF DISSONANCE RESULTS
Although there is a vast body of research supporting dissonance theory, the theory has not gone unchallenged. Bem (1967) proposed that findings such as those from Festinger and Carlsmith's $1/$20 experiment could be explained with **self-perception theory**, which holds that we infer our attitudes in the same way an outside observer would. From this perspective, the $1 subjects' attitudes changed because they observed themselves engage in behavior that indicated their underlying attitude was positive. The $20 subjects, in observing their behavior, could attrib-

ute it to the $20 and were not required to make any inferences about their own attitudes.

A number of researchers have attempted to determine whether cognitive dissonance or self-perception theory provides a better explanation of results such as those obtained in insufficient justification studies (e.g., Kiesler and Pallak, 1976; Ross and Schulman, 1973). In their reviews of these studies Fazio, Zanna, and Cooper (1977, 1979) have concluded that both theories are applicable to human behavior. They argue that dissonance theory applies best to judgments and inferences people make when they attempt to explain behavior that is in conflict with their attitudes, while self-perception theory applies best to judgments and inferences made about behavior that is consistent with one's attitudes.

Other theorists argue that the dissonance results can be explained as the product of experimental subjects' efforts to present themselves as consistent and stable individuals. According to **impression management theory**, subjects apparently change their attitudes because they try not to look bad in awkward situations created by experimenters (Tedeschi, Schlenker, and Bonoma, 1971). Indeed, studies have shown that when subjects are not under any impression management pressure to make a good impression—when, for instance, they believe that the experimenter can assess their true attitudes or their identity is concealed from the experimenter—behavior that is inconsistent with their beliefs may not lead them to change their attitudes (Gaes, Kalle, and Tedeschi, 1978; Malkis, Kalle, and Tedeschi, 1982).

Other psychologists have questioned whether cognitive dissonance really produces the unpleasant feelings and the motivation to resolve them that Festinger originally postulated. The research on this question is complicated, but a particular study (Higgins, Rhodewalt, and Zanna, 1979) illustrates the methods and findings produced by researchers interested in this issue. The researchers assumed that subjects whose behavior ran contrary to their attitudes or beliefs would experience some form of arousal. They also provided the subjects with possible attributions for that arousal. The subjects in each of five groups were given a pill (actually a placebo) and were told that it would produce a side effect. One group was told that the pill would make them feel "unpleasantly sedated." Others were told that the pill would make them feel "relaxed," "tense," "pleasantly excited," or would have no side effect. Thus, the subjects were given attributions that combined the elements pleasantness and unpleasantness, sedation and arousal. After taking the pill, the subjects did things that the researchers knew from earlier tests ran counter to their attitudes. Then, their attitudes were assessed again.

The researchers expected to see the least change in attitude among the subjects who could (mis)attribute the unpleasant arousal produced by cognitive dissonance to the pill they had been given. If subjects could not attribute unpleasant arousal to the pill, then the subjects were expected to show the usual pattern of attitude change. The researchers' hypothesis was borne out. As Table 16-5 shows, the results of the study strongly suggest that the primary component of cognitive dissonance is unpleasantness. Subjects who could attribute the unpleasantness they experienced to the pill showed the least change in attitude. Otherwise, the attributions did little in the way of changing people's attitudes.

TABLE 16-5 ATTITUDE CHANGE

Immediate Attitude Change for High-Choice Conditions

	Possible "Side Effects" of Placebo		
	Arousing	*Calming*	*No Side Effects (control condition)*
Sensation			
Pleasant	7.3	5.9	4.7
Unpleasant	1.7	0.4	

Source: Higgins, Rhodewalt, and Zanna, 1979.
Note: Attitude change scores for subjects in a placebo attribution study. Higher scores indicate greater acceptance of the counterattitudinal position.

As you can see, dissonance theory is alive and well, even though it has gradually been modified and qualified over the past 30 years. Dissonance theory no longer maintains the dominant position it once held. Today it is considered together with other theoretical approaches to attitude change as researchers try to determine the conditions under which dissonance, self-perception, and impression management influence how people form their attitudes (Baumeister and Tice, 1984; Tetlock and Manstead, 1985).

CHANGING ATTITUDES AND BEHAVIOR

Social psychologists are so interested in learning about how people form and change their attitudes ("I *will* vote Republican. No, come to think of it, I won't.") that some 1000 new studies of attitude change emerge every year (McGuire, 1985). In the following section, we discuss forms of communication designed to persuade people to change their attitudes and actions.

"But Mom, all the other kids are going to the party," you pleaded as a child. "Whatever you do, don't take statistics," you warn your roommate. You have probably tried to influence someone's behavior or change someone's attitude many, many times by presenting what you considered persuasive information. In fact, people often do change their attitudes in response to a persuasive communication, and so social psychologists have been interested in determining what makes a communication persuasive.

All communication, persuasive or otherwise, can be analyzed by its components: source, message, channel, receiver, and target.

The Communication Source

How much does it matter *who* communicates a message? The answer is that it can make a big difference. The credibility, attractiveness, power, and style of sources all influence the persuasiveness of their messages. What makes a source *credible* is primarily trustworthiness. Although it generally helps for a source to be knowledgeable, or expert, these characteristics are not always helpful (McGinnies and Ward, 1980) and

BOX 16-3
APPLYING RESEARCH ON PERSUASION TO ADVERTISING

Advertisers want to present an audience with commercials that contain the most information, are best remembered, and are as persuasive as possible. Might they accomplish this by simply squeezing more into their commercials?

There is substantial variability in the rate at which people normally speak, with an upper limit of about 180 words a minute and a lower limit of about 120 words (Monroe and Ehinger, 1974). Most people speak about 145 words per minute. Social

psychologists and market researchers have studied the effects of accelerated speech and have produced some surprising results. People's comprehension is virtually unaffected by the rate of speech until it reaches a supersonic 280 words a minute (Fairbanks, Guttman, and Miron, 1957; Wheeless, 1971). (Special electronic techniques allow recorded speech to be speeded up without distortion.) In one study to examine the relation between rate of speech and persuasiveness, researchers presented people with low-speed (111 words a minute), normal-speed (140 words a minute), or high-speed (195 words a minute) messages about the health dangers of coffee. They found that as the speed of the message increased, people agreed more strongly with the mes-

sage. On a 10-point scale, mean agreement was 5.7, 6.5, and 6.8 for the low-, normal-, and high-speed communications. The faster message apparently had been the most persuasive.

People also prefer accelerated speech. Researchers presented subjects with various samples of compressed speech, including a radio comment by Alistair Cooke, of Public Television's Masterpiece Theater, and a number of radio commercials. Listeners not only preferred and found more interesting those presentations that were 30 percent faster than normal, but also recalled more information about the products advertised (Miller, Maruyama, Beaber, and Valone, 1976).

---

may even backfire, as for instance, when an expert appears to have a personal involvement in an issue and therefore is perceived as less than objective (Harmon and Coney, 1982). A person's trustworthiness is perceived to vary according to his or her sincerity and disinterestedness (Wheeless and Grotz, 1977); whether he or she is arguing against his or her best interest (Walster, Aronson, and Abrahams, 1966); and whether he or she is arguing against an audience's obvious preferences (Eagly, Wood, and Chaiken, 1978).

The **attractiveness** of a person communicating a message may be based on physical appearance (Chaiken, 1979, Chaiken & Stanger, 1987; Horai, Naccari, and Fatoullah, 1974). It may be based on similarities between the sender and audience, such as racial similarities (Dembroski, Lasater, and Ramirez, 1978). It also may be based on similarities in attitude (Insko, Nacoste, and Moe, 1983). A communicator may become *powerful* if he or she can punish noncompliance and reward compliance (Galbraith, 1983). Communicators also may become powerful by their social status (Kipnis, 1976) or simply because there are many communicators conveying the same message (Tanford and Penrod, 1984). They may become powerful by arguing a position consistently (Moscovici, 1980). Certain speech *styles* also enhance the persuasiveness of a source. For example, rhetorical questions ("We all would like to see our country have a strong defense, wouldn't we?") can make a speaker more persuasive (Zillmann, 1972). Figurative speech, such as analogies ("This issue is the moral equivalent of war.") and metaphors ("It's time the President takes the helm of the ship of state and . . ."), and visual images ("I have *been* to the mountaintop.") also increase persuasiveness (Bowers and Osborn, 1966; McCroskey and Combs, 1969; Rossiter and Percy, 1983). All of these characteristics are thought to affect how well people pay attention to and process the persuasive communications (McGuire, 1985).

The Message

Although rhetoricians have been studying persuasive arguments since at least the time of Aristotle (who wrote a volume on **rhetoric**), psychologists' understanding of the persuasive effects of various types of messages derives largely from research conducted over the past 30 years. We can consider only a few of the many message characteristics that are known to influence message persuasiveness. For example, how effective are **fear appeals** (e.g., advertisements against smoking or favoring seatbelt use that incorporate information about negative consequences such as illness, injury, and death)? They can produce high immediate compliance but may lose their potency over time (Beck, 1979) and they are more effective if accompanied with information on how to avoid the threat (Leventhal, Singer, and Jones, 1965). Should a communicator draw conclusions or leave that to the audience? Research by Hovland and Mandell (1952) indicates an advantage for explicit conclusion drawing by the communication source, although some of this benefit may be lost on those members of the audience who could draw the conclusion themselves (Thistlewaite and Kamenetzky, 1955).

Should a speaker present both sides of an argument? Early research found that arguments presenting both sides of an issue were more persuasive than one-sided arguments (Hovland, Lumsdaine, and Sheffield, 1949). Furthermore, it was found that anticipating and refuting the arguments of the opposition actually "inoculates" an audience against the effects of the counterarguments (McGuire, 1964). Does repetition of an argument strengthen it or do people get sick of hearing the same old arguments time and again? The answer is yes to both positions. Several repetitions of an argument make a message more persuasive, but after about three repetitions the speaker runs some danger that further repetitions will reduce the impact of the message (Cacioppo and Petty, 1979; Krugman, 1972; Miller, 1976).

The Channel

There has been substantial research on the persuasiveness of specific channels, such as television, spoken communication, print, and nonverbal communication. But there has been little research to compare the effects of communications delivered over different channels, despite the fact that advertisers spend more than $50 billion a year (McGuire, 1985). Here we briefly consider research on the effectiveness of persuasive messages of television and note some of the differences among channels.

Television is unquestionably a prominent feature of American life. The television is on (though probably not attended to actively) nearly 7 hours a day in the average American home (Comstock et al., 1978). The average child sees 20,000 commercials a year, and the average high school graduate has watched over 20,000 hours of television by the time of graduation—more time than has been spent in the classroom (Adler et al., 1980)! Despite all this exposure to the advertising on television, research on the effects of television advertising reveal surprisingly small benefits for advertisers. Researchers who have examined the relation between advertising expenditures for a particular product and the share of the market secured by that product reveal little or no relation between expenditures and market share (Aaker, Carman, and Jackson, 1982; Assmus, Farley, and Lehmann, 1984). Studies of drug advertising and sales indicate only a weak relationship between expenditures and people's choices of drugs (Milavsky, Pekowsky, and Stipp, 1975).

In contrast, research on the effects of advertising on children indicates that it does influence children's desire for and preferences for products, although the effects, once again, are not dramatic (Gorn and Goldberg, 1982; Roberts, 1982; Roedder, Sternthal, and Calder, 1983; Wartella, 1980). One reason children may be more influenced than adults by advertising is that they generally do not understand the marketing intent of advertisements until they are 4 or 5 years old (Gaines and Esserman, 1981).

People use different channels, or media, for different purposes, and these media influence their message recipients in different ways. For example, people report getting more information from television than from other media (Lichty, 1982). But people remember more of what they read in print than they remember from television and remember radio communications least well (Chaiken and Eagly, 1976; Keating and Latane, 1976; Williams, 1975, 1977). Because television is such a strong attention-getter, it may be particularly effective in communicating simple messages, but when information becomes more complex, printed materials are superior (McGuire, 1985).

The Receiver

Certain personal characteristics make the receivers of a message more or less susceptible to its influence. Children, as you just saw, are likely to be more easily influenced by television commercials than are older people. The characteristic that has received the greatest research attention is gender differences, and the conclusions reached by researchers have changed fairly dramatically over the past 20 years. As recently as 1970, researchers seemed to agree that women are more readily influenced than men (Gergen and Marlowe, 1970; McGuire, 1969b). But more recent reviews of the research literature have produced different conclusions (Block, 1976; Eagly, 1978, 1983; Eagly and Carli, 1981; Maccoby and Jacklin, 1974). According to these reviews, in a high percentage of studies no gender differences could be detected in susceptibility to influence. (For example, there were no differences in 84 of 138 studies examined by Maccoby and Jacklin.) In some studies men turned out to be the more easily influenced.

In their review of nearly 150 studies Eagly and Carli (1981) concluded that overall, the studies indicated an extremely slight, even trivial tendency for women to be more readily influenced than men. But the researchers pointed out that this difference could be attributed to two factors. First, nearly 80 percent of research on influence had been conducted by men. Whereas their research showed gender differences, no such differences emerged from research conducted by women. Thus, the difference might be attributable to something that the researchers were doing. Second, many of the studies in which there were gender differences looked at attitude change regarding topics about which men would be more interested and informed and therefore potentially more resistant to influence. Indeed, men have been found to be more readily influenced on "women's issues" than women are (Karabenick, 1983).

The Target

The target or goal of most persuasive communications is to induce lasting changes in attitudes and behavior. Many factors have been shown to influence the durability of changes in attitudes (Cook and Flay, 1978). Thus, more durable attitude change is produced when a message emphasizes the inconsistencies between a person's behavior and their attitudes. Writing one's own counterattitudinal statement produces more durable change than reading someone else's (Watts, 1967; Huesmann, Eron, Klein, Brice, and Fischer, 1983). What people remember about a persuasive communication also influences the durability of their change in attitude. Thus, it is more important that the people remember the conclusions drawn from the communication than that he or she remember specific arguments within it (Watts and McGuire, 1964).

One of the most interesting phenomena associated with attitudes is the **sleeper effect** (Hovland, Lumsdaine, and Sheffield, 1949; Peterson and Thurstone, 1933). After showing films designed to change attitudes, the researchers found greater changes in attitudes after several weeks or months had passed than they found immediately after showing the films. More recent research indicates that sleeper effects occur when people are presented with a strongly persuasive message that is immediately discounted (for example, because the speaker is not credible), after which the message and the discounting cue are disassociated. Then the discounting cue is forgotten while the message content is remembered and produces attitude change (Cook, Gruder, Hennigan, and Flay, 1979; Greenwald et al., 1986; Pratkanis et al., 1985).

Cognitive Response Theory

Why do attitudes change? What goes on inside a person's head? One recent and influential answer to this question is supplied by **cognitive response theory**. According to this theory, how much a person's attitude will change depends on the thoughts (or cognitions) generated in the person in response to a message (Petty and Cacioppo, 1981). When a person thinks more about a communication, particularly when the per-

TABLE 16-6   INVOLVEMENT AND ATTITUDE CHANGE

Attitudes and Cognitive Responses in Relation to Involvement and Quality of Message Arguments

Item	Weak Arguments Involvement		Strong Arguments Involvement	
	Low	High	Low	High
Attitude	−0.24	−0.67	0.20	0.71
Counterarguments	2.11	3.28	2.05	1.33
Favorable thoughts	0.88	1.11	1.44	2.94

Source: After Petty and Cacioppo, 1979.
Note: The degree of attitude change, number of counterarguments generated, and number of favorable thoughts generated by people who heard an attitude-change message vary as a function of the people's involvement with the issue and the strength of the message. Higher score indicates greater change.

son forms arguments against the communication, the person is less likely to be persuaded. Evidence for the theory comes from several sources. For instance, it is known that forewarning receivers about the content of a persuasive communication or simply inducing receivers to think about the topic of the communication before receiving it increases their resistance to the communication (Petty and Cacioppo, 1977). Subjects who have been forewarned and asked to record their thoughts as the persuasive communication is presented generate more topic-relevant thoughts than subjects not forewarned.

Further evidence for the theory is supplied in research on the effects of personal involvement with an issue (Howard-Pitney, Borgida, and Omoto, 1986). According to cognitive response theory, people who feel personally involved with an issue are more likely to generate thoughts in response to persuasive messages about that issue than are people who feel less personally involved. To test how personal involvement affects attitude change, subjects heard strong or weak arguments in favor of a proposal that college seniors be required to take a comprehensive examination in their major before graduation (Petty and Cacioppo, 1979). The exam was proposed to go into effect at the students' own college (high involvement) or at another college (low involvement). Then the students wrote down their thoughts in response to the various arguments. As Table 16-6 shows, the more personally involved students produced more favorable thoughts and greater attitude change in response to strong arguments but more counterarguments and less attitude change in response to weak arguments.

BEHAVIOR AND ATTITUDES

Our discussions of attitude measurement and theories of attitude formation and change have implicitly assumed that attitudes are related to and can even be used to predict behavior. In fact, untangling the precise relationship between attitudes and behavior has proven a nettlesome problem for social psychologists. This difficulty is well illustrated in research conducted by LaPiere (1934). During the early 1930s LaPiere traveled extensively throughout the United States with a young Chinese couple whom LaPiere described as "personable" and "charming." During the 1930s attitudes toward Chinese people were fairly negative and discrimination fairly widespread. LaPiere expected to have trouble finding hotel and restaurant accommodations as they traveled the country. Instead, in over 10,000 miles of travel, LaPiere and the Chinese couple were refused service only once. LaPiere was surprised by their treatment and 6 months after his trip mailed questionnaires to the hotels and restaurants they had patronized. He asked the management whether it accepted Chinese people as guests. Over 90 percent of the respondents said no.

Problems in Predicting Behavior from Attitudes

A variety of explanations for the poor correspondence between people's expressed attitudes and their behavior have been offered. Some critics have noted that the staff LaPiere dealt with in person may not have been the same as those who responded about company policy to his questionnaire (Dillehay, 1973; Triandis, 1971). They also have suggested that when the staff was confronted with LaPiere and his friends, the staff may have reacted to the fact that LaPiere was Caucasian and ignored the race of his friends, something that they did not do on the questionnaire.

It is important to note that LaPiere did not conclude from his study that attitudes do not correspond to behavior. Rather, his conclusion was that attitudes measured on questionnaires may be too abstract, general, and distant from actual behavior to allow reasonable prediction of behavior. But later researchers have concluded that attitudes and behavior often are inconsistent. One reviewer of a large number of attitude behavior studies conducted since LaPiere's research concluded that these studies show a relatively weak correlation of .3 between attitudes and behavior and suggested that it is considerably more likely that attitudes will be unrelated or only slightly related to overt behaviors than that they will be closely related (Wicker, 1969). The reviewer suggested two basic reasons for these weak relationships: personal and situational factors.

At the personal level, people may hold other attitudes that are strongly related to their behavior, and they may have competing motives to behave in a particular way. At the situational level, people may fail to consider the influence of others or the influence of norms on their own behavior. (For instance, it may be easier or more acceptable to write "no service" on a questionnaire than it is to say the same thing face to face with someone.) Finally, people may not foresee events that will influence their actual behavior, and so they may profess prejudice against Chinese but act civilly when a Chinese couple is accompanied by a Caucasian.

Successful Prediction of Behavior

Critics of research on the relation between attitudes and behavior have improved in attitude-measurement techniques and specified more clearly the conditions under which attitudes predict behavior. Probably the

TABLE 16-7 ATTITUDES AND BEHAVIOR

Attitude Measure	*Correlation with Behavior*
1. Attitude toward birth control	.083
2. Attitude toward birth control pills	.323
3. Attitude toward using birth control pills	.525
4. Attitude toward using birth control pills during the next 2 years	.572

Source: After Davidson and Jaccard, 1979.
Note: The correlation between 244 women's attitudes toward the use of birth control pills and their behavior (their use of birth control pills during a 2-year period) for measures of attitude varying in specificity.

most systematic effort to find ways to improve the predictive value of attitudes is the work of Ajzen and Fishbein (1977, 1980; Fishbein and Ajzen, 1974, 1975). There are two important components to their work. The first is their notion of levels of correspondence: attitudes will correspond to behavior only if the attitudes are measured at the same level of specificity as the behavior. Thus, to predict general forms of behavior, one should assess general attitudes about that behavior and to predict specific forms of behavior, one should assess specific attitudes. The importance of levels of correspondence is illustrated in a study by researchers who measured, at varying degrees of specificity, women's attitudes toward the use of oral contraceptives and used those attitudes to predict the women's use of oral contraceptives over the 2-year period after the attitudes had been measured (Davidson and Jaccard, 1979). As Table 16-7 shows, as attitudes grew more specific with regard to actual use of oral contraceptives during the 2-year period, the correlation/correspondence between attitudes and behavior grew stronger.

The second component to Ajzen and Fishbein's research is their **theory of reasoned action** (see Figure 16-6). The theory assumes, first, that most people think about the implications of their behavior and that most of their behavior is under conscious control. Thus, in trying to predict someone's behavior, the most effective method is to assess a person's *intention* to perform that behavior. Psychologists assess intentions to act by breaking them down into two main variables: a person's attitudes toward the behavior and the person's subjective norms or perceptions of the social pressures to perform or not perform the behavior. Like the study of women and oral contraceptives described earlier, other research generally has proven quite successful in predicting behavior. For example, researchers tried to predict whether pregnant women would breast-feed or bottle-feed their infants (Manstead, Profitt, and Smart, 1983). The researchers measured the women's attitudes toward breast-feeding, assessed their intentions to breast- or bottle-feed, and assessed their subjective norms (that is, what their family members and friends thought about breast-feeding). The overall correlation between the women's attitudes and their behavior was quite high (.77).

In sum, Ajzen and Fishbein counsel that effective attitude measurement requires that attitudes be measured at a level of generality that is appropriate to the behavior of interest and that behavioral intentions be

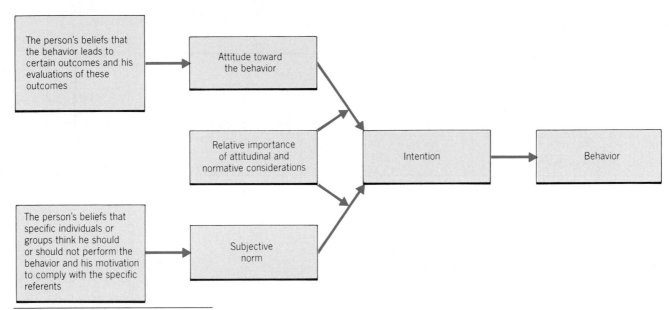

The person's beliefs that the behavior leads to certain outcomes and his evaluations of these outcomes

Attitude toward the behavior

Relative importance of attitudinal and normative considerations

The person's beliefs that specific individuals or groups think he should or should not perform the behavior and his motivation to comply with the specific referents

Subjective norm

Intention

Behavior

FIGURE 16-6   AJZEN AND FISHBEIN'S MODEL OF THE ATTITUDE BEHAVIOR RELATIONSHIP.

assessed using both attitudes toward the behavior and the actors' perceptions of norms regarding the behavior.

Behavior and Attitudes: A Reciprocal Relationship

One assumption behind in our discussion of attitudes, is that attitudes guide or direct people's behavior. This is a logical assumption, but it ignores some of the findings from other domains of attitude research that we have already examined. For instance, we have seen that when people act in ways that contradict their attitudes and beliefs, their attitudes may change. Thus, any complete model of attitudes and behavior must also take into account that people's behavior and attitudes affect each other reciprocally (Kelman, 1974).

These reciprocal effects are well illustrated in a study in which both attitudes and earlier behavior were tested as predictors of future behavior (Bagozzi, 1981). Shortly before a campus blood drive, the researcher questioned 95 students, faculty, and staff members toward their attitudes about donating blood, their personal norms and perceptions of social norms about donating, whether they had donated blood in the past, their intention to donate during the upcoming drive, and their beliefs about the consequences of donating blood. The researcher later found out whether these people donated blood during the campus blood drive that took place 1 week after the interviews and again during a second blood drive held 4 months later.

The results appear in Figure 16-7. The paths in the model can be thought of as correlation coefficients that reflect the strength of the relation among the attitudinal and behavioral predictors and blood donating after 1 week and 4 months. There are several notable features to these results. First, it turned out that people's social and personal norms were essentially unrelated to their intentions and behavior. Al-

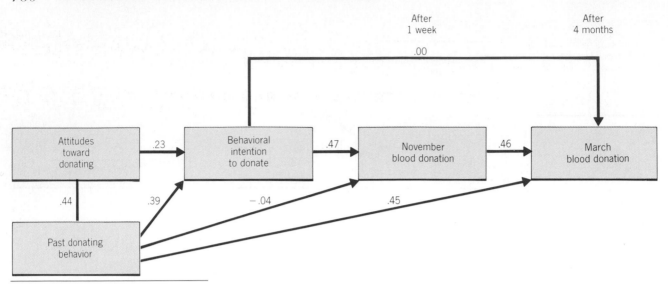

FIGURE 16-7 ATTITUDE-BEHAVIOR RELATIONSHIPS.
This figure shows the effects of people's earlier blood donations, their attitudes toward donations, their intentions to donate blood, and their actual donations of blood at two points in time. Numbers on the paths indicate the strength of the relationships and can range from −1 to 1 with a value of 0 indicating no relationship. (After Bagozzi, 1981.)

though norms have been shown to influence intentions and behavior in other studies, it may be that when it comes to donating blood, widely shared norms about the desirability of donating are less important determinants of behavior than are the consequences (inconvenience and discomfort) of donating. Second, intentions were strongly related to donations at 1 week but were unrelated to donations at 4 months. In fact, one of the common findings in studies of attitudes and behaviors is that measurements made just before the behavior tend to be better than measurements taken well before the behavior. Third, not only was people's earlier behavior an important determinant of their attitudes and intentions (which predicted behavior at 1 week), but earlier behavior also predicted later behavior, and there were strong links between behavior after 1 week and after 4 months.

People's earlier behavior has been shown to influence their attitudes in a number of ways. For example, when people's attitudes are based on their personal experience, they are held with greater conviction (Regan and Fazio, 1977), they produce more consistent behavior over time (Findlay, 1981; Sivacek and Crano, 1982), and they are more resistant to change (Kiesler, 1971). As self-perception theory would predict, people's past behavior provides them with compelling information about themselves. In short, attitudes do not simply cause behavior. In fact, there is a reciprocal relationship between attitudes and behavior—our behavior may change as a result of changes in attitude, but our attitudes also change in response to our behaviors.

SUMMARY

THE SELF

1. *The Self.* Though we may think of our "self" as a single, unified thing, William James argued that the self is composed of several different components including the physical body, a set of enduring personal values and beliefs, and a social self that is known by others. All of us also possess a

self-concept that develops out of our relationships with other people and reflects, in part, our perception of how others think about and evaluate us. When we think about our "self," we tend to think about our personal characteristics such as our age, sex, and occupation and characteristics that distinguish us from others.

2. *Self-schemas.* We all possess self-schemas or organized collections of knowledge and beliefs about ourselves. These schemas influence the ways in which we recognize, remember, and evaluate information about ourself. Self-schemas help us decide when information is relevant to ourself.

PERCEIVING THE SELF

3. *Self-perception Theory.* Self-perception theory contends that we learn about ourselves in much the same way that others learn about us—by observing our own behavior and inferring our attitudes, beliefs, and feelings from that behavior. In this view, we do not have any privileged access to inner thoughts or feelings and may not be able to introspectively determine the causes of our behavior. Studies of self-judgments of emotional states do indicate that we rely in part upon situational information and comparisons with others to gauge our own emotional states. When, for instance, the causes of emotional arousal are ambiguous, people may rely on external sources of information to determine the causes and nature of their emotional state.

4. *Objective Self-awareness.* We all vary in the degree to which we are self-aware or self-conscious. Sometimes we are acutely aware of ourself and our self-presentations even. At such times we may be hypercritical of ourselves and particularly eager to secure information about how well we are performing. At other times we may be so engaged in an activity that we lose awareness of ourself and do not engage in self-evaluation.

5. *Self-presentation.* The manner in which we present ourself to others has sometimes been likened to a theatrical production. We generally wish to present ourself in a positive light, to match our behaviors appropriately to the situation, to foster impressions that are consistent with our ideal self. To accomplish the goals we typically adopt self-presentational strategies designed to foster the desired impression.

6. *Self-monitoring.* Successful self-presentation requires that we be aware of impressions we make and that we regulate our behavior to make desired impressions. People vary in the degree to which they can self monitor or successfully evaluate social situations and shape their behavior to fit the situation. Those who are good at such monitoring (high self-monitors) are more socially adept, relaxed, and friendly in social situations.

PERCEIVING OTHERS

7. *Impression Formation.* We all quickly form general impressions of people when we first meet them, and the first pieces of information we receive about someone tend to carry greater weight than later pieces of information—the primacy effect. Furthermore, some types of information carry greater weight than others. Central traits (such as *cold* and *warm*) versus less central traits (such as *blunt* and *polite*) can have a much broader impact on our impressions of others.

8. *Implicit Personality Theories.* Although personality psychologists and laypersons have not reached a consensus about how people's personalities are organized, our everyday experiences in the world do lead most of us to form implicit personality theories or expectations about the traits that "go together" in people.

9. *Attribution.* In addition to forming impressions of others, we also typically try to explain their behavior. Basic distinctions can be made between dispositions and situations as explanations of behavior. When trying to decide whether to attribute someone's behavior to their dispositions or to situational causes, we might consider factors such as the actors' intentions and abilities. When making attributions to the person we typically seek a correspondent inference—we seek to label a person's actions and their disposition with the same term: for example, hostile acts from a hostile person, loving acts from a loving person.

10. *The Covariation Model.* Kelley argued that attributions of causation depend on judgments along three dimensions: we want to know whether a behavior is distinctive, whether the actor performs the behavior consistently, and whether the behavior is consensual—do most people behave the same way in a similar situation? Person attributions are most likely when a behavior is distinctive to an individual, the behavior is consistent across situations, and others do not regularly behave in the same way.

11. *Attributional Biases.* Our attributional judgments are not always made in the optimal manner. There appears to be a general inclination to attribute behavior to dispositions rather than situations—what has been termed the fundamental attribution error. Observers of behavior tend to attribute the behavior to actors' dispositions, whereas actors tend to attribute causation to

situational causes. People also have a tendency to underuse consensus or base rate information. In addition, in these cognitive biases, people's attributions also reflect motivational biases. Thus, we tend to assume that others will behave in the same way we do.

ATTITUDES AND BEHAVIOR

12. *Attitudes.* Attitudes have been defined in various ways (e.g., as predispositions to respond in a particular way and as a mixture of feelings, cognitions, and behavioral tendencies). Although there is no clear consensus on a definition, attitude has been one of the most important constructs in social psychology. Attitudes are measured in a variety of ways—with attitude scales such as the Semantic Differential and even with measures of physiological responses such as movements in facial muscles. Attitudes are acquired in a variety of ways. They can be learned through classical conditioning, operant conditioning, and observational learning.

13. *Consistency Theories.* Sometimes we discover that our attitudes about people and things are not entirely consistent with one another. In such situations balance theory postulates that we will experience an unpleasant state of tension that will promote a change in the attitudes. Festinger termed this conflict dissonance and studied the ways in which people reduce their dissonance. One of his classic studies demonstrated that when behaviors and attitudes are not consistent, attitudes can change in unexpected ways. If people behave in a manner that is inconsistent with their attitude, but have an insufficient justification for the behavior, their attitude may change.

Although alternative explanations based on self-perception theory and impression management can account for the results of some cognitive dissonance studies, the basic premise that dissonance produces an unpleasant state has been confirmed.

CHANGING ATTITUDES AND BEHAVIOR

14. *The Communication Source, Message, and Channel.* The source of a communication is more persuasive if he or she is credible or trustworthy. One of the many ways to increase trustworthiness is to argue against one's own interests. Attractive sources who are similar to their targets are more persuasive, as are powerful, high-status communicators. Among the features of a message that can make it more persuasive are appeals to fear accompanied by information on how to avoid the threat, drawing conclusions, presenting both sides of an argument, and a limited amount of repetition of arguments.

Although television advertisements do not appear to affect adult purchasing very dramatically, children, who are not so aware of the purposes of advertising, are more susceptible. Different message channels vary in the attention they attract (an advantage for television) and in the memorability of the information they convey (where the printed media excel).

15. *Persuasion in Advertising.* While the public image of the fast-talking salesperson may be negative, commercials in which the rate of speech has been increased (without a commensurate increase in the pitch of the speaker's voice) can be more persuasive, more interesting and better-remembered.

16. *The Receiver and Enduring Attitude Change.* Though early research suggested that women were easier to persuade than men, more recent research makes it clear there is no fundamental difference. Rather, males (and females) are more susceptible to influence in regard to matters that are less familiar to them.

Enduring changes in attitudes are most likely when the inconsistencies in a person's attitudes and behavior are called to their attention and when people remember the conclusions of the arguments they hear. Sleeper effects can occur when a discredited source makes a strong argument, but the identity of the discredited source is forgotten with the passage of time.

17. *Cognitive Response Theory.* This theory posits that the extent of attitude change produced by a message depends on the thoughts a person generates in response to a message. People who generate more counterarguments to a message (perhaps because they have been forewarned about the message or are more familiar with the arguments contained in the message) are less likely to be persuaded.

FURTHER READINGS

There are a number of widely available social psychology textbooks that consider in much greater detail the topics covered in Chapters 16 and 17 of this text. Among these texts are *Social Psychology* by Robert Baron and Donn Byrne (1987); *A Survey of Social Psychology* by Leonard Berkowitz (1986); *Social Psychology* by John Brigham (1986); *Social Psychology: The Second Edition* by Roger Brown (1986); *Social Psychology* by Kay Deaux and Lawrence Wrightsman (1987); *Social Psychology* by Kenneth Gergen and Mary Gergen (1986); *Social Psychology* by David G. Myers (1987); *Social Psychology* by Steven Penrod (1986); *Social Psychology* by David

Sears, Jonathon Freedman, and L. Anne Peplau (1985); and *Understanding Social Psychology* by Stephen Worchel, Joel Cooper, and George Goethals (1987).

More detailed treatments of the topics covered in Chapters 16 and 17 can also be found in *Advances in Experimental Social Psychology*, a series of 20 volumes edited by Leonard Berkowitz. Each volume contains chapter-length reviews of research on a variety of social psychological topics. The chapters are written by leading researchers and provide thoughtful overviews of prominent findings and theories. Among the reviews with special relevance to this chapter are "Mental Representations of the Self" by John Kihlstrom and Nancy Cantor (Vol. 17, 1984); "Theory of the Self: Impasse and Evolution" by Kenneth Gergen (Vol. 17, 1984); "Cognitive Theories of Persuasion" by Alice Eagly and Shelly Chaiken (Vol. 17, 1984); and "The Elaboration Likelihood Model of Persuasion" by Richard Petty and John Cacioppo (Vol. 19, 1986).

Another important source of review chapters is the two-volume *Handbook of Social Psychology* (3rd Ed.) edited by Gardner Lindzey and Eliot Aronson (1985). Among the relevant chapters are historical overviews of the development of social psychology by Gordon Allport (a reprint from an earlier edition of the *Handbook*) and by Edward Jones. The role of learning theory in social psychology is addressed in a chapter by Bernice Lott and Albert Lott, attitude and opinion measurement are covered in a chapter by Robin Dawes and Tom Smith, attribution and social perception research are reviewed by Michael Ross and Garth Fletcher, and William McGuire provides an integrative review of research on attitudes and attitude change.

Other excellent review series include the *Review of Personality and Social Psychology* which, in recent volumes, has examined issues concerning sex and gender (edited by Philip Shaver and Clyde Hendrick, 1987); the self and social behavior (edited by Philip Shaver, 1986); and emotions, relationships, and health (edited by Philip Shaver, 1984). In addition, the *Journal of Social Issues* regularly devotes entire volumes to a single topic.

Recent volumes that expand upon the topics covered in this chapter include *Public Appearances/Public Realities: The Psychology of Self-Monitoring* by Mark Snyder (1986); *An Attribution Theory of Motivation and Emotion* by Bernard Weiner (1986); *Social Cognition* by Susan Fiske and Shelley Taylor (1984); and *Attitude Change: Central and Peripheral Routes to Persuasion* by Richard Petty and John Cacioppo (1986).

784

17

SOCIAL INTERACTION

If you think back over the past 24 hours and the most memorable things you have done, chances are that the events you recall involve other people. Many of the most important events in people's lives arise from social interaction, either direct interaction with others or interaction between other people that affect them indirectly.

In this chapter we will examine various forms of social interaction. We will begin by discussing what causes people to be attracted, and attractive, to others. Along the way we will discuss mundane things such as the characteristics that make people attractive, and sublime things such as love and beauty. Then we shall turn our attention to broader aspects of social interaction and examine the behavior of individuals in group settings. We will pay particular attention to the ways in which groups affect the behavior of group members and the ways in which group members influence the group. In the third and fourth sections of the chapter, we will examine two especially important forms of social interaction: aggressive behavior and prosocial, or altruistic, behavior. We will closely examine the factors that increase and decrease these forms of behavior.

INTERPERSONAL ATTRACTION

Imagine that you have agreed to be a subject in a psychology experiment. When you enter the laboratory, you are greeted by a man dressed in a white laboratory coat who introduces himself as "Dr. Gregor Zilstein of the Medical School's Departments of Neurology and Psychiatry." Dr. Zilstein proceeds to explain to you that you will be participating in a study of the effects of electric shock. You are shown a room containing elaborate electrical equipment, and Dr. Zilstein tells you

> *Now, I feel I must be completely honest with you and tell you exactly what you are in for. These shocks will hurt, they will be painful. As you can guess, if, in research of this sort, we're to learn anything at all that will really help humanity, it is necessary that our shocks be intense.*

> *(Schachter, 1959, p. 13)*

At this point Dr. Zilstein tells you that you will have to wait outside for 10 minutes while the equipment is set up. You are asked whether you would prefer to wait by yourself or in a room with others. What is your preference?

Affiliative Behavior

After you have answered Dr. Zilstein's question, he takes off his white coat and tells you that he is not really Dr. Zilstein, but that the experiment is being conducted by Stanley Schachter, a social psychologist. The experimenter also tells you that you are not going to be shocked, but that the real purpose of the study is to examine people's tendency to affiliate with others when they are under stress. In fact, the experiment consists of two conditions. The first, to which you were assigned, was the

FIGURE 17-1 ANXIETY AND AFFILIATION.

Under conditions of heightened levels of anxiety people prefer the company of others to waiting alone. (After Schachter, 1959.)

FIGURE 17-1 ANXIETY AND AFFILIATION

	Number choosing to wait		
	Together	*Don't care*	*Alone*
High anxiety	20	9	3
Low anxiety	10	18	2

high-stress condition. In the second, or low-stress condition, the subjects were not shown the electrical equipment, and while they were told that they would be receiving shocks, "Dr. Zilstein" also informed the subjects that:

> *I assure you that what you will feel will not in any way be painful. It will resemble more a tickle or a tingle than anything unpleasant.*

> *(Schachter, 1959, pp. 13–14)*

Would a simple manipulation of this sort influence people's preference for waiting alone as opposed to waiting with someone else? As you can see in Figure 17-1, nearly two-thirds of the high-stress subjects preferred to wait with other people, whereas only one-third of the low-stress subjects preferred to wait with others.

Do people like company whenever they are distressed? No. Under some conditions, people who are stressed may prefer to be alone. In one study all the subjects, who were men, were led to believe that they were going to have to suck on infantile objects (such as baby bottles, oversized nipples, and pacifiers) for 2 minutes. These men preferred to wait alone (Sarnoff and Zimbardo, 1961). Thus it seems that certain types of stress increase the desire to affiliate with others, whereas other types of stress—such as those that may produce embarrassment—reduce this desire. Why are there such differences?

Social Psychological Theories of Affiliation

In Chapter 11 we discussed the motivation behind affiliation, and we particularly emphasized the attachments that develop between infants and their caretaker. From the social psychologist's viewpoint, affiliation is also an important form of behavior, and two major social psychological theories have been advanced to account for people's desire to affiliate with others, especially at times of stress. According to **social comparison theory** (Festinger, 1954), people seek to affiliate with others to evaluate their opinions and reactions in light of other people's reactions and opinions. Particularly when a situation or threat is ambiguous, people want the company of others because they can provide information that helps them assess or understand social reality (Rabbie, 1963). Similarly, people confronted by the ambiguous threat of shock in an experimental situation can use the responses of others to gauge just how threatening the shocks might be. Of course, in an unambiguous situation, such as the one in which the men had to suck on baby bottles and the like (Sarnoff and Zimbardo, 1961), the social comparisons provided by the presence of others would likely aggravate the embarrassment. To make social comparisons, people prefer to affiliate with others who are like them in appropriate ways (Goethals and Darley, 1977). For instance, research has shown that people prefer the company of others who are confronted by the same danger or threat as they, rather than others who are not faced with the threat or who have already experienced the threat (Schachter, 1959; Zimbardo and Formica, 1963). As Stanley Schachter put it: "Misery doesn't just love any kind of company. It loves only miserable company" (Schachter, 1959, p. 24).

The second theoretical perspective accounts for affiliative behavior as a **reduction of arousal**. This approach emphasizes that when people are under great stress, they seek out others to provide comfort, to distract them from the threat, and to supply models of relaxed behavior (Cottrell and Epley, 1977; Epley, 1974)—things that other subjects in the baby-bottle study (Sarnoff and Zimbardo, 1961) probably could not supply. As this theory would predict, Rabbie (1963) found that when people felt threatened and were given an opportunity to wait with another person who was calm, moderately fearful, or highly fearful, people (even very fearful ones) preferred not to wait with another very fearful person. Presumably, another fearful person would not provide comfort or reassurance and might aggravate the person's own fear. Social comparison and arousal-reduction theories are not inconsistent. Indeed we might qualify Schachter's statement by saying: misery loves company, as long as the company is not too miserable.

Theories of Interpersonal Attraction

Clearly we do not associate with people simply to reduce our anxieties, for humans are social animals who thrive on the companionship and love of their fellow humans. Unfortunately, simply saying that humans are social animals does not tell us *why* we like other people generally or *why* we develop long-lasting relationships with particular people. What is the social "glue" that keeps people together? Social psychologists have devoted many years to thinking about and conducting research on interpersonal attraction. Part of this work has involved the formulation of theories about why people are attracted to one another, part of it has been devoted to developing methods for measuring the quality and quantity of attraction (Box 17-1), and part of it has been devoted to the exploration of general factors or variables that influence interpersonal attraction. Let us start with three of the major theoretical perspectives that have dominated attraction research (Berscheid, 1985), for they provide a basis for integrating the empirical research we discuss in the next section.

REINFORCEMENT THEORY   One of the broadest theories about interpersonal attraction grew from the work of Theodore Newcombe (1956), who proposed that our attraction to another person is a function of the frequency with which they reward us and that the likelihood we will receive rewards from the other person is a function of the frequency with which we reward them. In essence, we are attracted to people who are reinforcing to us and, by implication, not attracted to those who are

Are you currently in love? Have you been in love before? How would you define love? To study love, psychologists need operational definitions, the very idea of which may offend you. In 1975, Senator William Proxmire denounced the expenditure of federal money on research in love. As he put it, "There are some things better left unstudied." Undaunted by such criticisms, social psychologists have forged ahead with research on love, and one of the major breakthroughs that has made this research possible was the development of scientific methods for the measurement of love. Much of the credit for this breakthrough must go to psychologist Zick Rubin, who, in 1973, published *Liking and Loving*. In that book, Rubin recounted his efforts to develop a scale to measure love.

Rubin began his research by postulating that love has three elements: (1) *caring* or feeling that another person is important; (2) *attachment* or the desire to be with another person and be approved of and cared for; and (3) *intimacy* or the close and confidential communication and bonds between people. Rubin composed a large set of "items" or questions that he thought reflected each of these components of love and administered the resulting questionnaire to dating couples at the University of Michigan. After careful analysis of the responses to his questionnaire, Rubin was able to construct two separate scales. One assesses "liking" and the other assesses "loving." Examples of his scale items are shown in Table 1.

Rubin's analysis of the dating couple's ratings of their lovers and friends revealed that friends and lovers were both well liked, but that, as expected, friends were not as well loved as lovers (see Table 2). Note, however, that males and females differ in the extent to which they love their friends. Perhaps as a result of their socialization, women reported they loved their friends more than men loved their friends.

BOX TABLE 1   SELECTED EXAMPLES OF LOVE-SCALE AND LIKING-SCALE ITEMS

Love Scale

1. If _____ were feeling bad, my first duty would be to cheer him (her) up.
2. I feel that I can confide in _____ about virtually everything.
3. If I could never be with _____, I would feel miserable.

Liking Scale

1. I think that _____ is usually well adjusted.
2. I have great confidence in _____'s good judgment.
3. _____ is the sort of person whom I myself would like to be.

Source: Rubin, 1973.

BOX TABLE 2   AVERAGE LOVE AND LIKING SCORES FOR DATING PARTNERS AND SAME-SEX FRIENDS

	Women	*Men*
Love for partner	90.57	90.44
Liking for partner	89.10	85.30
Love for friend	64.79	54.47
Liking for friend	80.21	78.38

Source: Rubin, 1973.

punishing to us. Furthermore, relationships are reciprocal, and we can influence the behavior of others through the rewards and punishments we deliver.

As you can see, reinforcement theories of attraction draw heavily from traditional learning theories and postulate that attraction to others is a product of the reinforcements and punishments we receive from the environment and from others. According to **reinforcement-affect model**, which builds on principles of secondary reinforcement, people like others who are associated with positive events and dislike those associated with negative events (Clore and Byrne, 1974). Indeed, the ancient practice of killing bearers of bad tidings finds a modern parallel in findings that people do not like strangers whom they meet under unpleasant circumstances as much as they like strangers met under pleasant circumstances (Griffit and Veitch, 1971; Veitch and Griffit, 1976).

EXCHANGE THEORY   One social psychologist has developed a theory of relationships that combines learning theory with economics (Homans, 1961a, 1980). **Social exchange theory**, like reinforcement theory, holds that attraction is influenced by rewards and punishments, but adds the qualification that judgments about attraction are influenced by the ratio of costs and benefits in a relationship. People are thought to follow a **minimax principle** in their relationships in that they most like relationships that provide maximum rewards at a minimum cost.

The rewards in relationships include love, money, status, goods, services, and information (Foa and Foa, 1974). The costs include time, effort, lost opportunities (to develop relationships with others), money, embarrassment, and so on. Rewards and costs cannot be calculated in the same way for everyone but depend on each person's needs and desires. Thus it is difficult to formulate precise predictions about the attraction arising from particular social exchanges.

Other social exchange theorists (Kelley and Thibaut, 1978; Thibaut and Kelley, 1959) have built upon this economic analysis to postulate that when people estimate their attraction to another person, they make two types of calculations. First, they assess **comparison level**—their sense of what they deserve in a relationship. If, based on past experience, they feel short-changed in a particular relationship (the outcomes fall below their comparison level), they are less likely to maintain that relationship than they are to maintain a relationship in which the outcomes are above their comparison level. A second calculation involves a **comparison level for alternatives**. Here the question is whether other relationships would offer better ratios of rewards to costs. Even if two relationships are above people's comparison levels, they are still likely to maintain or invest in those alternatives that have the highest ratios of benefits to costs.

EQUITY THEORY   The key notion of *equity theory* is not that both parties to a relationship should have equal rewards and costs, but that they should have equal *ratios* of rewards to costs. Thus, one person may invest a lot in a relationship, while the second invests very little. Equity still can be maintained if the first person receives the bulk of the rewards produced by the relationship. Equity theory postulates that an imbalance between the rewards and costs of the two members of a relationship motivates people to restore equity and that if equity cannot be restored, the relationship may fail. In contrast to exchange theory (which emphasizes the maximizing of rewards over costs), equity theory emphasizes a relative balance in rewards and costs. Research on intimate relationships confirms that equity does affect relationships (Hatfield and Traupmann, 1981; Kidder, Fagan, and Cohn, 1981).

The Antecedents of Attraction

Write down a list of ten people you like. What do you like about them? Why do you like those people in particular? These are among the questions that are addressed by research on the determinants of interpersonal attraction. This research has cast a wide net. Some has drawn upon folklore to generate hypotheses about interpersonal attraction (Do "birds of a feather flock together," or do opposites attract?) whereas other research has built upon theoretical insights into behavior. In any event, the research has revealed some surprising factors that influence attraction.

PROPINQUITY   If you look over your list of friends, you may find that many of them are people who have, in one way or another, been near to you or readily available as friends. They are people with whom you have had frequent opportunities to interact. If you live in a dormitory, you may find that the friends tend to come from your floor in the dorm, live closest to you on your floor, and may even be roommates. Many studies have confirmed that nearness affects attraction. These studies have examined friendship patterns in such diverse settings as married student housing (Festinger, Schachter, and Back, 1950); in housing projects for the elderly (Nehemow and Lawton, 1975); and in police academies (Segal, 1974).

SIMILARITY   Although for many years correlational evidence has suggested that people are attracted to those who are similar to them (Burgess and Wallin, 1943), the first compelling demonstration of a similarity effect was produced in a study of transfer students to the University of Michigan (Newcombe, 1961). These students, who were unlikely to know one another initially, were offered free rooms in a dormitory if they would complete a series of questionnaires during the semester. The students completed questionnaires on their attitudes and their perceptions of their fellow students. Early in the semester, proximity was the best predictor of liking, but as time went on, attitude similarity turned out to be the best predictor of liking. Many laboratory and field experiments also have demonstrated that similarity in attitudes is a determinant of attraction (Hill and Stull, 1981; Kandel, 1978).

Two primary explanations of similarity effects have been offered. First, someone whose attitudes are like one's own reinforces and validates one's attitudes, opinions, and beliefs and rewards the drive to be logical, consistent, and accurate in interpreting the world. Second, a person with similar attitudes is likely also to have other traits that we hold in high regard. People's attraction to a stranger has been shown to be a function of the number of desirable traits in the stranger rather than the number of traits which are like one's own.

FAMILIARITY   Not only do people like those who are similar to them, they also like people (and things) with which they are familiar. People, for example, prefer the art, music, words, and other things that are familiar to them. In one study, the more often people had been exposed to the photograph of another person, the more they liked the person in the photograph (Zajonc, 1968)—a phenomenon called the **mere exposure effect**. Other researchers have confirmed that mere exposure increases liking (Harrison, 1977; Moreland and Zajonc, 1979). How often people had encountered one another has been shown to be positively associated with their interest in interacting again and their willingness to disclose intimate information (Brockner and Swap, 1976). One reason is because familiarity also fosters the impression that another person is more similar (Moreland and Zajonc, 1982), and as we have already said, similarity promotes liking.

However, there may be limits to mere exposure effects. It may be possible to see a stimulus (even a person) so often that one's interest is at least temporarily reduced (Hill, 1978). There is even some evidence from studies—such as those of children raised in Israeli kibbutzim (Talmon, 1964)—that increased familiarity can reduce sexual attraction (Rosenblatt and Anderson, 1981).

PHYSICAL ATTRACTIVENESS Ellen Berscheid (1985) has observed that social psychologists once seemed especially reluctant to undertake research on the effects of physical attractiveness on social behavior, but that during the past 20 years they have overcome that reluctance "with a vengeance." It is safe to say that the research has shown physical attractiveness to be one of the strongest and most pervasive influences on social behavior ever examined. Physical attractiveness is clearly something worth possessing. The benefits of physical attractiveness begin to accrue early in a person's life. Attractive children are more popular with their classmates (Dion and Berscheid, 1974) and receive more support, better opportunities, and better evaluations from their teachers (Adams and LaVoie, 1974; Clifford and Walster, 1973; Vaughan and Langlois, 1983).

These benefits of physical attractiveness continue throughout life: attractive adults are more likely to receive job offers after interviews (Dipboye, Arvey, and Terpstra, 1977), to receive higher salaries (Jackson, 1983), to be recommended for higher status positions (Unger, Hilderbrand, and Maden, 1982), to receive more lenient treatment for transgressions (Efran, 1974), and to receive help from others (Benson, Karabenick, and Lerner, 1976). In addition, they are less likely to be diagnosed with and hospitalized for psychiatric disorders (Cash, Kehr, Polyson, and Freeman, 1977; Sussman and Muesser, 1983). A number of researchers have even found evidence that physical attractiveness can "rub off" onto the people who associate with attractive people. People are viewed more positively when they are accompanied by an attractive person, and the effect is most pronounced for men in the company of attractive females (Bar-Tal and Saxe, 1976; Kernis and Wheeler, 1981; Sigall and Landy, 1973).

ATTRACTIVENESS STEREOTYPES Attractive people also benefit from a number of stereotypes about "beautiful people." The physically attractive are believed by others to be better adjusted, more talented,

TABLE 17-1   ATTRACTIVENESS AND ASCRIBED CHARACTERISTICS

Ascribed Trait	Attractive Person	Average Person	Unattractive Person
Social desirability of personality	65.39	62.42	56.31
Occupational status	2.25	2.02	1.70
Marital competence	1.70	.71	.37
Parental competence	3.54	4.55	3.91
Social and professional happiness	63.7	6.34	5.28
Total happiness	11.60	11.60	8.83
Likelihood of marriage	2.17	1.82	1.52

Source: After Dion et al., 1972.
Note: Ratings of personality and other characteristics are generally more positive for attractive than for unattractive people. Higher scores indicate more of the ascribed characteristics.

happier, kinder, more interesting, more sexually responsive and sexually experienced, more moral, and more intelligent than less attractive people (Brigham, 1980; Goldman and Lewis, 1977; Maruyama and Miller, 1980; May and Hamilton, 1980). Attractive people also are regarded as more sociable (Dion, Berscheid, and Walster, 1972; see Table 17-1). In some instances, these beliefs do have a basis in fact. For example, attractiveness has been found to be related to the number and quality of social interactions experienced by both men and women (Berscheid, Dion, Walster, and Walster, 1971; Reis, Nezlek, and Wheeler, 1980). Attractive college women report falling in love more often and have more sexual experience than less attractive college women (Kaats and Davis, 1970). Attractive people also are more confident about their social skills (Abbott and Sebastian, 1981) and have higher self-esteem (Lerner and Karabenick, 1974). There may be a self-fulfilling quality to these differences, because attractive people are more likely to be approached for dates and therefore have more opportunities for social interaction (Sussman, Mueser, Grau, and Yarnold, 1983).

Lest the case for physical attractiveness be overstated, it is important to note that beauty is not always a benefit. For example, despite the usually positive stereotypes attributed to attractive people, attractive people are believed to be vain and more likely to have extramarital

TABLE 17-2   ATTRACTIVENESS AND PUNISHMENT

Crime	Defendant's Attractiveness		
	Attractive	Unattractive	Control
Swindle	5.45	4.35	4.35
Burglary	2.80	5.20	5.10

Source: After Sigall and Ostrove, 1975.
Note: This table shows the number of years mock jurors assigned to defendants accused of burglary and swindling. The mean sentence was less for an attractive defendant accused of burglary. But it was higher for an attractive defendant accused of swindling, for then it appeared that the defendant has used his attractiveness in perpetrating the crime, $n = 20$ per cell.

affairs (Dermer and Thiel, 1975). Attractive criminals may also be punished more harshly if they have used their physical appearance to further their crime (Sigall and Ostrove, 1975; see Table 17-2). Attractive people also seem to discount positive judgments that are made about them (Major, Carrington, and Carnavale, 1984). Perhaps they recognize the possibility that other people's judgments may be unduly influenced by their physical attraction.

THE MATCHING PRINCIPLE   In one of the very earliest experimental studies of interpersonal attraction, other students rated the attractiveness of a number of freshmen at the University of Minnesota (Walster, Aronson, Abrahams, and Rottmann, 1966). The experimenters also measured the freshmen's attitudes, intelligence, and personality characteristics. Then the students were invited to a "Welcome Week" dance at which they were led to believe that they had been computer matched with someone of the other sex. In fact, the researchers paired the students off randomly. Halfway through the dance, the students were asked how satisfied they were with their dance partners.

The researchers examined the students' measures of attitudes, intelligence, personality, and attractiveness to see which, if any, accounted for the students' ratings. The researchers had originally predicted that they would find similarity effects like those we discussed earlier. That is, they expected that the highest ratings would come from couples that were similar in physical attractiveness, a phenomena that sometimes has been termed **the matching principle**. This finding also would be predicted by equity theory, for if physical attractiveness is one of the "investments" that people bring to a relationship, and other "investments" are equal or unknown, as we might expect them to be in a random-paired first date, then the equitable preferences should be for someone of similar attractiveness. Instead, the researchers found that the physical attractiveness of the partner, and not similarity, most influenced the ratings of the students.

Other studies confirm that people prefer to date the most attractive people they possibly can (Huston, 1973). Of course, not everyone can date extremely attractive people, and field studies of actual dating behavior—studies that look at who actually approaches and who actually is approached for dates—confirm the matching principle. People do seem to ask for dates with, accept for dates, and even marry people who roughly match them in attractiveness (Berscheid et al., 1971; Cash and Derlaga, 1978; Folkes, 1982; McKillip and Reidel, 1983). If you examine the dating patterns of your friends, you are likely to find further confirmation of the matching principle.

SOCIAL INFLUENCE

Those of us who live in Western societies generally conceive of ourselves as rational, self-directed, and autonomous beings who govern our own behavior as we see fit. But we also recognize that we are strongly influenced by our social world. To some extent, we go along with the wishes and opinions of our family and friends, we wear the latest fashions, and comply with authority. Most social conformity is harmless enough, although we have heard about frightening forms of social conformity such as that in Nazi Germany, where otherwise ordinary people committed horrible atrocities against innocent victims.

Social psychologists have long struggled to understand how social or group pressures operate on individuals. Early theorists [Tarde (1890), Le Bon (1895), and Binet (1900)] in Europe actually believed that groups influenced individual behavior through processes they variously labeled as "hypnosis," "imitation," and "suggestion." Most of these early theories held that when individuals function in groups, their usual forms of thinking, feeling, and acting are modified in such a way that they are more susceptible to group influences. Thus, they held that a kind of "group mind" could emerge from group interaction and come to dominate the behavior of group members.

These theories may sound rather mystical to us today, but it was not until the mid-1930s that social psychological experiments began to reveal how group influences truly operate. The research and theories of group influence have made a distinction between **conformity**, in which a person yields to group pressure, and **obedience**, in which a person complies with destructive or immoral demands of authority. We shall first discuss the conformity research.

Conformity

Sometimes people conform to what others are saying, or doing, or thinking, because they wholeheartedly agree with those others or have been swayed by them. Sometimes people conform because they feel, for some reason, that they ought to, but inside they disagree with what others are saying or doing. There is an important difference between these two kinds of conformity (Deutsch and Gerard, 1955). In what has been called **informational social influence**, a person publicly *and* privately accepts a group's opinions. But in **normative social influence**, a person publicly conforms to social pressure but privately does *not* accept a group's opinion.

INFORMATIONAL SOCIAL INFLUENCE   A series of laboratory experiments showed the effects of informational influence (Sherif, 1935, 1936). These studies took advantage of an optical illusion known as the autokinetic effect: in a totally darkened room a small spot of light will appear to move about in various directions. In the absence of any visual cues to stabilize the light, small movements of the eye create an impression that the light is moving (see Chapter 3). Over a series of trials, the researcher had subjects repeatedly estimate how far the light moved. Some subjects made these estimates while they were alone in the room. Others made the estimates where they could hear others' estimates. The individual estimates varied widely from as little as 1 and 2 inches to as much as 80 feet!

Sherif was interested in the effect of the group judgments on individual judgments. He observed that when subjects made estimates alone, the estimates varied widely from one person to the next. People seemed

FIGURE 17-2 SOCIAL INFLUENCES ON PERCEPTION. When the individual judgments of subjects about how far a spot of light had moved in a dark room varied widely before they participated in group sessions, their responses gradually converged across group sessions (left). When the individual judgments were similar to begin with, they remained similar throughout the group sessions (right). (After Sherif, 1958.)

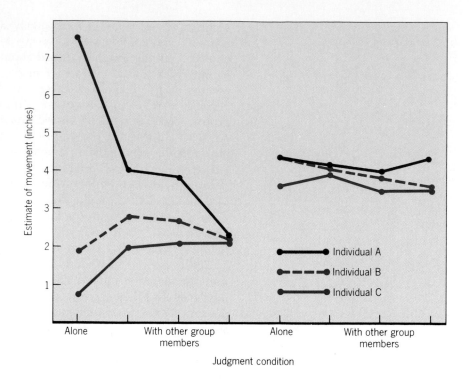

to have personal norms for making their estimates. However, when the estimates were made in the presence of others, the individual norms gradually gave way to group norms. Over a series of trials, the individuals tended to converge on estimates that were similar in length. This convergence took longer when subjects first made individual judgments and then joined a group, but a group norm still emerged (see Figure 17-2). Even when those individuals were removed from the group and again gave individual judgments, their judgments continued to be influenced by the group norms. Interestingly enough, most subjects were unaware that other group members had influenced their judgments.

NORMATIVE SOCIAL INFLUENCE   The people who had to judge how far the spot of light had moved in the dark room found themselves in an ambiguous situation, and so it was natural for them to rely on one another in making their estimates. But what if the situation had been unambiguous? Would the group still influence individual responses?

One researcher, Solomon Asch (1951), thought it unlikely that the group would have such an influence in an unambiguous situation and set up experimental groups consisting of one naive subject and six confederates. The subjects were presented with an unambiguous task in which they were to judge which of three lines that varied in length matched the length of a comparison line (see Figure 17-3). The subjects made judgments on a series of 18 trials, and the groups were arranged so that the true subject heard five or six of the confederates make their "judgments" before giving their own opinion. On the first two trials everything proceeded smoothly, but then the confederates began to give erroneous judgments. In fact, the confederates had all been coached to give the same wrong answer on 12 of the 18 trials.

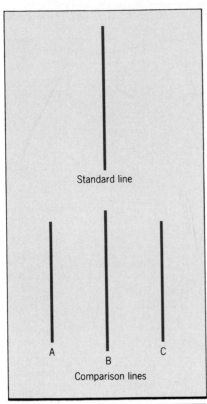

FIGURE 17-3 THE ASCH STIMULI.
An example of simple lines, the lengths of which were compared by subjects in the Asch (1955, 1956) experiments.

What did the real subjects do? Remember that the task was unambiguous. Anyone could provide the right answer quite easily. But to his surprise, the researcher found that the subjects frequently conformed to the group pressure. About one-third of the subjects changed more than 50 percent of their responses to fit the opinions of the confederates. Only 25 percent of the subjects fully resisted the group. Why had so many subjects distorted their responses?

One answer to this question is provided in the theories of the social psychologists who have suggested that group members conform to group norms to avoid social rejection. Members of the majority position in a group often turn their attention and their persuasion skills to "deviants" in the group in order to achieve unanimity. If those who disagree do not come around, then the majority grows to dislike and ostracize them. The possibility of **social rejection** can provide a strong incentive for conformity.

SITUATIONAL INFLUENCES ON CONFORMITY Imagine that you are in a small class with only seven students, and you are discussing a serious political issue—apartheid, say. One person in the class argues that apartheid is justifiable. The six others in the class stare in horror. One says, "Apartheid is never justifiable! It is an immoral system. Period!" A second student chimes in, "I agree. There have been a lot of economic arguments made about why apartheid is good for South African blacks, but these don't hold water." As more students jump in on the anti-apartheid side, the first student feels more and more uncomfortable. At some point, that student is likely to give in to the group pressure.

Many different factors within a situation are known to influence the degree to which people conform to group influence. Group *size* is one such factor. In the studies of judging line lengths described earlier, conformity to the group increased as the number of confederates increased up to four, and then began to level off (Asch, 1956; Gerard, Wilhelm, and Connolley, 1968; Tanford and Penrod, 1984; see Figure 17-4). But it is not simply the number of majority members who affect conformity (Wilder, 1977). It is the number of independent opinions they express that influences conformity. This effect may explain why simply increasing the number of majority group members beyond four does not substantially increase conformity. Perhaps dissenters tend not to see these additional majority group members as truly independent voices.

MINORITY INFLUENCE Before 1970, most social psychological research on influence processes examined conformity to majorities and ignored the possibility that minorities could also have influence on majorities (Nemeth, 1986). We know from experience that dissenters *can* influence the majority. History is full of examples of lone individuals and small groups who have produced profound changes in their societies—Christ, Luther, Gandhi, and many others. Minority influence depends heavily on the *style of behavior* adopted by the minority. For example, the *consistency* with which a minority argues its position affects its persuasiveness (Moscovici, Lage, and Naffrechoux, 1969). Sometimes a minority can influence others simply by repeating its position over and over in its

FIGURE 17-4 GROUP SIZE AND CONFORMITY.
Conformity to majority group pressure increases—though at a decreasing rate—as group size increases. (After Asch, 1951; Gerard, Wilhelmy, and Connolley, 1968.)

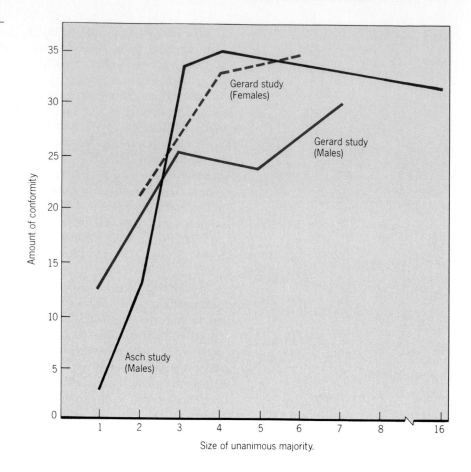

arguments, a technique known to be effective in producing attitude change (Cacioppo and Petty, 1979b).

Obedience

You probably have heard the story of Adolf Eichmann, the Nazi head of the Gestapo Jewish Section responsible for the deportation of millions of Jews to concentration camps, where they were murdered in gas chambers. Eichmann was apprehended in Argentina in 1960 by Israeli agents, taken to Israel, and tried for his war crimes. As part of his defense, Eichmann asserted that he had merely been following the orders of his superiors, who had led him to believe that what he was doing was both lawful and patriotic. Eichmann was convicted and hanged. Lt. William Calley, Jr., in his court martial for the 1968 massacre of 100 Vietnamese civilians by American soldiers, also claimed that he was merely following orders. Calley was convicted and served a 40-month sentence. Similarly, James W. McCord, a former FBI agent arrested as one of the Watergate burglars who broke into the Democratic Party national headquarters, justified his actions on the grounds that the break-in had been approved by the U.S. Attorney General.

The actions of Eichmann, Calley, McCord and many others who claim to carry out morally reprehensible acts "under orders" are disturbing in part because of the horrible consequences of the acts. But the acts also are disturbing because people like Eichmann, Calley, and McCord proved to be rather ordinary people. We all recognize that many ordinary people find themselves in situations where they are directed by people in authority to do things of questionable legality and morality. Why do people find it difficult to resist such pressure, even when the things they are asked or directed to do are horrible?

In one of the most provocative series of studies ever conducted by a social psychologist, Stanley Milgram (1963, 1965, 1974) devised a set of experiments on people's obedience to authority. Milgram's first experiment was conducted in New Haven, Connecticut, and his subjects were 40 adult men between the ages of 20 and 50 drawn from a wide variety of backgrounds (engineers, postal clerks, laborers, teachers, salesmen, and others). You can get the flavor of Milgram's experiments by reading Box 17-2. During their participation in the research, the subjects were encouraged by an authority figure to deliver a series of increasingly painful shocks to another person under the guise of a "learning experiment."

The critical question in Milgram's study was, of course, how severe a shock would you deliver to the learner before refusing to go on. Milgram surveyed large numbers of individuals, including undergraduates, psychologists, and psychiatrists, described the study to them and asked them to predict how many subjects would obey the experimenter. Survey respondents consistently underpredicted the levels of obedience. Table 17-3 gives a summary of the results. Milgram wanted to determine first of all the extent to which average people would be willing to do obviously unpleasant things to other, innocent people at the prodding of an authority figure. As Table 17-3 shows all the subjects were willing to administer at least 300 volts, and nearly two-thirds (26 out of 40) continued to deliver shocks all the way to 450 volts. Clearly these subjects were generally willing to obey the voice of authority. However, that is not to say that they obeyed eagerly or comfortably. Many of the subjects displayed extreme anxiety, trembled, sweated, and broke into nervous laughter. Three even appeared to experience seizures—so severe in one case that the experiment was terminated. But most subjects continued despite their discomfort. Even when Milgram moved the experiment from the Yale campus to a commercial building in Bridgeport, Connecticut, 50 percent of the subjects were still fully obedient.

The second important question Milgram addressed in his research concerned the conditions under which people would be more or less obedient to authority figures. To answer this question, Milgram conducted a series of studies in which he systematically varied his experimental conditions (1974). In one set of studies Milgram varied the proximity of the learner and the teacher. He found that as he moved the learner closer to the victim, obedience went down. When the learner was in a separate room and could only be heard, over 60 percent of the subjects delivered the 450 volt shock. When the learner was moved into the same room as the teacher and sat about 18 inches away, obedience dropped to 40 percent. When teachers were required to press the

BOX 17-2
THE MILGRAM EXPERIMENTS

Imagine for a moment that you have responded to a newspaper advertisement promising that you will be paid to come to the campus of Yale University and participate in a study. When you arrive, you are introduced to the experimenter and another subject and told that you will both be participating in a study of the effects of punishment (electric shock) on learning. You are further told

> *So, in this study we are bringing together a number of adults of different occupations and ages, and we are asking some of them to be teachers and some of them to be learners.*
>
> *We want to find out just what effect different people have on each other as teachers and learners, and also what effect* punishment *will have on learning in this situation.*
>
> *Therefore, I'm going to ask one of you to be the teacher here tonight, and the other one to be the learner.*
>
> *(Milgram, 1963, p. 373)*

At this point, you and the other subject draw lots to determine which of you will be the teacher and which will be the learner. You draw the teaching role. The experimenter gives you a sample of the 45-volt shock. The machinery and procedures have convinced you, as they convince the other subjects, that you really are delivering shocks to the learner. At this point the learner is led into a separate room where an electrode is attached to his wrist, and he is strapped into a chair (so he cannot escape the shocks). You are assured, "Although the shocks can be extremely painful,

they cause no permanent tissue damage" (Milgram, 1963, p. 373). The experimenter leads you to another room and explains to you and the learner that the learning task involves memorizing word pairs. As teacher, you will first read a series of word pairs to the learner. Then you will read the first word of a pair together with four alternative second words. The learner will select which of the four alternatives goes with the first by pressing one of four switches with his free hand.

You are shown your shock generator (see Box Figure 1), which has 30 switches indicating voltages ranging from 15 volts (labeled "slight shock") to 375 volts (labeled "danger—severe shock"), and, ultimately, to 450 volts (labeled "X X X"). You are instructed to administer 15 volts the first time the learner makes an error. Each time the learner makes another error, you are told to increase the voltage by 15

and to announce the new voltage to the learner before throwing the switch.

Milgram had arranged for the confederate to make periodic errors so that the teachers would have an opportunity to deliver the shocks. The confederate was to make a mild protest of the shocks at 75 volts. At 150 volts the protest would be louder; the confederate would scream loudly at 285 volts; and at 300 volts the learner would pound on the wall. After that he would stop answering questions. The experimenter told the teachers that not answering was to be treated as an error and that they should keep administering shocks. If teachers hesitated, the experimenter would say "please continue." If teachers hesitated again, the experimenter said "You have no other choice; you must go on." The experiment proceeded until a teacher delivered the 450-volt shock or refused to continue.

BOX FIGURE 1   THE MILGRAM MACHINE.
These pictures show the shock generator used in Milgram's obedience studies and actual experimental sessions. (Photos copyright Stanley Milgram, 1965.)

TABLE 17-3   SHOCK LEVELS IN MILGRAM'S OBEDIENCE STUDY

Verbal Designation and Voltage Indication	Number of Subjects for Whom This Was Maximum Shock	Verbal Designation and Voltage Indication	Number of Subjects for Whom This Was Maximum Shock
Slight shock		Intense shock	
15	0	255	0
30	0	270	0
45	0	285	0
60	0	300	5
Moderate shock		Extreme-intensity shock	
75	0	315	4
90	0	330	2
105	0	345	1
120	0	360	1
Strong shock		Danger—severe shock	
135	0	375	1
150	0	390	0
165	0	405	0
180	0	420	0
Very strong shock		XXX	
195	0	435	0
210	0	450	26
225	0		
240	0		

Source: After Milgram, 1963.

Note: Shock levels administered by subjects in Milgram's obedience study. The table indicates the number of subjects for whom each level was the maximum shock.

learner's hand onto a shock plate, the proportion of obedient subjects dropped to 30 percent.

The physical *presence of the experimenter* also strongly influenced obedience. When the experimenter simply gave initial directions and then left the room (ostensibly to answer a phone), the percentage of fully obedient teachers fell by about two-thirds. In addition, a number of teachers reduced the voltage of the shocks they administered. When the learner's suffering was emphasized, this too reduced obedience. Many of Milgram's findings have been replicated in other countries, including Germany and Australia (Kilham and Mann, 1974; Mantell, 1971).

Two important criticisms have been made of Milgram's research. The more important criticism concerns the ethics of the research. Many critics have viewed the research as inherently unethical because it subjected people to very intense pressures, deceived them, and may have humiliated them (Baumrind, 1964). Milgram (1974) responded to such criticisms by noting that only 2 percent of his more than 1000 subjects regretted participating in the research. Other critics have questioned the extent to which Milgram's findings can be generalized to the real world. But studies conducted outside of laboratories support the findings (Hofling et al., 1966). Criticisms aside, the point remains that under prodding from an authority, many ordinary people were willing to do extremely unpleasant and possibly lethal things to another person.

AGGRESSION

Aggression seems to be everywhere. Only 10 of 185 generations in the past five thousand years have lived in peace (Baron, 1983). Every year thousands of Americans are the victims of aggression and violence. The FBI reports that each year during the 1980s nearly 20,000 Americans have been murdered, nearly 80,000 raped, over 500,000 robbed, and over 600,000 assaulted (*Uniform Crime Reports,* 1985). The National Institute of Justice reports that each year, one in every four households is touched by crime and one in 20 by a violent crime (NIJ, 1985). In some ways, crime is more of a problem now than it was only 20 years ago: the murder rate in 1980 was twice that of 1960 and ten times that of 1903 (NIJ, 1983).

A substantial portion of crime is committed by people who are strangers to the victim, yet over half the murders and nearly half of all assaults are actually committed by acquaintances and relatives of the victim. Furthermore, it is widely believed that a large proportion of crimes committed by relatives are never reported to the authorities (NIJ, 1983), and a growing body of research evidence shows that a substantial amount of violence actually occurs in people's homes. Nationwide surveys of married couples reveal that 25 percent report having engaged in some type of physical violence during their marriage, and most of the assaults were committed by husbands (NIJ, 1983; Steinmetz and Straus, 1974; Straus, 1977). Recent surveys of families reveal that children were the targets of violence in 62 percent of the households surveyed (Sullivan, 1985). Although the most common forms of violence were slapping and spanking (55 percent of the households), in fully 10 percent of the households children had been the victims of extreme violence, having been hit with objects and fists, shot, or knifed. The researchers estimated that at least one million children are physically abused each year and that between 2000 and 5000 die from their injuries.

Why are aggression and violence so widespread? What can be done to reduce or eliminate them? These are the types of questions that have motivated social psychological research on aggression. Although this research has not led to a substantial reduction in the violence, it suggests strategies for doing so.

Defining and Measuring Aggression

As is always the case when psychologists begin research on a complex phenomenon, they have to begin with a firm definition of that phenomenon. In Chapters 10 and 11, we briefly discussed how to define aggression. Some psychologists have argued that it is often difficult to assess the intentions behind an aggressive act and have defined aggression in purely behavioral terms. For example, aggression has been defined as "a response that delivers noxious stimuli to another organism" (p. 1). Most researchers, however, have offered definitions of aggression that take account of the aggressor's intentions. According to one popular definition (and the one we will use in this chapter; Baron, 1977) aggression includes any behavior that is intended to harm another person who does not want to be harmed. This definition emphasizes four components of aggression: that humans are both the aggressors and the victims, that behavior can cause harm, that the intent is to cause harm, and that the victim is not a willing participant. Given this definition, are child abuse, warfare, boxing, or football aggressive acts?

Of course, forming this kind of definition is only a first step in scientific investigation, for then it is necessary to formulate an operational definition. Researchers have used several operational definitions of human aggression. One way some researchers measure aggression is with an "aggression machine" (Buss, 1961). These machines resemble the device that Milgram used in his obedience research (see Box Figure 1 for Box 17-2). Subjects are led to believe that they are using the machine to deliver electric shocks to another subject, who is actually a confederate of the experimenter and does not receive any shocks. Subjects usually are given a sample of the shocks that they are supposedly administering and then deliver the shocks as part of a "learning experiment." Often the subjects are allowed to deliver shocks at a strength and duration of their own choosing. This strength and duration over several "learning trials" serve as the measure of aggression.

Although the "aggression machine" has, as you shall see, been used quite often in laboratory experiments, it has been criticized as a measure of aggression. For example, some critics have argued that the machine is not a direct or reliable measure of aggression and have questioned the ethics of inducing people to deliver what they believe to be real shocks to other people (Baron and Eggleston, 1972). Others note that aggression machines do not measure what nonscientists mean by aggression and question whether laboratory findings based on such measures are externally valid or generalize to real-world aggression (Freedman, 1984). Defenders of these laboratory measures argue that laboratory situations need not closely resemble real-world situations, for the critical consideration is someone's belief that he or she can harm a victim (Berkowitz and Donnerstein, 1982). But some researchers have tried to use more direct measures of aggression—"Bobo dolls" that children punch or written measures of verbal aggression, for example. Of course, even these more direct measures of aggressive behavior are subject to questions about external validity, for they, too, are undertaken within controlled, experimental circumstances.

Theoretical Approaches to Aggression: The Frustration–Aggression Hypothesis

In Chapters 5, 10, and 11 we discussed instinctual, biological, and learning theories of aggression. Each provides an important perspective on aggression, but none explains it fully. It probably is true that human genetic makeup influences the types and patterns of human aggression. Clearly, human aggression involves the brain and hormonal systems. But we need further research before we can understand precisely how all these factors fit together to produce human aggression. In this chapter, we review research into the cultural and social influences on aggression.

People sit locked in a traffic jam, fuming about being late, and when the traffic starts to move, they drive as fast and as furiously as they can. The child trying desperately to learn to tie his shoelaces fumbles for the fifth time and bursts into tears of frustration and anger. For many years psychologists have considered aggression a consequence of frustration. One of the first and most influential scientific theories of aggression was developed a half century ago by John Dollard and his associates at Yale University (1939). They asserted that aggression is always a consequence of frustration and that frustration always leads to some kind of aggression. They defined **frustration** as anything that interferes with the achievement of a goal. Although most psychologists today would consider this hypothesis too broad, they would agree that some forms of frustration can lead to aggression. For example, in an early study, some children were allowed to enter a room full of appealing toys without any delay (Barker, Dembo, and Lewin, 1941). Others could look into the room but were not allowed to enter immediately. In other words they were deliberately frustrated. When the frustrated children were allowed to enter the room and play with the toys, they were much more likely to throw and smash the toys than were the children who had been allowed to enter immediately.

Frustration may often lead to aggression, but it does not always do so. People in many studies have not become aggressive after being frustrated (Gentry, 1970; Taylor and Pisano, 1971) or have become only mildly aggressive (Buss, 1963). As early as 1941, Neal Miller, one of Dollard's colleagues, saw that frustration does not always produce aggression. As others have shown, it may lead to other responses, such as depression, dependency, withdrawal, resignation, and even drug dependency (Bandura, 1973; Baron, 1977). In sum, the original frustration–aggression hypothesis was overstated on two grounds: although frustration may promote aggression, it does *not always* do so, and although aggression is often the product of frustration, it may be produced by *other causes*.

The Revised Frustration–Aggression Hypothesis

These limitations of the original frustration–aggression hypothesis led Leonard Berkowitz (1965, 1969) to revise it. Frustration, he has said, produces "a *readiness* for aggressive acts" (Berkowitz, 1965, p. 308). But the likelihood that people will act aggressively and the strength of their aggressive response both depend on the presence of environmental cues to aggression. Thus, Berkowitz stresses the relationship between environmental cues and internal emotional states in aggressive behavior.

AROUSAL AND READINESS FOR AGGRESSION   What, besides frustration, may increase a person's readiness to respond aggressively? *Anger.* People who feel angry are more likely to act aggressively than others, and that anger may make them even more likely to act aggressively than frustration does (Baron, 1972; Gentry, 1970; Rule and Hewitt, 1971;

TABLE 17-4 AROUSAL, INSULT, AND AGGRESSION

	Attack	*No Attack*
High arousal (exercise)	126.5	58.0
Low arousal (no exercise)	90.1	75.0

Source: After Zillmann and Bryant, 1974.
Note: This table shows the mean level of noise that people delivered to someone else after having been physically abused by exercise or not abused and then insulted.

Zillmann, 1979). For example, when people are provoked into anger by insults and physical attacks, they become more aggressive (Dengerink and Meyers, 1977; Taylor and Pisano, 1971; White and Gruber, 1982).

General arousal also plays a role in promoting aggression. According to the *excitation-transfer* theory of aggression, people can transfer the arousal produced by one situation to another arousing situation (Zillmann, 1971, 1982). Someone who has had a miserable day—lost a wallet, flunked an exam, got a rejection letter from a prospective college or employer—is likely to react much more aggressively and excitedly to spilling ketchup on his or her sweater than someone who has not had such a miserable day.

In a study of the transfer of excitation from one situation to another, researchers had some subjects ride an exercise cycle, which aroused them physically (Zillmann and Bryant, 1974). Other subjects were given a task that did not arouse them. Then, half of the subjects from each group were insulted, and they all were given a chance to deliver painful noises to a confederate. The people who had both been physiologically aroused *and* insulted were more aggressive than the people who had been insulted only, or aroused only (see Table 17-4). Although many people have shown the effects of transferring excitation from one situation to another (Bryant and Zillmann, 1979; Ramirez, Bryant, and Zillmann, 1982; Tannenbaum and Zillmann, 1975), it appears general arousal only promotes aggression when people misattribute the arousal to the source of the insult or provocation. If people believe the arousal is due to some innocuous cause, such as riding a bicycle, they are not likely to display increased aggressiveness.

SEXUAL AROUSAL AND AGGRESSION Not only have psychologists been interested in the connections between general arousal and aggression, but because of the prominence and controversy concerning the role of pornography in criminal behavior, they also have been interested in the connection between *sexual arousal* and aggression. The researchers usually use an experimental procedure in which people see sexually arousing films or books and then are insulted by the experimenter. For a while, the findings looked contradictory. Some researchers found that sexual arousal increased people's aggressiveness (Baron and Bell, 1973; Donnerstein, Donnerstein, and Evans, 1975; Meyer, 1972; Zillmann, 1971). But others found that sexual arousal actually reduced aggressiveness (Baron, 1974; Donnerstein et al., 1975; Frodi, 1977; Zillmann and Sapolsky, 1977).

More recently it has been suggested that these differences actually may result from the different levels of arousal provoked in each study (Baron, 1977; Baron and Bell, 1977; Donnerstein, 1983; Zillmann and Bryant, 1983). This mild sexual arousal, such as that induced by *Playboy* magazine, may reduce aggression, perhaps because the pleasant feelings associated with mild arousal are incongruent with aggression or because the arousal distracts people from their anger. But people are more likely to transfer more extreme sexual arousal, perhaps because extremely arousing material itself produces negative reactions (Ramirez, Bryant, and Zillman, 1982; White, 1979). (For a discussion of the long-term effects of aggressive-erotic material, see Box 17-3.)

SITUATIONAL DETERMINANTS OF AGGRESSION People often become aggressive because *situational factors* trigger their arousal and irritation (Malamuth, 1986). People who had been made angry and then heard a loud noise, delivered more intense shocks to a confederate than people who had not heard the noise (Donnerstein and Wilson, 1976). When researchers studied over 100 riots that had broken out over a period of some years in the United States, they found that the likelihood of a riot increased as air temperatures (and presumably irritation and discomfort) went up (see Figure 17-5) (Carlsmith and Anderson, 1979). Similarly, other researchers found a positive relation between high temperatures and violent crimes against people such as rape and murder, but no relation between high temperatures and crimes against property (Anderson and Anderson, 1984).

Alcohol and drugs are also associated with aggressive behavior. A study of nearly 5800 jail inmates showed that more than half had been drunk when they committed a crime. Sixty-two percent of those convicted for

FIGURE 17-5 AIR TEMPERATURE AND RIOTS.
After studying the weather conditions that prevailed during 102 riots in the United States, the researchers concluded that the likelihood of a riot increases along with the ambient air temperature. (Carlsmith and Anderson, 1979.)

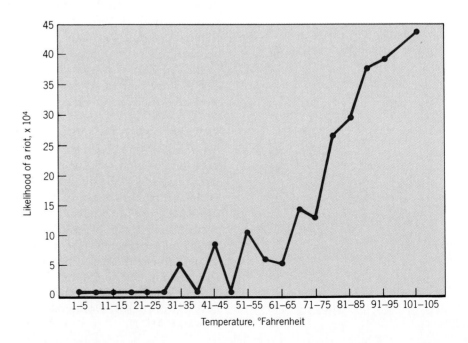

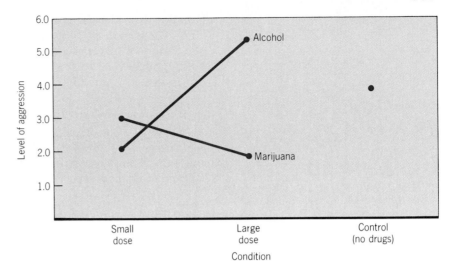

FIGURE 17-6 ALCOHOL, MARIJUANA, AND AGGRESSION. The effects of marijuana and alcohol on aggression. Subjects were given small or large doses of THC (the active ingredient in marijuana) or alcohol. Whereas subjects given large doses of alcohol became more aggressive, subjects given large doses of marijuana became less aggressive. (After Taylor et al., 1976.)

assault and 49 percent of those convicted of murder or attempted murder had been drinking at the time of the crime (NIJ, 1985). Laboratory studies show that small doses of alcohol inhibit aggression, but large doses increase it. In contrast, large doses of marijuana actually inhibit aggression (Myserscough and Taylor, 1985; Taylor, Gammon, and Capasso, 1976; Figure 17-6). In short, a variety of situational factors can promote aggressive behavior—either because they are directly irritating or make people more irritable.

CUES TO AGGRESSION One of the long-standing political debates in this country and abroad is whether private citizens should be allowed to carry guns and other weapons. On one side of the debate are those whose bumper stickers declare, "When guns are outlawed, only outlaws will have guns." On the other side are those who argue that the very presence of guns increases the level of violence in society. Some research in the psychology laboratory sheds light on this heated debate. This research has demonstrated a phenomenon called the **weapons effect** (Berkowitz and LePage, 1967). In one experiment, for example, people were led to believe that the experiment concerned reactions to stress. The task was for each subject and a partner (who actually was a confederate of the researchers) to generate ideas for a sales campaign and then evaluate one another's ideas.

In the first phase of the study, half the subjects were given a single electrical shock by their partner. The other half were given several shocks and a negative evaluation, all of which presumably increased their readiness to act aggressively. Then the subject and the confederate changed places, and the subject had the opportunity to deliver the shocks. But at this point, one-third of the subjects sat at a table that had nothing on it but the electrical switch for delivering the shocks. One-third had the switch and neutral objects like badminton equipment on their table. The final third had the switch, a revolver, and a shotgun. As the researchers had hypothesized (in the reformulated frustration-aggression hypothesis), the weapons became cues to aggression that would increase the number and duration of shocks the subjects administered and the subjects who had been given the most shocks would act the most aggressively. The findings, in fact, bear out the hypothesis. The weapons lying on the table did correspond to an increase in aggression. Although the study was later criticized on the grounds that subjects may have been aware of and influenced by the researchers' hypothesis (Page and Scheidt, 1971), the weapons effect has been tested under conditions that rule out this possibility (Page and O'Neal, 1977; Turner and Simons, 1974) and has been reproduced by a number of researchers (Cahoon and Edmunds, 1984; Frodi, 1975).

Social Learning and Aggression

Knowing something about the conditions under which people are likely to respond aggressively—when they are frustrated, aroused, targets of aggression themselves, and so on—is only part of understanding this aspect of social behavior. Knowing something about *how* humans learn aggression is just as important. The social learning theory of Albert Bandura (1973, 1977a), which we have described in several earlier chapters, addresses this question directly. Bandura argues that there is a continuous interaction between an individual and the social environment that controls all behavior—including aggression—and that whether a person behaves aggressively will depend upon the person's learning history, the reinforcements a person has received for past aggression, and the cues to aggression provided by the environment. The social learning approach to aggression emphasizes the role of both operant and observational learning of aggression.

OPERANT LEARNING OF AGGRESSION As you saw in Chapter 11, there have been many demonstrations that aggressive behavior can be shaped through reinforcements, that is, increased by rewards and decreased by punishment. The examples are everywhere (Cowan and Walters, 1963; Geen and Pigg, 1970; Geen and Stonner, 1971). Nursery schools have reduced the number of aggressive acts by 3- and 4-year-old boys by simply ignoring their aggression and attending to (reinforcing) their nonaggressive behavior. When researchers reinforced people who were giving electric shocks to someone else in an experiment, by saying such things as "You're doing fine" and "That's good," they found that these people administered more intense shocks than those who had not been encouraged (Geen and Pigg, 1970).

The effects of punishment on aggressive behavior are not always immediate or uncomplicated. Although directly punishing aggression sometimes can reduce it (Chasdi and Lawrence, 1955; Wilson and Rogers, 1975), there is good evidence that the deterrent effects of punishment are short-lived and may actually backfire, that is, promote aggression. For example, if people interpret the punishment as a provocation or if it angers them, they may immediately become more aggressive (Dyck and Rule, 1978; Harvey and Enzle, 1978). Furthermore, punishment may produce long-term increases in aggression. The more physical

FIGURE 17-7 MARITAL VIOLENCE.

FIGURE 17-7 MARITAL VIOLENCE.
The amount of violence within a marriage is systematically linked to the amount of violence the husbands and wives experienced as teenagers. (After Straus et al., 1980.)

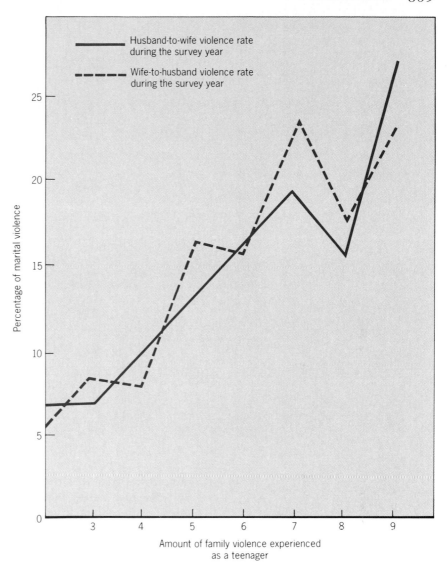

Husband-to-wife violence rate during the survey year

Wife-to-husband violence rate during the survey year

Percentage of marital violence

Amount of family violence experienced as a teenager

punishment that parents use, for example, the more aggressive their adolescent boys (Bandura and Walters, 1959). The more violence husbands and wives experienced as teenagers, the more violent they are likely to be as married couples (see Figure 17-7) (Straus, Gelles, and Steinmetz, 1980).

It is unquestionably true that our learning experiences influence our aggressive behavior, and although direct reinforcement of aggression may play a role in learning some aggressive behavior, most of us probably learn more through observation.

MODELING AND IMITATION OF AGGRESSION   One reason that punishing children may make them aggressive adults is because parents who use physical punishment serve as behavioral models for their children.

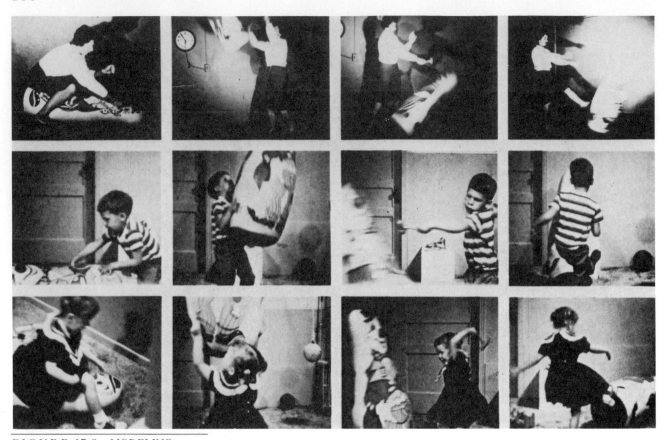

*FIGURE 17-8   MODELING
AGGRESSION.*

*Adults' aggressive behavior can serve
as a model for children's behavior.
Children imitated the aggressive play of
adults. (From Bandura, Ross, and Ross,
1963.)*

Children who see adults whom they admire behave aggressively are quite likely to imitate the aggressive behavior. For example, nursery school children worked on an interesting art project in one part of a classroom while an adult played quietly with some Tinker Toys in another part of the room (Bandura, Ross, and Ross, 1961, 1963). In one condition of the experiment, the adult played quietly with the Tinker Toys for 10 minutes.

In a second condition, the adult played with the Tinker Toys for 1 minute, then got up, and for 9 minutes treated a 5-foot inflatable Bobo doll aggressively (see Figure 17-8). The adult punched, sat on, and kicked the doll, threw things at it, and hit it with a mallet, while shouting such things as: "Kick him," "Pow," "Sock him in the nose," and "Hit him down." The children from both games were then taken to another room that contained very attractive toys. After being allowed to play with the toys for 2 minutes, they were interrupted and told that they could not play with the toys. Instead, they were taken to another room that contained toys including a 3-foot Bobo doll, a mallet, and a variety of nonaggressive toys. As Table 17-5 shows, the children who had seen the violent model displayed much more aggressive speech and actions than did the children who had seen a neutral model. Furthermore, their aggressive behavior clearly imitated the behavior of the violent adult.

TABLE 17-5 THE EFFECTS OF ADULT MODELS
OF AGGRESSION

	Mean Aggression	
Condition	Physical	Verbal
Violent model	12.73	8.18
Neutral model	1.05	0.35

Source: After Bandura, Ross, and Ross, 1961.
Note: This table shows the mean level of physical and verbal aggression directed at a Bobo doll by children who had watched either a violent or a neutral adult model.

Research by Bandura and others has demonstrated that a number of factors can enhance or reduce imitative aggression. Thus, children also are more likely to imitate models who have been rewarded for their aggression and less likely to imitate models who have been punished (Bandura, 1965; Hicks, 1965). Children are more likely to imitate people of their own sex and people of high status (Bandura et al., 1961; Turner and Berkowitz, 1972), and although realistic aggression seems to produce greater imitation than unrealistic aggression, even cartoon violence can increase imitative aggression (Bandura et al., 1963; Thomas and Tell, 1974).

In short, aggression, like other behaviors, can be strongly influenced by learning—both operantly and through observation. It has probably already occurred to you that children are exposed to quite a lot of aggressive behavior on television. Indeed, insights into the relation between learning and aggression has prompted many researchers and parents to worry about the effects of media violence on the behavior of viewers—a problem we consider in the next section.

Media Violence

Violence and aggression seem to be so contagious that people apparently imitate the aggression they see on television and in the movies. John Hinckley, the young man who shot President Ronald Reagan, was acting in imitation of a character in the extremely violent movie, *Taxi Driver.* Similarly, there was a rash of imitative suicides among people who had seen *The Deerhunter,* a film in which there is a scene involving a game of Russian roulette. There even is a measurable increase in homicides after highly publicized heavyweight boxing matches (Phillips and Hensley, 1984).

As you saw in Chapter 9, researchers have long been interested in the effects of television violence on children. In the early 1970s the Surgeon General of the United States commissioned research on the effects of televised violence. Although there was not much research to go on at the time, the Surgeon General's report (1972) tentatively concluded that televised violence did influence some children's behavior under some circumstances. This report precipitated hundreds of new studies of media violence, and in the early 1980s the National Institutes of Mental

Health commissioned a new review of this literature. The NIMH reviewers concluded that

> *The consensus among most of the research community is that violence on television does lead to aggressive behavior by children and teenagers who watch the programs. This conclusion is based on laboratory experiments and on field studies. Not all children become aggressive, of course, but the correlations between violence and aggression are positive. In magnitude, television violence is as strongly correlated with aggressive behavior as any other behavioral variable that has been measured. The research question has moved from whether or not there is an effect to seeking explanations for the effect. (p. 6)*

In one *longitudinal study*, the researchers interviewed 878 8-year-old children, their classmates, and their parents in 1960 (Eron and Huesmann, 1980; Eron, 1982; Huesmann, 1982, 1984, 1986; Huesmann,

FIGURE 17-9 CRIME AND TELEVISION.
The seriousness of the crimes that men at age 30 are convicted of varies as a function of boys' preference for television violence at age 8. (After Huesmann, 1986.)

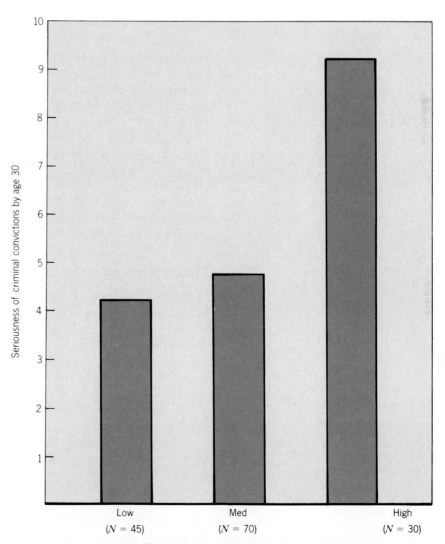

Eron, Lefkowitz, and Walder, 1984). Then, in 1982, the researchers again interviewed 632 of the original subjects, their spouses, and children and reviewed police, mental health, and motor vehicle records. One of their major findings was that peers' ratings of a child's aggressiveness—"Who is always getting into fights over nothing?"—in the third grade predicted serious antisocial behavior in adulthood. In other words, aggressive children tended to become aggressive adults, that is, adults who still were more aggressive than their peers according to themselves, their spouses, and their children. As adults, those who had been aggressive children also had more traffic violations and more criminal convictions, and were convicted of more serious crimes. These findings held true for both men and women. Furthermore, the researchers found a link between boys' watching violent television shows and their later aggression. Other researchers since have found a similar link for girls (see Figure 17-9). Boys who preferred violent television programs at age 8, as adults were convicted of more serious crimes than boys who liked less violent programs.

Of course, because such studies are correlational, the relationship does not, by itself, prove that watching television in childhood *causes* the aggressive behavior in adulthood. There are other possible explanations of the findings, after all. Children whose parents are poorly educated, or children from socially and economically disadvantaged families, or children with low IQs might prefer violent television *and* have more serious criminal records. However, the researchers were able to rule out many of these possible explanations. Their conclusion—which is the same conclusion reached by most other media researchers—is that televised violence *teaches* children to be violent.

Other large-scale longitudinal studies of children in the United States, Finland, Australia, Poland, the Netherlands, and Israel have shown sim-

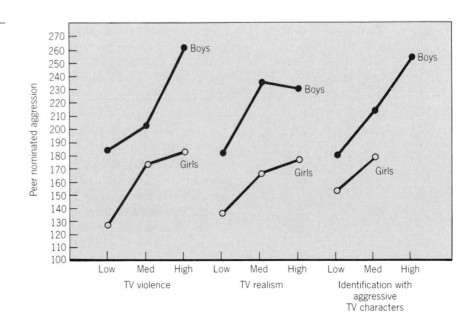

FIGURE 17-10   TELEVISION VIOLENCE AND CHILDHOOD AGGRESSION.
Children's aggressive behavior has been linked to the amount of violence they watch on television, the extent to which they believe televised violence is real, and the extent to which they identify with aggressive television characters. (After Eron, 1982.)

BOX 17-3
MEDIA VIOLENCE AGAINST WOMEN

In recent years, several prominent feminist writers have raised serious questions about the social effects of pornography and violence against women in the mass media. These writers generally distinguish between *erotica* and *aggressive* or *coercive pornography*. *Erotica* includes sexually explicit materials that depict men and women as equals and in a positive and humane light that shows respect for sexual relationships. *Aggressive* or *coercive pornography* depicts women as the targets of aggression and in subordinate and negative roles.

> *Look at any photo or film of people making love, really making love . . . there is usually a sensuality and touch and warmth, an acceptance, . . . a spontaneous sense . . . of shared pleasure. Now look at any depiction of sex in which there is clear force, or an unequal power that spells coercion. It may be very blatant, with weapons of torture or bondage, wounds and bruises, . . . humiliation. It may be much more subtle . . . In either case, there is no sense of equal choice or equal power.*
>
> (Steinem, 1980, p. 37)

Similarly, Susan Brownmiller (1975) argues that pornography promotes "a climate in which acts of sexual hostility directed against women are not only tolerated but ideologically encouraged" (p. 444).

We have already seen that sexual arousal coupled with negative affect can make people more aggressive, but the question here is whether depictions of sex plus aggression have especially negative consequences for women. These questions are raised at a time when sexually explicit materials that graphically depict a wide variety of sexual behavior are widely available. X-rated videocassettes, for example, are among the most popular tapes on the market. Images of aggression against women are widely available in advertisements in women's fashion magazines, in films, and on TV (Malamuth and Spinner, 1980; Smith, Check, and Henry, 1984).

In the past few years, researchers have conducted a number of laboratory studies to see whether aggressive pornography has any effect and, if so, what these effects might be (Donnerstein, Linz, and Penrod, 1987). They have found that sexually explicit aggression against women, particularly that in which the women seem to enjoy or become sexually aroused by

the aggression, can lead to changes in *men's* attitudes toward rape and behaviors toward women. The men may become increasingly aggressive toward women in the laboratory (Donnerstein, 1980, 1983; Donnerstein and Berkowitz, 1981; see Box Figure 1). They may have more fantasies about rape (Malamuth, 1981a), feel more willing to commit rape (Donnerstein, 1984; Malamuth, Haber, and Feshbach, 1980), more readily accept myths about rape, such as that some women want to be raped and that women who dress without bras are asking for trouble (Check, 1985; Check and Malamuth, 1982; Donnerstein, 1984), and become less sensitive to the plight of rape victims (Malamuth and Check, 1980; Malamuth, Haber, and Feshbach, 1980).

Over and over again, researchers find that aggressive sexual scenes in films change men's attitudes toward women and rape—for the worse. For example, college students of both sexes saw two popular, mass-release R-rated films (*The Getaway* and *Swept Away*) (Malamuth and Check, 1981). In each film, the female star is sexually assaulted by the male star, and later falls in love with him. After seeing the films, the male college students more readily accepted myths

ilar positive relations among the children's aggressiveness and (1) the amount of violence the children see on television, (2) the extent to which the children believe that televised violence is real, and (3) the extent to which they identify with the aggressive characters they see (see Figure 17-10) (reported in Eron, 1982, 1984). The lure of the television set (or the movie screen), with its fast action and powerful characters, is strong for children and adults alike. Yet violent television programs can lure people into acting violently themselves. The danger is especially great for children, who are less adept than adults at telling the difference between fiction and reality and who readily idolize the violent characters whom about rape (described in the previous paragraph) and violence against women. In a more extensive study, men volunteered to watch five commercially released films from one of three categories: (1) sexually explicit but nonviolent X-rated films; (2) R-rated extremely violent films in which women are the victims of graphic violence, often in an erotic context, and (3) R-rated nonviolent films (Linz, Penrod, and Donnerstein, 1985). Only the men who watched the violent R-rated films showed the changes in attitude just described. After they watched five of these films, the men became desensitized. They were less distressed by what they saw, thought the films contained less violence, and thought they were less degrading to women than they had after seeing just one film. Furthermore, when the men served as jurors in a mock trial involving a charge of rape, they were generally less sympathetic with rape victims and were less sympathetic with the victim in the case in particular. In contrast, when women volunteered for a similar study, they also became desensitized to filmed violence, but they continued to reject violence against women (Krafka, Penrod, and Donnerstein, 1987).

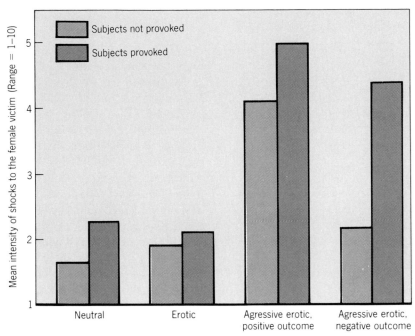

BOX FIGURE 1   THE EFFECTS OF AGGRESSIVE EROTICA.
After men watched an erotic film that showed a woman suffering as a result of aggression, only those men who also had been angered previously acted aggressively toward (gave shocks to) another woman. In contrast, when the woman in the aggressive erotic film did not appear to suffer, men who had been angered and men who had not been angered both acted more aggressively toward the second woman after they had seen the film. Neutral and erotic films with no aggression did not increase aggression. (After Donnerstein and Berkowitz, 1981.)

they see punching, slashing, and shooting their way across the flickering screen.

ALTRUISM

Late in the evening of March 13, 1964, a young woman, Kitty Genovese, was returning home from work when she was attacked in front of her apartment. Over a period of 35 minutes, her assailant attacked her three separate times. Kitty Genovese repeatedly screamed that she was being stabbed and called for help. Twice the assailant was apparently frightened away when neighbors turned on lights. Thirty-eight neighbors heard her screams, but no one went to her assistance, and no one called the police until 20 minutes after the assault ended. The police arrived at the scene in 2 minutes, but it was too late for Kitty Genovese. She died from her stab wounds.

In the summer of 1944, Swedish and Allied authorities sent Raoul Wallenberg to Hungary on a mission to save Jews from the Nazis. Over a period of a few months, Wallenberg issued Swedish passports to more than 20,000 Jews from Budapest and managed to place another 13,000 in "safe houses" under Swedish protection. Wallenberg's work placed him at great personal risk. He personally stood on a deportation train handing out Swedish papers to anyone who could reach them and insisted that everyone holding the papers be removed from the train. He literally pulled people out of death marches and brought them supplies when he ran out of passports (Lester and Werbell, 1980).

Heroes like Raoul Wallenberg and apathetic bystanders like Kitty Genovese's neighbors seem to be worlds apart. Why do people sometimes behave nobly and sometimes utterly ignobly? Just as philosophers have argued about the relation between human nature and aggression, they have argued about human nature and altruism. And as is the case with aggression, only recently have social psychologists and other researchers undertaken serious scientific research on the causes of prosocial, or altruistic, behavior.

Defining Altruism

Researchers often distinguish among *prosocial behavior, altruistic behavior,* and *helping behavior. Prosocial behavior* forms the broadest category of behavior and generally refers to behavior designed to help others without regard to the helper's motives (Rushton, 1980) or to behavior valued by a society. Prosocial behavior might include donating to charities, volunteering for military service, and cooperating with others. Of course, in that different societies value different kinds of behavior, contradictions can arise. For example, Nazi "Good Samaritan" laws that required German citizens to aid the government in the persecution of Jews certainly did not promote what an ethical person would consider prosocial behavior (Piliavin, Dovidio, Gaertner, and Clark, 1981).

Altruism, more narrowly defined than prosocial behavior, describes the motivation of helpers and the benefits to recipients. For example, altruism can be defined as behavior carried out to benefit another without anticipation of external rewards (Macaulay and Berkowitz, 1970, p. 3). A narrower definition emphasizes four components of altruism: an intention to help, some cost to the helper, no expectation of an external reward for the helper, and favorable consequences for the recipient (Batson and Coke, 1981). In contrast, *helping behavior* differs from altruistic behavior insofar as people may be externally rewarded for helping, *and* the helping behavior is defined as such by the helper rather than by the recipient.

In this section, we consider why people help others and behave altruistically. We will examine this question from several theoretical perspectives, including two that are quite familiar to us: the sociobiological perspective and the social learning perspective. In addition, we examine the influence of social and personal norms and the influence of situational and personal factors on prosocial behavior.

A Sociobiological Perspective on Altruism

Can there be a genetic basis for altruism? If evolution is based on the survival of the fittest, how can altruistic behavior—particularly when it costs the life of the helper—promote the survival of a gene for altruism? It would seem that natural selection should favor self-preserving behaviors. Yet studies of social insects like bees and ants clearly indicate that altruistic behaviors must have some selective advantage. How else can one explain the existence of sterile female worker bees who devote their lives to taking care of the queen bee and defending the hive, often at the expense of their own lives? How else can one explain the fact that in many animal species, warnings of danger by one animal actually put the animal that sounds the warning in danger? For example, Darwin (1871) himself observed the hind foot thumping by rabbits that makes them easier targets of prey. Why do dominant male baboons expose themselves to risk while their tribe moves away from danger (Hall, 1960), and why do parents in many species sacrifice themselves when their offspring are threatened (Wilson, 1975)?

Sociobiologists have sought to explain the existence and preservation of such altruistic behavior through a process of *kin selection*. Basically, they argue that what matters in evolution is the survival of genes and not necessarily the organism that carries the genes. Sociobiologists therefore talk about a "selfish gene" (Wilson, 1975). The worker bee that dies defending a hive helps to ensure that its genes—which it shares with the queen and its sister workers—will be passed on by the surviving queen. Similarly, the parent that dies for its offspring has helped to ensure that the genes they share (half of the offspring's genes are identical to those of either parent) will survive into future generations. Indeed, the parent that saves four offspring actually preserves twice as many of its own genes—including some genes for altruism—as it possesses itself!

Sociobiological theory of altruism has been criticized, however (Campbell, 1975, 1983). The question of whether behavior observed in other species can be generalized to humans aside for a moment, critics note that though altruism kinship selection can account for altruistic behavior among closely related animals, it cannot easily explain altruistic behavior that benefits strangers. Two general responses have been offered in response to this criticism. First, humans may have evolved under conditions in which it was generally difficult to tell who was a relative and who was not (Krebs, 1983; Krebs and Miller, 1985). However, altruistic responses might be based on more reliable cues such as familiarity, similarity, proximity, and in-group membership—all of which could favor the helping of nonrelatives. Second, altruism might have evolved through a reciprocal process (Trivers, 1971). If people help others, even strangers, and the benefit outweighs the cost to the helpers *and* if the helpers can expect reciprocal assistance in the future, in the long run, the genes of people who help others undergo a survival benefit.

Sociobiologists stress the genetic underpinnings of altruistic behavior. But, of course, every human also *learns* this kind of behavior. How do we learn altruism?

Learning to Behave Altruistically

The circumstances that people find themselves in and the people around them can strongly influence whether people do or do not behave altruistically. As in so many other areas of human behavior, if people are rewarded for altruism, they are more likely to behave altruistically and if they are punished or not rewarded for it, they are less likely to behave altruistically. Many researchers have demonstrated that helping can be operantly conditioned (Grusec, 1982). For example, shoppers who were asked to give directions were more likely to help a third person, who supposedly accidentally dropped a package, when they were thanked for giving directions than when the person who asked for directions said "OK" or gave some other neutral response or rebuffed them with "I can't understand what you are saying" (Moss and Page, 1972). In children, too, rewards increase altruistic behavior. Four-year-olds were more likely to share marbles when they were rewarded for their generosity (Fisher, 1963; Midlarsky and Bryan, 1967). Criticizing them made them less likely to share later on (Rushton and Teachman, 1978).

People imitate the standards of altruism they see other people upholding. For example, women college students interacted with a woman who was a confederate of the experimenters, ostensibly as part of an experiment (Rushton and Campbell, 1977). Then the student and the woman passed a table where people were soliciting blood donations. In half the cases the woman volunteered immediately to give blood. In half the cases she simply paused to speak with another person. When she volunteered to give blood, 67 percent of the students did too (and 33 percent ultimately gave the blood). But when she did not volunteer, only 25 of the subjects did and none actually gave blood. The studies of modeling and reinforcement clearly demonstrate that prosocial behavior can be learned and socially influenced. This kind of social influence may last for relatively long periods (Grusec, 1981) and they may generalize across situations (Grusec, Keczynstia, Rushton, and Simutis, 1978). These results raise the question of what people generally learn about social expectations or norms for prosocial behavior.

Social Norms

Societies could not operate unless their members agreed on certain rules, most of them unwritten and tacitly understood, about the right way to act in various social situations. In this society, for example, we have *social norms* about not staring at strangers, about not physically abusing others, about answering the telephone when it rings, and on and on. People must learn these norms, which represent society's expectations about their behavior. No one is born with this knowledge, after all. Through social learning, by being reinforced and punished for appropriate and inappropriate behavior and by watching how others behave, people *internalize* these norms and use them to guide their own behavior. Psychologists have identified a number of norms thought to influence prosocial behavior.

One unwritten social rule is the *social-responsibility norm,* which holds that we ought to help those who need help even when we have no expectation of benefiting. Everyday experience and research both confirm that people often help others even in the absence of social rewards, but their willingness to do so depends on the extent to which the person in need is responsible for his or her neediness. The unwritten rule seems to be something like "give people what they deserve."

An even more powerful norm is the *reciprocity norm,* which holds that people should help (and not hurt) those who have helped them (Gouldner, 1960). This norm, in fact, may be universal and operates in all societies. It is likely that people the world over learn to act according to the Golden Rule and its variants—to do unto others as they would have others do unto them, to avoid biting the hand that feeds them, to return favors, and so forth. Research confirms that people often reciprocate (Staub and Sherk, 1970; Pruitt, 1968). But their perceptions of a donor's motivations will affect their inclination to reciprocate (Dovidio, 1984). People are less likely to reciprocate when they believe that someone who helps them has selfish motives (Worchel, Andreoli, and Archer, 1976), when they feel pressured to reciprocate (Fraser and Fujitomi, 1972), and when the initial sacrifice is both small and expected by the recipient (Wilke and Lanzetta, 1970).

Equity theory has also been used to explain prosocial behavior, particularly to explain people's responses when they receive inequitable rewards. People who receive more than their due often seek to redistribute rewards (Leventhal, Weiss, and Long, 1969; Walster, Walster, and Berscheid, 1978) and may feel distressed if they cannot restore equity (Gross and Latane, 1974).

But norms are general, and they can go only so far in explaining altruistic behavior. Norms may say little about how people are to act in particular situations because sometimes conflicting norms govern the same situation—one is told to help others at the same time as one is told not to be a busybody—people do not always act consistently and do not always observe norms (Latane and Darley, 1970). It, therefore, can be more helpful to think in terms of *personal norms,* an individual's belief about how he or she ought to act in a particular situation (Schwartz, 1977). To know whether someone is likely to behave altruistically, then, it is helpful to know that person's own norms. It has been suggested that prosocial behavior develops in four stages. In the first stage a person must become aware of someone else's needs. The person must find out about the plight of the homeless. In the second stage the person must consider his or her *personal norms* and determine the obligations of the particular situation. "I should volunteer my time," the person thinks. In the third stage the person assesses possible responses and their consequences (including reasons against action or *defenses*). "If I volunteer, I won't have time for studying." In the fourth stage a person takes *action* if he or she has become aware enough, feels obligated enough, and has few defenses against helping (Schwartz, 1977; Schwartz and Howard, 1981).

Emergency Intervention

Knowing that people need help in the abstract and being present at an emergency are different kinds of situations and give rise to different kinds of responses from those involved. Prompted in part by reports of the failure of bystanders to intervene in emergencies such as the murder of Kitty Genovese, Bibb Latane and John Darley (1968, 1970) undertook a series of now classic studies in which they sought to identify the factors that influence whether people intervene in an emergency. They created a wide variety of emergency situations in their laboratory. In one study people entered a room either alone, with two others, or with two confederates of the experimenter. In the room they read a sign directing them to complete a questionnaire and then to wait for the experimenter. While they waited, the room began to fill with smoke. After 4 minutes, the smoke made it hard for them to see or breathe. People who were alone in the room generally walked around trying to figure out what was causing the smoke. Seventy-five percent of them left the room and reported the problem within 4 minutes. But people who waited with other naive subjects were much less likely to act; only 38 percent reported the smoke. Only 10 percent of the people who waited with passive confederates, who ignored the smoke and worked diligently, reported the situation.

In other studies, involving less ambiguous situations, people working alone or with others were confronted with a woman who screamed when she fell off a chair and cried out about her injured ankle (Latane and Darley, 1970), heard another person suffer an apparent seizure (Darley and Latane, 1968), or witnessed a crime (Latane and Darley, 1970). The people's responses followed a consistent pattern (see Figure 17-11): as the number of bystanders increased, the less likely it became that an individual would intervene. Even though the likelihood that a particular person will intervene declines as the number of bystanders increases, the likelihood that *someone* will intervene increases. This *bystander effect* has been observed in many different studies and in nearly 6000 subjects (Latane and Nida, 1981; Latane, Nida, and Wilson, 1981). On the average, people who are alone and become aware that someone needs help do intervene in about three-quarters of the cases. But in only half the cases do people intervene when others are present. When the bystanders can communicate, they are less likely to help a victim as their numbers increase. Why should the presence of others have this effect? Several explanations of the bystander effect have been offered.

A MODEL OF BYSTANDER INTERVENTION Before people run to rescue someone in trouble, they have to make five separate decisions (Latane and Darley, 1970). First, they have to *notice* that a situation may be an emergency. Second, they have to *interpret* the situation as an emergency. Third, they have to *assume* personal *responsibility* for acting in the situation. Fourth, they have to *decide* an appropriate *form* of assist-

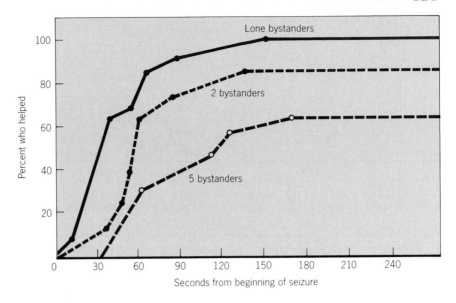

FIGURE 17-11 BYSTANDER INTERVENTION.
The percentage of students who intervened when they heard another person apparently suffering a seizure was strongly influenced by the number of bystanders present. When the students were alone, more than 90 percent intervened within the first 90 seconds. When five bystanders were present, fewer than 50 percent intervened within 90 seconds. (After Darley and Latane, 1968.)

ance. Finally, they would have to actually *provide* that assistance (see Figure 17-12). Whether other people are present can affect how people behave at each of the five steps. For example, in one of their experiments, in which people found themselves in a smoke-filled room, Latane and Darley (1968) observed that people who were waiting in groups attended closely to the questionnaires they were completing and took longer to *notice* the smoke. Similarly, when people are stimulated by busy, noisy streets, for example, their attention is distracted, and they are less likely to notice emergencies (Korte, Ypma, and Toppen, 1975; Weiner, 1976). A number of studies clearly indicate that the ambiguity of a situation also affects the likelihood of intervention. When people can clearly *interpret* a situation as an emergency, many of them—even those in groups—do intervene. For example, many people come to the aid of workers who have fallen and cried out in pain (Clark and Word, 1972) or asked for assistance (Yakimovitch and Saltz, 1971). Many stepped in when a man and woman were observed fighting, and the woman stated, "I don't know you!" (Shotland and Straw, 1976). Many also stepped in when a subway passenger carrying a cane fell as the train left the station (Piliavin, Rodin, and Piliavin, 1969). However, when a situation is ambiguous, the presence of others can produce what has been termed *pluralistic ignorance* (Latane and Darley, 1970). In these situations, people tend to rely on one another to interpret the situation as an emergency and to act appropriately. But onlookers may feel inhibited about taking action; they may worry about what others will think of them. No one wants to risk misinterpreting the situation, and no one wants to act like Chicken Little if the sky is not actually falling in. Of course, when everyone stands by waiting for someone else to act, no one acts at all.

Furthermore, when a number of people are present at an emergency there can be a *diffusion of responsibility.* The responsibility for action does not focus on a particular person, and so everyone looks to everyone else to assume responsibility. This reduced sense of personal responsibility is

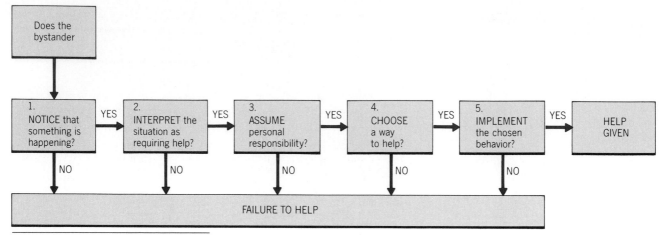

FIGURE 17-12 DARLEY AND LATANE'S 1970 FIVE-STEP MODEL OF EMERGENCY INTERVENTION.

precisely what researchers found when they interviewed witnesses to an emergency—80 percent of the witnesses who were not friends reported that they felt a personal obligation to intervene, but only 17 percent of those who were with friends reported this feeling of personal obligation (Schwartz and Gottlieb, 1980).

But other factors certainly influence whether people offer help in an emergency and increase their sense of responsibility even in the presence of others. People who are especially competent to respond to the situation are more likely to intervene than others (Schwartz, 1970). When researchers interviewed people who had actually intervened in dangerous crime situations such as armed robberies, bank holdups, and street muggings, they found that those who had some form of training in emergency procedures were much more likely to intervene than were people without such training (Figure 17-13) (Huston, Ruggerio, Conner, and Geis, 1981).

THE AROUSAL/COST–REWARD MODEL Assume that someone has noticed and appropriately interpreted a situation as an emergency, has

FIGURE 17-13 WHO INTERVENES IN VIOLENT CRIMES?
Comparisons of people who did and did not intervene in violent crimes revealed that those who intervened were not only heavier, taller, and considered themselves stronger, but also tended to have emergency training appropriate for the situation. (After Huston et al., 1981.)

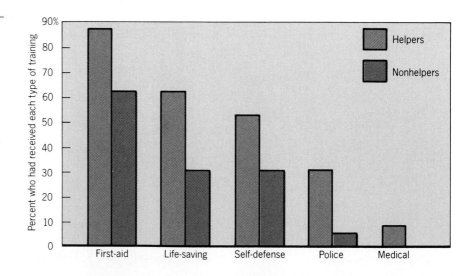

FIGURE 17-14   THE COSTS OF INTERVENTION.
Emergency intervention is most likely when the cost of helping is low and the cost of not helping is high. (After Clark, 1976.)

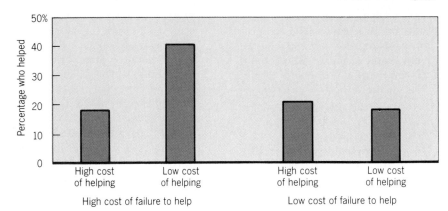

assumed some personal responsibility, and has formulated a plan for helping. What might prevent that person from offering help or prompt that person to act? The likelihood of intervention depends, it has been argued, on the person's level of emotional arousal and the costs or rewards of intervening (Piliavin, Dovidio, Gaertner, and Clark, 1981). According to the *arousal/cost–reward* model, onlookers experience arousal that is similar to but less than that of victims in an emergency. Onlookers are motivated to reduce this arousal in a manner that costs them less, and quickly calculate the relative costs of intervening or not intervening. Both intervening and not intervening carry personal costs and rewards. People who stop to help may lose time, may be inconvenienced, take the risk of earning others' disapproval and of being embarrassed. But they also stand to gain—others' approval, gratitude, pride in themselves, and other rewards. Similarly, the actions or inactions of onlookers also carry costs and rewards for the victim of an emergency, of course, which onlookers include in their calculations. People are more likely to intervene when they are quite aroused and when the balance of rewards and costs favors their intervention (Piliavin et al., 1981; see Figure 17-14). Furthermore, in clear, unambiguous emergencies, observers' levels of arousal may prompt them to intervene even in the face of extreme risks and low payoffs to themselves. Acts of extraordinary heroism do, in fact, seem to occur most often when heroes and heroines are extremely aroused.

SUMMARY

INTERPERSONAL ATTRACTION

1. *Affiliative Behavior.* Humans are social creatures and at times of stress appear to like the presence of others (unless the presence of others produces embarrassment). One theory of affiliation contends that the presence of others allows us to make social comparisons that help us to assess social reality. A second theory of affili- ation contends that the presence of others can help to reduce our arousal and anxiety.

2. *Reinforcement Theory of Attraction.* This theory postulates that we are attracted to specific people who are reinforcing to us. Exchange theorists contend that we like relationships in which we obtain the maximum rewards in exchange for the minimum costs. In this model attraction to others is based on comparison levels (what do we feel we deserve from the relationship?) and comparison levels for alternatives (what are the ratios or rewards to costs available in relationships with other people?). Equity theorists

argue that we are not strictly seeking to maximize the ratio of rewards to costs, but seek equitable relationships in which both members of the relationship enjoy similar reward-to-cost ratios.

3. *Antecedents of Attraction.* Among the many factors that are known to influence interpersonal attraction is propinquity—we tend to form friendships with people who are most accessible to us. We also tend to form relationships with people whose attitudes are similar to ours and with those who are more familiar to us.

One of the most important influences on interpersonal attraction and social interaction is physical appearance. Physically attractive people receive more social rewards such as popularity, job interviews, higher pay, and so on. Our stereotypes about attractive people are generally very positive, although attractive people are thought to be more vain and less faithful. Although intuitions may suggest that we tend to seek out the most attractive partners possible, in fact, people tend to seek out others who are similar in attractiveness—what has been termed the "matching principle."

SOCIAL INFLUENCE

4. *Conformity.* Conformity can be traced to two common causes. Sometimes people conform under informational social influence—in ambiguous situations we rely upon the judgments of others as a guide to assessing social reality. In other instances people may capitulate to the desires and judgments of others in response to normative social influences. When confronted with a group of other people who disagree with us, we may give way in order to avoid social rejection—even when we are fairly certain our judgments are correct.

5. *Obedience.* Dramatic social

events such as those in Nazi Germany and massacres supposedly executed in the name of higher authorities prompted social psychologists—notably Stanley Milgram—to investigate the causes of obedience to authority. These controversial studies demonstrated that a high proportion of ordinary people could be induced to do extraordinary things (deliver apparently dangerous shocks) to other people when prompted by authority figures. Obedience to the wishes of the authority were influenced by a number of situational factors such as the setting of the study, the proximity of the subject and confederate and the physical presence of the authority.

AGGRESSION

6. *Defining and Measuring Aggression.* Aggression and violence are widespread in our society and in our entertainment. Psychologists interested in the causes of aggression have examined "behavior that is intended to harm another person who does not want to be harmed." Studying aggression in experimental settings is obviously difficult for ethical reasons, and as a result laboratory researchers have often relied upon aggression machines that lead subjects to believe they are delivering shocks to other people—though in fact they are not.

7. *The Frustration–Aggression Hypothesis.* One of the most influential early theories of aggression postulated that any frustration in the achievement of a goal would lead to aggression. However it has been shown that frustration does not always lead to aggressions.

8. *The Revised Frustration–Aggression Hypothesis.* The revised frustration–aggression hypothesis takes account of the fact that frustration may increase the readiness

for aggression, but a variety of environmental and internal cues will determine whether frustration produces aggressive behavior. One emotional state, anger (which is often produced in laboratory research by having a confederate insult a subject), clearly increases aggressive behavior. General arousal can further facilitate aggression in people if they are angered. Other forms of arousal, such as sexual arousal, do not seem to increase aggression unless people have a negative reaction to the arousing material.

A number of situational factors have been shown to trigger irritation and arousal and promote aggression. These include the discomfort produced by hot weather and noxious noise. Similarly, alcohol—which may make people more irritable and less inhibited—is associated with greater aggression. When people learn aggressive behavior, they also learn a variety of cues to the aggression (such as the presence of weapons) that may later facilitate aggressive behavior.

9. *Social Learning and Aggression.* Many forms of aggressive behavior are undoubtedly learned—sometimes through direct reinforcement of aggressive behavior. Punishment—which is itself often aggressive—may actually promote aggression. People also learn aggressive behavior through observational learning. Models of aggressive behavior are most likely to be imitated when they are high in status, when they are the same gender as the observer, when the model's aggression has been rewarded, and when the aggression is realistic.

10. *Media Violence.* After more than two decades of scientific research, social psychologists have reached a general consensus that violence on television promotes aggression by children. This con-

clusion is based on laboratory research and on longitudinal studies of children over a period of more than 20 years. Recent research indicates that pornography that depicts aggression against women—particularly depictions in which the victims enjoy the aggression—can have a negative impact on viewers' attitudes. These effects are not limited to explicitly sexual materials, for similar attitude changes have been observed in males who viewed widely available R-rated films featuring aggression against women.

ALTRUISM

11. *Defining Altruism.* Narrowly defined, altruism refers to acts in which there is an intention to help, there is some cost to the helper, the helper has no expectation of an external reward, and the action produces favorable consequences for the recipient. There are a variety of explanations for why people behave altruistically.

12. *The Sociobiological Perspective.* Though natural selection would seem to favor selfish behavior, altruistic behavior is common across many species. Sociobiologists believe that such behaviors are maintained through kin selection and the survival of genes rather than the survival of the individual carriers of genes. When an animal or person performs an act that preserves another animal or person with whom the actor shares genes, the genes shared by the actor and the recipient of the altruistic act are preserved even though the altruist may not be.

13. *Learning Altruism and Social Norms.* As with other behaviors, altruism can be learned— through operant conditioning and through observation of altruistic acts performed by others.

Much of what we learn about altruism is in the form of social norms. The social-responsibility norm holds that we should give people what they deserve. The reciprocity norms hold that we should help and not hurt those who have helped us.

14. *Emergency Intervention.* Why do people sometimes respond altruistically to emergency situations and sometimes not? One explanation for inaction is the bystander effect. Laboratory and field experiments indicate that as the number of bystanders to an emergency situation increases, the likelihood that any one person will intercede declines.

Some factors promote intervention: people who possess skills that are appropriate for the emergency often feel more responsible and may have more effective plans of action. In addition, unambiguous emergencies, heightened states of arousal, and favorable balances between the rewards and costs of intervention may prompt bystanders to intervene.

FURTHER READINGS

In addition to the general resources mentioned at the end of Chapter 16, a number of volumes and chapters specifically address issues raised in this chapter. With regard to interpersonal attraction, some recent major volumes include *Personal Relationships,* a series of volumes edited by Stephen Duck and Robin Gilmour (1981–1984); *Intimate Relationships: Development, Dynamics, and Deterioration,* edited by Daniel Perlman and Stephen Duck (1986); *A New Look at Love* by Elaine Hatfield and Ellen Berscheid (1985); *The Physical Attractiveness Phenomena* by Gordon Patzer (1985); *Intimate Relationships* by Sharon Brehm (1985); and *Close Relationships* by Harold Kelley and his colleagues (1985).

Probably the classic work on social influence is *Obedience to Authority* in which Stanley Milgram discussed his series of research studies (1974). A more recent work on the topic is *Social Influence: Science and Practice* by Robert Cialdini (1985). *Social Influence* edited by Mark Zanna, James Olson, and Peter Herman (1987), includes a series of chapters by leading researchers. A chapter by Serge Moscovici in the *Handbook of Social Psychology* (3rd Ed., edited by Gardner Lindzey and Eliot Aronson, 1985) emphasizes social influence from the perspective of minorities. *Inside the Jury* by Reid Hastie, Steven Penrod, and Nancy Pennington (1983) provides a glimpse into social influence in operation in the courtroom.

Among the better general surveys of research on aggression are *Human Aggression* by Robert Baron (1977); *Aggression: Theoretical and Empirical Reviews* edited by Russell Geen and Edward Donnerstein (1983); Dennis Krebs and Dale Miller also discuss research on "Altruism and Aggression" in their *Handbook of Social Psychology* (1985) chapter. One of the most active areas of aggression research addresses the effects of violent and sexually explicit media. Among the recent volumes that review this research are *The Question of Pornography* by Edward Donnerstein, Daniel Linz, and Steven Penrod (1987); *Pornography and Sexual Aggression* edited by Neil Malamuth and Edward Donnerstein (1984); and an entire volume of the *Journal of Social Issues* edited by L. Rowell Huesmann and Neil Malamuth (1987).

In addition to these volumes that review research on altruism, the following works provide an overview of recent research and applications: *Altruistic Emotion, Cognition, and Behavior* by Nancy Eisenberg (1986); *New Directions in Helping: Help-Seeking,* edited by Bella DePaulo, Arie Nadler, and Jeffrey Fisher (1983); and *Emergency Intervention* by Jane Piliavin and her colleagues.

APPENDIX A

RESEARCH IN PSYCHOLOGY

THE RESEARCH METHODS OF PSYCHOLOGY

Psychologists study a wide range of phenomena, from the biochemistry of learning to international conflict, and therefore they have developed a broad set of methodological approaches that are of common interest and relevance to them in their various kinds of work. Just as psychologists share a general agreement about the assumptions and goals of scientific research, they also agree upon the value of a broad set of scientific research concepts and methods.

Hypothesis Generation and the Role of Theory

Theories of human behavior are among the most important accomplishments of psychology. Freud's psychoanalytic theory of human behavior, for example, profoundly altered the way that people think about such phenomena as unconscious motivation. The behaviorists' theory of stimulus and response, the sociobiologists' theory of the connection between genetic programs and social behavior, and social psychological theories about attitudes and behavior are just a few of the many theories within psychology. Theories are important first of all because they help psychologists to organize their knowledge about human behavior and provide coherent accounts of the causal relationships that govern that behavior. Theories also are important because they allow psychologists to make testable predictions about human behavior.

The process of theory development is in some ways circular (see Figure A-1). A good theory generates testable predictions. The results of tests of these predictions help psychologists to reevaluate our theories. If research results show the predictions were in error, then we go back to the theory and consider ways in which the theory can be reformulated to account for the error. If the research results show predictions were correct, then our confidence in the theory is increased, and we work to formulate additional tests of the theory.

Hypotheses are predictions that can be tested. For example, a psychologist might hypothesize that people who smile a lot are better liked than people who don't smile very much. Not all hypotheses are derived from theories. Sometimes psychologists are confronted with new phenomena that they do not really understand and therefore formulate some hypotheses as starting points for systematic research. Sometimes hypotheses are suggested by everyday experiences, popular knowledge and beliefs. Whatever their source, these theories must be subjected to systematic testing.

Null Hypothesis and Research

Suppose that we, as researchers, have formulated the hypothesis that people who smile a lot are better liked than people who don't smile very much. To test this hypothesis we might identify two acquaintances, one

FIGURE A-1   A
REPRESENTATION OF THE
COMPONENTS OF THE
SCIENTIFIC PROCESS.
[Adapted from Walter Wallace (Ed.),
Sociological Theory, 1969, p. ix.]

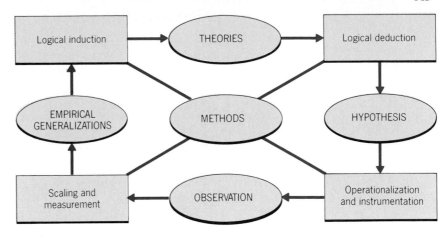

who smiles a lot and one who does not, and ask a number of people who know these two acquaintances to rate how well they like them (as we shall see, there are a number of problems with this method, but we will come to them shortly). We could then compare the ratings of the "smiler" with the ratings of the "nonsmiler." Our comparison of these ratings will actually allow us to evaluate two distinct hypotheses. The first hypothesis is termed the **null hypothesis** (*null* meaning "not any"). It states that any differences that we observe in the ratings of the smiler and the nonsmiler are not real differences but are due to chance or luck. In other words, according to the null hypothesis any differences in ratings do not reflect real, systematic differences in people's ratings of the smiler and nonsmiler. Perhaps the differences in ratings reflected the raters' feelings about something in the acquaintances' behavior other than their smiling, or perhaps they reflected extraneous feelings in the raters and had nothing to do with the smiling. Extraneous, random events are always at play in people's behavior, and researchers therefore must always distinguish between results that may have occurred by chance and those that may have occurred by the action of the behavior explicitly under study.

The second, or **research hypothesis**, states that the differences in the two facial expressions did influence the ratings of the people who made the ratings and the differences we have observed are not merely due to chance (see Figure A-2).

FIGURE A-2   RESEARCH
HYPOTHESES.
*The null and research hypotheses used in
a study of the effects of smiling on liking.*

NULL HYPOTHESIS: Any difference in the liking of Smilers and Non-smilers arises solely as a result of chance factors such as errors in measurement and natural variation in the raters themselves. Smiling in social interactions does not generally influence how well liked a person is.

RESEARCH HYPOTHESIS: Smiling influences the impressions that people make. All other things being equal, people who smile at other people will be better liked than people who do not smile at others. The differences in ratings of Smilers and Nonsmilers is *caused* by the differences in smiling.

Statistical Significance

The research hypothesis is supported only if we can rule out the null hypothesis. To rule out the null hypothesis, we must obtain a difference in ratings large enough that it cannot be attributed to chance events. For example, because we know that there are normally variations in people's reactions to others (whether or not the others smile a lot), we must find out whether the differences in ratings that we have observed might be due to the fact that we happened to question acquaintances of the "smiler" on a day when most of them happened to have especially warm feelings about all their friends. Thus, their high ratings might have had nothing to do with the fact the smiler smiles.

Researchers try to design their studies so carefully that they do not inadvertently contaminate their results with chance factors (a subject we discuss in the following section). They also rely on tests of **statistical significance** (discussed in the appendix to this textbook). A test of statistical significance is a test of probability. It is designed to answer how likely it is that an observed difference between groups could be produced by chance factors when there is no real difference between the groups. Only when a difference is so large that it is unlikely to have been produced by chance will a researcher be prepared to reject the null hypothesis and conclude there is some real difference between the two groups. In testing differences, most psychologists adopt the conventional level of statistical significance of $p < .05$. What this means is that the null hypothesis is rejected if the observed difference would appear fewer than 5 out of 100 times if the null hypothesis were true. In other words, psychologists reject the null hypothesis of "no difference" only when it is very unlikely to be true. Of course, because behavior is complex, even if psychologists find that the differences are large enough to warrant rejection of the null hypothesis, they unfortunately still cannot automatically assume that the research hypothesis is true. The difference might have been produced by a factor other than the one specified in the hypothesis.

Independent and Dependent Variables

In our study of one smiler and one nonsmiler, we researchers had no control over the smiling. We were interested in the effects of smiling on liking and, in essence, we hypothesized that smiling **caused** liking. In most instances researchers examine **variables** such as smiling and liking because they are interested in the causal relationships between those variables (Figure A-3). But unless researchers can **control** or **manipulate** their causal or **independent** variables and then examine the effects of these manipulations on the outcome or **dependent** variables, they can never be certain that causal variables are having the hypothesized effects on the outcome variables (Figure A-3). Researchers may be able to observe correlations or simultaneous changes in the two types of variables, but that would not prove one variable caused the other. Indeed, we might repeat our little study with a hundred pairs of smilers and nonsmilers and observe that smiling and liking are almost invariably linked. But, and this is an important but, we could never really be certain, using

FIGURE A-3   THE
RELATIONSHIP BETWEEN
INDEPENDENT AND DEPENDENT
VARIABLES.

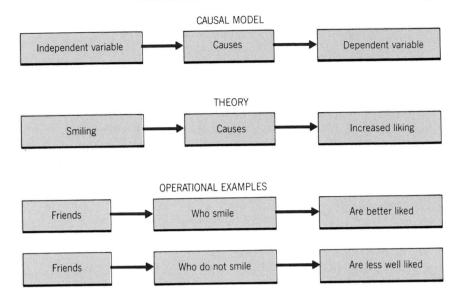

the method described above, that we did not have the causal relation reversed: maybe people who are well-liked are happier and therefore smile more! It may even be possible that some third variable (such as "success in life") causes people to smile *and* be liked. As it turns out, experimental methods give us a way to resolve such problems.

The Validity and Reliability of Variables

Earlier we discussed operational definitions—these are the operations or actions that embody the independent variable and the measures that embody the dependent variables. Sometimes it may be difficult to devise an effective operational definition. This is especially true in situations where researchers are working with highly abstract concepts. How, for instance, should researchers operationalize "stress"? How can and should "intelligence" be measured? When is behavior "aggressive"? What is "happiness"? One general answer to this type of question is that psychologists often try a variety of operational definitions. Subjects are, for instance, "stressed" in a variety of ways. Sometimes they are subjected to loud and unpredictable noises, sometimes they are crowded together in small, overheated rooms, sometimes they are asked to drink lots of coffee (caffeine is a stimulant), sometimes they are told that they are going to be making a public presentation to a large audience.

All of these operational definitions of stress possess some **face validity**. That is, most of us recognize that we would be stressed under the conditions described. But maybe these operations represent different things (arousal? discomfort?). Only by employing a number of alternative operational definitions can psychologists determine that some or all of these operational definitions produce similar effects on subjects. If the variables all seem to be related in terms of their effects, psychologists talk in terms of **construct validity**. This means that researchers have reached some agreement about what the underlying concept or construct ("stress") is and some agreement on how it should be operationalized and measured.

One other characteristic of variables ought to be mentioned. Have you ever had a bathroom scale that registered a different weight each time you stepped on it (even over a period of a few seconds)? That scale was probably a valid measure of weight, but it lacked **reliability**. A reliable measure is one that yields identical results when conditions are identical, for example, a wooden yardstick can produce reliable measures of your height.

Many psychological measures are not entirely reliable. Imagine, for instance, that you took an intelligence test this morning and then took the test again late this evening. Aside from the fact that you probably learned something about the test from taking it in the morning, you probably would not receive the same score in both sessions anyway. You might be fresher, more attentive, even more motivated in the morning than in the evening. A lower evening score certainly should not be the basis for concluding that you are losing IQ points as time goes by. In fact, the general assumption is that intelligence is fairly stable, although testing procedures introduce some unreliability into the measures. Similar reliability problems can obviously arise when measuring variables such as liking in our smiling studies.

Experimental Control: Manipulation of Independent Variables

In experimental studies, the researcher exercises control over the independent or causal variable and frequently can manipulate when or how much of the independent variable is present at any given time. Let's return to our hypothesis about the effects of smiling on people's liking of one another. We have postulated that all other things being equal, a person who smiles at others is going to be better liked than a person who maintains a neutral expression. We might test our hypothesis by conducting a true experiment. To do so we could set up a situation in which a single individual (someone who is collaborating with us in our research) interacts with a series of strangers. In order not to alert the strangers to the true purpose of our study (if we told them we were interested in the effects of smiling on liking, that knowledge might affect their behavior), we engage in a mild deception. We might characterize these interactions as a "get acquainted session." In order to assure that all strangers are treated essentially alike (remember, "all other things being equal"), our collaborator may have a fixed script to follow while interacting with these strangers.

To test our hypothesis about smiling experimentally, we must also manipulate our independent variable: smiling. Thus, we set up the "get acquainted" situation so that with half the subjects the collaborator smiles consistently, and with the other half the collaborator keeps a neutral facial expression. At the end of each session, we ask the stranger to privately rate the extent to which he or she liked the partner in this "get acquainted situation." Let's suppose that we do observe the differ-

FIGURE A-4   AN EXAMPLE OF THE DESIGN OF A RESEARCH EXPERIMENT THAT EXAMINES THE EFFECT OF SMILING ON LIKING.

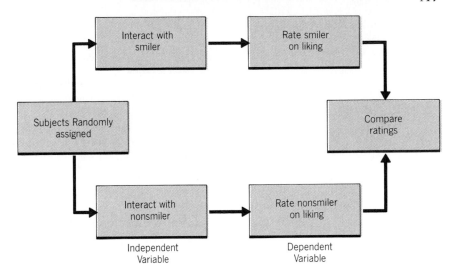

ence that we predicted: strangers liked the smiling collaborator better than the collaborator with the neutral expression and the difference is statistically significant (see Figure A-4). If we have designed our experiment properly and observed the experimental research guidelines that we discuss later, we may well be able to rule out the null hypothesis. But does this *prove* our research hypothesis? Unfortunately, it does not, for there are other grounds on which our conclusions can be questioned.

Internal Validity

Suppose that somebody comes along and challenges the **internal validity** of our study. Our study would be internally valid if our smiling manipulation truly had produced the rating differences. But our critic argues that we didn't successfully manipulate smiling (perhaps the confederate was not a very good actor), and so the results must be attributed to something else. What is more, says the critic, we inadvertently have provided support for a different research hypothesis. We have shown not that the difference observed between the two groups is directly caused by smiling but that a person who smiles also speaks in a more animated and attentive manner. The critic's **rival hypothesis** is that it is really the animation and attention that are producing the observed differences in liking.

The critic asserts that we have **confounded** or mixed up these variables so that we cannot accurately determine whether smiling or animation produced the results (see Figure A-5). Can you design an experiment in which smilers and nonsmilers are sometimes animated and sometimes not animated in order to eliminate the possible confound? As long as there are rival alternative hypotheses available, it is essentially impossible to prove the validity of the theory that generated the original research hypothesis. We may be able to effectively rule out rival alternative hypotheses by demonstrating in soundly designed experiments that the predictions made in those alternative hypotheses are not supported

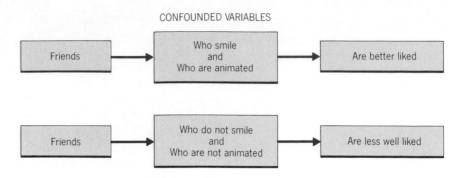

by experimental results, but we can never be entirely certain that someone else won't come along with a new theory and generate yet another plausible rival hypothesis.

Random Assignment of Subjects

Yet another critic might point out that our two groups of strangers were not really different from one another. Perhaps we unwittingly assigned males to the "smile" condition and females to the "nonsmile" condition. Our ratings might be attributable to a difference between males and females. You might react by saying, Well, I can see that we should have made sure that the two groups were as much alike as possible by **matching** the characteristics of subjects in both groups. Perhaps we should have identified every characteristic that could be related to liking others. We should have asked how attractive each subject is, how outgoing and personable each subject is, whether the subject is male or female, how mature the subject is, how similar the confederate is to the subject, and so on. But as you can see the problem with matching subjects in the two groups is that the list of matching variables quickly grows very long and it may become very difficult to find matches.

The alternative to matching is **random assignment** of subjects to the different experimental conditions. What happens if, as each subject enters our lab, we flip a coin and send all "heads" to be smiled at and all "tails" not to be smiled at? The answer is that by chance alone, approximately half the males, half the females, half the attractive people, half the mature subjects, indeed, half of every type of subject we can (and cannot) think of should end up receiving smiles, and half should end up not receiving smiles. By randomly assigning subjects to conditions, we have, in effect, assured that the two groups will not be significantly different.

External Validity

So far, so good. We have done everything right and are feeling confident about our results and the support it lends to our theory. But along comes another critic who argues, Your laboratory experiment is a nice demonstration that smiling *can* affect liking, but I doubt that your results

generalize to the real world. In other words, the study may be internally valid, but it is not **externally valid**. The challenge to external validity can take many forms. Some may argue that the laboratory study lacked realism and that its results would not generalize to settings and situations in which subjects had more at stake than a few post-session ratings. Some may argue that the results are true only for undergraduates and that if the experiment were run with more mature adults, smiling would not affect liking. Still others might argue that the results are solely attributable to some quirky characteristic in our confederate and that most people could not significantly affect the impressions they make by smiling or not smiling at strangers.

The most effective way to respond to critiques about the external validity of studies is to repeat or replicate the study using a wide variety of situations and settings, with a wide variety of confederates, a wide variety of subjects, and a wide variety of interrelated manipulations of the independent variable. A single experimental study is seldom regarded as conclusive evidence. Psychologists recognize that all studies and findings are strengthened by replications.

Experimental Settings

Experiments are conducted in laboratory settings and as **field experiments** outside of the laboratory. You probably know, for example, about true experiments that have been conducted with actual patients who have been randomly assigned to receive new experimental drugs and treatments. In order to evaluate psychotherapies, a number of experimental studies have been conducted in which patients are randomly assigned to receive different types of therapy. True field experiments also have been employed in schools to test new teaching techniques, and in the criminal justice system to evaluate different methods for instructing juries about the law. As with all experiments, researchers in these studies exercised control over the independent variable by determining, generally through random assignment, who received the drug, who would be taught in the new way, and who would receive the new form of legal instructions.

Threats to Experimental Research

Because conducting experimental research can be a complex affair, researchers must be sensitive to several additional research problems.

EXPERIMENTER EFFECTS   Whenever researchers are working with human subjects (and sometimes when working with nonhumans), it is important for the researchers to be aware that their behavior may influence the responses of their subjects. Researchers must be careful to respond to subjects in all experimental conditions in the same way. They must not smile or nod approvingly only at those in one condition. They must say the same things in the same ways, and behave to those in the experimental condition just as they behave to those in another. Research on experimenter effects (Rosenthal and Rosnow, 1969) has convincingly demonstrated that research subjects are very sensitive to what researchers say and do and that subjects' behavior can be influenced even by very subtle nonverbal cues, such as tone of voice, facial expression, and the like.

Careful researchers can avoid experimenter effects by doing such things as keeping the collaborators on the research team who come into contact with subjects in the dark or blind about research hypotheses or about which experimental group a subject is in. To avoid situations in which experimenters and subjects can influence outcomes, researchers frequently use **double-blind** research designs in which neither the experimenter nor the subject knows which experimental condition a subject is in or the hypothesized effects of the experiment.

SUBJECT EFFECTS   Much of the laboratory research conducted by psychologists makes use of volunteer undergraduate subjects. But does laboratory research on college students generalize well to other subject populations? Some psychologists have attempted to determine the answer to this question (Rosenthal and Rosnow, 1969, 1975). Among other differences, it is clear that volunteer subjects tend to be better educated, younger, less conventional, and more intelligent than the general population. Awareness of subject characteristics helps psychologists exercise caution when it comes to generalizing their findings.

Nonexperimental Research Methods

You will see throughout this textbook a large number of studies that have used nonexperimental methods. Psychologists and other scientists generally prefer to use experimental methods because the degree of control they allow also allows them to reach more definite conclusions about causal relationships. However, there are many instances in which it is impossible for researchers to conduct true experiments because the researchers cannot manipulate independent variables. For example, many psychologists are interested in the differences between males and females, but it is clearly impossible for researchers to randomly assign people to be males and females. Even though it is more difficult to make

TABLE A-1   A SUMMARY OF THE STRENGTHS AND WEAKNESSES OF RESEARCH METHODS

	Internal Validity	External Validity	Experimenter Control	Resistance to Experimenter Bias	Ethical Problems	Ease of Conducting Study
Content analyses	moderate	moderate	weak	moderate	few	very easy
Archival studies	weak	moderate	weak	strong	few	very easy
Case studies	weak	weak	weak	weak	many	moderate
Field observations	weak	weak	weak	weak	many	moderate
Surveys	moderate	moderate	moderate	moderate	some	moderate
Quasi-experiments	strong	moderate	moderate	moderate	few	most difficult
Lab experiments	strong	moderate	strong	moderate	some	moderate
Field experiments	moderate	strong	strong	moderate	some	most difficult

Adapted from Penrod, 1986.

unambiguous causal judgments using nonexperimental methods, such methods are nonetheless important tools for researchers. (For a look at the strengths and weaknesses of several research methods, see Table A-1.) Psychologists use a wide variety of nonexperimental methods.

ARCHIVAL STUDIES   **Archives** are places where public records and documents are stored. Researchers study archives to learn about natural patterns in behavior and events. Public records about the economy, for example, are invaluable to economists who want to understand the relationships between such things as government and private spending, inflation and unemployment, and so on. Archives also can serve as important sources of information about phenomena of interest to psychologists. For instance, psychologists have used public records to study a variety of social conditions such as marriage and divorce rates; crime, suicide, and hospitalization rates; mental health treatment; family size, employment rates of mothers; and (by consulting old public opinion polls) changes in public attitudes and values.

The archival method has the advantages of being unobtrusive and not requiring interaction with the people who originally supplied the data. Because it is unobtrusive, it eliminates the possibility that people's responses will be influenced by the fact that they have been asked to give a direct response to the researcher. Other advantages to the archival method are that the data already exist, may be readily available, may be highly reliable, and may provide a record spanning many years. But the method's disadvantages are that sometimes the appropriate data may not exist, may be hard to locate, and may take a lot of time to reduce to analyzable form.

CONTENT ANALYSES   One increasingly popular nonexperimental method is called **content analysis**. It is designed to allow researchers to evaluate systematically the qualitative aspects of documents and communications. The method can be illustrated with an example. Many psychologists have been interested in the effects of television violence on children's behavior and attitudes. Naturally, one of the questions that arises is how violent is television? Although psychologists can answer this question in part by polling people and asking them their opinions, a more systematic method is to record the acts of violence that appear on television. One researcher therefore might simply record the number of times each hour during prime time that someone is injured by another. A second researcher might record how many times an hour injury is just threatened or aggression rewarded. Content analyses allow researchers a way to quantify and to operationally define forms of behavior recorded in books, films, public documents, and other archives. Through careful description of the archival method used, researchers also can replicate one another's studies.

OBSERVATIONAL STUDIES   In an **observational** study, a researcher is typically on the scene and trying to record systematically the events she observes. The psychologists who go to a family's house to record the behavior of a mother and infant, who enter a school classroom to study the students, who record data on workers in offices and factories all are observers. There are a variety of observational methods. In a **case study**, a researcher or group of researchers may concentrate on a single person, group, or event for study. When researchers are part of the group or events being studied, they are called **participant observers**.

In one of the best-known participant observation studies conducted by psychologists, a group of researchers faked insanity in order to secure admission to mental hospitals (Rosenhan, 1973). The researchers were able to document a number of ways in which hospital procedures made it difficult for anyone to seem normal. One of the major problems with observational methods is that researchers may find it difficult to maintain an objective stance toward the people or events being studied. A second common problem arises when only one observer is used, because perhaps someone else would have seen things differently.

SURVEYS   The nonexperimental research method that is probably most familiar is the **survey**. Surveys are used to assess people's attitudes and to gather information from them about their behavior. Psychologists have used surveys to learn about such things as the sexual behavior of adults, personality characteristics, children's after-school activities, and the relation between an infant's intelligence and the number of stimulating objects in the house he or she lives in. So common are surveys that chances are very good that you have participated in more than one survey. Perhaps you have even assisted in conducting a survey. Surveys are conducted so that the researcher can learn about the characteristics of a particular **population**. The population can be very large (all eligible voters in the United States) or fairly small (all the members of your introductory psychology class). When the population is large, it is often inconvenient to survey everyone. In such circumstances, surveyors generally will take a **random sample** from the population—for example, select at random one of every ten names on a list of eligible voters. By surveying the population at random, the surveyors minimize the possibility that the people they survey are somehow unrepresentative of the population.

There are a number of survey techniques. Surveys can be conducted by telephone, or they can be conducted in personal interviews in which the surveyor speaks directly to the person being surveyed. Surveys also can be conducted by mail. No matter which method they use, surveyors must be aware of potential survey problems. Interviewers must be carefully trained so that they do not influence responses. Questionnaires have to be carefully worded so they are not confusing, not embarrassing ("What are your favorite sexual practices?"), and not biased ("When did you stop beating your dog?"). The sample of people surveyed has to be carefully constructed to assure that results will generalize to the intended population.

One type of questionnaire that you probably have encountered is the **personal inventory**. Personal inventories are self-report instruments commonly used to assess a person's aptitudes and interests. Psychologists can use them to determine whether someone is likely to be happy and successful as a pilot, psychologist, social worker, salesperson, or engineer. Personal inventories are also often used for purposes of clinical and personality assessment. Clinical inventories are used to determine whether a person is seriously depressed or suffering from some psychiatric disturbance. Personality inventories are used to assess normal personality traits such as dominance, achievement, and nurturance.

QUASI-EXPERIMENTS Although psychologists may not always be able to manipulate or control independent variables, in many situations they can take advantage of naturally occurring events in order to get one step closer to a true experiment. For example, some social psychologists have been interested in the deterrent effects of the death penalty. They wonder how to determine whether the death penalty deters crime. Certainly they cannot conduct a true experiment by randomly assigning convicted killers to be executed. An alternative is to compare crime rates in states that do and do not have a death penalty. Such nonexperimental studies have not convincingly demonstrated a deterrence effect, but there are, as we have seen, a number of ways to challenge the results of nonexperimental research. Another alternative is to look at crime rates in states before and after the death penalty has been instituted. These studies also have not convincingly demonstrated that the death penalty has a deterrent effect.

Quasi-experimental studies make use of naturally occurring manipulations. Although these natural manipulations do not achieve the kind of control characteristic of true experiments (among other things, subjects are not randomly assigned to experimental conditions), quasi-experimental methods do provide a stronger basis than nonexperimental methods from which to infer causal relationships. In addition, quasi-experimental methods can be used in almost any kind of setting: they are appropriate for evaluating the effects of new programs and procedures in schools, businesses, hospitals and clinics, courts and jails, and many other settings. Quasi-experimental research is often used to test whether laboratory research findings generalize to the everyday world beyond the laboratory walls.

Research Ethics

Not only does each research method have its particular advantages and disadvantages (see Table A-1), it may also raise particular ethical issues. For example, researchers who conduct clinical trials of a new drug's effect on disease must wrestle with ethical problems such as what to do if the drug harms patients, and what to do if those in the untreated group clearly are suffering harm from not receiving treatment. Researchers conducting observational studies must avoid invading the privacy of those they study or evoking harmful behavior from them. How is a researcher to study aggression without *causing* aggression? Researchers also must avoid injuries such as embarrassment or loss of self-esteem to subjects.

HARMFUL EFFECTS Some psychological research unquestionably has harmful consequences. Perhaps the best example of this is research on animals that may permanently damage or even kill them. Much of this research is conducted with rats, but some of it involves rabbits, dogs, cats, and primates, animals that readily evoke human sympathy. Researchers, no matter what type of subject they use, must consider the possibly harmful consequences of their research on their subjects. Whenever there are potential or real harmful consequences for subjects, psychologists determine whether there are alternative, less harmful, methods available. They also determine that any possibly harmful consequences are outweighed by the need for scientific knowledge, and make every effort to assure that subjects do not suffer unnecessarily.

DECEPTION AND INFORMED CONSENT We have already noted that the results from studies involving human subjects may be biased if subjects are aware of the purposes or hypotheses underlying the studies. The most common method researchers use to protect the integrity of experiments is to not advise subjects about the true intent of a study until the study is completed. Psychologists do not use deception unless it is necessary to assure the validity of the experiment, and they minimize the amount of deception they do engage in. Psychologists convey as much essential information as possible about a study before subjects begin participation.

People do not want to step into an experiment in which they might be hurt, insulted, or made to look foolish. Researchers construct their studies to minimize such risks. Researchers fully inform subjects about any known harmful consequences they might experience and request the subjects' **informed consent** to participate despite the risks. Without such knowledge, consent to participate can hardly be termed "informed." Risks or not, psychologists do not coerce subjects into participating. Finally, researchers fully **debrief** or inform subjects about the true nature of the study once the subjects have completed their participation.

Research is essential to the progress of psychology, and psychologists have endeavored to assure that their research and their research methods are ethically sound and worthy of public support. Virtually all researchers must submit their plans to institutional review boards for scrutiny and supervision. These boards are typically composed of members from the research community and from the public. They provide an invaluable service in protecting the public, in protecting research subjects, and in helping researchers to make ethical decisions.

SUMMARY

THE RESEARCH METHODS OF PSYCHOLOGY

1. *Hypothesis Testing.* Scientific tests of hypotheses require the evaluation of the null hypothesis, which states that any differences we observe in outcomes is the product of chance or luck, and the research hypothesis, which states that the differences we observe reflect true differences, rather than chance factors. Hypotheses are evaluated with tests of statistical significance. The null hypothesis is typically re-

jected and the research hypothesis accepted if observed differences would arise by chance alone fewer than 5 times in 100 ($p < .05$).

2. *Independent and Dependent Variables.* Psychologists examine independent variables in order to determine their causal effects on dependent variables.

3. *The Validity and Reliability of Variables.* Psychologists always seek reliable measures—measures that produce identical results under identical conditions. Operational definitions of constructs possess face validity if they appear to measure what they are intended to measure. If a set of alternative operational definitions intended to measure the same construct all seem to be related in their effects, the variables may be said to possess construct validity. If an experimenter has successfully manipulated a variable in the intended manner and any effects can be attributed to the manipulation, then the experiment possesses internal validity. And if the results of an experiment can appropriately be generalized to other people and other settings, researchers have greater confidence in the external validity of the experiment.

4. *Experimental Control.* Experimental studies require that a researcher manipulate or experimentally control independent variables. Experimental control fa-

cilitates the study of causal relationships.

5. *Random Assignment of Subjects.* Though it is desirable to perfectly match the characteristics of subjects in the different groups used in an experiment, it is usually impossible to match subjects on all possible characteristics. A practical alternative to matching is to randomly assign subjects to experimental conditions; this assures that there are no systematic differences between the groups.

6. *Threats to Experimental Research.* Experimenters must take steps to assure that they do not communicate their expectations about experiments to their subjects. Subjects in all experimental conditions should be treated in the same way. Under some circumstances it is desirable to use double-blind procedures in which neither the experimenter nor the subject knows the experimental condition into which the subject has been placed.

7. *Nonexperimental Research Methods.* A wide variety of nonexperimental research methods are employed by psychologists. Archival studies analyze public records and documents found in archives. Content analyses are quantitative studies of the contents of books, films, television, and other documents. Observational studies may be conducted by researchers who observe naturally occurring events; these observers

may even be participants in those events. Surveys are used to assess attitudes and learn about behavior. Common survey methods include public opinion polls and personal inventories. When researchers take advantage of naturally occurring events and treat these events as though they were experimental manipulations, the researchers are using quasi-experimental methods.

8. *Research Ethics.* Psychologists conduct their research in an ethical manner. This means that experimental subjects—whether humans or animals—are never subjected to unnecessary harms, studies are designed so they do not invade the privacy of subjects, and subjects are fully informed about the possible consequences of participation in research so they may exercise informed consent.

FURTHER READINGS

There are a number of highly readable volumes on research methods and design. These include *Research Methods in Social Relations* (5th Ed.) by Louise Kidder and Charles Judd (1986); *Essentials of Behavioral Research* by Robert Rosenthal and Ralph Rosnow (1984); *Research Methods in Psychology* (2nd Ed.) by David Elmes, Barry Kantowitz, and Henry Roediger (1985); and *Research Methods in Psychology* by John Shaughnessy and Eugene Zechmeister (1985).

APPENDIX B

STATISTICS

> *Some people use statistics the way a drunkard uses a lamppost—for support rather than illumination.*
>
> H. L. Mencken

As this quotation suggests, statistics are tools to help people shed light on what otherwise might be difficult to see. You probably already use statistics every day. When you read that a public opinion poll found that 52 percent of people favor, say, lower taxes, 40 percent oppose them, and 8 percent are undecided, you are using statistics. When you see a chart in a magazine showing how the inflation rate has increased or decreased over the past 20 years, you are using statistics. The purpose of statistics is to help people understand the results of observations they have made. In this appendix, we show you the basics of how statistics help people describe their observations and make inferences about them. It will help you to understand the information in this textbook and in newspapers, in magazines, and on television.

Let's begin with a simple example. Suppose that you are a clinical psychologist who has devised an insightful new treatment for people who have an eating disorder and who are severely underweight. (Disorders of this kind are discussed in Chapter 10.) Naturally, it is important for you and for your future patients to know whether your new treatment really works. So you design an experiment to test whether the outcome for patients who receive your new treatment is better than the outcome for patients who receive the standard treatment. To test this outcome you measure, among other things, the actual body weight of patients at the end of treatment. You find, to your pleasure, that many of the patients who received the new treatment weigh more at the end of the experiment than those who received the standard treatment. How will you describe this result to other clinical psychologists who may wish to use your new treatment or to future patients? They may want to know how much patients in each group weigh after treatment, the size of the difference between the two groups, whether some or all of the patients improve, and so on. **Descriptive statistics** are the tools that allow you to answer these questions concisely and precisely. They are methods for describing and summarizing a set of observations.

DESCRIPTIVE STATISTICS

To show your results, your first step might be to construct a simple table. For example, Table B-1 lists the body weights for patients in both groups at the end of treatment. A table of this sort is useful because now another psychologist can compare the actual final weights of patients in the two groups. But a table like this is a cumbersome way to describe results, especially if there are many observations. Imagine if there were 50 or 100 patients in each group! It might be more helpful to plot a frequency distribution for each treatment group.

TABLE B-1 HYPOTHETICAL RESULTS OF
WEIGHT-CONTROL TREATMENTS

Standard Treatment		*New Treatment*	
Patient	*Weight (lb)*	*Patient*	*Weight (lb)*
1	105	1	101
2	82	2	92
3	96	3	110
4	86	4	86
5	101	5	105
6	75	6	115
7	90	7	89
8	80	8	107
9	92	9	101
10	90	10	97
11	101	11	105
12	82	12	95
13	99	13	101
14	87	14	112
15	90	15	89
	Total (ΣX): 1356		Total (ΣX): 1505
	Mean $(\overline{X})$: 90.4		Mean $(\overline{X})$: 100.3

Note: Hypothetical body weights of patients given a standard treatment and patients given a new treatment for an eating disorder. The 30 patients would have been randomly assigned to each treatment condition at the beginning of the experiment so that the two groups initially consisted of patients who were similar in all important respects, such as age, sex, and initial body weight.

Frequency Distributions

A **frequency distribution** simply shows the number (frequency) of people with a particular score, in this case body weight. Figure B-1 graphs the frequency distributions of the information in Table B-1. The graph lets another person compare the two groups at a glance. When a frequency distribution appears as a bar graph, as in Figure B-1, it is called a *histogram*. When a frequency distribution appears as a graph in which the frequency values are connected with lines, as in Figure B-2, it is called a *polygon*.

The polygons in Figure B-2 illustrate some of the characteristic shapes of frequency distributions. For Neighborhood 1, annual incomes are fairly similar among the households. Most of the households earn between $25,000 and $40,000 a year, and the remaining households are distributed evenly to either side of the middle-income scores. This type of frequency distribution has a *symmetrical* shape. In Neighborhood 2, many households have relatively low incomes, and a few have high incomes. This type of distribution, with a peak to one side and a long tail, is a *skewed* distribution. In this example the distribution is skewed to the right. If the peak were on the right and the long tail were on the left (a wealthy neighborhood with a few poor households), the distribution would be skewed to the left. In Neighborhood 3, many households have relatively low incomes, many have high incomes, and a few are in be-

FIGURE B-1 FREQUENCY DISTRIBUTIONS OF THE BODY-WEIGHT SCORES FROM TABLE B-1.
Body weight is given on the horizontal axis (abscissa), and the number of patients with each weight is given on the vertical axis (ordinate).

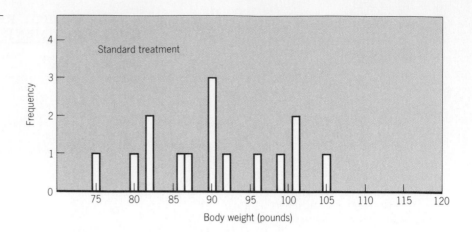

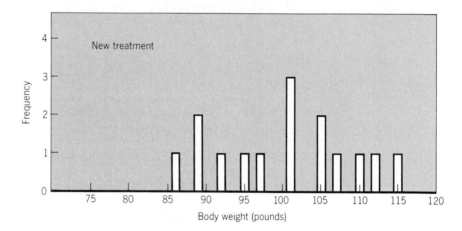

tween. This kind of distribution, with two peaks, is a *bimodal* frequency distribution.

Frequency distributions like those in Figures B-1 and B-2 are very useful for describing results, and you can see many such graphs throughout this book. But psychologists also have to be able to describe their results numerically. For example, in your experiment on treating eating disorders, you might like to summarize the patients' weights so that you can concisely and precisely tell colleagues what you found. Two different descriptive statistics provide such a summary. They are measures of central tendency and measures of variability.

Measures of Central Tendency

Measures of central tendency include measures of the mean, median, and mode of sets of figures. All of these measures describe the *center* of a set of scores. The most commonly used measure of central tendency is the familiar arithmetic average, or **mean**. To obtain the mean, first add all the scores.

$$\Sigma X = X_1 + X_2 + X_3 + \ldots$$

FIGURE B-2 CHARACTERISTIC SHAPES OF FREQUENCY DISTRIBUTIONS.

These frequency distributions represent hypothetical data for annual income of households in three different neighborhoods. The abscissa shows annual income in $5000 intervals (for example, $20,000 to $25,000, $25,000 to $30,000, and so on). The ordinate shows the number of households with each interval of income. There are three different shapes of distributions: symmetrical, skewed, *and* bimodal.

Neighborhood 1

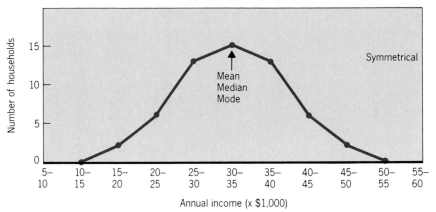

Neighborhood 2

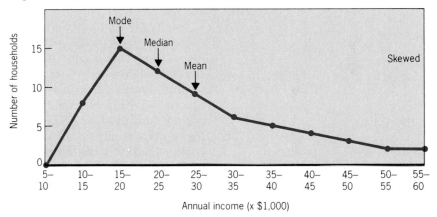

Neighborhood 3

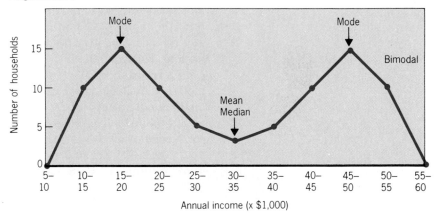

The Greek letter Σ, *sigma,* is a symbol that means *to sum.* The sum of the individual scores (ΣX) is divided by the total number of scores (N), and this gives the mean $(\overline{X})$.

$$\overline{X} = \frac{\Sigma X}{N}$$

For the results of your experiment shown in Table B-1, the mean weight of patients receiving the standard treatment is 90.4 pounds, and the mean weight of patients receiving the new treatment is 100.3 pounds. Now you can readily tell a colleague that, on average, patients receiving your new treatment weighed about 10 pounds more than those receiving the standard treatment.

Another common measure of central tendency is the **median**. It is the middle score of the set. Half the scores are higher than the median and half are lower. An easy way to find the median is to list the scores from lowest to highest and to count to the middle score. For the results in Table B-1, the median weight for patients in the Standard Treatment condition is 90 pounds and the median for the New Treatment condition is 100 pounds. If there is an even number of scores (for example, 14 instead of 15), the median is the score halfway between the two middle scores.

Scientists often prefer to use the mean over the median since, in calculating the mean the values of all scores are included, whereas the median reflects only the middle score and ignores the exact values of the high and low scores. But in some cases scientists do prefer to use the median. For example, consider what would happen if patient 9 in the Standard Treatment condition began to overeat and weighed in at 215 pounds instead of 92 pounds! The mean weight for the Standard Treatment group would be 98.6 pounds instead of 90.4 pounds. That figure of 98.6 pounds is somewhat misleading as a measure of *central* tendency, because it is influenced so much by one very extreme and atypical score. But the median is unaffected by this single atypical score; it remains 90 pounds. In general, when there are one or a few extreme scores in a distribution, the median reflects the central tendency better than the mean.

A third measure of central tendency is the **mode**, which is simply the most frequent score in a distribution. In the Standard Treatment condition, the mode is 90 pounds, and in the New Treatment condition it is 100 pounds. Scientists do not often use the mode because it can be misleading. For example, if there are relatively few scores in a distribution, even a relatively small change in one score can dramatically change the mode. Thus if patient 7 in the Standard Treatment condition weighed 101 pounds instead of 90 pounds, the mode would increase from 90 to 101 pounds. The mode does have some uses, though. For instance, for Neighborhood 3 in Figure B-2, we can say that annual income had two modes—of $15,000 to $20,000 and $45,000 to $50,000—which is more informative than saying that the mean or median income was $30,000 to $35,000.

As you can see in Figure B-2, the mean, median, and mode are the same for symmetrical distributions. However, they may differ considerably for other types of distributions. For example, if the distribution is skewed to the right (as in the middle distribution in Figure B-2), the value of the mean is higher than the median and the median is higher than the mode. Thus, when you are given a measure of central tendency, you need to know the shape of the distribution in order to interpret it properly.

Measures of Variability

Let's return now to your experiment comparing treatments for eating disorders. You want to tell people how consistent the results are from patient to patient and to say whether or not all patients given a particular treatment weigh about the same amount. **Measures of variability** provide the answer. They indicate the amount of spread of the scores around the center.

Perhaps the most obvious measure of variability is the **range**, the difference between the highest and lowest scores in the distribution. For the Standard Treatment condition, the range of body weights is 105 minus 75, or 30 pounds. For the New Treatment condition, the range is 115 minus 86, or 29 pounds. Although you can quickly and easily calculate the range, it reflects only the values of the two most extreme scores and does not reveal the spread of the other scores between the two extremes. Figure B-3 illustrates this problem. It clearly shows that the distributions of exam scores of two classes in introductory psychology are very different. In Class 1, all but a few scores are clustered around

FIGURE B-3 DIFFERENCES IN VARIABILITY.

Shown are hypothetical final exam scores obtained by students in two different Introduction to psychology classes. The abscissa shows exam scores in 5-point intervals. The ordinate shows the number of students with a score in each interval. The exam results are graphed separately for each psychology class. There are 96 students in Class 1 and, with only a few exceptions, they all got very similar scores. There are 114 students in Class 2, and their scores were much more variable.

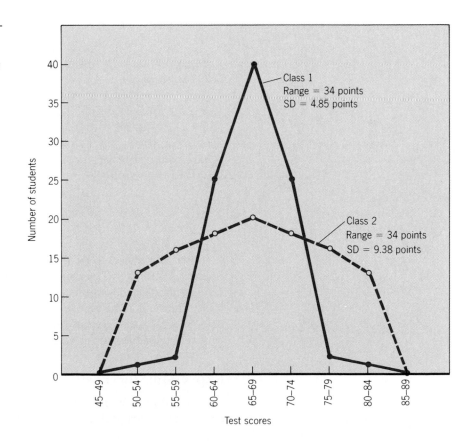

Class 1
Range = 34 points
SD = 4.85 points

Class 2
Range = 34 points
SD = 9.38 points

the center of the distribution. In Class 2, the scores are more dispersed. Yet the range ($84 - 50 = 34$ points) is exactly the same for both distributions.

How can we devise a measure of variability that will reflect the differences between the two distributions in Figure B-3? What we want is a measure of variability that takes all scores into account. So we might begin by determining the difference between each exam score (X) and the mean ($\overline{X}$) for the class:

$$X - \overline{X}$$

We might then determine the average of these differences by adding them up $[\Sigma(X - \overline{X})]$ and dividing by the total number of scores (N):

$$\frac{\Sigma(X - \overline{X})}{N}$$

At first glance, this average difference from the mean seems to be what we are looking for as a measure of variability that takes all scores into account. But notice that the sum of the differences between each score and the mean $[\Sigma(X - \overline{X})]$ always equals zero because the positive differences cancel the negative differences. Therefore $\Sigma(X - \overline{X})/N$ always equals zero. Clearly, this is not a very useful "measure" of variability. We can solve this problem by squaring each of the differences $[(X - \overline{X})^2]$ before adding them up. The resulting measure of variability is called the **variance (V)**.

$$V = \frac{\Sigma(X - \overline{X})^2}{N}$$

The problem with this measure is that the outcome is a squared number. For example, if we were to calculate the variance of body weights among patients in the Standard Treatment condition, we would obtain $V = 70.9$ square pounds. But people do not weigh square pounds. It is much more useful to have a measure of variability in the same unit of measure as the original scores. We can derive this measure by taking the square root of the variance that we have just calculated. The result is the **standard deviation (SD)**:

$$SD = \sqrt{\frac{\Sigma(X - \overline{X})^2}{N}}$$

Table B-2 shows how the standard deviation is calculated for the Standard and New Treatment conditions. The two distributions have similar standard deviations, as you might guess by looking at the variability in Figure B-1. In Figure B-3 the standard deviation for Class 2 (9.38 points) is about twice that for Class 1 (4.85 points), which also seems to reflect the differences in variability between the two classes.

Expressing the Position of a Score in a Distribution

Suppose that you are in one of the introductory psychology classes charted in Figure B-3, and you get a score of 75 points on the test. What

TABLE B-2 CALCULATING THE STANDARD DEVIATION

Standard Treatment

Patient	Weight (X)	Mean ($\overline{X}$)	(X − $\overline{X}$)	(X − $\overline{X}$)^2
1	105	90.4	14.6	213.16
2	82	90.4	− 8.4	70.56
3	96	90.4	5.6	31.36
4	86	90.4	− 4.4	19.36
5	101	90.4	10.6	112.36
6	75	90.4	−15.4	237.16
7	90	90.4	− 0.4	0.16
8	80	90.4	−10.4	108.16
9	92	90.4	1.6	2.56
10	90	90.4	− 0.4	0.16
11	101	90.4	10.6	112.36
12	82	90.4	− 8.4	70.56
13	99	90.4	8.6	73.96
14	87	90.4	− 3.4	11.56
15	90	90.4	− 0.4	0.16

$$SD = \sqrt{\frac{\Sigma(X - \overline{X})^2}{N}}$$

$$\Sigma(X - \overline{X})^2 = 1063.60$$

$$SD = \sqrt{\frac{1063.6}{15}}$$

$$SD = \sqrt{70.9}$$

$$SD = 8.42 \text{ lb}$$

New Treatment

Patient	Weight (X)	Mean ($\overline{X}$)	(X − $\overline{X}$)	(X − $\overline{X}$)^2
1	101	100.3	0.7	0.49
2	92	100.3	− 8.3	68.89
3	110	100.3	9.7	94.09
4	86	100.3	−14.3	204.49
5	105	100.3	4.7	22.09
6	115	100.3	14.7	216.09
7	89	100.3	−11.3	127.69
8	107	100.3	6.7	44.89
9	101	100.3	0.7	0.49
10	97	100.3	− 3.3	10.89
11	105	100.3	4.7	22.09
12	95	100.3	− 5.3	28.09
13	101	100.3	0.7	0.49
14	112	100.3	11.7	136.89
15	89	100.3	−11.3	127.69

$$SD = \sqrt{\frac{\Sigma(X - \overline{X})^2}{N}}$$

$$\Sigma(X - \overline{X})^2 = 1105.35$$

$$SD = \sqrt{\frac{1105.35}{15}}$$

$$SD = \sqrt{73.7}$$

$$SD = 8.58 \text{ lb}$$

letter grade will you receive for that score? In many courses, those in which the professor grades on a "curve," your letter grade will depend on how you did relative to other students in your class. In other words, your grade depends on the position of your test score in the overall frequency distribution of test scores for your class. If you are in Class 1, your 75 points is one of the highest scores in the class, and you will get an A. If you are in Class 2, you will only get a B because many other students scored higher than 75 points.

For assigning grades as well as for many other applications—your SAT scores, your height, your pitching ability relative to those of others—it is useful to have a statistic that precisely describes the position of a score in a distribution. One such statistic is the **percentile rank**, which indicates the percentage of all scores that lie below the score in question. For example, in Class 1, 96 students took the test, and 93 of them scored lower than your 75 points. Therefore, 97 percent (93/96) of the students had a lower score, and your score is in the 97th percentile for that class. In Class 2, 114 students took the test, and 85 of them scored lower than 75 points, so your score is in the 75th percentile for that class.

Converting scores into percentile ranks allows you to make direct comparisons between outcomes that would seem to defy comparison. For instance, if you can run 100 yards in 15 seconds, are you better at running or at introductory psychology? If your time score of 15 seconds places you in the 60th percentile for running 100 yards and your test score of 75 points places you in the 97th (or even the 75th) percentile for introductory psychology, we can say that you are better at introductory psychology than at running (at least for these comparison groups).

Another statistic for locating a score in a distribution is the **standard score** (also called the *z-score*). The z-score describes the position of a score in relation to the mean and standard deviation of a distribution. In fact, the z-score is simply the number of standard deviations the score in question is away from the mean:

$$z = \frac{(X - \overline{X})}{SD}$$

Thus, if the mean test score $(\overline{X})$ for Class 1 is 67 points and the standard deviation for that class is 4.85 points, the z-score for a score of 75 points is $(75 - 67)/4.85 = 1.65$. That is, a score of 75 points is 1.65 standard deviations above the mean. Because Class 2 has a standard deviation of 9.38 points, a score of 75 points has a z-score of $(75 - 67)/9.38 = 0.85$. In this class, 75 points is only 0.85 standard deviations above the mean.

The Normal Distribution

If we plotted all the IQ scores of the American population on a graph, the graph would look something like Figure B-4. As we mentioned, frequency distributions have different shapes, one of which is symmetrical (Figure B-2). Figure B-4 shows a special type of symmetrical distribution, called a **normal distribution** (or **normal curve**). Normal distributions are bell-shaped. Most scores cluster around the center (the mean), and fewer scores occur as they get farther from the center. For a normal dis-

FIGURE B-4   THE NORMAL DISTRIBUTION.
This is a frequency distribution in which particular percentages of scores occur within particular areas of the distribution. Thus, about 68 percent of the scores always fall within ± 1 standard deviation of the mean, about 95 percent fall within ± 2 standard deviations of the mean, and 99.7 percent fall within ± 3 standard deviations of the mean.

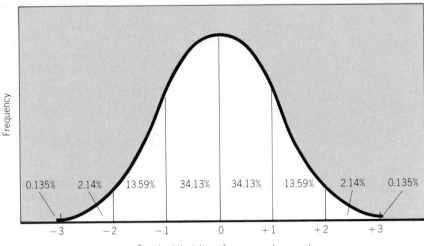

tribution, particular percentages of the scores occur within particular areas of the distribution and can be described as being certain numbers of standard deviations from the mean. For instance, in *all* normal distributions, exactly 34.13 percent of the scores occur between the mean score and the score that is 1 standard deviation above (or below) the mean, exactly 13.59 percent of the scores occur between the score that is 1 standard deviation above the mean and the score that is 2 standard deviations above the mean, and so on. Indeed, for *any* portion of the distribution defined in standard deviation units from the mean, the percentages of scores will be exactly the same in all normal distributions.

It may seem unlikely that distributions with these exact properties could occur very often. After all, how often could frequency distributions of variables take the shape of a normal curve? The answer is, very often. Mathematicians have shown that a normal distribution always occurs when the variable being measured is the combination of many independent influences. For example, an individual's intellectual abilities are determined by many different genes as well as by environmental factors (see Chapter 14). These many independent influences all combine to determine what psychologists label as intelligence. Frequency distributions of measures of intelligence—that is, IQ test scores—have the shape of a normal distribution. Similarly, an individual's height is determined by a combination of many different influences (genes, nutrition, and so on), and frequency distributions for height of men or women (but not both together) are normal curves. It turns out that the frequency distributions of many biological and psychological measures approximate a normal curve.

One advantage of the normal distribution is that when scores are known to have a normal distribution, psychologists can determine the percentile rank of a particular score simply by knowing the z-score. For example, suppose that you take the Stanford–Binet intelligence test and get an IQ score of 115. The overall frequency distribution of scores on this test is a normal curve with a mean of 100 and a standard deviation of about 15. Therefore, your score of 115 is 1 standard deviation above the mean, which corresponds to a z-score of 1 (that is, $115 - 100/15 = 1$). We can tell that your percentile rank for IQ is 84.13 because in a normal distribution 50 percent of the scores are below the mean and 34.13 percent of the scores are between the mean and a z-score of 1 (Figure B-4). Thus, about 84 percent of people tested have an IQ score lower than yours.

Describing the Relation between Two Scores

Let's return to your experiment on the effectiveness of the standard and new treatments for eating disorders. You probably measure more than just the body weight of patients in each treatment group. For example, you might also want to know whether patients who received the new treatment are happier and more satisfied with life than those who received the standard treatment. So you devise a questionnaire that gives a valid and reliable measure of happiness and life satisfaction and give it to your patients. Table B-3 shows hypothetical scores on this questionnaire along with the body-weight measures for each patient in the New Treatment condition.

It is natural for you to wonder whether there is any relationship between your patients' happiness and their body weight at the end of treatment. Do patients who are happier and more satisfied with life do better in terms of body weight (that is, do they weigh more) at the end of treatment than those who are less satisfied with life? When you ask this question, you are asking whether the two variables, or scores (life satisfaction and weight), are **correlated**—whether they tend to vary together.

TABLE B-3   HYPOTHETICAL QUESTIONNAIRE RESULTS

	New Treatment	
Patient	*Weight (lb)*	*Happiness and Life Satisfaction*
1	101	60
2	92	58
3	110	69
4	86	52
5	105	69
6	115	71
7	89	51
8	107	65
9	101	54
10	97	62
11	105	60
12	95	55
13	101	66
14	112	63
15	89	59

Note: A list of hypothetical scores on a happiness/life satisfaction questionnaire for patients in the New Treatment condition. The body weight scores from Table B-1 also appear here. Both measures would have been made at the end of treatment.

As you see throughout this textbook in descriptions of research results, psychologists often want to know whether two variables are correlated. For instance, they may want to know whether IQ is related to grades in college, whether the ability to see fine details (visual acuity) is related to the ability to see dim lights (brightness threshold), or whether the amount of violence children watch on television is related to the amount of violence children act out in the real world.

You could try to see whether happiness correlates with body weight by scanning the list in Table B-3 and comparing the pairs of scores. However, a much easier way to see if there is a relationship is to construct a **scatter plot** (or **scatter diagram**) such as the one in Figure B-5. In this diagram, one point is plotted for each patient. Each point represents both the body-weight score (horizontal axis) and the happiness/life satisfaction score (vertical axis) for that patient. You can see that the points cluster fairly tightly along a diagonal line, an indication that there *is* a correlation between the two variables: higher body weight *is* associated with greater happiness and life satisfaction. This relation is a **positive correlation**. As one variable increases the other increases too. Other variables may have a **negative correlation**. As one variable increases the other decreases. For example, increases in the number of cigarettes a person smokes each day are associated with decreases in the length of

FIGURE B-5   A SCATTER PLOT OF THE SCORES IN TABLE B-3. For each patient, a single point represents both the body weight and happiness/life satisfaction score. For example, for patient 12 in Table B-3, a point is plotted at 95 pounds on the horizontal axis and 55 on the vertical axis. (This point is shown as an "x" on the scatter plot.)

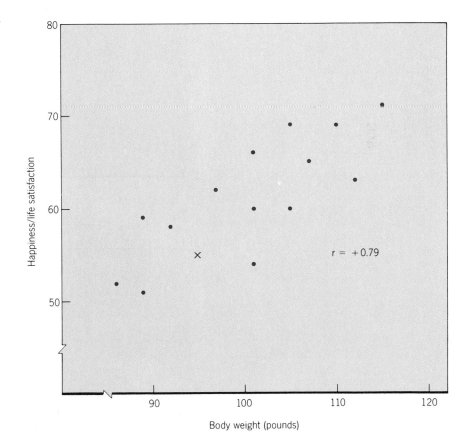

life. If the variables show no consistent pattern of relationship, they have no correlation. For example, there is no relation (no correlation) between shoe size and IQ scores.

Figure B-6 shows several different scatter plots for hypothetical data to illustrate different directions (positive and negative) and strengths of

FIGURE B-6 CORRELATIONS HAVE DIFFERENT STRENGTHS AND DIRECTIONS.
Shown are scatter plots for hypothetical data that have different types of relationships, or correlations. For Panel (a), there is no relation between the two measures plotted. The variables plotted in (b) and (c) are positively correlated, and the relationship is stronger in (c) than in (b). The variables plotted in (d), (e), and (f) are negatively correlated. The negative correlation in (e) is stronger than that in (d), and the negative correlation in (f) is perfect.

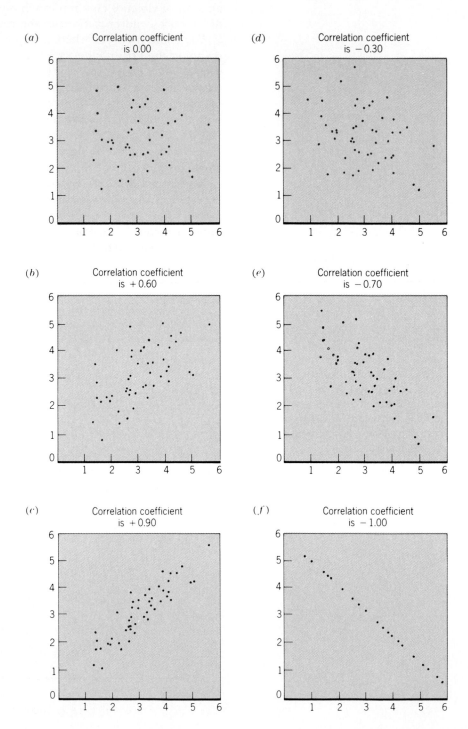

correlations. For the scatter plot in the upper left panel (*a*), there is no correlation between the two variables. The other two panels on the left of the figure show scatter plots for variables that are positively correlated. Notice that the points in Panel (*c*) cluster more tightly along a diagonal line than the points in Panel (*b*). This tighter clustering shows that there is a much stronger relation (and, hence, correlation) between the variables plotted in Panel (*c*) than Panel (*b*).

The three panels on the right of Figure B-6 show scatter plots for variables that are negatively correlated. Again, the strength of the relationship differs in each panel, from relatively weak [Panel (*d*)] to very strong [Panel (*f*)]. In fact, the correlation between the two measures in Panel (*f*) is perfect; all of the points lie along a diagonal line. It is difficult to think of a real-life example of two variables that have a perfect negative relationship, so here is a rather silly one. If we measured the distance between the floor and the top of the head (height) and the distance between the top of the head and the ceiling for 20 people, the scatter plot of the two measures would look like that in the lower right panel.

Statisticians have developed a concise and precise way to describe these different types of correlations. This descriptive statistic is the correlation coefficient.

THE CORRELATION COEFFICIENT   The **correlation coefficient (*r*)** is a number that reflects both the strength and the direction (positive or negative) of the relationship between two variables. The formula for the correlation coefficient is

$$r = \frac{\Sigma(X - \overline{X})(Y - \overline{Y})}{N(SD_X)(SD_Y)}$$

As in other formulas you have seen in this appendix, X represents the individual scores and $\overline{X}$ represents the mean of those scores for one of the measures (say, body weight). Y and $\overline{Y}$ represent the same statistics for the other measure (say, happiness and life satisfaction scores). Σ indicates that we add up the products of $(X - \overline{X})(Y - \overline{Y})$ for each pair of scores. N is the number of pairs of scores. SD_X and SD_Y are the standard deviations of the scores for the two measures. Thus the formula takes into account the variability of the scores (the standard deviations) and the relative difference of each score from its associated mean (the product of the difference scores for each pair). Table B-4 shows how the correlation coefficient is calculated for the two measures in your treatment experiment.

When calculated this way, correlation coefficients have either a positive (+) or a negative (−) sign. As you saw earlier, a positive correlation coefficient indicates that two variables have a positive relation—as in the relation of body weight and happiness/life satisfaction in your experiment and in Panels (*b*) and (*c*) of Figure B-6. A negative correlation coefficient indicates that two variables have a negative relation, as in Panels (*d*), (*e*), and (*f*) of Figure B-6. The absolute value—that is, the size of the number, independent of the sign of the correlation coeffi-

TABLE B-4 CALCULATING THE CORRELATION COEFFICIENT

Patient	Weight (lb) (variable X)	Happiness/Life Satisfaction (variable Y)	$(X - \overline{X})$	$(Y - \overline{Y})$	$(X - \overline{X})(Y - \overline{Y})$
		New Treatment			
1	101	60	0.7	− 0.9	− 0.6
2	92	58	− 8.3	− 2.9	24.1
3	110	69	9.7	8.1	78.6
4	86	52	−14.3	− 8.1	115.8
5	105	69	4.7	8.1	38.1
6	115	71	14.7	10.1	148.5
7	89	51	−11.3	− 9.9	111.9
8	107	65	6.7	4.1	27.5
9	101	54	0.7	− 6.9	− 4.8
10	97	62	− 3.3	1.1	− 3.6
11	105	60	4.7	− 0.9	− 4.2
12	95	55	− 5.3	− 5.9	31.3
13	101	66	0.7	5.1	3.6
14	112	63	11.7	2.1	24.6
15	89	59	−11.3	− 1.9	21.5

$$\overline{X} = 100.3 \qquad \overline{Y} = 60.9 \qquad \Sigma(X - \overline{X})(Y - \overline{Y}) = 612.3$$

$$SD_X = 8.58 \qquad SD_Y = 6.01$$

$$r = \frac{\Sigma(X - \overline{X})(Y - \overline{Y})}{N(SD_X)(SD_Y)}$$

$$r = \frac{612.3}{15(8.58)(6.01)}$$

$$r = \frac{612.3}{773.49}$$

$$r = 0.79$$

Note: Calculation of the correlation coefficient for the scores listed in Table B-3 and shown in Figure B-5. For each patient, we first determine the difference between the individual score and the mean score for each variable [$(X - \overline{X})$ and $(Y - \overline{Y})$]. Then multiply these two difference scores to give the product of the two difference scores for each patient [$(X - \overline{X})(Y - \overline{Y})$]. Then sum the products for all 15 patients [$\Sigma(X - \overline{X})(Y - \overline{Y})$]. Divide this sum by the product of the total number of patients and the standard deviations for both variables [$N(SD_X)(SD_Y)$]. The result is the correlation coefficient (r).

cient—indicates the strength of the relation. The absolute value of correlation coefficients can vary from 0.0 to 1.0. A correlation coefficient of 0.0 indicates no relation between two variables and 1.0 indicates a perfect relation between them. By combining the sign and the size of the correlation coefficient, we have an indication of both the direction and the strength of the relationship. Thus $r = -0.30$ [as in Panel (*d*) of Figure B-6] indicates a relatively weak negative relation between two variables; $r = +0.60$ [as in Panel (*b*)] indicates a fairly strong positive relation, and $r = -0.70$ [Panel (*e*)] indicates a stronger negative relation.

PREDICTION VERSUS CAUSATION Correlation coefficients tell researchers how well they can predict one measure if they know another. For example, Figure B-5 shows that if you know a patient's score on the happiness and life satisfaction questionnaire, you can fairly well predict his or her body weight at the end of treatment. If the patient's happiness and life satisfaction score is high (between 65 and 71, say), his or her body weight also is likely to be high (between 101 and 115 pounds). If the patient's happiness and life satisfaction score is low (between 51 and 55), his or her body weight is likely to be low (between 86 and 101 pounds). But knowing someone's shoe size does not help us predict his or her IQ because the correlation coefficient between these two variables is 0.0.

The higher the absolute value of the correlation coefficient (the closer to $+1.00$ or -1.00), the better the prediction one can make. In fact, if the correlation between two variables is $+1.00$ or -1.00, one can perfectly predict one variable from the other. For instance, if we know the distance between the floor and the top of someone's head (height), we can predict with perfect accuracy the distance between the top of his or her head and the ceiling (assuming we know the height of the ceiling). There is a perfect negative correlation of -1.00 between these two measures.

Although high correlations allow for fairly accurate predictions, *correlation does not imply causation.* Just because you can predict body weight fairly well from knowing a patient's happiness and life satisfaction score, you cannot conclude that happiness and satisfaction with life necessarily *caused* a patient to put on more weight during treatment. It is equally possible that putting on the weight caused the patient to be happier and more satisfied with life. It also is possible that some third variable caused both measures to increase together. For instance, perhaps the new treatment succeeded in getting patients to eat more, and eating more independently caused the patients to be happier and more satisfied with life and to weigh more. Another example of this extremely important point is a hypothetical study of liquor store profits and the church minister's income in a small town. Suppose that researchers find that there is a high positive correlation between the two. As liquor profits increase, so does the minister's income. Why? Does the owner of the liquor store put more money in the church collection plate as his profits rise? Does the minister buy more liquor as his income rises? As the economy improves, do people in the town have more money to donate to the minister's collection plate and more money to buy liquor? The last possibility is the most likely. But no one can know for sure just by plotting the correlation. The high correlation between liquor profits and the minister's income only allows us to predict how the two will vary; it does not tell us what *caused* what. As you saw in Appendix A, the only way to find out about causal relationships is to *control* or manipulate one variable (called the independent variable) and see if the manipulation produces changes in the other variable (the dependent variable).

MAKING INFERENCES ABOUT THE DATA

So far you have seen that statistics can be useful for describing or summarizing observations. They also can be useful in helping research-

TABLE B-5 SAMPLES FROM A POPULATION

80	95	74	99
76	93	104	111
105+	74	107	95*
118	101+	91	84
101*	115*	85	76
83	65	92+	107
121	84	100	82+
68	89*	106	96
82+	125	73	99+
90	95	97*	106
103	75+	94	109
92*	92	90+	101*
87	90+	97	73
89	99	102	87
96+	113	79	94
117	107*	69	112*
106	80+	71	109
86+	96	89	87+
117	87	101+	125
110*	101*	116	89*
86*	110	96	95
128	97	92	82
83	74	103	101
75	92	105*	90+
105*	95	117	93

Note: A list of hypothetical body weights of 100 people in a clinic for treating eating disorders. The mean weight for all 100 people is 95 pounds.

ers draw conclusions, or make inferences, from data. To see why, look again at the results of your experiment on treatments for eating disorders (Table B-1). Patients given the standard treatment weighed an average of 90.4 pounds at the end of the experiment, whereas patients given the new treatment weighed an average of 100.3 pounds. Can you conclude that the new treatment is superior to the standard treatment?

At first, this question seems silly. Of course the new treatment is superior, you might say: the patients weighed some 10 pounds more than those who received the standard treatment! But you really must ask: Is the difference between the two conditions really a result of the different treatments, or could it have occurred by luck or chance? Suppose that 100 people have an average weight of 95 pounds, as shown in Table B-5. If you randomly select 15 of these people (for example, those marked by + in the table), their average weight might be 90.4 pounds. If you randomly select another 15 people from the list (those marked by *), their average weight might be 100.3 pounds. Thus, just by chance, the randomly selected two groups have a difference in average weights of about 10 pounds. Is it possible that the 10-pound difference between patients in the Standard and New Treatment conditions similarly is due to chance? **Inferential statistics** help people to answer this question. To understand how, we have to take a small digression.

Populations and Samples

In statistics, a **population** is a complete set of observations or measures from all members of a specified group. For example, a population might be the IQ of every person in the world, the top speed of every car currently on the road, the body weight of all adults, or the body weight of all adults with an eating disorder. If we wanted some information about a population, the most accurate way to obtain it would be to make the desired measure (such as IQ, speed, or weight) on every member of the specified group—that is, to measure the entire population. But measuring every member of the group is rarely practical. How could anyone measure the IQ of every person in the world? As a substitute, researchers study a part of the population—a **sample**. Usually, the sample is selected randomly from the population, though other selection procedures may be used. The important thing is that the sample be selected in an unbiased way so that it gives the most accurate possible representation of the population as a whole. Thus, we may measure the top speed of a randomly selected fraction of the cars that are currently on the road, or we may measure the body weights of only 15 randomly selected patients in an eating disorders clinic.

Samples have several important characteristics. To illustrate them, we will define the 100 body weights shown in Table B-5 to be the population of interest. Now suppose we take three random samples of 15 people from this population. The mean weights for these three samples might be 90.4, 100.3, and 96.8 pounds. Although all three sample means are fairly close to the mean for the entire population, none is exactly 95 pounds. Furthermore, the three sample means are different from each other. Why? The samples do not accurately represent the entire population. The samples contain some error, or variability, referred to as **sampling error**.

Although a sampling error creeps in whenever people use a sample to estimate something about a population, the size of the sampling error diminishes if the sample is larger. For instance, if we take three random samples of 30 people from the population in Table B-5, the mean weights are 93.7, 94.6, and 95.8 pounds. Not only are all three estimates closer to the true population mean of 95 pounds than when our samples included only 15 people, but they also are closer to each other. To take an extreme example, you certainly would have more confidence in an estimate of the population mean if the estimate were based on a sample of 95 people than if it were based on a sample of only 5 people!

To go a step further, take a large number of random samples—say, 50 samples of 15 people each. Then calculate the mean of each sample and plot a frequency distribution of the 50 sample means. You find that the frequency distribution of sample means has approximately the shape of a normal distribution. The mean of this normal distribution (the mean of the means, or a kind of *grand mean*) will be very close to the true population mean and the 50 sample means will vary around it. Of course, you can determine the degree to which the sample means vary around the grand mean by calculating the standard deviation of the sample means. Fortunately, we don't actually have to take all 50 samples, calculate their means, and then calculate the standard deviation of these means. We can obtain a good estimate of the standard deviation of all the sample means from just one of the samples. This estimate is called the **standard error of the mean (SE)**. The formula for the standard error of the mean is

$$SE = \frac{SD}{\sqrt{N}}$$

where *SD* is the standard deviation of the single sample and *N* is the number of observations in that sample.

For example, we can calculate the standard error of the mean for the sample of 15 body weights marked by "+" in Table B-5. The standard deviation of this sample is 8.42 pounds. Therefore, the standard error of the mean is

$$SE = \frac{8.42}{\sqrt{15}}$$
$$SE = \frac{8.42}{3.87}$$
$$SE = 2.18 \text{ pounds}$$

This number is an estimate of the standard deviation of the means of a large number of samples. You can see that, as we have said, the variability of the sample means (their standard deviation, estimated from the standard error of the mean for a single sample) decreases as the size of the sample increases (as the denominator in the equation gets bigger). In addition, the standard error of the mean decreases as the variability in the sample (its standard deviation) decreases (as the numerator in the equation gets smaller).

Back to Making Inferences

With some basic concepts about taking samples from populations in hand, we can return now to see how statistics help researchers make inferences from samples.

HOW REPRESENTATIVE IS A MEAN?   Researchers take samples from a population so that they can make inferences about the population. For instance, suppose you want to know the mean IQ of all students in your college (the population). Rather than test every student, you test a random sample. Your purpose is to use the mean of the sample to infer the mean of the population. You might ask just how well the sample mean represents the true mean of the entire population.

You can answer this question from knowing of the standard error of the mean. Recall that the standard error of the mean, calculated for a single sample, is an estimate of the standard deviation of many hypothetical sample means that you might measure from the population. Recall also that the frequency distribution of many sample means is a normal distribution. Therefore, you know that some 68 percent of all hypothetical sample means fall within plus and minus one standard deviation of the population mean, about 95 percent fall within plus and minus two standard deviations, and so on (see Figure B-4). In other words, there is about a 68 percent chance that the mean calculated from a single sample lies within one standard error (calculated from that sample) of the true population mean, a 95 percent chance that the sample mean lies within two standard errors of the population mean, and so on.

You can see how this works in an example. Suppose that you take a random sample of 100 students from your college and measure their IQs. You find that the mean IQ of this sample is 115.5 points and the standard deviation is 15 points. You calculate that the standard error of the mean is 1.5 IQ points ($SE = 15/\sqrt{100} = 1.5$). From the standard error, you can infer that if you were to take many such samples from the college, about 68 percent of the measured sample means would be within 1.5 IQ points of whatever the true population mean is (that is, the mean IQ of every student in the college). In other words, there is a 68 percent probability that the sample mean of 115.5 that you have measured is within 1.5 points of the true mean IQ for the college population. Stated slightly differently, you can conclude (infer) that there is a 68 percent probability that an IQ range of 114 to 117 (that is, 115.5 ± 1.5) includes the true mean IQ of the college population.

The probability in the conclusion is referred to as the *level of confidence*. Thus you can say that you have a 68 percent level of confidence that the range of 114 to 117 includes the mean IQ for the college. The range of scores in the conclusion is called the *confidence interval*. Thus you have a 68 percent level of confidence that the confidence interval of 114 to 117 points includes the mean IQ for the college. This statement answers our question about how well the sample mean represents the true mean of the entire population.

What if your sample had been larger—say, 300 people? Assuming that the mean and standard deviation of the sample are the same as before, the standard error of the sample mean would be smaller: $SE = 15/\sqrt{300} = 0.87$ points. Now you can say that you have a 68 percent level of confidence that the confidence interval of 114.63 to 116.37 IQ points (115.5 ± 0.87) includes the true mean IQ for the college. Thus, with a larger sample size, the sample mean provides a better estimate of the population mean—the confidence interval becomes narrower.

In practice, researchers consider a 68 percent level of confidence too low to allow them to be reasonably sure of an inference they wish to make. Generally, researchers prefer a 95 percent level of confidence. Because 95 percent of scores fall within plus and minus two standard deviations of the mean of a normal distribution, a confidence interval based on two standard deviations (estimated from two standard errors of the sample mean) will provide the desired 95 percent level of confidence. In the example of a sample of 100 students from your college, two standard errors of the mean is 3.0 points. Therefore, based on this sample, you can have a 95 percent level of confidence that a confidence interval of 112.5 to 118.5 points (that is, 115.5 ± 3) includes the true mean IQ of the college population.

THE SIGNIFICANCE OF A DIFFERENCE Earlier we wanted to know the probability that the different mean weights for the Standard Treatment group (90.4 pounds) and the New Treatment group (100.3 pounds) occurred by chance or were the result of the different treatments. Now that you know about samples and populations, you can ask the question a little more precisely: What is the probability that these two sample means (one mean for the sample of 15 people in the Standard Treatment condition and one mean for the sample of 15 people in the New Treatment condition) actually come from the same population? That is, how likely is it that the two groups simply represent two random samples from the same population, and that the different mean weights for each sample occurred just by chance—as a result of sampling error—and not because of the different treatments? Inferential statistics will answer this question.

You can conceptualize the problem by looking at Figure B-7. The two frequency distributions on the top of the figure are from two random samples. Each distribution has a mean and some degree of variability, as indicated by the standard error of the mean calculated from that sample. The two means are different (100 for sample 1 and 105 for sample 2), but the scores of the two distributions overlap substantially. Do samples 1 and 2 actually come from the same population and differ only because of sampling error? We certainly do not have much confidence that they come from different populations. Remember that there is a 95 percent probability that the interval, or range of scores, between two standard errors of the mean of a sample includes the true population mean. Because the standard error of the mean is so large for each sample ($SE = 3$ for both samples), there is a reasonable probability that the true population mean for sample 1 also is the true population mean for sample 2. Using a 95 percent level of confidence, the confidence interval for sample 1 is 94 to 106 (that is, 100 ± 6). Therefore we have a 95 percent level of confidence that the range of 94 to 106 includes the true mean of the population from which sample 1 was taken. For sample 2, we have a 95 percent level of confidence that the range of 99 to 111 (that is, 105 ± 6) includes the population mean. Thus the confidence intervals for both samples overlap substantially and the mean of the population might well be the same for both samples.

Now look at the two frequency distributions in the middle of Figure B-7. These two samples have the same means as those at the top of the figure, but they have much less variability—that is, smaller standard errors ($SE = 1$ for both of these samples). It seems much more likely that these two distributions actually come from different populations. In fact, we have a 95 percent level of confidence that the range from 98 to 102 (that is, 100 ± 2) includes the mean of the population from which sample 1 was taken and a 95 percent level of confidence that the range from 103 to 107 (that is, 105 ± 2) includes the mean of the population from which sample 2 was taken. Thus it is unlikely that these two samples come from the same population.

Finally, the two distributions at the bottom of Figure B-7 have the same variability ($SE = 3$ for both samples) as those at the top, but their means are much farther apart. Again, we have much more confidence that the two samples represent two different populations. For sample 1, we have a 95 percent level of confidence that the range from 94 to 106

*FIGURE B-7   PAIRS OF
FREQUENCY DISTRIBUTIONS
WITH DIFFERENT MEANS AND
AMOUNTS OF VARIABILITY.*
The three pairs of frequency distributions
are for hypothetical samples. The
ordinate shows frequency of scores (the
actual numbers are not given), and the
abscissa shows the measure on some
hypothetical test (such as IQ scores from
two samples of college students or top
speeds of two samples of automobiles).
The mean and standard error of the
mean for each sample are given on the
right.

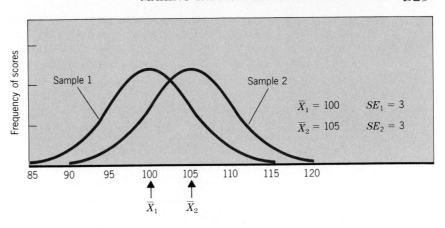

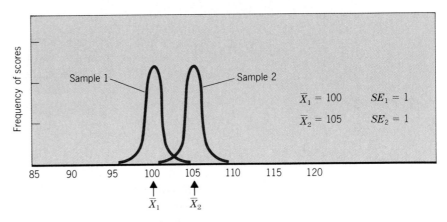

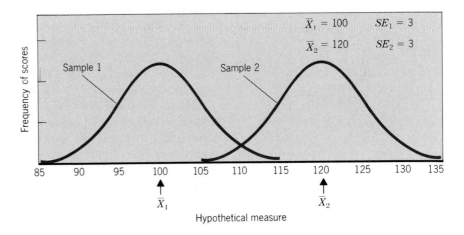

includes the population mean. For sample 2, we have a 95 percent level
of confidence that the range from 114 to 126 includes the population
mean.

In general, the further apart the sample means are and the less overlap between scores in the two samples, the more confident we can be that
the two samples come from different populations and are not just two

random samples from the same population. There is a way to measure this precisely. There is a mathematical statement that takes into account both the difference between the sample means and the degree of variability (the standard errors of the means). This statistic is called *t*.

$$t = \frac{\overline{X}_1 - \overline{X}_2}{\sqrt{(SE_1)^2 + (SE_2)^2}}$$

where $\overline{X}_1$ and $\overline{X}_2$ are the means of samples 1 and 2, and SE_1 and SE_2 are the standard errors of the means for the same two samples. The term $\overline{X}_1 - \overline{X}_2$ is the difference between the two sample means. The term $(SE_1)^2 + (SE_2)^2$ is called the *standard error of the difference between the means* and can be symbolized by SE_D. Thus, in simplified form the formula can be written as

$$t = \frac{\overline{X}_1 - \overline{X}_2}{SE_D}$$

Notice that the *t* statistic has the same general form as a *z*-score (standard score, discussed earlier). In fact, when the number of scores in each sample is large enough, the *t* statistic *is* a kind of *z*-score and has the same properties. Therefore, for large samples, we can rewrite the formula above as

$$z = \frac{\overline{X}_1 - \overline{X}_2}{SE_D}$$

If samples 1 and 2 come from the same population, the frequency distribution of *z*-scores is a normal distribution with a mean of zero and a standard deviation of 1 (see Figure B-4). Thus a *z*-score of 1 is one standard deviation above the mean of the population, a *z*-score of -1 is one standard deviation below the mean, and so on. Therefore, about 68 percent of all *z*-scores fall between values of $+1$ and -1, 95 percent fall between $+2$ and -2, and so on. In practice, researchers ignore the sign of the *z*-score and say that 68 percent of all *z*-scores have a value of 1 or less and 95 percent of all *z*-scores have a value of 2 or less.

These properties of *z*-scores help researchers determine if two samples are likely to have come from the same population. If we calculate the *z*-score for any two samples drawn from the same population, 68 percent of the time the *z*-score will be 1 or less just by chance (due to sampling error) and 95 percent of the time it will be 2 or less just by chance. Statisticians usually state these probabilities in reverse: A *z*-score will be *greater* than 2 by chance alone less than 5 percent of the time. Therefore, if we have two samples and use their means and standard errors to calculate the *z*-score for the samples, the *z*-score will be greater than 2 just by chance (that is, due to sampling error) less than 5 percent of the time. Thus if the *z*-score for two samples is greater than 2, the observed difference between the two samples probably was not a chance event that reflected sampling error. We can then infer that the two samples are *significantly different*—that they probably come from two different populations (that is, two populations with different means). Another way to say this is that the difference between the two samples is *statistically significant*.

You can see how this works for the three pairs of samples in Figure B-7. By using the values for the means and standard errors given in the figure, we find that the z-score for the top two samples is 1.18. Because this z-score is less than 2, we are reluctant to conclude that the two samples came from different populations. The difference between these two samples may well have come about by chance sampling errors. For the middle two sampling distributions, the z-score is 3.55. This number is much greater than 2, and so there is less than a 5 percent chance that the two samples came from the same population and differ only because of chance sampling error. We conclude that the two samples are significantly different and probably came from different populations (for example, two groups given different treatments). For the bottom two samples the z-score is 4.72. This number, too, is much greater than 2, so we conclude that the two samples are significantly different.

Finally, you can apply this analysis to your experiment on treatments for eating disorders (see Table B-2). For the Standard Treatment condition, the standard error of the mean is

$$SE = \frac{SD}{\sqrt{N}}$$

$$SE = \frac{8.42}{\sqrt{15}}$$

$$SE = 2.18$$

For the New Treatment condition, the standard error of the mean is

$$SE = \frac{8.58}{\sqrt{15}}$$

$$SE = 2.22$$

Now calculate the z-score, starting with the difference between the sample means:

$$\overline{X}_1 - \overline{X}_2 = 90.4 - 100.3$$
$$\overline{X}_1 - \overline{X}_2 = -9.9$$

The standard error of the difference between the means is

$$SE_D = \sqrt{(2.18)^2 + (2.22)^2}$$
$$SE_D = \sqrt{4.75 + 4.93}$$
$$SE_D = 3.11$$

And the z-score is

$$z = \frac{-9.9}{3.11}$$
$$z = -3.18$$

This z-score has a value much greater than 2 (ignoring the sign), which means that there is less than a 5 percent chance that the difference between the Standard Treatment and New Treatment samples is due to

As we have said, people use statistics every day. But all too often, by accident or by design, these statistics lie to us. Darrell Huff (1954) wrote a now classic book in which he described how people lie with statistics. Here are some of the things you should watch for.

THE WELL-CHOSEN AVERAGE

The mayor of Grandville points to the success of her economic programs by noting that the average annual income of people in Grandville is $20,000 per person whereas the average for neighboring Madton is only $10,000 per person. But the mayor of Madton disagrees and says that the average annual income is $10,000 per person in both cities. Who is lying? Neither, or both, depending on your point of view. The term *average* often

is used very loosely and may refer to the mean, the median, or the mode of distribution. As you saw in Figure B-2, if the frequency distribution is skewed, the mean, median, and mode may be very different. If Grandville has a few extremely rich residents, the mean income may be $20,000 per person whereas the median income is $10,000. Madton may have a more symmetrical distribution of incomes in which both the mean and the median income are $10,000 per person. The mayor of Grandville was referring to the mean income, which is much higher in Grandville than in Madton. The mayor of Madton was referring to the median income, which is the same for both cities. When you hear claims about "averages," it is important to know whether people are referring to the mean, median, or mode.

THE LITTLE FIGURES THAT ARE NOT THERE

We are told in a television commercial

that "80 percent of the doctors who responded to our survey recommend Feelwell aspirin over Painfree." This statement may be true, but it is nonetheless misleading. Doctors are busy people and most toss such surveys into the trashcan. Perhaps only 10 doctors actually answered the survey. If so, then 80 percent means 8 doctors. This sample is too small to be representative of the population of all doctors. The little figure that is not there in the television commercial is the sample size, but you need this little figure to interpret the statement.

THE SAMPLE WITH THE BUILT-IN BIAS

You also need to know *which* doctors filled out the survey for the television commercial. Suppose that the survey accompanied a letter that said that the makers of Feelwell aspirin wanted to know how many doctors recommend their product. Those doctors who recommended Feelwell may have taken the time to fill out the survey, but

chance sampling error. You therefore can infer that the two samples probably represent two different populations, one given the standard treatment and one given the new treatment. We conclude that the two samples are significantly different and that the new treatment probably does produce a population of patients with higher body weights.

Inferences Are Based on Probabilities

You have seen that when researchers infer that two groups (samples) are significantly different, they base their inference on the following: There is less than a 5 percent chance that the samples actually came from the same population and that the difference is due to sampling error. This is a statement of probability: Fewer than 5 times in 100 will a difference this large occur just by chance. Statisticians generally state these probabilities as decimal fractions rather than as percentages. For example, instead of saying that there is less than a 5 percent chance for a z-score of greater than 2, they say that the probability is less than 0.05 (that is, $5/100 = 0.05$).

those doctors who recommended other brands may not have taken the trouble to fill out a survey for the Feelwell company. So the surveys that are returned come from doctors who are biased in favor of Feelwell aspirin. Instead of being random, the sample has a built-in bias. Before you can interpret a statistical statement, you need to know how the sample was chosen.

MUCH ADO ABOUT PRACTICALLY NOTHING

Many companies sell books to help high school students prepare for the Scholastic Aptitude Test, and many colleges use the SAT in evaluating students for admission. Suppose that one company conducts a study and finds that students who used its book had a mean score of 525 on the SAT, compared to a mean score of 500 for students who did not use the book. The company announces, with some fanfare, that its book helps students score higher on the SAT. Let's also

suppose that the study was conducted properly. Should high school students rush out and buy the book? Without knowing the variability among the SAT scores for those who used the book and those who didn't, no one can really know if the book is worth its price. What if the range of scores for those who used the book was 375 to 675, whereas the range for students who did not use it was 300 to 700? There is substantial variability and overlap between the two groups, and some students who did *not* use the book actually did better than those who did. Before we can evaluate comparisons between groups, we need to know the degree of variability. Indeed, it is best if we know whether differences are statistically significant as well as the probability value from the statistical test that was used. Otherwise, we may wind up making much ado about practically nothing.

Even if two groups are significantly different, we still run the risk of making much ado about practically noth-

ing. For example, suppose that students who use the SAT-preparation book have a mean score of 502 on the SAT, whereas those who do not use the book have a mean score of 500. Suppose also that there is little variability or overlap between the two groups and that the difference is statistically significant. But is a difference of only 2 points on the SAT test meaningful? Are you willing to spend $30 for the book and hours studying it to improve your score by a scant 2 points? As Huff (1954) states, "Sometimes a big ado is made about a difference that is mathematically real and demonstrable but so tiny as to have no importance." In their research, psychologists strive to learn about phenomena that are psychologically significant as well as statistically significant.

Because inferences are based on probabilities, they *could* be wrong. If you flip a coin, the probability that it will come up heads is 1/2, or 0.5. If you flip the coin 10 times, the probability that it will come up heads 8 or more of the 10 times is about 0.05. It is unlikely, but it *could* happen. Similarly, when we say that the probability is less than 0.05 that a difference between two groups (samples) is due to sampling error, it is unlikely, but it could happen. If in fact the difference was due to sampling error, we will have made an incorrect inference.

By agreement, researchers generally consider a probability of 0.05 or less to be small enough to let them conclude that the observed difference between two samples did not occur by chance. If the probability is higher, say 0.1 (1 in 10) that the difference occurred by chance, careful researchers get nervous. A probability of 0.1 is just too high to make them conclude that the difference did not occur by chance, so they act conservatively and infer that the groups or samples are not significantly different. If the probability is lower, say 0.01 (1 in 100) that the difference occurred by chance, the researchers feel much more confident in concluding that the groups are significantly different.

But no matter how low the probability is that two samples came from the same population, researchers can never be absolutely certain that they came from different populations. Even if the probability were less than 0.000001 (1 in a million), there still is that slight possibility that the difference between the two groups was a chance occurrence. So we can never infer with certainty that two groups really are different—that they come from two different populations. We can only infer that they *probably* do.

Statistical Tests of Hypotheses

The z-score is one example of a **statistical test**—a statistic that allows researchers to test the probability that some outcome or observation has occurred by chance. Statistical tests are used for testing hypotheses (see Appendix A). When researchers carry out an experiment (for example, to determine whether a new treatment is better than a standard treatment), they formulate a **research hypothesis** that the two groups are different (for example, have different weights at the end of treatment). A **null hypothesis** states that the two groups are the same and that any observed difference is due to chance, or sampling error. A statistical test, then, is a test of the null hypothesis. It allows researchers to state the probability that the null hypothesis is true (that the difference between groups is due to chance). If the statistical test shows that this probability is low (say, less than 0.05), the researchers reject the null hypothesis and conclude that the research hypothesis is probably correct.

Psychologists and other scientists routinely apply many other statistical tests to their data. For instance, look back at the scatter plots and correlation coefficients in Figure B-6. When researchers find that there is some relation between two measures, expressed as a correlation coefficient, they like to know the probability that the relationship occurred just by chance. Looking at Figure B-6, they may feel confident that the relation shown in Panel (*c*) (correlation coefficient of +0.90) is strong and reliable. But how about the relationship shown in Panel (*b*) (correlation coefficient of +0.60) or Panel (*d*) (correlation coefficient of −0.30)?

Statistical tests are available that allow researchers to state the probability that a particular correlation coefficient (relationship between two measures) occurred by chance. The research hypothesis is that there is a relationship between two measures and the null hypothesis is that there isn't—that any apparent relationship is due to chance. If the statistical test shows that the probability of obtaining the correlation coefficient is less than 0.05, the researcher will reject the null hypothesis and conclude that the correlation is statistically significant.

SUMMARY

DESCRIPTIVE STATISTICS

1. *Frequency Distributions.* Descriptive statistics describe and summarize observations. Frequency distributions are graphs that show the number (frequency) of occurrences of each score and charac-

teristically have symmetrical, skewed, or bimodal shapes.

2. *Measures of Central Tendency and Variability.* Measures of central tendency describe the center of a set of scores. The arithmetic average, or mean, is a measure of central tendency obtained by adding up all the scores and dividing by the total number of scores. Another measure, the median, is the middle score of the set. The mode is the most frequent score in a distribution. Measures of variability indicate the amount of spread of the scores around the center. For example, the range is the difference between the highest and lowest scores in the distribution. The standard deviation is a measure of variability that takes all scores into account.

3. *Expressing the Position of a Score in a Distribution.* The percentile rank of a score describes its position in a distribution. The percentile rank indicates the percentage of all scores that lie below the score in question. The standard score (or z-score) describes the position of a score relative to the mean and standard deviation of a distribution.

4. *The Normal Distribution.* The normal distribution (or normal curve) is a special type of symmetrical distribution that is bell-shaped. Particular percentages of scores occur within areas of the normal distribution and can be specified in standard deviation units away from the mean. Therefore, in a normal distribution, the z-score indicates the percentile rank of a score. The frequency distributions of many biological and psychological measures approximate a normal distribution.

5. *Describing the Relation between Two Scores.* Two variables are correlated when they tend to vary together. A scatter plot (or scatter diagram) is a graph that readily displays the relation between two variables. The correlation coefficient mathematically describes the relation. The size of the correlation coefficient indicates the strength of the relationship. Correlation coefficients range from 0.0 (no relation between the two variables) to ±1.0 (a perfect relation). The sign of the correlation coefficient (+ or −) indicates the direction of the relation. In a positive correlation, one variable increases as the other increases. In a negative correlation, one variable decreases as the other increases.

MAKING INFERENCES ABOUT THE DATA

6. *Populations and Samples.* Researchers make inferences about a population (every member of a specified group) by studying a sample (a part of the population). But samples do not perfectly represent the entire population; inevitably there is some sampling error. A statistic called the standard error of the mean gives an estimate of the amount of sampling error. Researchers use the standard error of the mean to determine how well the mean of a sample represents the true mean of the entire population. Specifically, researchers determine the probability (their level of confidence) that some range of scores (the confidence interval) includes the true mean of the population.

7. *The Significance of a Difference.* Researchers use statistics to make inferences about whether differences between two samples—such as two groups of subjects given different treatments in an experiment—occurred from chance sampling error rather than from different treatments. For example, a z-score can be calculated from the mean and standard error of the mean for the two samples. The size of the z-score indicates the probability that the two samples came from the same population and differ only because of sampling error. If the z-score is large, it is unlikely that the observed difference between the two samples was a chance event due to sampling error. Researchers then conclude (make the inference) that the two samples are significantly different.

8. *Hypothesis Testing and Probabilities.* When researchers conduct an experiment, they formulate a research hypothesis that two samples in their experiment (such as groups of subjects given different treatments) are different. The null hypothesis states that the two samples are the same and that any difference observed is due to chance, or sampling error. A statistical test, such as the z-score, allows researchers to state the probability that the null hypothesis is true. If the statistical test shows that this probability is low, researchers reject the null hypothesis and conclude that the research hypothesis is probably correct. Thus statistical tests allow researchers to make inferences about hypotheses. But because the inferences are based on probabilities, they could be wrong. Researchers never can infer that two samples definitely are different, only that they probably are.

FURTHER READINGS

Many textbooks provide an introduction to statistics, and many are written with psychologists and other behavioral scientists in mind. Three such books that are especially well-written and clear are *Statistical Thinking* by Phillips (1982), *How to Use (and Misuse) Statistics* by Kimble (1978), and *Elements of Statistical Reasoning* by Minium and Clarke (1982).

Also highly recommended is *How to Lie with Statistics* by Huff (1954). This witty book illustrates many of the pitfalls to using statistics. It also provides a good overview of the concepts of descriptive and inferential statistics.

APPENDIX C

CAREERS IN PSYCHOLOGY

THE PRACTICE OF PSYCHOLOGY

One very concrete way to understand what psychology is all about is to examine what makes a person a psychologist and what psychologists actually do.

The Making of a Psychologist

What makes a person a psychologist? One simple answer to this question is training and education. A typical psychologist might have eight or more years of education beyond high school: A four-year undergraduate major in psychology, followed by a four- to six-year training program culminating in a Ph.D.—a doctorate—in psychology. During this training program the typical psychologist will have taken a large number of courses on general topics in psychology, courses in areas of special interest, and courses on research methods and statistics. The training will have included independent research for a master's degree thesis, some sort of comprehensive examination, and a large-scale independent re-

TABLE C-1 MEMBERSHIP INTERESTS IN THE AMERICAN PSYCHOLOGICAL ASSOCIATION

Division	*% of total*	*Division*	*% of total*
General	2.14		
Teaching of Psychology	1.72	History of Psychology	.59
Experimental	2.62	Community Psychology	1.35
Evaluation and Measurement	1.35	Psychopharmacology	.77
Physiological and Comparative	.95	Psychotherapy	2.76
Developmental	1.46	Psychological Hypnosis	.75
Society of Personality and Social Psychology	1.81	State Psychological Association Affairs	
SPSSI (Society for the Psychological Study of Social Issues)	1.70	Humanistic Psychology	.79
		Mental Retardation	.68
Psychology and The Arts	.75	Population and Environmental Psychology	.58
Clinical	5.64	Psychology of Women	2.83
Consulting	.64	PIRI (Psychologists Interested in Religious Issues)	1.53
Society for Industrial and Organizational Psychology, Inc.	4.66	Child, Youth, and Family Services	1.20
Educational	1.38	Health Psychology	1.75
School	2.84	Psychoanalysis	2.93
Counseling	3.40	Clinical Neuropsychology	1.87
Psychologists in Public Service	.77	Psychology—Law Society	.65
Military	.65	Psychologists in Independent Practice	5.43
Adult Development and Aging	1.16	Family Psychology	1.39
Society of Applied Experimental and Engineering Psychologists	.74	Society for the Psychological Study of Lesbian and Gay Issues	1.38
Rehabilitation Psychology	.63	Society for the Psychological Study of Ethnic Minority Issues	*
Consumer Psychology	.59		
Theoretical and Philosophical	.52	Media Psychology	*
Experimental Analysis of Behavior	1.31	Exercise & Sport Psychology	*

Source: Adapted from American Psychological Association, 1986.
*New divisions as of 1986

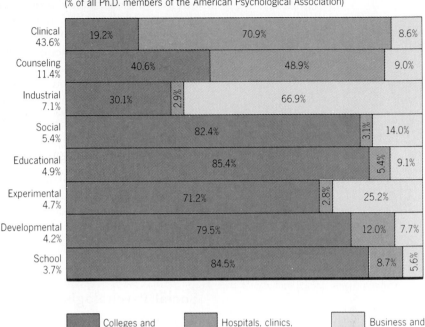

FIGURE C-1   WHERE PSYCHOLOGISTS WORK.
(Adapted from Stapp and Fulcher, 1983.)

search study for the doctoral dissertation. Many psychologists also spend another year or more in postdoctoral research or clinical training programs where they further improve their psychological skills.

After their training is completed, where do psychologists go? Of the estimated 260,000 plus psychologists in the world, over 100,000 live in the United States (Rosenzweig, 1984). In 1986 nearly 63,000 of these psychologists (and nearly 22,000 students) were members of the American Psychological Association (APA)—an organization founded in 1892 to encourage the scientific advancement of psychology. As of 1987 the APA is organized into 45 divisions, and most members belong to one or more of these divisions. Table C-1 shows the names of these divisions and their relative size.

What do these psychologists do? From Figure C-1 you can get a good sense of the general areas in which psychologists work and also the kinds of settings—universities, clinics, businesses, and so on—in which they work. In the event you are not familiar with the work of the different types of psychologists mentioned in Figure C-1, we provide a brief description of the work settings and activities of the most common types.

Clinical and Counseling Psychologists

As Figure C-1 makes clear, a majority of Ph.D. level psychologists classify themselves as clinical or counseling psychologists with clinicians outnumbering counselors by nearly four to one. Over a quarter of these psychologists are in private practice providing psychotherapy, assessing psychological functioning, and counseling on personal, family, career, and other problems. Many others work in hospitals, clinics, and human service agencies where they provide similar services. Their clients and patients range from those with severe psychological dysfunctions to those with minor and temporary difficulties. Their treatment programs also cover a wide range from individual and group therapy and hospitalization. A significant number of clinical and counseling psychologists also hold academic positions in which they teach and conduct research on clinical problems.

Industrial and Organizational Psychologists

Two out of three industrial and organizational psychologists work in industrial, government, and business settings. They are concerned with employer–employee relations, they measure employee aptitudes and interests, they develop programs to improve morale and productivity, they research effective ways to organize work groups, and they help to develop effective sales techniques.

Social Psychologists

Social psychologists are interested in the relationships between people. Over 80 percent are employed in academic settings. They are engaged in research on topics such as the causes of aggression and pro-social behavior, racism and conflict between groups, social influence and attitude change, romantic attraction and friendship, the influence of the mass media on behavior, the relationship between people and their environment, and the psychological aspects of medicine and law.

Experimental Psychologists

The term *experimental psychologist* is a catchall, for it includes psychologists with a wide variety of interests: sensation, perception, neuroscience, learning, memory, motivation, cognition, and even physiology. The vast majority of experimental psychologists hold positions in colleges and universities and engage in basic research. However, significant numbers of experimental psychologists also work in industry and government, where they apply research findings and, for example, solve problems involving the "human factor" such as finding ways that humans can most effectively use machines.

Developmental Psychologists

Most developmental psychologists hold academic positions, although a significant number also work in human services. Developmental researchers work with a broad array of theories and methods drawn from other areas of psychology. Developmental psychologists' interests range from physiological development to social development, and they study not only development in childhood, but development across the life span.

Educational Psychologists

Not too surprisingly, the vast majority of educational psychologists work in colleges and universities, where they conduct research on educational techniques and instruct future elementary and secondary school teachers.

School Psychologists

Over 60 percent of school psychologists work in primary and secondary schools. They mainly administer intelligence and aptitude tests, give career and education counseling, and consult on personal problems.

As we indicated earlier, despite the fact that psychologists can be found in a wide variety of work settings and are engaged in a wide variety of research and service activities, psychologists have a great many things in common. Perhaps the fundamental link between psychologists is their scientific orientation.

GLOSSARY

a-process According to opponent-process theory, an organism's initial emotional response to a motivationally significant stimulus.

A-State According to opponent-process theory, the emotional-motivational state that the organism is in when experiencing an a-process.

absolute threshold The minimum amount of energy that can produce a sensation.

accessible information Information that can be retrieved from memory—in contrast to information that is available but not retrievable.

accessory structure The part of a sense organ that serves to focus, amplify, or alter particular environmental stimuli.

accommodation (Piaget) In Piaget's theory, the process that occurs when people modify a scheme to include the new object or event.

accommodation (vision) The change in focus of the eye that results from changes in the shape of the lens.

achievement motivation The motivation to strive to attempt and complete moderately difficult tasks.

acoustic signals In speech perception, the particular stimulus frequencies and intensities associated with each phoneme.

acquired motivation The process through which a previously neutral stimulus attains motivational significance.

acquisition stage The stage of memory at which information is placed into memory.

action potential A brief, pulse-like change in voltage across the membrane of a neuron. This electrical signal propagates along the axon of the neuron and is a basic form of information transmission in the nervous system.

acquisition stage The stage of memory at which information is placed into memory.

actions Coordinated voluntary behaviors that replace reflexes during the first year of child development.

activational effects Effects of hormones that reveal latent sexual characteristics.

actor–observer bias The general tendency to overestimate the effects of dispositions on other people's behavior.

acute effects The immediate, direct effects of a drug on physiological systems.

adaptation The decrease in sensory system sensitivity that occurs during prolonged stimulation.

additive color mixture Color mixture in which different wavelengths of light are added together, such as when lights of different wavelengths are shined into the eye.

adipocytes Fat cells.

adoption studies A method for studying behavior genetics in which the behavior of adopted children is compared with that of their biological and adopted parents and siblings.

adrenal cortex The covering of the adrenal gland that is activated during stress reactions and releases steroids such as cortisol that promote healing.

affective component of attitudes A person's feelings and emotions (including physiological responses) toward an object.

affiliation motivation The motivation to remain close emotionally or physically to another creature because closeness brings pleasure and separation causes distress.

aggressive pornography Aggressive or coercive pornography depicts women as the targets of aggression and in subordinate and negative roles.

agoraphobia A type of phobia in which the individual fears open or public places. It is often accompanied by panic attacks.

algorithm A set of procedures that guarantees a particular solution to a problem. For example, you use your basic mathematical skills and apply an algorithm to get an exact answer to the product of 298×11.

altruism More narrowly defined than prosocial behavior, describes the motivation of helpers and the benefits to recipients.

Alzheimer's disease A type of dementia, thus it is characterized by severe memory loss, personality changes, and a profound inability to reason. Eventually persons suffering from this disorder become stuporous and die.

amblyopia Poor visual acuity caused by abnormalities in the brain. Commonly called "lazy eye."

amplitude In hearing, the greatest pressure of a sound wave.

ampulla A bulge at the end of each semicircular canal, in which receptors for the vestibular sense are located.

anal stage Stage of development in psychoanalytic theory during which there is a focus on the pleasures of elimination.

anal-expulsives In psychoanalytic theory anal-expulsives tend to be messy, highly emotional, and aggressively destructive.

analog representation People in the analog camp argue that visual information is represented in memory in a form that has physical features analogous to the images perceived.

androgens Hormones that influence sexual differentiation—one of which is testosterone.

androgyny The combination in the same person of certain traditional male and female sex-role characteristics and behavior.

angular gyrus A region of the brain. Damage to the angular gyrus can result in a difficulty in naming isolated objects and in reading although not in naming during conversational speech.

anhedonia A condition, often occurring in schizophrenia, in which the person is incapable of experiencing pleasure.

anorexia nervosa An eating disorder in which a person stops eating. The condition can be so severe that it may lead to death through starvation.

anterior pituitary The front part of the pituitary gland.

anterograde amnesia The failure to form new memories.

antigens Foreign cells or material that enters the body.

antisocial personality disorder A personality disorder in which the individual acts in an impulsive manner, taking risks and incurring long-term costs in order to obtain immediate gratification. The interpersonal relationships of the psychopathic individual are characterized by superficiality and opportunism. Also called *psychopathy*.

aphasia Disruptions of both spoken and written language. Aphasic speech is halting and telegraphic, punctuated by many pauses, and full of slips of the tongue.

apparent motion Instances in which stationary stimuli appear to move.

aqueous humor The watery fluid in the space between the cornea and the lens of the eye.

archetypes Jung believed that accumulated human experiences with objects such as "mother," "father," "death," and so on have produced inherited tendencies to respond to these objects in shared, often highly emotional ways.

archives Archives are places where public records and documents are stored. Researchers study archives to learn about natural patterns in behavior and events.

arousal/cost–reward model of helping This model postulates that onlookers experience arousal that is similar to but less than that of victims in an emergency. Onlookers are motivated to reduce this arousal in a manner that costs them less, and quickly calculate the relative costs of intervening or not intervening.

artificial intelligence The use of computers to simulate complex human thought processes.

assimilation In Piaget's theory, the process that occurs when people incorporate a new object or event into an existing scheme.

associative strength The capacity of the conditioned stimulus to elicit the conditioned response.

attention A mental function that brings certain information into conscious awareness and keeps other information out.

attentional processes In Bandura's social learning theory attentional processes determine whether a person observes behavior.

attitude Gordon Allport offered the following classic definition "an attitude is a mental and neural state of readiness, organized through experience, exerting a directive or dynamic influence upon the individual's response to all objects and situations with which it is related" (1935).

attribution The process by which the behavior of other people is explained—generally in terms of personal dispositions and environmental influences.

attribution theory A theory that holds that the emotional or motivational impact of an event depends upon an individual's beliefs about the cause of the event.

audition The sensation and perception of sound. Also called *hearing*.

auditory canal Part of the outer ear that funnels sound waves from the pinna to the eardrum.

auditory feature detectors Neurons in the brain that respond to particular patterns and features of sound, such as those in speech.

autokinesis A type of apparent motion in which a dim stationary point of light in a very dark room seems to move.

availability heuristic The tendency to estimate the likelihood of events on the basis of the ease with which they can be brought to mind.

available information Information that is in memory but cannot be retrieved. A distinction can be made between information that is available in memory and information that is accessible.

aversion therapy A behavior therapy technique in which an unpleasant stimulus is paired with a stimulus for which the client has an abnormal or excessive attraction. The intent is to reduce the appeal of the latter stimulus—to create an "aversion" to it.

avoidance training A reinforcement paradigm in which application of a punisher is delayed upon occurrence of a particular behavior.

axon sprouting Growth and formation of new connections by undamaged axons in response to damage of other axons.

B-cells Lymphocytes that attack antigens.

b-process According to opponent-process theory, an organism's secondary emotional response to a motivationally significant stimulus that counters the organism's initial emotional response (the a-process).

B-State According to opponent-process theory, the emotional-motivational state that the organism is in when experiencing a b-process.

babbling At about their third or fourth month, babies begin to babble—to make sounds that resemble the vowel and conso-

nant combinations of speech such as "pa" and "boo." Within a few weeks, these sounds may be repeated to form multisyllabic utterances such as "bababababababa."

backwards conditioning A form of Pavlovian conditioning in which the unconditioned stimulus precedes the conditioned stimulus in time, resulting in poor conditioning presumably because the conditioned stimulus does not serve as a good signal of the unconditioned stimulus.

balance theory Analysis of relationships among cognitive elements in models consisting of dyads (two elements) and triads (three elements). Triads can represent balanced and unbalanced relationships.

basal metabolism The amount of energy expended by the body to maintain basic physiological functions while in a resting state.

basic needs In Maslow's hierarchy basic needs such as physiological needs must be satisfied before needs at higher levels (metaneeds) can be addressed. At higher levels are psychological needs.

basilar membrane A long membrane in the cochlea upon which the auditory receptor cells sit.

Beck Depression Inventory (BDI) A test designed to index a person's level of depression.

behavior genetics The study of genetic bases of behavior.

behavior therapy A type of therapy, based on learning theory and research, that stresses that abnormal behavior is learned according to the same principles as is normal behavior.

Behavioral Activation System (BAS) The system, as proposed by Jeffrey Gray, that is activated by reward or the absence of expected punishment. Its activation increases approach behavior with respect to attractive incentive stimuli.

behavioral component of an attitude The behavioral component of an attitude consists of the mental and physical processes that prepare a person to respond in a particular way to an object.

Behavioral Inhibition System (BIS) The system, as proposed by Jeffrey Gray, that is activated by punishment, by frustrative nonreward, or by startling stimuli, and that results in freezing, arousal, and heightened attention. Phenomenologically, activation of the BIS feels like anxiety.

behaviorism A functionalist approach to behavior, that strongly rejects the introspectionist approach to psychology, and argues that only directly observable behavior is the proper subject for psychological study.

benzodiazepines Drugs such as Valium and Librium that are used to treat anxiety.

biases Imperfections of judgment that result when people rely upon rules of thumb.

binocular cues Visual depth cues that require the use of both eyes (binocular) to produce the perception of depth.

biogenic amines Neurotransmitters that contain a carbon chain and a nitrogen-hydrogen group; examples are dopamine and norepinephrine.

bipolar disorder A mental disorder characterized by bouts of mania. The affected individual may also experience bouts of depression as well.

blind spot The region of the retina where axons of the ganglion cells leave the eye and

become the optic nerve. Also called the *optic disc.*

blocking A procedure used in Pavlovian conditioning in which a conditioned stimulus 2 is paired with an unconditioned stimulus that is already signaled reliably by another conditioned stimulus 1. Conditioned stimulus 2 will be ineffective in acquiring the capacity to elicit a conditioned response because conditioning with it will be blocked by the preexisting relationship with conditioned stimulus 1.

blocking of retrieval Once a word has been used as a retrieval cue, it is likely to activate the same paths to information that is being sought and thus inhibit retrieval.

blood–brain barrier A barrier, formed by cells of the capillaries, between the blood and the brain.

bond A strong emotional attachment between two individuals, such as an infant and parent.

bottom-up theory States that people combine simple features in their perception of complex patterns, such as the auditory patterns in speech.

bound morpheme A bound morpheme is attached to and modifies the meaning of other morphemes. Bound morphemes include prefixes such as the *in* in incompetent, the *s* in dogs, and the *blue* and *berry* in blueberry.

brain stem The lower and back part of the brain, consisting of the midbrain, pons, medulla, and cerebellum.

brightness The visual experience that corresponds primarily to the intensity of light.

brightness constancy The perception that the brightness of an area remains the same even though its luminance (light intensity) changes.

Broca's aphasia An expressive disorder in which victims seem to know what they want to say but cannot find the words for it.

bulimia An eating disorder in which a person gorges on food in eating binges and later gets rid of the food either through regurgitation or through laxatives.

bystander effect As the number of bystanders increases, the less likely it becomes that an individual will intervene.

cardinal traits At the top of his trait hierarchy, Allport placed cardinal traits, the master motives or passions that pervade every aspect of life.

case study An observational research method. In a case study, a researcher or group of researchers may concentrate on a single person, group, or event for study.

castration anxiety Freud suggested that boys who worry that their fathers might retaliate for the boys' affection for the mother by cutting off the boys' penis suffer from castration anxiety.

categorical syllogism The premises in such syllogisms specify the relationships among categories and yield logical conclusions. The premises need not be factually true. In forming categorical syllogisms, four kinds of statements can be used—all, some, some not, and no.

cathexis Freud termed the expenditure of instinctual energies through an object, cathexis.

cell assemblies Hebb argued that behavioral, perceptual, and memory patterns are built up gradually through the connection of sets of cells called cell assemblies and that very complex behaviors were formed through the action of sets of cell assemblies.

center-to-periphery The pattern of early physical growth of the child; the center of the body grows more early in life, and the arms and legs grow more later. Also called *proximodistal*.

central nervous system The brain and spinal cord—everything inside the bony protection of the skull and spine (vertebral column).

central traits The notion that certain traits are more important than others in creating impressions.

central traits (Allport) In Allport's theory everyone has central traits such as neatness (or its opposite), thriftiness, industriousness, and the like. These represent a relatively small number of dispositions that have a broad influence on an individual's behavior.

cephalocaudal The pattern of early physical growth of the child; growth initially is more rapid in the head and upper body, and later growth occurs more in the lower body. Also called *head-to-foot*.

cerebral commissures Bundles of axons that carry information from neurons in one hemisphere to the other.

cerebral cortex A thin layer of tissue (about 3 millimeters thick) that covers the surface of the brain.

cerebral hemisphere The left or right half of the brain.

cerebrospinal fluid (CSF) A substance that fills the ventricles and the space between the meninges and the central nervous system.

cerebrum The large front part of the brain, consisting of the cerebral cortex, thalamus, hypothalamus, basal ganglia, and limbic system. Also called the *forebrain*.

characteristic features Properties of the concept that are not essential.

chemical transmitter A substance that is released by a presynaptic nerve terminal and has some effect on the postsynaptic cell, usually a change in permeability to one or more ions. Also called a *neurotransmitter*.

cholecystokinin A hormone released by the intestine that stimulates the vagus nerve and signals the brain to stop eating.

chromatic adaptation Change in the perception of the color of a light that occurs during prolonged exposure to that light.

chromatographic theory States that different odors are caused by different patterns of flow of odor molecules across the mucous layer covering the olfactory receptor cells.

chromosomes Structures in the nucleus of a cell that contain the genetic material.

chunking The capacity of short-term memory is between five and nine items. These items may be letters, numbers, nonsense syllables, or words. Items may also be chunked or linked together (as when seven letters form a single word) in short-term memory to increase its capacity.

circadian rhythms Biological rhythms that are generated from within the body and that have a complete cycle of about one day.

circular reactions Piaget's name for repetitious behaviors that seem to be produced for their own sake, simply for the sensorimotor experience.

class inclusion The ability to reason logically about the relationship between classes and subclasses.

classical conditioning A set of procedures that leads to relatively durable behavior change. A stimulus that produces no dra-

matic behavioral or physiological effects, a conditioned stimulus, is paired with a stimulus that reliably produces behavioral or physiological effects, an unconditioned stimulus. After repeated pairings, the conditioned stimulus by itself causes or elicits effects that are similar to those originally produced only by the unconditioned stimulus. Also called *Pavlovian conditioning*.

client-centered therapy Emphasizes that it is the client's view of himself or herself and the world that matters and that the therapist must see the world through the client's eyes.

cochlea The spiral-shaped part of the inner ear that contains the basilar membrane and auditory receptor cells.

code The representation of information about the world among neurons in the brain.

cognitive The cognitive component of an attitude consists of the cognitions (knowledge, facts, beliefs, and opinions) a person holds about an object.

cognitive biases So called because they seem to arise from the deficiencies in the collection and processing of social information.

cognitive development Development of knowledge about the world and how to manipulate it. Development of sensation and perception, of the ability to learn, to reason, and to solve problems.

cognitive dissonance Leon Festinger's theory—a major premise of which is that people are motivated to maintain consistency among the cognitive elements that make up their attitudes.

cognitive map A hypothetical representation of space/environment that guides an animal's learning or performance; for instance, in maze learning.

cognitive psychology The study of the mental processes involved in collecting, organizing, interpreting, remembering, and using information.

cognitive psychotherapies Those psychotherapies based on the belief that mental disorders or psychological problems arise from nonoptical, conscious, processing of information—for instance, incorrect attributions, bad assumptions, and selective attention to information.

cognitive response theory According to this theory, how much a person's attitude will change depends on the thoughts (or cognitions) generated in the person in response to a message.

cohort effects In studies of development, differences in performance that are due to common experiences rather than to age itself.

cohorts Groups of people who were born at different times and thus have different experiences.

collective unconscious In Jung's theory these are the "memory traces" of repeated human experiences that have accumulated over the millions of years of human development.

color constancy The perception that the color of an object remains the same despite changes in wavelength.

comparison level People's standard for what they deserve in a relationship. If, based on past experience, they feel short-changed in a particular relationship (the outcomes fall below their comparison level), they are less likely to maintain that relationship than they are to maintain a relationship in which the outcomes are above their comparison level.

comparison level for alternatives A calculation of whether other relationships would offer better ratios of rewards to costs.

complementary colors Two colors whose mixture produces white or an achromatic gray.

compound stimulus A procedure used in Pavlovian conditioning in which an unconditioned stimulus is paired with more than one conditioned stimulus.

concept learning Learning in which organisms learn about abstract relationships among stimuli. Also called *set learning*.

conditional syllogism Logical statement consisting of two premises and a conclusion.

conditioned taste aversion The avoidance of a particular taste that has been associated with illness.

conditions of worth In Rogers' theory, the notion that a child learns about external standards that ensure positive regard.

conduction aphasia If contact between Wernicke's and Broca's regions is damaged, a patient may be able to produce and understand speech, but have trouble repeating phrases (presumably because the information cannot be passed from Wernicke's area, where it is processed, to Broca's area, where it is produced).

cones A type of light receptor in the retina; cones are primarily responsible for people's ability to see colors and to see daylight or other high levels of light.

conflict hypothesis States that motion sickness is the result of a conflict between two sources of information about spatial orientation of the head and body.

conformity The tendency of individuals to act in ways that are in accord with the behavior of others in their group. The yielding to group pressure.

confounded Variables are confounded when they are mixed up in such a way that we cannot accurately determine whether one variable or the other produced the effects we observe.

conscience In Freud's theory, a part of the superego developed through punishments administered by parents. The conscience is primarily concerned with bad behavior, and it controls behavior by making a person feel worthless or bad.

conscious level In Freud's and other theories, the conscious level is everything that an individual is aware of at a given point in time, including perceptions, sensations, memories, and the like.

consciousness The sense of "I" or "self." An awareness of personal identity and an awareness of the relationship between the external world and self.

consensus In attribution theory, a judgment of whether most people act in the same way toward an entity.

conservation The recognition that irrelevant changes in the external appearance of an object have no effect on the object's quantity (weight, length, volume, or the like).

consistency (attributional) In attribution theory, the question of whether a person behaves in a particular way whenever a particular cause is present.

consistency (minority influence) In minority influence situations, the consistency with which a minority argues its position affects its persuasiveness.

consistency in behavior across situations The

question of whether or under what conditions behavior is consistent across situations.

consistency in personal traits over time The question of whether individual traits endure over long periods of time.

constitutional approach Sheldon's argument that a person's body type determines his or her personality and behavior.

construct validity A test of the extent to which variables that, on theoretical grounds, ought to be related to one another are in fact related. When construct validity is achieved, it means that researchers have reached some agreement about what a theoretical concept or construct is and some agreement on how it should be operationalized and measured.

content analysis Content analysis is designed to allow researchers to evaluate systematically the qualitative aspects of documents and communications.

content validity When validity is determined by evaluating whether the assessment device actually elicits those same behaviors or responses in which the assessor is interested.

context dependency Because people encode specifics about their internal body states and external environmental conditions along with other information, they can use the body state and environmental information or context as cues to retrieve additional material from memory.

contiguity The theory of Pavlovian conditioning that holds that the essential relationship between the conditioned stimulus and the unconditioned stimulus that leads to the acquisition of a conditioned response is that the two stimuli occur close together in time.

contingency The relationship between a behavior and its consequence.

continuous reinforcement A schedule of reinforcement in which every instance of a behavior is followed by a particular consequence.

contrast The difference in light intensity between the darkest and lightest parts of visual objects, such as the stripes of a grating.

convergent measures Assessments that are designed to measure the same thing—usually the same hypothetical construct.

coos Beginning at about 3 to 5 weeks, infants generate sounds called coos.

cornea The transparent bulge in front of the eye.

corollary discharge theory States that when motor areas of the brain command a movement, they send out an additional (corollary) signal (discharge) to other areas of the brain indicating that a movement is about to occur.

correlated Measures or scores that tend to vary together.

correlation coefficient A statistic that indicates both the strength and the direction (positive or negative) of the relationship between two measures. Correlation coefficients range from 0.0 (no relationship between the two measures) to ±1.0 (a perfect relation). The sign of the correlation coefficient (+ or −) indicates the direction of the relation.

correspondent inferences Inferences are correspondent when a person can label both the behavior and the disposition of an actor with the same term.

corticosterone Naturally occurring steroids released by the adrenal cortex during stress that help reduce inflammation and promote healing. Also called *cortisol*.

cortisol Naturally occurring steroids released by the adrenal cortex during stress that help reduce inflammation and promote healing. Also called *corticosterone*.

criterion The implicit rule used by an observer when deciding whether a particular level of sensory neural activity is due to noise alone or to signal-plus-noise.

criterion validity When validity is determined by evaluating whether the assessment device predicts an outcome in which the assessor is interested.

critical period (brain) A limited period of development during which the brain is susceptible to change as a result of environmental influences.

critical period (learning) A time during development when animals are capable of a particular type of learning that cannot be mastered during any other developmental period.

cross-adaptation The decrease in sensitivity to one stimulus that occurs during prolonged exposure to another, similar, stimulus.

cross-sectional experimental design A method of studying development in which groups of individuals of different ages are compared.

crystallized intelligence A term used to describe previously stored knowledge, and processes that allow such knowledge to be used, in the conduct of cognitive, intelligent acts. This aspect of intelligence is thought to increase over the life span.

cyclic adenosine 3′,5′-monophosphate (cAMP) An enzyme, inhibited by antipsychotic drugs, that normally helps action potentials occur if a neuron's receptors are stimulated.

dark adaptation The increase in sensitivity to light that occurs during time spent in the dark.

data Psychologists collect their observations or data through systematic observation.

death instinct (thanatos) In Freud's theory the striving to return to an inorganic state. The death instinct is one of the more controversial aspects of Freud's theory.

debriefing Researchers fully debrief or inform subjects about the true nature of the study once the subjects have completed their participation.

decay The erosion of information from long-term memory.

decibel (dB) sound pressure level (SPL) The most common unit of sound amplitude. The amplitude of sound pressure relative to the pressure of the weakest 1000-Hz tone that people can hear.

declarative knowledge Ideas, propositions, and declarations about the nature of the physical and social world.

deductive logic In deductive logic, people can reason, with certainty, from premises to conclusions. In deductive logic, logically valid syllogisms need not be factually true.

defense mechanisms In psychoanalytic theory defense mechanisms protect against anxiety. They may distort and falsify reality and exclude feelings of anxiety from consciousness.

defining features Defining features are essential to the definition of a word, whereas characteristic features describe properties of the concept that are not essential.

delirium tremens A symptom of chronic alcoholism and alcohol withdrawal in which the individual becomes confused and has hallucinations.

delusions A belief that diverges greatly from those of the rest of society and cannot be supported by cogent argument or evidence.

dementia Decline of mental status—decreased memory, reasoning ability, and personality change.

denial A refusal to recognize a threat—perhaps the most basic defense mechanism in psychoanalytic theory.

dermis The inner layer of the skin.

descriptive statistics Numerical methods for describing and summarizing a set of observations.

determinist The determinist point of view holds that all events are caused by other events.

developmental stages Relatively abrupt, qualitative changes in thought or behavior that occur in a particular sequence during development.

dichromats People who are partially color blind because they are missing one type of cone receptor in the retina.

dictionary theory of meaning This approach is based on a logical analysis of language and seeks to identify the various meanings that a single word may have.

difference threshold The least difference between two stimuli that is necessary for a person to be able to discriminate between them.

difference-reduction In problem solving, this is one version of the means–end strategy and is based on the idea that an operation should reduce the difference between the current state and the desired goal.

diffusion of responsibility When responsibility for action does not focus on a particular person, everyone looks to everyone else to assume responsibility. One explanation of bystander effects.

direct assessment An approach to assessment in which the assessor attempts to measure the very behavior or response in which the assessor is interested.

disconfirmation One strategy for determining decision making is to test and rule out or disconfirm incorrect hypotheses.

discounting principle People discount the role of a given cause in producing an effect if other plausible causes are also present.

discrimination A judgment about whether two stimuli are different.

discriminative stimulus A stimulus that signals when reinforcement is available.

dishabituator A stimulus that elicits exaggerated responding in an habituated organism. Dishabituators tend to be startling, and they cannot be the stimulus to which the organism was habituated.

displacement In psychoanalytic theory a defense mechanism that arises when people remove their impulses from someone or something unsatisfying to someone or something that may be satisfying.

displacement activity Seemingly purposeless behaviors that organisms emit when faced with conflicting motivations.

dissonance Discomfort produced when a person's cognitions—beliefs, opinions, self-perceptions, and the like—do not fit together harmoniously.

dissonance reduction Efforts to reduce dissonance—often through attitude change.

distinctiveness In attribution theory, the extent to which a behavior occurs only when a particular cause is present.

disulfiram (Antabuse) A drug used to treat alcoholism. It prevents the metabolism of alcohol, allowing a poison to build up when the alcoholic drinks alcohol, thereby making the alcoholic feel sick whenever he or she drinks.

divided attention Attending to two or more stimuli at the same time.

dizygotic (DZ) twins Twins that arise from two separate fertilized eggs and are no more alike genetically than any other siblings. Also called *fraternal twins.*

dominant gene The gene that determines the trait when two genes in a pair specify different traits.

dopamine A neurotransmitter, excesses of which have been implicated with schizophrenia, while deficits are implicated in the neurological condition, Parkinson's disease. In addition, it appears to be a major transmitter in brain reward systems that allow us to feel pleasure.

double-blind In double-blind research designs neither the experimenter nor the subject knows which experimental condition a subject is in or the hypothesized effects of the experiment.

Down syndrome A set of abnormalities usually caused by an error in cell division that results in three chromosomes in the 21st position rather than the normal two chromosomes. Down syndrome is characterized by moderate-to-severe mental retardation and unusual physical features—short, stubby fingers, slanting eyes, and short stature.

drugs of abuse Natural or synthetic chemicals that are habitually used by significant numbers of people for nonmedical purposes.

dual process theory Atkinson and Shiffrin's dual process distinction between short-term and long-term memory systems or stages.

dynamic monocular cues Visual depth cues that are based on features of moving (dynamic) objects and require only one eye (monocular) to produce the perception of depth.

dynamic psychotherapy A type of psychotherapy that is based on Freudian personality theory, but that is much shorter than psychoanalysis.

eardrum A thin membrane in the outer ear that vibrates to sound waves.

echoic memory A storage system that retains auditory information for a few seconds.

echolocation The ability to locate objects in space by sensing the echoes of sounds that are reflected from them.

ectomorphs In Sheldon's theory ectomorphs are slender and fragile with a lot of skin relative to their body weight.

effectors Muscles and glands that make it possible for organisms to have some effect on the world.

ego In psychoanalytic theory the psychic component that mediates between the id and reality. It is a kind of executive manager for the personality. The ego is rational and seeks to govern behavior in a manner that is consistent with social expectations.

ego instincts Freud distinguished between ego instincts, which are directed to self-preservation, and sexual instincts, which are directed to preservation of the species.

ego psychologists Erik Erikson and a number of other psychoanalysts argued against Freud's characterization of the ego as dependent on the id and insisted, instead, that the ego is largely autonomous (for which they are called ego psychologists).

ego-ideal A part of the superego developed through the rewards given by parents.

egocentric Viewing everything only from one's own perspective. The inability to take another person's point of view.

electric sense The sensation and perception of electric currents in water.

electroconvulsive therapy (ECT) A treatment in which electric current is passed through a client's brain, or one hemisphere of a client's brain, in order to alleviate depression. Although the treatment is often effective in reducing depression, the basis of its effectiveness is not understood.

electroencephalogram (EEG) Recordings of brain waves that represent the electrical activity of many cells. Usually recorded with large electrodes placed on the scalp.

embryonic stage The period between the second and the eighth weeks of prenatal development.

empiricism Scientific approach to building knowledge—scientists understand the world by directly and systematically experiencing and testing it.

empty nest The parent's household when the last child has grown up and left home.

encoding The processes by which information is prepared for storage in memory.

encoding specificity hypothesis The idea that whenever a person experiences an event, a number of aspects of the event are encoded (e.g., the time, the location, features of the setting, the people involved, the actions taken during the event, and so on). Retrieval cues will be more effective if they match these encodings.

endocrine glands Glands that secrete chemicals into the fluids around capillaries.

endogenous opioids Protein molecules manufactured by the body that have effects very similar to those of plant (alkaloid) opiates such as opium.

endomorphs In Sheldon's theory endomorphs are rounded and have protruding stomachs, and are relaxed in posture and movement.

endorphins Opiate-like substances that occur naturally in the nervous system. Also called *endogenous opioids.*

engram The site where learning supposedly takes place and a memory "trace" remains.

epidermis The protective outer layer of the skin.

epilepsy A disease in which the neurons in a particular region of the brain are too active.

episodic memory Memory for particular events in one's life.

equal loudness curve A graph that shows intensities at which sounds of different frequencies have the same perceived loudness.

equity theory The notion that both parties to a relationship should have equal ratios of rewards and costs, rather than equal rewards to costs.

erogenous zones Freud believed that over the course of development, people's (libidinal) energies are devoted to different interests and objects and parts of the body, or erogenous zones. Each area and its associated drives (hunger, elimination, and sex) give way to the next as the primary focus of a child's activities.

erotica Erotica includes sexually explicit materials that depict men and women as equals and in a positive and humane light that shows respect for sexual relationships.

escape training A reinforcement paradigm in which a punisher is removed upon the occurrence of a particular behavior.

estradiol An estrogen sex hormone that is partly responsible for the physical changes seen in girls during puberty. It has activational effects on their latent sexual characteristics.

ethologists Scientists who study the behavior of animals in their natural environments.

ethology A functional approach to the analysis of behaviors in which characteristic patterns of behavior are thought to reflect the end products of evolutionary pressures (natural selection). This approach emphasizes the study of species within their natural environments and uses comparisons across species to determine the functional significance of behaviors.

eugenics The theory or practice of regulating family size according to the traits of the parents.

excitation A hypothetical process that accounts for the conditioned stimulus acquiring the capacity to elicit the conditioned response.

excitation-transfer The theory that people can transfer the arousal produced by one situation to another arousing situation.

exhaustive searches Sternberg's short-term memory studies indicated that searches for newly learned information are exhaustive rather than self-terminating. That is, people seemed to search all the items in a set and then respond, rather than examining each item individually and responding as soon as a match was made.

existential anxiety Existentialists have argued that being is the ultimate objective of life and that being implies an awareness of nonbeing and the inevitability of death. From this awareness comes, inevitably, existential anxiety.

exocrine glands Glands that secrete chemicals through a duct.

expectancies The idea that behavior in pursuit of goals is governed by expectations of future rewards.

expressed emotion Communications in a family marked by high levels of hostility, criticism, and overinvolvement.

expressive disorder Broca's aphasia is sometimes characterized as an expressive disorder because one of its main symptoms is that victims seem to know what they want to say but cannot find the words for it.

external validity The challenge to external validity can take many forms. Some may argue that a laboratory study lacked realism and that its results would not generalize to other settings, other subjects, or other times.

extrasensory perception (ESP) Perceptual abilities, such as clairvoyance, precognition, and telepathy, that do not depend on known sensory systems.

extrastriate visual cortex Areas of the cortex that lie beyond striate cortex and are involved in vision. Also called *higher-order visual areas* of the cortex.

extravert In Eysenck's theory a typical extravert is sociable, exuberant, likes parties and craves excitement, and is frequently impulsive.

face validity When operational definitions of a construct possess an appearance of validity—when they look like what they purport to be.

factor analysis A statistical procedure in which the researcher attempts to discover how multiple variables are related to one another.

familiarity You identify a person or an object when there is a match between the information you are given and critical features of the information stored in your memory. But the degree of familiarity you experience depends upon the number of features that match.

fear appeals Fear appeals (such as advertisements against smoking or favoring seatbelt use that incorporate information about negative consequences such as illness, injury, and death) can produce high immediate compliance but may lose their potency over time.

feral children Children who have been discovered living in the wild, sometimes in the company of animals such as wolves—and deprived children who have been raised in isolation and without benefit of significant human contact.

fetal stage The period of prenatal development between the eighth week after fertilization until birth, which is usually 38 or so weeks after fertilization.

field experiments Experiments conducted outside the laboratory. For example, experiments that have been conducted with actual patients who have been randomly assigned to receive new experimental drugs and treatments.

fixated In psychoanalytic theory, if a child cannot solve the problems of development at a particular developmental stage, or if progress is interrupted by childhood traumas, he or she may become fixated or stuck at that stage.

fixed action pattern A sequence of specific behaviors that is elicited in exactly the same way each time the organism is exposed to a specific type of stimulus (a releasing stimulus).

fixed-interval schedule A reinforcement schedule in which a particular, set, amount of time must pass before a response will lead to reinforcement.

fixed-ratio schedule A reinforcement schedule in which a particular, set, number of responses is required before reinforcement is delivered.

flavor A complex sensation associated with food, based on the taste, temperature, texture, and especially smell of the food.

flooding therapy/implosion A behavior therapy technique used to reduce phobic fears in which the person is rapidly exposed to maximally fear-eliciting objects.

fluid intelligence A term used to describe those processes that are responsible for the ability to acquire new information and master novel problems. This aspect of intelligence is thought typically to increase through adolescence and to decline during middle-age and thereafter.

forebrain The large front part of the brain, consisting of the cerebral cortex, thalamus, hypothalamus, basal ganglia, and limbic system. Also called the *cerebrum*.

fovea A region at the center of the retina that is specialized for seeing color and fine details.

fraternal twins Twins that arise from two separate fertilized eggs and are no more alike genetically than any other siblings. Also

called *dizygotic twins*.

free association The uncensored reporting of thoughts as they occur.

free morpheme A word that stands on its own—dog, love, car, etc.; contrasts with bound morphemes.

free recall When subjects do not have to recall information in any particular order.

frequency In hearing, the number of complete cycles of a sound wave in a period of time; expressed as cycles per second, or Hertz (Hz).

frequency distribution A graph that shows the number (frequency) of observations with particular scores. Scores are plotted on the horizontal axis (abscissa) and the frequency of each score is plotted on the vertical axis (ordinate) of the graph.

frequency theory States that sounds of a particular frequency cause the basilar membrane to vibrate at that frequency, and that this vibration in turn stimulates receptor cells at the same frequency and causes the auditory nerve fibers to discharge action potentials at that frequency.

fricatives Consonants produced with a fricative or slowing of the air flow—e.g., both /f/ and /h/.

frustration Anything that interferes with the achievement of a goal.

functional analysis Assessments of the functional significance of behavior or biological characteristics. In Darwin's theory characteristics and behaviors are analyzed to determine their functional significance or role in promoting the survival of an organism and the reproduction of its genes.

functional fixedness The tendency to recognize the customary functions of objects in a particular situation and miss other functions the objects might serve.

fundamental attribution error Probably the most common cognitive error that people make is to overattribute causation to a person's disposition and underattribute it to situational factors.

g The general factor yielded by factor analysis that appears to account for much of the variance in performance on tests of cognitive ability (e.g., IQ tests).

gender role The mannerisms, perspectives, interests, and habits that are associated with a particular sex. This may be distinct from actual biological sexual features.

gene The unit of hereditary information.

general adaptation syndrome The three-stage pattern of reaction that Hans Selye thought characterized organisms' reactions to stressors. In the different stages, the alarm, resistance, and exhaustion stages, organisms have different abilities to adapt to new stressors and show different levels of physical effects of the stress.

general paresis Advanced neurosyphilis that produces cognitive and personality changes. Once a leading cause of hospitalization in mental asylums.

generalization The tendency for stimuli similar to a conditioned stimulus to elicit conditioned responses similar to those elicited by the conditioned stimulus.

generalize To extrapolate findings to the broader world.

generalized anxiety disorder A mental disorder in which the person suffers from chronic anxiety.

generate and test One straightforward problem-solving heuristic is to generate a possible solution to a problem and test it.

generation gap Large differences between parents' and peers' norms.

generator potential A change in voltage across the membrane of a sensory neuron.

genital stage In psychoanalytic theory the stage at which erotic impulses, which were primarily autoerotic before latency, surface with a new emphasis. Adolescents become interested in genital sexuality.

genotype The genes for a particular trait.

germinal stage The first two weeks of prenatal development after fertilization of the egg cell.

Gestalt school of psychology A group of psychologists who want to examine the whole of experience—the larger patterns, structure, and organization of behavior. Gestalt psychologists believe that the whole is different from the sum of its parts and that something essential is lost when only the parts are examined. For example, in studying perception, Gestalt psychologists believe that a perceived form has a unity that is greater than the sum of the elementary stimulus elements that make up the form.

gestation period The period of development that occurs within the mother's body; the period from conception to birth. Also called the *prenatal period*.

glia The supporting cells of the central nervous system.

global aphasia Global aphasics, who have sustained damage to both Broca's and Wernicke's regions, may show no evidence of language comprehension and may speak only a single word repetitively.

glucostats Sensors that measure the amount of glucose in the blood.

Golgi tendon organs Receptors on tendons that are stimulated by stretch or contraction of the muscles.

grammar Although people can generate an infinite number of sentences, these sentences follow a systematic and finite set of rules called a grammar. A grammar tells how such things as verbs, nouns, and their modifiers relate to one another. A grammar provides rules for linking words into meaningful sequences.

growth principle Horney rejected Freud's view that most of the important matters in development are settled in childhood. She replaced his pleasure and death instincts with her growth principle. It was her belief that people are born with a capacity for growth and strive to achieve their full potential.

gustation The sensation and perception of chemicals on the tongue and palate. Also called the sense of *taste*.

habit According to Hull, habit, along with drive and incentive value, determines motivation level. High habit strength is produced by numerous previous occasions in which a particular behavior is rewarded.

habitual responses The second level of Eysenck's personality hierarchy consists of habitual responses or characteristic patterns of behavior that are repeated in similar situations.

habituation Decreased response to a stimulus that is produced by repeated exposure to that stimulus.

hair cells Receptor cells that have tiny hairs, or cilia, protruding from them.

hallucinations Sensory experiences that have no basis in reality.

head-to-foot The pattern of early physical growth of the child; growth initially is more rapid in the head and upper body, and later growth occurs more in the lower body. Also called *cephalocaudal*.

hearing The sensation and perception of sound. Also called *audition*.

helping Helping behavior differs from altruistic behavior insofar as people may be externally rewarded for helping and the helping behavior is defined as such by the helper rather than by the recipient.

heritability coefficient This coefficient reflects the degree of genetic influence on personality or another characteristic.

Hertz (Hz) A measure of sound frequency. One cycle per second.

heterozygous When two genes in a pair specify different traits.

heuristic This is a general rule of thumb. A heuristic can be contrasted with an algorithm. For example, to estimate the product of 298 $\times$ 11 you might use a heuristic and round 298 to 300 and 11 to 10 so that you can multiply them in your head.

hidden observer A phenomenon in which a hypnotized person acts as if there were an internal observer who is aware of external reality.

higher order visual areas Areas of the cortex that lie beyond striate cortex and are involved in vision. Also called *extrastriate visual cortex*.

histamine A neurotransmitter.

histrionic personality disorder A personality disorder in which the individual acts dramatically and has emotional outbursts that seem designed to capture attention.

holophrastic speech During the child's second year words are generally used one at a time in what is called holophrastic speech (from the Greek *holos*, "whole" and *phrazein*, "to point out").

homeostasis A term that describes processes through which the body maintains a particular level of physiological functioning.

homozygous When two genes in a pair specify the same trait.

hormones The chemicals secreted by the endocrine glands.

hostile aggression Aggression that appears to be motivated by the aggressor's desire to hurt or injure the victim.

hue The visual experience that corresponds primarily to the wavelength of light. Commonly used as a synonym for *color*.

humanistic therapy An approach to psychotherapy based on the notion that humans are essentially good and will achieve psychological health if they are not fettered and their natural impulses are not distorted by society.

hypermnesia The remembering of more information with the passing of time. Improved memory during hypnosis.

hypnosis A condition in which a person experiences changes in perception, memory, and behavior in response to suggestions made by the hypnotist.

hypochondriasis A mental disorder in which a person chronically fears that he or she suffers from physical illness despite an absence of

physical evidence of disease. This differs from hysteria in that the hypochondriac fears that he or she has a specific disease, whereas the hysteric is more concerned with individual symptoms.

hypotheses Hypotheses are predictions that can be tested.

hypothetical construct A presumed state of nature or natural process that can be studied only indirectly.

hysteria A now dated term for a mental disorder, usually occurring in women, in which a person has numerous complaints of aches and pains but shows no physical evidence. It is important to note that the hysteric is not lying—he or she really believes there to be a physical problem.

iatrogenic illness An illness that is produced by a treatment.

icon A vivid but short-lived mental image of viewed stimuli.

id In psychoanalytic theory the instinctual side of mental life—the biological foundations of personality. It is the source of the energies for instinctual urges, such as aggression and sexuality. The id exercises no logic and no morals, is selfish and demanding, and seeks immediate and unrestrained gratification.

identical twins Two individuals that arise from the same fertilized egg and therefore have identical genotypes. Also called *monozygotic twins*.

identification (memory) When you recognize something, you have made a comparison between information provided to you and the information you find in your memory. The comparison can yield an identification or a sense of familiarity. You identify a stimulus when there is a match between the information you are given and critical features of the information stored in your memory.

identification (personality) Freud talked about identification as a defense mechanism in which a person, say a child, internalizes or assumes the characteristics of another person who is thought to be very powerful or otherwise desirable.

identity An individual's choices about the kind of person he or she wants to be and what his or her role will be in society.

identity confusion Erikson's term for a state in which adolescents cannot "find" themselves and never form a firm sense of identity.

idiographic An approach to personality based on intensive studies of individuals and descriptions of the unique characteristics of those individuals.

imipramine An antidepressant drug that appears to work, at least in part, because it reduces the activity of the neurotransmitter, norepinephrine.

immune system A collection of organs and cell types in the body whose main purpose is to fight off foreign invaders (such as bacteria) and reduce disease or the risk of disease.

implicit personality theories Peoples' expectations about how traits fit together.

impression management theory The theory that people change their attitudes because they try not to look bad in awkward situations.

imprinting A type of learning in which a young animal develops an intense and durable attachment to an object or animal to

which it has been exposed. Imprinting usually occurs only during a critical period of development. See also *critical period*.

inbred strains Strains of animals that are produced by mating brothers and sisters, and then mating brothers and sisters from the offspring, and so on.

incentives Goals that are sufficiently desirable or undesirable so that they can elicit motivated behavior.

independent variable Any variable that is expected to produce an effect on another variable—typically refers to the experimental variable under the control of the experimenter.

indirect assessment An approach to assessment in which the assessor does not attempt to measure the very behavior or response in which he or she is interested, but rather attempts to measure a sign or reflection of the behavior.

inductive logic Determining a general rule that covers a number of specific instances. In inductive logic we cannot reach conclusions with certainty. Contrasts with deductive logic.

infantile autism A mental disorder diagnosed in infancy in which the child cannot develop or sustain close interpersonal relationships or contact, has severe communication difficulties, often shows perceptual deficits characteristic of schizophrenia, and tends to be mentally retarded.

inferential statistics Numerical methods that help researchers draw conclusions from observations by indicating the probabilities of certain outcomes.

inferiorities Adler drew an anology between physical compensation for a disability and psychological compensation. He believed that someone who had psychological and social inferiorities might strive to overcome them.

informational social influence When a person publicly and privately accepts a group's opinions.

informed consent Researchers fully inform subjects about any known harmful consequences they might experience and request the subjects' informed consent to participate despite the risks.

inhibition A hypothetical process that accounts for the conditioned stimulus not eliciting the conditioned response following extinction; the conditioned response is inhibited.

insomnia A difficulty in getting to sleep or in staying asleep.

instinctive Due to genetic inheritance, not learned.

instinctive drift The tendency for operant behavior to change over time despite a lack of change in reinforcement contingencies. The change in behavior appears to occur because stimuli present during the operant behavior come to elicit instinctive, inborn, Pavlovian conditioned responses that interfere with the operant behavior.

instrumental aggression Aggression that appears to be motivated to secure some tangible reward or advantage.

instrumental learning Learning that is determined by the consequences of behavior. Also called *operant learning*.

insufficient justification Attitude change following the performance of counterattitudinal behavior may result when a person has insufficient justification for behavior.

intelligence quotient (IQ) Once literally a

quotient constituted of the relationship between chronical age and an estimate of mental age that was derived from performance on the Stanford-Binet test. Now a label used for a score yielded by any intelligence test. See also *mental age.*

interaural distortion differences A cue for sound localization that depends on the fact that sounds in different locations in space have different relative distortions as they enter each ear.

interaural intensity differences A cue for sound localization that depends on the fact that sounds in different locations in space have different relative intensities at each ear.

interaural time differences A cue for sound localization that depends on the fact that sounds in different locations in space arrive at each ear at different relative times.

interference Process in which newly learned material blocks the recall of other material.

internal consistency A method for assessing the reliability of a psychological test by determining whether the responses to individual items agree with one another.

internal lexicon The structure of the concepts and meanings stored in memory (the internal dictionary).

internal validity A measure of an experimenter's success in manipulating the variables that he or she intends to manipulate and in ruling out other explanations of the experimental results.

interstimulus interval The interval in time between a conditioned stimulus and an unconditioned stimulus in a Pavlovian conditioning procedure.

introspection Studies of people's sensations, feelings, and images produced by responses to simple stimuli such as sounds and colors.

introvert In Eysenck's personality model the typical introvert is shy, self-controlled, quiet, introspective, and inhibited rather than impulsive.

invariance The perception that different acoustic signals are the same phoneme.

iproniazid A drug that inhibits monoamine oxidase, an enzyme that breaks down neurotransmitters such as norepinephrine and dopamine, and results in elation. Because iproniazid inhibits this oxidase, it results in increased levels of neurotransmitters, suggesting that high levels of these transmitters produce elation.

iris The colored disc surrounding the pupil of the eye.

James–Lange theory A theory of emotion that holds that our subjective experience of emotions is produced through our sensing our peripheral physiological reactions that are reflexively elicited by motivationally significant external stimuli.

just noticeable difference (jnd) A physical difference between standard and comparison stimuli that can be discriminated 50 percent of the time.

kin selection In sociobiological theory the argument that what matters in evolution is the survival of genes and not necessarily the organism that carries the genes. Thus, the parent that dies for its offspring has helped to ensure that the genes they share will survive into future generations.

kinesthesis The sensation and perception of the positions of the limbs and joints.

Korsakoff's psychosis A condition, caused by chronic alcohol abuse, in which the alcohol-damaged brain does not function properly, and people lose the ability to store new information in long-term memory.

Korsakoff's syndrome A pattern of systematic loss of past memories (retrograde amnesia) and the failure to form new memories (anterograde amnesia).

language acquisition device Some nativists argue that as a result of evolutionary pressures, humans are biologically predisposed to learn language and have a built-in set of perceptual and cognitive abilities specialized to facilitate language learning and production.

language universals Patterns in speech development common to all environmental conditions.

latency period Between the ages of 5 and 6, children enter the latency period, which lasts until the ages of about 12 or 13 (the age of puberty). Freud believed that during the latency period, the sexual instincts are dormant.

lateral geniculate nucleus A group of neurons in the thalamus that receive inputs directly from the two eyes.

lateral inhibition The process of inhibitory neural interaction between cells of adjacent regions of a sensory surface, such as the retina.

law of effect The principle stated by Edward Thorndike that organisms tend to engage in acts that have pleasing consequences and cease in engaging in acts that have unpleasant consequences.

law of specific nerve energies States that gross sensory quality, such as light, sound, and touch, depends on which nerve is stimulated, not on how it is stimulated.

laws of organization Principles, formulated by the Gestalt psychologists, that explain why we perceive certain stimulus patterns as a unified group or form.

learned helplessness A condition produced by uncontrollable stress in which an animal becomes inactive and no longer tries to cope with environmental challenges.

lemniscal system Central nervous system pathways that carry information primarily about touch and pressure.

lens A structure in the eye that changes the focus of an image that enters the eye.

leucotomy A type of psychosurgery in which connections between the frontal lobes and the rest of the brain are severed.

libido In Freudian theory the energy that fuels motivated behaviors—procreation, eating, accomplishment.

life energy Jung viewed libido as a general life energy, of which sexual urges were just one aspect.

life instinct Freud subsumed the ego and sexual instincts into a single life instinct (eros) and its associated energy (libido).

light adaptation The decrease in sensitivity to light that occurs during time spent in bright light.

link method A mnemonic device that relies on forming links between items with mental images.

lithium carbonate A drug containing the mineral lithium that is effective in the treatment of bipolar affective illness.

lobotomy A type of psychosurgery in which the frontal lobes are removed.

locus ceruleus A nucleus in the brain that appears to be involved with anxiety states such as panic attacks and with drug withdrawal symptoms.

longitudinal experimental design A method of studying development in which performance of the same group of individuals is compared at different ages.

loudness The auditory experience that corresponds primarily to the amplitude of sound waves.

lymphocytes Cells of the immune system that are responsible for fighting disease by attacking antigens or by attacking the body's own cells that have been altered or damaged.

maintenance rehearsal The mental repeating of to-be-remembered information—holds information in short-term memory.

major depression A mental disorder characterized by hopelessness, an inability to experience pleasure, and profound sadness.

mands Mands are forms of verbal behavior controlled by listeners' responses (as in comMAND).

mania A state characterized by tremendous energy, elevated mood, and imprudent behavior. Mania is a necessary condition for the diagnosis of bipolar disorder.

manic episode A discrete period in which an individual has tremendous energy, an elevated mood, and engages in imprudent behavior.

manipulate Researchers seek to control or manipulate their causal or independent variable and then examine the effects of these manipulations on the outcome or dependent variables.

matching To assure that two groups are as much alike as possible they are matched on relevant characteristics.

matching principle The notion that people will be most attracted to other people who are similar in physical attractiveness.

mean A statistical measure of central tendency, obtained by dividing the sum of all scores by the number of scores. The arithmetic average.

means–end A heuristic strategy that requires that problem solvers identify the ends they seek to achieve and find a sequence of operations (the means) to that end.

measures of central tendency Statistics that describe the center of a set of scores. The mean, median, and mode are commonly used measures of central tendency.

measures of variability Statistics that describe the amount of spread of scores around the center of a set of scores. The range, variance, and standard deviation are commonly used measures of variability.

mechanization of thought Occurs when people develop a "set" or regular mental orientation to problems that impede their problem solving. Also called *set effect.*

median A statistical measure of central tendency; the middle score of a set of scores.

median forebrain bundle A section of the brain, in which dopamine is the principal neurotransmitter, that is activated by pleasurable incentives and that may mediate pursuit of the incentives.

meditation A practice that people engage in to alter consciousness by restricting their awareness to a single process.

menarche The onset of menstruation.

meninges Tough connective tissue that covers the central nervous system.

mental age The age at which most children can answer a question or a type of question on an intelligence test.

mental chronometry A method for the study of the structure and nature of mental events. Measurement of the time various mental events take or, more specifically, people's reaction times to stimuli.

mental retardation A mental disorder diagnosed in childhood characterized by subnormal intelligence and deficient adaptive behavior.

mere exposure effect People prefer things that are familiar to them. The more often people had been exposed to stimuli, the more they liked the stimuli.

mesomorphs In Sheldon's theory mesomorphs have a heavy, hard, rectangular shape; their muscles and bones dominate their frames.

metamemory An understanding of the variables that affect one's own memory performance and how performance can be improved.

metaneeds In Maslow's theory the highest level, psychological needs.

method of loci A mnemonic device in which to-be-remembered information is linked to locations in a mental map.

Millon Clinical Multiaxial Inventory (MCMI) A new objective test designed to yield information on a client's personality structure.

minimal pairs The phonemes used in a language are identified by examining pairs of words that are identical except for one sound. For example, "hat" and "bat" share the "at" sound, but /b/ and the /h/ change the meanings.

minimax principle People are thought to follow a minimax principle in their relationships in that they most like relationships that provide maximum rewards at a minimum cost.

Minnesota Multiphasic Personality Inventory (MMPI) A widely used objective test designed to yield information on diagnosis.

mnemonic A memory device used to enhance recall of information.

mode A statistical measure of central tendency; the most frequent score in a set of scores.

modus ponens A logical rule that specifies that when presented the proposition A implies B and given A, we may infer B.

modus tollens A logical rule that specifies that when presented the proposition A implies B and given B is false, we must infer that A is also false.

molar analysis Analysis of phenomena at a high level of abstraction. For example, the analysis of language as a social phenomenon.

molecular analysis Analysis of phenomena at the level of the smallest elements or component parts. For example, the analysis of language at the neural level.

monoamine oxidase inhibitors (MAO) Drugs intended to alleviate the symptoms of depression. Usually used only if tricyclic antidepressants have been found to be ineffective because of potential danger.

monochromats People who are completely color blind because they have only one type of cone receptor in the retina or, in some cases, no functioning cones.

monozygotic (MZ) twins Two individuals that arise from the same fertilized egg and therefore have identical genotypes. Also called *identical twins.*

moral anxiety In psychoanalytic theory an internally generated anxiety based on the feelings of guilt and shame produced by the conscience as it tries to punish the immoral impulses of the id.

morphemes The smallest units of language that carry meaning. Morphemes may be words or part of words.

morphophonemic rules The rules that govern the combination of morphemes within a language.

motivational biases Cognitive biases that seem to serve basic needs, such as self-protection.

motivational processes In Bandura's model rewards affect not only attention to behavior, but the actual performance of the learned behavior.

motor responses In Bandura's model these are the acts or steps that people must take to act on their symbolic, remembered representation of behavior.

narcolepsy–cataplexy syndrome A sleep disorder in which a person suddenly falls asleep at inappropriate times (narcolepsy), often associated with brief periods of muscle weakness or paralysis (cataplexy).

natural selection The process whereby characteristics that confer survival value on an organism help to assure that the organism's genes and the characteristics expressed by those genes will be passed along to the next generation.

nature Nature versus nurture; refers to effects of heredity on development. Genetically determined characteristics and abilities.

need In motivation theory it is the physiological requirements of the body produced by the operations of the body. In drive theory, need, or the sensation of need, produces drive.

negative color afterimage A phenomenon in which, after prolonged exposure to light of a given color, objects appear to be the complementary color.

negative correlation A relationship between two measures such that as values of one measure increase, values on the second measure decrease.

negative symptoms schizophrenia Schizophrenia characterized by an absence of normal functioning. There is an absence of appropriate emotional responsivity—flattened affect, and an absence of appropriate social relationships—social withdrawal. In addition, there is an absence of some of the more florid symptoms of schizophrenia: e.g., hallucinations and delusions. Compare with *positive symptoms schizophrenia.*

neo-Freudians Freud's followers who remained quite loyal to Freud and his intellectual legacy but found reasons to criticize and modify Freud's theory.

neuroleptic A drug that is intended to reduce the symptoms of schizophrenia.

neurons Specialized cells that are the basic units of communication within the nervous system.

neurotic anxiety Freud emphasized that anxiety is not always a response to an external threat. Neurotic anxiety arises out of the unconscious as a result of threats from the instincts.

neuroticism In Eysenck's theory people high in neuroticism tend to be emotionally unstable, easily aroused, worrisome, and frequently complain about anxieties and bodily aches.

neurotransmitter A substance that is released by a presynaptic nerve terminal and has some effect on the postsynaptic cell, usually a change in permeability to one or more ions. Also called a *chemical transmitter.*

neutral zone A range of skin temperatures around physiological zero within which changes in skin temperature cannot be felt.

nomothetic Nomothetic personality theories are based on studies of groups and broadly shared characteristics that describe the general and universal laws of personality.

non-REM Non-rapid eye movement sleep; the collective name for sleep stages 1 to 4.

noncommon effects People more easily and confidently make inferences when they can determine that a particular action has distinctive features or noncommon effects.

nonspectral colors Hues, such as purple, that do not correspond to a single wavelength on the visible spectrum and can be produced only by mixing two wavelengths of light.

norepinephrine A neurotransmitter that probably is involved in many different types of behaviors and emotions. Evidence suggests that it is involved in hostile aggression and that deficits in norepinephrine are associated with depression.

normal curve A bell-shaped frequency distribution in which most scores cluster around the center (the mean), and fewer scores occur as they get farther from the center. For a normal curve, particular percentages of the scores occur within particular areas of the distribution and can be described as being certain numbers of standard deviations from the mean. Also called a *normal distribution.*

normal distribution A bell-shaped frequency distribution in which most scores cluster around the center (the mean), and fewer scores occur as they get farther from the center. For a normal distribution, particular percentages of the scores occur within particular areas of the distribution and can be described as being certain numbers of standard deviations from the mean. Also called a *normal curve.*

normative social influence In normative social influence, a person publicly conforms to social pressure but privately does not accept a group's opinion.

nucleus A small structure inside a cell. Also, a group of neurons that have common functions.

null hypothesis In statistics, the hypothesis that any differences observed among treatment conditions (for example, groups in an experiment) are due to chance, or sampling error, and that there are no true differences among the conditions.

nurture Nature versus nurture; refers to effects of the environment on development. The influence of all the experiences people have during a lifetime.

obedience When a person complies with destructive or immoral demands of authority.

object constancy The knowledge that an object continues to exist even though it may be out of sight.

object permanence The concept that objects continue to exist even when they are out of sight, hearing, or touch.

object-relations A modern extension of Freudian theory emphasizing the importance of the development of a sense of self.

objective self-awareness Situations in which a person's awareness is focused on the self. People who are objectively self-aware focus intently on their own values, standards, and attitudes and critically evaluate the extent to which they meet their own expectations.

objective tests Psychological tests that are highly structured in that the test taker has only a limited number of options for answering the questions.

observational learning Learning that results from mere observation of behavior.

observational studies Studies in which a researcher is typically on the scene and trying to record systematically the events she observes.

obsessive-compulsive disorder A mental disorder in which a person is plagued by recurrent shocking or frightening thoughts, for instance, that he or she will harm someone or die. The victim acts on these obsessions by repeatedly performing a ritualistic act that is intended to stave off harm.

Oedipus complex Freud thought it is a universal and biologically based fact of life that a boy desires his mother, yet also fears punishment or retaliation from his father. Freud named this tangle of sexual wishes and fears after the hero of Sophocles' tragedy, Oedipus Rex, who unknowingly killed his father and committed incest with his mother.

olfaction The sensation and perception of odors. Also called the sense of *smell*.

olfactory bulb A structure at the base of the brain that receives inputs from the olfactory receptor cells and is involved in the sense of smell.

olfactory epithelium The layer of olfactory receptor cells and adjacent supporting cells that lines the inside of the nose.

omission training A reinforcement paradigm in which access to a reinforcer is delayed upon the occurrence of a particular behavior.

operant A term used by B. F. Skinner to signify a behavior that has a particular relationship with a consequence.

operant learning Learning that is determined by the consequences of behavior. Also called *instrumental learning*.

operational definitions Definitions that specify how a concept is to be measured.

operations In Piaget's theory mental actions or representations that are reversible.

opiate antagonist A drug that blocks the effects of endogenous opioids as well as those derived from the opium poppy such as morphine and heroin.

opponent-process theory (emotion) States that strong emotional or affective experiences are automatically opposed by emotional responses that neutralize or counter the initial emotional reaction.

opponent-process theory (vision) States that the perception of color is based on two retinal processes that respond in opposite ways to the complementary hue pairs red–green and blue–yellow.

optic chiasm The place where the optic nerves meet on their way to the brain, and axons

from half of each retina cross to the opposite side of the brain.

optic disc The region of the retina where axons of the ganglion cells leave the eye and become the optic nerve. Also called the *blind spot*.

optic nerve Name for the collection of axons that leave the eye, before they enter the brain.

optic tracts Name for the collection of axons from the eye after they have entered the brain.

oral stage In psychoanalytic theory the stage at which children derive great pleasure from taking things into their mouth.

organ of Corti A structure in the cochlea of the inner ear, consisting of the basilar membrane, tectorial membrane, and auditory receptor cells.

organizational effects Effects of hormones that exert permanent effects on sexual characteristics.

ossicles Three tiny bones in the middle ear that transfer sound pressure from the eardrum to the oval window. The malleus (hammer), incus (anvil), and stapes (stirrup).

oval window A thin membrane in the inner ear that vibrates to sound waves.

overextend Children overextend the meaning of a word when they use it to refer to a much broader set of events and objects than an adult would.

paired associates Pairs of numbers and words such as "27–tacks" used in memory studies.

panic disorder A mental disorder characterized by the occurrence of panic attacks—discrete episodes in which the person experiences autonomic nervous system symptoms (racing heart, sweatiness, and increased respiration) and typically has frightening thoughts (that the person is going crazy or is about to die).

papillae Ridges and valleys on the tongue that are lined with taste buds.

paradoxical directive A strategic therapist's instruction that appears absurd because it seems intended to produce effects opposite to those that are desired.

paranoid personality disorder A personality disorder in which the individual is chronically suspicious of others, yet does not have the flagrant communication or cognitive symptoms of paranoid schizophrenia.

parapsychology The field of psychology concerned with psychic phenomena such as extrasensory perception and psychokinesis.

parasomnia Sleep disorders in which sleeping and waking themselves are normal but people exhibit certain undesirable behaviors, such as sleepwalking or bed-wetting, as they sleep.

Parkinson's disease A neurological disorder characterized by motor disturbance (e.g., shuffling gait, tremor). Signs and symptoms of Parkinson's disease can be produced as a side effect of antipsychotic drugs.

participant observers When researchers are part of the group or events being studied, they are called participant observers.

Pavlovian conditioning A set of procedures that leads to relatively durable behavior change. A stimulus that produces no dramatic behavioral or physiological effects, a conditioned stimulus, is paired with a stimulus that reliably produces behavioral or phys-

iological effects, an unconditioned stimulus. After repeated pairings the conditioned stimulus by itself causes or elicits effects that are similar to those originally produced only by the unconditioned stimulus. Also called *classical conditioning*.

pegword A mnemonic device that uses a series of memorized number–word rhymes.

penis envy According to Freud the experiences of girls during the phallic stage are different from those of boys. Girls realize they do not have a penis and develop penis envy.

percentile rank A statistic that describes the position of a score in a distribution; the percentage of all scores that lie below the score in question.

perception Our experience of relatively complex events and the influence of factors such as attention and prior learning on our sensory experience.

peripheral nerves Bundles of axons or dendrites that link the sensory receptors, central nervous system (brain and spinal cord), and effectors (muscles and glands) throughout the body.

peripheral nervous system The part of the nervous system that is distributed throughout the body, outside the skull and spine.

person-centered therapy A humanistic psychotherapy developed by Carl Rogers that is aimed at allowing a person to achieve his or her full potential.

persona Jung believed that a person or social self develops as a shell around the ego. The persona is the self as presented to others.

personal inventory Self-report instruments commonly used to assess a person's aptitudes and interests.

personal norms An individual's belief about how he or she ought to act in a particular situation.

personal unconscious A personality component Jung believed to contain experiences that were once conscious but since have been repressed or forgotten. (This concept is roughly analogous to Freud's preconscious.)

phallic stage In psychoanalytic theory the stage at which the attention of children is directed to the genitals and the pleasures of genital stimulation.

phenomenology According to this view, if one is to understand another person, one must understand how he or she experiences and understands the world. People's experience of the world—including their experience of themselves—is seen to be the key to understanding the development and structure of their personality.

phenotype The actual physical characteristics that are displayed by an individual. The phenotype may or may not reflect the individual's genotype.

pheromones Odorous chemicals that are released by animals and cause specific reactions in other animals of the species.

phi phenomenon A simple case of stroboscopic movement in which two adjacent stationary lights flashing on and off in sequence produce apparent motion.

phobias Extreme and apparently irrational fears.

phobic disorders Mental disorders characterized by irrational fears that interfere with functioning or happiness.

phoneme The shortest segment of sound that

distinguishes one word from another. The minimal unit of speech in a language that distinguishes meanings in that language.

phonological The sound level of language.

photon A quantum of light (visible radiation). The energy released from a single electron.

phrase-structure Rules governing how words can be built into phrases and phrases combined into sentences.

phrenology The practice that arose in the 1800s and continued well into the 1900s in which assessments of a person's personality or intellect were attempted based on the skull structure.

physical dependence A physiological condition produced by prolonged exposure to a particular drug, inferred when a withdrawal syndrome occurs after the drug is discontinued.

physiological zero A reference skin temperature, usually about 32°C (90°F).

pictorial cues Visual depth cues that are based on features of stationary objects and require only one eye to produce the perception of depth. Also called *static monocular cues.*

pinna The fleshy outer part of the ear.

pitch The auditory experience that corresponds primarily to the frequency of sound waves.

pituitary gland The gland located at the base of the brain, just under the hypothalamus, which controls the output of hormones from many other glands of the body.

place theory States that different sound frequencies stimulate receptor cells at different locations along the basilar membrane. Consequently, only certain auditory nerve fibers (those connected to the stimulated receptors) are activated to signal the presence of specific stimulus frequencies.

placebo A procedure or substance that is administered to a patient or subject as if it were a treatment, but that is not intended to have an effect.

plasticity Changes in the connections and functions of neurons.

pleasure principle In psychoanalytic theory the id obeys the pleasure principle; it pursues pleasure and avoids pain.

pluralistic ignorance When a situation is ambiguous, the presence of others can produce what has been termed pluralistic ignorance. In these situations, people tend to rely on one another to interpret the situation as an emergency and to act appropriately.

polygenic traits Traits that depend on the combined effects of many pairs of genes.

population A complete set of observations or measures from all members of a specified group. The group can be very large (all eligible voters in the United States) or fairly small (all the members of your introductory psychology class).

positive correlation A relationship between two measures such that as values of one measure increase, values on the second measure also increase.

positive regard Rogers emphasized the child's need for positive regard or esteem from others.

positive symptoms schizophrenia Characterized by the presence of abnormal symptoms and signs—delusions, hallucinations, and extreme emotionality. Compare with *negative symptoms schizophrenia.*

postsynaptic potential The action potential that occurs in the neuron that is stimulated across the synapse.

postdecision dissonance After making a decision people appear to reduce dissonance by rating their choices more favorably or by devaluing the alternatives they have not selected.

posterior pituitary The back part of the pituitary gland.

posthypnotic amnesia A phenomenon in which people are given a suggestion during hypnosis so that when the hypnosis ends, they forget what happened while they were hypnotized.

practice effects Changes in performance that occur when the same individuals are tested repeatedly.

pragmatics The social rules of language use, such as varying language complexity to match the abilities of listeners.

preconscious Information or thoughts that a person is not presently aware of but that have been processed and are readily available to consciousness.

prenatal period The period of development that occurs within the mother's body; the period from conception to birth. Also called the *gestation period.*

preparedness The theory that animals are genetically equipped to associate particular classes of stimuli with one another. Because it has conferred a survival advantage, natural selection has resulted in animals' being able to learn associations between different classes of stimuli with few pairings of the two types of stimuli (e.g., tastes and illness) and with long periods of time separating the types of stimuli. Prepared associations are supposed to be quite durable.

presentation of self in everyday life Goffman's characterization of social interaction as a kind of theatrical ritual in which each participant acts out a role.

primacy effect (memory) A serial position effect in which people recall words from early in a list better than those in the middle.

primacy effects (impression formation) The tendency to give greater weight to traits presented early in a series of traits when forming an impression.

primary colors Three colors that when mixed together in appropriate amounts can produce any other color.

primary drives Drives that are directly produced by need (deprivation) or painful stimuli.

primary reinforcer A stimulus that can serve as an effective reinforcer (it can increase the rate of preceding behavior) without it's ever having been paired with another reinforcer. It is by itself reinforcing. Food is an example of a primary reinforcer.

primary visual cortex An area of cortex in the occipital lobe that receives inputs from the lateral geniculate nucleus of the thalamus and that is involved in vision. Also called the *striate cortex.*

primers Pheromones that produce physiological (usually hormonal) changes in the receiving animal, which then alter the animal's behavior.

priming Exposure of an organism to an incentive so that the organism pursues more of the incentive.

proactive interference When previously learned material impairs the recall of newly learned material.

problem space All the possible moves or problem "states" that are available from the beginning of a problem to its solution.

procedural knowledge The set of procedures, or cognitive skills, that people use to manipulate or transform information about the world.

procedural memory Knowledge of motor skills, such as bicycle riding, that are acquired through practice.

process schizophrenia A type of schizophrenia that arises early in life (typically in the teens), is associated with flattened affect, and tends to be chronic.

projection A primitive defense mechanism in which we (unconsciously) assume that thoughts and impulses come from outside of us.

projective tests Indirect assessment devices that are intended to reflect a person's unconscious motivations.

propositional representation People in the propositional camp argue that visual information is represented in memory by a set of rules—propositions—that can generate images.

prosocial behavior Behavior designed to help others without regard to the helper's motives or to behavior valued by a society.

prototype The most typical instance of a category.

proximodistal The pattern of early physical growth of the child; the center of the body grows more early in life, and the arms and legs grow more later. Also called *center-to-periphery.*

psychoanalysis The personality theory and a clinical method of treating emotionally disturbed patients developed by Sigmund Freud.

psychopathology The study of psychological difficulties.

psychokinesis The ability to manipulate or move objects mentally.

psychological dependence A drug user's obsessive concern with getting and using a nonmedical drug.

psychometric A term referring to measurement of psychological factors.

psychometric function A graph of the relationship between different values of a stimulus and a person's perception of those values.

psychopaths Disinhibited individuals who pursue pleasurable incentives while being seemingly unaware of the harm their behavior may cause themselves or others or the risks that they take.

psychopathy A personality disorder in which the individual acts in an impulsive manner, taking risks and incurring long-term costs in order to obtain immediate gratification. The interpersonal relationships of the psychopathic individual are characterized by superficiality and opportunism. Also called *antisocial personality disorder.*

psychophysical scaling Procedures for determining the relationship between changes in the intensity of a stimulus and people's perception of its intensity.

psychophysics Study of the relationships between physical stimuli and people's experience of them.

psychosomatic disease Disease whose origins

can best be understood in terms of psychological causes but that have observable physical consequences.

psychosurgery   Surgery on the brain that is done to alleviate a mental disorder despite the fact that there is no apparent pathology of brain tissue.

psychotherapies   Those treatments whose effects can best be understood in terms of effects on the mind; that is, their effects on the way an individual thinks or feels about things or in terms of the individual's personality.

puberty   The physical changes that result in sexual maturation.

punisher   A stimulus that decreases the future probability of the behavior that immediately precedes it.

pupil   The central opening of the eye, formed by the iris.

pure tone   A sound wave that has the form of a sine wave; the simplest type of sound wave.

random assignment   The alternative to matching is to randomly assign subjects to experimental conditions in such a way that each subject has an equal chance of being assigned to different conditions. This helps to assure that the two groups will not be significantly different to begin with.

random sample   When the population is large, researchers may select at random a portion of the population. In random selection everyone has an equal chance of being selected. This minimizes the possibility that respondents are somehow unrepresentative of the population.

range   A statistical measure of variability; the difference between the highest and lowest scores in a set of scores.

rapid eye movement (REM)   A stage of sleep that is characterized by rapid movements of the eyes under the closed lids.

rationalization   In psychoanalytic theory a defense mechanism in which people try to justify their behavior through plausible but inaccurate explanations.

reaction formation   In psychoanalytic theory a defense mechanism in which people convert an undesirable impulse into its opposite.

reaction range   The range of possible phenotypes for a given genotype.

reactive schizophrenia   A type of schizophrenia that arises relatively late in life (postadolescence), that is associated with great emotionality, and that seems to occur in discrete bouts—leaving the victim relatively unimpaired when not experiencing a bout.

real movement   The actual movement of stimuli.

reality anxiety   A response to an external threat. In contrast to neurotic anxiety.

reality principle   The ego operates according to the reality principle; it is practical and defers the gratification sought by the id until the person can achieve pleasure without incurring the costs of punishment or social reproach.

recency effect   A serial position effect in which words presented late in a list are recalled better than those presented in the middle.

receptive aphasia   Wernicke's aphasia is sometimes referred to as receptive aphasia because people with it have problems with comprehension.

receptive field   The area of sensory field, such as an area of the visual field or an area of the skin, within which stimulation affects the activity of a neuron.

receptor cell   A cell that is specialized to respond to certain kinds of external energy.

receptor potential   A voltage change across the membrane of a receptor cell that occurs in response to an external stimulus.

receptor sites   A molecule in the cell membrane that combines with specific chemical substances, such as neurotransmitters.

recessive gene   The gene that fails to determine the trait when two genes in a pair specify different traits.

reciprocal determinism   Bandura and other social learning theorists also have emphasized that social learning processes are a joint product of interactions between the organism and its environment—what Bandura terms reciprocal determinism.

reciprocity norm   A powerful norm that holds that people should help (and not hurt) those who have helped them.

reduction of arousal   A theoretical account for affiliative behavior that emphasizes that when people are under great stress, they seek out others to provide comfort, to distract them from the threat, and to supply models of relaxed behavior.

reductionism   The argument that a molecular analysis is sufficient to understand psychological phenomena.

reference group   Parents, teachers, and peers are important sources of attitudes for adolescents and young adults—they are important reference groups or models for children.

reflex   A behavioral or physiological response that invariably follows from a particular type of stimulation. An automatic reaction to a stimulus.

refractory period   The time during which the membrane of a neuron cannot produce a second action potential.

regeneration   Regrowth of a damaged axon.

rehearsal   Mental repetition of material we wish to retain in short-term memory.

reinforcement–affect model   According to this theory, which builds on principles of secondary reinforcement, people like others who are associated with positive events and dislike those associated with negative events.

reinforcer   A stimulus that increases the future probability of the behavior that immediately precedes it.

release from proactive interference   Interference arises when possible responses to retrieval cues compete. The presentation of new material that does not compete with old material can reduce this interference.

releasers   Pheromones that automatically trigger an immediate behavioral response from the receiving animal.

releasing stimulus   A stimulus that is effective in eliciting consistently a fixed action pattern—an invariant sequence of behaviors.

reliability   The extent to which a measure is repeatable, that is, will yield the same score if measuring the same thing across time.

reminiscence   Recalling newly learned material better after the passage of time than when being tested immediately.

repeated reproduction   Reproducing information several times.

repetition compulsion   A term used to describe an inefficient or disturbing pattern of behavior that a person repeats again and again because of unconscious motivational influences.

representativeness heuristic   Gauging the likelihood of an event according to its similarity to prototypes for the event.

repressed   Memories or intentions that are pushed into the unconscious because they are unpleasant or threatening.

repression   In psychoanalytic theory a basic defense mechanism in which unacceptable thoughts and wishes are forced into the unconscious.

research hypothesis   In statistics the hypothesis that any differences observed among treatment conditions (for example, groups in an experiment) are due to actual effects of the treatments rather than to chance.

reserpine   A drug once used to treat hypertension that produced depression, possibly because it depletes neurotransmitters like serotonin and norepinephrine.

resting potential   The voltage difference between the inside and outside of the neuron when the neuron is at rest.

retention processes   In Bandura's theory these processes determine whether a person remembers modeled behavior.

retina   A sheet of cells that covers most of the inner surface of the eyeball.

retrieval cues   Information that prompts people to remember by specifying the goal of the memory search and by directing the generation and evaluation of possible answers.

retrieval stage   The final stage of memory—refers to the process of bringing information out of memory.

retroactive interference   When learning new material impairs the recall of previously learned material.

retrograde amnesia   The loss of memories formed in the past.

rhetoric   The study of persuasive arguments.

rival hypotheses   Hypotheses that observed differences are the product of some cause other than the one manipulated by the experimenter.

rods   A type of light receptor in the retina; rods are sensitive to low light levels over a wide range of wavelengths.

Rorschach test   A projective test consisting of inkblots that a person is asked to view, thereafter reporting his or her reactions.

saccule   A structure in the inner ear that contains receptors for the vestibular sense.

sample   A part of a population.

sampling error   Variability, or error, that occurs when using a sample to estimate something about a population.

satellite cells   The supporting cells of the peripheral nervous system.

saturation   The visual experience that corresponds primarily to the purity of a single-wavelength light. Saturation distinguishes pale from vivid colors.

scatter diagram   A graph that shows the relation between two measures. Values of one measure are represented on the horizontal axis and values of the second measure are represented on the vertical axis. Each point in the graph represents a score on both measures. Also called a *scatter plot*.

scatter plot   A graph that shows the relation between two measures. Values of one measure are represented on the horizontal axis and values of the second measure are represented on the vertical axis. Each point in the graph represents a score on both measures. Also called a *scatter diagram*.

schedule of reinforcement The relationship between a behavior and its consequences with respect to the number of behaviors necessary to produce a consequence or the amount of time that must pass before a consequence is available.

schema Bartlett referred to memory for central facts and themes as the schema "an active organisation of past reactions, or of past experience." These are cognitive structures that contain organized knowledge and beliefs about a specific domain—such as the self—and serve to categorize and organize new information about that domain.

schemes A structured piece of knowledge, or concept, about a physical or mental interaction with the world.

schizoid personality disorder A personality disorder in which people are cold and aloof and have great difficulty maintaining close interpersonal relationships.

schizophrenia A mental disorder characterized by problems of communication, mood, and cognition. Typical symptoms and signs are attentional problems, unusual language use, and an inability to maintain close personal relationships. Actually, there may be multiple types of schizophrenia, each having different causes.

sclera A strong elastic membrane that forms the eyeball.

second signal system Pavlov referred to language as a second signal system because he recognized that words and their meanings could serve as Pavlovian stimuli (signals) just as can physical stimuli such as lights, sounds, and tactile stimuli.

secondary drives Drives that are produced by a stimulus that was once motivationally neutral but that has acquired motivational significance by being paired with other stimuli that elicit drives.

secondary retrieval cues The use of alternative retrieval cues when people cannot retrieve information from their memories because of blocking or cue overload.

secondary traits Allport identified a category of secondary traits that do not have a broad or consistent influence on behavior. These traits take the form of preferences and aversions.

selective attention The ability to process a single task or set of stimuli while ignoring others.

selective breeding A procedure in which animals that show an extreme of a particular trait are bred together, their offspring that show an extreme of the trait are bred together, and so on.

selective dropout effect A loss of particular types of subjects in studies of development that use the longitudinal experimental design.

self-actualization Rogers emphasized the human inclination to move past satisfaction of basic needs such as hunger and thirst, and develop from a simple to a complex person who is an independent and efficacious adult, self-expressive, and creative.

self-actualizing drive According to Carl Rogers' theory of client-centered therapy, the drive intrinsic to every creature to achieve its full potential.

self-based biases Attributional biases involving people's projections of their own attitudes onto others. For example, we generally assume that others will act as we would act.

self-concept An understanding that one is a separate and independent person.

self-efficacy A person's belief in his or her ability to perform particular acts and to control events. According to self-efficacy theory, the opportunity to demonstrate self-efficacy is a powerful motivational force.

self-monitors People who use information to carefully construct their own self-presentations. They are skillful at expressing or concealing their true feelings to behave in socially acceptable ways.

self-perception theory Theory that holds that we learn about our own attitudes, feelings, and other inner states in the same way that other people learn about them by inferring them from our own behavior.

self-predictions A direct assessment strategy in which an individual is asked how he or she will perform in a particular situation.

self-schemas Schemas that contain people's knowledge and beliefs about the specific roles that they play, about the specific people with whom they interact, about their personal characteristics and values, about the specific situations they encounter, the specific behaviors in which they engage, and so on.

self-terminating searches Memory searches that end once the desired information has been obtained.

self-theory Rogers was primarily concerned with the fit between two aspects of the self: the "actual self" and the "ideal self." The actual self is the self-concept or self perceived by the individual and need not consist of objectively correct perceptions. The ideal self is the self-concept to which the individual aspires.

semantic differential Measurement procedure in which people are simply presented a statement and asked to rate it on a series of bipolar adjectives good–bad, many–few, etc.

semantic encoding One way that people encode long-term memories is according to semantic encoding. Information is stored in a form that reflects its meaning.

semantic memory Memory for the meaning of words and concepts.

semantics The field concerned with the meaning of language.

semicircular canals Three loops in the inner ear that contain receptors for the vestibular sense.

senility Severe intellectual impairment in old age.

sensation The process by which we receive and experience relatively simple events in the external world.

sense organ A structure, such as the eye or ear, that is specialized to handle certain kinds of external energy.

sensitivity A measure of a person's ability to detect weak stimuli. The lower the stimulus intensity that can be detected, the higher the sensitivity to that stimulus.

sensitization A process that is inferred to occur during habituation on the basis of the observation that habituated organisms show exaggerated responses to new stimuli. Presumably, sensitization accounts for such exaggerated responding.

sensory neuron A neuron that is involved in processing and transmitting sensory information in the nervous system.

sensory receptors Specialized cells, located inside the body and on its surface, that respond to environmental stimulation and provide the nervous system with its inputs.

separation anxiety The fear and distress that occur when an infant is temporarily separated from the primary caregiver.

sequential experimental design A method of studying development that combines aspects of both cross-sectional and longitudinal designs. Specifically, groups of individuals of different ages are compared, and the comparison is repeated for the same individuals at two or more ages.

serial order Method in which memory is assessed in the serial order in which the information was learned.

serial position effects The differential in recallability of items presented early, in the middle, and late in a sequence of items.

serial reproduction The conveying of information from one person to another, from the second to a third, and so on.

set effect Occurs when people develop a "set" or regular mental orientation to the problems that impedes their problem solving. Also called *mechanization of thought*.

set learning Learning in which organisms learn about abstract relationships among stimuli. Also called *concept learning*.

set point A hypothesized value for a physical variable (for example, body weight) that the body attempts to achieve and defend.

sex roles The personality characteristics and behavior that one's culture defines as appropriate for males and females.

sex-linked traits Traits that are determined by genes on the sex chromosomes.

sex-role identity A person's inner belief that his or her interests and behavior conform to the norms of his or her culture.

sexual instincts For Freud sexual instincts are directed to preservation of the species and include not only sexual intercourse, but also affection for family, friends, and even community.

shape constancy The perception that forms or objects keep the same apparent shape despite changes in their orientation.

shaping A procedure in which successive approximations to a particular behavioral response are reinforced.

shift in meaning Changes in the meaning of words that result when they are combined with other words—as when "irresponsible"—a negative term—becomes even more negative when used in the phrase "irresponsible father."

signal detection theory States that an observer's detection of a stimulus depends on both the observer's sensitivity to the stimulus and the observer's criterion for responding. The theory includes procedures for estimating an observer's sensitivity independent of his or her criterion for responding.

simple phobias A type of phobia in which the person has an irrational fear of discrete objects such as snakes, dogs, or scissors.

simultaneous brightness contrast The perception that an area of a given luminance (light intensity) appears brighter when surrounded by a dark area than when surrounded by a light area.

simultaneous color contrast The perception that an area of a given wavelength appears a different color when surrounded by an area of one wavelength than when surrounded by an area of a different wavelength.

sine-wave gratings Repeating patterns of dark and light stripes in which intensity increases and decreases gradually as a sine-wave function of location.

single process model A memory model that offers an alternative single process account of the findings that are used to support the distinction between short-term and long-term memory.

single-cell recording A method in which tiny electrodes (called microelectrodes) are used to record the electrical activity of single neurons.

situational attributions Ascribing the causes of behavior to situational factors.

size constancy The perception that objects viewed at varying distances remain the same size.

skin senses The sensation and perception of touch, pressure, pain, and temperature on the skin.

sleep apnea An abnormal cessation of breathing during sleep.

sleeper effect When persuasive communications produce greater changes in attitudes after the passage time than they produce immediately.

smell The sensation and perception of odors. Also called *olfaction.*

social comparison theory Theory that people seek to affiliate with others to evaluate their opinions and reactions in light of other people's reactions and opinions.

social exchange theory Theory that attraction is influenced by rewards and punishments, with the qualification that judgments about attraction are influenced by the ratio of costs and benefits in a relationship.

social facilitation The beneficial effects produced by the presence of groups.

social norms These norms represent society's expectations about behavior. These norms are acquired through social learning. By being reinforced and punished for appropriate and inappropriate behavior and by watching how others behave, people *internalize* these norms and use them to guide their own behavior.

social phobias A type of phobia in which the person has an irrational fear of contact with other people or of being scrutinized or appraised by others. Public speaking anxiety is a common social phobia.

social rejection If those who disagree do not come around, then the majority grows to dislike and ostracize them. Such social rejection can provide a strong incentive for conformity.

social-learning theory States that socialization is learned as people interact with their environments. The learning occurs through observation, Pavlovian conditioning, and operant conditioning.

social-responsibility norm Norm that holds that we ought to help those who need help even when we have no expectation of benefiting.

socialization The process by which individuals acquire the attitudes, social skills, and behaviors that are expected by other members of their society.

sociobiology The sociobiological approach emphasizes the analysis of behavior at the

level of the gene. Sociobiologists attempt to explain even complex human behaviors such as aggression and altruism in genetic terms.

somatic sensory cortex The region of cortex in the parietal lobe that is involved in sensation and perception of touch, pressure, and kinesthesis.

somatic treatments Those treatments whose effects can best be understood in terms of effects on the body.

somatization disorder A mental disorder in which the person has numerous worries and complaints about his or her physical health, but shows no evidence of any physical disease. This is a modern diagnostic label for hysteria.

somatotypes Sheldon concluded that people have three basic body types, or somatotypes.

sone A unit of measurement of the perceived loudness of a sound.

sound localization The ability to determine the source of sounds around you.

sound spectrogram A graph in which the frequency of a sound stimulus is plotted on the vertical axis, time is plotted on the horizontal axis, and the amount of sound energy is indicated by the degree of darkness.

sound waves Vibrations, or pressure changes, in a medium such as air or water.

source traits According to Cattell these are the basic, underlying structures that provide coherence to personality and that explain behavior.

spatial contrast sensitivity The contrast (difference in intensity) that is necessary to detect sine-wave gratings of different spatial frequencies.

spatial frequency The number of dark and light stripe pairs (called cycles) that are present across a specified distance of a grating.

species-specific defense reactions Instinctive responses that are elicited by painful or threatening stimuli.

specific anosmia An inability to smell specific odors.

specific hunger A taste preference for substances that meet a biological need.

specific responses In Eysenck's personality theory people have specific responses or individual acts that may or may not be characteristic of them. These are at the lowest level of Eysenck's behavioral hierarchy.

spinal cord The part of the central nervous system that extends down through the center of the bony vertebral column (spine).

spinal reflexes Automatic movements that result from direct sensory inputs to the spinal cord; they require no participation by the brain.

spinothalamic system Central nervous system pathways that carry information primarily about pain and temperature.

split-half reliability A method for determining reliability by discovering whether one-half of the test produces scores that agree with those yielded by the other half of the test.

spreading activation In network models the process of retrieval is conceived in terms of one concept activating another concept. When one of the concepts in the network is activated, spreading activation to other concepts makes them easier to retrieve. Those concepts that are already most strongly associated with the original concept will be re-

trieved earliest.

standard deviation A statistical measure of variability that reflects the difference of each score from the mean of the set of scores. The square root of the variance.

standard error of the mean A statistic that provides an estimate, based on a single sample, of the standard deviation of many sample means around the true population mean.

standard score A statistic that describes the position of a score in a distribution; the number of standard deviations the score in question is away from the mean of the set of scores. Also called a *z-score.*

Stanford–Binet A test designed to yield an estimate of intelligence—an IQ test.

state-dependency Research indicates that recall (even more than recognition) improves when people try to retrieve information while they are in the same physiological state as they were when they first learned the information.

static monocular cues Visual depth cues that are based on features of stationary (static) objects and require only one eye (monocular) to produce the perception of depth. Also called *pictorial cues.*

statistical significance A test of statistical significance is a test of probability. It tests how likely it is that an observed difference between groups could be produced by chance factors when there is no real difference between the groups.

statistical test A procedure that allows researchers to determine the probability that some outcome or observation has occurred by chance.

stereochemical theory States that there are a small number of primary odor qualities such as musky, floral, minty, and putrid that are determined by the shape of the odor molecules.

Stevens' power law States that sensation magnitude is proportional to stimulus magnitude raised to some power.

stimulus Any kind of physical event or energy that can be detected by an organism.

stimulus substitution The theory espoused by Pavlov that holds that Pavlovian conditioning occurs because organisms learn to respond as if the conditioned stimulus were the unconditioned stimulus; the conditioned stimulus becomes a substitute for the unconditioned stimulus.

storage stage The second stage of memory, which involves the "warehousing" of the information that has been acquired.

strabismus A condition in which the two eyes do not point in the same direction.

stranger anxiety A fearful reaction to a stranger.

strategic therapy A type of family therapy based on the notion that psychological problems or mental disorders are caused, at least in part, by disturbed communication within the family. A goal of strategic therapy is to disrupt these old communication patterns and help the family develop new patterns.

stress The physiological, emotional, and behavioral state that exists when an organism is faced with an environmental challenge.

stress-induced analgesia A reduction in pain that results when people are under stress.

stretch receptors Receptors that are located directly on the muscle fibers and are stimulated when the muscle is stretched.

striate cortex An area of cortex in the occipital lobe that receives inputs from the lateral geniculate nucleus of the thalamus and that is involved in vision. Also called the *primary visual cortex.*

striving for superiority Adler's view that the basic motivation that we all share is the striving for superiority—not a striving to be better than the people around us, but a striving to improve ourselves.

stroboscopic movement A type of apparent motion produced by adjacent stationary lights that flash on and off in sequence.

structuralist One who is interested in the interrelationships of the various parts of the brain and how they operate together in sensation, perception, and conscious experience.

structured interviews An assessment strategy in which the assessor's questions of a client come from a predetermined list of questions that guide the assessor's investigation of a client's problems—usually directed at determining a client's diagnosis.

sublimate In psychoanalytic theory a defense mechanism in which libidinal energy is directed away from socially unacceptable behavior to acceptable behavior. This is done by finding a substitute for the real object of motivation. Also called *sublimation.*

sublimation In psychoanalytic theory a defense mechanism in which libidinal energy is directed away from socially unacceptable behavior to acceptable behavior. This is done by finding a substitute for the real object of motivation. Also called *sublimate.*

subliminal perception Sensory information that is perceived and potentially available to consciousness but that a person does not notice at the moment.

subtractive color mixture Color mixture in which pigments absorb (subtract) certain wavelengths from white light and reflect others, such as when paints are mixed.

successive approximations Behaviors that come closer and closer to an ideal behavior that an operant conditioner wishes an organism to produce.

superego In psychoanalytic theory instinctual needs are governed by the development of a conscience (the superego), which reflects the rules of society.

surface traits According to Cattell, surface traits are those traits that, to a casual observer, seem to "go together."

survey Surveys are used to assess people's attitudes and to gather information from them about their behavior.

syllogism An argument consisting of two premises (which are assumed to be true) and a conclusion.

synaptic cleft The space separating a presynaptic nerve terminal from the postsynaptic cell.

synaptic transmission Passage of a signal between two neurons, or between a neuron and muscle, at a synaptic contact.

synaptic vesicles Small sacs, in a presynaptic nerve terminal, that are filled with a chemical transmitter.

syndrome A collection of symptoms and signs that occur together. Presumably if certain symptoms and signs co-occur, they reflect a common disease process and should respond to the same treatment.

syntactic capacities The ability to compose symbols in such a way as to express meanings that are different from the sum of the meanings of the individual symbols.

syntax The rules for combining elements of language into meaningful utterances.

systematic desensitization A behavior therapy technique designed to reduce phobic fears. It involves the gradual exposure of the phobic person to the objects that he or she fears.

t statistic A number that reflects both the difference between two sample means and the variability in each sample.

T cells Lymphocytes that attack the body's own cells that have been altered or damaged by disease.

tacts Skinner defined tacts as verbal behavior under the control of objects or events in the environment.

tardive dyskinesia An iatrogenic illness characterized by writhing muscle movements that is a consequence of chronic antipsychotic drug administration.

taste The sensation and perception of chemicals on the tongue and palate. Also called *gustation.*

taste buds Structures in the papillae of the tongue that contain taste receptor cells.

taste modifiers Substances that alter the way other substances taste.

tectorial membrane A long membrane in the cochlea in which hairs of auditory receptor cells are embedded.

temperament The characteristic ways in which people respond to other people and events.

teratogens Drugs that can produce birth defects.

test–retest reliability A method for determining reliability by discovering the extent to which a test yields the same score when it is used on more than one occasion.

Thematic Apperception Test (TAT) A projective test that is supposed to elicit information about the test taker's motivations even when the test taker is unaware of them. The test consists of a series of pictures with no apparent meaning and the test taker must guess what story lies behind each picture.

theory of psychosocial development Erikson's theory, which states that individuals go through eight stages from birth to old age, and each stage is characterized by the need to resolve a developmental crisis that arises as the individual encounters the social environment.

theory of reasoned action The theory assumes that most people think about the implications of their behavior and that most of their behavior is under conscious control.

third force The phenomenological or humanist tradition meant to serve as an alternative to psychoanalytic and behavioral theories.

threshold of excitation The critical value of the voltage difference across the membrane at which an action potential is initiated in a neuron.

tip-of-the-tongue (TOT) phenomenon When one knows one has the wrong word but is close to retrieving the right one.

tolerance A decreased response to a drug after prolonged use.

top-down theory States that people's knowledge of the context of complex patterns, such as the auditory patterns in speech, de-

termines their perception of the simple features that make up the patterns.

topographic map The point-to-point representation of a sensory surface in the brain.

Tourette's tic syndrome A disorder starting in childhood in which the person produces verbal or motor (movement) tics—explosive sounds, hand flailing, and so on.

traits Basic characteristics—in personality theories people are thought to possess varying degrees of traits.

transduction The transformation of external energy into the electrochemical activity of nerve cells.

transference The process in which a client responds to a therapist as if the therapist were an important figure from the client's past—usually a parent.

transformations Modification of simple declarative sentences into questions, negations, and compound sentences.

transitivity The ability to make logical inferences on the basis of separate relationships.

trephination The practice of prehistoric humans in which holes were made in the skull presumably to release evil spirits.

trichromatic theory States that the sensation of color results from the relative activity of three receptors, each of which is most sensitive to one of three primary colors.

trichromats People who have three types of cone receptors in the retina and can match any hue with a mixture of three primary hues.

tricyclic antidepressant drugs Drugs shown to be effective in alleviating the symptoms of depression.

true score A hypothetical value that represents the score obtained when using perfect measurement procedures.

twin comparisons A method for studying behavior genetics in which the similarities in behavior of identical twins and fraternal twins are compared.

two-point discrimination threshold The least distance between two stimuli that people require to tell that there are two separate touches rather than one.

type A behavior pattern A pattern of behavior characterized by impatience, aggressiveness, ambitiousness, and striving. This behavior pattern has been associated with increased risk of heart disease.

types Characterizing people in broad terms thought to reflect the basic and stable structure of their personality.

unconditional positive regard Providing people with affection that is not conditioned upon the behavior of the recipient.

unconscious Generally considered to consist of memories, knowledge, and thought processes that are not readily available to consciousness but that nevertheless influence thought and action. In psychoanalytic theory, a level of the psyche that is the repository of the deep, inaccessible drives and urges that determine behavior.

underextend A child underextends a word when she applies it too narrowly, as when a child who has been given the label "sofa" for the soft piece of furniture she sees at a store may believe that the term applies only to sofas seen at stores.

unstructured interviews An assessment strategy in which the assessor's questions of a client are guided by the assessor's perspective and knowledge of personality and psychopathology and do not depend upon a preexisting set of questions.

utricle A structure in the inner ear that contains receptors for the vestibular sense.

vacuum behaviors Behaviors that organisms produce when they are faced with no strong motivational stimuli.

validity A concept referring to the extent to which a test or assessment device actually measures the variable or factor that it is supposed or intended to measure.

variable-interval schedule A reinforcement schedule in which a varying amount of time must pass before a response will lead to reinforcement.

variable-ratio schedule A reinforcement schedule in which a varying number of responses is required before reinforcement is delivered.

variables Factors that are measured and manipulated by researchers.

variance A statistical measure of variability that reflects the difference of each score from the mean of the set of scores.

vasopressin A hormone released by the pituitary that determines how much water is retained in the blood by the kidneys.

ventricles A series of interconnected cavities inside the brain.

vestibular sense The sensation and perception of the orientation of the head and body in space.

vestibulo-ocular reflex The automatic combination of eye movements that helps to keep visual images stable on the retina as the head turns.

vicarious learning Observers of behavior can be vicariously reinforced by observing the consequences of other people's behavior.

vigilance Sustained attention; the ability to remain attentive for long periods of time.

vision The sensation and perception of light.

visual acuity A measure of the finest detail that a person can see.

visual angle The separation between two visual stimuli, measured in degrees of arc.

vitreous humor A jellylike substance that fills the eyeball.

voiced The consonants produced with sounds generated in the glottis and sounds such as the hiss of an /s/ produced behind the teeth.

volley principle States that although individual auditory nerve fibers may not be able to follow the frequency of sound stimuli, successive waves of individual fibers can follow the stimuli.

weapons effect The notion that the very presence of weapons increases the level of violence in society.

Weber fraction The proportion by which a stimulus must be changed to be just noticeably different.

Weber's law States that the size of a just noticeable difference is a constant proportion of the size of the standard stimulus.

Wechsler Adult Intelligence Scale (WAIS) A test designed to yield an estimate of intelligence—an IQ test.

Wernicke's aphasia A form of aphasia in which people have problems with comprehension. In contrast to the halting speech of Broca's aphasics, Wernicke's aphasics produce fluent but unintelligible speech.

withdrawal syndrome Signs and symptoms that occur after cessation of a drug that has been taken habitually.

withdrawal training A reinforcement paradigm in which a reinforcer is removed upon the occurrence of a particular behavior.

Yerkes–Dodson Law The notion that there is an optimal, nonzero, level of arousal that is most pleasurable and that results in the best performance.

z-score A statistic that describes the position of a score in a distribution; the number of standard deviations the score in question is away from the mean of the set of scores. Also called a *standard score*.

REFERENCES

Aaker, D. A., Carman, J. M., & Jackson, R. (1982). Modeling advertising-sales relationships involving feedback: A time series analysis of six cereal brands. *Journal of Marketing Research, 19*, 116–125.

Abbott, A. R., & Sebastian, R. J. (1981). Physical attractiveness and expectations of success. *Personality and Social Psychology Bulletin, 7*, 481–486.

Abbs, J. H., & Sussman, H. M. (1971). Neurophysiological feature detectors and speech perception: A discussion of theoretical implications. *Journal of Speech Research, 14*, 23–36.

Abel, E. L. (1984). *Fetal alcohol syndrome and fetal alcohol effects.* New York: Plenum Press.

Abel, E. L. (1985). Late sequelae of fetal alcohol syndrome. In U. Rydberg, C. Alling, J. Engle, B. Pernow, L. A. Pellborn, & S. Rossner (Eds.), *Alcohol and the developing brain* (pp. 125–134). New York: Raven Press.

Abramson, L. Y., Metalsky, G. I., & Alloy, L. B. (in submission). The hopelessness theory of depression: a metatheoretical analysis with implications for psychopathology research. Manuscript submitted for publication.

Abramson, L. Y., Seligman, M. E. P., & Teasdale, J. D. (1978). Learned helplessness in humans: critique and reformulation. *Journal of Abnormal Psychology, 87*, 49–74.

Ackerman, B. P. (1985). Children's retrieval deficit. In C. J. Brainerd & M. Pressley (Eds.), *Basic processes in memory development: Progress in cognitive development research* (pp. 1–46). New York: Springer-Verlag.

Ackroyd, C., Humphrey, N. K., & Warrington, E. K. (1974). Lasting effects of early blindness. *Quarterly Journal of Experimental Psychology, 26*, 114–124.

Adair, J. G., & Spinner, B. (1981). Subject access to cognitive-processes-demand characteristics and verbal report. *Journal for the Theory of Social Behavior, 1*, 31–52.

Adam, K. (1980). Sleep as a restorative process and a theory to explain why. *Progress in Brain Research, 53*, 289–306.

Adams, G. R., & LaVoie, J. C. (1974). The effect of sex of child, conduct, and facial attractiveness of teacher expectancy. *Education, 95*, 76–83.

Adelson, E. H. (1978). Iconic storage: The role of rods. *Science, 201*, 544–546.

Adelson, E. H., & Jonides, J. (1980). The psychophysics of iconic storage. *Journal of Experimental Psychology: Human Perception and Performance, 6*, 486–493.

Adler, A. (1907). *Study of organ inferiority and its psychical compensation: A contribution to clinical medicine.* New York: Nervous and Mental Diseases Publishing Company.

Adler, R. P., Lesser, G. S., Meringoff, L. K., Robertson, T. S., & Ward, S. (1980). *The effects of television advertising on children.* Lexington, MA: D. C. Heath.

Agras, W. S., & Werne, J. (1977). Behavior modification in anorexia nervosa: research foundations. In *Proceedings of the First International Conference on Anorexia Nervosa.* New York: Raven Press.

Ahlstrom, W. M., & Havighurst, R. J. (1971). *400 Losers.* San Francisco: Jossy-Bass.

Ainsworth, M. D. S., & Bell, S. M. (1974). Mother–infant interaction and the development of competence. In K. Connolly and J. Bluener (Eds.), *The growth of completeness.* New York: Academic Press.

Ainsworth, M. D., Bell, S. M., & Stayton, D. C. (1971). Individual differences in a strange-situation behavior of one-year olds. In H. R. Schaffer (Ed.), *The origins of human social relations.* London: Academic Press.

Ainsworth, M. D. S., Blehar, M. C., Waters, E., & Wall, S. (1978). *Patterns of attachment: A psychological study of the strange situation.* Hillsdale, NJ: Lawrence Erlbaum.

Aitkin, L. M., Irvine, D. R. F., & Webster, W. R. (1984). Central neural mechanisms of hearing. In I. Darian-Smith (Ed.), *Handbook of physiology—The nervous system III* (pp. 675–737). Bethesda, MD: American Physiological Society.

Ajzen, I., & Fishbein, M. (1977). Attitude-behavior relations: A theoretical analysis and review of empirical research. *Psychological Bulletin, 84*, 888–918.

Ajzen, I., & Fishbein, M. (1980). *Understanding attitudes and predicting social behavior.* Englewood Cliffs, NJ: Prentice-Hall.

Ajzen, I., & Holmes, W. H. (1976). Uniqueness of behavioral effects in causal attribution. *Journal of Personality, 44*, 98–108.

Albers, J. (1975). *Interaction of color.* New Haven, CT: Yale University Press.

Albert, D. J., & Walsh, M. L. (1984). Neural systems and the inhibitory modulation of agonistic behavior: A comparison of mammalian species. *Neuroscience and Biobehavioral Reviews, 8*, 5–24.

Alberts, J. R. (1981). Ontogeny of olfaction: Reciprocal roles of sensation and behavior in the development of perception. In R. N. Aslin, J. R. Alberts, & M. R. Peterson (Eds.), *Development of perception* Vol. 1, pp. 321–357). New York: Academic Press.

Alicke, M. D., & Insko, C. A. (1984). Sampling of similar and dissimilar persons and objects as a function of the generality of attribution goal. *Journal of Personality and Social Psychology, 46*, 763–777.

Alker, H. A. (1972). Is personality situationally specific or intrapsychically consistent? *Journal of Personality, 40*, 1–16.

Allen, M. G. (1976). Twin studies of affective illness. *Archives of General Psychiatry, 33*, 1476–1478.

Allport, F. H. (1924). *Social psychology.* Boston: Houghton Mifflin.

Allport, G. W. (1935). Attitudes. In C. Murchison (Ed.), *A handbook of social psychology.* Worcester, MA: Clark University Press.

Allport, G. W. (1937). *Personality: A psychological interpretation.* New York: Holt, Rhinehart, & Winston.

Allport, G. W. (1961). *Pattern and growth in personality.* New York: Holt, Rhinehart, & Winston.

Allport, G. W., & Odbert, H. S. (1936). Trait names: A psycholexical study. *Psychological Monograph, 47*, 171–220.

Alper, J. (1986). Our dual memory. *Science 86, 7*, 44–49.

Amenson, C. S., & Lewinson, P. M. (1981). An investigation into the observed sex difference in prevalence of unipolar depression. *Journal of Abnormal Psychology, 90*, 1–13.

American Psychiatric Association. (1980). *Diagnostic and statistical manual of mental disorders* (3rd ed.). Washington, DC: Author.

Amoore, J. E. (1970). *Molecular basis of odor.* Springfield, IL: Charles C. Thomas.

Amoore, J. E. (1977). Specific anosmia and the concept of primary odors. *Chemical Senses and Flavor, 2*, 267–282.

Amoore, J. E., Johnston, J. W., Jr., & Rubin, M. (1964). The stereochemical theory of odor. *Scientific American, 210*, 42–49.

Anand, B. K., & Brobeck, J. F. (1951). Hypothalamic control of food intake. *Yale Journal of Biological Medicine, 24*, 123–140.

Anastasi, A. (1958). *Differential psychology* (3rd ed.). New York: Macmillan.

Anastasi, A. (1982). *Psychological testing.* New York: Macmillan.

Anderson, C. A. (1983). Motivational and performance deficits in interpersonal settings: The effects of attributional style. *Journal of Personality and Social Psychology, 45*, 1136–1147.

Anderson, C. A. (1985). Actor and observer attributions for different types of situations: Causal-structure effects, individual differences, and the dimensionality of causes. *Social Cognition, 3*, 323–340.

Anderson, C. A., & Anderson, D. C. (1984). Ambient temperature and violent crime: Tests of linear and curvilinear hypotheses. *Journal of Personality and Social Psychology, 46*, 91–97.

Anderson, J. R. (1985). *Cognitive psychology and its implications.* New York: Freeman.

Anderson, J. R., & Bower, G. H. (1972). Recognition and retrieval processes in free recall. *Psychological Review, 79,* 97–123.

Anderson, W. (Trans.) (1970). *Theophrastus: The character sketches.* New York: Holt, Rinehart, & Winston.

Andreasen, N. C. (1985). Positive vs. negative schizophrenia: A critical evaluation. *Schizophrenia Bulletin, 11,* 380–389.

Andreasen, N. C., Olson, S. A., Dennert, J. W., & Smith, M. R. (1982). Ventricular enlargement in schizophrenia: Relationship to positive and negative symptoms. *American Journal of Psychiatry, 139,* 297–302.

Andreasen, N. L. (1979). Affective flattening and the criteria for schizophrenia. *American Journal of Psychiatry, 136,* 944–947.

Andreasen, N. L. (1984). *The broken brain.* New York: Harper & Row.

Anglin, J. M. *Word, object, and conceptual development.* New York: Norton.

Angus, R. G., & Heslegrave, R. J. (1985). Effects of sleep loss on sustained cognitive performance during a command and control simulation. *Behavior Research Methods, Instrumentation, and Computers, 17,* 55–67.

Angus, R. G., Heslegrave, R. J., & Myles, W. S. (1985). Effects of prolonged sleep deprivation, with and without chronic physical exercise, on mood and performance. *Psychophysiology, 22,* 276–282.

Anstis, S., Giaschi, D., & Cogan, A. I. (1985). Adaptation to apparent motion. *Vision Research, 25,* 1051–1062.

Antell, S. E., & Caron, A. J. (1985). Neonatal perception of spatial relationships. *Infant Development and Behavior, 8,* 15–23.

Apkarian, P. A. (1983). Visual training after long term deprivation: a case report. *International Journal of Neuroscience, 19,* 65–84.

Arenberg, D. (1982). Changes with age in problem solving. In F. I. M. Craik & S. Trehub (Eds.), *Aging and Cognitive Processes* (pp. 221–235). New York: Plenum Press.

Arenberg, D., & Robertson-Tchabo, E. A. (1977). Learning and aging. In J. E. Birren & K. W. Schaie (Eds.), *Handbook of psychology of aging* (pp. 421–449). New York: Van Nostrand Reinhold.

Arkes, H. R. (1981). Impediments to accurate clinical judgment and possible ways to minimize their impact. *Journal of Consulting and Clinical Psychology, 49,* 323–330.

Arkin, R. M., Cooper, H., & Kolditz, T. (1980). A statistical review of literature concerning the self-serving attribution bias in interpersonal influence situations. *Journal of Personality, 48,* 435–448.

Arkin, R. M., Deichon, C. S., & Maruyama, G. M. (1982). Roles of attribution, affect, and cognitive interference in test anxiety. *Journal of Personality and Social Psychology, 43,* 1111–1124.

Arkin, R. M., & Maruyama, G. M. (1979). Attribution, affect, and college exam performance. *Journal of Educational Psychology, 71,* 85–93.

Armstrong, S. L., Gleitman, L. R., & Gleitman, H. (1983). What some concepts might not be. *Cognition, 13,* 263–308.

Arnsten, A. F. T., & Goldman-Rakic, P. S. (1985). Alpha$_2$-adrenergic mechanisms in prefrontal cortex associated with cognitive de-cline in aged nonhuman primates. *Science, 230,* 1273–1276.

Arvidson, K., & Friberg, U. (1980). Human taste: Response and taste bud number in fungiform papillae. *Science, 209,* 807–808.

Asberg, M., Thoren, P., Traskman, L., Bertilsson, L., & Ringberger, V. (1976). "Serotonin depression"—A biochemical subgroup within the affective disorders? *Science, 191,* 478–480.

Asch, S. (1946). Forming impressions of personality. *Journal of Abnormal and Social Psychology, 41,* 258–290.

Asch, S. E. (1955). Opinions and social pressure. *Scientific American, 103,* 31–35.

Asch, S. E. (1956). Studies of independence and conformity: A minority of one against a unanimous majority. *Psychological Monographs, 70,* 9, Whole No. 416.

Aschoff, J. (1969). Desynchronization and re-synchronization of human circadian rhythms. *Aerospace Medicine, 40,* 844–849.

Ashton, H., & Stepney, B. (1982). *Smoking: Psychology and pharmacology.* London: Tavistock.

Aslin, R. N. (1977). Development of binocular fixation in human infants. *Journal of Experimental Child Psychology, 23,* 133–150.

Aslin, R. N. (1981). Experiential influences and sensitive periods in perceptual development: A unified model. In R. N. Aslin, J. R. Alberts, & M. R. Peterson (Eds.), *Development of perception: Psychobiological perspectives.* Vol. 2: *The visual system.* New York: Academic Press.

Aslin, R. N., Alberts, J. R., & Peterson, M. R. (1981). *Development of perception: Psychobiological perspectives.* Vol. 2: *The visual system.* New York: Academic Press.

Aslin, R. N., Pisoni, D. B., & Jusczyk, P. W. (1983). Auditory development and speech perception in infancy. In M. M. Haith and J. J. Campos (Eds.), *Handbook of child psychology,* Vol. II (4th ed.): *Infancy and developmental psychology* (pp. 573–687). New York: John Wiley & Sons.

Assmus, G., Farley, J. U., & Lehmann, D. R. (1984). How advertising affects sales: Meta-analysis of econometric results. *Journal of Marketing Research, 21,* 65–74.

Atkinson, J. W., & Raynor, J. O. (1974). *Motivation and achievement.* Washington, DC: Winston.

Atkinson, R. C., & Joula, J. F. (1974). Search and decision processes in recognition memory. In D. H. Krantz, R. C. Atkinson, R. D. Luce, & P. Suppes (Eds.), *Contemporary developments in mathematical psychology.* San Francisco: W. H. Freeman Co.

Atkinson, R., & Shiffrin, R. M. (1968). Human memory: A proposed system and its control processes. In K. W. Spence & J. T. Spence (Eds.), *The psychology of learning and motivation* (Vol. 2). New York: Academic Press.

Atkinson, R. C., & Shiffrin, R. M. (1971). The control of short-term memory. *Scientific American, 225,* 82–90.

Atrens, D. M. (1985). The psychobiology of obesity. *Proceedings of the Nutrition Society of Australia, 10,* 78–87.

Atwood, M. E., & Polson, P. G. (1976). A process model for water jar problems. *Cognitive Psychology, 8,* 191–216.

Aubert, H. (1886). Die Bewegungsempfindung. *Archiv fur die Gesamte Physiologic des Menchen und der Tiere, 39,* 347–370.

Averill, J. R. (1983). Studies on anger and ag-gression: Implications for theories of emotion. *American Psychologist,* Nov., 1145–1160.

Awaya, S., Miyake, Y., Imayuni, Y., Shiose, Y., Kanda, T., & Komuro, K. (1973). Amblyopia in man, suggestive of stimulus deprivation amblyopia. *Japanese Journal of Ophthalmology, 17,* 69–82.

Ayllon, T., & Azrin, N. H. (1968). *The token economy: A motivational system for therapy and rehabilitation.* New York: Appleton-Century-Crofts.

Azrin, N. H., & Holz, W. C. (1966). In W. K. Honig (Ed.), *Operant behavior: Areas of research and application.* New York: Appleton-Century-Crofts.

Azrin, N. H., Hutchinson, R. R., & Hake, D. F. (1966). Extinction-induced aggression. *Journal of the Experimental Analysis of Behavior, 9,* 191–204.

Bachman, J. G. (1970). *Youth in Transition, Vol. 2. The impact of family background and intelligence on tenth-grade boys.* Ann Arbor, MI: Inst. Soc. Res. Univ. of Michigan.

Baddeley, A. D. (1982). Domains of recollection. *Psychological Review, 89,* 708–729.

Baddeley, A. D. (1983). Working memory. *Philosophical Transactions of the Royal Society, B302,* 311–324.

Baddeley, A. D. (1986). *Working memory.* New York: Oxford University Press.

Baddeley, A. D., & Ecob, J. R. (1973). Reaction-time and short-term memory: Implications of repetition for the high-speed exhaustive scan hypothesis. *Quarterly Journal of Experimental Psychology, 25,* 229–240.

Baddeley, A. D., & Hitch, G. (1974). Working memory. In G. H. Bower (Ed.), *The psychology of learning and motivation* (Vol. 8). London: Academic Press.

Baerends, G. P., Brouwer, R., & Waterbolk, H. T. (1955). Ethological studies on *Lebistes reticulatus (Peters):* I. An analysis of the male courtship patterns. *Behaviour, 8,* 249–334.

Bagozzi, R. P. (1981). Attitudes, intentions, and behavior: A test of some key hypotheses. *Journal of Personality and Social Psychology, 41,* 607–627.

Bahrick, H. P. (1984). Semantic memory content in permastore: Fifty years of memory for Spanish learned in school. *Journal of Experimental Psychology: General, 113,* 1–29.

Bahrick, H. P., Bahrick, P. O., & Wittlinger, R. P. (1975). Fifty years of memory for names and faces: A cross-sectional approach. *Journal of Experimental Psychology: General, 104,* 54–75.

Bahrick, H. P., Clark, S., & Bahrick, P. (1967). Generalization gradients as indicants of learning and retention of a recognition task. *Journal of Experimental Psychology, 75,* 464–471.

Baile, C. A., McLaughlin, C. L., & Della-Fera, M. A. (1986). Role of cholecystokinin and opioid peptides in control of food intake. *Physiological Reviews, 66,* 172–234.

Bailey, J. M., & Horn, J. M. (1986). A source of variance in IQ unique to the lower-scoring monozygotic line? Cotwin. *Behavior Genetics, 16,* 509–516.

Baker, L. J., Dearborn, M., Hastings, J. E., Hamburger, R. (1984). Type A behavior on women: A review. *Health Psychology, 3,* 477–497.

Baker, L. J., Hastings, J. E., & Hart, J. D. (1984). Enhanced psychophysiological responses of Type A coronary patients during Type A-relevant imagery. *Journal of Behavioral Medicine, 7,* 287–306.

Ballard, P. B. (1913). Oblivescence and reminiscence. *British Journal of Psychology Monograph Supplement, 1,* No 2.

Baltes, P. B, & Schaie K. W. (1976). On the plasticity of intelligence in adulthood and old age: Where Horn and Donaldson fail. *American Psychologist, 31,* 720–725.

Bandler, R. J., Madaras, G. R., & Bem, D. J. (1968). Self-observation as a source of pain perception. *Journal of Personality and Social Psychology, 9,* 205–209.

Bandura, A. (1965). Influence of models' reinforcement contingencies on the acquisition of imitative responses. *Journal of Personality and Social Psychology, 1,* 589–595.

Bandura, A. (1969). Social-learning theory of identificatory processes. In D. A. Goslin (Ed.), *Handbook of socialization theory and research* (pp. 213–262). Chicago: Rand McNally.

Bandura, A. (1973). *Aggression: A social learning analysis.* Englewood Cliffs, NJ: Prentice-Hall.

Bandura, A. (1977). Self-efficacy: Toward a unifying theory of behavioral change. *Psychological Review, 84,* 191–215. (a)

Bandura, A. (1977). *Social learning theory.* Englewood Cliffs, NJ: Prentice-Hall. (b)

Bandura, A. (1978). Reflections on self-efficacy. In S. Rachman (Ed.), *Advances in behavioral research and therapy* (Vol. 1). Oxford: Pergamon Press.

Bandura, A. (1982). Self-efficacy mechanism in human agency. *American Psychologist, 37,* 122–147.

Bandura, A. (1986). Fearful expectations and avoidant actions as coeffects of perceived self-inefficacy. *American Psychologist, 41,* 1389–1391.

Bandura A., & Adams, N. E. (1977). Analysis of self-efficacy theory of behavior change. *Cognitive Therapy and Research, 1,* 287–308.

Bandura, A., Adams, N. E., & Beyer, J. (1975). Cognitive processes mediating behavioral change. *Journal of Personality and Social Psychology, 35,* 125–139.

Bandura, A., Adams, N. E., Hardy, A. B., & Howells, G. N. (1980). Tests of the generality of self-efficacy theory. *Cognitive Therapy and Research, 4,* 39–66.

Bandura, A., Ross, D., & Ross, S. A. (1961). Transmission of aggression through imitation of aggressive models. *Journal of Abnormal and Social Psychology, 63,* 575–582.

Bandura, A., Ross, D., & Ross, S. A. (1963). Imitation of film-mediated aggression models. *Journal of Abnormal and Social Psychology, 66,* 3–11.

Bandura, A., Taylor, C. B., Williams, S. L., Mefford, I. N., & Barchas, J. D. (1985). Catecholamine secretin as a function of perceived coping self-efficacy. *Journal of Consulting and Clinical Psychology, 53,* 406–414.

Bandura, A., & Walters, R. H. (1959). *Adolescent aggression: A study of the influence of child-training practices and family interrelationships.* New York: Ronald.

Bandura, A., & Walters, R. H. (1963). *Social learning and personality development.* New York: Holt, Rinehart & Winston.

Banks, M. S., Aslin, R. N., & Letson, R. D. (1975). Sensitive period for the development of human binocular vision. *Science, 190,* 675–677.

Banks, M. S., & Salapatek, P. (1983). Infant visual perception. In P. H. Mussen (Ed.), *Handbook of child psychology: Infancy and developmental psychobiology* (pp. 435–571). New York: John Wiley & Sons.

Banyai, E. I., & Hilgard, E. R. (1976). A comparison of active-alert hypnotic induction with traditional relaxation induction. *Journal of Abnormal Psychology, 85,* 218–224.

Bar-Tal, D., & Saxe, L. (1976). Perceptions of similarly and dissimilarly attractive couples and individuals. *Journal of Personality and Social Psychology, 33,* 772–781.

Barber, T. X. (1979). Suggested ('hypnotic') behavior: The trance paradigm versus and alternative paradigm. In E. From & R. E. Shor (Eds.), *Hypnosis: Developments in research and new perspectives* (pp. 217–272). Chicago: Aldine.

Bargh, J. A. (1982). Attention and automaticity in the processing of self-relevant information. *Journal of Personality and Social Psychology, 43,* 425–436.

Barker, R., Dembo, T., & Lewin, K. (1941). Frustration and aggression: An experiment with young children. *University of Iowa Studies in Child Welfare, 18,* No. 1.

Barlow, H. B., & Levick, W. R. (1969). Changes in the maintained discharge with adaptation level in the cat retina. *Journal of Physiology, London, 202,* 699–718.

Barlow, H. B., & Mollon, J. D. (1982). *The senses.* Cambridge: Cambridge University Press.

Baron, R. A. (1972). Aggression as a function of ambient temperatures and prior anger arousal. *Journal of Personality and Social Psychology, 21,* 183–189.

Baron, R. A. (1974). The aggression-inhibiting influence of heightened sexual arousal. *Journal of Personality and Social Psychology, 30,* 318–322.

Baron, R. A. (1977). *Human aggression.* New York: Plenum.

Baron, R. A. (1983). The control of human aggression: An optimistic perspective. *Journal of Social and Clinical Psychology, 1,* 97–119.

Baron, R. A., & Bell, P. A. (1973). Effects of heightened sexual arousal on physical aggression. In *Proceedings of the 81st Annual Convention of the American Psychological Association, 8,* 171–172.

Baron, R. A., & Bell P. A. (1977). Sexual arousal and aggression by males: Effects of type of erotic stimuli and prior provocation. *Journal of Personality and Social Psychology, 35,* 79–87.

Baron, R. A., & Eggleston, R. J. (1972). Performance on the "aggression machine": Motivation to help or harm? *Psychonomic Science, 26,* 321–322.

Bartlett, F. C. (1932). *Remembering.* Cambridge: Cambridge University Press.

Basser, L. S. (1962). Hemiplegia of early onset and the faculty of speech with special reference to the effects of hemispherectomy. *Brain, 85,* 427–460.

Bates, E. (1976). *Language and context: The acquisition of pragmatics.* New York: Academic Press.

Batson, C. D., & Coke, J. S. (1981). Empathy: A source of altruistic motivation for helping? In J. P. Rushton & R. M. Sorrentino (Eds.), *Altruism and helping behavior.* Hillsdale, NJ: Lawrence Erlbaum.

Bauers, K. S. (1984). On being unconsciously influenced and informed. In K. S. Bowers & D. Meichenbaum (Eds.), *Unconscious reconsidered* (pp. 227–272). New York: John Wiley & Sons.

Baumeister, R. F., & Tice, D. M. (1984). Role of self-presentation and choice in cognitive dissonance under forced compliance: Necessary or sufficient causes. *Journal of Personality and Social Psychology, 43,* 838–852.

Baumeister, D. (1964). Some thoughts on the ethics of research: After reading Milgram's "Behavioral study of obedience." *American Psychologist, 19,* 421–423.

Baumrind, D. (1973). The development of instrumental competence through socialization. In A. D. Pick (Ed.), *Minnesota Symposia on Child Psychology* (pp. 3–46). Minneapolis: University of Minnesota Press.

Bayley, N. (1956). Individual patterns of development. *Child Development, 27,* 45–47.

Beach, F. (1969). It's all in your mind. *Psychology Today, 3,* 33–35.

Bear, D. M. (1979). The temporal lobes: An approach to the study of organic behavioral changes. In M. S. Gazzaniga (Ed.), *Handbook of behavioral neurobiology* (pp. 75–95). New York: Plenum Press.

Beck, A. T. (1967). *Depression: clinical, experimental, and theoretical aspects.* New York: Harper & Row.

Beck, A. T., & Emery, G. (1985). *Anxiety disorders and phobias.* New York: Basic Books.

Beck, A. T., Ward, C. H., Mendelson, M., Mock, J. E., & Erbaugh, J. K. (1962). Reliability of psychiatric diagnoses. 2: A study of consistency of clinical judgments and ratings. *American Journal of Psychiatry, 119,* 351–357.

Beck, K. H. (1979). The effects of positive and negative arousal upon attitudes, belief acceptance, behavioral intention, and behavior. *Journal of Social Psychology, 107,* 239–251.

Becker, J. A. (1986). Bossy and nice requests: Children's production and interpretation. *Merrill-Palmer Quarterly, 32,* 393–413.

Becker, J. A., & Smenner, P. A. (1986). The spontaneous use of *thank you* by preschoolers as a function of sex, socioeconomic status, and listener status. *Language Society, 15,* 537–546.

Beckwith, L. (1979). Prediction of emotional and social behavior. In J. D. Osofsky (Ed.), *Handbook of infant development* (pp. 671–706). New York: John Wiley & Sons.

Beecher, H. K. (1955). The powerful placebo. *Journal of the American Medical Association, 159,* 1603–1606.

Beecher, H. K. (1956). Relationship of significance of wound to the pain experienced. *Journal of the American Medical Association, 161,* 1609–1613.

Begg, I., & Denny, J. P. (1969). Empirical reconciliation of atmosphere and conversion interpretations of syllogistic reasoning errors. *Journal of Experimental Psychology, 81,* 351–354.

Beidler, L. M., & Smallman, R. L. (1965). Renewal of cells within taste buds. *Journal of Cell Biology, 27,* 263–272.

Békésy, G. von. (1960). *Experiments in hearing.* New York: McGraw-Hill.

Bell, A. P., & Weinberg, M. S. (1979). *Homosexualities: A study of diversity among men and women.* New York: Simon & Schuster.

Bell, S., & Ainsworth, M. D. (1972). Infant crying and maternal responsiveness. *Child Development, 43,* 1171–1190.

Bem, D. J. (1965). An experimental analysis of self-persuasion. *Journal of Experimental Social Psychology, 1,* 199–218.

Bem, D. J. (1967). Self-perception: An alternative interpretation of cognitive dissonance phenomena. *Psychology Review, 74,* 183–200.

Bem, D. J. (1972). Constructing cross-situational consistencies in behavior: Some thoughts on Alker's critique of Mischel. *Journal of Personality, 40,* 17–26. (a)

Bem, D. J. (1972). Self-perception theory. In L. Berkowitz (Ed.), *Advances in experimental social psychology* (Vol. 6). New York: Academic Press. (b)

Bem, D. J., & Allen, A. (1974). On predicting some of the people some of the time: The search for cross-situational consistencies in behavior. *Psychological Review, 81,* 506–520.

Bem, S. L. (1974). The measurement of psychological androgyny. *Journal of Consulting Clinical Psychology, 42,* 155–162.

Bem, S. L. (1984). Androgyny and gender schema theory: A conceptual and empirical integration. In T. B. Sondregger (Ed.), *Nebraska Symposium on Motivation: Psychological Gender* (pp. 179–226). Lincoln: University of Nebraska Press.

Bemis, K. M. (1978). Current approaches to the etiology and treatment of anorexia nervosa. *Psychological Bulletin, 85,* 593–617.

Benedict, H. (1979). Early lexical development: Comprehension and production. *Journal of Child Language, 6,* 183–200.

Benjamin, L. S., Foster, S. W., Giat-Roberto, L., & Estroff, S. E. (in press). Breaking the family code: Analyzing videotapes of family interactions by structural analysis of social behavior. In L. S. Greenberg & W. M. Pinsoff (Eds.), *Psychotherapeutic process: A research handbook.* New York: Guilford.

Benson, A. J. (1982). The vestibular sensory system. In H. B. Barlow & J. D. Mollon (Eds.), *The Senses* (pp. 333–368). New York: Cambridge University Press.

Benson, H. (1975). *The relaxation response.* New York: Morrow.

Benson, P. L., Karabenick, S. A., & Lerner, R. M. (1976). Pretty pleases: The effects of physical attractiveness, race, and sex on receiving help. *Journal of Experimental Psychology, 12,* 409–415.

Berger, R. J. (1969). The sleep and dream cycle. In A. Kales (Ed.), *Sleep: Physiology and pathology* (pp. 17–32). Philadelphia: Lippincott.

Berkley, M. (1978). Vision: Geniculocortical system. In R. B. Masterton (Ed.), *Handbook of Behavioral Neurobiology* (pp. 165–207). New York: Plenum.

Berkowitz, L. (1965). The concept of aggressive drive: Some additional considerations. In L. Berkowitz (Ed.), *Advances in experimental social psychology* (Vol. 2). New York: Academic Press.

Berkowitz, L. (1969). The frustration-aggression hypothesis revisited. In L. Berkowitz (Ed.), *Roots of aggression: A re-examination of the frustration-aggression hypothesis* (pp. 1–20). New York: Atherton.

Berkowitz, L. (1984). Human aggression. In N. S. Endler & J. M. Hunt (Eds.), *Personality and the behavioral disorders* (Vol. 1). New York: John Wiley & Sons.

Berkowitz, L., Cochran, S., & Embree, M. (1981). Physical pain and the goal of aversively stimulated aggression. *Journal of Personality and Social Psychology, 40,* 687–700.

Berkowitz, L., & Donnerstein, E. (1982). External validity is more than skin deep: Some answers to criticisms of laboratory experiments. *American Psychologist, 37,* 245–257.

Berkowitz, L., & Knurek, K. A. (1969). Label-mediated hostility generalization. *Journal of Personality and Social Psychology, 13,* 200–206.

Berkowitz, L., & LePage, A. (1967). Weapons as aggression-eliciting stimuli. *Journal of Personality and Social Psychology, 7,* 202–207.

Berlin, B. (1978). Ethnobiological classification. In E. Rosch & B. B. Lloyd (Eds.), *Cognition and categorization.* New York: John Wiley & Sons.

Berman, K. F., Zoc, R. F. K., & Weinberger, D. R. (1986). Physiological dysfunction of dorsolateral prefrontal cortex in schizophrenia: II. Role of neuroleptic treatment, attention, and mental effort. *Archives of General Psychiatry, 43,* 126–135.

Bermant, G., & Davidson, J. M. (1974). *Biological bases of sexual behavior.* New York: Harper & Row.

Bernheim, K. F., & Lewine, R. R. J. (1979). *Schizophrenia: Symptoms, causes, treatments.* New York: Norton.

Berry, J. W. (1980). Cultural universality of any theory of human intelligence remains an open question. *Behavioral and Brain Sciences, 3,* 584–585.

Berscheid, E. (1985). Interpersonal attraction. In G. Lindzey & E. Aronson (Eds.), *The handbook of social psychology* (Vol. II, 3rd ed.). New York: Random House.

Berscheid, E., Dion, K., Walster, E., & Walster, G. W. (1971). Physical attractiveness and dating choice: A test of the matching hypothesis. *Journal of Experimental Social Psychology, 7,* 173–189.

Bersoff, D. N. (1973). Silk purses into sow's ears. *American Psychologist, 28,* 892–899.

Bexton, W. H., Heron, W., & Scott, T. H. (1954). Effects of decreased variation in the sensory environment. *Canadian Journal of Psychology, 8,* 70–76.

Biederman, I., Mezzanotte, R. J., & Rabinowitz, J. C. (1982). Scene perception: Detecting and judging objects undergoing relational violations. *Cognitive Psychology, 14,* 143–177.

Bignami, A., Chi, N. H., & Dahl, D. (1986). The role of neuroglia in axonal growth and regeneration. In G. D. Das & R. B. Wallace (Eds.), *Neural transplantation and regeneration: Proceedings in life sciences* (pp. 229–244). Berlin: Springer-Verlag.

Biller, H. B. (1976). The father and personality development: Paternal deprivation and sex-role development. In M. E. Lamb (Ed.), *The role of the father in child development* (pp. 89–156). New York: John Wiley & Sons.

Bindra, D. (1959). *Motivation: A systematic reinterpretation.* New York: Ronald.

Bindra, D. (1974). A motivational view of learning, performance, and behavior modification. *Psychological Review, 81,* 199–213.

Bindra, D., & Spinner, N. (1958). Response to different degrees of novelty: The incidence of various activities. *Journal of the Experimental Analysis of Behavior, 1,* 341–350.

Binet, A. (1900). *La suggestibilité.* Paris: Schleicher.

Binet, A. (1910). *Les idées modernes sur les enfants.* Paris: E. Flammarion, cited in Jenson, 1980.

Birch, E. E., & Stager, D. R. (1985). Monocular acuity and stereopsis in infantile esotropia. *Investigative Ophthalmology and Visual Science, 26,* 1624–1630.

Bird, E. D., Spokes, E. G., & Iversen, L. L. (1979). Brain norepinephrine and dopamine in schizophrenia. *Science, 204,* 73–94.

Birren, J. E., & Schaie, K. W. (Eds.). (1985). *Handbook of the psychology of aging* (2nd ed.). New York: Van Nostrand Reinhold.

Björklund, A., & Stenevi, U. (1984). Intracerebral neural implants: Neuronal replacement and reconstruction of damaged circuitries. *Annual Review of Neuroscience, 7,* 279–308.

Blanchard, E. B., & Andrasik, F. (1985). *Management of chronic headaches: A psychological approach.* New York: Pergamon Press.

Blaney, P. H. (1986). Affect and memory: A review. *Psychological Bulletin, 99,* 229–246.

Blasi, A. (1980). Bridging moral cognition and moral action: A critical review of the literature. *Psychological Bulletin, 88,* 1–45.

Blehar, M. C., Lieberman, A. F., & Ainsworth, M. D. S. (1977). Early face-to-face interaction and its relation to infant-mother attachment. *Child Development, 48,* 182–194.

Blinkov, S. M., & Glezer, I. I. (1968). *The human brain in figures and tables.* New York: Plenum Press.

Block, J. (1971). *Lives through time.* Berkeley, CA: Bancroft.

Block, J. (1977). Advancing the psychology of personality: Paradigmatic shift or improving the quality of research. In D. Magnusson & N. S. Endler (Eds.), *Personality at the crossroads: Current issues in interactional psychology.* Hillsdale, NJ: Lawrence Erlbaum.

Block, J. H. (1976). Issues, problems, and pitfalls in assessing sex differences: A critical review of "The psychology of sex differences." *Merrill-Palmer Quarterly, 22,* 283–308.

Bloom, L., Merkin, S., & Wootten, J. (1982). Wh-questions: Linguistic factors that contribute to the sequence of acquisition. *Child Development, 53,* 1084–1092.

Blumstein, S. E. (1982). Language dissolution in aphasia: Evidence from linguistic theory. In L. Obler & L. Menn (Eds.), *Exceptional language and linguistics* (pp. 203–215). New York: Academic Press.

Bobrow, D. G. (1968). Natural language input for a computer problem-solving system. In M. Minsky (Ed.), *Semantic information processing.* Cambridge: MIT Press.

Bogardis, C., Lillioja, S., Ravussin, E., Abbott, W., Zawadzki, J. K., Young, A., Knowles, W. C., Jacobowitz, R., & Moll, P. P. (1986). Familial dependence of resting metabolic rate. *New England Journal of Medicine, 315,* 96–100.

Bogen, J. E. (1969). The other side of the brain. II. An appositional mind. *Bulletin of the Los Angeles Neurological Society, 34,* 135–162.

Bogen, J. E. (1977). Some educational implications of hemispheric specialization. In M. C. Wittrock (Ed.), *The human brain* (pp. 133–152). Englewood Cliffs, NJ: Prentice-Hall.

Bogen, J. E. (1986). One brain, 2 brains, or both. In F. Leporé, M. Ptito, & H. H. Jasper (Eds.), *Two hemispheres—One brain: Functions of the corpus callosum* (pp. 21–36). New York: Alan R. Liss.

Bolles, R. C. (1967). *Theory of motivation*. New York: Harper & Row.

Bolles, R. C. (1972). Reinforcement, expectancy, and learning. *Psychological Review, 79,* 394–409. (a)

Bolles, R. C. (1972). Species-specific defence reactions and avoidance learning. In M. E. P. Seligman & J. L. Hager (Eds.), *Biological boundaries of learning* (pp. 189–211). New York: Appleton-Century- Crofts. (b)

Boole, G. (1854). *An investigation into the laws of thought*. London: Walton and Maberly.

Boothe, R. G., Dobson, V., & Teller, D. Y. (1985). Postnatal development of vision in human and nonhuman primates. *Annual Review of Neuroscience, 8,* 495–546.

Borgida, E., & Nisbett, R. (1977). The differential impact of abstract versus concrete information on decisions. *Journal of Applied Social Psychology, 7,* 258–271.

Boring, E. G. (1923). Intelligence as the tests test it. *New Republic, 35,* 35–37.

Borjesou, M. (1976). The etiology of obesity in children. A study of 101 twin pairs. *Acta Paediatrica Scandinavia, 65,* 279–287.

Borkowski, J. G., & Maxwell, S. E. (1985). Looking for Mr. Good-g; general intelligence and processing speed. *The Behavioral and Brain Sciences, 8,* 221–222.

Botwinick, J. (1984). *Aging and behavior*. New York: Springer Publishing Company.

Bouchard, T. J., Heston, L., Eckert, E., Keyes, M., & Resnick, S. (1981). The Minnesota study of twins reared apart: Project description and sample results in the developmental domain. *Twin research 3: Intelligence, personality and development*. New York: Alan R. Liss.

Bourne, P. G. (1975). Polydrug abuse—status report on the federal effort. In E. Senay, V. Shorty, & H. Alksen (Eds.), *Developments in the field of drug abuse: National drug abuse conference* (pp. 197–226). Cambridge, MA: Schenkman.

Bousfield, W. A. (1953). The occurrence of clustering in the recall of randomly arranged associates. *Journal of General Psychology, 49,* 229–240.

Bower, G. H. (1981). Mood and memory. *American Psychologist, 36,* 129–148.

Bower, G. H., & Karlin, M. B. (1974). Depth of processing pictures of faces and recognition memory. *Journal of Experimental Psychology, 103,* 751–757.

Bower, G. H., & Trabasso, T. R. (1964). Concept identification. In R. C. Atkinson (Ed.), *Studies in mathematical psychology*. Stanford, CA: Stanford University Press.

Bowers, J. W., & Osborn, M. M. (1966). Attitudinal effects of selected types of concluding metaphors in persuasive speech. *Speech Monographs, 33,* 147–155.

Bowers, K. S. (1976). *Hypnosis for the seriously curious*. Monterey, CA: Brooks/Cole.

Bowers, K. S., & Meichenbaum, D. (Eds.). (1984). *The unconscious reconsidered*. New York: John Wiley & Sons.

Bowlby, J. (1969). *Attachment and loss: Vol. I: Attachment*. New York: Basic Books.

Bowmaker, J. K. (1983). How is colour perceived: The visual pigments of human cones. *Transactions of the Ophthalmological Society, 103,* 373–379.

Bradshaw, J. L., & Nettleton, N. C. (1981). The nature of hemispheric specialization in man. *Behavioral and Brain Sciences, 4,* 51–80.

Brainerd, C. J. (1985). Model-based approaches to storage and retrieval development. In C. J. Brainerd & M. Pressley (Eds.), *Basic processes in memory development: Progress in cognitive development research* (pp. 143–207). New York: Springer-Verlag.

Bransford, J. D., & Johnson, M. K. (1972). Contextual prerequisites for understanding: Some investigations of comprehension and recall. *Journal of Verbal Learning and Verbal Behavior, 11,* 717–721.

Breggin, P. R. (1980). Brain-disabling therapies. In E. S. Valenstein (Ed.), *The psychosurgery debate*. San Francisco: Freeman.

Brehm, J. W. (1956). Post-decision changes in desirability of alternatives. *Journal of Abnormal and Social Psychology, 52,* 348–389.

Bremer, F. (1937). L'activité cerebrale au cours du sommeil et de la narcose. Contribution à la l'etude du mecanisme du sommeil. *Bulletin de l'Academie Royale de Belgique, 4,* 68–86.

Brenner, C. (1957). *An elementary textbook of psychoanalysis*. Garden City, NY: Doubleday.

Breuer, J., & Freud, S. (1893/1974). *Studies on hysteria*. Harmondsworth, England: Pelican.

Brewin, C. R. (1985). Depression and causal attributions: What is their relation? *Psychological Bulletin, 98,* 297–309.

Briddell, D. W., & Wilson, G. T. (1976). Effects of alcohol and expectancy set on male sexual arousal. *Journal of Abnormal Psychology, 85,* 225–234.

Bridgeman, B., & Fishman, R. (1985). Dissociation of corollary discharge from gaze direction does not induce a straight-ahead shift. *Perception and Psychophysics, 37,* 523–528.

Brigden, R. (1933). A tachistoscopic study of the differentiation of perception. *Psychological Monographs, 44,* 153–166.

Briggs, G. E. (1957). Retroactive inhibition as a function of the degree of original and interpolated learnings. *Journal of Experimental Psychology, 53,* 60–67.

Brigham, J. C. (1980). Limiting conditions of the "physical attractiveness stereotype": Attributions about divorce. *Journal of Research in Personality, 14,* 365–375.

Brinley, J. F., Jovick, T. J., & McLaughlin, L. M. (1974). Age, reasoning, and memory. *Journal of Gerontology, 29,* 182–189.

Broadbent, D. E. (1954). The role of auditory localization and attention in memory span. *Journal of Experimental Psychology, 47,* 191–196.

Broadbent, D. E. (1958). *Perception and communication*. New York: Pergamon Press.

Broca, P. (1865). Sur le siège de la faculté du langage articulé. *Bulletin de la Société d'Anthropologie, 6,* 377.

Brockner, J., & Swap, W. C. (1976). Effects of repeated exposure and attitudinal similarity on self-disclosure and interpersonal attraction. *Journal of Personality and Social Psychology, 33,* 531–540.

Brody, E. B., & Brody, N. (1976). *Intelligence: Nature, determinants, and consequences*. New York: Academic Press.

Brooks, V. B., & Thach, W. T. (1981). Cerebral control of posture and movement. In V. B. Brooks (Ed.), *Handbook of physiology—The nervous system II* (pp. 877–946). Bethesda, MD: American Physiological Society.

Brooks-Gunn, J., & Lewis, M. (1984). The development of early visual self-recognition. *Developmental Review, 4,* 215–239.

Broverman, K., Vogel, S. R., Broverman, D. M., Clarkson, E., & Rosenkrantz, P. S. (1972). Sex-role stereotypes: A current appraisal. *Journal of Social Issues, 28,* 59–78.

Brown, G. L., Ballenger, J. C., Minichiello, M. D., & Goodwin, F. N. (1979). Human aggression and its relationship to cerebral spinal fluid, 5-hydroxyyindoleacetic acid, 3-methoxy-4-hydroxyphenylglycol and homovanillic acid. In M. Sandler (Ed.), *Psychopharmacology of aggression*. New York: Raven Press.

Brown, G. W., Carstairs, G. M., & Topping, G. G. (1958). Post hospital adjustment of chronic mental patients. *Lancet, 2,* 685–689.

Brown, G. W. K., Birley, J. L. T., & Wing, J. K. (1972). Influence of family life on the course of schizophrenic disorders: A replication. *British Journal of Psychiatry, 121,* 241–258.

Brown, J. (1958). Some tests of decay theory of immediate memory. *Quarterly Journal of Experimental Psychology, 10,* 12–21.

Brown, P. K., & Wald, G. (1964). Visual pigments in single rods and cones of the human retina. *Science, 144,* 45–52.

Brown, R. (1986). *Social psychology* (2nd ed.). New York: Free Press.

Brown, R., & Kulik, J. (1977). Flashbulb memories. *Cognition, 5,* 73–99.

Brown, R., & McNeill, D. (1966). The "tip of the tongue" phenomenon. *Journal of Verbal Learning and Verbal Behavior, 5,* 325–337.

Brown, T., Cazden, C. B., & Bellugi, U. (1969). The child's grammar from 1 to 3. In J. P. Hill (Ed.), *Minnesota symposium on child psychology* (Vol. 2). Minneapolis: University of Minnesota Press.

Brownell, H. H., Bihrle, A. M., & Michelow, D. (1986). Basic and subordinate level naming by agrammatic and fluent aphasic patients. *Brain and Language, 28,* 42–52.

Brownell, H. H., Potter, H. H., Bihrle, A. M., & Gardner, H. (1986). Inference deficits in right brain-damaged patients. *Brain and Language, 27,* 310–321.

Brownmiller, S. (1975). *Against our will: Men, women, and rape*. New York: Simon & Schuster.

Bruce, H. (1959). An exteroceptive block to pregnancy in the mouse. *Nature, 184,* 105.

Bruch, H. (1973). *Eating disorders*. New York: Basic Books.

Bruner, J. S., Goodnow, J., & Austin, G. A. (1956). *A study of thinking*. New York: John Wiley & Sons.

Brunswick, E. (1943). Organismic achievement and environmental probability. *Psychological Review, 50,* 255–272.

Bryan, J. H., Redfield, J., & Mader, S. (1971). Words and deeds about altruism and the subsequent reinforcement power of the model. *Child Development, 42,* 1501–1508.

Bryan, J. H., & Walbek, N. H. (1970). The impact of words and deeds concerning altruism upon children. *Child Development, 41,* 747–757.

Bryant, J., & Zillmann, D. (1979). Effect of intensification of annoyance through unrelated residual excitation on substantially delayed hostile behavior. *Journal of Experimental Social Psychology, 15,* 470–480.

Buck, R. (1985). Prime theory: An integrated view of motivation and emotion. *Psychological Review, 92,* 389–413.

Bugelski, B. R., & Alampay, D. A. (1961). The

role of frequency in developing perceptual set. *Canadian Journal of Psychology, 15,* 205–211.

Bullock, T. H. (1982). Electroreception. *Annual Review of Neuroscience, 5,* 121–170.

Bullock, T. H. (1984). Comparative neuroscience holds promise for quiet revolutions. *Science, 225,* 473–478.

Burchfield, S. R. (1985). Stress: An integrative framework. In S. R. Burchfield (Ed.), *Stress: Psychological and physiological interactions.* Washington, DC: Hemisphere Publishing.

Burgess, E. W., & Wallin, P. W. (1943). Homogamy in social characteristics. *American Journal of Sociology, 49*(2), 109–124.

Burgess, P. R., Wei, J. Y., Clark, F. O., & Simon, J. (1982). Signaling of kinesthetic information in peripheral sensory receptors. *Annual Review of Neurosciences,* 171–187.

Burisch, M. (1984). Approaches to personality inventory scale construction. *American Psychologist, 39,* 214–227.

Burton, R. V. (1963). Generality of honesty reconsidered. *Psychological Review, 70,* 481–499.

Buss, A. (1961). *The psychology of aggression.* New York: John Wiley & Sons.

Buss, A. H. (1963). Physical aggression in retaliation to different frustrations. *Journal of Abnormal Social Psychology, 67,* 1–7.

Butters, N., & Cermak, L. S. (1980). *Alcoholic Korsakoff's syndrome.* New York: Academic Press.

Cacioppo, J. T., & Petty, R. E. (1979). Attitudes and cognitive response: An electrophysiological approach. *Journal of Personality and Social Psychology, 37,* 2181–2199. (a)

Cacioppo, J. T., Petty, R. E., Losch, M. E., & Kim, H. S. (1986). Electromyographic activity over facial muscle regions can differentiate the valence and intensity of affective reactions. *Journal of Personality and Social Psychology, 50,* 260–268.

Cacioppo, J. T., Petty, R. E., & Morris, K. J. (1985). Semantic, evaluative, and self-referent processing: Memory, cognitive effort, and somatovisceral activity. *Psychophysiology, 22,* 371–384.

Cacioppo, J. T., & Petty, R. E. (1979). Effects of message repetition and position on cognitive response, recall, and persuasion. *Journal of Personality and Social Psychology, 37,* 97–109. (b)

Cahoon, D. D., & Edmunds, E. M. (1984). Guns/no guns and the expression of social hostility. *Bulletin of the Psychonomic Society, 22,* 305–308.

Cain, W. S., & Engen, T. (1969). Olfactory adaptation and the scaling of odor intensity. In C. Pfaffman (Ed.), *Olfaction and taste III* (pp. 127–141). New York: Rockefeller University Press.

Calder, B. J., & Staw, B. M. (1975). Self-perception of intrinsic and extrinsic motivation. *Journal of Personality and Social Psychology, 31,* 599–605.

Campbell, D. T. (1975). On the conflicts between biological and social evolution and between psychology and moral tradition. *American Psychologist, 30,* 1103–1126.

Campbell, E. (1983). Becoming voluntarily childless: An exploratory study in a Scottish city. *Social Biology, 30,* 307–317.

Campbell, R., Landis, T., & Regard, M. (1986). Face recognition and lipreading. *Brain, 109,* 509–521.

Campbell, S. S., & Tobler, I. (1984). Animal sleep: A review of sleep duration across phylogeny. *Neuroscience and Biobehavioral Reviews, 8,* 269–300.

Canestrari, R. E., Jr. (1963). Paced and self-paced learning in young and elderly adults. *Journal of Gerontology, 18,* 165–168.

Canestrari, R. E., Jr. (1968). Age changes in acquisition. In G. A. Talland (Ed.), *Human aging and behavior* (pp. 169–188). New York: Academic Press.

Cannon, D. S., Baker, T. B., Gino, A., & Nathon, P. E. (in press). Alcohol aversion therapy: Relationship between strength of aversion and abstinence. *Journal of Consulting and Clinical Psychology.*

Cannon, W. B. (1929). *Bodily changes in pain, hunger, fear and rage.* New York: Banford.

Cannon, W. B. (1972). The James–Lange theory of emotions: A critical examination of an alternative theory. *American Journal of Psychology, 39,* 106–124.

Canter, G. J., Trost, J. E., & Burns, M. S. (1985). Contrasting speech patterns of apraxia of speech and phonemic paraphasia. *Brain and Language, 24,* 204–222.

Cantor, N., Markus, H., Niedenthal, P., & Nurius, P. (1986). On motivation and the self-concept. In R. M. Sorrentino, & R. T. Higgins (Eds.), *Handbook of motivation and cognition.* New York: Guilford.

Capaldi, E. D., Hovancik, J. R., & Davidson, T. L. (1979). Learning about water by hungry rats. *Learning and Motivation, 10,* 58–72.

Caplan, D., Baker, C. & DeHaut, F. (1985). Syntactic determinants of sentence comprehension in aphasia. *Cognition, 21,* 117–175.

Caramazza, A., & Zurif, E. B. (1976). Dissociation of algorithmic and heuristic processes in language comprehension: Evidence from aphasia. *Brain and Language, 3,* 572–582.

Carew, T. J. (1985). The control of reflex action. In E. R. Kandel & J. H. Schwartz (Eds.), *Principles of neural science* (2nd ed., pp. 457–468). New York: Elsevier.

Carey, S. (1977). The child as word learner. In M. Halle, J. Bresnan, & G. A. Miller (Eds.), *Linguistic theory and psychological reality.* Cambridge, MA: MIT Press.

Carey, S. (1985). *Conceptual changes in adulthood.* Cambridge, MA: MIT Press.

Carlsmith, J. M., & Anderson, C. A. (1979). Ambient temperature and the occurrence of collective violence: A new analysis. *Journal of Personality and Social Psychology, 37,* 337–344.

Carlson, C. R., White, D. K., & Turkat, I. D. (1982). Night terrors: A clinical and empirical review. *Clinical Psychology Review, 2,* 455–468.

Carlson, N. R. (1986). *Physiology of behavior.* Boston: Allyn & Bacon.

Carrington, P. (1978). *Clinically Standardized Meditation (CSM) instructor's kit.* Kendall Park, NJ: Pace Educational Systems.

Carroll, J. B. (1985). The measurement of intelligence. In R. J. Sternberg (Ed.), *Handbook of human intelligence.* Cambridge: Cambridge University Press.

Cartwright, R. A. (1978). *A primer of sleep and dreaming.* Reading, MA: Addison-Wesley.

Case, R. (1985). *Intellectual development: Birth to adulthood.* Orlando, FL: Academic Press.

Cash, T. F., & Derlega, V. J. (1978). The matching hypothesis: Physical attractiveness among same-sexed friends. *Personality and Social Psychology Bulletin, 4,* 240–243.

Cash, T. F., Kehr, J. A., Ployson, J., & Freeman, V. (1977). Role of physical attractiveness in peer attribution of psychological disturbance. *Journal of Counseling and Clinical Psychology, 45,* 987–993.

Cattell, R. B. (1950). *Personality: A systematic theoretical and factual study.* New York: McGraw-Hill.

Cattell, R. B. (1956). A shortened 'basic English' (Form C) version of the 16 P. F. Questionnaire. *Journal of Social Psychology, 44,* 257–278.

Cattell, R. B. (1957). *Personality and motivation structure and measurement.* New York: Harcourt, Brace, and World.

Cattell, R. B. (1963). Theory of fluid and crystallized: A critical experiment. *Journal of Educational Psychology, 54,* 1–22.

Cattell, R. B. (1965). *The scientific analysis of personality.* Baltimore: Penguin.

Cattell, R.B. (1971). *Abilities: Their structure, growth, and action.* Boston: Houghton-Mufflin.

Cattell, R. B. (1986). The 16 PF Personality Structure and Dr. Eysenck. *Journal of Social Behavior and Personality, 1,* 153–160.

Cattell, R. B., Eber, H. W., & Tatsuoka, M. M. (1970). *Handbook for the Sixteen Personality Factor Questionnaire (16PF).* Champaign, IL: Institute for Personality and Ability Testing.

Cattell, R. B., & Kline, P. (1977). *The scientific analysis of personality and motivation.* New York: Academic Press.

Cattell, R. B., & Krug, S. E. (1986). The number of factors in the 16PF: A review of the evidence with special emphasis on the methodological problems. *Educational and Psychological Measurement, 46,* 509–522.

Cattell, R. B., & Nesselroade, J. R. (1967). Likeness and completeness theories examined by Sixteen Personality Factor Measures by stably and unstably married couples. *Journal of Personality and Social Psychology, 7,* 351–361.

Cavineso, V. S., & O'Brien, P. (1980). Current concepts: headache. *New England Journal of Medicine, 302,* 446.

Ceraso, J., & Provitera, A. (1971). Sources of error in syllogistic reasoning. *Cognitive Psychology, 2,* 400–410.

Cerella, J. (1985). Information processing rates in the elderly. *Psychological Bulletin, 98,* 67–83.

Cermak, L. S., O'Connor, M., & Talbot, N. (1986). Biasing of alcoholic Korsakoff patients' semantic memory. *Journal of Clinical and Experimental Neuropsychology, 8,* 543–555.

Chaiken, S. (1979). Communicator physical attractiveness and persuasion. *Journal of Personality and Social Psychology, 37,* 1387–1397.

Chaiken, S., & Stangor, C. (1987). Attitudes and attitude. In M. R. Rosenzweig & L. W. Porter (Eds.), *Annual review of psychology* (pp. 575–630). Palo Alto, CA: Annual Reviews.

Chaney, E. F., O'Leary, M. R., & Marlatt, G. A. (1978). Skill training with alcoholics. *Journal of Consulting and Clinical Psychology, 46,* 1092–1104.

Chapman, J., & McGhie, A. (1962). A comparative study of disordered attention in schizophrenia. *Journal of Mental Science, 108,* 487–500.

Chapman, L. J., & Chapman, J. P. (1959). Atmosphere effect reexamined. *Journal of Experimental Psychology, 58,* 220–226.

Chapman, L. J., & Chapman, J. P. (1967). The genesis of popular but erroneous psychodiagnostic observations. *Journal of Abnormal Psychology, 72,* 193–204.

Chapman, L. J., & Chapman, J. P. (1973). *Disordered thought in schizophrenia.* New York: Appleton-Century-Crofts.

Charness, N. (1981). Aging and skilled problem solving. *Journal of Experimental Psychology: General, 110,* 21–38. (a)

Charness, N. (1981). Search in chess: age and skill differences. *Journal of Experimental Psychology: Human Perception and Performance, 7,* 467–476. (b)

Charness, N. (1985). Aging and problem-solving performance. In N. Charness (Ed.), *Aging and human performance* (pp. 225–259). Chichester: John Wiley & Sons. (a)

Charness, N. (Ed.). (1985). *Aging and human performance.* New York: John Wiley & Sons. (b)

Chasdi, E. H., & Lawrence, M. S. (1955). Some antecedents of aggression and effects of frustration in doll play. In D. McClelland (Ed.), *Studies in motivation.* New York: Appleton-Century-Crofts.

Chase, W. G., & Ericsson, K. A. (1981). Skilled memory. In J. R. Anderson (Ed.), *Cognitive skills and their acquisition.* Hillsdale, NJ: Lawrence Erlbaum.

Chase, W. G., & Ericsson, K. A. (1982). Skill and working memory. In G. H. Bower (Ed.), *The psychology of learning and motivation* (Vol. 16). New York: Academic Press.

Check, J. V. P. (1985). Hostility toward women: Some theoretical considerations. In G. W. Russell (Ed.), *Violence in intimate relationships.* Jamaica, NY: Spectrum. (a)

Check, J. V. P. (1985). *The hostility toward women scale.* Unpublished doctoral dissertation. University of Manitoba, Winnipeg, Canada. (b)

Check, J. V. P., & Malamuth, N. M. (1982). *Pornography effects and self-reported likelihood of committing acquaintance versus stranger rape.* Paper presented at the meeting of the Midwestern Psychological Association, Minneapolis.

Cheng, P. W., Holyoak, K. J., Nisbett, R. E., & Oliver, L. M. (1986). Pragmatic versus syntactic approaches to training deductive reasoning. *Cognitive Psychology, 18,* 293–328.

Cherry, E. C. (1953). Some experiments on the recognition of speech with one and two ears. *Journal of the Acoustical Society of America, 25,* 975–979.

Chevrier, J., & Delorme, A. (1983). Depth perception in Pandora's box and size illusion: Evolution with age. *Perception, 12,* 177–186.

Chi, M. T. H., Feltovich, P. J., & Glaser, R. (1981). Categorization and representation of physics problems by experts and novices. *Cognitive Science, 5,* 121–152.

Chomsky, N. (1965). *Aspects of the theory of syntax.* Cambridge, MA: MIT Press.

Chomsky, N. (1968). *Language and mind.* New York: Harcourt, Brace, Jovanovich.

Chomsky, N. (1975). *Reflections on language.* New York: Pantheon Books.

Chomsky, N. (1980). *Rules and representations.* New York: Columbia University Press.

Chorover, S. L. (1980). The psychosurgery evaluation studies and their impact on the commission's report. In E. S. Valenstein (Ed.), *The psychosurgery debate.* San Francisco: Freeman.

Church, A. T., Katigbak, M. S., & Almario-Valazco, G. (1985). Psychometric intelligence and adaptive competence in rural Philippine children. *Intelligence, 9,* 317–340.

Clark, D. M., & Teasdale, J. D. (1982). Diurnal variation in clinical depression and accessibility of memories of positive and negative experiences. *Journal of Abnormal Psychology, 91,* 87–95.

Clark, D. M., & Teasdale, J. D. (1985). Constraints on the effects of mood on memory. *Journal of Personality and Social Psychology, 48,* 1595–1608.

Clark, H. H., & Chase, W. G. (1972). On the process of comparing sentences against pictures. *Cognitive Psychology, 3,* 472–517.

Clark, H. H., & Clark, E. V. (1977). *Psychology and language.* New York: Harcourt, Brace, Jovanovich.

Clark, R. D., III (1976). On the Piliavin and Piliavin model of helping behavior: Costs are in the eye of the beholder. *Journal of Applied Social Psychology, 6,* 322–328.

Clark, R. D., & Word, L. E. (1972). Why don't bystanders help? Because of ambiguity? *Journal of Personality and Social Psychology, 24,* 392–400.

Clarke, P. G. H. (1985). Neuronal death in the development of the vertebrate nervous system. *Trends in Neurosciences, 8,* 345–349.

Clarke-Stewart, A. (1982). *Daycare.* Cambridge, MA: Harvard University Press.

Clarke-Stewart, K. A. (1973). Interactions between mothers and their young children: Characteristics and consequences. *Monographs of the Society for Research in Child Development, 38,* (Serial No. 153).

Clausen, J. A. (1975). The social meaning of differential physical and sexual maturation. In S. E. Dragastin & G. H. Elder (Eds.), *Adolescence in the life cycle: Psychological change and social context* (pp. 25–47). New York: John Wiley & Sons.

Clifford, M. M., & Walster, E. (1973). The effect of physical attractiveness on teacher expectation. *Sociology of Education, 46,* 248–258.

Clore, G. L., & Byrne, D. (1974). A reinforcement-affect model of attraction. In T. L. Huston (Ed.), *Foundations of interpersonal attraction.* New York: Academic Press.

Coe, W. C., & Sarbin, T. R. (1977). Hypnosis from the standpoint of a contextualist. In W. F. Edmonston (Ed.), *Conceptual and investigative approaches to hypnosis and hypnotic phenomena* (pp. 2–13). New York: Annals of the NY Academy of Science.

Cohen, J., Dearnaley, E. J., & Hansel, C. E. M. (1958). The risk taken in driving under the influence of alcohol. *British Medical Journal, 1,* 1438–1442.

Cohen, S., & Syme, S. L. (1985). *Social support and health.* New York: Academic Press.

Cohen, S., & Wills, T. A. (1985). Stress, social support, and the buffering hypothesis. *Psychological Bulletin, 98,* 310–357.

Colby, A., Kohlberg, L., Gibbs, J., & Leiber-

man, M. (1983). Longitudinal study of moral judgment. *Monographs of Social Research in Child Development, 48.*

Coleman, J. (1980). Friendship and the peer group in adolescence. In J. Adelson (Ed.), *Handbook of adolescent development* (pp. 408–430). New York: John Wiley & Sons.

Coleman, J. C., & Hammen, C. L. (1974). *Contemporary psychology and effective behavior.* Glenville, IL: Scott, Foresman.

Collings, V. B. (1974). Human taste response as a function of locus of stimulation on the tongue and soft palate. *Perception and Psychophysics, 16,* 169–174.

Collins, A. M., & Loftus, E. F. (1975). A spreading-activation theory of semantic processing. *Psychological Review, 82,* 407–428.

Collins, A. M., & Quillian, M. R. (1969). Retrieval time from semantic memory. *Journal of Verbal Learning and Verbal Behavior, 8,* 240–248.

Collins, K. H., & Tatum, A. L. (1925). A conditioned salivary reflex established by chronic morphine poisoning. *American Journal of Physiology, 74,* 14–15.

Colquhoun, W. P. (1971). Circadian variations in mental efficiency. In W. P. Colquhoun (Ed.), *Biological rhythms and human performance* (pp. 39–107). New York: Academic Press.

Comarr, A. E. (1970). Sexual function among patients with spinal cord injury. *Urologia Internationalis, 25,* 134–168.

Comstock, G., Chaffee, S., Katzman, N., McCombs, M., & Roberts, D. (1978). *Television and human behavior.* New York: Columbia University Press.

Condiotte, M. M., & Lichtenstein, E. (1981). Self-efficacy and relapse in smoking cessation programs. *Journal of Consulting and Clinical Psychology, 49,* 648–658.

Conger, J. J. (1977). Parent–child relationships, social change, and adolescent vulnerability. *Journal of Pediatric Psychology, 2,* 93–97.

Conley, J. J. (1985). Longitudinal stability of personality traits: A multitrait-multimethod-multioccasion analysis. *Journal of Personality and Social Psychology, 49,* 1266–1282.

Conrad, R. (1964). Acoustic confusion in immediate memory. *British Journal of Psychology, 55,* 75–84.

Conrad, R. (1972). Speech and reading. In J. F. Kavanagh & I. G. Maddingly (Eds.), *The relationships between speech and reading.* Cambridge, MA: MIT Press.

Coo, C. L., Weiner, S. G., Rosenberg, L. T., & Levine, S. (1985). Endocrine and immune responses to separation and maternal loss in nonhuman primates. In M. Reite & T. Field (Eds.), *The psychobiology of attachment and separation.* New York: Academic Press.

Cook, T. D., & Flay, B. R. (1978). The temporal persistence of experimentally induced attitude change: An evaluative review. In L. Berkowitz (Ed.), *Advances in experimental social psychology* (Vol. 11). New York: Academic Press.

Cook, T. D., Gruder, C. L., Hennigan, K. M., & Flay, B. R. (1979). History of the sleeper effect: Some logical pitfalls in accepting the null hypothesis. *Psychological Bulletin, 86,* 662–679.

Cooke, N. M., Durso, F. T., & Schvaneveldt, R. W. (1986). Recall and measures of memory organization. *Journal of Experimental Psychology: Learning, Memory, and Cognition, 12,* 538–549.

Cooley, C. H. (1922). *Humane nature and the social order.* Glencoe, IL: The Free Press.

Coopen, A., Prange, A. J., Whybrow, P. L., & Noguera, R. (1972). Abnormalities of the indoleamines in affective disorders. *Archives of General Psychiatry, 26,* 474–478.

Cooper, L. M., & London, P. (1973). Reactivation of memory by hypnosis and suggestion. *International Journal of Clinical and Experimental Hypnosis, 21,* 312–323.

Corballis, M. C. (1986). Is mental rotation controlled or automatic? *Memory and Cognition, 14,* 124–128.

Coren, S., Porac, C., & Ward, C. M. (1984). *Sensation and perception.* Orlando, FL: Academic Press.

Cornblatt, B. A., & Erlenmeyer-Kimling, L. (1985). Global attentional deviance as a marker of risk for schizophrenia: Specificity and predictive validity. *Journal of Abnormal Psychology, 94,* 470–486.

Cornsweet, T. N. (1970). *Visual perception.* New York: Academic Press.

Corrigan, R. (1978). Language development as related to Stage 6 object permanence development. *Journal of Child Language, 5,* 173–189.

Corrigan, R. (1983). The development of representational skills. *New Directions for Child Development, 21,* 51–64.

Cortes, J. B., & Gatti, F. M. (1965). Physique and self-descriptions of temperament. *Journal of Consulting Psychology, 29,* 432–439.

Costa, P. T., Jr., McCrae, R. R., & Arenberg, D. (1980). Enduring dispositions in adult males. *Journal of Personality and Social Psychology, 38,* 793–800.

Côté, L., & Crutcher, M. D. (1985). Motor functions of the basal ganglion and diseases of transmitter metabolism. In E. R. Kandel & J. H. Schwartz (Eds.), *Principles of neural science* (2nd ed., pp. 523–535). New York: Elsevier.

Cotman, C. W. (Ed.). (1985). *Synaptic plasticity.* New York: Guilford Press.

Cotman, C. W., & Nieto-Sampedro, M. (1982). Brain function, synapse renewal, and plasticity. *Annual Review of Psychology, 33,* 371–402.

Cottrell, N. B., & Epley, S. W. (1977). Affiliation, social comparison, and socially mediated stress reduction. In J. Suls & R. L. Miller (Eds.), *Social comparison processes.* Washington, DC: Hemisphere/Halsted.

Cowan, P. A., & Walters, R. H. (1963). Studies of reinforcement of aggression: I. Effects of scheduling. *Child Development, 34,* 543–551.

Cowan, W. M. (1979). The development of the brain. *Scientific American, 241,* 113–133.

Cowan, W. M., Fawcett, J. W., O'Leary, D. D. M., & Stanfield, B. B. (1984). Regressive events in neurogenesis. *Science, 225,* 1258–1265.

Cowart, B. J. (1981). Development of taste perception in humans: Sensitivity and preference throughout the life span. *Psychological Bulletin, 90,* 43–73.

Cox, J. R., & Griggs, R. A. (1982). The effects of experience on performance in Wason's selection task. *Memory & Cognition, 10,* 496–502.

Coyne, J. C. (1976). Depression and the response of others. *Journal of Abnormal Psychol-ogy, 85,* 186–193.

Coyne, J. C. (1985). Studying depressed persons with strangers and spouses. *Journal of Abnormal Psychology, 94,* 231–232.

Craig, K. D. (1978). Social modeling influences on pain. *The Psychology of Pain,* 73–109.

Craig, K. D., & Prkachin, K. M. (1978). Social modeling influences on sensory decision theory and psychophysiological indexes of pain. *Journal of Personality and Social Psychology, 36,* 805–815.

Craig, K. D., & Weiss, S. M. (1971). Vicarious influences on pain-threshold determinations. *Journal of Personality and Social Psychology, 19,* 53–59.

Craik, F. I. M. (1977). Age differences in human memory. In J. E. Birren & K. W. Schaie (Eds.), *Handbook of the psychology of aging* (pp. 384–420). New York: Van Nostrand Reinhold.

Craik, F. I. M., & Byrd, M. (1982). Aging and cognitive deficits: The role of attentional resources. In F. I. M. Craik & S. Trehub (Eds.), *Aging and cognitive processes* (pp. 191–211). New York: Plenum Press.

Craik, F. I. M., & Lockhart, R. S. (1972). Levels of processing: A framework for memory research. *Journal of Learning and Verbal Behavior, 11,* 671–684.

Craik, F. I. M., & Tulving, E. (1975). Depth of processing and the retention of words in episodic memory. *Journal of Experimental Psychology: General, 104,* 268–294.

Cravioto, J., & DeLicardie, E. R. (1978). Nutrition, mental development, and learning. In F. Falkner & J. M. Tanner (Eds.), *Human growth* Vol. 3: *Neurobiology and nutrition* (pp. 481–511). New York: Plenum Press.

Crawford, H. J., MacDonald, H., & Hilgard, E. R. (1979). Hypnotic deafness: A psychophysical study of responses to tone intensity as modified by hypnosis. *American Journal of Psychology, 92,* 193–214.

Crease, I., Burt, D. R., & Snyder, S. H. (1976). Dopamine receptor binding predicts clinical and pharmacological potencies of antischizophrenic drugs. *Science, 192,* 481–483.

Creasey, H., & Rapoport, S. I. (1985). The aging human brain. *Annals of Neurology, 17,* 2–10.

Cremieux, J., Orban, G. A., & Duysens, J. (1984). Responses of cat visual cortical cells to continuously and stroboscopically illuminated moving light slits compared. *Vision Research, 24,* 449–457.

Crisp, A. H. (1984). The psychopathology of anorexia nervosa: Getting the "heat" out of the system. In A. J. Stunkard and E. Stellar (Eds.), *Eating and its disorders* (pp. 209–234). New York: Raven Press.

Crisp, A. H., Hall, A., & Holland, A. J. (1985). Nature and nurture in anorexia nervosa: A study of 34 pairs of twins, one pair of triplets, and an adoptive family. *International Journal of Eating Disorders, 4,* 5–28.

Crocker, J. (1981). Judgment of covariation by social perceivers. *Psychological Bulletin, 90,* 272–292.

Cronbach, L. J. (1984). *Essentials of psychological testing.* New York: Harper & Row.

Crouter, A. C., Belsky, J., & Spanier, G. B. (1984). The family context of child development—divorce and maternal employment. In G. J. Whitehurst (Ed.), *Annals of child development* (pp. 201–238). Greenwich: JAI Press.

Crow, T. J. (1980). Molecular pathology of schizophrenia: More than one disease process? *British Medical Journal, 280,* 66–68.

Crow, T. J. (1985). The two-syndrome concept: Origins and current status. *Schizophrenia Bulletin, 11,* 471–486.

Crow, T. J., MacMillan, J. F., Johnson, A. L., & Johnstone, E. C. (1986). II. A randomized controlled trial of prophylatic neuroleptic treatment. *British Journal of Psychiatry, 148,* 120–127.

Crowe, R. R. (1982). Recent genetic research in schizophrenia. In F. A. Henn & H. A. Nasrallah (Eds.), *Schizophrenia as a brain disease* (pp. 40–60). New York: Oxford University Press.

Curtiss, S. (1977). *Genie: A psycholinguistic study of a modern day "wild child."* New York: Academic Press.

Curtiss, S. (1981). Dissociations between language and cognition: Cases and implications. *Journal of Autism and Developmental Disorders, 11,* 15–30.

Curtiss, S., Fromkin, V., Krashen, S., Rigler, D., & Rigler, M. (1974). The linguistic development of Genie. *Language, 50,* 528–554.

Cutler, B., & Penrod, S. (1987). Context reinstatement and eyewitness identification. In G. Davies & D. Thomson (Eds.), *Memory in context: Context in memory.* Chichester: John Wiley & Sons.

Dahlstrom, W. G., Welsh, G. S., & Dalstrom, L. E. (1975). *An MMPI handbook.* Vol. II: *Research applications.* Minneapolis: University of Minnesota Press.

Damon, W., & Hart, D. (1982). The development of self-understanding from infancy through adolescence. *Child Development, 53,* 481–864.

Danheiser, P. R., & Graziano, W. G. (1982). Self-monitoring and cooperation as a self-presentational strategy. *Journal of Personality and Social Psychology, 42,* 497–505.

Darian-Smith, I. (1984). The sense of touch: Performance and peripheral neural processes. In I. Darian-Smith (Ed.), *Handbook of physiology—The nervous system III* (pp. 739–788). Bethesda, MD: American Physiological Society. (a)

Darian-Smith, I. (1984). Thermal sensibility. In I. Darian-Smith (Ed.), *Handbook of physiology—The nervous system III* (pp. 879–913). Bethesda, MD: American Physiological Society. (b)

Darian-Smith, I. (1984). *Handbook of physiology,* Section I: *The nervous system;* Volume III. *Sensory processes,* Part 2. Bethesda, MD: American Physiological Society. (c)

Darley, J. M., & Latane, B. (1968). Bystander intervention in emergencies: Diffusion of responsibility. *Journal of Personality and Social Psychology, 8,* 377–383.

Dartnall, H. J. A., Bowmaker, J. K., & Mollon, J. D. (1983). Microspectrophotometry of human photoreceptors. In J. D. Mollon & L. T. Sharpe (Eds.), *Colour vision: Physiology and psychophysics* (pp. 69–80). London: Academic Press.

Darwin, C. (1859). *On the origin of species by means of natural selection.* New York: A. L. Burt.

Darwin, C. (1871). *The descent of man, and selection in relation to sex.* London: John Murray.

Darwin, C. (1972). *The expression of emotions in man and animals.* London: Murray. Reprinted by the University of Chicago Press. (Original work published 1872).

Darwin, C. T., Turvey, M. T., & Crowder, R. G. (1972). An auditory analogue of the Sperling partial report procedure: Evidence for brief auditory storage. *Cognitive Psychology, 3,* 255–267.

Davidson, A. R., & Jaccard, J. (1979). Variables that moderate the attitude-behavior relation: Results of a longitudinal survey. *Journal of Personality and Social Psychology, 37,* 1364–1376.

Davidson, J. M., Camargo, C. A., & Smith, E. R. (1979). Effects of androgen on sexual behavior in hypogonadal men. *Journal of Clinical Endocrinology and Metabolism, 48,* 955–958.

Davidson, R. J., & Fox, N. A. (1982). Asymmetrical brain activity discriminates between positive and negative affective stimuli in human infants. *Science, 218,* 1235–1237.

Davidson, R. J., Schwartz, G. E., Saron, C., Bennett, J., & Goleman, D. J. (1979). Frontal versus parietal EEG asymmetry during positive and negative affect. *Psychophysiology, 16,* 202–203.

Davidson, T. L., Capaldi, E. D., & Campbell, D. H. (1985). Irrelevant incentive learning revisited: Associating flavors and exteroceptive cues with positive incentives. *Learning and Motivation, 16,* 288–300.

Davis, H. (1961). Some principles of sensory receptor action. *Physiological Reviews, 41,* 391–416.

Davis, J. M. (1980). Antipsychotic drugs. In H. I. Kaplan, A. M. Freedman, & B. J. Sadock (Eds.), *Comprehensive textbook of psychiatry,* (3rd ed.). Baltimore, MD: Williams & Wilkins.

Davis, J. M., & Cole, J. O. (1975). Antipsychotic drugs. In A. M. Freeman, H. I. Kaplan, & B. J. Sadock (Eds.), *Comprehensive textbook of psychiatry,* (2nd ed., Vol. 2). Baltimore, MD: Williams & Wilkins.

Davis, M., Parisi, T., Gcncdclman, D. 3., Tischler, M., & Kehne, J. H. (1982). Habituation and sensitization of startle reflexes elicited electrically from the brainstem. *Science, 218,* 688–690.

Davis, M. H., & Stephan, W. G. (1980). Attributions for exam performance. *Journal of Applied Social Psychology, 10,* 235–248.

Davison, G. C., & Neale, J. M. (1985). *Abnormal psychology.* New York: John Wiley & Sons.

Daw, N. W. (1984). The psychology and physiology of colour vision. *Trends in Neurosciences, 7,* 330–335.

Day, R. H., Stuart, G. W., & Dickinson, R. G. (1980). Size constancy does not fail below half a degree. *Perceptual Psychophysics, 28,* 263–265.

de Charms, R., & Moeller, G. H. (1962). Values expressed in American children's readers 1800–1950. *Journal of Abnormal and Social Psychology, 64,* 136–142.

de Vries, H., & Stuiver, M. (1961). The absolute sensitivity of the human sense of smell. In W. A. Rosenblith (Ed.), *Sensory communication* (pp. 159–167). Cambridge, MA: MIT Press.

DeBerry, M., & Timrots, A. (1986). *Criminal victimization 1985.* U.S. Department of Justice, Bureau of Justice Statistics. Washington, DC: U.S. Government Printing Office.

DeCasper, A. J., & Fifer, W. P. (1980). Of hu-

man bonding: Newborns prefer their mothers' voices. *Science, 208,* 1174–1176.

DeCasper, A. J., & Spence, M. J. (1986). Prenatal maternal speech influences newborns' perception of speech sounds. *Infant Behavior and Development, 9,* 133–150.

Deci, E. L. (1972). Intrinsic motivation, extrinsic reinforcement and inequality. *Journal of Personality and Social Psychology, 22,* 113–120.

Deci, K. L. (1975). *Intrinsic motivation.* New York: Plenum Press.

Delmonte, M. M. (1984). Meditation practice as related to occupational stress, health and productivity. *Perceptual and Motor Skills, 59,* 581–582.

Delmonte, M. M. (1985). Meditation and anxiety reduction: A literature review. *Clinical Psychology Review, 5,* 91–102. (a)

Delmonte, M. M. (1985). Biochemical indices associated with meditation practice: A literature review. *Neuroscience and Biobehavioral Reviews, 9,* 557–562. (b)

Delmonte, M. M., & Kenny, V. (1985). Models of meditation. *British Journal of Psychotherapy, 1,* 197–214.

DeLuca, J. R. (Ed.). (1981). *Alcohol and health: Fourth Special Report to the U.S. Congress.* Rockville, MD: Nat. Inst. Alcohol & Alcohol Abuse.

Dembroski, T. M., Lasater, T. M., & Ramirez, A. (1978). Communicator similarity, fear-arousing communications, and compliance with health care recommendations. *Journal of Applied Social Psychology, 8,* 254–269.

Dement, W. C. (1960). The effect of dream deprivation. *Science, 131,* 1705–1707.

Dement, W. C. (1974). *Some must watch while some must sleep.* New York: Freeman.

Dement, W. C., & Kleitman, N. (1957). Cyclic variations in EEG during sleep and their relations to eye movement, body motility, and dreaming. *Electroencephalography and Clinical Neurophysiology, 9,* 673–690. (a)

Dement, W. C., & Kleitman, N. (1957). The relation of eye movements during sleep to dream activity: An objective method for the study of dreaming. *Journal of Experimental Psychology, 53,* 339–346. (b)

Dement, W.C., Seidel, W., & Carskadon, M. (1984). Issues in the diagnosis and treatment of insomnia. In I. Hindmarch, H. Ott, & T. Roth (Eds.), *Sleep, benzodiazepines and performance: Experimental methodologies and research prospects* (pp. 11–43). Berlin: Springer-Verlag.

Dement, W. C., & Wolpert, E. (1958). The relation of eye movements, bodily motility, and external stimuli to dream content. *Journal of Experimental Psychology, 55,* 543–553.

Deneau, G., Yanagita, T., & Seevers, M. H. (1969). Self-administration of psychoactive substances by the monkey. *Psychopharmacologia, 16,* 30–48.

Denney, N. W. (1982). *Aging and cognitive changes* (pp. 807–827). Englewood Cliffs, NJ: Prentice-Hall.

Denney, N. W. (1985). A review of life-span research with the twenty questions task: A study of problem-solving ability. *International Journal of Aging and Human Development, 21,* 161–173.

Denney, N. W., & Denney, D. R. (1982). The relationship between classification and questioning strategies among adults. *Journal of Gerontology, 37,* 190–196.

Dennis, M., & Kohn, B. (1975). Comprehension

of syntax in infantile hemiplegics after cerebral hemidecortication: Left hemisphere superiority. *Brain and Language, 2,* 472–482.

Dennis, M., & Whitaker, H. A. (1976). Language acquisition following hemidecortication: Linguistic superiority of the left over the right hemisphere. *Brain and Language, 3,* 403–433.

Dennis, W. (1960). Causes of retardation among institutional children: Iran. *Journal of Genetic Psychology, 96,* 46–50.

Dennis, W., & Dennis, M. G. (1940). The effect of cradling practices upon the onset of walking in Hopi children. *Journal of Genetic Psychology, 56,* 77–86.

Dermer, M., & Thiel, D. L. (1975). When beauty may fail. *Journal of Personality and Social Psychology, 31,* 1168–1196.

Descartes, R. (1664/1972). *Treatise of man.* Cambridge: Harvard University Press.

Desimone, R., Albright, T. D., Gross, C. G., & Bruce, C. (1984). Stimulus-selective properties of inferior temporal neurons in the macaque. *The Journal of Neuroscience, 4,* 2051–2062.

Desmond, J. E., & Moore, J. W. (1982). A brain stem region essential for classically conditioned but not unconditioned nictitating membrane response. *Physiological Behavior, 28,* 1029–1033.

Desmond, J. E., & Moore, J. W. (1983). A supratrigeminal region implicated in the classically conditioned nictating membrane response. *Brain Research Bulletin, 10,* 765–773.

Deutsch, A. (1949). *The mentally ill in America.* New York: Columbia University Press.

Deutsch, J. A. (1978). The stomach in food satiation and the regulation of appetite. *Progressive Neurobiology, 10,* 135–153.

Deutsch, J. G., Larason, K. (1974). Model-oriented sexual behavior in surrogate-reared rhesus monkeys. *Brain Behavior and Evolution, 9,* 157–161.

Deutsch, M., & Gerard, H. G. (1955). A study of normative and informational social influence on individual judgment. *Journal of Abnormal and Social Psychology, 51,* 629–636.

DeValois, R. L., & Jacobs, G. H. (1968). Primate color vision. *Science, 162,* 533–540.

deVilliers, J. G., & deVilliers, P. A. (1973). A cross-sectional study of the acquisition of grammatical morphemes in child speech. *Journal of Psycholinguistic Research, 2,* 267–278.

deVilliers, J. G., & deVilliers, P. A. (1978). *Language acquisition.* Cambridge, MA: Harvard University Press.

deVilliers, P. A., & deVilliers, J. G. (1979). *Early language.* Cambridge, MA: Harvard University Press.

DeVoto, B. (1947). *Across the wide Missouri.* Boston: Houghton Mifflin.

Diaconis, P. (1978). Statistical problems in ESP research. *Science, 201,* 131–136.

Diamond, S. J. (1979). Symmetry and asymmetry in the vertebrate brain. In D. H. Oakley & H. C. Plotkin (Eds.), *Brain, behavior and evolution* (pp. 189–218). London: Methuen.

Diemer, E., & Iran-Nejad, A. (1986). The relationship in experience between various types of affect. *Journal of Personality and Social Psychology, 50,* 1031–1038.

Digman, J. M., & Inouye, J. (1986). Further specification of the five robust factors of personality. *Journal of Personality and Social Psy-*

chology, 50, 116–123.

Dillehay, R. C. (1973). On the irrelevance of the classical negative evidence concerning the effect of attitudes on behavior. *American Psychologist, 28,* 887–891.

Dion, K., Berscheid, E., & Walster, E. (1972). What is beautiful is good. *Journal of Personality and Social Psychology, 34,* 285–290.

Dion, K., & Berscheid, E. (1974). Physical attractiveness and peer perception among children. *Sociometry, 37,* 1–12.

Dipboye, R. L., Arvey, R. D., & Terpstra, D. E. (1977). Sex and physical attractiveness of raters and applicants as determinants of resume evaluations. *Journal of Applied Psychology, 62,* 288–294.

DiVesta, F. J. (1974). *Language learning and cognitive processes.* Monterey, CA: Brooks/Cole.

Dixon, N. R. (1981). *Preconscious processing.* New York: John Wiley & Sons.

Dobbing, J. (1974). The later development of the central nervous system and its vulnerability. In J. A. Davis & J. Dobbing (Eds.), *Scientific foundations of pediatrics* (pp. 565–577). London: Heineman.

Dobbing, J. (1985). Maternal nutrition in pregnancy and later achievement of offspring: A personal interpretation. *Early Human Development, 12,* 1–8.

Dollard, J., Doob, L. W., Miller, N. E., Mowrer, O. H., & Sears, R. R. (1939). *Frustration and aggression.* New Haven, CT: Yale University Press.

Dollard, J. & Miller, N. E. (1950). *Personality and psychotherapy.* New York: McGraw-Hill.

Donaldson, M. (1978). *Children's minds.* New York: Norton.

Donders, F. C. (1868–1869). On the speed of mental processes. Reprinted in *Acta Psychologica, 30* (1969), 412–431.

Donnerstein, E. (1980). Aggressive erotica and violence against women. *Journal of Personality and Social Psychology, 39,* 269–277.

Donnerstein, E. (1983). Erotica and human aggression. In R. Geen & E. Donnerstein (Eds.), *Aggression: Theoretical and empirical reviews.* New York: Academic Press.

Donnerstein, E. (1984). Pornography: Its effect on violence against women. In N. M. Malamuth & E. Donnerstein (Eds.), *Pornography and sexual aggression.* New York: Academic Press.

Donnerstein, E., & Berkowitz, L. (1981). Victims reactions in aggressive-erotic film as a factor in violence against women. *Journal of Personality and Social Psychology, 41,* 710–724.

Donnerstein, E., Donnerstein, M., Evans, R. (1975). Erotic stimuli and aggression: Facilitation or inhibition. *Journal of Personality and Social Psychology, 34,* 774–781.

Donnerstein, E., Linz, D., & Penrod, S. (1987). *The question of pornography.* New York: Free Press.

Donnerstein, E., & Wilson, D. W. (1976). Effects of noise and perceived control on ongoing and subsequent aggressive behavior. *Journal of Personality and Social Psychology, 34,* 774–781.

Dooling, D. J., & Christiaansen, R. E. (1977). Episodic and semantic aspects of memory for prose. *Journal of Experimental Psychology: Human Learning and Memory, 3,* 428–436.

Dorian, B., Garfinkel, P., Brown, G., (1982). Aberrations in lymphocyte subpopulations and function during psychological stress.

Clinical and Experimental Immunology, 50, 132–138.

Doty, R. L. (1981). Olfactory communication in humans. *Chemical Senses, 6,* 357–376.

Dovidio, J. F. (1984). Helping behavior and altruism: An empirical and conceptual overview. In L. Berkowitz (Ed.), *Advances in experimental social psychology* (Vol. 17). New York: Academic Press.

Dovner, G. (1968). Hormonal induction and prevention of female homosexuality. *Journal of Endocrinology, 40,* 163–164.

Dowling, J. E., & Ehinger, B. (1975). Synaptic organization of the amine-containing interplexiform cells of the goldfish and Cebus monkey retinas. *Science, 188,* 270–273.

Dudycha, G. J. (1936). An objective study of punctuality in relation to personality and achievement. *Archives of Psychology, 204,* 1–319.

Duffy, E. (1962). *Activation and behavior.* New York: John Wiley & Sons.

Dulit, E. (1972). Adolescent thinking a la Piaget: The formal stage. *Journal of Youth and Adolescence, 1,* 281–301.

Duncker, K. (1945). On problem-solving (L. S. Lees, Trans.). *Psychological Monographs, 58,* No. 270.

Duval, S., & Wicklund, R. A. (1972). *A theory of objective self-awareness.* New York: Academic Press.

Dweck, C. S., & Licht, B. (1980). Learned helplessness and intellectual achievement. In J. Garber & M. E. P. Seligman (Eds.), *Human helplessness.* New York: Academic.

Dyck, R. J., & Rule, B. G. (1978). Effect on retaliation of causal attributions concerning attack. *Journal of Personality and Social Psychology, 36,* 521–529.

Dywan, J., & Bowers, K. (1983). The use of hypnosis to enhance recall. *Science, 222,* 184–185.

Eagle, M. N. (1984). *Recent developments in psychoanalysis: A critical evaluation.* New York: McGraw-Hill.

Eagly, A. H. (1978). Sex differences in influenceability. *Psychological Bulletin, 85,* 86–116.

Eagly, A. H., & Carli, L. (1981). *Sex of researchers and sex-typed communications as determinants of sex differences in influenceability: A meta-analysis of social influence studies.* Unpublished manuscript, Purdue University.

Eagly, A. H., Wood, W., & Chaiken, S. (1978). Causal inferences about communicators and their effect on opinion change. *Journal of Personality and Social Psychology, 36,* 424–435.

Ebbinghaus, H. (1897). Uber eine neue methode zur prufung geistiger fahigkeiten und ihre anwendung bei schulkindern. *Zeitschrift für Psychologische und Physiologische Sinnesorgane, 13,* 401–459.

Ebbinghaus, H. (1964). *Memory: A contribution to experimental psychology.* (H. A. Ruger & C. E. Bussenius, Trans.) New York: Dover (Original work published 1885).

Edelman, B., Engell, D., Bronstein, P., & Hirsch, E. (1986). Environmental effects on the intake of overweight and normal-weight men. *Appetite, 7,* 71–83.

Edwards, C. P. (1982). Moral development in comparative cultural perspective. In D. A. Wagner & H. W. Stevenson (Eds.), *Cultural perspectives on child development* (pp. 248–279). San Francisco: Freeman.

Efran, M. G. (1974). The effect of physical appearance on the judgment of guilt, interpersonal attraction, and severity of recommended punishment in a simulated jury task. *Journal of Experimental Research in Personality, 8,* 45–54.

Ehrhardt, A. A., Evers, K., & Money, J. (1968). Influence of androgen and some aspects of sexually dimorphic behavior in women with the late-treated adrenogenital syndrome. *Johns Hopkins Medical Journal, 123,* 115–122.

Eibl-Eibesfeldt, I. (1971). *Love and hate.* New York: Holt, Rinehart & Winston.

Eibl-Eibesfeldt, I. (1973). The expressive behavior of the deaf-and-blind-born. In M. Von Cranach & I. Vine (Eds.), *Social communication and movement.* New York: Academic Press.

Eich, J. E. (1980). The cue-dependent nature of state dependent retrieval. *Memory and Cognition, 8,* 157–173.

Eichelman, B., Elliott, G. R., & Barchas, J. D. (1981). Biochemical, pharmacological, and genetic aspects of aggression. In D. A. Hamburg & M. B. Trudeau (Eds.), *Biobehavioral aspects of aggression.* New York: Liss.

Eichorn, D. H. (1979). Physical development: Current foci of research. In J. D. Osofsky (Ed.), *Handbook of infant development* (pp. 253–282). New York: John Wiley & Sons.

Eilers, R. E., Gavin, W. J., & Wilson, W. R. (1979). Linguistic experience and phonemic perception in infancy: A crosslinguistic study. *Child Development, 50,* 14–18.

Eilers, R. E., & Oller, D. K. (1985). Developmental aspects of infant speech discrimination: The role of linguistic experience. *Trends in Neurosciences, 8,* 453–456.

Eimas, P. D., & Corbit, J. D. (1973). Selective adaptation of linguistic feature detectors. *Cognitive Psychology, 4,* 99–109.

Eimas, P. D., Sigueland, E. R., Jusczyk, P., & Vigorito, J. (1971). Speech perception in infants. *Science, 171,* 303–306.

Eisen, S. (1979). Actor-observer differences in information inference and causal attribution. *Journal of Personality and Social Psychology, 37,* 261–272.

Eiser, J. R., & Sutton, S. R. (1977). Smoking as a subjectively rational choice. *Addictive Behaviors, 2,* 129–134.

Eiserer, L. A. (1978). Effects of food primes on the operant behavior of nondeprived rats. *Animal Learning & Behavior, 6,* 308–312.

Ekman, P. (1973). Cross-cultural studies in facial expression. In P. Ekman (Ed.), *Darwin and facial expressions: A century of research in review.* New York: Academic.

Ekman, P. (1983). Autonomic nervous system activity distinguishes among the emotions. *Science, 221,* 1208–1210.

Ekman, P., & Friesen, W. V. (1971). Constants across cultures in the face of emotion. *Journal of Personality and Social Psychology, 17,* 124–129.

Elam, M., Yoa, T., Thorne, P., Svensson, T. H. (1981). Hypercopnia and hypoxia: chemoreceptor-mediated control of locus ceruleus neurons and eplanchnic, sympathetic nerves. *Brain Research, 222,* 373–381.

Elder, G. H., Jr. (1980). *Family structure and socialization.* New York: Arno Press.

Elton, D., Stanley, G., & Burrows, G. (1983). *Psychological control of pain.* Orlando, FL: Grune & Stratton.

Emde, R., Gaensbauer, T., & Harmon, R.

(1976). Emotional expression in infancy: A biobehavioral study. *Psychological Issues, 10* (monogr. 37), 3–192.

Emory, R. E. (1982). Interparental conflict and the children of discord and divorce. *Psychological Bulletin, 92,* 310–330.

Endicott, J., Nee, J., Cohen, J., Fleiss, J. L., & Simon, R. (1986). Diagnosis of schizophrenia: Prediction of short-term outcome. *Archives of General Psychiatry, 43,* 13–19.

Epley, S. W. (1974). Reduction of the behavioral effects of aversive stimulation by the presence of companions. *Psychological Bulletin, 81,* 271–283.

Epstein, S. (1973). The self-concept revisited: Or a theory of a theory. *American Psychologist, 28,* 404–416.

Epstein, S. (1979). The stability of behavior: I. On predicting most people much of the time. *Journal of Personality and Social Psychology, 37,* 1097–1126. (a)

Epstein, S. (1979). Explorations in personality today and tomorrow: A tribute to Henry A. Murray. *American Psychologist, 34,* 649–653. (b)

Epstein, S. (1980). The stability of behavior: II. Implications for psychological research. *American Psychologist, 35,* 790–806.

Epstein, S. (1983). The stability of confusion: A reply to Mischel and Peake. *Psychological Review, 90,* 179–184.

Epstein, S. M. (1967). Toward a unified theory of anxiety. In *Progress in experimental personality research.* New York: Academic.

Erdberg, P., & Exner, J. E. (1984). Rorschach assessment. In G. Goldstein, & M. Hersen (Eds.), *Handbook of psychological assessment.* New York: Pergamon Press.

Erdelyi, M. H., & Becker, J. (1974). Hypermnesia for pictures: Incremental memory for pictures but not words in multiple recall trials. *Cognitive Psychology, 6,* 159–171.

Erdman, G., & Jahnke, H. (1978). Interaction between physiological and cognitive determinants of emotion: Experimental studies on Schachter's theory of emotions. *Biological Psychology, 6,* 61–64.

Erickson, R. P. (1984). On the neural bases of behavior. *American Scientist, 72,* 233–241.

Ericsson, K. A. (1985). Memory skill. *Canadian Journal of Psychology, 39,* 188–231.

Ericsson, K. A., & Chase, W. G. (1982). Exceptional memory. *American Scientist, 70,* 607–614.

Erikson, E. H. (1963). *Childhood and society* (2nd ed.). New York: Norton.

Erikson, E. H. (1968). *Identity, youth, and crisis.* New York: Norton.

Erlenmeyer-Kimling, L. (1968). Studies on the offspring of two schizophrenic parents. In D. Rosenthal & S. S. Katz (Eds.), *The transmission of schizophrenia.* New York: Pergamon.

Eron, L. D. (1965). Rorschach. In O. K. Buros (Ed.), *The sixth mental measurements yearbook.* Highland Park, NJ: Gryphon.

Eron, L. D. (1972). Thematic apperception test. In O. K. Buros (Ed.), *The seventh mental measurements yearbook* (Vol. 1). Highland Park, NJ: Gryphon.

Eron, L. D. (1982). Parent–child interaction, television violence, and aggression of children. *American Psychologist, 37,* 197–211.

Eron, L. D., & Huesmann, L. R. (1980). Adolescent aggression and television. *Annals of the New York Academy of Sciences, 347,* 319–331.

Errera, P., & Coleman, J. V. (1963). A long term follow-up study of neurotic phobic patients in a psychiatric clinic. *Journal of Nervous and Mental Disease, 136,* 267–271.

Evans, E. F. (1974). Neural processes for the detection of acoustic patterns and for sound localization. In F. O. Schmitt & F. G. Worden (Eds.), *The neurosciences: Third study program* (pp. 131–145). Cambridge, MA: MIT Press.

Evans, E. F. (1978). Place and time coding of frequency in the peripheral auditory system: Some physiological pros and cons. *Audiology, 17,* 369–420.

Evans, J. St. B. T. (1982). *The psychology of deductive reasoning.* London: Routledge & Kegan Paul.

Evans, T. G. (1968). A program for the solution of a class of geometry-analogy intelligence test questions. In M. L. Minsky (Ed.), *Semantic information processing.* Cambridge, MA: MIT Press.

Evarts, E. V. (1966). Pyramidal tract activity associated with a conditioned hand movement in the monkey. *Journal of Neurophysiology, 29,* 1011, 1027.

Evarts, E. V. (1973). Brain mechanisms in movement. *Scientific American, 229,* 96–103.

Evarts, E. V. (1981). Role of motor cortex in voluntary movements in primates. In V. B. Brooks (Ed.), *Handbook of physiology—The nervous system II* (pp. 1083–1120). Bethesda, MD: American Physiological Society.

Evarts, E. V., Kimura, M., Wurtz, R. H., & Hikosaka, O. (1984). Behavioral correlates of activity in basal ganglia neurons. *Trends in Neurosciences, 7,* 447–453.

Exner, J. E., & Weiner, I. B. (1982). *The Rorschach: A comprehensive system.* Vol. 3: *Assessment of children and adolescents.* New York: John Wiley & Sons.

Exner, J. E., & Wylie, J. R. (1977). Some Rorschach data concerning suicide. *Journal of Personality Assessment, 41,* 339–348.

Eyferth, K. (1961). Leistungen verscheidener gruppen von besatzunfskindern in Hamberg-Wechsler Intellgenztest fur kinder (HAWK). *Archiv für die Gesante Psychologie, 113,* 222–241.

Eysenck, H. J. (1947). *Dimensions of personality.* London: Routledge & Kegan Paul.

Eysenck, H. J. (1952). The effects of psychotherapy: An evaluation. *Journal of Consulting Psychology, 16,* 319–324.

Eysenck, H. J. (1967). *The biological basis of personality.* Springfield, IL: Charles C. Thomas.

Eysenck, H. J. (1970). *Readings in extraversion-introversion: Bearings on basic psychological processes* (Vol. 3). New York: Wiley.

Eysenck, H. J. (1975). *The inequality of man.* San Diego: Edits Publishers.

Eysenck, H. J. (1983). The effectiveness of psychotherapy: The specter at the feast. *The Behavioral and Brain Sciences, 6,* 290.

Eysenck, H. J. (1984). Personality and individual differences. *Bulletin of the British Psychological Society, 37,* 237.

Eysenck, H. J. (1986). Can personality study ever be scientific? *Journal of Social Behavior and Personality, 1,* 3–19.

Eysenck, H. J., & Eysenck, M. W. (1985). *Personality and individual differences.* New York: Plenum Press.

Eysenck, H. J., & Eysenck, S. B. G. (1968). A factorial study of psychoticism as a dimension of personality. *Multivariate Behavioral Research, Special Issue,* 15–31.

Eysenck, H. J., & Rachman, S. (1965). *The causes and cures of neurosis: An introduction to modern behavior therapy based on learning theory and the principles of conditioning.* San Diego: Knapp.

Fagot, B. I. (1978). The influence of sex of child on parental reactions to toddler children. *Child Development, 49,* 459–465.

Fairbanks, G., Guttman, N., & Miron, M. S. (1957). Effects of time-compression upon the comprehension of connected speech. *Journal of Hearing and Speech Disorders, 22,* 10–19.

Fairburn, C. G. (1984). Bulimia: Its epidemiology and management. In A. J. Stunkard and E. Stellar (Eds.), *Eating and its disorders* (pp. 235–258). New York: Raven Press.

Fantz, R. L. (1961). The origin of form perception. *Scientific American, 204,* 66–72.

Faris, B. E. L., & Dunham, H. W. (1939). *Mental disorders in urban areas: An ecological study of schizophrenia and other psychoses.* Chicago: University of Chicago Press.

Faust, I. M. (1984). Role of the fat cell in energy balance physiology. In A. J. Stunkard and E. Stellar (Eds.), *Eating and its disorders* (pp. 97–107). New York: Raven Press.

Faust, I. M., Johnson, P. R., & Hirsch, J. (1977). Surgical removal of adipose tissue alters feeding behavior and the development of obesity in rats. *Science, 197,* 393–396.

Faust, M. S. (1960). Developmental maturity as a determinant in prestige of adolescent girls. *Child Development, 31,* 173–184.

Fazio, R. H., Zanna, M. P., & Cooper, J. (1977). Dissonance and self-perception: An integrative view of each theory's proper domain of application. *Journal of Experimental Social Psychology, 13,* 464–479.

Fazio, R. H., Zanna, M. P., & Cooper, J. (1979). On the relationship of data to theory: A reply to Ronis and Greenwald. *Journal of Experimental Social Psychology, 15,* 70–76.

Feldman, M. P., & MacCulloch, M. J. (1971). *Homosexual behavior: Therapy and assessment.* Oxford, England: Pergamon.

Feldman, R. D. (1982). *Whatever happened to the Quiz Kids?* Chicago: Chicago Review Press.

Feldman, R. S., & Quenzer, L. F. (1984). *Fundamentals of neuropsychopharmacology.* Sunderland, MA: Sinauer Associates.

Felten, D. L., Overhage, J. M., Felten, S. Y., & Schmeditje, J. F. (1981). Noradrenergic sympathetic innervation of lymphoid tissue in the rabbit appendix: Further evidence for a link between the nervous and immune systems. *Brain Research Bulletin, 7,* 595–612.

Fenstermacher, J. D. (1985). Current models of blood-brain transfer. *Trends in Neurosciences, 8,* 449–452.

Ferguson, E. D. (1976). *Motivation: An experimental approach.* New York: Holt, Rinehart & Winston.

Ferguson, G. A. (1956). On transfer and the abilities of man. *Canadian Journal of Psychology, 10,* 121–131.

Fernandez, A., & Glenberg, A. M. (1985). Changing environmental context does not reliably affect memory. *Memory and Cognition, 13,* 333–345.

Festinger, L. A. (1954). A theory of social comparison processes. *Human Relations, 1,* 117–140.

Festinger, L. A. (1957). *A theory of cognitive dissonance.* Stanford, CA: Stanford University Press.

Festinger, L. A., & Carlsmith, J. (1959). Cognitive consequences of forced compliance. *Journal of Abnormal and Social Psychology, 58,* 203–210.

Festinger, L. A., Schachter, S., & Back, K. (1950). *Social pressures in informal groups: A study of a housing community.* New York: Harper.

Field, K. M., Woodson, R., Greenberg, R., & Cohen, D. (1982). Discrimination and imitation of facial expressions by neonates. *Science, 218,* 179–181.

Fields, H. L. (1981). Pain II: New approaches to management. *Annals of Neurology, 9,* 101.

Fields, H. L., & Levine, J. D. (1984). Placebo analgesia—a role for endorphins? *Trends in Neurosciences, 7,* 271–273.

Findahl, O., & Hoyer, B. (1985). Some characteristics of news memory and comprehension. *Journal of Broadcasting and Electronic Media, 29,* pp. 379–396.

Findlay, S. (1981). Most sex-ed classes don't alter behavior. *USA Today,* p. 10.

Fine, A. (1986). Transplantation in the central nervous system. *Scientific American, 255,* 52–58.

Fink, G. (1985). Homeostasis and hormonal regulation (neuroendocrine reflections of the brain). In C. W. Coen (Ed.), *Functions of the brain* (pp. 130–159). Oxford: Clarendon Press.

Finn, S. E. (1986). Stability of personality self-ratings over 30 years: Evidence for an age/cohort interaction. *Journal of Personality and Social Psychology, 50,* 813–818.

Fischer, K. W., & Lazerson, A. (1984). *Human development: From conception through adolescence.* New York: Freeman.

Fischer, K. W., & Silvern, L. (1985). Stages and individual differences in cognitive development. *Annual Review of Psychology, 36,* 613–648.

Fischer, M. (1973). Genetic and environmental factors in schizophrenia: A study of schizophrenic twins and their families. *Acta Psychiatrica Scandinavica,* Suppl. 238.

Fischhoff, B., Slovic, P., & Lichtenstein, S. (1977). Knowing with certainty: The appropriateness of extreme confidence. *Journal of Experimental Psychology: Human Perception and Performance, 3,* 552–564.

Fishbein, M., & Ajzen, I. (1974). Attitudes toward objects as predictors of single and multiple behavioral criteria. *Psychological Review, 81,* 59–74.

Fishbein, M., & Ajzen, I. (1975). *Belief, attitude, intention and behavior: An introduction to theory and research.* Reading, MA: Addison-Wesley.

Fisher, D. L. (1981). A three-factor model of syllogistic reasoning: The study of isolable stages. *Memory and Cognition, 9,* 496–514.

Fisher, E. B., Jr., Delamater, A. M., Bertelson, A. D., & Kirkley, B. G. (1982). *Journal of Consulting and Clinical Psychology, 50,* 993–1003.

Fisher, W. F. (1963). Sharing in preschool children as a function of amount and type of reinforcement. *Genetic Psychology Monographs, 68,* 215–245.

Fiske, D. W. (1949). Consistency of the factorial structures of personality ratings from different sources. *Journal of Abnormal Social Psychology, 44,* 329–344.

Fiske, S. T., & Taylor, S. (1984). *Social cognition.* Reading, MA: Addison-Wesley.

Flanagan, T. J., & McGarrell, E. F. (1986). *Sourcebook of criminal justice statistics—1985.* U.S. Department of Justice, Bureau of Justice Statistics. Washington, DC: U.S. Government Printing Office.

Flavell, J. H. (1982). On cognitive development. *Child Development, 53,* 1–10.

Flavell, J. H. (1985). *Cognitive development.* Englewood Cliffs, NJ: Prentice-Hall.

Flavell, J. H., Beach, D. R., & Chinsky, J. M. (1966). Spontaneous verbal rehearsal in a memory task as a function of age. *Child Develoment, 37,* 283–299.

Fletcher, H., & Munson, W. A. (1933). Loudness: Its definition, measurement, and calculation. *Journal of the Acoustical Society of America, 5,* 82–108.

Floderus-Myrhed, B., Pederson, N., & Rasmuson, I. (1980). Assessment of heritability for personality, based on a short-form of the Eysenck Personality Inventory: A study of 12,898 twin pairs. *Behavioral Genetics, 10,* 153–162.

Foa, U. G., & Foa, E. B. (1974). *Societal structures of the mind.* Springfield, IL: Charles C. Thomas.

Fodor, J. A., Garrett, M., & Bever, T. G. (1968). Some syntactic determinants of sentential complexity: 2. Verb structure. *Perception & Psychophysics, 3,* 453–461.

Folkard, S. (1982). Circadian rhythms and human memory. In F. M. Brown & R. C. Graeber (Eds.), *Rhythmic aspects of behavior* (pp. 241–272). Hillsdale, NJ: Erlbaum.

Folkard, S., & Monk, T. H. (1980). Circadian rhythms in human memory. *British Journal of Psychology, 71,* 295–307.

Folkard, S., & Monk, T. H. (1983). Chronopsychology—circadian rhythms and human performance. In A. Gale & J. A. Edwards (Eds.), *Physiological correlates of human behavior.* Vol. II: *Attention and performance* (pp. 57–78). London: Academic Press.

Folkes, V. S. (1982). Forming relationships and the matching hypothesis. *Personality and Social Psychological Bulletin, 8*(4), 631–636.

Folkman, S., & Lazarus, R. (1986). Stress processes and depressive symptomatology. *Journal of Abnormal Psychology, 95,* 107–113.

Folkman, S., Lazarus, R. S., Dunkel-Schetter, C., DeLongis, A., & Gruer, R. J. (1986). Dynamics of a stressful encounter: Cognitive appraisal, coping, and encounter outcomes. *Journal of Personality and Social Psychology, 50,* 992–1003.

Ford, C., & Beach, F. *Patterns of sexual behavior.* New York: Harper & Row.

Forem, J. (1973). *Transcendental Meditation: Maharishi Mahesh Yogi and the science of creative intelligence.* New York: Dutton.

Fosshage, J. L. (1983). The psychological function of dreams: A revised psychoanalytic perspective. *Psychoanalysis and Contemporary Thought, 6,* 641–669.

Foucault, M. (1965). *Madness & Civilization.* New York: Vintage.

Fowles, D. C. (1980). The three arousal model: Implications of Gray's two-factor learning theory for heart rate, electrodermal activity, and psychopathy. *Psychophysiology, 17,* 87–104.

Fowles, D. C. (1982). Arousal: Implications of behavior theories of motivation. Paper presented as part of a Symposium honoring John I. and Beatrice C. Lacey. Minneapolis, MN, October 20, 1982.

Fox, N. A., & Davidson, R. J. (1984). Hemispheric substrates of affect: A developmental model. In N. A. Fox & R. J. Davidson (Eds.), *The psychology of affective development.* Hillsdale, NJ: Erlbaum.

Fox, R., Lehmkuhle, S. W., & Westendorf, D. (1976). Falcon visual acuity. *Science, 192,* 263–265.

Fox, R., Patterson, R., & Francis, E. L. (1986). Stereoacuity in young children. *Investigative Ophthalmology and Visual Science, 27,* 598–600.

Frank, J. D. (1974). *Persuasion and healing.* New York: Schocken Books.

Fraser, S. C., & Fujitomi, I. (1972). Perceived prior compliance, psychological reactance and altruistic contributions. *Proceedings of the 80th Annual Convention of the American Psychological Association, 7,* 247–248.

Frazier, L., & Rayner, K. (1982). Making and correcting errors during sentence comprehension: Eye movements in the analysis of structurally ambiguous sentences. *Cognitive Psychology, 14,* 178–210.

Freed, W. J., de Medinaceli, L., & Wyatt, R. J. (1985). Promoting functional plasticity in the damaged nervous system. *Science, 227,* 1544–1552.

Freedman, B., & Chapman, L. (1973). Early subjective experience in schizophrenic episodes. *Journal of Abnormal Psychology, 82,* 46–54.

Freedman, L. Z. (1984). Social impact of attack on a president: Its public reverberations. *Behavioral Sciences and the Law, 2,* 195–206.

Freedman, R. (1985). Neurochemical, neuroendocrine, and psychopharmacological factors in mental illness. In R. C. Simons (Ed.), *Understanding human behavior in health and illness* (3rd ed.). Baltimore, MD: Williams & Wilkins.

Freud, S. (1900/1955). *The interpretation of dreams.* (J. Strachey, Trans. & Ed.) New York: Basic Books.

Freud, S. (1923). *The ego and the id.*

Freud, S. (1926). *Inhibitions, symptoms, and anxiety.* (Standard Edition, Vol. 20). London: Hogarth, 1959.

Freud, S. (1950). *Beyond the pleasure principle.* (J. Strachey, Trans.). New York: Liveright. (Original work published 1920).

Freund, H.-J. (1984). Premotor areas in man. *Trends in Neurosciences, 7,* 481–483.

Frick, R. W. (1985). Communicating emotion: The role of prosodic features. *Psychological Bulletin, 97,* 412–429.

Friedman, L. J., Thornton, J. E., & Pugh, E. N., Jr. (1985). Cone antagonism along visual pathways of red/green dichromats. *Vision Research, 25,* 1647–1654.

Friedman, M., & Rosenman, R. H. (1974). *Type A behavior and your heart.* Greenwich, CT: Fawcett-Crest.

Frisby, J. P. (1980). *Seeing: Illusion, brain and mind.* Oxford: Oxford University Press.

Frodi, A. (1975). The effect of exposure to weapons on aggressive behavior from a cross-cultural perspective. *International Journal of Psychology, 10,* 283–292.

Frodi, A. (1977). Sexual arousal, situational restrictiveness, and aggressive behavior. *Journal of Research in Personality, 11,* 48–58.

Fromkin, V., Krashen, S., Curtiss, S., Rigler, D., & Rigler, M. (1974). The development of language: a case of language acquisition beyond the "critical period." *Brain and Language, 1,* 81–107.

Gaes, G. G., Kalle, R. J., & Tedeschi, J. T. (1978). Impression management in the forced compliance situation: Two studies using the bogus pipeline. *Journal of Experimental Social Psychology, 14,* 493–510.

Gage, F. H., Björklund, A., Isacson, O., & Brudin, P. (1986). Uses of neuronal transplantation in models of neurodegenerative diseases. In G. D. Das & R. B. Wallace (Eds.), *Neural transplantation and regeneration: Proceedings in life sciences* (pp. 103–124). Berlin: Springer-Verlag.

Gaines, L., & Esserman, J. F. (1981). A quantitative study of young children's comprehension of television programs and commercials. In J. F. Esserman (Ed.), *Television advertising and children: Issues, research and findings.* New York: Child Research Service.

Galaburda, A. M. (1984). Anatomical asymmetries. In N. Geschwind & A. M. Galaburda (Eds.), *Cerebral dominance: The biological foundations* (pp. 11–25). Cambridge, MA: Harvard University Press.

Galanter, E. (1962). Contemporary psychophysics. In R. Brown, E. Galanter, E. H. Hess, & G. Mandler (Eds.), *New Directions in Psychology. I.* (pp. 106–156). New York: Holt, Rinehart & Winston.

Galbraith, J. K. (1983). *The anatomy of power.* Boston: Houghton-Mifflin.

Galton, F. (1869). *Hereditary genius: An inquiry into its laws and consequences.* London: Macmillan.

Garcia, J., Hankins, W. G., & Rusiniak, K. W. (1974). Behavioral regulation of the milieu interne in man and rat. *Science, 185,* 824–831.

Gardner, B. T., & Gardner, R. A. (1971). Two-way communication with an infant chimpanzee. In A. M. Schrier & F. Stollnitz (Eds.), *Behavior of non-human primates* (pp. 119–184). New York: Academic Press.

Gardner, B. T., & Gardner, R. A. (1975). Evidence for sentence constituents in the early utterances of child and chimpanzee. *Journal of Experimental Psychology: General, 104,* 244–267.

Gardner, H. (1975). *The shattered mind.* New York: A. A. Knopf.

Gardner, M. (1981). *Science: Good, bad and bogus.* New York: Prometheus.

Gardner, M. B., & Gardner, R. S. (1973). Problem of localization in the median plane: Effect of pinnae cavity occlusion. *Journal of the Acoustical Society of America, 53,* 400–408.

Gardner, R. A., & Gardner, B. T. (1978). Comparative psychology and language acquisition. *Annals of the New York Academy of Sciences, 809,* 37–76.

Garfield, S. L. (1983). Effectiveness of psychotherapy: The perennial controversy. *Professional Psychology: Research and Practice, 14,* 35–43.

Garfield, S. L. (1984). Psychotherapy: efficacy, generality, and specificity. In J. B. W. Williams, & R. L. Spitzer (Eds.), *Psychotherapy research: Where are we and where should we go?* New York: Guilford.

Garfield, S. L. (1986). Problems in diagnostic classification. In T. Million & G. L. Klerman (Eds.), *Contemporary directions in psychopathology.* New York: Guilford.

Garmezy, N. (1970). Process and reactive schizophrenia: Some conceptions and issues. *Schizophrenia Bulletin, 2,* 30–74.

Garvey, C. (1975). Requests and responses in children's speech. *Journal of Child Language, 2,* 41–63.

Gascaly, S. A., & Borges, C. A. (1979). The male physique and behavioral expectancies. *Journal of Psychology, 101,* 97–102.

Gay, W. I. (Ed.). (1986). *Health benefits of animal research.* Washington, DC: Foundation for Biomedical Research.

Geen, R. G., & Pigg, R. (1970). Acquisition of an aggressive response and its generalization to verbal behavior. *Journal of Personality and Social Psychology, 15,* 165–170.

Geen, R. G., & Stonner, D. (1971). An extended apparatus for measuring aggression in humans. *Behavior Research Methods and Instrumentation, 3,* 197–198.

Geldard, F. A. (1972). *The human senses* (2nd ed.). New York: John Wiley & Sons.

Gelfand, D. M., & Hartmann, D. P. (1980). The development of prosocial behavior and moral judgment. In R. L. Ault (Ed.), *Developmental perspectives.* Santa Monica, CA: Goodyear.

Gentner, D., & Gentner, D. R. (1983). Flowing waters or teeming crowds: Mental models of electricity. In D. Gentner & A. L. Stevens (Eds.), *Mental models.* Hillsdale, NJ: Lawrence Erlbaum.

Gentry, W. D. (1970). Effects of frustration, attack, and prior aggressive training on overt aggression and vascular processes. *Journal of Personality and Social Psychology, 16,* 718–725.

Gerard, H. B., Wilhelmy, R., & Connolley, E. (1968). Conformity and group size. *Journal of Personality and Social Psychology, 8,* 79–82.

Gergen, K. J., & Marlow, D. (1970). *Personality and social behavior.* Reading, MA: Addison-Wesley.

Gergen, K. J., & Wishnov, B. (1965). Others' self-evaluations and interaction anticipation as determinants of self-presentation. *Journal of Personality and Social Psychology, 2,* 348–358.

Geschwind, N. (1965). Disconnection syndromes in animals and man. *Brain, 88,* 237–294, 585–644.

Geschwind, N. (1979). Specializations of the human brain. *Scientific American, 241,* 180–201.

Geschwind, N., & Levitsky, W. (1968). Human brain: left–right asymmetries in temporal speech region. *Science, 161,* 186–187.

Getchell, T. V., Margolis, F. L., & Getchell, M. L. (1985). Perireceptor and receptor events in vertebrate olfaction. *Progress in Neurobiology, 23,* 317–345.

Ghez, C. (1985). Voluntary movement. In E. R. Kandel & J. H. Schwartz (Eds.), *Principles of neural science* (2nd ed., pp. 487–501). New York: Elsevier.

Ghez, C., & Fahn, S. (1985). The cerebellum. In E. R. Kandel & H. Schwartz (Eds.), *Principles of neural science* (pp. 502–522). New York: Elsevier.

Giambra, L. M., & Arenberg, D. (1980). Problem solving, concept learning and aging. In L. W. Poon (Ed.), *Aging in the 1980s* (pp. 253–259). Washington, DC: American Psychological Association.

Gibbens, T. C. N. (1963). *Psychiatric studies of Borstal lads.* London: Oxford University Press.

Gibson, E. H., & Walk, R. M. (1960). The 'visual cliff.' *Scientific American, 202,* 64–71.

Gibson, J. J. (1950). *The perception of the visual world.* Boston: Houghton Mifflin.

Gibson, J. J. (1966). *The senses considered as perceptual systems.* Boston: Houghton Mifflin.

Gick, M. L., & Holyoak, K. J. (1980). Schema induction and analogical transfer. *Cognitive Psychology, 12,* 306–355.

Gilman, S. L. (1982). *Seeing the insane.* New York: John Wiley & Sons.

Gilovich, T., Vallone, R., & Tversky, A. (1985). The hot hand in basketball: On the misconception in random sequences. *Cognitive Psychology, 17,* 295–314.

Glanzer, M., & Cunitz, A. R. (1966). Two storage mechanisms in free recall. *Journal of Verbal Learning and Verbal Behavior, 5,* 351–360.

Glass, A. L., & Holyoak, K. J. (1986). *Cognition.* New York: Random House.

Glass, D. C. (1977). *Behavior patterns, stress and coronary disease.* New York: Lawrence Erlbaum.

Gleitman, H. (1981). *Psychology.* New York: Norton.

Glenberg, A. (1984). A retrieval account of the long-term modality effect. *Journal of Experimental Psychology: Learning, Memory, and Cognition, 10,* 16–31.

Glenberg, A., Smith, S. M., & Green, C. (1977). Type I rehearsal: Maintenance and more. *Journal of Verbal Learning and Verbal Behavior, 16,* 339–352.

Glenn, H. D. (1975). Psychological well-being in the postparental stage: Some evidence from national surveys. *Journal of Marriage and the Family, 37,* 105–110.

Glucksberg, S., & Cowen, G. N., Jr. (1970). Memory for nonattended auditory material. *Cognitive Psychology, 1,* 149–156.

Glucksberg, S., & Weisberg, R. W. (1966). Verbal behavior and problem solving: Some effects of labeling in a functional fixedness problem. *Journal of Experimental Psychology, 71,* 659–664.

Glueck, S., & Glueck, E. (1956). *Physique and delinquency.* New York: Harper.

Goddard, H. H. (1912). *The Kallikak family, a study in the heredity of feeble-mindedness.* New York: Macmillan.

Godden, D. R., & Baddeley, A. D. (1975). Context-dependent memory in two natural environments: On land and underwater. *British Journal of Psychology, 66,* 325–332.

Goethals, G. R., & Darley, J. M., Jr. (1977). Social comparison theory: An attributional approach. In J. M. Suls & R. L. Miller (Eds.), *Social comparison processes: Theoretical and empirical perspectives.* Washington, DC: Hemisphere.

Goffman, E. (1955). On face work: An analysis of ritual elements in social interaction. *Psychiatry, 18,* 213–231.

Goffman, E. (1959). *The presentation of self in everyday life.* New York: Doubleday.

Goffman, E. (1967). *Interaction ritual.* Garden

City, NY: Doubleday.

Goffman, E. (1971). *Relations in public*. New York: Basic Books.

Goldberg, G. (1985). Supplementary motor area structure and function: Review and hypotheses. *Behavioral and Brain Sciences, 8*, 567–587.

Goldberg, S. (1983). Parent–infant bonding: Another look. *Child Development, 54*, 1355–1382.

Goldberger, M. E., & Murray, M. (1985). Recovery of function and anatomical plasticity after damage to the adult and neonatal spinal cord. In C. W. Cotman (Ed.), *Synaptic plasticity* (pp. 77–110). New York: Guilford.

Goldfoot, D. A. (1977). Rearing conditions which support or inhibit later sexual potential of laboratory-born rhesus monkeys: Hypotheses and diagnostic behaviors. *Laboratory Animal Science, 27*, 548–556.

Goldgaber, D., Lesman, M. I., McBride, O. W., Saffiotti, U., & Gajdusek, D. C. (1987). Characterization and chromosomal localization of a cDNA encoding brain amyloid of Alzheimer's disease. *Science, 235*, 877–880.

Goldman, R. D., & Hewitt, B. N. (1976). The Scholastic Aptitude Test "explains" why college men major in science more often than college women. *Journal of Counseling Psychology, 23*, 50–54.

Goldman, R. D., & Slaughter, R. E. (1976). Why college grade-point average is difficult to predict. *Journal of Educational Psychology, 68*, 9–14.

Goldman, W., & Lewis, P. (1977). Beautiful is good: Evidence that the physically attractive are more socially skillful. *Journal of Experimental Social Psychology, 13*, 125–130.

Goldman-Rakic, P. S. (1984). The frontal lobes: Uncharted provinces of the brain. *Trends in Neurosciences, 7*, 425–429.

Goldstein, D. B. (1983). *Pharmacology of alcohol*. New York: Oxford.

Goldstein, E. B. (1984). *Sensation and perception*. Belmont, CA: Wordsworth.

Goldstein, M. J. (1983). Family interaction: Patterns predictive of the onset and course of schizophrenia. In H. Stierlin, L. C. Wynne, & M. Wirsching (Eds.), *Psychosocial intervention in schizophrenia*. Berlin: Springer-Verlag.

Goldstein, M. J., Baker, B. L., & Jamison, K. R. (1986). *Abnormal psychology: Experiences, origins, and interventions*. Boston: Little, Brown.

Goldston, D. B., Hinrichs, J. V., & Richman, C. L. (1985). Subjects' expectations, individual variability, and the scanning of mental images. *Memory and Cognition, 13*, 365–370.

Goleman, D. (1977). *The varieties of the meditative experience*. New York: E. P. Dutton.

Goodenough, D. R. (1978). Dream recall: History and current status of the field. In A. M. Arkin, J. S. Antrobus, & J. S. Ellman (Eds.), *The mind in sleep: Psychology and psychophysiology* (pp. 113–141). Hillsdale, NJ: Lawrence Erlbaum.

Goodenough, F. L. (1932). Expression of the emotions in a blind-deaf child. *Journal of Abnormal and Social Psychology, 27*, 328–333.

Goodglass, H., & Baker, E. (1976). Semantic field, naming, and auditory comprehension in aphasia. *Brain and Language, 3*, 359–374.

Goodwin, D. W. (1976). *Is alcoholism hereditary?* New York: Oxford University Press.

Goodwin, D. W., & Guze, S. B. (1984). *Psychiatric diagnosis*. New York: Oxford.

Goodwin, D. W., Powell, B., Bremer, D., Hoine, H., & Stern, J. (1969). Alcohol and recall: State dependent effects in man. *Science, 163*, 1358.

Goodwin, F. K. (1978). Human aggression linked to chemical balance. *Science News, 356*.

Goodwin, F. K., Post, R. M., Dunner, D. L., & Gordon, E. K. (1973). Cerebrospinal fluid amine metabolites in affective illness: The probenacid technique. *American Journal of Psychiatry, 130*, 73–79.

Goodwin, J. S., Bromberg, S., Staszak, C., (1981). Effect of physical stress on sensitivity of lymphocytes to inhibition by protaglandin E2. *Journal of Immunology, 127*, 518–522.

Gordon, C. (1968). Self-conceptions: Configurations of content. In C. P. Gordon & K. P. Gergen (Eds.), *The self in social interaction*. New York: John Wiley & Sons.

Gorenstein, E. E., & Newman, J. P. (1980). Disinhibitory psychopathology: A new perspective and a model for research. *Psychological Review, 87*, 301–315.

Gorn, G. J., & Goldberg, M. E. (1982). Behavioral evidence of the effects of televised food messages on children. *Journal of Consumer Research, 9*, 200–205.

Gorski, R. A., Gordon, J. H., Shryne, J. E., & Southam, A. M. (1978). Evidence for a morphological sex difference within the medial preoptic area of the rat brain. *Brain research, 148*, 333–346.

Gottesman, I. I. (1963). Genetic aspects of intelligent behavior. In N. Ellis (Ed.), *Handbook of mental deficiency* (pp. 253–296). New York: McGraw-Hill.

Gottesman, I. I., & Shields, J. (1972). *Schizophrenia and genetics: A twin study vantage point*. New York: Academic Press.

Gould, J. L. (1982). *Ethology. The mechanisms and evolution of behavior*. New York: Norton.

Gould, S. J. (1981). *The mismeasure of man*. New York: Norton.

Gouldner, A. W. (1960). The notion of reciprocity: A preliminary statement. *American Sociological Review, 25*, 161–178.

Gouras, P. (1984). Color vision. In N. N. Osborne & G. J. Chader (Eds.), *Progress in retinal research* (pp. 227–262). Oxford: Pergamon Press.

Gouras, P., & Zrenner, E. (1981). Color vision: A review from a neurophysiological perspective. In E. Ottoson (Ed.), *Progress in sensory physiology* (pp. 139–179). Berlin: Springer-Verlag.

Goy, R. W., & McEwen, B. S. (1980). *Sexual differentiation of the brain*. Cambridge, MA: MIT Press.

Grace, A. A., & Bunney, B. S. (1985). Dopamine. In M. A. Rogawski & J. L. Barker (Eds.), *Neurotransmitter actions in the vertebrate nervous system* (pp. 285–320). New York: Plenum Press.

Graesser, A. C., & Mandler, G. (1978). Limited processing capacity constrains the storage of unrelated sets of words and retrieval from natural categories. *Journal of Experimental Psychology: Human Learning and Memory, 4*, 86–100.

Graham, C. H., & Hsia, Y. (1958). Color defect and color theory. *Science, 127*, 675–682.

Granrud, C. E., Yonas, A., & Opland, E. A. (1985). Infants' sensitivity to the depth cue of shading. *Perception and Psychophysics, 37*, 415–419.

Gray, J. A. (1975). *Elements of a two-process theory of learning*. London: Academic Press.

Gray, J. A. (1982). *The neuropsychology of anxiety*. Oxford: Oxford University Press. (a)

Gray, J. A. (1982). The neuropsychology of anxiety. *The Behavioral and Brain Sciences, 5*, 469–534. (b)

Gray, J. J., & Ford, K. (1985). The incidence of bulimia in a college sample. *International Journal of Eating Disorders, 4*, 201–210.

Green, D. G., & Powers, M. K. (1982). Mechanisms of light adaptation in rat retina. *Vision Research, 22*, 209–216.

Green D. M. (1985). Temporal factors in psychoacoustics. In A. Michelsen (Ed.), *Time resolution in auditory systems: Proceedings in life sciences* (pp. 122–140). Berlin: Springer-Verlag.

Green, D. M., & Swets, J. A. (1966). *Signal detection theory and psychophysics*. New York: John Wiley & Sons.

Green, R. (1974). *Sexual identity conflict in children and adults*. Baltimore, MD: Penguin.

Greenberg, B. S. (1972). Children's reactions to TV blacks. *Journalism Quarterly, 49*, 5–14.

Greenblatt, D. J., & Shader, R. I. (1978). Pharmacotherapy of anxiety with benzodiazepine and β-adrenergic blockers. In M. A. Lipton, A. DiMascio, & K. F. Killan (Eds.), *Psychopharmacology: A generation of progress*. New York: Raven Press.

Greene, R. L. (1986). A common basis for recency effects in immediate and delayed recall. *Journal of Experimental Psychology: Learning, Memory, and Cognition, 12*, 413–418. (a)

Greene, R. L. (1986). Sources of recency effects in free recall. *Psychological Bulletin, 99*, 221–228. (b)

Greenfield, P. M. (1976). Cross-cultural research and Piagetian theory: Paradox and progress. In K. F. Riegel & J. A. Meacham (Eds.), *The developing individual in a changing world* (pp. 322–333). Chicago: Aldine.

Greeno, J. G. (1974). Hobbits and orcs: Acquisition of a sequential concept. *Cognitive Psychology, 6*, 270–292.

Greenwald, A. G., & Pratkanis, A. R. (1985). The self. In R. S. Wyer & T. K. Srull (Eds.), *Handbook of social cognition*. Hillsdale, NJ: Lawrence Erlbaum.

Greenwald, A. G., & Pratkanis, A. R., Leippe, M. R., & Baumgardner, M. H. (1986). Under what conditions does theory obstruct research progress? *Psychological Review, 93*, 216–229.

Greer, K. (1984). Physiology of motor control. In M. M. Smyth & A. M. Wing (Eds.), *Psychology of human movement* (pp. 76–46). London: Academic Press.

Gregory, R. L. (1963). Distortion of space as inappropriate constancy scaling. *Nature, 199*, 678–680.

Gregory, R. L. (1970). *The intelligent eye*. New York: McGraw-Hill.

Gregory, R. L. (1977). *Eye and brain: The psychology of seeing* (3rd ed.). New York: McGraw-Hill.

Greif, E. B., & Ulman, K. J. (1982). The psychological impact of menarche on early adolescent females: A review of the literature. *Child Development, 53*, 1413–1430.

Greist, J. H., Jefferson, J. W., & Spitzer, R. L. (1982). *Treatment of mental disorders*. New York: Oxford University Press.

Grier, J. W. (1984). *Biology of animal behavior*.

St. Louis: Times Mirror/Mosby.

Griffin, D. R. (1958). *Listening in the dark. The acoustic orientation of bats and men.* New Haven: Yale University Press.

Griffit, W., & Veitch, R. (1971). Hot and crowded: Influences of population density and temperature on interpersonal affective behavior. *Journal of Personality and Social Psychology, 17,* 92–98.

Griffith, J. D., Cavanaugh, J., Held, J., (1972). Dextroamphetamine: Evaluation of psychotomimentic properties in man. *Archives of General Psychiatry, 26,* 97–100.

Groos, G. A. (1983). Circadian rhythms and the circadian system. *Advances in Biological Psychiatry, 11,* 1–9.

Gross, A. E., & Latane, J. G. (1974). Receiving help, reciprocation, and interpersonal attraction. *Journal of Applied Social Psychology, 4,* 210–223.

Gross, C. G. (1973). Inferotemporal cortex and vision. In E. Stellar & J. Sprague (Eds.), *Progress in physiological psychology* (pp. 77–123). New York: Academic Press.

Gross, C. G., Rocha-Miranda, C. E., & Bender, D. B. (1972). Visual properties of neurons in inferotemporal cortex of the macaque. *Journal of Neurophysiology, 35,* 96–111.

Gross, R. T. (1984). Patterns of maturation—Their effects on behavior and development. In M. D. Levine & P. Satz (Eds.), *Middle childhood: Development and dysfunction* (pp. 47–62). Baltimore: University Park Press.

Grossman, L., & Eagle, M. (1970). Synonymity, antonymity, and association in false recognition responses. *Journal of Experimental Psychology, 83,* 244–248.

Grossman, M., Carey, S., Zurif, E., & Diller, L. (1986). Proper and common nouns: Form class judgments in Broca's aphasia. *Brain and Language, 28,* 114–125.

Grossman, S. P. (1984). Contemporary problems concerning our understanding of brain mechanisms that regulate food intake and body weight. In A. J. Stunkard and E. Stellar (Eds.), *Eating and its disorders* (pp. 5–13). New York: Raven Press.

Gruenewald, P. J., & Lockhead, G. R. (1980). The free recall of category examples. *Journal of Experimental Psychology: Human Learning and Memory, 6,* 225–240.

Gruneberg, M. M., & Monk, J. (1974). Feeling of knowing and cued recall. *Acta Psychologica, 38,* 257–265.

Grunt, J. A., & Young, D. C. (1952). Differential reactivity of individuals and the response of male guinea pigs to testosterone proprionate. *Endocrinology, 51,* 237–248.

Grusec, J. E. (1981). Socialization processes and the development of altruism. In J. P. Rushton & R. M. Sorrentino (Eds.), *Altruism and helping behavior: Social, personality, and developmental perspectives.* Hillsdale, NJ: Lawrence Erlbaum.

Grusec, J. E. (1982). The socialization of altruism. In N. Eisenberg (Ed.), *The development of prosocial behavior.* New York: Academic Press.

Grusec, J. E., Kuczynski, L., Rushton, J. P., & Simutis, Z. M. (1978). Modeling, direct instruction, and attributions: Effects on altruism. *Developmental Psychology, 14,* 51–57.

Guilford, J. P. (1959). *Personality.* New York: McGraw-Hill.

Guilford, J. P. (1964). Zero correlations among tests of intellectual abilities. *Psychological Bul-*

letin, 61, 401–404.

Guilford, J. P. (1982). Cognitive psychology's ambiguities: Some suggested remedies. *Psychological Review, 89,* 48–59.

Guillery, R. W. (1986). Neural abnormalities of albinos. *Trends in Neuroscience, 9,* 364–367.

Gunderson, J. G., Autry, J. H., III, & Mosher, L. R. (1974). Special report: Schizophrenia. *Schizophrenia Bulletin, 9,* 16–54.

Guth, L., Reier, P. J., Barrett, C. P., & Donati, E. J. (1983). Repair of the mammalian spinal cord. *Trends in Neurosciences, 6,* 20–24.

Haber, R. N., & Alpert, R. (1958). The role of situation and picture cues in projective measurement of the achievement motive. In J. W. Atkinson (Ed.), *Motives in fantasy, action, and society.* Princeton, NJ: Van Nostrand.

Haley, J., & Hoffman, L. (1967). *Techniques of family therapy.* New York: Basic Books.

Hall, C. S. (1954). *A primer of Freudian psychology.* New York: World Publishing.

Hall, E., Perlmutter, M., & Lamb, M. E. (1982). *Child psychology today.* New York: Random House.

Hall, J. G. (1985). Letter to the editor (emotion and immunity). *Lancet, 2,* 326–327.

Hall, K. R. L. (1960). *The hidden dimension.* Garden City, NY: Doubleday.

Hall, S. M., Rugg, D., Tunstall, C., & Jones, R. T. (1984). Preventing relapse to cigarette smoking by behavioral skill training. *Journal of Consulting and Clinical Psychology, 52,* 372–382.

Hallam, R. S. (1985). *Anxiety: Psychological perspectives on panic and agoraphobia.* London: Academic Press.

Hansel, C. E. M. (1980). *ESP and parapsychology: A critical evaluation.* Buffalo, NY: Prometheus Books.

Harlap, S., & Shiono, P. H. (1980). Alcohol, smoking, and incidence of spontaneous abortions in the first and second trimester. *The Lancet,* 173–176.

Harlow, H. F. (1971). *Learning to love.* San Francisco: Albion.

Harlow, H. F., Harlow, M. K., & Mayer, D. R. (1950). Learning motivated by a manipulation drive. *Journal of Experimental Psychology, 40,* 228–234.

Harlow, H. F., & Zimmerman, R. R. (1959). Affectional responses in the infant monkey. *Science, 130,* 421–432.

Harmon, R. R., & K. A. Coney (1982). The persuasive effects of source magnification of cognitive effort on attitudes: An information-processing view. *Journal of Personality and Social Psychology, 40,* 401–413.

Harris, J. E. (1980). Memory aids people use: Two interview studies. *Memory and Cognition, 8,* 31–38.

Harris, R. S., & Martin, R. (1984). Specific depletion of body fat in parabiotic partners of tube-fed, obese rats. *American Journal of Physiology, 247,* R380–R386.

Harrison, A. H. (1977). Mere exposure. In L. Berkowitz (Ed.), *Advances in experimental social psychology* (Vol. 10). New York: Academic Press.

Hart, B. (1968). Role of prior experience on the effects of castration on sexual behavior of male dogs. *Journal of Comparative and Physiological Psychology, 66,* 719–725.

Harter, S. (1983). Developmental perspectives on the self-system. In P. H. Mussen & E. M.

Hetherington (Eds.), *Handbook of child psychology: Socialization, personality, and social development* (pp. 275–385). New York: John Wiley & Sons.

Hartline, H. K., & Ratliff, F. (1957). Inhibitory interaction of receptor units in the eye of Limulus. *Journal of General Physiology, 40,* 357–376.

Hartshorne, H., & May, M. S. (1928). *Studies in the nature of character: Studies in deceit* (Vol. 1). New York: Macmillan.

Hartshorne, H., & May, M. S. (1929). *Studies in the nature of character: Studies in self-control* (Vol. 2). New York: Macmillan.

Hartup, W. W. (1983). The peer system. In P. H. Mussen & E. M. Hetherington (Eds.), *Handbook of child psychology: Socialization, personality, and social development* (pp. 103–196). New York: John Wiley & Sons.

Harvey, J. H., Town, J. P., & Yarkin, K. L. (1981). How fundamental is "The fundamental attribution error"? *Journal of Personality and Social Psychology, 40,* 346–349.

Harvey, M. D., & Enzle, M. E. (1978). Effects of retaliation latency and provocation level on judged blameworthiness for retaliatory aggression. *Personality and Social Psychology Bulletin, 4,* 579–582.

Hasher, L., & Griffin, M. (1978). Reconstructive and reproductive processes in memory. *Journal of Experimental Psychology: Human Learning and Memory, 4,* 318–330.

Hatfield, E., & Traupmann, J. (1981). Intimate relationships: A perspective from equity theory. In S. Duck and R. Gilmour (Eds.). *Personal relationships* (Vol. 1). New York: Academic Press.

Hawke, C. C. (1950). Castration and sex crimes. *American Journal of Mental Deficiency, 55,* 220–226.

Hay, L. (1984). The development of movement control. In M. M. Smyth & A. M. Wing (Eds.), *Psychology of human movement* (pp. 241–268). London: Academic Press.

Hayes, J. R. (1985). Three problems in teaching general skills. In S. F. Chipman, J. W. Segal, & R. Glaser (Eds.), *Thinking and learning skills* (pp. 391–405). Hillsdale, NJ: Lawrence Erlbaum.

Hayes, K. J., & Hayes, C. (1951). Intellectual development of a home-raised chimpanzee. *Proceedings of the American Philosophical Society, 95,* 105–109.

Healy, W., Bonner, A. F., & Bowers, A. M. (1930). *The structure and meaning of psychoanalysis.* New York: Knopf.

Heath, R. G. (1963). Electrical self-stimulation of the brain in man. *American Journal of Psychiatry, 120,* 571–577.

Heath, R. G. (1964). Pleasure response of human subjects to direct stimulation of the brain: Physiologic and psychodynamic considerations. In R. G. Heath (Ed.), *The role of pleasure in behavior* (pp. 219–243). New York: Hoeber, Harper & Row.

Heaton, R. K., Nelson, L. M., Thompson, D. S., Burks, J. S., & Franklin, G. M. (1985). Neuropsychological findings in relapsing-remitting and chronic-progressive multiple sclerosis. *Journal of Consulting and Clinical Psychology, 53,* 103–110.

Hebb, D. O. (1949). *The organization of behavior.* New York: John Wiley & Sons.

Hebb, D. O. (1966). Drives and the C.N.S. (conceptual nervous system). In D. Bindra &

J. Stewart (Eds.), *Motivation*. Baltimore, MD: Penguin.

Hecaen, H., & Albert, M. L. (1978). *Human neuropsychology*. New York: John Wiley & Sons.

Hecht, E. R., Shlaer, S., & Pirenne, M. H. (1942). Energy, quanta, and vision. *Journal of General Physiology, 25*, 819–840.

Hecht, S., & Shlaer, S. (1938). An adaptometer for measuring human dark adaptation. *Journal of the Optical Society of America, 28*, 269–275.

Heckhausen, H., Schmalt, H.-D., & Schneider, K. (1985). *Achievement motivation in perspective*. Orlando, FL: Academic.

Heider, F. (1944). Social perception and phenomenal causality. *Psychological Review, 51*, 358–374.

Heider, F. (1946). Attitudes and cognitive organization. *Journal of Psychology, 21*, 107–112.

Heider, F. (1958). *The psychology of interpersonal relations*. New York: John Wiley & Sons.

Heider, F., & Simmel, M. (1944). An experimental study of apparent behavior. *American Journal of Psychology, 57*, 243–259.

Heilman, K. M. (1979). Neglect and related disorders. In K. M. Heilman & E. Valenstein (Eds.), *Clinical neuropsychology* (pp. 268–307). New York: Oxford University Press.

Helzer, J. E., Clayton, P. J., Pambakian, R., Reich, T., Woodruff, R. A., & Reveley, M. A. (1977). *Reliability of psychiatric diagnosis, 34*, 136–141.

Helzer, J. E., Robins, L. N., McEvoy, L. T., Spitznagel, E. L., Stoltzman, R. K., Farmer, A., & Brockington, I. F. (1985). A comparison of clinical and diagnostic interview schedule diagnoses. *Archives of General Psychiatry, 42*, 657–666.

Henderson, N. D. (1982). Human behavior genetics. *Annual Review of Psychology, 33*, 403–440.

Hendrickson, A. E., & Youdelis, C. (1984). The morphological development of the human fovea. *Ophthalmology, 91*, 603–612.

Henry, J. P., Stephens, P. M., & Santisteban, G. A. (1975). A model of psychosocial hypertension showing reversibility and progression of cardiovascular complications. *Circulation Research, 36*, 156–164.

Herink, R. (1980). *The psychotherapy handbook: The A to Z guide to more than 250 therapies in use today*. New York: New American Library.

Herman, C. P., & Polivy, J. (1984). A boundary model for the regulation of eating. In A. J. Stunkard and E. Stellar (Eds.), *Eating and its disorders* (pp. 141–156). New York: Raven Press.

Herrnstein, R. J. (1971). I. Q. *Atlantic Monthly, 228*, 43–64.

Herschel, J. (1972). A scaled ratio of body weight to brain weight as a comparative index of relative importance of brain size in mammals of widely varying body mass. *Psychological Reports, 31*, 84–86.

Hershey, D. (1974). *Lifespan—and factors affecting it*. Springfield, IL: C. C. Thomas.

Hess, E. H. (1958). "Imprinting" in animals. *Scientific American, 198*, 81–90.

Hess, E. H. (1972). Imprinting in a natural laboratory. *Scientific American, 227*, 24–31.

Hess, E. H. (1973). Comparative sensory processes. In D. A. Demsbury & D. A. Rethlingshafer (Eds.), *Comparative psychology: A modern survey* (pp. 344–394). New York: McGraw-Hill.

Heston, L. L. (1976). Psychiatric disorders in foster home reared children of schizophrenic mothers. *British Journal of Psychiatry, 112*, 819–825.

Hetherington, A. W., & Ranson, S. W. (1940). Hypothalamic lesions and adiposity in the rat. *Anatomical Record, 78*, 149–172.

Hetherington, E. M. (1972). Effects of father absence on personality development in adolescent daughters. *Developmental Psychology, 7*, 313–326.

Hetherington, E. M. (1983). *Handbook of child psychology* (4th ed.). Socialization, personality and social development. New York: John Wiley & Sons.

Heuser, J. E. (1977). Synaptic vesicle exocytosis revealed in quick-frozen frog neuromuscular junctions treated with 4-amino-pyridine and given a single electrical shock. In W. M. Cowan & J. A. Ferrendelli (Eds.), *Society for neuroscience symposia* (pp. 215–239). Bethesda, MD: Society for Neuroscience.

Hicks, D. J. (1965). Imitation and retention of film-mediated aggressive peer and adult models. *Journal of Personality and Social Psychology, 2*, 97–100.

Hicks, R. E., & Kinsbourne, M. (1978). Human handedness. In M. Kinsbourne (Ed.), *Asymmetrical function of the brain* (pp. 523–549). Cambridge: Cambridge University Press.

Higgins, E. T., Rhodewalt, F., & Zanna, M. (1979). Dissonance motivation: Its nature, persistence, and reinstatement. *Journal of Experimental Social Psychology, 15*, 16–34.

Hikscher, J. A., & Herman, C. P. (1977). Obesity, dieting, and the expression of 'obese' characteristics. *Journal of Comparative Physiology and Psychology, 91*, 374–380.

Hildum, D. C., & Brown, R. W. (1956). Verbal reinforcement and interviewer bias. *Journal of Abnormal and Social Psychology, 53*, 108–111.

Hilgard, E. R. (1965). *Hypnotic susceptibility*. New York: Harcourt Brace Jovanovich.

Hilgard, E. R. (1977). *Divided consciousness*. New York: John Wiley & Sons.

Hilgard, E. R., & Hilgard, J. R. (1983). *Hypnosis in the relief of pain*. Los Altos, CA: Kaufman.

Hill, C. T., & Stull, D. E. (1981). Sex differences in effects of social and value similarity in same-sex friendship. *Journal of Personality and Social Psychology, 41*, 488–502.

Hill, T. D., Reddon, J. R., & Jackson, D. N. (1985). The factor structure of the Wechsler scales: A brief review. *Clinical Psychology Review, 5*, 287–306.

Hill, W. F. (1978). Effects of mere exposure on preference in nonhuman mammals. *Psychological Bulletin, 85*(6), 1177–1198.

Hilton, D. J., & Slugoski, B. R. (1986). Knowledge-based causal attribution: The abnormal conditions focus model. *Psychological Review, 93*, 75–88.

Hinchcliffe, R. (1962). The anatomical locus of presbycusis. *Journal of Speech and Hearing Disorders, 27*, 301–310.

Hirst, W., Johnson, M. K., Kim, J. K., Risse, G., Phelps, E. A., & Volpe, B. T. (1986). Recognition and recall in amnesics. *Journal of Experimental Psychology: Learning, Memory, and Cognition, 12*, 445–451.

Hoch, S. J. (1986). Counterfactual reasoning and accuracy in predicting personal events. *Journal of Experimental Psychology: Learning, Memory, and Cognition, 11*, 719–731.

Hochberg, J. E. (1971). Perception. In J. W. Kling & L. A. Riggs (Eds.), *Experimental psychology* (pp. 396–550). New York: Holt, Rinehart & Winston.

Hoelscher, T. J., Lichstein, K. L., & Rosenthal, T. L. (1986). Home relaxation practice in hypertension treatment: Objective assessment and compliance induction. *Journal of Consulting and Clinical Psychology, 54*, 1217–1221.

Hofling, C. K., Brotzman, E., Dalrymple, S., Graves, N., & Pierce, C. M. (1966). An experimental study in nurse-physician relationships. *Journal of Nervous and Mental Diseases, 143*, 171–180.

Hofmann, F. G. (1983). *A handbook on drug and alcohol abuse*. New York: Oxford University Press.

Hogan, R., DeSoto, L. B., & Solano, C. (1977). Traits, tests, and personality research. *American Psychologist, 32*, 255–264.

Hohman, G. W. (1966). Some effects of spinal cord lesions on experienced emotional feelings. *Psychophysiology, 3*, 143–156.

Holden, C. (1980). News and comment: Identical twins reared apart. *Science, 207*, 1323–1328.

Holding, D. H., & Reynolds, R. I. (1982). Recall or evaluation of chess positions as determinants of chess skill. *Memory & Cognition, 10*, 237–242.

Hollingshead, A. B., & Pedlich, F. L. (1958). *Social class and mental illness: A community study*. New York: John Wiley & Sons.

Hollister, L. E. (1980). Dependence on benzodiazepines. In S. J. Szara & J. P. Ludford (Eds.), *Benzodiazepines: A review of research results* (pp. 70–82). Washington, DC: Superintendent of Documents.

Hollon, J. D., Tuason, V. B., Weiner, M. J., de Rubers, R. J., Evans, M. D., & Garvey, M. (1983). Combined cognitive-pharmacotherapy vs. cognitive therapy alone in the treatment of depressed outpatients: Differential treatment outcome in the CPT project. Association for the Advancement of Behavior Therapy, Washington, DC, Dec. 10, 1983.

Hollon, S. D., & Beck, A. T. (1979). Cognitive therapy of depression. In P. C. Kendall & S. D. Hollon (Eds.), *Cognitive-behavioral interventions: Theory, research, and procedures*. New York: Academic Press.

Holmes, D. S. (1984). Meditation and somatic arousal reduction: A review of the experimental evidence. *American Psychologist, 39*, 1–10.

Holmes, D. S. (1985). To meditate or to simply rest, that is the question: A response to the comments of Shapiro. *American Psychologist, 40*, 722–725. (a)

Holmes, D. S. (1985). To meditate or rest? The answer is rest. *American Psychologist, 40*, 728–731. (b)

Holmes, T. H., & Rahe, R. H. (1967). The social readjustment rating scale. *Journal of Psychosomatic Research, 11*, 213–218.

Holway, A. H., & Boring, E. G. (1941). Determinants of apparent visual size with distant variant. *American Journal of Psychology, 54*, 21–37.

Homans, G. C. (1958). Social behavior and exchange. *American Journal of Sociology, 63*, 597–606.

Homans, G. C. (1961). *Social behavior: Its elementary forms.* New York: Harcourt Brace. (a)

Homans, G. C. (1961). *The human group.* New York: Harcourt, Brace. (b)

Horai, J., Naccari, N., & Fatoullah, E. (1974). The effects of expertise and physical attractiveness upon opinion agreement and liking. *Sociometry, 37,* 601–606.

Horn, J. L., & Donaldson, G. (1976). On the myth of intellectual decline in adulthood. *American Psychologist, 31,* 701–719.

Horn, J. L., & Donaldson, G. (1980). Cognitive development in adulthood. In O. G. Brim, Jr., & J. Kagan (Eds.), *Constancy and change in human development.* Cambridge, MA: Harvard University Press.

Horn, J. L., & Knapp, J. R. (1973). On the subjective character of the empirical base of Guilford's structure-of-intellect model. *Psychological Bulletin, 80,* 33–43.

Horne, J. A. (1978). A review of the biological effects of total sleep deprivation in man. *Biological Psychology, 7,* 55–102.

Horne, J. A. (1979). Restitution and human sleep; a critical review. *Physiological Psychology, 7,* 115–125.

Horne, J. A. (1985). Sleep function, with particular reference to sleep deprivation. *Annals of Clinical Research, 17,* 199–208.

Horne, J. A., Brass, C. G., & Pettitt, A. N. (1980). Circadian performance differences between morning and evening 'types.' *Ergonomics, 23,* 29–36.

Horne, J. A., & Pettitt, A. N. (1985). High incentive effects on vigilance performance during 72 hours of total sleep deprivation. *Acta Psychologica, 58,* 123–139.

Hovland, C., Lumsdaine, A., & Sheffield, F. (1949). *Experiments on mass communication.* Princeton, NJ: Princeton University Press.

Hovland, C., & Mandell, W. (1952). An experimental comparison of conclusion-drawing by the communicator and the audience. *Journal of Abnormal and Social Psychology, 47,* 581–588.

Howard-Pitney, B., Borgida, E., Omoto, A. M. (1986). Personal involvement: An examination of processing differences. *Social Cognition, 4,* 39–57.

Hubel, D. H., & Wiesel, T. N. (1962). Receptive fields, binocular interaction and functional architecture in the cat's visual cortex. *Journal of Physiology, London, 160,* 106–154.

Hubel, D. H., & Wiesel, T. N. (1970). The period of susceptibility to the physiological effects of unilateral eye closure in kittens. *Journal of Physiology, London, 206,* 419–436.

Hudspeth, A. J. (1985). The cellular basis of hearing: The biophysics of hair cells. *Science, 230,* 745–752.

Huesmann, L. R. (1982). Television violence and aggressive behavior. In D. Pearl, L. Bouthilet, & J. Lazar (Eds.), *Television and behavior: Ten years of scientific progress and implications for the 80s.* (pp. 126–137). Washington, DC: U.S. Government Printing Office.

Huesmann, L. R. (1984). *TV violence and aggression: Long term effects.* Presentation at the Society of Experimental Social Psychology meetings, Snowbird, Utah.

Huesmann, L. R. (1986). Psychological processes promoting the relation between exposure to media violence and aggressive behavior by the viewer. *Journal of Social Issues, 42,* 125–139.

Huesmann, L. R., Eron, L. D., Klein, R., Brice, P., & Fischer, P. (1983). Mitigating the imitation of aggressive behaviors by changing children's attitudes about media violence. *Journal of Personality and Social Psychology, 44,* 899–910.

Huesmann, L. R., Eron, L. D., Lefkowitz, M. M., & Walder, L. O. (1984). Stability of aggression over time and generations. *Developmental Psychology, 20,* 1120–1134.

Huff, D. (1954). *How to lie with statistics.* New York: Norton.

Hugdahl, K., & Ohman, A. (1977). Effects of instruction on acquisition and extinction of electrodermal responses to fear relevant stimuli. *Journal of Experimental Psychology: Human Learning and Memory, 3,* 608–618.

Hulicka, I. M. (1967). Age differences in retention as a function of interference. *Journal of Gerontology, 22,* 180–184.

Hull, C. L. (1952). *A behavior system.* New Haven, CT: Yale University Press.

Humphrey, L. L., Apple, R. F., & Kirschenbaum, D. S. (1986). Differentiating bulimic-anorexic from normal families using interpersonal and behavioral observational systems. *Journal of Consulting and Clinical Psychology, 54,* 190–195.

Humphreys, L. G. (1957). Characteristics of type concepts with special reference to Sheldon's typology. *Psychological Bulletin, 54,* 218–228.

Humphreys, L. G. (1971). Theory of intelligence. In R. Cancro (Ed.), *Intelligence: Genetic and environmental influences* (pp. 31–55). New York: Grune & Stratton.

Hunt, E., & Love, T. (1972). How good can memory be? In A. W. Melton & E. Martin (Eds.), *Coding processes in human memory.* New York: Holt.

Hunt, E., Lunneborg, C., & Lewis, J. (1975). What does it mean to be high verbal? *Cognitive Psychology, 7,* 194–227.

Hunt, W. A., Wittson, C. L., & Hunt, E. B. (1953). A theoretical and practical analysis of the diagnostic process. In P. H. Hoch & J. Zubin (Eds.), *Current problems in psychiatric diagnosis.* New York: Grune & Stratton.

Hupp, S. C., & Mervis, C. B. (1982). Acquisition of basic object categories by severely handicapped children. *Child Development, 53,* 760–767.

Husch, J., & Knittle, J. L. (1970). Cellularity of obese and nonobese human adipose tissue. *Federation Processes, 29,* 1516–1521.

Huston, A. C. (1983). Sex typing. In P. H. Mussen & E. M. Hetherington (Eds.), *Handbook of child psychology: Socialization, personality, and social development* (pp. 387–467). New York: John Wiley & Sons.

Huston, T. L. (1973). Ambiguity of acceptance, social desirability and dating choice. *Journal of Experimental Social Psychology, 9,* 32–42.

Huston, T. L., Ruggiero, M., Conner, R., & Geis, G. (1981). Bystander intervention into crime: A study based on naturally occurring episodes. *Social Psychology Quarterly, 44,* 14–23.

Hutchings, B., & Mednick, S. A. (1977). Criminality in adoptees and their adoptive and biological parents: A pilot study. In S. A. Mednick & K. O. Christiansen (Eds.), *Biosocial bases of criminal behavior.* New York: Gardner.

Huttenlocher, J., & Smiley, P. (1987). Early word meanings: The case of object names. *Cognitive Psychology, 19,* 63–89.

Huttenlocker, P. R., de Courten, C., Garey, L. J., & van der Loos, H. (1982). Synaptogenesis in human visual cortex—evidence for synapse elimination during normal development. *Neuroscience Letters, 33,* 247–252.

Huxley, A. (1946). *Brave new world.* New York and London: Harper & Brothers.

Hyde, T. S., & Jenkins, J. J. (1969). Differential effects of incidental tasks on the organization of recall of a list of highly associated words. *Journal of Experimental Psychology, 82,* 472–481.

Hyman, F. C. (1979). Tissue restoration function of sleep. *Biological Psychology Bulletin, 5,* 127–139.

Hyvärinen, J. (1982). *The parietal cortex of monkey and man.* New York: Springer-Verlag.

Ickes, W. J., & Barnes, R. D. (1977). The role of sex and self-monitoring in unstructured dyadic interactions. *Journal of Personality and Social Psychology, 35,* 315–330.

Ickes, W. J., Wicklund, R. A., & Ferris, B. C. (1973). Objective self awareness and self esteem. *Journal of Experimental Social Psychology, 9,* 202–219.

Iggo, A. (1985). Sensory receptors in the skin of mammals and their sensory functions. *Revue Neurologique, 141,* 599–613.

Ince, L. P., Brucker, B. B., & Alba, A. (1978). Reflex conditioning in a spinal man. *Journal of Comparative Physiological Psychology, 92,* 796–802.

Inhelder, B., & Piaget, J. (1955/1958). *The growth of logical thinking from childhood to adolescence.* New York: Basic Books.

Inhelder, B., & Piaget, J. (1959/1964). *The early growth of logic in the child.* New York: Harper & Row.

Insko, C. A. (1965). Verbal reinforcement of attitude. *Journal of Personality and Social Psychology, 2,* 621–623.

Insko, C. A., & Cialdini, R. B. (1969). A test of three interpretations of attitudinal verbal reinforcement. *Journal of Personality and Social Psychology, 12,* 333–341.

Insko, C. A., Nacoste, R. W., & Moe, J. L. (1983). Belief congruence and racial discrimination: Review of the evidence and critical evaluation. *European Journal of Social Psychology, 11,* 153–174.

Intons-Peterson, M. J., & Fournier, J. (1986). External and internal memory aids: When and how often do we use them? *Journal of Experimental Psychology: General, 115,* 267–280.

Isager, T., Brinch, M., Kreiner, S., & Tolstrup, K. (1985). Death and relapse in anorexia nervosa: Survival analysis of 151 cases. *Journal of Psychiatric Research, 19,* 515–521.

Isbell, H., Fraser, H. G., Wikler, A., Belleville, R. E., & Eisenman, A. J. (1955). An experimental study of the etiology of 'run fits' and delirium tremens. *Quarterly Journal of Studies of Alcohol, 16,* 1–33.

Ishihara, S. (1980). *Tests for colour-blindness.* Tokyo: Kanehara & Co., Ltd.

Ito, M. (1984). The modifiable neuronal network of the cerebellum. *The Japanese Journal of Physiology, 34,* 781–792.

Iversen, S. D. (1984). Behavioural effects of manipulation of basal ganglia neurotransmitters. In D. Evered & M. O'Connor (Eds.), *Functions of the basal ganglia* (pp. 183–200). London: Pitman Publishing Ltd.

Iversen, S. D., & Iversen, L. L. (1981). *Behavioral pharmacology.* New York: Oxford University Press.

Iwamura, Y., Tanaka, M., Sakamoto, M., & Hikosaka, O. (1985). Vertical neuronal arrays in the postcentral gyrus signaling active touch—a receptive field study in the conscious monkey. *Experimental Brain Research, 58,* 412–420.

Izard, C. E. (1972). *Patterns of emotions: A new analysis of anxiety and depression.* New York: Academic Press.

Izard, C. E. (1978). On the ontogenesis of emotions and emotion-cognition relationships in infancy. In M. Lewis & L. A. Rosenblum (Eds.), *The development of affect.* New York: Plenum Press.

Jacklet, J. W. (1985). Neurobiology of circadian rhythms generators. *Trends in Neurosciences, 8,* 69–73.

Jackson, C. M. (1929). Some aspects of form and growth. In W. J. Robbins, S. Brody, A. F. Hogan, etc. (Eds.), *Growth* (pp. 111–140). New Haven, CT: Yale University Press.

Jackson, D. N. (1971). The dynamics of structured personality tests. *Psychological Review, 78,* 229–248.

Jackson, J. E. (1983). Election night reporting and voter turnout. *American Journal of Political Science, 27,* 615–635.

Jackson, R. L., Alexander, J. H., & Maier, S. F. (1980). Learned helplessness, inactivity, and associative deficits: Effects of inescapable shock on response choice escape learning. *Journal of Experimental Psychology: Animal Behavior Processes, 6,* 1–20.

Jacobs, H. L. (1967). Taste and the role of experience in the regulation of food intake. In M. R. Kare & O. Maller (Eds.), *The chemical senses and nutrition* (pp. 187–200). Baltimore: Johns Hopkins Press.

Jacobs, J. (1887). Experiments on "prehension." *Mind, 12,* 75–79.

Jacobs, R. C., & Campbell, D. T. (1961). The perpetuation of an arbitrary tradition through successive generations of a laboratory microculture. *Journal of Abnormal and Social Psychology, 62,* 649–658.

Jacobson, A., & McKinney, W. T. (1982). Affective disorders. In J. H. Greist, J. W. Jefferson, & R. L. Spitzer (Eds.), *Treatment of mental disorders.* New York: Oxford University Press.

Jacobson, E. (1938). *Progressive relaxation.* Chicago: University of Chicago Press.

James, W. (1890). *The principles of psychology.* New York: Holt, Rinehart, and Winston.

Janicek, P. G., Davis, J. M., Gibbons, R. D., Ericksen, S., Chang, & Gallagher, P. (1985). Efficacy of ECT: A meta-analysis. *American Journal of Psychiatry, 142,* 297–302.

Jefferson, L. (1984). *These are my sisters.* Tulsa, OK: Vickers Publishing Co.

Jeffries, R. P., Polson, P. G., Razran, L., & Atwood, M. (1977). A process model for missionaries–cannibals and other river-crossing problems. *Cognitive Psychology, 9,* 412–440.

Jenkins, J. G., & Dallenbach, K. M. (1924). Obliviscence during sleep and waking. *American Journal of Psychology, 35,* 605–612.

Jensen, A. R. (1965). Rorschach. In O. K. Buros (Ed.), *The sixth mental measurements yearbook.* Highland Park, NJ: Gryphon.

Jensen, A. R. (1969). How much can we boost IQ and scholastic achievement? *Harvard Educational Review, 39,* 1–123.

Jensen, A. R. (1980). *Bias in mental testing.* New York: The Free Press.

Jensen, A. R. (1985). The nature of the black–white difference on various psychometric tests: Spearman's hypothesis. *The Behavioral and Brain Sciences, 8,* 193–219.

Jerison, H. J., & Pickett, R. M. (1964). Vigilance: The importance of the elicited observing rate. *Science, 143,* 970–971.

Job market opens up for the 68-cent woman. (1987, July 26). *The New York Times,* p. 6.

Johansson, R. S., & Vallbo, A. B. (1983). Tactile sensory coding in the glabrous skin of the human hand. *Trends in Neurosciences, 6,* 27–32.

Johnson, C. H., & Hastings, J. W. (1986). The elusive mechanism of the circadian clock. *American Scientist, 74,* 29–37.

Johnson, C. J., Pick, H. L., Siegel, G. M., Cicciarelli, A. W., & Garber, S. R. (1981). Effects of interpersonal distance on children's vocal intensity. *Child Development, 52,* 721–723.

Johnson, W. F., Emde, R. N., Scharer, K. R., & Klinnert, M. D. (1986). Recognition of emotion from vocal cues. *Archives of General Psychiatry, 43,* 280–283.

Johnson-Laird, P. (1983). *Mental models: Towards a cognitive science of language, inference, and consciousness.* Cambridge, MA: Harvard University Press.

Johnson-Laird, P. N., Legrenzi, P., & Legrenzi, M. (1972). Reasoning and a sense of reality. *British Journal of Psychology, 63,* 395–400.

Johnson-Laird, P. N., & Steedman, M. (1978). The psychology of syllogisms. *Cognitive Psychology, 10,* 64–99.

Johnston, D., & Davidson, J. M. (1972). Intracerebral androgen and sexual behavior in the male rat. *Hormones and Behavior, 3,* 345–351.

Jolicoeur, P. (1985). The time to name disoriented natural objects. *Memory and Cognition, 13,* 289–303.

Jolicoeur, P., & Landau, M. J. (1984). Effects of orientation on the identification of simple visual patterns. *Canadian Journal of Psychology, 38,* 80–93.

Jones, D. G. (1983). Development, maturation, and aging of synapses. In S. Fedoroff & L. Hertz (Eds.), *Advances in cellular neurobiology* (pp. 163–222). Orlando, FL: Academic Press.

Jones, E. E., & Davis, K. E. (1965). A theory of correspondent inferences: From acts to dispositions. In L. Berkowitz (Ed.), *Advances in experimental and social psychology* (Vol. 2). New York: Academic Press.

Jones, E. E., Gergen, K. J., & Davis, K. E. (1962). Some determinants of reactions to being approved or disapproved as a person. *Psychological Monographs, 76.*

Jones, E. E., & Harris, V. A. (1967). The attribution of attitudes. *Journal of Experimental Social Psychology, 3,* 1–24.

Jones, E. E., & McGillis, D. (1976). Correspondent inferences and the attribution cube: A comparative reappraisal. In J. H. Harvey, W. J. Ickes, & R. F. Kidd (Eds.), *New directions in attribution research* (Vol. 1). Hillsdale, NJ: Lawrence Erlbaum.

Jones, E. E., & Nisbett, R. E. (1972). The actor and the observer: Divergent perceptions of the causes of behavior. In E. E. Jones et al., *Attribution: Perceiving the causes of behavior.* Morristown, NJ: General Learning Press.

Jones, L. V. (1984). White–black achievement differences. *American Psychologist, 39,* 1207–1213.

Jordan, N. (1953). Behavioral forces that are a function of attitudes and of cognitive organization. *Human Relations, 6,* 273–288.

Jost, A. (1985). Sexual organogenesis. In N. Adler, D. Pfaff, & R. W. Goy (Eds.), *Handbook of behavioral neurobiology.* Vol. 7: *Reproduction* (pp. 3–20). New York: Plenum Press.

Jung, R. (1974). Neuropsychologie und Neurophysiologie des Kontur—und Formsehens in Zeichnung und Malerei. In H. H. Wieck (Ed.), *Psychopathologie musischer Gestaltungen* (pp. 29–88). Stuttgart: Schatlaner Verlag.

Kaats, G. R., & Davis, K. E. (1970). The dynamics of sexual behavior of college students. *Journal of Marriage and the Family, 32,* 390–399.

Kagan, J., Kearsley, R., & Zelazo, P. (1978). *Infancy: Its place in human development.* Cambridge, MA: Harvard University Press.

Kahn, R. J., McNair, D. M., Lipman, R. S., Covi, L., Rickels, K., Downing, R., Fisher, S., & Frankenthales, L. M. (1986). Imipramine and chlordiazepoxide in depressive and anxiety disorders: II. Efficacy in anxious outpatients. *Archives of General Psychiatry, 43,* 79–85.

Kahneman, D. (1973). *Attention and effort.* Englewood Cliff, NJ: Prentice-Hall.

Kahneman, D., & Tversky, A. (1972). Subjective probability: A judgment of representativeness. *Cognitive Psychology, 3,* 430–454.

Kahneman, D., & Tversky, A. (1973). On the psychology of prediction. *Psychological Review, 80,* 237–251.

Kahneman, D., & Tversky, A. (1982). The simulation heuristic. In D. Kahneman, P. Slovic, & A. Tversky (Eds.), *Judgment under uncertainty: Heuristics and biases.* Cambridge: Cambridge University Press.

Kaimowitz, G. (1980). My case against psychosurgery. In E. S. Valenstein (Eds.), *The psychosurgery debate.* San Francisco: Freeman.

Kallman, F. J. (1952). A comparative twin study of the genetic aspects of male homosexuality. *Journal of Nervous and Mental Disease, 115,* 283–298.

Kalra, S. P., & Sawyer, C. H. (1970). Blockage of copulation-induced emulation in the rat by anterior hypothalamic deafferentiation. *Endocrinology, 87,* 1124–1128.

Kaltwinkel, E. E. (1949). Death due to cardiac disease following the use of emetine hydrochloride in conditioned-reflex treatment of chronic alcoholism. *New England Journal of Medicine, 240,* 995–997.

Kamin, L. J. (1974). *The science and politics of I.Q.* Potomac, MD: Erlbaum.

Kandel, D. B. (1978). Similarity in real-life adolescent friendship pairs. *Journal of Personality and Social Psychology, 36,* 306–312.

Kandel, E. (1979). Small systems of neurons. *Scientific American, 241,* 66–89.

Kandel, E. R. (1985). Brain and behavior. In E. R. Kandel & J. H. Schwartz (Eds.), *Principles of neural science* (pp. 3–12). New York: Elsevier.

Kandel, E. R., & Schwartz, J. H. (1985). *Principles of neural science* (2nd ed.). New York:

Elsevier.

Kanfer, F. H., & Saslow, G. (1965). Behavioral analysis: An alternative to diagnostic classification. *Archives of General Psychiatry, 12,* 529–538.

Kanfer, F. H., & Saslow, G. (1969). Behavior diagnosis. In C. M. Franks (Ed.), *Behavior therapy: Appraisal and status.* New York: McGraw-Hill.

Kanizsa, G. (1976). Subjective contours. *Scientific American, 234,* 48–52.

Kanner, A. D., Coyne, J. C., Schaefer, C., & Lazarus, R. S. (1981). Comparison of two modes of stress measurement: Minor daily hassles and uplifts vs. major life events. *Journal of Behavioral Medicine, 4,* 1–39.

Kaplan, B. (1964). *The inner world of mental illness.* New York: Harper & Row.

Karabenick, S. A. (1983). Sex-relevance of content and influenceability: Sistrunk and McDavid revisited. *Personality and Social Psychology Bulletin, 9,* 243–252.

Karchmer, M. A., & Winograd, E. (1971). Effects of studying a subset of familiar items on the recall of the remaining items: The John Brown effect. *Psychonomic Science, 25,* 224–225.

Karson, C. N., Kleinman, J. E., & Wyatt, R. J. (1986). Biochemical concepts of schizophrenia. In T. Million & G. Klerman (Eds.), *Contemporary directions in psychopathology.* New York: Guilford.

Kasa, P. (1986). The cholinergic systems in brain and spinal cord. *Progress in Neurobiology, 26,* 211–272.

Kashani, J., & Simonds, J. F. (1979). The incidence of depression in children. *American Journal of Psychiatry, 136,* 1203–1205.

Katcher, A. H., Solomon, R. L., Turner, L. H., LoLordo, V. M., Overmier, J. B., & Rescorla, R. A. (1969). Heart-rate and blood pressure responses to signaled and unsignaled shocks: Effects of cardiac sympathectomy. *Journal of Comparative and Physiological Psychology, 68,* 163–174.

Katz, J. J., & Fodor, J. A. (1963). The structure of a semantic theory. *Language, 39,* 170–210.

Katz, J. J., & Postal, P. M. (1964). *An integrated theory of linguistic description.* Cambridge, MA: MIT Press.

Katz, M., Keusch, G. T., & Mata, L. (Eds.). (1975). Malnutrition and infection during pregnancy: Determinants of growth and development of the child. *American Journal of Diseases of Children, 29,* 419–463.

Keating, J. P., & Latane, B. (1976). Politicians on TV: The image is the message. *Journal of Social Issues, 32,* 116–132.

Keesey, R. E., & Powley, T. L. (1975). Hypothalamic regulation of body weight. *American Scientist, 63,* 558–565.

Keesey, R. E., & Powley, T. L. (1986). The regulation of body weight. *Annual Review of Psychology, 37,* 109–134.

Keeton, W. T. (1971). Magnets interfere with pigeon homing. *Proceedings of the National Academy of Science USA, 68,* 102–106.

Kelley, H. H. (1950). The warm–cold variable in first impressions of persons. *Journal of Personality, 18,* 431–439.

Kelley, H. H. (1967). Attribution theory in social psychology. In L. Levine (Ed.), *Nebraska Symposium on Motivation.* (Vol. 15). Lincoln, NB: University of Nebraska Press.

Kelley, H. H. (1971). *Attribution in social interaction.* Morristown, NJ: General Learning Press.

Kelley, H. H. (1972). *Causal schemata and the attribution process.* Morristown, NJ: General Learning Press.

Kelley, H. H., & Michela, J. L. (1980). Attribution theory and research. *Annual Review of Psychology, 31,* 457–501.

Kelley, H. H., & Thibaut, J. W. (1978). *Interpersonal relations: A theory of interdependence.* New York: Wiley-Interscience.

Kellogg, W. N., & Kellogg, L. A. (1933). *The ape and the child.* New York: McGraw-Hill.

Kelly, D. H., & Shannon, D. C. (1979). Periodic breathing in infants with near-miss sudden infant death syndrome. *Pediatrics, 63,* 355–360.

Kelly, J. P. (1985). Cranial nerve nuclei, the reticular formation, and biogenic amine-containing neurons. In E. R. Kandel & J. H. Schwartz (Eds.), *Principles of neural science.* (2nd ed., pp. 539–561). New York: Elsevier.

Kelly, J. S., & Rogawski, M. A. (1985). Acetylcholine. In M. A. Rogawski & J. L. Barker (Eds.), *Neurotransmitter actions in the vertebrate nervous system* (pp. 143–200). New York: Plenum Press.

Kelman, H. C. (1974). Attitudes are alive and well and gainfully employed in the sphere of action. *American Psychologist, 29,* 310–335.

Kemp, S. (1985). Modern myth and medieval madness: Views of mental illness in the European middle ages and renaissance. *New Zealand Journal of Psychology, 14,* 1–8.

Kenshalo, D. R. (1976). Correlations of temperature sensitivity in man and monkeys: A first approximation. In Y. Zotterman (Ed.), *Sensory functions of the skin in primates with special reference to man* (pp. 305–330). Oxford, England: Pergamon Press.

Kenshalo, D. R., & Scott, H. H., Jr. (1966). Temporal course of thermal adaptation. *Science, 151,* 1095–1096.

Kerkhof, G. A. (1985). Inter-individual differences in the human circadian system—A review. *Biological Psychology, 20,* 83–112.

Kernis, M. H., & Wheeler, L. (1981). Beautiful friends and ugly strangers: Radiation and contrast effects in perception of same-sex pairs. *Personality and Social Psychology Bulletin, 7,* 617–620.

Kerpelman, J. P., & Himmelfarb, S. (1971). Partial reinforcement effects in attitude acquisition and counterconditioning. *Journal of Personality and Social Psychology, 19,* 301–305.

Kesner, R. P., & Baker, T. B. (1980). Neuroanatomical correlates of language and memory: A developmental perspective. In R. Ault (Eds.), *Developmental perspectives.* Santa Monica, CA: Good Year Publishing Co.

Keverne, E. B. (1982). Chemical senses: Smell. In H. B. Barlow & J. D. Mollon (Eds.), *The senses* (pp. 409–427). New York: Cambridge University Press. (a)

Keverne, E. B. (1982). Chemical senses: Taste. In H. B. Barlow & J. D. Mollon (Eds.), *The senses* (pp. 428–447). New York: Cambridge University Press. (b)

Kidder, L. H., Fagan, M. A., & Cohn, E. S. (1981). Giving and receiving: Social justice in close relationships. In M. J. Lerner & S. C. Lerner (Eds.), *The justice motive in social behavior: Adapting to times of scarcity and change* (pp. 235–259). New York: Plenum Press.

Kieras, D. E. (1981). Component processes in the comprehension of simple prose. *Journal of Verbal Learning and Behavior, 20,* 1–23.

Kiesler, C. A. (1971). *The psychology of commitment.* New York: Academic Press.

Kiesler, C. A., & Pallak, M. S. (1976). Arousal properties of dissonance manipulations. *Psychological Bulletin, 83,* 1014–1025.

Kihlstrom, J. F. (1984). Conscious, subconscious, unconscious—a cognitive perspective. In K. S. Bowers & D. Meichenbaum (Eds.), *Unconscious reconsidered* (pp. 149–211). New York: John Wiley & Sons.

Kihlstrom, J. F. (1985). Hypnosis. *Annual Review of Psychology, 36,* 385–418.

Kihlstrom, J. F., & Evans, F. J. (1979). Memory retrieval processes in postsynaptic amnesia. In J. F. Kihlstrom & F. J. Evans (Eds.), *Functional disorders of memory* (pp. 179–218). Hillsdale, NJ: Lawrence Erlbaum.

Kilham, W., & Mann, L. (1974). Level of destructive obedience as a function of transmitter and executant roles in the Milgram obedience paradigm. *Journal of Personality and Social Psychology, 29,* 696–702.

Kimble, G. (1978). *How to use (and mis-use) statistics.* Englewood Cliffs, NJ: Spectrum Books.

Kimmel, D. C., Price, K. F., & Walker, J. W. (1978). Retirement choice and retirement satisfaction. *Journal of Gerontology, 33,* 575–585.

Kinney, D. K., & Jacobson, B. (1978). Environmental factors in schizophrenia: New adoption study evidence and its implications for genetic and environmental research. In L. C. Wynne, R. L. Cromwell, & S. Matthysse (Eds.), *The nature of schizophrenia.* New York: John Wiley & Sons.

Kinsbourne, M. (1975). Cerebral dominance, learning, and cognition. In G. P. Mykebust (Ed.), *Progress in learning disabilities.* New York: Grune & Stratton.

Kinsey, A. C., Pornesay, W. B., & Martin, C. E. (1948). *Sexual behavior in the human male.* Philadelphia: Saunders.

Kintsch, W. (1974). *The representation of meaning in memory.* Hillsdale, NJ: Lawrence Erlbaum.

Kintsch, W., & Keenan, J. M. (1973). Reading rate and retention as a function of the number of propositions in the base structure of sentences. *Cognitive Psychology, 5,* 257–274.

Kinzey, S. L. (1975). The effects of extended spaceflight on hematologic and immunologic systems. *Journal of the American Medical Women's Association, 30,* 218–232.

Kipnis, D. (1976). *The powerholders.* Chicago: University of Chicago Press.

Kirschvink, J. L. (1982). Birds, bees and magnetism: A new look at the old problem of magnetoreception. *Trends in Neurosciences, 5,* 160–167.

Klaus, K. M. H., & Kennell, J. H. (1976). *Maternal-infant bonding.* St. Louis: Mosby.

Klein, D. F., & Rabkin, J. G. (1984). Specificity and strategy in psychotherapy research and practice. In J. B. W. Williams & R. L. Spitzer (Eds.), *Psychotherapy research: Where are we?* New York: Guilford.

Klein, K. E., Wegman, H. M., & Hunt, B. M. (1972). Desynchronization of body temperature and performance circadian rhythm as a result of out-going and home-going transmeridian flights. *Aerospace Medicine, 43,* 119–132.

Klein, S. B. (1982). *Motivation: Biosocial approaches.* New York: McGraw-Hill.

Kleitman, N. (1963). *Sleep and wakefulness.* Chicago: University of Chicago Press.

Klerman, G. L. (1986). Historical perspectives

on contemporary schools of psychopathology. In T. Million & G. L. Klerman (Eds.), *Contemporary directions in psychopathology*. New York: Guilford.

Klerman, G. L., & Cole, J. O. (1965). Clinical pharmacology of imipramine and related antidepressant compounds. *Pharmacological Review, 17*, 100–141.

Klima, E. S., & Bellugi, U. (1979). *The signs of language*. Cambridge, MA: Harvard University Press.

Kline, J., Shrout, P., Stein, Z., Susser, M., & Warburton, D. (1980). Drinking during pregnancy and spontaneous abortion. *The Lancet*, 176–180.

Kline, P. (1981). *Fact and fantasy in Freudian theory* (2nd ed.). London: Methuen.

Klinger, E. (1975). Consequences of commitment to and disengagement from incentives. *Psychological Review, 82*, 1–25.

Klingman, A., Melamed, B. G., Cuthbert, M. I., Hermecz, D. A. (1984). Effects of participant modeling on information acquisition and skill utilization. *Journal of Consulting and Clinical Psychology, 52*, 414–421.

Klopfer, B., & Kelley, D. (1942). *The Rorschach technique*. Yonkers, NY: World Book.

Knittle, J. L., & Hirsch, J. (1968). Effect of early nutrition on the development of rat epididymal fat pads: Cellularity and metabolism. *Journal of Clinical Investigation, 4*, 2091–2098.

Knox, R. E., & Inkster, J. A. (1968). Postdecision dissonance at post-time. *Journal of Personality and Social Psychology, 8*, 319–323.

Knox, V. J., Morgan, A. H., & Hilgard, E. R. (1974). Pain and suffering in ischemia: The paradox of hypnotically suggested anesthesia as contradicted by reports from the 'hidden observer.' *Archives of General Psychiatry, 30*, 840–847.

Kohlberg, L. (1969). Stage and sequence: The cognitive-developmental approach to socialization. In D. A. Goslin (Ed.), *Handbook of socialization theory and research* (pp. 347–480). Chicago: Rand McNally.

Kohlberg, L. (1976). Moral stages and moralization: The cognitive-developmental approach. In T. Likona (Ed.), *Moral development and behavior: Theory, research, and social issues* (pp. 31–53). New York: Holt, Rinehart & Winston.

Kohlberg, L. (1981). *The philosophy of moral development: Moral stages and the idea of justice:* Vol. 1 *Essays on moral development*. San Francisco: Harper & Row.

Kohlberg, L. (1984). *The psychology of moral development: The nature and validity of moral stages: Essays on moral development*. San Francisco: Harper & Row.

Kohler, W. (1969). *The task of Gestalt psychology*. Princeton, NJ: Princeton University Press.

Koriat, A., Lichtenstein, S., & Fischhoff, B. (1980). Reasons for confidence. *Journal of Experimental Psychology: Human Memory and Learning, 6*, 107–118.

Kornhuber, H. H. (1983). Chemistry, physiology and neuropsychology of schizophrenia—towards an earlier diagnosis of schizophrenia—I. *Archiv fur Psychiatrie und Nervenkrankheiten, 233*, 415–422.

Korte, C., Ypma, I., & Toppen, A. (1975). Helpfulness in Dutch society as a function of urbanization and environmental input level. *Journal of Personality and Social Psychology, 32*, 996–1003.

Kosslyn, S. M. (1975). Information representation in visual images. *Cognitive Psychology, 7*, 341–370.

Kosslyn, S. M., Ball, T. M., & Reiser, B. J. (1978). Visual images preserve metric spatial information: Evidence from studies of image scanning. *Journal of Experimental Psychology: Human Perception and Performance, 4*, 47–60.

Kosson, D. S., & Newman, J. P. (1986). Psychopathy and the allocation of attentional capacity in a divided-attention situation. *Journal of Abnormal Psychology, 95*, 257–263.

Kovacs, M., Rush, A. J., Beck, A. T., & Hollon, S. D. (1981). Depressed outpatients treated with cognitive therapy or pharmacotherapy: A one-year follow-up. *Archives of General Psychiatry, 38*, 33–39.

Kozlowski, L. T. (1977). Effects of distorted auditory and rhyming cues on retrieval of tip-of-the-tongue words by poets and nonpoets. *Memory and Cognition, 5*, 482–490.

Kraepelin, E. (1919). *Dementia praecox and paraphrenia*. Edinburgh: E. S. Livingstone.

Krafka, C., & Penrod, S. (1985). Reinstatement of context in a field experiment on eyewitness identification. *Journal of Personality and Social Psychology, 49*, 58–69.

Krafka, C., Penrod, S., & Donnerstein, E. (1987). *Sexually explicit, sexually aggressive, and violent media: The effect of naturalistic exposure on females*. Unpublished manuscript, University of Wisconsin-Madison, Madison, WI.

Kraut, R. E., & Lewis, S. H. (1982). Person perception and self-awareness: Knowledge of one's influences on one's own judgements. *Journal of Personality and Social Psychology, 42*, 448–460.

Krebs, D. L. (1983). Commentaries and critiques. In D. Bridgeman (Ed.), *The nature of prosocial development. Interdisciplinary theories and strategies*. New York: Academic Press.

Krebs, D. L., & Miller, D. T. (1985). Altruism and aggression. In G. Lindzey, & E. Aronson (Eds.), *Handbook of social psychology* (Vol. 2). New York: Random House.

Krech, D., & Crutchfield, R. S. (1948). *Theory and problems of social psychology*. New York: McGraw-Hill.

Kreutzer, M. A., Leonard, C., & Flavell, J. H. (1975). An interview study of children's knowledge about memory. *Monographs of the Society for Research in Child Development, 40*.

Kringlen, E. (1967). Heredity and social factors in schizophrenic twins: An epidemiological-clinical study. In J. Romano (Ed.), *The origins of schizophrenia*. New York: Excerpta Medica Foundation.

Kroll, N. E. A., Schepler, E. M., & Angin, K. T. (1986). Bizarre imagery: The misremembered mnemonic. *Journal of Experimental Psychology: Learning, Memory, and Cognition, 12*, 42–53.

Kruglanski, A. W. (1977). The place of naive contents in a theory of attributions: Reflections on Calder's and Zuckerman's critiques of the endogenous-exogenous partition. *Personality and Social Psychology Bulletin, 3*, 592–605.

Krugman, H. E. (1972). The impact of television advertising: Learning without involvement. *Public Opinion Quarterly, 29*, 349–356.

Kuffler, S. W., Nicholls, J. G., & Martin, A. R. (1984). *From neuron to brain* (2nd ed.). Sunderland, MA: Sinauer.

Kuhar, M. J., Pert, C. B., & Snyder, S. H. (1973). Regional distribution of opiate receptor binding in human and monkey brain. *Nature, 245*, 447–450.

Kuhl, P. K., & Meltzoff, A. N. (1982). The bimodal perception of speech in infancy. *Science, 218*, 1138–1141.

Kukla, A. (1972). Foundations of an attributional theory of performance. *Psychological Review, 79*, 454–470.

Kulik, J. A., Sledge, P., & Mahler, H. (1986). Self-confirmatory attribution, egocentrism, and the perpetuation of self-beliefs. *Journal of Personality and Social Psychology, 50*, 587–594.

Kupferman, I. (1985). Hemispheric asymmetries and the cortical localization of higher cognitive and affective functions. In E. R. Kandel & J. H. Schwartz (Eds.), *Principles of neural science* (pp. 673–687). New York: Elsevier.

Kurichara, K., Kurichara, Y., & Beidler, L. M. (1969). Isolation and mechanism of taste modifiers: Taste-modifying protein and gymnemic acids. In C. Pfaffman (Ed.), *Olfaction and taste III* (pp. 450–469). New York: Rockefeller University Press.

Kusanin, J., Knight, E., & Sage, P. (1934). The parent–child relationship in schizophrenia: I. Overprotection–rejection. *Journal of Nervous and Mental Disease, 72*, 249–263.

Lacey, J. I. (1967). Somatic response patterning and stress: Some revisions of activation theory. In M. H. Appley & R. Trumbull (Eds.), *Psychological stress: Issues in research*. New York: Appleton.

Lader, M. H. (1981). Benzodiazepine dependence. In R. Murray, A. H. Ghodse, C. Harris, D. Williams, & P. Williams (Eds.), *The misuse of psychotropic drugs*. London: Gaskell.

Lamb, M. E. (1982). Early contact and maternal/infant bonding: A decade later. *Pediatrics, 70*, 763–768.

Lamb, M. E., Pleck, J. H., & Levine, J. A. (1985). The role of the father in child development—the effects of increased paternal involvement. In B. B. Lahey & A. E. Kaezdin (Eds.), *Advances in clinical child psychology* (pp. 229–266). New York: Plenum.

Land, E. H. (1983). Recent advances in retinex theory and some implications for cortical computations: Color vision and the natural image. *Proceedings of the National Academy of Science, USA, 80*, 5163–5169.

Landman, J. T., & Dawes, R. M. (1982). Psychotherapy outcome: Smith and Glass' conclusions stand up under scrutiny. *American Psychologist, 37*, 504–516.

Lang, A. R., Goeckner, D. J., Adesso, V. J., & Marlatt, G. A. (1975). Effects of alcohol on aggression in male social drinkers. *Journal of Abnormal Psychology, 84*, 508–518.

Lang, P. J. (1984). Cognition in emotion. In C. Izard, J. Kagan, & R. B. Zajonc (Eds.), *Emotions, cognition, and behavior*. New York: Cambridge University Press.

Lang, P. J., Lewin, D. N., Miller, G. A., & Kozak, M. J. (1983). Fear behavior, fear imaging, and the psychophysiology of emotion: The problem of affective response integration. *Journal of Abnormal Psychology, 92*, 276–306.

Lang, P. J., & Melamed, B. G. (1969). Case report: Avoidance conditioning therapy of an infant with chronic ruminative vomiting. *Journal of Abnormal Psychology, 74*, 1–8.

Lange, C. (1967). The emotions. Translation of Lange's 1885 monograph. In C. J. Lange & W. James (Eds.), *The emotions*. New York: Hafner.

Langfeldt, G. (1937). The prognosis in schizophrenia and the factors influencing the course of the disease. *Acta Psychiatrica et Neurologica Scandinavica*, Suppl. 13.

Lanzetta, J. T., Sullivan, D. G., Masters, R. D., & McHugo, G. J. (1985). Viewers' emotional and cognitive responses to televised images of political leaders. In S. Kraus & R. M. Kerloff (Eds.), *Mass media and political thought: An information processing approach*. Beverly Hills, CA: Sage.

LaPiere, R. T. (1934). Attitudes vs. action. *Social Forces, 13*, 230–237.

Larsson, K., & Hermer, L. (1964). Mating behavior of male rats after lesions in the preoptic area. *Nature, 202*, 413–414.

Lasagna, L., Von Felsinger, J. M., & Beecher, H. K. (1955). Drug induced mood changes in man. I. Observations of healthy subjects, chronically ill patients and "post addicts" *Journal of the American Medical Association, 157*, 1006–1020.

Lashley, K. (1950). In search of the Engram. In *Symposium of the Society for Experimental Biology* (Vol. 4). New York: Cambridge University Press.

Latane, B., & Nida, S. (1981). Ten years of research on group size and helping. *Psychological Bulletin, 89*, 308–324.

Latane, B., & Darley, J. M. (1968). Group inhibition of bystander interventions in emergencies. *Journal of Personality and Social Psychology, 10*, 215–221.

Latane, B., & Darley, J. M. (1970). *The unresponsive bystander: Why doesn't he help?* New York: Appleton-Century-Crofts.

Latane, B., Nida, S. A., & Wilson, D. W. (1981). The effects of group size and helping behavior. In J. P. Rushton & R. M. Sorrentino (Eds.), *Altruism and helping behavior: Social, personality, and developmental perspectives*. Hillsdale, NJ: Lawrence Erlbaum.

Laudenslager, M. L., Ryan, S. M., Dungan, R. C., Hyson, R. L., & Maier, S. F. (1983). Coping and immunosuppression: Inescapable but not escapable shock suppresses lymphocyte proliferation. *Science, 221*, 568–570.

Lazarus, R. S. (1977). Psychological stress and coping in adaptation and illness. In Z. J. Lipowski, D. R. Lippsitt, & P. C. Shybrow (Eds.), *Psychosomatic medicine: Current trends and clinical applications*. New York: Oxford University Press.

Le Bon, G. (1895). *Psychologie des foules*. Paris: F. Olean.

Lechtenberg, R. (1982). *The psychiatrists' guide to diseases of the nervous system*. New York: John Wiley & Sons.

Leckman, J. F., Merikangas, K. R., Pauls, D. L., Prusoff, B. A., & Weissman, M. M. (1983). Anxiety disorders and depression; contradictions between family study data and DSM-III conventions. *American Journal of Psychiatry, 140*, 880–882.

Leeper, R. W. (1948). A motivational theory of emotion to replace "emotion as disorganized response." *Psychological Review, 55*, 5–21.

Leff, J. P. (1976). Schizophrenia and sensitivity to the family environment. *Schizophrenia Bulletin, 2*, 566–574.

Leff, J., & Vaughn, C. (1981). The role of maintenance therapy and relatives' expressed emotion in relapse of schizophrenia: A two-year follow-up. *British Journal of Psychiatry, 139*, 102–104.

Lefkowitz, M. M. (1981). Smoking during pregnancy: Long-term effects on offspring. *Developmental Psychology, 17*, 192–194.

Lehman, D. R., Ellard, J. H., & Wortman, C. B. (1986). Special support for the bereaved: Recipients' and providers' perspectives on what is helpful. *Journal of Consulting and Clinical Psychology, 54*, 438–446.

LeMasters, E. E. (1957). Parenthood as crisis. *Marriage and Family Living, 19*, 352–355.

Lenneberg, E. H. (1964). Language disorders in childhood. *Harvard Educational Review, 34*, 152–177.

Lenneberg, E. H. (1967). *Biological foundations of language*. New York: John Wiley & Sons.

Lenneberg, E. H., Rebelsky, F. G., & Nichols, I. A. (1965). The vocalizations of infants born deaf and hearing parents. *Human Development, 8*, 23–37.

Leporé, F., Ptito, M., & Jasper, H. H. (1986). *Two hemispheres—one brain: Functions of the corpus callosum*. New York: Alan R. Liss.

Lerner, R. M., & Karabenick, S. A. (1974). Physical attractiveness, body attitudes, and self-concept in late adolescents. *Journal of Youth Adolescence, 3*, 307–316.

Lester, E., & Werbell, F. E. (1980). The lost hero of the holocaust. *The New York Times Magazine*, March 30, pp. 112–117; 128–131.

Leventhal, G. S., Weiss, T., & Long, G. (1969). Equity, reciprocity, and reallocating the rewards in the dyad. *Journal of Personality and Social Psychology, 13*, 300–305.

Leventhal, H. (1974). Emotions: A basic problem for social psychology. In C. Nemeth (Ed.), *Social psychology: Classic and contemporary integrations*. Chicago: Rand McNally.

Leventhal, H., & Cleary, P. D. (1980). The smoking problem: A review of the research and theory in behavioral risk modification. *Psychological Bulletin, 88*, 370–405.

Leventhal, H., Singer, R., & Jones, S. (1965). The effects of fear and specificity of recommendation upon attitudes and behavior. *Journal of Personality and Social Psychology, 2*, 20–29.

Leventhal, H., & Tomarken, A. J. (1985). Emotions: Today's problems. M. R. Rosenzweig & L. W. Porter (Eds.), *Annual Review of Psychology*. Palo Alto, CA: Annual Reviews.

Levine, J. D., Gordon, N. C., & Fields, H. L. (1979). The role of endorphins in placebo analgesia. In J. J. Bonica, J. C. Liebeskind, & D. Albe-Fessard (Eds.), *Advances in pain research and therapy* (Vol. 3). New York: Raven Press.

Levine, M. (1966). Hypothesis behavior by humans during discrimination learning. *Journal of Experimental Psychology, 71*, 331–338.

Levy, J., Trevarthen, C., & Sperry, R. W. (1972). Perception of bilateral chimeric figures following hemispheric deconnection. *Brain, 95*, 61–78.

Levy-Agresti, J., & Sperry, R. W. (1968). Differential perceptual capacities in major and minor hemispheres. *Proceedings of the National Academy of Science, U.S.A., 61*, 1151.

Lewin, K. (1935). *A dynamic theory of personality*. New York: McGraw-Hill.

Lewinsohn, P. M., Hoberman, H., Teri, L., & Hautzinger, M. (1985). In S. Reiss, & R. R. Bootzin (Eds.), *Theoretical issues in behavior therapy*. New York: Academic Press.

Lewis, C. C. (1981). The effects of parental firm control: A reinterpretation of findings. *Psychological Bulletin, 90*, 547–563.

Lewontin, R. C. (1970). Race and intelligence. *Bulletin of the Atomic Scientists, 26*, 2–8.

Lewontin, R. C., Rose, S., & Kamin, L. J. (1984). *Not in our genes*. New York: Pantheon.

Lichtenstein, S., Fischhoff, B., & Phillips, L. D. (1982). Calibration of probabilities: The state of the art to 1980. In D. Kahneman, P. Slovic, & A. Tversky (Eds.), *Judgment under uncertainty: Heuristics and biases*. Cambridge: Cambridge University Press.

Lichty, L. W. (1982). Video versus print. *Wilson Quarterly, 6*(5), 48–57.

Lieberman, P. (1967). *Intonation, perception, and language*. Cambridge, MA: MIT Press.

Lieberman, P. (1984). *The biology and evolution of language*. Cambridge, MA: Harvard University Press.

Lieberman, P. (1985). On the evolution of human syntactic ability. Its pre-adaptive bases—motor control and speech. *Journal of Human Evolution, 14*, 657–668.

Liebert, R. M. (1986). Effects of television on children and adolescents. *Journal of Developmental and Behavioral Pediatrics, 7*, 43–48.

Liebowitz, M. R., Fyer, A. J., McGrath, P., & Klein, D. F. (1981). Clonidine treatment of panic disorder. *Psychopharmacology Bulletin, 17*, 122–124.

Liebowitz, M. R., Gorman, J. M., Fyer, A. J., et al. (1985). Lactate provocation of panic attacks: II. Biochemical and physiological findings. *Archives of General Psychiatry, 42*, 709–719.

Linberg, K. A., & Fisher, S. K. (1986). An ultrastructural study of interplexiform cell synapses in the human retina. *The Journal of Comparative Neurology, 243*, 561–576.

Lindsay, P. H., & Norman, D. A. (1977). *Human information processing*. New York: Academic Press.

Lindsley, J. R. (1975). Producing simple utterances: How far ahead do we plan? *Cognitive Psychology, 7*, 1–19.

Linton, R. (1945). *The cultural background of personality*. New York: Appleton-Century.

Linton, R. (1950). Problems of status personality. In S. S. Sargent, & M. W. Smith, (Eds.), *Culture and personality* (pp. 163–173). New York: Viking Fund.

Linz, D. (1985). *Sexual violence in the media: Effects on male viewers and implications for society*. Unpublished doctoral dissertation, University of Wisconsin, Madison.

Lisowski, F. P. (1967). Prehistoric and early historic trepanation. In D. Brothwell & A. T. Sandison (Eds.), *Diseases in antiquity*. Springfield, IL: Charles C. Thomas.

Lissmann, H. W. (1963). Electric location by fishes. *Scientific American, 208*, 50–59.

Little, K. B., & Schneidman, E. S. (1959). Congruencies among interpretations of psychological test and anamnestic data. *Psychological Monographs, 73*, (6 Whole No. 476).

Locke, E. A., Shaw, K. N., Saari, L. M., & Latham, G. P. (1981). Goal setting and task performance: 1969–1980. *Psychological Bulletin, 90*, 125–152.

Locke, S. E., Kraus, L., Laserman, J., Hurst, M. W., Heisel, S., & Williams, R. M. (1984). Life change stress, psychiatric symptoms, and natural killer cell activity. *Psychosomatic Medicine, 46,* 441–453.

Loeb, M., & Binford, J. R. (1963). Some factors influencing the effective auditory differences in men. *Journal of the Acoustical Society of America, 35,* 884–891.

Loehlin, J. C., & Nichols, R. C. (1976). *Heredity, environment, and personality: A study of 850 sets of twins.* Austin: University of Texas Press.

Logue, A. W. (1985). Conditioned food aversion learning in humans. In N. S. Braveman & P. Bronstein (Eds.), *Experimental assessments and clinical applications of conditioned food aversions* (pp. 316–329). New York: New York Academy of Sciences.

Long, G. M., & Sakitt, B. (1980). Target duration effects on iconic memory: The confounding role of changing stimulus dimensions. *Quarterly Journal of Experimental Psychology, 32,* 269–285.

Longo, L. M. (1982). The health consequences of maternal smoking: Experimental studies and public policy recommendations. In *Alternative dietary practices and nutritional abuses in pregnancy. Proceedings of a workshop* (pp. 135–159). Washington, DC: National Academy Press.

Lopes, L. L. (1982). Decision making in the short run. *Journal of Experimental Psychology: Human Memory and Learning, 7,* 377–385.

Lopes, L. L. (1983). Doing the impossible: A note on induction and the experience of randomness. *Journal of Experimental Psychology: Learning, Memory, and Cognition, 8,* 626–636.

Lorayne, H., & Lucas, J. (1974). *The memory book.* New York: Ballantine Books.

Lorch, R. F., Jr. (1981). The role of two types of semantic information in the processing of false sentences. *Journal of Verbal Learning and Verbal Behavior, 21,* 468–492.

Lorenz, K. (1966). An energy model of instinctive actions. In D. Bindra & J. Stewart (Eds.), *Motivation: Selected readings.* New York: Penguin.

Lovaas, O. I. (1977). *The autistic child.* New York: Lexington Books.

Lowell, E. L. (1952). The need for achievement in learning and speed of performance. *Journal of Psychology, 33,* 31–40.

Luborsky, L. (1984). *Principles of psychoanalytic psychotherapy.* New York: Basic Books.

Luborsky, L., Mellon, J., Ravenswaay, Pv., Childress, A. R., Cohen, K. D., Hole, A. V., Ming, S., Crits-Christopl, P., Levine, F. J., & Alexander, K. (1985). A verification of Freud's grandest clinical hypothesis: The transference. *Clinical Psychological Review, 5,* 231–246.

Luborsky, L., Singer, B., & Luborsky, L. (1975). Comparative studies of psychotherapies: Is it true that "Everyone has won and all must have prices"? *Archives of General Psychiatry, 32,* 995–1008.

Luchins, A. (1957). Primacy-recency in impression formation. In C. Hovland, W. Mandell, E. Campbell, T. Brock, A. Luchins, A. Cohen, W. McGuire, I. Janis, R. Feierabend, & N. Anderson (Eds.), *The order of presentation in persuasion.* New Haven, CT: Yale University Press.

Luchins, A. S. (1942). Mechanization in problem solving. *Psychological Monographs, 54,* No. 248.

Ludwig, D., Franco, J. N., & Malloy, T. E.

(1986). Effects of reciprocity and self-monitoring on self-disclosure with a new acquaintance. *Journal of Personality and Social Psychology, 50,* 1077–1082.

Lung, C., & Dominowski, R. L. (1985). Effects of strategy instructions and practice on nine-dot problem solving. *Journal of Experimental Psychology: Learning, Memory, and Cognition, 11,* 804–811.

Luria, A. R. (1968). *The mind of a mnemonist.* New York: Basic Books.

Lykken, D. T. (1982). Research with twins: The concept of emergenesis. *Psychophysiology, 19,* 361–373.

Lyman, B. J., & MacDaniel, M. A. (1986). Effects of encoding strategy on long-term memory for odours. *The Quarterly Journal of Experimental Psychology, 38A,* 753–765.

Lynch, J. C. (1980). The functional organization of posterior parietal association cortex. *Behavioral and Brain Sciences, 3,* 485–534.

Lytton, H. (1977). Do parents create, or respond to, differences in twins? *Developmental Psychology, 13,* 456–459.

Macaulay, J. R., & Berkowitz, L. (1970). *Altruism and helping behavior.* New York: Academic Press.

Maccoby, E. F., & Jacklin, C. N. (1974). *The psychology of sex differences.* Stanford, CA: Stanford University Press.

MacFarlane, A. (1975). Olfaction in the development of social preferences in the human neonate. In Ciba Foundation Symposium, *Parent–infant interaction* (pp. 103–117). Amsterdam: Elsevier.

MacKenzie, B. (1984). Explaining race differences in IQ. *American Psychologist, 39,* 1214–1233.

MacKey, A. V. P. (1980). Positive and negative schizophrenic symptoms and the role of dopamine: Discussion, 1. *British Journal of Psychiatry, 137,* 379–383.

MacKinnon, D. W., & Dukes, W. (1962). Repression. In L. Postman (Ed.), *Psychology in the making.* (pp. 662–774). New York: Knopf.

Mackworth, N. H. (1950). Researches on the measurements of human performance. *Medical Research Council (Great Britain), Special Report Series (SRS-268).*

Maclay, H., & Osgood, C. E. (1959). Hesitation phenomena in spontaneous English speech. *Word, 15,* 19–44.

MacMillan, J. F., Gold, A., Crow, T. J., Johnson, A. L., & Johnstone, E. C. (1986). IV. Expressed emotion and relapse. *British Journal of Psychiatry, 148,* 133–143.

Maddi, S. R. (1980). *Personality theories: A comparative analysis.* Homewood, IL: The Dorsey Press.

Maier, N. R. F. (1931). Reasoning in humans. *Journal of Comparative Psychology, 12,* 181–194.

Major, B. (1980). Information acquisition and attribution processes. *Journal of Personality and Social Psychology, 39,* 1010–1023.

Major, B., Carrington, P. I., & Carnavale, P. J. D. (1984). Physical attractiveness and self-esteem: Attributions for praise from an other-sex evaluator. *Personality and Social Psychology Bulletin, 10,* 43–50.

Malamuth, N. (1981). Rape fantasies as a function of exposure to violent and sexual stimuli. *Archives of Sexual Behavior, 10,* 33–47.

Malamuth, N. M. (1986). Predictors of naturalistic sexual aggression. *Journal of Personality and Social Psychology, 50,* 953–962.

Malamuth, N. M., & Check, J. V. (1980). Penile tumescence and perceptual responses to rape as a function of victim's perceived reactions. *Journal of Applied Social Psychology, 10,* 528–547.

Malamuth, N. M., & Check, J. V. (1981). The effects of mass media exposure on acceptance of violence against women: A field experiment. *Journal of Research in Personality, 15,* 436–446.

Malamuth, N. M., Haber, S., & Feshbach, S. (1980). Testing hypotheses regarding rape: Exposure to sexual violence, sex differences, and the "normality," of rapists. *Journal of Research in Personality, 14,* 121–137.

Malamuth, N. M., & Spinner, B. A. (1980). Longitudinal content analysis of sexual violence in the best-selling erotic magazines. *Journal of Sex Research, 16,* 226–237.

Malkis, F. S., Kalle, R. J., & Tedeschi, J. T. (1982). Attitudinal politics in the forced compliance situation. *Journal of Social Psychology, 117,* 79–91.

Malmo, R. B. (1966). Studies of anxiety: Some clinical origins of the activation concept. In C. D. Spielberger (Ed.), *Anxiety and behavior.* New York: Academic.

Malone, R. B. (1966). Studies of anxiety: Some clinical origins of the activation concept. In C. D. Spielberger (Ed.), *Anxiety and behavior.* New York: Academic Press.

Mandler, G. (1983). Consciousness: Its function and construction. *Presidential address to the Division of General Psychology, APA.*

Mandler, G. (1985). *Cognitive psychology: An essay in cognitive science.* Hillsdale, NJ: Lawrence Erlbaum.

Mangan, G. L., & Golding, J. (1978). An 'enhancement' model of smoking maintenance? In R. E. Thornton (Ed.), *Smoking behaviour: Physiological and psychological influences.* Edinburgh: Churchill, Livingstone.

Mann, M. D. (1984). The growth of the brain and skull in children. *Developmental Brain Research, 13,* 169–178.

Mansky, P. A. (1978). Opiates: Human psychopharmacology. In L. L. Iversen, S. D. Iversen, & S. H. Snyder (Eds.), *Handbook of psychopharmacology.* New York: Plenum Press.

Manstead, A. S. R., Profitt, C., & Smart, J. L. (1983). Predicting and understanding mothers' infant-feeding intentions and behavior: Testing the theory of reasoned action. *Journal of Personality and Social Psychology, 44,* 657–671.

Mantell, D. M. (1971). The potential for violence in Germany. *Journal of Social Issues, 27,* 101–112.

Marcus, S. L., & Rips, L. J. (1979). Conditional reasoning. *Journal of Verbal Learning & Verbal Behavior, 18,* 199–223.

Margolese, M. S., & Janiger, O. (1973). Androsterone/etiocholanolone ratios in male homosexuals. *British Medical Journal, 3,* 207–210.

Marks, I. M., & Herst, E. R. (1970). A survey of 1,200 agoraphobics in Britain. *Social Psychiatry, 5,* 16–24.

Marks, W. B., Dobelle, W. H., & MacNichol, E. F. (1964). Visual pigments of single primate cones. *Science, 143,* 1181–1183.

Markus, H., Crane, M., Berstein, S., & Siladi,

M. (1982). Self-schemas and gender. *Journal of Personality and Social Psychology, 42,* 38–50.

Marrackd, P., & Kappler, J. (1986). The T-cell and its receptor. *Scientific American, 254,* 36–45.

Marshall, J. F. (1985). Neural plasticity and recovery of function after brain injury. In J. R. Smythies & R. J. Bradley (Eds.), *International review of neurobiology* (pp. 201–248). Orlando, FL: Academic Press.

Martin, J., & Venables, P. H. (1980). *Techniques in psychophysiology.* New York: John Wiley & Sons.

Martin, R. C., & Blossom-Stach, C. (1986). Evidence of syntactic deficits in a fluent aphasic. *Brain and Language, 28,* 196–234.

Martone, M., Butters, N., Payne, M., Becker, J. T., & Sax, D. S. (1984). Dissociations between skill learning and verbal recognition in amnesia and dementia. *Archives of Neurology, 41,* 965–970.

Maruyama, G., & Miller, N. (1980). Physical attractiveness, race, and essay evaluation. *Personality and Social Psychology Bulletin, 6,* 384–390.

Maslach, C. (1979). Negative emotional biasing of unexplained arousal. *Journal of Personality and Social Psychology, 37,* 953–969.

Maslow, A. H. (1970). *Motivation and personality* (2nd ed.). New York: Harper & Row.

Masson, M. E. J. (1984). Memory for the surface structure of sentences: Remembering with and without awareness. *Journal of Verbal Learning and Verbal Behavior, 23,* 579–592.

Masters, W. H., & Johnson, V. E. (1970). *Human sexual inadequacy.* Boston: Little, Brown.

Matarazzo, J. D. (1972). *Wechsler's measurement and appraisal of adult intelligence* (5th ed.). Baltimore: Williams & Wilkins.

Matarazzo, R. G., & Matarazzo, J. D. (1984). Assessment of adult intelligence in clinical practice. In P. McReynolds & G. J. Chelune (Eds.), *Advances in psychological assessment.* San Francisco: Jossey-Bass.

Mathews, D., & Edwards, D. A. (1977). Involvement of the ventromedial and anterior hypothalamic nuclei in the hormonal instruction of receptivity in the female rat. *Physiology and Behavior, 19,* 319–326.

Matin, L., & MacKinnon, G. E. (1964). Autokinetic movement: Selective manipulation of directional components by image stabilization. *Science, 143,* 147–148.

May, J. L., & Hamilton, P. A. (1980). Effects of musically evoked affect on women's interpersonal attraction toward and perceptual judgements of physical attractiveness of men. *Motivation and Emotion, 4,* 217–228.

Mayer, D. J., & Watkins, L. R. (1984). Multiple endogenous opiate and nonopiate analgesia systems. In L. Kruger & J. C. Liebeskind (Eds.), *Neural mechanisms of pain: Advances in pain research and therapy* (pp. 253–276). New York: Raven Press.

Mayer, D. L., & Dobson, V. (1980). Assessment of vision in young children: A new operant approach yields estimates of acuity. *Investigative Ophthalmology and Visual Science, 19,* 566–570.

Mayer, J. (1955). Regulation of energy intake and the body weight: The glucostatic theory and the lipostatic hypothesis. *Annual New York Academy of Science, 63,* 15–43.

McArthur, L. A. (1972). The how and what of why: Some determinants and consequences of causal attribution. *Journal of Personality and Social Psychology, 22,* 171–193.

McBurney, D. H. (1984). Taste and olfaction: Sensory discrimination. In I. Darian-Smith (Ed.), *Handbook of physiology—The nervous system III* (pp. 1067–1086). Bethesda, MD: American Physiological Society.

McBurney, D. H., & Gent, J. I. (1979). On the nature of taste qualities. *Psychological Bulletin, 86,* 151–169.

McCabe, M. P., Collins, J. K., & Burns, A. M. (1978). Hypnosis as an altered state of consciousness: I. A review of traditional theories. *Australian Journal of Clinical and Experimental Hypnosis, 6,* 39–54.

McCabe, M. P., Collins, J. K., & Burns, A. M. (1979). Hypnosis as an altered state of consciousness. II. A review of contemporary theories and empirical evidence. *Australian Journal of Clinical and Experimental Hypnosis, 7,* 7–25.

McCall, R. B. (1977). Childhood IQ's as predictors of adult educational and occupational status. *Science, 197,* 482–483.

McClearn, G. E. (1970). Genetic influences on behavior and development. In P. H. Mussen (Ed.), *Carmichael's manual of child psychology* (Vol. 1, 3rd ed. pp. 39–76). New York: John Wiley & Sons.

McClelland, D. C. (1951). *Personality.* New York: Holt, Rinehart, & Winston.

McClelland, D. C. (1961). *The achieving society.* Princeton, NJ: Van Nostrand.

McClelland, D. C. (1965). Achievement and entrepreneurship: A longitudinal study. *Journal of Personality and Social Psychology, 1,* 389–392.

McClelland, D. C. (1973). Testing for competence rather than for "intelligence." *American Psychologist, 28,* 1–14.

McClelland, D. C., Atkinson, J. W., Clark, R. W., & Lowell, E. L. (1953). *The achievement motive.* New York: Appleton-Century-Crofts.

McClintock, M. K. (1971). Menstrual synchrony and suppression. *Nature, 229,* 244–245.

McCollough, C. (1965). Color adaptation of edge detectors in the human visual system. *Science, 149,* 1115–1116.

McConnell, S. R. (1983). Retirement and employment. In D. S. Woodruff & J. E. Birren (Eds.), *Aging: Scientific perspectives and social issues* (pp. 333–350). Monterey, CA: Brooks/Cole.

McCormick, D. A., & Thompson, R. F. (1984). Cerebellum: Essential involvement and regulation of presynaptic nerve terminals. In W. Y. Cheung (Ed.), *Calcium and cell function.* New York: Academic Press.

McCroskey, J. C., & Combs, W. H. (1969). The effects of the use of analogy on attitude change and source credibility. *Journal of Communication, 19,* 333–339.

McDaniel, M. A., & Einstein, G. O. (1986). Bizarre imagery as an effective memory aid: The importance of distinctiveness. *Journal of Experimental Psychology: Learning, Memory, and Cognition, 12,* 54–65.

McDougall, W. (1908). *An introduction to social psychology.* London: Methuen.

McDowell, J. (1979). Effects of encoding and retrieval cuing on recall in Korsakoff patients. *Memory and Cognition, 7,* 156–164.

McGeer, P. L., & McGeer, E. G. (1981). Neurotransmitters in the ageing brain. In A. M. Davidson & R. H. S. Thompson (Eds.), *The molecular basis of neuropathology* (pp. 631–648). London: Edward Arnold.

McGeoch, J. A. (1942). Forgetting and the law of disuse. *Psychological Review, 39,* 352–370.

McGinnies, E., & Ward, C. D. (1980). Better liked than right: Trustworthiness and expertise as factors in credibility. *Personality and Social Psychology Bulletin, 6,* 467–472.

McGlashan, T. H. (1986). The Chestnut Lodge follow-up study. *Archives of General Psychiatry, 43,* 20–30.

McGrath, M. J., & Cohen, D. B. (1978). REM sleep facilitation of adaptive waking behavior: A review of the literature. *Psychological Bulletin, 85,* 24–57.

McGue, M., Gottesman, I. I., & Rao, D. C. (1986). The analysis of schizophrenia family data. *Behavior Genetics, 16,* 75–88.

McGuire, W. J. (1964). Inducing resistance to persuasion: Some contemporary approaches. In L. Berkowitz (Ed.), *Advances in experimental social psychology* (Vol. 1). New York: Academic Press.

McGuire, W. J. (1969). The nature of attitudes and attitude change. In G. Lindzey & E. Aronson (Eds.), *Handbook of social psychology* (Vol. 3 2nd ed., pp. 136–314). Reading, MA: Addison-Wesley.

McGuire, W. J. (1985). Attitudes and attitude change. In G. Lindzey & E. Aronson (Eds.), *Handbook of social psychology* (Vol. 2). New York: Random House.

McGuire, W. J., & Padawer-Singer, A. (1976). Trait salience in the spontaneous self-concept. *Journal of Personality and Social Psychology, 33,* 743–754.

McHugh, R. R., & Slavney, P. R. (1983). *The perspectives of psychiatry.* Baltimore: Johns Hopkins University Press.

McHugo, G. J., Lanzetta, J. T., Sullivan, D. G., Masters, R. D., & Englis, B. G. (1985). Emotional reactions to a political leader's expressive displays. *Journal of Personality and Social Psychology, 49,* 1513–1529.

McKenna, R. J. (1972). Some effects of anxiety level and food cues on the eating behavior of obese and normal subjects. *Journal of Personality and Social Psychology, 22,* 311–319.

McKillip, J., & Reidel, S. L. (1983). External validity of matching on physical attractiveness for same and opposite sex couples. *Journal of Applied Social Psychology, 13,* 328–337.

McKoon, G., & Ratcliff, R. (1979). Priming in episodic and semantic memory. *Journal of Verbal Learning and Verbal Behavior, 18,* 463–480.

McKoon, G., Ratcliff, R., & Dell, G. S. (1986). A critical evaluation of the semantic-episodic distinction. *Journal of Experimental Psychology: Learning, Memory, and Cognition, 12,* 295–306.

McNeil, E. (1967). *The quiet furies.* Englewood Cliffs, NJ: Prentice-Hall.

McNeil, T. F., & Kaij, M. D. (1978). Obstetric factors in the development of schizophrenia: Complications in the births of preschizophrenics and in reproduction by schizophrenic parents. In L. C. Wynne, L. Cromwell, & S. K. Matthysse (Eds.), *Schizophrenia: New approaches to research and treatment.* New York: John Wiley & Sons.

McNemar, Q. (1942). *The revision of the Stanford-Binet Scale.* Boston: Houghton-Mifflin.

McNemar, Q. (1964). Lost: Our intelligence. Why? *American Psychologist, 19,* 871–882.

Mead, G. H. (1934). *Mind, self, and society.* Chicago: University of Chicago Press.

Megargee, E. I. (1966). Undercontrolled and overcontrolled personality types in extreme antisocial aggression. *Psychological Monographs, 80,* 13, Whole No. 611.

Mehrabian, A., & Russell, J. A. (1974). An approach to environmental psychology. Cambridge, MA: MIT Press.

Mello, N. K., & Mendelson, J. H. (1978). Alcohol and human behavior. In L. L. Iversen, S. D. Iversen, & S. H. Snyder (Eds.), *Handbook of psychopharmacology.* New York: Plenum Press.

Melzak, R., & Wall, P. D. (1965). Pain mechanisms: A new theory. *Science, 150,* 971–979.

Memmelstein, R., Cohen, S., Lichtenstein, E., Baer, J S., & Kararck, T. (1986). Social support and smoking cessation and maintenance. *Journal of Consulting and Clinical Psychology, 54,* 447–453.

Meredith, N. (1986). Testing the talking cure. In *Science, 86,* 7 (June), 31–37.

Mervis, C. B., & Rosch, E. (1981). Categorization of natural objects. *Annual Review of Psychology, 32,* 89–115.

Metalsky, G. I., Abramson, L. Y., Seligman, M. E. P., Semmel, A., & Peterson, C. (1982). Attributional style and life events in the classroom: Vulnerability and invulnerability to depressive novel reactions. *Journal of Personality and Social Psychology, 43,* 612–617.

Metcoff, J. (1978). Association of fetal growth with maternal nutrition. In F. Falkner & J. M. Tanner (Eds.), *Human growth.* Vol. 1: *Principles and prenatal growth* (pp. 415–460). New York: Plenum Press.

Meyer, M. B., Jonas, B. S., & Tonascia, J. A. (1976). Perinatal events associated with maternal smoking during pregnancy. *American Journal of Epidemiology, 103,* 464–476.

Meyer, T. P. (1972). The effects of sexually arousing and violent films on aggressive behavior. *Journal of Sex Research, 8,* 324–331.

Michael, C. R. (1978). Color vision mechanisms in monkey striate cortex: Simple cells with dual opponent-color receptive fields. *Journal of Neurophysiology, 41,* 1233–1249. (a)

Michael, C. R. (1978). Color-sensitive complex cells in monkey striate cortex. *Journal of Neurophysiology, 41,* 1250–1266. (b)

Michel, A. E., & Garey, L. J. (1984). The development of dendritic spines in the human visual cortex. *Human Neurobiology, 3,* 223–228.

Midlarsky, E., Bryan, J. H., & Brickman, P. (1973). Aversive approval: Interactive effects of modeling and reinforcement on altruistic behavior. *Child Development, 44,* 321–328.

Miklowitz, D. J., Strachan, A. M., Goldstein, M. J., Doane, J. A., Snyder, K. S., Hogarty, G. E., & Falloon, I. R. H. (1986). Expressed emotion and communication deviance in the families of schizophrenics. *Journal of Abnormal Psychology, 95,* 60–66.

Milavsky, J. R., Pekowsky, B., & Stipp, H. (1975). TV drug advertising and proprietary and illicit drug use among teenage boys. *Public Opinion Quarterly, 43,* 457–480.

Miles, F. A. (1984). Sensing self-motion: Visual and vestibular mechanisms share the same frame of reference. *Trends in Neurosciences, 7,* 303–304.

Milgram, S. (1963). Behavioral study of obedience. *Journal of Abnormal and Social Psychology, 67,* 376.

Milgram, S. (1965). Liberating effects of group pressure. *Journal of Personality and Social Psychology, 1,* 127–134.

Milgram, S. (1974). *Obedience to authority.* New York: Harper & Row.

Millar, W. S. (1972). A study of operant conditioning under delayed reinforcement in early infancy. *Monographs of the Society for Research in Child Develop- ment, 37.*

Miller, A. G. (1976). Constraint and target effects in the attribution of attitudes. *Journal of Experimental and Social Psychology, 12,* 325–329.

Miller, A. G., Jones, E. E., & Hinkle, S. (1981). A robust attribution error in the personality domain. *Journal of Experimental Social Psychology, 17,* 587–600.

Miller, A. K. H., Alston, R. L., & Corsellis, J. H. N. (1980). Variation with age in the volumes of grey and white matter in the cerebral hemispheres of man: Measurements with an image analyzer. *Neuropathology and Applied Neurobiology, 6,* 119–132.

Miller, B. C., & Sollie, D. L. (1980). Normal stresses during the transition to parenthood. *Family Relations, 29,* 459–465.

Miller, C. H. (1975). Dreams and dreaming: The current state of the art. *American Journal of Psychoanalysis, 35,* 135–146.

Miller, D. T., & Ross, M. (1975). Self-serving biases in the attribution of causality: Fact or fiction? *Psychological Bulletin, 82,* 213–225.

Miller, G. A. (1956). The magic number seven, plus or minus two: Some limits on our capacity for processing information. *Psychological Review, 63,* 81–97.

Miller, G. A. (1962). *Psychology: The science of mental life.* New York: Harper & Row.

Miller, G. A., & Isard, S. (1963). Some perceptual consequences of linguistic rules. *Journal of Verbal Learning and Verbal Behavior, 2,* 217–228.

Miller, M., Pasik, P., & Pasik, T. (1980). Extrageniculostriate vision in the monkey. VII. Contrast sensitivity functions. *Journal of Neurophysiology, 43,* 1510–1526.

Miller, N., Maruyama, G., Beaber, R. J., & Valone, K. (1976). Speed of speech and persuasion. *Journal of Personality and Social Psychology, 34,* 615–625.

Miller, N. E. (1948). Studies of fear as an acquirable drive: 1: Fear as motivation and fear-reduction as reinforcement in the learning of new responses. *Journal of Experimental Psychology, 38,* 89–101.

Miller, N. E. (1985). The value of behavioral research on animals. *American Psychologist, 40,* 423–440.

Miller, N., & Dollard, J. (1941). *Social learning and imitation.* New Haven, CT: Yale University Press.

Millon, T. (1984). Interpretive guide to the Millon Clinical Multiaxial Inventory. In P. McReynolds & G. J. Chelune (Eds.), *Advances in psychological assessment* (Vol. 6). San Francisco: Jossey-Bass.

Millon, T. (1986). On the past and future of the DSM-III: Personal recollections and projections. In T. Millon & G. Klerman (Eds.), *Contemporary directions in psychopathology.* New York: Guilford.

Mills, A. W. (1958). On the minimum audible angle. *Journal of the Acoustical Society of America, 30,* 237–246.

Milner, B. (1970). Memory and the medial temporal regions of the brain. In K. H. Pribram & D. E. Broadbent (Eds.), *Biology of memory* (pp. 29–50). New York: Academic Press.

Milner, B., Corkin, S., & Teuber, H.-L. (1968). Further analysis of the hippocampal amnesia syndrome: 14-year follow-up study of H.M. *Neuropsychologia, 6,* 215–234.

Milner, B., & Petrides, M. (1984). Behavioural effects of frontal-lobe lesions in man. *Trends in Neurosciences, 7,* 403–407.

Mineka, S., Keir, R., & Price, V. (1980). Fear of snakes in wild- and lab-reared rhesus monkeys. *Animal Learning and Behavior, 8,* 653–663.

Mineka, S., & Suomi, S. J. (1978). Social separation in monkeys. *Psychological Bulletin, 85,* 1376–1400.

Minium, E. W., & Clarke, R. W. (1982). *Elements of statistical reasoning.* New York: John Wiley & Sons.

Mirsky, A. F., & Orzack, M. H. (1980). Two retrospective studies of psychosurgery. In E. S. Valenstein (Ed.), *The psychosurgery debate.* San Francisco: Freeman.

Mischel, W. (1961). Delay of gratification, need for achievement, and acquiescence in another culture. *Journal of Abnormal and Social Psychology, 62,* 543–552.

Mischel, W. (1968). *Personality and assessment.* New York: John Wiley & Sons.

Mischel, W. (1970). Sex typing and socialization. In P. H. Mussen (Ed.), *Carmichael's manual of child psychology* (pp. 3–72). New York: John Wiley & Sons.

Mischel, W. (1972). Direct versus indirect personality assessment: Evidence and implications. *Journal of Consulting and Clinical Psychology, 38,* 319–324.

Mishkin, M., & Appenzeller, T. (1987). The anatomy of memory. *Scientific American, 256,* 80–89.

Mishkin, M., & Petri, H. L. (1984). Memories and habits: Some implications for the analysis of learning and retention. In L. R. Squire & N. Butters (Eds.), *Neuropsychology of memory.* New York: Guilford.

Mishkin, M., Ungerleider, L. G., & Macko, K. A. (1983). Object vision and spatial vision: Two cortical pathways. *Trends in Neurosciences, 6,* 414–416.

Mitchell, D. E., & Timney, B. (1984). Postnatal development of function in the mammalian visual system. In I. Darian-Smith (Ed.), *Handbook of physiology—the nervous system III* (pp. 507–555). Bethesda, MD: American Physiological Society.

Mitchell, D. D., Harlow, H. F., Griffin, G. A., & Miller, G. W. (1967). Repeated maternal separation in the monkey. *Psychonomic Science, 8,* 197–198.

Moncrieff, R. W. (1956). Olfactory adaptation and odour likeness. *Journal of Physiology, London, 133,* 301–316.

Money, J. (1961). Components of eroticism in man: I. The hormones in relation to sexual morphology and sexual desire. *Journal of Nervous and Mental Disease, 132,* 239–248.

Money, J., & Ehrhardt, A. (1972). *Man and*

woman, boy and girl. Baltimore: Johns Hopkins University Press.

Money, K. E., & Myles, W. S. (1975). Motion sickness and other vestibulo-gastric illnesses. In R. F. Maunton (Ed.), *The vestibular system*. New York: Academic Press.

Monjan, K. A., & Collector, M. I. (1977). Stress-induced modulation of the immune response. *Science, 196*, 307.

Monroe, A. H., & Ehinger, D. (1974). *Principles and types of speech communication* (7th ed.). Glenview, IL: Scott Foresman.

Monson, T. C., & Snyder, M. (1977). Actors, observers, and the attribution process. *Journal of Experimental Social Psychology, 13*, 89–111.

Moore, R. Y., & Bloom, F. E. (1978). Central catecholamine neuron systems: anatomy and physiology of the dopamine systems. *Annual Review of Neuroscience, 1*, 129–169.

Moore, R. Y., & Bloom, F. E. (1979). Central catecholamine neuron systems: anatomy and physiology of the norepinephrine and epinephrine systems. *Annual Review of Neuroscience, 2*, 113–168.

Moore-Ede, M. C., Czeisler, C. H., & Richardson, G. S. (1983). Circadian timekeeping in health and disease. Part 2. Clinical implications of circadian rhythmicity. *The New England Journal of Medicine, 309*, 530–536.

Moreland, R. L., & Zajonc, R. B. (1979). Exposure effects may not depend on stimulus recognition. *Journal of Personality and Social Psychology, 37*, 1085–1089.

Moreland, R. L., & Zajonc, R. B. (1982). Exposure effects in person perception: Familiarity, similarity and attraction. *Journal of Experimental Social Psychology, 18*, 395–415.

Morell, P., & Norton, W. T. (1980). Myelin. *Scientific American, 242*, 88–119.

Morris, J. L. (1966). Propensity for risk taking as a determinant of vocational choice: An extension of the theory of achievement motivation. *Journal of Personality and Social Psychology, 3*, 328–335.

Morruzzi, G., & Magoun, H. W. (1949). Brain stem reticular formation and activation of the EEG. *Electroencephalography and Clinical Neurophysiology, 1*, 455–473.

Moscovici, S. (1980). Toward a theory of conversion behavior. In L. Berkowitz (Ed.), *Advances in experimental social psychology* (Vol. 13, pp. 209–239). New York: Academic Press.

Moscovici, S., Lage, E., & Naffrechoux, M. (1969). Influence of a consistent minority on the responses of a majority in a color perception task. *Sociometry, 32*, 365–379.

Moss, M. K., & Page, R. A. (1972). Reinforcement and helping behavior. *Journal of Applied Social Psychology, 2*, 360–371.

Moulton, D. G. (1977). Minimum odorant concentrations detectible by the dog and their implications for olfactory receptor sensitivity. In D. Muller-Schwarze & M. M. Mozelle (Eds.), *Chemical signals in vertebrates* (pp. 455–464). New York: Plenum Press.

Mountcastle, V. B. (1984). Central nervous mechanisms in mechanoreceptive sensibility. In I. Darian-Smith (Ed.), *Handbook of physiology—the nervous system III* (pp. 789–818). Bethesda, MD: American Physiological Society.

Mower, O. H., & Jones, H. M. (1945). Habit strength as a function of the pattern of rein-

forcement. *Journal of Experimental Psychology, 35*, 293–311.

Moyer, K. E. (1976). *The psychobiology of aggression*. New York: Harper & Row.

Mozell, K. M. (1970). Evidence for a chromatographic model of olfaction. *Journal of General Physiology, 56*, 46.

Mueller, C. G., & Rudolph, M. (1966). *Light and vision*. New York: Time-Life Books.

Mueller, C. W., Lisman, S. A., & Spear, N. E. (1983). Alcohol enhancement of human memory: Tests of consolidation and interference hypotheses. *Psychopharmacology, 80*, 226–230.

Mullen, B., Futrell, D., Stairs, O., Tice, D. M., Baumeister, R. F., Dawson, K. E., Riordan, C. A., Radloff, C. E., Goethals, G. R., Kennedy, J. G., & Rosenfeld, P. (1986). Newscasters' facial expressions and voting behavior of viewers: Can a smile elect a president? *Journal of Personality and Social Psychology, 51*, 291–295.

Muller, J. (1840). *Handbuch du physiologie des Menschen*. Coblenz: Holscher.

Murdock, B. B. (1961). The retention of individual items. *Journal of Experimental Psychology, 62*, 618–625.

Murdock, B. B. (1962). The serial position effect of free recall. *Journal of Experimental Psychology, 64*, 482–488.

Murray, D. J. (1983). *A history of Western psychology*. Englewood Cliffs, NJ: Prentice-Hall.

Murray, E. J. (1964). *Motivation and emotion*. Englewood Cliffs, NJ: Prentice-Hall.

Murray, H. A. (1938). *Explorations in personality*. New York: Oxford University Press.

Mussen, P., Eichorn, D. H., Honzik, M. P., Bieher, S. L., & Meredith, W. (1980). Continuity and change in women's characteristics over four decades. *International Journal of Behavioral Development, 3*, 333–347.

Mussen, P. H., Conger, J. J., Kagan, J., & Huston, A. C. (1984). *Child development and personality* (6th ed.). New York: Harper & Row.

Myers, B. J. (1984). Mother–infant bonding: Rejoinder to Kennell and Klaus. *Developmental Review, 4*, 283–288.

Myers, N. A., & Perlmutter, M. (1978). Memory in the years from two to five. In P. A. Ornstein (Ed.), *Memory development in children* (pp. 191–218). Hillsdale, NJ: Lawrence Erlbaum.

Myers, R. E. (1976). Comparative neurology of vocalization and speech: Proof of a dichotomy. In S. R. Harnad, H. D. Steklis, & J. Lancaster (Eds.), *Annals of the New York Academy of Sciences, 280*, 745–757.

Myserscough, R., & Taylor, S. P. (1985). The effects of marijuana on human physical aggression. *Journal of Personality and Social Psychology, 49*, 1541–1546.

Nagoshi, C. T., & Johnson, R. C. (1986). The ubiquity of *g*. *Personality and Individual Differences, 7*, 201–207.

Nahemow, L., & Lawton, M. P. (1975). Similarity and propinquity in friendship formation. *Journal of Personality and Social Psychology, 32*, 205–213.

Naitoh, P. (1976). Sleep deprivation in human subjects: A reappraisal. *Waking and Sleeping, 1*, 53–60.

Najinski, V. (1936). *The diary of Vaslav Najinski*.

New York: Simon & Schuster.

Naranjo, C., & Ornstein, R. E. (1971). *On the psychology of meditation*. New York: Penguin.

National Institutes of Mental Health. (1982). *Television and behavior: Ten years of scientific progress and implications for the eighties*. Vol. 1: *Summary Report*. Washington, D.C.: PHHS Publ. No. (ADM) 82–1195.

Natsoulas, T. (1978). Consciousness. *American Psychologist, 33*, 906–914.

Natsoulas, T. (1983). Addendum to 'consciousness.' *American Psychologist, 38*, 121–122.

Neale, J., & Oltmanns, T. F. (1980). *Schizophrenia*. New York: John Wiley & Sons.

Nebes, R. D. (1974). Hemispheric specialization in commisurotomized man. *Psychological Bulletin, 81*, 1–14.

Neimark, E. D. (1982). Cognitive development in adulthood: Using what you've got. In T. M. Field, A. Huston, H. C. Quay, & L. Troll (Eds.), *Review of human development* (pp. 435–446). New York: Wiley-Interscience.

Neisser, U. (1967). *Cognitive psychology*. Englewood Cliffs, NJ: Prentice-Hall.

Neisser, U. (1976). *Cognition and reality: Principles and implications*. San Francisco: Freeman.

Neisser, U., & Becklen, R. (1975). Selective looking: Attending to visually-specific events. *Cognitive Psychology, 7*, 480–494.

Nelson, J. D., Gelfand, D. M., & Hartmann, D. (1969). Children's aggression following competition and exposure to an aggressive model. *Child Development, 40*, 1085–1097.

Nelson, K. (1973). Some evidence for the cognitive primacy of categorization and its functional basis. *Merrill-Palmer Quarterly of Behavior and Development, 19*, 21–39.

Nelson, K. E., & Kosslyn, S. M. (1976). Recognition of previously labeled or unlabeled pictures by 5-year-olds and adults. *Journal of Experimental Child Psychology, 21*, 40–45.

Nelson, T. O. (1977). Repetition and depth of processing. *Journal of Verbal Learning and Verbal Behavior, 16*, 151–172.

Nelson, T. O., McSpadden, M., Fromme, K., & Marlatt, G. A. (1986). Effects of alcohol intoxication on metamemory and on retrieval from long-term memory. *Journal of Experimental Psychology: General, 115*, 247–254.

Nelson, T. O., & Rothbart, R. (1972). Acoustic savings for items forgotten from long-term memory. *Journal of Experimental Psychology, 93*, 357–360.

Nemeth, C. J. (1986). Differential contributions of majority and minority influence. *Psychological Review, 93*, 23–32.

Nesbitt, R. E., & Schachter, S. (1966). Cognitive manipulation of pain. *Journal of Experimental and Social Psychology, 2*, 227–236.

Neugarten, B. L. (1970). Dynamics of transition of middle age to old age. Adaptation and the life cycle. *Journal of Geriatric Psychiatry, 4*, 71–87.

Nevo, S. (1985). Bulimic symptoms: Prevalence and ethnic differences among college women. *International Journal of Eating Disorders, 4*, 151–168.

Newcomb, T. (1943). *Personality and social change*. New York: Dryden.

Newcomb, T. (1956). The prediction of interpersonal attraction. *American Psychologist, 11*, 575–586.

Newcomb, T. (1961). *The acquaintance process*. New York: Holt, Rinehart & Winston.

Newell, A., & Simon, H. (1972). *Human problem solving.* Englewood Cliffs, NJ: Prentice-Hall.

Newman, J. D. (1978). Perception of sounds used in species-specific communication: The auditory cortex and beyond. *Journal of Medical Primatology, 7,* 98–105.

Newman, J. D., & Wollberg, Z. (1973). Multiple coding of species-specific vocalizations in the auditory cortex of squirrel monkeys. *Brain Research, 54,* 287–304.

Newman, J. P., & Kosson, D. S. (1986). Passive avoidance learning in psychopathic and non-psychopathic offenders. *Journal of Abnormal Psychology, 95,* 252–256.

Newman, J. P., Widom, C. S., & Nathan, S. (1985). Passive-avoidance in syndromes of disinhibition: Psychopathy and extraversion. *Journal of Personality and Social Psychology, 48,* 1316–1327.

Newtson, D. (1974). Dispositional inference from effects of actions: Effects chosen and effects forgone. *Journal of Experimental Social Psychology, 10,* 489–496.

Newtson, D., & Czerlinsky, T. (1974). Adjustment of attitude communications for contrasts by extreme audiences. *Journal of Personality and Social Psychology, 30,* 829–837.

Nicholls, J. G. (1984). Achievement motivation: Conceptions of ability: Subjective experience, task choice, and performance. *Psychological Review, 91,* 328–346.

Nichols, R. (1978). Twin studies of ability, personality, and interests. *Home, 29,* 158–173.

Nichols, S. L., & Newman, J. P. (1986). Effects of punishment on response latency in extraverts. *Journal of Personality and Social Psychology, 50,* 624–630.

Nickerson, R. S., & Adams, M. J. (1979). Long-term memory for a common object. *Cognitive Psychology, 11,* 287–307.

Niedenthal, P. M., Cantor, N., & Kihlstrom, J. F. (1985). Prototype-matching: A strategy for social decision-making. *Journal of Personality and Social Psychology, 48,* 575–584.

Nilsson, L., Furuhjelm, M., Ingelman-Sundberg, A., & Wirsen, C. (1977). *A child is born.* New York: Delacorte Press/Seymour Laurence.

Nilsson, L., Lindberg, J., Ingvar, D., Nordfeldt, S., & Pettersson, R. (1974). *Behold man.* Boston: Little, Brown.

Nisbett, R. E., & Wilson, T. (1977). The halo effect: Evidence for unconscious alteration of judgments. *Journal of Personality and Social Psychology, 35,* 250–256.

Nolen-Hoeksema, S., Girgus, J. S., & Seligman, M. E. P. (1986). Learned helplessness in children: A longitudinal study of depression, achievement, and explanatory style. *Journal of Personality and Social Psychology, 51.*

Norgren, R. (1984). Centural neural mechanisms of taste. In I. Darian-Smith (Ed.), *Handbook of physiology—the nervous system III* (pp. 1087–1128). Bethesda, MD: American Physiological Society.

Norman, D. A. (1968). Toward a theory of memory and attention. *Psychological Review, 75,* 522–536.

Norman, W. T. (1963). Toward an adequate taxonomy of personality attributes: Replicated factor structure in peer nomination personality ratings. *Journal of Abnormal and Social Psychology, 66,* 574–583.

Norman-Jackson, J. (1982). Family interactions, language development, and primary reading achievement of Black children in families of low income. *Child Development, 53,* 349–358.

Novin, D., & VanderWeele, D. A. (1977). Visceral involvement in feeding: There is more to regulation than the hypothalamus. In J. M. Spague & A. N. Epstein, *Progress in psychobiology and physiological psychology* (193–241). New York: Academic Press.

Noyes, R., Clancy, J., Hoenk, P. R., & Slymen, D. J. (1980). The prognosis of anxiety neurosis. *Archives of General Psychiatry, 37,* 173–178.

Nunnally, J. C. (1978). *Psychometric theory.* New York: McGraw-Hill.

O'Brien, C. P. (1976). Experimental analysis of conditioning factors in human narcotic addictions. *Pharmacological Reviews, 27,* 533–543.

O'Brien, D. F. (1982). The chemistry of vision. *Science, 218,* 961–966.

O'Brien, M., & Huston, A. C. (1985). Development of sex-typed behavior in toddlers. *Developmental Psychology, 21,* 866–871.

O'Hara, M. W. (1986). Social support, life events, and depression during pregnancy and the puerperium. *Archives of General Psychiatry, 43,* 569–573.

O'Hara, M. W., Behm, L. P., & Campbell, S. B. (1982). Predicting depressive symptomatology: Cognitive-behavioral models and postpartum depression. *Journal of Abnormal Psychology, 91,* 457–461.

Oakley, D. A., & Eames, L. C. (1985). The plurality of consciousness. In D. A. Oakley (Ed.), *Brain and mind* (pp. 217–251). London: Methuen.

Obrist, W. D. (1976). Problems of aging. In G. E. Chatrian & G. C. Lairy (Eds.), *Handbook of electroencephalography and clinical neurophysiology* (pp. 6A275–6A292). Amsterdam: Elsevier.

Ohman, A., Dimberg, U., & Ost, L. G. (1984). Animal and social phobias: Biological constraints on learned fear responses. In S. Reiss & R. Bootzin (Eds.), *Theoretical issues in behavior therapy.* New York: Academic Press.

Oldenberg, B., Perkins, R. J., & Andrews, G. (1985). Controlled trial of psychological intervention of myocardial infarction. *Journal of Consulting and Clinical Psychology, 53,* 852–859.

Oldfield, S. R., & Parker, S. P. A. (1984). Acuity of sound localisation: A topography of auditory space. I. Normal hearing conditions. *Perception, 13,* 581–600. (a)

Oldfield, S. R., & Parker, S. P. A. (1984). Acuity of sound localisation: A topography of auditory space. II. Pinna cues absent. *Perception, 13,* 601–618. (b)

Olds, J., & Milner, P. (1954). Positive reinforcement produced by electrical stimulation of septal area and other regions of the rat brain. *Journal of Comparative and Physiological Psychology, 47,* 419–427.

Oller, D. K., & Eilers, R. E. (1982). Similarity of babbling in Spanish- and English-learning babies. *Journal of Child Language, 9,* 565–577.

Olson, L. (1985). On the use of transplants to counteract the symptoms of Parkinson's disease: Background, experimental models, and possible clinical applications. In C. W. Cotman (Ed.), *Synaptic plasticity* (pp. 485–505). New York: Guilford.

Olton, D. S. (1984). In L. R. Squire & N. Butters, (Eds.), *Neuropsychology of memory* (pp. 367–373). New York: Guilford.

Olweus, D. (1977). A critical analysis of the "modern" interactionist position. In D. Magnusson & N. S. Endler (Eds.), *Personality at the crossroads: Current issues in interactional psychology.* Hillsdale, NJ: Lawrence Erlbaum.

Olweus, D. (1979). The stability of aggressive reaction patterns in human males: A review. *Psychological Bulletin, 85,* 852–875.

Orne, M. T. (1972). Can a hypnotized subject be compelled to carry out otherwise unacceptable behavior? *International Journal of Clinical and Experimental Hypnosis, 20,* 101–117.

Orne, M. T. (1979). The use and misuse of hypnosis in court. *International Journal of Clinical and Experimental Hypnosis, 27,* 311–341.

Orne, M. T., Sheehan, P. W., & Evans, F. J. (1968). Occurrence of posthypnotic behavior outside the experimental setting. *Journal of Personality and Social Psychology, 9,* 189–196.

Osgood, C. E. (1965). Cross cultural comparability of attitude measurement via multilingual semantic differentials. In I. S. Steiner & M. Fishbein (Eds.), *Recent studies in social psychology.* New York: Holt, Rinehart, & Winston.

Osgood, C. E., Suci, G. J., & Tannenbaum, P. H. (1957). *The measurement of meaning.* Urbana: University of Illinois Press.

Osterberg, G. (1935). Topography of the layer of rods and cones in the human retina. *Acta Ophthalmologica. Klh., Supplement, 6,* 1–106.

Ottoson, J.-O. (1985). Use and misuse of electroconvulsive treatment. *Biological Psychiatry, 20,* 933–946.

Oviatt, S. L. (1980). The emerging ability to comprehend language: An experimental approach. *Child Development, 51,* 97–106.

Paccia-Cooper, J., & Cooper, W. E. (1981). The processing of phrase structures in speech production. In P. D. Eimas, & J. L. Miller (Eds.) *Perspectives in the study of speech* (pp. 311–336). Hillsdale, NJ: Lawrence Erlbaum.

Pack, G. T., & McNeer, G. (1943). Total gastrectomy for cancer: Collective review of literature and original report of twenty cases. *International Abstracts of Surgery, 77,* 265–299.

Page, D., & O'Neal, E. (1977). "Weapons effect" without demand characteristics. *Psychological Reports, 41,* 29–30.

Page, M. M., & Scheidt, R. J. (1971). The elusive weapons effect: Demand awareness evaluation apprehension, and slightly sophisticated subjects. *Journal of Personality and Social Psychology, 20,* 304–318.

Paivio, A. (1971). *Imagery and verbal processes.* New York: Holt, Rinehart, & Winston.

Paivio, A., & Csapo, K. (1973). Picture superiority in free recall: Imagery or dual coding? *Cognitive Psychology, 5,* 176–206.

Palkovitz, R. (1985). Fathers' birth attendance, early contact, and extended contact with their newborns: A critical review. *Child Development, 56,* 392–406.

Panksepp, J., & DeEskinazi, F. G. (1980). Opiates and homing. *Journal of Comparative and Physiological Psychology, 94,* 650–663.

Panksepp, J., Meeker, R., & Bean, N. J. (1980). The neurochemical control of crying. *Pharmacology Biochemistry & Behavior, 12,* 437–443.

Panksepp, J., Sivig, S. M., & Normansell, L. A. (1985). Brain opioidy and social emotions. In M. Reite & T. Field (Eds.), *The psychobiology of attachment and separation* (pp. 3–49). New York: Academic Press.

Papausek, H. (1967). Experimental studies of appetitional behavior in human newborns and infants. In H. W. Stevenson, E. H. Hess, & H. L. Rheingold (Eds.), *Early behavior* (pp. 249–277). New York: John Wiley & Sons.

Parasuraman, R. (1984). Sustained attention in detection and discrimination. In R. Parasuraman & D. R. Davies (Eds.), *Varieties of attention* (pp. 243–271). Orlando, FL: Academic Press.

Parasuraman, R., & Davies, D. R. (Eds.). (1984). *Varieties of attention.* Orlando, FL: Academic Press.

Pare, W. P., Krothfeld, B., Isom, K. E., & Varady, A. (1973). Cholesterol synthesis and metabolism as a function of unpredictable shock stimulation. *Physiology and Behavior, 11,* 107–110.

Parke, R. D., & Tinsley, B. R. (1981). The father's role in infancy: Determinants of involvement in caregiving and play. In M. E. Lamb (Ed.), *The role of the father in child development* (pp. 429–457). New York: John Wiley & Sons.

Parker, D. E. (1980). The vestibular apparatus. *Scientific American, 243,* 118–135.

Parloff, M. B. (1986). Placebo controls in psychotherapy research: A sine qua non or a placebo for research problems. *Journal of Consulting and Clinical Psychology, 54,* 79–87.

Parmalee, A. H., Jr., & Sigman, M. D. (1983). Perinatal brain development and behavior. In P. H. Mussen (Ed.), *Handbook of child psychology,* Vol. II.
Infancy and developmental psychobiology (pp. 95–155). New York: John Wiley & Sons.

Parmalee, A. H., Jr., Wenner, W. H., & Schulz, H. R. (1964). Infant sleep patterns: From birth to 16 weeks of age. *Journal of Pediatrics, 65,* 576–582.

Parry, B. L., & Rush, A. J. (1979). Oral contraceptives and depressive symptomatolgy: Biologic mechanisms. *Comprehensive Psychiatry, 20,* 347–358.

Patel, A. J. (1983). Undernutrition and brain development. *Trends in Neurosciences, 6,* 151–153.

Patterson, F. (1978). The gestures of a gorilla: Sign language in another pongid species. *Brain and Language, 5,* 72–97.

Patterson, F., & Linden, E. (1981). *The education of Koko.* New York: Holt, Rinehart, & Winston.

Patterson, G. R. (1971). *Families: Applications of social learning to family life.* Champaign, IL: Research Press.

Patterson, G. R., Littman, R. A., & Bricker, W. (1967). Assertive behavior in children: A step toward a theory of aggression. *Monographs of the Society for Research in Child Development, 32,* No. 5.

Paul, G. L. (1966). *Insight vs. desensitization in psychotherapy.* Stanford, CA: Stanford University Press.

Paunonen, S. V., & Jackson, D. N. (1985). Idiographic measurement strategies for personality and prediction: Some unredeemed promissory notes. *Psychological Review, 92,* 486–511.

Pavlov, I. P. (1960). *Conditioned reflexes.* New York: Dover. (Originally published, 1927).

Payne, D. G. (1987). Hyperamnesia and reminiscence in recall: A historical and empirical review. *Psychological Bulletin, 101,* 5–27.

Payne, M., & Cooper, W. E. (1985). Paralexic errors in Broca's and Wernicke's aphasia. *Neuropsychologica, 23,* 571–574.

Penfield, W. (1958). Functional localization in temporal and deep sylvian areas. *Research Publication of the Association for Research on Nervous and Mental Disease, 36,* 210–226. (a)

Penfield, W. (1958). *The excitable cortex in conscious man.* Liverpool: University of Liverpool Press. (b)

Penfield, W., & Jasper, H. H. (1954). *Epilepsy and the functional anatomy of the human brain.* Boston: Little Brown.

Penfield, W., & Rasmussen, T. (1952). *The cerebral cortex of man.* New York: Macmillan.

Penrod, S. (1986). *Social psychology.* Englewood Cliffs, NJ: Prentice-Hall.

Penrose, L. S., & Penrose, R. (1958). Impossible objects: A special type of illusion. *British Journal of Psychology, 49,* 31–33.

Perachio, A. A., Marr, C. D., & Alexander, M. (1979). Sexual behavior in male rhesus monkeys elicited by electrical stimulation of preoptic and hypothalamic area. *Brain Research, 177,* 127–144.

Perin, C. T. (1942). Behavioral potentiality as a joint function of the amount of training and the degree of hunger at the time of extinction. *Journal of Experimental Psychology, 30,* 93–113.

Perl, E. R. (1984). Characterization of nociceptors and their activation of neurons in the superficial dorsal horn—1st steps for the sensation of pain. In L. Kruger & J. C. Liebeskind (Eds.), *Neural mechanisms of pain: Advances in pain research and therapy* (pp. 23–52). New York: Raven Press.

Perlmutter, M., & Hall, E. (1985). *Adult development and aging.* New York: John Wiley & Sons.

Perry, M. A., & Furukawa, M. J. (1986). Modeling methods. In F. H. Kanfer & A. P. Goldstein (Eds.), *Helping people change: A textbook of methods.* New York: Pergamon.

Persons, J. B., & Rao, P. A. (1981). *Cognitions and depression in psychiatric inpatients.* Unpublished manuscript, University of Pennsylvania, cited in Peterson & Seligman, 1984.

Pervin, L. A. (1984). *Current controversies & issues in personality* (2nd ed.). New York: John Wiley & Sons.

Peters, A., Palay, S. L., & Webster, H. de F. (1976). *The fine structure of the nervous system: The neurons and supporting cells.* Philadelphia: Saunders.

Peterson, C., & Seligman, M. E. P. (1984). Causal explanations as a risk factor for depression: Theory and evidence. *Psychological Review, 91,* 347–374.

Peterson, R. C., & Thurstone, L. L. (1933). *The effect of motion pictures on the social attitudes of high school children.* Chicago: University of Chicago Press.

Petti, T. A. (1981). *Active treatment of childhood depression.* In J. F. Clarkin & H. I. Glazer (Eds.), *Depression: Behavioral and directive intervention strategies.* New York: Garland STPM Press.

Petty, R. E., & Cacioppo, J. T. (1977). Fore-

warning, cognitive responding, and resistance to persuasion. *Journal of Personality and Social Psychology, 35,* 645–655.

Petty, R. E., & Cacioppo, J. T. (1979). Effects of forewarning of persuasive intent and involvement on cognitive responses and persuasion. *Personality and Social Psychology Bulletin, 5,* 173–176.

Petty, R. E., & Cacioppo, J. T. (1981). *Attitudes and persuasion: Classic and contemporary approaches.* Dubuque, IA: Brown.

Pfaff, D. W. (1980). *Estrogens and brain function: Neural analysis of a gonmone-controlled mammalian reproductive behavior.* New York: Springer-Verlag.

Pfaffman, C., Frank, M., Bartoshuk, L. M., & Snell, T. C. (1979). Coding gustatory information in the squirrel monkey chorda tympani. *Progress in Psychobiology and Physiological Psychology, 6,* 1–27.

Phillips, D. P., & Brugge, J. F. (1985). Progress in neurophysiology of sound localization. *Annual Review of Psychology, 36,* 245–274.

Phillips, D. P., & Hensley, J. E. (1984). When violence is rewarded or punished: The impact of mass media stories on homicide. *Journal of Communication, 34,* 101–116.

Phillips, J. L., Jr. (1982). *Statistical thinking: A structural approach* (2nd ed.). San Francisco: Freeman.

Piaget, J. (1932/1965). *The moral judgment of the child.* New York: The Free Press.

Piaget, J. (1936/1952). *The origins of intelligence in children.* New York: International Universities Press.

Piaget, J. (1971). The theory of stages in cognitive development. In D. R. Green, M. P. Ford, & G. B. Flamer (Eds.), *Measurement and Piaget* (pp. 1–11). New York: McGraw-Hill.

Piaget, J. (1983). Piaget's theory. In W. Kessen (Ed.), *Handbook of child psychology* (4th ed.). *History, theory, and methods* (pp. 103–128). New York: John Wiley & Sons.

Piaget, J., & Inhelder, B. (1948/1967). *The child's conception of space.* New York: Norton.

Piliavin, I., Rodin, J., & Piliavin, J. (1969). Good Samaritanism: An underground phenomenon? *Journal of Personality and Social Psychology, 13,* 288–299.

Piliavin, J. A., Dovidio, J. F., Gaertner, S. L., & Clark, R. D., III. (1981). *Emergency intervention.* New York: Academic Press.

Piotrowski, Z. (1957). *Percepanalysis.* New York: Macmillan.

Pirenne, M. H. (1967). *Vision and the eye.* London: Chapman & Hall.

Pirke, K. M., & Ploog, D. (1986). Psychobiology of anorexia nervosa. In R. J. Wurtman and J. J. Wurtman (Eds.), *Nutrition and the brain* (Vol. 7, pp. 167–198). New York: Raven Press.

Pitts, F. N., Jr., & McClure, J. N., Jr. (1967). Lactate metabolism in anxiety neurosis. *New England Journal of Medicine, 277,* 1328–1336.

Plomin, R., Willerman, L., & Loehlin, J. C. (1976). Resemblance in appearance and the equal environments assumption in twin studies of personality? *Behavior Genetics, 6,* 43–52.

Plotnick, R., Mir, D., & Delgado, J. M. R. (1971). Aggression noxiousness and brain stimulation in unrestrained rhesus monkeys. In B. E. Eleftheriou & J. P. Scoh (Eds.), *The physiology of aggression and defeat.* New York: Plenum Press.

Plutchik, R. (1980). *Emotion: A psychoevolutionary synthesis*. New York: Harper & Row.

Pohorecky, L. A. (1977). Biphasic action of ethanol. *Biobehavioral Reviews, 1*, 231–240.

Pollack, I., & Pickett, J. M. (1964). The intelligibility of excerpts from conversational speech. *Language and Speech, 6*, 165–171.

Pomeranz, B. (1982). Acupuncture and the endorphins. *Ethos, 10*, 385–393.

Poon, L. W. (1985). Differences in human memory with aging: Nature, causes, and clinical implications. In J. E. Birren & K. W. Schaie (Eds.), *Handbook of the psychology of aging* (pp. 427–462). New York: Van Nostrand Reinhold.

Posner, M. I. (1973). *Cognition: An introduction*. Glenview, IL: Scott, Foresman.

Posner, M. I. (1985). Chronometric measures of *g*. *The Behavioral and Brain Sciences, 8*, 237–238.

Post, R. M. (1986). Does limbic system dysfunction play a role in affective illness? In B. K. Doane & K. E. Livingston (Eds.), *Limbic system—functional organization and clinical disorders* (pp. 229–250). New York: Raven Press.

Postman, L., Stark, K., & Fraser, J. (1968). Temporal changes in interference. *Journal of Verbal Learning and Verbal Behavior, 7*, 672–694.

Potkay, C. R., & Allen, B. P. (1986). *Personality: Theory, research, and applications*. Belmont, CA: Brooks/Cole.

Poznanski, E., Mokvos, H. B., Grossman, J., & Freeman, F. N. (1985). Diagnostic criteria in childhood depression. *American Journal of Psychiatry, 142*, 1168–1173.

Prather, J., & Fidell, L. S. (1975). Sex differences in the content and style of medical advertisements. *Social Science of Medicine, 9*, 23–26.

Pratkanis, A. R., Greenwald, A. G., Leippe, M. R., & Baumgardner, M. H. (1985). *In search of reliable persuasion effects: III. The sleeper effect is dead. Long live the sleeper effect*. Manuscript submitted for publication.

Premack, A. J., & Premack, D. (1972). Teaching language to an ape. *Scientific American, 227*, 92–99.

Premack, D. (1971). Language in chimpanzee? *Science, 172*, 808–822.

Price, J. S. (1978). Chronic depressive illness. *British Medical Journal, 1*, 1200–1201.

Price-Williams, D. (1981). Concrete and formal operations. In R. H. Monroe, R. L. Monroe, & B. B. Whiting (Eds.), *Handbook of Cross-cultural Human Development* (pp. 403–422). New York: Garland STM Press.

Prioleau, L., Murdock, M., & Brody, N. (1983). An analysis of psychotherapy versus placebo studies. *The Behavioral and Brain Sciences, 6*, 275–310.

Pruitt, D. G. (1968). Reciprocity and credit building in a laboratory dyad. *Journal of Personality and Social Psychology, 8*, 143–147.

Puccetti, R. (1981). The case for mental duality: Evidence from split-brain data and other considerations. *Behavioral and Brain Sciences, 4*, 93–123.

Puccetti, R., & Dykes, R. W. (1978). Sensory cortex and the mind-brain problem. *Behavioral and Brain Sciences, 1*, 337–343.

Pylyshyn, Z. W. (1979). Imagery theory: Not mysterious—just wrong. *Behavioral and Brain Sciences, 2*, 561–563.

Pylyshyn, Z. W. (1981). The imagery debate: Analogue media versus tacit knowledge. *Psychological Review, 88*, 16–45.

Pylyshyn, Z. W. (1984). *Computation and cognition: Toward a foundation for cognitive science*. Cambridge, MA: MIT Press.

Quillian, M. R. (1967). Word concepts: A theory and simulation of some basic semantic capabilities. *Behavioral Science, 12*, 410–430.

Quinsey, V. L., Chaplin, T. C., & Upfold, D. (1984). Sexual arousal to nonsexual violence and sadomasochistic themes among rapists and non-sex-offenders. *Journal of Consulting and Clinical Psychology, 52*, 651–657.

Rabbie, J. M. (1963). Differential preference for companionship under threat. *Journal of Abnormal and Social Psychology, 67*, 643–648.

Rabbitt, P. (1977). Changes in problem solving in old age. In J. E. Birren & K. W. Schaie (Eds.), *Handbook of the psychology of aging* (pp. 606–625). New York: Van Nostrand Reinhold.

Rabbitt, P. M. A. (1985). Oh *g* Dr. Jensen! or, *g*-ing up cognitive psychology. *The Behavioral and Brain Sciences, 8*, 238–239.

Rachman, S. J., & Wilson, G. T. (1980). *The effects of psychological therapy* (2nd ed.). Homewood, IL: Dorsey.

Rahe, R. H., Rubin, R. T., & Arthur, R. J. (1974). The three investigators study: Serum uric acid, cholesterol, and cortisol variability during stresses of everyday life. *Psychosomatic Medicine, 36*, 258–268.

Ramirez, J., Bryant, J., & Zillmann, D. (1982). Effects of erotica on retaliatory behavior as a function of level of prior provocation. *Journal of Personality and Social Psychology, 43*, 971–978.

Rand, G., & Wapner, S. (1967). Postural states as a factor in memory. *Journal of Verbal Learning and Verbal Behavior, 6*, 268–271.

Randi, J. (1978). The psychology of conjuring. *Technology Review, 80*, 56–63.

Rapaport, D., Gill, M., & Schafer, R. (1945, 1946). *Diagnostic psychological testing* (Vol. I & II). Chicago: Yearbook Publishers.

Raphael, B. (1976). *The thinking computer*. San Francisco: Freeman.

Raps, C. S., Peterson, C., Reinhard, K. S., Abramson, L. Y., & Seligman, M. E. P. (1982). Attributional style among depressed patients. *Journal of Abnormal Psychology, 91*, 102–108.

Rawlins, J. N. P. (1985). Associations across time: The hippocampus as a temporary memory store. *Behavioral and Brain Sciences, 8*, 479–496.

Raynor, J. O. (1970). Relationships between achievement-related motives, future orientation, and academic performance. *Journal of Personality and Social Psychology, 15*, 28–33.

Razran, G. H. S. (1940). Conditioned responses: A classified bibliography. *Psychological Bulletin, 37*, 481.

Razrin, G. (1965). Evolutionary psychology: Levels of learning and perception and thinking. In B. Wolman (Ed.), *Scientific psychology: Principles and approaches*. New York: Basic Books.

Read, J. D., & Bruce, D. (1982). Longitudinal tracking of difficult memory retrievals. *Cognitive Psychology, 14*, 280–300.

Redel, W. H., & Andrykowski, M. A. (1982). Behavioral intervention in cancer treatment: Controlling aversion reactions to chemotherapy. *Journal of Consulting and Clinical Psychology, 50*, 1018–1029.

Reed, S. K., Dempster, A., & Ettinger, M. (1985). Usefulness of analogous solutions for solving algebra word problems. *Journal of Experimental Psychology: Learning, Memory, and Cognition, 11*, 106–125.

Reese, H. W., & Rodeheaver, D. (1985). Problem solving and complex decision making. In J. E. Birren, & K. W. Schaie (Eds.), *Handbook of the psychology of aging* (pp. 474–499). New York: Van Nostrand Reinhold.

Regan, D. T., & Fazio, R. (1977). On the consistency between attitudes and behavior: Look to the method of attitude formation. *Journal of Experimental Social Psychology, 13*, 28–45.

Regan, D. T., & Totten, J. (1975). Empathy and attribution: Turning observers into actors. *Journal of Personality and Social Psychology, 32*, 850–856.

Reichlin, S. (1978). Introduction. In S. Reichlin, R. J. Baldessarini, & J. B. Martin (Eds.), *The hypothalamus* (pp. 1–14). New York: Raven Press.

Reier, P. J., Stensaas, L. J., & Guth, L. (1983). The astrocytic scar as an impediment to regeneration in the central nervous system. In C. C. Kao, R. P. Bunge, & P. J. Reier (Eds.), *Spinal cord reconstruction* (pp. 163–195). New York: Raven Press.

Reis, H. T., Nezlek, J., & Wheeler, L. (1980). Physical attractiveness in social interaction. *Journal of Personality and Social Psychology, 38*, 604–617.

Reitman, J. S. (1976). Skilled perception in Go: Deducing memory structures from inter-response times. *Cognitive Psychology, 8*, 336–356.

Rescorla, R. A. (1967). Pavlovian conditioning and its proper control procedures. *Psychological Review, 74*, 71–80.

Rest, J. R., Davison, M. L., & Robbins, S. (1978). Age trends in judging moral issues: A review of cross-sectional, longitudinal, and sequential studies of the Defining Issues Test. *Child Development, 49*, 263–279.

Restak, R. (1984). *The brain*. New York: Bantam Books.

Revusky, S. (1967). Hunger level during food consumption: Effects on subsequent preferences. *Psychonomic Science, 7*, 109–110.

Reymond, L. (1985). Spatial visual acuity of the eagle Aquila audax: A behavioural, optical and anatomical investigation. *Vision Research, 25*, 1477–1491.

Reynolds, A. G., & Flagg, P. W. (1983). *Cognitive psychology* (2nd ed.). Boston: Little, Brown.

Reynolds, D. V. (1969). Surgery in the rat during electrical analgesia induced by focal brain stimulation. *Science, 164*, 444–445.

Rheingold, H. L., & Eckerman, C. O. (1971). Departures from the mother. In H. R. Schaffer (Ed.), *The origins of human social relations*. New York: Academic Press.

Rhodewalt, F., & Agustsdottir, S. (1986). Effects of self-presentation on the phenomenal self. *Journal of Personality and Social Psychology, 50*, 47–55.

Richardson, P. H., & Vincent, C. A. (1986).

Acupuncture for the treatment of pain—a review of evaluative research. *Pain, 24,* 15–40.

Richardson, P. M., Aguayo, A. J., & McGuinnes, U. M. (1983). Role of sheath cells in axonal regeneration. In C. C. Kao, P. Bunge, & P. J. Reier (Eds.), *Spinal cord reconstruction* (pp. 293–304). New York: Raven Press.

Rickels, K. (1979). Psychopharmacological approaches to treatment of anxiety. In W. E. Fann, I. Karacan, A. D. Pokorny, & R. L. Williams (Eds.), *Phenomenology and treatment of anxiety.* New York: Spectrum.

Riegel, K. F., & Riegel, R. M. (1972). Development, drop and death. *Developmental Psychology, 6,* 306–319.

Riley, V., & Spackman, D. (1974). Modifying effects of a benign virus on the malignant process and the role of physiological stress on tumor incidence. In Fogarty International Center Proceedings No. 28 (DHEW Publication No. 77–893). Washington, DC: U.S. Government Printing Office.

Rips, L. J., & Marcus, S. L. (1977) Suppositions and the analysis of conditional sentences. In M. A. Just & P. A. Carpenter (Eds.), *Cognitive processes in comprehension.* Hillsdale, NJ: Lawrence Erlbaum.

Rips, L. J., Shoben, E. J., & Smith, E. E. (1973). Semantic distance and the verification of semantic relations. *Journal of Verbal Learning and Verbal Behavior, 12,* 1–20.

Roberts, D. F. (1982). Children and commercials: Issues, evidence, interventions. *Prevention in Human Services, 2,* 19–36.

Robinson, D. A. (1976). Adaptive gain control of vestibulo-ocular reflex by the cerebellum. *Journal of Neurophysiology, 39,* 954–969.

Rodin, J. (1981). Current status of the internal-external hypothesis for obesity. What went wrong? *American Psychologist, 36,* 361–372.

Roedder, D. L., Sternthal, B., & Calder, B. J. (1983). Attitude-behavior consistency in children's responses to television advertising. *Journal of Marketing Research, 20,* 337–349.

Roeder, K. D. (1963). *Nerve cells and insect behavior.* Cambridge, MA: Harvard University Press.

Roediger, H. L. (1984). Does current evidence from dissociation experiments favor the episodic/semantic distinction? Commentary on Tulving, E., *Precis of elements of episodic memory: The behavioral and brain sciences, 7,* 252–254.

Roffwarg, H. P., Munzio, J. N., & Dement, W. C. (1966). Ontogenic development of the human sleep-dream cycle. *Science, 152,* 604–619.

Rogawski, M. A. (1985). Norepinephrine. In M. A. Rogawski & J. L. Barker (Eds.), *Neurotransmitter actions in the vertebrate nervous system* (pp. 241–284). New York: Plenum Press.

Rogel, M. J. (1978). A critical evaluation of the possibility of higher primate reproductive and sexual pheromones. *Psychological Bulletin, 85,* 810–830.

Rogers, C. (1951). *Client-centered therapy: Its current practice, implication, and theory.* Boston: Houghton Mifflin.

Rogers, C. R. (1959). A theory of therapy, personality, and interpersonal relationships, as developed in the client-centered framework. In S. Koch (Ed.), *Psychology: A study of a sci-*

ence (Vol. 3). New York: McGraw-Hill.

Rogers, C. R. (1980). *A way of being.* Boston, MA: Houghton Mifflin.

Rogers, C. R., & Stevens, B. (1967). *Person to person.* Walnut Creek, CA: Real People Press.

Rogers, T. B. (1977). Self reference in memory: Recognition of personality items. *Journal of Research in Personality, 11,* 295–305.

Rogers, T. B. (1981). A model of the self as an aspect of human information processing. In N. Cantor & J. Kihlstrom (Eds.), *Personality, cognition, and social interaction.* Hillsdale, NJ: Lawrence Erlbaum.

Roland, P. E., & Friberg, L. (1985). Localization of cortical areas activated by thinking. *Journal of Neurophysiology, 53,* 1219–1243.

Roland, P. E., Larsen, B., Lassen, N. A., & Skinhoj, E. (1980). Supplementary motor area and other cortical areas in organization of voluntary movements in man. *Journal of Neurophysiology, 43,* 118–136.

Rosch, E. (1973). On the internal structure of perceptual and semantic categories. In T. E. Moore (Ed.), *Cognitive development and the acquisition of language.* New York: Academic Press.

Rosch, E. (1975). Cognitive representations of semantic categories. *Journal of Experimental Psychology: General, 104,* 192–223.

Rosch, E., Mervis, C. B., Gray, W., Johnson, D., & Boyes-Braem, P. (1976). Basic objects in natural categories. *Cognitive Psychology, 8,* 382–439.

Rosen, C. M. (September 1987). The eerie world of reunited twins. *Discover,* 36–46.

Rosenberg, M. (1986). Self-concept from middle childhood through adolescence. In J. Suls, A. G. Greenwald (Eds.), *Psychological perspectives on the self* (pp. 107–136). Hillsdale, NJ: Lawrence Erlbaum.

Rosenberg, S., Nelson, C., & Vivekananthan, P. S. (1968). A multidimensional approach to the structure of personality impressions. *Journal of Personality and Social Psychology, 9,* 283 291.

Rosenblatt, P. C., & Anderson, R. M. (1981). Human sexuality in cross-cultural perspective. In M. Cook (Ed.), *The bases of human sexual attraction* (pp. 215–250). London and New York: Academic Press.

Rosenfeld, P., Giacalone, R., & Tedeschi, J. T. (1983). Cognitive dissonance vs. impression management. *Journal of Social Psychology, 120,* 203–211.

Rosenhan, D. L. (1973). On being sane in insane places. *Science, 179,* 250–258.

Rosenhan, D. L., & Seligman, M. E. P. (1984). *Abnormal psychology.* New York: Norton.

Rosenthal, R., & Rosnow, R. L. (1969). The volunteer subject. In R. Rosenthal & R. Rosnow (Eds.), *Artifact in behavioral research.* New York: Academic Press.

Rosenthal, R., & Rosnow, R. L. (1975). *The volunteer subject.* New York: John Wiley & Sons.

Rosenzweig, M. R. (1984). Experience, memory, and the brain. *American Psychologist, 39,* 365–376.

Rosenzweig, M. R., & Leiman, A. L. (1982). *Physiological psychology.* Lexington, MA: D. C. Heath.

Ross, B. H. (1981). The more the better? Number of decisions as a determinant of memorability. *Memory & Cognition, 9,* 23–33.

Ross, E. D. (1984). Right hemisphere's role in

language, affective behavior and emotion. *Trends in Neurosciences, 7,* 342–346.

Ross, K. G., & Fletcher, D. J. (1985). Comparative study of genetic and social structure in two forms of the fire ant *Solenopsis invicta* (Hymenoptera: Formicidae). *Behavioral Ecology and Sociobiology, 17,* 349–356.

Ross, L. (1977). The intuitive psychologist and his shortcomings: Distortions in the attribution process. In L. Berkowitz (Ed.), *Advances in experimental social psychology* (Vol. 10). New York: Academic Press.

Ross, L., Amabile, T. M., & Steinmetz, J. L. (1977). Social roles, social control, and bias in social-perception processes. *Journal of Personality and Social Psychology, 35,* 485–494.

Ross, L., Greene, D., & House, P. (1977). The "false consensus effect": An egocentric bias in social perception and attribution processes. *Journal of Experimental Social Psychology, 13,* 270–301.

Ross, M., & Schulman, R. (1973). Increasing the salience of initial attitudes: Dissonance versus self-perception theory. *Journal of Personality and Social Psychology, 28,* 138–144.

Rossiter, J. R., & Percy, L. (1983). Visual communication in advertising. In R. J. Harris (Ed.), *Information processing research in advertising.* Hillsdale, NJ: Lawrence Erlbaum.

Roth, E. M., & Shoben, E. E. (1983). The effect of context on the structure of categories. *Cognitive Psychology, 15,* 346–379.

Routtenberg, A. (1978). The reward system of the brain. *Scientific American, 239,* 154–165.

Rowland, N. E., & Antelman, S. M. (1976). Stress-induced hyperphagia and obesity in rats: A possible model for understanding human obesity. *Science, 191,* 310–312.

Rubin, L. (1979). *Women of a certain age: The midlife search for self.* New York: Harper & Row.

Rubin, Z. (1973). *Liking and loving: An invitation to social psychology.* New York: Holt, Rinehart & Winston.

Ruchalla, E., Schalt, E., & Vogel, F. (1985). Relations between mental performance and reaction time: New aspects of an old problem. *Intelligence, 9,* 189–205.

Rule, B. G., & Hewitt, L. S. (1971). Effects of thwarting on cardiac response and physical aggression. *Journal of Personality and Social Psychology, 19,* 181–187.

Rumbaugh, D. (Ed.), (1977). *Language learning in a chimpanzee.* New York: Academic Press.

Rundus, D. (1971). Analysis of rehearsal processes in free recall. *Journal of Experimental Psychology, 89,* 63–77.

Rundus, D., & Atkinson, R. C. (1970). Rehearsal processes in free recall: A procedure for direct observation. *Journal of Verbal Learning and Verbal Behavior, 9,* 99–105.

Runnig, H. (1972). Psychological studies of Kalahari Bushmen. In L. J. Cronbach & P. J. D. Drenth (Eds.), *Mental tests and cultural adaptation.* The Hague: Monton.

Rushton, J. P. (1975). Generosity in children: Immediate and long-term effects of modeling, preaching and moral judgment. *Journal of Personality and Social Psychology, 31,* 459–466.

Rushton, J. P. (1980). *Altruism, socialization and society.* Englewood Cliffs, NJ: Prentice-Hall.

Rushton, J. P., & Campbell, A. C. (1977). Modeling, vicarious reinforcement and extraversion on blood donating in adults: Immediate and long-term effects. *European Journal of Social Psychology, 7,* 297–306.

Rushton, J. P., Jackson, D. N., & Paunonen, S. V. (1981). Personality: Nomothetic or idiographic? A response to Kenrick and Stringfield. *Psychological Review, 88,* 582–589.

Rushton, J. P., & Teachman, G. (1978). The effects of positive reinforcement, attributions, and punishment on model induced altruism in children. *Personality and Social Psychology Bulletin, 4,* 322–325.

Rushton, W. A. H. (1962). Visual pigments in man. *Scientific American, 207,* 120–132.

Rushton, W. A. H. (1975). Visual pigments and color blindness. *Scientific American, 232,* 64.

Russeck, M. (1971). Hepatic factors and the neurophysiological mechanisms controlling feeding behavior. In S. Ehrenpries (Ed.), *Neurosciences research* (Vol. 4, pp. 213–282). New York: Academic Press.

Russell, M. J. (1976). Human olfactory communication. *Nature, 260,* 520–522.

Russell, M. J., Switz, G. M., & Thompson, K. (1980). Olfactory influence on the human menstrual cycle. *Pharmacology, Biochemistry and Behavior, 13,* 737–738.

Rutter, M. (1971). Parent–child separation: Psychological effects on the children. *Journal of Child Psychology and Psychiatry, 12,* 233–260.

Ryan, C., & Butters, N. (1984). Alcohol consumption and premature aging: A critical review. In M. Galanter (Ed.), *Recent developments in alcoholism* (Vol. 1). New York: Plenum Press.

Ryback, R. S., & Lewis, O. F. (1971). Effects of prolonged bed rest on EEG sleep patterns in young, healthy volunteers. *Electroencephalography and Clinical Neurophysiology, 51,* 395–399.

Sabel, B. A., Dunbar, G. L., Fass, B., & Stein, D. G. (1985). Gangliosides, neuroplasticity, and behavioral recovery after brain damage. In B. E. Will, P. Schmitt & J. C. Dalrymple-Alford (Eds.), *Brain plasticity, learning, and memory* (pp. 481–493). New York: Plenum Press.

Sachs, J. S. (1967). Recognition memory for syntactic and semantic aspects of connected discourse. *Perception and Psychophysics, 2,* 437–442.

Sackheim, H. A., Winman, A. L., Gur, L. C., Greenberg, M., Hungerbuhler, J. P. (1982). Pathological laughing and crying: Functional brain asymmetry in the expression of positive and negative emotions. *Archives of Neurology, 39,* 210–218.

Sacks, O. (1985). *The man who mistook his wife for a hat.* New York: Summit.

Safer, M. A., & Leventhal, H. (1977). Ear differences in evaluating emotional tones of voice and verbal content. *Journal of Experimental Psychology: Human Perception and Performance, 3,* 75–82.

Saghir, M. T., & Robins, E. (1973). *Male and female homosexuality: A comprehensive investigation.* Baltimore: Williams & Wilkins.

Sakitt, B. (1976). Iconic memory. *Psychological Review, 83,* 257–276.

Sakitt, B., & Long, G. M. (1979). Spare the rod and spoil the icon. *Journal of Experimental Psychology: Human Perception and Performance, 5,* 19–30.

Salapatek, P., & Kessen, W. (1966). Visual scan-

ning of triangles by the human newborn. *Journal of Experimental Child Psychology, 3,* 155–167.

Samuels, A. B. (1981). Phonemic restoration: Insights from a new methodology. *Journal of Experimental Psychology: General, 110,* 474–494.

Sanders, R. J. (1985). Teaching apes to ape language: Explaining the imitative and nonimitative signing of a chimpanzee (Pan troglodytes). *Journal of Comparative Psychology, 99,* 197–210.

Sandler, J. (1986). Aversion methods. In F. H. Konfer & A. P. Goldstein (Eds.), *Helping people change.* New York: Pergamon.

Sanford, A. J. (1985). *Cognition and cognitive psychology.* New York: Basic Books.

Santrock, J. W., & Warshak, R. A. (1979). Father custody and social development in boys and girls. *Journal of Social Issues, 35,* 112–125.

Sappey, P. (1889). *Traite d'anatomie descriptive.* Paris: Delalgaye Lecrosnier.

Sarason, I. G., & Sarason, B. R. (1984). *Abnormal psychology.* Englewood Cliffs, NJ: Prentice-Hall.

Sarnoff, I., & Zimbardo, P. (1961). Anxiety, fear and social affiliation. *Journal of Abnormal and Social Psychology, 62,* 356–363.

Satinoff, E., & Henderson, R. (1977). Thermoregulatory behavior. In W. K. Honig & J. E. R. Staddon (Eds.), *Handbook of operant behavior* (pp. 153–173). Englewood Cliffs, NJ: Prentice-Hall.

Satir, V. (1967). A family of angels. In J. Haley & L. Hoffman (Eds.), *Techniques of family therapy.* New York: Basic Books.

Savage-Rumbaugh, E. S., Pate, J. L., Lawson, J., Smith, S. T., & Rosenbaum, S. (1983). Can a chimpanzee make a statement? *Journal of Experimental Psychology: General, 112,* 457–492.

Savage-Rumbaugh, E. S., Rumbaugh, D. M., & Boysen, S. L. (1978). Symbolic communication between two chimpanzees (Pan troglodytes). *Science, 201,* 641–644.

Savage-Rumbaugh, E. S., Rumbaugh, D. M., & Boysen, S. L. (1980). Do apes use a language? *American Scientist, 68,* 49–61.

Sawyer, J. (1966). Measurement *and* prediction, clinical *and* statistical. *Psychological Bulletin, 66,* 178–200.

Sayegh, Y., & Dennis, W. (1965). The effect of supplementary experiences upon the behavioral development of infants in institutions. *Child Development, 36,* 81–90.

Scanzoni, L., & Scanzoni, J. (1976). *Men, women and change: A sociology of marriage and the family.* New York: McGraw-Hill.

Scarr, S. (1966). Genetic factors in activity and motivation. *Child Development, 37,* 663–673.

Scarr, S., & Carter-Saltzman, L. (1979). Twin method: Defense of a critical assumption. *Behavior Genetics, 9,* 527–542.

Scarr, S., & Carter-Saltzman, L. (1985). Genetics and intelligence. In R. J. Sternberg (Ed.), *Handbook of human intelligence.* Cambridge: Cambridge University Press.

Scarr, S., & Kidd, K. K. (1983). Developmental behavior genetics. In M. Haith & J. Campos (Eds.), *Mussen handbook of child psychology* (pp. 345–433). New York: John Wiley & Sons.

Scarr, S., Pakstis, A. J., Katz, S. H., & Barker, W. B. (1977). The absence of a relationship

between degree of white ancestry and intellectual skills within a black population. *Human Genetics, 39,* 69–86.

Scarr, S., & Weinberg, R. A. (1976). IQ test performance by black children adopted by white families. *American Psychologist, 31,* 726–739.

Schachter, S. (1959). *The psychology of affiliation.* Stanford, CA: Stanford University Press.

Schachter, S. (1971). Some extraordinary facts about obese humans and rats. *American Psychologist, 26,* 129–144.

Schachter, S., Goldman, R., & Gordon, A. (1968). Effects of fear, food deprivation, and obesity on eating. *Journal of Personality and Social Psychology, 10,* 91–97.

Schachter, S., & Latane, B. (1964). Crime, cognition, and the autonomic nervous system. *Nebraska Symposium on Motivation, 12,* 221–275.

Schachter, S., & Singer, J. (1962). Cognitive, social, and physiological determinants of emotional state. *Psychological Review, 69,* 379–399.

Schaffer, C. E., Davidson, R. J., & Saron, C. (1983). Frontal and parietal electroencephalogram asymmetry in depressed and nondepressed subjects. *Biological Psychiatry, 18,* 753–762.

Schaie, K. W. (1977). Quasi-experimental research designs in the psychology of aging. In J. E. Birren & K. W. Schaie (Eds.), *Handbook of the psychology of aging* (pp. 39–58). New York: Van Nostrand Reinhold.

Schaie, K. W., & Willis, S. L. (1986). Can decline in adult intellectual functioning be reversed? *Developmental Psychology, 22,* 223–232.

Scheier, M. F., & Carver, C. S. (1983). Self-directed attention and the comparison of self with standards. *Journal of Experimental Social Psychology, 19,* 205–222.

Scheres, K. R. (1979). Nonlinguistic vocal indicators of emotion and psychopathology. In C. E. Izard (Ed.), *Emotions in personality and psychopathology* (pp. 495–529). New York: Plenum Press.

Schiffman, S. S., & Erickson, R. P. (1980). The issue of primary tastes versus a taste continuum. *Neuroscience and Biobehavioral Reviews, 4,* 109–117.

Schiller, P. H. (1984). The superior colliculus and visual function. In I. Darian-Smith (Ed.), *Handbook of physiology—the nervous system III. Sensory processes.* Part 1 (pp. 457–505). Bethesda, MD: American Physiological Society.

Schleifer, S. J., Keller, S. E., Camerino, M., Thornton, J. C., & Stein, K. M. (1983). Suppression of lymphocyte stimulation following bereavement. *Journal of the American Medical Association, 250,* 374–377.

Schneider, W., Dumais, S. T., & Shiffrin, R. M. (1984). Automatic and control processing and attention. In R. Parasuraman & D. R. Davies (Eds.), *Varieties of Attention* (pp. 1–27). Orlando, FL: Academic Press.

Schneirla, T. C. (1959). An evolutionary and developmental theory of biphasic processes underlying approach and withdrawal. In M. R. Jones (Ed.), *Nebraska symposium on motivation.* Lincoln, NE: University of Nebraska Press.

Schober, F. W. (1952). Uber die Abhangigkeit der oberen Horgrenze vom Lebensalter.

Acustica, 2, 219–224.

Schranger, J. S., & Osberg, T. M. (1981). The relative accuracy of self-predictions and judgments by others in psychological assessment. *Psychological Bulletin, 96,* 322–351.

Schrober, D. P. (1955). *Memoirs of my nervous illness.* London: William Dawson & Sons.

Schulsinger, F. (1977). Psychopathy: Heredity and environment. *International Journal of Mental Health, 1,* 190–206.

Schuurman, T. (1981). *Endocrine processes underlying victory and defeat in the male rat.* Doctoral dissertation, University of Groningen, Haren.

Schwartz, B. (1984). *Psychology of learning and behavior.* New York: Norton.

Schwartz, E. L., Desimone, R., Albright, T. D., & Gross, C. G. (1983). Shape recognition and inferior temporal neurons. *Proceedings of the National Academy of Science, USA, 80,* 5776–5778.

Schwartz, G. E., Weinberger, D. A., & Singer, J. A. (1981). Cardiovascular differentiation of happiness, sadness, anger, and fear following imagery and exercise. *Psychosomatic Medicine, 43,* 343–364.

Schwartz, M. F., Saffran, E. M., & Marin, O. S. M. (1980). The word-order problem in agrammatism I: Comprehension. *Brain and Language, 2,* 420–433.

Schwartz, S. (1977). Normative influences on altruism. In L. Berkowitz (Ed.), *Advances in experimental social psychology* (Vol. 10). New York: Academic Press.

Schwartz, S. H. (1970). Elicitation of moral obligation and self-sacrificing behavior: An experimental study of volunteering to be a bone marrow donor. *Journal of Personality and Social Psychology, 15,* 283–293.

Schwartz, S. H., & Gottlieb, A. (1980). Bystander anonymity and reactions to emergencies. *Journal of Personality and Social Psychology, 39,* 418–430.

Schwartz, S. H., & Howard, J. A. (1981). A normative decision-making model of altruism. In J. P. Rushton & R. M. Sorrentino (Eds.), *Altruism and helping behavior.* Hillsdale, NJ: Lawrence Erlbaum.

Schweickert, R., & Boruff, B. (1986). Short-term memory capacity: Magic number or magic spell? *Journal of Experimental Psychology: Learning, Memory, and Cognition, 12,* 419–425.

Schweitzer, L., & Adams, G. (1979). The diagnosis and management of anxiety for primary care physicians. In W. E. Fann, I. Karacan, A. D. Pokorny, & R. L. Williams (Eds.), *Phenomenology and treatment of anxiety.* New York: Spectrum.

Scott, B. S., Becker, L. E., & Petit, T. L. (1983). Neurobiology of Down's syndrome. *Progress in Neurobiology, 21,* 199.

Scott, D. W. (1986). Anorexia nervosa: A review of possible genetic factors. *International Journal of Eating Disorders, 5,* 1–20.

Segal, M. W. (1974). Alphabet and attraction: An unobtrusive measure of the effect of propinquity in a field setting. *Journal of Personality and Social Psychology, 30,* 654–657.

Seidenberg, R. (1971). Drug advertising and perception of mental illness. *Mental Hygiene, 55,* 21–31.

Seidman, L. J. (1983). Schizophrenia and brain dysfunction: An integration of recent neurodiagnostic findings. *Psychological Bulletin, 94,* 195–238.

Sekuler, R., & Blake, R. (1985). *Perception.* New York: Knopf.

Seligman, M. E. P. (1975). *Helplessness.* San Francisco: Freeman.

Seligman, M. E. P., & Maier, S. F. (1967). Failure to escape traumatic shock. *Journal of Experimental Psychology, 74,* 1–9.

Seligman, M. E. P., Peterson, C., Kaslow, N. J., Tannebaum, R. L., Alloy, L. B., & Abramson, L. Y. (1984). Explanatory style and depressive symptoms among children. *Journal of Abnormal Psychology, 93,* 235–238.

Selkoe, D. J., Bell, D. S., Podlisny, M. B., Price, D. L., & Cork, L. C. (1987). Conservation of brain amyloid proteins in aged mammals and humans with Alzheimer's disease. *Science, 235,* 873–877.

Selmanowitz, O. J., Rizer, R. L., & Orentreich, N. (1977). Aging of the skin and its appendages. In C. E. Finch & L. Hayflick (Eds.), *Handbook of the biology of aging* (pp. 496–509). New York: Van Nostrand Reinhold.

Selvini-Palazzoli, M., & Prata, G. (1983). A new method for therapy and research in the treatment of schizophrenic families. In H. Stierlin, L. C. Hynne, & M. Wirsching (Eds.), *Psychosocial intervention in schizophrenia.* Berlin: Springer-Verlag.

Selye, H. (1950). *The physiology and pathology of exposure to stress.* Montreal: Acta, Inc.

Selye, H. (1952). *The story of the adaptation syndrome.* Montreal: Acta, Inc.

Selye, H. (1956). *The stress of life.* New York: McGraw-Hill.

Semenza, C., & Goodglass, H. (1985). Localization of body parts in brain injured subjects. *Neuropsychologia, 23,* 161–175.

Shaffer, D. (1985). *Developmental psychology: Theory, research, and applications.* Monterey, CA: Brooks/Cole.

Shaffer, D. R., Smith, J. E., & Tomarelli, M. (1982). Self-monitoring as a determinant of self-disclosure reciprocity during the acquaintance process. *Journal of Personality and Social Psychology, 43,* 163–175.

Shah, S. (1978). Dangerousness: A paradigm for exploring some issues in law and psychology. *American Psychologist, 33,* 224–238.

Shand, M. A. (1982). Sign-based short-term coding of American sign language signs and printed English words by congenitally deaf signers. *Cognitive Psychology, 14,* 1–12.

Shapiro, B. E., & Danly, M. (1985). The role of the right hemisphere in the control of speech prosody in propositional and affective contexts. *Brain and Language, 24,* 204–222.

Shapiro, D. A. (1985). Recent applications of meta-analysis in clinical research. *Clinical Psychological Review, 5,* 13–34.

Shapiro, D. H., Jr. (1980). *Meditation: Self-regulation strategy and altered state of consciousness.* Chicago: Aldine.

Shapiro, D. H., Jr. (1982). Overview: Clinical and physiological comparison of meditation with other self-control strategies. *American Journal of Psychiatry, 139,* 267–274.

Shapiro, D. H., Jr. (1985). Clinical use of meditation as a self-regulation strategy: Comments on Holmes's conclusions and implications. *American Psychologist, 40,* 719–722.

Shapley, R., & Lennie, P. (1985). Spatial frequency analysis in the visual system. *Annual Review of Neuroscience, 8,* 547–583.

Sharp, G. L., Cutler, B. L., & Penrod, S. D. (in press). Performance feedback improves the resolution of confidence judgments. *Organizational behavior and human decision-making.*

Shasby, G., & Kingsley, R. F. (1978). A study of behavior and body type in troubled youth. *Journal of School Health, 48,* 103–107.

Shatz, M. (1983). Communication. In J. Flavell & E. Markman (Eds.), *Cognitive development.* New York: John Wiley & Sons.

Shatz, M., & Gelman, R. (1973). The development of communication skills: Modification in the speech of young children as a function of listener. *Monographs of Society for Research in Child Development, 38* (Serial No. 152).

Shaver, P., & Rubenstein, C. (1980). Childhood attachment experience and adult loneliness. *The Review of Personality and Social Psychology, 1,* 42–73.

Sheils, M. (1983). A portrait of America. *Newsweek,* January 17.

Shepard, R. N. (1967). Recognition memory for words, sentences, and pictures. *Journal of Verbal Learning and Verbal Behavior, 6,* 156–163.

Shepard, R. N., & Metzler, J. (1971). Mental rotation for three-dimensional objects. *Science, 171,* 701–703.

Sherif, M. (1935). An experimental study of stereotypes. *Journal of Abnormal and Social Psychology, 29,* 371–375.

Sherif, M. (1936). *The psychology of social norms.* New York: Harper & Row.

Sherif, M. (1958). Superordinate goals in the reduction of intergroup conflict. *American Journal of Sociology, 63,* 349–356.

Sherman, S. M., & Spear, P. D. (1982). Organization of visual pathways in normal and visually deprived cats. *Physiological Reviews, 62,* 738–855.

Shields, J. (1976). Heredity and environment. In H. J. Eysenck & G. D. Wilson (Eds.), *A textbook of human psychology.* Baltimore: University Park Press.

Shimamura, A. P., & Squire, L. R. (1986). Memory and metamemory. A study of the feeling-of-knowing phenomenon in amnesic patients. *Journal of Experimental Psychology: Learning, Memory, and Cognition, 12,* 452–460.

Shoben, E. J., Westcourt, K. T., & Smith, E. E. (1978). Sentence verification, sentence recognition, and the semantic/episodic distinction. *Journal of Experimental Psychology: Human Learning and Memory, 4,* 304–317.

Shotland, R. L., & Straw, M. K. (1976). Bystander response to an assault: When a man attacks a woman. *Journal of Personality and Social Psychology, 34,* 990–999.

Shurrager, R. S., & Culler, E. (1940). Conditioning in the spinal dog. *Journal of Experimental Psychology, 26,* 133–159.

Sigall, H., & Landy, D. (1973). Radiating beauty: The effects of having a physically attractive partner on person perception. *Journal of Personality and Social Psychology, 28,* 218–224.

Sigall, H., & Ostrove, N. (1975). Beautiful but dangerous: Effects of offender attractiveness and nature of the crime on juridic judgment. *Journal of Personality and Social Psychology, 31,* 410–444.

Signorielli, N., Gross, L., & Morgan, M. (1982). Violence in television programs: Ten years later. In D. Perel, L. Bouthilet, & J. Lazar

(Eds.), *Television and behavior: Ten years of scientific progress and implications for the eighties* (pp. 158–173). Washington, DC: US Government Printing Office.

Silberglied, J. (1979). Communication in the ultraviolet. *Annual Review of Ecological Systems, 10,* 373–398.

Silverton, L., Finello, K. M., Mednick, S. A., & Schulsinger, F. (1985). Low birth weight and ventricular enlargement in a high-risk sample. *Journal of Abnormal Psychology, 94,* 405–409.

Simmons, J. A., Howell, D. J., & Suga, N. (1975). Information content of bat sonar echoes. *American Scientist, 63,* 204–215.

Simon, B. (1974). *The politics of educational reform, 1920–1940.* London: Lawrence-Wishart.

Simon, H., & Reed, S. (1976). Modeling strategy shifts in a problem-solving task. *Cognitive Psychology, 8,* 86–97.

Simons, A. D., Murphy, G. E., Levine, J. L., & Wetzel, R. D. (1986). Cognitive therapy and pharmacotherapy for depression: Sustained improvement over one year. *Archives of General Psychiatry, 43,* 43–48.

Simpson, G. M., & May, P. R. A. (1982). Schizophrenic disorders. In J. H. Greist, J. W. Jefferson, & R. L. Spitzer (Eds.), *Treatment of mental disorders.* New York: Oxford.

Sines, L. K. (1959). The relative contributions of four kinds of data to accuracy in personality assessment. *Journal of Consulting Psychology, 243,* 483–492.

Singer, J. H. (1976). *Androgyny: Toward a new theory of sexuality.* Garden City, NY: Anchor.

Singer, W. (1977). Control of thalamic transmission by corticofugal and ascending reticular pathways in the visual system. *Physiological Reviews, 57,* 396–420.

Sivacek, J., & Crano, W. D. (1982). Vested interest as a moderator of attitude-behavior consistency. *Journal of Personality and Social Psychology, 43,* 210–221.

Skinner, B. F. (1957). *Verbal behavior.* New York: Appleton-Century-Crofts.

Skinner, B. F. (1964). Behaviorism at fifty. In T. W. Wann (Ed.), *Behaviorism and phenomenology* (pp. 79–108). Chicago: University of Chicago Press.

Skinner, B. F. (1974). *About behaviorism.* New York: Knopf.

Sklar, L. S., & Anisman, H. (1979). Stress and coping factors influence tumor growth. *Science, 205,* 513–515.

Skman, P., Levenson, R. W., & Friesen, W. V. (1983). Autonomic nervous system activity distinguishes among emotions. *Science, 221,* 1208–1210.

Skolnick, A. (1981). Married lives: Longitudinal perspectives on marriage. In D. H. Eichron, J. A. Clausen, N. Haan, & M. P. Honzik (Eds.), *Present and past in middle life* (pp. 269–298). New York: Academic Press.

Skov, R. B., & Sherman, S. J. (1986). Information-gathering processes: Diagnosticity, hypothesis-confirmatory strategies, and perceived hypothesis confirmation. *Journal of Experimental Social Psychology, 22,* 93–121.

Slimp, J. C., Hart, B. L., & Goy, R. M. (1978). Heterosexual and social behavior of adult male rhesus monkeys with medial preoptic-anterior hypothalamic lesions. *Brain Research, 142,* 105–122.

Sloane, R. B., Staples, F. R., Cristol, A. H.,

Yorkston, N., & Whipple, K. (1975). *Psychotherapy versus behavior therapy.* Cambridge, MA: Harvard University Press.

Slobin, D. I. (1971). *Psycholinguistics.* Glencoe, IL: Scott, Foresman.

Slobin, D. I. (1973). Cognitive prequisites for the development of grammar. In C. A. Ferguson & D. I. Slobin (Eds.), *Advances in psycholinguistics* (pp. 175–208). New York: Holt.

Slobin, D. I. (1982). Universal and particular in the acquisition of language. In E. Wanner & L. R. Gleitman (Eds.), *Language acquisition: The state of the art* (pp. 128–170). Cambridge: Cambridge University Press.

Smith, C. (1985). Sleep states and learning: A review of the animal literature. *Neuroscience and Biobehavioral Reviews, 9,* 157–168.

Smith, C. B. (1984). Aging and changes in cerebral energy metabolism. *Trends in Neurosciences, 7,* 203–207.

Smith, D. V. (1985). The neural representation of gustatory quality. In M. J. Correia & A. A. Perachio (Eds.), *Contemporary sensory neurobiology* (pp. 75–98). New York: Alan R. Liss.

Smith, E. E., Shoben, E. J., & Rips, L. J. (1974). Structure and process in semantic memory: A featural model for semantic decisions. *Psychological Review, 81,* 214–241.

Smith, G. F., & Warren, S. T. (1985). The biology of Down syndrome. In G. F. Smith (Ed.), *Molecular structure of the number 21 chromosome and Down syndrome* (pp. 1–10). New York: Annals of the New York Academy.

Smith, G. P. (1984). Gut hormone hypothesis of postpranchal satiety. In A. J. Stunkard & E. Stellar (Eds.), *Eating and its disorders* (pp. 67–75). New York: Raven Press.

Smith, M. A., Check, J. V. P., & Henry, M. J. (1984). *Sexual violence in the mass media: A content analysis of feature-length films.* Paper presented at the meeting of the Canadian Psychological Association, Ottawa, Ontario.

Smith, M. C. (1983). Hypnotic memory enhancement of witnesses: Does it work? *Psychological Bulletin, 94,* 387–407.

Smith, M. L., Glass, G. V., & Miller, T. I. (1980). *The benefits of psychotherapy.* Baltimore: Johns Hopkins University Press.

Smith, R. J. (1979). Study finds sleeping pills overprescribed. *Science, 204,* 287–288.

Smith, R. P., Warm, J. S., & Alluisi, E. A. (1966). Effects of temporal uncertainty on watchkeeping performance. *Perception and Psychophysics, 1,* 293–299.

Smith, S. (1985). A sound memory. *American Journal of Psychology, 98,* 591–603.

Snarey, J. R. (1985). Cross-cultural universality of social-moral development: A critical review of Kohlbergian research. *Psychological Bulletin, 97,* 202–232.

Snyder, A. W., Bossomaier, T. R. J., & Hughes, A. (1986). Optical image quality and the cone mosaic. *Science, 231,* 499–501.

Snyder, F. (1970). The phenomenology of dreaming. In L. Madow & L. H. Snow (Eds.), *The psychodynamic implications of the physiological studies on dreams* (pp. 124–151). Springfield, IL: Charles C. Thomas.

Snyder, K. G., & Gangestad, S. (1986). On the nature of self-monitoring: Matters of assessment, matters of validity. *Journal of Personality and Social Psychology, 51,* 125–139.

Snyder, M. (1974). Self-monitoring of expressive behavior. *Journal of Personality and Social Psychology, 30,* 526–537.

Snyder, M. (1979). Self-monitoring processes. In L. Berkowitz (Ed.), *Advances in experimental social psychology* (Vol. 12). New York: Academic Press.

Snyder, M. (1981). "Seek and ye shall find . . ." In E. T. Higgins, C. P. Herman, & M. P. Zanna (Eds.), *Social cognition: The Ontario symposium on personality and social psychology.* Hillsdale, NJ: Lawrence Erlbaum.

Snyder, M. (1986). *Public appearances/private realities: The psychology of self-monitoring.* New York: Freeman.

Snyder, M., Gangestad, S., & Simpson, J. A. (1983). Choosing friends as activity partners: The role of self-monitoring. *Journal of Personality and Social Psychology, 45,* 1061–1072.

Snyder, M., & Simpson, J. A. (1984). Self-monitoring and dating relationships. *Journal of Personality and Social Psychology, 47,* 1281–1291.

Snyder, M., Simpson, J. A., & Gangestad, S. (1986). Personality and sexual relations. *Journal of Personality and Social Psychology, 51,* 181–190.

Snyder, M., & Uranowitz, S. W. (1978). Reconstructing the past: Some cognitive consequences of person perception. *Journal of Personality and Social Psychology, 36,* 941–950.

Snyder, S. H. (1980). *Biological aspects of mental disorder.* New York: Oxford.

Snyder, S. H. (1982). Neurotransmitters and CNS disease: Schizophrenia. *Lancet, 2,* 970–974.

Snyder, S. H. (1984). Drug and neurotransmitter receptors in the brain. *Science, 224,* 22–31.

Soal, S. G., & Bateman, F. (1954). *Modern experiments in telepathy.* New Haven, CT: Yale University Press.

Sobell, M. B., Schaeffer, H. H., & Mills, R. C. (1972). Differences in baseline drinking behaviors between alcoholics and normal drinkers. *Behaviour Research and Therapy, 10,* 257–268.

Solomon, G. F., Amkraut, A. A., & Rubin, R. T. (1985). Stress, hormones, neuroregulation, and immunity. In S. R. Burchfield (Ed.), *Stress: Psychological and physiological interactions.* Washington, DC: Hemisphere Publishing.

Solomon, R. L. (1977). An opponent-process theory of acquired motivation: The affective dynamics of addiction. In J. D. Maser & M. E. P. Seligman (Eds.), *Psychopathology: Experimental models.* San Francisco: Freeman.

Sonnentino, R. M., & Higgins, E. T. (1986). *Handbook of motivation and cognition.* New York: Guilford.

Sontag, L. W. (1941). The significance of fetal environmental differences. *American Journal of Obstetrics and Gynecology, 42,* 996–1003.

Sontag, L. W. (1944). War and fetal maternal relationship. *Marriage and Family Living, 6,* 3–5, 16.

Sontag, S. (1977). The double standard of aging. In L. R. Allman & D. R. Jaffe (Eds.), *Readings in adult psychology: Contemporary perspectives* (pp. 285–294). New York: Harper & Row.

Spanos, N. P. (1982). A social psychological approach to hypnotic behavior. In G. Weary & H. L. Mirels (Eds.), *Integrations of clinical and social psychology* (pp. 231–271). New York: Oxford. (a)

Spanos, N. P. (1982). Hypnotic behavior: A cognitive, social psychological perspective. *Research communications in psychology, psychiatry and behavior, 7,* 199–213. (b)

Sparks, D. L. (1986). Translation of sensory signals into commands for control of saccadic eye movements: Role of primate superior colliculus. *Physiological Reviews, 66,* 118–171.

Spear, P. D. (1985). Neural mechanisms of compensation following neonatal visual cortex damage. In C. W. Cotman (Ed.), *Synaptic plasticity* (pp. 111–167). New York: Guilford.

Spearman, C. (1923). *The nature of "intelligence" and the principles of cognition.* London: Macmillan.

Spelke, E. S., & Cortelyou, A. (1981). Perceptual aspects of social knowing: Looking and listening in infancy. In M. E. Lamb & L. R. Sherrod (Eds.), *Infant social cognition: Empirical and theoretical considerations.* Hillsdale, NJ: Lawrence Erlbaum.

Spence, J. T., Helmreich, R. L., & Stapp, J. (1975). Ratings of self and peers on sex-role attributes and their relation to self-esteem and conceptions of masculinity and femininity. *Journal of Personality and Social Psychology, 32,* 29–39.

Sperling, G. (1960). The information available in brief visual presentations. *Psychological Monographs, 74,* 1–29.

Sperry, R. W. (1961). Cerebral organization and behavior. *Science, 133,* 1749.

Sperry, R. W. (1968). Mental unity following surgical disconnection of the cerebral hemispheres. *The Harvey Lectures, Series 62* (pp. 293–323). New York: Academic Press.

Sperry, R. W. (1974). Lateral specialization in the surgically separated hemispheres. In F. O. Schmitt & F. G. Worden (Eds.), *The neurosciences: Third study program* (pp. 5–19). Cambridge, MA: MIT Press.

Sperry, R. W. (1982). Some effects of disconnecting the cerebral hemispheres. *Science, 217,* 1223–1226.

Sperry, R. W. (1984). Consciousness, personal identity and the divided brain. *Neuropsychologia, 22,* 661–674.

Sperry, R. W., Stamm, J., & Miner, N. (1956). Relearning tests for interocular transfer following division of optic chiasma and corpus callosum in cats. *Journal of Comparative and Physiological Psychology, 49,* 529–533.

Spiegel, D., Cutcomb, S., Ren, C., & Pribram, K. (1985). Hypnotic hallucination alters evoked potentials. *Journal of Abnormal Psychology, 94,* 249–255.

Spitzer, R. L., & Fleiss, J. L. (1974). A reanalysis of the reliability of psychiatric diagnosis. *British Journal of Psychiatry, 125,* 341–347.

Squire, L. R. (1982). The neuropsychology of human memory. *Annual Review of Neuroscience, 5,* 241–273.

Squire, L. R. (1986). Mechanisms of memory. *Science, 232,* 1612–1619.

Squire, L. R., & Cohen, N. J. (1984). Human memory and amnesia. In G. Lynch, J. McGaugh, & N. M. Weinberger (Eds.), *Neurobiology of learning and memory* (pp. 3–64). New York: Guilford.

St. George-Hyslop, P. H., et al. (1987). The genetic defect causing familial Alzheimer's dis-

ease maps on chromosome 21. *Science, 235,* 885–890.

Staats, A. W., & Staats, C. K. (1957, 1958). Attitudes established by classical conditioning. *Journal of Abnormal and Social Psychology, 57,* 37–40.

Standing, L. (1973). Learning 10,000 pictures. *Quarterly Journal of Experimental Psychology, 25,* 207–222.

Stanton, M. D. (1981). Strategic approaches to family therapy. In A. S. Gurman & D. P. Kniskern (Eds.), *Handbook of family therapy.* New York: Brunner/Mazel.

Stapp, J., & Fulcher, R. (1983). The employment of APA members. *American Psychologist, 36,* 1263–1314.

Stark, L., & Bridgeman, B. (1983). Role of corollary discharge in space constancy. *Perception and Psychophysics, 34,* 371–380.

Staub, E., & Sherk, L. (1970). Need for approval, children's sharing behavior, and reciprocity in sharing. *Child Development, 41,* 243–252.

Stein, A. H., & Friedrich, L. K. (1975). Impact of television on children and youth. In E. M. Hetherington, J. W. Hagen, R. Kron, & A. H. Stein (Eds.), *Review of child development research* (pp. 183–256). Chicago: University of Chicago Press.

Stein, D. G., Labbe, R., Attella, M. J., & Rakowsky, H. A. (1985). Fetal brain tissue transplants reduce visual deficits in adult rats with bilateral lesions of the occipital cortex. *Behavioral and Neural Biology, 44,* 266–277.

Stein, L., Wise, C. D., & Belluzzi, J. D. (1977). Neuropharmacology of reward and punishment. In L. L. Iversen, S. D. Iversen, & S. H. Snyder (Eds.), *Handbook of psychopharmacology,* Vol. 8. *Drugs, neurotransmitters and behavior.* New York: Plenum Press.

Stein, Z., Susser, M., Saenger, G., & Marolla F. (1972). Nutrition and mental performance. *Science, 173,* 708–713.

Steinem, G. (1980). Erotica and pornography: A clear and present difference. In L. Lederer (Ed.), *Take back the night: Women on pornography.* New York: Morrow.

Steiner, J. E. (1977). Facial expressions in response to taste and smell stimulation. In H. W. Reese & L. P. Lipsitt (Eds.), *Advances in child development and behavior* (Vol. 13, pp. 257–296). New York: Academic Press.

Steinmetz, S. K., & Straus, M. A. (1974). *Violence in the family.* New York: Dodd, Mead.

Stellar, J. R., & Stellar, E. (1985). *The neurobiology of motivation and reward.* New York: Springer-Verlag.

Stern, J. A., Brown, M., Ulett, G., & Sletten, I. (1977). A comparison of hypnosis, acupuncture, morphine, valium, aspirin, and placebo in the management of experimentally induced pain. *Annals of the New York Academy of Science, 296,* 175–193.

Stern, J. S. (1984). Is obesity a disease of inactivity? In A. J. Stunkard & E. Stellar (Eds.), *Eating and its disorders* (pp. 131–139). New York: Raven Press.

Stern, L. (1985). *The structures and strategies of human memory.* Homewood, IL: The Dorsey Press.

Stern, W. C., & Margane, P. J. (1974). Theoretical view of REM sleep function: Maintenance of catecholamine systems in the central nervous system. *Behavioral Biology, 11,* 1–32.

Sternberg, R. J. (Ed.). (1984). *Mechanisms of cognitive development.* New York: Freeman.

Sternberg, R. J. (1985). *Beyond IQ.* Cambridge: Cambridge University Press. (a)

Sternberg, R. J. (1985). *Handbook of human intelligence.* Cambridge: Cambridge University Press. (b)

Sternberg, S. (1966). High-speed scanning in human memory. *Science, 153,* 652–654.

Sternberg, S. (1967). Retrieval of contextual information from memory. *Psychonomic Science, 8,* 55–56.

Sternberg, S. (1969). The discovery of processing stages: Extensions of Donder's method. In W. G. Koster (Ed.), *Attention and performance II* (pp. 276–315). Amsterdam: North Holland.

Stevens, C. F. (1979). The neuron. *Scientific American, 741,* 54–65.

Stevens, J. K., Emerson, R. C., Gerstin, G. L., Kallos, T., Neufeld, G. R., Nichols, S. W., & Rosenquist, A. C. (1976). Paralysis of the awake human: Visual perceptions. *Vision Research, 16,* 93–98.

Stevens, S. S. (1956). The direct estimation of sensory magnitudes—loudness. *American Journal of Psychology, 69,* 1–25.

Stevens, S. S. (1961). To honor Fechner and repeat his law. *Science, 133,* 80–86.

Stevens, S. S. (1962). The surprising simplicity of sensory metrics. *American Psychologist, 17,* 29–39.

Stevens-Long, J. (1984). *Adult life: Developmental processes* (2nd ed.). Palo Alto, CA: Mayfield.

Stewart, J. (1984). Reinstatement of heroin and cocaine self-administration behavior in the rat by intracerebral application of morphine in the ventral tegmental area. *Pharmacology Biochemistry & Behavior, 20,* 917–923.

Stewart J., de Wit, H., & Eikelboom, R. (1984). Role of unconditioned and conditioned drug effects in the self-administration of opiates and stimulants. *Psychological Review, 91,* 251–268.

Stewart, J. W., McGrath, P. J., Liebowitz, M. R., Harrison, W., Quitkin, F., & Rabkin, J. G. (1985). Treatment outcome validation of DSM-III depressive subtypes: Clinical usefulness in outpatients with mild to moderate depression. *Archives of General Psychiatry, 452,* 1148–1153.

Stewart, R. M., & Rosenberg, R. N. (1979). Physiology of glia—glial-neuronal interactions. *International Review of Neurobiology, 21,* 275–310.

Stiles, W. B., Shapiro, D. A., & Elliott, R. (1986). "Are all psychotherapies equivalent?" *American Psychologist, 41,* 165–180.

Stones, M. J., & Kozma, A. (1985). Physical performance. In N. Charness (Ed.), *Aging and human performance* (pp. 261–291). Chichester: John Wiley & Sons.

Storandt, M., Grant, E. A., & Gordon, B. C. (1978). Remote memory as a function of age and sex. *Experimental Aging Research, 4,* 365–375.

Storms, M. D. (1973). Videotape and the attribution process: Reversing actors' and observers' points of view. *Journal of Personality and Social Psychology, 27*(2), 165–175.

Straus, M. (1977, March). Normative and behavioral aspects of violence between spouses: Preliminary data on a nationally representative USA *sample.* Paper presented at the Symposium on Violence in Canadian Society, Simon Fraser University.

Straus, M., Gelles, R., & Steinmetz, S. (1980). *Behind closed doors: Violence in the American family.* Garden City, NY: Doubleday.

Strauss, J., Carpenter, W. T., & Bastko, J. (1974). The diagnosis and understanding of schizophrenia: III. Speculations on the processes that underlie schizophrenic symptoms and signs. *Schizophrenia Bulletin, 1,* 61–69.

Streissguth, A. P., Martin, D. C., Barr, H. M., Sandman, B. M., Kirchner, G. L., & Darby, B. L. (1984). Intrauterine alcohol and nicotine exposure: Attention and reaction time in 4-year-old children. *Developmental Psychology, 20,* 533–541.

Stricker, E. M. (1983). Brain neurochemistry and the control of food intake. In E. Satinoff & P. Teitelbaum (Eds.), *Handbook of behavioral neurobiology* (Vol. 6, pp. 329–366). New York: Plenum Press.

Strupp, H. H. (1984). The Vanderbilt psychotherapy research project: past, present, and future. In J. B. W. Williams & R. L. Spitzer (Eds.), *Psychotherapy research: Where are we and where should we go?* New York: Guilford.

Stunkard, A. J., Sorensen, T. I. A., Harris, C., Teasdale, T. W., Chakraborty, R., Schull, W. S., & Schusinger, F. (1986). An adoption study of human obesity. *New England Journal of Medicine, 314,* 193–198.

Suga, N. (1984). The extent to which biosonor information is represented by the auditory cortex of the mustached bat. In G. M. Edelman, W. E. Gall, & W. M. Cowan (Eds.), *Dynamic aspects of neocortical function* (pp. 315–373). New York: John Wiley & Sons.

Suinn, R. M. (1982). Intervention with Type A behaviors. *Journal of Consulting and Clinical Psychology, 50,* 933–949.

Sullivan, D. A. (1985). The ties that bind: Differentials between seasonal and permanent migrants to retirement communities. *Research on Aging, 7,* 235–250.

Summers, W. V., Horton, D. L., & Diehl, V. A. (1985). Contextual knowledge during encoding influences sentence recognition. *Journal of Experimental Psychology: Learning, Memory, and Cognition, 11,* 771–779.

Sunderland, S. (1978). *Nerves and nerve injuries* (2nd ed.). Edinburgh: Churchill Livingston.

Suomi, S. J., Collins, M. L., Harlow, H. F., & Ruppenthal, G. C. (1976). Effects of maternal and peer separations on young monkeys. *Journal of Child Psychology and Psychiatry, 17,* 101–112.

Surgeon General's Scientific Advisory Committee on Television and Social Behavior (1972). *Television and growing up: The impact on televised violence.* Washington, DC: U.S. Government Printing Office.

Sussman, S., & Mueser, K. (1983). Age, socio-economic status, severity of mental disorder, and chronicity as predictors of physical attractiveness. *Journal of Abnormal Psychology, 92,* 225–258.

Sussman, S., Mueser, K., Grau, B. W., & Yarnold, P. (1983). Stability of females' facial attractiveness during childhood. *Journal of Personality and Social Psychology, 44,* 1231–1233.

Swaab, D. F., & Fliers, E. (1985). A sexually dimorphic nucleus in the human brain. *Science, 228,* 1112–1115.

Swart, C., & Berkowitz, L. (1976). The effect of a stimulus associated with a victim's pain on later aggression. *Journal of Personality and Social Psychology, 33,* 623–631.

Swets, J. A. (1977). Signal detection theory applied to vigilance. In R. R. Mackie (Ed.), *Vigilance: Theory, operational performance, and physiological correlates* (pp. 705–718). New York: Plenum Press.

Tafler, W. H., & Kennedy, D. (1965). *The biology of organisms.* New York: John Wiley & Sons.

Talmon, Y. (1964). Mate selection in collective settlements. *American Sociological Review, 29,* 491–508.

Tanabe, T., Iino, M., & Takagi, S. F. (1975). Discrimination of odors in olfactory bulb, pyriform amygdaloid areas and orbito-frontal cortex of the monkey. *Journal of Neurophysiology, 38,* 1284–1296.

Tanford, S., & Penrod, S. (1984). Social Influence Model: a formal integration of research on majority and minority influence processes. *Psychological Bulletin, 95,* 189–225.

Tanji, J. (1984). The neuronal activity in the supplementary motor area of primates. *Trends in Neurosciences, 7,* 282–285.

Tannenbaum, P. H., & Zillman, D. (1975). Emotional arousal in the facilitation of aggression through communication. In L. Berkowitz (Ed.), *Advances in experimental social psychology* (Vol. 8). New York: Academic Press.

Tanner, J. M. (1978). *Foetus into man: physical growth from conception to maturity.* Cambridge, MA: Harvard University Press.

Tanner, J. M., & Whitehouse, R. H. (1976). Clinical longitudinal standards for height, weight, height velocity, weight velocity, and the stages of puberty. *Archives for Disease in Childhood, 51,* 170–179.

Taplin, J. E., & Staudenmayer, H. (1973). Interpretation of abstract conditional sentences in deductive reasoning. *Journal of Verbal Behavior, 12,* 530–542.

Tarde, G. (1890). *Les lois de l'imitation. Etude sociologique.* Paris: Alcan.

Tartter, V. C. (1986). *Language processes.* New York: Holt, Rinehart, and Winston.

Taussig, H. B. (1962). A study of the German outbreak of phocomelia. The thalidomide syndrome. *Journal of the American Medical Association, 180,* 1106–1114.

Taylor, R. L. (1949). *W. C. Fields: His follies and fortunes.* New York: Doubleday and Co.

Taylor, S. P., Gammon, C. B., & Capasso, D. R. (1976). Aggression as a function of alcohol and threat. *Journal of Personality and Social Psychology, 34,* 938–941.

Taylor, S. P., & Pisano, R. (1971). Physical aggression as a function of frustration and physical attack. *Journal of Social Psychology, 84,* 261–267.

Tebecis, A. K., Provins, K. A., Farnbach, R. W., & Pentony, P. (1975). Hypnosis and the EEG: A quantitative investigation. *Journal of Nervous and Mental Diseases, 161,* 1–17.

Tedeschi, J. T., Schlenker, B. R., & Bonoma, T. V. (1971). Cognitive dissonance: Private ratiocination or public spectacle? *American Psychologist, 26,* 685–695.

Tedin, K. L. (1974). The influence of parents on the political attitudes of adolescents. *American Political Science Review, 68,* 1579–1592.

Teghtsoonian, R. (1971). On the exponents in Stevens' law and the constant in Ehrman's law. *Psychological Review, 78,* 71–80.

Teller, D. Y. (1981). The development of visual acuity in human and monkey infants. *Trends in Neurosciences, 4,* 21–23.

Teller, D. Y. (1982). Scotopic vision, color vision, and stereopsis in infants. *Current Eye Research, 2,* 199–210.

Terman, L. M. (1921). Intelligence and its measurement, Part II. *Journal of Educational Psychology, 12,* 127–133.

Terrace, H. S. (1979). *Nim.* New York: Knopf.

Terrace, H. S., Pettito, L. A., Sanders, R. J., & Bever, T. G. (1979). Can an ape create a sentence? *Science, 206,* 891–902.

Terry, R. D. (1976). Dementia. *Archives of Neurology, 33,* 1.

Tetlock, P. (1980). Explaining teacher explanations of pupil performance: A self-presentational interpretation. *Social Psychology Quarterly, 43,* 283–290.

Tetlock, P. E., & Kim, J. I. (1987). Accountability and judgment processes in a personality prediction task. *Journal of Personality and Social Psychology, 52,* 700–709.

Tetlock, P. E., & Manstead, A. S. (1985). Impression management versus intrapsychic explanations in social psychology: A useful dichotomy? *Psychological Review, 92,* 59–77.

Teuber, H.-L. (1975). Recovery of function after brain injury in man. In R. Porter & D. W. Fitzsimons (Eds.), *Outcome of severe damage to the central nervous system. Ciba Foundation Symposium No. 34* (pp. 159–186). Amsterdam: Elsevier/Excerpta Medica.

Teuber, H.-L., Corkin, S. H., & Twitchell, T. E. (1977). Study of cingulotomy in man: A summary. In W. H. Sweet, S. Obrador, & J. G. Martin-Rodriguez (Eds.), *Neurosurgical treatment in psychiatry, pain, and epilepsy.* Baltimore: University Park Press.

Thibaut, J. W., & Kelley, H. (1959). *The social psychology of groups.* New York: John Wiley & Sons.

Thistlewaite, D. L., & Kamenetzky, J. (1955). Attitude change through refutation and elaboration of audience counterarguments. *Journal of Abnormal and Social Psychology, 51,* 3–9.

Thoits, P. A. (1985). Social support and psychological well-being: Theoretical possibilities. In I. G. Sarason & R. B. Sarason (Eds.), *Social support: Theory, research and applications* (pp. 51–72). The Hague, The Netherlands: Martinus, Nijhoff.

Thoits, P. A. (1986). Social support as coping assistance. *Journal of Consulting and Clinical Psychology, 54,* 416–423.

Thomas, A., & Chess, S. (1977). *Temperament and development.* New York: Brunner/Mazel.

Thomas, A., & Chess, S. (1980). *The dynamics of psychological development.* New York: Brunner/Mazel.

Thomas, D., Campos, J. J., Shucard, D. W., Ransay, D. S., & Shucard, J. (1981). Semantic comprehension in infancy: A signal detection approach. *Child Development, 52,* 798–803.

Thomas, M. H., & Tell, P. M. (1974). Effects of viewing real versus fantasy violence upon interpersonal aggression. *Journal of Research in Personality, 8,* 153–160.

Thompson, A. M., Billewicz, N. Z., & Passmore, R. (1961). The relation between caloric intake and body-weight in man. *Lancet, 1,* 1027–1028.

Thompson, J. K., Jarvis, G. J., Labrey, B. B., & Cureton, K. J. (1982). Exercise and obesity: Etiology, physiology, and intervention. *Psychological Bulletin, 91,* 55–79.

Thompson, N. L., McCandless, B. R., & Strickland, B. R. (1971). Personal adjustment of male and female homosexuals and heterosexuals. *Journal of Abnormal and Social Psychology, 78,* 237–240.

Thompson, R. F. (1967). *Foundations of physiological psychology.* New York: Harper & Row.

Thompson R. F. (1986). The neurobiology of learning and memory. *Science, 233,* 941–947.

Thorndike, E. L. (1911). *Animal intelligence.* New York: Macmillan. (Originally published, 1898.)

Thorndike, R. L. (1933). The effect of the interval between test and retest on the constancy of the IQ. *Journal of Educational Psychology, 24,* 543–549.

Thurstone, L. L. (1946). Comment. *American Journal of Sociology, 52,* 39–40.

Tienari, P., Sorri, A., Naarala, M., Lahti, I., Pohjola, J., Bostrom, C., & Wahlberg, K.-E. (1983). The Finnish adoptive family study: Adopted-away offspring of schizophrenic mothers. In H. Stierlin, L. C. Wynne, & M. Wirsching (Eds.), *Psychosocial intervention in schizophrenia.* Berlin: Springer-Verlag.

Tiffany, S. T., Martin, E. M., & Baker, T. B. (1986). Treatments for cigarette smoking: An evaluation of the contributions of aversion and counseling procedures. *Behaviour Research and Therapy, 24,* 437–452.

Timrots, A., & Rand, M. (1987). *Violent crime by strangers and nonstrangers.* U.S. Department of Justice, Bureau of Justice Statistics. Washington, DC: U.S. Government Printing Office.

Tinbergen, N. (1952). Derived activities: Their causation, biological significance, and origin and emancipation during evolution. *Quarterly Review of Biology, 27,* 1–32.

Tompkins, C. A., & Mateer, C. A. (1985). Right hemisphere appreciation of prosodic and linguistic indications of implicit attitude. *Brain and Language, 24,* 185–203.

Torgersen, S. (1986). Genetic factors in moderately severe and mild affective disorders. *Archives of General Psychiatry, 43,* 222–226.

Trabasso, T. R. (1975). Representation, memory, and reasoning: How do we make transitive inferences? In A. D. Pick (Ed.), *Minnesota Symposium on Child Psychology* (pp. 135–172). Minneapolis: University of Minnesota Press.

Tranel, D. T., Fijsher, A. E., & Fowles, D. C. (1982). Magnitude of incentive effects on heart rate. *Psychophysiology, 19,* 514–519.

Treisman, A. M. (1964). Selective attention in man. *British Medical Bulletin, 20,* 12–16.

Treisman, A. M., & Davis, A. (1973). Divided attention to ear and eye. In S. Kornblum (Ed.), *Attention and performance IV* (pp. 101–117). New York: Academic Press.

Triandis, H. C. (1971). *Attitude and attitude change.* New York: John Wiley & Sons.

Trivers, R. L. (1971). The evolution of reciprocal altruism. *Quarterly Review of Biology, 46,* 35–37.

Trope, Y. (1986). Identification and inferential processes in dispositional attribution. *Psychological Review, 93,* 239–257.

Tryon, R. C. (1940). Genetic differences in maze-learning ability in rats. *Yearbook of the National Society for the Study of Education, 39,* 111–119.

Tryon, R. C. (1942). Individual differences. In F. A. Moss (Ed.), *Comparative psychology* (pp. 330–365). Englewood Cliffs, NJ: Prentice-Hall.

Tsukahara, N., & Murakami, F. (1983). Axonal sprouting and recovery of function after brain damage. In J. E. Desmedt (Ed.), *Motor control mechanisms in health and disease: Advances in neurology* (pp. 1073–1084). New York: Raven Press.

Tulving, E. (1967). The effects of presentation and recall of materials in free-recall learning. *Journal of Verbal Learning and Verbal Behavior, 6,* 175–184.

Tulving, E. (1972). Episodic and semantic memory. In E. Tulving & W. Donaldson (Eds.), *Organization and memory.* New York: Academic Press.

Tulving, E. (1981). Similarity relations in recognition. *Journal of Verbal Learning and Verbal Behavior, 20,* 479–496.

Tulving, E. (1985). How many memory systems are there? *American Psychologist, 40,* 385–398.

Tulving, E., & Thompson, D. M. (1973). Encoding specificity and retrieval processes in episodic memory. *Psychological Review, 80,* 353–373.

Turek, F. W. (1985). Circadian neural rhythms in mammals. *Annual Review of Physiology, 47,* 49–63.

Turner, C. D. (1960). *General endocrinology.* Philadelphia: Saunders.

Turner, C. W., & Berkowitz, L. (1972). Identification with film aggressor (covert role taking) and reactions to film violence. *Journal of Personality and Social Psychology, 21,* 256–264.

Turner, C. W., & Simons, L. S. (1974). Effects of subject sophistication and evaluation apprehension on aggressive responses to weapons. *Journal of Personality and Social Psychology, 30,* 341–348.

Tversky, A., & Kahneman, D. (1973). Availability: A heuristic for judging frequency and probability. *Cognitive Psychology, 5,* 207–232.

Tversky, A., & Kahneman, D. (1974). Judgment under uncertainty. Heuristics and biases. *Science, 815,* 1124–1131.

Tversky, A., & Kahneman, D. (1978). Causal schemata in judgments under uncertainty. In M. Fishbein (Ed.), *Progress in social psychology.* Hillsdale: Lawrence Erlbaum.

Ulrich, R. E., & Azrin, N. H. (1962). Reflexive fighting in response to aversive stimulation. *Journal of the Experimental Analysis of Behavior, 5,* 511–520.

Underwood, B. J. (1948). Retroactive and proactive inhibition after five and forty-eight hours. *Journal of Experimental Psychology, 38,* 29–38. (a)

Underwood, B. J. (1948). "Spontaneous recovery" of verbal associations. *Journal of Experimental Psychology, 38,* 429–439. (b)

Underwood, B. J. (1949). Proactive inhibition as a function of time and degree of prior learning. *Journal of Experimental Psychology, 39,* 24–34.

Underwood, B. J. (1957). Interference and forgetting. *Psychological Review, 64,* 49–60.

Unger, R. L., Hilderbrand, M., & Maden, T. (1982). Physical attractiveness and assumptions about social deviance: Some sex-by-sex comparisons. *Personality and Social Psychology Bulletin, 8,* 293–301.

United States Department of Health, Education, and Welfare (1979). *Smoking and Health: A Report of the Surgeon General—DHEW publication no. (PHS) 79-50066.* Washington, DC: U.S. Government Printing Office.

Uttal, W. R. (1973). *The psychobiology of sensory coding.* New York: Harper & Row.

Vaillant, G. E. (1983). *The natural history of alcoholism.* Cambridge, MA: Harvard University Press.

Valenstein, E. S. (1973). *Brain control.* New York: John Wiley & Sons.

Valenstein, E. S. (1980). Historical perspective. In E. S. Valenstein (Ed.), *The psychosurgery debate.* San Francisco: Freeman. (a)

Valenstein, E. S. (1980). Review of the literature on postoperative evaluation. In E. S. Valenstein (Ed.), *The psychosurgery debate.* San Francisco: Freeman. (b)

Valenstein, E. S. (1986). *Great and desperate cures.* New York: Basic Books.

Valins, S. (1972). Persistent effects of information about internal reactions: Ineffectiveness of debriefing. In H. London & R. E. Nisbett (Eds.), *The cognitive alteration of feeling states.* Chicago: Aldine.

Van Dis, H., & Larsson, K. (1971). Induction of sexual arousal in the castrated male rat by intracranial stimulation. *Physiology and Behavior, 6,* 85–86.

Van Essen, D. C., & Maunsell, J. H. R. (1983). Hierarchical organization and functional streams in the visual cortex. *Trends in Neurosciences, 6,* 370–374.

Vanden Bos, G. R. (1986). Psychotherapy research: a special issue. *American Psychologist, 41,* 111–112.

Vandenberg, S. G., & Vogler, G. P. (1985). Genetic determinants of intelligence. In B. B. Wolman (Ed.), *Handbook of intelligence.* New York: John Wiley & Sons.

Vargha-Khadem, F., O'Gorman, A. M., & Watters, G. V. (1985). Aphasia and handedness in relation to hemispheric side, age at injury and severity of cerebral lesion during childhood. *Brain, 108,* 677–696.

Vaugh, C. E., Snyder, K., Jones, S., Freeman, W. B., & Falloon, I. R. H. (1984). Family factors in schizophrenic relapse: A replication in California of British research on expressed emotion. *Archives of General Psychiatry, 41,* 1169–1177.

Vaughan, B. E., & Langlois, J. H. (1983). Physical attractiveness has a correlate of peer status and social competence in preschool children. *Developmental Psychology, 19,* 561–567.

Veitch, R., & Griffit, W. (1976). Good news: Affective and interpersonal effects. *Journal of Applied Social Psychology, 6,* 69–76.

Vernon, P. E. (1950). *The structure of human abilities.* New York: John Wiley & Sons.

Vilberg, T. R., & Keesey, R. E. (1984). Reduced energy expenditure after ventromedial hypothalamic lesions in female rats. *American Journal of Physiology, 247,* R183–R188.

Voegtlin, W. L. (1940). The treatment of alcoholism by establishing a conditioned reflex. *American Journal of Medical Science, 199,* 802–809.

Vogel, G. W. (1975). A review of REM sleep deprivation. *Archives of General Psychiatry, 32,* 749–761.

Volgyesi, F. A. (1954). "School for patients" hypnosis-therapy and psychoprophylaxis. *British Journal of Medical Hypnotism, 5,* 8–17.

von Baeyer, C. L., Sherk, D. L., & Zanna, M. P. (1979). *Impression management: Female job applicants, male (chauvinist) interviewer.* Paper presented at the Meeting of the APA, New York.

von Holst, E. (1954). Relations between the central nervous system and the peripheral organs. *British Journal of Animal Behaviour, 2,* 89–94.

von Senden, M. (1960). *Space and sight.* New York: Free Press.

Vonnegut, M. (1975). *The Eden express.* Toronto: Bantam Books.

Wada, J., Clarke, R., & Hamm, A. (1975). Cerebral hemisphere asymmetry in humans. *Archives of Neurology, 32,* 239–246.

Wade, T. C., & Baker, T. B. (1977). Opinions and use of psychological tests: A survey of clinical psychologists. *American Psychologist, 32,* 874–882.

Wade, T. C., Baker, T. B., & Hartmann, D. P. (1979). Behavior therapists' self-reported views and practices. *The Behavior Therapist, 2,* 3–6.

Wagenaar, W. A. (1970). Subjective randomness and the capacity to generate information. In A. F. Sanders (Ed.), *Attention and performance III, Acta Psychologica, 33,* 233–242.

Wagner, H. L., MacDonald, C. J., & Manstead, A. S. R. (1986). Communication of individual emotions by spontaneous facial expressions. *Journal of Personality and Social Psychology, 50,* 737–743.

Walcott, C. (1974). The homing of pigeons. *American Scientist, 62,* 542–552.

Walcott, C., Gould, J. L., & Kirschvink, J. L. (1979). Pigeons have magnets. *Science, 205,* 1023–1029.

Wald, G. (1950). Eye and camera. *Scientific American, 183,* 32–41.

Walker, L. J. (1986). Experiential and cognitive sources of moral development in adulthood. *Human Development, 29,* 113–124.

Wall, P. D. (1978). The gate control theory of pain mechanisms. *Brain, 101,* 1–18.

Wall, P. D. (1979). On the relation of injury to pain. *Pain, 6,* 253–264.

Wallace, W. (1969). *Sociological theory.* New York: Aldine.

Walsh, D. A. (1983). Age differences in learning and memory. In D. S. Woodruff & J. E. Birren (Eds.), *Aging: Scientific perspectives and social issues* (pp. 149–177). Monterey, CA: Brooks/Cole.

Walsh, W. B., & Betz, N. E. (1985). *Tests & assessment.* Englewood Cliffs, NJ: Prentice-Hall.

Walster, E., Aronson, E., & Abrahams, D. (1966). On increasing the persuasiveness of a low prestige communicator. *Journal of Experimental Social Psychology, 2,* 325–342.

Walster, E., Aronson, E., Abrahams, D., & Rottman, L. (1966). Importance of physical attractiveness in dating behavior. *Journal of Personality and Social Psychology, 4,* 508–516.

Walster, E., Walster, G. W., & Berschied, E. (1978). *Equity: Theory and research.* Boston: Allyn & Bacon.

Warm, J. S., & Jerison, H. J. (1984). The psychophysics of vigilance. In J. S. Warm (Ed.), *Sustained attention in human performance* (pp. 15–60). New York: John Wiley & Sons.

Warren, R. M. (1970). Perceptual restoration of missing speech sounds. *Science, 167,* 392–393.

Warrington, E. K. (1986). Memory for facts and memory for events. *British Journal of Clinical Psychology, 25,* 1–12.

Wartella, E. (1980). Individual differences in children's responses to television advertising. In E. L. Palmer & A. Dorr (Eds.), *Children and the faces of television: Teaching, violence, selling* (pp. 307–322). New York: Academic Press.

Wason, P. C. (1960). On the failure to eliminate hypotheses in a conceptual task. *Quarterly Journal of Experimental Psychology, 12,* 129–140.

Wason, P. C. (1966). Reasoning. In B. M. Foss (Ed.), *New horizons in psychology.* Harmondsworth: Penguin.

Wason, P. C. (1968). On the failure to eliminate hypotheses in a conceptual task: A second look. In P. C. Wason and P. N. Johnson-Laird (Eds.), *Thinking and reasoning.* Middlesex, England: Penguin.

Wason, P. C., & Johnson-Laird, P. N. (1972). *Psychology of reasoning: Structure and content.* London: Batsford; Cambridge, MA: Harvard University Press.

Wason, P. C., & Shapiro, D. (1971). Natural and contrived experience in a reasoning problem. *Quarterly Journal of Experimental Psychology, 23,* 63–71.

Waters, E. (1978). The reliability and stability of individual differences in infant–mother attachment. *Child Development, 49,* 483–494.

Watkins, L. R., & Mayer, D. J. (1982). Organization of endogenous opiate and non-opiate pain control systems. *Science, 216,* 1185–1192.

Watson, J. B. (1913). Psychology as the behaviorist views it. *Psychological Review, 20,* 158–177.

Watson, J. B. (1930/1966). *Behaviorism.* Chicago: Phoenix Books.

Watson, W. E. (1974). Physiology of neurologia. *Physiology and Behavior, 54,* 245–271.

Watts, W. A. (1967). Relative persistence of opinion change induced by active compared to passive participation. *Journal of Personality and Social Psychology, 5,* 4–15.

Watts, W. A., & McGuire, W. M. (1964). Persistence of induced opinion change and retention of inducing message content. *Journal of Abnormal Social Psychology, 68,* 233–241.

Waugh, N. C., & Barr, R. A. (1982). Encoding deficits in aging. In F. I. M. Craik & S. Trehub (Eds.), *Aging and cognitive processes* (pp. 183–190). New York: Plenum Press.

Waugh, N. C., & Norman, D. A. (1965). Primary memory. *Psychological Review, 72,* 89–104.

Waxenberg, S. E., Drellich, M. G., & Sutherland, A. M. (1959). The role of hormones in human behavior: I. Changes in female sexuality after adrenalectomy. *Journal of Clinical Endocrinology and Metabolism, 19,* 193–202.

Weaver, T. R. (1946). The incidence of maladjustment among mental defectives in military environments. *American Journal of Mental Deficiency, 51,* 238–246.

Webb, W. B. (1975). *The gentle tyrant.* Englewood Cliffs, NJ: Prentice-Hall.

Webb, W. B. (1979). Are short and long sleepers different? *Psychological Reports, 44,* 259–264.

Webb, W. B., & Agnew, H. W., Jr. (1973). Effects on performance of high and low energy-expenditure during sleep deprivation. *Perceptual and Motor Skills, 37,* 511–514.

Webb, W. B., Agnew, H. W., Jr. & Williams, R. L. (1971). Effect on sleep of a sleep period time displacement. *Aerospace Medicine, 42,* 152–155.

Webb, W. B., & Cartwright, R. D. (1978). Sleep and dreams. *Annual Review of Psychology, 29,* 223–252.

Weber, E. H. (1834). *De Pulsu, Resorptione, Auditu et Tactu: Annotationes Anatomicae et Physiologicae.* Leipzig: Koehler.

Wechsler, D. (1981). *Manual for the Wechsler Adult Intelligence Scale—Revised.* New York: Psychological Corporation.

Wei, L. Y. (1979). Scientific advance in acupuncture. *American Journal of Chinese Medicine, 7,* 53–75.

Weinberger, D. R., Berman, K. F., & Eec, R. F. (1986). Physiologic dysfunction of dorsolateral prefrontal cortex in schizophrenia: I. Regional cerebral blood flow evidence. *Archives of General Psychiatry, 432,* 114–124.

Weiner, B. (1985). An attribution theory of achievement motivation and emotion. *Psychological Review, 92,* 548–573. (a)

Weiner, B. (1985). *Human motivation.* New York: Springer-Verlag. (b)

Weiner, B. (1986). Attribution, emotion, and action. In Sorrentino, R. M., & Higgins, E. T. (Eds.), *Handbook of motivation and cognition.* New York: Guilford.

Weiner, F. H. (1976). Altruism, ambience, and action: The effects of rural and urban rearing on helping behavior. *Journal of Personality and Social Psychology, 34,* 112–124.

Weingarten, H. P. (1985). Stimulus control of eating: Implications for a two-factor theory of hunger. *Appetite, 6,* 387–401.

Weinstein, E. A. (1980). Clinical features of hemi-inattention. *The Behavioral and Brain Sciences, 3,* 518–520.

Weinstein, S. (1968). Intensive and extensive aspects of tactile sensitivity as a function of body part, sex, and laterality. In D. R. Kenshalo (Ed.), *The skin senses* (pp. 195–218). Springfield, IL: Charles C. Thomas.

Weiss, J. M. (1971). Effects of coping behavior in different warning signal conditions on stress pathology in rats. *Journal of Comparative and Physiological Psychology, 77,* 1–13.

Weitzman, E. D. (1981). Sleep and its disorders. *Annual Review of Neuroscience, 4,* 381–418.

Weizenbaum, J. (1966). ELIZA: A computer program for the study of natural language communication between man and machine. *Communications of the Association for Computing Machinery, 9,* 36–45.

Wellman, H. M., & Lempers, J. D. (1977). The naturalistic communicative abilities of two-year-olds. *Child Development, 48,* 1052–1057.

Wenger, M. A., Jones, F. N., & Jones, M. H. (1956). *Physiological psychology.* New York: Holt, Rinehart & Winston.

Werner, E. E., & Smith, R. S. (1982). *Vulnerable but invincible.* New York: McGraw-Hill.

Werner, J. S., & Perlmutter, M. (1979). Development of visual memory in infants. In H. W. Reese & L. P. Lipsitt (Eds.), *Advances in child development and behavior* (pp. 1–56). New York: Academic Press.

Werner, J. S., & Wooten, B. R. (1985). Unsettled issues in infant color vision. *Infant Behav-*

ior and Development, 8, 99–108.

Wernicke, C. (1874). Der aphasische symptomen-complex. Breslau: Franck U. Weigart.

Wertheimer, M. (1912). Experimentelle Studien uber das Sehen von Bewegung. Zeitschrift fur Psychologie, 61, 161–265.

Wertheimer, M. (1958). Principles of perceptual organization. In D. S. Beardslee & M. Wertheimer (Eds.), Readings in perception (pp. 115–137). Princeton, NJ: Van Nostrand.

Wever, E. G. (1949). Theory of hearing. New York: John Wiley & Sons.

Wever, R. A. (1975). The circadian multi-oscillator system of man. International Journal of Chronobiology, 3, 19–55.

Wever, R. A. (1979). The circadian system of man. Results of experiments under temporal isolation. New York: Springer-Verlag.

Wheeless, L. R. (1971). Some effects of time-compressed speech on persuasion. Journal of Broadcasting, 15, 415–420.

Wheeless, L. R., & Grotz, J. (1977). The measurement of trust and its relationship to self-disclosure. Human Communication Research, 3, 250–257.

White, J. W., & Gruber, K. J. (1982). Instigative aggression as a function of past experience and target characteristics. Journal of Personality and Social Psychology, 42, 1069–1075.

White, L. A. (1979). Erotica and aggression: The influence of sexual arousal, positive affect, and negative affect on aggressive behavior. Journal of Personality and Social Psychology, 37, 591–601.

Whitsel, B. L., Dreyer, D. A., & Holins, M. (1978). Representation of moving stimuli by somatosensory neurons. Federation Proceedings, 37, 2223–2227.

Wickelgren, W. A. (1974). How to solve problems. San Francisco: Freeman.

Wickens, D. D. (1972). Characteristics of word encoding. In A. W. Melton & E. Martin (Eds.), Coding processes in human memory. Washington, DC: Winston.

Wicker, A. W. (1969). Attitudes versus actions: The relationship of verbal and overt behavioral responses to attitude objects. Journal of Social Issues, 25(4), 41–78.

Wicklund, R. A. (1975). Objective self-awareness. In L. Berkowitz (Ed.), Advances in experimental social psychology (Vol. 8). New York: Academic Press.

Wicklund, R. A., & Frey, D. (1980). Self-awareness theory: When the self makes a difference. In D. M. Wegner & R. R. Vallacher (Eds.), The self in social psychology. New York: Oxford University Press.

Wiesel, T. N., & Hubel, D. H. (1965). Comparison of the effects of unilateral and bilateral eye closure on cortical unit responses in kittens. Journal of Neurophysiology, 28, 1029–1040.

Wiggins, J. S. (1973). Personality and prediction. Reading, MA: Addison-Wesley.

Wightman, F. L., Kistler, D. J., & Perkins, M. E. (1987). A new approach to the study of human sound localization. In W. A. Yost & G. Gourevitch (Eds.), Directional hearing (pp. 26–48). Berlin: Springer-Verlag.

Wightman, F. L., & Green, D. M. (1974). The perception of pitch. American Scientist, 62, 208–215.

Wikler, A., & Pescor, R. W. (1953). Psychiatric aspects of drug addiction. American Journal of Medicine, 14, 566–570.

Wilcox, M. J., & Webster, E. J. (1980). Early discourse behavior: An analysis of children's responses to listener feedback. Child Development, 51, 1120–1125.

Wild, H. M., Butler, S. R., Carden, D., & Kulikowski, J. J. (1985). Primate cortical area V4 important for colour constancy but not wavelength discrimination. Nature, 313, 133–134.

Wilder, D. A. (1977). Perception of groups, size of opposition, and social influence. Journal of Experimental Social Psychology, 13, 253–258.

Wilke, H., & Lanzetta, J. T. (1970). The obligation to help: The effects of amount of prior help on subsequent helping behavior. Journal of Experimental Social Psychology, 6, 488–493.

Wilkinson, R. T. (1965). Sleep deprivation. In O. G. Edholm & A. L. Bacharach (Eds.), Physiology of human survival (pp. 399–430). London: Academic Press.

Williams, E. (1975). Medium or message: Communications medium as a determinant of interpersonal evaluation. Sociometry, 38, 119–130.

Williams, E. (1977). Experimental comparisons of face-to-face and mediated communication: A review. Psychological Bulletin, 84, 963–976.

Williams, M. D. (1976). Retrieval from very long-term memory. Unpublished doctoral dissertation. University of California, San Diego.

Williams, S. B. (1938). Resistance to extinction as a function of the number of reinforcements. Journal of Experimental Psychology, 23, 506–521.

Willis, W. D., Jr. (1985). The pain system. New York: Karger.

Willmuth, M. E., Leitenberg, H., Rosen, J. C., Fondacaro, K. M., & Gross, J. (1985). Body size distortion in bulimia nervosa. International Journal of Eating Disorders, 4, 71–78.

Willner, P. (1985). Depression: A psychobiological synthesis. New York: John Wiley & Sons.

Wilson, E. O. (1975). Sociobiology: The new synthesis. Cambridge, MA: Harvard University Press.

Wilson, G. T., & Lawson, D. M. (1976). Effects of alcohol on sexual arousal in women. Journal of Abnormal Psychology, 85, 587–594.

Wilson, L., & Rogers, W. (1975). The fire this time: Effects of race of target, insult, and potential retaliation on Black aggression. Journal of Personality and Social Psychology, 32, 857–864.

Wimer, R. E., & Wimer, C. C. (1985). Animal behavior genetics: A search for the biological foundations of behavior. Annual Review of Psychology, 36, 171–218.

Winocur, G., Kinsbourne, M., & Moscovitch, M. (1981). The effect of cuing on release from proactive interference in Korsakoff-amnesic patients. Journal of Experimental Psychology: Human Learning and Memory, 7, 56–65.

Winograd, E., & Soloway, R. M. (1986). On forgetting the locations of things stored in special places. Journal of Experimental Psychology: General, 115, 366–372.

Winston, P. H. (1977). Artificial intelligence. Reading, MA: Addison-Wesley.

Wise, R. A. (1983). Brain neuronal systems mediating reward processes. In J. E. Smith & J. D. Lane (Eds.), Neurobiology of opiate reward processes (pp. 405–438). Amsterdam: Elsevier.

Wise, S. P., & Strick, P. L. (1984). Anatomical and physiological organization of the nonprimary motor cortex. Trends in Neuroscience, 7, 442–446.

Wolbarsht, M. L., Wagner, H. G., & Ringo, J. L. (1985). Retinal mechanisms for improving visual acuity. In A. Fein & J. S. Levine (Eds.), Visual system: MBL Lectures in Biology (pp. 167–187). New York: Alan R. Liss.

Wolman, B. B., Dale, L. A., Schmeidler, G. R., & Ullman, M. (Eds.). (1977). Handbook of parapsychology. New York: Van Nostrand Reinhold.

Wolpe, J. (1958). Reciprocal inhibition therapy. Stanford, CA: Stanford University Press.

Woodworth, R. S. (1938). Experimental psychology. New York: Henry Holt.

Woodworth, R. S. (1940). Psychology. New York: Holt.

Woodworth, R. S., & Sels, S. B. (1935). An atmospheric effect in formal syllogistic reasoning. Journal of Experimental Psychology, 18, 451–460.

Woody, C. D. (1986). Understanding the cellular basis of memory and learning. Annual Review of Psychology, 37, 433–493.

Woolsey, C. N. (1958). Organization of somatic sensory and motor areas of cerebral cortex. In H. F. Harlow & C. N. Woolsey (Eds.), Biological and biochemical bases of behavior (pp. 63–81). Madison: University of Wisconsin Press.

Woolsey, C. N. (1961). Organization of the cortical auditory system. In W. A. Rosenblith (Ed.), Sensory communication (pp. 235–257). New York: John Wiley & Sons.

Worchel, S., Andreoli, V., & Archer, R. (1976). When is a favor a threat to freedom: The effects of attribution and importance of freedom on reciprocity. Journal of Personality, 44, 294–310.

Wyburn, G. M., Pickford, R. W., & Hirst, R. J. (1964). Human senses and perception. Toronto: University of Toronto Press.

Wyer, R. S., & Bodenhausen, G. V. (1985). Event memory: The effects of processing objectives and time delay on memory for action sequences. Journal of Personality and Social Psychology, 49, 301–316.

Yakimovitch, D., & Saltz, E. (1971). Helping behavior: The cry for help. Psychonomic Science, 23, 427–428.

Yakoviev, P. I., & Lecours, A. R. (1967). The mylogenetic cycles of regional maturation of the brain. In A. Minkowski (Ed.), Regional development of the brain in early life (pp. 3–70). Oxford: Blackwell.

Yamamoto, T. (1984). Taste responses of cortical neurons. Progress in Neurobiology, 23, 273–316.

Yarbus, A. L. (1967). Eye movements and vision. New York: Plenum Press.

Yates, J., & Taylor, J. (1978). Stereotypes for somatotypes: Shared beliefs about Sheldon's physiques. Psychological Reports, 43, 777–778.

Yeo, C. H., Hardiman, M. J., & Glickstein, M. (1984). Discrete lesions of the cerebellar cortex abolish the classically conditioned nictitating membrane response of the rabbit. Behavioral Brain Research, 13, 261–266.

Yerkes, R. M., & Dodson, J. D. (1908). The relation of strength of stimulus to rapidity of habit formation. Journal of Comparative Neurology and Psychology, 18, 459–482.

Yonas, A. (1981). Infants' responses to optical information for collision. In R. N. Aslin, J. R. Alberts, & M. R. Petersen (Eds.), *Development of perception* (pp. 313–334). New York: Academic Press.

Yonas, A., Granrud, C. E., & Pettersen, L. (1985). Infants' sensitivity to relative size information for distance. *Developmental Psychology, 21,* 161–167.

Young, L. R. (1984). Perception of the body in space: Mechanisms. In I. Darian-Smith (Ed.), *Handbook of physiology—the nervous system III* (pp. 1023–1066). Bethesda, MD: American Physiological Society.

Young, P. T. (1961). *Motivation and emotion.* New York: John Wiley & Sons.

Yu, B., Zhang, W., Jing, Q., Peng, R., Zhang, G., & Simon, H. A. (1985). STM capacity for Chinese and English language materials. *Memory and Cognition, 13,* 202–207.

Zaidel, E. (1976). Auditory vocabulary of the right hemisphere following brain bisection or hemidecortication. *Cortex, 12,* 191–211.

Zajonc, R. B. (1968). Attitudinal effects of mere exposure. *Journal of Personality and Social Psychology. Monograph Supplement, 9,* 1–27.

Zajonc, R. B. (1985). Emotion and facial efference: A theory reclaimed. *Science, 228,* 15–21.

Zanna, M. P., Kiesler, C. A., & Pilkonis, P. A. (1970). Positive and negative attitudinal effect established by classical conditioning. *Journal of Personality and Social Psychology, 14,* 321–328.

Zeki, S. M. (1983). Color coding in the cerebral cortex: The reaction of cells in monkey visual cortex to wavelengths and colours. *Neuroscience, 9,* 741–766.

Zepelin, H., & Rechtschaffen, P. (1974). Mammalian sleep, longevity, and energy metabolism. *Brain, Behavior and Evolution, 10,* 425–470.

Zhang, G., & Simon, H. A. (1985). STM capacity for Chinese words and idioms: Chunking and acoustical loop hypotheses. *Memory and Cognition, 13,* 193–201.

Zigler, E., & Seitz, V. (1985). Social policy and intelligence. In R. Sternberg (Ed.), *Handbook of human intelligence.* New York: Cambridge University Press.

Zillmann, D. (1971). Excitation transfer in communication-mediated aggressive behavior. *Journal of Experimental Social Psychology, 7,* 419–434.

Zillmann, D. (1972). Rhetorical elicitation of agreement, in persuasion. *Journal of Personality and Social Psychology, 21,* 159–165.

Zillmann, D. (1979). *Hostility and aggression.* Hillsdale, NJ: Lawrence Erlbaum.

Zillmann, D. (1982). Transfer of excitation in emotional behavior. In J. T. Cacioppo & R. E. Petty (Eds.), *Social psychophysiology.* New York: Guilford Press.

Zillmann, D., & Bryant, J. (1974). Effects of residual excitation on the emotional response to provocation and delayed aggressive behavior. *Journal of Personality and Social Psychology, 30,* 782–791.

Zillmann, D., & Bryant, J. (1983). Pornography and social science research: . . . higher moralities. *Journal of Communication, 33,* 111–114.

Zillmann, D., & Sapolsky, B. S. (1977). What mediates the effects of mild erotica on annoyance and hostile behavior in males? *Journal of Personality and Social Psychology, 35,* 587–596.

Zimbardo, P. G., & Formica, R. (1963). Emotional comparison and self esteem as determinants of affiliation. *Journal of Personality and Social Psychology, 16,* 669–680.

Zingg, R. M. (1940). Feral man and extreme cases of isolation. *American Journal of Psychology, 53,* 487–517.

Zola-Morgan, S., & Squire, L. R. (1986). Memory impairment in monkeys following lesions limited to the hippocampus. *Behavioral Neuroscience, 100,* 144–160.

Zola-Morgan, S., Squire, L. R., & Amaral, D. G. (1986). Human amnesia and the medial temporal region: Enduring memory impairment following a bilateral lesion limited to field CA1 of the hippocampus. *Journal of Neuroscience, 6,* 2950–2967.

Zuckerman, M. (1979). Attribution of success and failure revisited: or The motivational bias is alive and well in attribution theory. *Journal of Personality, 47,* 245–287.

Zuckerman, M., Mann, R. W., & Bernieri, F. J. (1982). Determinants of consensus estimates: Attribution, salience, and representativeness. *Journal of Personality and Social Psychology, 42,* 839–852.

Zylman, R. (1968). Accidents, alcohol and single cause explanations. *Quarterly Journal of Studies on Alcohol,* 212–233.

PHOTO CREDITS

Chapter 1
Opener: Alice Kandell/Photo Researchers. Figs. 1.1 and 1.2: The Bettmann Archive. Fig. 1.3: Alinari/Art Resource, NY. Figs. 1.4–1.8: The Bettmann Archive. Fig. 1.9: Courtesy The American Museum of Natural History. Fig. 1.10: Nina Leen/Life Magazine. © Time, Inc. Fig. 1.11: Courtesy Teachers College, Columbia University. Figs. 1.12 and 1.13: The Bettmann Archive. Fig. 1.14: Kathy Bendo. Fig. 1.15: Max Halberstadt. Fig. 1.16: Ted Polumbaum. Fig. 1.17: Antony Di Gesu/Delacorte Press. Fig. 1.18: Bill Anderson/Monkmeyer. Fig. 1.19: Wide World Photos.

Chapter 2
Opener: Jim Harrison/Stock, Boston. Fig. 2.1: Photo by Lennart Nilsson. From *Behold Man,* Little, Brown & Company, Boston. Fig. 2.3: © Dan McCoy/Rainbow. Fig. 2.5: Courtesy Dr. Chris Gall, University of California at Irvine, Dept. of Anatomy. Fig. 2.7: Courtesy Terence H. Williams. Fig. 2.8: Courtesy Peter Spear. Fig. 2.13: (b) Courtesy Alan Peters, Ph.D., Boston University School of Medicine, Dept. of Anatomy. Fig. 2.14: (b) Courtesy Dr. John E. Heuser of Washington University School of Medicine, St. Louis, Mo. Fig. 2.20: Courtesy Dr. A. P. Roland, Karolinska Hospital, Sweden. American Psychological Society. Fig. 2.21: (top left) From *Human Neuropsychology,* Hecaen and Albert, John Wiley & Sons, 1978, p. 104; (bottom left) From "The Functional Organization of Posterior Parietal Association Cortex," by James C. Lynch, in *The Behavioral and Brain Sciences,* Vol. 3, p. 519. © 1980 Cambridge University Press. Reprinted by permission. (a) (b) and (c) Anton Räderscheidt/VAGA.

Chapter 3
Opener: Henri Cartier-Bresson/Magnum. Fig. 3.8: Photo by Lennart Nilsson. From *Behold Man,* Little, Brown & Company, Boston. Fig. 3.15: Courtesy Dr. Nigel Daw, Dept. of Cell Biology and Physiology, Washington University School of Medicine, Mo. Fig. 3.17: Courtesy Dr. Robert Shapley, Rockefeller Medical Center. Fig. 3.18: Courtesy F. W. Campbell, Physiological Laboratory, Cambridge, England. Fig. 3.22: Courtesy Kaiser Porcelain Ltd. Fig. 3.29: Courtesy U.S. Geological Survey, Dept. of the Interior. Fig. 3.30: Caspar David Friedrich: Hochgebirge, um 1824, im Krieg Vernichtet/Art Resource, NY. Fig. 3.31: From *Sensation and Perception,* 2nd edition, by E. Bruce Goldstein. © 1984 by Wadsworth, Inc. Used by permission. Fig. 3.34: © 1971 Scott Ransom/Taurus Photos. Fig. 3.35: (b) M. C. Escher, *Waterfalls,* 1961, Collection Escher Foundation, Coll. Haags Gemeentemuseum. Fig. 3.37:

Courtesy Macbeth, a division of Kollmorgen Corp. Fig. 3.38: Life Science Library/*Light and Vision.* Photography by John Zimmerman. © 1966 Time-Life Books, Inc. Fig. 3.39: Courtesy Kodak. Fig. 3.45: Courtesy Richmond Products, Boca Raton, Fl. Fig. 3.48: Enrico Ferorelli/DOT.

Chapter 4
Opener: James Carroll. Fig. 4.10: Courtesy Professor E. F. Evans, Dept. of Communications and Neurosciences, University of Keele, England. Fig. 4.16: © Raleigh Souther. Fig. 4.24: Courtesy Dr. Thomas Eisner, Cornell University.

Chapter 5
Opener: Mark Godfrey/Archive Pictures. Fig. 5.4: From Yarbus, *Eye Movements and Vision,* Plenum Publishing Company, 1966. Fig. 5.15: © 1982 Michal Heron/Woodfin Camp and Associates. Fig. 5.16: Courtesy Dr. William C. Dement, Stanford University Medical School. Fig. 5.20: © 1976 Ray Ellis/Rapho-Photo Researchers. Fig. 5.21: Culver Pictures, Inc.

Chapter 6
Opener: George W. Gardner. Fig. 6.1: The Bettmann Archive. Fig. 6.2: (a) Culver Pictures, Inc. (b) From Kimble, et al., *Psychology,* Fig. 8.2, John Wiley & Sons, 1984. Fig. 6.12: Sybil Shelton/Monkmeyer Press Photo Service. Fig. 6.14: (a) Elliot Erwitt/Magnum Photos. (b) Courtesy Thomas M. Waller, The Wisconsin State Journal. Fig. 6.16: Courtesy Dr. Nathan Azrin, Nova University, Ft. Lauderdale, Fl. Fig. 6.20: UPI/Bettmann Newsphotos. Fig. 6.21: From Wolfgang Köhler, *The Mentality of Apes,* 1925. Fig. 6.24: (top) Leonard Freed/Magnum Photos; (bottom) Hella Hamid/Photo Researchers. Box 6.3: Courtesy Primate Laboratory, University of Wisconsin, Madison. Fig. 6.25: Courtesy Animal Behavior Enterprises, Inc. Fig. 6.28: (a) Stephen Dalton 1973/National Audubon Society/Photo Researchers. (b) Steve Raye 1981/FPG International.

Chapter 7
Opener: Ulrike Welsch. Fig. 7.15: Courtesy Dr. Endel Tulving, University of Toronto, Canada.

Chapter 8
Opener: Owen Franken/Stock, Boston.

Chapter 9
Opener: Jim Anderson/Woodfin Camp and Associates. Fig. 9.1: (a) Bob Kalman/The Image Works, Inc. (b) Michael Hayman/Photo Researchers. Fig. 9.2: Photo by Lennart Nilsson

from *Behold Man,* Little, Brown & Company, Boston. Fig. 9.3: From Paul H. Mussen, ed., *Handbook of Child Psychology,* 4th edition, pp. 358–9, John Wiley & Sons, 1983. Fig. 9.6: Bruce Roberts/Photo Researchers. Fig. 9.10: (a,d) Lennart Nilsson, *Behold Man,* Little, Brown & Company, Boston, (b,c) Lennart Nilsson, *A Child is Born,* Dell Publishing Company, NY. Fig. 9.15: (a) Alice Kandell/Photo Researchers. (b) © 1984 Dean Abramson/ Stock, Boston. Fig. 9.16: Courtesy Safra Nimrod. Fig. 9.17: (a) © 1979 Frank Siteman/The Picture Cube. (b) Michael Hayman/Photo Researchers. Fig. 9.18: AP/Wide World Photos. Fig. 9.19: Brad Hess/Monkmeyer Press Photo Service. Fig. 9.20: Monkmeyer Press Photo Service. Fig. 9.23: Zimbel/Monkmeyer Press Photo Service. Fig. 9.25: Sam Falk/The New York Times Pictures. Fig. 9.31: Therese Frare/The Picture Cube. Fig. 9.32: Courtesy Primate Laboratory, University of Wisconsin, Madison. Fig. 9.33: (a) Renee Lynn/Photo Researchers. (b) Suzanne Szasz/Photo Researchers. Fig. 9.34: (a) Elizabeth Crews/The Image Works. (b) Guy Gillette/Photo Researchers. Fig. 9.35: Joseph Szabo/Photo Researchers. Fig. 9.36: Elizabeth Crews/Stock, Boston. Fig. 9.37: (a) Lionel J-M Delevingne/Stock, Boston. (b) Ulrike Welsch. (c) Bernard Pierre Wolff/Photo Researchers.

Chapter 10
Opener: Ulrike Welsch. Fig. 10.1: Dr. B. Grzimek, Tierbilder Okapia/Photo Researchers. Fig. 10.5: From *Nerve Cells and Insect Behavior* by K. D. Roeder (rev. ed. 1963), Harvard University Press. Photo by Frederic A. Webster. Fig. 10.6: Nina Leen/Life Magazine. © Time, Inc. Fig. 10.7: Illustration by John Langley Howard in "Imprinting in Animals" by Eckhard H. Hess, *Scientific American,* March 1958, p. 82. Fig. 10.9: Credit unknown. Fig. 10.15: Reproduced from unpublished doctoral thesis by J. N. P. Rawlins, Oxford University. Dissection by J. N. P. Rawlins. Photo by J. P. Broad. Fig. 10.18: © John Lei, 1987/Omni-Photo Communications. Fig. 10.23: M. Borjesan, M.D., "The Aetiology of Obesity in Children: A Study of 101 Twins," Acta Paediatrica Scandajavia (1976), Vol. 65, pp. 282–3. Fig. 10.24: Courtesy Professor P. Teitelbaum, University of Pennsylvania. Box 10.1, Fig. 1: Robert V. Eckert, Jr./EKM-Nepenthe. Fig. 10.27: Movie Star News. Fig. 10.28: Alinari/Art Resource, NY. Figs. 10.29–31: By permission of Henry J. Baker, Bowman Gray School of Medicine. Courtesy Audio-Visual Services, Wisconsin Regional Primate Research Center Library. Photo by Bob Dodsworth.

Chapter 11
Opener: Tim Carlson/Stock, Boston. Fig. 11.3: G. Ronald Austing/Photo Researchers. Fig. 11.4: Henry Miller/FPG International. Fig. 11.5: From *Psychology Today*, "Pain and Aggression" by Nathan H. Azrin, Ph.D., May 1967, p. 30. Fig. 11.6: Courtesy Professor E. H. Hess, University of Chicago. Fig. 11.7: F. Jillson/FPG International. Fig. 11.8: (a) © 1987 Erika Stone. (b) Toni Angermayer/Photo Researchers. Fig. 11.9: Courtesy Primate Laboratory, University of Wisconsin, Madison. Fig. 11.10: Ulrike Welsch/Stock, Boston. Fig. 11.11: From *Thematic Apperception Test* by Henry A. Murray, Harvard University Pess. © 1953 by the President and Fellows of Harvard College. Reprinted with permission of the publishers. Fig. 11.14: Courtesy New York Public Library. Fig. 11.15: Courtesy Dr. Tiffany M. Field, University of Miami. Fig. 11.16: Courtesy Dr. Paul Ekman, Human Interaction Laboratory, University of California at San Francisco. Fig. 11.17: Courtesy Richie Davidson, University of Wisconsin. Fig. 11.19: From *Traité d'Anatomie Descriptive* by P. Sappey, Delahaye Lecrosnier, Paris, 1888/89. Fig. 11.20: Courtesy Dr. Paul Ekman, Human Interaction Laboratory, University of California at San Francisco. © 1983. Actor: Tom Harrison. Fig. 11.23: Courtesy New York Public Library. Fig. 11.24: From *The Story of Adaptation Syndrome* by H. Seyle, ACTA Press, 1952. Fig. 11.27: A. G. Farr, S. K. Anderson, P. Marrack, and J. Kappler (1985). Fig. 11.30: Courtesy Dr. Jay M. Weiss, Duke University Medical Center.

Chapter 12
Opener: Charles Harbutt/Archive Pictures. Fig. 12.2: Courtesy New York Public Library. Fig. 12.3: UPI/Bettmann Newsphotos. Figs. 12.5 and Fig. 12.7: Credit unknown. Fig. 12.10: The Bettmann Archive. Fig. 12.11: From *Atlas of Men* by Dr. William Sheldon, Hafner Publishing Company, 1970. Fig. 12.13: Bob Sacha, *Discover Magazine*. © 1987. Fig. 12.14: Culver Pictures, Inc. Fig. 12.16: The Bettmann Archive. Fig. 12.17: Bildarchiv Preussischer Kulturbesitz, Berlin. Fig. 12.18: The Bettmann Archive. Fig. 12.19: UPI/Bettmann Newsphotos. Fig. 12.20: Courtesy Albert Bandura.

Chapter 13
Opener: Arthur Tress/Photo Researchers. Figs. 13.1–2: UPI/Bettmann Newsphotos. Fig. 13.3: The University Museum, University of Pennsylvania, Philadelphia. Fig. 13.4: Courtesy Sander Gilman. From *Seeing the Insane* by Sander Gilman, John Wiley & Sons, 1982. Fig. 13.5: Courtesy Yale Medical Library. Fig. 13.6: Courtesy History of Science Collections, Cornell University Libraries. Fig. 13.7: The Bettmann Archive/BBC Hulton. Fig. 13.8: Benyas-Kaufman/Black Star. Fig. 13.9: Courtesy Sander Gilman. From *Seeing the Insane* by Sander Gilman, John Wiley & Sons, 1982. Fig. 13.10: Courtesy Daniel R. Weinberger, M.D., NIMH, Washington, D.C. Fig. 13.12: From *Phobia* by John Vasso, Friede Covici, Inc., 1931, Special Collections, The Research Libraries, The New York Public Library. Fig. 13.13: Courtesy Dr. Dennis Solkoe Center for

Neurological Diseases, Boston, Ma. Fig. 13.14: © 1987 Allan Grant.

Chapter 14
Opener: Derek Berg. Fig. 14.8: From *The Kallikak Family, A Study in the Heredity of Feeble-Mindedness* by H. H. Goddard, p. 121, Macmillan © 1931. Box 14.2, Fig. 1: By permission of Quiz Kids, Inc., Los Angeles, Ca. Photo courtesy Joan Bishop.

Chapter 15
Opener: Bernard Pierre Wolff/Magnum. Fig. 15.1: (a) Movie Star News. (b) AP/Wide World Photos. (c) Culver Pictures, Inc. Fig. 15.2: Will McIntyre/Photo Researchers. Fig. 15.5: Courtesy Dr. Elliot S. Valenstein. Fig. 15.6: Courtesy Dr. Elliot S. Valenstein and M. Hunter Brown. Fig. 15.9: Courtesy Dr. Daniel R. Weinberger, M.D., NIMH, Washington, D.C. Box 15.2, Fig. 1: Courtesy Photographic Media Center, University of Wisconsin—Extension.

Chapter 16
Opener: Charles Harbutt/Archive Pictures. Box 16.2, Fig. 1: Gregory J. McHugo, Dartmouth College.

Chapter 17
Opener: André Kertész/Archive Pictures. Fig. 17.8: Courtesy Albert Bandura. Box 17.2, Fig. 1: From the film *Obedience* by Stanley Milgram, © 1965, distributed by The New York University Film Library.

SUBJECT INDEX